The Billboard Book of

NUMBER ONE Country HITS

Tom Roland

BILLBOARD BOOKS

An imprint of Watson-Guptill Publications/New York

ABOUT THE AUTHOR

Born and raised in Des Moines, Iowa, Tom Roland moved to Nashville and edited the country section of *Cash Box* magazine. He then worked in New York as the writer and associate producer of the Unistar Radio Network's *Solid Gold Country*. Tom's articles have appeared in *Country Song Roundup, Tune-In, Airplay, Country News, Collectibles Illustrated* and *Country Rhythms*. He currently resides in Nashville.

Edited by Fred Weiler
Senior Editor: Tad Lathrop
Book and Jacket Design: Bob Fillie
Production Manager: Ellen Greene

First published 1991 by Billboard Books, an imprint of Watson-Guptill Publications, a division of BPI Communications, Inc. 1515 Broadway, New York, NY 10036.

Library of Congress Cataloging-in-Publication Data

Roland, Tom.
　　The Billboard book of number one country hits / Tom Roland.
　　　　p.　　　cm.
　　ISBN 0-8230-7553-2
　　1. Country music—discography.　2. Country musicians.
　I. Billboard.　II. Title.　III. Title: Billboard book of
　number 1 country hits.
　ML156.4.C7R64　1991
　016.78242'1642'0266—dc20　　　　　　　　90-15588
　　　　　　　　　　　　　　　　　　　　　　　　　　　CIP

Manufactured in the United States of America
First printing, 1991

1　2　3　4　5　6　7　8　9　/96　95　94　93　92　91

To Donald and Rosemary Roland,
for instilling independence, self-confidence and love;
and to Jeffrey Rosenblum,
for providing the final push.

Acknowledgments

In 1985, Billboard Books released *The Billboard Book of Number One Hits*, in which author Fred Bronson profiled every pop record that hit number one during the rock era, along with the performers who made them. I frequently turned to it for answers to specific questions, to learn more about some of my favorite records, and as a research tool in my own work.

After contemplating the idea of doing a similar treatment of country music, I approached Billboard Books in the summer of 1988, and began work on the project shortly thereafter. My editor warned me that the book would undoubtedly require more work than I envisioned. The book took *much* more.

The required research sometimes seemed overwhelming, but various little events helped to lighten the load—hanging out on Willie Nelson's bus, breakfast with Mickey Gilley, a Christmas card from Sonny James, a call at home from George Strait. A huge thanks goes out to all those creative individuals who took the time to answer my questions—approximately 250 recording artists, songwriters, producers and musicians who personally divulged their recollections of the creative processes.

For every artist or writer, though, there were many more people behind the scenes who helped set up the interviews or locate research materials. A hearty thanks to the booking agents, publishers, publicists, managers and record company personnel who made *The Billboard Book of Number One Country Hits* a priority in their hectic schedules.

Thanks go as well to ASCAP, BMI, SESAC, the Country Music Association, the Grand Ole Opry, Pam Green, Belinda Pruyne, Lydia Dixon-Harden and the Nashville Songwriters Association, who were all helpful in locating many of the people (including one I thought was dead!) that I interviewed for the book.

Thanks to Don Roy for his help in tracking down information on Jerry Wallace, and to Alan Mayor for his photographs. Thanks also to the Country Music Foundation, for its endless stream of resource materials, and John Morthland's *The Best of Country Music*. I'm also indebted to Jeff Rosenblum, whose specialized computer program made researching and retaining much of the information possible.

Robyn Wells, Jonathan Pillot, Denise Oliver and Janet Bozeman deserve special recognition for their assistance in pre-production detail work and/or emotional support. Everyone at the Unistar Radio Network also receives applause for overlooking the days when I was "stressed out" and for accommodating my unusual schedule—particularly Ed Salamon, Kevin Rider, Rich Rosenfeld, Mike Fitzgerald, Steve O'Brien, Mikal Ross, Charlie Cook, Peter Shamin and Cindy Sivak.

I'd be remiss to overlook the invaluable contributions of my editors, Tad Lathrop and Fred Weiler, who probably hung up the phone on many occasions and said, "He's worried about this?" Tad, in particular, put my mind at ease after the first deadline, when I really began to feel the pressures that drive many writers to distraction.

Finally, there are those people who, though not directly involved with the book, fall under the heading "when the student is ready, the teacher appears." They include James Eklof, Mark Baumgardner, Leigh Fleming, Margaret Jensen, Gene Cotton, Jim Sharp, Jennifer Bohler, Robert Mulloy, Dr. Donald Taylor, Rev. Robert Williams, Lisa Kennedy, Lisa Nixon, Dana Behrendsen, Wendy Bowman, Marla Stewart, Ann-Marie Scesney, Juanita Butler, Lori Rolet-Pinkerton and John Brejot. Ted Roland, in particular, helped me put the book into perspective during the final months of work.

Contents

Introduction

Although this account of country music's most popular records picks up in the late '60s, the music itself has a rich history, with roots that run deep into the soil of America's beginnings. Drawing on British and Scottish folk ballads brought to America by the early settlers, country music came to life in the rural South. Impoverished farmers and backwoodsmen would sing, *a cappella*, their tales of hardship and tragedy, and hand them down from generation to generation. From such humble beginnings—and common themes like doomed love and poverty—country music has undergone an enormous transformation. It has evolved from a regionally-specialized sound into an idiom that 60 percent of Americans now listen to on a regular basis.

By the 1920s, the picture of country music looked something like this: the banjo and fiddle were being played at country dances, social gatherings, and fiddlers' contests; black railroad workers were popularizing the guitar in mountain areas; and bright, church-inspired harmonies were springing up alongside the doleful tones of traditional folk music. In 1922, the first country record, Eck Robertson and Henry Gillilard's "Sally Goodin'"/"Arkansaw Traveller," appeared; surprisingly, that opening salvo was produced in the urban confines of New York City. Five years later, in Bristol, Tennessee, Ralph Peer recorded the Carter Family and Jimmie Rodgers on the same day.

Record companies didn't even know what to call this rustic brew, so they labeled it "familiar tunes," "old-time southern songs," or "hill-country melodies." But regardless of what it was called, the music establishment looked on it derisively as crude corn-pone. While songwriters in other fields earned income for the public performances of their songs, country writers—like their rhythm & blues counterparts—made money only from the sale of sheet music. Since no one else would perform their songs, country writers had to, so that the typical country performer also wrote his own material. Those writers who weren't performers composed only in their spare time, after working during the day at their primary jobs.

The establishment may have scoffed at "hillbilly music" (as it was dubbed in 1925), but American farmers and the working class embraced it. Thanks to radio and the phonograph, distinctive regional styles started melding together. The Grand Ole Opry—originally just another local radio show—brought performers like "Uncle" Dave Macon and Roy Acuff to the entire eastern half of the United States every weekend. In the pre-television '20s and '30s, families starved for entertainment would gather round their only radio every Saturday night to hear the "barn dances" beamed live from Nashville.

Advances in recording technology were altering the music itself. The advent of sensitive microphones meant that voices could be picked up more easily, so that the emphasis in recorded country music began shifting toward harmonies and vocal nuances. In addition, during the '40s, changes in the structure of the music business made it possible for country writers to eventually collect royalties for the performance of their creations. Songwriters started turning out more sophisticated, high-quality compositions.

At the same time, country performers were becoming more visible and their successes more conspicuous. A case in point is Jimmie Rodgers, "The Singing Brakeman." Rodgers' earnings of $100,000 a year (at the peak of his career) sent a signal to other performers that, indeed, there was money to be made in this endeavor. Singing cowboys like Gene Autry and Tex Ritter, fabricated by Hollywood, lent respectability to country music, though what they sang veered closer to Tin Pan Alley pop than rough-hewn rural sounds. Nonetheless, these singing cowboys inspired hordes of aspiring country and even pop stars to pick up a guitar.

New markets opened up, new faces entered the country derby, and new musical forms like Western Swing, bluegrass, and honky-tonk emerged. Western Swing, pioneered by Bob Wills, blended country instrumentation with other styles—Dixieland then big-band jazz, fiddle-guitar duets, blues, polka, and Cajun/Tex-Mex music. Bill Monroe's music, later dubbed bluegrass, featured quicksilver fingerwork on the guitar, mandolin, fiddle, and banjo, overlaid with high vocal harmonies. As its name suggests, honky-tonk came from rough-and-tumble Texas bars, where performers needed electric amplification to be heard over crowd noise—thus Ernest Tubb's groundbreaking work in bringing the electric guitar into the country framework.

No one influenced the growth of country music more than Hank Williams. Signed in 1946 to Nashville's first publishing company, Acuff-Rose, Hank rapidly became the genre's first superstar, and within a scant six years, he redefined the boundaries of country music. His songs were covered by pop performers like Tony Bennett and Jo Stafford, enlarging American appreciation for such chillingly plaintive songs as "I'm So Lonesome I Could Cry" and "Your Cheatin' Heart."

As a result of Williams' success, country music broke open in the '50s. Artists like Ernest Tubb, Webb Pierce and Lefty Frizzell continued to play a honky-tonk sound, while Eddy Arnold and Marty Robbins broadened the music's influence. Ironically, a performer from the ranks of country music almost single-handedly killed off the format. Elvis Presley made his initial impact in country music, but once RCA bought his contract from Sun Records, his explosive blend of country, rockabilly, and R & B threatened to put an end to the "pure" (i.e. Grand Ole Opry-endorsed) country music that had drawn musicians and businessmen to Nashville. Steered toward Hollywood by his manager, Colonel Tom Parker, Elvis all but ignored country music for a decade and a half.

With rock and roll taking the country by storm, country suffered a lull in the latter part of the '50s. At the same time, however, *hybrid* forms of country were making inroads. Johnny Cash followed a path similar to Presley's, gaining mass appeal with his distinctive brand of rockabilly on the Sun label. Jerry Lee Lewis made waves with his pumping piano—a sound rooted in black boogie-woogie from the wrong side of the tracks—and the Everly Brothers' sweet harmonies, suffused with the "high and lonesome" bluegrass sound, had a sweeping influence on pop performers everywhere.

The following decade saw the peak of country's "glitter" era, as the rhinestone suits of Porter Wagoner and Bill Anderson, among many others, sparkled both on concert stages and national television shows. Ray Price, meanwhile, strove for a more adult/contemporary sound, adding a string section to some of his recordings. Likewise, the efforts of record producers Owen Bradley, Don Law and Chet Atkins helped to create a nebulous style called The Nashville Sound.

"The Nashville Sound" refers more to the way country records were made than to the music itself. A group of session players would lay down an unobtrusive instrumental bed with the singer performing live; the producer would then "sweeten" the tracks with strings, choirs, horns, whatever, as an overdub. At its best, this system brought smoothness and sophistication to country music; at its worst, it substituted the raw, heartfelt vitality of "white man's blues" with a slick pop sheen, just to make the music more palatable for pop/easy listening audiences. The Nashville Sound came to dominate—and, for many listeners, epitomize—country music for much of the '60s and early '70s.

Several major trends have waxed and waned since then, many of them in reaction to The Nashville Sound. Honky-tonk made a brief comeback in the early '60s, with The Bakersfield Sound spearheaded by Buck Owens and Merle Haggard restoring some of country's grit. At one point, thanks to Bob Dylan's *Nashville Skyline*, it was fashionable for every self-respecting rock artist to record in Nashville; soon groups like the Byrds, Poco, and the Eagles were crafting the hybrid called country rock. There was the rough sound of the "outlaw" movement, led by Willie Nelson and Waylon Jennings, as well as the slick approach of the *Urban Cowboy* period. More recently, the back-to-basics stance of the New Traditionalist movement seems to be the order of the day.

Despite the fluctuations of styles and the year-to-year swings in the overall sales of country music, the format has experienced a fairly steady growth in its 70-year history. *Billboard* started measuring the sales of individual records in 1944 with the publication of its country chart. By that time, Ernest Tubb had persuaded the industry to drop the "hillbilly" monicker, in favor of "country & western." Eventually, Nashville regarded even "C & W" as a disparaging label, and the format was dubbed "country." The National Academy of Recording Arts and Sciences officially changed its Grammy category from "country & western" to "country" for the 1968 eligibility year—which is why *The Billboard Book of Number One Country Hits* kicks off in 1968.

Readers familiar with *The Billboard Book of Number One Hits* will soon discover that country artists make records in a different context than their Top 40 counterparts. More often than not, performers do not write their own songs. They tour more frequently than other musicians do, and that forces most of them to rely on people who can devote a greater portion of their time to writing. Thus, thousands of writers are centered in Nashville, struggling to land songs with maybe a hundred recording artists. They shop their songs through a "demo tape," a not-for-sale recording that can feature anything from a simple guitar-and-vocal arrangement to a full-blown production job, complete with strings. The artists then sift through the hundreds or thousands of demos they receive, and pick material to record for an album. From there, a lucky two or three songs become singles, and only a tiny fraction of the singles that come out each year make it all the way to number one.

Thus, the songwriter commands more respect in Nashville than his/her peers in Los Angeles or New York. Tunesmiths like Harlan Howard, Bob McDill or Hank Cochran have made lifetime careers out of chronicling very basic human emotions and situations. Their stories are as integral to a study of individual country records as the stories of the musicians themselves.

Since much of country music emanates from Nashville, the community has become unusually—and understandably—protective of its product. The city, its journalists, and its fans, have grown almost obsessive in defining the country sound. Radio stations often feel forced to evaluate a record's validity by identifying its instruments—"Is that a steel guitar in there?"—and Music City has mixed feelings about artists "crossing over" from country airplay into the pop field. On the one hand, the record labels want their music to reach as many people as possible, generating more income; the artists themselves frequently want to expand their audiences. But on the other

hand, the industry seems to demand that crossover success occur by accident: the audience, and the business, views an artist who concentrates on a pop career skeptically, as if he or she has abandoned country altogether. Thus, artists whose wide-ranging musical tastes cannot be rigidly defined or pigeonholed—people like Ronnie Milsap or Dolly Parton—must handle their careers almost as delicately as one would handle a glass figurine.

Those country artists who have been successful over the long haul—as well as those who have had only fleeting glory—are all contained in *The Billboard Book of Number One Country Hits*. The stories behind these songs seem to mirror the very basic emotions they try so desperately to capture—from the tragic to the humorous, from the mundane to the bizarre. Taken as a whole, these number one singles might well represent every emotion known to man.

A few notes about the entries in *The Billboard Book of Number One Country Hits:*

On occasion, a few records have hit the top with the benefit of airplay on both sides. In that instance, *Billboard* has frequently listed both titles on the chart, separated simply by a slash, and I've done the same thing. (For this type of entry, a slash also separates the respective writers and producers for "A" and "B" sides.) In some instances, however, two sides from the same single achieved different peak positions. Nonetheless, both are listed here, with the side that reached number one listed first. Conway Twitty has the one exception: both "Touch The Hand" and "Don't Cry Joni" received heavy airplay, but they didn't make their chart runs simultaneously. Only "Touch The Hand" is listed.

Janie Frickie remained something of an enigma until the closing weeks of the editing process. She started her career spelling her name "Fricke," but changed it when even her fellow performers had trouble pronouncing it correctly off the cue cards at awards shows. Since she now goes under the "Frickie" spelling, all references to Janie use the "–ie" ending, even though all but her last number one single used the original spelling.

Number One Country Hits

1
SING ME BACK HOME
MERLE HAGGARD
& THE STRANGERS

Capitol 2017
Writer: Merle Haggard
Producer: Ken Nelson
January 20, 1968 (2 weeks)

In December of 1957, Merle Haggard was convicted of an offense that earned him a spot in *The Book of Lists #3*, among "19 Stupid Thieves." Haggard and a friend, Micky Gorham, tried to break into a restaurant in California after hours. As it turned out, the establishment was actually still open; Merle was caught and served time at San Quentin.

His incarceration was a pivotal event. In the midst of his sentence, he endured seven days of isolation for making moonshine, and he emerged from his cell determined to turn his life around. Upon his release in 1960, he turned to music as a legitimate vocation.

Haggard had been a member of the audience for one of Johnny Cash's appearances at San Quentin [see 40—"A Boy Named Sue"], and Cash later convinced Haggard to be candid with the public about his prison experiences. It was a wise piece of advice, and prison themes underscored each of Merle's first three number one singles.

The first, "I'm A Lonesome Fugitive," was written by Liz and Casey Anderson [see 78—"You're My Man"], and reached the top on March 4, 1967. On September 2, Merle returned to number one with his own composition, "Branded Man." "Sing Me Back Home" followed in the same vein, though the title is not quite so obviously linked to prison.

"Sing Me Back Home" is the tale of a Death Row prisoner, bound for execution, whose last request is a song that will remind him of home. It was based on a man Haggard knew in San Quentin, Jimmy "Rabbit" Hendricks. Hendricks had escaped and killed a policeman on the outside, and a San Francisco court handed down a death sentence.

"Even though the crime was brutal and the guy was an incorrigible criminal, it's a feeling you never forget when you seen someone you know make that last walk," Haggard told Bob Eubanks in *Billboard*. "They bring him through the yard, and there's a guard in front and a guard behind—that's how you know a death prisoner.

"They brought 'Rabbit' out, and a bunch of guys who knew him were sitting around as he came through the yard. That was a strong picture that was left in my mind. Later, one time when we were driving through North Carolina, the 'Sing Me Back Home' thing came out of it."

2
SKIP A ROPE
HENSON CARGILL

Monument 1041
Writers: Jack Moran, Glenn D. Tubb
Producer: Don Law
February 3, 1968 (5 weeks)

When Henson Cargill became an "overnight sensation" in 1968, it was the perfect melding of a castaway song and a castaway artist.

Already established in Las Vegas, Cargill had made two previous trips to Nashville, attracting absolutely no interest. On his third trip, he met up with record producer Don Law, who took a different viewpoint. Law wasn't interested in any of Cargill's material, but he did see potential in the Oklahoma City native.

The night before their first recording session, Cargill ran into another former Oklahoman, Tom Hartman, who had once been a disk jockey in the Sooner State capital. Hartman was pitching songs for Tree Publishing, and he played Cargill a song called "Skip A Rope," which had already made the rounds in Nashville without catching a single taker.

Cargill liked "Skip A Rope," and the next day, he and Law recorded it, although even then it seemed destined to fall by the wayside. Johnny Cash had taken an interest, but he was willing to let Cargill take the first crack at it, and Law made an arrangement with the publishers that gave him 90 days to secure a record deal before any other artists could record it.

Once again, the Nashville establishment was hesitant to take on "Skip A Rope," which blamed such problems as dishonesty and racism on parents. "Nobody ever stepped on anybody's toes in country music," Cargill later told Covey Bean in the *Sunday Oklahoman*. "It was a heavy lyric to put out in a country market, and they didn't think it would work."

The one company willing to give it a shot was Monument Records, and it proved a wise investment. Cargill signed with absolutely no advance, and within 90 days of the song's release, "Skip A Rope" had sold more than 500,000 copies. It stayed at number one on the *Billboard* country charts for five straight weeks and also hit number 25 on the pop charts. One year later, Cargill scored his only other Top Ten single, "None Of My Business."

Cargill's family tree was actually quite impressive. His grandfather had been the mayor of Oklahoma City, and his father was a prominent attorney. In fact, Cargill had worked as a deputy sheriff before establishing himself in Las Vegas. After his successful peak in Nashville, he returned to Oklahoma City, where he opened a nightclub called Henson's, now located in nearby Norman.

3
TAKE ME TO YOUR WORLD
TAMMY WYNETTE
Epic 10269
Writers: Billy Sherrill, Glenn Sutton
Producer: Billy Sherrill
March 9, 1968 (1 week)

Ever since Tammy Wynette first entered the *Billboard* country chart on December 10, 1966, with "Apartment #9," journalists have struggled to find the perfect description of her unique vocal delivery. Perhaps author Joan Dew said it best in her book *Singers and Sweethearts: The Women in Country Music*, when she described Tammy's "tearful" style as "the voice of every heartbreak a woman has ever known."

Heartbreak has been, in fact, a dominant feature of Wynette's lifestyle—both before her rise to popularity and since—but the early years of her career read more like a fairy tale.

Born Virginia Wynette Pugh, in Itawamba County, Mississippi, on May 5, 1942, she first met producer Billy Sherrill because his secretary was away from her desk. Wynette sang with a guitar in his office that day, and Sherrill said if she could find the right song, he'd record her. The next time she appeared at the office, he played a tape of "Apartment #9" for her, and suggested she use "Tammy" for a stage name. Sherrill also promised to put her hometown on the map.

That happened almost immediately. She followed "Apartment #9" with "Your Good Girl's Gonna Go Bad" (number three) in 1967, and when she teamed with David Houston on

Henson Cargill

"(My) Elusive Dreams" [see 9—"Have A Little Faith"], she went to number one for the very first time on September 16.

"I Don't Wanna Play House," written by Sherrill with Glenn Sutton, brought her to number one as a solo vocalist one month later, and "Take Me To Your World," *again* written by Sherrill and Sutton, achieved the same peak position.

"'Take Me To Your World' was a song that was written for another girl with the name Beverly Byrd," explains Sutton. "I had signed her, and I cut it on her, and Billy wanted to write the strings for it, so he did the string arrangement after I did the rhythm track on it." After the tracks were laid down, though,

Sherrill decided it would work better if they had Wynette record it.

"I remember thinking 'Oh, no, don't put strings on it,'" says Tammy. "That was the first song I had that had strings on it, and I thought, 'Oh, you're going to ruin me; that's so pop-sounding, and everyone will think I'm going pop.'"

4

A WORLD OF OUR OWN
SONNY JAMES

Capitol 2067
Writer: Tom Springfield
Producer: George Richey
March 16, 1968 (3 weeks)

By the time Sonny James appeared at number one on March 16, 1968, "A World Of Our Own" was part of a growing legend in country music. James made his very first appearance on the *Billboard* chart exactly a dozen years earlier (March 14, 1956) with "For Rent," a single that peaked at number 12.

When "A World Of Our Own" reached the top of that list, it marked James' eighth trip to number one. His prior successes (and the dates they first reached number one) were:

"Young Love" (Feb. 16, 1957; 7 weeks)
"You're The Only World I Know" (Jan. 23, 1965; 4 weeks)
"Behind The Tear" (Oct. 9, 1965; 2 weeks)
"Take Good Care Of Her" (June 18, 1966; 2 weeks)
"Need You" (Apr. 29, 1967; 2 weeks)
"I'll Never Find Another You" (Aug. 5, 1967; 4 weeks)
"It's The Little Things" (Nov. 18, 1967; 5 weeks)

"A World Of Our Own" continued a streak James started with "Need You"—it was his fourth consecutive single to reach number one. It was also his second cover of a song that was originally a pop hit for the Seekers.

Hailing from Australia, the Seekers were a folk group that gained a worldwide audience after moving to England in 1964. Their biggest recording was "Georgy Girl," a number two single from 1966, but that was their third entry on the *Billboard* Hot 100. "I'll Never Find Another You" was their first Top Ten single; in 1965, they followed it with "A World Of Our Own," which reached number 19.

Sonny remade both of their first two chart singles, and both were written by Englishman Tom Springfield, who journeyed to Nashville to accept songwriter awards for the two compositions after Sonny recorded them. It was Springfield's first opportunity to talk with James in person.

"When we met, he was talking about how when he first heard the records, he liked them," James recalls. "He said he never dreamed when he wrote the song that that kind of arrangement could work. He said he really liked it—that it was a fresh approach to the song.

"He's an excellent writer, but when he came here to win those awards, you'd think he'd never won one before. I was so happy to get the songs, I thought *I* should be the one that was jumping up and down."

5

HOW LONG WILL MY BABY BE GONE
BUCK OWENS & HIS BUCKAROOS

Capitol 2080
Writer: Buck Owens
Producer: Ken Nelson
April 6, 1968 (1 week)

Buck Owens has often compared the early years of his life to the John Steinbeck novel *The Grapes of Wrath*, and the analogy is quite appropriate. He was born Alvis Edgar Owens, Jr., on August 12, 1929—just a couple of months before the stock-market crash on October 29.

Owens grew up in Sherman, Texas, where he chose his own nickname, asking his parents to call him "Buck," after one of their horses. Like the Joad family in *The Grapes of Wrath*, the Owens clan fell on hard times during the Depression and set off for California. The car broke down in Arizona, though, and they decided to settle in Mesa.

At age 20, Owens moved to Bakersfield to work as a musician on the local club scene. He played for seven steady years at The Blackboard, and became one of the most in-demand musicians in the area, playing on records by Tennessee Ernie Ford, Sonny James and Tommy Sands. He also took Ferlin Husky's place as a member of Tommy Collins' band.

In 1959, Owens emerged as a co-writer, with Harlan Howard, of Kitty Wells' Top Five record, "Mommy For A Day." By the end of the year, he notched his own Top Five single, "Under Your Spell Again." In 1963, he hit the number one position with "Act Naturally," the first of 21 chart-toppers.

Through the next six years, Buck racked up such number one releases as "Love's Gonna Live Here" (which stayed at the top for 16 weeks), "My Heart Skips A Beat," "Together Again," and his best-seller, "I've Got A Tiger By The Tail." With the release of "Buckaroo" in 1965, he credited his backing band on the label of each of his singles. He continued to reach the top regularly, with "Waitin' In Your Welfare Line" and "Think Of Me," among others.

"How Long Will My Baby Be Gone" was the sixteenth in Owens' collection of number one singles. "It's just a song I wrote," Owens says modestly of the rhythmic composition. "I thought it was a different approach and a different thing, and it turned out all right."

6

YOU ARE MY TREASURE
JACK GREENE
Decca 32261
Writer: Cindy Walker
Producer: Owen Bradley
April 13, 1968 (1 week)

"You Are My Treasure" was the third number one record for Jack Greene, who had already spent a dozen weeks at the top in 1966 and 1967.

"There Goes My Everything" became Greene's first single to hit number one—it reached that position in December 1966. The song was written by Dallas Frazier, and Jack's first wife insisted that Greene record it. The Jordanaires helped him change the melody on the last line. Recorded in three takes, "Everything" went on to a seven-week run at the top.

Half a year later, Greene followed up by remaking a Mel Tillis composition, "All The Time." Owen Bradley had produced another version of the song for Kitty Wells in 1959, which reached number eighteen on *Billboard*'s country charts as the "B" side of her number five recording, "Mommy For A Day."

When Greene released "All The Time" as an "A" side, another Frazier song, "Wanting You But Never Having You," was picked as its "B" side, and it charted as well. "At that session," Greene remembers, "we didn't do the three or

Jack Greene

four sides that we normally do. Those were the only two records that we had in the can that we felt were good at all. We felt that to make this follow-up record strongest, both of them were 'A' sides, and Owen said, 'Let's put both of them on the same record.'"

Buoyed by a "concerto"-type piano sound from Floyd Cramer, "All The Time" emerged at number one for five weeks starting on June 17, 1967. In December, *Billboard* named it the number one country single of the entire year.

Greene peaked at number two with his next single, "What Locks The Door," but he returned to the top with "You Are My Treasure." The tune was written specifically for him by Cindy Walker, who had heard Jack on Nashville's WSM radio in an interview with Ralph Emery. "She said that I had a certain quality in my voice when I talked," notes Greene, "and she wanted to write a song around that and do a recitation."

After Walker sent the song to Bradley, he asked if he could record it with Bill Anderson, well-known for his long line of recitations. Walker declined, insisting that "Treasure" was designed only for Greene, and Bradley recorded it with 30 musicians (including a string section) all present in the studio at the same time.

7

FIST CITY
LORETTA LYNN
Decca 32264
Writer: Loretta Lynn
Producer: Owen Bradley
April 20, 1968 (1 week)

Many of Loretta Lynn's biggest records—especially in the early years of her career—were based on real-life experiences involving her husband, O. V. Lynn (often called "Mooney" or "Doo"), who is credited with pushing her into an entertainment career.

"That's enough to kill him for," laughs Loretta. "He got me in the business, and after about a year and a half, or two years, he said, 'You're a big girl now; you're on your own.'"

"Fist City," one of Lynn's most underrated compositions, revolved around Mooney. She wrote it about a woman who lived five miles away from them in Nashville. That lady would often show up at clubs where Lynn was appearing, making a play for Loretta's husband while

Loretta was on stage. The song was a bit of a personal message, advising her competitor to back off, or be ready to fight.

"Fist City" was Lynn's second number one single, following "Don't Come Home A-Drinkin' (With Lovin' On Your Mind)," a controversial 1966 record that was banned on several radio stations, including Chicago's WJJD. Earlier that year, Loretta came close with "You Ain't Woman Enough," which stalled at number two behind David Houston's "Almost Persuaded" [see 9—"Have A Little Faith"].

"Loretta's style was based on defying her husband or anybody else that got in her way," suggests producer Owen Bradley. " 'Fist City' sort of says it all. When we cut that, we were finishing up an album, and she came into town just to do that. We had a terrible snow—she barely got out of town, and she barely got back to Nashville the next day."

"Fist City" brought Lynn's total to a dozen Top Ten country singles in a career that dated back to 1960. Her very first record, "Honky Tonk Girl" (released on Norm Burley's Seattle-based Zero Records), reached number 14. Burley paid for Loretta and Mooney to drive across country to promote the record to radio stations; during that trip, they met a Tucson disk jockey named Waylon Jennings.

Loretta first appeared on the Grand Ole Opry on October 15, 1960, and two years later, she became a permanent member. That same year, she signed with Decca Records, and her debut Decca single, "Success," became her first Top Ten release. Other successes followed, including "Wine, Women And Song," "Blue Kentucky Girl" and "If You're Not Gone Too Long."

8

THE LEGEND OF BONNIE AND CLYDE
MERLE HAGGARD & THE STRANGERS
Capitol 2123
Writer: Merle Haggard
Producer: Ken Nelson
April 27, 1968 (2 weeks)

"I got into everything I could get into, just for the excitement of it sometimes," recalls Merle Haggard, describing his youth. "I never hurt anybody, though; I might have inconvenienced a few people, but I sure wasn't no Bonnie and Clyde."

That didn't stop him from singing about those two infamous characters, though. In 1967, Warren Beatty and Faye Dunaway starred in *Bonnie and Clyde*, which earned ten Academy Award nominations. Haggard saw the film six times, and it inspired him to write his own ode to the criminal couple.

"My idols were the wrong people," he explained to Alanna Nash in *Behind Closed Doors*. "I idolized Jesse James, Bonnie and Clyde, and those people, I presume because of the movies and the way that people like that were dramatized and made out to be heroes."

Haggard & The Strangers recorded "The Legend Of Bonnie And Clyde" at the Capitol Studios, located at 1750 North Vine Street in Hollywood. That same studio had also yielded such hits as Al Martino's "Spanish Eyes," Bobbie Gentry's "Ode To Billie Joe" and Glen Campbell's "By The Time I Get To Phoenix" [see 10—"I Wanna Live"].

Campbell, in fact, played both guitar and banjo, and provided back-up vocals on "The Legend Of Bonnie And Clyde." A longtime studio session player, Campbell had amassed an incredible resumé as a hitmaker. He participated in Elvis Presley's "Viva Las Vegas," Frank Sinatra's "Strangers In The Night" and the Monkees' "I'm A Believer," but his relationship with Haggard was particularly special.

Campbell had brought a copy of "By The Time I Get To Phoenix" to Haggard in the Capitol Studios just after recording it. Though Capitol would ship the single, Merle offered to send out copies of the record as well, along with his own mailing of "Sing Me Back Home" [see 1]. "By The Time I Get To Phoenix" offered stiff competition, peaking at number two. "Merle jokes with Glen," laughs Haggard's steel player, Norm Hamlet, "and says, 'That's the last time I send your record out.'"

The "B" side of "The Legend Of Bonnie And Clyde" was "Today I Started Loving You Again" [see 72—"Help Me Make It Through The Night"]. Though Haggard's version never charted, it became a country standard, recorded by more than 100 different artists.

9
HAVE A LITTLE FAITH
DAVID HOUSTON
Epic 10291
Writers: Billy Sherrill, Glenn Sutton
Producer: Billy Sherrill
May 11, 1968 (1 week)

David Houston is responsible for a couple of firsts in the record business. On October 19, 1963, his "Mountain Of Love" entered the *Billboard* country charts, making it the first hit released by Epic Records, a sister label of Columbia. "Mountain Of Love" eventually peaked at number two, but on August 13, 1966, David's "Almost Persuaded" began a nine-week stay at number one, making it the first song written and/or produced by Billy Sherrill to reach the top.

Winning two Grammy awards (for Best Country Vocal Performance by a Male and Best Song), "Almost Persuaded" occurred as a fluke. Houston was scheduled to record "We Got Love" at 8:00 A.M., and took a room at the Sam Davis Hotel in Nashville. The day before the session, he still needed a "B" side, and Sherrill and Glenn Sutton worked down to the wire on material.

"They had a verse and a chorus written," Houston recalls. "Billy wouldn't come up in that hotel 'cause it didn't have an elevator, and he was afraid the thing was going to catch on fire. He'd send Glenn up there with the song. They had a verse and chorus of it finished at 12:00 at night."

Sherrill and Sutton finished the second verse overnight, and Houston recorded "Almost Persuaded" that morning, with Hargus "Pig" Robbins providing a simple but crucial keyboard line. The record shipped with "We Got Love" as the hit, but Mac Curtis flipped it over during a morning radio show on WPLO in Atlanta, and audience response guaranteed "Almost Persuaded"'s success.

In July of 1967, "With One Exception" took Houston to number one again, and on September 16, Houston appeared once more at the top with "(My) Elusive Dreams," a duet with Tammy Wynette. One week later, Houston & Wynette remained at number one, while Houston entered the chart with a solo single, "You Mean The World To Me." Based on a classical piece titled "Lieberstrong," it likewise spent two weeks at the top in November.

"Have A Little Faith," with back-up vocals by the Jordanaires, was Houston's fifth chart-topping single. Johnny Cash had used trumpets on "Ring Of Fire" in 1963, but "Have A Little Faith" is believed to be the first single ever to use brass in unison with a steel guitar.

"Have A Little Faith" reached number one three days after the death of George D. Hay. Known as "The Solemn Old Judge," Hay originated "The WSM Barn Dance," which he later re-dubbed the Grand Ole Opry.

Bobby Goldsboro

10

I WANNA LIVE

GLEN CAMPBELL

Capitol 2146
Writer: John D. Loudermilk
Producer: Al De Lory
May 18, 1968 (3 weeks)

Glen Campbell had been recording for Capitol Records for seven years when his star finally shone for the first time. He hit *Billboard*'s Hot 100 in 1961, with "Turn Around, Look At Me," and sporadically charted during the next six years on both the country and pop charts.

In the meantime, he became one of the most respected studio musicians on the West Coast, commanding an annual income of $50,000 to $70,000. His goal was to make his own hits, though, and frustration began to take its toll. "I'd given up, and was going into commercial work with Chuck Blore," he told *Billboard*'s Ron Tepper in 1970, "and then it happened."

"It" was a meteoric rise to national prominence, beginning in 1967. Campbell recorded John Hartford's "Gentle On My Mind," which went to number 30 (15 months later, he re-released it, reaching number 44). The follow-up was "By The Time I Get To Phoenix," which peaked at number two.

Just six months later, Glen earned his very first chart-topping single with ace songwriter John D. Loudermilk's "I Wanna Live." Later inducted into the Nashville Songwriters Hall of Fame, Loudermilk wrote the number one country singles "Then You Can Tell Me Goodbye" [see 18], by Eddy Arnold; "Abilene," by George Hamilton IV; "Waterloo," by Stonewall Jackson; and "Talk Back Trembling Lips," by Ernie Ashworth. He also wrote "Indian Reservation," a number one pop hit for Paul Revere & The Raiders.

After debuting on April 13, 1968, "I Wanna Live" reached the number one position in its sixth week on the chart. Bobby Goldsboro's "Honey" [see 11] took over the top spot the following week, and three weeks later, Campbell returned to number one for another two-week run.

Notes Glen: "I just liked it because of what it said: 'I want to live, live and let live/I want all the love that life has to give,' and I still hold on to that principle, too. 'I want to live, and let you live some, too'—I wish the world was like that."

11

HONEY

BOBBY GOLDSBORO

United Artists 50283
Writer: Bobby Russell
Producer: Bob Montgomery
May 25, 1968 (3 weeks)

Before 1968, Bobby Goldsboro had never appeared on the country chart. A one-time member of Roy Orbison's band, he gained his first hit as a solo performer in 1964, with "See The Funny Little Clown," a self-penned single that reached number nine on the pop chart. Bobby failed to return to the Top Ten, though, until 1968, when "Honey" went to number one on both the Hot 100 and the country chart.

Goldsboro and producer Bob Montgomery had to make a deal to record the song in the first place. Songwriter Bobby Russell had produced it with former Kingston Trio member Bob Shane, and Russell only allowed Goldsboro and Montgomery to cut it with the promise that it couldn't be released without his approval.

"The session on 'Honey' was unreal," Bobby told Jim Bickhart of *Billboard*. "We cut it right the first take, tried it again just to see if something was wrong, and it came out just as well the second time, so we went with the second take."

The session took place on January 30, 1968, at RCA's Nashville studios, and, in a rare situation, all of the musicians stayed long enough to hear the playback. "All of us that played that night knew it was going to be a big record," says piano player Larry Butler. "In fact, most of us called our wives at home so we could play it for them over the phone."

Shane's record was still in release, though, and Montgomery had to stick by his agreement to keep the Goldsboro version "in the can," until he received a call from a promotion man who was working the record. According to Montgomery, "Bob Holiday called me and said, 'If you call Russell right now, he'll tell you to put that record out 'cause he's pissed off at Decca over something. If you catch him right now he'll tell you to put it out.' So I did, and sure enough, he said, 'I don't give a damn what you do.'"

UA rush-released "Honey," and Goldsboro's version sold a million copies in its first three weeks, on its way to global sales of more than six million. It was the best-selling record worldwide for the entire year.

Goldsboro's only other Top Ten country single came three years later, with "Watching Scotty Grow."

12

D-I-V-O-R-C-E

TAMMY WYNETTE

Epic 10315
Writers: Bobby Braddock, Curly Putman
Producer: Billy Sherrill
June 29, 1968 (3 weeks)

Prior to life as an entertainer, Tammy Wynette held a wide range of vocations, working in a shoe factory, a doctor's office, the cotton fields and a hair salon. She acted as a spelling teacher, though, in her 1968 classic "D-I-V-O-R-C-E," a song that capitalized on the common parental trick by which Mom or Dad spells out words to keep secrets from the kids.

In 1966, Bobby Braddock played piano on the road as a member of Marty Robbins' band, but the following year, he signed with Tree Publishing in Nashville, and one of the first songs he wrote at the time started out as "I L-O-V-E Y-O-U (Do I Have To Spell It Out For You)." "Somehow it turned into 'D-I-V-O-R-C-E,'" says Braddock, "and I did a demo on it, but I was never able to get anybody to record it."

In the early part of 1968, Tree song plugger Curly Putman noted that "D-I-V-O-R-C-E" was "too happy for such a sad song," and Braddock, in fact, characterizes the original melody as simply "goofy."

"Basically, most of the words were there," recalls Curly. "We might have changed a line here or there, but I worked with him to smooth the song out a little bit and changed the melody." Putman wanted no part of the royalties, but Braddock insisted he get a piece of the earnings. "The song had never stirred up that much interest until Curly made those changes," Braddock explains, "and what he did just really brought it to life."

On February 29, Wynette earned a Grammy award for her performance on "I Don't Wanna Play House" [see 3—"Take Me To Your World"], and that same night, Braddock told producer Billy Sherrill about his new song. The following day, Putman and Braddock delivered it personally to Sherrill at the Epic offices.

"I just went ba-na-nas," Sherrill relates. Tammy had the same reaction.

"I remember thinking when I first heard the song, 'How ridiculous that I didn't write this song, because how many times have I spelled out words in front of my kids?' I was doing it at the time—it went right along with my life."

13

FOLSOM PRISON BLUES
JOHNNY CASH
Columbia 44513
Writer: Johnny Cash
Producer: Bob Johnston
July 20, 1968 (4 weeks)

"Folsom Prison Blues" provided a link between Johnny Cash's Sun days and his peak years with the Columbia label. Legally born J.R. Cash (the military wouldn't accept initials, so he chose John as his first name), he first came to national notice in 1955 on Sam Phillips' Memphis-based label, with "Cry, Cry, Cry."

For the next two-and-a-half years, Cash held a dominant position in country music, with 15 Top Ten singles. Four of them—"I Walk The Line," "There You Go," "Ballad Of A Teenage Queen" and "Guess Things Happen That Way"—went all the way to number one.

Sun, in fact, was the first label to release "Folsom Prison Blues," a song he wrote a few months after "Cry, Cry, Cry" landed on the *Billboard* chart. Cash was to catch a plane out of Memphis, but, with a few hours to kill before departure, he ducked into a movie theater to pass the time. The film just happened to be *Inside the Walls of Folsom Prison*, and Johnny was instantly caught up in the tale of its primary character, a convict.

Once on the plane, he put pencil to paper, refused the complimentary meal, and crafted the lyrics in less than an hour. After another hour, he invented the melody, and the following day, he worked up the arrangement with guitarist Luther Perkins and bassist Marshall Grant.

Johnny recorded "Folsom Prison Blues" in late 1955, but Phillips judged it inappropriate for the Christmas season. He delayed its release until the following year, when it peaked at the number four position.

Cash signed with Columbia on August 1, 1958, and almost ten years later, "Folsom" re-emerged as an even bigger live recording. In the meantime, Johnny had racked up three more number one singles: "Don't Take Your Guns To Town," "Ring Of Fire" and "Understand Your Man."

The live *Folsom Prison* album was recorded in his second appearance at the institution, and the title track spent four weeks at number one.

"By doing a prison concert, we were letting inmates know that somewhere in the free world was somebody who cared for them as human beings," Cash wrote in his autobiography, *Man in Black*. "With fewer crimes in our land, on our streets, as our aim, maybe when those men were paroled back into society's mainstream, there'd be less hostility knowing someone had cared."

14

HEAVEN SAYS HELLO
SONNY JAMES
Capitol 2155
Writer: Cindy Walker
Producer: Kelso Herston
August 17, 1968 (1 week)

Born James Loden on May 1, 1929, Sonny James grew up in a musical family on a farm near Hackleburg, Alabama, a community of about 700. Nicknamed "Sonny," he started playing guitar when he was just three years old, using a homemade instrument fashioned with the bottom of a molasses bucket.

In 1933, James made his stage debut with the Loden family band in a Birmingham folk contest. Singer Kate Smith reportedly presented the youngster with a silver dollar that day, and predicted a bright future for Loden. By age ten, in fact, those predictions were already coming true, as he racked up five different fiddle championships in the Mid-South.

A straight-A high school student, James was offered a college scholarship, but turned it down to further his budding musical career. It was briefly short-circuited by the Korean War, as Loden spent 15 months overseas. Upon his return, he made his way to Nashville, where he spent a week as a guest of Chet Atkins, then working for RCA Records.

Ken Nelson, from the competing Capitol label, came over to visit, and Loden sang a few songs for Nelson in Chet's den. As a result, Loden earned a recording deal with Capitol, and Nelson suggested they drop his real last name and just use "Sonny James."

That name was a veritable fixture on the *Billboard* country charts by 1968, when James scored his fifth consecutive number one single with "Heaven Says Hello." He picked up the tune from longtime friend Cindy Walker, who also wrote "You Don't Know Me" [see 440] and "Cherokee Maiden" [see 265], among others.

Perhaps the most notable element of the tune was the vocal counter-rhythm provided by Millie Kirkham, whose angelic performance was perfect for "Heaven."

"Every song that I used to get, I would go over it many times when I was on the road before I'd ever go in the studio," says James, "and I'd always have this arrangement in my mind. It wasn't written down; it was in my head. I just heard this, and it's really crazy how those arrangements come about. You hear a song, and say, 'How best can I come up with an arrangement without destroying the song?'"

ALREADY IT'S HEAVEN
DAVID HOUSTON
Epic 10338
Writers: Billy Sherrill, Glenn Sutton
Producer: Billy Sherrill
August 24, 1968 (1 week)

D avid Houston hails from rather impressive stock. Born December 9, 1938, in Bossier (pronounced "BO-zhur") City, Louisiana, his ancestors include both Sam Houston, from his father's lineage, and General Robert E. Lee, from his mother's side of the family.

At the age of twelve, Houston auditioned across the river in Shreveport for the "Louisiana Hayride" radio show, and became a regular

David Houston

a few years later, after Slim Whitman paid for his first recording session in 1952. Through the "Hayride," he met Tillman Franks, who managed Johnny Horton. "I was in the car with them on the way to Nashville when they wrote 'Honky Tonk Man,'" Houston notes, "and Grady Martin played my guitar on the session." Houston's own records didn't garner much attention.

After high school, he attended Centenary College in Shreveport. The choir director refused him a position in the choir, so Houston dropped out, returning to spot recording work. Among his sessions at the time was a tune called "Sherry's Lips," recorded with Fred Carter and Bob Montgomery at Sam Phillips' studios in Memphis. The engineer was Billy Sherrill.

Houston then spent several years as an insurance underwriter, and a phone call from Franks prompted him to record "Mountain Of Love" [see 9—"Have A Little Faith"] in Dallas. Franks sold the master to Epic, and Sherrill took over as producer at that point.

"Billy has one way of doing things: his way," Houston says respectfully. "He'd rather have you sit on a stool until it's time to sing, and not voice a lot of opinions. I tried to give my opinion, and it didn't work. He'd go take a piss, and not come back for two hours. He reminds me of George Patton."

Sherrill produced a Coca-Cola commercial with Houston, but they encountered phrasing problems with their sixth number one country single, "Already It's Heaven." Houston's vocals and Pete Drake's steel guitar overlapped, and multiple takes were needed to fix the timing.

"It was a hard record to cut," Houston recalls. "I never have cut an easy hit. They all sound easy, 'cause a hit's supposed to be a song anybody can sing—but it ain't."

16

MAMA TRIED

MERLE HAGGARD & THE STRANGERS

Capitol 2219
Writer: Merle Haggard
Producer: Ken Nelson
August 31, 1968 (4 weeks)

In 1958, 21 was the "legal age," a time when a youngster could legally vote and drink; but when Merle Haggard's twenty-first birthday

arrived, he was in a cell at San Quentin Prison [see 1—"Sing Me Back Home"]. Ten years later, Haggard discussed that circumstance with his band, the Strangers, and it provided a starting point for "Mama Tried."

Much of the song was based on Haggard's own experiences, although he admitted to Wayne Bledsoe of the *Knoxville News-Sentinel* that he took a few liberties: "Instead of life in prison I was doing one-to-fifteen years—I just couldn't get that to rhyme." In all, Merle served two years and nine months at San Quentin; his stay tempered his rebellious attitude. "I look back at it now," he says, "and I wouldn't trade the experience. I did a lot of thinking then; I learned a lot in prison that I might never have known otherwise."

Part of his personal reflection involved the impact of his confinement on his family—particularly on his mother, Flossie, who became the family's sole provider when her husband, James, died from a stroke. Merle was just nine at the time.

"When my father passed away, she had never done anything except be a housewife and raise a garden and can foods so we could make it through the winter, and that type of thing," Haggard explained to Bob Eubanks in *Billboard*. "Fortunately, she had a good education and she stepped out into the world and took a job as a bookkeeper for a meat company. She was lucky enough to make fairly good money for a woman at that time.

"She had a boy who was more than wild. I don't know what I'd have done with me if I had been the parent. I was a child that needed two parents, and there was a period that came up that my mother just couldn't handle. My dad wasn't there and my older brother tried to step in, and, of course, I resented that. It just got all confused and messed up. Mama certainly did try."

As with "The Legend Of Bonnie And Clyde" [see 8], Haggard recruited Glen Campbell for the "Mama Tried" session, and the song appeared in the movie *Killers Three*. Ironically, Haggard played a cop in the film.

17

HARPER VALLEY P.T.A.

JEANNIE C. RILEY

Plantation 3
Writer: Tom T. Hall
Producer: Shelby Singleton, Jr.
September 28, 1968 (3 weeks)

Two summers after Jeannie C. Riley moved from Anson, Texas, to Nashville, with her husband, two kids and a U-Haul trailer in tow, she became a prime example of the old adage about being in the right place at the right time.

Riley performed on demos for several companies in Music City. Although her office skills were hardly up to snuff, her interest in the music business was so keen that songwriter Jerry Chestnut gave her a secretarial job anyway. One of her demos crossed the desk of Shelby Singleton, Jr., and he decided her voice was perfect for "Harper Valley P.T.A.," a song he had picked up from Tom T. Hall six months earlier. The tune was about a sassy woman who'd lived a few miles away from Hall's hometown in Kentucky, and he updated her fight with the local P.T.A. after her child had been spanked in school.

"The song pretty much is true with the exception of the miniskirt, because they didn't wear them in those days," Hall told Dorothy Horstman in *Sing Your Heart Out, Country Boy.*

Jeannie felt insecure about the song. She knew "Harper Valley P.T.A." would score well on the pop charts, but she had doubts about its country potential. Nevertheless, she signed with Plantation Records on a Thursday night, and recorded the song on Friday. Singleton settled on the second take, and within hours, Ralph Emery was playing it on Nashville's WSM-AM.

"I knew that I'd cut a hit before I ever left the studio that night," Riley has said. "I rushed home and phoned Mama in Texas and told her I'd just cut the nation's next number one single."

In fact, two months after her July 26 session, the record did hit number one on *Billboard's* country chart, one week after it topped the Hot 100. Reportedly, it sold 1.6 million copies in its first ten days of release, and has sold eight million to date.

Riley racked up five more Top Ten singles in the next three years, including "The Girl Most Likely," "There Never Was A Time," "Country Girl," and "Good Enough To Be Your Wife." In 1972, she became a born-again Christian. Due in great part to the overnight success of "Harper Valley P.T.A.," Jeannie had been thrown into a rollercoaster existence, as documented in her autobiography *From Harper Valley to the Mountain Top.*

"Harper Valley P.T.A." went on to become the basis for a movie and a television series, with Barbara Eden starring in both.

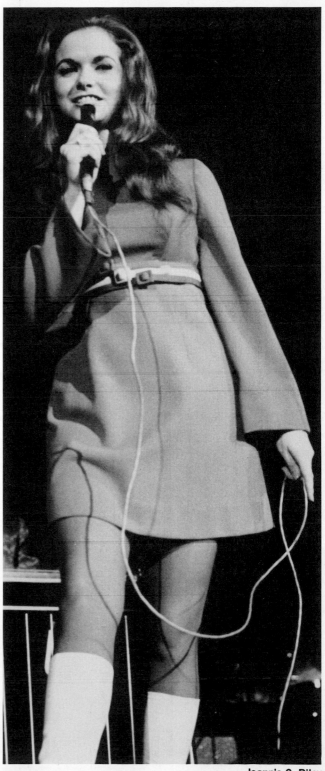

Jeannie C. Riley

18

THEN YOU CAN TELL ME GOODBYE

EDDY ARNOLD

RCA 9606
Writer: John D. Loudermilk
Producer: Chet Atkins
October 19, 1968 (2 weeks)

Eddy Arnold was hardly a stranger to number one when "Then You Can Tell Me Goodbye" became his twenty-eighth single to reach that position. His first number one hit came more than twenty years earlier, with 1947's "What Is Life Without Love?"

Born on May 15, 1918, near Henderson, Tennessee, Arnold sang and played guitar at Pinson High School, but left school to help out on the family farm. In 1936, he made his radio debut, singing live on a station in Jackson, Tennessee, then moved on to several more stations before signing with RCA Records in 1944. Because of his rural background, Arnold was dubbed "The Tennessee Plowboy." After he hit number one for the thirteenth time in 1955, with "The Cattle Call," he shifted his priorities and devoted most of his energies to raising his family.

Arnold still recorded 11 more Top Ten records over the next decade. By 1965, he had earned a new nickname—"The Ambassador of Country Music"—as a softer approach brought him success in both pop and easy-listening formats.

"I decided to take a good, simple song and add violins," he explained to Jim Ruth of the *Lancaster Sunday News*. "I made some other records with violins before, but everything just seemed to gel."

As a result, Arnold earned seven more number ones in a two-and-a-half-year period, beginning with "What's He Doin' In My World" (his first number one record in ten years) and "Make The World Go Away," and ending with "Then You Can Tell Me Goodbye," composed by ace songwriter John D. Loudermilk.

"[Loudermilk] was a very interesting personality—and still is," notes producer Chet Atkins. "One week, John would be a Communist, and the next week, he'd belong to the John Birch Society. He rode around with the cops, he'd go out to haunted houses—he was just wild. I love him like a brother."

On February 23, 1970, RCA Records honored Eddy at New York's Waldorf-Astoria for sales of more than 60 million records; he has since topped the 80-million mark.

In 1980, Eddy Arnold enjoyed a brief resurgence when he hit the Top Ten again with "Let's Get It While The Gettin's Good" and "That's What I Get For Loving You." Eddy still lives just outside of Nashville.

Eddy Arnold

19

NEXT IN LINE

CONWAY TWITTY

Decca 32361
Writers: Wayne Kemp, Curtis Wayne
Producer: Owen Bradley
November 1, 1968 (1 week)

Conway Twitty can thank songwriter Wayne Kemp for his first three bona fide country successes. Kemp, a struggling artist, went to visit Twitty at his home in Oklahoma City, where both lived at the time. Close to bankruptcy, Kemp offered to sell Twitty a song titled "The Image Of Me" for $500 in an effort to scrape up some quick cash and keep his electricity on.

Twitty agreed that it was a hit, but insisted that Kemp retain his publishing rights. Conway loaned him $500, and promised that if Wayne's own recording of the song on Jab Records proved unsuccessful, then he'd cut it.

After three months in release, Kemp's record had yet to chart, and Twitty took it into the studio. On March 23, 1968, "The Image Of Me" debuted in *Billboard*, and it became Twitty's first Top Five country record. Kemp had already had several successes as a writer—George Jones' "Love Bug" reached the number six position in 1965.

Though Kemp sweated out its release for several months, "Image" came together in a burst of creative energy. "I wrote it early one morning," he recalls. "I got up, drank a cup of coffee at the kitchen table. It just came to me all of a sudden. It's the quickest song I ever wrote."

You can't argue with success, and Twitty returned to Kemp for his follow-up single, "Next In Line," a song that Wayne co-wrote with his bass player, Curtis Wayne.

" 'Next In Line' was a hard song," says Kemp. "We had this melody for a long time. We couldn't find any words for it, and we had it all wrote except the title, 'Next In Line,' and the last line of the verse we couldn't get. It took us about six months to find a title for it."

"Next In Line" was apparently the right title. The song became a milestone in Twitty's career, his first single to top *Billboard*'s country chart. Not surprisingly, Conway again turned to his Oklahoma City neighbor at the end of 1968. Kemp's "Darling You Know I Wouldn't Lie," co-authored with Red Lane, brought Twitty to number two.

20
I WALK ALONE
MARTY ROBBINS
Columbia 44633
Writer: Herbert Wilson
Producer: Bob Johnston
November 9, 1968 (2 weeks)

Martin David Robinson was one of country music's most revered entertainers ever, but he coined his stage name to avoid the wrath of his family. Growing up outside of Phoenix in Glendale, Arizona, Marty Robbins lived in a working-class household. He feared his parents might not approve of his carefree style of employment, so he began appearing at clubs under the assumed name.

Robbins was a poor student, and his early interests in music were cultivated by his cowboy hero, Gene Autry, and his grandfather, "Texas" Bob Heckle, following his birth on September 26, 1925. An older sister gave him a second-hand guitar in his mid-teens, and a few years later, Marty prayed regularly that he might become a singer. By that point, he had become something of an enigma to the family: he'd tangled with the police on several occasions, and seemed unable to keep a job. "At one point," he later recalled for a record-company bio, "I had eight jobs in six months and quit them all."

A spot on radio station KPHO in Phoenix changed his lack of dedication to a career. Calling himself "Marty Robbins," he was soon hosting a television program called "Western Caravan." One of his guests was Little Jimmy Dickens, who was impressed by the local talent and suggested that Columbia Records sign Robbins. In 1952, Marty released his first single, "Love Me Or Leave Me Alone," and on January 19, 1953, he made his first appearance on the Grand Ole Opry. Two months later, his first Top Ten single, "I'll Go On Alone," debuted on the *Billboard* country charts, and Robbins was soon among Nashville's major performers.

From 1956 to 1967, Robbins put together ten number one singles, including "Singing The Blues," "A White Sport Coat (And A Pink Carnation)," "Devil Woman," and the Gordon Lightfoot composition "Ribbon Of Darkness." His classic "El Paso" was the third single to win the Grammy for Best Country & Western Performance (preceded by the Kingston Trio's "Tom Dooley" and Johnny Horton's "The Battle Of New Orleans"); "Don't Worry" earned the distinction of being the first record to use a distorted guitar, when Grady Martin's performance was recorded incorrectly.

"I Walk Alone," with its slow, bluesy rhythms, became the eleventh of Marty Robbins' number one recordings, debuting on October 10, 1968, and reaching its chart pinnacle a scant five weeks later—just days after the nation elected Richard Nixon as president.

21

STAND BY YOUR MAN
TAMMY WYNETTE

Epic 10398
Writers: Billy Sherrill, Tammy Wynette
Producer: Billy Sherrill
November 23, 1968 (3 weeks)

Hardly a story is written about Tammy Wynette in which her association with "Stand By Your Man" isn't mentioned. Following a three-week run at number one, the song became her second Grammy-winner on March 11, 1970. It was so closely linked with Tammy that it was used as the title for her 1979 biography.

The idea for "Stand By Your Man" belonged to producer Billy Sherrill, who carried the title in his pocket on a piece of paper for more than a year. He put it to use during a recording session in Columbia Studio B on August 26, 1968. After cutting two songs, Sherrill gave the musicians (including the Jordanaires and steel guitarist Pete Drake) a 20-minute break, and went upstairs with Wynette to write one more tune. Sherrill suggested "Stand By Your Man," and Tammy had an instant affinity for the concept.

"We just sat down, and after a couple of lines, it just came to us," Wynette recalled to Katy Bee in *Tune-In* magazine. "It was one of the fastest songs to ever come to me. It was almost as if it was meant to be."

The antagonistic response from the nation's feminists actually helped gain publicity for the song after its release. In Dorothy Horstman's *Sing Your Heart Out, Country Boy*, Sherrill even admitted that he intended "Stand By Your Man" as a song for the women who wanted no part of the women's movement.

"I wanted . . . a song for the truly liberated woman," he explained, "one who is secure enough in her identity to enjoy it. Even though to some skeptics it may hint of chauvinism, as far as I'm concerned, they can like it or lump it. 'Stand By Your Man' is just another way of saying 'I love you—without reservations.' "

"Stand By Your Man" was the stand-out track in a quintet of Wynette songs used in the Jack Nicholson movie *Five Easy Pieces*. The notes from the tune's melody were also used in the design of the "burglar bars" on the windows of Tammy's Nashville home, purchased in 1974.

According to Tammy, Sherrill told her that the melody was actually borrowed from a "public domain" work created by classical composer Richard Strauss. "I guess we steal from everybody," she confesses. "There's not a whole lot of original melodies left."

22

BORN TO BE WITH YOU
SONNY JAMES

Capitol 2271
Writer: Don Robertson
Producer: Kelso Herston
December 14, 1968 (1 week)

On November 28, 1968, Sonny James became the second country artist to appear in the Macy's Thanksgiving Day Parade [see 25—"Until My Dreams Come True"], riding a buckboard float down Broadway in New York City. He sang "Born To Be With You," his then-current single, to a national audience over NBC-TV, and two weeks later, the record became his sixth consecutive number one single.

"Born To Be With You" had originally been recorded by the Chordettes, who took a ballad version of the song to number five on *Billboard*'s Hot 100 in 1956. James adapted the song to his own special needs, speeding up the tempo of the original and at the same time providing a contrast to his prior release. "I always had sort of an idea that when I was bringing out records, I didn't want to lull everybody to sleep with a ballad," he explains. "If I had a ballad out, I'd follow it with something medium or something really uptempo."

"Heaven Says Hello" [see 14] was a rather quiet ballad, and "Born To Be With You" marked a return to the uptempo feel of two earlier James singles, "I'll Never Find Another You" and "A World Of Our Own" [see 4]. James also foresaw the tune as a radio winner.

"That was always on my mind," he admits. "If one of my records was a hit, I knew that the men and the ladies that were on the air were playing it every day on their three-hour shift, and I never wanted them to say, 'Oh, it's another one.' I wanted to add a little something and still hold on to my identity, so the only way I could do that was to change complete ideas of songs. I was writing a lot at the time, but I felt that I needed outside songs to give me that variety, and this is why I did things like 'Born To Be With You.' "

Even as he mixed up styles and tempos,

though, James retained a distinctive sound. By 1967, he was sufficiently popular to be picked by the Country Music Association to co-host its very first awards show with Bobbie Gentry, at the Municipal Auditorium in downtown Nashville.

23
WICHITA LINEMAN
GLEN CAMPBELL
Capitol 2302
Writer: Jimmy Webb
Producer: Al De Lory
December 21, 1968 (2 weeks)

"I think Jimmy Webb writes probably the best melodies and chord progressions of anybody that I've ever heard, including the greats. He's my very favorite writer of all time."

Coming from Glen Campbell, that statement is hardly a surprise. Campbell has frequently turned to Webb for many of his records. The list includes "By The Time I Get To Phoenix" [see 10—"I Wanna Live"], "Galveston" [see 30], "Honey Come Back," "Still Within The Sound Of My Voice" and his original recording of "Highwayman" [see 633]. Campbell's recording of Webb's "Wichita Lineman" provided him with his first Top Five pop hit, as well as his second number one country record.

"We carted Jimmy's organ out of his house and brought it down to the studio and set it up, just to get the effect of 'Wichita Lineman,'" Campbell remembers. "I think it's a marvelous song."

Campbell's "Wichita" success coincided with his emergence as a Hollywood commodity. He was chosen to host a summer replacement series for "The Smothers Brothers Comedy Hour" in 1968; the program proved so popular that on January 29, 1969, "The Glen Campbell Goodtime Hour" began a three-year run on CBS. The show featured such regulars or semi-regulars as Dom DeLuise, Mel Tillis, Jerry Reed [see 79—"When You're Hot, You're Hot"] and John Hartford. Hartford's "Gentle On My Mind" [see 10—"I Wanna Live"] was used as the theme song. Ultimately, the "Goodtime Hour" closed its prime-time history on June 13, 1972, following programming differences between Campbell and the network.

"I got some memos," Campbell recalls, "saying, 'You got to cut down the country acts, and you got to cut down the black acts.' That stuck in my craw, so that was the end of 'The Glen Campbell Goodtime Hour.'"

Popular reports cite Campbell as the seventh son of a seventh son, although he's actually the seventh son of a *second* son, born April 22, 1936, in Delight, Arkansas. His parents gave him his first guitar, a $5.00 instrument from the Sears & Roebuck catalog, when he was four years old. Borrowing musically from guitarists Django Reinhardt and Barney Kessel, he eventually dropped out of school at age 15 to play in a Southwestern band led by his uncle, Dick Bills. When he was 24, he left for Los Angeles, where his skills on recording sessions led to a solo contract.

Glen Campbell

24

DADDY SANG BASS

JOHNNY CASH

Columbia 44689
Writer: Carl Perkins
Producer: Bob Johnston
January 4, 1969 (6 weeks)

On February 29, 1968, Johnny Cash and June Carter announced their plans to be married in March. The Grammy awards were presented that evening, and when Ferlin Husky gave them a trophy for "Jackson," he called it "the perfect wedding gift."

A member of the legendary Carter Family, June grew up in music. She wrote "Ring Of Fire" [see 13—"Folsom Prison Blues"] for Cash, and she is generally credited as an influence in helping him combat his narcotic addiction of the '60s.

"He's probably the strongest, nicest, neatest man I've ever known in my life," says Carter. "The only thing that has ever been rough for him has been the fact that he's a chemically dependent person.

"It hurts you so bad. I mean, you either want to be a little hero and help them out, or you manipulate things to make excuses for them so they can continue to do what they're doing. There comes a time when you have to learn to deal with it."

Carter played an important role in "Daddy Sang Bass," a song that stayed at number one for six weeks, longer than any other Cash recording. It was written by Johnny's friend and bandmember, Carl Perkins, a labelmate during the Sun years.

"I started with the Johnny Cash Show in 1965," recalls Perkins. "I really went to just do two dates with John, and it wound up being ten years. I was on all of his records, the *Folsom Prison* album, the *San Quentin* album—that's me on 'A Boy Named Sue' [see 40] chicken-plucking on that old guitar."

As he did with Patsy Cline's "So Wrong," Perkins started writing "Daddy Sang Bass" in a concert-hall dressing room. "Johnny Cash walked in," he remembers. "I said, 'John, pardon me, I've got a thing started that you could do. You'd hit the low notes—"Daddy sang bass"—and June could say, "Mama sang tenor," and the Statlers [Cash's back-up singers] say, "Me and little brothers with John right in there." ' He said, 'Hey, man, I like that,' so I finished that song."

Perkins borrowed from the refrain of the Carter Family's "Will The Circle Be Unbroken," and sang it for Johnny and June during a car ride, to secure her approval. With June's okay, "Daddy Sang Bass," featuring an all-star line-up, reached number one in just five weeks.

25

UNTIL MY DREAMS COME TRUE

JACK GREENE

Decca 32423
Writer: Dallas Frazier
Producer: Owen Bradley
February 15, 1969 (2 weeks)

Standing more than six feet tall, Jack Greene earned the nickname "The Jolly Giant," and by the end of 1967, he'd likewise become a gigantic presence in country music. On November 23 of that year, he became the first of Nashville's major stars to appear in the Macy's Thanksgiving Day Parade, and exactly one month later, he earned membership in the Grand Ole Opry.

Many called him an overnight success, but Greene's stature was actually hard-won over a period of more than 20 years. Born January 7, 1930, in Maryville, Tennessee, he first picked up the guitar at age eight. He made his professional debut in 1944, singing on radio station WGAP in Tennessee while still a high school freshman.

In 1948, Jack took up the bass, and two years later, after moving to Atlanta, he added the drums to his growing list of capabilities. It wasn't until June of 1962, though, that Greene got his first big break, when Ernest Tubb hired him as a member of the Troubadors.

Owen Bradley signed Greene to Decca Records because of his vocal performance on one of Tubb's singles, "The Last Letter," and then gave the singer a back-handed compliment. "He told me early on in my career that a good singer is a liability," Greene recalls. "He said, 'The guy that sings on key and does it right, you've got to have a great song every time—but with a stylist like Ernest Tubb, you can take a *pretty good* song and have a hit with it.' "

Greene's fourth number one single was once again produced by Bradley, and like "There Goes My Everything" [see 6—"You Are My Treasure"], "Until My Dreams Come True" came from the pen of Dallas Frazier.

"On this particular song, Dallas was on vacation in Florida," notes Greene. "I called [song plugger] Ray Baker, and said 'I'm going into the studio in the morning, and I need a song.' He found Dallas, Dallas drove thirty miles to rent a tape recorder, wrote the song, and got it to me the next morning in Nashville, rushed it by air. We learned it at the session and cut it that day."

26
TO MAKE LOVE SWEETER FOR YOU
JERRY LEE LEWIS
Smash 2202
Writers: Glenn Sutton, Jerry Kennedy
Producer: Jerry Kennedy
March 1, 1969 (1 week)

Country music proved a haven for Jerry Lee Lewis, who had been embraced and summarily cast aside by the rock and roll industry in its formative years. Twenty months after Elvis Presley left Sun Records for mega-stardom with RCA, Lewis first entered the *Billboard* country chart on June 12, 1957, with "Whole Lotta Shakin' Goin' On."

Though his pumping piano was considered a revolutionary rock sound, Jerry Lee's early material actually fared better on the country list than on the Hot 100. "Whole Lotta Shakin' Goin' On" reached number three on the pop chart, while his follow-up, "Great Balls Of Fire," managed to hit number two. But each stayed at number one on the country chart for two weeks. In 1958, Lewis added two more Top Ten releases: "Breathless" and "High School Confidential." "The Killer"'s momentum soon dissipated when his marriage to his thirteen-year-old second cousin, Myra Gail Brown (his third marriage), became public knowledge.

Concerts were canceled and editorials were written, and it took eight years for Lewis to finally find a home once more. He signed with Smash Records in 1964, and two years later, he committed himself to recording specifically for the country market. In 1968, he reached number four with "Another Place, Another Time," and he followed up with three Glenn Sutton compositions. "What's Made Milwaukee Famous (Has Made A Loser Out Of Me)" and "She Still Comes Around" both went to number two, and "To Make Love Sweeter For You" finally brought him back to the top, eleven years after his last number one.

"That was a thing that I had a great lyric on and a horrible melody," says Sutton. "When I took it in to [producer] Jerry Kennedy, he said, 'I like it, but that melody is terrible, let me work on the melody,' and I said, 'Sure, be my guest,' so he came up with the melody for it." "To Make Love Sweeter For You" was the only number one record on which Kennedy augmented his usual production role to contribute as a writer.

"I remember that was a daytime session," Kennedy notes, "because Jerry Lee had to sing so high on it. I'm glad that we caught him early in the day."

27
ONLY THE LONELY
SONNY JAMES
Label: Capitol 2370
Writers: Roy Orbison, Joe Melson
Producer: Kelso Herston
March 8, 1969 (3 weeks)

Though he established his home in Nashville, Roy Orbison never actually hit the *Billboard* country chart until 1980, when he wrote and recorded "That Lovin' You Feelin' Again," a duet with Emmylou Harris from the *Roadie* soundtrack. Instead, he was a mainstay of pop music two decades earlier, accruing nine Top Ten singles between 1960 and 1964.

Born April 23, 1936, in Vernon, Texas, Orbison first charted with "Ooby Dooby," released in 1956 on Sam Phillips' Sun label. He became friends at that time with Sonny James, often opening for "The Southern Gentleman" when he toured in the West Texas area. Roy's first bona fide hit was "Only The Lonely," a song he once hoped the Everly Brothers would cut. Instead, he recorded it and went to number two on the Hot 100 in 1960. James introduced it as a country single almost nine years later.

"I thought 'Only The Lonely' was an excellent song," says James, "and I felt that it would just fit right in with country.

"In my group, going back to 'Young Love,' I'd use the group singing a counter-rhythm. When I was singing 'Young love,' they'd sing, 'You're my love, first love'—it was like a chant. On 'Only The Lonely,' Roy had written it with the girls singing in back of him, so it had that background that was tailor-made to what I was doing."

Buck Owens

After "Only The Lonely" reached number one, James considered recording "Blue Bayou." Instead, he put it on the shelf with every intention of cutting it later, but he never quite got to it. Linda Ronstadt recorded it, though, and it went to number two in 1977.

Several other Orbison songs also achieved notable success. Don McLean's revival of "Crying" went to number six on the pop chart in 1981, and Mickey Gilley & Charly McClain hit number five in 1984 with "Candy Man" [see 541—"Paradise Tonight"]. In addition, "Dream Baby (How Long Must I Dream)" (written by Cindy Walker, but made famous by Orbison) succeeded in two remakes: by Glen Campbell (number seven, 1971) and Lacy J. Dalton (number nine, 1983).

On December 7, 1988, Orbison died from a massive heart attack, just as his career was on an upswing. A couple of months later, Virgin Records issued *Mystery Girl*, which finally brought him onto the country charts as a solo performer—"You Got It" peaked at number seven.

28

WHO'S GONNA MOW YOUR GRASS
BUCK OWENS
& HIS BUCKAROOS
Capitol 2377
Writer: Buck Owens
Producer: Ken Nelson
March 29, 1969 (2 weeks)

In 1968, Buck Owens came close to scoring his seventeenth number one single, stopping at number two with "Sweet Rosie Jones." "Let The World Keep On A-Turnin'," a duet with his son, Buddy Alan, reached number seven; "I've Got You On My Mind Again" went to number five; and Buck finally hit big with "Who's Gonna Mow Your Grass."

In the meantime, Owens got a firsthand view of the lawn at 1600 Pennsylvania Avenue in Washington, D.C., in September of 1968. His performance was reportedly the first ever by a country entertainer at the White House.

"You'd think that it was eventful," reports Owens, "but it was really *un*eventful. It was a thrill to get to go there and play, but I also got to play a lot of other interesting places: the Empire State Building, the old Madison Square Garden, Carnegie Hall, the Astrodome, Prince Royal Albert Hall. There were just a lot of places I was able to do all that."

It was appropriate that Owens should be the first country star to play the White House. Three years earlier, amidst the unrest caused by American involvement in Vietnam, Owens sported a red, white and blue guitar. It became a trademark, although he received quite a backlash in the press in an age of anti-government sentiments. "I never was one for following the crowd," quips Buck.

That statement certainly applied to "Who's Gonna Mow Your Grass." "I put a fuzz tone on that record, and I thought the country music community was gonna lynch me. I'm an old-time closet rock and roller. I love good music of any kind, but my very favorites are good country and good rock and roll."

Owens' experiment with fuzz tone was hardly new. In fact, Marty Robbins was the first to use the effect, when Grady Martin's guitar was accidentally distorted during the recording sessions of Robbins' 1961 single "Don't Worry" [see 20—"I Walk Alone"]. If the Nashville establishment had grown to hate that sound, though, country fans loved it.

" 'Who's Gonna Mow Your Grass' was just a fun song," says Owens. "It was almost like a jazz waltz when I got through with it. I just sang it twice—one time pretty good and one time pretty bad—and put them together and said, 'That'll do it.' "

29

WOMAN OF THE WORLD (LEAVE MY WORLD ALONE)
LORETTA LYNN

Decca 32439
Writer: Sharon Higgins
Producer: Owen Bradley
April 12, 1969 (1 week)

How coincidental that Loretta Lynn attained stardom—her mother named her after Loretta Young, a movie star whose picture was taped on the walls of their home in Butcher Holler, Kentucky.

Loretta was born April 14, 1935, near Van Lear, the second of eight children in the poverty-stricken Webb family. Often, the family subsisted on a meal of bread and gravy, made from brown flour and water. Bologna was considered a luxury, and government-supplied cabbage and grapefruit was definitely an improvement.

At age 13, Loretta married O.V. Lynn [see 7—"Fist City"], who took her across the country from Kentucky to Washington state. Though most country stars begin singing in their teen years, Loretta's musical career actually began in her twenties. O.V. (a.k.a. Mooney) believed that she had some talent, and bought her a guitar for her birthday to encourage her. Making her first record changed her entire world.

"By the time I was 17, I had four kids, and I had never been anywhere," Lynn explains. "It was very, very rough and hard on me. I was a mother and a housewife for 13 years, and bein' a singer was somethin' that really had never entered my mind. Just rockin' and singin' the babies to sleep was about the only thing I ever did. Crystal [Gayle] and my little brother had a little radio show, and she was just a little, tiny girl. I think they were all singin' before me."

Starting late was no problem for Loretta, though. In 1967, she was named the Female Vocalist of the Year in the very first Country Music Association awards presentation, and after "Fist City" became her second number one single the following year, it took only a year to rack up her third. "You've Just Stepped In (From Stepping Out On Me)" reached number two, "Your Squaw Is On The Warpath" hit number three, and "Woman Of The World (Leave My World Alone)" returned her to the top.

"There was a girl from Missouri that come in with the song," she recalls, "and I helped her with it, because I had to rearrange a song to fit me if somebody else was writin' on it."

Lynn followed up with three more Top Ten singles in the next 20 months, plus "Wings Upon Your Horns" (one of her controversial compositions), which peaked at number 11.

30

GALVESTON
GLEN CAMPBELL

Capitol 2428
Writer: Jimmy Webb
Producer: Al De Lory
April 19, 1969 (3 weeks)

Two simple lines about "cannons flashing" and cleaning a gun led many listeners to associate "Galveston" with the Vietnam War.

"Because of the time that the song was written, it took on an anti-war feeling," songwriter Jimmy Webb told Ed Galeno in *Tune-In* magazine. "The truth is, when I was writing it, I wasn't thinking about Vietnam too much. I was thinking about outlaws, about the whole country/western field. But when I got further into it, I realized that there was some symbolism in it. It really did represent something that was happening to guys my age at that time."

Having already provided Glen Campbell with a couple of major hits [see 23—"Wichita Lineman"], Webb naturally had Campbell in mind for "Galveston." "I wrote it as a Glen Campbell record. I definitely wrote it for him as an artist in a series of things that we were doing. I figured it would be a hit for him. That's honestly the reason I wrote it." Webb's hunch paid off with Campbell's third number one single in the spring of 1969.

Glen's career was expanding at an astronomical rate. His previous acting experience consisted of a single appearance as a guitar player in an episode of "The F.B.I.," but he emerged in 1969 as a major personality. His own TV show held down a Wednesday night time slot, and he appeared in his first motion picture, *True Grit*.

"I was so bad," he confesses. "I made John Wayne look so good that he won his only Oscar. I'm the only guy that can make the statement, 'I was with him in his Oscar-winning role.' "

The film also brought Campbell a Top Ten single with the title track. His next two records, "Try A Little Kindness" and "Honey Come Back," both stopped at number two.

He made another movie in 1970, co-starring with Joe Namath in *Norwood*, but the experience soured him on Hollywood, even though he nabbed yet another hit with the Mac Davis-penned "Everything A Man Could Ever Need." Campbell's remakes of "It's Only Make Believe" and "Dream Baby" also reached the Top Ten, but the hits became sporadic for several years. "Manhattan, Kansas" turned the trick in 1972, as did "Bonaparte's Retreat" in 1974.

31

HUNGRY EYES

MERLE HAGGARD
& THE STRANGERS

Capitol 2383
Writer: Merle Haggard
Producer: Ken Nelson
May 10, 1969 (1 week)

"There was a black preacher I heard one time who said, 'The best thing you can do for the poor is not to be one of them.' I think there's a lot more truth to that than I first realized."

Merle Haggard made that statement to Wayne Bledsoe of the *Knoxville News-Sentinel*, many years after he had escaped the trappings of poverty in Bakersfield, California. A converted boxcar served as home for a youthful Haggard. His parents (Jim and Flossie) and two siblings (Lowell and Lillian) migrated from Oklahoma in 1934, three years prior to Merle's birth, in a '26 Chevy. Many of the Okies who wound up in California actually fared worse than the Haggards, and their plight became a part of "Hungry Eyes," which featured Glen Campbell on backing vocals [see 8—"The Legend Of Bonnie And Clyde"].

In the summer of 1946, Merle's mother took him to Hughson, near Modesto, to visit relatives, and when he stepped off the train, he saw the canvas-covered shacks of a labor camp for the first time. That image provided the first line of "Hungry Eyes."

"Around Bakersfield, a lot of people worked in the fields and lived in labor camps," says Norm Hamlet of Haggard's band, the Strangers. "They just got along the best they could. They didn't really have a lot of success in life, they just got by. A lot of people think the songs [Merle's] done are experiences he's had. Some of them are not necessarily personal experiences, but experiences of seeing other people in the same situation.

"He never lived in any labor camps, but he remembers his own adventures, and he remembers those old camps like that, and people working hard and doing labor in the fields. He just wrote it thinking of his mother."

Before "Hungry Eyes," Haggard had adapted his experiences riding freight trains in extolling the virtues of a hobo. The single "I Take A Lot Of Pride In What I Am" notched a number three peak position in early 1969. On February 22, "Hungry Eyes" debuted on the *Billboard* country chart, and in its twelfth week, it edged its way to number one.

In the interim, Haggard's compositions set a precedent that remains unmatched in the Academy of Country Music Awards. Three of his songs were among the five finalists in both the Song of the Year *and* Top Single categories: "The Legend Of Bonnie And Clyde", "I Take A Lot Of Pride In What I Am" and "Mama Tried" [see 16].

32

MY LIFE (THROW IT AWAY IF I WANT TO)

BILL ANDERSON

Decca 32445
Writer: Bill Anderson
Producer: Owen Bradley
May 10, 1969 (2 weeks)

Thanks in great part to the syndicated television offering "The Bill Anderson Show," Anderson might have been the most recognizable country performer of the '60s.

Bill's work on the tube followed an extremely successful recording career that began in 1959, with his release "That's What It's Like To Be Lonesome." In the decade that followed, he racked up 15 Top Ten singles on the *Billboard* country chart. Three of those— "8 × 10," "Wild Weekend" and "Happy State Of Mind"—stalled at number two. Four more went to number one, including "Mama Sang A Song," in 1962; "I Get The Fever," in 1966; and his duet with Jan Howard, "For Loving You," in 1967.

His biggest record, though, was his 1963 recording, "Still." The song was inspired by an old girlfriend, who eventually married a weatherman at an Atlanta television station. Anderson was set for an interview at that station one morning, and as he drove into the parking lot, his ex-girlfriend, whom he hadn't seen in five years, was standing in the doorway.

Haunted by the memory of their relationship, the incident stuck with Bill all day, and he finally wrote "Still" at 3:00 the following morning. "Still" stayed at number one for three weeks, beginning April 13, 1963.

Billboard named "Still" the top country single for 1963, and "My Life (Throw It Away If I Want To)" gained similar recognition, as the number one record for 1969. Characterized by Anderson as his most cynical release, it was the result of a divorce.

"My wife told me that if I left her, I'd be throwing away my life," he recalls, "whereupon I replied, 'Well, it's my life—I guess I can throw it away if I want to.' As soon as I said the line, my songwriter's antenna went up, and it didn't take me long to write the song. I thought it turned out to be pretty clever, but the humor and poignancy were totally lost on my wife's divorce lawyer."

Bill Anderson

33

SINGING MY SONG

TAMMY WYNETTE

Epic 10462
Writers: Billy Sherrill, Tammy Wynette, Glenn Sutton
Producer: Billy Sherrill
May 31, 1969 (2 weeks)

"Stand By Your Man" [see 21] brought Tammy Wynette recognition from a wider audience when it surprised even her by crossing over onto the *Billboard* Hot 100, where it peaked at number 19. The follow-up was crucial, and Tammy admits quite frankly that it sounded very much like "Stand By Your Man."

"It wasn't intentional," she says. "We were so in awe as to what 'Stand By Your Man' had done, and we were just at our wits' end as to what to do for a follow-up. We knew we couldn't beat it, and we wanted so badly to have something as good, or something that the people would enjoy."

Wynette had recently moved to Lakeland, Florida, and was playing in Atlanta when producer Billy Sherrill called her in March of 1969 to tell her that they had nothing ready for her next session. Sherrill asked her to come to Nashville a couple of days early to try and write some material for the session. "Stand By Your Man" was the first song they co-wrote; they needed Glenn Sutton's help to finish "Singing My Song," which had an unusual twist.

"We had the entire song written, and we couldn't think of what to call it," Tammy recalls. "We just had to call it 'Singing My Song.' There was really no punchline in it, except for one line—'That's why I keep singing my song.'

"We had the whole song written without the title, and I don't think that's ever happened to me. Usually you have a title to begin with, and

you work from that. An idea usually comes from a title, but not this time."

In addition to the notoriety that "Stand By Your Man" brought her, Tammy's personal life had also changed drastically: her move to Florida was prompted by her marriage to country legend George Jones. The two had first sung together on stage while touring with David Houston [see 9—"Have A Little Faith"], and a romance quickly blossomed. They announced that they were married on August 22, 1968, although the event didn't actually take place until February 16, 1969, in Ringgold, Georgia. The couple was instantly hailed as "Mr. & Mrs. Country Music."

34
RUNNING BEAR
SONNY JAMES

Capitol 2486
Writer: J.P. Richardson
Producer: Kelso Herston
June 14, 1969 (3 weeks)

Sonny James on "The Ed Sullivan Show"

After a plane crash claimed the life of Buddy Holly on February 3, 1959, that date went down in music annals as "the day the music died." Alongside him were two other recording stars: Ritchie Valens and "The Big Bopper," J.P. Richardson.

Born October 24, 1930, in Sabine Pass, Texas, Richardson earned a place in the Beaumont broadcasting community on radio station KTRM. After a one-year stint in the Army, he returned to Beaumont, gaining notoriety by setting a new world record with a "Jape-A-Thon"—122 straight hours on the air.

The Big Bopper earned a number three pop record with "Chantilly Lace" [see 96] in 1958. Beaumont entertainment entrepreneur Harold W. "Pappy" Daily was affiliated with the Big Bopper, as well as country singer George Jones, and just three months after the release of "Chantilly Lace," Jones released Richardson's "Treasure Of Love," which peaked at number six. On March 15, 1959—about six months after the Big Bopper's passing—Jones debuted in *Billboard* with Richardson's "White Lightning," which went all the way to number one. In 1961, Hank Snow went to number five with his recording of another Big Bopper composition, "Beggar To A King."

Later that year, Johnny Preston recorded another Richardson composition, "Running Bear," which reached number one on the Hot 100. Sonny James resurrected the tune in 1969, and it became a number one country single in its sixth week on the *Billboard* chart.

"When 'Running Bear' came out, there wasn't anything on the market like it," James explains. "It was really different, and it was uptempo."

Another major aid came with James' exposure on "The Ed Sullivan Show" in May. "I was fortunate enough at that time to do 'Ed Sullivan' a couple of times a year," he says. "He'd do it with taste, even though it was a country artist and country wasn't seen that much. With 'Running Bear,' I remember he had Peter Generro do choreography with his group, and they did a good job.

"There were one or two other network shows I sang it on at that time. I think with that exposure—plus they were hearing it on the air—the image that you would see had such a great impact, and I think that had a great deal to do with the success of it."

Alongside "Young Love," "Running Bear" became one of James' trademark tunes, and soon emerged as his traditional closing number.

35

STATUE OF A FOOL
JACK GREENE
Decca 32490
Writer: Jan Crutchfield
Producer: Owen Bradley
July 5, 1969 (2 weeks)

Though his record easily reached number one after its release, Jack Greene held on to "Statue Of A Fool" for seven years before he finally issued it. Originally titled "Name It After Me," "Statue" was only recorded when a change of title fooled Owen Bradley, who had passed on it several times before.

In 1961, while working at an Atlanta show called "Dixie Jubilee," Greene was approached by RCA executive Sam Wallace about the possibility of recording for the label with a new "Dynagroove" technology. Jack went to Nashville and spent the day with Teddy Wilburn, who gave him several songs, including "Name It After Me," but the RCA deal never came off.

Once Greene was signed to Decca Records, he repeatedly tried to record the song, but Bradley turned him down every time. The key to its success came when Greene ran into Doyle Wilburn. "He grabbed me by the arm," Greene recalls, "and said, 'Somewhere there she be, for the all the world to see, the statue of a fool.' He recited the whole song to me before he turned me loose and said, 'That's a great lyric, isn't it? Go home and sit down with your guitar, and live with that song, and make it a Jack Greene song.'"

For months, Greene devoted much of his free time to molding the song into a new shape. He made a couple of changes, slowed the tempo down, and played it once more for Bradley, who now liked the number. Asked for the title, Greene said it didn't have one, and gave Bradley the option of naming it. Bradley settled on "Statue Of A Fool." "I never told Owen till it went number one that it was 'Name It After Me.'"

Greene followed up "Statue" with "Back In The Arms Of Love" (number four). At the end of 1969, he released a duet with Jeannie Seely, "Wish I Didn't Have To Miss You," which hit number two. He remained with Decca (which became MCA) until 1975, and has continued to record for various labels, including Frontline and Step One.

His career took an unusual twist for seven years when an impersonator (Lawrence Irving

Taylor) claimed to be Jack Greene, taking money from elderly couples and running up unpaid bills at hotels. On June 17, 1988, Taylor was apprehended after trying to buy a $700,000 horse farm in Kentucky.

36
I LOVE YOU MORE TODAY
CONWAY TWITTY
Decca 32481
Writer: L.E. White
Producer: Owen Bradley
July 19, 1969 (1 week)

In 1970, Conway Twitty appointed L.E. White to run Twitty Bird Music, a publishing company that represented all of Conway's material. White had an important role: to write for Twitty, screen his material and find new songwriters to sign for Conway's publishing venture. Though L.E. was not expecting this move, it represented the culmination of White's personal songwriting education.

"I studied Conway a long time before I ever met him, and thought his singing sounded exactly like what I could write," notes White. "He sounded country like I like, and I wrote ten songs and went to Knoxville and introduced myself. I studied him about eight months before I wrote the ten songs and demoed them.

"He was staying in town that night and heard 'em, and I thought he was puttin' me on. I didn't know him at the time, but he said, 'No, these two right here will be my next two singles.'"

Twitty invited L.E. to his next recording session, where he cut one of the two songs, "I Love You More Today." The record reached number one in the summer of 1969—one day before Man first walked on the moon. At the turn of the decade, Twitty gave White his permanent publishing position.

A Knoxville native, White already had a distinguished musical background. Having first written in high school, he performed on a radio show hosted by Archie Campbell (later with TV's "Hee Haw"). White journeyed to Nashville in 1953, where he played fiddle and sang with bluegrass legend Bill Monroe.

L.E. remained with Conway for thirteen years, finally leaving in 1983. During that period, he watched Twitty Bird Music expand from one to three publishing companies, overseen by Tree Publishing. Twitty recorded more than 65 of White's compositions, including "To See My Angel Cry" [see 44] and "After The Fire Is Gone" [see 74].

Twitty produced several solo singles for White in 1972, although L.E. charted only twice. Both were duet singles recorded with Lola Jean Dillon [see 266—"Somebody Somewhere"], also signed at the time with Twitty Bird Music. One of the White/Dillon duets, "You're The Reason Our Kids Are Ugly," was remade by Conway and Loretta Lynn as the "B" side of "From Seven Till Ten" [see 221—"Feelins'"].

37
JOHNNY B. GOODE
BUCK OWENS
& HIS BUCKAROOS
Capitol 2485
Writer: Chuck Berry
Producer: Ken Nelson
July 26, 1969 (2 weeks)

"I've always thought that Chuck Berry might have had a rock and roll heart, but he had a country soul."

That's how Buck Owens explains his choice of material from one of rock music's seminal figures. Owens is hardly the only country performer who has notched a hit with a Berry original. Other remakes include "Maybellene," by George Jones & Johnny Paycheck; "Too Much Monkey Business," by Freddy Weller; "Promised Land," by both Weller and Elvis Presley; "Brown-Eyed Handsome Man," by Waylon Jennings; "Memphis," by Fred Knoblock; and "(You Never Can Tell) C'est La Vie," by Emmylou Harris.

Owens was the first to tap Berry's catalog, though, releasing a live rendition of "Johnny B. Goode" recorded at London's Palladium. It was a natural inclusion in Buck's stage shows, since he started playing it in 1958 during his days at The Blackboard [see 5—"How Long Will My Baby Be Gone"] in Bakersfield.

"In this honky-tonk, we played country and we played Little Richard," he recalls, "and we played mambos and sambas and tangos. We played lots and lots of Bob Wills. We played 'Cherry Pink And Apple Blossom White,' we played all those songs. It was a wonderful experience, and they became my influences. Rodney Crowell says that John Lennon and Buck Owens were his influences. I'd always thought that Bob Wills and Little Richard were my influences, as far as the Bakersfield Sound, and the hard-driving type of country music."

As with the distorted guitar on "Who's Gonna Mow Your Grass" [see 28], "Johnny B. Goode" elicited negative comments from some Nashville quarters.

"I never thought of 'Johnny B. Goode' as being a rock and roll song," Buck insists. "I saw 'Johnny B. Goode' as being about a little boy playing a guitar sitting by a railroad track, and that's pretty country to me. I never did care about the flak, and I still don't care, and I ain't gonna care tomorrow."

Whether or not the record went over well in Music City, "Johnny B. Goode" earned top marks with the general public. The single entered the *Billboard* country chart on May 24, 1969. Two months later, "Johnny B. Goode" began a two-week run at number one.

38

ALL I HAVE TO OFFER YOU (IS ME)
CHARLEY PRIDE
RCA 0167
Writers: A.L. Owens, Dallas Frazier
Producers: Chet Atkins, Jack Clement,
Bob Ferguson,
Felton Jarvis
August 9, 1969 (1 week)

With the tenth single of his career, Charley Pride made recording history—when "All I Have To Offer You (Is Me)" made him the first black vocalist to top the country chart.

Pride's ascent in the midst of a racially tense period was a potential bombshell, and RCA Records went to unusual lengths to hide his "uniqueness" for as long as possible. When his first single, "The Snakes Crawl At Night," shipped on December 28, 1965, disk jockeys received their copies without the usual accompanying photograph and bio. The label hoped to draw attention to Charley's vocal quality before he gained attention for his color.

The concern was understandable. So sensitive were minority issues that on April 6, 1968, the Grand Ole Opry canceled a show for the first time due to racial tensions following the murder of Martin Luther King two days earlier in Memphis.

Four noted producers were all credited on the label of Pride's first records, even though Jack Clement was the only producer who entered the studio with Pride.

"With the uniqueness of me being the first colored/Negro/black coming into the country music field," Pride explains, "they thought it was essential that the deejays would see those names out there: Chet Atkins, Bob Ferguson, Felton Jarvis and Jack Clement. Those are four legitimate names that would make sure that the people realized, once they found out the color of my skin, that it was no hoax—this was for real."

For extra emphasis, each of the first five singles credited the artist as "*Country* Charley Pride." The third, "Just Between You And Me," was the first to chart, reaching number nine in 1966. Each successive release slightly improved his chart standing, with "The Easy Part's Over" peaking at number two in 1968. Three records later, "All I Have To Offer You" brought him to the top.

Charley's first nine singles were written primarily by Clement or the team of Jerry Foster and Bill Rice, but "All I Have To Offer You" was the first Pride record penned by another successful duo, Dallas Frazier and "Doodle" Owens. The title popped out of a conversation they had while driving around Nashville, and the actual writing took very little time at all.

Likewise, it took little time for Pride to find success with it—the record hit number one in its ninth week on the chart.

39

WORKIN' MAN BLUES
MERLE HAGGARD
& THE STRANGERS
Capitol 2503
Writer: Merle Haggard
Producer: Ken Nelson
August 16, 1969 (1 week)

"I'm not a dyed-in-the-wool fan of many people," Merle Haggard said in his autobiography, *Sing Me Back Home*, "but I'm a true [Johnny] Cash fan. There's a certain magic that must have been born in him. He can grab an audience and hold them right till the last chorus."

The first time Haggard saw the Man in Black was when Cash played San Quentin [see 40—"A Boy Named Sue"] in 1958, and the next time they crossed paths, both appeared on a television show in Chicago. Nowhere did Haggard try to emulate his hero more than in writing "Workin' Man Blues."

Johnny Cash

Merle was traveling in his bus on Interstate 10, just outside of Tucson, when he decided he wanted to cut something that would have the same impact as Cash's "Folsom Prison Blues" [see 13]. The perfect song would be one that the ordinary working man could relate to, and it took 30 minutes maximum to create "Workin' Man Blues."

"It was a good session," remembers steel-playing Stranger Norm Hamlet. "It was really an uptempo thing and everybody was getting into it, 'cause I think at one point or another everybody feels the same way. They might not be making too much, but they go to work every day, maybe go have a drink after they get off work, and that makes the world go around."

"Workin' Man Blues" entered the *Billboard* country chart on July 5, 1969—one day after Independence Day—and by the time Labor Day rolled around, it was already on its way back down, having peaked at number one on August 16.

Though the work of a traveling musician has been glamorized, Hamlet points out that the career can be just as demanding as any other. "It's kind of like any other job in a way. People have to go to school to be what they need to be. With musicians, it's the same thing. You don't learn everything overnight, but a lot of people don't take that into consideration when they're thinking how easy this looks.

"Of course, we're not working at a job that we don't like—and there's a lot of people that have to do that."

40
A BOY NAMED SUE
JOHNNY CASH
Columbia 44944
Writer: Shel Silverstein
Producer: Bob Johnston
August 23, 1969 (5 weeks)

Discounting Elvis Presley, Ricky Nelson and Brenda Lee—who were all primarily pop/rock performers during significant portions of their careers—Johnny Cash has appeared on *Billboard*'s Hot 100 more times than any other country artist in history. Beginning in 1956, Cash landed on the pop chart 48 times, and the most successful of his "crossover" releases was "A Boy Named Sue."

"Sue" was the only single to emerge from his second prison album, recorded live at San

Quentin. A novelty song written by Shel Silverstein [see 92—"One's On The Way"], the record was certified a million-seller on August 14, 1969. Nine days later, it ascended to number one on the *Billboard* country chart, peaking that same week at number two on the pop chart—just behind the Rolling Stones' "Honky Tonk Women."

"The week before I went to play San Quentin, we had a party at my house, a guitar pull," Cash told Bill Flanagan of *Musician*. "One right after the other, Bob Dylan sang 'Lay, Lady, Lay,' Graham Nash sang 'Marrakesh Express,' Joni Mitchell sang 'Both Sides Now,' Kris [Kristofferson] sang 'Me And Bobby McGee,' and Shel Silverstein sang 'A Boy Named Sue.' I asked Shel to write down the lyrics to it.

"When I went to San Quentin, June [Carter Cash] asked if I had it. I said, 'Yeah, but I haven't had a chance to rehearse it, I can't do it.' She said, 'Take the lyrics, put it on the music stand and read it off as you sing it. They'll love it.'"

Though Cash was undergoing a spiritual reformation at the time, he read the lyrics word-for-word in that performance, and the phrase "son of a bitch" was bleeped out on the record.

"It was taking a little while for a cleaner language to catch up with my new nature," he explained in his autobiography, *Man in Black*. "I should have remembered that when I made a mistake, the whole world will know about it."

The San Quentin appearance continued a long tradition for Cash, who started performing for prison crowds in 1957, at a state facility in Huntsville, Texas. He first played San Quentin the following year, and a young Merle Haggard was in the audience.

On July 12, 1970, Cash presented an autographed gold record to South Dakota judge Sue Hicks. Contrary to legend, Silverstein insists that Hicks was *not* the catalyst for the song.

41

TALL DARK STRANGER
BUCK OWENS
& HIS BUCKAROOS
Capitol 2570
Writer: Buck Owens
Producer: Ken Nelson
September 27, 1969 (1 week)

Among the biggest events in country music during 1969 was the debut of "Hee Haw" on June 15. The series was a corny, country version of "Rowan & Martin's Laugh-In," but after its entry onto national television, a *Billboard* reporter wrote that it "set country music back 20 years."

"They took it pretty seriously," remembers Buck Owens, "but, hell, it wasn't supposed to be serious. 'Hee Haw' was fun. It had a lot of pretty girls, and had a lot of ugly old fat guys, and people took it the wrong way."

Owens backed into the series, which he co-hosted with Roy Clark [see 129—"Come Live With Me"] until 1986. He was taping "The Jonathan Winters Show" in December of 1968 when he was approached by a hopeful TV executive, and Buck agreed to host the pilot, doubting that he'd ever hear from the man again. In February, CBS advanced the producers enough money to shoot the pilot, and by May, "Hee Haw" received a thirteen-week contract.

"Hee Haw" stayed on CBS until 1971, when the network pulled it off the airwaves in an effort to reel in more viewers in large urban markets. The show immediately went into syndication, where it has remained ever since. During his 17 years with the program, Owens watched his record sales drop dramatically.

"They can see you every week on television," he explains. "Television is the quintessential culprit of removing any mystique from a singer."

In the wake of "Hee Haw"'s debut, however, Buck earned his nineteenth number one single. He wrote "Tall Dark Stranger" around a phrase he'd often heard from his grandmother.

"I was around her a considerable amount," he recalls. "My grandmother said that when someone was tall, dark and handsome, they were someone to be looked upon carefully, and if they were a tall, dark, handsome *stranger*, you'd get the women and the kids in, to where no one would run off with the tall, dark stranger."

Owens toyed with the idea for a lengthy period of time, and when he sat down to write the number prior to a show in Las Vegas, it literally flowed. "I could see the thing happening as I was writing the song. It was just one of those songs that I couldn't write it down fast enough. Usually, when that kind of thing happens, you've got something worth looking at."

That was certainly true of "Tall Dark Stranger," which edged into the top spot on September 27, 1969, in its eighth week on the chart.

42

SINCE I MET YOU BABY
SONNY JAMES

Capitol 2595
Writer: Ivory Joe Hunter
Producer: Kelso Herston
October 4, 1969 (3 weeks)

On April 9, 1965, the city of Houston made history by opening the Astrodome. Built at a cost of $20.5 million, the stadium covers 9.5 acres, and serves as the home for the Astros baseball team, the Oilers football team, and the annual Houston Livestock and Rodeo Show. In August of 1969, Sonny James became the first man ever to record an album at the spacious facility—*The Astrodome Presents Sonny James*—and the LP's single fulfilled a promise made more than ten years earlier.

James had begun his long-running series of appearances on "The Ed Sullivan Show" during the late '50s, and performed "Young Love" on one particular show dedicated to the top hits of 1957. On that same program, rhythm & blues vocalist Ivory Joe Hunter sang "Since I Met You Baby," a number 12 recording on *Billboard*'s Hot 100. Backstage at rehearsal, James was struck by the tune, and suggested to Hunter that it could be done as a country song.

"He said, 'Someday, why don't you do it?'" James recalls, "and I said 'I will.' He had those gold teeth in the front, and he smiled a lot, and I said, 'One of these days I'll do it,' and he said he was going to hold me to it."

As he did in "Heaven Says Hello" [see 14], James used Millie Kirkham to enhance parts of "Since I Met You Baby." "I started using this real high voice [on my records], and a lot of people over the years would hear this voice. I tried not to overdo it, but I'd use it when it fit— sparingly—on introductions. A lot of people thought it was an instrument, her voice was that beautiful. It was so high, and I'd get her at her peak, without straining."

James reappeared on "The Ed Sullivan Show" in the autumn of 1969 and sang "Since I Met You Baby," which occupied the top of the *Billboard* country chart throughout most of October.

"I guess people just liked it because it was such a simple song," James conjectures. "The lyric is very short, and the whole story is in the first line: 'Since I met you baby, my whole life is changed.'"

43

THE WAYS TO LOVE A MAN
TAMMY WYNETTE

Epic 10512
Writers: Billy Sherrill, Glenn Sutton,
Tammy Wynette
Producer: Billy Sherrill
October 25, 1969 (2 weeks)

On June 15, 1969, "Hee Haw" made its television debut at 9:00 EST on CBS [see 41— "Tall Dark Stranger"]. Hosted by Roy Clark and Buck Owens, the program presented a special musical guest each week, and the first week brought an illustrious twosome: George Jones & Tammy Wynette.

Country music fans embraced the concept of two top-name performers in a star-studded marriage, even if it was the third marriage for each of them. Quite naturally, they often assumed that George and Tammy were singing about each other on their records, and that helped propel Tammy's "The Ways To Love A Man" to number one for a couple of weeks beginning October 25. It was her fourth consecutive single to reach the top of the *Billboard* chart.

Earlier that month, Wynette had been a prominent participant at the Country Music Association awards. For the second year in a row, she picked up the award for Female Vocalist of the Year, and she was also nominated for Song of the Year and Album of the Year, both in recognition of "Stand By Your Man" [see 21].

After "The Ways To Love A Man" reached number one, Tammy followed up with "I'll See Him Through," which debuted at number 34 on January 31, 1970. It reached number two in its seventh week on the chart, where it remained for two weeks, kept out of number one by Merle Haggard's "Fightin' Side Of Me" [see 50].

The accolades continued to pour in, and on April 16, 1970, Wynette received a gold album from the Recording Industry Association of America, certifying her *Greatest Hits* for sales of 500,000 copies. It wasn't until 1976 that the RIAA certified platinum LPs (sales of one million units). But Tammy achieved that figure before then, reportedly the first woman to do so in Nashville—thus her nickname, "The First Lady of Country Music."

"We knew it and the label knew it and people in the business knew it," she says, "but there

was no big thing about it, because nobody certified that those things happened other than the company."

When the RIAA finally established the platinum album awards, Crystal Gayle became the first lady "officially" recognized for selling a million copies. Her award came for *We Must Believe in Magic* [see 292—"Don't It Make My Brown Eyes Blue"] on February 15, 1978.

44
TO SEE MY ANGEL CRY
CONWAY TWITTY

Decca 32546
Writers: L.E. White, Carlton Haney, Conway Twitty
Producer: Owen Bradley
November 8, 1969 (1 week)

Conway Twitty first appeared on *Billboard*'s country singles chart on March 26, 1966, with "Guess My Eyes Were Bigger Than My Heart." It reached number 18, although it took two years before he could eclipse that peak with "The Image Of Me" [see 19—"Next In Line"].

In the meantime, "Guess My Eyes Were Bigger Than My Heart" helped to build his reputation on the country stage. Concert promoter Carlton Haney heard the record, and gave Conway a spot opening for George Jones in Little Rock. Over the next several weeks, Twitty opened for Buck Owens and Loretta Lynn, gaining standing ovations at each show.

Twitty and Haney understandably maintained close business ties for a number of years, and in 1969, Carlton provided Conway with the basis for a number one single, "To See My Angel Cry."

"It was [Carlton's] idea," explains songwriter L.E. White. "Me and Conway wrote it, then called [Haney] and told him he wrote it. He wasn't even there, but he had the idea for it." "To See My Angel Cry" appeared at number one on November 8, 1969, just a few weeks after Conway began a short-lived business venture—the Twitty Burger, originally created in 1960.

Fast food was the side order of the day in Nashville, a trend that began in 1967 with Minnie Pearl's Fried Chicken. In her footsteps, Eddy Arnold (chicken), Little Jimmy Dickens (smoked meats), Hank Williams, Jr. (barbecue) and Tennessee Ernie Ford (steak and biscuits) all established their own chains.

Conway's enterprise—a family-style operation that gained financial backing from Merle Haggard, Sonny James, Harlan Howard [see 591—"I Don't Know A Thing About Love"] and former Oklahoma governor J. Howard Robinson—flew with the slogan "Tweet Yourself To A Twitty Burger." Billed as "the hamburger with a Polynesian Punch," Twitty's concoction incorporated a quarter-pound of charcoal-broiled chopped sirloin, three slices of bacon, and a slice of pineapple—all dipped in batter and deep fried. For kids, the restaurant offered the Itty Bitty Twitty Burger.

The Twitty Burger proved to be a bust. The business went under, but instead of declaring bankruptcy, Conway personally repaid each of his investors. "It took twelve years and an awful lot of money out of my life," he told Peer J. Oppenheimer in *Family Weekly*. "That's when I decided to stick to what I know. And it isn't Twitty Burgers. It's country music."

45

OKIE FROM MUSKOGEE
MERLE HAGGARD & THE STRANGERS
Capitol 2626
Writers: Merle Haggard, Roy Burris
Producer: Ken Nelson
November 15, 1969 (4 weeks)

Besides its status as the inspiration for his biggest career hit, Muskogee, Oklahoma, holds a great deal of personal importance for Merle Haggard. His father lived in Checotah (about 20 miles south of Muskogee) before bringing the family to California [see 31—"Hungry Eyes"] just three years before Merle's birth.

"My father worked hard on his farm, was proud of it, and got called white trash once he took to the road as an Okie," Haggard explained to Nat Hentoff in the *Village Voice*. "There were a lot of other Okies from around there, proud people whose farms and homes were foreclosed by Eastern bankers, and who then got treated like dirt. Listen to that line: 'I'm proud to be an Okie from Muskogee.' Nobody had ever said that before in a song."

Haggard was on tour with his band, the Strangers, when they saw a sign along the interstate that read: "Muskogee 19 miles." One of the Strangers commented that the citizens of Muskogee probably didn't smoke marijuana, and Haggard and drummer Roy Burris began feeding off of that line. "It started as a joke," Haggard told Wayne Bledsoe of the *Knoxville News-Sentinel*, "but it only lasted about three seconds before we realized the importance of it."

It took less than 20 minutes total to finish "Okie," which garnered a huge amount of attention—from both supporters and dissidents—for its decidedly right-wing political stance. President Richard Nixon sent Haggard a letter expressing his personal congratulations; in fact, Nixon liked the song so much he asked Johnny Cash to perform it at the White House [see 63—"Sunday Mornin' Comin' Down"].

"The main message in 'Muskogee' was pride," says Merle, "and the patriotism was evident."

The first version of "Okie From Muskogee" entered the *Billboard* country chart on October 11, 1969. "We made a mistake," Haggard notes, "and put it on a studio cut first, and it did very well. But then the live version came out, and it just kind of stunted that sales figure."

The record ascended to number one in its sixth week. "Okie" was certified as a million-seller on October 2, 1970, and on October 15 (nearly a year to the day after its chart entry), the Country Music Association named it the Single of the Year, duplicating an earlier honor from the Academy of Country Music.

46

(I'M SO) AFRAID OF LOSING YOU
CHARLEY PRIDE
RCA 0265
Writers: A.L. Owens, Dallas Frazier
Producer: Jack Clement
December 13, 1969 (3 weeks)

"(I'm So) Afraid Of Losing You" represented Charley Pride's second consecutive number one single written by A.L. "Doodle" Owens and Dallas Frazier.

"It took all day long to write that one," notes Doodle. "We were on Dallas' boat, and we were going up and down the lake and just floating around. We had our guitar, and Dallas just started strumming and came up with the first line, and it just went on from there, but it took all day to do it. We just had to fish for lines all day long to get it right."

Owens and Frazier reeled in a hit, though,

once the song was finished. They knew instinctively as they worked on it that it would suit Pride quite well, and his recording was released on October 14, 1969. It debuted on the *Billboard* country chart on November 8, and skipped to number one in a quick six weeks.

It proved to be a very merry Christmas for Pride. "(I'm So) Afraid Of Losing You" held on to the top position for three weeks, and on December 20, *The Best of Charley Pride* climbed to number one on the country album chart, a position it occupied for 13 weeks.

Pride's success was particularly satisfying because he overcame so much opposition just to get a series of breaks. The first opportunity came in 1963, when he sang for Red Foley backstage at a concert in Montana. When Foley first met Pride, he was concerned that the young black man was trying to stir up racial controversies. When Charley started singing, however, Foley was impressed, and arranged for a session in Nashville.

In Music City, Pride met Jack D. Johnson, a public relations man for Cedarwood publishing, who'd been looking for someone like Charley for some time. "I used to ask shoeshine guys if they knew anybody black that sang country music," Johnson told Vernell Hackett in *Country Song Roundup*. "I'd see a nice-looking black guy on the street, and I might stop him and ask if he liked country music. I sure got lots of funny looks, too!"

Johnson signed Pride to a management deal on March 4, 1964; seventeen months later, Charley secured a record contract and did his first session for the label.

47

BABY, BABY (I KNOW YOU'RE A LADY)
DAVID HOUSTON
Epic 10539
Writers: Norro Wilson, Alex Harvey
Producer: Billy Sherrill
January 3, 1970 (4 weeks)

David Houston's seventh and final trip to number one was also the first for a burgeoning singer/songwriter. Norro Wilson entered the *Billboard* country charts with three different singles during 1969 as a recording artist for Smash Records. None of them was able to pass number 44, and Wilson continued to double as

a songwriter and song plugger for Al Gallico Music in Nashville.

With the turn of the decade, Wilson's songwriting fortunes began to improve. "Baby, Baby (I Know You're A Lady)" started out as a guitar riff built around a D chord, and it eventually grew into a single that spent four weeks at number one.

"I used to go into Billy Sherrill's office," remembers Wilson, "and I'd sit there and talk to him—loafing, of course. I had this little guitar lick, and he'd say, 'What is that you're playing?' Later, Alex Harvey was over visiting me when I was representing Al Gallico Music, and he thought it was interesting, too. Then we came up with the title, 'Baby, Baby,' and we kept fudging it."

Wilson had thoughts of using the song for his own recording career, but fate intervened when he appeared at the Landmark Hotel in Las Vegas, with Danny Davis & The Nashville Brass, Mel Tillis and Diana Trask. "While I was gone, they had David Houston cut the record. Al Gallico called me up while I was working in Vegas, and said I had a monster."

Houston's momentum carried him through several more years of Top Ten records, as he added ten more hits for Epic through the end of 1974. Included were "A Woman Always Knows" and "Good Things," both of which peaked at number two; and "After Closing Time," a 1970 duet with Barbara Mandrell that represented her first Top Ten recording.

A member of the Grand Ole Opry since 1971, Houston recorded for several other labels during the remainder of the decade, but was hampered by medical difficulties throughout the '80s. He developed cartilage problems in an elbow and both knees, and had ear trouble that impaired his hearing. In 1987, he remarried, and now makes his home in Prescott, Arkansas.

48

A WEEK IN A COUNTRY JAIL
TOM T. HALL
Mercury 72998
Writer: Tom T. Hall
Producer: Jerry Kennedy
January 31, 1970 (2 weeks)

He's been rightfully labeled a "reluctant star." Tom T. Hall didn't move to Nashville to make records. He went to write songs, and his tunes have supplied other performers with a bevy of hits: "Harper Valley P.T.A.," by Jeannie Riley [see 17]; "The Pool Shark," by Dave Dudley [see 54]; "D.J. For A Day," by Jimmy C. Newman; "That's How I Got To Memphis," by Bobby Bare; and "I'm Not Ready Yet," by George Jones. That's just a partial list.

After moving to Nashville on January 1, 1964, Hall penned a massive number of compositions—songs that were admired, but seemingly ill-suited for the existing artists. Producer Jerry Kennedy convinced Tom to sign with Mercury to get his songs recorded. Little more than a year passed between Hall's first single and his first Top Five tune, "Ballad Of Forty Dollars," which debuted in 1968. A year after that, he released "A Week In A Country Jail," the first of seven to top the *Billboard* country chart.

Inspiration for the record came from Hall's Brentwood, Tennessee neighbor Stonewall Jackson, who had two number one singles of his own: 1959's "Waterloo" and 1964's "B.J. The D.J." Jackson requested a prison song for a concept album, but when Hall tried to write one, he lamented to his wife, Miss Dixie, that he'd never been to prison—only to jail.

"Miss Dixie always had these very logical answers for me," Hall wryly notes, "and she said, 'Well, write about being in jail.' So I got to thinking, 'Which time would be the most interesting time?' I never robbed a bank or anything, so I'm not laying any claim to too much in that regard.

"But I remember being in Kentucky, and they kept me locked up because the judge's grandmother died, and nobody got out of jail till he got back. He went to the funeral, and, of course, he went to the wake, and it was out of town, and he was gone. I was in there for about a week, so I wrote a song about 'A Week In A Country Jail.'"

Once the record hit, Hall used its autobiographical approach as a foundation for future successes. "I thought, 'Well, if people are interested in that sort of thing, I've led an interesting and varied life.' So I started writing about places I'd been and things I've done."

Tom T. Hall

49

IT'S JUST A MATTER OF TIME

SONNY JAMES

Capitol 2700
Writers: Clyde Otis, Brook Benton,
Belford Hendricks
Producer: George Richey
February 14, 1970 (4 weeks)

His real name was Benjamin Franklin Peay, but American pop audiences knew him better as Brook Benton. Born in Camden, South Carolina, on September 19, 1931, Benton learned to sing with a local gospel group, and started working at age 12, delivering milk. After moving to New York, he pushed carts of clothing through the city's garment district, and then became a truck driver, all the while writing songs on the side.

"It's Just A Matter Of Time," produced by Clyde Otis in 1958, became Brook's breakthrough composition. The song was the first of eight Benton singles that would reach the Top Ten on *Billboard*'s Hot 100 through 1970.

Several of his recordings would resurface on the country charts when other artists provided new versions. Don Williams took "The Ties That Bind" to number five in 1974, and Hank Williams, Jr., went to number 13 that same year with "Rainy Night In Georgia." The first successful cover of a Benton tune, though, came with Sonny James' remake of "It's Just A Matter Of Time."

Benton had gained his first inspiration for the song in his sleep, and, quite amazingly, he retained the idea after awakening the next morning. He told Otis of it at a later date, and they collaborated with Belford Hendricks to finish the composition.

More than ten years later, "It's Just A Matter Of Time" became James' tenth consecutive number one single. "I was looking for a ballad," James explains. "I'd had some uptempos, and I didn't have anything like 'Matter Of Time,' and I'd also heard a little lick that I could do on my guitar. I was going for a good song, that put the style of guitar that I played out front, and I just felt the song. Of course, it turned out to be a good one for me."

As with many of his singles, Sonny performed "Matter Of Time" on "The Ed Sullivan Show" on January 11, 1970, and again on "Hee Haw" ten days later. Beginning on Valentine's Day, James occupied the top of *Billboard*'s country chart for exactly four weeks. Iron-

ically, the last week that the record stayed at number one, Benton peaked for the last time in the pop chart's Top Ten with "A Rainy Night In Georgia."

50

THE FIGHTIN' SIDE OF ME

MERLE HAGGARD
& THE STRANGERS

Capitol 2719
Writer: Merle Haggard
Producer: Ken Nelson
March 14, 1970 (3 weeks)

Coming at a time when the Vietnam War, the sexual revolution and rock and roll fiercely divided generations, Merle Haggard's "Okie From Muskogee" [see 45] and "The Fightin' Side Of Me" were both a blessing and a burden.

"I didn't intend for 'Okie' to be taken as strongly from my lips as it was," he says. "Now, I'm not saying that I'm not proud of the song or that I'm in disagreement with the song, but I think those songs actually hurt me. At the time I released them, there was such a strong movement in this country in the opposite direction that it alienated me from a lot of people who might otherwise have been fans of mine."

"The Fightin' Side Of Me" was worded particularly strongly. Haggard called America's pacifists "squirrely" and advised "If you don't love it, leave it." Picket lines were formed outside some of his concerts by groups opposing the Vietnam War.

"A lot of people might have misinterpreted those songs, particularly 'Fightin','" he reflects. "I'm not saying you can't stand up and say what you believe in. That's one of the most important rights we have, and that's what *I'm* doing. But I am saying—and I am attacking—anything that might destroy democracy. If we hadn't defended our way of living, our American way of life, in the past—well, there wouldn't be anything to tear up today."

If the liberal segment of society disapproved, enough of the right wing supported "The Fightin' Side Of Me" to keep it at number one for three weeks, beginning March 14, 1970. One month later, the Academy of Country Music also supported Hag, giving him five "Hat" awards, including Male Vocalist of the Year, and Best Band (awarded to the Strangers).

Merle also received a special request from Alabama governor George Wallace. Apparently a country fan [see 112—"My Man"], Wallace asked Haggard to campaign for his re-election; Merle declined.

51

TENNESSEE BIRDWALK
JACK BLANCHARD & MISTY MORGAN
Wayside 010
Writer: Jack Blanchard
Producer: Little Richie Johnson
April 4, 1970 (2 weeks)

The teaming of Jack Blanchard & Misty Morgan—as a married couple and as a performing duo—brimmed with coincidences. Both were born in the month of May

Jack Blanchard & Misty Morgan

(Blanchard on May 8, 1941; Morgan on May 23, 1945) and both deliveries occurred at Millard Fillmore Hospital in Buffalo, New York.

Blanchard and Morgan each had parents named John and Mary, each had a sister named Virginia, and both had blue eyes and brown hair. To top it off, both families moved to Tonawanda, New York, and then to southern Ohio, and yet the couple didn't actually meet until both were living in Hollywood, Florida. "We were working in different nightclubs on the same street," Blanchard once told writer Jim Roden, "both playing the piano. Then one night when I was off, she dropped in at the place I was working and auditioned for my job."

Misty didn't get the job, but she did end up with Blanchard when they later married in Kingsland, Georgia. In spite of their obvious musical similarities, it took yet another five years before they began working together. "It just happened that the band I was with broke up," he notes, "so Misty and I decided to try it

as a team. It was that or starve."

In the meantime, Blanchard applied his writing talents to a comic strip and several books, in addition to a newspaper column in central Florida, appropriately titled "Misty Voices." Still, it was both of their voices that brought them national acclaim.

A Florida disk jockey brought the duo to the attention of New Mexico record producer Little Richie Johnson, who signed them to Wayside Records with their first single, "Bethlehem Steel." "Big Black Bird" finally charted in 1969, and the following year, "Tennessee Birdwalk," with its novelty focus on bird baths and fowl in underwear, hit the top spot.

"Humphrey The Camel" followed it to number five four months later, but it proved to be the last of Blanchard & Morgan's bona fide hits. They moved to Mega Records in 1971, and to Epic in 1973, last appearing on the *Billboard* charts in the early part of 1976.

52

IS ANYBODY GOIN' TO SAN ANTONE?
CHARLEY PRIDE
RCA 9806
Writers: Glenn Martin, Dave Kirby
Producer: Jack Clement
April 18, 1970 (2 weeks)

Born in Texas and raised in Albuquerque, Dave Kirby moved to Nashville to become a songwriter. He earned a spot among the most prolific session guitarists for several years, playing on such records as "Lucille" [see 280], "Jolene" [see 152] and "I Believe In You" [see 397]. Kirby also fared well as a songwriter, creating "There Ain't No Good Chain Gang," "Memories To Burn" and the Grammy-nominated "Is Anybody Goin' To San Antone?," among others.

The latter tune originated at a Nashville recording session, when someone leaving the studio asked that very question while walking out the door. "We started working on it when we'd be together, or when we'd talk on the phone," recalls co-writer Glenn Martin. "I had to go to Atlanta on a trip, and [Kirby] went, and we finished it up on the way. I think it's the most equally co-written song I've ever written."

Pride didn't really have a lot of time to get the lyrics down, though. "Most of the time I like to get my music and live with it for quite

some time," he explains. "This was brought to me about 15 minutes prior to recording. They said, 'We just wrote this song,' and I said, 'Okay, I don't like taking it like that,' but I had about 15 or 20 minutes to learn this song."

The writers promised Pride an exclusive on the number, but the publishing company was sold, and in the confusion, the song was pitched to New York Jets football player Bake Turner. "I get back home," says Charley, "and I lay down in my bed, and I looked at Johnny Carson, and there's Bake Turner. He's on Johnny Carson, doing that particular song, and I said, 'Oh, my goodness, how could they just have written that thing and here he is doing it on Johnny Carson?'"

Though he had no recording deal, Turner announced that he was releasing "Is Anybody Goin' To San Antone?" as a single, and Pride was miffed about the situation. "We didn't know a thing," Martin insists. "Obviously, we wouldn't pitch a song knowing Charley was gonna come out with it."

Pride tried recording several other songs in hopes of finding a replacement single, but nothing worked as well as "San Antone," and he released the record anyway. Turner never charted, but Pride went on to notch his third straight number one single.

53

MY WOMAN, MY WOMAN, MY WIFE
MARTY ROBBINS
Columbia 45091
Writer: Marty Robbins
Producer: Bob Johnston
Date: May 2, 1970 (1 week)

The eighteen months that transpired between Marty Robbins' eleventh and twelfth number one singles proved a significant period in his career. Three intervening releases—"It's A Sin," "I Can't Say Goodbye" and "Camelia"— all earned Top Ten status, but the most important event took place on August 1, 1969.

While traveling by bus to a show in Greenville, Ohio, Robbins felt chest pains near Cleveland. It took an hour to find a doctor, who informed the entertainer that he was having a heart attack. Marty refused to believe him, took some pain pills and went on to play the show anyway.

He did accept the next diagnosis, though, which showed that three of the four arteries to his heart were almost totally blocked. He was given a 50-50 chance of survival, and on January 27, 1970, he underwent open-heart surgery in a five-and-a-half hour operation in Nashville conducted by Dr. William Stoney, Jr. Eight years later, he told an audience at the Grand Ole Opry that he had actually seen Christ while he was clinically dead during the course of the operation. Appropriately, his next number one single blended a spiritual air with the love of a lady.

Robbins performed his first Opry show after the operation on March 30, 1970, nine days after entering the *Billboard* country chart with "My Woman, My Woman, My Wife." He'd written the song specifically for Marizona Baldwin, whom he had married in June 1945.

Six weeks after it appeared, the record moved to number one. During its chart run, Robbins was honored by the Academy of Country Music, which named him Artist of the Decade for the '60s. On March 16, 1971, Marty picked up his second Grammy award, when "My Woman, My Woman, My Wife" earned the trophy for Best Country Song.

Doctors had told him to slow down after his heart surgery, but Robbins was soon going at

full speed again. "I don't think he should have told me that," Robbins later remarked to Stacy Harris in *Country Song Roundup*. "It really floored me for a while, but not for long. I really come alive when I'm on stage."

54

THE POOL SHARK
DAVE DUDLEY
Mercury 73029
Writer: Tom T. Hall
Producer: Jerry Kennedy
May 9, 1970 (1 week)

Born May 3, 1928, as David Darwin Pudraska, he's better known to most as Dave Dudley, "The High Priest of Diesel Country."

Raised in Stevens Point, Wisconsin, Dudley first set his sights on baseball, but an arm injury in semi-pro ball ended that career. In the fall of 1950, he found a new vocation while visiting a friend at radio station WTMT. Dudley played along with a record in the studio, and ended up with his own morning show. He moved to stations in Waterloo; Charles City, Iowa; and St. Paul. All the while, he worked with several different bands in various nightclubs, eventually taking a slot as emcee at The Flame in Minnesota.

After work on December 3, 1960, Dave was hit and nearly killed by an automobile. When the insurance company paid him $14,000, he invested the money in the record business, creating his own label—Golden Wing Records—and cutting a song called "Six Days On The Road."

The investment paid huge dividends. The record soared to number two on the *Billboard* country chart in 1963, establishing Dudley as the truckers' spokesman. By the end of the '60s, Dudley had amassed nine Top Ten singles, including "Cowboy Boots," "Truck Drivin' Son-Of-A-Gun" and "What We're Fighting For."

Ironically, the truckin' king scored his only number one single with "The Pool Shark," Dudley's first release of the '70s. Tom T. Hall wrote the song, calling upon memories of a period when he played billiards quite regularly in West Virginia. He combined that knowledge with a fascination for Paul Newman's role as "Fast Eddie" Felson in *The Hustler*. The song told the story of a would-be hustler who meets up with a pro and loses his shirt.

STEREO SR 61276
PLAYABLE ON MODERN MONAURAL EQUIPMENT

THE POOL SHARK
featuring "THIS NIGHT AIN'T FIT FOR NOTHING BUT DRINKING"

dave dudley

mercury

"When I recorded a demo for Dudley," recalls Hall, "I was hoarse from laryngitis. I'm not sure that Dave knew I had laryngitis when I recorded it, or if he thought that was part of the character when I was doing the narrative. He picked up on some of that and did some real rough talking, a Mafia dialect, or somethin'."

A year later, Dudley mustered his last two Top Ten singles. In 1978, he returned for a time to radio work, holding down a slot on WSM out of Nashville. He continues to hold an annual country festival every August at his lodge in Dudleyville, Wisconsin.

55

MY LOVE
SONNY JAMES

Capitol 2782
Writer: Tony Hatch
Producer: Kelso Herston
May 16, 1970 (3 weeks)

"My Love" became Sonny James' eleventh consecutive number one single. It was a significant achievement, but especially striking when compared to earlier chart runs. Before James, only five streaks had been achieved that went beyond two back-to-back chart-toppers:

- Buck Owens, 1966-67 ("Think Of Me," "Open Up Your Heart," "Where Does The Good Times Go," "Sam's Place," "Your Tender Loving Care")
- Elvis Presley, 1955-56 ("I Forgot To Remember To Forget," "Heartbreak Hotel," "I Want You, I Need You, I Love You," "Don't Be Cruel"/"Hound Dog")
- Buck Owens, 1963-64 ("Act Naturally," "Love's Gonna Live Here," "My Heart Skips A Beat"/"Together Again," "I Don't Care")
- Buck Owens, 1965 ("I've Got A Tiger By The Tail," "Before You Go," "Only You [Can Break My Heart]")
- Jim Reeves, 1966 ("Distant Drums," "Blue Side Of Lonesome," "I Won't Come In While He's There")

One of the keys to James' streak was his dedication to variety. "I believe it's like vanilla ice cream," he explains. "Regardless of how well you like it, if you don't have a little something else, it gets old. I think you can go to the watering trough too often."

James went to a Petula Clark recording in the case of "My Love." It was written by her producer, Tony Hatch, on a transatlantic flight, and Petula's version peaked at number one on the *Billboard* Hot 100 in 1966. James was able to adapt it to a country audience just four years later.

"I wanted something fast, like a bluegrass song," James notes. "I'm a big bluegrass fan, and I wanted something that I could really go with. I hadn't featured the Southern Gentlemen, my group, that much. I'd been kind of holding them back, but on this one, I brought them right out front."

As with many of his singles, James sang "My Love" on national television a couple of times: April 8, on "The Johnny Cash Show"; and May 10, on "The Ed Sullivan Show" (his third appearance of the year). "My Love" reached the top of the country chart in only six weeks, and stayed at number one for three more weeks.

A dozen years later, the song's original performer, Petula Clark, made an attempt at a country career. She went as far as number 20 in 1982 with "Natural Love."

56

HELLO DARLIN'
CONWAY TWITTY

Decca 32661
Writer: Conway Twitty
Producer: Owen Bradley
June 6, 1970 (4 weeks)

"Hello Darlin'" existed for an entire decade before the public ever heard it. During the days that his career embraced rock and roll, Conway Twitty frequently wrote country songs but had no outlets to get them recorded. As a result, he simply dropped cassette copies into a huge box and put them in storage.

After he signed a contract with Decca Records' country division, Twitty frequently culled material from that box of unheard oldies. In 1969, he brought out a piece that he had written in 1960 and played it for producer Owen Bradley. It had no discernible chorus or hook line; Conway viewed it as a "left field" number.

Bradley liked the tune, however, and they decided to do a little work on it. For starters, they titled it "Hello Darlin'," copping the first line—heard only once in the entire song—as the title. Owen suggested that Conway simply speak those two words instead of singing them. They also changed the arrangement to highlight an electric piano.

"That was very unusual for country music at that time," recalls keyboard player Larry Butler. "I was playing regular piano, and I kept looking over against the wall, and there was this little old Wurlitzer piano sittin' over there, and we were tryin' to figure out somethin' different for the intro. I suggested to Owen Bradley that I try this. They listened to it, Conway liked it, and that was it."

"Hello Darlin'" entered *Billboard*'s country chart at number 31 on April 25, 1970, and in its seventh week, it reached number one, holding down the top spot for the entire month of June.

Five years after its release, the record made history far outside the earth's atmosphere. Brigadier General Thomas P. Stafford contacted Twitty on March 27, 1975, about music that the astronauts could take along on an Apollo/Soyuz space mission. Engineer David Barnes suggested they record one of Twitty's songs in Russian, and Twitty secured an Oklahoma University professor to assist in translating "Hello Darlin'" to "Privet Radost."

Twitty was on hand at Cape Kennedy to witness the historic launch on July 15, 1975, and when the U.S. and Soviet crews linked in space two days later, he watched the global telecast from a hotel room in Oakland. Playing in the background was "Privet Radost."

57
HE LOVES ME ALL THE WAY
TAMMY WYNETTE
Epic 10612
Writers: Norro Wilson, Carmol Taylor, Billy Sherrill
Producer: Billy Sherrill
July 4, 1970 (3 weeks)

On April 13, 1970, Tammy Wynette picked up her first and only Top Female Vocalist award from the Los Angeles-based Academy of Country Music. About six weeks later, on May 23, 1970, the ACM winner appeared on the *Billboard* country chart with yet another showcase of her talents, albeit one with a very deliberate purpose.

"We wanted an uptempo something to get away from the sameness in what we had written before," she says. "Everything seemed to be about the same, tempo-wise. We didn't have a whole lot of variety in the tempo and we were trying to get something a little bit more 'up' and a little more happy."

As usual, the tune was co-written by producer Billy Sherrill, who summoned Norro Wilson and Carmol Taylor from his stable of associates to help out. Born September 5, 1931, Taylor grew up in Brilliant, Alabama, about 40 miles southeast of Wynette's birthplace. An aspiring performer, his best showing as a solo artist was "I Really Had A Ball Last Night," which peaked at number 23 in 1976.

Carmol fared much better as a writer for Al Gallico Music, penning such tunes as "The Grand Tour" [see 176] and "There's A Song On The Jukebox" (recorded by David Wills). Taylor died from lung cancer on December 5, 1986, but the work he left behind included two number one records for Tammy, "My Man (Understands)" [see 112] and "He Loves Me All The Way."

Both songs were, for Wynette, atypically uptempo releases. "The easiest thing to get done from a radio level is something energetic," notes Wilson. "They tend to play it quicker than a ballad. I think ballads are always the hardest thing in the world to get to happen, and that's understandable, because they have to be so great. 'He Loves Me All The Way' is one of those things that we went in and tried to hammer, nail, manufacture. We were doing it our way—the same way that some of these young guys are doing it now."

Their way brought prosperity on Independence Day in 1970, when "He Loves Me All The Way" began a three-week command of the number one position.

58
WONDER COULD I LIVE THERE ANYMORE
CHARLEY PRIDE
RCA 9855
Writer: Bill Rice
Producer: Jack Clement
July 25, 1970 (2 weeks)

Having operated for the first five years of his career from Helena, Montana, Charley Pride moved closer to Nashville in June of 1969, settling in Dallas. Texas' central location made it easier for him to tour, and, as a sports buff, Pride was also attracted by the various professional and collegiate events in the city.

"Most of my kids were born in the Rockies," he told *Billboard*'s Edward Morris, outlining the major reasons for moving. "I lived up there during the '60s, the turbulent years of the civil rights crisis. I didn't want my children being exposed to any more prejudice. Nashville at that time was more segregated. Plus, I knew if I moved to Nashville I would never be away from the hustle and bustle of the business."

Home was the central theme of "Wonder Could I Live There Anymore," Pride's second number one single of the '70s. The song contemplates a trip back to the family farm, where Mom and Dad are locked into a day-to-day routine. Appropriately, Bill Rice wrote it after a vacation, and it's the only number one single he wrote without his usual partner, Jerry Foster.

Foster was concurrently interested in a performing career, and when he was given a chance to work on the song with Rice, he went out on tour instead. Publisher Bill Hall encouraged Rice to write the tune on his own, and Rice originally turned it in as "I Wouldn't Want To Live There Anymore" before Pride altered the title.

"I actually went in and tried to give half of the [credit for the] song to Foster," Rice says, " 'cause we were tryin' to build a team. Hall wouldn't hear of it. In fact, he said, 'Whenever the statement comes in, I'm gonna show Foster how much you made on that song.' Bill was trying to make a point that Foster's writing career was much more important than wantin' to be a star, so he used that as a tool."

While "Wonder Could I Live There Anymore" occupied the top of the country singles chart for two weeks, Pride made the top of the album chart a home of his own during 1970. He spent a total of 30 weeks at number one with three different releases: *The Best of Charley Pride*, *Just Plain Charley* and *Charley Pride's 10th Album*.

Sonny James

59
DON'T KEEP ME HANGIN' ON
SONNY JAMES
Capitol 2834
Writers: Carole Smith, Sonny James
Producer: George Richey
August 8, 1970 (4 weeks)

Sonny James was a competent songwriter, but it was rarely evident from his hits—not because they lacked anything, but because he wrote so few of his own recordings.

Sonny wrote his second number one single, "You're The Only World I Know" [see 4—"A World Of Our Own"], with Bob Tubert, netting a Grammy nomination for Country Song of the Year in 1965. They also teamed up for "I'll Keep Holding On" (number two, 1965), and James co-authored "True Love's A Blessing" (number three, 1966) with Carole Smith. It took four more years before he released another self-penned single, "Don't Keep Me Hangin' On."

"I was always writing," Sonny notes, "and [Capitol's] Ken Nelson used to mention some of the songs that I wrote or co-wrote, and I'd say, 'Ken, I honestly can't give you an opinion on it because I'm too close to it.' It's hard for me to give an opinion on something that I'm close to, because I could be biased. Ken would say, 'I feel real strong about this, Sonny; I think we should go with it.' He would be the one really to pick the songs out that I wrote."

Such was the case with "Don't Keep Me Hangin' On," another tune co-written with Smith, a songwriter from St. Petersburg.

"Carole and I had written a lot of story songs," James says. "She's a great lyric writer, and I owe her so much because a lot of my albums were filled with her lyrics. Basically, she was a lyric writer mostly, but she always thought that I wrote the melodies that seemed to fit her lyrics better than some that she would do, so consequently we wrote a lot of songs together. 'Don't Keep Me Hangin' On' was one of them."

Widely regarded as a perfectionist, James credits Capitol Records—he spent 14 years with the label—for keeping up his enthusiasm. "I was fortunate in working with a record company that believed in me, and that was because of Ken Nelson. They had such a positive attitude, and you knew that if you gave them something, they'd go with it. I think they got the most out of everything I ever did."

60

ALL FOR THE LOVE OF SUNSHINE
HANK WILLIAMS, JR. WITH THE MIKE CURB CONGREGATION
MGM 14152
Writers: Lalo Schifrin, Harkey Hatcher, Mike Curb
Producers: Jim Vienneau, Mike Curb
September 5, 1970 (2 weeks)

Given the same name as his legendary father, Hank Williams, Jr., carried quite a weight on his shoulders for years. He was born May 26, 1949, in Shreveport, Louisiana. The senior Hank was working in Shreveport as a performer on the "Louisiana Hayride," sent there by the talent agents at the Grand Ole Opry. They knew that Hank had a problem with chemical dependency, and told him if he could stay straight for a year, they would give him membership on the Opry.

Once he became an Opry member, the elder Williams eventually nicknamed his son "Bocephus." That name originally belonged to a wooden dummy, the handheld prop of Opry comedian Rod Brasfield.

Following his father's death [see 385—"You Win Again"], Bocephus took up the banner, first appearing on stage in Swainsboro, Georgia, at the age of eight. "I walked out on that stage," he recalls, "with my hands stuffed into the pockets of my little black suit, and I sang 'Lovesick Blues' in my little eight-year-old voice. The audience loved it. They went crazy,

shouting about 'Hank's little boy.' "

The boy first recorded at age 14, singing 13 songs on the soundtrack to *Your Cheatin' Heart*, a biographical MGM movie in which George Hamilton played Hank, Sr. The film also brought the younger Williams his first country hit, "Long Gone Lonesome Blues."

Two years later, Bocephus wrote his first song, "Standing In The Shadows," about the strain of living up to his father's name. It, too, became a Top Five recording. Three more singles equaled that status until he earned his first number one single with "All For The Love Of Sunshine," a ballad that MGM president Mike Curb placed in the James Garner militia movie *Kelly's Heroes*. "It was out in the middle of a battle scene," laughs Hank's manager, Merle Kilgore. "He's singing 'All for the love of sunshine'—boom! It was unbelievable."

Hank's basic vocals were recorded in Nashville, and the Mike Curb Congregation added back-up vocals in Los Angeles. The Congregation also earned a pop hit out of the same film, with "All Those Burning Bridges."

Curb, who took the MGM job at age 25, was instrumental in building the careers of Donny and Marie Osmond [see 147—"Paper Roses"], and was voted Lieutenant Governor of California in the late '70s. He currently owns Curb Records.

61

FOR THE GOOD TIMES/GRAZIN' IN GREENER PASTURES
RAY PRICE
Columbia 45178
Writer: Kris Kristofferson/Ray Pennington
Producer: Don Law
September 19, 1970 (1 week)

When Ray Price reached the top of the *Billboard* country chart with "For The Good Times" in 1970, it ended a ten-year absence of number one records for a man who has experimented with a number of musical styles. Noted initially for the walking bass of his country shuffles, Price had opted for a more urbane sound, enhanced by a bevy of strings. When that texture met with Kris Kristofferson's composition, the resulting "For The Good Times" not only reached number one in country music, but also soared to number 11 on the Hot 100.

Kristofferson started the song in 1968 during a drive from Nashville to the Gulf of Mexico, where he piloted helicopters for offshore oil rigs. He hated the trip, and on this particular drive, he developed the first verse and chorus of a song about a final sexual encounter between a man and woman who were breaking up.

"After a while, the melody really got to me," Kris said in *The Tennessean*. "I couldn't wait to get to a guitar. I was riding along thinking about that part where it says, 'Hear the whisper of the raindrops blowin' soft against the window . . .,' and I wondered what the chords were. Hell, I wondered if I could play it. I wrote only the first part of the lyrics then. A while went by before I finished it, I can't remember how long. But I do remember who I wrote it about."

Ray Pennington—who worked for Buckhorn Music, publisher of "For The Good Times"—thought the song might do well for Price, who was touring at the time. Pennington got hold of Price's schedule and sent a copy of the demo to a club in Odessa, Texas, where Price would appear. Ray listened to it between shows and decided to cut it.

Initially, Columbia released "For The Good Times" as the "B" side of "Grazin' In Greener Pastures," despite Price's contention that "For The Good Times" would be more successful. The label shifted its emphasis after Wayne Newton also cut "For The Good Times," and Price ended up selling 11 million copies.

In March of 1971, Price won his only Grammy award for the tune. That same year, the Academy of Country Music cited "For The Good Times" as Song of the Year and Single Record of the Year. The *For The Good Times* LP earned Album of the Year honors.

Jerry Lee Lewis at Nashville's Mercury Studio, 1970

62
THERE MUST BE MORE TO LOVE THAN THIS
JERRY LEE LEWIS
Mercury 73099
Writers: William E. Taylor, LaVerne Thomas
Producer: Jerry Kennedy
September 26, 1970 (2 weeks)

Once he remolded himself as strictly a country act [see 26—"To Make Love Sweeter For You"], Jerry Lee Lewis earned huge marks in the field. He became a model of consistency, and as his Smash/Mercury singles reached the Top Five, Sun Records reissued some of his material from their vaults, taking his older songs into the Top Ten during the same period.

Three Sun re-releases made the Top Ten in a nine-month stretch during 1969–70: "Invitation To Your Party," "One Minute Past Eternity" and "I Can't Seem To Say Goodbye." Concurrently, Mercury had success with "One Has My Name (The Other Has My Heart)" (number three), "She Even Woke Me Up To Say Goodbye" (number two) and "Once More With Feeling" (number two). In addition, Jerry Lee and younger sister Linda Gail Lewis scored a Top Ten duet in 1969 with a remake of "Don't Let Me Cross Over."

On August 22, 1970, Lewis entered the *Billboard* country chart with "There Must Be More To Love Than This," written in part by Bill Taylor, who played trumpet in the Killer's band at the time. "I didn't believe in the thing," confesses producer Jerry Kennedy. "I wasn't really in love with that song, not until Jerry laid it down." Obviously, Lewis knew what it needed, and in its sixth week, it emerged at number one for a two-week run.

Jerry Lee Lewis was born September 29, 1935, in Ferriday, Louisiana, where his companions were cousins Jimmy Swaggart and Mickey Gilley [see 245—"Don't The Girls All Get Prettier At Closing Time"]. Many of the events of Lewis' youth pitted the fundamentalist religious attitudes of his upbringing against his energetic musical fervor. His mother preached at the local Assembly of God Church, and Jerry Lee would often play the piano during the service. When he was a teenager, though, a church in Texas bounced him out of Bible school when he applied his pumping piano to "My God Is Real."

Lewis briefly pursued life in the ministry, although he quickly left that to Swaggart, and devoted his attentions to music full-time. His first Sun recordings came in 1956, with "End Of The Road" and "Crazy Arms," and his financial success during that period ultimately inspired Mickey Gilley to chase a similar musical career.

63
SUNDAY MORNING COMING DOWN
JOHNNY CASH
Columbia 45211
Writer: Kris Kristofferson
Producer: Bob Johnston
October 10, 1970 (2 weeks)

The 1969 Country Music Association awards show belonged almost exclusively to Johnny Cash. Cash was named Entertainer of the Year, Male Vocalist of the Year, and (along with June Carter) Vocal Group of the Year. *Johnny Cash at San Quentin* brought him his second straight Album of the Year award, and "A Boy Named Sue" [see 40] earned Single of the Year honors.

Along with Glen Campbell [see 23—"Wichita Lineman"], television had made Cash the most recognizable performer of that era. "The Johnny Cash Show" premiered on June 7, 1969 (his first guests were Bob Dylan and Joni Mitchell) as a summer series. Renewed in January, the program broadcast to 23,000,000 viewers each week until May of 1971.

At the height of his popularity, Johnny received a call from White House aide H.R. Haldeman, who asked Cash to perform at the White House on April 17, 1970. Cash accepted the invitation, but declined to perform two of the three songs on President Richard Nixon's "wish list," including "Okie From Muskogee" [see 45]. Cash *did* play the requested "A Boy Named Sue" plus his controversial anti-Vietnam release "What Is Truth." That single eventually peaked at number three.

In May, Cash took time out to film *A Gunfighter*, with Kirk Douglas, and on September 5, he appeared in *Billboard* with his next single, "Sunday Morning Coming Down." Kris Kristofferson wrote the song while he lived in a dilapidated tenement following a divorce. Kris first met Cash while working at Columbia Recording Studios [see 135—"Why Me"].

"They told him if he pitched his songs to me while I was recording, they would fire him," Cash recalled to Bill Flanagan in *Musician*. "Then one Sunday, he landed in my yard in a helicopter and brought me 'Sunday Morning Coming Down.' That's true. He fell out of that helicopter with a beer in one hand and a tape in the other and said, 'By God, I'm gonna get a song to you one way or another.' I said, 'Well, you just did, let's go in and hear it.'"

After Cash cut the song, it remained at number one for two weeks. During that period, the CMA named it Song of the Year on October 16; coincidentally, the Nashville Songwriters Association formed its Hall of Fame on October 12. Kristofferson was inducted on October 9, 1977.

64
RUN, WOMAN, RUN
TAMMY WYNETTE
Epic 10653
Writers: Dan Hoffman, Ann Booth, Duke Goff
Producer: Billy Sherrill
October 24, 1970 (2 weeks)

Beginning July 26, 1970, Tammy Wynette was scheduled for an extended vacation, designed to keep her off the road until she delivered the first baby from her marriage to George Jones. That break didn't last all that long, though—she performed on stage when she was still eight months pregnant.

During the final trimester, Tammy hooked

one more hit, a song that appropriately celebrated the importance of perseverance in making a marriage work. Though "Run, Woman, Run" proved successful, producer Billy Sherrill hardly considers it among the best songs Tammy recorded: "It was the lesser of all the evils that came in that day," he says.

Tammy, however, disagrees. "I thought it was a very pretty song, and kind of different, melody-wise, from what I had been doing. I used to get on stage and say, 'I'm gonna do my new record, "One Woman One."' It's so tongue-twisting to say 'Run, Woman, Run,' but I really did like that song. It said about the same thing as what I had been saying—it just said it a little bit different."

The song was so close in content to "Stand By Your Man" [see 21] that Epic Records feared it might trigger a similar outrage in feminist quarters. To introduce the tune, Epic took out a full-page ad in *Billboard* announcing the release of "Run, Woman, Run" "with apologies to the women's liberation movement."

"We kind of got in trouble with women's lib," Tammy admits, "but I have to be very honest. That was the way I was born and raised. That was the South back then, and when a man said something, that was the gospel. He was the head of the house, and you just did so, and you didn't think twice about doing it. It was our way of life, and I had no idea that I was saying something controversial."

When "Run, Woman, Run" reached number one on October 24, it put the cap on an incredible month for Tammy. On October 15, she earned her third Country Music Association award as Female Vocalist of the Year. Ten days earlier, she gave birth to a girl, whose name was taken from both Mommy and Daddy: Tamala Georgette.

65
I CAN'T BELIEVE THAT YOU'VE STOPPED LOVING ME
CHARLEY PRIDE
RCA 9902
Writers: A.L. Owens, Dallas Frazier
Producer: Jack Clement
November 7, 1970 (2 weeks)

Following "All I Have To Offer You (Is Me)" [see 38] and "(I'm So) Afraid Of Losing You" [see 46], "I Can't Believe That You've Stopped

Loving Me" became the third of Charley Pride's five number one singles written by A.L. "Doodle" Owens and Dallas Frazier.

"When I first came to Nashville, I had my family with me," remembers Owens. "We rented a motel room, and we were waiting to get into a house, and I went in from the pool one day and I wrote that title down. A long time later, I told Dallas about it, and we did it."

Fortunately for both writers, their songs fit Pride almost perfectly. "I think Jack Clement had a lot to do with it," Doodle explains. "I think he liked the feel of the songs and the tempo of the songs, and the phrasing and everything for Charley."

Nicknamed "Cowboy" when he performed on a Memphis radio show in the mid-'50s with Dickey Lee [see 229—"Rocky"] and future Crystal Gayle producer Allen Reynolds, Clement figured prominently in some of country music's biggest successes. He produced Jerry Lee Lewis' first single, "Crazy Arms," while working as an engineer for Sam Phillips, and he wrote Johnny Cash's number one records "Ballad Of A Teenage Queen" and "I Guess Things Happen That Way." He also produced Cash's classic "Ring Of Fire." Approached by manager Jack D. Johnson, Clement produced the demo tape that eventually secured Pride's deal with RCA.

"Jack Clement was the one who suggested a recording session for me," Pride told *Billboard*. "They gave me seven or eight songs to learn while I was on vacation and visiting my father in Mississippi. I was supposed to mail them back, but I drove them up in person instead. Jack Clement had me sing the songs there, with a guitar, after he had asked me if I was ready. I sang the songs, and Clement looked over at Johnson and said, without hesitation, 'He's ready.'"

Clement produced Pride's first session on August 16, 1965, then tried to secure a recording deal for Charley.

"I played the tape for Chet Atkins first," says Clement, "but he turned it down. Everybody turned it down, and I was on the verge of pressing it up myself. One day I ran into Chet down by the water cooler at RCA, and he said, 'What have you done with that black boy's record?' I said, 'Well, I ain't had no luck; I'm thinking about pressing it up myself.'

"He said, 'Well, I been thinking about that—we might be passing up another Elvis Presley.'"

Chet signed Pride to RCA on September 28, 1965.

66

FIFTEEN YEARS AGO
CONWAY TWITTY
Decca 32742
Writer: Raymond Smith
Producer: Owen Bradley
November 21, 1970 (1 week)

Conway Twitty picked up his fifth number one country single from a broadcaster in Greenville, Tennessee—thanks to another station in nearby Knoxville.

Raymond Smith first started writing country songs during his early teens, but in 1969, he managed a "beautiful music" station. He returned to writing when he watched a Jack Greene concert.

"I stood up on the hill and listened to him sing a while," remembers Smith, "listenin' to that steel guitar moan, and that pure-bred country, and thought, 'Gosh, that sounds good,' and that's when I started working on 'Fifteen Years Ago.' Most of it was written the following day. I just kind of got inspired with a good melody and good storyline. Where that came from I don't know."

Smith paid for his own recording session, and released "Fifteen Years Ago" as a single on Sugarhill Records, a subsidiary of the Chart label that first signed Lynn Anderson [see 69—"Rose Garden"]. The song performed well in a handful of markets, including Dallas, Philadelphia and Knoxville, where WIVK played it.

When Twitty played a Knoxville nightclub, one of the station's disk jockeys approached him and suggested that he listen to Raymond's record, which had failed to chart nationally. The deejay then offered to send a copy to Conway's office. "I said, 'No, no, no, no, let's call the radio station right now and get somebody to bring it out here,'" Twitty notes. "Usually when you let somethin' like that go, it never happens. I got that record that night, and found me a record player and listened to it, and that's all it took."

Twitty placed a call to Smith in the groggy hours of the morning to tell him how much he liked it and to ask for permission to record it. "I said, 'Well, good . . . I think,'" laughs Smith. "I was courteous to him and all that, but I really didn't know what that meant."

Smith attended the recording session in Bradley's Barn, however, and the meaning began to sink in. The song went to number one in November of 1970, and was re-recorded by several other artists. Its most notable reappearance came in 1971, when Ben Colder (a.k.a. Sheb Wooley) parodied "Fifteen Years Ago" with his composition "Fifteen Beers Ago."

67

ENDLESSLY
SONNY JAMES
Capitol 2914
Writers: Clyde Otis/Brook Benton
Producer: George Richey
November 28, 1970 (3 weeks)

Following up on the earlier success of "It's Just A Matter Of Time" [see 49], Sonny James reached number one on the *Billboard* country chart with an old Brook Benton tune for the second time during 1970. He did it with "Endlessly," a song Benton had written about a love that goes on and on into infinity.

Though he sang it, it wasn't James' original idea to record it. Benton's producer, publisher and frequent co-writer, Clyde Otis, had suggested "Endlessly" after "It's Just A Matter Of Time" reached number one. On top of that, a disk jockey took the time to write James a letter, which echoed Otis' sentiment.

"He knew I liked 'It's Just A Matter Of Time,'" James remembers, "and mentioned the success I'd had with 'I'll Never Find Another You' and those fast songs, and said that 'Endlessly' would be right down my alley.

"I thought, 'Here's Clyde Otis, and here's this fellow in radio who writes, and isn't connected with the song in any way, they may be right.' I got out my guitar, and I worked something up, and I did 'Endlessly' and kept the guitar work all the way through the song. After that, I knew I had to do that one."

James earned the nickname "The Southern Gentleman," and with good reason. He's one of the most thoughtful and patient men who has ever worked in the country music business, and, true to form, he had every intention of phoning the deejay who wrote the letter to thank him for the suggestion.

"It's one of those cases that I'm gonna get back to him, and you have it there on your desk with five hundred other things," laments James. "My desk is always messed up. Somehow or other, either somebody in the office tried to straighten up or something, and I couldn't find it. I never did know where I could call the guy and thank him."

Benton passed away in New York on April 16, 1988 from a combination of spinal meningitis, pneumonia and diabetes.

His song brought landmark results for Sonny James. After three weeks at number one, James had garnered a total of 17 number one records to date. Altogether, he'd spent 54 weeks—more than a year!—at the top of the *Billboard* country chart.

68

COAL MINER'S DAUGHTER
LORETTA LYNN

Decca 32749
Writer: Loretta Lynn
Producer: Owen Bradley
December 19, 1970 (1 week)

"**C**oal Miner's Daughter" is the most significant record of Loretta Lynn's career. An autobiographical sketch, it's become her nickname; the title of a book, co-authored by the *New York Times*' George Vecsey; and the title of a movie, starring Sissy Spacek. Loretta's bus carries a "Coal Miner" insignia, and she also uses that phrase as her CB handle.

Loretta had actually wanted to write a song about her youth for many years, and she got the opportunity while waiting to do some work on a television show at the WSIX studios in Nashville. With nothing better to do, she headed for the dressing room and began writing off the top of her head. Within a few hours, she had fashioned "Coal Miner's Daughter" with nine verses.

Only six made it to vinyl, though. Three verses—about the interior-decorating scheme at the Webb log-cabin home, the frequent Kentucky floods, and "hog-killing day"—were left out. No changes were made to the first line, "I was borned a coal miner's daughter," despite its grammatical problems.

"'Borned'?" questions producer Owen Bradley. "Well, that sounds like Loretta to me. She speaks her own language. She has her own tongue. She has a lot of those goodies like that, and I have always felt that she shouldn't be corrected to the point that you spoil that. I think that's her charm. I may be wrong, but if she did 'em all perfect, she'd sound like a whole lot of other people."

Lynn felt that "Coal Miner's Daughter" was

Loretta Lynn

too personal for a single release, and held it back for a year. She recorded it with two other songs on October 1, 1969, and these other two were released first. "Wings Upon Your Horns" [see 29—"Woman Of The World"] went to number 11 and "You Wanna Give Me A Lift" peaked at number six. "Coal Miner's Daughter" finally shipped as a single on October 5, 1970, and reached number one just before year-end.

Among its accomplishments: "It told everybody," Loretta said in *Coal Miner's Daughter*, "that I could write about something else besides marriage problems."

69

ROSE GARDEN

LYNN ANDERSON

Columbia 45252
Writer: Joe South
Producer: Glenn Sutton
December 26, 1970 (5 weeks)

Joe South's first appearance on the *Billboard* album charts came on February 8, 1969, with *Introspect*. Though it was never a "monster" seller, it developed an impressive track record, yielding his hits "Games People Play" and "Walk A Mile In My Shoes."

That album also attracted the attention of Lynn Anderson, a 21-year-old vocalist at Nashville's Chart Records. On May 4, 1969, Anderson married songwriter/record producer Glenn Sutton. By the following year, she had left Chart and signed with Columbia, going to number three with "Stay There 'Til I Get There." She kept insisting that Sutton allow her to record a song from *Introspect* titled "Rose Garden," but he repeatedly turned her down.

"The reason they objected to my recording it was the line 'I could promise you things like big diamond rings,'" Anderson recalls. "It was not a line that a woman would say to a man; they thought, therefore, that it could not be a female vocal on that particular song."

Finally, one of her recording sessions was finished earlier than usual, and they had an extra 15 minutes with nothing planned. "We simply cut it because we didn't have anything else that they considered better," she laughs. The first take didn't work, and the session musicians (including Charlie McCoy and Jerry Kennedy) came up with a different pattern, later dubbed "The Rose Garden Shuffle." "Actually Bill Anderson started that years before 'Rose Garden,'" says Kennedy. "It's what they called the old bluebeat, or ska. We cut a record called 'Blue Beat' in '62 or '63 that had that beat, and Owen [Bradley] used that beat on several Bill Anderson records in the early '60s."

Initially, Columbia's country division planned another song for release, but label president Clive Davis, in town for a convention, heard Sutton mixing "Rose Garden" in Studio B. After a second listen, Davis pronounced that it would be the next single.

While "Rose Garden" vaulted toward number one on the *Billboard* country chart, it simultaneously went to number three on the Hot 100. Both the single and the *Rose Garden* album sold in excess of one million copies. In 1989, the song made a unique appearance on the pop charts once again—excerpts from Anderson's performance were lifted from "Rose Garden" and inserted into "I Beg Your Pardon," a dance record by Kon Kan.

70

FLESH AND BLOOD

JOHNNY CASH

Columbia 45269
Writer: Johnny Cash
Producer: Bob Johnston
January 30, 1971 (1 week)

"Let's face it," Johnny Cash told Neil Pond of the *Music City News* in 1987, "for thirty-one years I've been staying in the finest hotels and traveling first class. But my roots are in the working man. I can remember very well how it is to pick cotton ten hours a day, or to plow, or how to cut wood. I remember it so well, I guess, because I don't intend to ever try to do it again."

A working-class family outing provided the impetus for "Flesh And Blood," Johnny's twelfth number one single. Cash, wife June Carter, and daughters Carlene and Rosie Carter ventured into the countryside in DeKalb County, Tennessee, for a simple picnic. They built a fire by the banks of a creek and roasted hot dogs during the afternoon hours.

Johnny's senses were inundated by the sights and sounds of Mother Nature: the rippling waters, the shade of a willow tree, birds resting on a cliff. Despite the peace and beauty of the location, it occurred to Cash that the love of his wife was even more important. The sentiment inspired him to write "Flesh And Blood" and propelled the song from its December 19, 1970, debut to chart-topping stature six weeks later.

It took more than five years for Cash to return to number one [see 249—"One Piece At A Time"], partially because he devoted much of his time to outside ventures. In March of 1972, 20th Century-Fox released his movie, *Gospel Road*, filmed on location in the Holy Land. The film was later picked up by Billy Graham. In 1975, he released his autobiography, *Man in Black*.

His consistently black apparel is a trademark for Cash, and he followed "Flesh And Blood" with "Man In Black," in which the color became a symbol for many social ills. "Man In Black" surged to number three in 1971, and the following year, Cash watched three consecutive records stop at number two.

"A Thing Called Love" was held out of number one by Freddie Hart's "My Hang-Up Is You" [see 95]. "Kate" was beat out by Donna Fargo's "Happiest Girl In The Whole U.S.A." [see 99] and Sonny James' "That's Why I Love You Like I Do" [see 100]. "Oney" peaked beneath Tammy Wynette's "My Man (Understands)" [see 112] and Charley Pride's "She's Too Good To Be True" [see 113]. "Any Old Wind That Blows" went to number three in 1973.

71

JOSHUA
DOLLY PARTON
RCA 9928
Writer: Dolly Parton
Producer: Bob Ferguson
February 6, 1971 (1 week)

Dolly Parton began her recording career at age 13, when she took a Greyhound bus from her Tennessee mountain home to Lake Charles, Louisiana, where an uncle had rented studio time. Young Dolly recorded "Puppy Love," a composition of her own.

Even at that early age, her mind was set on a career in country music, and on May 30, 1964—one day after she graduated from high school—Parton moved to Nashville. Along with her uncle, Bill Owens, she began a prolific period of writing, and her first success came when Bill Phillips went to number six in 1966 with their composition, "Put It Off Until Tomorrow."

Shortly afterward, Dolly signed a recording deal with Fred Foster's Monument Records, and on January 21, 1967, she made her first appearance on the *Billboard* country chart, with "Dumb Blonde." "Something Fishy" took her to number 17 later that summer, but a pivotal event occurred on October 16, 1967, when she debuted as a member of the Porter Wagoner Show [see 181—"Please Don't Stop Loving Me"].

Wagoner was instrumental in securing Parton a contract with RCA, and, while their duets found immediate acceptance, it took a little

longer for Dolly's solo records to take hold. She didn't reach the Top Ten until her seventh solo RCA release, "Mule Skinner Blues," in 1970. "Joshua," her next single, debuted on December 12, and took her all the way to number one two months later.

Like her later song, "Applejack," "Joshua" was written about a reclusive man from her youth. "There was an old gentleman that lived alone when we were growing up," Dolly explains. "He played the banjo, and he was just real special, especially to me. They're two totally different songs—'Applejack' and 'Joshua'—'cause [in "Joshua"] I had the love interest, but I just let my imagination run wild, and made it into a good song. There was certainly never any romance between us, although I loved him deeply."

"Applejack" later served a specific purpose for Dolly. It was included on the *New Harvest . . . First Gathering* album, her first after siding with new management in Los Angeles [see 202—"The Bargain Store"]. As if to prove she was holding on to her country roots, Dolly included appearances on "Applejack" by Roy Acuff, Chet Atkins and Grandpa Jones, among others.

72

HELP ME MAKE IT THROUGH THE NIGHT
SAMMI SMITH
Mega 0015
Writer: Kris Kristofferson
Producer: Jim Malloy
February 13, 1971 (3 weeks)

Bobby Bare was among the early believers in Kris Kristofferson, and, in fact, Bare had two Kristofferson-penned hits: "Please Don't Tell Me How The Story Ends" [see 177] and "Come Sundown." At one point, he intended to release "Help Me Make It Through The Night" as well.

"I was fixing to release it," he recalls, "and I was doing a show in Philadelphia. Sammi Smith was on, and she said, 'It's my next record.' She beat me out with it, but, of course, I had recorded it different. Mine might not have been a hit."

"Help Me Make It Through The Night" started when Kristofferson conceived the first line of the tune. That's all he had for some time, but the inspiration for the rest of the song came while he was working as a helicopter pilot at an offshore oil rig in the Gulf of Mexico. To pass the time one evening, Kris sat in his copter on the platform, strumming a 12-string guitar. As he gazed at the stars, the rest of the tune came to him quite quickly. The song's title was based on an interview he had once read in which Frank Sinatra talked about using a bottle or a woman to get through the night.

The first person to cut "Help Me Make It Through The Night" was an artist named Bill Nash, but his version went largely overlooked,

Sammi Smith

partially because radio programmers felt the song was too controversial. Dottie West also thought it a bit risqué, and she refused to even cut the song. Sammi Smith, however, appreciated its frankness.

"I never did see anything scandalous about that song," she told Robert Oermann in *Country Song Roundup*. "For me, it was just a very tender, moving song. I honestly don't see anything distasteful about the song."

The general public agreed. In addition to hitting the top of the country charts, "Help Me Make It Through The Night" reached number eight on *Billboard*'s Hot 100, and earned a gold record on April 26, 1971. It netted Single of the Year honors from the Country Music Association, and claimed the Grammys for Best Country Song and Best Country Female.

Smith earned only two more Top Ten hits—with her follow-up, "Then You Walk In," and her 1975 recording of "Today I Started Loving You Again." She also wrote Waylon Jennings' 1971 hit "Cedartown, Georgia," which reached number 12.

73

I'D RATHER LOVE YOU
CHARLEY PRIDE
RCA 9952
Writer: Johnny Duncan
Producer: Jack Clement
March 6, 1971 (3 weeks)

Charley Pride's show welcomed a new addition in 1970: a struggling performer named Johnny Duncan. Duncan had been signed a few years earlier by Columbia [see 281—"It Couldn't Have Been Any Better"], but still hadn't been able to connect with a single that could break his own career open. Pride, however, saw promise in the vocalist and allowed him to use his own band, the Pridesmen, on tour.

"I was an added artist," Duncan explains. "I wasn't out there except as an artist in my own right. I didn't front the band, as many people thought—I was just an added part of the show.

"At that time, Alec Houston, the ventriloquist/comedian, was a part of the show, so it was myself and Alex, and Pride was becoming a superstar. Then there'd be Waylon Jennings or Mel Tillis or different people [who] would be brought in to different cities. I don't guess I ever saw a show during that two-and-a-half or three years with Pride that you couldn't bring your mother and your sister and your family to. We didn't do anything but family shows, and I'm still proud of that."

Pride took a particular interest in Duncan's work as a writer, and recorded a number of his songs during the period they toured together. The album *I'm Just Me* is a prime example—Duncan placed three songs in the package, including "I'd Rather Love You," written after a show at the Tri-State Fair in Amarillo, Texas.

"That particular night, it was an early show, and I'd finished," recalls Duncan. "One of the guys who was helping with the fair, said 'Would you like to just go on back over to the hotel?' and I said, 'Sure,' so I got back early with nobody around, and I sat down and wrote the song there in about 20 minutes at the motel in Amarillo."

Duncan first recorded the song himself, with Bob Montgomery producing. Columbia had decided on a different Pride single, but when Charley heard "I'd Rather Love You," he asked if he could record it. "Charley just really flipped out over it," notes Duncan, "and I said, 'Yeah, you can have it, sure.' As a matter of fact, it was the beginning of much better times financially, and I bought Mama and the kids a new house and everything."

Charley Pride

74

AFTER THE FIRE IS GONE
CONWAY TWITTY
& LORETTA LYNN
Decca 32776
Writer: L.E. White
Producer: Owen Bradley
March 27, 1971 (2 weeks)

Conway Twitty and Loretta Lynn spent a great deal of time together when England hosted the first Wembley Country Music Festival in the late '60s. While the Wembley concerts have since become huge annual events, that first one was particularly special, because it marked the beginning of the Twitty/Lynn duets.

The two sang together quite often during that trip, discovering they had similar musical tastes. Twitty swapped road stories with both Lynn and her husband, Mooney, and it became apparent that their personalities were quite compatible.

"We decided we'd have to do some tracks together," says Conway, "and when we got back to the States we started recording. Our styles were close anyway, so we just went through material we had and picked songs that would be good for singles. The fan reaction was immediate. We felt it from the beginning. I think our first single sold over 400,000 copies."

Producer Owen Bradley calls that first single a "tremendous title," but songwriter L.E. White, signed to Twitty's publishing company at the time, remembers that he composed "After The Fire Is Gone" long before his employer expressed an interest in it.

"I was in Gatlinburg looking at a fireplace where the fire was out," remembers White, "and somebody said, 'Boy, it looks cold in there, don't it?' Writers are always trying to study everything, and I thought that something about that sounded like a song—'There's nothing colder than ashes after the fire is gone.'

"That was about all there was to that, so I wrote it and showed it to Conway and he didn't like it at all for about a year. Then he called me one night about 2:00 in the morning and said, 'Boy, I found this song that'd be good for me and Loretta. We're gonna record Monday, and this could be a big hit for us.'"

They actually cut the song on a Wednesday—November 10, 1970—and released it just after New Year's. It debuted on *Billboard*'s country chart on February 6, peaking at number one in its eighth week. On March 14, 1972, the National Academy of Recording Arts And Sciences rewarded the duo's efforts with a Grammy award for Best Country Vocal Performance by a Group.

"After The Fire Is Gone" has been recorded by approximately 40 artists, including Willie Nelson and unrelated Tracy Nelson, who took it to number 17 in 1974.

75
EMPTY ARMS
SONNY JAMES
Capitol 3015
Writer: Ivory Joe Hunter
Producer: George Richey
April 10, 1971 (4 weeks)

Just as "Endlessly" [see 67] represented Sonny James' second number one remake of a Brook Benton tune, "Empty Arms" was his second number one originally recorded by blues musician Ivory Joe Hunter.

Having met Hunter on "The Ed Sullivan Show," James took an immediate liking to him, and when "Since I Met You Baby" [see 36] proved successful, Sonny had a natural inclination to do more of Hunter's songs.

"I've always been really blues-oriented, anyway," James maintains. "I love the blues and country blues. I think a great deal of it is because I played guitar, and most guitar players and piano players love to play the blues. I've yet to meet one that didn't like to play the blues. I think it's our form of just letting your hair down and playing. I like any form of the old-fashioned, real gutbucket kind of blues."

Like some of his earlier hits, "Empty Arms" featured Millie Kirkham's soprano, and James indicates that the record's appeal stems from simplicity.

"Most of the lyrics, if you'll check anything I've ever done, they were very simple—just

like conversation. Nearly every lyric I ever did, I'd look at it, and if it didn't sound good reading it, then I would pass on the lyric. For me, it was just like conversation with a melody, and that explains the closeness of 'Since I Met You Baby' and 'Empty Arms.'"

After both of those records attained their number one peaks, James played a show in Monroe, Louisiana. Hunter was in attendance at that particular performance, and went backstage afterward to visit.

"He said that since I'd done them, he was just getting records all over the place," recalls James. "He sent me quite a few of his songs on tape; it wasn't probably more than a year before he died [November 8, 1974, from lung cancer], but I've still got the tape."

Since Hunter and James had first met on "The Ed Sullivan Show," it's ironic that the program was on its last legs as "Empty Arms" reached its peak. Five weeks after the record ended its four-week run at number one, Sullivan's show bowed out, on June 6, 1971.

76
HOW MUCH MORE CAN SHE STAND
CONWAY TWITTY
Decca 32801
Writer: Harry Compton
Producer: Owen Bradley
May 8, 1971 (1 week)

Harold Lloyd Jenkins chose an unusual stage name by pairing the names of two towns on a map: Conway, Arkansas, and Twitty, Texas. Conway Twitty first furrowed a niche for himself in rock and roll music, garnering a number one record in 1958 with "It's Only Make Believe" [see 248—"After All The Good Is Gone"]. The Twitty monicker decorated rock record labels and marquees through 1964, but Conway could no longer go on with his charade—in his heart, he really wanted to sing country music.

His first country success came in 1962, when Ray Price recorded a Twitty composition, "Walk Me To The Door," taking it to number seven. Two years later, Conway closed out his rock career during an eight-week engagement at a New Jersey club. His manager had promised he could start doing country shows when that booking ended, but instead sent Conway a new set of contracts for another rock tour. Twitty walked off the stage—with the club owner's blessing—and never looked back.

Conway knew that country radio programmers would view his conversion suspiciously, and Twitty purposely spent years grinding out hardcore country records to prove his sincerity. Even by 1971, traditional sounds continued to dominate his seventh chart-topping release, "How Much More Can She Stand."

The song was written by Harry Compton, one-half of the Compton Brothers, a St. Louis act whose biggest single was 1969's "Haunted House," which peaked at number 11. They introduced "How Much More Can She Stand" to Conway prior to a show in Wisconsin.

"One of the Compton Brothers got me off in the dressing room back there," Conway remembers, "and said, 'Boy, we got a song here that we wrote, and we really believe in, and we pitched it to everybody in Nashville and everybody hates it. We think it's good, and we value your opinion and'd like to see what you think about it.' So they sang this song to me, and I said, 'You mean to tell me that everybody in Nashville turned this song down? Well, I'm glad, 'cause I'm not turnin' it down—it's gonna be my next single.'"

Twitty highlighted Harry on high tenor harmonies, and the single spent a week at number one in May of 1971.

77
I WON'T MENTION IT AGAIN
RAY PRICE
Columbia 45329
Writers: Cam Mullins, Carolyn Jean Yates
Producer: Don Law
May 15, 1971 (3 weeks)

Among the more ironic events of Ray Price's career was a live appearance with the Dallas Symphony in the early '70s. Price turned to the musicians during the show and told them they were the best country band that had ever accompanied him. Price's use of strings had long been a point of controversy.

He first used symphonic enhancement during the late '50s on a gospel album titled *Faith*. It was more successful than anyone had predicted, and Price used strings again in later years on his secular country singles. "Burning Memories," a 1964 release, was the first, and it reached number two. Even more dramatic was his recording of "Danny Boy" in 1967.

"I was fighting with the so-called establishment over the new sound," he says. "I've been punished pretty severely over that. They got on my back on 'Danny Boy,' but it was a big, big record. They all said that I'd gone pop, but, of course, that wasn't true at all. They had to have somebody to shoot at, I guess."

Once "For The Good Times" became successful, however, the opposition quieted down. Cam Mullins had arranged the string parts on all of Price's records since the release of "Danny Boy," including "For The Good Times" [see 61], and Mullins wrote the follow-up. He used "Good Times" as a pattern, and when "I Won't Mention It Again" reached the top of the charts, it marked the first time in his career that Price had achieved back-to-back number one singles.

Ray's first appearance in *Billboard* came in 1952 with "Talk To Your Heart," which peaked at number three. He quickly earned widespread fame two years later with a double-sided release: "I'll Be There (If You Ever Want Me)" (sometimes called "Ain't No Chain") went to number two, and "Release Me" earned a number six peak.

"Crazy Arms" was the first of Price's patented four/four shuffles, and his first number one record. It stayed at the top of the country chart for ten weeks in 1956. "My Shoes Keep Walking Back To You" hit number one the following year, "City Lights" [see 195] reached the top in 1958, and "The Same Old Me" did likewise in 1959.

78
YOU'RE MY MAN
LYNN ANDERSON
Columbia 45356
Writer: Glenn Sutton
Producer: Glenn Sutton
June 5, 1971 (2 weeks)

Born September 26, 1947, in Grand Forks, North Dakota, Lynn Anderson spent her formative years in California. Her mother, Liz Anderson, gained a reputation as a songwriter, thanks to the Merle Haggard recordings "(All My Friends Are Gonna Be) Strangers" and "I'm A Lonesome Fugitive" [see 1—"Sing Me Back Home"]. Lynn's father, Casey Anderson, also wrote songs.

In fact, one of her father's jobs was to sell used cars at a dealership in Sacramento.

Among his fellow workers at the lot were Jack McFadden, who quit that job to manage Buck Owens; and Curt Sapaugh, who wrote Glen Campbell's "Try A Little Kindness."

During her teen years, Anderson was primarily interested in horses, winning more than 100 trophies, as well as the title of California Horse Show Queen at the State Fair. Nevertheless, she entered a singing contest sponsored by a local television show, "Country Corners." By the time of her twentieth birth-

Jerry Reed

day, she already had a contract with "The Lawrence Welk Show" as the only country singer on network television.

"I never had considered myself a great singer," she says. "I was really kind of surprised by it. I was in the right place at the right time, and I always felt like 'Make the most of this and get all you can out of it, because one of these days, these people are going to realize that you don't know what you're doing.' It took me a long time to finally accept the fact that show business is my life."

In spite of her track record, many still thought of Anderson as a new artist when "Rose Garden" came out, and husband/producer Glenn Sutton wrote "You're My Man" as a follow-up. "That was written specifically by him about him for me to sing about him," she chuckles. "Talk about an in-house project. That was Glenn specifically writing a song in the vein of 'Rose Garden.'"

"You're My Man" was one of three Sutton compositions to hit number one for Anderson, and as her producer, he came under a great deal of criticism in Nashville for recording his own material. "Back then, there weren't as many great songs as there are now," Sutton explains, "and generally, we'd just go with the best record. [Other songwriters] used to jump and say, 'You won't put nothing out but something you write,' but if it's the best song, we gotta go with it."

79
WHEN YOU'RE HOT, YOU'RE HOT
JERRY REED
RCA 9976
Writer: J.R. Hubbard
Producer: Chet Atkins
June 19, 1971 (5 weeks)

On April 18, 1970, RCA Records placed an ad in *Billboard* in which Chet Atkins, vice president of the label's country division, put his job on the line. Atkins called Jerry Reed "one of the greatest undeveloped talents I have ever known," at a time when Reed had yet to crack the Top Ten. "If Jerry doesn't make it big in the near future," Chet continued, "I will probably quit my job, because, if that is true, I do not know talent." Atkins probably had a sense of what was about to happen: by the end of the year, Reed was one of the hottest-selling acts in the business.

The record that turned things around was "Amos Moses," which debuted on October 24, 1970. Prior to that, Reed's highest position came when he hit number 11 with "Are You From Dixie (Cause I'm From Dixie, Too)." "Amos Moses," in fact, reached only number 16, but it fared better on the *Billboard* Hot 100, peaking at number eight on February 27, 1971. The single was also certified for sales of one million copies.

His follow-up was even bigger. Reed was a regular on "The Glen Campbell Goodtime Hour," and during the course of a show, he forgot one of his lines. Stuck, he simply ad-libbed "When you're hot, you're hot," and the audience went crazy. Reed was quick to recognize that he was on to something, and wrote an entire song based on that line when he got home.

He incorporated the phrase into a crap game, and the song's storyline concluded with an appearance in court. Between the sassy female vocalists, Reed's sloppy rap and the grinding guitar work, "When You're Hot, You're Hot" took on a bit of a party atmosphere.

"I like to have fun," Reed explained to *Country Song Roundup*. "I don't think [music] should be political, left- or right-wing. I just want people to stomp their feet and grin. They get enough of this other stuff in newspapers. I want to entertain people, and I want them to forget all that."

His approach paid off quite handsomely. "When You're Hot, You're Hot" spent five weeks at the top of the *Billboard* country chart, and peaked at number nine on the Hot 100. It also brought Jerry Reed Hubbard a Grammy for Best Country Vocal Performance by a Male.

In 1971, James' band, the Southern Gentlemen, included Gary Robbles, Jack Galloway, Lonnie Webb and Milo Liggett. Because of James' heavy touring schedule, friendship played a key role in the group's success. "We were on the bus going from one date to another one afternoon," Sonny remembers, "and we always had one guitar, and everything else was down below in the luggage compartment. You joke and have a lot of fun on tour, and most of the time, we just had this small gut-string guitar that we'd be playing.

"One afternoon, we were just knocking around and I was playing some blues. Jack gave me a vamp, and I started playing it, and then he started singing, 'Bright lights, big city, gone to my baby's head.' We were just knocking ourselves out playing it, and when we finished, I asked Jack how old the song was, and he started talking about it. I decided I'd record the song, because if we enjoyed the song that much, I thought other people would."

The country audience liked it enough to give James his fifteenth consecutive number one single and nineteenth overall. His biggest hit, though, was his first, "Young Love." James acquired it through a rather simple process: Atlanta publisher Bill Lowery sent it to producer Ken Nelson on an acetate, and Nelson thought it was perfect for his artist.

"It fit what we wanted to do," James recalls, "which was a strumming style of guitar playing. That laid the foundation for the future records that I would do. I would say that on 90 percent of the records I released after 'Young Love,' you could hear my guitar as a predominant part of the record. It established a sound. I believe that played a great part in the success I had."

80

BRIGHT LIGHTS, BIG CITY
SONNY JAMES

Capitol 3114
Writer: Jimmy Reed
Producer: George Richey
July 24, 1971 (1 week)

Jimmy Reed first recorded "Bright Lights, Big City" back in 1961, taking it to number 58 on the *Billboard* Hot 100. Reed was a noted blues musician, and Sonny James was familiar with him and the song, although he'd never tied the two together until a fateful day on the bus.

81

I'M JUST ME
CHARLEY PRIDE

RCA 9996
Writer: Glenn Martin
Producer: Jack Clement
July 31, 1971 (4 weeks)

"Most songwriters come to town and have to sleep in their cars for the first three or four months," says songwriter Glenn Martin. "I don't have no good stories like that. I came to town in a Cadillac, and had enough money to sustain me for two or three years. I didn't have to worry about making a living. I could just work on my writing."

Martin owned an instrument store in suburban Smyrna, Georgia, that worked out an association with an Atlanta club called The Playroom. Country performers headlined The Playroom for an entire week at a time, and Glenn's store would invite each entertainer to drop by on Saturday for a special promotion. Almost invariably, the performer would show up, and end up playing with a band that was set up at the store.

Through that promotion, Martin met most of the biggest stars of the '60s, and when he met Jeannie Seely, he started a friendship with her husband, songwriter Hank Cochran [see 111—"It's Not Love"]. On Cochran's advice, Martin sold his share of the business and moved to Nashville in 1968.

Charley Pride was another performer whom Glenn had met through his Smyrna operation, and, after beginning his career as a writer, Martin gained an opportunity to spend a few days with Pride in the Carolinas. During that trip, he fashioned "I'm Just Me" specifically for Pride.

"I also had another song that I played for Charley that he really liked," says Martin. "That's the one he really wanted to cut, so I put it down on a little old tape recorder for him at the hotel. I did that, and then I did 'I'm Just Me.'

"He said he wanted to record them both. I went into the studio, and they'd already started recording. The other thing's the one he really wanted to cut, and it turned out, he did 'I'm Just Me' and he never did do the other one."

When the chorus kicked off with "I was born to be exactly what you see," it became apparent that "I'm Just Me" would work almost as a theme song for Pride. "It just fit the image of myself," Charley remarks matter-of-factly. "I have no gimmicks or anything, it's just me, it's just what you see. I'm an open book, and the lyrics kind of fit me."

82

GOOD LOVIN' (MAKES IT RIGHT)
TAMMY WYNETTE

Epic 10759
Writer: Billy Sherrill
Producer: Billy Sherrill
August 28, 1971 (2 weeks)

After scoring six number one records out of her previous seven singles, Tammy Wynette just missed the top with two consecutive releases in 1970 and 1971, although both of them still made the Top Five.

The first near-miss was "The Wonders You Perform," a gospel number written by Jerry Chesnut during a thunderstorm. Chesnut had just helped in the birth of a baby calf, and inspired by the miracle of life, he sat under an umbrella on his tractor and scribbled down the words to the song while the rain poured down around him. The single peaked at number five, and Tammy notes that, except for " 'Til I Can Make It On My Own" [see 242], "The Wonders You Perform" is her favorite among her own recordings. "Not only does it strengthen the way I believe and help me keep my faith," she says, "it just reminds me of where I came from and how I got started. Gospel to me was—and still is—just the greatest music in the world."

Wynette's next release, "We Sure Can Love Each Other," stopped at number two, where it remained for three weeks just behind Sonny James' "Empty Arms" [see 75]. The song was conceived by her record producer, Billy Sherrill, who wrote it with Tammy after seeing Johnny Carson read the line "We sure can hurt each other" from a greeting card on "The Tonight Show."

Finally, Wynette returned to number one on August 28, 1971, with "Good Lovin' (Makes It Right)," in which she continued her frequent exploration into a woman's role in her husband's (in)fidelity. It's the only chart-topper that Sherrill ever wrote without the aid of a co-writer (Sherrill is the sole writer on "Too Far Gone," a song that *didn't* reach number one, although it did become a hit twice—for Joe Stampley and Emmylou Harris). "I'm not that proud of ["Good Lovin' "]," Sherrill says, noting that it was written in a rush just before the recording session. "It's not exactly 'Moon River.' You write because you need somebody to come in and play you a hit song. If they don't, you're up against the wall and you've got to do something. Most of my writing was out of panic, or out of necessity to have *something* to produce."

That circumstance put pressure on Wynette before each session. "In the first five years of my career, I never went in with all my songs," she notes. "It was just habit, and I had to learn the melody or the lyrics or both 30 minutes prior to the session. It was always 'panic time.'"

83

EASY LOVING
FREDDIE HART

Capitol 3115
Writer: Freddie Hart
Producer: George Richey
September 11, 1971 (3 weeks)

"There's number one songs, and there's trunk-of-the-tree songs," explains Freddie Hart. " 'I Can't Stop Loving You' and 'Release Me' are trunk-of-the-tree songs—songs that other songs take from. Other songs are branches, even though they get to be number one, but 'Easy Loving' was a trunk-of-the-tree song like 'Big Bad John.' "

"Easy Loving" was also a bit of a fluke.

Hart had been recording for more than 18 years, but his top showing on the *Billboard* charts at that point had been logged back in 1959, when he reached number 17 with "Chain Gang," and followed up with a number 18 single, "The Key's In The Mailbox."

In 1970, he released the album *California Grapevine*, but when the title track stalled as a single at number 68, Capitol summarily dropped him. "They put it back on the shelf," Hart remembers, "but all of a sudden, Jim Clemens at WPLO in Atlanta started playing 'Easy Loving,' and it just busted wide open. In fact, I think it was number one before I even got back on Capitol Records again. I wasn't even under contract."

Originally, Hart wrote "Easy Loving" under

Freddie Hart

the working title "Easy Loving Teenage Hearts," although it was eventually shortened and the age references disappeared. "I wanted to write something that every man would like to say and every woman would like to hear, and it came out that way. I think it was just something fresh. You write something special, and you don't even know that until it goes out and grabs people."

In fact, "Easy Loving" was the first number one country hit to use the word "sex." "When I was writing it, I started to take the line 'so sexy-looking' out, because I didn't think it would pass censorship."

Hart left the line in, though. In the recording studio, guitarist Billy Sanford and steel guitarist George Green played a unison line that provided the instrumental theme; the track was completed in just two takes.

84

THE YEAR THAT CLAYTON DELANEY DIED
TOM T. HALL
Mercury 73221
Writer: Tom T. Hall
Producer: Jerry Kennedy
September 18, 1971 (2 weeks)

"I used to get all fired up," remembers record producer Jerry Kennedy, "when Tom [T. Hall] would call and say, 'Hey, I got a batch of new things I'd like to play for you.' It was like opening things at Christmas.

"I knew out of that batch there were gonna be some killers; there always were. It was just like watching a movie when I'd hear these things—you could actually see the story unfolding."

Appropriately, Hall earned the nickname "The Storyteller," and one of his best-known stories, "The Year That Clayton Delaney Died," fell under his autobiographical career plan [see 48—"A Week In A Country Jail"].

"[Clayton] was my childhood hero, and a real good picker," says Hall. "He died when he was about 19 or 20 [of an undiagnosed lung disease], but a lot of people think it's about an old man. I was about seven or eight, but he was the only real live guitar player [in the area], and I learned a lot from him."

Delaney played regularly at the Buckeye Gardens in Connersville, Indiana, and when

Tom T. first took up performing after the armed services, he started at that same club. Clayton Delaney was a pseudonym, each name taken from a different road leading to his country home.

"There's a valuable lesson that I learned from Clayton Delaney," T. suggests, "although at first it irritated me—he wouldn't imitate anybody. He would sing like Clayton Delaney. He would sing an Ernest Tubb song, and I'd think, 'Well, that doesn't sound like Ernest Tubb,' and when he would sing a Hank Williams song, 'Well, that doesn't sound like Hank Williams.' So after he died and I was about 12 or 13, I thought I'd start singing like myself."

Hall was hardly enamored with his own vocal skills, but he did well enough to convey his story songs quite effectively. During the year before "Clayton Delaney," he hit number eight with "Shoeshine Man," and matched that feat with "Salute To A Switchblade," based on his years with the military in Germany.

On the heels of "Clayton Delaney," he returned to number eight once again with "Me And Jesus," a message of personal belief.

85

HOW CAN I UNLOVE YOU
LYNN ANDERSON
Columbia 45429
Writer: Joe South
Producer: Glenn Sutton
October 16, 1971 (3 weeks)

Like "Rose Garden," [see 69] "How Can I Unlove You" came from a Joe South record.

"I used to call that my 7-Up song," says Lynn Anderson. "Here was the idea of 'unlove' during the Uncola campaign. I thought that was a great song; I really love Joe South's writing. I really think some of his songs from that period are still just as valid now as they were 20 years ago. He's just a classic writer."

Also like "Rose Garden," the record used a walking bass and shuffle rhythm on its trip to number one, and it became Lynn's third chart-topping effort in three releases. Glenn Sutton, her producer and husband, hired an arranger for "some lush, big-time stuff" with the strings, and the result was the most ambitious string arrangement to reach number one.

"Cam Mullins was doing the arranging at the time," Anderson notes, "and he came up with some real great licks. That was during that period that Ray Price and I and Sammi Smith and Anne Murray were able to take country music over onto the pop charts. The feeling at that time was that you had to have strings—that made the difference between a country record and a pop record."

Unlike "Rose Garden," the intentional crossover approach had unspectacular results: "How Can I Unlove You" stopped at number 63 on *Billboard*'s Hot 100.

Though the record was not a big pop hit, Lynn continued to make great strides in country. She had won the Academy of Country Music award for Top Female Vocalist earlier in the year, and she also picked up the Country Music Association trophy while "Unlove" was at number one.

Unfortunately, none of the following year's releases achieved the top spot. "Cry" [see 693] stopped at number three, while "Listen To A Country Song" and "Fool Me" both peaked at number four.

One of Glenn Sutton's compositions went to number four for a labelmate in 1972, and Sutton points to that success as an example of the type of problem he and Lynn faced in their marriage. "She got mad about 'There's A Party Goin' On' with Jody Miller. I said, 'Look, it's Billy Sherrill's artist, he cut it on her, I wrote it with him, there's nothing I can do.'"

"Occasionally, it caused a little friction," Lynn concedes.

Lynn Anderson

86

HERE COMES HONEY AGAIN
SONNY JAMES
Capitol 3174
Writers: Carole Smith, Sonny James
Producer: George Richey
November 6, 1971 (1 week)

"I think as much effort as we put forth, I always considered that there was a much higher power taking care of me and my thoughts, because I wasn't that intelligent," says Sonny James of his string of sixteen consecutive number one country singles. "I don't think anybody really is, when you get down to it, and I always considered that a big factor in any success that I've had."

"Here Comes Honey Again" was the final record in James' winning streak, and it was one of the rare instances in which he tried to duplicate part of an earlier single.

"When 'Here Comes Honey Again' hit, I wanted a really, really simple ballad," he explains. "I wanted it to be just straightforward, and I wanted it to be in the area of 'Take Good Care Of Her' [see 4—"A World Of Our Own"] because it had been so successful for me, and I loved that song.

"I wanted something in that same tempo, but something that's really simply written, so Carole Smith and I wrote that song on the phone. Consequently, it turned out to be a good recording for me . . . 'Take Good Care Of Her' and 'Here Comes Honey Again' were nothing alike at all; the message is entirely different, but they have that same flow."

When "Here Comes Honey Again" became his sixteenth straight number one record, James set a mark that would last nearly fourteen years. Sonny's chart run stretched from

April 29, 1967, through November 26, 1971, and his achievement went uncontested until Alabama notched its seventeenth straight number one record (not counting a Christmas single) on August 3, 1985, with "Forty Hour Week" [see 631].

During his four-and-a-half-year reign, James spent a total of 45 weeks at number one. He finally broke his streak with a remake of the 1962 Gene Pitney hit "Only Love Can Break A Heart." Debuting on January 15, 1972, it peaked at number two on February 26, blocked from the top by Faron Young's "It's Four In The Morning" [see 93], Tammy Wynette's "Bedtime Story" [see 94] and Freddie Hart's "My Hang-Up Is You" [see 95].

87
LEAD ME ON
CONWAY TWITTY & LORETTA LYNN
Decca 32873
Writer: Leon Copeland
Producer: Owen Bradley
November 13, 1971 (1 week)

Conway Twitty and Loretta Lynn recorded "Lead Me On," their second duet single, in November of 1970, one day after cutting their first [see 74—"After The Fire Is Gone"]. It remained in the Decca Records vaults, however, until its release on September 6, 1971.

"Lead Me On" encountered no resistance from radio or the public at large in ascending to number one just two months later. Loretta did, however, have problems with her management, and as a result, the single's release coincided with the formation of a new booking agency.

Founded in September, United Talent was co-owned by Twitty and Lynn, with a two-person staff headed by Jimmy Jay, who had previously handled Twitty's dates for the Bob Neal Agency. By 1977, the now-defunct company coordinated tours for 25 different performers, including Mickey Gilley, Billy "Crash" Craddock and Moe Bandy. "The agency was formed just to handle bookings for Lynn and Twitty," Jay told Billboard in 1977. "At the time, we never dreamed it would develop into what it is today. We operate differently from any talent agency I know of. We have no contracts with any of our acts—we work strictly on a handshake basis—and most of them have been with us for many, many years."

In one of their first headlining appearances after the agency's debut, Conway and Loretta performed "Lead Me On" with memorable results.

"Conway used to be real bashful," Loretta explains. "When I found out he was bashful, I liked to pull things on him. I had a gown made with Velcro, and it was made with shorts, and a top hooked together, and the skirt come around with Velcro on it. Course it was a long skirt, looked like a long gown, and he didn't know the difference.

"When 'Lead Me On' first come out, we got to the microphone, started to sing it, and he sang his part, and when it come to me singin' 'Lead Me On,' I took my skirt and just went like it was rippin'. He almost passed out, and he's never forgotten that one."

The Lead Me On album was never forgotten, either—ten years after its release, it was finally certified gold on October 29, 1981.

88
DADDY FRANK (THE GUITAR MAN)
MERLE HAGGARD & THE STRANGERS
Capitol 3198
Writer: Merle Haggard
Producer: Ken Nelson
November 20, 1971 (2 weeks)

Merle Haggard engendered a great deal of controversy for his political commentary [see 45—"Okie From Muskogee" and 50—"The Fightin' Side Of Me"] during 1969 and 1970. If marijuana and Vietnam weren't enough to tackle, he wanted to release "Irma Jackson," a song about an interracial romance, as a follow-up. His record company had other ideas.

"Capitol allowed me to do 99 percent of everything I set out to do," Haggard told Todd Everett in Billboard, "and on those couple of exceptions, they turned out to be right. My producer, Ken Nelson, felt that I shouldn't release it. I think that Ken was probably right at the time. Later on, we re-cut the song and put it on an album."

In its stead, Merle released an instrumental—practically a jam session—called "Street Singer." Despite its lack of a "hook," Haggard was so popular that it still hit number nine. He closed out 1970 with "Jesus, Take A Hold" and "I Can't Be Myself," both of which peaked at number three.

The following year, "Soldier's Last Letter" also went to number three, while "Someday We'll Look Back" spent two weeks at number two, held out of the top spot by Charley Pride's "I'm Just Me" [see 81].

"Daddy Frank (The Guitar Man)" returned Hag to number one, though it was a far cry from the socially relevant themes of his two previous chart-toppers. "Daddy Frank" was the fictitious leader of a family band: he was blind, and "Momma," who was deaf, drove the group's pickup truck.

"He changed it around and made it different, but he got the inspiration from the Maddox Brothers & Sister Rose," says Norm Hamlet of the Strangers. "He just took the idea that they were a family traveling around, and he sort of changed it around with Daddy Frank being blind, just gave it a gimmick."

Recorded in Buck Owens' studio in Bakersfield, "Daddy Frank" was one of the first Haggard recordings to feature the Strangers without any additional session musicians. The only "outsider" on the record was the backing chorus, which comprised children from Haggard's and manager Fuzzy Owen's families.

The ultimate result: Merle Haggard, the guitar man, had his tenth number one single.

89

KISS AN ANGEL GOOD MORNIN'
CHARLEY PRIDE
RCA 0550
Writer: Ben Peters
Producer: Jack Clement
December 4, 1971 (5 weeks)

On October 10, 1971, Charley Pride was the big winner at the Country Music Association awards show, picking up the trophies for Entertainer of the Year and Male Vocalist of the Year. Ironically, the votes were cast even before Pride reached the zenith of his recording career.

On September 28, he released "Kiss An Angel Good Mornin'," and thirteen days after his CMA haul, the record made its debut on the *Billboard* country chart at a modest number 57. In its seventh week, "Kiss An Angel" vaulted into the number one position, a place it held for five weeks in a row, giving it the longest tenure at the top among all of Pride's records.

Songwriter Ben Peters had a newborn infant named Angela that inspired "Angel," and he says that his wife, Jackie, also played a part in its content. "I could not wait to get into the studio to do that particular song," Pride notes. Charley cut "Kiss An Angel" in the RCA recording studio on July 28, 1971, although he had already recorded it in Jack Clement's studios. "I used to get him in my studio a few days before we'd go in, and we'd do the records in demo form," says Clement. "That's how we worked out the 'Kiss An Angel Good Mornin' arrangement. It was worth it to me to work out the intros and all that before we got there. It made him learn the song a little better and stuff."

The arrangement kicked off with a familiar piano lick provided by Charles Cochran, who has since played on most of Don Williams' and Crystal Gayle's records. Despite its mainstream country sound, "Kiss An Angel" managed to cross over onto the *Billboard* Hot 100, peaking at number 21. It was certified gold on March 8, 1972.

"I had no idea that it would do what it did do," Pride explains, "because at that time, other stations like MOR [middle-of-the-road] and pop stations weren't nearly as lenient about playing a good country record as country was at playing pop artists. But enough of them played it, and a million people went out and bought it."

90

WOULD YOU TAKE ANOTHER CHANCE ON ME/ME AND BOBBY MCGEE
JERRY LEE LEWIS
Mercury 73248
Writers: Jerry Foster, Bill Rice/Kris Kristofferson, Fred Foster
Producer: Jerry Kennedy
January 8, 1972 (1 week)

By any accounting, Jerry Lee Lewis' life hasn't been a pretty picture. After the story of his intra-family marriage broke in 1958 [see 26—"To Make Love Sweeter For You"], tragedy struck again when his three-year-old son, Steve, drowned in a swimming pool. After 13 years of marriage, Myra left him in 1970, then his mother died of cancer, and his son, Jerry Lee, Jr., was killed in a 1973 car accident.

In 1971, Lewis married his fourth wife, Jaren; in spite of the personal turmoil that surrounded him, his recording efforts continued to satisfy listeners. "Touching Home" reached number three in 1971, and he kicked off '72 with another number one, "Would You Take Another Chance On Me," a song Jerry Foster and Bill Rice originally intended for Jack Greene.

"Jerry Lee was going through a real personal time," Rice remembers. "I think he and Myra had gotten their divorce, or were getting their divorce. Hargus 'Pig' Robbins was hired to play the session with Jerry Lee. [Lewis] just took a hand mike and sat down on the piano stool beside Pig, and he was very emotional about it."

"That was the very first time he used that phrase 'Think about it, darlin','" adds producer Jerry Kennedy. "It was real tender at that time."

The Lewis legacy has continued with its usual series of ups and downs. He notched one more chart-topper in 1972 [see 96—"Chantilly Lace"], as well as eight more Top Ten singles over the following decade, including "I'll Find It Where I Can," "Middle Age Crazy," "Over The Rainbow" and "39 And Holding."

Merle Haggard

Merle Haggard

In 1981, Lewis was hospitalized with a perforated stomach, and doctors gave him only a 50-50 chance of survival. He underwent two operations that lasted a total of 12 hours, and Jerry Lee surprised many by escaping death.

However, his fourth wife, Jaren, drowned in 1982, and his fifth wife, Shawn Michelle Stephens, died from a drug overdose in 1983, three months after the wedding. In 1984, Jerry Lee married for the sixth time, although that wedding ended in divorce.

In 1989, Dennis Quaid starred as the Killer in the movie *Great Balls of Fire*, based on Myra's book of the same name.

91
CAROLYN
MERLE HAGGARD & THE STRANGERS
Capitol 3222
Writer: Tommy Collins
Producer: Earl Ball
January 15, 1972 (3 weeks)

Bakersfield, California [see 790—"Streets Of Bakersfield"], has often been called "Nashville West" because of the outgrowth of a long line of successful country musicians. Among the performers who have graduated from the city's club circuit are Buck Owens, Merle Haggard, Ferlin Husky and Tommy Collins. Journalists have repeatedly lumped them together as purveyors of "The Bakersfield Sound."

"I always felt like everybody out here wanted to dance," offers Owens, "and if they wanted to dance and drink, the next thing you know, you've got to have some drums and a bass. I always felt like our sound was much more of a driving sound, not as laid-back. I think that might go along with the rest of California; we might be just a half-a-mile faster than some of the other folks."

Tommy Collins' career brushed those of both Owens and Haggard in Bakersfield. Born Leonard Raymond Sipes [see 238—"The Roots Of My Raising"] in Oklahoma City on September 28, 1930, Collins moved to California in 1952. He employed Buck as a guitarist, and began his own recording career in 1953, earning four Top Ten records during the next two years. As a writer, he also picked up a hit when Faron Young covered "If You Ain't Lovin' (You Ain't Livin')" [see 797].

Collins moved into the ministry from 1961 to 1964, but in the meantime, he became friends with Haggard. "I heard him on the radio singing 'Sing Me A Sad Song,'" recalls Collins, "and I started asking questions about him. I looked him up, and Merle and I really got acquainted fishing on the Kern River. Then he started recording some of my songs. The first one, 'Sam Hill,' was when he was on Tally Records [in 1964]."

Eight years later, Haggard took another Collins composition, "Carolyn," all the way to number one. Sung to a woman named Carolyn, it suggests a trip of desperation by a married man to a brothel.

"It was an indirect way of talking to someone," Collins reflects. "I wanted to come in the side door rather than the front door. It happened to be my wife, and I wanted to say something to her, as if I was talking to someone else."

"Carolyn" was the last of Haggard's hits to employ Glen Campbell as a backing vocalist [see 8—"The Legend Of Bonnie And Clyde"].

92
ONE'S ON THE WAY
LORETTA LYNN
Decca 32900
Writer: Shel Silverstein
Producer: Owen Bradley
February 5, 1972 (2 weeks)

In 1987, Loretta Lynn attended a White House dinner with a group of scientists and inventors, where she received an Outstanding Achievement Award. Humbled, she told her intellectual dinner mates, "All I ever did was invent kids."

In fact, at the age of 31, she became a grandmother for the first time, one year after her twins, Peggy and Patsy, were the last two additions to the family. Neither of them particularly liked her fifth number one single: "One's On The Way" closed with Loretta's wish, "I hope it ain't twins again."

"One's On The Way" was a humorous piece on motherhood, in which an average, ordinary housewife compares her conditions to the glamorous lives of Debbie Reynolds and Elizabeth Taylor. Shel Silverstein concocted the tune, and sent it to producer Owen Bradley.

"Shel gave me that for somebody else, Jeannie Seely or somebody," recalls Bradley, "but

whoever it was, they didn't like it, and I kept it around. Loretta didn't need any songs. She had plenty of songs."

That situation changed when Loretta left the Wil-Helm agency, and her managers, Doyle and Teddy Wilburn. Lynn had signed some lifetime contracts with the Wilburn brothers, and since the deals would provide them royalties from any new songs that she would write, she declined to write any new ones. Yet "One's On The Way" sounded like she could have written it.

"Owen Bradley felt there was no one in country music that could get by with that song but me," she laughs. "I had the kids to kind of prove it, and he thought I would make a hit out of it, and we did."

Decca mistakenly released the record on November 15, 1971, with the title "Here In Topeka," and had to re-service radio stations with a correctly titled copy. According to Loretta, "People still holler at my shows, 'Here In Topeka'!"

"One's On The Way" was her third solo single to debut on the *Billboard* chart during 1971. "I Wanna Be Free" reached number three, and "You're Lookin' At Country" peaked at number five. "One's On The Way" started 1972 off in fine fashion when it topped the chart for two straight weeks. In January, Loretta's *Greatest Hits* LP became her first gold album.

93
IT'S FOUR IN THE MORNING
FARON YOUNG
Mercury 73250
Writer: Jerry Chesnut
Producer: Jerry Kennedy
February 19, 1972 (2 weeks)

For two decades, Faron Young was among the most consistent performers in country music. He first charted in 1953 with "Goin' Steady," which reached number two, and by the end of 1974, he'd racked up 42 Top Ten singles. Among them were five number one records: "Live Fast, Love Hard, Die Young" (1955), "Alone With You" (1958), "Country Girl" (1959), Willie Nelson's "Hello Walls" (1961)—and "It's Four In The Morning."

The latter number was born out of determination. Faron was involved in a car accident in 1970 that severely damaged his tongue. After four operations, he could sing once again,

Faron Young

but when songwriter Jerry Chesnut expressed an interest in writing for him, Young requested a tune that avoided the letter "S," because he still lisped from the accident. Chesnut came back with "It's Four In The Morning," a song in three-quarter time.

"Faron wanted to take it out of waltz time," remembers producer Jerry Kennedy, who grew up with Young in Shreveport. "There was a theory for a long time that waltzes wouldn't sell. I'm really thankful I won that argument."

Young was pleased, too, when the single reached number one for two weeks in a row. In fact, the achievement coincided with his fortieth birthday, February 25, 1972.

Faron Young made his first record in 1951, at the age of nineteen, and his musical fortunes were aided by the Korean War. He entered the military in the fall of 1952, and won an Army talent contest on national television. For two

years, he performed for troops all over the globe and worked on the Army's radio recruitment show, with announcer Leonard Nimoy.

By the end of the decade, Young had begun a film career that included eleven movies. The first, *Hidden Gun*, also featured Angie Dickinson, and his role as a deputy inspired his nickname "The Young Sheriff."

"Back then, you had Ernest Tubb, the Texas Troubadour, or Hank Thompson, the Singing Ranger," Faron explains. "They ended up running a contest and calling me Faron Young, the Young Sheriff. I later changed that from Young Sheriff to Singing Sheriff—I figured when I hit 35, it was time to change it."

In addition to being an entertainer, Young is also an astute businessman. He built the Young Executive Building when Nashville's Music Row was in its formative years, and founded the *Music City News*.

94

BEDTIME STORY

TAMMY WYNETTE

Epic 10818
Writers: Billy Sherrill, Glenn Sutton
Producer: Billy Sherrill
March 4, 1972 (1 week)

"Bedtime Story" was something of a hybrid between two of Tammy Wynette's earlier classics. Several of the instrumental riffs are almost carbon copies of those in "Stand By Your Man" [see 21], and the children's theme parallel the ideas behind "I Don't Wanna Play House" [see 3—"Take Me To Your World"].

In fact, a few of the circumstances behind "Bedtime Story" were similar to "I Don't Wanna Play House" as well. Just before Tammy cut the latter song in 1967, she had walked into Billy Sherrill's office to find nursery-rhyme books scattered all over the floor. Sherrill co-wrote "I Don't Wanna Play House" with Glenn Sutton, and in 1971, Sherrill and Sutton used children's books once again to research the verses of "Bedtime Story."

"We were working on that and got stuck," Sutton recalls, "so Billy sent me to the book-store to buy 10 or 15 bedtime-story books. I went and bought all these bedtime stories, and we spent a couple of hours reading bedtime stories. After we read those books and every-thing, we sat down and just jotted notes down and finished it up. Most of them would have a king and a queen and a castle, and we just took the generalities of about 20 bedtime stories and said, 'Okay, here's what should be in a bedtime story.'"

At a time when most country records ran about two-and-a-half minutes in length, the label on "Bedtime Story" reads "4:15."

"That was real long," notes Sutton, "and I remember when we were cutting it, somebody mentioned it in the session. I think it was Pete Drake, who was playing steel at the time; he said, 'Isn't that thing awful long? Isn't it four or five minutes long?' and I remember Billy say-ing, 'I don't care if it's ten minutes long—I like it.'"

Tammy liked the record for more personal reasons.

"It came along at the time Georgette [see 64—"Run, Woman, Run"] was a little baby," she says, "and that meant a lot to me. It was almost as if I was doing a song for my new baby, so it was very special."

Despite its length, the record earned high marks with the public, too. "Bedtime Story" entered the *Billboard* country chart on New Year's Day of 1972 and claimed its number one ranking two months later.

95

MY HANG-UP IS YOU

FREDDIE HART

Capitol 3261
Writer: Freddie Hart
Producer: Earl Ball
March 11, 1972 (6 weeks)

Freddie Hart was re-signed by Capitol Rec-ords once "Easy Loving" [see 83] became a huge success in 1971, and Hart quickly moved from one of the valleys in his professional life to instant superstar status.

"Easy Loving" earned Grammy nomina-tions for Best Country Song and Best Country Vocal Performance by a Male; it picked up the Country Music Association's Song of the Year honors two years in a row; and it was named Single of the Year, Album of the Year and Song of the Year by the Academy of Country Music. The Recording Industry Association of Amer-ica eventually certified "Easy Loving" as a million-selling single on October 23, 1972, and *Billboard* named it the number one country single of 1971.

Hart quickly proved his success was no fluke—his follow-up, "My Hang-Up Is You," spent half-a-dozen weeks at the top spot. Like "Easy Loving," it became *Billboard*'s top coun-try single for the entire year, giving Hart that honor two years in a row.

Says Hart of the writing process: "They had a thing going around—'my hang-up is this' and 'my hang-up is that'—but most of them were bad hang-ups. I wanted to make it a pretty thing.

"I remember right after I wrote that, and I had an appearance in Atlanta, Georgia. We had over 22,000 people, and I sang 'Easy Loving' 11 times. After the show, I sang 'My Hang-Up' on my bus for some deejays and some re-porters, and they said they were sure it would be a hit. That's a wonderful feeling; nothing's any good unless you can share it with some-body. Whether it's a painting or a song or a book, you want to share it with somebody. It's no good if you keep it to yourself."

The lead and steel guitars made use of the

same instrumental riff that wove its way through "Easy Loving," and Hart's slippery tenor performance was strong enough that the ACM named him both the Entertainer of the Year and Top Male Vocalist.

96

CHANTILLY LACE/ THINK ABOUT IT DARLIN'
JERRY LEE LEWIS
Mercury 73273
Writers: J.P. Richardson/Jerry Foster, Bill Rice
Producer: Jerry Kennedy
April 22, 1972 (3 weeks)

"Chantilly Lace" was a cover of the original 1958 record by the Big Bopper [see 162—"Running Bear"], and after the initial "Hello-o-o, you good lookin' thing," Jerry Lee Lewis further personalized his version with the words, "This is the Killer speaking."

In fact, Jerry Lee did quite a lot of talking during the recording session, although only a portion of it actually appears on the single. Listed officially on the record at a time of 2:50, "Chantilly Lace" was recorded in a single take, but the track lasted about eight minutes in total.

"It was so great, I did not want to stop it," says producer Jerry Kennedy. "It was a party, is what it was. Everybody got into this thing so great. There was not even a 'take number' on the thing. We put one take down, and listened back to it, and that was the record. There's no way we could make it any better."

The powers-that-be at Mercury Records considered releasing the full-length version at one point, but too much of the recording was viewed as questionable, and it's likely that the public will never hear the entire take.

"At that point in time, people weren't making dirty records," Kennedy notes. "There used to be—it wasn't really a war—but it was like a silent thing between all the string players and the rhythm section. It was like an unspoken thing that neither associated with the other.

"At a certain point in that record, the arranger wasn't turned around facing me to see that I was having a good time listening to this thing. He started talking to the string section, and Jerry heard him talking when there was a break, and he got nutso.

"In his rage, he was saying like 'Well, I don't give a damn about what's happening there/I'm hangin' in/Like Gunga Din, Chantilly Lace . . .' all in rhythm, and everybody in the studio hit it on the word 'lace' after he'd had this big fit. It was just phenomenal. It just blew me totally away, and we let him go another two or three minutes."

"Chantilly Lace" entered the *Billboard* country chart on March 11, 1972, and reached number one just six weeks later. It remained in the top spot for three weeks total—longer than any other Jerry Lee Lewis single.

97

GRANDMA HARP/ TURNIN' OFF A MEMORY
MERLE HAGGARD & THE STRANGERS
Capitol 3294
Writer: Merle Haggard
Producer: Ken Nelson
May 13, 1972 (2 weeks)

"What I play doesn't have much to do with commerciality," Merle Haggard told writer Greg Oates in 1980. "I try more every day to look at my music as an art form and try to do it the way I feel it should be done, regardless of the penalties or prizes."

His art in 1972 took on a very personal form of self-expression, as Haggard paid homage to his mother's mother, who had passed away the previous year at the age of 93. Merle led into the song with a 56-second recitation, recalling many of "Grandma Harp"'s strong points, and the tone of his voice displayed just how much his subject moved him.

When "Grandma Harp" slipped into the number one slot on May 13, 1972, it marked his twelfth number one single as a recording artist, and tenth as a songwriter.

Haggard explained his writing process to Bob Eubanks in *Billboard*: "If it's a good song, if it's one that pans out all the way and goes on to be recorded, it usually comes all at one time. I mean, in a matter of ten minutes, the whole thing will be done. Some of them I spend a lot of time on to get a melody that I am satisfied with. The words usually come first—the idea, the construction of the song is probably similar to a movie or whatever. You get a thought or idea that's worth spending a lot of time on."

Had Grandma Harp lived another year, she would have been proud of Merle. A dozen years after his discharge from San Quentin [see 1—"Sing Me Back Home"], he received a letter dated March 14, 1972, from California governor Ronald Reagan. After eight months of consideration, Reagan cited him as a "fully rehabilitated member of society" and granted a full pardon for his criminal offenses.

Haggard was born April 6, 1937, and after the death of his father [see 16—"Mama Tried"], he became a "problem child." He hopped trains on several occasions, once riding all the way to Texas, but one highlight came in 1951, when he saw Lefty Frizzell perform in Bakersfield. Frizzell told the audience it was the first time he ever played "Always Late" in public.

"I felt," wrote Haggard in his autobiography, *Sing Me Back Home*, "like I was being included in country music history in some way."

Conway Twitty

98

(LOST HER LOVE) ON OUR LAST DATE
CONWAY TWITTY
Decca 32945
Writers: Conway Twitty, Floyd Cramer
Producer: Owen Bradley
May 27, 1972 (1 week)

Floyd Cramer is the best-known session pianist in country music history. After Cramer's work on the "Louisiana Hayride" radio show, Chet Atkins summoned him to Nashville, where Floyd introduced his unique style to records by the Everly Brothers, Elvis Presley and Jim Reeves, among many others. He developed his seminal piano sound by mimicking the bending of guitar strings—in effect, utilizing a series of grace notes—and thus appeared on many of the records that created "The Nashville Sound."

Cramer became one of the few session players to gain fame with the general public after signing a recording contract with RCA. He recorded a series of instrumental singles and albums, and "Last Date" became the most popular.

Cramer had already written and recorded it before he gave it a title, deciding on "Last Date" because of the song's melancholy nature. It peaked at number 11 on the country chart, but fared much better on *Billboard*'s Hot 100, spending four weeks at number two in late 1960. The number one record at that time was Elvis Presley's "Are You Lonesome Tonight?," which, coincidentally, featured Cramer on piano.

"I was in Canada, playin' some concerts, the first time I heard 'Last Date,'" Conway Twitty recalls. "It was just beautiful, and within three weeks, I had written my own words to it, using his melody."

Twitty had no country connections at the time, and simply put the song in a box of tunes [see 56—"Hello Darlin'"]. Even as Cramer's record peaked, however, Boudleaux Bryant added *his* own lyrics to the melody, and Skeeter Davis took "My Last Date (With You)" to number five. Conway thus had no chance of immediate success with his version.

"The next time I did a session in Nashville, Floyd Cramer happened to play piano on my rock and roll sessions," notes Conway. "I called him over there and told him this story, and he said, 'Well, come on over to the piano—I'd like to hear it.' I sang these words for him, and he said, 'My God, that's absolutely beautiful words.' I just had to wait and bide my time."

Twitty played his version in concert and received overwhelming response. He decided to cut it, and, despite the doubts of producer Owen Bradley, "(Lost Her Love) On Our Last Date" achieved a number one peak position. Emmylou Harris returned the song to number one more than a decade later [see 503].

99

THE HAPPIEST GIRL IN THE WHOLE U.S.A.
DONNA FARGO
Dot 17409
Writer: Donna Fargo
Producer: Stan Silver
June 3, 1972 (3 weeks)

"One of my dreams was to be a teacher," says Donna Fargo, "and the other was to be a singer." By her mid-twenties, she was pursuing both of those dreams at the very same time—living in California, she taught English as Mrs. Stan Silver and played on weekends as Donna Fargo.

Her first single earned regional success on Ramco Records (it was Ramco who gave Fargo, named Yvonne Vaughan at birth, her stage name), and she also appeared on the Challenge label with "Daddy." In the early '70s, she began to shake things up when Silver took her to Nashville during Easter vacation to record four sides, one of which was her own composition, "The Happiest Girl In The Whole U.S.A." "It really started out to be 'Happiest Girl In The World'," she recalls, "but the rhyme scheme got to be too unnatural, so I changed it to 'U.S.A.' It just kind of wrote itself after that."

Silver pitched the demo to all of Nashville's major labels, and legend has it that Billy Sherrill wanted to cut "The Happiest Girl" with newcomer Tanya Tucker. Tucker turned it down, but Fargo insists she never would have let them record it in the first place. "I was real interested in becoming a singer," she says, "and I only became a writer so I could become a singer."

Eventually, Dot Records gave Fargo a contract, and the record made the grade on the country charts while she continued assigning homework and testing students in California. As it hit number one in June of 1972, though, she quit her job, and the Silvers moved to Nashville. Once in their new home, they were overwhelmed with awards. "The Happiest Girl" sold a million copies, brought her a Grammy, and earned Single of the Year honors from both the Country Music Association and the Academy of Country Music.

Fargo notes that it also earned international acclaim. "I remember thinking that if it became a hit it wouldn't be a hit outside the U.S. because of the title, but I was wrong about that. It was a hit in Canada, Australia and New Zealand."

100

THAT'S WHY I LOVE YOU LIKE I DO
SONNY JAMES
Capitol 3322
Writers: Jack Morrow, Kelso Herston
Producer: Kelso Herston
June 24, 1972 (1 week)

After "Only Love Can Break A Heart" broke Sonny James' streak of sixteen consecutive number one singles [see 86—"Here Comes Honey Again"], he had little choice but to start up a new streak. His next release was "That's Why I Love You Like I Do," which returned him to the number one position. It was his last number one single in a 14-year association with Capitol Records, yet it was originally recorded as the "B" side to his *first* number one single, "Young Love" [see 80—"Bright Lights, Big City"].

Originally, "That's Why I Love You Like I Do" was titled "You're The Reason (I'm In Love)." Many people suggested that if James had saved the song, he could have used it to follow up "Young Love," instead of featuring it as the "B" side of "Young Love." "I figured that since so many people liked that, I had to do it sometime when it was the 'A' side," he says.

In 1961, he was ready to record it again, but Bobby Edwards released a country hit entitled "You're The Reason," and James put his record on hold to avoid confusion. In 1963, he felt the time was right again, but Bobby Darin released a pop hit, "You're The Reason I'm Living," and James put it off once more.

James' contract—only a page-and-a-half

long—had almost run out by 1971, and Nashville was filled with rumors that CBS Records president Clive Davis had approached James about signing with Columbia. During October, Capitol president Ken Nelson confided to James that he was retiring—more or less suggesting that Sonny accept Columbia's offer.

Nevertheless, James had one more record left to fulfill his contract with Capitol, so he proffered "You're The Reason (I'm In Love)." He also suggested they change the name of the song to "That's Why I Love You Like I Do," a phrase that appeared often in the lyric.

It wasn't the only thing different from the original recording. The new version included trumpets best described (by Sonny) as "junior high schoolish," and moved at a faster tempo; unlike the original, it was also recorded in stereo!

The single entered the *Billboard* country chart on May 13, 1972. Two days later, Clive Davis announced Sonny's signing at a huge gathering at the Vanderbilt Holiday Inn in Nashville.

Hank Williams, Jr., before his accident

101

ELEVEN ROSES
HANK WILLIAMS, JR.
MGM 14371
Writers: Lamar Morris, Darrell McCall
Producer: Jim Vienneau
July 1, 1972 (2 weeks)

Hank Williams, Jr., earned his first number one record [see 60—"All For The Love Of Sunshine"] at the youthful age of 21. Not surprisingly, many of the songs he recorded or performed up to that point were things he was talked into doing.

As he matured, however, he gained a clearer picture of music and himself. " 'Eleven Roses' was when he really started getting into the business, and recording, and songs," suggests current manager Merle Kilgore. "He really took an interest, and started recognizing a hit song. He got turned on to songs, really, right in that area of time."

"Eleven Roses" came out of Bocephus' own publishing company. "Darrell McCall and Lamar Morris were working for Hank," Kilgore explains, "and they wrote that song in the back of the bus on tour, and sung it for Hank, and he said, 'Boys, that's it, I'm cutting that song.' That's one of my all-time favorites."

Hank, Jr., was already on a successful path. In 1969, his name was added to the Walkway of Stars at the Country Music Hall of Fame, laid next to his father's star. That year alone, he released six different albums, either as Hank, Jr., or as Luke the Drifter, Jr. One of them, *Live at Cobo Hall*, was recorded in Detroit on May 4, 1969. That package show, which Johnny Cash headlined, set a record at the time as the highest-grossing country concert in history.

Through 1974, he'd amassed 13 Top Ten records, but his success was hardly fulfilling. "I had been [told], more or less, 'Go out there and clone your daddy—don't think about doing anything on your own,' " Williams told *Billboard*'s Gerry Wood. "Hell, that had to end."

He moved to Cullman, Alabama, where he recorded the *Friends* album, which included appearances by Charlie Daniels, Toy Caldwell of the Marshall Tucker Band, and Chuck Leavell of the Allman Brothers Band. It signaled a new—and controversial—direction for Bocephus' music, but it took more than a year for the album to be released.

In the meantime, Hank suffered a huge setback. He fell more than 500 feet while mountain-climbing in Montana on August 8, 1975. He was given little chance of living, and when he recovered, the doctors told him he was put on earth for a purpose.

102

MADE IN JAPAN

BUCK OWENS & HIS
BUCKAROOS

Capitol 3314
Writers: Bob Morris, Faye Morris
Producer: Ken Nelson
July 15, 1972 (1 week)

After "Tall Dark Stranger" [see 41] reached the top in 1969, it took eight solo singles and nearly three years for Buck Owens to return to number one. In the meantime, he hit on three different cities with his consecutive releases "Big In Vegas," "The Kansas City Song" and "I Wouldn't Live In New York City (If They Gave Me The Whole Dang Town)."

He covered Simon & Garfunkel's "Bridge Over Troubled Water" and peaked at number two with "Rollin' In My Sweet Baby's Arms," finally gaining his twentieth number one single on "Made In Japan," written by Bob Morris and his wife, Faye.

"Bob actually had been in the Navy and had been in Japan during the Korean conflict," Owens notes. "Bob has since passed away from cancer, but he presented me that song, and when I heard 'My transistor radio . . .' I knew I wanted to do the song."

Buck and Don Rich played a guitar harmony line based on the Oriental pentatonic scale, and Rich overdubbed a similar fiddle part that provided an authentic Japanese feel. That effect contributed to the record's number one showing in the summer of 1972.

A year later, Buck dropped the "Buckaroos" credit from the label of his records, although they remained his road group. He gained four more Top Ten singles in 1973–74: "Big Game Hunter," "On The Cover Of The Music City News," "(It's A) Monster's Holiday" and "Great Expectations."

In 1976, he moved from Capitol Records to Warner Bros., where he emerged with the cleverly-titled *Buck 'Em* album, featuring Steve and LaDonna Gatlin on backing vocals. Labelmate Emmylou Harris covered "Together Again" [see 244] that year, and three years later, Buck reached number 11 in a duet with Emmylou, "Play Together Again Again."

His stay on Warners was a disappointment, though. By January of 1980, Owens had become disenchanted with the creative direction of country music and retired from recording and performing.

He still appeared, however, as the co-host of "Hee Haw" for six more years, and continued to work in an executive position as the owner of his own complex in Bakersfield. In addition, he owned a number of radio stations, including KNIX in Phoenix, which was named in 1987 as the Country Station of the Year by both the Country Music Association and the Academy of Country Music.

103

IT'S GONNA TAKE A
LITTLE BIT LONGER

CHARLEY PRIDE

RCA 0707
Writer: Ben Peters
Producer: Jack Clement
July 22, 1972 (3 weeks)

Charley Pride has often told reporters he's been "blessed" with the voice that's created his success, and in 1972, his faith entered into his recording career in more obvious ways. On February 19, he appeared on the *Billboard* country chart with "All His Children," a Henry Mancini composition that celebrated both spirituality and equality with a folksy approach. The single peaked on April 1 at number two, held out of the top spot by Freddie Hart's "My Hang-Up Is You" [see 95].

On March 14, Charley won his first two Grammys, both coming in gospel categories. *Did You Think to Pray* picked up the award for Best Sacred Performance, and "Let Me Live" took the nod for Best Gospel Performance.

"I think religious beliefs help in any given direction," Pride notes. "When you believe in the all-Creator, I believe definitely that has helped all the way around—not only in my career, but in my whole life. I don't go to church that much, but I'm a believer, from being brought up in a Baptist church. My dad was a deacon of a Baptist church for more than 45 years, so I'm a believer."

Pride's quasi-gospel foray, "All His Children," appeared in the movie *Sometimes a Great Notion*, and in the meantime, he prepared a new album, *A Sunshiny Day with Charley Pride*. The album's "It's Gonna Take A Little Bit Longer," recorded in Nashville on January 12, returned him to number one for three weeks in the summer of 1972.

In February of 1974, *A Sunshiny Day* was

the first record named Favorite Country Album in the American Music Awards, as the Pride juggernaut rolled on, despite reported differences between Pride and producer Jack Clement.

"One time I calculated that I was getting $20,000 an hour—or was it a day?—for every time I went in the studio with him," Clement recalls. "We'd cut an album in two or three days.

"I loved the guy, and still do. We argued, but it was man to man. He's hard-headed and that kind of stuff. He wants to produce and he wants to be everything. It got to eating at him that the producer was getting too important in this thing. I got through 21 albums with him, with 10 or 12 songs from them. That's a lot of wax."

ple began saying it more and more in conjunction with Freddie Hart on stage. "A lot of people would use it," he recalls, "and it's quite a compliment when someone copies you in some way or develops a saying."

Hart was born December 22, 1933, in a house on dead man's curve in Lochapoka, Alabama. He was one of fifteen children (ten boys and five girls) in a sharecropping family, and he'd grown accustomed to picking cotton, corn and peanuts by the age of five. At that time, his Uncle Fletcher made Freddie his first guitar out of a wooden cigar box and the copper coil from a Ford Model T.

That guitar provided a foundation, and Hart spent a great deal of his youth playing guitar, writing simple melodies and listening to the radio. "I always loved music," he recalls, "and we never missed the Grand Ole Opry on Saturday night."

104
BLESS YOUR HEART
FREDDIE HART
Capitol 3353
Writers: Freddie Hart, Jack Lebsock
Producer: Earl Ball
August 12, 1972 (2 weeks)

"Bless Your Heart" became Freddie Hart's third number one single as a recording artist, but it was actually his fourth as a songwriter. Carl Smith performed on the first, taking "Loose Talk" to number one for seven weeks, beginning January 8, 1955.

"I was in a room with some people and a bunch of kids were out in the street playing," remembers Hart of the inspiration. "Someone said 'Get those brats out of the street before a car runs over them.' A woman right next to us says, 'You know, there's a lot of loose tongues wagging around us today,' and out of that I got 'Loose Talk.'"

"Loose Talk" was recorded by more than 50 other performers, and Hart went on to gain several other valuable cuts. Patsy Cline featured his "Lovin' In Vain" on the "B" side of "I Fall To Pieces," and he also earned hits when Porter Wagoner recorded "Skid Row Joe" (number three, 1966) and George Jones did "My Tears Are Overdue" (number 15, 1964).

"I love to write," says Hart. "To me, a song is very real; it's people put to music."

In the case of "Bless Your Heart," it was the artist's name that provided the basis for the record. The title is a common phrase, but peo-

105
IF YOU LEAVE ME TONIGHT I'LL CRY
JERRY WALLACE
Decca 32989
Writers: Gerald Sanford, Hal Mooney
Producer: Joe Johnson
August 26, 1972 (2 weeks)

In some respects, Jerry Wallace's career paralleled Conway Twitty's. Both started out making pop hits, shifted their attentions to country in the mid-'60s, and topped the country chart for the first time with Decca Records.

Born December 15, 1933, in Kansas City, Missouri, Wallace grew up in both the Show Me State and Glendale, Arizona. He displayed an affinity for country music during his youth, and worked at music and acting. He also proved adept at impersonating other entertainers, an ability he often incorporated into his concerts.

Wallace first recorded for the Allied label in 1951. He emerged with Challenge Records in 1958, reaching number 11 on Billboard's Hot 100 with "How The Time Flies." A year later, "Primrose Lane" went to number eight. "In The Misty Moonlight" hit number 19 in 1964.

In 1965, Jerry resurfaced in country music, but he failed to crack even the Top Ten until he cut a song for an episode of Rod Serling's "Night Gallery." Universal Studios needed someone to record "If You Leave Me Tonight

I'll Cry." The vocalist would have to sound like Nat King Cole, and Wallace got the job. "Nat King Cole was my idol," he told Skip Hess of the *Indianapolis News*, "and it made me feel wonderful that Universal chose me as the one who sounded most like Nat King Cole." Only a portion of the record appeared in the "Night Gallery" episode, titled "The Tune in Dan's Cafe." That portion played several times, though: the needle in the jukebox kept stopping at " 'til death . . .'til death . . .'til death."

Thanks to a huge response from viewers around the country, the cut became a single from Wallace's Decca album *To Get to You*. It

Don Gibson

sold 800,000 copies and spent two weeks at number one on *Billboard*'s country chart.

Jerry's follow-up, "Do You Know What It's Like To Be Lonesome," hit number two in 1973, just behind Merle Haggard's "I Wonder If They Ever Think Of Me" [see 119]. "Don't Give Up On Me" and "My Wife's House" also reached the Top Ten, but Wallace ran into litigation with his management in 1975 and didn't record for two years. He never regained his momentum.

Wallace supplemented his music career with acting jobs, appearing in character roles on many different shows. He also recorded music for TV shows like "Flipper" and Richard Boone's "Hec Ramsey."

106

WOMAN (SENSUOUS WOMAN)

DON GIBSON

Hickory 1638
Writer: Gary S. Paxton
Producer: Wesley Rose
September 2, 1972 (1 week)

"Woman (Sensuous Woman)" portrayed a lustful affair in which a man goes outside of his marriage repeatedly to a woman who holds him in a spell. References to craving her body and losing control conjure up a picture of love as an addiction—how ironic, since "Woman" is the only number one record that Don Gibson recorded after conquering his own addiction.

Born in Shelby, North Carolina, on April 3, 1928, Gibson gained his first real break while playing a nightclub in Knoxville, Tennessee. He was spotted by Mel Foree, who brought publisher Wesley Rose from Nashville to hear the singer. Gibson sang his own composition, "Sweet Dreams" [see 269], on stage that evening, and Rose signed Gibson as a writer.

Gibson earned his first trip to number one in 1958 with his RCA recording "Oh Lonesome Me," which also featured "I Can't Stop Loving You" [see 108] on the flip side. He followed with another number one single, "Blue Blue Day," and over the next eight years, he garnered a dozen more Top Ten recordings. Included were "Just One Time," "Sea Of Heartbreak" and "Lonesome Number One," each of which stopped at number two.

That period brought the seeds of Gibson's addiction. He was plagued by personal problems and put on too many pounds. A doctor gave him pills to help bring his weight back down, but Gibson began swallowing as many as 25 at a time. "It's the worst thing that ever happened to me," he told *Country Song Roundup* in 1975. "I lost track of time. I lived from day to day. I was on pep pills and tranquilizers—never the hard stuff, just the pills. They were trouble, and I lived with trouble." In 1967, Gibson married Bobbi Patterson, whom he credits with ending his chemical dependency.

At the close of the decade, Gibson left RCA to sign with Hickory Records, a division of the Acuff-Rose publishing firm. With that move, his publisher also took on the production role in his recordings. "Without Wesley Rose," Gibson told *Billboard*, "I wouldn't know how to operate."

It took a couple of years for Rose to get Gibson back near the top of the *Billboard* country chart. In late 1971, he reached number five with an Eddy Raven composition, "Country Green," and two records later, "Woman (Sensuous Woman)" became Don's third number one single as a performer.

107
WHEN THE SNOW IS ON THE ROSES
SONNY JAMES
Columbia 45644
Writers: Larry Kusick, Eddie Snyder, Ernest Bader, Hans Last
Producer: George Richey
September 16, 1972 (1 week)

When Clive Davis signed Sonny James to a Columbia recording contract [see 100— "That's Why I Love You Like I Do"], it was a major deal partially because it was the only time that Davis *personally* signed a country act to the label.

After becoming head of the label in the '60s, Davis helped turn Columbia into a premier rock and roll label by signing such acts as Janis Joplin, Blood Sweat & Tears, and blues guitarist Johnny Winter. Having been so involved in the deal, it was certain that Davis would pay close attention to James' career, and things certainly started on the right foot with Sonny's first Columbia single.

"When The Snow Is On The Roses" had first been recorded by Ed Ames, and after its debut on the *Billboard* country chart on July 22,

1972, James' version hit number one in its ninth week. He followed up with "White Silver Sands," which reached number five; and "I Love You More And More Everyday," which went to number four.

Unfortunately, Davis was fired on May 29, 1973, amidst charges of misuse of company funds. The dismissal was a controversial one throughout the entire music business, but it was particularly disheartening to James.

"I was just in hog heaven," Sonny recalls. "They had given me a good financial agreement, guaranteed, and here was my first album, off and running, and boom, all this blew up about Clive. I always thought he had to take the blame for something.

"I was blown out of the sky 'cause I was signed by him. They had told me that to start with, they were going to double my album sales. That's one of the reasons I went with them."

With Davis out of the picture, James' next single, "If She Just Helps Me Get Over You," managed a peak position of number 15. He waited until the spring of 1974 to release his next single.

Davis, meanwhile, recovered from his ouster. In 1974, he took over Bell Records, changing its name to Arista. He returned to the top of the pop world by signing acts like Barry Manilow, Whitney Houston and Air Supply. On May 8, 1989, Davis announced the opening of a Nashville division of Arista.

108
I CAN'T STOP LOVING YOU
CONWAY TWITTY
Decca 32988
Writer: Don Gibson
Producer: Owen Bradley
September 23, 1972 (1 week)

To call it a productive afternoon would be a major understatement. At one point in the '50s, Don Gibson spent a winter's day writing songs in his trailer off the Clinton Highway in Knoxville. Gibson simply sat on his bed, singing lyrics into his tape recorder as he composed them, but two of his compositions still stand more than three decades later.

One of the day's creations was originally titled "Ole Lonesome Me." Once he turned it in to his publisher, Acuff-Rose, it was altered to "*Oh* Lonesome Me," and that title took

Gibson to number one on the country chart on April 14, 1958.

The "B" side of "Oh Lonesome Me" also charted, hitting number seven, but over time, it outstripped the "A" side's achievements. "I Can't Stop Loving You" developed out of a conscious attempt to write a ballad of lost love. After working up a first draft, Gibson looked back over his work and one particular line stood out. Using that phrase as a title, he started over again, and "I Can't Stop Loving You" ultimately became his most recorded composition.

While Gibson's own version gained airplay, Kitty Wells simultaneously took it to number three on the country chart. Four years later, Ray Charles introduced it to an even larger audience, earning a number one single on the *Billboard* Hot 100. Conway Twitty duplicated that feat in country music when he remade it ten years after Charles' recording.

"I had started doin' it on stage," recalls Twitty. "I had my own arrangement of it, and I got so much reaction from this song, and the way I did it, I went to [producer] Owen Bradley and told him I was goin' to do it for an album, but I thought it could be a single. We got that much reaction from it out there, and that's what I listen to. I don't listen to people in the business—I listen to those fans out there.

"Owen said, 'Everybody in the business has recorded this song, it's on every album.' I said, 'Nope, it's not on a Conway Twitty album. There's a lot of Conway Twitty fans out there. I appreciate your point, and you do have one—but I think I do, too.'"

On July 29, 1972, Twitty's version of "I Can't Stop Loving You" debuted at number 45, and after summer officially ended, the record became his tenth number one country single.

Mel Tillis

109

I AIN'T NEVER
MEL TILLIS
MGM 14418
Writers: Mel Tillis, Webb Pierce
Producer: Jim Vienneau
September 30, 1972 (2 weeks)

Before Mel Tillis ever found success as a recording artist, he established himself as a talented songwriter in Nashville. He first sojourned to Music City in June of 1956, but found that competition for recording contracts was already stiff. Several people told him, however, that songs were always in short supply; Mel took a Greyhound bus back to Florida.

There, he continued working as a singer, and honed his skills as a writer. When Ray Price appeared in the area, Tillis played a few songs for him, and Price took one, "I'm Tired," back to Nashville. He introduced it to Webb Pierce, who cut it without Tillis' knowledge. It went to number three in 1957.

That warranted a return to Nashville on a permanent basis, and Tillis found a ready market for his songs. He wrote a steady line of hits, including the Grammy-winning "Detroit City" and the Kenny Rogers & The First Edition classic, "Ruby, Don't Take Your Love To Town."

Other successful Tillis compositions included "Honey (Open That Door)" [see 571], Jack Greene's "All The Time" [see 6—"You Are My Treasure"], and three Ray Price hits—"Heart Over Mind," "One More Time" and "Burning Memories."

Webb Pierce remained Mel's biggest supporter, though, in part because he was able to persuade then-"green" Tillis to cut him in on the financial arrangements. Pierce hit number one with "Honky Tonk Song," and also scored Top Ten singles with "Tupelo County Jail," "No Love Have I" and "I Ain't Never."

As an artist, Tillis didn't have a Top Ten hit himself until 1968's "Who's Julie." He racked up eight more Top Ten records—including a remake of "Heart Over Mind"—before he achieved his first number one single, another remake of a self-penned song, "I Ain't Never."

"We just thought that was a good idea to try that song," says producer Jim Vienneau. "We thought it was ready for rebirth, so we did it, and it worked out pretty good."

Vienneau, who took over as the head of MGM's country division in 1965, had produced number one pop records for Connie Francis, Mark Dinning and Conway Twitty, and had also helped Sheb Wooley and Hank Williams, Jr., to chart-topping country hits. In this instance, Vienneau's hunch was good enough to land Tillis' first number one record, 15 years after Mel's first session.

because he always wore a beard. It was just kind of a little song to him in a way."

"Funny Face" also proved to Fargo that simple songs are the best songs. "That was one of the first songs I ever wrote, but I always thought it was too simple, and I kept trying to change it. I wrote 16 verses to it, trying to complicate it and make it real different. I finally just wound up using the first two verses I wrote for it, and just went with my gut feeling about it, and I'm glad I did."

At one time, Fargo had pitched "Funny Face" to comedian George Lindsey (a.k.a. "Goober" from "The Andy Griffith Show"), who had expressed interest in recording a song of hers after he heard her earlier Challenge release "Daddy" on a Burbank station. Lindsey turned "Funny Face" down, and Donna's version surfaced on its own after "Happiest Girl" broke out.

"It started getting requests out of the album, and it just kind of happened. It wasn't like, 'Well, what are we going to put out next?' It was almost like there was no other choice because of the requests. You just pray for those kinds of things. I was really lucky—besides being 'The Happiest Girl' I was also the luckiest girl."

Since Stan Silver doubles as her husband and producer, Fargo is also lucky to have an immediate sounding board with an opposite personality. "My goal was to please us both with a song. I knew that if I could please us both, then I was reaching the population."

110

FUNNY FACE
DONNA FARGO
Dot 17429
Writer: Donna Fargo
Producer: Stan Silver
October 14, 1972 (3 weeks)

For those who thought "The Happiest Girl In The Whole U.S.A." [see 99] might have been a fluke, "Funny Face" laid any doubts to rest about Donna Fargo's talent. When it crossed the million mark, she became the first female country star to have back-to-back gold singles, and the *Happiest Girl in the Whole U.S.A.* album likewise went gold.

While it followed "Happiest Girl" in release, "Funny Face" had actually been written earlier. "It was a natural song for me to write," Fargo says, " 'cause my husband used to call me 'funny face' and I used to call him 'fuzzy face'

111

IT'S NOT LOVE (BUT IT'S NOT BAD)
MERLE HAGGARD & THE STRANGERS
Capitol 3419
Writers: Hank Cochran, Glenn Martin
Producer: Fuzzy Owen
November 4, 1972 (1 week)

"It's Not Love (But It's Not Bad)" received a nomination from the Country Music Association for Song of the Year in 1973, though its beginning was hardly auspicious. Glenn Martin started the song for laughs, writing about a personal situation that songwriter Hank Cochran was in at the time.

"It was just a little ditty," says Martin, "and the next time I was around Hank, I was gonna play it for him. When I got to the part where the line came, 'It's not love, but it's not bad,' I thought that this might be more than a joke."

With some of the work already done, he got in touch with Cochran and offered him a chance to help finish it. It sat around unfinished for some time, though, until Merle Haggard provided them with an added incentive.

"Merle called Hank from Florida and told him he was gonna be in town the next day, and he needed one good song," Martin remembers. "He didn't care who wrote it or who published it, he just needed one good song. Hank and I got together, and he wrote the last verse, and then we tightened it up a little bit, and Haggard came in town the next day, and we played it for him."

Recorded at Columbia Studios in Nashville, Haggard's rendition with the Strangers featured Hargus "Pig" Robbins on piano, and both Martin and Cochran were present at the recording session. They were hardly finished, though.

Sometime earlier, Haggard had cut another Martin/Cochran composition titled "Montego Bay" in California. It had been designated as a single, and Cochran left California to come back to Nashville. In the meantime, Haggard wrote another song, and "Montego Bay" was bumped.

"This time, Hank got on the bus with Merle and stayed with him," says Martin. "On the way to California, Merle wrote that thing 'I Wonder If They Ever Think Of Me' [see 119] about the prisoners being released. He really wanted to come out with that, because it was a timely-type thing, but to keep Merle from bumping our song, Hank stuck with him until our thing came out."

Cochran's persistence paid huge dividends. In addition to netting a CMA nomination, "It's Not Love" reached number one in its tenth week on the *Billboard* chart.

112

MY MAN (UNDERSTANDS)
TAMMY WYNETTE

Epic 10909
Writers: Carmol Taylor, Norro Wilson,
Billy Sherrill
Producer: Billy Sherrill
November 11, 1972 (1 week)

Billy Sherrill's CBS associate, Glenn Sutton, had a proclivity for writing songs for women

to sing about their man [see 190—"What A Man, My Man Is"]. So at first glance, one might have expected that Sutton co-wrote "My Man (Understands)" with Sherrill. In fact, the credit goes to two other writers from Sherrill's stable at the Al Gallico publishing house, Carmol Taylor and Norro Wilson.

"My Man (Understands)" came on the heels of "Reach Out Your Hand," a Sherrill composition written in tandem with Tammy Wynette. "Reach Out" peaked at the number two slot on the *Billboard* country chart during the summer of 1972, edged out of number one by Charley Pride's "It's Gonna Take A Little Bit Longer" [see 103].

"Reach Out Your Hand" first entered the chart the week that ended May 20, and Tammy and her husband George Jones brushed closely with American history. They were scheduled to appear that week in Florida on the campaign trail in support of presidential hopeful George Wallace. On May 15, however, Wallace was shot in a Maryland shopping mall, and eventually withdrew from the race. Wallace's Florida appearance—thus George & Tammy's—was necessarily canceled.

At the time, Jones owned a theme park in Lakeland, Florida: Old Plantation Country Music Park. By the time "My Man (Understands)" reached number one in November, Jones had sold off the park, and the couple moved back to Nashville, where their careers were based in the first place.

"My Man," in fact, is characterized by Norro Wilson as an example of songwriting as a day-to-day job, much like any other. "There are songs that have some funny things taking place," he notes, "but this one was more like 'I went to work this morning, went in the office, made three phone calls, fixed my coffee and we wrote,' and that's kind of how that is."

"I've done so few uptempo songs," adds Tammy, "but that song said exactly what I wanted to say, and I think it says what a woman in love likes to say about her man. 'Maybe he doesn't rule over me, but he's got me in the palm of his hand or wrapped around his little finger,' and that's what that song said in a happy sort of way, instead of a sad way."

"My Man (Understands)" debuted on the *Billboard* country chart at number 57 on September 16. When "My Man" reached number one eight weeks later on November 11, it had a strange political irony in light of Tammy's ties to Governor Wallace. Four days before the song topped the chart, Richard M. Nixon was re-elected President.

113
SHE'S TOO GOOD TO BE TRUE
CHARLEY PRIDE
RCA 0802
Writer: Johnny Duncan
Producer: Jack Clement
November 18, 1972 (3 weeks)

Billboard named Charley Pride the top country singles artist for the year 1972, and his third single to hit number one during the calendar year came with "She's Too Good To Be True." It was the tenth number one single of his career, and the second written by Johnny Duncan, who left Pride's show during the fall of 1972 [see 73—"I'd Rather Love You"].

"I wrote the song in Texas," Duncan remembers. "I grew up in Dublin, and I was back home with my mom and dad when I got the idea. It was in the wee hours of the night. I scribbled down most of the lyrics, and then took it back and finished it in Nashville. It was about a particular person in my life at that time, somebody other than my wife, I'm sorry to say. That was one of the better-written songs during that stretch."

Pride agreed, and recorded "She's Too Good To Be True" on August 17. Another person who agreed was songwriter A.L. Owens, who had already earned three number one singles with Pride. "I had a great compliment from 'Doodle' Owens," says Duncan. "Doodle and Dallas Frazier wrote so many great songs. Doodle came to me at the BMI banquet and said, 'That's the best song this year.' That was the greatest compliment I'd had as a songwriter, especially from people of that caliber."

"She's Too Good To Be True" debuted at a modest number 74 on October 7, hitting number one six weeks later.

Though Duncan left the Charley Pride Show to work more on his own, he still maintained a friendship with Pride, and in 1975, Pride recorded another of his songs as a single. "I Ain't All Bad" peaked at number six.

Charley has never written any of the songs he's recorded, though he has long predicted that he'll come up with a few before his career is over. "I do write," he insists. "I've only written a couple of things, and now I'm starting to write. I always said I would end up in reverse of people like Roger Miller, Kris Kristofferson, Tom T. Hall. They wrote first and were artists second. I'm an artist first, and I'll write second."

114
GOT THE ALL-OVERS FOR YOU
FREDDIE HART & THE HEARTBEATS
Capitol 3453
Writer: Freddie Hart
Producer: Earl Ball
December 9, 1972 (3 weeks)

With the release of "Got The All-Overs For You," Freddie Hart started a new precedent in his recording career. It was the first of his singles to credit his touring band, the Heartbeats, on the label.

"I wanted to make them feel good," he says, "and I had one of the finest bands in the country anyway. I kept them for eight or nine years, and they were unusually good. A lot of times you can take a good road band, but they're not studio musicians. There's a difference; it's hard to tell *them* that, but there is quite a difference."

Like "Loose Talk" [see 104—"Bless Your Heart"], "The All-Overs" came out of a conversation. "Wade Pepper was the head of Capitol Records," recalls Hart, "and I was in his office. He said, 'Freddie, I've got a girl in the office, and every time she hears one of your songs, she gets the all-overs.' I said, 'Wade, I'm going to write a song about that.'"

True to his word, Hart came up with a winner, as "The All-Overs" spent three weeks at the top of *Billboard*'s country singles chart. It also followed the "sexy" theme that "Easy Loving" [see 83] had first established. "That was the thing I was doing," Freddie admits, "putting a woman on a pedestal, which ain't a bad idea, either. I think everybody wants to be wanted."

That was certainly true in the case of Hart, who wanted to become a country performer so badly that he ran away from home at age twelve, telling his parents upon his return that he had appeared on the Grand Ole Opry.

"I walked those streets so much, I believe there's as many tears of mine on the sidewalks of Nashville as anybody's. I used to sit outside the old Ryman Auditorium and look inside and watch them entertaining. I'd walk away with my heart in my hands, and I wanted something good to say, so I'd tell them I was on the Grand Ole Opry."

Eventually, his parents sent Freddie to a Civilian Conservation Corps camp, and his mother lied about his age so that he could join

Ray Price

forming at local country clubs, and in 1948, he made his first appearance on radio station KRBC.

A year later, Ray was a regular on the "Big D Jamboree" show on KRLD in Dallas, which eventually brought him a national audience on the CBS radio network. From there, it was a short step to membership in the Grand Ole Opry in 1952, and a recording contract from Columbia Records.

During those years, he became friends with Hank Williams, and the two shared a house (Williams lived upstairs, Price lived downstairs) on Natchez Trace in Nashville after Hank and Audrey had separated.

In a manner of speaking, Price represents a direct link from those early pioneers to contemporary country. Hank's friend also employed a huge number of future performers in his own Cherokee Cowboy band, including Willie Nelson, Roger Miller, Johnny Paycheck (then known as Donnie Young) and Johnny Bush. Those friendships would later pay off when Nelson joined Price on a duet album, *San Antonio Rose*, and when Nelson and Miller featured him on their single "Old Friends."

On eight different occasions, *Billboard* named Price the top Male Vocalist of the Year, owing in part to a total of eight number one records, and nine more that peaked at number two. Among the "also-rans" are "I've Got A New Heartache," "Heartaches By The Number" and "Burning Memories." Two more hit the number two position in 1972: Kris Kristofferson's "I'd Rather Be Sorry" and Mac Davis' "The Lonesomest Lonesome."

"She's Got To Be A Saint," with its gospel-inflected lyric, brought Ray back to number one at the end of 1972.

"It was given to me out in California by a publisher, Al Gallico, who was a real hotshot promoter, too," says Price. "Al brought it in and promised me that if I'd cut it, it would be a number one record, and that's exactly what happened."

the Marines. After four years in the service, Hart finally got his musical career off to a start in 1949.

115
SHE'S GOT TO BE A SAINT
RAY PRICE

Columbia 45724
Writers: Joe Paulini, Mario J. DiNapoli
Producer: Don Law
December 30, 1972 (3 weeks)

Born January 12, 1926, Ray Noble Price became a country singer almost by mistake. Raised on a farm in Cherokee County, Texas, he pursued a veterinary degree at North Texas Stage Agricultural College in Abilene. At night, he supplemented his studies by per-

---

116
SOUL SONG
JOE STAMPLEY

Dot 17442
Writers: George Richey, Norro Wilson, Billy Sherrill
Producer: Norro Wilson
January 20, 1973 (1 week)

Especially in a subjective medium like music, encouragement is a motivating factor during the early years of development, and Joe Stampley couldn't have asked for a better motivator than the legendary Hank Williams.

Stampley was born June 6, 1943, in Springhill, Louisiana, just a mile from the Arkansas borderline. He grew up on a steady diet of country music, and for several years, his family lived in Texas. There, at the age of seven, he happened to meet Williams in Baytown.

"We lived right down the road from a country radio station," Stampley remembers, "and he and Johnny Horton were doing some shows in Houston. They were at the radio station, and I went down and got to meet both of them." Joe told his idol that he knew all of his songs and could imitate him rather well; Williams encouraged the youngster to develop his own style. Stampley has held on to that advice throughout his career.

At 13, Stampley convinced his father to purchase a tape recorder so he could hear himself played back and try to improve his work. Two years later, he had returned to Louisiana, where Springhill disk jockey Merle Kilgore [see 448—"All My Rowdy Friends (Have Settled Down)"] helped Stampley secure his first recording contract with Imperial Records.

In 1961, Joe moved on to Chicago's Chess Records, but it took another nine years before he finally connected with Nashville. He sent songs to publisher Al Gallico, who lined up a recording contract for him with Paramount Records. Joe's first single was "Quonette McGraw From Smackover, Arkansas."

Dot bought out Paramount, and Stampley debuted on the *Billboard* country charts on February 20, 1971, with "Take Time To Know Her." A year later, Norro Wilson took over production chores and brought Joe his first Top Ten single, "If You Touch Me (You've Got To Love Me)."

The follow-up, "Soul Song," was conceived by keyboard player George Richey, who developed the chorus and had Wilson and Billy Sherrill fill out the verses. Teenager Tanya Tucker recorded it first, but when it failed to become a hit single, Stampley covered it. Joe's version of "Soul Song" debuted in *Billboard* on November 11, 1972, at number 44. Ten weeks later, the record carried Stampley to number one for the first time in his career. It also reached number 37 on *Billboard*'s Hot 100.

"I was kind of amazed," Stampley admits, "but it sounded like a crossover record to me."

117
(OLD DOGS, CHILDREN AND) WATERMELON WINE

TOM T. HALL

Mercury 73346
Writer: Tom T. Hall
Producer: Jerry Kennedy
January 27, 1973 (1 week)

As historians frequently note, the 1968 Democratic National Convention in Chicago was a disaster. Mayor Daley's police force attacked demonstrators on national TV, and the whole fiasco became an embarrassment for the party. In an effort to divert attention during

Tom T. Hall

the 1972 convention, Tom T. Hall took part in a music festival in Miami Beach. He was joined at Flamingo Park by George Jones and Tammy Wynette, already tied to one of the year's major political stories [see 112—"My Man (Understands)"].

"This was just across the street from the convention center," Hall recalls, "so these young people became more interested in the music than in the politics. They all came over, and brought a case of beer and fired up a joint and sat around in the grass, and we played music for them. They left the convention alone."

After the show, Hall went back to his hotel. The place was quiet, since most of the registrants were back at the convention, and Tom T. headed into the lounge. "The rest of it," he says, "is in the song."

The song was "(Old Dogs, Children And) Watermelon Wine," Hall's recounting of a conversation with an old man he met in the bar.

"He was a grand old gentleman. He was wiping the tables and killin' time. I figured out later that the old man in the song was retired. He said, 'I turned 65, by the way, a few months ago,' and what he was telling me was he didn't need this job. He was on Social Security. You know, I'd written this song and it took me two years to figure out what that line was about.

"The classic bartender was standing wiping a glass, and I don't know why they do that, but he had this one glass, and he was wearin' it out wiping it, and watching 'Ironside' on TV."

Hall wrote the lyrics—more than four minutes' worth—on an airsickness bag during his return flight to Tennessee.

"He had flown back to Nashville for a 10:00 A.M. session," says producer Jerry Kennedy. "His plane was late gettin' there, and he walked in with that song written. He didn't even have a melody finished for it. All of that was finished right on the date, and to me, that's one of the best songs he's ever written."

118
SHE NEEDS SOMEONE TO HOLD HER (WHEN SHE CRIES)
CONWAY TWITTY
Decca 33033
Writer: Raymond Smith
Producer: Owen Bradley
February 3, 1973 (2 weeks)

"She Needs Someone To Hold Her (When She Cries)" marked the second number one single for Raymond Smith, a part-time songwriter from eastern Tennessee [see 66—"Fifteen Years Ago"]. It was also the second he penned for Conway Twitty.

"If you ever watch 'Wheel of Fortune,'" says Smith, "there are times you get off on the wrong track and your mind can't solve the simplest puzzle. Other times, it automatically comes right to your mind. It's kind of the way songs go. The good ones come easy—you almost know what the next line's gonna be. It's just natural for it to say what it says."

It's even more natural when the writer lives what he writes about, and Conway believes that was the case with "She Needs Someone To Hold Her." "I think Raymond was goin' through some problems at the time," he says. "I figured that had something to do with the way he wrote that song. It usually does."

At the time he submitted the song, Smith had no conception of its potential. "Somehow or another, I've always had trouble distinguishing my own hits," he explains. "I write songs and I can tell very little difference in them to begin with. After I set them aside for a while and then go back to them, I can kind of do that.

"When I wrote 'She Needs Someone To Hold Her,' I didn't really know that that was a smash. I sent it in with two other songs to my publisher—all three of which, incidentally, were recorded. L.E. White was runnin' the publishing for Conway, and kind of screened the songs for his next sessions."

"I think L.E. called me and played it for me over the phone late one night," Conway continues. "He said, 'Do you want me to play it again?' and I said, 'Nope, you don't need to play it again. I only need to hear that once. That's gonna be my next single.'"

"She Needs Someone To Hold Her (When She Cries)" did quite well for Conway, debuting higher than any other new single on December 2, 1972. The record appeared at number 51, just one notch higher than "(Old Dogs, Children And) Watermelon Wine" [see 117]. It progressed to the top spot two months later.

Smith never did pursue songwriting on a full-time basis, and currently owns a pair of radio stations—WGRV-AM and WIKQ-FM—in Greenville, Tennessee.

Conway followed up "She Needs Someone To Hold Her" with "Baby's Gone," which stopped at number two on June 2, nudged out of number one by the Jeanne Pruett single "Satin Sheets" [see 131].

119
I WONDER IF THEY EVER THINK OF ME
MERLE HAGGARD & THE STRANGERS

Capitol 3488
Writer: Merle Haggard
Producer: Fuzzy Owen
February 17, 1973 (1 week)

Proclaiming that America had achieved "peace with honor," President Richard Nixon announced on January 23, 1973, that he had approved a treaty which would end American involvement in Vietnam. The first U.S. "advisers" had lost their lives in 1959, but the height of the war stretched from 1965 to 1972.

During that time, 45,000 American soldiers died, two million medals were awarded and more than six million tons of bombs were dropped in Southeast Asia. All but one of the remaining prisoners of war were freed by March 29, 1973, but 1,359 were listed as Missing In Action.

On behalf of the POWs, Merle Haggard wrote "I Wonder If They Ever Think Of Me," although its release was delayed a couple of months [see 111—"It's Not Love"].

"I don't recall a specific event occurring," says Merle of the song's inspiration, "except the issue of the prisoner of war has always been a big issue, and especially in wartime. The Vietnam War was such a strange and misunderstood war."

Ironically, "I Wonder If They Ever Think Of Me" crept up the *Billboard* chart as America's involvement in the war was waning. The record reached number one on February 17, just five days after the first group of prisoners left Hanoi.

A month later, Haggard brought the Strangers to the center of America's political machine, playing the White House for First Lady Patricia Nixon's sixty-first birthday. It was quite an initiation for piano player Mark Yeary, who made his first appearance as a member of the band on that show.

"You talk about nervous," says steel player Norm Hamlet, "he was *real* nervous. But everything worked fine. We went in and played the White House, and little did we know at that

Merle Haggard at the White House with President Nixon

time, though, that they [all the President's men] had a meeting and were upstairs talking about the Watergate thing—at least that's what we were told."

The Watergate issue later found its way into another Haggard recording. Merle lamented Nixon's public stance in "Are The Good Times Really Over (I Wish A Buck Was Still Silver)" [see 467—"Big City"].

120
RATED "X"
LORETTA LYNN
Decca 33039
Writer: Loretta Lynn
Producer: Owen Bradley
February 24, 1973 (1 week)

On the evening of October 16, 1972, Loretta Lynn picked up the Country Music Association's Female Vocalist of the Year award. That trophy wasn't particularly surprising to those in attendance, but she did pull off a real coup that evening with another award.

Lynn was the first woman ever nominated for the CMA's Entertainer of the Year honors, but no one gave her a chance of winning; even her husband went hunting because he didn't want to see her lose. Instead, a shocked Loretta heard her name called when the envelope was opened. Her position as the first woman to win Entertainer of the Year was appropriate—she had also been the first to step out of the subservient female role.

"She was the opposite of Kitty Wells," says producer Owen Bradley. "Kitty was the mistreated housewife, and Loretta was the housewife who wasn't gonna take anything off of anybody. This sort of was really like an accident. I wish to hell I could say I was smart enough to have planned it, but at least I didn't say 'No, we don't wanna do that 'cause it won't work.'"

Lynn also earned a reputation for making records that were banned by different radio stations, including "Rated 'X,'" her first release following the CMA presentation. The single called up images of Linda Lovelace and Xaviera Hollander, making some programmers a little skittish.

"I wrote that song about a woman that had been married and was divorced," explains Loretta. "This was about the time that all you heard about was them movies comin' out that

were rated X, and I thought, 'Hmmm, I'll just write about a divorced woman,' 'cause I had about eight songs banned, and every time I had a song banned, it went number one, so I didn't worry about it anymore.

"No one listened to see if it was dirty or not, but it wasn't dirty at all. When they finally started listening to it, they made it a number one record, even though they first started off bannin' it."

Bradley views it as a typical Loretta Lynn single. "I'd say that was pretty much in the groove of what we were trying to get across," he offers. "We were maybe running it in the ground a little bit, but we did it again, and got away with it, I guess."

121
THE LORD KNOWS I'M DRINKING
CAL SMITH
Decca 33040
Writer: Bill Anderson
Producer: Walter Haynes
March 4, 1973 (1 week)

In addition to writing most of his own songs, Bill Anderson has attained a huge degree of success by supplying hits for many of his fellow Nashville artists. On six different occasions, his compositions have reached number one in the hands of other performers.

Two different versions of "City Lights" [see 195] have hit the top, along with "Once A Day," by Connie Smith, in 1964; "Saginaw, Michigan" [see 199—"It's Time To Pay The Fiddler"], by Lefty Frizzell, also in 1964; "I May Never Get To Heaven" [see 353], by Conway Twitty; and Cal Smith's recording of "The Lord Knows I'm Drinking."

The latter tune, a controversial composition in which Anderson grappled with the judgmental nature of many "religious" people, stemmed from a dinner date with his wife at a restaurant near their church.

"We were enjoying a glass of wine with our meal," Anderson explains, "when suddenly I looked up and several of the staunchest members of the congregation were coming in the door. My first reaction was to slide my glass of wine behind a menu which was standing up on the table so the church members wouldn't see it.

"Becky saw what I was about to do and would have no part of it. 'Hey, the Lord knows

I'm drinking,' she said. I nearly fell headfirst into the mashed potatoes reaching for a paper napkin to write down her line. While Becky calmly finished her meal, I sat there and wrote the entire song."

Several performers turned it down, but it finally came to prominence in the hands of Cal Smith, a longtime performer whose first bona fide hit coincided one year earlier with his fortieth birthday. Smith's remake of "I've Found Someone Of My Own," a 1971 pop hit for Free Movement, had taken him to number four. The follow-up, "For My Baby," was a disappointment, but "The Lord Knows I'm Drinking" became his very first number one record.

"I recorded the song in the same session I recorded 'Someone Of My Own,'" Smith said in the "Ramblin' Rhodes" column of Georgia's *Augusta Herald.* "Immediately, I felt the song would be a hit. I talked my producer, Walter Haynes, into putting the song on an album, and after 'Someone Of My Own' became a hit, disk jockeys started playing 'The Lord Knows I'm Drinking' from the album."

122
'TIL I GET IT RIGHT
TAMMY WYNETTE
Epic 10940
Writers: Red Lane, Larry Henley
Producer: Billy Sherrill
March 10, 1973 (1 week)

Tammy Wynette has been married five different times, and in 1973, she was with her third husband, George Jones. The fact that four marriages failed has often been a source of sorrow for Tammy, but she has joked on occasion that the opening line of " 'Til I Get It Right" is the story of her life.

"When I heard it, I thought, 'Gosh, how many stupid mistakes I've made,'" she recalls, "and here's a song that says, 'I'm gonna keep on'—not only 'falling in love,' but I took it as life in general—" 'til I get it right.'"

The inspiration for the tune belonged to songwriter Larry Henley, a one-time member of the Newbeats, who went to number two on *Billboard*'s Hot 100 in 1964 with "Bread And Butter." Henley was shifting from a pop career to country when he conceived " 'Til I Get It Right."

"I thought of the idea while I was riding back

on a plane from London with the Newbeats," he says. "I thought while I was gone I should have tried to come up with some song ideas. I thought of that on the plane and toyed around with it in my mind, until I got back and got with Red Lane."

Henley and producer Billy Sherrill have different stories about how " 'Til I Get It Right" arrived at Sherrill's office. Sherrill claims that he first heard it during a "guitar pull" on the Cumberland River.

Notes Sherrill: "Red Lane got up and sang it, and I said, 'Red, who has got a hold on that song?' and he said, 'Nobody, I just wrote it.' I said, 'I've got to have it for Tammy.' We cut it that week."

Henley's version of the story is one in which neither Sherrill nor Tammy were particularly interested.

"Red was taking flying lessons at the time," Henley explains, "and we had just written the song the night before. Red wanted to go flying that day, but Tammy was recording, and I said, 'Red, why don't we go play this song for Tammy and then go fly.' Billy nor Tammy, neither one liked the song. George Jones was there. They cut it because *he* liked it, not because they did, really."

Whether Jones or Sherrill made the decision, it was a good one. " 'Til I Get It Right" became Tammy's twelfth solo single to hit number one.

123
TEDDY BEAR SONG
BARBARA FAIRCHILD
Columbia 45743
Writers: Don Earl, Nick Nixon
Producer: Jerry Crutchfield
March 17, 1973 (2 weeks)

Born November 12, 1950, Barbara Fairchild started on the road to music when she was just five years old, singing "Peter Cottontail" and "Easter Parade" at a school talent contest in Arkansas. It took her seven years to finally win the competition, but she was never able to shake her cutesy/youthful image.

Her family moved to St. Louis when she was 13, and two years later, she cut her first record, "A Brand New Bed Of Roses," for Norman Records. Another two years down the line, Barbara met record producer Jerry Crutchfield while cutting through a parking lot

Barbara Fairchild

in Nashville. That happenstance led to a contract with Kapp Records at age 17.

Shortly afterward, Fairchild moved to Columbia Records, where she earned her first real hit four years later. "Teddy Bear Song" was written by two friends who had also moved to Nashville from St. Louis: former homicide detective Don Earl and recording artist Nick Nixon.

Recorded with the Jordanaires on back-up vocals, "Teddy Bear Song" was included on an album entitled *A Sweeter Love*. "Thanks For The Memories" and the title track were released first, but Jim Clemens, a disk jockey at WPLO in Atlanta, started playing "Teddy Bear Song" off the album. After he reported its local success to Crutchfield, the song became a single, entering the *Billboard* country chart on December 30, 1972.

"Teddy Bear Song," Fairchild's first hit and only number one record, brought her a nomination for the Academy of Country Music's Top Female Vocalist of the Year award. Unfortunately, the song's youthful thrust was difficult to live down. "We got sent songs about Yogi Bear and *everything* to do with that kind of thing," she told Robert K. Oermann of *The Tennessean*, "but that's not the type of bag you can stay in eternally, because it gets awfully monotonous."

She pulled two more hits out of the children's "bag"—"Kid Stuff," which hit number two in 1973, and "Baby Doll," which peaked at number six the next year. Breaking away from the mold, however, didn't help. She never reached the Top Ten again, and in 1980, she moved to Texas.

In 1986, Barbara signed with Capitol Records. She had only one single for the label, produced by Don Williams and Allen Reynolds.

KEEP ME IN MIND
LYNN ANDERSON
Columbia 45768
Writers: Glenn Sutton, George Richey
Producer: Glenn Sutton
March 31, 1973 (1 week)

"In her time, my mom was one of only three ladies who were writing," says Lynn Anderson of her mother, Liz Anderson. "Cindy Walker and Felice Bryant were the only other ladies that I know of; for her time, Mama was fantastic."

Though her mother was ahead of the Equal Rights movement, Lynn reached her career peak at a time when women were coming into their own in the music business. In fact, she was introduced to both the performing and financial aspects of the industry in the late '60s by doubling as a recording artist and a secretary for Chart Records. "I was taking orders for my own records," she laughs, "and if Handleman Distributing would call and order 1,000 copies, I'd tell them they were selling like crazy. Usually, I sold some product that way."

Still, once she signed up with Columbia, husband/producer Glenn Sutton handled most if not all of her business decisions, leaving her free to work on her performances. A good example is her fourth number one single, "Keep Me In Mind."

"That was probably the most difficult song to sing that I've ever done," she states. " 'Keep Me In Mind' had a tremendous range. There were some notes in there that were kind of at the dog-whistle stage."

Much of the work was already done by the time she even knew the song existed. Sutton and George Richey wrote "Keep Me In Mind"—plus a Joe Stampley single, "I'm Still Loving You"—at Columbia Studio A.

"George was sitting at the piano playing," Glenn remembers, "and I came in. He was just playing a melody or something. I said, 'When you got time, let's try something with it,' so we just started from scratch, and within about an hour and a half, we had 'Keep Me In Mind.'

"I don't think I ever played it to Lynn. I was doing some tracks and she didn't feel good and didn't get to the session, and we just did four tracks. Janie Frickie was a background singer at the time; she did the vocals for me, for Lynn to learn them from. I took it home and played it to her, and she loved it."

SUPER KIND OF WOMAN
FREDDIE HART & THE HEARTBEATS
Capitol 3524
Writer: Jack Lebsock
Producer: Bob Morris
April 7, 1973 (1 week)

Country music took on a "superior" tone during the week of April 14, 1973: Freddie Hart's "*Super* Kind Of Woman" and Donna Fargo's "*Super*man" [see 127] both rested in the Top Five. Of his six number one singles, "Super Kind Of Woman" is the only one that Hart didn't write. Jack Lebsock had co-written "Bless Your Heart" [see 104] in 1972, and Lebsock would later go on to record under the name Jack Grayson, reaching number 18 in 1982 with his remake of "When A Man Loves A Woman."

Hart had several other influential musical associations during his early years in the business. The first came in 1949 when he met Hank Williams. They struck up something of a friendship, although Hart basically ran errands and picked up sandwiches for Williams.

"He gave me a lot of pointers," recalls Hart. "He said when you're writing a song to make believe that it's the last song you're ever going to write or you're ever going to sing. He said that a song is real, that it's life—little episodes of your life and my life—put to music."

It was Lefty Frizzell, though, who gave Hart his first break in the industry, and Hart remained a member of his backing band for 11 years. The two met while Hart was working in a Phoenix, Arizona, cotton-seed mill. Frizzell helped Freddie get his first recording contract with Capitol Records, and, as a result, Hart's first single, "Butterfly Love," was released in 1952. The following year, Freddie became a regular on the "Town Hall Party" show, a West Coast version of the Grand Ole Opry that ran on Saturday nights for a three-year period.

By 1959, Hart had moved to Columbia Records, and he shifted in 1965 to Kapp; his first Kapp release, "Hank Williams' Guitar," peaked at number 23. In 1970, he made his second appearance at Capitol, setting up the *California Grapevine* album that eventually yielded "Easy Loving" [see 83].

Building on the success that "Easy Loving" established, "Super Kind Of Woman" became Hart's fifth consecutive number one single.

His new-found success brought a host of opportunities, including appearances on "The Merv Griffin Show" and "The Dinah Shore Show," an engagement at the White House for President Nixon, and a special performance for Alabama governor George Wallace.

Ultimately, "Shoulder" fared well enough as a commercial effort. It rested at number 64 when it first appeared on the *Billboard* chart on February 10, 1973. Nine weeks later, it slipped into number one for one week.

126
A SHOULDER TO CRY ON
CHARLEY PRIDE
RCA 0884
Writer: Merle Haggard
Producer: Jack Clement
April 14, 1973 (1 week)

On top of the 38 number one singles he has recorded as a solo artist and in duets, Merle Haggard has registered two chart-topping records when other performers covered his material. In all, Haggard has written five songs that have become hits six different times.

"Today I Started Loving You Again" [see 8—"The Legend Of Bonnie & Clyde"] went to number nine for Sammi Smith in 1975 and also reached number 16 when Charlie McCoy released an instrumental version in 1972. Conway Twitty scored a number four peak with "I Wonder What She'll Think About Me Leaving" in 1971, and Hank Williams, Jr., also climbed to number four in 1969 with "I'd Rather Be Gone." Haggard's two number one efforts came with George Jones' cover of "I Always Get Lucky With You" [see 530]—and Charley Pride's rendition of "A Shoulder To Cry On."

"There's a song which shouldn't have been a single," Pride says in retrospect. "I kind of got caught feeling an obligation to Merle in the way I had committed myself in doing the song. I was out in Las Vegas and I went up on stage, and he pitched it to me right on stage. I told him I did like it and I ended up recording it. He said he was going to cut some things I published, which he never got around to doing. That's one of those deals."

If he had it to do over, Pride insists he would have released a song written by Ben Peters instead. "It came down to 'My Love Is Deep, My Love Is Wide,'" he says, "whether it would be that one or 'Shoulder To Cry On.' I liked Merle's song, but I think 'My Love Is Deep, My Love Is Wide' should have been the single. I think 'My Love Is Deep, My Love Is Wide' was a much better song and came off as a much better commercial single than 'Shoulder To Cry On.'"

127
SUPERMAN
DONNA FARGO
Dot 17444
Writer: Donna Fargo
Producer: Stan Silver
April 21, 1973 (1 week)

Superman first hit the streets in Action Comics #1 in April of 1938, thanks to writer Jerry Siegel and artist Joe Shuster. With movies, cartoons and television adding to his stature, the Man of Steel has reached mythical proportions over the years, and Donna Fargo likewise needed super material to combat the "sophomore jinx" in 1973.

"Sophomore jinx" is a record industry cliché which posits that if an artist has overwhelming success with a first project, the next is bound to be a disappointment. Complicating matters in the music business is the tendency to pigeonhole performers into a specific style. Yet Fargo escaped both the sophomore jinx and the stereotyping with her second album, cleverly titled *My Second Album*.

If any pressure existed to equal the success of "Happiest Girl In The Whole U.S.A." [see 99] and "Funny Face" [see 110], it never quite hit home at the time. "If I knew then what I know now," Fargo asserts, "I would have felt more pressure, but I don't think I did. I was just writing songs, doing what I wanted to do, playing it by ear."

As it was, she was already trying to accomplish a number of goals with "Superman." "I pushed for that song to be a single because I didn't want to be 'typed,'" she recalls. "You can listen to the radio and someone will have a hit on something and then come out with a song just like it, except a few changes of lyrics. I didn't want to do that as a writer.

"I also wanted to show the gutsy side of an independent woman. I wanted to show the complexity of people, because we can be entirely positive—like with 'Happiest Girl' and 'Funny Face'—but you can also have an independent spirit and the kind of attitude that's in 'Superman.'"

Aptly enough, "Superman" reached its peak position in April of 1973—on the Caped Crusader's 35th birthday.

128
BEHIND CLOSED DOORS
CHARLIE RICH
Epic 10950
Writer: Kenny O'Dell
Producer: Billy Sherrill
April 28, 1973 (2 weeks)

In 1958, Sun Records founder Sam Phillips suggested that Charlie Rich was the only artist he had signed who could potentially rival Elvis Presley. Occasionally, Rich seemed on the verge of approaching that potential, but it wasn't until "Behind Closed Doors" came along that the dam burst and accolades came flooding in.

Signed five years earlier by Epic Records, Rich languished over the right approach to his music. Influenced by a variety of musical styles, his sound was simply too wide-ranging for many radio programmers to feature.

"The jocks had been complaining that he was too bluesy for country, and others said he was too country for anything else," producer Billy Sherrill told *Billboard*'s Bill Williams. "We just needed the right song, and nobody really knows what's the right song until it comes along. It's like a pretty woman. No one can say what it takes to make her pretty, but when you see her, you know."

Sherrill found the "right song" in the hands of Kenny O'Dell, who had written Rich's first Top Ten country single, "I Take It On Home." Sherrill encouraged O'Dell to come up with more material for Rich, and at the end of 1972, O'Dell brought him "Behind Closed Doors."

"It was just a title I had written down," says Kenny, "and I had a little guitar riff that I'd carried with me for a couple of years. The chorus was pretty much a little deviation on that."

During his Sun days, Rich had often played piano on some of Jerry Lee Lewis' recording sessions; likewise, Charlie turned over the keyboard duties on his own records to Hargus "Pig" Robbins, who developed a classic bluesy opening riff. O'Dell played guitar on the session, in which they also recorded "The Most Beautiful Girl" [see 148]. Sherrill later decided to change a couple of lines at the end of the

Donna Fargo

second verse, and Rich overdubbed the new lyrics.

Initially branded by some radio stations as "dirty," "Behind Closed Doors" soon proved to be the "right song" Rich needed. It spent two weeks at the top of *Billboard*'s country chart, hit number 15 on the Hot 100, and sold a million copies by September.

"Behind Closed Doors" netted four awards from the Country Music Association and a pair of Grammy awards.

Roy Clark

129
COME LIVE WITH ME
ROY CLARK
Dot 17449
Writers: Boudleaux Bryant, Felice Bryant
Producer: Jim Foglesong
May 12, 1973 (1 week)

He's a singer, film star, ambassador and comedian—yet Roy Clark is best known to many as the host of "Hee Haw." While filming that program, in fact, he was introduced to the only number one single of his career.

Clark reported on a Friday morning to the TV studio and headed to "Hee Haw" producer Sam Lovello's office, where songwriter Boudleaux Bryant was already seated with a song he had written the previous night. Bryant and his wife, Felice, were one of the hottest songwriting teams in Nashville: their collaborations included "All I Have To Do Is Dream," "Bye Bye Love," "A Hole In My Pocket" and "Rocky Top."

"Come Live With Me" was tailor-made for Clark, and after its chart entry on February 17, 1973, it took three months to reach number one. It was the most successful of his nine Top Ten singles, which also included two records that went to number two (1973's "Somewhere Between Love And Tomorrow" and 1976's "If I Had To Do It All Over Again"). Another, "Yesterday When I Was Young," reached number nine on the country chart and peaked at number 19 on *Billboard*'s Hot 100.

Born April 15, 1933, in Meherrin, Virginia, Roy first encountered a musical instrument in the form of a guitar which his father built from a cigar box, a ukulele neck and four strings. His first interest, though, was sports. At 18, he was offered a tryout with the St. Louis Browns baseball team, and at 19, he boxed in 15 different matches in the Washington, D.C., area.

In 1954, he had his own band in the nation's capitol, but he left the group to join Jimmy Dean's band. After two years, Dean fired him for his lack of punctuality, and Clark hooked up with Wanda Jackson shortly thereafter. In 1963, he earned his first recording contract with Capitol Records, gaining a Top Ten single with "Tips Of My Fingers."

Ultimately, Roy Clark has become one of the most honored country figures of his era. He won Entertainer of the Year trophies twice from the Academy of Country Music and once from the Country Music Association, and picked up a Grammy award as an instrumentalist. Clark also has a star in the Hollywood Walk of Fame, and became the first country star to stand in for Johnny Carson as guest host of "The Tonight Show." He has toured the Soviet Union twice.

130
WHAT'S YOUR MAMA'S NAME
TANYA TUCKER
Columbia 45799
Writers: Earl Montgomery, Dallas Frazier
Producer: Billy Sherrill
May 19, 1973 (1 week)

Country music has long been considered an adult medium, due in part to the mature themes that dominate so many of the genre's records. Still, in 1972, a 13-year-old Tanya Tucker surprised the entire Nashville community with her entree, "Delta Dawn."

Billy Sherrill signed the teenager on the basis of a demo tape she made in Las Vegas, and it seemed rather obvious that a youngster like Tucker would sing about topics that related to her youthful experience. Instead, Sherrill came up with the adult viewpoint of "Delta Dawn," after seeing Bette Midler perform it on "The Tonight Show."

Nashville legend holds that Sherrill first played "The Happiest Girl In The Whole U.S.A." [see 99] for Tucker, and that she turned it down before choosing "Delta Dawn," although he disputes that story.

"I never pitched that to Tanya," he maintains. "I never pitched anything to Tanya; I *told* her to cut it. I heard 'Happiest Girl In The Whole U.S.A.' riding down the street in L.A. It was Donna Fargo's record, and I called Al Gallico and he bought half the publishing on it."

Tucker counters: "He knows it happened, because Al Gallico came in and had the song, and it was already a record. I said, 'That's just not my song, Billy,' and he looked at Al and said, 'You heard what she said.'"

After the success of "Delta Dawn," Tucker went to number five with a double-sided single, "Love's The Answer" and "Jamestown Ferry," following that with her first number one record, "What's Your Mama's Name."

"I thought it was a mediocre song until the very last line," says Sherrill. "In fact, I wasn't even gonna cut it until I heard, 'and her eyes are Wilson green' [the song's main character is

Buford Wilson], and I went bananas. That was the reason we cut that song, that one line."

Sherrill recorded it with George Jones first, but it was Tanya's version that came out as a single. "The first time I heard it, Peanut Montgomery played it for me at the deejay convention in Nashville in 1972," Tanya notes. "He played it for me at his house, and I said, 'That song's for me.' It's such a great story, and a mature story at that."

131
SATIN SHEETS
JEANNE PRUETT
MCA 40015
Writer: John Volinkaty
Producer: Walter Haynes
May 26, 1973 (3 weeks)

Jeanne Pruett didn't actually sleep on satin sheets during 1973, although she did use a satin pillowcase when she turned in at nights. By the middle of the year, "Satin Sheets" proved as important to Pruett as the glass slipper proved to Cinderella.

Actually, the creation of "Satin Sheets" was quite a Cinderella story for songwriter John Volinkaty. He was an amateur writer from Minneapolis, and the song was the first he had ever had recorded—in fact, it was the first song he had ever written. He was shopping in a Red Owl grocery store when the idea hit, and 30 minutes later, the entire song was written. "Satin Sheets" was copyrighted by MCA Music in 1970, and three years later, it found its way to Pruett, who was recording for the label.

While "Satin Sheets" was Volinkaty's first attempt, Pruett had been working in the record industry for quite some time. Named Norma Jean Bowman upon her birth (January 30, 1937) in Pell City, Alabama, she married Jack Pruett and moved to Nashville in 1956. Jack spent 14 years as a guitar player for Marty Robbins, and in 1963, Norma Jean began writing specifically with Robbins in mind.

Her composition "Count Me Out" went to number 14 for Robbins in 1966, and five years later, Pruett grabbed her own recording deal. Four singles failed to attract much attention, but her fifth, "Satin Sheets," was an overwhelming success. It jumped from number eight to number one on May 26, 1973, where it stayed for two weeks before falling. Two weeks later, it returned for another week at

Jeanne Pruett

the top. In the meantime, it also went to number 28 on the *Billboard* Hot 100.

"Satin Sheets" sold more than 800,000 copies. In July, Porter Wagoner and Dolly Parton announced to the audience at the Grand Ole Opry—to Jeanne's surprise—that she had become the latest Opry member.

Pruett followed up the record with "I'm Your Woman," which peaked at number eight, while Robbins simultaneously earned a number nine single with one of her songs, "Love Me."

It took six years for Pruett to reach the Top Ten again, although she did so three times in succession, with "Back To Back," "Temporarily Yours" and "It's Too Late" on independent IBC Records.

132

YOU ALWAYS COME BACK (TO HURTING ME)

JOHNNY RODRIGUEZ

Mercury 73368
Writers: Johnny Rodriguez, Tom T. Hall
Producer: Jerry Kennedy
June 9, 1973 (1 week)

The story of Johnny Rodriguez's lucky break is one of the most bizarre tales in country music history. At age 17, he was with several friends at a beer party when they decided to barbecue a goat. They had to steal the animal, and cooked it at a state park. When they were caught in the early morning hours, Rodriguez took the blame.

Rodriguez was surprised to find the offense was a felony, and he was sentenced to three-to-seven years in a county jail. To pass the time, he sang songs in his cell, and one of the Texas Rangers who served as his jailer was impressed by the teenager's vocal abilities. He put Rodriguez in touch with entertainment executive Happy Shahan, who then employed his new discovery in a show at his theme park, Alamo Village.

On Labor Day in 1970, Bobby Bare and Tom T. Hall heard Johnny, and Hall suggested that some day, he might be able to join up with the Storytellers. Shortly afterward, Johnny's father died from cancer, and his oldest brother was killed in a car accident. A shaken Rodriguez decided it was time to head to Tennessee.

He stepped off a plane in Nashville with $14,

two pairs of pants, three shirts and a guitar wrapped in cellophane. After checking in downtown at the Sam Davis Hotel, Rodriguez called Hall's office, and Tom T. picked him up in a black limousine. As it turned out, Hall had just lost a guitar player, and he gave Rodriguez the job.

Hall later introduced Rodriguez to Roy Dea at Mercury Records, and Dea signed him immediately. At age 20, Johnny released his first single in 1972, reaching number nine with "Pass Me By (If You're Only Passing Through)." His next, "You Always Come Back (To Hurting Me)"—co-written with Hall—became his first number one.

"That was about the first song that we co-wrote," Rodriguez remembers. "I used to play the secretary on the road for him while I was playing guitar. He'd be writing songs, and I'd actually write them down on paper. [With "You Always Come Back,"] I just got an idea while he was writing one, and wrote it down."

133
KIDS SAY THE DARNDEST THINGS
TAMMY WYNETTE
Epic 10969
Writers: Billy Sherrill, Glenn Sutton
Producer: Billy Sherrill
June 16, 1973 (1 week)

With her early number one singles "I Don't Wanna Play House" [see 3—"Take Me To Your World"] and "D-I-V-O-R-C-E" [see 12], Tammy Wynette offered a children's perspective on domestic problems. Though these numbers helped provide her a special niche in country music, she hardly noticed their similarities at the time.

"I never thought about it until we came out with 'Stand By Your Man' [see 21]," she says. "I was so green to the business and knew so little about it, that I really didn't think about doing so many things that you could place in one category. I had children, and I was a mother raising my children alone. They just seemed to really fit my life, and I liked what they said."

Producer Billy Sherrill liked the results of those particular singles, and he returned to the children's theme often. In 1973, he borrowed the title of Art Linkletter's "Kids Say the Darndest Things" to concoct another num-

ber one single. "I just thought that song was so cute," Tammy remembers. "It was such a clever way of getting out of a tight situation without making it so serious."

Sherrill was quite serious, though, in his concerns about copyright infringement. The song might never have been written if it weren't for a ruling from the CBS legal department.

"Billy was doing all those kid songs," reports co-writer Glenn Sutton, "and he wanted to call the album *Kids Say the Darndest Things*. He checked with legal, because of the Art Linkletter thing, and the legal people at CBS said we could do it if we had a song called 'Kids Say The Darndest Things' in it. We wrote the song just so Billy could use the title."

They took it one step further, though. After they wrote the song, they went ahead and approached Linkletter personally for his permission.

"He had 'Kids Say the Darndest Things' all wrapped up," Tammy recalls. "He had the TV show and he had the book, so we sweated a little while about getting that cleared to use as a song. Billy has the original—and I have a copy—of a letter from Art Linkletter's company signed by him stating that they would give us permission to use that."

The song became a legitimate number one record in June of 1973.

134
DON'T FIGHT THE FEELINGS OF LOVE
CHARLEY PRIDE
RCA 0942
Writer: John Schweers
Producer: Jack Clement
June 30, 1973 (1 week)

"Don't Fight The Feelings Of Love" represents the first number one single for a then-struggling songwriter named John Schweers. Schweers moved to Nashville on June 23, 1972, having already placed a song with Merle Haggard's guitarist, Bobby Wayne. Unfortunately, by the time Schweers hit town, Wayne had been dropped by Capitol.

Instead of giving up, Schweers worked throughout the summer in Nashville, and eventually signed with Charley Pride's newly formed Pi-Gem Music Publishing. Tom Col-

Kris Kristofferson

lins, who managed the company, repeatedly encouraged Schweers to write uptempo songs, and "Don't Fight The Feelings Of Love" emerged from those attempts.

"'Don't fight the feeling' was just a saying that was going around at that time," Schweers recalls, "and I had an upstairs apartment rented at $100 a month. I got a feel going on the guitar, and started playing this thing, and my landlady came and knocked on the door, because I'd been playing this thing and banging my foot just keeping time with it. I had an infectious melody going, and she thought I was nailing something on the wall. I said, 'No, I'm writing songs,' and she said, 'You're a songwriter?!'—I think to her horror—she just found that out too late, after I'd moved in."

Collins had Schweers do a couple of rewrites to improve "Don't Fight The Feelings," and when the publisher was satisfied, Schweers put together a demo tape. He then went home to Texas to go hunting with his father and brother.

"I got a tape in the mail back in San Antonio, and my father brought it out to me at the ranch," he laughs. "It said on it, 'Here's your Christmas present.' I had a little cheap amplifier and a little cheap tape recorder, and I played it again, and thought 'What did they redemo my tune for?' About half-way through it, I said, 'Who's that singing?' I started it over, and said, 'That's Charley Pride! That's Charley Pride!' I was about ten feet up in the air. I'd been trying to get a Charley Pride session all summer, and this was about my first cut in Nashville."

RCA released "Don't Fight The Feelings" as a single on April 17, 1973, and more than two months later, Schweers had even more cause for celebration. The record landed at number one on the final day of June.

135

WHY ME

KRIS KRISTOFFERSON

Monument 8571
Writer: Kris Kristofferson
Producer: Fred Foster
July 7, 1973 (1 week)

"I don't know why anyone would want to hear me. I sound like a damned frog."

Kris Kristofferson made that statement near the beginning of his career, and though he's hardly at the top of anyone's list among country music's vocalists, Kristofferson is almost uniformly considered one of the genre's best songwriters.

Thanks in great part to his honesty with the sexual topics of "For The Good Times" [see 61] and "Help Me Make It Through The Night" [see 72], Kristofferson is cited by many as the first "outlaw" [see 237—"Good Hearted Woman"]. Surprising to some, "Why Me" was a humble, introspective treatment of a gospel subject.

Kristofferson was inspired to write the song after going to church, where Larry Gatlin sang "Help Me" [see 203—"I Just Can't Get Her Out Of My Mind"] for the congregation. On the way home, Kristofferson started composing "Why Me" in his car, and he included the single on his album *Jesus Was a Capricorn*. Kristofferson's rough performance, recorded on July 8, 1972, was supported vocally by Gatlin and Kris' wife-to-be, Rita Coolidge. Kris and Rita married on August 19, 1973, and divorced on December 2, 1979.

Reaching number one on July 7, 1973—one year, almost to the day, after he recorded it—"Why Me" became Kristofferson's only hit as a solo artist, although he later returned to the top as one-fourth of the quartet in "Highwayman" [see 633]. "Why Me" was certified gold on November 11, 1973.

Kristofferson officially lists Brownsville, Texas, as his hometown, although he's lived in a number of cities since his birth on June 22, 1936. His father, a two-star general, moved the family a number of times during his youth. Kristofferson pursued creative writing at Pomona College in California, earning a Rhodes scholarship to study at England's Cambridge University.

After taking up a brief military career, Kristofferson turned down an opportunity to teach at West Point, heading instead to Nashville in 1965. He worked by day as a bartender at Nashville's Tally Ho Tavern and by night as a janitor at Columbia Recording Studios, finally winning over the city's recording artists with songs like "Me And Bobby McGee" [see 90], "Please Don't Tell Me How The Story Ends" [see 177] and "Sunday Mornin' Comin' Down" [see 63].

Kristofferson has augmented his musical career with a series of acting roles. His movies include *Alice Doesn't Live Here Anymore, A Star Is Born, Convoy* [see 233], and *Big Top Pee-Wee*, as well as the TV mini-series *Amerika*.

136
LOVE IS THE FOUNDATION
LORETTA LYNN
MCA 40058
Writer: William C. Hall
Producer: Owen Bradley
July 14, 1973 (2 weeks)

From 1944 to 1958, *Billboard* published a fluctuating series of country charts, designating separate numbers based on information for jukeboxes, best-sellers and disc jockeys. The magazine finally consolidated the numbers into one country chart on October 20, 1958. Initially, the chart listed the Top 30 singles in the nation, but on January 11, 1964, it expanded to include 50 titles. On October 15, 1966, 75 records were highlighted weekly, and on July 14, 1973, *Billboard* printed its first country chart to feature 100 records.

Occupying the top position that week was a Loretta Lynn single, "Love Is The Foundation."

"A boy from Ohio wrote that song, and he writes for me right now," she says. "He's in my publishing company, and it was a very long song when I found it. It was in a box of songs that I was listenin' to, and it was real long. I thought it was a great song, so I took some verses out of it, and recorded it, and it went to number one. I'm very proud of that song, too." Songwriter William C. Hall, incidentally, should not be confused with Bill Hall [see 58—"Wonder Could I Live There Anymore"], one of Nashville's former publishing moguls.

Lynn followed up "Love Is The Foundation" with two more Top Five successes. "Hey Loretta," written by Shel Silverstein [see 120—"One's On The Way"], hit number three, while "They Don't Make 'Em Like My Daddy" went to number four.

Loretta's own daddy played a large role in her life, though he stood a mere five-foot-seven. Half Cherokee, Teddy Webb mined the Van Lear coal mines in Kentucky, and he purchased the Philco radio that introduced Loretta to the Grand Ole Opry. Suffering from black lung, he moved the family to Wabash, Indiana, but only after Loretta and her husband had moved to Washington. He passed away on February 22, 1959, and, though father and daughter were separated by more than 2,000 miles, Lynn had two dreams the night before in which she received a premonition of her father in a casket.

Teddy Webb would have been proud of his daughter in 1973. On October 27, *Love is the Foundation* became her fifth record to reach the top of the *Billboard* country album chart.

137
YOU WERE ALWAYS THERE
DONNA FARGO
Dot 17460
Writer: Donna Fargo
Producer: Stan Silver
July 28, 1973 (1 week)

She was once labeled "one of the world's great upbeat optimists," but a couple of severe blows have tested Donna Fargo's usually cheery outlook. One of those was the death of her mother just before "The Happiest Girl In The Whole U.S.A." [see 99] was released, and that tragedy provided the impetus for her fourth consecutive number one record.

A native of Mt. Airy, North Carolina, Fargo had grown up on a tobacco farm, and when she reached high school, she devoted much of her time to her studies, her friends and cheerleading. She attended High Point College, and the day of her graduation, she immediately moved to California. Throughout all of that, Fargo took her mother's presence for granted, and after her passing, it occurred to Donna that she had never really gotten to know her mother.

"I thought, this probably happens to a lot of people," she surmises. "All of a sudden, they're gone and you haven't really sat down and talked about what her favorite color is, what she was like when *she* was growing up, and did her mother and father treat her well."

Fargo felt that her experiences might be of benefit to her listeners, and for that reason, she specifically wanted "You Were Always There" to be released as a single. "I think that people relate to music, especially the lyrics in country music. I didn't want to get on any high horse and preach, but I think sometimes you can learn things from songs, and I thought that maybe somebody who didn't have a good relationship with their parents would get together with them before it was too late."

As it turned out, that's exactly what happened with one of her fans. She took the message to heart and repaired a bad relationship with her mother, who passed away shortly thereafter.

"You Were Always There" was the last in a streak of four consecutive number one records for Fargo, but her records still performed well. "Little Girl Gone" entered the *Billboard* charts on September 29, 1973, and peaked at number two, while "I'll Try A Little Bit Harder" went to number six in the spring of 1974.

138
LORD, MR. FORD
JERRY REED
RCA 0960
Writer: Dick Feller
Producer: Chet Atkins
August 4, 1973 (1 week)

As the U.S. experienced its first major oil crisis, Jerry Reed capitalized on public frustrations with his single "Lord, Mr. Ford." Citing the costs of gas, insurance, monthly payments, maintenance and all the other incidentals, Reed demonstrated that a $4,000 car could actually cost its owner $14,000.99! Few could say it with such humor as Reed.

"Jerry was just a wild man," notes producer Chet Atkins, "and Dick Feller was writing for Jerry at that time, and he was havin' some luck with novelties, so we did that."

"Lord, Mr. Ford" made its chart debut during Memorial Day weekend, on May 26, 1973, one day before the scheduled Indianapolis 500. Eleven weeks later, Reed crossed the finish line with his second number one record.

Reed hailed originally from Atlanta, where he was born March 20, 1937. He claims that his very first thoughts as a kid revolved around music, and he never finished school because of it. He first signed with Capitol Records in 1955, and went on the road with Ernest Tubb for a month. He tried to finish his education through night school, but he couldn't concentrate in the classroom. Instead, his thoughts drifted toward new guitar licks.

Reed ended up in Nashville, where he became a studio guitar player throughout the early '60s. In addition, he developed skills as a songwriter. Some of his more successful compositions included "Misery Loves Company" [see 392—"Cowboys And Clowns"], which went to number one for Porter Wagoner in 1962; "A Thing Called Love," by Johnny Cash; and two Elvis Presley singles, "U.S. Male" and "Guitar Man" [see 416].

Reed finally got his break as a recording

artist when Chet Atkins signed him to RCA in 1965. Atkins helped bring out Reed's wilder side on record, and unlocked the energy that is a natural part of his personality.

Following "Lord, Mr. Ford," Reed diversified his routine with a foray into films. He racked up credits in *W.W. & the Dixie Dancekings, Gator, Smokey and the Bandit, Hot Stuff,* and *Bat 21.* The *Smokey* soundtrack yielded another success in 1977 when he released "East Bound And Down," co-written with Feller, who penned "Lord, Mr. Ford." "East Bound" stopped at number two for two weeks, kept out of the top spot by the Kendalls' "Heaven's Just A Sin Away" [see 295].

139
TRIP TO HEAVEN
FREDDIE HART & THE HEARTBEATS
Capitol 3612
Writer: Freddie Hart
Producer: Bob Morris
August 11, 1973 (1 week)

Freddie Hart is quite open about the Christianity that guides many of his decisions, and his sixth consecutive number one single was crafted on a Biblical image.

"Sometimes people think 'Trip To Heaven' was a gospel thing, which it's not," says Hart of the record's romantic theme. "I have written a lot of gospel songs, though, and I've got a whole gospel album. I don't usually play a place unless I can play a gospel song; that's part of life, too.

" 'Trip To Heaven' was just kind of a play on words. People were always talking about 'This is Heaven' and 'That is Heaven,' so I just thought about taking a trip to heaven and you didn't even have to die."

The record represented Hart's final trip to number one, although he continued to build hit records for several years. "If You Can't Feel It (It Ain't There)," "The Want-To's" and "My Woman's Man" all earned high marks; in fact, following "This Is Heaven," his next seven singles all cracked *Billboard*'s Top Five through 1976. Among them were "Hang In There Girl" (a 1974 song about his wife) and his 1975 single "The First Time," both of which peaked at number two. His last appearance in the Top Ten came in early 1977 on "When Lovers Turn To Strangers."

Freddie remained with Capitol Records through 1979, but at the turn of the decade, he moved to independent Sunbird Records, garnering a minor hit in the process on "Sure Thing." In 1986, he marketed a double album, *From Hart to Hearts,* on the Nashville Network.

Hart has continued to tour steadily, splitting his personal time between a home in California and one in Nashville. Outside of music, he absorbs himself in oil painting, carpentry, antiques and the martial arts, where he holds a black belt in Judo.

"I'll always be in the business," he promises. "People think I still have a chance to come back, but if I don't, I've had a wonderful dream come true. I might go into producing or management or publishing. My hands and my heart will always be in the business."

140
LOUISIANA WOMAN, MISSISSIPPI MAN
LORETTA LYNN & CONWAY TWITTY
MCA 40079
Writers: Becki Bluefield, Jim Owen
Producer: Owen Bradley
August 18, 1973 (1 week)

Loretta Lynn and Conway Twitty first met each other in producer Owen Bradley's recording studio in 1967, due in part to Twitty's foresight. Conway resided in Oklahoma City at the time, but he had a habit of driving to Nashville early for his sessions to hang out at Bradley's Barn. He assumed that by making an early appearance, he could meet session players or recording artists who were ending a session before his.

After arriving in Music City, he quietly entered the recording studio on this occasion only to discover that Loretta was working. Several times, she had indicated to Bradley that she wanted to meet Twitty, and the producer brought Conway right up behind her, unseen to Loretta.

Bradley reminded her of the conversations about Conway, and then instructed her to turn around. Lynn was so startled that she jumped, as Twitty describes, "like a cartoon character."

"I didn't know it," he told *Billboard*, "but she was a Conway Twitty fan. She wasn't a rock and roll fan, but she loved 'It's Only Make Believe.'

**Loretta Lynn &
Conway Twitty**

She had a big Conway Twitty poster she kept in her house before she even got in the business."

When they first decided to record together two years later [see 74—"After The Fire Is Gone"], Twitty and Lynn met with surprising opposition. Having witnessed previous collaborations with other artists, their associates worried that the budding friendship would sour with a clash of egos in the studio.

"It made sense to us and Mooney [her husband], but not to anybody else," Conway told Wilbur Cross and Michael Kosser in *The Conway Twitty Story.* "Everybody else fought us on it. Of course, I was my own boss and stood firm. As for Loretta, she finally just had to tell

everybody, 'Hey, we're going to do it and that's the way it is.'"

Their intuitions won out, and Mississippi-born Twitty and Kentucky native Lynn reaped their first number one duet album with *Louisiana Woman, Mississippi Man* on September 15, 1973. Four weeks earlier, the title track became their third chart-topping single. Mooney gets credit for recognizing its potential.

"Somebody came into my office and let my husband listen to his song," Loretta reports, "and he said, 'Hey, let me keep this song. I'm gonna see if I can get Conway Twitty and Loretta to do it,' and that was his idea."

EVERYBODY'S HAD THE BLUES
MERLE HAGGARD & THE STRANGERS

Capitol 3641
Writer: Merle Haggard
Producer: Fuzzy Owen
August 25, 1973 (2 weeks)

"The emotions and the moods that I have in my life come out in songs," Merle Haggard once told New York writer Mark Rose. "I've covered most of my main emotions in one song or another, and I think if everybody in the world could write songs, I'm sure that most of the same emotions that I covered would also be covered by other people."

Sorrow seemed to be a key emotion for Haggard in 1973. Following his song for Vietnam POWs, "I Wonder If They Ever Think Of Me" [see 119], he reached number three on May 12, with "The Emptiest Arms In The World." His next single, a live rendition of "Everybody's Had The Blues," returned Merle to number one. The single debuted on June 30 at number 55, and peaked in its ninth week.

"That song," he explains, "I started for Dean Martin. I was trying to come up with something that was like 'Everybody Loves Somebody Sometime' [see 506—" 'Til I Gain Control Again"]. I'd written a song that Dean had done, 'I Take A Lot Of Pride In What I Am' [see 31—"Hungry Eyes"], and I've always been a Dean Martin fan. I was trying to write him a hit, but as things would have it, we wound up doing it on a live album in New Orleans before we saw Dean Martin."

Even if the subject matter of "Everybody's Had The Blues" was a "downer," his life offstage hardly reflected it. "There was a hell of a lot of fast living all along the way," Haggard told writer Bob Allen. "In fact . . . it seems kinda foggy now when I try and remember it."

Haggard sometimes refers to the early '70s as "the big party," but if it's sketchy in his memory, steel player Norm Hamlet and drummer Biff Adam remember it a little better. They were in large part responsible for keeping the party on the highway.

"I wasn't much of a partier," notes Hamlet. "I was a bandleader trying to take care of business and everything. Where the rest of them would go out and have a drink and get halfshot, we had to get everybody up the next morning, so we had to stay pretty straight."

YOU'VE NEVER BEEN THIS FAR BEFORE
CONWAY TWITTY

MCA 40094
Writer: Conway Twitty
Producer: Owen Bradley
September 8, 1973 (3 weeks)

Conway Twitty has always insisted—and, no doubt, always will—that "You've Never Been This Far Before" had more honorable intentions than many believe. Yet no matter how often he repeats himself, he has always had his detractors—and always will.

Even before the song's release, the Twitty camp discussed the ramifications of the sexual message that some listeners would read into it. "I worried that it might hurt Conway's reputation," admits producer Owen Bradley, "but I guess it didn't. We talked about it while we were doing it, and he strongly felt that there wasn't anything bad about it. But you can argue those things. It depends on which way you want it to go, and he wanted it to go. Hell, he was the star—it was his record, and his life, so that's what we did."

The expected controversy swelled as soon as "You've Never Been This Far Before" hit the marketplace. Three heavyweight stations—Atlanta's WPLO, Nashville's WSM and Forth Worth's WBAP—all refused to play it, although WPLO later added the single after it achieved hit status.

"The line that really got 'em," says Conway, "was, 'As my trembling fingers touch forbidden places,' but I still don't think it's a dirty song. Women understood what I meant by that line. It was about stepping outside the boundaries of marriage for the first time, about how just holding hands would have been forbidden."

Twitty also defended the song to LaWayne Satterfield of the *Music City News*: "It's not about a girl who's a virgin, or anything like that. It's about a married woman. These two people have thought a lot about each other for a long time. The guy in the song has thought a lot of this woman for years, but she was married to somebody else, and she thought a lot of him. It had been a situation like that for a long time. There's a line in the song that says 'I don't know and I don't care what made you tell him you don't love him anymore.' That means the situation has changed, and she is not with her husband anymore."

Tanya Tucker

The controversy didn't actually hurt the record at all. Neither did the secondary "buh, buh, buh" hook. "You've Never Been This Far Before" became one of Twitty's biggest country singles, and also reached number 22 on the *Billboard* Hot 100.

143

BLOOD RED AND GOIN' DOWN
TANYA TUCKER
Columbia 45892
Writer: Curly Putman
Producer: Billy Sherrill
September 29, 1973 (1 week)

The title of "Blood Red And Goin' Down" has often been the subject of some rather off-color humor, but its success is no laughing matter to either songwriter Curly Putman or Tanya Tucker. The phrase actually refers to a Georgia sunset, and Putman is the first to admit it's a "strange-sounding title."

"I was always a big fan of Erskine Caldwell books," he explains. Caldwell wrote primarily of poor Southern whites in novels like *Tobacco Road* and *Trouble in July*, and his work influenced a number of Putman's tunes.

"When I write a story song, I build it around a Southern Delta-ish town, or a Georgia town, but 'Blood Red And Goin' Down' just sounded different. It was a strange title, but when it was sung, it kind of set up a mood for a lonely-looking part of the day. When the sun is going down, you can see that redness in the sky, so I did that mostly to set up a thing in Georgia where a little boy or a girl is going with their dad to find their mother who had gone off with somebody."

Putman took the song to producer Billy Sherrill, thinking he would use it for one of the male artists he was working with at CBS Records. Instead, Sherrill picked it as a Tanya Tucker tune.

"I just loved it," says Tucker. "The minute I heard it, I knew it was for me. Again, it was a story song, which I was really into. From 'Delta Dawn' to 'Jamestown Ferry' to 'What's Your Mama's Name' [see 130] to 'Blood Red' were all story songs, and I really, really liked that. Of course, I liked the ending, too."

The finale actually comes as a surprise—the jealous father murders both his unfaithful wife and her willing companion.

"Most of my songs during that time, I was

killing people off," Putman remembers. "I always thought that was a good ending, although you have to handle it very carefully. The father leaves them both 'soaking up the sawdust on the floor.' It didn't come right out and say it."

144
YOU'RE THE BEST THING THAT EVER HAPPENED TO ME
RAY PRICE
Columbia 45889
Writer: Jim Weatherly
Producer: Don Law
October 6, 1973 (1 week)

"You're The Best Thing That Ever Happened To Me" is one of two songs written by Jim Weatherly to enjoy success as a country single and also find a home in pop music with Gladys Knight & The Pips. The first was "Neither One Of Us (Wants To Be The First To Say Goodbye)." Bob Luman recorded a country version, entering *Billboard* on January 27, 1973, and eventually reaching number seven. The Pips debuted with the same song the same week, but managed to peak at number two in the Hot 100.

Gladys Knight again hit the Top Five with "You're The Best Thing" in 1974, but her rendition of the song was released six months after Ray Price conquered the country chart.

" I wrote it in about '71," Weatherly reports. "Just like I always do when I write, I tried to come up with an idea or a title, and it dawned on me that I'd never heard a song called 'You're The Best Thing That Ever Happened To Me,' and yet it was something that you heard people say about five or six times a week, either on television, or in movies, or people you're talking to.

"I thought it was really strange that nobody'd written a song with that title—possibly somebody had, but I'd never heard it—so I just sat down and let this stream of consciousness happen. I basically wrote it in a very short period of time, probably 30 minutes or an hour."

Danny Thomas, the father-in-law of Weatherly's manager at the time, was the first to record "You're The Best Thing"—as a Christmas present for his wife. Though Weatherly wrote it in Los Angeles, he was on hand for Price's recording session at Nashville's Columbia Studio.

"I did it on the first take, and [Weatherly] didn't understand why we didn't work on it for a day or two," Price recalls. "I learned years ago that you can work on a song for a hundred years, and it just gets worse. It doesn't improve a bit. If you've got to gimmick one up, it's not worth the effort."

Price was obviously impressed by Weatherly's writing—each of his next six singles were Weatherly compositions.

145
RIDIN' MY THUMB TO MEXICO
JOHNNY RODRIGUEZ
Mercury 73416
Writer: Johnny Rodriguez
Producer: Jerry Kennedy
October 13, 1973 (2 weeks)

Johnny Rodriguez set a country music precedent when "You Always Come Back (To Hurting Me)" [see 132] established him as the first Mexican-American to garner a number one record on the *Billboard* charts.

Born December 10, 1951, Rodriguez grew up in Sabinal, Texas, about 90 miles from the Mexican border. Johnny was the next-to-youngest of ten children in the family, living in a four-room shack, and his growing years were split between the violent street life of the Chicano neighborhood and the middle-American standards set in the white school system.

Chameleon-like, Rodriguez functioned well in both environments. He gained A's and B's at school and served as captain of his junior high school football team, but he also landed in jail four times before his eighteenth birthday. His Mexican-American heritage has often led him to record with both English and Spanish lyrics in the same song, but while "Ridin' My Thumb To Mexico" displayed an obvious link to his background, it was cut entirely in English.

"That was the very first one that I wrote myself," he says of his second number one single. "I wrote that on the bus when I was riding down the road. That song's mainly about the summer when I was growing up in south Texas. I used to hitchhike all over the place and go to Mexico sometimes, and that's what inspired that song."

"I think that thing went out 30 minutes after we finished mixing it," adds producer Jerry Kennedy. "I really felt like we had a hit record; so did everybody in Chicago, which is where

[Mercury's] home office was at that time. I remember calls coming in from all of the brass in Chicago, talking about what a great record it was, and they were going to work it pop."

The label did try to push it to Top 40 stations, but it managed to reach only number 70 on *Billboard*'s Hot 100. Nevertheless, it did go to number one on the country chart on October 13, 1973. Two days later, with only three singles under his belt, Johnny Rodriguez was voted one of five finalists for the Country Music Association's Male Vocalist of the Year award.

146
WE'RE GONNA HOLD ON
GEORGE JONES & TAMMY WYNETTE
Epic 11031
Writers: George Jones, Earl Montgomery
Producer: Billy Sherrill
October 19, 1973 (2 weeks)

When George Jones & Tammy Wynette tied the knot in February of 1969 [see 33—"Singing My Song"], they were already working the road as a duo, and they had a desire to record together. Unfortunately, they were on separate labels.

Jones wanted out of his Musicor deal, but he had three years left on the contract, and the label refused to budge. Reportedly, Jones finally paid $100,000 and gave up all rights to his Musicor royalties to get out of the deal. On October 1, 1971, he emerged, predictably, on the Epic roster, where he could cut material freely with his bride and labelmate.

On Christmas Day, George & Tammy appeared on the *Billboard* chart in a duet remake of Jones' 1965 hit "Take Me." That single peaked at number nine, while their follow-up, "The Ceremony," reached number six.

The union was already in trouble, however, and on August 1, 1973, Tammy filed for D-I-V-O-R-C-E, for the first time. The central problem was Jones' drinking, and he had just returned from a binge that lasted several days when he introduced Tammy to the hook of "We're Gonna Hold On."

He met up with Tammy and his friend, Earl "Peanut" Montgomery, at a Holiday Inn on the road. "He knew I was mad," she says. "He knew I was very upset with him, and he got out the guitar, and all he would do was strum it and sing, 'We're gonna hold on, we're gonna hold on . . .'

"That was the last thing that I wanted to hear, because I wanted to be mad. I wanted to get it out, and he just kept on and on and on and on. He had the melody and everything, but he wasn't thinking 'song' for quite a while."

Finally, Jones put some words down on a piece of paper at the hotel. After they drove to the show, he cleaned up in the dressing room, and before taking his shower, he handed the guitar to Montgomery and asked him to finish it.

Publicly, Jones & Wynette projected a happy image as they waved to on-lookers and TV cameras on Thanksgiving Day, riding a turtle float at the Macy's Day Parade. "We're Gonna Hold On" wafted from the float's speakers that day, one month after the record reached number one on the *Billboard* chart.

147
PAPER ROSES
MARIE OSMOND
MGM 14609
Writers: Janice Torre, Fred Spielman
Producer: Sonny James
November 10, 1973 (2 weeks)

The last thing the music world needed in 1973, or so it seemed, was another Osmond. Utah's five-member family group, the Osmonds, made its national debut on "The Andy Williams Show," and had progressed to making pop records that built a substantial following of teenage girls.

Outside the group setting, Donny Osmond became a solo star, and even Little Jimmy Osmond, the youngest member of the family, made a couple of records. MGM executive Mike Curb thought it might be wise to go to the well one more time, and asked the Osmonds' mother, Olive, if 13-year-old Marie could sing. Olive responded in the affirmative, but added that Marie tended toward country.

That made perfect marketing sense to Curb, who knew that he would have a tough time selling another Osmond in the pop market. The next task was to find a producer to create country songs that would pass the family's strict lyrical tests. A friend of Curb felt Sonny James made sense. Not only was Sonny sensitive about lyrics; he also had some free time off the road.

Marie Osmond
with Sonny James

James wanted to hear a tape before he committed to producing Marie, and received a two-song demo that included her recording of Dolly Parton's "Coat Of Many Colors." "When I heard it, her voice didn't sound that different," James remembers. "She sounded good. She was a child, you could tell, but I'd hear, every once in a while, this cutting sound. It wasn't consistent all the way through, but it was just cutting, what I considered a real ear-catcher."

James decided to work on the project, and MGM flew Marie into Nashville to cut the album at Jack Clement's studio. She sang all the tracks live with the musicians, and strings were added later. James personally chose "Paper Roses" as the first single, and it added the Osmond name to country playlists, hitting number one exactly four weeks after Marie's fourteenth birthday.

"Paper Roses" also brought Ms. Osmond into the same pop territory as her brothers.

The record peaked at number five on the *Billboard* Hot 100—as did Anita Bryant's 1960 version of the same song.

148

THE MOST BEAUTIFUL GIRL

CHARLIE RICH

Epic 11040
Writers: Norro Wilson, Billy Sherrill,
Rory Bourke
Producer: Billy Sherrill
November 24, 1973 (3 weeks)

The same year that Charlie Rich signed with Epic Records [see 128—"Behind Closed Doors"], the foundation was laid for the biggest song of his career. It took half a decade for

"The Most Beautiful Girl" to make its mark.

In 1968, Norro Wilson was struggling as a new artist for Smash Records. Oddly enough, he turned to one of the label's promotion men, 26-year-old Rory Bourke, and asked Bourke to write a song that might "break" him. Together, they concocted "Hey, Mister," in which the singer goes out searching for a woman who has left him.

"Rory had the verse, 'I woke up this morning/Realized what I had done,'" Wilson recalls. "Not even attemptin' to be a writer in those years, I'm wakin' up from a night out that we'd had, and thinkin' what's next to be said." Norro felt the jilted man would need to describe the woman he was looking for, but as he and Bourke considered different physical attributes, it became apparent that characterizing the lady as tall, skinny or blonde might limit the song's appeal.

"Everybody's got a most beautiful girl or guy," Norro explains. "Whoever that person is, is the most beautiful in the world to somebody."

Wilson cut "Hey, Mister" on an album for Smash, but he also pitched the song repeatedly to producer Billy Sherrill. Later, he pitched another song titled "Mama McCluskey" to Sherrill, who decided that combining both tunes would produce a winner. They took a line or two from "Mama McCluskey," injected it into "Hey, Mister," and changed the title to "The Most Beautiful Girl."

Wilson and Sherrill agreed it was a better song, and Norro had Joe Stampley record a version of it about the same time that he produced Joe's "Soul Song" [see 116]. Wilson and Sherrill could have used "The Most Beautiful Girl" as Stampley's follow-up to "Soul Song," but instead chose "Bring It On Home (To Your Woman)."

Charlie Rich got hold of "The Most Beautiful Girl," which was selected as the second single from *Behind Closed Doors*. Eighteen days after "Behind Closed Doors" became a gold single, "The Most Beautiful Girl" debuted on *Billboard*'s country chart. A week later, it showed up on the Hot 100 and simultaneously vaulted to the top of both lists. It sold more than two million copies by the end of 1974.

149
AMAZING LOVE
CHARLEY PRIDE

RCA 0073
Writer: John Schweers
Producer: Jack Clement
December 15, 1973 (1 week)

After songwriter John Schweers earned his first number one single with "Don't Fight The Feelings Of Love" [see 134], his second came with Charley Pride's follow-up to that release, "Amazing Love." Schweers actually wrote "Amazing Love" first, in the fall of 1972, but it went through almost a year's worth of alterations before the final version saw the light of day.

"I had taken a song into [publisher] Tom Collins," Schweers explains, "and the song wasn't called 'Amazing Love.' It was the hook in the last verse; I don't even know what the song was called. Tom didn't like the song, but he thought I ought to write a song called 'Amazing Love,' so I did. I took it in there, and it was a positive song, but the man is leaving in the song and he leaves a rose on the pillow for his wife to find. The trouble I was having with it, was that it seemed as if the man was leaving for good."

"Amazing Love" became Schweers' pet project for an entire month. He rewrote it a number of times, constructing more than 25 different verses before settling on the final two. Pride recorded it on April 17, 1973, the same day RCA released "Don't Fight The Feelings Of Love."

One snag in the project, though, came with a bluesy major-seventh chord that Schweers had incorporated. "They were a little bit afraid of that," notes Schweers. "Charley had really just done straight chords, and he was noted as being a hard country singer, and that's what they wanted. They were having tremendous success at that time, so they didn't want to upset the apple cart with my one little chord."

During the late summer, RCA decided not to release "Amazing Love" as a single, and Schweers' publisher sent the song over to Ray Price's office for his consideration. In the interim, though, producer Jack Clement came up with a new plan for the song.

While Pride was out of town, Clement stripped down the instrumental tracks, leaving just Pride's vocals and the drums from the original recording. He replaced them with a new arrangement, courtesy of Charles Cochran [see 89—"Kiss An Angel Good Mornin'"], that changed the chord structure. The final version of "Amazing Love" was released on September 18.

150

IF WE MAKE IT THROUGH DECEMBER

MERLE HAGGARD & THE STRANGERS

Capitol 3746
Writer: Merle Haggard
Producer: Ken Nelson
December 22, 1973 (4 weeks)

The Christmas season has yielded a plethora of country classics that get dusted off once a year at radio stations all around the nation. Alabama's "Christmas In Dixie," Dolly Parton's "Hard Candy Christmas," Willie Nelson's "Pretty Paper" and Buck Owens' "Daddy Looked A Lot Like Santa" represent only a handful of the special yuletide recordings.

Because the records gain airplay the day after Thanksgiving—at the earliest—and go off the air the day after Christmas, they have a rather short lifespan in a given year, yet three holiday singles were strong enough to reach number one in their limited period.

The first two—Gene Autry's "Rudolph, The Red Nosed Reindeer" and Ernest Tubb's "Blue Christmas"—were both released in 1949. The other, Merle Haggard's "If We Make It Through December," dates back to 1973.

Though it mentions the holiday, Haggard's single isn't really a pure Christmas record. Economics are as much a factor in the storyline as the yuletide season, and it actually first appeared on the *Billboard* chart on October 27, 1973, debuting at number 57. With that head start, "If We Make It Through December" was able to pick up enough momentum to reach the top a few days before Christmas.

The impetus for the song, though, came from neither Christmas nor the economy. Guitar player Roy Nichols had been married several times, and his divorces always seemed to come late in the year. As another year-end approached, Haggard asked about Nichols' outlook, and the response was, "If we just make it through December . . ."

If the song was special to the public, it meant even more to guitarist Ronnie Reno. The son of Don Reno, he was previously a member of the Osborne Brothers, who had opened for Haggard at a White House concert [see 119—"I Wonder If They Ever Think Of Me"]. Reno had since left the Osbornes, and joined the Strangers shortly after.

" 'If We Make It Through December' was my first session with Merle," says Reno. "In fact, it was the first song I recorded with Merle, and naturally, I was a little nervous. He was doing a Christmas album. I remember we did it in July maybe, and we recorded it in Buck Owens' old studio there in Bakersfield."

151

I LOVE

TOM T. HALL

Mercury 73436
Writer: Tom T. Hall
Producer: Jerry Kennedy
January 19, 1974 (2 weeks)

Once a journalism student in Roanoke, Tom T. Hall has applied his pen to many kinds of projects besides country songs. He has written a number of books, including *The Storyteller's Nashville, The Laughing Man of Woodmont Coves, Christmas in the Old House* and *Acts of Life*. In 1973, he earned a Grammy award for writing the liner notes to his *Greatest Hits* album, and he also created ad copy for a Virginia radio station where he used to work on the air. In the case of "I Love," Hall picked up his biggest hit by writing out a list.

A psychiatrist friend ("I wasn't a patient, but I could have been on occasion") suggested to Tom T. that one could overcome a sense of unhappiness by making a list of all the things that are out of place in one's life. In most cases, it would end up a short list.

"I thought that was a negative exercise," Tom remarks "so one morning I thought I'd make a list of all the things I love. I started making a list, and from force of habit, I started singing it as I went along. I wrote the song in about five minutes, but it is a list of some things that I really care about."

In many ways, the song structure is similar to that of *The Sound of Music*'s "My Favorite Things." Hall's favorites include such unusual and diverse elements as squirrels, onions and pickup trucks.

"Then I got to perform on TV, on NBC," says Hall, "and 'bourbon in a glass and grass,' they took the 'grass' out because they thought I was talking about marijuana. I said, 'No, I've got 35 head of cattle, and hay is $3.50 a bale—I *love* grass.' They didn't buy that, because it was so close to 'bourbon.' "

"I Love" became the only legitimate "crossover" hit of Tom's career, peaking at number 12 on the *Billboard* Hot 100 and reaching number one on the country chart. "I Love" also boosted his standing with the Carter Family—not Mother Maybelle's, but Mother Lillian's. As the late Billy Carter explained in liner notes to a Hall LP: "She knew she could trust Tom because a man that could sing about baby ducks the way he did loved animals. And a man that loved animals had to love people and life."

Dolly Parton

152

JOLENE
DOLLY PARTON
RCA 0145
Writer: Dolly Parton
Producer: Bob Ferguson
February 2, 1974 (1 week)

Trailing "Joshua" [see 71] by three years, Dolly Parton's second number one single, "Jolene," was also the first to place her on *Billboard*'s Hot 100 chart.

"There was no conscious effort to go pop," she told *Billboard*'s Bob Kirsch. "Every song has its own personality and this one just happened to have a pop flavor to it. I've always hoped to have something that might go either way, but I'd never compromise my material to do it."

In the period following "Joshua," Dolly displayed occasional flashes of brilliance, continuing her solo career alongside her series of duets with mentor Porter Wagoner [see 181—"Please Don't Stop Loving Me"]. "Coat Of Many Colors," which she still cites as her favorite self-penned song, carried her to number four in 1971. The follow-up, "Touch Your Woman," peaked at number six in 1972, and she celebrated her birthplace with the concept album *My Tennessee Mountain Home*. The title track went to number 15 as a single.

In September of 1973, Dolly released her next solo album, *Bubbling Over*, but it seemingly fizzled out before RCA could swing into action with a single. "We were planning on releasing 'Bubbling Over' as the single," Dolly noted, "but after the LP was finished, we had some other sessions scheduled and 'Jolene' came out of these. We simply thought it was the strongest thing for a single."

Though the Jolene in the song was a husband-stealing beauty, the real Jolene was an 11- or 12-year-old fan. They met one night after a concert, as Dolly signed autographs on stage, and the youngster proffered a photo of herself in a Girl Scout outfit. Scrawled on the back was "Love, Jolene."

Dolly had never heard the name before, and was intrigued by it. She put the photo in a drawer, but one night, while she was writing, the name kept coming back to her. After the song was written, Dolly had Jolene's picture enlarged and placed in a personal scrapbook.

"Jolene" only reached number 60 on the pop charts, but it was enough to raise eyebrows in

Nashville. "I'm glad to be getting some pop action with 'Jolene,'" she stated, "but I'm country and always will be. Hopefully, I'll simply be accepted as Dolly Parton someday and not be placed in any one musical category."

153
WORLD OF MAKE BELIEVE
BILL ANDERSON
MCA 40164
Writers: Pee Wee Maddux, Marion
Carpenter, Pete McCord
Producer: Owen Bradley
February 9, 1974 (1 week)

After three records stalled at number two [see 32—"My Life"] during the first decade of his career, Bill Anderson racked up several more near-misses. "But You Know I Love You" [see 430] almost made the top in 1969, as did three consecutive singles in 1972-73: "Don't She Look Good," "If You Can Live With It" and "The Corner Of My Life."

Finally, Anderson followed that trio with his fifth number one, "World Of Make Believe." "I first heard this song in the late '50s, when a soul artist named Johnny Bragg recorded it for Decca," Anderson relates. "*He* had heard it on a small record label out of Mobile.

"At the time I pictured the song as too 'pop' for me to ever think about singing, but in later years, as country began to lean more toward the middle-of-the-road, I remembered the song and mentioned it to Owen Bradley. He had produced the Johnny Bragg record and remembered the song well. We thought it was just an album cut when we recorded it, but radio stations started playing it off the album, and we released it as a single."

Anderson was born November 1, 1937, in Columbia, South Carolina, although he grew up primarily in Georgia. He attended high school in Avondale, a suburb of Atlanta. There he played first base on a team that won the state championship, and Anderson received an offer to train with the Chicago Cubs.

His parents had other ideas, though, and convinced Bill to enter college first. "I went to [the University of] Georgia fully intending to play pro ball after graduation," he told Margaret Dick in *Country Song Roundup*, "but I started hanging around with musicians. It got to where I liked playing music more than I liked playing ball."

Anderson started working clubs with local bands during his freshman year in college, finally graduating with a degree in broadcast journalism. He had covered high school sports for the *Atlanta Constitution*, later working at a radio station in Commerce, Georgia. His writing skills eventually paved the way for his entertainment career, bringing him a number one single with "City Lights" [see 195] when Ray Price topped the chart for 13 weeks beginning October 20, 1958.

154
THAT'S THE WAY LOVE GOES
JOHNNY RODRIGUEZ
Mercury 73446
Writers: Sanger D. Shafer, Lefty Frizzell
Producer: Jerry Kennedy
February 16, 1974 (1 week)

Johnny Rodriguez picked up his third consecutive number one single when he covered a song penned by Lefty Frizzell. Having first appeared on *Billboard*'s country chart in October of 1950 [see 260—"If You've Got The Money, I've Got The Time"], Frizzell built up a long list of hits in more than two decades of recording. Sadly, Rodriguez's single was the last number one that Lefty would achieve as a songwriter prior to his death on July 19, 1975.

Rodriguez first heard the song at the very same time as one of his fellow performers, and the timing was such that he got the first crack at it.

"Me and Merle Haggard and Lefty Frizzell and Whitey Shafer and Dallas Frazier and Lewis Talley were all sitting in a motel room in Nashville called the Continental Inn one night," Rodriguez explains. "We'd been playing songs to each other, and the very last song of that night, Lefty was fixing to go home. He said, 'I got one more song I want to play,' and it was 'That's The Way Love Goes.'

"Merle wanted to cut it, but he'd just finished doing an album. Whitey Shafer, who co-wrote it with Lefty, brought it down to the studio the next day where I was recording, and I went in and recorded it. The good thing about it was that exactly ten years later, Merle Haggard had a number one record on it, too [see 556], so it worked out real good."

Considering the traditional country image of both Frizzell and Shafer, Rodriguez's next release was a 180-degree turn, as he covered the

Beatles' "Something." Still, it made sense for Rodriguez, who was a teenager at the time of the British Invasion in the mid-'60s. Several of his friends were also inspired by the group, and noting the success of the Beatles' long hair as a gimmick, they formed their own band with a rather strange twist. In honor of their favorite TV program, "Star Trek," they all donned pointed ears and called themselves the Spocks.

"Something" went to number six for Rodriguez in 1974, and he followed up with a number two single, "Dance With Me (One More Time)," and a number three performance, "We're Over."

155
ANOTHER LONELY SONG
TAMMY WYNETTE
Epic 11079
Writers: Billy Sherrill, Norro Wilson,
Tammy Wynette
Producer: Billy Sherrill
February 23, 1974 (2 weeks)

"To me, that was one of the special songs that we've written," says Norro Wilson, noting the "little pop overtones" of "Another Lonely Song."

"I grew up in Kentucky listening to the Four Freshman and the Four Aces and the Ames Brothers, the McGuire Sisters. Nat King Cole was my favorite in the world. I like the way the old melodies were written and the old harmonies.

"I would think, too, that melodies tend to be my forté. I can give myself some credit about some good lyrics in good songs, but I really think my forté is more musical than lyrical. There's nothing wrong with that. Hal David is not musical; Burt Bacharach is. They didn't do too bad."

Wilson didn't do too bad either, when he teamed up with Tammy Wynette and producer Billy Sherrill to write the very melodic "Another Lonely Song," the fourteenth number one single of Wynette's solo career. Still, for all of the tuneful sounds on the record, Tammy's greatest concern came from its lyrics, which grappled with the issues of religion and interpersonal fidelity.

"I especially remember the line 'and though I shouldn't give a damn,' " she recalls. "I was so upset, because I was raised very strict, and I

thought 'damn' was the worst thing in the world for somebody to say in a song, especially a lady."

Sherrill let her cut it twice, once with the questionable line, and once with a replacement line: "and though I shouldn't feel this down." She took a copy of the tape home to play for George Jones, and he wasn't happy with the "damn" line, either.

Tammy shed tears over it that night, and put in a panicked call to Wilson, but he convinced her to wait until the next morning. They had a meeting at that time, and when they played it again, the record elicited a different response. "George looked at Sherrill," she notes, "and said, 'Well, I guess it's still in good taste,' and that was the end of it."

Wynette followed "Another Lonely Song" with "Woman To Woman" and "(You Make Me Want To Be) A Mother," both of which peaked at number four. When her next single, "I Still Believe In Fairy Tales," stopped at number 13, it halted an eight-year string of hits. From 1967 to 1975, Tammy had racked up 21 consecutive Top Ten solo releases.

156
THERE WON'T BE ANYMORE
CHARLIE RICH
RCA 0195
Writer: Charlie Rich
Producer: Chet Atkins
March 9, 1974 (2 weeks)

On March 16, 1974, a longstanding country tradition took on a new setting as the Grand Ole Opry moved from the Ryman Auditorium in downtown Nashville to a stage at the burgeoning Opryland complex that already included the Opryland amusement park. President Richard Nixon appeared at the induction ceremonies, playing three songs on piano, dancing to a bluegrass rendition of "Hail To The Chief" and joining Roy Acuff in a routine that involved Acuff's trademark yellow yo-yo.

Even as a new setting invigorated a country landmark, the top country single in the nation was a ten-year-old recording enhanced by new packaging. Charlie Rich wrote and recorded "There Won't Be Anymore" under the watchful eye of Chet Atkins, but RCA never reaped success from the cut until Rich hit it big with "Behind Closed Doors" [see 128] and "The Most Beautiful Girl" [see 148].

"I was very impressed by Charlie's talent," says Chet. "I thought he was one of the greatest I'd ever encountered, and I was really unhappy I didn't make more hits with him. They were tryin' out a new label when he came with us. They started a new label called Groove. That hurt us a lot, because the label never did really make it."

Many of his RCA masters were repackaged once Rich rose to popularity on Epic, and *There Won't Be Anymore* was the first of several compilation albums timed by the label to capitalize on his status.

The public apparently had a huge appetite for his records, too: "There Won't Be Anymore" was one of two simultaneous Rich hits. While that song remained at number one, Charlie soared into the Top 30 with "A Very Special Love Song" [see 159].

A Billy Sherrill-produced remake of "There Won't Be Anymore" also appeared on Rich's *Very Special Love Songs* album. Though never released by Epic as a single, it, like the RCA cut, earned scattered airplay. Both versions were fairly similar, the primary difference being the types of licks provided by the different keyboard players—Floyd Cramer [see 98—"(Lost Her Love) On Our Last Date"] on the RCA record, and "Pig" Robbins in the Epic recording.

157

THERE'S A HONKY TONK ANGEL (WHO'LL TAKE ME BACK IN)
CONWAY TWITTY

MCA 40173
Writers: Troy Seals, Denny Rice
Producer: Owen Bradley
March 23, 1974 (1 week)

In 1960, while still working the rock and roll club circuit [see 76—"How Much More Can She Stand"], Conway Twitty made a Hamilton, Ohio, bar called Frog's a frequent stomping ground when he played the Cincinnati area. He became friends with a band that regularly played Frog's, and at least three of its members have been involved in national records. Guitarist Lonnie Mack earned a Top Ten pop record in 1963 with his instrumental version of "Memphis"; Denny Rice picked up work as one of the Twitty Birds; and Troy Seals moved to Nashville, where he helped build Quadraphonic

Charlie Rich

Sound Studio and played bass on a number of records, including "Country Bumpkin" [see 163].

About that time, Seals began to develop as a songwriter, and his first number one single came in a pairing with his former bandmate, Rice, on "There's A Honky Tonk Angel."

"We had this song," Troy recalls. "At that time it was called 'Marlene.' It was about Denny's wife, and he was having an unhappy marriage at the time. So we got it out and worked with it, and we got it switched around from the title that we had. We worked on it for a couple of days, and Dobie Gray was cuttin' his first album in Nashville, and he cut it."

While Gray was recording *Drift Away*, Twitty heard "There's A Honky Tonk Angel," and he also recorded his own version. Ironically, though he was friends with Seals (Troy met his wife, Joanne, through Conway), he didn't realize that Troy had written the song. He didn't even know Seals had moved to Nashville until he saw the lyric sheet on the day he recorded it.

"I picked it as my next single," Conway remembers. "The next thing I know, the president of MCA Records at that time, Mike Maitland, happened to be out there on the road with us. We was doin' somethin', and he happened to tell me, 'We got that same title, Dobie Gray, that's his next single as well as yours.' I said, 'You got to be kiddin' me.' When the smoke cleared away, Dobie's record was pulled."

Twitty's version reached number one in March of 1974, and the song appeared on Dobie Gray's *Loving Arms* album. Five years later, an Elvis Presley rendition—released two years after his passing—reached number six.

158

WOULD YOU LAY WITH ME (IN A FIELD OF STONE)

TANYA TUCKER

Columbia 45991
Writer: David Allan Coe
Producer: Billy Sherrill
March 30, 1974 (1 week)

David Allan Coe is an imposing physical presence. Covered almost entirely by tattoos, Coe is an ex-convict who once spent time on Death Row. His image has been further cultivated from public appearances with a set of leather-clad bodyguards in tow, and he's notorious for a couple of X-rated albums.

By the same token, Coe has achieved a certain notoriety on a musical level, reaching the Top Ten with "You Never Even Called Me By My Name," "The Ride" and "Mona Lisa's Lost Her Smile." He also wrote two number one singles, "Take This Job And Shove It" [see 300] and "Would You Lay With Me (In A Field Of Stone)," a song that started out as a poem for his brother's wedding.

"It was called 'Tell Me Lady, Can You Pray,'" recalls producer Billy Sherrill, "and he eventually put a tune to it, and played it for me one day. 'Tell Me Lady, Can You Pray' didn't even make sense. Of course, David's done a lot of things that didn't make sense."

Particularly confusing was the first line, "Would you lay with me in a field of stone," and Sherrill admitted that he didn't understand it. Coe explained it as a vow for eternal unity: "Live with me all your life, and then, when I die and you die, we'll be buried together."

"It's a great idea," notes Sherrill, "even though it's a bit ethereal for country music."

Sherrill liked it, but insisted that he would only cut the song if Coe would change the title from "Tell Me Lady Can You Pray" to "Would You Lay With Me." "You know that takes guts," Sherrill laughs, "to tell that to a man with all that hair and those tattoos looking at you."

Tanya Tucker was a bit tentative about the song, but she trusted Sherrill's judgment enough to record it anyway. The single ended with a dramatic "round," and it generated a lot of attention on its way to number one.

"It was my first really controversial song," she explains. "A couple of radio stations banned it because of my age and the content of the song, but when you realize what it was written about, it makes much more sense. It's a very intriguing song. If you were going to get married, that would be a great wedding vow."

159

A VERY SPECIAL LOVE SONG

CHARLIE RICH

Epic 11091
Writers: Billy Sherrill, Norro Wilson
Producer: Billy Sherrill
April 6, 1974 (3 weeks)

"A Very Special Love Song" was a very unique song for Charlie Rich. The melody of each verse derived from an interweaving pattern, meshing Rich's vocal work with an eight-note keyboard pattern that also appeared in the record's intro and between verses. Unless the listener is specifically looking for it, it's almost a subliminal effect, but it was enough to distinguish his fourth number one single in less than a year.

"That little melodic thing was inspired by the theme from *The Summer of '42*," admits songwriter Norro Wilson. "I don't think I stole from them at all, but that's my favorite theme of all time. There's not a similarity, and yet, you can understand what I was thinking about and where I was coming from."

Wilson doodled with that pattern for some time, and on one particular occasion, it caught producer Billy Sherrill's attention.

"He loved that," Wilson remembers, "and he said, 'That's very special.' We needed something for Charlie, and he said, 'Let's write for him a very special love song.' I think Billy's the most magnificent, creative person I've ever known."

Rich must have agreed. He signed with Epic—despite better financial offers from other labels—specifically to work with Sherrill, who had engineered some of his sessions when Rich recorded for Sun Records [see 128—"Behind Closed Doors"]. Charlie, in fact, included a "key man" clause in his contract: if Sherrill left the company, Rich was free to leave as well.

A native of Phil Campbell, Alabama, Sherrill honed his musical skills playing piano for his father's traveling ministry. When he formed a band in Kentucky, the group played on stage during a shooting at a club.

At Epic, Sherrill produced Tammy Wynette, George Jones, Tanya Tucker, Lacy J. Dalton and Johnny Paycheck, among many others. He has also written such hits as "Stand By Your Man" [see 21], "The Most Beautiful Girl" [see 148], "Too Far Gone" and "Sweet And Innocent."

After Sherrill helped propel "The Silver Fox" to stardom, Rich accomplished a remarkable feat while "A Very Special Love Song" resided at number one. Beginning April 20, 1974, Charlie's *There Won't Be Anymore* [see 156], *Behind Closed Doors* and *Very Special Love Songs* occupied the top three slots on the *Billboard* country album chart for six consecutive weeks.

Hank Snow

160

HELLO LOVE
HANK SNOW
RCA 0215
Writers: Betty Jean Robinson,
Aileen Muich
Producers: Ronny Light, Chet Atkins
April 27, 1974 (1 week)

Chet Atkins once credited Hank Snow with a "special quality that makes him sound good even on a bad jukebox." Snow displayed that quality on 43 Top Ten singles that spanned four different decades.

Hank Snow was born in Nova Scotia, and his parents divorced when he was eight. His mother remarried, but his stepfather beat him and abused him many times before kicking him out of the house at age 12. During his teens, Hank supported himself by selling newspapers and Fuller brushes. Eventually, he earned $5.95 unloading salt from a freighter, and used it to purchase his first guitar. By age 15, he was singing in the streets for pocket change.

Snow moved on to radio station CHNS in Halifax, holding down his own show under the name "Hank, The Singing Ranger." He first recorded for Victor in Canada during 1936, but set his sights on a career in the U.S. In the mid-'40s, he started playing live dates in America, and in 1949, he charted in *Billboard* for the first time with his Top Ten recording "Marriage Vow."

Hank's next release, "I'm Moving On" [see 503—"(Lost His Love) On Our Last Date"], spent an incredible 21 weeks at number one in 1950. He topped the chart with his next two singles, "The Golden Rocket" and "Rhumba Boogie," and spent another 20 weeks at the top in 1954 with "I Don't Hurt Anymore." "Let Me Go, Lover" reached number one for Snow in 1955, but it took nearly eight years before "I've Been Everywhere," a virtual litany of American cities, returned him to the top of the charts.

Snow had been absent from the number one position for nearly a dozen years when "Hello Love" rejuvenated his career. After debuting in *Billboard* on February 9, 1974, it topped the chart on April 27. The following week, with Snow approaching age 60, RCA announced that it had renewed his contract for 13 more years. If the deal had gone through, he would have been with the label for more than 50 years. But the contract never reached its finale—in 1980, Hank's tenure with RCA was ended after 44 years.

On October 8, 1979, Hank Snow was inducted into the Country Music Hall of Fame.

Garrison Keillor later used "Hello Love" as the theme song for his radio show, "The Prairie Home Companion."

161
THINGS AREN'T FUNNY ANYMORE
MERLE HAGGARD
& THE STRANGERS
Capitol 3830
Writer: Merle Haggard
Producer: Ken Nelson
May 4, 1974 (1 week)

Ken Nelson played an important role in the development of Merle Haggard, signing him to Capitol Records in 1965 after the Tally release "(My Friends Are Gonna Be) Strangers" reached number 10.

Nelson got his start in the business at age 14, as a vocalist on a live radio show. From 1935 to 1946, he was one of the most influential men in Chicago's broadcast market, but he left radio to work for Capitol Records. In 1948, he moved to California, becoming the head of the label's country department four years later.

Perhaps his biggest mistake came when he turned down an opportunity to record "The Ballad Of Davy Crockett," but Ken did plenty of other things right. Heading the Capitol operations, he produced performers like Hank Thompson, Buck Owens, Sonny James and Haggard. His primary philosophy was to sign performers with a clear sense of vision about their work.

"He would just sit back there and let the artist do what he was best at doing," remembers Haggard's steel player, Norm Hamlet. "He was just there to lend a helping hand to anybody who needed it. He was always in the control room, and he would listen and if anybody made a mistake or they were out of tune, he'd say so. He had a great ear."

"When you were recording, he'd just doodle on a piece of paper," Haggard confirmed, in Alanna Nash's *Behind Closed Doors*. "He'd say, 'All right, Master 45,265, Take One.' And he'd go to doodling. And then when the song was over, he'd either say, 'Merle, I think we should do it one more time,' or he'd say, 'It's a master and a joy to behold—come in and be proud.' He always used those words, you know."

Nominated in 1989 for a spot in the Country Music Hall of Fame, Nelson produced *Merle Haggard: His 30th Album*, which yielded "Things Aren't Funny Anymore." As with his previous single [see 150—"If We Make It Through December"], Haggard wrote the song after a conversation with guitarist Roy Nichols. In this instance, Nichols complained that the touring life was no longer fun. With a little imagination, it became "Things Aren't Funny Anymore," Haggard's seventeenth number one single.

162
IS IT WRONG (FOR LOVING YOU)
SONNY JAMES
Columbia 46003
Writer: Warner McPherson
Producer: George Richey
May 11, 1974 (1 week)

Warner McPherson—better known as Warner Mack—earned eleven Top Ten records between 1957 and 1969, including a number one single in 1965, "The Bridge Washed Out." His very first hit was a self-written composition that peaked at number nine, and in 1974, Sonny James took that same song, "Is It Wrong (For Loving You)," all the way to number one.

James and Mack shared the same manager, Bob Neal, and the two quite naturally became friends. Initially, Sonny recorded "Is It Wrong" simply as an album cut, but popular demand more or less forced its release as a single.

"A lot of people from different parts of the country mentioned that song," he says. "I didn't ask their opinion. They just volunteered it, and that's a good sign, if someone at a personal appearance or a radio personality will say, 'Sonny, you ought to consider this song for a single.' It doesn't have to be too many before you decide there's something there, or these people wouldn't be volunteering."

"Is It Wrong" was James' last number one single, but it was hardly his final hit. He placed seven more singles in *Billboard*'s Top Ten through 1977, including remakes of "What In The World's Come Over You" and "You're Free To Go," as well as "A Little Bit South Of Saskatoon," which appeared in the Paul Newman movie *Slap Shot*.

Known for wearing blue in his personal appearances ("I feel good when I'm wearing it," he once told writer Sherry Woods), Sonny earned acclaim for three different projects in the mid-'70s. The *In Prison, In Person* LP was the first album ever recorded with a cast of inmates as the supporting musicians; his rendition of "Just A Closer Walk With Thee" earned a Grammy nomination; and his Bicentennial retrospective *200 Years of Country Music* netted an Album of the Year nomination from the Country Music Association.

In 1979, James recorded a couple of singles for Monument Records, and two years later, he signed up with Dimension, an association that lasted until 1983. Altogether, he spent 63 weeks of his career at number one on the *Billboard* country chart, with 23 different singles.

163

COUNTRY BUMPKIN
CAL SMITH
MCA 40191
Writer: Don Wayne
Producer: Walter Haynes
May 18, 1974 (1 week)

"Country Bumpkin" was built by songwriter Don Wayne on the frequently held belief that the quiet, laid-back lifestyle of a rural existence is preferable to the frenzied pace of an urban environment. The song told the story of a country boy who visits a bar, wins the heart of a sophisticated city girl and takes her

back to the country, where they settle down and raise a family.

Wayne had already written a couple of hits, including "Saginaw, Michigan" [see 121—"The Lord Knows I'm Drinking"], by Lefty Frizzell; and "Hank," which peaked at number 12 for Hank Williams, Jr., in 1973. Wayne was writing for Tree Publishing when he got the idea for "Country Bumpkin," although Tree never got the chance to publish it.

"Don said they hadn't done much for him," Cal Smith told Jim Roden in the *Dallas Times-Herald*. "One day, he happened to overhear one of their people say, 'We don't want that country bumpkin-type stuff of his.' Don left, and as he was riding in his car, he thought up 'Country Bumpkin.'"

By the time it arrived in Smith's hands, though, the vocalist already had enough songs for the album he was working on. Producer Walter Haynes played "Country Bumpkin" for him the day before their recording session.

"I told him that ['Country Bumpkin'] has to be one of the finest songs I've ever heard," said Smith. "The song just hit me right away. Coming off a farm myself, I know the meaning of it. All country people know what a country bumpkin is."

Intrigued by the song, Smith scrapped one of the other tunes he had planned to record in his session and cut "Country Bumpkin" instead. It was so successful that he made it the title track for the album, and it also became the biggest record of his career. After entering the *Billboard* country chart on March 9, 1974, it reached number one in its eleventh week.

The Country Music Association named "Country Bumpkin" the Song of the Year and Single Record of the Year at the CMA's 1974 awards show, and the Academy of Country Music doled out similar kudos at its 1975 celebration. The CMA also nominated *Country Bumpkin* as the Album of the Year.

164

NO CHARGE
MELBA MONTGOMERY
Elektra 45883
Writer: Harlan Howard
Producer: Pete Drake
May 25, 1974 (1 week)

In 1914, Congress passed a special resolution designating the second Sunday of each May

Melba Montgomery

as Mother's Day. Sixty years later, Melba Montgomery celebrated the occasion with a very special release appropriate for the holiday. "No Charge" presented the heart-tugging story of a young boy who submits a bill to his mother for the nagging household chores he has been required to perform. In response, his mother lists her many duties on his behalf, all attended to at "no charge."

The song was written by Harlan Howard, whose numerous credits include "I Fall To Pieces" [see 282—"She's Got You"], "The Blizzard," "I Don't Know A Thing About Love (The Moon Song)" [see 591] and "Why Not Me" [see 600].

"After all these years," says Howard, "I have just a handful of real favorites—songs that I just couldn't ever possibly write better, and there's nothing to change, and I've never heard a song like it. 'The Blizzard' is one of my favorites, and 'No Charge' fits in that category. I've never written a song that moves people so much. I've had guys tell me they almost wrecked their truck when they heard it 'cause it made them cry.

"I had a lot of delightful records in many different languages on that song, but I guess that's probably my favorite song as far as impact is concerned."

"No Charge" was the only number one single for Melba Montgomery, who hails from Iron City, Tennessee (birthdate: October 14, 1938). She entered a number of talent contests as a teenager, but the most important was a 1958 win in a Pet Milk-sponsored contest at the WSM studios in Nashville. Following that performance, she spent several years as a member of Roy Acuff's band.

Melba first charted on the United Artists label in 1963, in a duet with George Jones, "We Must Have Been Out Of Our Minds." The record reached number three. She continued to put out singles as a solo performer, and with duet partners Gene Pitney and Charlie Louvin, but it took "No Charge" to return Montgomery to the Top Ten.

The record, incidentally, was the first to reach number one for the country division of Elektra Records. The only other "Mother's Day special" to even approach the success of "No Charge" is Jimmy Dean's 1976 recording, "I.O.U." That single peaked at number nine.

165

PURE LOVE

RONNIE MILSAP

RCA 0237
Writer: Eddie Rabbitt
Producer: Tom Collins
June 1, 1974 (1 week)

When Ronnie Milsap landed his first number one record with "Pure Love," it marked the end of a lengthy search. He tried to make it in both Atlanta and Memphis before his move to Nashville, experimenting with several styles. In fact, his first records actually charted as rhythm and blues singles for New York-based Scepter Records in the mid-'60s.

In Memphis, Milsap had played regularly at a nightclub called T.J.'s [see 345—"Nobody Likes Sad Songs"], where he was heard by an East Tennessee teacher named Tom Collins in the summer of 1971. Collins, who hoped to land a job in the record industry, told Milsap he should consider cutting country records, and when he went to work for Charley Pride's publishing company a year later, Collins received a call from Ronnie.

On December 26, 1972, Milsap moved to Music City, where he started playing piano at Roger Miller's King of the Road Motel. Pride and partner Jack D. Johnson saw Ronnie perform and offered him a management contract. Collins produced a demo tape; RCA signed Ronnie to a recording contract in April of 1973.

"I Hate You," Milsap's first country single, hit the Top Ten in the summer of 1973. A follow-up, "That Girl Who Waits On Tables," reached number 11. "Pure Love," an advertiser's delight, followed. Eddie Rabbitt wrote it for his future wife, Janine, with a 99⁴⁴/₁₀₀ percent allusion to Ivory soap and a reference to Cap'n Crunch, which ultimately became Milsap's C.B. handle.

"There's a verse in there about being in the park and swingin' on the swings," notes Eddie, "but when Milsap cut it, they knocked one of the verses out—it was too long, I guess. I was in a phase at that time when I was eating a lot of Cap'n Crunch and half-and-half. It was real good, but it was real fattening, too."

Collins heard Rabbitt perform "Pure Love" at a live show in Nashville, but Pride, who had first shot at it, suggested that Milsap record it.

Because of Milsap's wide-ranging musical background, Collins went to great lengths to ensure a "country" production. Joe Zinkan played an upright bass, rather than an electric one, and Lloyd Green played steel guitar on the session. The whole song was cut in less than 40 minutes.

166

I WILL ALWAYS LOVE YOU

DOLLY PARTON

RCA 0234
Writer: Dolly Parton
Producer: Bob Ferguson
June 8, 1974 (1 week)

"I always loved to sing," Dolly Parton once told *Billboard*'s Gerry Wood, "but my songwriting was the thing that made me feel like I had something to say. That's my heart, my joy, and that's what got me out of the Smokies . . . It kept me sane—it was therapy, but it also was a job. And it was always a very personal thing to me."

Dolly has a natural ability to take the personal events and circumstances of her life and portray them in a manner that many others can understand. "I Will Always Love You" is a perfect example.

At the time she wrote the song, she was contemplating a departure from Porter Wagoner's entourage [see 181—"Please Don't Stop Loving Me"]. Writing was probably quite therapeutic, as she took those basic feelings of sorrow and tried to incorporate them into a more commercial method of saying goodbye. In addition, she dredged up memories of some of her high school sweethearts, and the emotions that surrounded her move from the Smoky Mountains to Nashville [see 71—"Joshua"]. All of those inspirations combined to form one monumental ballad, "I Will Always Love You."

With the Wagoner/Parton relationship on its final legs, the sessions had grown increasingly difficult. Porter viewed Dolly as an employee, and he wanted to produce her records his own way. Dolly, on the other hand, wanted more of her own input, and Bob Ferguson, who received the actual label credit as producer, had to serve as a mediator.

"I leaned on him a great deal," says Dolly, "more than Porter even knew or would have wanted me to. Porter did a great job on the records. Porter was more aggressive than Bob, but Bob had a lot of creative control. He was great at keeping order in the studio, which often got out of order because of Porter's temper with the musicians. Bob had a nice, easy way of keeping things in perspective, and he also had a lot of wonderful, creative ideas, more than he ever did really get credit for."

Recorded at Nashville's RCA Studios, "I Will Always Love You" was included on the *Jolene* [see 152] album. Selected as the second single, it entered the *Billboard* chart at number 87 on April 6, 1974, slipping into the top position in its tenth week. Eight years later, it would return to number one [see 490].

167

I DON'T SEE ME IN YOUR EYES ANYMORE

CHARLIE RICH

RCA 0260
Writers: Bennie Benjamin,
George David Weiss
Producer: Chet Atkins
June 15, 1974 (1 week)

A member of the Country Music Hall of Fame, Chet Atkins is reluctant to accept the title "Father of the Nashville Sound." Along with producers like Don Law, Ken Nelson and Owen Bradley, Atkins helped to take country music to a new mass of people during the '60s.

A proficient guitarist, Atkins made his first appearance on the Grand Ole Opry in 1946. He started working with the Carter Family and making his own records, and in 1949, Steve Sholes appointed him as the primary guitarist for RCA sessions. Eventually, Atkins began producing records in the mid-'50s, becoming the head of RCA's Nashville wing from 1957 to 1974. His efforts resulted in more than 30 number one records (plus countless other hits) as a producer, including classics by Eddy Arnold, Jim Reeves, Don Gibson and Jerry Reed.

Despite Chet's work with Charlie Rich, none of his successes with "The Silver Fox" came until late in Atkins' division-leading tenure. Included is Rich's fifth number one single—and second for RCA—"I Don't See Me In Your Eyes Anymore."

"I like that song a lot," says Chet. "I was recording about 30 artists in those days, so I don't remember much about it. We tried to make a good record on it. I still think it's a good song. I've got his gold record hangin' in my bathroom, and I see that every day."

Atkins wasn't the first to see the potential of "I Don't See Me In Your Eyes Anymore." Perry Como recorded it during 1949. Songwriters Bennie Benjamin and George David Weiss were a fairly potent team. Their collective resumé includes such titles as "I Don't Want To Set The World On Fire," "The Lion Sleeps Tonight," "Surrender" and "Can't Help Falling In Love."

Rich's recording of "I Don't See Me In Your Eyes Anymore" debuted on the country chart on May 4, 1974. In its seventh week—25 years after Como introduced it—the song reached number one.

On July 2, Charlie made his first Las Vegas appearance at the Hilton Hotel. He shared the bill that night with a lady making her own debut: Australia's Olivia Newton-John.

168

THIS TIME

WAYLON JENNINGS

RCA 0251
Writer: Waylon Jennings
Producer: Waylon Jennings
June 22, 1974 (1 week)

Waylon Jennings had been signed to RCA Records for nine years before he finally earned his first number one record as a country artist with "This Time."

His first contract actually came in 1963, with Herb Alpert's A & M Records, but that relationship yielded just one album. Alpert saw Jennings as a pop vocalist, in the vein of Al Martino, and that basic difference in philosophy prevented them from flourishing as a team.

After seeing Waylon play at JD's in Phoenix, Bobby Bare helped Jennings secure his RCA deal, convincing Chet Atkins to give him a chance. Things progressed slowly, however, after Jennings moved to Nashville in 1965. His first record, "That's The Chance I'll Have To Take," went to a mere number 49, and Jennings had to wait until his fifth RCA release, "(That's What You Get) For Lovin' Me," to reach the Top Ten.

A dozen more singles attained the same status in the ensuing years, including "Only Daddy That'll Walk The Line" (number two in 1968) and "I Got You," a duet with Anita Carter. He also picked up a Grammy with the Kimberlys in 1970 for "MacArthur Park."

Initially, Jennings relied on Atkins as a producer, but continually expressed discomfort with the standard Nashville recording methods. In November of 1972, attorney Neil Reshen exploited a loophole in Jennings' RCA contract to gain Waylon more money and artistic control over his records. Producing himself, Jennings finally notched that first number one single 19 months later with "This Time," a song he had written five years earlier.

Most of the *This Time* album was co-produced by Waylon and Willie Nelson, but "This Time" was one of the few tracks in which Nelson didn't participate.

"That thing almost didn't happen," says Waylon. "I was in the studio and was doing this album, and said, 'Let me try this song,' so I put it in there and started recording it, and it's got a real tricky meter to it. I said, 'Aw, hell, this thing ain't no good,' and I started to throw it away, and Richie Albright, my drummer, said, 'No, do it one more time, and I think it'll work.' So we did it one more and it worked, but that one almost didn't happen."

Waylon Jennings

169

ROOM FULL OF ROSES
MICKEY GILLEY
Playboy 50056
Writer: Tim Spencer
Producer: Mickey Gilley
June 29, 1974 (1 week)

"Room Full Of Roses" first appeared on the *Billboard* country charts on July 15, 1949, when George Morgan's original recording began a run toward number four. Twenty-five years later, the song served as Mickey Gilley's first national number one single, even though it emerged almost by accident.

Gilley's club in Pasadena, Texas, was already doing good business in the Houston area, and Gilley also had a local television program. He had his own Astro record label, and, in 1973, cut four tracks simply to promote his endeavors in the area. He recorded "She Called Me Baby" [see 188] specifically for a local jukebox operator who wanted a copy of the song, and also cut "Abilene" (a number one record for George Hamilton IV in 1963) and "When Two Worlds Collide" (first recorded by Jim Reeves).

Mickey did "Room Full Of Roses" at the same session, with every intention of making it the "B" side of "She Called Me Baby." Houston disk jockeys, however, got a copy of the single, flipped it over, and turned "Roses" into a local mega-hit. Gilley shopped the record around Nashville, but every major label turned him down. Instead, independent Playboy Records, based in Los Angeles, bought the master tape, and Gilley's "B" side became the beginning of a major career.

The single introduced Gilley with a piano style reminiscent of his cousin, Jerry Lee Lewis. "That was my first thought, when I made the arpeggio down the piano and started singing it," recalls Gilley. "I stopped about 16 bars into the song." Convinced by others at the session that his imitation of the Killer was perfect for the tune, Gilley launched into the song once more, running through the piece in its entirety twice. The first take is the one that was released in spite of several mistakes.

Gilley momentarily got lost during the piano solo in the middle, and somehow managed to come out of it in sync with the studio band. The steel guitar was also mixed louder than Gilley wanted, and was treated with an excessive amount of "echo" to hide the fact that it was recorded out of tune. Gilley also muffed the lyrics at one point, switching the "I"'s and "you"'s around in the first verse. "It really didn't make sense," he confesses, "but it was one of those things that had that particular sound that made it work."

170

HE THINKS I STILL CARE
ANNE MURRAY
Capitol 3867
Writer: Dickey Lee
Producer: Brian Ahern
July 6, 1974 (2 weeks)

"There are only two things I know about Canada: hockey and Anne Murray." Those are the words of pop superstar Elton John, who on July 13, 1974, resided in *Billboard*'s Hot 100 with "Don't Let The Sun Go Down On Me," just two spaces ahead of Murray's "You Won't See Me."

The flip side of Anne's single, "He Thinks I Still Care," topped the country chart the week before. It marks the only time in history that an artist achieved those levels on both the pop and country charts with opposite sides of the same record. "He Thinks I Still Care" also made Murray only the second Canadian to top *Billboard*'s country list [see 160—"Hello Love"].

Murray was raised in the Nova Scotia mining town of Springhill, where her musical tastes were shaped by her parents' love for standard vocalists like Perry Como and Rosemary Clooney. Those influences were balanced by the rock sounds she picked up on her radio.

"The only country music I listened to were the songs that ended up on the pop charts at the time," she notes. "People like Brenda Lee, Elvis Presley, Buddy Holly and Buddy Knox were on the pop charts, even Sonny James. All those tunes were Top 40 at that time, but they all had a real country flavor."

"He Thinks I Still Care" was the first pure country song that she learned to sing. She picked it up backstage at "Singalong Jubilee," a TV show out of Halifax that represented her first shot at the big time. "We all used to just sit around in the dressing room and sing," Anne remembers, "and when it came to putting together the *Danny's Song* album, that song just kind of came up."

The record had come up in country circles a dozen years earlier, when George Jones first took it to number one [see 176—"The Grand Tour"]. Dickey Lee [see 229—"Rocky"] wrote it about a break-up with one of his first girlfriends while he was still in college. "I really didn't think of it as a hit," Lee says.

Publishers Jack Clement and Bill Hall did. They got it to Jones, and *Billboard* eventually named it among the five biggest country singles for 1962. Over time, it's been recorded by more than 200 artists, including Kenny Rogers, Dan Seals and Elvis [see 291—"Way Down"].

171

MARIE LAVEAU
BOBBY BARE
RCA 0261
Writers: Shel Silverstein, Baxter Taylor III
Producer: Not listed
July 20, 1974 (1 week)

"I don't ever do something really weird just to get attention," says Bobby Bare. "It's too obvious. I always look for songs that entertain me, and if they entertain me, hopefully, I can relay that to everybody else. But I've never done anything specifically for shock value."

Despite that claim, Bare's track record is filled with slightly offbeat singles. At the top of the list is "Marie Laveau," a tale about a witch, and a record that has the distinction of being the only number one country single with a shriek or scream on it.

If Bare's records are peculiar, his entry into the business is just as strange. A native of Ironton, Ohio, Bare was drafted by the military just after he moved to Los Angeles in the late '50s. He headed back home, and a couple of days before his induction, he went into King Recording Studios in Cincinnati with a friend named Bill Parsons.

During the last 30 minutes of their session, they quickly laid down a song called "The All-American Boy," with Bare singing lead. King Records sold the demo to Fraternity Records for $500, with Bare earning ten percent. "The

All-American Boy," mistakenly listing Parsons as the vocalist, became a number two record in *Billboard*'s pop charts during 1959.

After his enlistment, Bare signed with RCA Records in Nashville, and his second country single, "Detroit City," won the Grammy award for Best Country & Western Recording for 1963. Bare dotted the country charts with eight more Top Five singles over the next decade, including "500 Miles Away From Home," "Miller's Cave" and "Daddy, What If," which featured his six-year-old son, Bobby, Jr., and peaked at number two just before the release of "Marie Laveau."

"Marie Laveau" also continued Bare's association with songwriter Shel Silverstein, who wrote Bare's 1972 single, "Sylvia's Mother," as well as "Daddy, What If." In 1975, Bare cut a double album of Silverstein's material, *Lullabyes, Legends and Lies*, and his last hit was a 1980 recording of Silverstein's "Numbers."

Bare became a cable television host for the Nashville Network in 1983, with a songwriter showcase titled "Bobby Bare and Friends."

172

YOU CAN'T BE A BEACON (IF YOUR LIGHT DON'T SHINE)

DONNA FARGO

Dot 17506
Writer: Marty Cooper
Producer: Stan Silver
July 27, 1974 (1 week)

Exactly one year after her fourth number one single [see 137—"You Were Always There"], Donna Fargo scored her fifth with a gospel tune. Marty Cooper was a friend of both Fargo and husband/producer Stan Silver, and had approached them about recording a few other songs before.

In those instances, the couple had passed, but Silver eventually called Cooper to request a gospel number. "In a few days," Donna recalls, "he gave me the song. I was getting ready to go into a recording session, and I just played it and learned it right there almost."

The lyrical flavor of "You Can't Be A Beacon (If Your Light Don't Shine)" followed quite closely a Biblical passage (Matthew 5:16): "Let your light so shine before men that they may see your good works, and glorify your Father."

Good works were hardly the order of the day, though, since the Watergate scandal was in its waning moments. It affected Fargo as strongly as anyone, and, ever the optimist, she tried to counter the negative mood of the nation with her next single, "U.S. Of A."

"The thing I remember most about 'U.S. Of A.' was the Nixon thing, and a 'What can we do?' kind of attitude. I wanted it to go higher on the charts ["U.S. Of A." peaked at number nine], but one of the problems was that the record company pulled it. They said it was too long, and they pulled the recitation out and put the record back out, but that killed it."

After "You Can't Be A Beacon," it would be three more years before Fargo could reach the

top again. In 1975, she released four more singles, but only one of them, "It Do Feel Good," managed to reach the Top Ten on the *Billboard* charts. In 1976, she re-emerged on Warner Bros., while her ABC/Dot remake of Stonewall Jackson's "Don't Be Angry" hit number three; 1977 got off to a good start when her Warners single "Mockingbird Hill" reached number nine.

173

RUB IT IN
BILLY "CRASH" CRADDOCK
ABC 11437
Writer: Layng Martine, Jr.
Producer: Ron Chancey
August 3, 1974 (2 weeks)

The nickname "Crash" is one that has often been misinterpreted, thanks to Billy Craddock's interests in auto racing. He first picked up the name playing running back on the high school football team. Weighing just 135 pounds, he would dart for a hole on the line and try to shimmy through it to avoid being tackled by the larger defensive players. By avoiding collisions, he became known as "Crash."

Still, the name didn't become permanent until he signed with Columbia Records in 1959. "They wanted to establish a personality instead of a record," he says. "It sounded weird to me back then—although the guys on the football team used to call me 'Crash' a lot, I'd never been called 'Crash' before in public. I thought it was a pretty good gimmick and it just might work."

It did work, although not in America. Craddock picked up three Top Ten records as a pop artist in Australia, but only reached number 94 on *Billboard*'s Hot 100 in the U.S. with "Don't Destroy Me."

Fifteen years later, he finally earned his first number one record—not as a pop star, but as a country performer. "Rub It In" had already been cut by three other artists with no success, but Craddock thought it was "cute," and took it into the studio. After its release, he was surprised to find that many stations across the country refused to play it.

"We didn't know why," he remembers, "so I had to call disk jockeys around the country and find out why they weren't playing it, and they told me it was a little risqué. I asked them all to go back to that song again. I said, 'We're talking

Billy "Crash" Craddock

about suntan lotion, and if you still think it's risqué, then don't play it.' Evidently, they all went back and listened to it, and it was the biggest record we ever had."

"Rub It In" brought Craddock back to the pop charts, peaking at number 16 on the *Billboard* Hot 100. Its upbeat tempo and lyric also provided a unique contrast to the news of the day, since "Rub It In" resided at the top of the country charts the same week that President Richard Nixon announced his resignation.

The song made a bit of a comeback in 1986, when Absorbine Jr. hired Craddock to cut the song as a commercial.

174
AS SOON AS I HANG UP THE PHONE
LORETTA LYNN
& CONWAY TWITTY
MCA 40251
Writer: Conway Twitty
Producer: Owen Bradley
August 17, 1974 (1 week)

When Conway Twitty and Loretta Lynn began recording together, they purposely agreed to make their duets a special event, releasing only one album or single per year. They also made an effort to stagger their singles, so that a Conway & Loretta duet didn't have to compete for airplay with a Twitty solo record and a Lynn single.

"We felt the duet could be so strong, it might actually hurt us as individual acts," Twitty explained in the liner notes of one of their *Greatest Hits* LPs. "We try to think of the fans, too," Lynn told *Billboard*. "The fans only have so much money. They go out and buy my records, they buy his records, so we don't want to make it too hard on them."

The one-record-a-year philosophy kept "As Soon As I Hang Up The Phone" "in the can" for more than a year. They recorded "Louisiana Woman, Mississippi Man" [see 140] on March 6, 1973, and released it that same year. "As Soon As I Hang Up The Phone," recorded one day later, was held back until the following year.

A novelty record that embraces a telephone conversation, the single was cut with Conway placing a call from a booth in the studio. Loretta was so absorbed in the song that when Twitty put down the receiver after the first take, she stormed in the booth and chastised him for hanging up on her. Lynn considers it her favorite among their duets.

"It starts with the phone ringing," she said in her autobiography, *Coal Miner's Daughter*, "and Conway, in a choking kind of voice, tries to tell me goodbye. Now, for a while, I don't pay any attention to what he's saying, but he keeps bringing the subject back to him leaving. Finally, he says it's true and I sing, 'Ohhh, nooo . . .'

"Now, how many people have gotten bad news on the phone about their man or woman? Lots. And I bet most of 'em react the way I do in that song. Well, that song started being played on the jukeboxes over and over again because it was real."

It was particularly real to those listeners who incorrectly thought the two were married. "Conway got a lot of letters from upset people after we did 'As Soon As I Hang Up The Phone,'" Loretta laughs.

175
OLD MAN FROM THE MOUNTAIN
MERLE HAGGARD
& THE STRANGERS
Capitol 3900
Writer: Merle Haggard
Producer: Fuzzy Owen
August 24, 1974 (1 week)

One can hardly accuse Merle Haggard of being a nine-to-five songwriter. He's gone through lengthy droughts on many occasions, and, in fact, had suffered a six-month dry spell before writing "If We Make It Through December" [see 150] during a bus ride that produced a total of five Christmas songs.

"When something hits me, that's when it starts to come," he once explained to Mark Rose. "It's kind of like one of these teletype machines. I'm watching one of them and all of a sudden it starts working. That's kind of the way my writing is. I have no idea when that machine's going to start."

A man named Dean Harrington triggered the machine in 1974. The owner of a construction company in Bellflower, California, Harrington shared similar musical tastes with Hag. "He was a good friend of ours," says ex-Stranger Ronnie Reno. "He was just a rowdy old man, and he would come up to Tahoe and Reno and Las Vegas and stay with us until we were through. He was actually from Oklahoma and loved Bob Wills, so Merle just wrote a song about him. We used to call him 'The Old Man From The Mountain,' and that's where the song came from: Dean Harrington."

"The Old Man From The Mountain" debuted in *Billboard* on June 29, 1974, with a modest number 78 entry position. Two months later, it made a one-week appearance at number one.

"We stopped in Dallas and cut 'The Old Man From The Mountain,'" Haggard told Todd Everett in *Billboard* during 1977. "There was a bass player there who used to play on all the old country records in the 1950s—the old upright, slap-type bass. Johnny Gimble, who had played in the Strangers and still plays on a lot of my records, knew where he was living, so we went down there to cut the single."

By the time the single reached its peak position, the flip side was garnering a substantial amount of airplay as well. Titled "Holding Things Together," it featured Reno and Bonnie Owens as supporting vocalists.

Owens, the one-time wife of Buck Owens, became Haggard's second wife in 1965, and is credited for getting many of his songs down on paper. Nineteen seventy-four proved a pivotal year in their relationship, as she gave up the road.

176

THE GRAND TOUR
GEORGE JONES
Epic 11122
Writers: Norro Wilson, Carmol Taylor, George Richey
Producer: Billy Sherrill
August 31, 1974 (1 week)

"Step right up, come on in . . ."

With that familiar phrase, George Jones offered an open invitation in "The Grand Tour" to take a stroll through the rooms of a home that had once held so many private and personal memories. Though the song was fictitious, it seemed appropriate; his own personal life had often become a source of public speculation.

Jones was born in East Texas on September 12, 1931, and he earned money in his youth by singing on the streets in downtown Beaumont. When his father got drunk, the senior Jones often forced George and his sister, Doris, to perform unwillingly at home.

Music was George's overriding passion nonetheless, and he was so consumed by it that he dropped out of school in the seventh grade. A few years later, he went to work at a Houston radio station, where he had the chance to meet his idol, Hank Williams. Ironically, Jones made his first record in 1953, the same year that Williams died.

"Why Baby Why" [see 508] became Jones' first bona fide hit in 1955, and he finally reached number one in 1959, with "White Lightning." Jones again reached the top in 1961 with "Tender Years," and in 1962 with "She Thinks I Still Care" [see 170]. "Walk Through This World With Me" went to number one in 1966, and he had endured an eight-year absence from the top as a solo artist when his friend and frequent session pianist, George Richey, provided Jones with his fifth chart-topping single.

"I was driving from Memphis over the weekend, and I had this idea for the song which started, 'Step right up, come on in,' reminiscent of a carnival barker," Richey remembers. "My now-late wife wanted to listen to the radio and I had this tune driving me crazy. I think it was a Saturday, and Jones was gonna cut on Tuesday, so I got as far as I could get, trying to write this song with the radio playing." That Monday, he completed "The Grand Tour" with Norro Wilson and Carmol Taylor, just in time for Jones' Tuesday session.

"As I recall, when George cut that song, it was the most talked-about record he'd had in an awfully long time," says Wilson. "We've written some things that are hokey as all get-out, but 'The Grand Tour' is one of my proudest moments."

177

PLEASE DON'T TELL ME HOW THE STORY ENDS
RONNIE MILSAP
RCA 0313
Writer: Kris Kristofferson
Producers: Tom Collins, Jack D. Johnson
September 7, 1974 (2 weeks)

During his years in Memphis [see 165—"Pure Love"], Ronnie Milsap had the opportunity to work with record producer Chips Moman, who produced the Elvis Presley "comeback" sessions that yielded "Suspicious

Minds" and "In The Ghetto." Milsap played piano on Elvis' rendition of "Gentle On My Mind," and also sang back-up on "Kentucky Rain."

Appropriately, Ronnie cut both of his first two number one singles—"Pure Love" and "Please Don't Tell Me How The Story Ends"—on Presley's thirty-ninth birthday, January 8, 1974. Both tunes were recorded in RCA's Nashville studios, the same site where Elvis recorded "It's Now Or Never," "Guitar Man" [see 416] and "A Big Hunk O' Love," among many others.

Kris Kristofferson wrote "Please Don't Tell Me" in a single evening, about a relationship he knew would never last. Bobby Bare was the first to have a hit with it, releasing the single in 1971. His version went to number eight, and was his follow-up to "Come Sundown," another Kristofferson composition that reached the Top Ten.

Milsap had also cut "Please Don't Tell Me" once before while recording with producer Dan Penn, for Warner Bros. Records. RCA was required to obtain a release from Warners to remake it, since five years had not yet elapsed since the first record was made.

"We went in and cut it," recalls producer Tom Collins, "and Ronnie did a little falsetto lick on there, which I felt really made the song shine. It was one of those when the track and everything just felt right. Thankfully, we were given that release, and people were just startin' to take notice of Ronnie."

Milsap recorded the song live with the band, but the single wasn't without its problems. "[Arranger] Bergen White had wrecked his car comin' in that mornin'," Collins recalls. "We did the strings in Studio B, and he was 30 or 40 minutes late. Yet we got all the tracks done with strings and it was a hit."

In fact, it was a very important hit for Ronnie. After debuting on July 20, 1974, at a modest number 84, "Please Don't Tell Me How The Story Ends" soared to number one in its eighth week. On March 1, 1975, the record netted Milsap his first Grammy award, for Best Country Vocal Performance by a Male.

178
I WOULDN'T WANT TO LIVE IF YOU DIDN'T LOVE ME
DON WILLIAMS

Dot 17516
Writer: Al Turney
Producer: Don Williams
September 21, 1974 (1 week)

Don Williams had a two-year history as a country recording artist when he picked up his first number one single with "I Wouldn't Want To Live If You Didn't Love Me."

"It's a great story," says Don's long-time associate, Garth Fundis. "It's one of those stories that a lot of people want to hear, 'cause there's just a shred of hope that somethin' spectacular could happen at any moment."

The moment that made "I Wouldn't Want To Live" so special occurred at a Red Ace service station in Nashville. Don stopped in to put gas in his tank, and, when he went to pay for it, the attendant recognized his name on the credit

Don Williams

card. The "pump boy," a struggling songwriter named Al Turney, asked if Williams could check out a few of his songs. Don replied in the affirmative, and received a tape with four different compositions. He fell in love with one of the songs, and recorded "I Wouldn't Want To Live If You Didn't Love Me" for his third album, naturally titled *Volume III*.

Dot Records released it as Williams' first single under a new recording contract, and when it appeared on the chart, the company took out a congratulatory ad in *Billboard* which read: "Don, we at Dot believe that your first single for our label is the greatest. 'I Wouldn't Want To Live If You Didn't Love Me' will be a giant record. We believe in it, and we believe in you."

The last line is almost prophetic, since "I Believe In You" [see 397] became his biggest career hit five years later. The ad proved prophetic in the short run, too—after debuting at a meager number 90 on July 6, 1974, "I Wouldn't Want To Live" ascended to number one in its twelfth week.

One more single from *Volume III*, a remake of Brook Benton's "The Ties That Bind," hit number four.

Williams, born May 27, 1939, in Floydada, Texas, grew up in Portland, near Corpus Christi. His mother taught him his first five or six chords on guitar, and during his teen years—the formative era for rock and roll—Don would pick out songs after hearing them on the radio. He made his professional debut at age 17.

179

I'M A RAMBLIN' MAN
WAYLON JENNINGS
RCA 10020
Writer: Ray Pennington
Producers: Waylon Jennings,
Ray Pennington
September 28, 1974 (1 week)

"I kind of call that my bubblegum country song," Waylon Jennings says of "I'm A Ramblin' Man." "It's kind of like rock and roll."

Actually, it started out more like "back-porch blues," songwriter Ray Pennington's description of a style patterned after Jimmy Reed. Pennington, who worked for King Records when he wrote the song in the mid-'50s,

built it specifically for a band he was moonlighting with. "When there wasn't sufficient stuff on the radio, I'd just write one," Pennington notes. "In that one, I tried to put in as many big cities as I could think of. I was kind of fond of Virginia, and I was living in Cincinnati, and I knew Chicago was a swinging place, so I got all of them in there."

In 1967, Pennington changed the arrangement, downplaying the blues element, and put out his own recording on Capitol Records, taking it to number 29. "Everytime I'd see him," says Pennington, "Waylon would tell me how much he liked it and that he was gonna record it. That went on for eight years."

"I loved his record of it," Waylon confirms, "and when we got into the studio, he had another song I wanted, 'Oklahoma Sunshine.' That was the one I really wanted, and I said, 'Ray, if you'll let me do that song, I'll do *this* song and let you produce 'em.'"

Waylon recorded "I'm A Ramblin' Man" on February 8, 1974, at RCA's Nashville studios. On the previous album, *This Time* [see 168], he'd stirred up controversy by recording at a different studio, owned by Tompall Glaser, and RCA had refused the masters, suggesting it would cause problems for the company with the electricians' union. Eventually, the label solved the problem and accepted the masters for *This Time*. Most of *The Ramblin' Man* was once again recorded at Glaser Sound.

"I'm A Ramblin' Man," buoyed by Dave Kirby's snappy rhythm guitar, became Jennings' second number one single. It also provided a basis for the first of several disagreements between Waylon and the Country Music Association. On October 14, 1974, Jennings was set to perform on the CMA awards show, where he was nominated for Male Vocalist of the Year. The day of the show, producers told him he'd have to cut his performance of "Ramblin' Man" down to two minutes. Concerned it would damage the song, he walked off the set.

180

I LOVE MY FRIEND
CHARLIE RICH
Epic 20006
Writers: Billy Sherrill, Norro Wilson
Producer: Billy Sherrill
October 5, 1974 (1 week)

Born December 14, 1932, in Colt, Arkansas, Charlie Rich chose his own musical course from a melting pot of influences. His parents, Baptist missionaries, exposed him to white gospel; the radio piped in the sounds of the Grand Ole Opry; and C.J. Allen, a plantation worker on his father's farm, taught him the blues.

An all-state wide receiver in high school, Charlie soon turned from football to music, and after a three-year stint in the military, he took up farming.

He played regularly on weekends at The Sharecropper, a Memphis club that paid out just $10 a night. A friend named Bill Justis (known for a 1957 instrumental hit, "Raunchy") helped him secure a recording deal with Sun. Moving from label to label, Charlie managed only two moderate pop hits prior to his country career: 1960's "Lonely Weekends" and 1965's "Mohair Sam."

Rich might have been part of the problem. His strict religious upbringing created an enormous amount of guilt about earning his living as a musician—especially when he played nightclubs. He had a bout with alcoholism, and feared the trappings of stardom.

"Maybe I really didn't want success all those years," he told Carol Ollen at the height of his popularity. "I probably was avoiding it, and I'll tell you why: because I knew what it would do. I knew it would take me away from my family."

"It's unbelievable," he elaborated to Peter Guralnick in *Lost Highway*. "Everyone connected with the rise of Charlie Rich and 'Behind Closed Doors' [see 128] is having trouble with their personal lives and with their marriage, and I don't except Margaret Ann and myself. You just can't imagine the disruption that it causes in people's lives."

Appropriately, two people with shattered personal lives were the topic of "I Love My Friend." "We wondered when we said 'I love my friend' if we were offering some strange message," says songwriter Norro Wilson. "If it sounded that way, it wasn't meant to. We thought it was very delicate, and if anybody listens to it closely, I think it has a lot of clever stuff to say. It was kind of a left-field thing."

Rich got to first base with the song on August 10, 1974, when it debuted on the *Billboard* country chart at number 89. He brought it home eight weeks later, on October 5, giving him half a dozen number one singles.

On September 10, Charlie's son, Allan Rich, gave his first performance, at a Memphis club called High Cotton.

181

PLEASE DON'T STOP LOVING ME

PORTER WAGONER & DOLLY PARTON

RCA 10010
Writers: Porter Wagoner, Dolly Parton
Producer: Bob Ferguson
October 12, 1974 (1 week)

Among duos that consist of two performers who also work as solo artists, Porter Wagoner & Dolly Parton have reached the *Billboard* country chart more times than any other act. Of their 21 charted singles, 14 established yet another record for duos as Top Ten hits.

The Porter & Dolly association began when Wagoner needed a new face for his syndicated

Dolly Parton & Porter Wagoner

television program, "The Porter Wagoner Show." Norma Jean was the "girl singer" in his act for seven years, but when she chose to pursue a solo career in 1967, Parton had the difficult task of following in her footsteps.

For some time, she was heckled from the audience at concerts, as many called out for Norma Jean. She won over country listeners, though, with her bubbly personality and a series of duets that teamed her with her employer.

The first Wagoner/Parton effort was cut in October of 1967, "The Last Thing On My Mind." It earned a number seven peak position, and they systematically added to the list with such successes as "We'll Get Ahead Someday," "Just Someone I Used To Know" and "If Teardrops Were Pennies." Finally, on October 12, 1974, "Please Don't Stop Loving Me" became their only number one duet.

The event was rather ironic. Parton's solo career was upward bound, and when she made it clear that she intended to leave Porter's show, they fought often in the recording studio. On April 21, 1974, she performed for the last time as a member of the Wagoner show in Salina, Kansas.

Though he earned much more than Parton in their working arrangement, Wagoner had been quite lavish in rewarding her. For example, he gave her a pair of diamond earrings and a custom-made El Dorado for Christmas in 1972. He was hurt by the split, and eventually sued her.

Part of the settlement included the release of a duet album by RCA in 1980, and Porter & Dolly returned to number two with "Making Plans." Eventually, the two smoothed things over. Wagoner appeared on her TV show in 1988; the next year, he shared the stage with her for the season-opening concert at her Dollywood amusement park.

Wagoner had two number one records as a solo performer: 1955's "A Satisfied Mind," and 1962's "Misery Loves Company" [see 392— "Cowboys And Clowns"].

182
I SEE THE WANT TO IN YOUR EYES
CONWAY TWITTY
MCA 40282
Writer: Wayne Carson
Producer: Owen Bradley
October 19, 1974 (2 weeks)

When Wayne Carson earned a number one country single with "I See The Want To In Your Eyes," he was hardly a newcomer to the record business. Through his association with record producer Chips Moman, Carson played on many of the pop sessions that emanated from Memphis in the late '60s, and wrote the Box Tops hits "The Letter," "Neon Rainbows" and "Soul Deep."

Simultaneously, Carson first topped the country chart as a songwriter on Eddy Arnold's 1966 single "Somebody Like Me." With the turn of the decade, Wayne's songs increasingly found greater acceptance in country music. Waylon Jennings went Top 20 with "(Don't Let The Sun Set On You In) Tulsa," Elvis Presley equaled that performance with "Always On My Mind" [see 471] and Johnny Paycheck earned a Top Ten single with "Slide Off Of Your Satin Sheets." Carson's "No Love At All" went Top 20 twice—on the country chart, for Lynn Anderson, and on the pop chart, for B.J. Thomas.

Carson earned perhaps his greatest support, though, from Gary Stewart, who reached number one with Carson's "She's Actin' Single (I'm Drinkin' Doubles)" [see 207]. Stewart's first hit was also a Carson composition, "Drinkin' Thing," a Top Ten record in the summer of 1974. Carson's "I See The Want To In Your Eyes" appeared on the flip side.

"I was talking to some gal somewhere," says Carson of the latter tune. "It was one of those things where you know that it ain't never gonna happen, but you sure do see the want-to, and it's just little thoughts, most of it. Some of it is based on something that I saw or heard, but most of it just comes right out of my little pea brain. I sit around and imagine how somebody would react in a certain situation, how somebody is being treated, or how somebody *should* have been treated."

Conway Twitty heard "The Want To" while driving that summer. "This song just flat blew my hat off," he recalls. "I had to pull over to the side of the road and stop. They mentioned the artist, and I'd never heard of him. When I got back to the office, I called that radio station and quizzed 'em about that particular song. It took them a while to figure out what I was talkin' about, and they said, 'Aw, yeah, yeah, yeah. It's by a boy named Gary Stewart. Nothin's gonna happen with it.'"

Convinced that Stewart's recording would never be a single, Conway took the song into the recording studio. His version secured the top spot for two weeks.

I OVERLOOKED AN ORCHID
MICKEY GILLEY
Playboy 6004
Writers: Carl Story, Shirly Lyn, Carl Smith
Producer: Eddie Kilroy
November 2, 1974 (1 week)

With the success of "Room Full Of Roses" [see 169], Mickey Gilley created the kind of problem that many people only dream about. Between the nightclub he co-owned with manager Sherwood Cryer and a 30-minute local television program sponsored by a furniture store, he hadn't *needed* a hit record.

"I had to make up my mind whether I was going to travel or try to stay and participate in what I had going in the local area," he remembers. "The club was successful, and the TV show was beginning to pay off for us. I knew the record companies weren't going to be interested in a person that's just sitting around down in Houston. Country record sales weren't something a company would flip over backwards for, if you weren't going to help promote it."

Gilley had been trying for years to come up with a hit record. In 1959, he garnered a hit in Houston with his remake of Warner Mack's "Is It Wrong" [see 162], which featured Kenny Rogers as a bass player. In 1964, he found success in Houston once more with "Lonely Wine," and in 1968, his "Now I Can Live Again," on Paula Records, reached number 68 on the *Billboard* country charts.

Mickey had finally given up on a recording career when he cut "Room Full Of Roses." "I had relaxed and I wasn't trying to be a recording artist anymore," he states. "When I didn't *have* to have it anymore, I relaxed, and began to come through—as far as Mickey Gilley and his personality—on the record."

After that first number one, he decided to give the record business one more shot, and Playboy Records encouraged him to find something in a similar vein as "Room Full Of Roses" for a follow-up. The choice was "I Overlooked An Orchid," a song he had sung as a youngster, and the company had to dig up the sheet music because Gilley no longer knew all the words. It had the same "flower" theme as "Roses," and the same Jerry Lee Lewis-style piano. "I Overlooked An Orchid" also had the same peak position, reaching number one on November 2, 1974.

LOVE IS LIKE A BUTTERFLY
DOLLY PARTON
RCA 10031
Writer: Dolly Parton
Producer: Bob Ferguson
November 9, 1974 (1 week)

"I liken myself to a butterfly," says Dolly Parton. "I think they're very colorful, and very gentle. They go about their business, just wanting to add some joy and some beauty to people's lives, and they're basically harmless."

With "Love Is Like A Butterfly," Dolly captured the insect's fluttering, lilting quality almost perfectly—not only with her picturesque lyrics and skipping melody, but also with her gentle vocal rendition. "Ever since I was a little child, I've been fascinated with butterflies," she notes. "I always say I was chasing dreams and butterflies."

As a youngster, Parton would skitter through the fields, following a single monarch or viceroy from bush to bush, and on one occasion, she ended up lost in the woods after dark.

"They tell me that everybody was out looking for me, and everybody was screaming for me," she recalls, "but I didn't know my way home. We had an old milking cow named Bessie, and she had a cowbell on, so I heard Bessie in the woods. She was going home for milking time, 'cause that's just how cows do, and so I followed her to the barn, and that's how I found my way home."

The butterfly became a symbol for Dolly. Just as Porter Wagoner wore rhinestone suits with flashing wagon wheels, Dolly commissioned her own outfits with beaded butterflies, and the American public took to the association wholeheartedly. Many fans sent butterfly replicas through the mail for her collection, and some of her friends referred to her as "Butterfly" as well.

One European fan, Butch Rutter, went so far as to have the *Love Is Like a Butterfly* album artwork tattooed on his back, with Dolly's own personal autograph (she signed just above the picture) tattooed as well. Rutter spent twelve hours having the complex graphics inked into his skin.

Parton also had an oval window custom-designed for her tour bus featuring a stained-glass butterfly. Eventually, Dolly sold the bus to concert promoter C.K. Spurlock. His associate, Mickey Baker, loaned it to Sawyer

Brown [see 620—"Step That Step"] when their bus had a fire. After that group used it, C.K. Spurlock sold the bus to the Forester Sisters.

185

COUNTRY IS
TOM T. HALL
Mercury 73617
Writer: Tom T. Hall
Producer: Jerry Kennedy
November 16, 1974 (1 week)

In its December 7, 1974, issue, *Billboard* ran a story titled "What Is Country Music? Charts Reflect Confusion." The article pointed to a division among country radio programmers about how to deal with the influx of artists from the pop charts, including John Denver, Olivia Newton-John, Gordon Lightfoot and Poco.

Performers had straddled multiple charts for years, but the issue had suddenly become controversial. In reaction, some stations took a hardline stance against records perceived as "non-country" (most continued to program "countrypolitan" sounds). Likewise, 50 Nashville performers formed the Association of Country Entertainers (ACE). The organization's initial, confused attempts to promote country actually alienated several performers, especially Newton-John.

The question of "What is country?" was already being handled at that time, though, by the astute Tom T. Hall, who reached number one during the peak of the controversy with "Country Is."

"It was the fashion to write liner notes," says Hall, explaining the song's origins, "and having this bent toward prose, I used to write liner notes for my albums all the time. I was gonna write a liner note, 'Country Is,' and there again, it turned into a song, like the list I made in 'I Love' [see 151]. I was just trying to define country music, but Kristofferson said it best: 'If it sounds country, it's country.'"

With the single before "Country Is," Tom T., in fact, had tested country's limits with his infectious composition "That Song Is Driving Me Crazy." Hall ended the song with a Dixieland ensemble, hardly a traditional kind of country arrangement. In fact, that experimental twist propelled his song to number two. Tom T. resigned from the Grand Ole Opry at

the time, claiming that he wouldn't be allowed to perform with horns on stage.

As it was, critics could hardly question Hall's status as a country performer. Born May 25, 1936, in poverty-stricken Olive Hill, Kentucky, he used to get up in the wee hours of the morning at age four to hear the Grand Ole Opry on the radio, and he wrote his first song by the age of nine.

Hall dropped out of school at age 15 to work in a garment factory by day and in a bluegrass band by night. Today, he owns two farms near Nashville.

186

TROUBLE IN PARADISE
LORETTA LYNN
MCA 40283
Writer: Kenny O'Dell
Producer: Owen Bradley
November 23, 1974 (1 week)

On March 28, 1974, Loretta Lynn began a three-year reign when the Academy of Country Music named her the Top Female Vocalist. That same month, the Nashville Songwriters Association cited Kenny O'Dell and Kris Kristofferson as Songwriters of the Year. Just three months later, two of those award-winners hooked up when Lynn recorded O'Dell's song, "Trouble In Paradise."

The title itself was hardly a new idea. The Crests, best known for "16 Candles," went to number 20 on *Billboard*'s pop chart with a song called "Trouble In Paradise" in 1960. In 1985, Huey Lewis & The News would resurrect the title with their contribution to the *We Are the World* album. O'Dell's "Trouble In Paradise," however, is the only one to reach the top of any chart.

"I had reservations about using that title, even though I had a different slant on it," notes O'Dell. "I just hate it when people use titles that have already been songs, but, nonetheless, I made myself go ahead and write it, and I wrote it as a country shuffle."

O'Dell took his song to Bill Haynes, who ran Lynn's Coal Miners Music publishing company. Haynes made an appointment for O'Dell to meet with Loretta, and after hearing the song, she agreed to record it, though she gave it a more straightforward arrangement. "They did it in a different little vein," O'Dell assesses. "It was more of a rock mode, it wasn't the country shuffle way that I'd presented it on my demo. Nonetheless, I was real tickled to get a Loretta Lynn cut, 'cause I've always enjoyed her work."

Both enjoyed a number one single as a result, but it wasn't the only list to put Loretta at the top. A Gallup poll cited her as as the best-known and most respected female entertainer in the U.S.

Not one to rest on laurels, she hardly slowed down with that honor. Lynn followed up "Trouble In Paradise" with "The Pill," another of her controversial recordings, centering on contraception. The conservative Grand Ole Opry decided to let her sing it on stage, although some radio stations remained touchy about the subject and kept the record off the airwaves. It still reached number five. Loretta also earned Top Ten status with her 1975 single "Home."

187
BACK HOME AGAIN
JOHN DENVER
RCA 10065
Writer: John Denver
Producer: Milton Okun
November 30, 1974 (1 week)

"My music and my work stem from the conviction that people everywhere are intrinsically the same," says John Denver. "Parents are the same, lovers are the same, families are the same. It's that shared experience to which my music is directed. When I write a song, I want to take the personal experience or observation I have and express it in as universal a way as possible. I absolutely believe there is

John Denver

something in all of us that binds us together."

The commonality of family provided a backdrop for John's first number one country hit, "Back Home Again," the title track from an album released on June 23, 1974. Denver recorded the album in a tension-and-release pattern. He worked in a Los Angeles studio from 10 A.M. to midnight for four consecutive days, took some time off, then returned to the same schedule. *Back Home Again* required a total of only fifteen studio days to complete.

It was his first album to gain total acceptance in country music. Denver actually broke out initially on *Billboard*'s Hot 100 in 1971, with "Take Me Home, Country Roads," which peaked at number two. It went only to number 50 on the country chart.

Neither "Rocky Mountain High" nor "Sunshine On My Shoulders" managed a large degree of country play, but that changed with *Back Home Again*. The first single, "Annie's Song," reached number nine during the summer months, and "Back Home Again" finally propelled him to number one. A third single, "Sweet Surrender," climbed to number seven, and *Back Home Again* also included the studio recording of "Thank God I'm A Country Boy" [see 210]. The following October, the Country Music Association proclaimed "Back Home Again" the Song of the Year.

Denver was a New Year's present for his parents when he was born December 31, 1943, in Roswell, New Mexico. His father was a military man, and the family moved quite frequently during his youth. John learned to play on a 1910 model Gibson guitar, and later abandoned his pursuit of an architectural degree to make music his career.

Denver beat out 250 candidates to take Chad Mitchell's place in the Chad Mitchell Trio for three years, during which time he wrote "Leaving On A Jet Plane." The song became a number one pop record for Peter, Paul & Mary, laying a strong foundation for future success.

188

SHE CALLED ME BABY
CHARLIE RICH
RCA 10062
Writer: Harlan Howard
Producer: Chet Atkins
December 7, 1974 (1 week)

Harlan Howard was a happy man in 1974. Finally, more than a dozen years after he wrote it, "She Called Me Baby" became a hit, and went all the way to number one.

"To show you how music's changed," says Howard, "my songwritin' buddies back then accused me of writing dirty songs. I said, 'Hell, that's just a couple of kids at a drive-in movie on Friday night—I don't see anything dirty about that,' but they did.

"I thought it was intimate. It wasn't nearly as intimate as some of that Kristofferson stuff not too many years later. The thought was a little sexier, but it was just a neat love song."

Maybe "She Called Me Baby" had to wait until the post-Kristofferson era. Ferlin Husky considered recording it in 1961, just after Howard composed it. Harlan cut it that year for Capitol Records, although it met with little success. "I blew the whole album 'cause I was nervous," Howard admits. "I was so intimidated by all these great musicians, like Grady Martin and Floyd Cramer and all these guys. They were just starin' at me like I come out of the woodwork or somethin'—at least I thought they were. They all later became friends of mine, but I was totally intimidated."

"She Called Me Baby" gained several more chances. A slew of artists recorded it, including Patsy Cline, Dick Curless, Carl Smith and Mickey Gilley [see 169—"Room Full Of Roses"], among many others. Charlie Rich's previously-unreleased RCA version emerged in 1974, about ten years after he cut it with Chet Atkins.

After the record went to number one, Rich slowed down on his touring the following year. He introduced three more Top Five singles— "My Elusive Dreams," "Every Time You Touch Me (I Get High)" and "All Over Me." In addition, he produced a pair of hits for David Wills, "There's A Song On The Jukebox" and "From Barrooms To Bedrooms."

Rich met tragedy, however, in October of 1975. His wife of twenty-four years, Margaret Ann, left him and filed for divorce, although they patched things up by November. On the Country Music Association awards show, October 13, Charlie, apparently drunk, flicked his Bic and torched the winning certificate when John Denver was named Entertainer of the Year. He apologized to his fans several days later in a letter to his fan club. His explanation: doctors had given him medication for a misdiagnosed insect bite. It turned out to be a fractured foot. Ironically, Rich cast his own vote for Entertainer for Denver.

189

I CAN HELP

BILLY SWAN

Monument 8621
Writer: Billy Swan
Producers: Chip Young, Billy Swan
December 14, 1974 (2 weeks)

"I Can Help" was a marvelous "groove" record, powered by a cascading guitar riff, a singable melody and a prominent organ passage. In fact, it was the keyboard part that launched the entire composition for Billy Swan, after Kris Kristofferson and then-wife Rita Coolidge presented him with a portable RMI organ for a wedding present. Swan had tied the knot with a woman who lived in his apartment building named Marlu.

Born May 12, 1943, in Cape Girardeau, Missouri, Swan was mesmerized first by the country music of Hank Williams and Lefty Frizzell, later coming under the influence of rockabilly stars like Jerry Lee Lewis and Buddy Holly. At the age of 16, he wrote his first song, "Lover Please," which became a Top Ten pop hit in 1962 for ex-Drifter Clyde McPhatter.

Swan boarded with Elvis Presley's uncle, Travis Smith, in Memphis for several years, but he later moved to Nashville, where he picked up work as an assistant at Columbia Studio B. He quit that job while Bob Dylan was in the process of recording the *Blonde on Blonde* album, and Columbia replaced him with Kristofferson.

Billy later picked up work at Combine Music Publishing, where he and Kristofferson actually worked together for the first time. He was responsible for helping the firm's songwriters make demo recordings, and among the songs he worked on was Kristofferson's "Me And Bobby McGee." In 1970, Kristofferson formed his own group, and hired Swan as the bass player for the band. "I was, and am, a terrible bass player," Billy later admitted to Judy Raphael in *Country Song Roundup*. As a result, he switched over to rhythm guitar and vocals.

Swan finally became a frontman in his own right with the release of "I Can Help," and he left Kristofferson briefly to form his own touring band. He likewise went to work behind Billy Joe Shaver and Kinky Friedman, but returned ultimately to Kristofferson's crew. "I'd have to have a lot of hit records before I'd want to get out of Kris' band and on my own," he

Billy Swan

noted. "I really enjoy being a back-up singer and musician."

Swan has continued to record sporadically, although nothing has approached "I Can Help," which earned certification for selling a million copies on December 2, 1974, and which has reportedly sold more than five million copies worldwide.

190

WHAT A MAN, MY MAN IS

LYNN ANDERSON

Columbia 10041
Writer: Glenn Sutton
Producer: Glenn Sutton
December 28, 1974 (1 week)

"What A Man, My Man Is" carried a familiar theme for Lynn Anderson, since "You're My Man" [see 78] also celebrated a successful marital relationship.

"That's the same thing," she acknowledges. "It's [husband] Glenn [Sutton] writing a song for me to sing about Glenn. It sounds kind of egotistical when you put it that way, but I felt that way about him, and I didn't mind singing a song that was singing his praises."

Though it might have summed up their relationship at the time, Sutton says he had other thoughts in mind when he first composed "What A Man." "I wrote it for the Lennon Sisters. In fact, I flew to Vegas, and met with them, and had an arrangement written for it and everything. Then, their whole deal with Atlantic Records fell through, so I used the thing on Lynn."

It became her last number one single, following on the heels of three Top Ten records released during 1973-74. After "What A Man" peaked at the end of the year, Anderson had to wait until 1979 to see the Top Ten again, with the release of "Isn't It Always Love."

In the meantime, her personal life took precedence over her career. She divorced Sutton in 1977, and married oilman Harold "Spook" Stream the following year. She briefly retired to look after her children (one by Sutton, two from Stream), but divorced Stream in 1981.

Finally, in 1983, she returned to the business once again with her album *Back*, on Permian Records. "It's a big challenge to try and work at this business again, with everybody knowing what you could do and what your faults are," she says of her comeback. "The number one problem was credibility. There's a lot of time and expense that goes into making somebody a 'star,' and having the company put all that effort into me, just to have me walk away from it, they were understandably shy about putting all their guns behind me again."

Anderson did net a Top Ten single in 1984 in a duet with Gary Morris, "You're Welcome To Tonight," but Permian folded and MCA ended up with Anderson's contract. She eventually split with that label and moved to Mercury Records in 1987.

191

THE DOOR
GEORGE JONES
Epic 50038
Writers: Billy Sherrill, Norro Wilson
Producer: Billy Sherrill
January 4, 1975 (1 week)

"If you're gonna sing a sad song, or ballad, you've got to have lived it yourself," George Jones said in a 1984 tour program. "You can think back to anything that made you sad—anything. Maybe your little dog died, and you think about that while you're singing, and pretty soon, it makes you sad. You become lost in the song, and before long, you're just like the people in the song."

"The Door" provided Jones with a plethora of sadness—images of bombs exploding, earthquakes, and mothers crying, and, of course, the sound of the door closing as a loved one walks away.

"I love that song," says songwriter Norro Wilson. "That's a hokey one. We went out and rented a damned door and slammed it [to create the sound effect]. The song idea is good, but you just kind of get a chuckle out of some of those things."

Actually, Wilson and producer Billy Sherrill went to a great deal of trouble for their chuckle. They couldn't mike a full door properly, and they rented a miniature door to provide the actual sound effect. "I remember 'and the slamming of the door'—boom—and we all laughed," Wilson recalls. "If people laughed at some of the things we've written, well, great, 'cause we laughed, too."

Actually, "The Door" brought more tears than laughter, and its timing was rather ironic. It entered the *Billboard* country chart on October 26, 1974, and cracked the Top Ten the same week that Jones left Tammy Wynette [see 274—"Near You"]. It reached number one on January 4, 1975, four days before she filed for divorce.

The remainder of the decade was a painful period for Jones. He followed "The Door" with "These Days (I Barely Get By)," a Top Ten single that Tammy had written specifically for him. In 1976, George reached number three with "Her Name Is . . .," a novelty recording that most listeners associated with his ex-wife. In 1978, he went to number six with James Taylor's "Bartender Blues."

George filed for bankruptcy that same year, and was also charged for assault with intent to murder after shooting at his best friend, Earl "Peanut" Montgomery. A manager reportedly forged his signature on a number of documents, Jones consistently failed to appear at many of his scheduled concerts, and his weight dropped to below 100 pounds. With rumors of alcohol and cocaine abuse swirling around him, Jones voluntarily checked into an Alabama rehabilitation center in 1979.

192
RUBY, BABY
BILLY "CRASH" CRADDOCK
ABC 12036
Writers: Jerry Leiber, Mike Stoller
Producer: Ron Chancey
January 11, 1975 (1 week)

Born June 16, 1939, Billy "Crash" Craddock grew up with country music in Greensboro, North Carolina. Craddock would head to the barn and use a broomstick as a prop, putting on his own Grand Ole Opry shows while imitating Hank Williams, Faron Young and Carl Smith.

By the time he was ten, he and his brothers were playing country music at talent shows, but once Columbia got hold of him and tried to mold him into a pop star [see 173—"Rub It In"], Billy earned a reputation as a rocker. "I don't think people know how much I love hard country music," he says. "If it's a good hard country song, I'd rather hear that than any other kind of song."

Adding to the confusion, Craddock first made waves in country music by remaking pop hits. His first single, a cover of Dawn's "Knock Three Times," appeared in 1971. "I hadn't heard it," he notes, "and some people mentioned it to me, so I went out and bought it. I listened to it and thought we'd put some Cajun fiddles on it and have a good country record." Other hits followed, including "Dream Lover," "You Better Move On," "Ain't Nothin' Shakin'," "I'm Gonna Knock On Your Door," "'Til The Water Stops Runnin'," "Sweet Magnolia Blossom" and, finally, "Rub It In."

To follow "Rub It In," Craddock once again returned to a remake of a pop number—Dion's 1963 hit "Ruby, Baby."

"My brother Ronald and I used to ride around in a car with some friends," recalls Craddock, "and we'd have a guitar. We'd go to these drive-ins and get us a Coke and a hot dog, and we'd start singing that song, and the people in the cars heard us doing it. We'd get through, then they'd start applauding. I got to thinking that if they liked the song that well back then, maybe if we recorded "Ruby, Baby," it could be a hit all over again."

Thanks to the remakes and his propensity for uptempo material, Craddock was dubbed "Mr. Country Rock," and he hit the Top Ten three more times during 1975, with "Still Thinkin' 'Bout You," "I Love The Blues And The Boogie Woogie" and "Easy As Pie."

193
KENTUCKY GAMBLER
MERLE HAGGARD & THE STRANGERS
Capitol 3974
Writer: Dolly Parton
Producers: Ken Nelson, Fuzzy Owen
January 18, 1975 (1 week)

On December 21, 1974, Dolly Parton placed three different songs on the *Billboard* country chart as a writer: Porter Wagoner's "Carolina Moonshine," her own "Love Is Like A Butterfly" [see 184] and Merle Haggard's recording of "Kentucky Gambler." When "Gambler" topped the chart a month later, it became her only number one single as a writer on someone else's record.

Other Parton songs that have found success with different artists include "To Daddy," by Emmylou Harris; "Put It Off Until Tomorrow," by the Kendalls; "Two Doors Down" [see 309—"It's All Wrong, But It's Alright"], by Zella Lehr; and "Waltz Me To Heaven," by Waylon Jennings.

" 'Kentucky Gambler' is a song I wrote based on the story of my Grandpa Parton," Dolly explains. "They tell me that in my Grandpa's younger days, he was quite a gambler. They say he used to go away from home a lot, and he used to lose what little money that he had accumulated."

On more than one occasion, Haggard himself has lost over $100,000 in a single evening playing blackjack in Nevada casinos. "I went through a period where I really thought that I was a professional gambler," he notes. "I had a tremendous streak of luck that lasted about three years, and I had a little gambling account that nobody knew about. I had about $300,000 in that account, and 'Kentucky Gambler' came right about the time that I lost the $300,000 plus probably another $300,000. Dolly happened to have correctly described the era that I was going through."

Merle first met Dolly when he performed in her hometown during the early '60s; she was on the bill as local talent. "Gambler" pre-dated their most extensive collaborations, as Dolly and her Travellin' Family Band shared the bill with Haggard on a series of dates during 1974–75.

"I didn't write 'Kentucky Gambler' for Merle," she says, "and I wasn't on the road with Merle when I wrote the song. I guess I was on the road with him by the time he recorded it, but it was just a song that I thought was good, and I pitched it to Merle because I've always loved his singing and his songwriting."

Haggard hoped that Dolly loved more than that, and he wrote his next single [see 204—"Always Wanting You"] for her.

194

(I'D BE) A LEGEND IN MY TIME
RONNIE MILSAP
RCA 10112
Writer: Don Gibson
Producers: Tom Collins, Jack D. Johnson
January 25, 1975 (1 week)

When the Country Music Association presented its annual awards in 1972, Ronnie Milsap kept track in his Memphis living room via television. The following year, he sat in the audience, and when the envelopes were opened on October 15, 1974, he picked up the trophy as Male Vocalist of the Year. That November, he returned to the recording studio to work on his next album. The first single and title track, "(I'd Be) A Legend In My Time," coincidentally used awards, trophies and fame to weave a tale of heartache.

Don Gibson wrote the song in 1960 while traveling with fellow Acuff-Rose songwriter Mel Foree to Knoxville. Gibson was thumbing through the pages of a magazine when he hit upon an article about an entertainer who wanted to be a legend in his own time. The song was recorded dozens of times over the ensuing years; Gibson, in fact, included it on his 1974 release *Country Green*.

Milsap had always had a fondness for Gibson, since they came from the same area. Gibson made frequent radio appearances in the mid-'50s on "The Mid-Day Merry-Go-Round" over Knoxville's WNOX. Milsap heard the broadcasts in his Smoky Mountain home, and continued to follow Gibson's career after he began having hits with "Oh, Lonesome Me" [see 108—"I Can't Stop Loving You"] in 1958.

"My wife and I both had thought that at some point on one of the sessions I'd record 'Legend In My Time,'" Ronnie says, "but it was originally done as a waltz. I took it out of 3/4 and moved it to 4/4, just to bring some kind of a change to the song." Milsap applied an even more dramatic alteration when manager Jack D. Johnson suggested he adapt an ar-

rangement he had been using in his live shows on a Glen Campbell tune titled "Houston." Ronnie jumped an octave to a "fourth-octave A-flat or A" at the end of the song.

On November 30, "Legend" debuted on the *Billboard* country chart, eventually reaching number one two months later. Ronnie followed up with "Too Late To Worry, Too Blue To Cry," a song he recorded at the same session; it peaked at number six.

On October 13, 1975, the CMA honored Milsap once more. *A Legend in My Time* picked up the trophy for Album of the Year.

195

CITY LIGHTS
MICKEY GILLEY
Playboy 6015
Writer: Bill Anderson
Producer: Eddie Kilroy
February 1, 1975 (1 week)

Like "Room Full Of Roses" [see 169], "City Lights" had already been to the Top Five before Mickey Gilley brought it to the top in 1975. In fact, Ray Price's original version went to number one on October 20, 1958, and stayed there for thirteen consecutive weeks before Jim Reeves' recording of "Billy Bayou" unseated it.

Price's recording broke open the career of a young Bill Anderson, who was still living in a three-story hotel in Commerce, Georgia, when he wrote the song in 1957.

"Often on hot summer nights, I would leave my room and take my guitar up to the roof of the hotel where it was cooler," Anderson recalls. "I'd sit up there and sing my songs out into the night.

"On this particular night, there must have been a million stars in the sky, and as I looked up at the stars and down upon the lights of the town, I began comparing in my mind the difference between the God-made stars and the man-made lights. I actually began writing the song with what turned out to be the second verse, the part about God making the stars and questioning whether or not He also made the 'City Lights.'

"My dad told me after I'd finished the song that he knew from that moment on, that I had the imagination it took to be a great songwriter if I could look down on Commerce, Georgia, and picture a 'great white way.' About all Commerce had was a couple of traffic lights, and even they didn't work half the time!"

Nearly two decades later, Gilley patterned his initial version of "City Lights" after the "pumping piano" in Jerry Lee Lewis' "Crazy Arms." Gilley was uncomfortable with the first recording of "City Lights," though, which was paced a little quicker than he desired.

"I went back to the hotel, and I kept thinking about that song," he notes. "I knew it was a hit song, but I didn't think it was recorded properly to be a number one record, or even a Top Ten record. So the next morning I walked back in the studio and told Eddie Kilroy that if we did it the same as Jerry Lee did 'Another Place, Another Time,' I thought we'd have a much better recording."

That slight alteration produced Gilley's third consecutive number one release.

Mickey Gilley

196
THEN WHO AM I
CHARLEY PRIDE
RCA 10126
Writers: A.L. "Doodle" Owens,
Dallas Frazier
Producer: Jerry Bradley
February 8, 1975 (1 week)

One of the most successful songwriting teams in Nashville during the '70s was A.L. "Doodle" Owens and Dallas Frazier. Owens, who earned his nickname during his youth from a family friend who called him "Doodlebug," is a former sign painter who took up writing in 1964.

Frazier wrote the number one pop record "Alley Oop," and moved on to a formidable country career in 1963, resulting in such classics as "There Goes My Everything" [see 6—"You Are My Treasure"], "Elvira" [see 427] and "Fourteen Carat Mind" [see 454]. Frazier eventually gave up the record industry to pursue the ministry, but he left behind a trail of Frazier & Owens compositions that includes four number one singles for Charley Pride. The last was "Then Who Am I."

"Dallas had been working on that idea for a long time," reports Owens. "He had it in the back of his mind, and one night we went up to the cabin on the hill to write a song. Dallas, it was like he wrote that first verse in just a minute. He's still one of the greatest writers that ever lived—if he had something to write,

he knew what to do with it."

"Then Who Am I" was the first number one record produced by Jerry Bradley. Bradley had produced a few singles for Nat Stuckey, as well as Johnny Russell's "Red Necks, White Socks And Blue Ribbon Beer," and had stepped in as Pride's producer when Jack Clement parted ways with Charley.

"I was running RCA, and Charley, [manager] Jack Johnson and I went to dinner at Mario's," remembers Bradley. "I was there in the capacity of the man that ran the company, and Charley and Jack felt like Jack Clement and Charley—this is my interpretation of what happened—they were ready for a change. Unfortunately, I delivered the news to Clement."

Bradley was picked as a successor, and as the transition was made, two of Pride's singles—"We Could" and "Mississippi Cotton Pickin' Delta Town"—peaked at number three on the *Billboard* country chart. Following Charley's one-year absence from the top, "Then Who Am I" returned him to number one on February 8, 1975.

197
DEVIL IN THE BOTTLE
T.G. SHEPPARD
Melodyland 6002
Writer: Bobby David
Producers: Jack Gilmer, Bill Browder,
Ray Ruff
February 15, 1975 (1 week)

"I was a promotion man at that time in Memphis," says T.G. Sheppard, thinking back to 1974, "and I'd pretty much given up on being an artist. It goes to show you that when you least expect it, that's when things come toward you."

The good fortune that came across Sheppard's path was a recitation about a married man who pays more attention to liquor than to his wife. A Nashville publishing representative named Dan Hoffman brought "Devil In The Bottle" to Sheppard's office. Many other executives had heard the song and turned it down, yet Sheppard was an immediate believer. His company, Umbrella Promotions, was also affiliated with a publishing firm, and it was there that "Devil"—and Sheppard's career as an artist—began to take shape.

"I held onto the song for many, many months," he notes. "Late one night, I was demoing some songs for the publishing company, and I had time for one more song, and I didn't have one. I ran upstairs and started searching for that tape, and strange enough, it was sitting right on my desk. I opened it up, put the reel on, we did a great demo with it, and it turned out so well. I had spent my own money on it, and every major record company turned it down."

Sheppard pitched the record to nearly every label in town, receiving 13 "thumbs down" responses, including one from Atlantic Records. As it turned out, Berry Gordy's Motown label had formed a country branch, and that company's headquarters was in the same Nashville office as Atlantic.

"They heard it through the wall," says Sheppard. "Atlantic turned it down, and as I was leaving, someone from Melodyland grabbed me and said, 'Wait a minute; that's a hit.'"

Janie Frickie sang back-up on the record, which includes one vocal flaw (Sheppard pronounced "escaping" as "excaping"). Eleven weeks after it first hit the country chart, "Devil In The Bottle" reached number one on February 15, 1975. Ironically, the same day that that issue of *Billboard* arrived in his mailbox, T.G. also received a rejection letter from another record company, which said the material wasn't "commercial enough."

198
I CARE/SNEAKY SNAKE
TOM T. HALL
Mercury 73641
Writer: Tom T. Hall
Producer: Jerry Kennedy
February 22, 1975 (1 week)

Today, Tom T. Hall wishes that he had released "I Care" and "Sneaky Snake" as separate singles, but in late 1974, the two were paired on the only single from a children's album.

"The people out of Chicago at Mercury Records thought I was crazy," Hall remembers. "'This guy's famous for a lot of stuff, but not singin' kids' songs,' you know. Infamous might be a better word."

Hall wrote both songs. "I Care" mirrored "I Love" [see 151] in some respects, both in its simplicity and its "list" approach. "Sneaky Snake" was a novelty record, built with a child's imagination. "I had my two little nephews on the farm at the time," Hall notes. "They'd do things with me, and we'd fish, and there was an old boat there, and I turned it over, and an old water snake ran out. So we fabricated this whole fantasy around 'Sneaky Snake.'"

It's been suggested that the record has a sexual secondary meaning, a notion that Hall refutes.

"When it hit the airwaves, there must have been 300 truck drivers whose handle on the CB was 'Sneaky Snake.' It meant something to a lot of people that the song had nothing to do with. I guess it was 'huggin' and kissin' and sneakin' around and dancin' and stealin' beer.'"

The sexual interpretation is especially ironic in light of Hall's goal with the children's album. He felt that kids who listened to country music probably didn't relate too much to songs about cheatin' or drinkin' or drivin' trucks. "We tried to put together a great little collection of songs that you could give kids for Christmas," explains producer Jerry Kennedy.

Kennedy deserves partial credit for Tom T.'s success—as the man who signed him to Mercury in 1967. Growing up in Shreveport, Jerry won a Bob Wills talent contest at age ten, and played on the "Louisiana Hayride" during his teens. He went on the road with Johnny Horton, but moved to Nashville in 1961, where he played guitar on such hits as "Harper Valley P.T.A." [see 17] and "Rose Garden" [see 69].

Kennedy headed Mercury's Nashville division for more than a decade, producing nearly 30 number one records.

199
IT'S TIME TO PAY THE FIDDLER
CAL SMITH
MCA 40335
Writers: Don Wayne, Walter Haynes
Producer: Walter Haynes
March 1, 1975 (1 week)

"Cal [Smith] really seems to have the voice and register for my songs," songwriter Don Wayne told Christopher Cabot of the *Asheville Times* in October of 1974. That comment proved to be an understatement a scant six months later.

Wayne and Smith combined their respective skills on the number one single "Country Bumpkin" [see 163], but Smith's follow-up, "Between Lust And Watching TV," managed to reach only number 11. Cal turned to Wayne's material again, though, when he recorded "It's Time To Pay The Fiddler," which became his third and final number one single in 1975.

Born in Gans, Oklahoma, on April 7, 1932, Smith moved with his family to Oakland when he was eleven. He dropped out of school in the ninth grade to ride broncos with the rodeo, but he found himself as the assistant for Tom Mason, a sideshow performer who threw knives at him and used a bullwhip to flick cigarettes from the youngster's lips. Eventually, Cal pursued a safer line of work as a disk jockey at KEEN in San Jose, where he also performed at the Remember Me Cafe—for $1.50 a night plus all he could eat.

His idol was Ernest Tubb, and on December 26, 1962, Smith became a member of Tubb's Texas Troubadours, staying with the band until July 9, 1968. Tubb, in fact, was the first to greet his former protegé backstage at the CMA awards in 1974 when Smith claimed honors for "Country Bumpkin."

"I remember riding down the road in the bus with Ernest one time," Cal once told Tom Carter of the *Tulsa Daily World*. "Nobody was talking, and all of a sudden, Ernest turns in his

Cal Smith

seat and says, 'Smith, your singing don't show me a thing.' I thought he was going to fire me, but he told me I sang too mechanical and told me to start singing one word at a time, with feeling. It was his constructive criticism. And Ernest was right. Look what happened—I never would have been anything without Ernest Tubb."

"It's Time To Pay The Fiddler" was Smith's last Top Ten single, although he came close on several more occasions. "She Talked A Lot About Texas" reached number 13 in 1975, while "Jason's Farm" followed it to number 12. Two years later, "I Just Came Home To Count The Memories" took him to number 15.

Lynn Anderson single in 1967. Twitty eventually won the court battle, but it took four years of litigation.

200

LINDA ON MY MIND

CONWAY TWITTY

MCA 40339
Writer: Conway Twitty
Producer: Owen Bradley
March 8, 1975 (1 week)

" 'Linda On My Mind' was a gigantic record for me," says Conway Twitty, "and you can't imagine how many times I've been asked, 'Conway, who's Linda?' That'll forever remain part of the mystique. That's what helps make it a hit."

No matter who Linda was—if she even existed at all—she helped to create the second of Conway's controversial hits [see 142—"You've Never Been This Far Before"]. The protagonist in the song sleeps with one woman while dreaming of another, and some listeners apparently took offense.

"I don't understand the reaction to this song," Twitty told Bill Morrison of the *Raleigh News & Observer*. "It never comes right out and says anything. The guy's in bed with his wife and thinking of another woman. We all write about situations like that. There are tons of songs like that. You can't take [sex] out of country music—if you did, it wouldn't be country music. But you can tell the story without being vulgar, and I don't think I was vulgar."

But the song was confusing, according to producer Owen Bradley. "There was a line in there that always drove me crazy," Bradley explains, "and I couldn't get Conway to change it. It was confusing as hell to me, but it wasn't to Conway. I said, 'You could make that so much better,' but he wouldn't touch it. And I guess he was right; that record did all right."

The line in question was "next to me, my soon-to-be, the one I left behind." "Owen's really easy-goin'," adds Conway, "so he didn't put up too much of a fuss, but for him to say anything was a lot. Even years later, he said 'I still don't understand it.'"

Twitty wrote "Linda" on his tour bus, en route to a show in California. Once recorded, it kicked off the New Year for Conway as the highest-debuting single on *Billboard*'s January 11, 1975, chart. It peaked at number one in its ninth week of release.

Two years later, songwriter Gene Hood filed suit against Conway, claiming that parts of "Linda On My Mind" were borrowed from his composition "Too Much Of You," a minor

201

BEFORE THE NEXT TEARDROP FALLS

FREDDY FENDER

Dot 17540
Writer: Vivian Keith, Ben Peters
Producer: Huey P. Meaux
March 15, 1975 (2 weeks)

During the latter part of the '60s, Ben Peters worked as a professional manager for Fingerlake Music Publishing in Nashville, and, at the time, he shuffled his paperwork through a secretary named Vivian Keith. In addition to doing office work, Peters was writing songs for the company (including a number one Eddy Arnold record, "Turn The World Around" [see 18]), and one evening Keith suggested he do something around the title "Before The Next Tear Falls."

"I said 'okay,'" Peters recalls, "and I went home that night and wrote most of what I call 'Before The Next Tear*drop* Falls.' I finished it up the next day."

Before Freddy Fender got hold of it, "Teardrop" had already earned a rather long history. Duane Dee cut it for Capitol Records in 1967, but he was drafted for military service while it was in release, and the record peaked on *Billboard*'s country chart at number 44. A total of 32 people eventually recorded the song before Fender came up with the definitive version.

Ironically, Fender didn't want to cut the song at all. A relative unknown, he was recording a rhythm and blues album in September of 1974 when producer Huey Meaux approached him with the instrumental tracks to "Teardrop" already recorded. All Fender had to do was supply the vocals.

Freddy was admittedly opposed to anything country, but he obliged Meaux just to get it out of the way. "That's what motivated me," he says. "I said, 'Well, as soon as I get through with this, I can get back to some *real* music.' In 20 minutes I put the voice on there, and that song is still selling."

It first appeared on *Billboard*'s country chart on January 11, 1975, at number 96—the worst debut ever for a number one record. Eleven weeks after hitting the top of the country charts, the record also reached number one on the Hot 100 on May 31, 1975. In between, it was certified gold by the Recording Industry Association of America for sales of a million copies on May 22.

"I was surprised," Fender says of the record's success, "but I didn't have much time to enjoy it, because as soon as that happened, I started getting bookings every day for the next three years."

202

THE BARGAIN STORE
DOLLY PARTON
RCA 10164
Writer: Dolly Parton
Producer: Bob Ferguson
March 29, 1975 (1 week)

" 'The Bargain Store' has always been one of my favorite songs that I've ever written," says Dolly Parton, adding it to a list that includes "Coat Of Many Colors" and "I Will Always Love You" [see 166]. "Every songwriter has his favorites. I have some that I can't stand, and I have some that I love to sing, and some that never grow old to me. I just thought 'Bargain Store' was a great idea for a song.

"Of course, we've all felt that we've been used at times, but also knowing all the time that there's still more love where that came from, and I just thought it was a good idea."

"The Bargain Store" became Dolly's fifth number one record as a solo artist, her fourth in a row. Still, several radio stations refused to play it, citing a questionable lyric.

"When I said the bargain store is open, come inside, I just meant my life is open, come into my life," she told Chet Flippo in *Rolling Stone*, "so I wasn't even thinkin' of it as a dirty thing. I just felt at that time I had been probably kicked around some . . . me and Porter [Wagoner], we just kind of said things, hurt each other's feelings and, you know, trampled around on territory that was real sensitive, cut each other about songs. I felt black and blue, and I just wanted to heal back up and mend myself back together and get on with my life."

Dolly's life was ready for some very major changes. Three more singles went Top Ten in the next two years: "The Seeker," "We Used To" and "All I Can Do." She hosted her own syndicated TV show, "Dolly," which lasted only 52 episodes.

And within a month after winning the Country Music Association's Female Vocalist of the Year award, she ruffled Nashville feathers with her announced intention to seek new management in Los Angeles.

"Dolly knew exactly what she wanted to be," says Jerry Bradley, then head of RCA's country division. "She sat right on my couch one day and said, 'When you son-of-a-bitches learn how to sell a female Elton John with long hair and big boobs that dresses like a freak, then we'll make some money.' "

203

I JUST CAN'T GET HER OUT OF MY MIND
JOHNNY RODRIGUEZ
Mercury 73659
Writer: Larry Gatlin
Producer: Jerry Kennedy
April 5, 1975 (1 week)

Larry Gatlin earned a reputation in his early Nashville days as one of the city's best songwriters, and even though he signed a recording deal with Monument Records in 1973, other vocalists at first fared better with his material. In late 1974, Gatlin reached number 14 with "Delta Dirt," but in the meantime, Elvis Presley took his gospel song "Help Me" all the way to number six. Johnny Rodriguez was the second performer to earn a Gatlin hit, when he cut "I Just Can't Get Her Out Of My Mind," and it became the first Gatlin song to reach number one.

"I was in Terre Haute, Indiana," says Gatlin of the tune's genesis. "I used to tell a little story about how there's not a heck of a lot to do in Terre Haute. They've got a World War II fighter plane sitting out there at the courthouse, and that's about it. The folks in Terre Haute got a little hot about that. It's a nice town.

"The CBS pressing plant was in Terre Haute, and I went up there a couple times to sing at the CBS Christmas party. One night after I went back to the Holiday Inn, the bar was closed—everything was just kind of closed down. I went to my room and wrote this song, and the next day, I sang it for Tex Davis, who was the national promotion man at that time for Monument Records. He said, 'Man, that sounds like a hit.' It seems like I had just finished an album and wasn't going to record for a while. Rodriguez was really hot at the time, and I had just met him, so I gave it to him."

Rodriguez was knocked out by the song, but he was also entranced by Gatlin's voice. "When I first heard that thing, I was talking to my producer, Jerry Kennedy, and I said, 'What's this guy doing singing the demo? He ought to be recording.'"

One year later, Gatlin's "Broken Lady" became his first Top Five single [see 303—"I Just Wish You Were Someone I Love"]. He didn't stop pitching material to Rodriguez, though; in 1977, they hooked up again when Gatlin wrote another Top Five single for Johnny, "If Practice Makes Perfect."

Johnny Rodriguez

204
ALWAYS WANTING YOU
MERLE HAGGARD & THE STRANGERS
Capitol 4027
Writer: Merle Haggard
Producer: Fuzzy Owen
April 12, 1975 (2 weeks)

Merle Haggard fell head over heels for Dolly Parton. The two were paired together on several concert tours during 1974-75 [see 193—"Kentucky Gambler"], and during that time, they spent large blocks of time together. Traveling from show to show, she would ride on his bus, or he would ride on hers, and they talked a great deal about music and their personal goals.

Haggard expressed his desires for a more intimate relationship on several occasions, but Dolly insisted throughout that it could never work, that she still in fact loved her husband, Carl Dean. His desires persisted.

"I couldn't get her off my mind," he wrote in *Sing Me Back Home: My Own Story*. "I'd see her when I walked out on stage, when I lay down at night, and when I woke up in the morning. I'd try to blot her out of my mind with all the well-known blotters. Nothing worked."

He did get a song out of it, though. Merle wrote "Always Wanting You" specifically for the object of his desire. Proud of his accomplishment, and hoping that it could possibly sway her, he phoned Dolly from Reno to wake her at 3:00 A.M. and play the song for her. Once again, she explained her inability to get involved, and eventually, after she heard the song, he allowed her to drift back to sleep.

The episode became a matter of public record after its inclusion in Merle's book, and Parton handled it with her usual grace. "It didn't really embarrass me," she says, "because I actually was more flattered than anything. I would have probably been embarrassed had there been a major romance between us, and had there been scandal or something, but he didn't claim that we had a love affair. He just said that he loved me, so why wouldn't I be flattered? I loved him, too. I think Merle is very special, and I thought that it was very bold and sweet of him to say that he cared that much."

Though written for Dolly, "Always Wanting You" was the first and only number one single to feature Louise Mandrell. She toured with

Haggard's band for six months, and when he recorded at Jack Clement Studios in Nashville, she joined Ronnie Reno as a supporting vocalist.

205
BLANKET ON THE GROUND
BILLIE JO SPEARS
United Artists 584
Writer: Roger Bowling
Producer: Larry Butler
April 26, 1975 (1 week)

Billie Jo Spears was set to begin work on a new album in 1975, and the day before the first session, producer Larry Butler was still looking for a few more tunes. Roger Bowling was in Butler's office, and had already played several songs when his producer, Paul Richey, suggested he pitch "Blanket On The Ground." The song had been around Nashville for about three years, but invariably producers turned it down because of a line in the chorus about married people "slippin' around."

Bowling expected the same reaction this time, but when he picked up a guitar and played the song, Butler said: "We'll take it."

"Blanket On The Ground" was one of 19 songs that Spears was to learn inside and out prior to the session, but it was the only one that she didn't bother to work on. "I thought it might be a little controversial," she confesses, "and I didn't think Larry would cut it." Instead, out of the 19, Butler decided that "Blanket" would be the first, and, despite Billie Jo's unfamiliarity with the tune, they nailed it on the second take.

As it turned out, the controversy never materialized. Actually, the line in question wasn't about slipping around with an outside lover, but about marital partners slipping around with each other. "Once we began to do it in the studio," she says, "I began to realize that it wasn't really controversial, and I thought, 'Well, how great; what a clever idea.'"

Spears was born January 14, 1938, in Beaumont, Texas. She earned her first record deal after a performance at Yvonne's Night Club, when a talent scout named John Rhodes persuaded her to move to Nashville. Billie Jo signed with United Artists Records, who were convinced that they had "the female George Jones."

Spears then moved to Capitol, where she scored her first hit with "Mr. Walker, It's All Over" (number four, 1969). Butler re-signed her with U.A. in 1974, where she remained until 1981, scoring three more Top Ten records: "What I've Got In Mind," "Misty Blue" and "If You Want Me."

206
ROLL ON BIG MAMA
JOE STAMPLEY
Epic 50075
Writer: Danny Darst
Producer: Norro Wilson
May 3, 1975 (1 week)

Joe Stampley got a fresh start in 1975 in more ways than one. After releasing six Top Ten singles from 1972 to 1975 for ABC/Dot, he signed with Epic Records, and he started out the new association in dramatic fashion with his second number one record.

By the same token, the single had a surprising start, fueled by the sound of an actual semi. "Roll On Big Mama" was written by Danny Darst, who submitted a demo that has been favorably compared to some of the old Hank Snow truckin' records. The demo caught the ear of producer Norro Wilson, who wanted the single to capture the feel of the road.

"I went in with the intention of just making this big, rhythmic, pounding record with bass guitars, trying to paint a picture of this big truck," Wilson remembers. He still had to convince the artist, though. "I didn't want to cut that song," Stampley admits. "I thought the song was meant for somebody else."

Joe relented, however, and Chuck Napier, one of Darst's friends, helped Wilson develop his plan. "He was doing TV stuff for *Overdrive* magazine," notes Wilson, "and he was acquainted with all these big trucking systems, like Peterbilt. We decided we would record a truck coming down the highway with the horns going. We got in the back alley behind CBS Studio B, and [recording engineer] Lou Bradley set up mikes at three different spots in the alleyway.

"We ended up with a guy who's not even a truck driver, he blows this big horn out there and goes through all the gears, zipping through the alley. What we got on tape was awesome, but we were only able to use the sound of the horn, and you hear it start up, but we couldn't get some of those great shift changes."

If Stampley took convincing, he wasn't alone. *Billboard*'s weekly review section is divided into "Picks," which are deemed to have the most chart potential, and "Recommended," which have a lesser degree of potential. The magazine tabbed "Roll On Big Mama" for a "Recommended" write-up ("They called it a 'so-so trucking song,'" notes Stampley), but it became Joe's second chart-topping single.

207

SHE'S ACTIN' SINGLE (I'M DRINKIN' DOUBLES)

GARY STEWART

RCA 10222
Writer: Wayne Carson
Producer: Roy Dea
May 10, 1975 (1 week)

Gary Stewart

It's somehow appropriate that Gary Stewart's only number one record would come with "She's *Actin*' Single," since he was named by his mother for *actor* Gary Cooper.

Stewart was born one of nine children in Letcher County, Kentucky, on May 28, 1944, and the family moved to Florida when he was twelve. He was playing professionally on the road by age 16, and eventually, Mel Tillis caught his set one night at The Wagon Wheel in Okeechobee. Tillis suggested that Gary take up songwriting and move to Nashville. Jerry Bradley signed him to a contract with Forrest Hills Publishing, and Stewart wrote two hits for Billy Walker, both of which peaked at number three in 1970.

In 1971, Stewart moved back to Florida, but before leaving, he cut a demo tape featuring country versions of Motown classics. The tape found its way to producer Roy Dea, who signed him with RCA Records in 1973.

"I never knew anybody who blowed me away like Gary," Dea told *Village Voice* writer Jimmy McDonough in 1988, "and I seen Elvis, Hank Williams, all of 'em. You get hooked on Stewart—he's like a damn drug." Indeed, Stewart's erratic vibrato and snarling renditions were a unique presence in country music, bringing three Top Ten hits: "Drinkin' Thing" [see 182—"I See The Want To In Your Eyes"] hit number ten in the summer of 1974; "Out Of Hand" followed it to number four; and "She's Actin' Single" soared all the way to the top, three weeks before his thirtieth birthday.

The late Pete Drake provided a key steel guitar part in Stewart's only number one single, the making of which was rather confusing, according to Gary. "It was a real unusual session. We took off instruments and put on instruments, and, for what all we did to it, it still sounded like it went down live."

Stewart secured six more Top 20 singles through 1978, though the highest-charting among them, "Your Place Or Mine," stopped at number 11. Later, Stewart put together a couple of duet albums with songwriter Dean Dillon. In 1983, the two co-wrote "Leave Them Boys Alone"—a salute to some of country music's wilder characters—with Tanya Tucker and Hank Williams, Jr.

In spite of Gary's success, his life soon became turbulent, due to a drug problem, a brief separation from his wife and his son's suicide in 1987. The 1988 *Village Voice* story seemed to revitalize interest in his career, though, and Stewart re-emerged with an album on High-Tone Records, *Brand New*.

208

(HEY WON'T YOU PLAY) ANOTHER SOMEBODY DONE SOMEBODY WRONG SONG

B.J. THOMAS

ABC 12054
Writers: Chips Moman, Larry Butler
Producer: Chips Moman
May 17, 1975 (1 week)

"(Hey Won't You Play) Another Somebody Done Somebody Wrong Song" marked pop star B.J. Thomas' first appearance on the *Billboard* country chart, but it was hardly a case of a rock and roller trying to invade a medium he knew nothing about.

Billy Joe Thomas was born in Oklahoma and raised near Houston. He grew up a fan of Jackie Wilson and Little Richard, but was just as enamored by Ernest Tubb and Hank Williams. In fact, his first Top Ten hit was a 1966 pop version of Hank's classic "I'm So Lonesome I Could Cry."

Thomas returned to the pop chart's Top Ten three more times through 1970, with "Hooked On A Feeling," "Raindrops Keep Fallin' On My Head" and "I Just Can't Help Believing." Almost five years passed before his next success, "Hey Won't You Play," provided a rebirth.

Producer Chips Moman wrote it in 20 minutes at home one evening with friend and fellow producer Larry Butler. Chips had had the original idea, and decided to cut the record with Thomas. "I was trying to talk Chips into letting me produce it on somebody else," Butler admits. "I'm glad Chips talked me out of it."

Apparently, Moman wasn't all that confident about it, though. Most of the *Reunion* album had already been cut when he finally introduced the song to B.J., and even then, it took some coaxing.

Explains B.J., "Chips was embarrassed, and he didn't know if it was a good song. Bobby Emmons played organ on the song, and convinced Chips' to play it. He played it rather badly, but we could just tell it was a great song."

The session included the same basic group that Moman employed on Elvis Presley's "Suspicious Minds." "Hey Won't You Play" hit number one on *Billboard*'s Hot 100 on April 26, 1975; on May 17, it repeated the feat on the country chart. Six days later, it was certified as Thomas' third million-selling single.

Jessi Colter

209

I'M NOT LISA

JESSI COLTER

Capitol 4009
Writer: Jessi Colter
Producer: Ken Mansfield,
Waylon Jennings
May 24, 1975 (1 week)

The first four notes of "I'm Not Lisa," when put to a slightly different rhythmic pattern, are the same as the notes in Don Ho's Hawaiian version of "Tiny Bubbles." Jessi Colter never made that connection, though, when she conceived the melody in a music-theory class years before she actually wrote a "romantic fantasy based on life." "I worked out a rhythm pattern, and I just put this little melody to it to take to my teacher," she remembers. "I put it away in my mind, and when I sat down to write this song, it came in about five minutes."

The protagonist in Colter's storyline was not

Lisa, but Julie—a name Colter's husband, Waylon Jennings, had used in his own work. "He had written a song before called 'Julie' that was about somebody from his past, and it seemed like the girl in this song," Colter notes. "I don't know where the name Lisa came from, but it was told kind of from Julie's aspect."

Session pianist Larry Muhoberac played a dramatic instrumental role in "I'm Not Lisa," but part of the record's magic stemmed from its honest portrayal of the Jennings/Colter marriage. The ceremony took place on October 26, 1969. She had been married for seven years to rock guitarist Duane Eddy; Jennings had been married twice before.

"Waylon and I hadn't been hooked up too long together," Colter recalls, "and I think it's a common thing that when you've been married before, you always ponder 'How much are they still into that relationship and that person?' Waylon in his own song has said he's 'lost somewhere in his lonesome past.' That's what occurred to me very strongly.

"I was a very different kind of woman from what he had had before. I didn't quite know how to take him, and he didn't know how to take me either. Part of all that was in there."

Colter (born Miriam Johnson) earned two Grammy nominations for "I'm Not Lisa": for Best Country Vocal Performance by a Female, and Best Country Song. The record also went into the Top Five on *Billboard*'s Hot 100. The follow-up single, "What's Happened To Blue Eyes," became her only other Top Five solo performance on the country chart, although she was one of four artists featured on the landmark album *Wanted: The Outlaws* [see 237—"Good Hearted Woman"].

210
THANK GOD I'M A COUNTRY BOY
JOHN DENVER
RCA 10239
Writer: John M. Sommers
Producer: Milton Okun
May 31, 1975 (1 week)

Henry John Deutschendorf, Jr., is hardly the kind of name a disk jockey wants to see on the label of a record. That was pretty obvious from the start of John Denver's career, but it wasn't something he relinquished easily.

"Nobody, even now, pronounces the name correctly," he says. "It's a difficult name, and I wasn't gonna let that be in the way of doing what I wanted to do. I really went through a difficult time about it. People kept suggesting names to me, and the only one that rang for me was Denver."

That name was familiar enough by 1975 that ABC-TV made him the centerpiece of an Emmy-winning special, "An Evening with John Denver." The title of the special coincided with his two-record live album, recorded at the Universal Amphitheater in California. The bulk of the material was credited to Denver, the classic singer/songwriter, but ironically, the lone single was written by a member of the band.

"Thank God I'm A Country Boy" was edited for radio play, and though the album earned gold status in February of 1975, the single performed with even greater success. Certified gold on June 26, it hit the top spot on the country chart five days later, and then reached number one on the *Billboard* Hot 100 the following week.

With its lyrics surrounding farm life, country cooking and the mountain fiddle, "Thank God I'm A Country Boy" is certainly a celebration of country lifestyles. In fact, with reference to the song "Sally Goodin'," the single provides an interesting link of country's past with its present. "Sally Goodin'" is one of two songs recorded by Eck Robertson and Henry Gilliland in 1922; along with its flip side, "Arkansaw Traveller," the Victor recording is recognized as the very first country record. Both tunes have become country "standards" of sorts.

In spite of "Country Boy"'s obvious country flavor, Denver swirled in controversy less than five months later when the Country Music Association named him Entertainer of the Year. A provincial segment of Nashville expressed its displeasure with the fact that a "crossover" performer could take the CMA's most prestigious award.

Denver, however, had grown up under the tutelage of his father, an avowed country fan. The influence was rather distinct, and eventually, Denver achieved a lifetime dream when he performed on the Grand Ole Opry for the very first time, on November 12, 1976.

"Country Boy"'s success kept Denver on the road; he spent the entire summer of 1975 away from his Aspen, Colorado, home. "I wanted to see how much I could do in new creative areas without blowing my home and family," he told *Billboard*. "But it turned out I bit off more than I could chew."

WINDOW UP ABOVE
MICKEY GILLEY

Playboy 6031
Writer: George Jones
Producer: Eddie Kilroy
June 7, 1975 (1 week)

After writing the song, George Jones first recorded "Window Up Above" in 1960. Released on Mercury Records, it debuted on *Billboard*'s country chart on Sunday, November 13. It peaked at number two after the first of the year, and remained on the charts a phenomenal 34 weeks.

In its re-emergence, the tune became Mickey Gilley's fourth consecutive number one record, as well as his fourth consecutive "cover."

"One of the reasons why we did so many remakes at that particular point was that nobody really took me seriously," Gilley laments. "The record company never really took me serious, Nashville didn't take me serious. They just thought that here was another little copy, and that when Jerry Lee Lewis got ready to come back, he'd knock Mickey Gilley out of the saddle and that would be the end of it."

With very few new songs coming in, Gilley continued to revive older chestnuts. "Window Up Above," a neo-voyeuristic cheatin' tune, was written while Jones was in the living room of his home in Vidor, Texas. Floyd Cramer played piano on the original, but Gilley gave it his own special keyboard flair for Playboy Records.

In 1975, Mickey was strapped for material, so producer Eddie Kilroy suggested that Gilley cut a few songs that he had played on stage a few years earlier at a Pasadena, Texas, club called The Ranch House. "Window Up Above" was one that Gilley performed often, and it emerged as a single, debuting on *Billboard*'s country chart on March 15. A dozen weeks later, the record became his fourth straight number one single.

Following "Window Up Above," Gilley returned once more to the "FTD-approved" themes of "Room Full Of Roses" [see 169] and "I Overlooked An Orchid" [see 183]. "Bouquet Of Roses" was, perhaps, too much "flower power," as it peaked at number 11. Gilley released a duet with labelmate Barbi Benton, and ended 1975 with a risqué tune, "Overnight Sensation," which peaked at number seven.

WHEN WILL I BE LOVED
LINDA RONSTADT

Capitol 4050
Writer: Phil Everly
Producer: Peter Asher
June 14, 1975 (1 week)

"I didn't set out to become a star," Linda Ronstadt told *Rolling Stone*'s Peter Herbst, "I set out to become a singer. I would have sung no matter what. The star part is just something that they made up in Hollywood in 1930."

Hailing from Tucson, Arizona, Ronstadt has achieved her stardom in a variety of musical formats, due in part to the musical diversity that surrounded her youth. Her father was of Mexican descent, and her grandfather used to arrange theatrical music.

Those sounds influenced her musical vocabulary, as did the works of Hank Williams, Elvis Presley and the Everly Brothers. In fact, she has re-recorded material first made by each of those performers, and one single—"When Will I Be Loved"—earned even higher marks for her than when the Everlys cut it. They first recorded it as the follow-up to "Cathy's Clown" [see 827], achieving a number eight peak position on the *Billboard* pop chart in 1960. Fifteen years later, it became Ronstadt's only solo number one country single.

Four months earlier, she earned her only number one on the Hot 100 with "You're No Good." Her diversity was apparent even then: the flip side, her Grammy-winning version of Hank Williams' "I Can't Help It (If I'm Still In Love With You)," rose to number two on the country chart.

Ronstadt's fortunes first turned toward stardom when she organized a group in Los Angeles called the Stone Poneys. They took "Different Drum" to number 13 in 1967, but 1975 marked her major breakthrough year. She quickly earned recognition as one of the most potent female vocalists in rock and roll, while she continued to maintain a simultaneous country success. Her rendition of Neil Young's "Love Is A Rose" made the Top Ten, as did "Crazy," "Blue Bayou" [see 27—"Only The Lonely"] and "I Never Will Marry."

Since 1980, Linda's career has been a study in experimentation. Her *Mad Love* album reflected an interest in New Wave, she cut three albums' worth of pop standards with arranger

Nelson Riddle, and she touched on her Mexican roots in 1987's *Canciones de mi Padre*. She also appeared with Rex Smith on Broadway, in *The Pirates of Penzance*.

Ronstadt returned to number one on the country chart in 1987 by teaming up with Dolly Parton and Emmylou Harris [see 721—"To Know Him Is To Love Him"].

213
YOU'RE MY BEST FRIEND
DON WILLIAMS
ABC/Dot 17550
Writer: Wayland Holyfield
Producer: Don Williams
June 21, 1975 (1 week)

"You're My Best Friend," Don Williams' second number one single, catapulted him to international recognition, particularly in Great Britain, where the English once voted "You're My Best Friend" their favorite all-time country record. By the end of the '70s, the United Kingdom's *Country Music People* magazine cited Williams as the Artist of the Decade. Even in Africa's Ivory Coast, he has been named that country's All-Time Favorite Artist.

"We're all basically the same," says Williams, appreciative of his global successes. "I've talked with people from Soviet Bloc countries, and Australians, Swiss—there's no difference. We all have the same feelings, the same desires and questions."

"You're My Best Friend" embraced one of those common needs, celebrating the love—and friendship—of a long-term romantic partner. "It was written about my wife," concedes songwriter Wayland Holyfield, "but also about a lot of people's wives, and girlfriends. As a romantic, I love to be able to do a song like that and have people respond to it.

"When I played it for Don, I was really insecure with it, just like any young songwriter who's new at the craft. You think, 'The kid's nice-lookin', but what are the other people gonna think?'"

Holyfield actually played it for Williams many times over, since he wrote for Don's publishing company. "It was a pretty regular thing for us to bounce songs off of each other in the shaping and polishing of the song," Don explains. "Wayland had this thought, and ran it by me, and I would tell him what I thought, and he'd go work on it, and this went on for the better part

of a year. The last time he brought it to me, I said, 'Well, that's it. She's finished now.'"

After releasing it as a single, Don found his audiences picked up all the lyrics very quickly, and it grew into a major sing-along section of his live show. "Best Friend" reached the top of the chart ten weeks after its *Billboard* debut, Holyfield's first hit composed without a co-writer.

"It really was great when that thing went up the charts and became number one," says Wayland. "What it did for me was prove to myself that I can do this. You do it once by yourself, maybe you can do it again."

214
TRYIN' TO BEAT THE MORNING HOME
T.G. SHEPPARD
Melodyland 6006
Writers: Red Williams, T.G. Sheppard, Elroy Kahanek
Producers: Jack Gilmer, Bill Browder, Ray Ruff
June 28, 1975 (1 week)

Although he later had his name legally changed, T.G. Sheppard was originally Bill Browder, and it was under that name that he first established himself in the record business. Browder was a promotion man for Stax Records, RCA, and later his own independent company, Umbrella Promotions.

Based in Memphis, Browder helped break a number of classic records at pop radio stations. A partial listing includes:

"These Eyes"—The Guess Who
"Take Me Home, Country Roads"—John Denver
"When You're Hot, You're Hot"—Jerry Reed [see 79]
"It's Impossible"—Perry Como
"The Letter"—The Box Tops
"Light My Fire"—Jose Feliciano
"The Good, The Bad, And The Ugly"— Hugh Montenegro
"Suspicious Minds"—Elvis Presley

When "Devil In The Bottle" [see 197] hit number one under the Sheppard moniker, he still continued to call radio stations as Bill Browder, and most of his contacts didn't realize he was the same person. Knowing the odds against making it in the business, Sheppard

T.G. Sheppard

wisely held onto his $200,000-a-year promotion job until he had a second legitimate hit. That second hit was also a number one single, and it's the only one Sheppard wrote.

"We couldn't find that magic song to follow up 'Devil In The Bottle,'" he says. "We knew it was important to have another one, so Elroy Kahanek and Red Williams—a disk jockey and a technician for WMC in Memphis—the three of us sat down one night, and somebody hollered out something about 'Tryin' To Beat The Morning Home.' It sounded like a song title, so we wrote it."

It wasn't Sheppard's last stab at composing, although it's the only major success he's attained. "I'm not really a writer, per se; I think there's one or two ideas that are hits in everyone. Maybe that's my one idea."

With the success of "Tryin' To Beat The Morning Home," Browder gave up his day job to devote his full attentions to his new career as a recording artist. He had been friends with Elvis Presley since 1961, and it was only with the second hit that Browder admitted to the King that *he* was T.G. Sheppard.

Contributing to Sheppard's new-found career, Presley presented his friend with two gifts: a Silver Eagle touring bus, and a diamond "TCB" pendant, signifying one of Elvis' favorite phrases: "takin' care of business."

215

LIZZIE AND THE RAINMAN

TANYA TUCKER

MCA 40402
Writers: Kenny O'Dell, Larry Henley
Producer: Snuff Garrett
June 13, 1975 (1 week)

While the rest of her classmates in Las Vegas went to school dances and gossiped about boyfriends, Tanya Tucker had a nightclub act to keep her extracurricular hours full by the time she was in the ninth grade. She dropped out, and continued to build on a series of records that already included three number one singles.

Following "Would You Lay With Me (In A Field Of Stone)" [see 158], she enjoyed one more Billy Sherrill-produced hit, "The Man That Turned My Mama On," and then signed with MCA Records the day she turned sweet sixteen.

MCA hoped that Tucker could "cross over" onto the pop charts, and they teamed her with Los Angeles producer "Snuff" Garrett, whose resumé included pop records by Gary Lewis & The Playboys, Cher and Vicki Lawrence. The very first song that Tucker recorded with Garrett was "Lizzie And The Rainman," based on the movie *The Rainmaker*.

"We disguised it a little bit," admits songwriter Larry Henley. "We didn't make it sound like it was really the movie, but it was taken from the essence of the movie. We had to have the character of old Starbuck in there. Lizzy Currie was the name of the main character in the movie; we called her Lizzie Cooper in the song."

The song was written around 1971; Alex Taylor (brother of James Taylor) and the Hollies both cut "Lizzie" before Tanya picked it up. "I think I submitted the tune at one time to Snuff Garrett for Cher," says O'Dell, "but don't hold me to that."

"Lizzie" never quite generated the pop success that MCA hoped for, although it did reach number 37 on *Billboard*'s Hot 100. It became Tanya's fourth number one country single, but she didn't relish working in Los Angeles. As a result, she did only one album with Garrett.

"It was a totally different experience for me," she says of the sessions. "I didn't really care for recording in L.A. It was kind of impersonal, and I was used to recording the way Billy had taught me how. That was what I was comfortable with, going and recording with the musicians live, but this time I was recording everything over the tracks. I didn't even see the musicians.

"Snuff did a great job, and I'm real proud of the record, but I just felt uncomfortable."

216

MOVIN' ON
MERLE HAGGARD & THE STRANGERS
Capitol 4085
Writer: Merle Haggard
Producer: Fuzzy Owen
July 12, 1975 (1 week)

For a songwriter who works primarily from inspiration, Merle Haggard faced one of the challenges of his career in creating "Movin' On." The producers for the "Movin' On" television series commissioned Haggard to write a theme song, forcing him to adapt his writing to someone else's work.

"There was quite a bit of pressure," he explained to Bob Eubanks in *Billboard*, "because they paid me half the money in front and the other half would come if I was able to write the song. I told them, 'I don't know whether I can do it or not.' I'm not that type of writer.

"I went down and watched the pilot of 'Movin' On,' with Claude Akins. It was a difficult thing for me to do, 'cause the title 'Movin' On' [see 160—"Hello Love"] had already been written and had been a big hit. The title 'Movin' On,' of course, was the name of Hank Snow's big song. I thought, 'How in the hell am I gonna write something about movin' on?' So I just tried to re-create what I saw on the screen and paid tribute to Will and Sonny, the characters of the series, as best I could."

Haggard's theme first appeared on network television on September 12, 1974, when the series premiered on NBC. Akins co-starred with Frank Converse as a pair of truck drivers looking for adventure all across the country. After the first year, "Movin' On" introduced two new drivers, Moose and Benjy, portrayed by former football player Rosey Grier and Art Metrano.

President Gerald Ford counted himself among the show's fans, but Haggard fared better in *Billboard* than the program did in the Nielsen ratings. "Movin' On" failed to crack the Top 25 among weekly network offerings, and the show made its last appearance on September 14, 1976.

Merle, on the other hand, debuted on May 24, 1975, at number 78. "Movin' On" cruised into the top position in a scant eight weeks. It was actually his fourth contribution to a visual production: he composed the "Killers Three Theme" and "Mama Tried" [see 16] for the movie *Killers Three* in 1968, and two years later, contributed "Turn Me Around" to the John Wayne film *Chisum*.

217

TOUCH THE HAND
CONWAY TWITTY
MCA 40407
Writers: Conway Twitty, Ron Peterson
Producer: Owen Bradley
July 19, 1975 (2 weeks)

"Touch The Hand" represents one-half of a very unusual single for Conway Twitty. Two-sided hits have emerged many times in music history, including "Don't Be Cruel"/ "Hound Dog" [see 275—"Moody Blue"], by Elvis Presley; "Oh, Lonesome Me"/"I Can't Stop Loving You" [see 108], by Don Gibson;

and "My Heart Skips A Beat"/"Together Again" [see 244], by Buck Owens; and "Bird Dog" [see 827—"Cathy's Clown"]/"Devoted To You," by the Everly Brothers.

Traditionally, successful "A" and "B" sides have charted at the same time, but the two hits that emerged from Conway's single rose one right after the other, rather than simultaneously.

MCA Records released "Touch The Hand" on May 1, 1975, and three weeks later, on May 24, it made its first appearance on the *Billboard* country chart, debuting at number 70. In its ninth week, it slipped into the number one position. On August 16, just as "Touch The Hand" slipped out of the Top 40, the flip side, "Don't Cry Joni," debuted at number 75, eventually peaking at number four on October 11.

"Don't Cry Joni" represents the most successful record made by one of Twitty's offspring. His daughter, Kathy, recorded in 1976 as Jesseca James; and his oldest son, Mike, cut records under the name Charlie Tango. "Don't Cry Joni," featuring 16-year-old Joni Lee Twitty, was the only one of these efforts to become a hit.

Recorded in a December 1974 session, the duet was written by Twitty about ten years earlier, as a gift to Joni. After years of disinterest, she suddenly decided at high school graduation that she wanted to be an entertainer, and Conway thought an appearance on an album cut might provide some encouragement.

"She was scared to death when we recorded it," laughs Conway. "Her knees were knockin'—you could hear 'em. Then when we got ready to release the album and the single, I thought, 'Well, why not just put this on the "B" side? It's a good song, and she can go and put a quarter in the jukebox and play this thing, and that might help her,' so I did that and forgot about it."

Instead, it became a hit when radio stations flipped "Touch The Hand." It also racked up surprising sales in the Spanish-speaking Mexican market.

Even as "Joni" surged forward, however, songwriter Ron Peterson sued Conway for copyright infringement on "Touch The Hand." Though maintaining his innocence, Twitty admits the similarities of his composition to Peterson's "blew my mind." On his attorney's advice, he settled out of court, and subsequent releases have credited Peterson as a co-writer.

218

JUST GET UP AND CLOSE THE DOOR
JOHNNY RODRIGUEZ
Mercury 73682
Writer: Linda Hargrove
Producer: Jerry Kennedy
August 2, 1975 (1 week)

Born February 3, 1951, Linda Hargrove was discovered by the late Pete Drake, when he played steel guitar on a 1971 Sandy Posey recording session. Hargrove played guitar on that session, during which they cut a song she'd written, and he signed her to his publishing company. Hargrove earned a handful of hits as a writer, including Olivia Newton-John's "Let It Shine," which went to number six, and George Jones' "Tennessee Whiskey," which made number two. Her first chart-topper, though, was Johnny Rodriguez's "Just Get Up And Close The Door."

"Pete Drake played on most of my number one records," notes Rodriguez, "and Linda was writing songs for him and learning how to use the control board at Pete Drake's studio in Nashville. Linda now is writing gospel music more than anything, but at that time, she was just learning, and I caught her at the right time, too, because she was just on a crest of getting some things like that going."

"Just Get Up And Close The Door" was Rodriguez's fifth number one single under the direction of producer Jerry Kennedy. "I believe [Kennedy] kind of had a real good feel for me from the very start," says Johnny, "because I got to meet him when I was just fresh in town and he pretty much knew my personality. I think that had a lot to do with our success."

Rodriguez had earned attention in Hollywood by 1975, making appearances on the TV series "Adam-12" and in the movie *Rio Diablo*. There were a lot of obligations and responsibilities that went along with his newfound status, and Johnny has even admitted that he didn't handle it well. Kennedy says, though, that outside interests didn't affect their creative efforts.

"I think his singing speaks for itself, so that was no problem," notes Kennedy. "The hardest part of Johnny's career was going on outside of the studio. He had people tugging at him, and when you're a success that young, it can be really confusing. But we never let that come into the studio."

219

WASTED DAYS AND WASTED NIGHTS
FREDDY FENDER
ABC/Dot 17558
Writer: Baldemar Huerta, Wayne Duncan
Producer: Huey P. Meaux
August 9, 1975 (2 weeks)

Born June 4, 1937, in San Benito, Texas, Freddy Fender grew up in a poor Hispanic community. The son of migrant workers, he dropped out of high school at age 16, joining the military for three years. Much of that time was spent in the brig, and in 1956, he was discharged from the service.

The following year, he began to make an impact in Texas and Mexico on Falcon Records with Spanish versions of Elvis Presley's "Don't Be Cruel" and Harry Belafonte's "Jamaica Farewell." During that time, he billed himself under his real name—Baldemar Huerta, "El Beebop Kid."

In spite of the success, he wanted more, and when he signed with Imperial Records, he used the brand name on his guitar to form a new stage monicker, Freddy Fender. By avoiding his Spanish name, he hoped to appeal to the wider "gringo" audience, and the move paid off in 1959 when several cities played his singles "Holy One" and "Wasted Days And Wasted Nights."

Re-recorded in 1975 with a similar arrangement, "Wasted Days" is Fender's only self-composed number one hit. During one of many low points in his life, Fender was playing The Starlight Club in Harlingen, Texas, when he came up with an initial idea of "Lonely Days And Lonely Nights."

"I didn't even have the money to rent a room," he recalls, "and I was staying in a little room at the bar where I was playing. I was feeling very sorry for myself, my marriage was on the rocks, and I was separated. Finally I settled on '*Wasted* Days And *Wasted* Nights.'

"It's a very simple song; the grammar is right on the edge of being bad grammar, but it isn't. The first verse, 'Wasted days and wasted nights, I have left for you behind,' has a lot to do with my Hispanic roots, because I don't think that an Anglo-American would come out with a line like that. But in Spanish, it would be very correct."

If his days in The Starlight Club were bad, there was still more tragedy to come. On May 13, 1960, he was arrested for possession of

Freddy Fender

two joints in Baton Rouge, and he remained in Angola State Prison until July of 1963. It would take a dozen years before he could recapture the momentum he had built on Imperial Records.

220

RHINESTONE COWBOY
GLEN CAMPBELL
Capitol 4095
Writer: Larry Weiss
Producers: Dennis Lambert, Brian Potter
August 23, 1975 (3 weeks)

Glen Campbell calls "Rhinestone Cowboy," the tale of a country boy trying to make it in the big city, his "philosophy song." He can also call it the biggest single release of his recording career.

"Rhinestone Cowboy" was written by Larry Weiss, a Los Angeles songwriter who had moved out from New York in 1971. "The idea for the song was a crying-out of myself," Weiss told Kelly Delaney of *American Songwriter*. "It was the spirit of a bunch of us on Broadway, where I started out. Neil Diamond, Tony Orlando—we all had dreams of making it."

He combined the hope and frustration of the road to stardom with the image of the "Rhinestone Cowboy," two words that someone else had used in a conversation. "I heard the phrase and thought, 'Boy, I like that title.' I put my own meaning to it and wrote the song. I'll always be a kid at heart, and 'Rhinestone Cowboy' was sort of a summation of all my childhood cowboy movie heroes—particularly Hopalong Cassidy."

Weiss recorded "Rhinestone Cowboy" on his own *Black and Blue Suite* album for 20th Century Records, envisioning success as a recording artist. Instead, the track received only a smattering of airplay. Fortunately, one of those "plays" reached the ears of Glen Campbell.

"I heard that on the radio at KNX, I think, in Los Angeles," notes Campbell, "and I took a demo of it to Australia in '74. The airlines were on strike, so we got to drive around the freeways of Australia—actually, they were two-lane roads, and pretty curvy at that. They followed a snake trail from Sydney to Brisbane, I think, but that's where I learned 'Rhinestone Cowboy.'

"I got back to Capitol Records, and Al Coury

said, 'You got to cut this song.' He put on 'Rhinestone Cowboy,' and I laughed—that was the one I had brought in for him to hear."

"Rhinestone Cowboy" sold more than two million copies by the end of 1975, en route to distinction as *Billboard*'s number one country single for the entire year. It earned Song of the Year honors from both the Academy of Country Music and the Country Music Association. The ACM also honored it as the Single Record of the Year.

Nine years later, it served as the inspiration for the Dolly Parton/Sylvester Stallone movie *Rhinestone* [see 585—"Tennessee Homesick Blues"].

221

FEELINS'
LORETTA LYNN
& CONWAY TWITTY
MCA 40420
Writers: Troy Seals, Don Goodman,
Will Jennings
Producer: Owen Bradley
September 6, 1975 (1 week)

"Feelins'" is the only number one country single authored by Will Jennings, a versatile songwriter whose track record includes such wide-ranging material as Dionne Warwick's "I Know I'll Never Love This Way Again," Barry Manilow's "Looks Like We Made It," Steve Winwood's "Higher Love" and the Joe Cocker & Jennifer Warnes duet, "Up Where We Belong."

Recorded on April Fools' Day in 1975, "Feelins'" became the fifth number one duet for Conway Twitty & Loretta Lynn, making them the only duo composed of two solo vocalists to top the chart that many times. They also topped the country album chart on three different occasions—with *Louisiana Woman, Mississippi Man* [see 140] in 1973, *Country Partners* in 1974, and *United Talent* (named for their booking agency [see 87—"Lead Me On"]) in 1976.

Though they toured and recorded together infrequently, the Twitty/Lynn partnership lasted a full decade, and the period made them the most honored duo in history. *Feelins'* secured the Academy of Country Music's Album of the Year award, while the ACM honored them as Vocal Group of the Year three times. The Country Music Association cited Conway

& Loretta as Vocal Duo of the Year four years in a row, beginning in 1972. They garnered the same recognition in the fan-voted *Music City News* awards for eight straight years beginning in 1971, winning ten times in all in eleven years. They continued to receive nominations for several years even after they stopped recording together.

Following "Feelins'," Twitty & Lynn earned seven more Top Ten records through 1981: "The Letter" (number three), "I Can't Love You Enough" (number two), "From Seven Till Ten" (number six), "You Know Just What I'd Do" (number nine), "It's True Love" (number five), "Lovin' What Your Lovin' Does To Me" (number seven) and "I Still Believe In Waltzes" (number two).

When they sang together on the ACM awards April 30, 1981, it marked their first public performance as a duet since the American Music Awards in January of 1977.

Following a five-year absence from recording, Conway & Loretta cut a special album for a television marketing campaign in 1988, and also released another, *Making Believe*, through traditional channels. Their albums *We Only Make Believe* and *The Very Best of Conway & Loretta* were both certified gold in November of that year.

Conway Twitty & Loretta Lynn

222

DAYDREAMS ABOUT NIGHT THINGS
RONNIE MILSAP

RCA 10335
Writer: John Schweers
Producers: Tom Collins, Jack D. Johnson
September 20, 1975 (2 weeks)

In 1975, Ronnie Milsap put the word out in Nashville that he wanted to record "uptempo, positive" material, in stark contrast to the stereotype of country music at that time. "Daydreams About Night Things" perfectly fit into that vein, although songwriter John Schweers never thought of Milsap when he wrote it.

"It was a saying that my grandfather had," Schweers explains. "He'd say, 'I'm havin' daydreams about night things in the middle of the afternoon,' and it just so happened that I'd met a girl, and I was definitely havin' daydreams about night things in the middle of the afternoon, so it was a pretty easy song to write. It's kind of the story of my wife and I. She wasn't my wife yet—but I married her later that year."

When Schweers first composed "Daydreams," writing songs was hardly a lucrative

venture. He took a sideline job selling real estate, and he actually wrote the first few lines of the lyric on a multiple listings page while calling prospective clients. The Country Music Hall of Fame later put that page on display.

Schweers wrote "Daydreams" and "She's Just An Old Love Turned Memory" [see 278] within a two-week span of time. He first pitched "Daydreams" to Charley Pride, sending "She's Just An Old Love" to Milsap. Each artist turned down the song Schweers sent to him, later recording the other one. Milsap, in fact, called Schweers while he was out showing a house to tell John he was cutting "Daydreams."

Making the record was an expensive proposition. The session was the first at RCA Studios using a brand new console, and everything sounded fine during the recording process. Later, engineer Al Pachucki and producer Tom Collins discovered the tracks were distorted, a loss of $3,000. RCA absorbed the cost, and Milsap had to re-cut the track.

"We went back there in a little small room in the RCA building called Studio C," says Collins, "and it's probably not as big as anybody's living room. We had all the musicians in there on top of each other. We had the Jordanaires singing, and it's a very tiny room, but that's where we played 'Daydreams.'"

On the same session, Milsap also recorded "Just In Case." "Daydreams" went to number one, and "Just In Case" followed it, hitting number six.

223
BLUE EYES CRYING IN THE RAIN
WILLIE NELSON
Columbia 10176
Writer: Fred Rose
Producer: Willie Nelson
October 4, 1975 (2 weeks)

Willie Nelson first moved to Nashville in 1960, but it took fifteen years and a return to Texas before he finally connected with the public in a big way. He had his first chart successes in 1962, hitting the Top Ten with "Touch Me" and "Willingly"—the latter a duet with then-wife Shirley Collie—but Nelson failed to follow through on that early promise.

He made a number of albums for RCA and Atlantic in the ensuing years, but on-lookers said he was "ahead of his time" or that he

played "too many chords." Moving to Austin in 1971, he found his audience—a mixture of hippies and rednecks—through the Armadillo World Headquarters, where he first appeared on August 12, 1972. A year later, he held the first quasi-annual Willie Nelson Picnic on the Fourth of July, but as he established his niche, Atlantic closed its country division. Willie bought out his contract in 1974 and signed with Columbia, where he was given "creative control."

He had no idea what to do with that control, though, until a drive from Colorado to Texas. He and his wife, Connie, formulated a concept album about a preacher in the Old West based around the song "Red Headed Stranger," which Willie first heard while working as a disk jockey in the mid-'50s. The album mixed older songs with several Willie wrote to tie the story together, and he cut it in three days for $20,000 at Autumn Sound in Garland, Texas. Columbia was less than thrilled with the results.

"They thought it wasn't finished," Willie told Frederick Burger in *Billboard*. "They thought it was underproduced, too sparse, all those things. Even though they didn't like it, they had already paid me a bunch of money for it, so they had to release it under my contract. And since they had money in it, they had to promote it."

Released in May of 1975, it surprised nearly everyone when "Blue Eyes Crying In The Rain," already 30 years old, emerged as a number one country record and hit number 21 on the *Billboard* Hot 100. On February 28, 1976, the single that Columbia didn't want to release brought Nelson a Grammy award.

Ultimately, *Red Headed Stranger* sold 2.5 million copies, and Willie turned it into a movie, co-starring Morgan Fairchild and Katharine Ross, in 1987.

224
HOPE YOU'RE FEELIN' ME (LIKE I'M FEELIN' YOU)
CHARLEY PRIDE
RCA 10344
Writers: Bobby David, Jim Rushing
Producers: Jerry Bradley, Charley Pride
October 18, 1975 (1 week)

Charley Pride orchestrated some pretty significant career changes in 1974 and 1975 that gave him more control over his own career.

First was his separation from Jack Clement [see 196—"Then Who Am I"], which left Pride credited as a co-producer on his material with Jerry Bradley.

Then, in March of '75, he ended his ten-year tenure with manager Jack D. Johnson. In the process, Johnson severed all ties to the Pi-Gem publishing venture [see 134—"Don't Fight The Feelings Of Love"]. Pride established a new talent agency called Chardon with Don Keirns, and Gary Stewart [see 207—"She's Actin' Single"] was the first performer to sign on.

Stewart toured as part of the Charley Pride Show, as did Dave & Sugar [see 253—"The Door Is Always Open"]. Ronnie Milsap, who had previously served as Pride's opening act, remained a part of Jack Johnson's organization.

Keirns had an unusual set-up—he was responsible for working as Pride's booking agent *and* as his road manager—but he also played an instrumental role in "Hope You're Feelin' Me (Like I'm Feelin' You)." "That was written by Bobby David," reports Pride. "Bobby David was a friend of his, and that song was pitched to me through Don—I ended up cutting it." RCA shipped "Hope You're Feelin' Me" on July 15, and it went on to become Charley's fifteenth chart-topping release.

Pride, in the meantime, has become one of country music's more astute businessmen. At various points, his portfolio has included radio stations, oil investments, a stake in the First Texas State Bank, Dallas' Cecca Recording Studio and an office complex. He has also purchased a large amount of real estate, including the 120-acre farm in Sledge, Mississippi, where he used to pick cotton.

Pride was born on that farm on March 18, 1938. His mother named him Charley Frank Pride, though the midwife mistakenly wrote down "Charl." His father worked as a sharecropper, and young Charley was also employed, as were his ten siblings, picking cotton for just $3.00 per 100 pounds. His dad taught him to be thorough in his work during those early years, and that lesson has helped Charley Pride build his business empire.

Tanya Tucker

225

SAN ANTONIO STROLL
TANYA TUCKER
MCA 40444
Writer: Peter Noah
Producer: Snuff Garrett
October 25, 1975 (1 week)

"I never had been to San Antonio, and never have been," admits one-time songwriter Peter Noah. "I don't know why that phrase 'San Antonio Stroll' popped into my head, but it did, and I just made up that whole little story to kind of go along with it."

Noah first wrote "San Antonio Stroll" in Chicago during the spring of 1972, more than three years before Tanya Tucker released it as a single. He was taking college courses by day and performing at small clubs by night; he started the song in the parking lot of one of those clubs. Eventually, Peter moved out to Los Angeles to be part of a band. He demoed a version of the song in his living room, and after the group broke up, he did some studio work for one of his former bandmates.

"In return for that, we recorded two of my songs as well," he says, "and 'San Antonio Stroll' was one of them. We basically worked from my original demo, and added bass and drums but kept the mandolin figure, and I think I added a banjo about half the way through it. The engineer on the session had a connection with Chappell Music and brought the song there."

Nothing happened with "San Antonio Stroll" for more than 18 months, and, though he kept writing songs, Noah also latched onto a job writing questions for a Hawaii-based TV game show called "Diamondhead." While in Hawaii, Noah discovered that "Snuff" Garrett intended to record the song with Tanya Tucker.

"Snuff called me while I was in Hawaii," Noah remembers. "He said he loved the song, but it was too long, and he wanted to cut it, and he needed it by the next morning. I said, 'Okay,' and wrote the version that she wound up recording, which basically combined the second and third verses."

The single followed Tanya's "Lizzie And The Rainman" [see 215] to number one. Noah was then 24 years old, and, though the song was successful, "San Antonio Stroll" was his only hit as a songwriter. Five years later, he decided to drop songwriting, and turned his attentions toward television.

It was a wise move. The former songwriter has earned writer/producer credits in several half-hour series, including "Mr. Sunshine," "Amen," "Mr. President," "Dear John" and "Anything But Love."

226

(TURN OUT THE LIGHT AND) LOVE ME TONIGHT

DON WILLIAMS

ABC/Dot 17568
Writer: Bob McDill
Producer: Don Williams
November 1, 1975 (1 week)

Don Williams sowed the seeds of his solo career in the fertile fields of JMI Records.

"I've never seen anything like the creative force at JMI," Don told Billboard's Gerry Wood, "and I probably never will again. The creative energy and effectiveness so far outran the administrative ability that it started coming down around our ears."

JMI stood for Jack Music, Inc., so named by its owner—music business veteran Jack "Cowboy" Clement [see 65—"I Can't Believe That You've Stopped Loving Me"]. His conglomerate included the record company, publishing concerns and Jack Clement Studios, with most of these ventures run by Allen Reynolds, a songwriter and singer who also produced Williams' first two albums.

Beginning in 1972, Don released five JMI singles. Four sides hit the Top 20 of the Billboard country chart, a stellar showing for an independent record label. The best performer was 1974's "We Should Be Together," which peaked at number five.

Don worked both as a song plugger and songwriter for Clement's publishing company, but he was frustrated in both areas. He pitched quality songs for JMI all over Nashville, but producers frequently told him that he should record them himself.

Williams reluctantly agreed, and from the beginning, one of his frequent suppliers was fellow JMI writer Bob McDill. Through time, McDill contributed a dozen hits to Don's resumé, including his third number one single, "(Turn Out The Light And) Love Me Tonight."

"I remember thinkin' that was just a little song," says McDill. "I wasn't excited about it at all, and Chuck Neese, who was pitchin' songs for us at the time, really jumped up and down about it and said, 'That's a smash.' Sure enough, we played it for Don, and it all came out just as Chuck predicted it would."

"Bob and I have been together on so many things," Williams adds. "When Bob writes somethin' that hits me, it hits me pretty hard, and that's just one of countless songs that Bob has brought to me that really affected me."

It affected the general masses just as much. "(Turn Out The Light And) Love Me Tonight" blanketed the top spot on November 1, 1975, after a dozen weeks on the Billboard chart.

227

I'M SORRY

JOHN DENVER

RCA 10353
Writer: John Denver
Producer: Milton Okun
November 8, 1975 (1 week)

At the height of his popularity, John Denver released an ecologically aware album in 1975 titled *Windsong*. The first single had the same title as an old Brenda Lee hit, "I'm Sorry," and it became his third number one country hit within the space of a year.

Windsong, meanwhile, provided Denver with a new career avenue. It became the name of his self-owned, RCA-distributed record company, and the label found success in 1976 when Denver's friends, Bill and Taffy Danoff, led the Starland Vocal Band to number one on the *Billboard* Hot 100 with "Afternoon Delight."

Denver appeared the following year in his first motion picture, co-starring with George Burns in *Oh, God!*. He likewise contributed time and energy to a host of social and ecological programs, including the Windstar Foundation, the National Space Institute, Save The Children, Friends of the Earth and the Human/Dolphin Foundation.

In 1984, John became the first American in more than seven years to perform publicly in the Soviet Union, and in 1986, he sunk $500,000 into a video for "What Are We Making Weapons For?," even though he recognized its political message left little chance for commercial success.

Denver concedes that he has probably sacrificed many personal successes to see his projects succeed. "I'd love to have a hit record," he says. "I'd love to be in the movies, all of this stuff, and maybe I can still do that. I'm certainly still working on it, and at the same time, there is this other thing which really has my heart in it, and my spirit and my vision, my dreams and desires for my children."

His celebrated marriage to Annie Martell ended in 1983, but on August 12, 1988, he remarried, to actress Cassandra Delaney.
couple of singles have broken through to hit status. "Some Days Are Diamonds (Some Days Are Stone)" reached number 10 in 1981, and "Dreamland Express" achieved a number nine peak in 1986. He has also had two successful duets: "Fly Away," featuring Olivia Newton-John, went to number 12 in 1975, and "Wild Montana Skies," with Emmylou Harris, propelled him to number 14 in 1983.

His celebrated marriage to Annie Martell ended in 1983, but on August 12, 1988, he remarried, to actress Cassandra Delaney, in

Denver has left an incredible mark in music. His first *Greatest Hits* album earned a special award from RCA Records for selling more than 10 million copies worldwide, and one source lists him among the five best-selling recording artists in history.

ARE YOU SURE HANK DONE IT THIS WAY/BOB WILLS IS STILL THE KING
WAYLON JENNINGS
RCA 10379
Writer: Waylon Jennings
Producers: Waylon Jennings,
Jack Clement, Ray Pennington
November 15, 1975 (1 week)

Waylon Jennings' third number one single could easily have been his fourth. "Rainy Day Woman" stopped at number two in 1975 behind Cal Smith's "It's Time To Pay The Fiddler" [see 199], and the follow-up, "Dreaming My Dreams With You," reached number 10. Waylon's return to number one was a double-sided hit which used country-music pioneers to convey Jenning's barbs at both the establishment (on one side of the record) and a friend (on the other side).

The "A" side, "Are You Sure Hank Done It This Way," made reference to Hank Williams while implying that Nashville had grown stagnant. "Anytime we were on the road," Jennings notes, "and there'd be something wrong, like a flat on the bus, or anything like that, you'd look at each other and say, 'Hmmm, are you sure Hank done it just like this? You sure Hank done it this way?'"

Waylon basically had just two lines to start with when he drove from his home to Jack Clement's recording studio. With one hand on the wheel, he jotted down the rest of the song on the back of an envelope, completing it before arriving at the studio on Belmont Boulevard. Placing the envelope on a music stand, Jennings recorded it that same day.

"About two weeks later," says Waylon, "a guy that worked for me brought me the envelope, and said, 'Waylon, do you care if I have this?' and I said, 'Well, what is it?' He says, 'This is your original lyrics on "Hank,"' and I said, 'Well, let me see it,' and I couldn't read a damn word of it, not one word. I don't know how I did it, I guess it was just fresh on my mind."

The "B" side, "Bob Wills Is Still The King," was written on a plane between Dallas and Austin, where he recorded it in concert on September 27, 1974. Jennings actually intended it as a message to Willie Nelson, spurred by anger over a booking arrangement the two had worked out. The dispute didn't last, but the song did, although Waylon almost gave it away to Tompall Glaser. Ironically, Wills passed away on May 13, 1975, between the time that Jennings recorded it and released it as a single.

Both sides were packaged on *Dreaming My Dreams*, Waylon's first album to reach number one on the *Billboard* album chart.

229

ROCKY
DICKEY LEE
RCA 10361
Writer: Jay Stevens
Producers: Roy Dea, Dickey Lee
November 22, 1975 (1 week)

Many country fans might have been surprised by the emergence of Dickey Lee, a former pop artist, on *Billboard*'s country charts in 1971.

Lee first attracted national attention when "Patches" took him to number six on the Hot 100 on October 6, 1962. Growing up in Mem-

phis, though, he had long held an interest in country music; once "The Mahogany Pulpit" appeared on the country chart, he was finally able to pursue that interest as a performer.

Born September 21, 1941, Dickey Lipscomb got his first break from disk jockey Dewey Phillips—the first man to play an Elvis Presley single [see 275—"Moody Blue"]—in 1954. Phillips introduced the artist to Jack Clement, the engineer at Sun Records. Lee made his first record at WHBQ radio's studio, and it went to number two locally, beat out only by Presley's "Teddy Bear."

In the meantime, Lee was offered a boxing scholarship to Memphis State, and he divided his time between college and music until "Patches" appeared, bringing a large measure of success.

A couple of other singles fared well on the pop charts, but Lee was unable to equal "Patches," and after signing with RCA in 1970, he persuaded Chet Atkins to let him make country singles. Lee had written "She Thinks I Still Care" [see 170], and when Atkins consented, "The Mahogany Pulpit" was his first country release. He followed with "Never End-

Dickey Lee

ing Song Of Love," which hit number eight, but Dickey didn't score big again until a publisher sent him a previously-released record called "Rocky."

"They had put the song out in a pop version," remembers Lee. "It was really good, but I thought it was just the demo."

As it turned out, that version, by Austin Roberts, picked up steam and became a Top Ten pop recording on October 4, 1975. Six weeks later, Lee took the same song to the top of the country charts. (Roberts later moved to Nashville, and has since written songs with Lee.)

Lee garnered two more Top Ten singles in 1976, with "Angels, Roses And Rain" and "9,999,999 Tears," but after a disappointing period with Mercury Records, he chose to pursue songwriting exclusively in 1981. That venture proved successful, as he penned number one singles like "You're The First Time I've Thought About Leaving" [see 517], "Let's Fall To Pieces Together" [see 584] and "I've Been Around Enough To Know" [see 594].

230
IT'S ALL IN THE MOVIES
MERLE HAGGARD & THE STRANGERS
Capitol 4141
Writer: Merle Haggard
Producer: Fuzzy Owen
November 29, 1975 (1 week)

"I'm a periodic writer," Merle Haggard once told *Billboard*'s Pat Nelson. "Sometimes I'll go for months and not write anything that's worth a damn. Then I'll finally come up with something. Hopefully, a person gets more critical with each piece of material he writes, and I keep searching and trying to write more quality than quantity."

On November 28, 1975, the Grand Ole Opry celebrated its fiftieth anniversary [see 156—"There Won't Be Anymore"], but the record Merle took to number one that same week had more to do with Hollywood than Nashville. "It's All In The Movies" drew on the romanticism and famous final scenes of the motion picture industry to create an analogy for love.

"I think we did that on the same session that we did 'If We Make It Through December' [see 150]," recalls guitar player and backing vocalist

Ronnie Reno. "A lot of times we would do the songs and they'd stay in the can for a year or so before we'd come out with them.

"I did a unison line with him, and Merle played the guitar in the acoustic break on that, too."

"I was going through a strange period in my life," Haggard elaborates. "I had a problem with my cervical nerve—it runs from your elbow to your little finger and the one next to it—and those two fingers were like they were asleep, and I couldn't feel anything. For a couple of years, I only had two fingers to play guitar with, and I played the lead on that with two fingers."

The instrumental break also featured a bluesy saxophone performance by Don Markham, who brought a tinge of jazz to the record. "It's All In The Movies" debuted in *Billboard* on October 4, 1975, heading to number one in its ninth week.

Merle himself has had an unusual relationship with the silver screen and television. He turned down several opportunities to host his own TV show, and once walked out on "The Ed Sullivan Show," refusing to do a choreographed dance sequence. During 1975, Merle hosted "Death Valley Days"; he also made brief appearances on such programs as "Doc Elliot" and "The Waltons." In addition, Haggard had parts in the mini-series *Centennial* and the Clint Eastwood film *Bronco Billy* [see 387—"Bar Room Buddies"].

231
SECRET LOVE
FREDDY FENDER
ABC/Dot 17585
Writers: Sammy Fain,
Paul Francis Webster
Producer: Huey P. Meaux
December 6, 1975 (1 week)

When Freddy Fender was released from prison in 1963 [see 219—"Wasted Days And Wasted Nights"], he had to start his once-promising recording career from ground zero again. He took menial jobs by day and played clubs in New Orleans by night, and, in the meantime, he went back to high school to get his diploma (he had dropped out in the eighth grade).

At the time that "Before The Next Teardrop Falls" [see 201] took off, Freddy was earning

$1.85 an hour at a car wash back in Texas. Suddenly, his career exploded, and in November of 1975, *Newsweek* hailed him as "The Tex-Mex Troubadour."

That same month, Fender was on his way to his third consecutive number one record, a remake of a 1953 Doris Day performance. Introduced in the movie *Calamity Jane*, "Secret Love" won an Academy Award for Best Song, and in 1954, Slim Whitman reached number three with the first country rendition. The Fender version appeared in *Billboard* at number 70 on October 11, 1975, two days before "Before The Next Teardrop Falls" earned Freddy an award from the Country Music Association. "Secret Love" topped out during the first weekend of December.

The months leading up to "Secret Love" were a flurry of activity for Fender. "Teardrop" and "Wasted Days" both sold a million copies, and the *Before the Next Teardrop Falls* album also went gold. Along with Johnny Rodriguez and comedian Freddie Prinze, Fender was one of a handful of Hispanics making inroads in the entertainment field, and he was inundated with media attention. In the midst of the clamor, the record label wanted another album, and producer Huey Meaux obliged them with *Are You Ready for Freddy*, all of which was hand-picked and pre-produced by Meaux before Fender ever got to the recording studio to add his vocals.

"I just got in there, and boom, boom, boom," says Fender of the recording process. "["Secret Love"] was a very challenging song. It's in the key of G, but I'm very fortunate in that I can sing bass all the way up to the top. I'm no Roy Orbison, but if I was to quit smoking, maybe I would give a real good tribute to Roy on the high notes.

"To this day, if I'm having a hard show, and the people are not into it, as soon as I hit 'Secret Love,' you can hear a pin drop. That song is such a beautiful song that any singer with a good voice can get a very receptive result."

232
LOVE PUT A SONG IN MY HEART
JOHNNY RODRIGUEZ
Mercury 73715
Writer: Ben Peters
Producer: Jerry Kennedy
December 13, 1975 (1 week)

The last of Johnny Rodriguez's six number one singles came from ace songwriter Ben Peters. "Love Put A Song In My Heart" was Peters' attempt to write a song for European audiences after he had taken a trip across the Atlantic. "I had listened to a lot of music in different countries in Europe," he says, "and they like that repetitious thing in the songs. I was trying to write something that reflected the European flair. I still hope that we'll get a record over there on that particular song someday."

Like Waylon Jennings, Peters lived in Rodriguez's neighborhood, and he used a personal touch in supplying Johnny with a demo tape. "I think their houses were backed up to each other," producer Jerry Kennedy remembers, "and he left it in the mailbox or knocked on his door or something, and Johnny brought it into the office."

The tape included both "Love Put A Song In My Heart" and "Daytime Friends" [see 294]. Rodriguez liked both, but, keeping an eye toward family harmony, he cut only the first song. "At the time, I was married," Johnny explains. "My wife didn't like ["Daytime Friends"], because it sounded like I was cheating on her, so I passed on that one and recorded the other one. I said, 'This is a little more positive, isn't it?'"

"Love Put A Song In My Heart" certainly produced positive results. Bill Justis, who reached number two on *Billboard*'s Hot 100 in 1958 with "Raunchy," arranged the strings on the record, and he cut the entire session live in the studio.

The Rodriguez/Kennedy collaboration lasted three more years, netting seven additional Top Ten singles through 1978, including "I Couldn't Be Me Without You" (number three), "I Wonder If I Ever Said Goodbye" (number two), and the original version of "We Believe In Happy Endings" [see 788]. In 1979, Rodriguez moved to Epic Records, reaching number six with "Down On The Rio Grande." Unfortunately, a narcotic addiction brought both Johnny's career and his personal life to its lowest ebb.

In 1981, Johnny reported to a Denton, Texas, rehabilitation center. With a new exuberance, he briefly regained his form in 1983 when two singles—"Foolin'" and "How Could I Love Her So Much"—reached the Top Ten with Lynn Anderson on back-up vocals. Leaving Epic in 1986, Johnny re-emerged on Capitol in 1987, hitting number 12 with "I Didn't (Every Chance I Had)."

233

CONVOY

C.W. McCALL

MGM 14839
Writers: Bill Fries, Chip Davis
Producers: Don Sears, Chip Davis
December 20, 1975 (6 weeks)

Bill Fries of Audobon, Iowa, was working as a $40,000-a-year advertising executive for Bozell & Jacobs in Omaha when he first developed the characters of C.W. McCall and the truck-stop waitress, Mavis. Their commercials for Old Home bread won a Clio award, and the song, "Old Home Filler-Up An' Keep On-A-Truckin' Cafe," rose to number 19 on the *Billboard* country charts in 1974.

Fries continued to work for Bozell & Jacobs, but he also pursued his secondary musical career, reaching number 12 with "Wolf Creek Pass" and number 13 with "Classified." In June

of 1975, he was listening to his CB radio when he got the idea for "Convoy," taking advantage of a growing fad. Nine months later, some 3.5 million CB operators were transmitting signals across the U.S., and some of them no doubt picked up on the trend after hearing McCall's hit.

The record's success was phenomenal. It debuted on the country chart on November 29, 1975, hit number one in its fourth week, and remained at the top for six full weeks. At the same time, it earned a position on *Billboard*'s Hot 100, reaching the top spot on January 10, 1976.

"Convoy" ultimately sold more than seven million copies, and *Billboard* named it the number one country single of the year for 1976. Two years later, it provided the basis for the movie *Convoy*, starring Kris Kristofferson and Ali McGraw.

It wasn't the last of McCall's country hits. In 1977, he went to number two one more time with "Roses For Mama," another recitation

C.W. McCall

record, written by a Nashville disk jockey.

Country music was hardly Fries' first calling. He was born November 15, 1929, to parents who played music to accompany silent movies in theaters. Developing his musical interests at home, Bill studied classical music at the University of Iowa, although he found music theory tedious and dropped out. He worked as a journalist for a period of time before he finally ended up with his award-winning advertising career.

After his music career ended, C.W. McCall became mayor of Olathe, Colorado, where one of his first administrative challenges concerned deer that were nibbling flowers and hedges on citizens' lawns.

Chip Davis, who co-wrote "Convoy," organized many of the musicians from that session to form a New Age act, Mannheim Steamroller.

234

THIS TIME I'VE HURT HER MORE THAN SHE LOVES ME
CONWAY TWITTY
MCA 40492
Writers: Earl Thomas Conley, Mary Larkin
Producer: Owen Bradley
January 31, 1976 (1 week)

Conway Twitty and Earl Thomas Conley were both literally on the move while "This Time I've Hurt Her More Than She Loves Me" developed as Conway's twentieth number one single, and Conley's first as a writer. Just prior to their big moment, Conley worked out of Huntsville, Alabama, while Twitty had long been established in Norman, Oklahoma. Both became residents of Nashville within a year of each other.

Conley earned his first Top 20 record in 1975, when Mel Street recorded his song "Smokey Mountain Memories" on the GRT label. Even before that, Earl had started work on "This Time I've Hurt Her More Than She Loves Me," written about the marriage of his future producer, Nelson Larkin.

"Nelson's wife had gotten this idea," says Conley, "so I wrote on this thing for a couple of years. It was written wrong, and after I'd written 'Smokey Mountain Memories' for Mel Street and moved to Nashville, then it just came out one day like [it is now]."

"We recorded it, I think, did a demo, kind of a 'spec track' on it. I still wasn't real comfortable in the studio, so we decided to pitch it to Conway. We took it over to Conway's office. He cut it right away, and it went to number one, so I was able to sustain myself for a couple more years."

Twitty, still living in Oklahoma, heard the song on a trip to Nashville, where L.E. White, of Twitty Bird Publishing, had set it aside. "I listened to it over and over that day," recalls Conway. "I told L.E., 'Man, I love the song, but I damn sure love his singin', too. Has he got a deal anywhere? Is anybody tryin' to help him? Call him, see what his deal is. Maybe we can help get him with a label or something—this guy sings his butt off.' "

The call was made, but nothing much came of it. In August of 1975, Twitty moved to Nashville; three months later, "This Time . . ." made its chart debut, with White and Carol Lee Cooper lending vocal support.

On January 31, 1976, Conway picked up his first number one single since moving to his new Music City home.

235

SOMETIMES
BILL ANDERSON & MARY LOU TURNER
MCA 40488
Writer: Bill Anderson
Producer: Owen Bradley
February 7, 1976 (1 week)

Thanks to his long string of quiet recitations, Bill Anderson earned the nickname "Whisperin' Bill," and he has whispered with two separate female duet partners on number one singles. The first was Jan Howard, who joined him on "For Loving You" [see 32—"My Life"] in 1967.

A native of West Plains, Missouri, Howard had replaced Jean Shepard as the regular female on "The Bill Anderson Show" during the '60s, expanding on her solo work, which included a number five recording in 1966, "Evil On Your Mind." Anderson & Howard followed "For Loving You" with three more Top Five singles through 1971, including their remake of the Supremes' "Someday We'll Be Together." Jan also wrote Anderson's 1970 hit, "Love Is A Sometime Thing."

Jan Howard left "The Bill Anderson Show"

in 1973, and 200 replacements were considered before Bill settled on Mary Lou Turner. After his "World Of Make Believe" [see 153] climbed to number one in 1974, Anderson earned a Top Ten release with "Every Time I Turn The Radio On," but was unable to crack that position again until he finally recorded a duet with Turner.

The vehicle was "Sometimes," a song he wrote while riding a bus during a tour of England. "I was reading a review of the movie *Shampoo*," he recalls, "and the reviewer had written about a part in the movie where one of the characters asked another if they were married. The character had replied 'Sometimes.'

"It struck me as a great idea for a duet between a man and a woman. Since there was no paper to write on in the bus, I tore a page out of the magazine I was reading and began writing the song as we rode along. I finished it before we got to the town where we'd be working."

Anderson taught it to Turner at the sound check that evening. "The blend of our voices wasn't the greatest I had ever heard," he admits, "but I felt from the beginning that the song was a hit. I didn't think it mattered who sang it, so I kept it for us."

They followed up "Sometimes" with one more Top Ten hit, "That's What Made Me Love You." Meanwhile, Anderson's work as a solo performer and as a songwriter [see 353—"I May Never Get To Heaven"] would yield further dividends.

Cledus Maggard

236

THE WHITE KNIGHT
CLEDUS MAGGARD
& THE CITIZEN'S BAND
Mercury 73751
Writer: Jay Huguely
Producers: Leslie Advertising
February 14, 1976 (1 week)

A fifteen-year veteran of the theater, Jay Huguely had acted in Shakespearean performances and performed in productions of *The Music Man* and *Man of La Mancha*. He had also made brief appearances on television's "The Saint" and "The Avengers." But nothing prepared him for the overwhelming success of "The White Knight," a novelty record based on the jargon heard daily on CB radio.

Huguely wasn't even aware of the citizen's band until he went to work at the Leslie Advertising Agency in Greenville, South Carolina. Company president Bill Leslie suggested the CB craze had advertising possibilities, but Huguely was unfamiliar with the entire movement. Leslie suggested he borrow a CB and park by the interstate to get a feel for it.

"I went out on I-85 and listened for about an hour," Jay told the *Fresno Bee*. "Then I came back in and asked Bill, 'Would you please tell me what all that stuff means?'" Leslie provided him with a CB dictionary that explained the terminology, and Huguely built the story-line from there.

"The whole thing started at three in the afternoon by the highway and ended that midnight," he said to Bill Morrison of the *Raleigh News & Observer*. "I actually wrote the song in 15 minutes. The rest of the time was spent putting the record together."

Originally, it was pitched to Sears & Roebuck as a commercial idea, but when Sears nixed it, 2,000 copies were pressed for local distribution. A Greenville radio station played the record, and all 2,000 sold out in a week. Mercury Records purchased the master, and Huguely suggested a new name for the label.

"About twenty years ago, I worked at a radio station and performed skits on the air," he explained at the time. "One of the continuing characters was Cledus Maggard. When 'The White Knight' was going to be released, I thought 'Jay Huguely' didn't sound right for a person doing that kind of record, and 'Cledus Maggard' popped into my mind."

It became a number one single, although Huguely never earned another country hit. He eventually resumed his acting career, performing in the 1982 Broadway show *Play Me a Country Song*. He wrote scripts for the short-lived TV program "Tales of the Gold Monkey," and he also worked as a story editor for "Magnum, P.I."

237

GOOD HEARTED WOMAN
WAYLON & WILLIE
RCA 10529
Writers: Waylon Jennings, Willie Nelson
Producers: Ray Pennington,
Waylon Jennings
February 21, 1976 (3 weeks)

"The outlaw movement?" former RCA division head Jerry Bradley queries rhetorically. "There wasn't no outlaw movement. It was a damn album cover called *The Outlaws*, but folklore made it into this great story."

Wanted: The Outlaws was packaged as a sampler, a series of eleven songs (eight of them previously released), featuring the talents of Waylon Jennings, Willie Nelson, Jessi Colter and Tompall Glaser. Each performer contributed two solo cuts to the project, and Waylon added three duets.

The "outlaw" label had been floating around for several years. Jennings cut Lee Clayton's "Ladies Love Outlaws" in 1972, but Glaser's publicist, Hazel Smith, generally receives credit for first encouraging its use by a North Carolina radio station to refer to the progressive edge of country.

The *Outlaws* album coincided with a media barrage touting the "outlaws," and both phenomena intertwined to raise the image to new heights. In the process, the album became the first Nashville package certified platinum by the Recording Industry Association of America for sales of a million copies. It yielded two hits: Waylon & Jessi's "Suspicious Minds" and Waylon & Willie's "Good Hearted Woman."

Jennings and Nelson wrote the latter in 1969 in a Fort Worth motel room, during a poker game. "I'd been reading an ad for Ike and Tina Turner," Waylon recalls, "and it said, 'Tina Turner singing songs about good-hearted women loving good-timing men.' I thought, 'What a great country song title that is!'" Willie contributed only two lines, though he received half of the royalties, and the twosome dictated lyrics to Nelson's wife, Connie, as they continued the game (they lost, incidentally).

"I think Connie and Jessi both were the object of that song," Willie reports. "Naturally, we started thinking about the ones who were having to put up with us at that particular time."

Jennings released "Good Hearted Woman" as a solo single in 1972, hitting number three, and later cut it on his album *Waylon Live*. His concert version provided the basis for the duet. "I just took my voice off and put Willie's on in different places," Waylon says. "Willie wasn't within 10,000 miles when I recorded it." Jennings also played with the applause, adding "canned" audience in several spots, including the part in which he calls "Willie!"

Ironically, after her ad inspired the song, Tina Turner later cut "Good Hearted Woman" on an album of her own.

**"The Outlaws":
Tompall Glaser,
Waylon Jennings,
Jessi Colter,
Willie Nelson**

THE ROOTS OF MY RAISING
MERLE HAGGARD
& THE STRANGERS
Capitol 4204
Writer: Tommy Collins
Producers: Ken Nelson, Fuzzy Owen
March 13, 1976 (1 week)

When "The Roots Of My Raising" reached the top of the country chart, it marked Merle Haggard's ninth straight number one single, giving him 14 number ones among his last 15 singles. It was also his second chart-topping hit written by Tommy Collins [see 91—"Carolyn"].

"I was writing that about my folks," says Collins, of "Roots"'s nostalgic feel. "I felt that the simple way of life was sort of disappearing with the modernization of things, so I just went back to the days in Oklahoma when I grew up in a rural area, on a farm.

"I wanted to capture something of those precious, simple days when we didn't have to lock our house, you didn't worry about people

stealing. You picked people up on the road and gave them a ride without the fear of having a gun pulled on you; if a neighbor's barn burned down, or his house, the other neighbors got together and built him another one. It was a great life."

Haggard and then-wife Bonnie Owens visited Collins at his home in Bakersfield when "The Roots Of My Raising" was still a work in progress. Even in its unfinished state, Merle wanted to record it, and when the whole thing was finished, it easily became the twenty-third number one single of Haggard's career, with Leona Williams providing the female voice.

In 1981, Haggard expressed his appreciation for Collins in a very personal way, writing and recording a single titled "Leonard." Haggard wrote the song during a bus trip to Gatlinburg with Leona (that same trip also yielded their duet hit "The Bull And The Beaver"), but he never told Collins about his creation. Instead, it came as a surprise.

"Months later," notes Collins, "I found out that he was gonna record. I went to his recording session, and I didn't mean to stay the entire session. I started to leave about halfway through it, and one of the musicians said Merle wanted me to stay for the session because he had a surprise for me.

"So I was there when he recorded 'Leonard,' and I feel like it's a very great honor that Merle would do that. It also told my real name [Leonard Sipes], which I appreciated."

239
FASTER HORSES (THE COWBOY AND THE POET)
TOM T. HALL
Mercury 73755
Writer: Tom T. Hall
Producer: Jerry Kennedy
March 20, 1976 (1 week)

"There was a fellow who won a Nobel Prize for something," says Tom T. Hall. "When they asked him about his philosophy of life, he said, 'Well, I'm like Tom T. Hall—faster horses, younger women, older whiskey and more money.' I thought that was kind of neat for a Nobel Prize winner to have that philosophy."

The Nobel winner's philosophy came straight from Tom T.'s composition "Faster Horses (The Cowboy And The Poet)."

"I was in New York," recalls Hall, "and a friend of mine was with me, and he said, 'Boy, this is a tough town.' I said, 'Yeah, I'll tell you what New York's about—it's about faster horses, younger women, older whiskey and more money.' That rolled off my tongue so cleverly that I wrote it down."

It remained on Hall's notepad for some time, until Bobby Bare informed him that he wanted to cut a concept album about cowboys. Hall decided the "faster horses" phrase would work as a cowboy's motto, and he wrote the song for that project.

Bare's version was never released as a single, and producer Jerry Kennedy decided Hall should record it. They sped up the tempo and threw in a horn arrangement, and Tom T. collected his seventh number one single. The motto was so catchy that it also popped up around the country as a silk-screened emblem.

"A lot of people now think that I'm singing about belt buckles and hat bands and bumper stickers," Hall laments, "but those came along *after* the song."

T. earned two more Top Ten hits with Mercury Records over the following year—the bluegrass standard "Fox On The Run" and "Your Man Loves You Honey"—before signing with RCA in 1977. Through the next five years, he went to the Top Ten only twice, with "What Have You Got To Lose" and "The Old Side Of Town." Eventually, he returned to Mercury, hitting number eight in 1984 with a remake of a Rudy Vallee number, "P.S. I Love You."

Tom T. continues to tour, but he has turned his interests from writing songs to writing books [see 151—"I Love"]. Hall has no regrets about his decline as a performer, either, since he was always a reluctant artist. "There's something about being over 50 and still wigglin' your butt," he says. "You have to realize who you are and what time it is anyway."

240
TILL THE RIVERS ALL RUN DRY
DON WILLIAMS
ABC/Dot 17604
Writers: Wayland Holyfield,
Don Williams
Producer: Don Williams
March 27, 1976 (1 week)

It should come as no surprise that a song of enduring commitment like "Till The Rivers

All Run Dry" should come from a confirmed romantic.

"It's a little embarrassing sometimes," Don Williams confesses, "because I can be watching somebody [on TV] find Lassie, and it almost brings tears to my eyes. She used to just tear me up. I mean, if she got lost, and then when they found her or whatever—I can get so emotionally moved by some of the silliest things."

Embarrassing though it might be, that sentimental side flowed in a very warm rendition on "Till The Rivers All Run Dry," co-written with Wayland Holyfield. "Wayland had pretty much the chorus in its entirety and was just havin' some trouble with what to say to go along with the chorus," Don recalls. "I pretty much wrote the verses to it. We sat down and did it together, but I guess that was my major contribution to it, where to go with the verses and what to say."

"I remember workin' on that song," notes Wayland. "Don had a little camper-type recreational vehicle that he traveled in at the time, and I remember workin' on that song in that rec-vee, 'cause it's real hot in the summer.

"In the studio, he did such a good job. But after it was recorded, Bobby Bare was in our office, 'cause Don had played him the album when it was new. After they came to that song, all Bobby said was, 'When do you ship that? That dog will hunt.'"

With Holyfield joining Williams on back-up vocals, the dog got off to a head start with its *Billboard* debut on January 31, 1976. Two months later, "Till The Rivers All Run Dry" broke free from the pack as the top country single of the week.

"This was new stuff to me, and I wasn't sure what does work and what doesn't work," Holyfield recalls, "but I loved that song, and a lot of people used it at weddings and still do."

241
YOU'LL LOSE A GOOD THING
FREDDY FENDER
ABC/Dot 17607
Writer: Huey P. Meaux
Producer: Huey P. Meaux
April 3, 1976 (1 week)

With Freddy Fender's career recharged, GRT Records brought out some of his older recordings during the course of 1975, and while "Secret Love" [see 231] shimmied upward, GRT had a simultaneous Top Ten success with "Since I Met You Baby" [see 42]. In 1976, the label reached number 13 with Freddy's version of "Wild Side Of Life," while one month later, ABC/Dot gave Fender his fourth number one single.

Once again, "You'll Lose A Good Thing" was a remake, having been introduced by Barbara Lynn in 1962. Recorded on the Jamie label by producer Huey Meaux, the original went all the way to number eight on the *Billboard* Hot 100. Meaux likewise produced Fender's version, which became the last of their four chart-topping efforts.

"Freddy was a novelty," Meaux told Bob Allen in *Country Song Roundup* in 1981. "He doesn't sing like nobody else. He's got that pain, that cry in his voice. And he stood out. He looked like the fun-lovin' guy that everybody wanted to be their buddy."

Freddy cut "You'll Lose A Good Thing"— and his other Meaux-produced hits—in Huey's Houston-based Sugar Hill Studios, a reconstructed facility that had previously yielded hits for George Jones, B.J. Thomas and Bobby Bland. The studio was also the site for the Big Bopper's "Chantilly Lace" [see 96].

Fender was able to muster only three more Top Ten singles after "You'll Lose A Good Thing": "Vaya Con Dios" (number seven, 1976), "Living It Down" (number two, 1976) and "The Rains Came" (number four, 1977). His career became muddled when a former manager left him with income tax problems, and he also developed a dependency on alcohol and several narcotics. On August 26, 1985, he was admitted to the Chemical Dependency Unit of South Texas, in Corpus Christi. The popular belief is that his dependency stemmed from his overnight success.

"I would like to say that," Freddy suggests. "That would make me look good, but regardless whether I'd have had trouble or not, I would have found troubles. If I didn't have a reason to do it, I would have found one. I used to use my career as an excuse, but not anymore."

Sober ever since, Fender recorded with Boston-based Critique Records in 1988, and in the meantime, he found a secondary career in films. His first role was a cameo appearance in *Short Eyes*, and he followed that with a spot in the Robert Redford-directed *The Milagro Beanfield War*. He has also been featured in two other movies, *She Came to the Valley* and *Always Roses*.

242

'TIL I CAN MAKE IT ON MY OWN
TAMMY WYNETTE

Epic 50196
Writers: Tammy Wynette, Billy Sherrill,
George Richey
Producer: Billy Sherrill
April 10, 1976 (1 week)

Tammy Wynette

Tammy Wynette calls " 'Til I Can Make It On My Own" her favorite of all the songs she's written. As with much of her material, the writing process began during a recording session. Piano player George Richey brought up an idea about how a person just divorced might gradually become independent.

Richey told Tammy of the title, and since she had just ended her marriage with George Jones, she related well to the topic. They didn't get too far at the session, though, and producer Billy Sherrill suggested they put the song aside until a later date.

Tammy visited Richey one Saturday night, and his wife Sheila fixed popcorn while the two worked on the song. They worked late into the evening and finished up most of " 'Til I Can Make It On My Own," but it still needed two more lines.

"We got Billy over to my house on Sunday," Richey recalls, "and we had televisions going in every den in the house and every bedroom, because he loved to bet the ballgames. He'd run from one room to another watching all the ballgames, and as soon as the ballgames were over, he came into the room where we were writing at the piano, and knocked out the two lines immediately."

In 1976, " 'Til I Can Make It On My Own" reached number one in its first fling at the chart. Three years later, Kenny Rogers & Dottie West took it to number three. Tammy sang back-up on their record.

Richey married Tammy on July 6, 1978. He has since been referred to as "Mr. Tammy Wynette" on occasion, but he is quite a figure in country music as well. Richey played piano on many of the records by Wynette, Jones and Charlie Rich, as well as on Johnny Paycheck's "Take This Job And Shove It" [see 300]. The former head of Capitol Records, George produced many of Sonny James' hits and Freddie Hart's "Easy Lovin'" [see 83]. He has also written many others, including "Soul Song" [see 116], "The Grand Tour" [see 176] and "A Picture Of Me (Without You)."

243

DRINKIN' MY BABY (OFF MY MIND)
EDDIE RABBITT

Elektra 45301
Writers: Eddie Rabbitt, Even Stevens
Producer: David Malloy
April 17, 1976 (1 week)

Born in Brooklyn on November 27, 1944, and raised in East Orange, New Jersey, Eddie Rabbitt is hardly the typical country artist. The son of an Irish immigrant, he learned his first handful of guitar chords during a Boy Scout hike, but his exposure to and love for country music had to filter through the urban/suburban environs of New York's metro area.

He learned his lessons well, though. Rabbitt memorized tons of trivia from country record labels: writers, producers, record times, publishers, "B" sides, and so on. He also got a chance to tap his reservoir at Elizabeth, New Jersey's Six Steps Down for $12 a night.

Scraping together as much as he could save, Rabbitt arrived in Nashville in 1968 with $1,000 in his back pocket. His car died when he reached his apartment on 17th Avenue, and he walked or hitched around Music City for more than a year.

Eddie's first successes came as a songwriter: he penned three songs for Elvis Presley, including "Kentucky Rain." In 1974, his composition "Pure Love" [see 165] provided Ronnie Milsap with his first number one single.

A few months later, "You Get To Me" marked Rabbitt's debut as an artist on the *Billboard* country chart. Two successive singles, "Forgive And Forget" and "I Should Have Married You," reached the Top 20. His next single, "Drinkin' My Baby (Off My Mind)," took him to number one.

"It's just a fun song," says Rabbitt, "one of those songs that's kind of a compilation of all the drinkin' songs in country. I never wrote a serious song about drinkin'. It was kind of imitating the art."

Johnny Bush was actually the first to record "Drinkin' My Baby," which Eddie composed during a three-day writing spree with frequent collaborator Even Stevens. That week's efforts also yielded "Two Dollars In The Jukebox," which Rabbitt took to number three in late 1976.

Rabbitt and Stevens were innovators, using a two-track machine at home to build demos, bouncing material from one track to another, adding new parts as they went along. They worked up "Drinkin' My Baby (Off My Mind)" on the machine, with a host of sound effects.

"We had beer cans bein' opened and fizzin' and pourin' into a glass," Stevens recalls, "and then it kicked in the rhythm and everything. When we got in the studio, we tried doin' that, but we realized it was corny, so we eliminated that part."

244
TOGETHER AGAIN
EMMYLOU HARRIS
Reprise 1346
Writer: Buck Owens
Producer: Brian Ahern
April 24, 1976 (1 week)

Country Music magazine once called her "the keeper of the country flame." It's an apt description for Emmylou Harris, whose love of tradition first flickered in 1975, with the release of her remake of the Louvin Brothers' "If I Could Only Win Your Love." The single soared to number four, and the *Pieces of the Sky* album went to number one.

Her respect for traditional music was relatively new at that time. Born April 2, 1947, in Birmingham, she grew up primarily in Virginia, a cheerleader, valedictorian and beauty contest winner. During high school, she leaned toward the folk of Pete Seeger and Bob Dylan. After a brief fling at drama at the University of North Carolina, she hit the road playing coffeehouses.

Emmylou lived for two years in New York, where she cut a folk album, then she ran away to Nashville for six months in 1970. Ultimately, she landed in Washington, D.C., where her return to the club scene brought her into contact with former Byrd and Flying Burrito Brother Gram Parsons. She joined his touring band and worked on two albums with Parsons before his death on September 19, 1973, of a drug overdose.

From Parsons, Harris acquired an appreciation for the Louvins, Charley Pride and Merle Haggard, and she followed their trail once she recovered from the shock of Parsons' passing.

Once established, Harris followed up *Pieces of the Sky* with the *Elite Hotel* album, and the album's first single represented the first number one—both for Emmylou and for Warner Bros.' country division. Appropriately, it was another of her remakes—a version of Buck Owens' "Together Again."

Owens wrote the song in 15 minutes at 3:00 A.M. years earlier. Terming it a "throwaway song," he featured it on the "B" side of "My Heart Skips A Beat," and both became number one records [see 5—"How Long Will My Baby Be Gone"] in 1964.

"I think it's very hard to write a happy song that isn't corny," opines Harris, "and that's just a brilliant example. You just sort of know that the people that are being sung about in this song have gone through a lot. Yet it doesn't talk about that; it just talks about the moment of being back together again. I think it sums up all that country music tries to be—incredibly simple, yet very poignant and moving."

Emmylou's "Together Again" his number one in 1976, a dozen years after Buck's. Three years later, Buck and Emmylou teamed up on a derivative duet, "Play Together Again Again."

245
DON'T THE GIRLS ALL GET PRETTIER AT CLOSING TIME
MICKEY GILLEY
Playboy 6063
Writer: Baker Knight
Producer: Eddie Kilroy
May 1, 1976 (1 week)

"Every time I find a song I like, it doesn't do worth a darn," Mickey Gilley told Jennifer Boeth of the *Dallas Times-Herald* in 1982. "But if it's one I don't care for, and somebody talks me into doing it, it does great. My taste in things has gotten to the point where I don't really know what's good."

That self-appraisal was based in part on his hesitation to record "Don't The Girls All Get Prettier At Closing Time." Producer Eddie Kilroy played a very basic guitar/vocal demo for Gilley made by songwriter Baker Knight.

"I had come to Nashville about six or eight months ahead of doing that particular session," Gilley recalls. "I wish I still had a copy of the demo, because it was great. I didn't pay that much attention to the melody, or anything, but I was totally intrigued with the lyrics. I thought it was a great song."

Nevertheless, Gilley felt it wasn't right for him, and passed on it. "It was demoed 2/4 time," he explains, "and it didn't have that boogie flavor to it or anything."

Kilroy was persistent, though, and his belief in "Don't The Girls" paid off. At the next session, Eddie pulled it out again, and, against Mickey's protests, played it once more. Finally, Kilroy made Gilley sit down at the piano and play his trademark boogie patterns, and with Gilley's fingers plunking out the rhythms, Kilroy sang the melody as he imagined it.

"It will work," agreed a now-convinced Gilley, "let's cut it."

Born March 9, 1936, Gilley grew up in Ferriday, Louisiana, where he hung out with his cousins, Jerry Lee Lewis and Jimmy Swaggart. His mother saved up money from her meager income as a waitress to buy Gilley his first piano before he hit the age of 12. Once he emerged as a national talent, it became clear that all three cousins had learned their craft the same way.

"I've always given Jerry Lee credit for being the best talent in the family," says Gilley. "It was his piano style that he created, and it rubbed off on me and Jimmy."

Charley Pride

246
MY EYES CAN ONLY SEE AS FAR AS YOU
CHARLEY PRIDE
RCA 10592
Writers: Naomi Martin, Jimmy Payne
Producer: Jerry Bradley
May 8, 1976 (1 week)

"I think a great bit of my success is because of how I try to deliver a song and put the feeling in it," Charley Pride told Alanna Nash in *Behind Closed Doors*. "I am in the business of selling lyrics. I don't think anyone should just . . . sing to be singing a song. If you just open your mouth and say the words without any emotion, it's pointless to try to sing the song."

Pride's attitudes about particular songs have not always been consistent, though. For whatever reason, Pride passed on "My Eyes Can Only See As Far As You" the first time he heard it. "I thought it was a hit," says producer Jerry Bradley, "but he didn't like it. Six months later when he came in, I played it to him again and he loved it. He didn't remember the song."

"It turned out to be one of the finest singles that we've had," Pride confirms. "He had pitched that song to me once before, and I do think it is a pretty song."

"My Eyes Can Only See As Far As You" was actually the second single from Pride's *The Happiness of Having You* album, recorded at RCA's "Nashville Sound" Studios. The title track had peaked at number three earlier in the year. "My Eyes" made its *Billboard* debut on March 13, just five days before Pride's thirty-eighth birthday. It was probably a good omen for Pride, who holds a fascination with astrology.

Charley has been known to present friends with a special necklace he designed himself. It incorporates a pair of fish—the symbol for his sign, Pisces—surrounding the letters "GID," his personal motto, "Get It Done." Pride often guesses the signs of mere acquaintances with an uncanny accuracy, at times pinpointing their actual birthdays.

"Everybody's psychic, you know, and sometimes I do that," he says nonchalantly. "You can just feel it. I've told people they're Libras or Tauruses, and they'll say, 'What? What?' It's a psychic thing. You miss sometimes, and then you hit."

Pride definitely hit with "My Eyes Can Only See As Far As You." It reached number one, eight weeks after securing a berth in the *Billboard* country chart.

247

WHAT GOES ON WHEN THE SUN GOES DOWN
RONNIE MILSAP
RCA 10593
Writer: John Schweers
Producers: Tom Collins, Jack D. Johnson
May 15, 1976 (1 week)

Both Ronnie Milsap and producer Tom Collins call *20/20 Vision* their favorite album among their collaborations. The title, of course, plays

upon the fact that Milsap has been blind since birth, from congenital glaucoma. His parents divorced when he was one, and left him in the care of his grandparents. They enrolled him, at age six, in the Morehead School for the Blind in Raleigh, North Carolina.

His blindness has fascinated the public and journalists alike, though Milsap has understandably grown weary of talking about it. After all, he gets along quite well as he is. He once kept up a bowling average of 161, he is able to go jogging along the interstate while on tour, and he even drives (with assistance) every now and then in open fields.

20/20 Vision came on the heels of Milsap's most successful single to date, "Daydreams About Night Things" [see 222]. It included liner notes by Marie Ratliff, who, a decade later, became the manager of *Billboard*'s country singles chart. The first single from *20/20*, "What Goes On When The Sun Goes Down," was written by John Schweers, who also penned "Daydreams."

"I was so ecstatic about the reaction to 'Daydreams,' and the kind of success that it had, I asked him to write another song like that," Milsap admits. "I hate to do that to a writer—'Go clone the last record.'"

Schweers, in fact, refers to "What Goes On" as "Son Of 'Daydreams.'"

"My wife found 'What Goes On When The Sun Goes Down,'" says John. "I think it was just some kind of advertisement for a nightclub or somethin' she got out of a magazine. She said, 'This'll be a good title,' and I wrote it down and just worked on it.

"I nearly threw it away. I got disgusted with it. I had written about four or five more tunes, and I took 'em in and played 'em for Tom and Ronnie and this was the last one I played. They started jumpin' up and down about this one, so I thought, 'Boy, I'm glad I brought it in.'"

"What Goes On When The Sun Goes Down" made its *Billboard* debut on March 20, 1976. Eight weeks later, it became Milsap's fifth number one single.

248

AFTER ALL THE GOOD IS GONE
CONWAY TWITTY
MCA 40534
Writer: Conway Twitty
Producer: Owen Bradley
May 22, 1976 (1 week)

Conway Twitty represents a confluence of musical styles. As a youngster, in Friar's Point, Mississippi, he was drawn to the Grand Ole Opry radio broadcasts via WSM in Nashville, the blues music of an unnamed black man, and the gospel he heard at church.

Returning to the U.S. following a stint in the military in Japan, Conway heard Elvis Presley singing "Mystery Train" for the first time, and he decided to follow Elvis' lead and pursue a rock and roll career. In that role, he created a standard titled "It's Only Make Believe," a 1958 million-seller that remains Twitty's concert-closer more than three decades later. His 1976 composition, "After All The Good Is Gone," harkens back to that pioneering era.

" 'After All The Good Is Gone' is that country, bluesy thing, real bluesy," he explains. "It was about twice as long as what you hear—maybe not twice, but it was a lot longer than what finally came out. We got in the studio, and Owen Bradley made me take out a bunch of it.

"That's the best of both worlds from Conway Twitty. That's country, and that's rock and roll, and it's the blues thing. It's even got some gospel feel in it. It's everything that I grew up singin'."

A new recording of "It's Only Make Believe" appeared on the record's "B" side. Released twenty years after Conway's first recording sessions at the Sun Studios in Memphis, "After All The Good Is Gone" debuted in *Billboard* on April 3, 1976. The record reached number one in just eight weeks.

Conway achieved his conversion from rock to country with the help of legendary Nashville songwriter Harlan Howard [see 591—"I Don't Know A Thing About Love"]. Howard encouraged Conway, and pitched the demo tape to Owen Bradley that eventually led to Twitty's signing as a country artist. Recorded in Muscle Shoals, many of those songs had the same problem as "After All The Good Is Gone": their length.

"His songs were always eight or ten minutes long," Howard remembers. "And I'm into commercial. I'd time 'em with a watch, and I know three minutes is pretty long. We had Conway make up a tape of all these incredibly long songs, and then you have to do 'em several times.

"I remember falling asleep in this big leather couch, and I don't think he even knew it. [When I woke up] this same song was going on, but it did show Conway really singin' very pure country-type songs, and 'Hello Darlin' ' [see 56] was one of them."

249

ONE PIECE AT A TIME
JOHNNY CASH
Columbia 10321
Writer: Wayne Kemp
Producers: Charlie Bragg, Don Davis
May 29, 1976 (2 weeks)

When Johnny Cash took "One Piece At A Time" to number one, it marked a comeback for The Man in Black, who hadn't had a chart-topping record for more than five years [see 70—"Flesh And Blood"].

"Man has only so much creative energy," Cash, then 44, told *Billboard*, "and I was working on a TV show, movies and a book. I got lazy about recording. That's a mistake a lot of artists my age make. I even took some soundtrack tapes from my TV show and released them as records. I should have gone into the studio and carefully recorded them."

The vehicle for his return was a novelty record in which an assembly-line worker steals an entire Cadillac piece by piece over a twenty-year period.

"That was a difficult song," says writer Wayne Kemp of "One Piece At A Time." "I worked on that two years trying to get it together. My wife gave me the idea. I came in from Georgia, and sat at the table drinking a cup of coffee, and I couldn't find the common denominator to tie it all together. It had a bunch of words going in all different directions, and she finally mentioned to me that none of these parts would fit if they were stolen over the years. That's what I was looking for—then I realized that if nothing would fit, it would be an ugly car."

In connection with the record, Cash was given one of those ugly cars: an automobile built with parts from a one-decade span of time, pieced together at Nashville's Hilltop Auto Sales. Life imitated art in one other instance, too. In the record, the title to the car weighed 60 pounds, and Kemp's lyric sheet was also quite lengthy.

"It's seven pages hand-written," he says, "and it's four pages typed. There's a lot of words in it."

Cash remained with Columbia Records for another decade, before moving to the Mercury roster. In the interim, he managed two more Top Ten solo singles, 1979's "(Ghost) Riders In The Sky" and 1981's "The Baron." He went to number two with Waylon Jennings in

1978, on "There Ain't No Good Chain Gang," and contributed to a number one quartet in 1985 on "Highwayman" [see 633].

In 1980, Cash was inducted into the Country Music Hall of Fame.

250

I'LL GET OVER YOU
CRYSTAL GAYLE
United Artists 781
Writer: Richard Leigh
Producer: Allen Reynolds
June 12, 1976 (1 week)

"Good things come to those who wait." It's a time-worn cliché, but in the case of Crystal Gayle, it's one that certainly applies. She debuted on *Billboard*'s country chart on September 19, 1970, with "I Cried (The Blues Right Out Of My Eyes)," written by her sister, Loretta Lynn. It took almost half a dozen years for Crystal to finally reach number one.

Her first record to reach the Top Ten came in late 1974. "Wrong Road Again" climbed to number six, and it took a full year before she could return to that chart level, reaching number eight with "Somebody Loves You." During that period of time, she had the good fortune of meeting Richard Leigh, then a student at Richmond's Virginia Commonwealth University.

Johnny Cash

"I met him in a telethon in Bristol, Tennessee," Crystal recalls. "He was a songwriter, and I was just starting out, and then he goes to Nashville . . ."

That first trip was an eye-opener for Leigh. He picked up some new ideas about his writing, and during his last semester at VCU, he wrote and demoed a fresh batch of songs. Armed with his new collection, Leigh returned to Music City, re-connecting with Gayle.

"On that first trip, I'd met [producer] Allen Reynolds and [pianist/arranger] Chuck Cochran and a bunch of guys who were affiliated with Crystal Gayle," says Leigh. "I called them up again and told 'em I was back in town. Allen listened to the tape of six songs and got to 'I'll Get Over You.' He stopped the tape and said it was a hit song, that he'd like to cut it—originally, he said, on me."

Leigh had other ideas. He asked Reynolds to play it for Crystal, who took to it immediately. "We cut that song one day on the second half of a session," Reynolds reports, "and we kind of got it goin', but it didn't please me. I said, 'We'll do this tomorrow or the next day'—we had the same band back, and the next day it was no problem. We just walked right in to that performance."

Among the vocalists on the session was a still unknown and unsigned Janie Frickie. Crystal took them to dinner at Nashville's T.G.I. Friday's after the session, but no one realized the celebration's significance—they had all just recorded Crystal's first chart-topping single.

picture *Raiders of Old California*, which starred Faron Young [see 93—"It's Four In The Morning"]; 1973's *Guns of a Stranger*, with Chill Wills; and the 1963 movie *Ballad of a Gunfighter*, based on Robbins' recordings "San Angelo" and "El Paso."

With Spanish guitar licks by Grady Martin and back-up vocals by Tompall & The Glaser Brothers [see 586—"You're Gettin' To Me Again"], "El Paso" was a landmark recording in country music. It ran over four minutes in length, and occupied the top slot on the *Billboard* country chart for seven consecutive weeks. It also topped the pop chart for two weeks, becoming the first number one pop single of the '60s.

"El Paso City" was a sequel to the original, with its lyrics making frequent reference to Robbins' earlier classic. "Every time I flew over El Paso, I was usually getting some sleep," he once told Bob Allen in *Country Song Roundup*. "It never failed that I would always wake up about five seconds before the pilot would say, 'And off to the left is the city of El Paso.' One time, I asked the stewardess for a pen and paper, and I had that song written before we even got across the state of New Mexico."

Robbins later wrote yet another sequel, "The Mystery Of El Paso City," although he never recorded it.

"El Paso City" was also the first single Robbins recorded under the guidance of producer Billy Sherrill. "We argued like cats and dogs," recalls Sherrill. "He'd say, 'You little red-headed bastard, you don't know anything—you steal songs more than I do.' He was an absolute pleasure to work with."

251
EL PASO CITY
MARTY ROBBINS
Columbia 10305
Writer: Marty Robbins
Producer: Billy Sherrill
June 19, 1976 (2 weeks)

Once country music drifted away from the "country & western" concept, Marty Robbins remained one of the few artists who continued to use Western cowboy tales as a primary element of his repertoire.

Gene Autry had been a source of inspiration during Robbins' formative years [see 20—"I Walk Alone"], and Marty went on to appear in a number of Westerns of his own. Among at least eleven films, his credits include the 1957

252
ALL THESE THINGS
JOE STAMPLEY
ABC/Dot 17624
Writer: Naomi Neville
Producer: Norro Wilson
July 3, 1976 (1 week)

With his change of record labels [see 206—"Roll On Big Mama"] in 1975, Joe Stampley barraged the *Billboard* country charts with material for two successive years. ABC/Dot put three Stampley singles in circulation during 1975, while the new Epic label released four.

During the Bicentennial year, Stampley hit the charts eight more times—four on each label. With that glut of material, only one single cracked the Top Ten, but it eventually went all the way to the top.

Art Neville, of the Neville Brothers, was the first to cut "All These Things" in 1961; Stampley found his way onto *Billboard*'s Hot 100 in 1966, when his pop group, the Uniques, released the song on Shreveport's Paula Records. Adding strings to the original recording, Paula reissued the single in 1972, but "All These Things" finally found its mark when Stampley re-cut it as a country song.

"It went number one country for me and thrilled me to death," says Stampley. "Also, it was voted the number one two-step dance song of the year in Texas."

It wasn't the last time that Stampley would record "All These Things," though. In 1981, he remade it as a ballad for Epic, but it only reached number 62.

After a brief dip in 1977, Stampley returned to *Billboard*'s Top Ten the following year with "Red Wine And Blue Memories," "If You've Got Ten Minutes (Let's Fall In Love)" and "Do You Ever Fool Around." In 1979, he augmented his solo career by teaming up with Moe Bandy [see 355—"Just Good Ol' Boys"], and notched another solo hit that year, "Put Your Clothes Back On."

That same year, his eighteen-year marriage to his high school sweetheart ended in divorce, but in 1981, he remarried. Joe also had another Top Ten single, "I'm Gonna Love You Back To Loving Me Again." He failed to reach that level again until 1984, when he covered "Double Shot (Of My Baby's Love)," a number 17 pop hit for the Swingin' Medallions in 1966.

Stampley continues to reside and record in Nashville, where his son, Tony, also works as a songwriter.

253

THE DOOR IS ALWAYS OPEN
DAVE & SUGAR

RCA 10625
Writers: Bob McDill, Dickey Lee
Producers: Jerry Bradley, Charley Pride,
Dave Rowland
July 10, 1976 (1 week)

"That story of class conflict, of a girl leaving her lover for a rich man, is an age-old tale,"
says songwriter Bob McDill, "but the public never tires of it. I think there's at least one hit every couple years with a variation of that same theme."

McDill went to number one with that theme by writing the chorus and the first verse to "The Door Is Always Open." Songwriting partner Dickey Lee contributed the second verse, and the song was cut by Tennessee Pulleybone, a group that would later become Bobby Bare's backing band.

Waylon Jennings also recorded the song for one of his albums, and it was that version that producer Jerry Bradley played for Dave Rowland, the male vocalist with Dave & Sugar. As became a standard practice with the trio, they shifted the song around, leading off with the chorus and dropping off any instrumental introduction; in record industry jargon, they started in "cold."

"I thought it was a great song," remembers Rowland. "I thought it would really work for us with our combination, and especially for the harmonies and the chorus, 'cause it's such a power chorus." That hunch proved correct when "The Door Is Always Open" became Dave & Sugar's second single and first number one record.

Born January 26, 1942, in Anaheim, California, Rowland was the one who basically put together the Sugar act. Skilled on piano, trumpet, drums, bass and guitar, he played in a military band during his enlistment, and later ended up a member of the Four Guys, who went on tour with Charley Pride. Rowland was eventually dropped from the Four Guys, shortly after going into debt for a new house, furniture, a piano and a new car. He took several short-term jobs, including work as a singing waiter in an Italian restaurant at the 100 Oaks Shopping Mall, vocal work in a commercial studio, and a loading-dock job at UPS. Meanwhile, he put together another quartet, Wild Oats, with three guys and a girl, but when that act folded, Rowland decided on a two girl/ one guy unit.

Dave & Sugar was courted by both Pride and Tammy Wynette, who were looking for opening acts. Rowland decided to work with Pride because of their prior association, and debuted in Oklahoma City on April 19, 1975. That summer in Pennsylvania, Bradley caught the show and laid the groundwork for a contract backstage. Bradley and Rowland agreed on "Queen Of The Silver Dollar" as a first single, setting up the success of the follow-up, "The Door Is Always Open."

TEDDY BEAR

RED SOVINE

Starday 142
Writers: Dale Royal, Billy Joe Burnette,
Tommy Hill, Red Sovine
Producer: Tommy Hill
July 17, 1976 (3 weeks)

He was named for a U.S. President and followed in the footsteps of a country giant, yet Woodrow Wilson "Red" Sovine earned a reputation on his own with a handful of songs about truck drivers.

Born July 7, 1918, in Charleston, West Virginia, Sovine joined his first band at age 17, appearing on radio WCHS. In 1947, he formed the Echo Valley Boys, which played at "The Louisiana Hayride." When Hank Williams left the show in 1949, Sovine moved into his spot as the Hayride's main attraction.

In 1955, he made his first appearance on *Billboard*'s country charts, and in March of 1956, Red earned his first number one single in a duet with Webb Pierce on "Why Baby Why" [see 508]. His first number one as a solo act came ten years later, when "Giddyup Go" spent six weeks in the top slot. In 1967, he went to number nine with "Phantom 309."

Like "Giddyup Go" and "Phantom 309," "Teddy Bear" was a recitation that embraced a trucker's theme, as a young, crippled boy gets on a CB radio from his home and pours out a heart-wrenching tale to many of the drivers passing by his town.

"If a motorist is in trouble, the truck driver is usually the first one to stop," one-time driver Sovine once told *Country Song Roundup*. "He'll be on that CB rounding up some help. The story told in 'Teddy Bear' is typical of the good deeds truckers perform every day."

Dale Royal, one of four writers listed on the single, was a truck driver as well. His CB handle was "The Storyteller," and "Teddy Bear" was a handle he assigned to the young boy in the song. Conceived on the road, it became the first song he ever had published and recorded.

The recitation spent three weeks at number one, beginning July 17, 1976, and on August 28, the *Teddy Bear* LP became Sovine's only record to top the country album chart.

Sovine died April 4, 1980, from injuries sustained in a car accident.

GOLDEN RING

GEORGE JONES
& TAMMY WYNETTE

Epic 50235
Writers: Bobby Braddock, Rafe VanHoy
Producer: Billy Sherrill
August 7, 1976 (1 week)

Producer Billy Sherrill calls "Golden Ring" a "Cinderella record." In fact, few records have ever developed from start to finish as quickly.

George Jones and Tammy Wynette had divorced the prior year, and they had decided to record together again. The marquee value of a reunion (on record, at least) was so powerful that whatever they recorded had the potential to become a monster. Songwriter Bobby Braddock felt he had the perfect concept.

"I had seen a TV show about the story of the life of a handgun," Braddock says. "The first person to buy it was a hunter, and a policeman had it, and somebody robbed a liquor store with it, and it finally ended up where somebody bought it to protect their home, and it showed a two-year-old standing up on a chair getting it and aiming it at his head."

Braddock decided to use the same concept to follow the life of a wedding ring. He tried to infuse the song with a country/gospel style in the vein of the Chuck Wagon Gang, and, though he had most of it developed, he couldn't seem to finish it.

Braddock knew George and Tammy were due to record within a couple of days, so he called Rafe VanHoy at 8:00 A.M. and asked for some help. "We got together in about an hour," VanHoy remembers. "My mother at that time worked at a wholesale jewelry place, and I remember calling her up and talking to her to find out all the details about rings and where they were made, different terminology— anything about them, just to have any kind of input that we could."

The next day, Braddock went out of town, and VanHoy was left to piece together a demo at Tree Publishing's four-track studios. VanHoy played it for Tree executive Buddy Killen, who was convinced it was a hit, and called Sherrill to tell him the demo was on its way over.

Sherrill heard it that day, and cut it in about 15 minutes a few days later, with George Richey on piano and the Gatlin Brothers on backing vocals. The Gatlins had no bass singer, though, so George Jones provided the final bass note.

The single was released within the next two weeks, debuted on the *Billboard* chart on June 5, 1976, and reached number one on August 7.

256

SAY IT AGAIN

DON WILLIAMS

ABC/Dot 17631
Writer: Bob McDill
Producer: Don Williams
August 14, 1976 (1 week)

With a birthday on April 4, 1944—4/4/44—Bob McDill represents an interesting case study for disciples of *Cheiro's Book of Numbers*. His effect on country music is even more interesting.

Hailing from Beaumont, Texas, McDill graduated from Lamar University and hitched up with the Army before heading to Memphis for a couple of years. There, he wrote songs for Sam the Sham & The Pharaohs, and for Perry Como, but the successes were fewer and in smaller degrees than he preferred.

He had a strong folk background, and when his friend, Allen Reynolds, suggested he move to Nashville, McDill hesitated before making the cross-state trek in 1969. He admittedly had to learn to like country music before he could start writing it seriously, and his first success didn't come until 1972, when Johnny Russell took his "Catfish John" to number 12.

A year later, Russell brought McDill his first Top Five single, with "Red Necks, White Socks And Blue Ribbon Beer," beginning an odyssey that yielded 39 Top Ten hits in the ensuing 16 years. Included were "Amanda" [see 346], "Louisiana Saturday Night," "Baby's Got Her Blue Jeans On" [see 608], "Song Of The South" [see 805] and "Don't Close Your Eyes" [see 781].

A dozen singles came through Don Williams releases, including "Rake And Ramblin' Man," "Good Ole Boys Like Me," "If Hollywood Don't Need You" [see 509] and "Say It Again," Don's fifth number one single.

"It's just one of those McDill songs," Williams says. "I don't think I had to do anything to it to make it work for me. There's so many songs I have to change up to make them work for me, but that song's just really pretty much straight-ahead."

McDill treats songwriting as anyone else would treat a more usual pursuit. He works fairly rigid daily hours in a publisher's cubicle on Music Row in Nashville, and any memories of "Say It Again" have blurred with the hundreds of other tunes he has composed there.

His efforts have been well-rewarded, and not just in a financial sense. Any industry discussions of the town's best songwriters invariably include his name, and in 1985, McDill received induction into the Nashville Songwriters Hall of Fame.

257

BRING IT ON HOME TO ME

MICKEY GILLEY

Playboy 6075
Writer: Sam Cooke
Producer: Eddie Kilroy
August 21, 1976 (1 week)

As a teenager in the early '50s, Mickey Gilley shared with his white schoolmates an interest in country music, and acquired a great deal of reverence for the early country stars. By the same token, Mickey would also visit the segregated black side of town with his cousins Jerry Lee Lewis and Jimmy Swaggart, where they took in the blues and boogie at a club called Haney's Big House.

With that early appreciation for soul sounds, it's not surprising that Gilley would find success on occasion by remaking R & B standards like "Bring It On Home To Me." The original version was recorded by Sam Cooke, reaching number 13 on *Billboard*'s Hot 100 during 1962. Featuring Lou Rawls on backing vocals, it followed such Cooke staples as "You Send Me," "Chain Gang," "Cupid" and "Wonderful World."

When Gilley cut "Bring It On Home To Me," he toyed with it several times in the recording studio before he settled on the final version.

"We had made a demo on the tune at the end of one of the sessions," he remembers. "We did it just to see what it needed, and at the time, Eddie Kilroy and I were putting all the arrangements to the tunes. I was up in the Faron Young Building, and they had a little piano set up on the side. I went over to the piano and started playing 'Bring It On Home' and we came up with the modulation in it, and Eddie said that was the way we needed to record it."

"Bring It On Home To Me" was included on the album *Gilley's Smokin'*, which also featured

"Don't The Girls All Get Prettier At Closing Time" [see 245]. In 1977, Gilley's efforts were rewarded with five trophies at the Academy of Country Music awards. "Bring It On Home" was named Single Record of the Year; "Don't The Girls" earned Song of the Year; and *Smokin'* became Album of the Year. Gilley was also honored as Top Male Vocalist and Entertainer of the Year.

Sam Cooke's "Bring It On Home To Me" influenced Motown artist Smokey Robinson, who used the song as a model when he wrote "You've Really Got A Hold On Me" in a New York hotel room. In 1983, Gilley cut Robinson's song, peaking at number two.

Mickey Gilley

258
(I'M A) STAND BY MY WOMAN MAN
RONNIE MILSAP
RCA 10724
Writer: Kent Robbins
Producers: Tom Collins, Jack D. Johnson
August 28, 1976 (2 weeks)

According to U.S. statutes, a publisher cannot copyright a title. For that reason, many records have similar-sounding titles. "He Got You" [see 491] sounds a lot like "She's Got You" [see 282]; Johnny Horton's "Honky Tonk Man" is identical to Marty Robbins' "Honkytonk Man"; and the Judds' "Young Love" [see 815] is comparable to the Sonny James classic [see 100—"That's Why I Love You Like I Do"].

Likewise, "(I'm A) Stand By My Woman Man" is quite reminiscent of the Tammy Wynette classic "Stand By Your Man" [see 21], a fact not lost on Al Gallico, who owned the publishing rights to that Billy Sherrill composition. Adding to the coincidence, Hargus "Pig" Robbins, who frequently played on Sherrill productions for Charlie Rich [see 128—"Behind Closed Doors"], Wynette and George Jones, also appeared on Ronnie Milsap's record.

"I accuse Pig today of playin' me into a lawsuit," laughs producer Tom Collins. "I said, 'Now, Pig, give me some licks like you would have done on a Billy Sherrill or Tammy Wynette session.' Of course, he played 'em, and it helped make the production of the record sound like 'Stand By Your Man' [though Milsap points to "Behind Closed Doors"]. That was my first lawsuit over a song. The rule of thumb when I first did that was: if every four bars is

different, you're okay. Of course, that's never been in writing."

Songwriter Kent Robbins (no relation to Pig) hadn't even intended to write "(I'm A) Stand By My Woman Man." That phrase was originally the second line of another song, and Collins, who published it, suggested he dump the original idea and make that line the centerpiece.

"I'd just been married for about three years," Robbins remembers. "We'd had our first little girl and everything, so the emotions in that are true. But it was something that got written and rewritten a few times before the final version came out."

"(I'm A) Stand By My Woman Man" took Milsap to number one in August of 1976. Six weeks later, the Country Music Association named him Male Vocalist of the Year for the second time. On February 19, 1977, the National Academy of Recording Arts and Sciences gave him his second Grammy for "(I'm A) Stand By My Woman Man."

I DON'T WANT TO HAVE TO MARRY YOU

JIM ED BROWN & HELEN CORNELIUS

RCA 10711
Writers: Fred Imus, Phil Sweet
Producer: Bob Ferguson
September 11, 1976 (2 weeks)

"I Don't Want To Have To Marry You" combined a struggling newcomer and a country music veteran. Jim Ed Brown (born April 1, 1934) first gained acceptance as a member of the Browns, a family trio that teamed him with his sisters Bonnie and Maxine.

The Browns reached number six in 1956 with "I Take The Chance," and earned their only number one record with "The Three Bells," which began a ten-week run at the top on August 31, 1959. Their follow-up, "Scarlet Ribbons," peaked at number seven, but that was the last of their Top Ten releases. In the mid-'60s, both sisters quit to devote more time to their families; Jim Ed went on to a solo career that produced four Top Ten singles, including "Pop A Top" (number three, 1967) and "Morning" (number four, 1970).

In 1975, Brown's career needed a shot in the arm, and he told producer Bob Ferguson that he was looking for a female singer to add to his show. Ferguson suggested Helen Cornelius (born December 6, 1941), from Mark Twain's hometown of Hannibal, Missouri. Brown thought their voices were incompatible, though, and the subject was dropped.

Nearly a year later, Ferguson approached Brown with "I Don't Want To Have To Marry You." Brown was interested in the song, especially when Ferguson told him he envisioned it as a duet. Brown thought it would provide a recorded reunion with sister Maxine, but instead, Ferguson suggested Cornelius. Not yet convinced, Brown consented.

The two vocalists had never met until they went in the studio to record the song, and that first collaboration became a monster success. "I Don't Want To Have To Marry You" debuted on the *Billboard* country chart on the nation's Bicentennial, and reached number one in September. In 1977, they earned Vocal Duo of the Year honors from the Country Music Association.

**Jim Ed Brown &
Helen Cornelius**

Jim Ed and Helen earned six more Top Ten singles—including "Saying Hello, Saying I Love You, Saying Goodbye" and "Lying In Love With You" (both number two) and "Fools" (number three)—before splitting at the end of 1980. Cornelius went on to headline her own solo tours and co-starred with Dave Rowland, of Dave & Sugar, in a road production of *Annie Get Your Gun*. Brown, meanwhile, became the host of the Nashville Network's "You Can Be A Star." In 1988, they made amends and returned to touring as a duo.

260

IF YOU'VE GOT THE MONEY, I'VE GOT THE TIME
WILLIE NELSON
Columbia 10383
Writers: Lefty Frizzell, Jim Beck
Producer: Willie Nelson
September 25, 1976 (1 week)

On October 11, 1982, the Country Music Hall of Fame added Lefty Frizzell to its roster. In a 14-year period, Frizzell netted 17 Top Ten singles and six number one records, the first with "If You've Got The Money, I've Got The Time."

Frizzell wrote the song after a friend asked if he wanted to take a ride, and Lefty replied, "If you've got the money, I've got the time." It instantly hit a nerve, and Frizzell parlayed the song into a three-week ride at number one in 1950.

Born William Orville Frizzell, Lefty picked up his interest in country music by listening to Jimmie Rodgers, Ernest Tubb and Roy Acuff. Around age 10, he made his first appearance on the radio, and in his late teens, he became a regular performer at local honky-tonks. He also tried boxing on the side.

"A lot of people say he got [his nickname] from being left-handed, boxing at the Golden Gloves," says his brother, David. "My mother told me that he got it from some of the local boys in the neighborhood. Lefty had a reputation for being a rough street fighter."

Lefty's successes included "Always Late," "Mom And Dad's Waltz," "The Long Black Veil" and "Saginaw, Michigan," but he was uncomfortable with his fame. He continued to record and write, however, and in the mid-'70s, he earned a number one single when

Johnny Rodriguez cut "That's The Way Love Goes" [see 154]. In the summer of 1975, he nabbed a Top Ten single when Moe Bandy recorded "Bandy The Rodeo Clown."

Four weeks after that record's chart debut, Lefty died on July 19, 1975, of a massive stroke. Exactly one year later, Willie Nelson's version of "If You've Got The Money, I've Got The Time" appeared in *Billboard*, eventually rising to number one. Another year later, Nelson released a tribute album, *To Lefty from Willie*, which yielded a Top Ten single with "I Love You A Thousand Ways."

"Actually, I had in mind to do that album earlier," notes Willie, "but then when Lefty died, I held on to that idea for a while. I didn't want anybody to think that I was tryin' to take advantage of the fact that he had died."

261

HERE'S SOME LOVE
TANYA TUCKER
MCA 40598
Writers: Richard Mainegra, Jack Roberts
Producer: Jerry Crutchfield
October 2, 1976 (1 week)

Though it earned her two number one singles, Tanya Tucker's first attempt at recording in Los Angeles was a disappointment [see 215—"Lizzie And The Rainman"], and she quickly returned to the familiar territory of Nashville to record her next MCA album.

Lovin' & Learnin' paired her with Jerry Crutchfield, an independent record producer who had worked with Barbara Fairchild [see 123—"The Teddy Bear Song"] and with Dave Loggins, on his Grammy-nominated pop single "Please Come To Boston." That first album with Crutchfield brought Tanya two hits, "Don't Believe My Heart Can Stand Another You," which reached number four; and the Loggins-penned "You've Got Me To Hold On To," which peaked at number three.

The second Tucker/Crutchfield collaboration yielded the album *Here's Some Love*, and the title track was selected as a first single. "I really liked the song," she recalls, "and I liked the way Jerry worked. We really got along together well, and the song came off great." In fact, it did well enough to become her sixth single to top the *Billboard* country charts, reaching its peak position on October 2, 1976. Five weeks later, the LP became her first and only record to top the *Billboard* country album chart.

Throughout the rest of the '70s, Tanya's successes became more sporadic. In 1977, "It's A Cowboy Lovin' Night" reached number seven, and on November 1, 1978, she made a controversial appearance on the stage of the Grand Ole Opry. Displaying a rock and roll attitude, she was booed for her covers of Elvis Presley and Buddy Holly material, although she won over the audience by the end, performing her yet-to-be-released single "Texas (When I Die)." The tune debuted in *Billboard* later that month, peaking at number five.

In the meantime, Tanya's *Greatest Hits* on Columbia became her first gold album in December of 1978, and the *TNT* LP went gold the following February. *TNT* also soared to number two on the country album chart in March of 1979, surpassed only by Kenny Rogers' *The Gambler* [see 330].

"I think it was just a searching period," says Tucker of her experiments with rock textures. "It was experimental. I wasn't leaving country music, because that's my roots, but I was searching and trying to cut bigger and better records."

262
THE GAMES THAT DADDIES PLAY
CONWAY TWITTY
MCA 40601
Writer: Conway Twitty
Producer: Owen Bradley
October 9, 1976 (1 week)

"I think any singer or songwriter worth his salt is very sensitive not only to things that happen to you, but to things that happen to people around you," says Conway Twitty. "I was well aware of that kind of thing."

"That kind of thing" was the topic of "The Games That Daddies Play," a situation in which a man fathers a son and leaves the mother to care for the boy alone. Twitty wrote it originally for Cal Smith, whose recording didn't quite hit the mark.

"I wrote it with some holes in it so you could put in some fresh [instrumental] licks," Conway explained to Jack Hurst of the *Chicago Tribune*. "I should've done a dub of the way I thought it should be done before I took it to Cal and Loretta [Lynn], but I firmly believed it was a hit song—so I decided to do it myself."

Twitty's version included some plucky fiddle parts and a unique triplet roll on steel guitar. The record became another success for Conway, slipping into the top spot in its eighth week on the *Billboard* country chart.

"I really liked Cal's singin'," Conway continues. "He's a friend, and that's just one of the things he turned down. I [found] another one for him. I called him and said, 'Cal, come down here, I got a smash for ya.'"

Cal passed on that record, too—it was "The Gambler" [see 330].

Two years later, Twitty and Smith became business partners—along with Jerry Reed and the Oak Ridge Boys' Richard Sterban, among others—in the Nashville Sounds, Music City's first minor-league baseball team in fifteen years.

Twitty (a.k.a. Harold Jenkins) held a long-time fascination with the nation's pastime. Nicknamed "Harold the Hawk," he was offered a pro contract by the Philadelphia Phillies after high school, although he was sidetracked by the Korean War. Even in the service, Conway played for the Army Engineers at Yokohama in Japan, although music bypassed baseball as his primary interest.

Owning the Sounds, Twitty was able to stay involved in the sport, and at one point, he even considered purchasing 42 percent of the Minnesota Twins. In 1988, Conway decided the ball team—plus other business interests—were taking too much time away from his music, so he sold his stock.

263
YOU AND ME
TAMMY WYNETTE
Epic 50264
Writers: Billy Sherrill, George Richey
Producer: Billy Sherrill
October 16, 1976 (2 weeks)

Tammy Wynette's sixteenth number one record as a solo star came with "You And Me," a song that Billy Sherrill checked out of the hospital to finish. Sherrill was in for an overnight physical, but he phoned George Richey to talk about a session that was coming up that week. Richey told Sherrill that he had a good idea to work with.

"He said, 'If you think we can write it, I can get out for two hours,'" Richey remembers.

Sherrill did check out that Sunday afternoon, but they ran into a snag trying to find the right words for part of the melody.

"It's the exact same story with Norro Wilson and me on 'A Very Special Love Song' [see 159], which has a counter-melody," says Sherrill. "On 'You And Me,' we tried to write a lyric to the melody, we worked, had lunch, had a couple of beers, came back, and it was just impossible.

"Then I thought of 'A Very Special Love Song,' and said, 'Wait a minute, George. Let's don't write the words to this thing. Let that melody be the answer to the words—"I can hear the rain is falling softly," *then* the melody.' Fifteen minutes later, we had the song, and it wrote itself."

They finished the tune that afternoon, and Sherrill checked back in to the hospital. The following day, he checked out, they recorded it, and it was released later that week.

Wynette recorded six more Top Ten singles through 1982, including "One Of A Kind," "Womanhood," "They Call It Making Love" and "Another Chance." She cut one more in a duet with Mark Gray in 1985, "Sometimes When We Touch."

Tammy gained more attention, though, in other areas of her life. After her 1978 marriage to Richey [see 242—"'Til I Can Make It On My Own"], she was abducted from a parking lot in Nashville and left beaten on an interstate in south Tennessee. Her captors were never identified.

In 1979, Tammy published her autobiography, *Stand By Your Man* [see 21], which became a TV movie in 1981. She underwent a series of operations, and checked into the Betty Ford Center after becoming addicted to a prescription drug. Appropriately, she appeared briefly in 1986 on a TV soap opera, "Capitol."

264

AMONG MY SOUVENIRS
MARTY ROBBINS
Columbia 10396
Writers: Edgar Leslie, Horatio Nicholls
Producer: Billy Sherrill
October 30, 1976 (1 week)

Marty Robbins

Marty Robbins was hardly the first person to sing "Among My Souvenirs." Four different people had released it in 1928, and Connie Francis revived it in 1959, taking it to number seven on *Billboard*'s pop chart.

The single opened with an alternating duet between Marty and a classically-inspired fiddle performance, culminating in a smooth, well-crafted ballad. "I loved 'My Souvenirs,'" producer Billy Sherrill recalls. "Marty hated the idea, but we put it out anyway. He wanted it for an album cut, and I finally talked him into putting it out as a single because we didn't have anything else. He thought it was a stupid record; the way we kicked it off was kind of schmaltzy."

"Among My Souvenirs" first appeared in *Billboard* at number 63 over Labor Day weekend in 1976, working its way to number one around Halloween. Robbins followed "Souvenirs" with four more consecutive Top Ten singles, the last coming with "Return To Me" in 1978, but when he decided to produce his own material, his success waned.

Marty was a survivor, though, both musically and in his personal life. His hobby was auto racing, and he competed in well over 50 events during the course of his lifetime (he drove the pace car at the Indianapolis 500 in 1976). In October 1974, he hit a wall at the Charlotte Speedway at 160 mph; he broke two ribs and a tailbone, and needed 37 stitches in his face. On New Years Day in 1981, Robbins suffered a second heart attack [see 53—"My Woman, My Woman, My Wife"], and in 1982, he mounted a comeback with his first Top Ten release in four years, "Some Memories Just Won't Die."

Unfortunately, the title provided the press with his eulogy, as he passed away December 8, 1982, six days after sustaining his third heart attack. Just two months earlier, on October 11, Tammy Wynette had presented him with a plaque at the Country Music Association awards show, signifying his induction into the Country Music Hall of Fame. The week of his passing, the Clint Eastwood film, *Honkytonk Man*, was released, with Marty singing the title track.

On May 7, 1983, he was honored when the Music City 420 NASCAR race was changed to the Marty Robbins 420. In 1988, Marty Robbins Enterprises released a series of four black-and-white videos compiling 12 episodes of "The Drifter," a mid-'60s TV series starring Robbins that had aired in only a handful of markets.

265

CHEROKEE MAIDEN/WHAT HAVE YOU GOT PLANNED TONIGHT DIANA

MERLE HAGGARD & THE STRANGERS

Capitol 4326
Writers: Cindy Walker/Dave Kirby
Producers: Ken Nelson, Fuzzy Owen
November 6, 1976 (1 week)

Though many people may not have subscribed to his political viewpoints in "Okie From Muskogee" [see 45] and "The Fightin' Side Of Me" [see 50], no one could dispute Merle Haggard's patriotism. When the Bicentennial year rolled around, it was no surprise that he released "Here Comes The Freedom Train," highlighting historic American figures like George Washington and Thomas Jefferson with a railroad theme.

"Freedom Train" peaked at number 10 over the Fourth of July, and Haggard's next release hit number one just four days after Jimmy Carter defeated incumbent Gerald Ford in the first election of the nation's third century. "Cherokee Maiden," like "Freedom Train," had a historic ring, since it was first recorded by Texas swing pioneer—and Haggard hero—Bob Wills.

"Bob Wills & The Texas Playboys was just a part of life in California if you were a transplanted Okie," explains Haggard. "To me, he was a big name, just like President Roosevelt."

So great was Wills' influence that in 1970, at the height of Haggard's career, he took a commercial risk in paying homage to his mentor with *A Tribute to the Best Damn Fiddle Player in the World (My Salute to Bob Wills)*. Merle took exhaustive measures to ensure the project was performed correctly. He visited the Texas hospital where Wills was bed-ridden with a heart ailment to interview the swing king; he spent hours listening to radio transcriptions of the original Playboys; and he practiced fiddle intensely for six months, sometimes as much as twelve hours a day.

"I remember one time," says Haggard, "I came to Nashville and stayed up 48 hours playing the fiddle. I wore out every damned guitar player in town."

He recorded that album with six of the original Playboys, and in 1976, another Playboy contributed to his number one Wills remake. "'Cherokee Maiden' we used to do on the show a lot because of Tiny Moore," states former Stranger Ronnie Reno. "Tiny played with Merle for so long, and Tiny had arranged it for Wills."

"Cherokee Maiden" was actually a two-sided hit. The "B" side, "What Have You Got Planned Tonight Diana," was written by then-Stranger Dave Kirby.

Four days after the record reached number one, Haggard's second wife, Bonnie Owens, filed for divorce.

266

SOMEBODY SOMEWHERE (DON'T KNOW WHAT HE'S MISSIN' TONIGHT)

LORETTA LYNN

MCA 40607
Writer: Lola Jean Dillon
Producer: Owen Bradley
November 13, 1976 (2 weeks)

Four years after the Country Music Association gave her the Entertainer of the Year award, Loretta Lynn picked up the same honor from the Academy of Country Music in 1976. Already one of the top ladies in the business for a full decade, her career picked up a boost through a meeting with songwriter Lola Jean Dillon.

Dillon earned her first writing contract without ever visiting Nashville, when a friend sent a tape of three songs to Harlan Howard [see 591—"I Don't Know A Thing About Love (The Moon Song)"]. Howard responded by picking up the publishing rights, so Dillon made her move to Music City. Dolly Parton had recorded one of her songs on an album, but with no singles, Lola Jean's income wasn't exactly substantial. She began answering the phone at Howard's company while he was between secretaries.

"I didn't do a good job at answerin' the phone," she confesses, "but I was sittin' there one day, sort of thinkin' how I could get somethin' to Loretta and make sure she heard it. I'd been sendin' stuff over to her office, and I felt like she hadn't been hearin' it."

She called Owen Bradley's secretary at MCA Records for advice, but her friend put Dillon on hold. The next voice on the line was an unfamiliar one, and Lola Jean thought she'd be chewed out. Instead, it was Loretta, who told her to bring a tape over right away. Lynn recorded one of the songs, "When The Tingle Becomes A Chill," which made it to number two on the *Billboard* country chart in 1975.

Once she cut "Tingle," Lynn signed Dillon to her own Coal Miners Music publishing company. Six months after the ACM honors, Loretta cut a second Dillon composition, "Somebody Somewhere (Don't Know What He's Missin' Tonight)," a tune Dillon wrote a year after signing with Loretta.

"When she recorded it, she called me up to the motel room and played it back for me," Dillon recalls, "and tears came to my eyes. It was really good the way she did it, and that's probably what made her put it out as a single, 'cause I think she figured if it touched me that much it'd touch everybody else that much."

"I just thought," Loretta adds, "that if that wasn't a great jukebox song, somebody somewhere wasn't listenin' too good."

Loretta Lynn

267

GOOD WOMAN BLUES

MEL TILLIS

MCA 40627
Writer: Ken McDuffle
Producers: Mel Tillis, John Virgin
November 27, 1976 (2 weeks)

Mel Tillis has established an entire public identity based in great part on a speech impediment. His name has appeared on marquees and record albums as M-M-M-Mel, and he's so comfortable with the problem that he titled his 1984 autobiography *Stutterin' Boy*.

Tillis acquired his handicap at the age of three when he contracted malaria. The stutter was an embarrassment, but everyone assumed it would go away as he got older. It didn't, although the stutter vanished when he sang. "Singing is a kind of mechanical helper," he explains. "With the various instruments playing along, the rhythm and everything moving, my voice just seems to flow with it . . . like following the bouncing rubber ball."

Though he now seems at ease with the condition, he remained unable to accept it until the late '50s. "I couldn't meet people, was afraid to get up in front of an audience. I even had a fear of answering the telephone. But let me tell you, it's much better to face the stuttering than to run away from it."

Tillis worked more often as a songwriter and sideman during the early part of his career, playing on shows with Minnie Pearl and Webb Pierce. He was featured as a vocalist during the Pearl dates, but she had to encourage him to speak to the audience. He discovered that his stutter actually enhanced his natural sense of humor, and he became more outgoing.

In 1968, Mel became a regular on TV's "The Porter Wagoner Show." After a disagreement, Wagoner fired him; the next day, he received an invitation to join "The Glen Campbell Goodtime Hour." There, his abilities as a guitarist, singer, songwriter and comedian all came to prominence, heightening his image in the minds of country fans.

The exposure helped build seven more Top Ten hits after "I Ain't Never" [see 109] went to number one. In fact, two of those records—"Sawmill" and "Midnight, Me And The Blues"—stopped at number two.

His recording efforts, when combined with his TV exposure and humorous disposition, helped Tillis capture the Country Music Association Entertainer of the Year award on October 11, 1976. One week earlier, his "Good Woman Blues" debuted on *Billboard*'s country charts; on December 4, it became his second chart-topping single.

268

THINKIN' OF A RENDEZVOUS

JOHNNY DUNCAN

Columbia 10417
Writers: Sonny Throckmorton,
Bobby Braddock
Producer: Billy Sherrill
December 11, 1976 (2 weeks)

Johnny Duncan had been making records for Columbia for almost a full decade before he finally found his way to number one. First appearing on the *Billboard* charts on August 12, 1967, he recorded with Don Law and Frank Jones for several years before hooking up with Billy Sherrill.

"The beginning with Billy actually came in the winter of '73," Duncan remembers. "My contract was up in '72, and I said, 'If I re-sign, the only smart thing for me to do is work with the number one man, and that of course is Billy Sherrill.'"

Sherrill produced one Top Ten single, "Sweet Country Woman," but when he couldn't re-create that success, Duncan grew discouraged with his career progress. His wife left him in 1975, and he moved back home to Texas. It took a single phone call to get Duncan to record again.

"Larry Gatlin called me," he recalls, "and said, 'John, other than me and Ray Price, you're the best singer in country music—why aren't you cutting records?' Larry and I got together in a couple of months and recorded 'Jo And The Cowboy,' and introduced the world to Janie Frickie."

"Jo And The Cowboy" peaked at number 26, hardly an illustrious showing, but it did set a precedent, and when Duncan teamed up with Sherrill again in 1976, Frickie became an integral part of the records. The first single in the new situation was "Stranger," a Kris Kristofferson tune that Johnny had heard on the radio while driving from Texas to Nashville. It went to number four on the *Billboard* chart, although Duncan was still not satisfied.

" 'Stranger' was a monster hit, even though it didn't go to number one," he says. "I thought if we could do it again, then it was legitimate."

The follow-up, "Thinkin' Of A Rendezvous," took him to number one in an ironic situation. Years earlier, songwriter Sonny Throckmorton had recorded a few songs in New Mexico with producer Norman Petty. The first song he cut was written by Duncan. With "Thinkin' Of A Rendezvous," they had reversed roles: Throckmorton penned Duncan's first chart-topping hit.

269
SWEET DREAMS
EMMYLOU HARRIS
Reprise 1371
Writer: Don Gibson
Producer: Brian Ahern
December 25, 1976 (2 weeks)

Rarely has a song performed so well on so many different occasions as "Sweet Dreams." Songwriter Don Gibson released it twice, hitting number nine in 1956, and number six in 1961. Faron Young was the first artist to have a hit with it, reaching number two in 1956, and Patsy Cline took it to the Top Ten in 1963.

The list also includes charted versions by Troy Seals and Reba McEntire, and a recording by Tommy McLain that reached number 15 on *Billboard*'s Hot 100 in 1966. But Emmylou Harris is the only person to take it to number one. She cut the song in Los Angeles on June 21, 1975—two weeks before "If I Could Only Win Your Love" [see 244—"Together Again"] first charted.

"That was the end of the first Hot Band tour," she says. "We wanted to capture that energy on tape, so we went in to the Roxy and recorded three days there. That was quite an experience."

A self-avowed "song collector," Emmylou was joined on vocals by Herb Pedersen (now of the Desert Rose Band) and Rodney Crowell. "When Rodney joined the band, he and I would sit around thinkin' of stuff to do," Harris remembers. "I had a lyric book. I'd write down every song that I really liked, and we would just thumb through them, and say, 'Oh, here's one.' We would just sit and sing, and 'Sweet Dreams' was definitely worked up singing with Rodney."

The Hot Band's first line-up, like those that have followed, was quite impressive. Included were ex-Eagle Bernie Leadon, drummer John Ware, Hank DeVito (who wrote Juice Newton's "Queen Of Hearts") and former Elvis Presley sidemen James Burton, Glen D. Hardin and Emory Gordy.

"The Hot Band was pretty hot," recalls Gordy, "and, I must say, arrogant. We were all very arrogant, and we didn't know what the hell we were doing, I don't think. We thought maybe we were playing country—we didn't realize at that time that country music didn't sound that way. But that's the way we thought it ought to be."

Apparently, the general country audience thought so, too. Just prior to "Sweet Dreams," Harris reached number three with "One Of These Days." She followed "Sweet Dreams" with three more Top Ten singles: "(You Never Can Tell) C'est La Vie," "Making Believe" and "To Daddy."

270
BROKEN DOWN IN TINY PIECES
BILLY "CRASH" CRADDOCK
ABC/Dot 17659
Writer: John Adrian
Producer: Ron Chancey
January 8, 1977 (1 week)

With his position as "Mr. Country Rock" [see 192—"Ruby Baby"] already established, Billy "Crash" Craddock made an effort in mid-career to widen his appeal and release more ballads. Accordingly, he led off 1976 with "Walk Softly" before releasing an ode to "Rub It In" [see 173] titled "You Rubbed It In All Wrong."

The latter tune was one of four hits written for Craddock by John Adrian, and the second became Billy's final number one single, "Broken Down In Tiny Pieces." A gentle, solemn release, the song featured a whispered reprise of the title by session singer Janie Frickie.

After his performance, Craddock had one special request: "When we finished, and listened to the playback, I said: 'Excuse me, but I've never asked for anything; I've never said release this song or release that one. I want this to be my next single—that is a hit record.' I just fell in love with the song when I heard it."

Following its *Billboard* chart debut on October 23, 1976, "Broken Down" took eleven

Crystal Gayle

weeks to finally reach number one. Craddock rounded out 1977 with two more ballads on ABC, "A Tear Fell" and the Adrian-penned "The First Time," but by the dawn of 1978, he had picked up a new contract with Capitol Records.

In the process, Craddock ended his association with producer Ron Chancey. Ron had co-founded Cartwheel Records (which released Craddock's first five singles) in 1970 with Dale Morris, a former pharmaceutical salesman often credited with discovering Craddock.

"Ron was hungry and I was hungry," says Craddock of the association. "I'm not hard to work with, because if there's a producer who's really set on a song, and I dislike the song, I'll do it anyway. I've always had a saying: 'Give me the right song, you do your part and I'll do mine, and it'll come out a hit.'"

After his move to Capitol, Craddock teamed with Dale Morris as producer, and the collaboration yielded two more hits: "I Cheated On A Good Woman's Love" and "If I Could Write A Song As Beautiful As You" (once again, written by Adrian).

Craddock's last Capitol album was released in 1982, and three years later, Billy appeared briefly on the Dot label. Still a Greensboro resident, he was eventually persuaded by his associates to drop "Billy" from his billing—he now appears only as "Crash" Craddock.

271
YOU NEVER MISS A REAL GOOD THING (TILL HE SAYS GOODBYE)
CRYSTAL GAYLE
United Artists 883
Writer: Bob McDill
Producer: Allen Reynolds
January 15, 1977 (1 week)

"If I had as many romantic break-ups as the characters in my songs do," Crystal Gayle told *USA Today*, "I'd be a regular on 'People's Court.'"

Instead, she has been a regular contributor to country music since the mid-'70s, with the admitted help of her sister, Loretta Lynn. Born Brenda Gail Webb on January 9, 1951, in Paintsville, Kentucky, Crystal grew up in an entirely different atmosphere than the "Coal Miner's Daughter" [see 68].

The family moved to Wabash, Indiana, when

Brenda was just four, and she was eight when Loretta cut her first record [see 7—"Fist City"]. Young Brenda was attracted to everything from Patsy Cline to Leslie Gore to the Beatles, and her musical tastes reflected that diversity.

Lynn, in fact, urged Brenda to make records that distinguished the two of them stylistically. "There's only one Loretta Lynn," Crystal explained to *TV Guide*'s Neil Hickey. "If I were real country, I probably wouldn't do as well because people would say, 'She's just trying to sound like her sister.'"

Songwriter Bob McDill contributed heavily to Gayle's sound on the 1976 album *Crystal*. Producer Allen Reynolds had persuaded McDill to move from Memphis to Nashville in earlier years, and McDill's publisher, Bill Hall, sent Reynolds a tape with three songs that ended up on the *Crystal* album.

"I called Bill on the weekend," Reynolds recalls, "and said, 'Bill, this is the best tape I've ever gotten.' It had 'You Never Miss A Real Good Thing' and 'I'll Do It All Over Again,' and a song called 'Right In The Palm Of Your Hand' that Crystal sang for years. At the time, we were into an album and strugglin' for material, so I could have killed to get that tape."

"You Never Miss A Real Good Thing" emerged as the album's second single, and Crystal's second number one record, though McDill doesn't even remember writing it. He describes it, quite accurately, as a "very progressive" record, a feel derived in part from the burning guitar work of the late Jim Colvard.

"I'll Do It All Over Again" was released as a follow-up, but stopped at number two, blocked from the top by Waylon Jennings' "Luckenbach, Texas" [see 286]. Interestingly, the third song on McDill's tape, "Right In The Palm Of Your Hand," also saw success as a single for Mel McDaniel [see 608—"Baby's Got Her Blue Jeans On"].

272

I CAN'T BELIEVE SHE GIVES IT ALL TO ME
CONWAY TWITTY

MCA 40469
Writer: Conway Twitty
Producer: Owen Bradley
January 22, 1977 (1 week)

Conway Twitty's litmus test for potential material is rather simple.

"I try to find a song that says something I know a man would like to say to a woman, but doesn't know how," he explains. "If you can make it easy for him—where all he has to do is go pick up an album, or drop a quarter in a jukebox, and just kinda give her a squeeze when he hears those words—then you've made a fan of the man, too. He appreciates the fact that you've said it for him."

Naturally, the songs Conway writes himself fit his criteria, and "I Can't Believe She Gives It All To Me" is no exception. "Again, a Conway Twitty melody," he evaluates, "a Conway Twitty-type story, that doesn't put a woman down, that's always got somethin' nice to say about the lady. I prefer to do 'em that way. You can find songs that talk about how rotten they are, and that kind of thing, but not for me."

The song brought Twitty his twenty-third number one country record, debuting November 20, 1976. Its rise to the top coincided with Jimmy Carter's Inauguration the following January.

Twitty's success came with the aid of producer Owen Bradley, who first signed him to Decca Records in 1965 [see 248—"After All The Good Is Gone"]. Born October 21, 1915, Bradley ranks among the most influential men in country music history.

A staff pianist with WSM in Nashville during the '20s, Owen served during World War II with legendary Boston Red Sox slugger Ted Williams. After the military, he played on Red Foley's "Chattanoogie Shoeshine Boy," marking his start with Decca Records. In 1950, Owen and his brother, session guitarist Harold Bradley, built the Quonset Hut, which became Columbia Studio B once they sold it to CBS. After an apprenticeship with Paul Cohen, Owen became the head of Decca's Nashville division, producing records for Kitty Wells, Loretta Lynn, Patsy Cline, Jack Greene, Ernest Tubb and Bill Anderson, to name a few. In all, Owen Bradley produced more than 70 number one singles, including such standards as "I Fall To Pieces," "I'm Sorry" and "My Special Angel."

Two noteworthy events occurred for Bradley during 1974. In October, he was named to the Country Music Hall of Fame. A couple of months earlier, his son, Jerry Bradley, was named the director of RCA's Nashville wing. It marked the only time in history that a father and son headed two rival labels.

273
LET MY LOVE BE YOUR PILLOW
RONNIE MILSAP
RCA 10843
Writer: John Schweers
Producers: Tom Collins, Ronnie Milsap
January 29, 1977 (1 week)

The only performer ever to win four Country Music Association awards for Album of the Year is Ronnie Milsap. In 1977, he won the second of those trophies with *Ronnie Milsap Live*, recorded at the same location in which the CMA bestows its honors: the Grand Ole Opry House.

Milsap spent two days rehearsing for the concert in a Nashville recording studio. Producer Tom Collins had a 24-track tape machine transported by van to the Opry, where Ralph Emery emceed two afternoon shows. In the end, Milsap culled the bulk of the album from the second performance.

Songwriter John Schweers collected his third number one record for Milsap with the only single pulled from the album, "Let My Love Be Your Pillow."

"I had that title," Schweers recalls, "but those kinds of things, you need a hook with it. I would sit down and write a page of hooks for that one line, and finally one of 'em would stand out. This one, it took me about two or three days to come up with 'Let my love be your pillow, and let me turn your life into a beautiful dream.' The 'dream' kind of refers back to 'pillow.'"

Schweers finished the song during the two days that Milsap was holed up in rehearsal, and he submitted it for Collins' inspection. Collins in turn called Milsap at home and told him that John was coming out with a last-minute addition. Ronnie liked it, too, but during rehearsals, he decided the second verse required a rewrite. Schweers had packed his writing notebook in his car, and retrieved the original notes on the song. He found a quiet alcove in the studio and went to work.

"I had about 15 pages, I guess, and I started lookin' at it, and finally the last verse came together. He liked 'Let my arms be your blanket when you sleep.'"

"Let My Love Be Your Pillow" first appeared at number 65 on November 27, 1976, covering the number one slot nine weeks later. On October 16, 1979, the live album became Milsap's third gold record.

274
NEAR YOU
GEORGE JONES & TAMMY WYNETTE
Epic 50314
Writers: Francis Craig, Kermit Goell
Producer: Billy Sherrill
February 4, 1977 (2 weeks)

On June 26, 1968, Edwin Craig passed away in Nashville. Craig was the chairman of the board of the National Life And Accident Insurance Company in 1925, when its subsidiary, WSM-AM, went on the air. A few months later, he gave final approval to a new program called "The WSM Barn Dance," which evolved into "The Grand Ole Opry."

Edwin Craig was a cousin of Francis Craig, who in 1947 wrote and performed "Near You." The following year, it became the theme song of "The Milton Berle Show."

On December 12, 1974, that same song became the very last that George Jones & Tammy Wynette would record as husband and wife. Their tumultuous six-year union had reached an all-time low, and the sessions at Columbia Studio B were hardly easy.

"They really weren't speaking then," says producer Billy Sherrill. "We just barely got through the cuts. It was bad. Toward the end, Jones wouldn't sing anything the same way twice for Tammy, and it was hard for her to phrase with him and all that. They just carried on. It made it miserable to try to do, and I thought, God, this needs to stop."

It did stop, and rather abruptly. That night, they returned to their home on Franklin Road about midnight. As they went to sleep, Jones promised that everything would work out all right, but the next morning, shortly after Wynette left the house for a dental appointment, Jones moved out for good.

That was December 13, 1974. The following March 13, the divorce became final, and she didn't see Jones again until October 13. "Near You" was held "in the can" for several years, but six months after "Golden Ring" [see 255] reached number one, "Near You" was released and sailed to the top as well.

"I always say that he nipped and I nagged," explains Wynette, summarizing the major problem with their marriage. "I guess we were both very good at it."

"Southern California" was chosen as a follow-up to "Near You," and it proceeded to a

number five peak in the fall of 1977. In the early part of 1980, Jones & Wynette teamed up for a reunion album, and it netted one last hit: "Two Story House" peaked at number two.

275

MOODY BLUE/SHE THINKS I STILL CARE

ELVIS PRESLEY

RCA 10857
Writers: Mark James/Dickey Lee
Producers: Elvis Presley/Felton Jarvis
February 19, 1977 (1 week)

He's acknowledged as the King of Rock and Roll, yet Elvis Aron Presley made his mark first in country music. After Elvis cut his earliest tracks at Sun Studios on July 5, 1954, his star was sighted by Memphis disk jockey Dewey Phillips, who played "That's All Right" and "Blue Moon Of Kentucky" repeatedly.

Presley gave his first performance later that month, and soon became a regular on "The Louisiana Hayride," acquiring a new manager, Colonel Tom Parker. The Colonel had previously guided the careers of Eddy Arnold and Hank Snow.

Elvis' chart debut came on July 6, 1955, with "Baby Let's Play House"; he reached number 10 on *Billboard*'s country list. On February 25, 1956, his Sun recording of "I Forgot To Remember To Forget" became his first number one single, also on the country chart, and on St. Patrick's Day, "Heartbreak Hotel" brought Presley his first number one with the RCA label. Following Carl Perkins' "Blue Suede Shoes," "Heartbreak Hotel" is also acknowledged as the second single ever to place on *Billboard*'s pop, country and R & B charts simultaneously.

"I Want You, I Need You, I Love You," "Don't Be Cruel"/"Hound Dog," "Teddy Bear" and "Jailhouse Rock" all attained number one stature on the country chart as well, but Elvis' induction into the Army on March 24, 1958, brought a major change. Following his return to civilian life, Presley seemed more intent on the glitter of Hollywood and the rock charts, leading to a thirteen-year absence from the Top Ten on *Billboard*'s country list.

"Suspicious Minds," "In The Ghetto" and "Kentucky Rain" would all prove successful country fare in later years, but they failed to dent even the upper 30 positions during their peak. Following his 1972 success with "Burning Love," Presley re-focused his attention on the country audience.

Three two-sided hits reached country's Top Ten in 1974, and after "Hurt" did likewise two years later, "Moody Blue" became Elvis' first number one country single since December 2, 1957. "Moody Blue" and its "B" side, "She Thinks I Still Care" [see 170], were recorded

more than a year before they hit number one. Cut February 2-4, 1976, they were, like most of the material on *Moody Blue*, laid down in the living room at Graceland Mansion.

276
SAY YOU'LL STAY UNTIL TOMORROW
TOM JONES
Epic 50308
Writers: Roger Greenaway, Barry Mason
Producer: Gordon Mills
February 26, 1977 (1 week)

When Tom Jones debuted on *Billboard*'s country chart on Christmas Day, 1976, about

Tom Jones

the only person who wasn't surprised was Jones.

Born June 7, 1940, in Pontrypridd, Wales, Jones first came to prominence in the U.S. as the deep-throated vocalist on "It's Not Unusual" in 1965. Through the next six years, he earned four more Top Ten singles on the Hot 100, including "What's New Pussycat?" and "She's A Lady," which peaked at number two.

In the meantime, his live concerts and his two-year network variety show, "This Is Tom Jones," earned him a reputation as an energetic, sexual entertainer. Jones commanded one of the highest salaries in Las Vegas, but his country side was lost in the process.

His father was a coal miner, and Tom compares his Welsh musical heritage to that of America's Loretta Lynn. "It's a slightly different music than Loretta would listen to," he said in 1983, "but coal miners sing. It's still in your roots. You come from the same kind of working-class community, and all those things rub off."

Jones developed his own working-class resume on construction crews by day, meanwhile playing the local clubs at night. After working in a trio called the Senators, he advanced to a solo career in England in 1964. In 1966-67, Jones reached the American Hot 100 on four different occasions with remakes of country hits: "Green, Green Grass Of Home," "Detroit City," "Funny, Familiar Forgotten Feelings" and "Sixteen Tons."

"Say You'll Stay Until Tomorrow" reconnected Jones with those country roots. It became a multi-format hit, climbing to number 15 on *Billboard*'s Hot 100 and number three on the adult/contemporary chart. Its best showing came in country music, reaching number one three months after it first hit the chart.

Written by Barry Mason (who had written "Delilah"), "Say You'll Stay" also brought a new phase to Tom's career. In 1981, he emerged on Mercury Records with a solid country album, *Darlin'*, and he followed with several more country LPs, as well as his Top Ten country single, "Touch Me (I'll Be Your Fool Once More)."

After his country deal ran out, Tom returned to the Hot 100 in 1989 with the Art Of Noise on a remake of Prince's "Kiss." "I'm relieved that contract is finished," a frustrated Jones told Bob Claypool of the *Houston Post*, referring to his Mercury contract. "They *only* wanted me to do country music, but once you did that, other kinds of stations wouldn't play your records. It was very confining."

277

HEART HEALER
MEL TILLIS
MCA 40667
Writers: Tom Gmeiner, John Greenebaum
Producers: Mel Tillis, Jimmy Bowen
March 5, 1977 (1 week)

Through his numerous appearances in Las Vegas, Mel Tillis became friends with Frank Sinatra. That makes it rather appropriate that Tillis was the first Nashville artist to use the services of Jimmy Bowen, who produced the Sinatra classics "Strangers In The Night," "That's Life" and "Somethin' Stupid."

Tillis agreed to work with Bowen on *Love's Troubled Waters*. They finalized the agreement while Mel was in the middle of sessions for the *Heart Healer* album, and Tillis persuaded Bowen to begin the association a little early.

"I was about to leave town," Bowen explains, "and one of his kids called up and wanted a new car. Somebody else called up with a lawsuit, and somebody else this and that. Mel looked at me, and he was like, 'I ain't got time for this,' and he said, 'Well, Bowen, would you . . . cut, uh, do this album?' And I said, 'Well, sure, if you like—have you got any songs picked?' His desk was covered with demos. There had to be 300, and he said, 'Uh, there's some in here.' That was about 4:00, and we had 'til 6:00."

Tillis insisted that they record a song called "Heart Healer." It debuted on January 15, 1977; seven weeks later, "Heart Healer" became Tillis' third number one record, and the first of more than sixty for Bowen. It was hardly without its problems.

Bowen had fought tooth and nail with Sinatra during the session for "That's Life," and he didn't pull any punches on this session, either. He had commentary and criticism for many of the musicians, and upset the entire cast.

"I didn't know that they had a bandleader down here," Bowen reasons, "and that's the person that kind of dictates the arrangement. I didn't know that. The reason I pissed off the whole band was that I took this guy's role, which I didn't know I was doin'."

Tillis was upset, too, when the album came in at $36,000—twice the budget of his previous release. "But," says Bowen, "the biggest album that cost $18,000 sold 40,000, and this album, fortunately for me, sold 140,000, so the increased cost was justified for him."

278

SHE'S JUST AN OLD LOVE TURNED MEMORY

CHARLEY PRIDE

RCA 10875
Writer: John Schweers
Producers: Jerry Bradley, Charley Pride
March 12, 1977 (1 week)

A couple of his favorite writers took Charley Pride out of the Bicentennial year and into 1977. His final single for 1976 came from Ben Peters, who literally woke up one morning and decided he had a whole lot of things to sing about. "A Whole Lotta Things To Sing About" soared to number two, peaking just behind Marty Robbins' "Among My Souvenirs" [see 264].

Pride's first 1977 single came from his own publishing company, as Pi-Gem writer John Schweers supplied "She's Just An Old Love Turned Memory." Schweers worked on the song for about eight months, but for most of that time, he merely had the title and a waltz rhythm. Finally, while writing one day, the whole thing fell into place.

"Charley turned down 'She's Just An Old Love Turned Memory' as well as 'Daydreams About Night Things' [see 222]," notes Schweers, "so I took it and pitched it to Nick Nixon [see 123—"The Teddy Bear Song"]. He held it for six months and then recorded it, and he got a really great cut on it."

Released in late 1975, Nixon's version managed only a number 64 showing on the *Billboard* country chart, but it inspired new recordings.

"Tammy Wynette heard it on the radio," says Schweers, "and then she cut it. We heard that it was going to be a single on Tammy, and about two weeks later, they called and said it wasn't going to be a single on Tammy. In the meantime, Charley had heard Nick Nixon's cut on it on the radio, and he decided he liked it, so the next time he recorded, he cut 'She's Just An Old Love Turned Memory.'"

Pride earned a number one single with the record, but he had his share of problems in the studio—all with the first line.

"It was 'I phoned her today,'" laughs producer Jerry Bradley, "and he kept singing like 'I honed her today,' and I said we should say 'called.' We got into a big argument as to whether it was 'phoned' or 'called,' and a buddy of mine that sold Wrangler boots at the time

came walking in the door. We were kind of joking, and I played it for this guy. We stopped the tape, and he looked at me and said, 'I *honed* her today?'"

Naturally, Pride's record says "called."

279

SOUTHERN NIGHTS

GLEN CAMPBELL

Capitol 4376
Writer: Allen Toussaint
Producer: Gary Klein
March 19, 1977 (2 weeks)

Thanks to the overwhelming success of "Rhinestone Cowboy" [see 220], Glen Campbell was able to flesh out his second wave of hit records during the mid-'70s. His next two singles, "Country Boy (You Got Your Feet In L.A.)" and a medley of "Don't Pull Your Love" and "Then You Can Tell Me Goodbye" [see 18], both returned him to the Top Five. In 1977, Glen found his fifth number one single through his buddy, Jimmy Webb [see 23—"Wichita Lineman"].

"'Southern Nights' is a song that I just loved when I heard it," Campbell recalls. "I was out at Jimmy Webb's house looking for songs, and I said, 'Has anybody else written any songs that you like—that you think is good poetry, good music?' He played me Allen Toussaint's record of 'Southern Nights.'"

Campbell in turn sent a copy to producer Gary Klein, who loved the music but found the lyrics totally indecipherable. "It had a real happy-go-lucky sound to it," says Klein, "a great melody. I didn't have a clue to what Allen was singing."

Klein also credits Campbell with inventing the dancing ten-second guitar lick that kicks off the record.

"When he picks up his guitar," Klein explains, "he comes up with the best ideas. I had to encourage him to pick up the guitar more often. He's just funny like that. He doesn't realize how great he is, and he needs a little encouragement now and then. He'd pick up a guitar to show me how he wanted something to go, and I'd say, 'Why don't you play it?' and he'd say, 'No, not me, I can't play that.' Of course, he'd just played it."

Like "Rhinestone Cowboy," "Southern Nights" reached number one on the *Billboard* Hot 100 in addition to topping the country

chart. Glen followed up with Neil Diamond's "Sunflower," reaching number four in the summer of 1977, but his hits became more sporadic from that point on.

After a three-year drought for Campbell, the theme from *Any Which Way You Can* reached number 10 in 1980. Four years later, Glen scored with "Faithless Love," "A Lady Like You" and "It's Just A Matter Of Time" [see 49, 845]. "The Hand That Rocks The Cradle," "Still Within The Sound Of My Voice" and "I Have You" also hit the Top Ten in 1987-88.

280

LUCILLE
KENNY ROGERS
United Artists 929
Writers: Roger Bowling, Hal Bynum
Producer: Larry Butler
April 2, 1977 (2 weeks)

The rags-to-riches tale of Kenny Rogers has been termed an "all-American story," one that hinges on "Lucille." The lead singer of the

First Edition, Rogers had earned notoriety with two Top Ten pop singles—"Just Dropped In (To See What Condition My Condition Was In)" and "Ruby, Don't Take Your Love To Town."

When the group disbanded in 1975, Kenny signed a solo deal with United Artists Records in Nashville. He needed an advance from the label just to keep a band together, and his first three singles did little more than establish his name on country radio. But "Lucille," the second single from Rogers' second solo album, proved a monster.

Hal Bynum started the song at a time when he was trying to keep a failing marriage together. One of his wife's female friends wanted to have an affair with him, and when his wife went out of town, Bynum feared that he would give in either to the other woman or to an alcoholic binge. As his wife prepared for her trip, he said to himself, "You picked a fine time to leave me."

Initially, Bynum turned that line into the story of a blind guitar player, but songwriter Roger Bowling stepped into the picture and helped Hal convert the tune to a barroom situation. Bowling then took "Lucille" to producer Larry Butler, who played it for two UA artists, both of whom turned it down.

Butler slipped it in among 30 songs he wanted Rogers to consider for his second album, and after several days of recording, they had 15 minutes left on their final session at American Studios. Kenny felt they were out of time, but Butler insisted they could learn "Lucille."

"Literally," Larry says, "I ran the song down with the band, played it for them one time, we rehearsed it one time, we turned the machines on, and the first playback is the cut we used. We cut the song in 15 minutes."

Rogers' raspy performance captivated not just the country market, but the public at large. While "Lucille" spent two weeks atop *Billboard*'s country chart, it also ascended to number five on the Hot 100, sold a million copies and led to seven awards combined between the Grammys, the Country Music Association and the Academy of Country Music.

Ironically, Kenny's mother was named Lucille.

Johnny Duncan

281

IT COULDN'T HAVE BEEN ANY BETTER

JOHNNY DUNCAN

Columbia 10474
Writer: Ray Griff
Producer: Billy Sherrill
April 16, 1977 (1 week)

With the success of "Stranger" and "Thinkin' Of A Rendezvous" [see 268], Johnny Duncan developed an affinity for sexual themes, and he found a perfect encore by soliciting material from a friend.

"I was in Memphis at a baseball game," he recalls. "We had a baseball team with Gene Ferguson, from CBS, and Ray Griff and I were down there. It seems like we were playing the Memphis Blues, and I told Ray at the game that I needed him to write something to follow 'Rendezvous.' I said, 'Make it just as sleazy as this last record.' So he went back to Nashville, and a couple of weeks later he had the song 'It Couldn't Have Been Any Better.'"

Like Johnny's two previous singles, this one featured Janie Frickie in a supporting vocal role. Lyrically, his material contrasted with the family concerts he wanted to give.

"I told a promoter one time that the raunchiest thing you'll see in a Duncan show is the lyrics to his songs," he says. "There've been some Sunday afternoon concerts where I kind of mumbled the words a little bit, but if you're gonna compete and be successful, you can't sing 'It's a beautiful spring/The flowers are blooming, the moon is blue.' After Kristofferson and 'Help Me Make It Through The Night' [see 72], then you had to say something."

Born October 5, 1939, Duncan convinced his mother, who played guitar, to teach him the instrument when he turned 12. A B+ high school student, he majored in English and speech at Texas Christian University, but dropped out after a couple of years.

"I had a new Belle Aire Chevrolet and a guitar, and women were looking at me kind of sideways, and I said 'Who needs this?' "

In 1959, Duncan moved to Clovis, New Mexico, where he worked with Norman Petty, who had produced Buddy Holly. He recorded in both London and New York, but a pop approach didn't seem to work, and by the mid-'60s, he was performing live on WSM Radio in Nashville. It was then that he received a call from Don Law and got the chance to record for Columbia.

282

SHE'S GOT YOU
LORETTA LYNN
MCA 40679
Writer: Hank Cochran
Producer: Owen Bradley
April 23, 1977 (1 week)

When Loretta Lynn moved to Nashville in 1960, her first real friend was Patsy Cline. Patsy heard Loretta singing "I Fall To Pieces" on the radio from Ernest Tubb's Record Shop, and summoned the youthful vocalist to the hospital where Cline was recuperating from an auto accident.

Both were at different points in their careers, but they had one thing in common: neither was financially set. Loretta was just beginning to establish herself, while Cline had already earned a couple of hits with "I Fall To Pieces" (number one) and "Walkin' After Midnight" (number two). Unfortunately, a shady business deal had left her with practically no income from those two singles.

Cline racked up a total of eight Top Ten records in her short-lived career. The Willie Nelson-penned "Crazy" peaked at number two in 1961, and she gained her second number one single with "She's Got You," which spent a total of five weeks in the top spot, including three weeks in April of 1962.

"The first time I heard this song," says Loretta, "I was down on the floor waxin' . . . and I had the radio sittin' on the floor. I told my sister, Peggy Sue, 'This is gonna be a smash record,' and it wasn't too long before it was number one."

Loretta recorded her own version of "She's Got You" for her 1977 tribute album, *I Remember Patsy*, and it reached number one in April of

that year—exactly 15 years after Cline's version achieved the feat. Loretta followed up with a remake of Patsy's "Why Can't He Be You," peaking at number seven.

Born September 8, 1932, in Winchester, Virginia, Cline was named Virginia Patterson Hensley at birth. She first performed in public—tap dancing at an amateur talent contest—at the age of four, but her real break came on January 21, 1957, when she appeared on "Arthur Godfrey's Talent Scouts," singing "Walkin' After Midnight." That appearance led to a recording contract with Decca.

The Patsy Cline story was cut short on March 5, 1963, when she died in a plane crash in Tennessee, along with Cowboy Copas and Hawkshaw Hawkins. That was hardly the end of her influence, though. She was inducted into the Country Music Hall of Fame on October 15, 1973, and her marriage with Charlie Dick provided the basis for the 1985 movie *Sweet Dreams*.

283

SHE'S PULLING ME BACK AGAIN
MICKEY GILLEY
Playboy 6100
Writers: Jerry Foster, Bill Rice
Producer: Eddie Kilroy
April 30, 1977 (1 week)

When Mickey Gilley came out the big winner at the Academy of Country Music Awards in May of 1977 [see 257—"Bring It On Home To Me"], he was riding on the heels of his seventh number one single.

At the end of 1976, he released his remake of Lloyd Price's "Lawdy Miss Clawdy," taking the soul classic to number three on *Billboard*'s country chart. He followed up with "She's Pulling Me Back Again," a tune written by the team of Jerry Foster and Bill Rice. Foster and Rice had already developed such hits as "Wonder Could I Live There Anymore" [see 58], by Charley Pride; "Someone To Give My Love To," by Johnny Paycheck; and "When You Say Love" (a former Budweiser commercial), by Bob Luman.

"She's Pulling Me Back Again" debuted on February 19, 1977, and hit number one ten weeks later, a few weeks before Mickey's ACM triumph. Foster and Rice later wrote and/or produced several Gilley hits, none of which equaled the success of this one.

"I'd always thought that 'Here Comes The Hurt' was a better record, a better song than 'She's Pulling Me Back Again,' " notes Gilley. "For some reason, 'Pulling Me Back' happened to have something to it, I guess, that would catch with the girls. It was a pretty clever song."

Gilley followed "She's Pulling Me Back Again" with "Honky Tonk Memories," "Chains Of Love" and "The Power Of Positive Drinkin'," all of which reached *Billboard*'s Top Ten. They were his final Playboy singles, though, as he signed a new agreement with Epic Records.

It was then that Foster and Rice stepped in again. Mickey believed that most of Nashville's songwriters usually held back their best material from him, but he sensed a rapport with Foster and Rice. "I heard some songs that were pretty good, but I would go in and ask for the *good* songs, and I think the only ones that ever shot totally straight with me were Foster and Rice," says Gilley.

They wrote "Here Comes The Hurt Again," his first Epic single, which peaked at number nine in 1978. They also produced his next four singles: "The Song We Made Love To," "Just Long Enough To Say Goodbye," "My Silver Lining" and "A Little Getting Used To." Only two of the four scratched the Top Ten, though, and Gilley entered the '80s in need of new blood.

284

PLAY, GUITAR, PLAY
CONWAY TWITTY
MCA 40682
Writer: Conway Twitty
Producer: Owen Bradley
May 7, 1977 (1 week)

Nearly ten years after Bobbie Gentry spun the mystery of the Tallahatchee Bridge in "Ode To Billie Joe," Conway Twitty took her cue with his intriguing "Play, Guitar, Play." Conway's suspense revolved around a musician whose concert tours served a dual purpose: a chance to bring his songs to a series of different cities, and a way to escape some "awful thing" in his past.

"The mystery thing in 'Billie Joe' was in my mind," Conway admitted to the *Chicago Tribune*'s Jack Hurst. "People all over the country are wondering what that [awful thing] was. No matter what the song is, fans always wonder, 'Did Conway really live this? Is this part of his life?' "

While Twitty confessed that he did have something to hide, he left listeners to "read between the lines in my song."

"That's kind of like 'Linda On My Mind' [see 200]," he says. "The mystique in that song will always be there, because I'll never talk about it, but it came from the hip, because it's about what I do—sittin' there talkin' to a friend that's been there with me since I was four years old, the guitar. There'll always be my secret between me and my guitar in that song."

Unlocking the secret of making it work in the studio proved a lengthy and difficult proposition. Conway first recorded the song in 1975, but the results were less than pleasing. He wasn't satisfied with the guitar work, or with the chorus, shortened at the suggestion of producer Owen Bradley. Twitty didn't release that first version. But nearly two years later, he re-cut it, getting the results he had wanted in the first place.

"I don't read music," he explains, "and I don't talk that language that these pickers talk in this town. Most of the pickers, they realize that we got a communication problem.

"This particular song, I wanted a certain sound and a certain lick that was a little simple. It seemed like it took forever for me to get it across to Grady Martin, who was playin' a gut-string on this one, to get that unique sound. These guys are so good, especially a guy like Grady Martin, and if you get too simple, they don't know what you're talkin' about."

The second attempt worked, propelling "Play, Guitar, Play" to number one in 1977.

285

SOME BROKEN HEARTS NEVER MEND
DON WILLIAMS
ABC/Dot 17683
Writer: Wayland Holyfield
Producer: Don Williams
May 14, 1977 (1 week)

Hailing from Little Rock, Wayland Holyfield didn't set out to become one of Nashville's finest songwriters. Instead, he earned a B.A. degree in marketing at the University of Arkansas, a credential he's never had to use.

Holyfield toured the South in a number of bands, moving to Nashville in 1972, where he joined Jack Clement's stable of writers [see 226—"Love Me Tonight"]. Wayland moved on to write for Don Williams Music, and became one of the most prolific writers in town. He has landed nearly 25 records in the Top Ten, including "You're The Best Break This Old Heart Ever Had" [see 462], "I'll Do It All Over Again," "Tears Of The Lonely," "Could I Have This Dance" [see 400] and "You'll Be Back (Every Night In My Dreams)." Holyfield penned five singles for Williams, including "She Never Knew Me," which peaked at number two in December of 1976, behind "Thinkin' Of A Rendezvous" [see 268].

Wayland also did Don's follow-up, "Some Broken Hearts Never Mend."

"Although it's got a bit of a negative lyric," says Holyfield, "I like to think that that song still feels good, so that what you end up with is a little hope after hearing 'Some broken hearts will never mend,' which is kind of a downer if you just read the lyric. When it's all together, it seems to work."

Holyfield wasn't alone in that evaluation. After debuting at number 61 on March 12, 1977, "Some Broken Hearts Never Mend" jumped 28 positions in its second week. In its tenth week, the single became Williams' sixth number one record.

"When the musicians were in there playing, there was somethin' magical about that darn track," Wayland recalls. "What you want is to have one plus one equal five in this business. We can all do 'one plus one is two,' but there was some magic with that thing. Don nailed it, the musicians nailed it."

The track was featured on Williams' *Visions* album, which also included two more Holyfield tunes that became hits—for other performers. Janie Frickie found success in 1981 with "I'll Need Someone To Hold Me (When I Cry)," and Rex Allen, Jr., went Top Ten with "I'm Getting Good At Missing You" at the same time "Some Broken Hearts" was in release.

286
LUCKENBACH, TEXAS (BACK TO THE BASICS OF LOVE)
WAYLON JENNINGS
RCA 10924
Writers: Chips Moman, Buddy Emmons

Producer: Chips Moman
May 21, 1977 (6 weeks)

"The best way to plug a song to me," suggests Waylon Jennings, "is to say, 'Here's a song that you can't do, but I'd like for you to hear anyway.' I'm a fool for that."

That's the method that producer Chips Moman used to introduce Jennings to "Luckenbach, Texas." Moman felt that Waylon probably wouldn't want to record it, because it mentioned him by name, as well as Willie Nelson, Hank Williams and songwriter Mickey Newbury.

Of course, other performers had mentioned themselves on their own records—particularly Loretta Lynn, in "Hey, Loretta" [see 136—"Love Is The Foundation"], and David Allan Coe, in "You Never Even Called Me By My Name" [see 158—"Would You Lay With Me"]. Jennings responded immediately to "Luckenbach," and recorded it at Moman's American Studio in Nashville for his album *Ol' Waylon*. In a spur-of-the-moment decision, Willie Nelson added his voice to the final verse, providing a couple of his own lyrical alterations.

"Willie stumbled in the studio," Waylon explains, "and I said, 'Why don't you sing with me on this?' I was cuttin' it, and he came in and put his voice on it. That's the way all those things were. They were inspirational, you might say."

On April 16, 1977, "Luckenbach, Texas (Back To The Basics Of Love)" made *Billboard* history when it became the first single ever to debut in the top half of the 100-position country chart. A handful of records had debuted in the 50s before, but "Luckenbach" hit number 48 in its first week.

RCA claimed sales of 100,000 copies in the first seven days, and the *Ol' Waylon* album was certified gold on June 6, going platinum on October 7. The record spent thirteen weeks at the top of *Billboard*'s country album chart. "Luckenbach" was one of only three records to spend six weeks at number one on the singles chart during the '70s [see 95—"My Hang-Up Is You" and 233—"Convoy"], and it also reached number 25 on the Hot 100.

Suddenly, the town of Luckenbach—a wide spot in the road 80 miles west of Austin—was besieged by network camera crews and reporters, and more than 100 city-limits signs have been stolen since then.

"The funny thing," notes Waylon, "is that Chips and Bobby Emmons had never been to Luckenbach, Texas, and neither have I."

287

THAT WAS YESTERDAY

DONNA FARGO

Warner Bros. 8375
Writer: Donna Fargo
Producer: Stan Silver
July 2, 1977 (1 week)

"That Was Yesterday" was a mistake.

When Donna Fargo first cut it, she felt it sounded too much like a Patsy Cline record. "It sounded too smooth," she told Patsi Cox of *Country Song Roundup*. "Now I loved Patsy's music, but it was *Patsy's* music. I'm more a writer/interpreter when it comes to a song."

The money had already been spent on the tracks, though, so Fargo tried to come up with a way to utilize what they had already done.

Donna Fargo

She took a tape of the session home and wrote some prose that might enhance it. Initially, she intended to alternate between the spoken part and the already-existing vocal. As it turned out, that didn't work either, and "It Was Yesterday" became a solid, wall-to-wall recitation.

It was slated as an album cut for *Fargo Country*, but a single disk jockey spurred its eventual rise to number one. The label resisted his suggestion that they put it out as a single, but he continued to call in to the record company, and over time, several other stations began playing "That Was Yesterday" as well. Warner Bros. saw the song's potential, and released it; "That Was Yesterday" hit the *Billboard* charts on April 30, 1977, and took only eight weeks to reach number one.

"Recitations really have to be from the heart," says Fargo. "You've really got to feel them. You can't just sit down and say, 'I'll make this a recitation,' because they sound phony if you try to do that. That would be hard work if it weren't something deep down inside you."

Fargo wrote another recitation in tribute to Elvis Presley on the day that he died; coincidentally, his former keyboard player, David Briggs, played piano on that record (as well as on all of her records except "The Happiest Girl In The Whole U.S.A.").

Donna scored four more Top Ten singles through 1979, but in June of 1978, she was diagnosed with multiple sclerosis. It was the ultimate test of her positive attitude toward life, keeping her out of work for four months. "We try to do the dates now so that they're not so stressful. It's hard 'cause I'm a real high-strung, energetic kind of a person. I have to kind of choke myself to keep myself down."

288

I'LL BE LEAVING ALONE

CHARLEY PRIDE

RCA 10975
Writers: Dickey Lee, Wayland Holyfield
Producers: Jerry Bradley, Charley Pride
July 9, 1977 (1 week)

Dickey Lee and Wayland Holyfield wrote "I'll Be Leaving Alone" at Lee's house over a period of several days. A pledge of fidelity in the face of temptation, the song admittedly baffled both writers, and they weren't quite sure who to approach about recording it. Lee recorded it under his RCA contract [see 229—

"Rocky"], but division head Jerry Bradley thought it might be appropriate for one of Lee's labelmates.

"Jerry loved it and sent it to Charley Pride and [his wife] Rozene," recalls Holyfield. "I think that Charley was initially not all that fired up about it, but Rozene had a large influence on him to do it. She loved it. She loved that idea of 'There's someone in Dallas [the Prides live in Dallas] waiting for me,' and I don't blame her."

Rozene wielded her influence during the quiet hours of the night. "She said, 'I got a song I want to play for you,'" remembers Charley, "and I said, 'Well, I'll listen to it.' She said, 'No, I want you to hear it *now*.' This was about two in the morning! She played it for me, so I said, 'Okay, I'll cut it.'"

That morning, Pride called Lee at home, waking him up around 6:00 or 7:00. When Dickey picked up the phone, Pride started singing the song through the receiver, and started the day off by promising to record it. There was some doubt, however, that it would ever make it as a single.

Says Lee: "I remember all the wheels at RCA were going, 'That's not going to be the single; I don't think that's it.' All the time, Rozene was saying, 'Don't sweat it, that's going to be the record'—and it was."

In addition to her influence on Pride's recording career, Rozene also has a huge impact on the family finances. When they first married, Charley spent just about every dime he earned, while, unknown to him, his wife put back much of the money she picked up as a beautician. One evening, he complained that they needed a down payment for a new car; the next day, she took the money out of her savings account and gave it to him. She's been in charge of the checkbook ever since.

289
IT WAS ALMOST LIKE A SONG
RONNIE MILSAP
RCA 10976
Writers: Archie Jordan, Hal David
Producers: Tom Collins, Ronnie Milsap
July 16, 1977 (3 weeks)

In 1978, RCA presented the first gold album ever inscribed in Braille to Ronnie Milsap for *It Was Almost Like a Song*. It was the first of three Milsap recordings to spend three weeks atop the country singles chart, and his first

"crossover" hit. It reached number 16 on *Billboard*'s Hot 100.

The song's raw materials were lodged in the mind of a little-known South Carolina songwriter, Archie Jordan, who had caught the ear of producer/publisher Tom Collins. Collins arranged through ASCAP to have Jordan collaborate with Hal David through the mail. (David had garnered fame writing a host of pop standards with Burt Bacharach such as "Alfie," "Raindrops Keep Fallin' On My Head" and "What The World Needs Now Is Love.") Jordan sent a tape with a handful of melodies to David. Two weeks later, David called him with the lyrics to "It Was Almost Like A Song."

"I pitched it all over Nashville," notes Jordan, "and I couldn't get anybody to record it. Finally, Tom pitched it to Jim Foglesong for Roy Clark, and Roy did cut it. I got very excited; it was my first cut. Then Roy canned it."

Milsap held onto a copy of the song for about six months, but wasn't particularly impressed with the song until around Christmas of 1976, when he worked up a new arrangement at the piano in his living room.

"I used 'Legend In My Time' [see 194] kind of as the pattern for the end of that song," Ronnie explains. "There again, you go up and hit the high A-flat. I called Tom Collins on the phone and had him come over, and I played it on the piano using the arrangement that I'd worked up."

"You don't ever want to sound like a cliché," Collins continues, "but I said, 'Ronnie, that's a smash. That sounds like a Grammy.' I called up Archie Jordan—I think it was at 12:00 at night—and told him I'd just heard a performance on his song and said, 'If it's not a Grammy, I'll be really surprised.'"

It didn't win a Grammy, but it did net two nominations. *It Was Almost Like a Song* brought Milsap his third Album of the Year award from the Country Music Association.

290
ROLLIN' WITH THE FLOW
CHARLIE RICH
Epic 50392
Writer: Jerry Hayes
Producer: Billy Sherrill
August 6, 1977 (2 weeks)

After "I Love My Friend" [see 180] reached number one in October of 1974, it took nearly three years for Charlie Rich to return to the top of the *Billboard* country charts with new material [see 188—"She Called Me Baby"].

"The Silver Fox" wasn't without his successes through the period. Three records reached the Top Five in 1975, and in 1976, he went to number 10 with "Since I Fell For You." Rich's return to number one came when producer Billy Sherrill found "Rollin' With The Flow" on the "B" side of a T.G. Sheppard record.

"I changed one word in that song," says Sherrill. "Not to applaud myself, but I think it was a key word. We had a real good feel on it, but the one line always bothered me. He said, 'I've got a lot of crazy friends, and One forgives me of my sins,' meaning Jesus. I thought, 'This just don't sit with me at all. Let's just say "I've got a lot of crazy friends and *they* forgive me of my sins." ' Charlie said, 'I like that better.'

"I think the song was improved drastically with that change. It was offensive the other way. It brought this religious connotation. I wasn't gonna cut that thing with it written like that. I don't think it bothered Charlie, but he liked it better this way."

"Rollin' With The Flow" still made references to "Jesus Loves Me," but that religious aside was hardly upsetting. After its debut over Memorial Day weekend, the record brought Rich back to the top in August of 1977.

The following year, Rich signed with United Artists Records for a reported $750,000. Larry Butler produced a Top Ten record on "Puttin' In Overtime At Home." One more Epic solo single followed, and "Beautiful Woman" also reached the Top Ten.

During the early '80s, Rich went into semi-retirement in Memphis, where he built a recording studio behind his house. He was fully capable of taking the time off financially. Though an investment in the Memphis franchise of the short-lived World Football League fared poorly, he had made several shrewd moves, acquiring interests in a bank and in Wendy's.

In October of 1989, Charlie made an appearance on the "Nashville Now" TV show, and announced his intent to return to the music business.

Elvis Presley

291

WAY DOWN/PLEDGING MY LOVE
ELVIS PRESLEY
RCA 10998
Writers: Layng Martine, Jr./Fats
Washington, Don Robey
Producers: Elvis Presley/Felton Jarvis
August 20, 1977 (1 week)

By 1977, the formerly slim movie star who had thrilled women as Elvis Presley had deteriorated into an overweight reminder of an earlier era. His concerts still consistently sold out, and the King gave plenty of shows until June 26. That night, he performed at the Market Square Arena in Indianapolis, but it proved to be the final appearance of his legendary career.

A day earlier, Presley's "Way Down" debuted on the *Billboard* country chart. Recorded in the living room at Graceland Mansion, it concluded with an ungodly low note, coaxed from J.D. Sumner of the Stamps Quartet. In late July, several former bodyguards released the book *Elvis: What Happened?*, accusing the King of a drug problem, among other things. Presley was hurt by the book, but he continued to enjoy success with his latest single, "Way Down." On August 16, he played racquetball with several associates, including girlfriend Ginger Alden, but at 2:30 that afternoon, she discovered him on the floor of the bathroom, adjacent to his bedroom at Graceland Mansion.

Presley's death at age 42 came as a shock to an adoring public, and thousands flocked to Memphis overnight to pay homage to their expired hero. More than 25,000 people viewed his body, standing in line for hours through first a light rain, and later the grueling heat of summer. Around 4:00 A.M. on August 19, two women were killed when a car plowed into the crowd gathered outside the mansion's gates.

Presley left an incredible legacy. Included were 33 movie appearances, a string of classic recordings and thousands of unanswered questions. His *Aloha from Hawaii via Satellite* concert set a record when it achieved a worldwide audience estimated at one billion viewers, and it earned distinction as the first quadraphonic album certified gold for sales of one million units. His enlistment, as Pvt. US 53310761, was the most publicized in military history, and *Billboard* proclaimed Elvis the first artist ever to sell one billion records worldwide.

Upon his death, record stores immediately sold all their existing Presley stock, and RCA kept its Indianapolis plant open 24 hours a day, pressing only material by the King to meet the demand. Meanwhile, producer Felton Jarvis was already at work enhancing material recorded during Presley's final concert tour for release as a two-record set, *Elvis in Concert*. Beginning September 3, Presley occupied the top spot on *Billboard*'s country album chart for 15 consecutive weeks. *Moody Blue* held the position the first ten weeks, followed by the live LP.

292
DON'T IT MAKE MY BROWN EYES BLUE
CRYSTAL GAYLE
United Artists 1016
Writer: Richard Leigh
Producer: Allen Reynolds
August 27, 1977 (4 weeks)

Few people would be disappointed with a number one record, but "I'll Get Over You" [see 250] sent songwriter Richard Leigh into a huge funk. The song was recorded even before he had a publisher, and went on to become a number one single and secure a Country Music Association nomination as Song of the Year. When two more songs were recorded with little success, Leigh feared his career was already over.

He lived in a Nashville duplex, next door to songwriter Sandy Mason, and when his depression seemed to wear on, she asked producer Allen Reynolds to drop by and give Leigh some encouragement. When Reynolds appeared, they all sat on the floor in Mason's apartment and went over material.

"He sang me some of his songs," says Reynolds, "and he mentioned this other song that they were gonna send to Shirley Bassey. He sang it, and my mouth dropped open, and I said, 'Shirley Bassey?! Hell, I got to have that song.'"

The song was "Don't It Make My Brown Eyes Blue," and Crystal Gayle had to tackle it with a substitute keyboard player. Her usual pianist, Charles Cochran, was recovering from a mild stroke, and Reynolds had Hargus "Pig" Robbins fill in. Robbins had played on "Behind Closed Doors" [see 128], and developed the same kind of bluesy feel for "Brown Eyes."

Once the arrangement was in place, the song was recorded live the first time that engineer Garth Fundis turned on the tape machine. "I wanted to re-sing it," Crystal confesses, "and actually, I did go in and try, but you needed to be in there with the band, 'cause it just all flowed."

"Brown Eyes" brought Leigh his second CMA Song of the Year award, and netted two Grammys. It was Gayle's only million-selling single, stayed atop the country chart for an entire month, and hit number two on *Billboard*'s Hot 100. *We Must Believe in Magic* became the first platinum album certified by the Recording Industry Association of America for a Nashville-based female.

The song has an unfortunate postscript. Leigh wrote it while his dog, Amanda, sat at his feet, staring up at him with her big, brown eyes. In later years, a trash collector threw rocks at the dog, and hit it in the eye. Amanda developed cataracts, and her brown eye literally turned blue.

293

I'VE ALREADY LOVED YOU IN MY MIND
CONWAY TWITTY
MCA 40754
Writer: Conway Twitty
Producer: Owen Bradley
September 24, 1977 (1 week)

Conway Twitty's twenty-fifth number one country single was also his ninth in a row, a string that began three years earlier with "I See The Want To In Your Eyes" [see 182]. "I've Already Loved You In My Mind" peered into the realm of fantasy, and the song allowed fantasy to become reality.

"That's one of my personal favorites, of all the things I've written," he says. "You know, President Jimmy Carter almost got kicked out of office for sayin' that. And he was just bein' truthful. There ain't a man walkin' that ain't had a thought like that cross his mind when he sees a pretty lady walk by.

"A lot of writers have dealt with that particular thing right there, but I don't ever remember hearin' one that said it just right. When I got through with this one, I thought, 'Yeah, I said it just right. It's not ever gonna offend a woman.' If I thought it would, I wouldn't have put it in there."

When "I've Already Loved You In My Mind" reached number one in September of 1977, it represented the final chart-topping hit that Owen Bradley produced for Conway. Bradley was behind the glass for each of Twitty's next four singles, but all of them failed to reach number one.

"Georgia Keeps Pulling On My Ring," "Boogie Grass Band" and "Your Love Had Taken Me That High" all reached the Top Five. "The Grandest Lady Of Them All," Conway's salute to the Grand Ole Opry, stopped at number 16. Though most performers would have

been pleased, it was the worst stretch for Conway in more than a decade.

He insists that his subsequent split from Bradley had nothing to do with the numbers, that he had already been contemplating a new approach. Owen encouraged Conway to do what he felt was necessary when they discussed the plan. "I was very careful about the way I made the break," Twitty said in his autobiography. "He gave me his blessing, but I could see that it really hurt him deeply. Loretta Lynn and I had stayed with Owen for many years."

Though difficult, Twitty's parting yielded favorable results: his next single, "Don't Take It Away" [see 342], brought Conway back to number one.

294

DAYTIME FRIENDS
KENNY ROGERS
United Artists 1027
Writer: Ben Peters
Producer: Larry Butler
October 1, 1977 (1 week)

"Kenny never worked a day in his life," "Mr." Rogers' mother, Lucille, once told *Billboard*. "That boy just kept on singin'."

Born August 21, 1938, in Houston, Kenny showed his business smarts early, when he sold newspapers at a local corner. Shrewdly, he sublet the location to a classmate and made money without touching the newsprint. As a high school senior, he formed his first band, the Scholars.

Though he tried selling office equipment for two years, music called. He earned a gold single in 1958 for "That Crazy Feeling," played stand-up bass with the Bobby Doyle Trio, and migrated to the New Christy Minstrels in 1966. A year later, four Minstrels formed the First Edition.

Harvard graduate Ken Kragen managed the group, and when it broke up in 1975, he retained Rogers as a client. After Kenny had joined United Artists [see 280—"Lucille"], the resulting association with producer Larry Butler provided a crucial piece of the puzzle for his later successes.

"I was trying to organize my life," says Kenny. "I didn't have a band. I didn't know how I was gonna pay anybody. I didn't know what I was gonna do with my life. I could very easily have had to get out of the business, had someone not come along and believed in me.

"Larry gave me an advance of $15,000 an album, and a two-album-a-year guarantee, so that was $30,000. I knew that if I had that kind of money coming in that I could now hire a band for six months.

"It's the domino theory. You have to get that first domino moving before you can move the second domino, and Larry allowed me to get that first domino."

Another came with "Lucille," and "Daytime Friends" fell in line behind it—a gift from songwriter Ben Peters, who drummed up the tune after a TV weatherman reported on "daytime highs and nighttime lows." Elvis Presley intended to record "Daytime Friends," although he passed away before he got a chance. Kenny had already cut it and released it as a single, anyway.

Butler gave the song an unusual treatment, too. He copied the guitars onto extra tracks to "fatten" the sound, and ended up with 18 guitars—4 electric and 14 rhythm—in the final product. It likewise fattened Kenny's cache, providing him with his second number one record.

HEAVEN'S JUST A SIN AWAY
THE KENDALLS
Ovation 1103
Writer: Jerry Gillespie
Producer: Brien Fisher
October 8, 1977 (4 weeks)

The Kendalls achieved an unusual success with "Heaven's Just A Sin Away." A gigantic single, it emerged from an album that was recorded in a single day.

"We had our material ready, so we went in and cut the LP in three sessions," Royce Kendall told *Billboard*'s Sally Hinkle. "In the hour in between each session, I would go in and put extra harmony on. Then the next night, we mixed the final takes. So, it actually took us one day and a night to complete the project."

Royce and daughter Jeannie Kendall found "Heaven's Just A Sin Away" a couple of months before that fateful day. Songwriter Jerry Gillespie approached them at a Nashville recording studio with a song he thought would be right for them. They had to wait to record it,

The Kendalls

since they were unsigned at the time. Once the Ovation label added them to its roster, the Kendalls pulled out "Heaven's Just A Sin Away" for that first day of recording.

"We'd only played the thing once, and we remembered it," notes Royce. "We could sing the melody right then, having only listened to it once. That's a good sign, so that's the reason we cut it."

During the session, keyboard player Ron Oates suggested they add a funky clavinet, and the sound became a hallmark of future Kendalls hits.

Ovation didn't foresee "Heaven's Just A Sin Away" as a hit. Instead, "Making Believe" was tapped as the album's first single. About the same time, Emmylou Harris released her version of that song [see 269—"Sweet Dreams"], ending any hopes for the Kendalls. The label selected "Live And Let Live" as a second single and relegated "Heaven's Just A Sin Away" to the "B" side.

Several stations started playing the latter cut, though, and Ovation went to work on it. The record entered *Billboard* at number 77 on August 6, 1977. Nine weeks later, it began a one-month run at the top. Ironically, though it embraced a "cheatin'" theme, "Heaven's Just A Sin Away" also gained heavy airplay on many gospel radio stations.

During the course of 1978, the record brought the Kendalls a Grammy award and the Country Music Association trophy for Single of the Year. On November 30, 1982, the album they recorded in one day was certified gold for selling 500,000 copies.

296
I'M JUST A COUNTRY BOY
DON WILLIAMS
ABC/Dot 17717
Writers: Fred Hellerman, Marshall Baker
Producer: Don Williams
November 5, 1977 (1 week)

In 1964, Don Williams formed the Pozo-Seco Singers, a folk trio that took its name from a Tex-Mex phrase meaning "dry well." Joining Susan Taylor and Lofton Kline, Williams was reluctantly nominated as the primary vocalist and group leader, and the Pozo-Seco Singers successfully plied their folk-musical trade for about seven years.

The trio earned six charted singles on *Bill-*

board's Hot 100 during 1966-67, paced by "Time," which hit number 47. Two more, "I Can Make It With You" and "Look What You've Done," reached number 32. Once the Pozo-Seco Singers disbanded in 1971, Don decided to give up music and briefly went into the furniture business with his father-in-law before he returned to Nashville.

Once his solo career took hold, his folk background came to the fore again when Williams called on "I'm Just A Country Boy," written in part by Fred Hellerman, an original member of the Weavers. That group also included Ronnie Gilbert, Lee Hays and Pete Seeger, whose basement served as the original meeting place for the group.

The Weavers debuted at The Village Vanguard in New York in 1949, and within a year, their presence was felt across the nation. In 1950, they joined Gordon Jenkins on his double-sided monster hit "Goodnight, Irene"/"Tzena, Tzena, Tzena." A year later, they teamed with folkie Terry Gilkyson to record another million-seller, "On Top Of Old Smoky," which peaked at number eight on the *Billboard* country chart. The Weavers fell apart during the Communist witch hunts of the McCarthy era, but still made a future impact as songwriters. Along with Leadbelly, they wrote "Kisses Sweeter Than Wine," a 1958 pop and country hit for Jimmie Rodgers.

"I've lived with 'I'm Just A Country Boy' for the better part of my life, and always loved it," Don explains. "Every once in a while I'll drag up a song like that, like 'The Ties That Bind'— I had lived with that song 20 years or better. 'Country Boy' is one of those classics, in my mind. I just wanted to bring it forward and see if people would still feel the same way about it."

297
MORE TO ME
CHARLEY PRIDE
RCA 11086
Writer: Ben Peters
Producers: Jerry Bradley, Charley Pride
November 12, 1977 (1 week)

"Most of the stories behind most of my songs," says songwriter Ben Peters, "are simply hunger."

A 1980 inductee to the Nashville Songwriters Hall of Fame, Peters has tasted success many times since first moving to Nashville in 1966. His songs have been played more than 10 million times on American radio stations, and at one point, he estimated that one of his songs started playing somewhere every 15 seconds. His compositions have been recorded by more than 140 artists, including Conway Twitty, the Oak Ridge Boys, Johnny Mathis, Ray Charles and the Ink Spots.

Peters has placed more of his songs with Charley Pride than with any other artist. "He's cut over 40 of them," Ben notes. "His manager was a good friend of ours, and after he cut two or three of them, they'd let me know, 'Hey, Pride's coming up to record again, you got anything?' and I'd check into it. If I didn't have anything, I'd make an effort to sit down and write something. I seemed to have been in a kind of groove there that just kind of fit Charley."

Of the Peters songs that Pride has recorded, at least seven have been released as singles. "The man's just a good writer," says Pride," and a lot of his songs came off good enough, out of all the other things we cut, that they ended up being singles. It's the song and the writer and the way the song comes out once you go in the studio, and it just warrants coming out as a single."

Peters' first successful single was Roy Drusky's recording of "If The Whole World Stopped Lovin'," which reached number 12 in 1967. His first number one came with Eddy Arnold's "Turn The World Around." Since then, he has earned a total of eight chart-topping records, including four of Pride's.

Hailing from the Mississippi Delta, Peters became a professional musician at age 14, playing sax and keyboards in a variety of local bands. Music paid his way through the University of Southern Mississippi, where he earned a business administration degree.

While in the Navy, Ben grew weary of nightclubs and set his sights on a job he could do at home. Songwriting fit the bill, and has paid off quite handsomely—"More To Me" became the third of his four chart-topping Charley Pride records.

298

THE WURLITZER PRIZE
(I DON'T WANT TO GET OVER YOU)/
LOOKIN' FOR A FEELING
WAYLON JENNINGS

RCA 11118
Writers: Chips Moman, Buddy Emmons/
Waylon Jennings
Producer: Chips Moman
November 19, 1977 (2 weeks)

On November 21, 1877, Thomas Edison announced that he had mistakenly invented the first system for sound reproduction. Edison had actually been working to create the telegraph, but within a month he applied for a patent on his "talking machine."

Initially, the phonograph was a novelty item: for a quarter, customers could speak into the machine and hear their voices played back on tin foil. In 1888, wax cylinders replaced the old foil, providing a higher quality and greater longevity. On November 23, 1889, the jukebox was born, when Louis Glass attached a coin slot to one of Edison's machines, located in San Francisco's Palais Royale Saloon. The gizmo was originally called "Nickel-In-The-Slot," and, after years of evolution, the jukebox reached its peak in popularity in the post-Depression era.

Exactly 100 years after the phonograph's invention, Waylon Jennings hit number one on the country chart with a song that hinged on the jukebox, "The Wurlitzer Prize." Like "Luckenbach, Texas" [see 286], it was written by producer Chips Moman and Buddy Emmons.

"I learned a big lesson from that thing," Waylon admits, "because when I started singing it on stage, I turned around to my drummer and said, 'Remind me that if I ever put out a single again, I have to sing the son of a bitch every day of my life.' So now I ask myself, 'Is this something I want to sing?' I think I wore ["The Wurlitzer Prize"] out. I loved it when I first heard it, you know, but I get bored quick."

Jennings spent more time recording it than he wanted. They built it up once, and then stripped off all the instrumental tracks except for the drums and rebuilt it. "I never could get really satisfied with it," he laments.

Just before the single's first *Billboard* appearance on October 10—at number 33, a temporary record for the highest debut ever [see 317—"Only One Love In My Life"]—Jennings swirled in controversy. A cocaine charge became national news on August 24, and, for the second year in a row, he stirred Nashville with his refusal to participate in the Country Music Association awards. In 1976, Waylon declined a chance to perform, but still won two trophies. The next year, he and Willie Nelson both asked to be removed from nominations, not wanting to compete with their fellow entertainers. Their names weren't removed—but they didn't win, either.

299
HERE YOU COME AGAIN
DOLLY PARTON
RCA 11123
Writers: Barry Mann, Cynthia Weil
Producer: Gary Klein
December 3, 1977 (5 weeks)

Dolly Parton couldn't have faced more pressure than when she deliberately scooted off to Los Angeles for new management and a shot at pop music. Her detractors resented her "snubbing" Nashville, and they predicted that Hollywood's wolves would tear apart everything that she had built up.

"I'm not leaving country," she insisted. "I am just taking it with me."

She first took it to "The Tonight Show with Johnny Carson," beginning January 19, 1977. Her self-deprecating commentary about her appearance helped to solidify her image with those who hadn't heard her country hits, and later that year, she introduced them to her music with a different-sounding "Here You Come Again."

Producer Gary Klein first heard the song on B.J. Thomas' eponymous album, and gave Thomas a call. When B.J. said he had no intention of releasing it as a single, Klein persuaded Dolly to cut it. The session prompted an unusual and much-imitated recording technique when Klein dampered the piano keys with freezer tape.

Once Klein produced a final mix, however, Dolly became edgy. She feared that "Here You Come Again" would confirm Nashville's suspicions that she had "gone Hollywood," and begged the producer to add a steel guitar. "She heard a hit," Klein remembers. "She knew it was a hit, and she had these terrible misgivings about the record because there wasn't a smack of 'real country' in it." Klein called in steel player Al Perkins to provide the needed parts, prominently enough to assuage any doubters.

"She wanted people to be able to hear the steel guitar," Klein explains, "so if someone said it isn't country, she could say it is and prove it. She was so relieved. It was like her life sentence was reprieved."

"Here You Come Again" did everything Dolly wanted. It spent five weeks at the top of the country chart, and brought her to number three on *Billboard*'s Hot 100, sandwiched between the Bee Gees and Rod Stewart. Two days after Christmas, 1977, it brought Parton her first gold album, which quickly went platinum as well. "Here You Come Again" also became Dolly's first gold single.

The record netted a Grammy award, and the California-based Academy of Country Music named Parton the Entertainer of the Year. In October of 1978, even the Nashville-based Country Music Association recognized that Dolly had not abandoned the city, and also voted her Entertainer of the Year.

300
TAKE THIS JOB AND SHOVE IT
JOHNNY PAYCHECK
Epic 50469
Writer: David Allan Coe
Producer: Billy Sherrill
January 7, 1978 (2 weeks)

It's ironic that a man named "Paycheck" would gain his only number one single with "Take This Job And Shove It."

Though it's closely identified with Johnny Paycheck, the song was actually written by David Allan Coe [see 158—"Would You Lay With Me (In A Field Of Stone)"]. Coe had been asked during a conversation if he would ever want to be a fireman, and he responded, "They can take that job and shove it." He wrote the song initially as a joke, but the longer he worked with it, the more confident he felt about it.

Coe took the tune to producer Billy Sherrill, who decided it was just what he needed for Paycheck, whom Epic had all but given up on. It was one of the easiest songs Paycheck ever recorded, and it became an anthem for working people everywhere. "Take This Job And Shove It" yielded Paycheck his second Grammy nomination (the other came for "She's All I Got") and became the title for a film.

Johnny Paycheck isn't the artist's real name. He was actually born Donald Eugene Lytle on May 31, 1941, in Greenfield, Ohio. He took his stage name from a former Golden Gloves boxer from Des Moines in 1965. Prior to that, however, he had been quite successful as a musician and supporting vocalist for Nashville artists like Porter Wagoner, Faron Young, George Jones and Ray Price.

Johnny began recording in 1959 for Decca, but his first Top Ten record, 1966's "The Lovin' Machine," was on Little Darlin' Records. A few years later, he was playing small clubs in the Los Angeles area when Sherrill spotted him and signed him with Epic.

Paycheck's first Epic single, "She's All I Got," went to number two in 1971, and he earned four more hits in the next two years. Including "Take This Job," he racked up four more in 1977-78, plus a Top Ten duet with George Jones on "Mabellene."

His recording successes were the "ups," though, in a rollercoaster career filled with more than a handful of "downs." At least a half-dozen times, Johnny has gone to court on a variety of charges, from burglary to verbal abuse. The most serious was an aggravated assault charge, stemming from a barroom shooting in Hillsboro, Ohio, on December 19, 1985. It resulted in a nine-and-a-half-year prison sentence.

Johnny Paycheck

301

WHAT A DIFFERENCE YOU'VE MADE IN MY LIFE

RONNIE MILSAP

RCA 11146
Writer: Archie Jordan
Producers: Tom Collins, Ronnie Milsap
January 21, 1978 (1 week)

At the time of its release, neither Ronnie Milsap nor songwriter Archie Jordan made any efforts to disclose the original intent of "What A Difference You've Made In My Life." They didn't need to—many listeners saw through the veil and recognized it as a gospel song.

"My wife and I were at a Bible study one night at a friend's house," explains the aptly-named Jordan. "There were about 30 people there, I guess, and this one guy got up at the end of the Bible study and gave his testimony.

"He told how he had been an alcoholic and been through a bad marriage, and in and out of jail. He'd had all kinds of problems, and right at the end of his testimony, he said, 'And then I found the Lord, and what a difference he's made in my life.'

"It just hit me like a ton of bricks. I said, 'Man, how many people feel that way?' And not only about the Lord, but about their parents or their wife or their child. So I thought about it that night. When I woke up the next morning, it really kind of jumped out all together, the melody and the lyric."

Milsap had Jordan rewrite a couple of lines out of the song, then took it into the recording studio with a special instrumental arrangement. Producer Tom Collins rented a second grand piano, and both Milsap and Jordan played dueling keyboards on the record, though Jordan went uncredited on the liner notes.

"The day we were recordin' it," Collins adds, "there was one musician that was havin' some personal problems. It was a real struggle in the studio. We edited it a lot, yet it worked."

It didn't take long for listeners to recognize the song's spiritual inspiration. Shortly after its release, gospel artists called in large numbers about recording it. Among those who did release Christian versions were Amy Grant and B.J. Thomas.

"What A Difference You've Made In My Life" made an impressive debut, appearing at number 40 on November 19, 1977. It winged its way to number one in its tenth week.

302

OUT OF MY HEAD AND BACK IN MY BED

LORETTA LYNN

MCA 40832
Writer: Peggy Forman
Producer: Owen Bradley
January 28, 1978 (2 weeks)

In 1976, Loretta Lynn's life story made its way to the bestseller list through *Coal Miner's Daughter* [see 68], an autobiography co-written with George Vecsey of the *New York Times*. Documenting her childhood in the Kentucky hills, her recording history and her volatile marriage to O.V. Lynn [see 7—"Fist City"], the book was an immediate success, selling 15,000 copies every two weeks. One year later, it appeared in paperback.

With her profile renewed, Loretta continued her dominating ways, taking the American Music Award for Favorite Female Vocalist in 1977 and 1978. She also captured her eleventh number one single in 1978, with "Out Of My Head And Back In My Bed," which she calls "a fun song."

"Out Of My Head" was written by Peggy Forman, a songwriter with Conway Twitty's Hello Darlin' Music who charted as a recording artist six different times between 1977 and 1982.

Later in the year, Lynn became the 1,693rd person to receive a star on the Hollywood Walk of Fame. Universal Pictures turned out a script to take *Coal Miner's Daughter* to the silver screen. Location shooting began in Nashville during April of 1979, at the Grand Ole Opry and Ernest Tubb's Record Shop. On March 4, 1980, the movie premiered in Nashville.

"It didn't show how much we fight," Loretta told Michiko Kakutani of the *New York Times*, explaining the on-screen portrayal of her marriage. "If they'd have done that, it would have been a thirty-year movie."

On May 1, 1980, the Academy of Country Music named Lynn the Artist of the Decade. Her decade had closed during 1978-79 with three more Top Ten singles, following "Out Of My Head And Back In My Bed": "We've Come A Long Way, Baby," "I Can't Feel You Anymore" and "I've Got A Picture Of Us On My Mind." She returned to the Top Ten in 1982 with "I Lie."

Though hit records have become a fleeting ideal for her, Loretta continues to work the road while adding to her accolades. In 1983, *Ladies' Home Journal* named her among America's 100 most important women, while the Nashville Songwriters Association inducted her into its Hall of Fame. She later became a member of the Country Music Hall of Fame, in October of 1988.

303

I JUST WISH YOU WERE SOMEONE I LOVE

LARRY GATLIN WITH BROTHERS & FRIENDS

Monument 234
Writer: Larry Gatlin
Producers: Larry Gatlin, Fred Foster
February 11, 1978 (1 week)

Born to an oil driller in West Texas, the Gatlin brothers grew up primarily in Odessa, where their first opportunities to perform came in the local church. Larry (born May 2, 1948) made his first attempts at writing songs by using pop melodies and replacing the original words with religious lyrics. Joined by Steve (April 4, 1951) and Rudy (August 20, 1952), they performed weekly for two years on an Abilene television show hosted by Slim Willet, and in their teens, they cut their first album, a gospel LP for Sword & Shield Records in Arlington.

Larry majored in English while attending the University of Houston, and his brothers went to Texas Tech in Lubbock. After graduation, Larry took pre-law, but his education ended when he earned a chance to sing in Las Vegas with the Imperials. There, Dottie West heard him singing in a dressing room, and, impressed by his abilities, eventually gave him airfare to Nashville.

Meanwhile, Steve and Rudy went on the road with their sister, LaDonna, as members of Tammy Wynette's backing band. But when "Broken Lady" introduced Larry to the Top Ten in 1976, they became part of his act, supporting him on his subsequent hits "Statues Without Hearts," "I Don't Wanna Cry" and "Love Is Just A Game."

Finally, "I Just Wish You Were Someone I Love" became their first number one single. That same week, Johnny Lee called Larry at The Golden Nugget, where he was working, to ask why he hadn't received some kind of recognition for his part in writing it.

As it turned out, Lee had given Gatlin the song's title during Darrell Royal's Golf Tournament in Houston. Gatlin, who has since given up liquor, had been too drunk to remember the episode when he came across the title.

"I had written it down on a little matchbook and forgotten it," he says. "I found it in my pocket two or three days later and wrote the song and never did associate it with Johnny Lee. After he got to telling me about it, I profusely apologized, and to make it up to him, I gave him the idea for a song I couldn't write."

304

DON'T BREAK THE HEART THAT LOVES YOU

MARGO SMITH

Warner Bros. 8508
Writers: Benny Davis, Ted Murray
Producer: Norro Wilson
February 18, 1978 (2 weeks)

Although she harbored dreams of a musical career as a youngster, Bette Lou Smith made music a classroom occupation before attempting it as a recording artist. A native of Dayton, Ohio, she decided at age 18 to get a teaching degree and build her self-confidence, and it wasn't until she was 33 that she made a concerted attempt at a musical career.

"I needed the fulfillment of graduating, going to college and being successful," Smith remembers. "I came from a broken home. My aunt and uncle adopted me at the age of two, I never knew my real mother until I was 19, my adopted father died when I was 13, and my real father died when I was 14. My childhood was traumatic and I really needed some success."

She found that success using music as a reward for her kindergarten classes until she was ready to handle the inevitable line of rejections that goes hand-in-hand with the record business. Her first record did well regionally, although she dropped "Bette Lou" (the label said it was "too goody two-shoes" and suggested "Peaches") and used the assumed name of "Margo."

Against the advice of her friends, she signed with 20th Century-Fox Records in 1975, where her first single, "There I Said It," made Billboard's Top Ten. The following year, she moved to Warner Bros., where she cut two more Top Ten releases before covering a song that Connie Francis took to number one on the pop charts in 1962.

"I had this babysitter at the time named Judy," Smith recalls. "Judy came with a record in her hand and said, 'This song that Connie Francis had would suit your voice to a tee.' I had never heard 'Don't Break The Heart That Loves You' before, so she played the song for me, and I thought it was great. I really liked it."

Judy proved to be correct: with a nostalgic break provided by sax player Bill Puett, "Don't Break The Heart That Loves You" spent two weeks at the top near Valentine's Day of 1978.

Margo Smith

305

MAMMAS, DON'T LET YOUR BABIES GROW UP TO BE COWBOYS/I CAN GET OFF ON YOU
WAYLON & WILLIE
RCA 11198
Writers: Ed Bruce, Patsy Bruce/
Waylon Jennings, Willie Nelson
Producer: Chips Moman
March 4, 1978 (4 weeks)

After the success of "Good Hearted Woman" [see 237], a duet album featuring both Waylon Jennings and Willie Nelson was a logical step, although the record required a bit of wheeling and dealing between RCA, Columbia and Neil Reshen, who managed both Waylon and Willie. By the time the album came out, two singles had already emerged. Jennings' "The Wurlitzer Prize" [see 298] went to number one, as did their duet, "Mammas, Don't Let Your Babies Grow Up To Be Cowboys," released a couple weeks ahead of the album.

"Mammas" was actually a remake of an Ed Bruce recording which peaked at number 15 in early 1976, just as "Good Hearted Woman" was on its way to number one. Bruce also wrote the song, with the help of then-wife Patsy Bruce, starting it on a drive home from a jingle session.

"I had just left the studio and everybody was knocked out with what I did," he remembers. "I was good at what I did, but nobody really knew, and my first thought was, 'Mammas, Don't Let Your Babies Grow Up To Play Guitars.' Then I changed it to 'Don't Let 'Em Grow Up To Be Cowboys' and worked in guitars."

Bruce thought about pitching the song to both Jennings and Nelson, ultimately keeping it for himself instead. In September of 1977, though, he placed a call to Waylon in hopes of getting him to cut a new version.

"We exchanged some pleasantries," Bruce explains, "and I said, 'Why don't you cut "Mammas"?' and he said, 'I did about two weeks ago!' He and Chips had gotten together to screen material, and each of them had brought in my album with 'Mammas' on it with the idea of presenting it to the other saying, 'Why don't we cut this?'"

Initially, Jennings recorded it as a solo artist.

"Later on," says Waylon, "me and Willie were talking about recording again, and I said, 'Willie, I cut this thing, but I ain't sure about it.'

I said, 'It don't sound right, but it might be a great duet.' The whole record was finished, and I just took part of my voice off and put his on."

The result was magic. The single went to number one and earned a Grammy award. The double-platinum *Waylon & Willie* album also yielded a solo Willie hit, "If You Can Touch Her At All."

306
READY FOR THE TIMES
TO GET BETTER
CRYSTAL GAYLE

United Artists 1136
Writer: Allen Reynolds
Producer: Allen Reynolds
April 1, 1978 (1 week)

Riding behind a monster, the obvious move for Crystal Gayle would have been to imitate "Don't It Make My Brown Eyes Blue" [see 292] with her next single. Instead, she segued from that bluesy record into the haunting sound of "Ready For The Times To Get Better."

"We always were ones to release different things," she offers. "We wouldn't follow the rules, because we knew how to make number one songs. It never failed. Everytime someone would have a number one song, their next single would almost sound exactly like that song, but it wasn't as good, and that used to bother me."

"Ready For The Times" wasn't a usual choice. Not only did it differ significantly from "Brown Eyes," it wasn't even from the same album, *We Must Believe in Magic*. Instead, United Artists dipped back into the previous *Crystal* album [see 271—"You Never Miss A Real Good Thing"]. Breaking another of Nashville's long-sacred rules, the song was written in a minor key.

"Ready For The Times To Get Better" is one of five Top Ten singles that producer Allen Reynolds has written. The others include Crystal's "Wrong Road Again" and "Somebody Loves You," Waylon Jennings' "Dreaming My Dreams With You" [see 228—"Are You Sure Hank Done It This Way"] and Don Williams' "We Should Be Together."

Reynolds wrote "Ready For The Times" during a three-hour period at a friend's house.

He had gone to water the plants during his friend's vacation, and ended up "noodling" at the keyboard. The song came at the end of that session. "I stood up and took two or three steps from the piano, and that song was just there in my head," he notes. "I don't play the piano that much, but I spun around and sat down at the piano, went exactly to the chord that I was hearing in my head, and it was a dissonant chord.

"The first part of that song just came really fast. I could barely find paper and get it down. I couldn't help myself. It was certainly what I was feeling at the moment, and it just popped out."

Doubting his objectivity about his own songs, Reynolds was reluctant to play "Ready For The Times" for Crystal. Those doubts were erased on April Fools' Day in 1978, when it became her fourth number one record.

307
SOMEONE LOVES YOU HONEY
CHARLEY PRIDE

RCA 11201
Writer: Don Devaney
Producers: Jerry Bradley, Charley Pride
April 8, 1978 (2 weeks)

Charley Pride met his wife-to-be while playing baseball for the Memphis Red Sox in the American Negro League. A friend introduced them after a game, leading to a five-month courtship. On December 28, 1956, they were married by a justice of the peace in Hernando, Mississippi.

Rozene Pride stuck with Charley through his military enlistment, several more years of his baseball pursuits and through the early years of a musical career in which he earned a grand total of $138 for his first record.

"As long as it's not detrimental to your family or you, you have to follow your dream," she told Diane Jennings in the *Dallas Morning News*. "I always felt he could make it as a singer. Dumb me, I never realized there hadn't been a black country singer until I saw it in print one day, and I said, 'Pride, is that true?'"

For those who have met the couple, even briefly, it's not hard to picture "Someone Loves You Honey" as a song that fits them well. Written by Canadian Don Devaney, it was recorded first by Brenda Lee, whose version caught the attention of producer Jerry Bradley. "It sparkled," he says, "and I knew Charley could do it. It just was a triple A-rated song."

It became Pride's twentieth number one record, after debuting on the *Billboard* country chart just three days before Valentine's Day in 1978.

"If you listen to my songs, most people feel that I sing them to my wife," Pride admits. "But it's nothing conscious; it just seems like it comes out that way. Many people think that's who I sing my songs to, and I guess I do. I sing them to anyone that's in love—and I guess after more than 30 years, we've been in love quite a bit."

Pride followed up "Someone Loves You Honey" with two more singles to round out 1978. "When I Stop Leaving (I'll Be Gone)" reached a peak position of number three during the fall, and the nostalgic "Burgers And Fries" spent three weeks at number two in December, unable to dislodge Kenny Rogers' "The Gambler" [see 330].

308

EVERY TIME TWO FOOLS COLLIDE
KENNY ROGERS & DOTTIE WEST
United Artists 1137
Writers: Jan Dyer, Jeff Tweel
Producer: Larry Butler
April 22, 1978 (2 weeks)

"**D**uets serve a couple of different purposes," theorizes Kenny Rogers. "First of all, I think there's a chemistry that happens when you're in the studio. When you go in as an

**Kenny Rogers &
Dottie West**

individual and you sing the best you think you're capable of, the moment someone else gets in there and they sing a little better than you do, you realize there's a little more in that well that you can reach for.

"But also, I think it's important for a career, because it's a way to have a release out without beating your sound into the ground. My sound, you hear six or eight or ten records in a row, and you say, 'Okay, enough, enough.'"

Important though duets might be, Kenny's first one came about by accident. Producer Larry Butler had a recording session with Dottie West at Sound Emporium Studios, scheduled to finish at 6:00. Kenny had time booked with Butler beginning at 7:00, and he decided to drop in early and visit with Dottie.

When he arrived, she stood alone in the studio, working on overdubs for a song called "Every Time Two Fools Collide." After one take, she took off the headphones and walked back into the control room to hear a playback.

"I was just singin' along with it," Kenny remembers, "and she said, 'Well, that sounds great.' I said, 'You know, we need to do a duet some time just for the fun of it,' and she said, 'Well, go out there and sing and see how it sounds.' So that's exactly what happened. I went out there and sang the second verse, and everybody loved it."

The following day, the duet idea began to snowball. Rogers' manager, Ken Kragen, contacted Dottie and signed her to a management contract. Kenny incorporated her show within his own concerts, and the record led to an entire duet album.

"Every Time Two Fools Collide" entered the *Billboard* country chart at number 65 on February 18, 1978. On March 5, Rogers and West hosted "The World's Largest Indoor Country Music Show" at the Silver Dome in Pontiac, Michigan, and a month later, the concert became an NBC-TV "Big Event" special. The same month, the song became Kenny's third number one record, and Dottie's first.

Their next duet, "Anyone Who Isn't Me Tonight," peaked at number two.

309
IT'S ALL WRONG, BUT IT'S ALL RIGHT/TWO DOORS DOWN
DOLLY PARTON

RCA 11240
Writer: Dolly Parton
Producer: Gary Klein
May 6, 1978 (2 weeks)

Dolly Parton's ongoing struggle with her weight (it's ranged from 105 pounds to 157) has provided frequent fodder for the grocery-store gossip papers. "I never was a heavy person 'til I got to be where I was making enough money to afford to get fat," she laughs, "'cause I was eating everything I wanted, stopping at every truckstop, and going out to eat with everybody."

In 1977, her battle with the bulge produced a prolific night of writing in a Howard Johnson's hotel room. Two of the songs from that evening occupied each side of a double-sided hit.

"When I was about 30, I was really getting to be a little porker," she giggles, "so I would start going on all these crazy diets. At the time I wrote these two songs, I had been on that old liquid protein diet for about four weeks. I'd lost a lot of weight, maybe 25, 27 pounds, but I was starved to death.

"I love those fried clams at Howard Johnson's, so I was in my room and all the band was out just partying and eating and having a big time, and I couldn't go out, because I knew if I went out that I'd want to eat.

"So I was in my room feeling sorry for myself, drinking that old, yucky liquid protein, and I could smell those old clams coming through the window from the restaurant. I thought, 'Well, I've got to do something or I'm gonna go crazy,' so I thought I'd write some songs.

"I started writing 'Two Doors Down,' 'cause they were literally two doors down at the Howard Johnson's and laughing and drinking and having a party."

Dolly had trouble sleeping, so she ordered some black coffee, and the caffeine kept her wired long enough to continue her writing spree. As a result, she also composed "It's All Wrong, But It's All Right."

In December, while Dolly sat at number one with "Here You Come Again" [see 299], RCA labelmate Zella Lehr released her own version of "Two Doors Down," which became her only Top Ten record. The same week that Lehr peaked, Dolly entered the chart with "Two Doors Down" as the "B" side of her release. While "It's All Wrong" received the dominant country play, "Two Doors Down" propelled Parton to number 19 on the *Billboard* Hot 100.

310

SHE CAN PUT HER SHOES UNDER MY BED (ANYTIME)

JOHNNY DUNCAN

Columbia 10694
Writers: Aaron Schroeder, Bob Halley
Producer: Billy Sherrill
May 20, 1978 (1 week)

Nine months after Elvis Presley passed away [see 291—"Way Down"], one of the King's former associates earned his very first number one country record. Aaron Schroeder had already hit the top spot on the pop charts by writing three Presley singles—"A Big Hunk O' Love," "It's Now Or Never" and "Good Luck Charm"—and had also netted such significant cuts as "Stuck On You," "I Got Stung" and "I Was The One" (the "B" side of "Heartbreak Hotel" [see 352]).

At the time of Presley's passing, Duncan was on his way up the *Billboard* charts with his Top Five "A Song In The Night," and he duplicated his showing with a Janie Frickie duet, "Come A Little Bit Closer," toward the end of the year. Around the same time, Schroeder approached Duncan's producer with "She Can Put Her Shoes Under My Bed (Anytime)."

"The demo came in to Billy Sherrill in 1977," Duncan relates, "and the quality of the demo was so bad that I couldn't even make out what he was saying and just pushed it aside. About a month or six weeks later, Billy said I should listen to it again, and there was something about the tone of his voice that told me I was missing something. Sure enough, when I really concentrated on it, I could see what Billy was talking about."

Duncan earned three more Top Ten singles as an artist over the next two years, and Jim Ed Brown & Helen Cornelius likewise went to number three with his composition, "Fools," but Johnny's records began slipping with the turn of the decade.

His father, Isaac Collins Duncan, passed away in 1981, and Johnny went back to Texas to be with his children. "It took me several years to get over the pressure of raising kids, and the politics of CBS, and the grind of the road out there," he assesses. "The over-used term 'burnout' would fit. When you walk out and you're smiling and you don't mean it, you cheat everybody."

The burnout eventually disappeared, as

Duncan married Connie Smith, of Resaca, Georgia, and had a son, John Isaac, in October of 1984.

311

DO YOU KNOW YOU ARE MY SUNSHINE

THE STATLER BROTHERS

Mercury 55022
Writers: Don Reid, Harold Reid
Producer: Jerry Kennedy
May 27, 1978 (2 weeks)

Hailing from Staunton (pronounced "Stanton"), Virginia, the Statler Brothers had to wait more than a dozen years after their first appearance on the *Billboard* country charts before they finally earned their first number one single.

"Flowers On The Wall," written by founding tenor Lew DeWitt, provided their initial entry, debuting on September 25, 1965. The group traveled at the time as a part of the Johnny Cash Show [see 24—"Daddy Sang Bass"], and it wasn't until they got hold of a chart that they even knew they had gained any airplay. By the time the record was through, "Flowers On The Wall" had peaked at number two on the country list and at number four on the Hot 100.

After several more years with Cash, the Statlers signed up with Mercury Records, recording with producer Jerry Kennedy for the first time in September of 1970. They put together seven more Top Ten hits prior to 1978, coming close to the top with the Grammy-winning "Do You Remember These" (a number two recording in 1972) and "I'll Go To My Grave Loving You" (number three, 1975).

Finally, the Statlers topped the charts with a song whose inspiration came from routine interaction with fans from the bandstand. Concertgoers would approach the stage to make requests, and one particular girl caught the attention of bass vocalist Harold Reid by asking "Do you know 'You Are My Sunshine'?"

"We were between songs," remembers Don Reid, "and Harold said, 'I just got a great idea for a song.' We carried the idea around, we were in Nashville recording later, and our session got snowed out. We were snowed in the hotel for a whole day, so we sat down, wrote the song that day, and recorded it the next day.

It was still 'wet' when we recorded it."

"Do You Know You Are My Sunshine" is the only single to reach number one featuring the title of another song within its own title. It's also the only chart-topping release to feature the original Statler line-up: Don Reid (born June 5, 1945), Harold Reid (August 21, 1939), Philip Balsley (August 8, 1939) and Lew DeWitt (March 8, 1939).

312

GEORGIA ON MY MIND

WILLIE NELSON

Columbia 10704
Writers: Hoagy Carmichael,
Stuart Gorrell
Producer: Booker T. Jones
June 10, 1978 (1 week)

Though he couldn't buy a hit a few years earlier, Willie Nelson commanded a juggernaut in the mid-'70s. The *Red Headed Stranger* album [see 223—"Blue Eyes Crying In The Rain"] succeeded against the accepted logic, and Willie's penchant for the unusual was widely embraced by the general public.

His long hair, bandana and earring would hardly have been accepted from a more traditional figure, but Willie did things his own way, and that in itself engendered respect. The series of Waylon & Willie hits [see 237—"Good Hearted Woman," 286—"Luckenbach, Texas" and 305—"Mammas, Don't Let Your Babies Grow Up To Be Cowboys"] further enhanced that reputation, branding Nelson with an "outlaw" label.

As they had with *Red Headed Stranger*, Columbia Records resisted Willie's 1978 concept: *Stardust*, an album with ten of his all-time favorite songs, most of which were written before 1950. The label felt he should come up with new material, but Willie thought it was a perfect way to create an even larger audience. His younger fans would treat them like they were new songs; older listeners would appreciate hearing some of their long-time favorites.

Willie recorded Hoagy Carmichael's "Stardust" first, and also added Carmichael's "Georgia On My Mind," written and recorded by Hoagy in 1930. Ray Charles gave the song a new reading in 1960, and Nelson's version revived national interest in Carmichael, who also wrote "Heart And Soul," "Ole Buttermilk Sky" and "I Get Along Without You Very Well,"

among others. A former law student, Carmichael died on December 27, 1981.

"Georgia On My Mind" yielded Willie's fifth number one single, and secured a Grammy award on March 15, 1979. It was also named the official state song of Georgia, replacing Carmichael's earlier rendition. CBS-TV's "Designing Women" adopted "Georgia On My Mind" as its theme song.

Nelson has since released three more standard-packed collections: *Somewhere Over the Rainbow, Without a Song* and *What a Wonderful World*. He explained his fascination with the pop classics to *USA Today*'s David Zimmerman: "All of us songwriters try to write songs of this same caliber, but it's difficult if not impossible to do. It's amazing how strong the lyrics and melodies are and how many millions of people are affected by them."

313

TWO MORE BOTTLES OF WINE

EMMYLOU HARRIS

Warner Bros. 8553
Writer: Delbert McClinton
Producer: Brian Ahern
June 17, 1978 (1 week)

Fans of Top 40 radio might know Delbert McClinton for his 1981 hit "Giving It Up For Your Love," but he had actually been working steadily for two decades. In 1962, he played harmonica on Bruce Channel's number one pop record "Hey! Baby." That same year, backstage at an early Beatles concert, he taught John Lennon the harmonica licks that appeared on "Love Me Do." And years later, he added Emmylou Harris to his growing cadre of admirers.

"I got turned on to Delbert from that [1975] album he did called *Victim of Life's Circumstances*," she notes. "I remember putting it on and just being sort of knocked out. His writing, his singing, his playing on the album, it was so much energy. It was like something that nobody else was doing, and I just couldn't believe that nothing grand happened for him."

Determined to find a McClinton song that could be performed from a woman's point of view, Emmylou settled on "Two More Bottles Of Wine." "We changed the rhythm quite a bit," she says, "and came up with something different, but still kept the spirit of the song—that 'we're gonna rise above it' kind of attitude."

Emmylou Harris

I'LL BE TRUE TO YOU

THE OAK RIDGE BOYS

ABC 12350
Writer: Alan Rhody
Producer: Ron Chancey
June 24, 1978 (1 week)

On August 6, 1945, America dropped the first atomic bomb on Hiroshima. The event brought World War II to an end in the Pacific theater, and brought a burgeoning community in eastern Tennessee, known as Oak Ridge, to prominence.

Just three years earlier, the town didn't even exist. Government-employed construction workers first appeared at the site on November 22, 1942, and they suggested the town's name. Within two years, the population of Oak Ridge swelled to 75,000: the atomic bomb was being perfected as part of the top-secret "Manhattan Project." Once President Truman decided to display the bomb's power, Oak Ridge gained its notoriety.

As the town grew to fame, so did Wally Fowler's gospel act, the Georgia Clodhoppers. Wally capitalized on the event, changing the group's name to the Oak Ridge Quartet, and a number of different line-ups existed throughout the ensuing years. Finally, during the '60s, the Quartet became the Oak Ridge Boys.

More changes occurred until 1973, when the line-up stabilized with Bill Golden, Duane Allen, Richard Sterban and Joe Bonsall. The act engendered controversy in the gospel world, since the band would play with long hair, turtleneck shirts and a drummer. When opposition grew, the Oak Ridge Boys became disenchanted with the gospel industry and edged their way into country music.

At first, the move was quite unsuccessful. In one year, they lost $100,000, and only the support of Johnny Cash—both verbal and financial—kept them going. Finally, in 1977, they secured a country recording deal with ABC/Dot. Record producer Ron Chancey went on the road with the Oaks and analyzed the strong points of their road show.

He captured the same enthusiasm on record, and their first single for the label, "Y'all Come Back Saloon," soared to number three. Another, "You're The One," brought them to number two, and "I'll Be True To You" improved one more notch, hitting number one.

"I was the last person to consent to record

As with all of the material from that period, Harris recorded "Two More Bottles Of Wine" with then-husband/producer Brian Ahern at their home near Beverly Hills. Ahern converted a semi into a mobile studio, and ran cables from the Enactron Truck into the house. The musicians each played in separate rooms while Ahern used the truck as a control booth.

"The house looked like something out of an Esther Williams movie," recalls Emmylou. "I mean it was the volcanic rock, and the swimming pool with swans, and the fountains and crushed glass poodles on the sliding doors of the closets, and butterflies, and a terrible white grand piano with gold pheasants on it. This is a rental house, and so I just stuck a picture of Dolly Parton on top of the fireplace, and I sort of focused on her."

Luckily, the set-up also put some distance between Ahern and the musicians.

"If he was mad," explains bassist Emory Gordy, "he had to run out of the truck and into the living room. By the time he got there, he wasn't mad anymore, not that he was given to fits of madness."

it," admits Allen. "I got the lead on it, and Ron kept telling me, 'You gotta record this song, 'cause it's a hit.' I didn't want to record it, because the woman gets killed off at the end, and I didn't think I wanted a single record with a woman dyin' off. Especially that early in our career.

"However, Ron Chancey was right, and I was wrong."

"It's time to stop and smell the roses," she says. "If you can afford it, I think it's sad to wait so long to enjoy your life. I always want to do TV and do some shows, if something comes up, but I don't want to be tied down and be responsible for eight people or something like that. I was always so frustrated, and I don't want that anymore. I'm going to enjoy my life."

315
IT ONLY HURTS FOR A LITTLE WHILE
MARGO SMITH
Warner Bros. 8555
Writers: Mack David, Fred Spielman
Producer: Norro Wilson
July 1, 1978 (1 week)

Margo Smith's two number one records were both cut at the very same session, and, as it happens, both were remakes. She had already recorded "Don't Break The Heart That Loves You" [see 304] and "Little Things Mean A Lot" (number three later that same year), and time was running out in the studio.

At an earlier date, Smith and Norro Wilson had both expressed an interest in the old Ames Brothers recording, "It Only Hurts For A Little While." Unfortunately, neither could remember all of the words, and they couldn't find a copy of the original in any music store.

"At the very end of the session," Margo notes, "somebody came running in with the sheet music to 'It Only Hurts For A Little While.' We didn't have much time at all, but everything we cut that day was right in the groove."

That single day was the climax of her career. She scored two more Top Ten hits in 1979, with "Still A Woman" and "If I Give My Heart To You," and in 1980, she gained a minor hit when she teamed up with Rex Allen, Jr., on "Cup Of Tea." Smith moved to Nashville in 1982 and continued to put out singles on several independent labels with little success. She continues to tour, although she sold her bus and appears with less frequency.

Margo used the money from her advances at Warner Bros. to put her children through college, began a designer sweatshirt business in 1987, and made a commitment to spend more time with her family.

316
I BELIEVE IN YOU
MEL TILLIS
MCA 40900
Writers: Buddy Cannon, Gene Dunlap
Producer: Jimmy Bowen
July 8, 1978 (1 week)

Hailing from Lexington, Tennessee, Buddy Cannon moved to Nashville to be a bass player. After stints with Bob Luman and Mel Tillis, however, he found songwriting and publishing a more lucrative arena and went to work in Tillis' company. Cannon has sung back-up on traditional records like George Strait's "Marina Del Rey" and "A Fire I Can't Put Out" [see 535], as well as on Reba McEntire's album *My Kind of Country*; yet the first number one record he ever wrote was the most progressive of Tillis' career.

Cannon wrote "I Believe In You" with Gene Dunlap in 1976, and played it for Tillis. Mel liked it, but felt it needed some work. "He asked us to go and do some rewrites on it," Cannon recalls, "and we did two or three different versions of the song. Mel pitched the original version to Glen Campbell, and Glen passed on it."

Tillis kept it in the back of his mind, however, and about 18 months after he heard it first, he recorded the original version of the song with producer Jimmy Bowen.

"I wanted him to step out," notes Bowen, "and so did he. It was a very difficult song to sing. We must have recorded it three or four times to finally get it, 'cause it was so different for him."

"Different" is an understatement. Bowen hired L.A. woodwind player Jim Horn to play flute on the record while Tillis was on tour, and added a full string section.

"He didn't know what to think of it," Bowen laughs.

Neither did country radio, and initially, many stations resisted the record. The stations that did add it, garnered positive results, and the record ultimately built enough momentum to reach number one. The *I Believe in You* album also netted a Top Five follow-up with "Ain't No California," on which Horn also played saxophone.

"When I started working with [Tillis]," says Bowen, "he had a five-piece band and himself. It wasn't much. Two years later, he called me one day, and said, 'Uh, Bowen, don't put any more things on my records.' I said, 'Why's that?' He said, 'Because you're about to, uh, break me. I'm up to two buses and a 15-piece band. Don't add one more thing.'"

317
ONLY ONE LOVE IN MY LIFE
RONNIE MILSAP
RCA 11270
Writers: John Bettis, R.C. Bannon
Producers: Tom Collins, Ronnie Milsap
July 15, 1978 (3 weeks)

On October 10, 1977, Ronnie Milsap completed a triple play at the Country Music Association awards show, collecting the trophies for Entertainer of the Year and Male Vocalist of the Year, as well as Album of the Year, for his live project [see 273—"Let My Love Be Your Pillow"].

When accepting the "biggie," for Entertainer, he went onstage with his wife, Joyce, and spoke about how much assistance and inspiration she had provided in helping him to attain his dream. That same night, R.C. Bannon watched the proceedings from his living room in Nashville, along with songwriter John Bettis. Touched by Milsap's acceptance speech, they wrote "Only One Love In My Life" especially for Ronnie and Joyce.

Quite often, such tailor-made songs fail to impress the artist they were written about, but in this instance, Milsap was immediately drawn in. The following month, he took the song into the recording studio, although it failed to generate any magic. Undaunted, he tried again in January, and within several months, that particular version was on the streets.

On June 3, 1978, "Only One Love In My Life" debuted at number 32, higher than any previous single on the *Billboard* country chart, later upstaged by "Every Which Way But Loose" [see 335]. By mid-summer, it became

Milsap's tenth number one single. In October, the album became his second gold record.

It was the first major success for Bannon, whose real name was Dan Shipley. He devised "R.C. Bannon" as an on-air name when he went to work for a Seattle radio station in 1968, taking the initials from RC Cola.

In July of 1976, Bannon signed with Warner Bros. Music as a writer, and a year later, he released his first single as a recording artist for Columbia Records. During Fan Fair in 1978, R.C. met labelmate Louise Mandrell, and on February 26, 1979, they exchanged wedding vows. His biggest success as a performer came when they teamed on a duet that summer: "Reunited" went to number 13.

Bannon wrote or produced Mandrell's biggest solo records, including "Save Me," "I Wanna Say Yes" and "Maybe My Baby." He also composed or arranged most of the music for the "Barbara Mandrell & The Mandrell Sisters" TV show [see 478—"'Til You're Gone"], and wrote Barbara's "One Of A Kind Pair Of Fools" [see 545].

318
LOVE OR SOMETHING LIKE IT
KENNY ROGERS
United Artists 1210
Writers: Kenny Rogers, Steve Glassmeyer
Producer: Larry Butler
August 5, 1978 (1 week)

Of his Top Ten country hits, Kenny Rogers receives songwriter credits on only four. On two of them—"Love Will Turn You Around" [see 485] and "Crazy" [see 613]—he played a somewhat minor role. The other two were released within ten months of each other.

Kenny cut "Sweet Music Man" on his album *Daytime Friends* [see 294], reaching number nine in December of 1977. Following an impromptu duet with Dottie West [see 308—"Every Time Two Fools Collide"], he released the title track of *Love or Something Like It*, written with Steve Glassmeyer, a member of his band.

"We were actually working at Las Vegas at the time," recalls Kenny, "doing three or four shows a night. We were working in the lounge at the Golden Nugget, and we had so much time off between shows with literally nothing else to do. I had just heard some song on the radio, I don't know what it was, it was kind of a gimmick type of song, a beer-drinkin' kind of song.

"We just started playing around really out of boredom, and we stumbled into a couple verses and the hook of 'Love or somethin' damn near like it,' and just liked it and had no intentions of recording it at the time."

It was exactly the kind of song Rogers needed for his Vegas act, and he later played it for producer Larry Butler, who was attracted to its island feel. "Love Or Something Like It" recounted a tale of a barroom seduction, and though other records have generated backlashes for suggestive lyrics [see 372—"I'd Love To Lay You Down"], "Love" received nary a complaint from radio.

"Usually," says Kenny, "people get offended when they think it's blatant, or that it's information that a younger group of people shouldn't have at their disposal. I think I'm real careful about that."

"I think," adds Butler, "it was one of those cases where the people were diggin' the record before they knew what it was sayin'."

Debuting at number 44 on June 3, 1978, "Love Or Something Like It" made it to number three six weeks later, but spent another two weeks stalled at number two behind Ronnie Milsap's "Only One Love In My Life" [see 317]. It finally slipped into the top spot on August 5.

Eddie Rabbitt

319
YOU DON'T LOVE ME ANYMORE
EDDIE RABBITT
Elektra 45488
Writers: Alan Ray, Jeff Raymond
Producer: David Malloy
August 12, 1978 (1 week)

When Sammi Smith recorded her album *Help Me Make It Through the Night* [see 72] in 1970, producer Jim Malloy enlisted two men to write liner notes—Kris Kristofferson, who wrote the title track, and Eddie Rabbitt, who Malloy felt was bound for future importance.

His prediction came true, with help in part from Malloy's son, David, who became Rabbitt's producer once the deal with Elektra Records was signed. Growing up, the younger Malloy disliked much of the country music his father listened to, and he vowed to change it when he matured.

"A lot of the music we were doing was very innovative," says David, "and you had a lot of old country deejays who were really opposed to our type of music. They were frightened by it. They didn't want any change.

"I enjoyed raising everybody's dander. Part of that was the frustration of wanting to do more than a country song, and having to figure out how to get through the country charts, over to the adult/contemporary charts, to have 'em cross over to the pop charts. What I tried to do, basically, was make pop records that could be acceptable to country radio."

The second number one single for both Rabbitt and Malloy follows along those lines. "You Don't Love Me Anymore" came from songwriters Jeff Raymond and Alan Ray, whom Rabbitt, Malloy and Even Stevens briefly considered signing to their DebDave publishing house. The record debuted at number 53 on *Billboard*'s Hot 100, and Malloy calls it "the first country song to have synthesized syndrums on it." Malloy also added a couple of "oohs" right before the chorus, inspired by something he heard on Elton John's *Madman Across the Water* album.

"You Don't Love Me Anymore" trailed Rabbitt's first number one single, "Drinkin' My Baby (Off My Mind)" [see 243], by more than two years. In the interim, he amassed five Top Ten singles. Two of them—"I Can't Help Myself" and "Hearts On Fire"—stopped at number two.

Rabbitt's efforts were recognized by his peers on April 27, 1978, when the Academy of Country Music named him Top New Male Vocalist.

320

TALKING IN YOUR SLEEP
CRYSTAL GAYLE
United Artists 1214
Writers: Roger Cook, Bobby Wood
Producer: Allen Reynolds
August 19, 1978 (2 weeks)

"Talking In Your Sleep"—Crystal Gayle's fifth number one single—represented the first country chart-topper for both Bobby Wood and Roger Cook. Wood's first real success as a writer came with Billy "Crash" Craddock's "Still Thinkin' 'Bout You" [see 192—"Ruby Baby"]. Later hits included "Half The Way" [see 375—"It's Like We Never Said Goodbye"], "He Got You" [see 491] and Merle Haggard's "A Better Love Next Time."

Wood was better known as a pianist, though. He contributed to a host of Memphis recordings, including Elvis Presley's "Suspicious Minds" and "In The Ghetto" plus Danny O'Keefe's "Goodtime Charlie's Got The Blues."

Cook originated the melody of "Talking In Your Sleep"'s chorus one day at his farmhouse in Franklin, Tennessee, and invited Wood to join him. "I sang it to him over the phone, and he got it on tape," remembers Cook. "He had this little place out in Brentwood, and a couple nights later, I went out there and we sat down. It's as simple as that."

"We were talkin' about dreams, sleep and everything," Wood adds, "and we were also talkin' about 'If You Talk In Your Sleep,' that a friend of mine, Red West, had written [for Elvis]. We decided to turn the idea around and

write 'You've Been Talking In Your Sleep,' make a different idea out of it."

That was on New Year's Eve, 1976. For the next 18 months, business partner Ralph Murphy pitched the song all over Nashville with disappointing results. Producer Allen Reynolds liked it and played it for Crystal during sessions for *We Must Believe in Magic*, but she turned it down.

"During the following year," Reynolds reports, "I pitched that song to several different producers—Larry Butler and Billy Sherrill. Sherrill was sayin', 'That's a hell of a song; I ought to cut that on Tammy.'"

Sherrill never did. In the meantime, RCA sent Wood a recording contract based on the demo. The papers were still on Bobby's desk when Reynolds called to tell him Crystal had changed her mind and did want to cut it. Wood decided that she would do better with the song than he would, and declined his recording deal.

Though it took 18 months to get it recorded, "Talking In Your Sleep" was an immediate success. It spent two weeks atop the country chart, and also peaked at number 18 on *Billboard*'s Hot 100.

321

BLUE SKIES
WILLIE NELSON
Columbia 10784
Writer: Irving Berlin
Producer: Booker T. Jones
September 2, 1978 (1 week)

Two events helped to shape Willie Nelson's monumental *Stardust* album [see 312—"Georgia On My Mind"]. One was the October 14, 1977, death of Bing Crosby, a vocalist whom Nelson had long admired. His passing caused Willie to re-examine his own career, and he naturally focused on the classics from Crosby's era.

The other event was more personal. Nelson bought a condominium in Malibu, and discovered that his upstairs neighbor was Booker T. Jones, best known for his work on "Green Onions" with Booker T. & The MG's. Willie asked him to create some arrangements for "Stardust" and "Moonlight In Vermont," and when the "charts" came out to his liking, Nelson asked Jones to co-produce an entire album.

"I wasn't really sure in my mind how well I

could do these songs because of my limited musical ability, as far as writing down songs of this caliber," Nelson told Chet Flippo in *Rolling Stone*. "These are complicated songs; they have a lot of chords in them. I needed someone like Booker to write and arrange. Once I got with him, it was easy to do the album."

Willie recorded the entire project with Brian Ahern's Enactron Truck, in Emmylou Harris' Hollywood Hills home [see 313—"Two More Bottles Of Wine"]. "It always felt relaxed when we were workin' around that place over there," says Willie. "It was a great studio."

Released in May of 1978, *Stardust* yielded a second chart-topping single with "Blue Skies," written by the legendary Irving Berlin, whose output included "God Bless America," "Puttin' On The Ritz," "There's No Business Like Show Business" and "White Christmas," among hundreds of tunes.

Later in the year, "All Of Me," also from the *Stardust* album, went to number three. The LP spent eleven weeks at number one on the *Billboard* country album chart that year, but its biggest distinction came on August 11, 1988, when CBS Records toasted Willie with a black-tie reception at the Opryland Hotel in Nashville. *Billboard*'s Gerry Wood presented Willie with a platinum trophy celebrating 520 weeks (10 years!) on the magazine's country album chart. By October of 1990, *Stardust* had logged more than 540 weeks on the chart.

In 1979, Willie released another concept album, *Willie Nelson Sings Kristofferson*. He peaked at number three with "Help Me Make It Through The Night" [see 72].

322
I'VE ALWAYS BEEN CRAZY
WAYLON JENNINGS
RCA 11344
Writer: Waylon Jennings
Producers: Richie Albright,
Waylon Jennings
September 9, 1978 (3 weeks)

On September 26, 1978, Waylon Jennings set his second sales precedent. *Wanted: The Outlaws* was the first Nashville album certified platinum, once the Recording Industry Association of America introduced that award in 1976, recognizing million-selling albums. In 1978, *I've Always Been Crazy* became the first country album ever to "ship gold," meaning

that 500,000 copies were ordered before it ever went to market.

By that point in time, the title track had already spent three weeks at the top of *Billboard*'s country singles chart.

"That was a little waltz," Waylon says, while admitting embarrassing details about its creation. "I was in the studio with some of the musicians, and they got in my cocaine, and did it all. It made me mad, so the next day I came in and did all of theirs, and I got really messed up, and I rewrote that song while I was trying to record it.

"It was eight minutes long when I got through with it. I had most of the lyrics, but I changed it into an upbeat, uptempo song. I think that's one of the best songs that I've written, 'cause it says some good things. My favorite line—and still, I guess, my favorite line I've ever written—is 'I've never intentionally hurt anyone.'"

One person who might disagree, though, was the trumpet player who added a few choice lines just before the record's fade-out. "That poor old guy," laughs Waylon. "I had him come in there, and like I say, the track was almost eight minutes long. I had that poor horn player come in and play it all the way through, and then play all the way through in harmony, and when he left there, his lips were all swollen and everything. I never saw him again, and I hope I never do, because I only used those horns in about three places after all that hard work he did."

"I've Always Been Crazy" was Waylon's third hit of 1978, though only his first solo record. He hit number one with Willie Nelson on "Mammas, Don't Let Your Babies Grow Up To Be Cowboys" [see 305]," and he peaked at number two during the summer with his friend, and one-time roommate, Johnny Cash, on "There Ain't No Good Chain Gang."

323
HEARTBREAKER
DOLLY PARTON
RCA 11296
Writers: David Wolfert,
Carole Bayer Sager
Producers: Gary Klein, Dolly Parton
September 30, 1978 (3 weeks)

"I always liked the look of our hookers back home," Dolly Parton once told Cliff Jahr in

Ladies' Home Journal. "Their big hairdos and makeup made them look *more*. When people say that less is more, I say more is more. Less is less. I go for more.

"I look one way and am another. It makes for a good combination. I always think of 'her,' the Dolly image, like a ventriloquist does his dummy. I have fun with it. I think, 'What will I do with *her* this year to surprise people? What'll *she* wear, what'll *she* say?'"

Apparently, her fun approach to fashion didn't sit well with everyone. In 1978, she was at the top of Blackwell's annual list of the Worst Dressed Celebrities. Likewise, that year's *Heartbreaker* brought a poor reaction from music critics, although it became her third gold album within a month of release.

The title track—and first single—was written by David Wolfert, a friend of producer Gary Klein. "David was in a band in the late '60s or early '70s in New York," Klein notes, "and I worked with him and his little band, and then we lost touch for years. I went out to L.A. to record, and I went in the studio and I saw David. Many years had passed since I'd last seen him, and the last person I expected to see hanging out in a studio lounge in Hollywood was David.

"David's a fabulous guitar player. He'd been in Janis Ian's band, and they'd been to Japan and all over the place. I was thrilled to see him, and told him I was about to record Dolly, and he ended up arranging so much of what I recorded with Dolly, playing guitar and—in this case— writing a song."

Extremely melodic, "Heartbreaker" debuted at number 38 on August 19. It ascended to number one in only its seventh week, and when it remained there for three weeks, it surpassed all of her records—except for "Here You Come Again" [see 299]—in its longevity at the top.

324

TEAR TIME
DAVE & SUGAR
RCA 11322
Writer: Jan Crutchfield
Producers: Jerry Bradley, Dave Rowland,
Charley Pride
October 21, 1978 (1 week)

Following the Bicentennial success of "The Door Is Always Open" [see 253], the thick, gospel harmonies of Dave & Sugar became an

Dave & Sugar

almost constant presence on the *Billboard* charts. "I'm Gonna Love You" reached number three at the end of 1976, and a trio of records hit the Top Ten in 1977: "Don't Throw It All Away," "That's The Way Love Should Be" and "I'm Knee Deep In Loving You."

Sugar returned to the number one spot two years after first topping the charts with "Tear Time," a tune they had had almost since their inception.

"We looked at this song and thought about releasing it as our very first single," suggests Dave Rowland, "but it being a ballad, Jerry Bradley and I thought we really needed to come out with an uptempo song for our first record. Jerry gave it to me when we went overseas for an Australian tour with Charley Pride, so I listened to it, and started working with it there. We kept it in the back of our minds, and when the time was right for a ballad, we went in and did that one."

Vicki Hackeman, the wife of Charley Pride's bass player, Ron Baker, was the first voice on the record, followed by a solo part for Rowland, and a strong performance by Sue Powell, who by then had replaced original member Jackie Frantz. "We have always switched off on the verses," says Rowland, "with each of the girls doing the lines, and me doing the lines, and in the choruses, I don't sing the melody. One of the girls would sing the melody, and I would always do a harmony part. We were a *sound*, and we wanted to continue that way because we were successful with it."

One piece of misleading information on many Sugar recordings was Charley Pride's billing as a co-producer. "He was there for our very first record," explains Rowland, "which was 'Queen Of The Silver Dollar,' but he also was a busy man, taking care of his career."

Rowland was also associated with the late Elvis Presley, when he joined the Stamps Quartet shortly after the *Aloha from Hawaii via Satellite* album. He toured with the King for two years, and appeared as a back-up vocalist on a number of his singles, including "My Boy," "Promised Land" and "Help Me."

325
LET'S TAKE THE LONG WAY AROUND THE WORLD
RONNIE MILSAP
RCA 11369

Writers: Archie Jordan, Naomi Martin
Producers: Tom Collins, Ronnie Milsap
October 28, 1978 (1 week)

Following the overwhelming success of "It Was Almost Like A Song" [see 289], Ronnie Milsap and Archie Jordan enjoyed an ongoing series of artist/writer collaborations. Milsap cut "What A Difference You've Made In My Life" [see 301] in 1977, and hit number six in 1979 with "In No Time At All." In between, he earned a number one single with "Let's Take The Long Way Around The World," which Jordan co-wrote with Naomi Martin.

"She'd actually lost her husband [Jim] the summer before in a drowning accident in [at Watts Bar Lake in Tennessee]," relates Milsap. "It was a very special story with all that, and the song had a powerful impact." "We were tryin' to say that people don't spend enough time together," Jordan adds.

Jim and Naomi had talked about taking a cruise just before his death. Using that as a starting point, Jordan and Martin wrote the tune in ten minutes specifically for Ronnie, who developed an arrangement reminiscent of "It Was Almost Like A Song."

"We had a much larger piano on 'Let's Take The Long Way Around The World,'" he says. "On 'Almost Like A Song,' we did some fourteen, fifteen takes until we could get one that Tom [Collins] and I liked. By that time, I had knocked the fifth octave E on the piano slightly out of tune from playing it so many times. It's not much, but it's just a little bit. We beat all that when we did 'Let's Take The Long Way Around The World.'"

The record used syndrums, frequently heard during that period on disco records. "Now those syndrums make me want to run off the road," laughs Collins. "It sounds like the War of 1812 on one of those licks, which I enjoyed at the time."

Jordan, a music composition major in college, also wrote Sylvia's "Drifter" [see 419]; "Happy Birthday Dear Heartache," for Barbara Mandrell; "It's All I Can Do" [see 438— "No Gettin' Over Me"], for Anne Murray; and a number one adult/contemporary record for Orsa Lia, "I Never Said I Love You." He has also worked as an arranger on records by Mandrell and Jim Ed Brown & Helen Cornelius, plus on both of Michael Johnson's number one singles: "Give Me Wings" [see 703] and "The Moon Is Still Over Her Shoulder" [see 720]. In 1989, Archie provided the musical score for the Disney cable movie *Caddie Woodlawn*.

326

SLEEPING SINGLE IN A DOUBLE BED

BARBARA MANDRELL

ABC 12362
Writers: Kye Fleming, Dennis Morgan
Producer: Tom Collins
November 4, 1978 (3 weeks)

She wasn't expected to live. In a Houston hospital in 1948, a pregnant Mary Mandrell went into convulsions. Doctors felt that with surgery they could save her, but told her husband, Irby, that they doubted the baby would make it. As it turned out, Irby ran into a doctor in the hospital whom he had known for years, and that medic gave special attention to the case. When both mother and daughter survived, the birth of Barbara Mandrell made a very special Christmas Day present.

From the outset, Irby foresaw a musical career for his child. Barbara read music before she read English, and studied music feverishly outside of school. The Mandrell family put together a band, and she toured at age 13 with Johnny Cash, June Carter and Patsy Cline. In 1967, she married Ken Dudney, the band's drummer, who soon went overseas as an Air Force pilot. The next year, Irby took Barbara to the Grand Ole Opry, and in the middle of the show, she turned to her father and asked him to manage her as an entertainer.

On March 1, 1969, Barbara signed her first deal with Columbia Records, and on July 8, 1972, became an Opry member. In a six-year career with Columbia, Mandrell managed four Top Ten records, two of them duets with David Houston. In 1975, she signed with ABC/Dot, and she was pregnant with her second child when she made her first record for the label. "Standing Room Only" hit number five.

Barbara Mandrell

Three more Top Ten singles later, Barbara recorded her first number one single, "Sleeping Single In A Double Bed," nearly a decade after signing with Columbia. Record producer/publisher Tom Collins initiated the idea for the song. His wife's grandparents slept together on a small bed, and it seemed to him they were "sleepin' double on a single bed." He passed the idea along to songwriters Kye Fleming and Dennis Morgan, and Kye turned the idea around to "Sleeping Single."

The song was pitched all over Nashville, with no takers, so Collins cut it on Mandrell. The record is buoyed by a Michael McDonald-like keyboard riff that Collins also used on several more of her singles. Ultimately, "Sleeping Single" spent three weeks at number one, and when the record company threw a "number one" party, Mandrell gave a diamond necklace to Fleming and a diamond ring to Morgan.

327
SWEET DESIRE/ OLD FASHIONED LOVE
THE KENDALLS
Ovation 1112
Writers: Jeannie Kendall/M.R. Martin, Mitch Johnson
Producer: Brien Fisher
November 25, 1978 (1 week)

When Royce and Jeannie Kendall teamed up to form the Kendalls, it was actually the second duo in the family tree. A decade before, Royce and his brother, Floyce, had performed together in California, but Royce gave up music to establish a more stable home environment for his daughter Jeannie.

Royce brought Jeannie and his wife, Melba, back to St. Louis, where the parents worked as barber and beautician, respectively. Her kindergarten teacher had suggested that Jeannie might succeed as an opera singer, but, though she had obvious musical talent, she didn't harmonize with her father until she was 15, in 1969.

Family friends encouraged them to move to Nashville, where Melba supported the family by working as a beautician at England's in suburban Madison. Steel-guitar player Pete Drake signed the father-daughter duo to Stop Records, where they cut a handful of singles.

They moved on to Dot, and then to United Artists, but along the way, a record executive tried to turn Jeannie into a solo artist.

Jeannie felt that her solo efforts took away the very textures that made the Kendalls act unique, and they took a six-month hiatus from recording. Once they re-signed with Ovation Records, however, the Kendalls' career took off with "Heaven's Just A Sin Away" [see 295]. They followed with a new album, *Old Fashioned Love*, which yielded two Top Ten singles, "It Don't Feel Like Sinnin' To Me" and "Pittsburgh Stealers."

Jeannie wrote the third single, "Sweet Desire," between shows during a road date in their former hometown, St. Louis. "We still had a motor home," she remembers. "We didn't have a bus, and we were outside in the motor home.

"We needed more songs for the album. We needed an uptempo, and it's kind of a desperation thing. So I was tryin' to think of a song that had some of the same style that I thought was working, but with something else a little different. I just came up with it, and I sung it to daddy, got out the guitar, played it, and that was it."

"Sweet Desire" first appeared in *Billboard* on September 23, 1978, and reached number one nine weeks later, during the Thanksgiving holiday. In December, Jeannie married the band's guitar player, Mack Watkins.

328
I JUST WANT TO LOVE YOU
EDDIE RABBITT
Elektra 45531
Writers: Eddie Rabbitt, Even Stevens, David Malloy
Producer: David Malloy
December 2, 1978 (1 week)

It's no surprise—Eddie Rabbitt's longtime writing partner wasn't originally named Even Stevens. An Ohio native, Bruce Stevens served as a radio operator for the Coast Guard prior to life in the music business, and many of his correspondents gave him the rhyming nickname, "Even." He didn't particularly like the name, but when he started writing for Ray Stevens (no relation), he decided Even would be more memorable than Bruce.

Even's rise to prominence is a classic songwriter tale. He went to visit Nashville on the advice of an uncle who played drums in a hole-in-the-wall bar on lower Broadway. The first night he was in town, Stevens went to hear his relative play, and after the last set, he played one of his compositions on a guitar that was laying around.

Webb Pierce happened into the bar, and heard Stevens singing "Fair Weather Friends." He offered Stevens a writer's contract, and Even was in town to stay. For a year, he lived in a former mail truck that had been converted for civilian use. Once he met Rabbitt, Stevens moved into one side of a duplex; Eddie lived on the other side, and they wrote together frequently, sometimes 18 hours a day.

After Rabbitt emerged on Elektra Records, Stevens remained his primary collaborator, although much of their material was written at the last minute during the recording sessions. "I Just Want To Love You" is a good example.

"We went into the studio and recorded the actual song with only about half of a verse and half of an actual chorus," notes Rabbitt. "We had partially written it about 15 minutes before in an office, waiting for 6:00 studio time to happen. We went into the studio excited about it, laid out the format to the guys, and said, 'We don't have this song written, but it goes something like this.'"

"That song was a composite of three other songs," adds Stevens. "We had started a couple different songs, and knew we had something good with parts of them. We tried recording a couple of 'em, but the songs weren't good enough, so we wrote another section, the chorus of 'I Just Want To Love You,' and used the verses and the bridges from these other ideas we had and made up the song."

329

ON MY KNEES
CHARLIE RICH WITH
JANIE FRICKIE
Epic 50616
Writer: Charlie Rich
Producer: Billy Sherrill
December 9, 1978 (1 week)

Janie Frickie had released three solo records by the time that "On My Knees" was released, but when she recorded it, she hadn't yet committed herself to a solo career. Frickie had recorded a few duets with Johnny Duncan, including "Thinkin' Of A Rendezvous" [see

268], a record that first brought her to the attention of country listeners.

Frickie was involved as a session singer on innumerable hits during the '70s. Among them were T.G. Sheppard's "Devil In The Bottle" [see 197], Moe Bandy's "It's A Cheatin' Situation," Conway Twitty's "I'd Love To Lay You Down" [see 372], Elvis Presley's "My Way," Mel Tillis' "I Got The Hoss," Vern Gosdin's "Till The End" and England Dan & John Ford Coley's "I'd Really Love To See You Tonight."

Her work in "On My Knees" was somewhat routine. "Billy Sherrill and Charlie Rich called me and asked me to come into the studio and do a harmony part on that," she recounts, "but they had already done the tracks. Billy and Charlie were there in the studio with me, and they kind of just told me what lines they wanted me to sing and what to do. But it was an overdub session."

"On My Knees" became Rich's third number one single as a writer. His first was "The Ways Of A Woman In Love," released by Johnny Cash in 1958, and his second was "There Won't Be Anymore" [see 156].

Rich explained his writing process to Peter Guralnick in *Feel Like Going Home*: "I don't really go in with a program to write about. I may get a melody, and that's what's the toughest. After I get a nice melody, the words come along pretty much by themselves. I don't try to write like a computer. I have to feel it and think it."

The same month that "On My Knees" went to number one, Rich made his first on-screen film appearance in *Every Which Way But Loose* [see 335]. The film brought him a hit with "I'll Wake You Up When I Get Home." Rich had previously provided music for the movies *Benji* and its sequel, *For the Love of Benji*. He also had a role in the 1981 movie *Take This Job and Shove It* [see 300].

330

THE GAMBLER
KENNY ROGERS
United Artists 1250
Writer: Don Schlitz
Producer: Larry Butler
December 16, 1978 (3 weeks)

August 1976. A struggling songwriter in his early 20s works the "graveyard shift" as a computer operator at Vanderbilt University.

After a couple of hours' sleep in the morning, he showers, dresses and wearily hits Nashville's Music Row.

It's a common type of story in country music's capital, but this particular version belongs to Don Schlitz. His story has a happy ending. Bob McDill was among the few people whose door was open to Schlitz, and on one particular visit, McDill demonstrated a new "open D" tuning on the guitar.

"I was really fascinated with the droning sound of it," says Don, "I didn't have a car. I walked from Bob's office to my apartment, which was a couple of miles away, and I sat down in front of the typewriter and wrote three songs in two hours. One of the songs was 'The Gambler.'"

Well, most of "The Gambler."

Schlitz left the song unfinished, and six weeks later, he played some of his tunes for fellow songwriter Jim Rushing, who listened patiently while Don ran through his repertoire. When Schlitz stopped, Jim asked if he had anything else, so Don played "The Gambler." "That," said Rushing, "is the one you ought to finish."

In a few more weeks, Schlitz added the final eight lines. Don cut a demo on the song, but when no one would record it, his publisher printed up copies of the demo and released them on the Crazy Mamas label. Capitol picked up his master. Meanwhile, Conway Twitty's son, Charlie Tango, cut it, as did Hugh Moffatt. Schlitz's version fared best, hitting number 65.

Producer Larry Butler was quite familiar with Schlitz's record, but he figured that Don would have a hit on his own with the song, and forgot about it. A day before a session with Kenny Rogers, however, Merlin Littlefield brought a copy of it to Butler. When he discovered that Don's record had fizzled out, Butler relayed the song to Kenny, who had heard Schlitz's version before.

After changing a couple of words and adding a key change, Rogers had his fifth number one record, and a signature song that provided the basis for several TV movies. "The Gambler" led directly to two Grammy awards, two Academy of Country Music awards and a trio of Country Music Association trophies.

331
TULSA TIME
DON WILLIAMS

ABC 12425
Writer: Danny Flowers
Producers: Don Williams, Garth Fundis
January 6, 1979 (1 week)

When the Country Music Association named him the Male Vocalist of the Year on October 9, 1978, Don Williams was surprised—perhaps with good reason. For one thing, the record business thrives all too often on glitz and hype, something he shies away from. It's probably cost him in terms of media recognition, but it's also made his music seem more honest and real.

For another, Williams didn't have the kind of year chartwise that he had previously enjoyed. Each of the three years prior, Don hit the top spot twice. In 1978, he failed to achieve that position, although he did fare nicely with "I've Got A Winner In You," which peaked at number seven, and "Rake And Ramblin' Man," number three.

On the heels of the CMA win, however, Don returned to number one with "Tulsa Time," a flagrant rock groove created by Danny Flowers, the guitarist for Williams' then-unnamed Scratch Band.

"I had waited for that song a long time," Don says. "I hadn't necessarily waited for it from Danny, but see, growing up, I made that transition from listening strictly to country music to what became rock and roll. And a lot of us changed without even knowing that there was really a change taking place. It was just a music that started happening, and we went with it. So there's a lot of rhythms and sounds that I just love."

It was the first of Don's singles to feature longtime engineer Garth Fundis as co-producer, and Williams invited him out to the house to check out a scratch tape that Flowers had submitted.

"It was a real rough demo," Garth recalls. "Danny just did it on a little cassette deck at home. It was kind of a funky little demo, but you could hear that it was just somethin' different, and it was somethin' different for Don, too."

After it reached number one, "Tulsa Time" brought several more accolades for Williams. Tulsa Mayor James Inhofe presented him a key to the city and declared February 4, 1979, as Don Williams Day in Tulsa. That spring, the Academy of Country Music cited "Tulsa Time" as the Single of the Year.

The record also appeared in the 1980 movie *Smokey and the Bandit II*. Eric Clapton took it to number 30 that same year on *Billboard*'s Hot 100.

332

LADY LAY DOWN
JOHN CONLEE
ABC 12420
Writers: Rafe VanHoy, Don Cook
Producer: Bud Logan
January 13, 1979 (1 week)

John Conlee is the only licensed mortician ever to have a number one country record. Born August 11, 1946, in Versailles (pronounced "Ver-SALES"), Kentucky, Conlee grew up on a farm, and, although he developed a lifelong interest in music, he didn't sign his first recording contract until he was 30 years old.

In the meantime, he set his sights on several other occupations, including work as a farmer and a stint at a Kentucky funeral parlor. Conlee performed at some of the memorial services, handled embalming and, on occasion, drove an ambulance. Even though he has since gone on to a new line of work, accruing number one records in the process, he still has his mortician's license.

"I'm proud of having been a part of that profession," he says. "It took three years to

get, and it's simple to renew, so why not keep it up? That way, it's in my pocket if I need it. You don't anticipate going back there, but you never know."

Conlee's career exploded in 1978 with the release of "Rose Colored Glasses," a self-penned composition of romantic self-deceit. The record peaked at number five, and "Lady Lay Down," the first of seven number one singles, came on the heels of that introductory signature piece.

"'Lady Lay Down' essentially was a shoo-in," Conlee notes. "It's a great song, but the success of 'Rose Colored Glasses' set up 'Lady Lay Down' so that when we released it, essentially stations went on it 'out-of-the-box,' as they say. It's special because it was our first number one, but a lot of people are amazed about 'Glasses' not being a number one record."

It was also the first number one single in a collaboration between Don Cook and Rafe Van-Hoy, a duo that would earn another number one on "Somebody's Gonna Love You" [see 544]. All told, Cook and VanHoy have amassed eight Top Ten singles as co-writers, including "Cryin' Again," by the Oak Ridge Boys; "Tonight," by Barbara Mandrell; and "I Wish That I Could Hurt That Way Again," by T. Graham Brown.

"Lady Lay Down" was one of their first creations. "The first night we ever got together to write, we wrote about four songs, which was real unusual for me," VanHoy recalls. "Don and I had a real natural collaborative team that seemed fun and easy."

333

I REALLY GOT THE FEELING/ BABY I'M BURNIN'
DOLLY PARTON
RCA 11420
Writers: Billy Vera, Dolly Parton
Producers: Gary Klein, Dolly Parton
January 20, 1979 (1 week)

Dolly Parton's peak years occurred with the help of two teams of associates. First, Sandy Gallin took over management of her career, highly recommended by her friend (also a client) Mac Davis.

Second, Dolly teamed up with the Entertainment Company, a unique production firm owned by Charles Koppelman, with Gary

Klein as its sole producer. Both Koppelman and Klein were involved in finding material, Koppelman with a view toward the overall picture (promotions, album packaging, budgets, and so on) and Klein handling the details of the recording process.

Klein's credentials were already quite impressive even before he went to work with Dolly. His production credits included Glen Campbell's "Southern Nights" [see 279], Johnny Cash's "The Lady Came From Baltimore," Mac Davis' "Stop And Smell The Roses" and Barbra Streisand's "My Heart Belongs To Me."

A Long Island resident, Gary had to split his time between home and Sound Labs in Hollywood.

"I was literally commuting on a weekly, semi-weekly, monthly basis," Klein reflects. "I had three kids at home, it got crazy. I would fly home on a Friday night, cut back to L.A. Sunday night, and record Monday morning. That was really a difficult situation, very tiring—but as Dolly would say, you gotta make hay while the sun shines."

Klein was the sole producer on the *Here You Come Again* album [see 299], but when Dolly followed with *Heartbreaker*, she took on a co-production role. "I wrote more of the songs, and I wanted to stay true to Dolly," she says. "I was afraid of getting too far away from who I am, so I was more involved in that on the production end."

The Entertainment Company published "I Really Got The Feeling," the first hit written by Billy Vera, who gained prominence in 1987 with his number one pop record, "At This Moment." Entering the *Billboard* country chart over Thanksgiving weekend in 1978, "I Really Got The Feeling" worked its way to number one.

The flip side, "Baby, I'm Burnin'," with its "Fourth of July" effects, managed a number 48 country peak, while moving to number 25 on the Hot 100. Says Dolly of the writing process: "I thought it was just a very commercial idea. I remember just kind of roaming around through the house, thinking about the hook. It wasn't new, it certainly wasn't original, but it seemed like a very good idea at the time."

Dolly Parton

334
WHY HAVE YOU LEFT THE ONE YOU LEFT ME FOR

CRYSTAL GAYLE
United Artists 1259
Writer: Mark True
Producer: Allen Reynolds
January 27, 1979 (2 weeks)

"I think one of the main things you've got to try to do," opines producer Allen Reynolds, "is to maintain the surprise element as you put out singles and not try to clone the previous big hit."

Thanks to "Don't It Make My Brown Eyes Blue" [see 292] and "Talking In Your Sleep" [see 320], Crystal Gayle was bombarded by songwriters offering songs that worked the same ballad territory. "Why Have You Left The One You Left Me For," one that presented Crystal with tongue-twisting trouble, provided a welcome respite from the flood.

It was the first success for Mark True, an "Air Force brat" who was born in England, lived in a number of American states and eventually studied music composition at the University of Tennessee. After winning a spot in an Opryland production in 1974, he transferred to tiny Belmont College, a Baptist institution near Nashville's Music Row that developed a rare music business program. True helped build the college's first recording studio, and cut the first session at the educational facility.

Mark signed his first songwriting contract at age 18 with ABC Music. Once the deal was up, Crystal's arranger, Charles Cochran, put him in touch with Roger Cook, who signed him to his Pic-A-Lic firm. It was under that agreement that True hit paydirt with "Why Have You Left The One," a song he wrote in five minutes about his wife's ex-fiancé.

"He kept tryin' to get her back," says True. "He would write her poems and send her cards, and I was at home one day tryin' to write songs and the mailman comes and brings this book of poems that her ex-fiancé had written for her, and I got to thinkin', 'What if she *did* decide to go back with him? What would he say to her?' That line just popped out, 'Why have you left the one you left me for,' and I said to myself, 'If you mess this one up, it's your own fault.'"

Gayle and Reynolds had already recorded eleven songs for the *When I Dream* album, but when they heard True's demo, they made room for an extra song. Crystal had trouble getting the words in the right order as she learned it, and they cut the song twice: once with a studio group, and, in the final version, with her own road band.

335
EVERY WHICH WAY BUT LOOSE
EDDIE RABBITT
Elektra 45554
Writers: Steve Dorff, Milton Brown, Snuff Garrett
Producer: Snuff Garrett
February 10, 1979 (3 weeks)

Eddie Rabbitt's "Every Which Way But Loose" was a monumental record. The title track to a Clint Eastwood motion picture, it's the only Rabbitt single to stay at number one longer than one week. On December 23, 1978, it debuted in *Billboard* at number 18, establish-

ing a new record for the highest first-week entry, a mark that still stands today.

The movie was the first of several Eastwood films in which Thomas "Snuff" Garrett received responsibility for the soundtrack. Garrett had his own production company to develop material specifically for the movie, and two of his staff writers provided the title track.

"The funniest thing about that song was that we wrote it so fast," explains Steve Dorff. "I called Milton Brown, who wrote the lyric with the title, and he was in Mobile, Alabama. I told him that there was a Clint Eastwood movie, and all I knew about it, having not read the script, was that he rode around with a monkey as a compatriot. At the time, the only name that had been mentioned about singing it was Jerry Lee Lewis. I told Milton to write the kind of lyric that Jerry Lee Lewis would sing.

"He called me back about 30 minutes later with the finished lyric, and we wrote the song over the phone."

Once shooting had already begun on the movie, Eastwood was talking with some people from Elektra Records about the soundtrack. Someone suggested Rabbitt, and Clint gave the idea his personal endorsement. Garrett shipped a tape of the song to Nashville for Eddie to learn, and he flew out to Los Angeles and cut it live within two hours.

Rabbitt made a couple of changes in the song in the process, including the addition of the drumbeats that lead up to the chorus.

"I also made them slow it down on the part, 'While you're turnin' me'" says Rabbitt. "We slowed that down and kind of built up to the chorus. The chorus had a fairly catchy melody, but it needed something."

In 1981, Eastwood filmed a sequel, once again co-starring Clyde the Orangutan. Rabbitt turned down an opportunity to record the theme song for *Any Which Way You Can*, and passed on an acting role in the picture as well.

336
GOLDEN TEARS
DAVE & SUGAR
RCA 11427
Writer: John Schweers
Producers: Jerry Bradley, Dave Rowland
March 3, 1979 (3 weeks)

The last of Dave & Sugar's three number one records was a highly coincidental release.

"I've always had a Chevrolet," relates Dave Rowland. "The song starts out 'From a Chevy to a Lincoln,' and oddly enough, I had just bought a new Lincoln. We couldn't afford a bus, so that's how we were traveling, and I said, 'Hey, this has got to be a hit.' I used to race cars at a drag strip, and I had a '49 Chevy for my first car. I had a '55 Chevy and a '57 Chevy, and I thought 'Golden Tears' had to be for us."

His prophecy was right, and "Golden Tears" became the only Dave & Sugar release to top the charts for three weeks. A tale of life in the fast lane, it supported the adage "it's lonely at the top."

"Success in life can change things around," notes Rowland. "People change sometimes when success comes. 'Golden Tears' is sort of a success story with an unsuccessful ending."

Dave & Sugar could never equal that success again. Two more records reached Top Ten levels in 1979, and in 1981, they moved to Elektra Records, scoring another hit with "Fool By Your Side."

Elektra then asked for a Dave Rowland solo album. "We were having some problems in the studio," he recalls, "and I got a call from James Stroud, who was producing us. They wanted to make it a solo album. I didn't want a solo album, but I really didn't have a choice."

Shortly after the solo album (appropriately titled *Sugar-Free*) was released, Dave & Sugar were dropped from the roster when Elektra and Warner Bros. merged in 1983. In 1984, Rowland toured with Helen Cornelius in a road production of *Annie Get Your Gun*, and in 1985, Dave & Sugar released an album on Dot.

"I always kept the girls with me," he adds, alluding to the solo LP. "We always did all of the group songs, I always kept the girls up front with me; I didn't put them on a stool behind the drums. The girls have always been a major part of the group."

337
I JUST FALL IN LOVE AGAIN
ANNE MURRAY
Capitol 4675
Writers: Steve Dorff, Gloria Sklerov, Harry Lloyd, Larry Herbstritt
Producer: Jim Ed Norman
March 24, 1979 (3 weeks)

In 1978, *Billboard* gave Anne Murray a special award for Artist Resurgence of the Year.

Anne Murray

Her career took a dip in the mid-'70s, thanks to a self-imposed hiatus.

Murray's first five years in the record business were filled with successes, but they came inconsistently. Her first single, 1970's "Snowbird," reached number 10 on the country chart, selling one million copies. "Danny's Song" equaled "Snowbird"'s chart peak in 1972, and three more singles reached the Top Five in 1974: the Grammy-winning "Love Song," "He Thinks I Still Care" [see 170] and "Son Of A Rotten Gambler."

Murray needed a break, though. She wanted to consider whether or not to continue the career, and she wanted to raise a family. The latter concern began to take shape when she married Bill Langstroth, on June 20, 1975—the same date as her thirtieth birthday.

"It was purely coincidental," she says of the timing. "I was married on the twentieth of June; my husband was divorced on the seventeenth. The divorce came through, and you need three days before you get married. It was nothing cutesy-pie, like 'I think it's neat to get married on my birthday,' or anything like that. It happened to be my thirtieth birthday.

"Three or four years after we were married, Bill found his family bible, and in it he found out that his parents were married on June 20, 1925—fifty years to the day earlier. He had no idea of that, either."

They had a son in August of 1976, and about a year later, her passion for recording returned. She enlisted producer Jim Ed Norman, and began her comeback in 1978 with a cover of the Everly Brothers' "Walk Right Back," reaching number four. "You Needed Me" (which hit number one on the Hot 100 and earned a pop Grammy) topped out at number four on the country chart. She picked up her second number one country record with "I Just Fall In Love Again," previously recorded by both the Carpenters and Dusty Springfield.

"I didn't think it would be number one on the country charts," she confesses, "because I felt the piano playing took a very classical-type approach to the song. I didn't think of it as even remotely country."

Nevertheless, it became *Billboard*'s top country single for the entire year.

338

(IF LOVING YOU IS WRONG) I DON'T WANT TO BE RIGHT

BARBARA MANDRELL
ABC 12451
Writers: Homer Banks, Raymond Jackson, Carl Hampton
Producer: Tom Collins
April 14, 1979 (1 week)

"To me, R & B music and country are so closely related," Barbara Mandrell told Douglas B. Green in *Billboard*. "Not the style—I mean, there's a soulful style and a country style—but as far as the material, the songs, we're talking about strong lyrics that deal with life, and the simplicity of it is the beauty of it."

Mandrell put a number of rhythm and blues songs to use in her country career from the very beginning. Her third charted single, 1971's "Do Right Woman, Do Right Man," was a remake of an Aretha Franklin release, and it gave her band the name the Do-Rites. She also covered Otis Redding's "I've Been Loving You Too Long," Joe Tex's "Show Me," Denise La Salle's "Married But Not To Each Other" and Shirley Brown's "Woman To Woman." The soul-music-as-country-music theory reached its zenith with "(If Loving You Is Wrong) I Don't Want To Be Right," which originally hit number three on the *Billboard* Hot 100 for Luther Ingram in 1972.

"We felt that that idea was a great country idea," notes producer Tom Collins. "We felt if we would do our own arrangement of it, it would hopefully be accepted by the country audience. We were bein' played on R & B stations, even out of New York. When we did it, Barbara's career was really in high gear, and it ended up bein' a really good record for us."

It easily followed "Sleeping Single In A Double Bed" [see 326] to number one, and also hit number 31 on the Hot 100, her only single to hit the pop Top 40.

In addition to continuing her tradition of R & B remakes, "I Don't Want To Be Right" extended Mandrell's track record of "cheatin'" hits. Despite her insistence that she has never strayed in her own marriage (*People* magazine called her "The Snow White of Country Music"), Mandrell frequently sang of infidelity in her hits. In fact, her 1973 single "Burning The Midnight Oil" was the first in which a woman—rather than a man—steps out on her spouse.

As she told British writer Stan Sayer: "Any performer who hasn't the theatrical ability to put herself into lyrics for a few minutes must have something missing—like talent."

339

ALL I EVER NEED IS YOU

KENNY ROGERS & DOTTIE WEST

United Artists 1276
Writers: Jimmy Holiday, Eddie Reeves
Producer: Larry Butler
April 21, 1979 (1 week)

After Kenny Rogers & Dottie West picked up the Country Music Association award for Vocal Duo of the Year, they set to work on an album called *Classics*, their versions of previous hits like "Together Again" [see 244], "(Hey, Won't You Play) Another Somebody Done Somebody Wrong Song" [see 208] and "You've Lost That Lovin' Feelin'." One of the last additions for the project was "All I Ever Need Is You."

"We had ballads, but we didn't have a song with that sing-along feel," explains producer Larry Butler, "a swing beat, or whatever you want to call it. It just was a good variety cut, so we went for it."

About eight years earlier, Eddie Reeves had put the song together with Kenny in mind . . . with some pushing. He had started the song, but was a little embarrassed about it. He shared a Los Angeles apartment with former recording artist Kris Jensen, who prodded Reeves to play it for a girlfriend one evening.

Reeves decided to take it to Jimmy Holiday, a fellow writer at United Artists Music. Holiday, who wrote "Put A Little Love In Your Heart," added a couple of verses. Then Reeves cut a demo of the song as a "mournful ballad" (his own description), mimicking Kenny's delivery in "Ruby, Don't Take Your Love To Town."

Rogers turned it down, and Ray Charles became the first to record "All I Ever Need Is You." Reeves, meanwhile, secured a recording contract with Kapp Records in 1971. When label president Johnny Musso discovered that Eddie wasn't planning to cut the song himself, he sent Charles' copy to producer Snuff Garrett, who recorded it on Sonny & Cher within the week. They had just introduced their television show two months earlier, and "All I Ever Need Is You" became their first hit together in nearly five years.

UA Music's Jimmy Gilmer reminded Butler of the song just in time for the *Classics* sessions, and it became Rogers & West's second number one single as a duet.

"It was always ironic in my mind that when I wrote this little love ballad," says Reeves, "I did a demo imitating Kenny Rogers, and he turned it down, and it comes around to him and he eventually does record it."

One other track from the album, a remake of Tammy Wynette's "'Til I Can Make It On My Own" [see 242], reached number three.

340

WHERE DO I PUT HER MEMORY

CHARLEY PRIDE

RCA 11477
Writer: Jim Weatherly
Producers: Jerry Bradley, Charley Pride
April 28, 1979 (1 week)

Some of Charley Pride's advisors were a little concerned when he cut Jim Weatherly's "Where Do I Put Her Memory." "It never bothered me," says producer Jerry Bradley, "but a lot of people were uncomfortable with Charley Pride singing, 'I cleaned out her drawers.'"

The drawers were innocent enough. They went along with the pillow, closet and curlers that represented a lost love.

"I was visiting my mother in Mississippi," Weatherly explains, "and I used to always try to write when I was down there. My head would get cleared out and there wouldn't be a whole lot going on.

"I remember just looking around the room to see if there was anything that helped me lock into a song. I saw pictures and a chest of drawers, just things, and it just kind of dawned on me that those were the kinds of things that you could get rid of, but you can never get rid of a memory. That's basically how the song came about."

Weatherly has settled into life as a songwriter, dividing his time between Nashville and Los Angeles. Writing was his original goal, but he spent several years pursuing a solo career as a recording artist. He hit number 11 on the *Billboard* Hot 100 in 1974 with his dramatic rendition of "The Need To Be," a song he had originally written for a Marlo Thomas TV special. The following year, he reached number nine on the country chart with "I'll Still Love You."

Weatherly is probably best known, though, for a series of songs that succeeded for Ray Price and Gladys Knight in the early '70s. Included are "You're The Best Thing That Ever Happened To Me" [see 144], "Midnight Train

John Conlee

To Georgia" and "Neither One Of Us (Wants To Be The First To Say Goodbye)." In 1984, he wrote Glen Campbell's "A Lady Like You."

A couple of coincidences underscored the success that Weatherly enjoyed with Pride. Weatherly's March 17th birthday falls one day before Pride's, and Jim grew up in Pontotoc, Mississippi, only 30 miles from Charley's mother-in-law.

Pride never envisioned "Where Do I Put Her Memory" as a single, but it emerged when he became dissatisfied with a few songs he'd just recorded. "Jerry Bradley and I went back and listened to some other things we had done," he recalls. "I think we added a guitar or something, and that ended up being the single."

341
BACKSIDE OF THIRTY
JOHN CONLEE
MCA/ABC 12455
Writer: John Conlee
Producer: Bud Logan
May 5, 1979 (1 week)

John Conlee has written only two of his own hit records. The first was "Rose Colored Glasses" [see 332—"Lady Lay Down"], and the second was "Backside Of Thirty," a tune about a divorced man trying to re-establish a life for himself.

"I wrote that in 1976, probably within a month of 'Rose Colored Glasses,'" says Conlee. "I had never been married before, and consequently not divorced, but I had been in a couple of relationships that had gotten pretty heavy and didn't work out. There's no piece of paper to tear apart, but still, a break-up is a break-up, and to that degree, I felt those things in the song.

"As a matter of fact, I was going through a break-up at the time, and I'm sure that break-up had a lot to do with the writing of both 'Backside Of Thirty' and 'Rose Colored Glasses.' It brought forth some emotion in me, but as far as the details of the song, that's observation. So many friends go through what that song talks about—the break-up of the home—and I was just on the other side of thirty when I wrote it."

Actually, "Backside Of Thirty" needed two attempts to attain hit status. Conlee secured his recording contract with ABC Records in 1976 through Dick Kent, a disk jockey at WLAC-FM in Nashville, where Conlee was working in the same capacity. Kent introduced John to ABC executive Jim Foglesong, who signed him and released three singles by July of 1977. None of them charted, but the label decided to re-release "Backside Of Thirty," which followed "Lady Lay Down" as Conlee's second number one single.

A couple of significant events were closely tied to "Backside." MCA Records absorbed ABC on March 5, 1979, two days after Conlee's single entered the *Billboard* country chart. His record was the last ABC release to hit number one. That same week, the Academy of Country Music named him the Best New Male Vocalist.

It would take more than four years before Conlee returned to number one, although he came close on several occasions. In the interim, he earned seven Top Ten singles, and four of them—"Before My Time," "Friday Night Blues," "She Can't Say That Anymore" and the mysterious "Miss Emily's Picture"— peaked at number two.

342
DON'T TAKE IT AWAY
CONWAY TWITTY
MCA 41002
Writers: Troy Seals, Max D. Barnes
Producers: Conway Twitty, David Barnes
May 12, 1979 (1 week)

After his break from record producer Owen Bradley [see 293—"I've Already Loved You In My Mind"], Conway Twitty enjoyed a new musical freedom. His first attempt apart from his mentor was 1979's *Cross Winds* album, on which he displayed a tougher, soul-edged style.

Conway picked David Barnes, of his road band, to arrange and co-produce the record. He also hired a number of the musicians who played on Elvis Presley's Memphis sessions with Chips Moman, including keyboard player Bobby Wood, bassist Mike Leech, and guitarists Reggie Young and Johnny Christopher.

For the first single, Conway chose a pleading, gut-wrenching ballad, "Don't Take It Away," written by his longtime buddy, Troy Seals [see 157—"There's A Honky Tonk Angel"]. "That was the first song that Troy and I

ever wrote together," recalls Max D. Barnes, "and it was shortly after I met him. He had the idea, and we sat down and wrote it."

That was in 1975. Several other acts cut it before Conway. Jody Miller charted modestly with it in 1975, and a black New York group, the Meadows Brothers, did a version as well. Barnes and Seals also picked up a recording from England's Don Stanton.

Twitty's soul-tinged rendition gave his career a little kick, showing off a facet of his musical personality which had largely been ignored. "Don't Take It Away" debuted at number 52 on St. Patrick's Day in 1979, and two months later, his stylistic fine-tuning paid off with a number one single.

"I never make a change, either in my career or in my personal life, without giving it a lot of thought," he offers. "I believe in change. It's the only thing I know of that's constant. When things stop changin', they die. When I began to produce myself, it was because I felt like I needed to change.

"I believe in being versatile and I've got a lot of different musical backgrounds I can draw from. I wanted to start using all this, but I have never wanted to alienate one country fan—not one. But I did want to pick up some new ones, and I think I've accomplished that."

343
IF I SAID YOU HAVE A BEAUTIFUL BODY WOULD YOU HOLD IT AGAINST ME
THE BELLAMY BROTHERS
Warner Bros. 8790
Writer: David Bellamy
Producer: Michael Lloyd
May 19, 1979 (3 weeks)

In 1976, the Bellamy Brothers established themselves quite handily with a gigantic pop record called "Let Your Love Flow." Howard Bellamy was a roadie for Jim Stafford when he sang lead on the session in November of 1975. It ascended to number one on the *Billboard* Hot 100, but just as quickly as Howard and brother David earned national recognition, they seemed destined for "one-hit wonder" status.

The Bellamys lost all control of their management situation, and instead of creating a new career, they found themselves in debt, signed to a record label that wouldn't even return their phone calls. Fortunately, they were able to work in Europe, and while earning their income overseas, they also edged their way into country music, where they had really wanted to be in the first place.

"'Let Your Love Flow' came along at a time when pop and country were all changing," David says. "I often thought if 'Let Your Love Flow' had been a couple years later, it would have been a big country hit."

As it was, "Let Your Love Flow" reached number 21 in country music, and during 1978, the Bellamy Brothers placed four more singles on the *Billboard* country chart. The last one, "Lovin' On," peaked at number 16. Howard and David completed their transition from pop to country with their next single, the light-hearted "If I Said You Have A Beautiful Body Would You Hold It Against Me."

"'Beautiful Body' came from hearing Groucho Marx," says David, who wrote it. "I was watching the old 'You Bet Your Life' show in Los Angeles. We lived out there for about four years, and I was watching one of the old re-runs and I heard him say that. It must have been back in the '50s when he said it, and I was thinking at that time that it would make a good song title."

"Beautiful Body" reached number one and stayed there for three weeks, securing a Grammy nomination in the process. It also outsold every other country single during 1979 in England, where it established an unusual mark as the longest title to ever hit the British pop chart. Its predecessor? Paul Evans' 1959 recording, "Seven Little Girls Sitting In The Back Seat Hugging And Kissing With Fred."

344

SHE BELIEVES IN ME
KENNY ROGERS
United Artists 1273
Writer: Steve Gibb
Producer: Larry Butler
June 9, 1979 (2 weeks)

During their five-year association, Kenny Rogers and producer Larry Butler earned a reputation for quick work. As a rule, Butler screened material for their albums and narrowed the field down to about thirty songs. Kenny then made a decision based on one or two listenings.

"Working quick allows me not to get burned out on songs," Kenny explains. "I love going in the studio and getting excited about a song, recording it and getting out. That way when it comes out, it's still fresh to me."

That left pre-production solely in the hands of Butler, who worked out most of the details (arrangements, keys, and so on) prior to the sessions. Things moved fairly quickly once the musicians were "on the clock."

"I think that the main thing we're supposed to do is create an emotion," says Larry. "If we make people laugh or cry over our records, we've done our job. If we don't, we've failed. So, consequently, you can't elaborate on an emotion very long—it either happens or it doesn't."

It happened in a big way with the album *The Gambler* [see 330]. Propelled by the title track, the LP sold a million copies within three months of release. Another two months later, in April of 1979, "She Believes In Me" emerged as the second single. Butler had already picked the material for the album when he first heard the song—at 2:30 A.M., while working very late at the office.

"When I heard 'She Believes In Me' I literally got tears in my eyes, and I stopped the tape and rewound it and listened to it over again," he says. "I was tryin' to decide if I liked it so much because it was an inside—so to speak—song, about a songwriter. Then I decided that that story could apply to anybody, any occupation, and so we cut it."

"She Believes In Me" was a cinch as a number one country record, and it also ascended to number five on *Billboard*'s Hot 100, selling a million copies in the process. Butler's late nights at the office paid off in other ways, too. The following year, he became the only Nashville producer to win the Grammy for Producer of the Year.

345

NOBODY LIKES SAD SONGS
RONNIE MILSAP
RCA 11553
Writers: Bob McDill, Wayland Holyfield
Producers: Ronnie Milsap, Tom Collins
June 23, 1979 (1 week)

On December 16, 1978, Ronnie Milsap appeared on the *Billboard* country charts with "Back On My Mind Again," which eventually made its way to number two. It stayed there for three weeks, held back from the top by Eddie Rabbitt's "Every Which Way But Loose" [see 335]. Even though it broke Milsap's streak of seven number one singles, the record was an obvious success.

It also bought Ronnie extra time to work on his next LP. *Images* was the first album he made in his own studio, purchased from Roy Orbison, who had simply called it US Recording Studios. Milsap re-dubbed it GroundStar Lab. "The laboratory thing started off as kind of a joke," chief engineer Ben Harris explained to *Billboard*'s Robyn Wells. "Ronnie would say in this accent, 'I'm going into my la-bor-atory to work now.' The name just stuck."

Images made RCA a little squeamish. Milsap took six months to make it—an unusual amount of time for a country artist—as he experimented with his new facility.

Finally, in April of 1979, RCA tapped "Nobody Likes Sad Songs" as the first single from Milsap's new playground. Bob McDill and Wayland Holyfield had started it from a working title, "I Hate Sad Songs." After "a lot of hard hours," as Wayland puts it, the two shaped the story of a club performer whose repertoire mirrors his personal life.

"It was reminiscent of working in a nightclub in Memphis called T.J.'s," Ronnie recalls. "I worked there for about two-and-a-half years when I started living in Memphis. We had to work six, seven sets a night on some nights— it was kind of a struggle. The guy who ran the place was always on your back, saying, 'You gotta do this, and you gotta do that,' so I kind of remembered that a little bit. I believe that's what drew me to that song."

Milsap recorded "Nobody Likes Sad Songs" in December of 1978, even as "Back On My Mind Again" made its debut. "Sad Songs" eventually found its way to number one the following June. He followed it up with "In No Time At All," a song he recorded at the same session. Along with the flip side, "Get It Up," it peaked at number six that fall.

346
AMANDA
WAYLON JENNINGS
RCA 11596
Writer: Bob McDill
Producer: Waylon Jennings
June 30, 1979 (1 weeks)

Ronnie Milsap

In 1979, Waylon Jennings was scheduled to release a new album, titled *Tennessee Waltz*, but everyone involved in the project agreed that it didn't have a hit single. In order to meet the schedule, RCA pulled the album, but used the same cover on a *Greatest Hits* release. It was one of the first "best of" packages to feature a single that had not yet been issued.

The song was "Amanda," a tune Jennings recorded in 1974 for his album *I'm a Ramblin' Man*. "It's the same cut," says Waylon. "The first time I did it—'I'm nearly 30 and still wearin' jeans'—I updated it to 40. I re-recorded that part, but the rest of it was the same."

Jennings' *Ramblin' Man* version wasn't "Amanda"'s first appearance, though. Don Williams recorded it as the "B" side of his 1973 single "Come Early Morning." The "A" side went to number 12, while "Amanda" earned airplay as well, reaching number 33. Songwriter Bob McDill describes the song as "an apology to my wife," but even before Williams' recording attracted attention, McDill had approached Waylon with it.

"I took that over to Waylon's office," he recalls, "and he was out or something, so I couldn't see him. But I left that there on the desk, and I told the girl to make sure he heard it, and he never did.

"About the time the disk jockeys started turning it over, he started hearing [Don's version] on the radio, and he called me up and said, 'Hoss, that's the story of my life. Why didn't you give me that song?' I said, 'Well, if you look on your receptionist's desk, I'll bet you'll find a copy of it. I tried my best.' He said, 'Well, I'm gonna cut it some day, anyway,' and I guess he was true to his word."

Waylon's *Greatest Hits* album, meanwhile, enjoyed an unusual chart life. The record debuted in *Billboard* on May 5, 1979, reaching number one on June 2. It remained in the Top Five through July 5, 1980. The album spent fifteen weeks at number one during 1979, and on May 31, 1980, it returned to the top of the chart more than a year after its release. In 1984, Jennings' *Greatest Hits* became the first country album to sell four million copies.

347
SHADOWS IN THE MOONLIGHT
ANNE MURRAY
Capitol 4716
Writers: Rory Bourke, Charlie Black
Producer: Jim Ed Norman
July 21, 1979 (1 week)

Adding their accomplishments together, Rory Bourke and Charlie Black have accounted for more than 25 Top Ten country hits. Six of those songs were tunes they wrote together, and their partnership started off in December of 1978, when they composed "Shadows In The Moonlight."

At the time, Bourke was working for Chappell Music, which had signed Black a few months earlier. Charlie had penned a couple of hits for Tommy Overstreet some years back, and Chappell's Henry Hurt wanted him to try writing with several of the company's other tunesmiths. It took a simple phone call from Bourke to bring immediate results.

"Rory was already a big-time established songwriter," says Black of their first writing

session, "and I thought, 'Gosh, I need to have something, I need to be prepared.' I had a couple of ideas laying around, little bits and pieces of tunes and ideas. I had a few lines and a few things that went together in the chorus of 'Shadows.' "

"He showed up at my house," Bourke continues, "and played me part of the chorus on 'Shadows In The Moonlight,' and said, 'What do you think?' I said, 'I think we better write this right away.' We wrote that song in the afternoon, and as they say in show business, it became the beginning of a beautiful relationship."

Together, Bourke and Black have written such hits as "Do You Love As Good As You Look" [see 415], by the Bellamy Brothers; "I Know A Heartache When I See One," by Jennifer Warnes; and "Lonely But Only For You," by Sissy Spacek. They have also been responsible for five different Anne Murray hits, including "Lucky Me," "Blessed Are The Believers" [see 431], "Another Sleepless Night" and "A Little Good News" [see 547].

Despite the now-obvious compatibility, Murray had to be coaxed into recording "Shadows" by producer Jim Ed Norman.

"When we were doing the background vocals, I was really happy that he'd convinced me," she says, "because sometimes you have to live with these tunes. My brother Bruce, Debbie Schaal, who travels with me now, and myself were doing the background vocals, and it solidified the tune so much. I kind of had a feeling that it might do well."

The record also got an extra kick from the guitar solo by Bob Mann (he later joined James Taylor's band) and a saxophone part during the fade-out by Don Thompson.

348
YOU'RE THE ONLY ONE
DOLLY PARTON
RCA 11577
Writers: Carole Bayer Sager,
Bruce Roberts
Producers: Dean Parks, Gregg Perry
July 28, 1979 (2 weeks)

"I don't think I'm a very good singer," Dolly Parton once told Leo Janos in *Cosmopolitan.* "I know how to put a song over, but my voice ain't what I call pleasin'. At least, not to me. I love it, though, and it's real joyful to me to belt out a good song. My heart is always true, but the notes that come out ain't."

She couldn't have been talking about her performance on "You're The Only One," a song she picked up from pop writer Carole Bayer Sager, who married Burt Bacharach in 1982. Sager's credentials include the Mindbenders' "A Groovy Kind Of Love," Carly Simon's "Nobody Does It Better" and Dionne Warwick & Friends' "That's What Friends Are For."

Debuting on June 9, 1979, "You're The Only One" became Dolly's tenth number one record in its eighth week on the *Billboard* country chart, and held on a second week. It marked the first of several Parton singles produced by her keyboard player, Gregg Perry.

"Actually, Gregg Perry was very involved in my career," Dolly notes. "And on the song '9 To 5' [see 409], a lot of people think that Mike Post produced that, and he did not. He did most of the other songs on the album, and a lot of people thought that he did '9 To 5.'

"That was always a heartbreaker for Gregg Perry. He worked very hard and did a great job on that particular song, and I always felt like Gregg didn't get his just dues on producing that."

Eventually, Perry left Parton's employ to study medicine.

"You're The Only One" was included on Parton's *Great Balls of Fire* LP, which also featured an unusual countrified version of the Beatles' "Help!" with Ricky Skaggs and Herb Pedersen (now of the Desert Rose Band) on back-up vocals. The twenty-fifth solo album of her career, *Great Balls of Fire* became Dolly's fourth gold album on November 13, 1979.

Two weeks earlier, "Sweet Summer Lovin'," the album's second single, peaked at number seven, the first Parton recording in two-and-a-half years that didn't reach number one. The flip side of "Summer" received a fair amount of airplay, although some of it proved quite unusual—though released at 45 RPM, "Great Balls Of Fire" was sometimes played at 33⅓.

349

SUSPICIONS
EDDIE RABBITT
Elektra 46053
Writers: Eddie Rabbitt, David Malloy,
Even Stevens, Randy McCormick
Producer: David Malloy
August 11, 1979 (1 week)

"**S**uspicions" stands among the most unlikely number one country hits ever made. Eddie Rabbitt's fifth chart-topping release, the record bore more resemblance to an R & B single than traditional country. In fact, it even appeared briefly on the soul charts.

Even more so than "I Just Want To Love You" [see 328], "Suspicions" was a last-minute addition to a Rabbitt album. *Loveline* was recorded in Muscle Shoals and Los Angeles, and the basic tracks were all completed.

"We were working at Wally Heider's Studio Four," recalls producer David Malloy, "which is adjacent to a famous Italian restaurant called Martoni's. In fact, you could smell the garlic comin' through the walls."

Malloy gave the musicians a lunch break, and stayed in the studio with Rabbitt and songwriter Even Stevens. Thirty minutes later, Randy McCormick came back and took his place at the Fender Rhodes piano.

"He had a great feel for somethin'," reports Stevens, "and he started playin', and we started makin' up words to it. Within five minutes, we had this song pretty well mapped out. Everybody was throwin' out lines, and I was writin' 'em down."

Fortunately, Malloy had the presence of mind to ask engineer Peter Granet to turn on a two-track tape machine to capture the song as they wrote it. The two-track wasn't set up to record, though. Unknown to the musicians, Granet instead recorded their performance through the 24-track console. It was so perfect that they used that take as the basis for the entire record.

"The track is actually Randy playing, and [drummer] Roger [Hawkins] playing, not knowing the machine was loaded," says Malloy, "just playing along with no headphones from the other side of the room, listening to the piano."

Rabbitt had to take a 7:00 A.M. flight out of L.A., and at 2:30 that morning, he threw on a vocal for Malloy to use as a guide in building the record. He sang it once, hearing only the piano and drums, and never heard it again until the record was finished, complete with a heavy bass from David Hungate and an unusual flute solo by Ernie Watts.

"'Suspicions' hasn't got a major chord in it," notes Rabbitt. "The record company told me I shouldn't put it out because it's not country."

Rabbitt insisted, however, and the record debuted at number 48 on June 16, 1979. It reached number one eight weeks later, on August 11.

350

COCA COLA COWBOY
MEL TILLIS
MCA 41041
Writers: Sandy Pinkard, Steve Dorff,
Bud Dain, Sam Atchley
Producer: Jimmy Bowen
August 18, 1979 (1 week)

Mel Tillis apparently isn't satisfied to hold down just one kind of role. After establishing his musical abilities, he expanded into acting, with roles in the movies *The Villain*, *Smokey and the Bandit* and *Uphill All the Way* (which he also produced). In the fall of 1979, he guested on an episode of "The Dukes of Hazzard." Just a few months earlier, he had picked up his fifth number one single, from another movie he appeared in—*Every Which Way But Loose* [see 335].

After Tillis agreed to be in the film, he met in San Diego with Snuff Garrett, hired by Clint Eastwood to produce the soundtrack. Garrett played him a couple of songs, neither of which particularly interested Mel.

Tillis offered instead to write a couple of his own. Garrett insisted, however, that Mel would have to cut both songs or forget about appearing in the movie. Tillis paused.

"You mean I have to do those or I can't be in the movie?"

"That's right," Garrett replied.

"Well, they sound better already!"

Mel cut both songs and made his appearance in the film. The first, "Send Me Down To Tucson," debuted on the *Billboard* country chart on January 13, 1979. It was strong enough to reach number two, but it remained there for three weeks, unable to dislodge Dave & Sugar's "Golden Tears" [see 336]. The second was "Coca Cola Cowboy," a song that was almost finished when songwriter Sandy Pinkard brought it into Steve Dorff's office.

"I specifically came up with the augmented chord," says Dorff, "which is the hook musically in the verse of the song."

Despite his dislike for the song in the movie, Tillis recorded "Coca Cola Cowboy" a second time for the *Mr. Entertainer* album.

"He didn't want to re-cut it for a record, either," notes producer Jimmy Bowen, "but he had to, because before he left California, he promised Snuff that he'd do it. I didn't like it, either. I thought it was the dumbest song I'd heard in my life. I couldn't stand it. Of course,

it went to number one, and I changed my mind."

Pinkard, who intended "Coca Cola Cowboy" as a silly song, went on to become half of Pinkard & Bowden, a duo specializing in song parodies like "Drivin' My Wife Away" [see 391] and "Mama, He's Lazy" [see 580].

351

THE DEVIL WENT DOWN TO GEORGIA
THE CHARLIE DANIELS BAND
Epic 50700
Writers: Charlie Daniels, Tom Crain,
Taz DiGregorio, Fred Edwards,
Charlie Hayward, Jim Marshall
Producer: John Boylan
August 25, 1979 (1 week)

Anyone who's seen *Damn Yankees* knows well the classic tale of a baseball fan who sells his soul to Satan for a chance to bring a World Series victory to the Washington Senators. That same theme was captured far from the lights of Broadway in Nashville's Woodland Studios when the Charlie Daniels Band cut "The Devil Went Down To Georgia."

In actuality, Daniels drew his inspiration not from the theater, but from a Roaring Twenties poem titled "Mountain Whippoorwill," by Stephen Vincent Benet. "We were recording our *Million Mile Reflections* album," he told Dorothy Horstman in *Sing Your Heart Out, Country Boy*, "and after completing the majority of the tracks, realized that we needed a fiddle tune. I just worked on the idea at home one night. We all liked it immediately, but really had no idea it would become one of our biggest hits."

The song actually represented a major change for the CDB. Earlier releases like "Uneasy Rider," "The South's Gonna Do It" and "Long Haired Country Boy" gained acceptance with pop and rock radio stations, but were unable to gain much response from country listeners. Labeled a part of the Southern Rock movement, the band finally broke the country market with the fiddle-heavy message of "The Devil Went Down To Georgia."

Two versions were actually released, which Daniels refers to as the Methodist Version and the Baptist Version. The latter includes an overdub, changing "son of a bitch" to "son of a gun." Both the single and the *Million Mile*

The Charlie
Daniels Band

Reflections album sold more than a million copies, and "The Devil Went Down To Georgia" also earned a Grammy for Best Country Performance by a Duo or Group With Vocal.

The summer of '79 actually proved a double winner for Daniels, who played fiddle on Hank Williams, Jr.'s "Family Tradition." Daniels has also recorded with Bob Dylan (on *Nashville Skyline*), Johnny Lee ("Cherokee Fiddle"), George Jones, Alabama and the Oak Ridge Boys.

The following summer proved successful for the CDB as well, as "In America" (a song inspired by the Iranian hostage crisis) reached number 13. Political themes also characterized 1982's "Still In Saigon" and 1985's "American Farmer," although neither garnered a large chart response.

The CDB returned to country music's Top Ten again in 1986 with "Drinkin' My Baby Goodbye," and in 1988, with "Boogie Woogie Fiddle Country Blues."

352
HEARTBREAK HOTEL
WILLIE NELSON & LEON RUSSELL
Columbia 11023
Writers: Mae Boren Axton,
Tommy Durden, Elvis Presley
Producers: Willie Nelson, Leon Russell
September 1, 1979 (1 week)

When Elvis Presley emerged in 1955, a Jacksonville teacher named Mae Axton became a friend and promised to write his first million-selling single. She made good on that promise when her frequent writing partner, Tommy Durden, showed her an article about a man who committed suicide and left a note: "I walk a lonely street." They put a "heartbreak hotel" at the end of that street, and 22 minutes later, they had completed Presley's first million-seller, recorded in January of 1956.

A year later, Axton headed to the Northwest to do publicity for an upcoming Hank Snow tour. At Vancouver radio station KVAN, she submitted to an on-air interview with a disk jockey who impressed her with his knowledge of her work. His name was Willie Nelson. Years later, Nelson and Leon Russell cut an upbeat version of "Heartbreak Hotel" for their 1979 duet album, *One for the Road.*

"That was Leon's idea," says Willie. "I liked the song, and I liked the writer, but he was the one that said we should do 'Heartbreak Hotel.'

"It was one of those weeks where we recorded and filmed at the same time, I think, a hundred and four or five tracks at Leon's place there in L.A. So every time we'd get through with one song, we'd say, 'Well, now what do you want to do?'

"One of those times, Leon suggested 'Heartbreak Hotel.' It was Leon's feel that we used on that particular record. He was playin' piano at the time, and I sort of followed his lead. Usually, the one who suggested the song had to set feel."

Russell, a one-time cohort of rock singer Joe Cocker, might have seemed an unlikely country singer. He had attracted attention for his pop hits "Tight Rope" and "Lady Blue," and for writing George Benson's "This Masquerade." Add to that a load of session work with Gary Lewis & The Playboys, Frank Sinatra and the Rolling Stones.

But Leon was also exposed, naturally, to country music while growing up in Oklahoma. In 1973, he surprised his rock audience by releasing *Hank Wilson's Back,* a country album that played on Hank Williams' name. Russell released a second "Hank Wilson" album a decade later.

Leon was the first person to sign Willie's heavily-autographed guitar.

353

I MAY NEVER GET TO HEAVEN
CONWAY TWITTY
MCA 41059
Writers: Bill Anderson, Buddy Killen
Producers: Conway Twitty, David Barnes
September 8, 1979 (1 week)

In 1975, the Nashville Songwriters Association admitted Bill Anderson into the Nashville Songwriters Hall of Fame. Unlike the Pro Football Hall of Fame or the Baseball Hall of Fame, Music City's hall for composers doesn't recognize its constituents only when a career is over. Often, induction comes while a writer is still enjoying the fruits of his/her labor.

Such is the case with Anderson. A year after that honor, he started a new series of successful recordings with producer Buddy Killen. Four singles, including "Peanuts And Diamonds," "Liars One, Believers Zero" and "Head To Toe," reached Top Ten status. "I Can't Wait Any Longer," which soared to number four in 1978, earned the distinction of being the first country record played in American discotheques.

Anderson's friendship with Buddy Killen went back more than two decades. Roger Miller, one of Killen's discoveries, had introduced the two, and Bill wrote several songs with Buddy, including "I May Never Get To Heaven."

"I wrote the lyrics to this song in 1959 when I broke up for a short while with a girl I had been dating," Anderson recalls. "I showed the lyric to Buddy one day while I was hanging out at Tree Publishing, and he sat down at the piano and put a beautiful melody to it.

"Don Gibson immediately recorded it, but it was the 'B' side of one of his big uptempo hits. Between 1959 and 1979, the song must have been recorded a dozen times—Aretha Franklin even cut it!—but it never became a hit."

"I had that song back when I was singin' rock music," adds Conway, who first heard Gibson's version. "I always loved this thing. That's one of those that I just kept in this little box, and when I figured the time was right, I went in there and recorded it.

"Buddy Killen just came unglued. As a writer, he figured he'd written a really good one, and nothin' had ever happened with it, so he was beside himself to hear it the way he wanted it done, and for it to become a number one record."

Though his hits have tailed off, Anderson has remained active throughout the '80s. He has been involved with the Nashville Network as a host and/or producer on several shows, including "Fandango."

In 1989, Longstreet Press published his autobiography, *Whisperin' Bill,* which centered on an October 13, 1984, accident that nearly killed his wife, Becky. Anderson continues to make regular concert appearances at the Grand Ole Opry, and is also the national spokesman for PoFolks, a family-style restaurant chain that has the same name as one of his very first hits.

354
YOU'RE MY JAMAICA
CHARLEY PRIDE
RCA 11655
Writer: Kent Robbins
Producers: Jerry Bradley, Charley Pride
September 15, 1979 (1 week)

Island rhythms appropriately permeate the strains of Charley Pride's "You're My Jamaica," which also holds the distinction as the first number one country hit ever recorded on the island of England.

"I undoubtedly wrote that in the winter," says songwriter Kent Robbins. "I'm a big island buff. I've been to the Bahamas and Bermuda and Hawaii, and I was just going through my notebook, where I jot down little ideas. I had a little piece of something, 'When it gets colder, you're my . . . something.' 'Blanket' or 'furnace' wouldn't have been very good, and Jamaica sort of jumped in there, and I just went, 'Wow! that's the idea.'

"I called it 'You're My Jamaica' and ran down to the travel agency and got some folders on the island so I wouldn't have the wrong images in there as far as the color of the sand, or the kind of drinks they drink, or whatever. I just put together a nice, sort of reggae-feeling, summery song in the middle of winter."

Ray Stevens' brother, John Ragsdale, was the first to record "You're My Jamaica." The single didn't do much, but Pride heard it and decided to cut his own version of the song.

In the meantime, RCA's corporate division decided Pride should record an entire album in Great Britain. The company thought he might increase his audience in the United Kingdom if he had the "English sound," so producer Jerry Bradley took keyboard player David Briggs overseas and hired British musicians to record a dozen tracks at the Audio International and Pye Recording Studios in London.

Most of those cuts remain in the label's vaults. After the album was recorded, RCA never bothered to release it in England, and "You're My Jamaica" was the only take salvaged for his next stateside album. It became the title track and first single, debuting in Billboard on July 14, 1979, reaching number one in its tenth charted week.

Pride followed "You're My Jamaica" with another cut from the album, this one recorded in Nashville's Music City Music Hall Studio. "Missin' You" went to number two.

355
JUST GOOD OL' BOYS
MOE BANDY & JOE STAMPLEY
Columbia 11027
Writer: Ansley Fleetwood
Producer: Ray Baker
September 22, 1979 (1 week)

Moe Bandy remembers that in 1979, Joe Stampley was "a hamburger freak," and that fact provided a starting point for the series of "Good Ol' Boys" duets. They were performing at London's annual Wembley Country Music Festival, and ran into each other in a hotel lobby. Stampley suggested they take the wives out, setting the scene for a history-making dinner at the Hard Rock Cafe.

At dinner, Stampley noted that "Moe & Joe" was as catchy as "Waylon & Willie," and the comment led to more serious discussion about a duet album. They planned to release the Johnny Horton classic "Honky Tonk Man" as the first single, but they shelved that idea in

**Moe Bandy &
Joe Stampley**

favor of a song written by Stampley's piano player.

Ansley Fleetwood had been at the same dinner in London, and inspired by the possibilities, he wrote "Just Good Ol' Boys" specifically for the album. "We listened to the song and we tried to sing it," remembers Bandy, "and it was like two brothers—I mean, our harmonies were just perfect. 'Good Ol' Boys' set the theme: we automatically became good ol' boys, and we automatically became hell-raisers."

The results were overwhelming. Moe and Joe won Vocal Duo of the Year awards in 1980 from both the Academy of Country Music and the Country Music Association, and lent their names to an entrepreneur who renamed his honky-tonks "Moe & Joe's." They followed with several more wild and woolly records; two of them ("Honky Tonk Queen" and "Where's The Dress") made Moe and Joe the first act to score hits about transvestites.

Ultimately, the success of the duets put a damper on both performers' solo careers. "The last stuff we did together was in '84 or '85," says Stampley, "and even now, when they come to my show, they expect to see Moe with me." "It was great for us," adds Bandy. "We made a lot of money, and traveled and did a lot of fun things. But to get back to our individual careers was really something. I think that's about the end of it. I hate to say 'never,' but . . ."

356

IT MUST BE LOVE
DON WILLIAMS
MCA 41069
Writer: Bob McDill
Producers: Don Williams, Garth Fundis
September 29, 1979 (1 week)

Don Williams' *Expressions* album represented a major change in his career, as he added Garth Fundis as a co-producer. Fundis had been there in the beginning, engineering Williams' first two albums, recorded with producer Allen Reynolds.

At that time, Garth worked as the staff engineer for Jack Clement Studios, although he later went independent, and, in fact, engineered "Don't It Make My Brown Eyes Blue" [see 292]. When he first went indie, he missed work on Williams' *Volume III* [see 178—"I

Wouldn't Want To Live If You Didn't Love Me"], but Williams hired him to engineer every album after that.

"It was pretty much him and me in the studio," Fundis notes. "He'd be out there singin' and I'd be in the control room. I've got a musical background. I was a music education major in college. I studied voice, so I'd help him— 'You're a little flat here,' or 'a little sharp,' just tryin' to help—and so at one point, it became obvious that I was much more than just an engineer. So he invited me to make this a co-production."

The *Expressions* album provided an excellent first outing for Fundis as a producer. "Tulsa Time" [see 331] hit number one, "Lay Down Beside Me" went to number three, and "It Must Be Love" returned Williams to the top spot.

Fundis and Williams did all of the harmony vocals on the latter song, another page out of the Bob McDill songbook [see 256—"Say It Again"].

"Whenever we're gettin' ready to record," says Garth, "there's always a call to McDill: 'Whaddya got?' But at the same time, through the year, even when we're not recording, McDill will write some new stuff and he'll automatically send a lot of it to Don first to see if he's interested before he plays it for anybody else."

"'It Must Be Love' is just a fun little ditty, fun to sing," McDill adds. "That was very innovative at the time, the way Don recorded that. It was really funky. It was kind of the cutting edge in country music at the time, musically."

His work with Williams has given Fundis greater respect in Nashville, and he has gone on to produce records for Mac Davis, New Grass Revival and Keith Whitley.

357

LAST CHEATER'S WALTZ
T.G. SHEPPARD
Warner Bros. 49024
Writer: Sonny Throckmorton
Producer: Buddy Killen
October 6, 1979 (2 weeks)

The latter part of the '70s was a frustrating period for T.G. Sheppard, who had given up a lucrative six-figure career for a recording vocation that at times brought in a mere $25,000 annually. After "Devil In The Bottle" [see 197] and "Tryin' To Beat The Morning Home" [see 214] both established him, his deal with Motown's country division quickly eroded.

"Melodyland closed their label down," he says, "and my contract was still tied up in litigation for two or three years, so it really was a dead period."

"Motels And Memories" and "Show Me A Man" brought two more Top Ten singles with Motown, and in 1977, Warner Bros. bought out the rest of T.G.'s contract. After a couple of lackluster singles, he teamed up with producer Buddy Killen, and immediately found a groove, collecting four straight Top Ten singles: "When Can We Do This Again," "Daylight," a remake of the Turtles' "Happy Together," and "You Feel Good All Over." More than four years after his second number one, Sheppard finally reached the top again with his next release, "Last Cheater's Waltz."

Credit for the song's plaintive melody belongs solely to songwriter Sonny Throckmorton, who was remodeling his house when he first started building "Last Cheater's Waltz." "I had a hammer or a saw in my hand, and I started singing the chorus," recalls Throckmorton. "I didn't have any words—just the melody—and for two or three days, I'd just sit around and sing it over and over and over.

"It started out to be the 'Strawberry Waltz,' and I could see these people meeting at a cherry festival or a strawberry festival, and dancing through the night. The melody tended to have a sad ending to it, and I wrestled with 'The Strawberry Waltz' for a long time. It didn't do any good, and eventually I had to get something that denotes a real sad ending.

" 'Last Cheater's Waltz' somehow came to me, and it was like a revelation, because of the way that it ended."

The song became the title track of an album that Throckmorton cut for Mercury Records in 1978. Released as a "B" side of "Smooth Sailin'," the songwriter's version peaked at number 47 in March of 1979.

358

ALL THE GOLD IN CALIFORNIA
LARRY GATLIN & THE GATLIN BROTHERS BAND
Columbia 11066
Writer: Larry Gatlin
Producers: Larry Gatlin, Steve Gatlin, Rudy Gatlin
October 20, 1979 (2 weeks)

Larry Gatlin was on a roll by 1979. With a number one record [see 303—"I Just Wish You Were Someone I Love"] under his belt, he added "Night Time Magic" (which peaked at number two) and "I've Done Enough Dyin' Today" to his string of successes in 1978. With his contract up for renewal, a bidding war ensued, and a trip to Los Angeles during the negotiations process inspired the Gatlins' signature song, "All The Gold In California."

Larry Gatlin & the Gatlin Brothers Band

Gatlin was between meetings with United Artists Records and Warner Bros., and had slowed to a stop on the Hollywood Freeway. "I was stuck in a traffic jam right in front of the Hollywood Bowl," he remembers, "and I looked at the truck in front of me and it looked like the family out of *The Grapes of Wrath*. I thought, 'These poor Okies have moved out here to California to get rich and California is just beating them up, 'cause they think all the gold is out here.'

"One thing led to another, and I wrote it in seven minutes. By the time I got to the next record meeting, I had the song finished, went back to Houston a couple days later and played it for my brothers and the band, and we just knew that it was a hit."

"All The Gold In California" was the first single to bill the group as a band, and their first for Columbia Records. The Academy of Country Music named it the Single of the Year, and also named *Straight Ahead* (their first gold LP) the Album of the Year.

With its frequent repetition and tight, family harmony, "All The Gold" is also the perfect example of the Gatlin philosophy about songs. Larry explains: "The songs that we've had that have been hits, I start out with the chorus— something that everybody can sing right in the front—then write a little verse part in the middle that explains it and then sing that chorus part again. It kind of became a Gatlin trademark. You sing that big harmony thing up front.

"The verses aren't what sells the record, and I'm a firm believer that if you don't capture their attention in the first 15 or 20 seconds of the song, you might as well forget it."

359

YOU DECORATED MY LIFE
KENNY ROGERS
United Artists 1315
Writers: Debbie Hupp, Bob Morrison
Producer: Larry Butler
November 3, 1979 (2 weeks)

In 1977, songwriter Johnny MacRae introduced fellow writer Bob Morrison to a new collaborator named Debbie Hupp. Having tried to "make a go" of writing once before, Hupp had moved back to Kentucky and started a family, working in store security for a liquor distillery.

They collaborated primarily through the mail or via telephone, and wrote their first big record together about six months after the partnership began. It took two years for that song, "You Decorated My Life," to pay off.

"That was one of those songs that I never even expected to get recorded," says Morrison. "When Debbie and I finished it, a lot of people said, 'Decorated? Come on, man.' It is unusual with respect to that word.

"It's a little bit wimpy—one of those sobby-dobby, sweetish, syrupy kind of ballads. But it worked, and that proved that I didn't know anything, 'cause I didn't think the song would get cut."

Actually, Morrison was the first to record it, for Monument Records. His version went nowhere. Then his publisher pitched "Decorated" to producer Larry Butler to record with Dottie West. Dottie turned it down, but Butler decided instead to make a record with Kenny Rogers.

"When Larry and I would listen to songs," says Kenny, "we would take these songs and put them into stacks of Yes, Maybe and No. The No's we would throw away. I kept taking this song, and I kind of liked it, but it was a little saccharine for me at first. I kept putting it in the Maybe stack, and I found out later that Larry kept sticking it on the bottom of the Yes stack, so we would always listen to it."

Butler pulled that stunt for a year until Rogers finally caved in and recorded "Decorated," releasing it as the first single from his album *Kenny*. It debuted on the *Billboard* chart on September 15, 1979, at number 48. Just seven weeks later, it climbed into the number one position. It rose simultaneously to number seven on the Hot 100, and earned Morrison and Hupp a Grammy for Best Country Song.

The album *Kenny* logged 24 weeks atop the country album chart, longer than any other Rogers album. The runners-up: *The Gambler* (23 weeks) and *Eyes That See in the Dark* (16 weeks).

360

COME WITH ME
WAYLON JENNINGS
RCA 11723
Writer: Chuck Howard
Producer: Richie Albright
November 17, 1979 (2 weeks)

For those who liked Waylon Jennings for his rough and rowdy ways, 1979 helped to position him as a vocalist of wider emotional range. Providing a stark contrast to the outlaw image [see 237—"Good Hearted Woman"] that surrounded him, Waylon released a pair of ballads in succession: "Amanda" [see 346] and "Come With Me."

Jennings came out subdued and thoughtful this time, enhanced by a female voice that some probably mistook as his wife, Jessi Colter.

"I tried to use that as a springboard to help Carter Robertson," he says. "She was the girl on there. I liked that song, but it was mainly to try and get her a deal [she'd had one with ABC, but had been let go prior to Waylon's *What Goes Around Comes Around* album]. I knew it could be a hit song, too. I think it was a good song, but I was trying to bring attention to her. She worked with us at the time, her and her husband. She did vocals and her husband did piano, Cliff Robertson."

"Come With Me" debuted in *Billboard* at number 40 on September 22, 1979, and reached the Top Ten in its fifth charted week. Three weeks later, "Come With Me" began a two-week run at number one. On March 3, 1980, *What Goes Around Comes Around* earned honors as Waylon's ninth gold album.

Jennings hails from Littlefield, Texas, a rural community outside of Lubbock, where he was born June 15, 1937. His father worked as a farm laborer and at a service station, and Waylon was the oldest of four boys.

He worked at a lumberyard at one point, but Waylon got started in his chosen profession at the age of 14, holding down a show on a local radio station, KVOW. The station's format featured alternating 15-minute blocks of music; one block might feature pop music, the next country, the next polkas. Through that musical education, Waylon learned to appreciate a wide range of musical styles, and one of his personal musical goals is to help break down the record industry's strict adherence to labels. It's that attitude that helped, in part, to define the progressive country—or outlaw—movement.

361
BROKEN HEARTED ME
ANNE MURRAY
Capitol 4773

Writer: Randy Goodrum
Producer: Jim Ed Norman
December 1, 1979 (1 week)

"I got on a roll and that was it," says Anne Murray of her third consecutive number one single. "Sometimes you get the feeling that you could put out something in Chinese and it would happen."

Part of the reason for her "roll" was the fact that she and producer Jim Ed Norman had simply been able to find solid songs to highlight her voice.

"You can really pretty much find a thread that runs through the kinds of songs that Anne and I did in our tenure together," observes Norman. "There was a kind of soft-spoken quality, there was a nice romance about them."

That assessment is particularly true in the case of "Broken Hearted Me," written by Randy Goodrum. Goodrum had written "You Needed Me" [see 337—"I Just Fall In Love Again"], and has fashioned a long list of country hits, including "It's True Love," by Conway Twitty & Loretta Lynn; "A Lesson In Leavin'" [see 376], by Dottie West; and "Fallin' In Love," by Sylvia.

Randy has also found pop successes with Michael Johnson's "Bluer Than Blue," Steve Perry's "Oh, Sherrie" and Chicago's "If She Would Have Been Faithful." "Broken Hearted Me" first appeared on the England Dan & John Ford Coley album *Dr. Heckle and Mr. Jive*.

"I remember a period there of going through just song after song after song from Randy," says Norman. " 'Broken Hearted Me' was the first song that came along after 'You Needed Me' that there was some real fascination for on Anne's part."

At the time they cut the record, Murray was pregnant with her daughter, Dawn, and she had a cold to boot. "The vocals on that record were a little bit more involved," says Norman. "Carrying the baby like she was, she had a reduced lung capacity, so she was taking these big breaths, because she's always sung with a tremendous amount of diaphragmic support."

Norman envisioned "Broken Hearted Me" in the same Phil Spectorish "wall of sound" style as the Beatles' "The Long And Winding Road." He hired a whole chorus of vocalists, but when the track was completed, he cut back on the effect, instinctively concerned that country radio wouldn't accept it. Radio and its listeners welcomed his final mix, though, and "Broken Hearted Me" climbed into the country top spot in December of 1979.

I CHEATED ME RIGHT OUT OF YOU

MOE BANDY

Columbia 11090
Writer: Bobby Barker
Producer: Ray Baker
December 8, 1979 (1 week)

"I never advocated cheatin'," insists Moe Bandy, who often used it as a theme for many of his early hits. "I was always the guy that did it, and messed up everything. We certainly didn't brag about it."

Moe Bandy

Bandy first hit the *Billboard* charts on March 30, 1974, with "I Just Started Hatin' Cheatin' Songs Today," and after that early success, country songwriters were quick to send him more tunes about sordid affairs. He became a consistent presence in country music's Top Ten, and peaked at number two with "Hank Williams, You Wrote My Life" (in 1976) and with "It's A Cheatin' Situation" (in 1979). "I Cheated Me Right Out Of You" finally brought him to the top later that same year.

"It was just a good ol' country song," Bandy says of the record. "It just laid right in there; it felt really good."

Bandy was born on Lincoln's birthday, 1944, in the town of Meridien, Mississippi, where his grandfather had once worked alongside country legend Jimmie Rodgers on the railroad.

While Moe was still a youngster, the Bandys moved to San Antonio, and in 1972, he met producer Ray Baker, who agreed to cut a record with him—but only if Bandy would pay for the sessions. Moe hocked his furniture a year later for $900, and after "I Just Started Hatin' Cheatin' Songs Today" was released, it still took a while for Bandy to get out of debt.

For years, Bandy was one of the few performers holding tightly to country music's traditions, and for his efforts, the Texas State Legislature named him the official King of Honky-Tonk. His string of hits continued until 1983, when they began to tail off. Finally, on July 4, 1986, Moe signed a new contract with MCA onstage during a concert in Oklahoma. With new producer Jerry Kennedy, he turned toward more positive songs, and returned again to country music's Top Ten.

"I hate to go out and record songs that make you think you have to have an image," he says. "I feel like now I'm more natural, more myself."

HAPPY BIRTHDAY DARLIN'

CONWAY TWITTY

MCA 41135
Writer: Chuck Howard
Producers: Conway Twitty, David Barnes
December 25, 1979 (3 weeks)

The third number one single from Conway Twitty's album *Cross Winds* represented a new level of achievement. "Happy Birthday

Darlin'" was his twenty-eighth chart-topping record, tying him with Eddy Arnold [see 18—"Then You Can Tell Me Goodbye"] at the top of *Billboard*'s all-time list. Stylistically, Conway's deep-throated romantic commentary brought him perhaps closer to soul lovemaster Barry White.

"Happy Birthday Darlin'" came from the pen of Chuck Howard, who also wrote Waylon Jennings' "Come With Me" [see 360] and Merle Haggard's "I'm Always On A Mountain When I Fall." "Happy Birthday Darlin'" had already been released once before when Conway heard it through his booking agent, Jimmy Jay [see 87—"Lead Me On"]. "I was in his office," remembers Twitty, "and every once in a while, he'd pitch me a song that somebody had left there or he'd heard or something. They were always awful—I mean, *bad*."

This time was different. Jay played some material recorded by an artist the booking agency had just signed. The performer was okay, but Conway was enamored with the song, "Happy Birthday Darlin'." After a little background research, it became apparent that the first version of the song had run its course with little success, and Twitty decided to release his own rendition.

"What a unique little song," he says. "I used basically the same arrangement. I think we improved on it a little bit, but it was really a unique, unusual little arrangement behind the song—unusual for a country music thing, especially a Conway Twitty thing. But I was doin' my own stuff then, so I had a little more freedom to do what I wanted to do."

Conway added his own "Hello Darlin'" [see 56] as an opening line, and by connecting his past with a reinvigorated present, he cinched its number one peak.

His new musical style wasn't the only change in evidence for Conway during 1979. That January, Jimmy Jay persuaded him to see a new hair stylist, Jacque King. She performed a major overhaul on his 'do, siphoning off the grease and plumping up new curls.

The new hairstyle did wonders for his public image. Twitty garnered as much publicity as he'd had in a decade or more, and he promptly dubbed it "The Curl Heard 'Round the World."

364
COWARD OF THE COUNTY
KENNY ROGERS

United Artists 1327
Writers: Roger Bowling,
Billy Edd Wheeler
Producer: Larry Butler
January 5, 1980 (3 weeks)

Billy Edd Wheeler earned a brief bit of glory in 1964 by hitting number three on the *Billboard* country chart with "Ode To The Little Brown Shack Out Back." Though he continued his recording career, he has been more successful as a songwriter.

In 1963, the Kingston Trio picked up a pop hit with Wheeler's "Reverend Mr. Black," and Billy has since penned several country hits, including Johnny Cash's "Jackson" (a Grammy-winning duet with June Carter) and "Blistered"; Elvis Presley's "It's Midnight"; and "Coward Of The County," a song he and co-writer Roger Bowling targeted for Kenny Rogers from the outset.

The song started during a drive along a mountain road, as Bowling hummed a chorus he had titled "The Promise." It was a pledge from a son to his father, with religious overtones.

"It's the idea that turning the other cheek is not a sign of weakness," Wheeler explained to Frye Gaillard of the *Charlotte Observer*. "It really has to do with Jesus' example, and I guess it's ingrained in all of us. I know it was when I was growing up in the mountains—'Be a good neighbor,' people used to say, 'but carry a big stick.'"

Wheeler felt that a story song with an underdog theme might work, and he and Bowling tried to fit that idea with "The Promise." It proved a difficult task, and they wrote three different versions before they finally created a storyline they were happy with. In fact, they continued making changes until just before Rogers recorded it for the album *Kenny*.

"Coward Of The County" caused problems for Larry Gatlin. The song implicated three fictitious Gatlin boys in a rape sequence.

"It was a really great song," says Larry, "but [even] my mother came home one day and said she heard a song that accused her boys of rapin' somebody. It did kind of make me mad. I think they could have showed a little good taste, and used somebody else's name."

Kenny hadn't considered the implication, and he made it up to the Gatlins by including them in his road show.

"Coward" hit number one on the country chart, reached number three on the pop chart, and sold a million copies.

365

I'LL BE COMING BACK FOR MORE

T.G. SHEPPARD

Warner Bros. 49110
Writers: Curly Putman, Sterling Whipple
Producer: Buddy Killen
January 26, 1980 (2 weeks)

A native of Eugene, Oregon, Sterling Whipple at one time followed in his father's footsteps by enrolling in law school. He found that career course uninspiring, though, and eventually, against the advice of his parents, moved to Nashville in June of 1974.

Unfortunately, his father never lived long enough to witness his success—ironic indeed, since Whipple's first hit was "Blind Man In The Bleachers," a composition about a football player whose father sees him play for the first time only after death. Kenny Starr recorded the song and took it to number two in 1975, while David Geddes simultaneously released a pop version (retitled "The Last Game Of The Season"), which peaked at number 18 on *Billboard*'s Hot 100.

Whipple charted three country singles as a vocalist (none peaked higher than number 25), but his biggest successes came as a writer. He penned "Prisoner Of Hope," by Johnny Lee; "Ain't No California," by Mel Tillis; and "In Some Room Above The Street," by Gary Stewart. He wrote for Buddy Killen's Tree Publishing, notching Sheppard's "Show Me A Man" [see 357—"Last Cheater's Waltz"] and "I'll Be Coming Back For More." Whipple's only number one single, "Coming Back" developed when he happened to wander by Curly Putman's office at an opportune moment.

"I don't like to make appointments to write songs," explains Putman. "If a friend of mine comes by and sits down for a little while and we kick around a title, we sometimes write it.

"Sterling and I had a good idea and decided to work on it. I had the title, and I wanted a T.G. Sheppard–style of song. We sat down and knocked it out in probably 30 minutes or an hour. We had T.G. in mind because he was working with [Killen] at the time, and we knew we had an outlet for something like that. It was a little sex-oriented, and it worked out real good."

"I'll Be Coming Back For More" was in some ways a distillation of Sheppard's career at that point. He had started with two recitations before advancing to songs that were predominantly sung. Likewise, "I'll Be Coming Back For More" opened with a spoken verse.

"I never really thought of myself as a singer until 'Last Cheater's Waltz' and 'Coming Back For More,'" Sheppard confesses. "Those first five years there were just an apprenticeship."

366

LEAVING LOUISIANA IN THE BROAD DAYLIGHT

THE OAK RIDGE BOYS

MCA 41154
Writers: Rodney Crowell,
Donivan Cowart
Producer: Ron Chancey
February 9, 1980 (1 week)

Shortly after "I'll Be True To You" [see 314] became their first number one record, the Oak Ridge Boys ascended to elite status in the country music business. The Country Music Association named them the Vocal Group of the Year in 1978. The following spring, the Academy of Country Music accorded them similar honors, and cited *Y'all Come Back Saloon* as the Album of the Year.

The Oaks accrued four more Top Ten singles as well: "Cryin' Again," "Come On In," "Sail Away" (which stopped at number two) and "Dream On." They returned to number one with "Leaving Louisiana In The Broad Daylight," a track pulled from the album *The Oak Ridge Boys Have Arrived*. "Leaving Louisiana" represented the first number one record written by former Emmylou Harris associate Rodney Crowell [see 269—"Sweet Dreams"].

Crowell wrote "Louisiana" with Donivan Cowart, a recording engineer who had moved from Texas to Nashville along with Crowell a few years before. They were working on a country album with "Mary Hartman, Mary Hartman" star Mary Kay Place when they created it.

"[Mary Kay] can just string words together for days," Crowell notes. "She's really a fine writer, with a real sense of poetry and meter and rhyme, so we just started talking to each other, kind of in clipped rhyme, and the whole approach to writing that song was basically around that. There's a lot of words—'Mary took to runnin' with a travelin' man'—almost like kids who jump a rope, and the kid jumps in the middle, and they have little words and sayings that they do, that kind of thing."

Emmylou included the song on her album *Quarter Moon in a Ten Cent Town,* and the Oaks eventually heard it on a tape of three Crowell songs. Also on the tape were "Bluebird Wine," which Harris featured on *Pieces of the Sky*; and "Never Together (But Close Sometimes)," which the Oaks cut in 1988 for *Monongahela* [see 792—"Gonna Take A Lot Of River"].

"Leaving Louisiana" first appeared on the *Billboard* country chart at number 51 on December 1, 1979. Ten weeks later, it edged into the top spot.

367

LOVE ME OVER AGAIN

DON WILLIAMS

MCA 41155
Writer: Don Williams
Producers: Don Williams, Garth Fundis
February 16, 1980 (1 week)

Originally, Don Williams moved to Nashville to pursue songwriting as a career. He harbored doubts about his own voice as a commercial vehicle, and likewise was reluctant to play the "star" game. After accepting a role as a

recording artist, however, his writing gradually went on the backburner until at one point in the mid-'80s, he went two years without writing anything.

"These days," says co-producer Garth Fundis, "there's so many people offerin' us material that he doesn't sit down and write much anymore. After you get busy and go out on the road doin' concerts and come home and try to find time with your family, Don says about the last thing you want to do is sit down and write by yourself, and try to pull somethin' out and say somethin'.

"The original reason he wrote songs was that he wanted to say somethin' he couldn't find anywhere else. Now he's findin' a lot of things that he wants to say in other people's songs."

The last Williams composition to hit number one was "Love Me Over Again," which debuted in *Billboard* on December 8, 1979, and peaked in its eleventh week.

"I have a little house across the road that I've used primarily for writing," Williams said from his home outside of Nashville, "and it was a song that I wrote over there.

"The songs that are the best for me are songs where I sit down with my guitar. If I get into a certain kind of groove, and I'm doing something with the guitar that's interesting to me, it starts dictating a mood. If the interest is there and I stay there long enough to where I can start talkin' about it, then I'll write a song, and that was one of those songs. The little thing that I was doin' on the guitar just felt a little different to me, and that song was the result of it."

Don wasn't sure of the song's value until he played it for Fundis, who decided they should definitely include it on the *Portrait* album. Williams followed "Love Me Over Again" with "Good Ole Boys Like Me," a semi-autobiographical Bob McDill composition, written in celebration of the South. That record spent three weeks at number two, unable to dislodge Ronnie Milsap's "My Heart" [see 381].

368

YEARS
BARBARA MANDRELL
MCA 41162
Writers: Kye Fleming, Dennis Morgan
Producer: Tom Collins
February 23, 1980 (1 week)

Kye Fleming and Dennis Morgan were the most prolific Nashville songwriting team of the early '80s. From 1978 through 1983, they racked up 20 Top Ten singles on the *Billboard* country chart, with seven of them hitting number one.

They started by fairly similar methods. Morgan grew up in Tracy, Minnesota, leaving high school in his junior year to pursue music. He played the coffeehouse circuit all over the country in the early '70s, finally settling in Nashville. After writing a few advertising jingles, he earned a contract in 1976 to write for Charley Pride's Pi-Gem Music, a company headed by Tom Collins.

Fleming grew up in numerous towns, thanks to the requirements of her father's position in the Navy. When she was 12, the family finally settled in Arkansas, and in the ninth grade, she started writing songs. Like Morgan, she played coffeehouses for much of the '70s, until she met Elvis Presley's bass player, Jerry Scheff, who got her an appointment with Pi-Gem. In January of 1978, she and Morgan wrote together for the first time.

Many of their songs were written to order. Collins produced Ronnie Milsap, Barbara Mandrell, Steve Wariner and Sylvia, among others, and when he needed material, he frequently gave the writers a title or a framework

he hoped to explore. They wrote and rewrote, pushed and pulled at their songs until they had exactly what was needed for the artist. "Years," a song recorded by Mandrell, differed from their usual approach.

" 'Years' is one of my favorites," says Fleming. "It's really from the heart, not that the actual experience has to be true. It's just that you reach in and you try to get something that moves you, for whatever reason."

When Collins produced the song, he felt it was too long to be a single. Mandrell's drummer, Randy Wright, provided an "answer voice" on the chorus, but Collins also brought in a session singer who did a more elaborate performance. When he had to turn in the album, he still hadn't remixed it with the new vocalist; since "Years" was not planned as a single, they left Wright on the record.

Radio started playing "Years" as an album cut, though, and MCA released it on December 7, 1979. Two months later, "Years," featuring Do-Rite Wright, hit number one.

369

I AIN'T LIVING LONG LIKE THIS
WAYLON JENNINGS
RCA 11898
Writer: Rodney Crowell
Producer: Richie Albright
March 1, 1980 (1 week)

Once the outlaw label [see 237—"Good Hearted Woman"] was affixed to Waylon Jennings, he spent a great deal of time and energy trying to fight the association. Though pleased with the attention to his music, Jennings didn't want to be stereotyped. At the end of 1978, he put his feelings into a Top Five single, "Don't You Think This Outlaw Bit's Done Got Out Of Hand."

Nevertheless, "I Ain't Living Long Like This" actually helped to promote the outlaw image. Rifles, lawmen and the jailhouse were all mentioned in the song, which had appeared earlier on an Emmylou Harris LP and as the title track of Rodney Crowell's first solo album.

Jennings' single version faded out after three-and-a-half minutes, though the album cut lasted five minutes.

"That is one take," Waylon says, "first take, and that's it. It's the only time I ever did it, but we all loved that damn song so much before I cut it, and it just came off, and I could never change it. I was gonna redo the vocal in a couple of places where it bothered me a little bit, but I could never lay it in there again like I did that one time."

Crowell called on part of his youth in writing "I Ain't Living Long Like This." Raised in Houston, he mentioned Wayside Drive, a street at the end of a fifty-mile channel that stretches from Galveston.

"There's an intersection there," he notes, "and that's where all of the old sailors and merchant marines and seamen would get off the boat. My grandfather was a nightwatchman at the ship channel, so he would take me off to get a haircut. There was a bar next door, and he would slip into the bar next door and start wetting his whistle. When I would get through, I would go out over there and watch my grandpa play shuffleboard with old sailors with a patch over their eye."

Crowell wrote "I Ain't Living Long" in Hermosa Beach, California, in 1976. Rodney had disobeyed the city's leash laws with his dog, Banjo, and in the middle of writing the song, the authorities incarcerated him briefly for nonpayment of the fines. When he returned to the song, he felt even closer to its jailhouse imagery.

"I Ain't Living Long Like This" was Crowell's second number one single, coming just three weeks after the first, "Leaving Louisiana In The Broad Daylight" [see 366].

Waylon Jennings

370
MY HEROES HAVE ALWAYS BEEN COWBOYS
WILLIE NELSON
Columbia 11186
Writer: Sharon Vaughan
Producers: Willie Nelson, Sydney Pollack
March 8, 1980 (2 weeks)

On December 21, 1979, Willie Nelson first appeared on the silver screen, when *The Electric Horseman* opened to national audiences. Willie co-starred with Robert Redford and Jane Fonda, and received outstanding reviews from his co-workers.

"Any man," said Redford in a CBS bio, "who can ad-lib a line on camera like 'I'm gonna get me a bottle of tequila, one of them Keno girls who can suck the chrome right off a trailer hitch, and kick back' deserves to be in movies, writing songs, or in jail."

Nelson might have been the only person who thought he should be in movies at first. He had tried—unsuccessfully at that time—to convert *Red Headed Stranger* [see 223—"Blue Eyes Crying In The Rain"] into a film, and literally talked his way into his role in *Horseman*. Initially, director Sydney Pollack promised Nelson only an acting part, but by volunteering to work on the soundtrack, Willie provided a new promotional avenue, since a hit single would generate interest in the picture.

Waylon Jennings played a role in the film's biggest song, "My Heroes Have Always Been Cowboys." Sharon Vaughan wrote it when boyfriend Bill Rice (now her husband) asked for a cowboy song for a Bobby Bare album. Bare didn't care for it, but Waylon subsequently recorded it for the *Outlaws* album [see 237—"Good Hearted Woman"]. When he ran into Willie before *Horseman* went into production, Jennings told him "My Heroes Have Always Been Cowboys" should be the theme song.

Pollack produced the record as well as the movie, and "Heroes" emerged with an unusual arrangement, including French horns, muted trumpets and harp.

"He did have some good ideas," notes Willie. "Also David Grusin, the musical director—I'm not sure exactly how that happened, but David is a very good musician, and I'm sure that if he heard this horn or that horn in there, he'd go ahead and put it in, regardless of whether it was a country song or not. David heard all these things and said they should go in there; Sydney was smart enough to leave 'em in."

"Heroes" was one of two Nelson singles to emerge from *Horseman*. After it hit number one, Columbia released Willie's version of the Allman Brothers' "Midnight Rider," which went to number six.

371
WHY DON'T YOU SPEND THE NIGHT
RONNIE MILSAP
RCA 11909
Writer: Bob McDill
Producers: Ronnie Milsap, Rob Galbraith
March 22, 1980 (1 week)

"When I was growing up in the late '50s, R & B, country and rock co-existed well together," reminisces Ronnie Milsap. "On the radio, where I grew up in North Carolina, they would play Little Richard followed by Ray Price, or they'd play Jim Reeves followed by Fats Domino or Pat Boone or Elvis. It was okay to like them all. Later, it became critical to only like one element."

Thus, in 1979, Ronnie broke his stride with "Get It Up," a semi-disco, semi-blues release featured as the "B" side of "In No Time At All" [see 345—"Nobody Likes Sad Songs"]. Promoted to pop radio, "Get It Up" reached number 45 on the *Billboard* Hot 100.

"I know that a lot of my fans were shocked by 'Get It Up,'" he admitted to *Billboard*'s Kip Kirby. "But I'd reached the point in my career with tunes like 'Only One Love In My Life' [see 325], 'Almost Like A Song' [see 289] and 'In No Time At All,' where I felt I was being fenced into a predictable mold. Once you start having hit singles, people kind of expect you to stay in that same groove."

Milsap found a niche somewhere between "Get It Up" and his signature ballads with the release of "Why Don't You Spend The Night." The album, *Milsap Magic*, was his first country LP recorded without the aid of longtime producer Tom Collins. Instead, Ronnie cut the entire project with Rob Galbraith, who had previously worked with Harry Chapin on the demo sessions for "Taxi."

Galbraith had become a key figure in Milsap's stable, and later headed up his publishing companies. His name was first introduced in Milsap's credits on "Nobody Likes Sad Songs" [see 345].

Despite an innovative production job, "Why Don't You Spend The Night" encountered a bit of difficulty. St. Petersburg's WSUN refused to play it, calling it "too suggestive." Remembers Milsap: "I talked to them on the phone and said, 'What about Conway singing "I'd Love To Lay You Down" [see 372]?' They said, 'Well, that indicates that the two of them are married.' I said, 'Well, what in the hell difference does that make?' They never did go for the record."

It was the only station, though, to take that stance, and the single hit number one on March 22, 1980.

372
I'D LOVE TO LAY YOU DOWN
CONWAY TWITTY
MCA 41174
Writer: Johnny MacRae
Producers: Conway Twitty, David Barnes
March 29, 1980 (1 week)

In 1980, Paul Harvey told Nashville's annual Country Radio Seminar that much of the material in circulation was "porno"-country. One of the then-current hits he apparently pointed to as an example was "I'd Love To Lay You Down."

Harvey wasn't alone in his assessment. Several country stations refused to play the record, despite Conway Twitty's defense. "It's not risqué," he told *Billboard*, "and it's certainly not a cheating song." "I would never touch anything that's filthy or without class," he further elaborated to the *Nashville Banner*'s Bill Hance. "But ["I'd Love To Lay You Down"] is not an off-color song. It's a love song about a couple who have been married for several years. I think the women who listen to the song recognize this fact. The men don't, and that's why some of the stations aren't playing it—the men are making the decisions."

When songwriter Johnny MacRae wrote it, he and frequent collaborator Bob Morrison had tried unsuccessfully to write a song for Johnny Duncan, who had earned some of his biggest successes with suggestive titles [see 281—"It Couldn't Have Been Any Better"]. Following a writing session, MacRae drove the 30-mile trip home, and in the privacy of his car, came up with the first verse and chorus of "I'd Love To Lay You Down."

The following morning, MacRae created the remainder of the song while jogging. He suggested that Morrison add a new melody, but Bob insisted that MacRae should keep what he had. He placed it with Conway, and, despite pockets of radio resistance, it still managed to hit number one.

"I think that probably a lot of women would like for somebody to feel that sentiment," MacRae suggests. "Love gets a little bit stale at times, and I think women just want to feel that they can still turn the guy on, even bein' a housewife. It's just about a guy still bein' in love.

"The title is just enough to catch attention. That's really all it serves. I think it goes deeper than something that's just a little smutty-assed title. It has more depth to it than that."

The record gave Conway the all-time lead when it became his twenty-ninth single to top *Billboard*'s country chart. His reward for the song? On occasion, he has been bombarded with women's underwear while singing it on stage.

373

SUGAR DADDY
THE BELLAMY BROTHERS
Warner Bros. 49160
Writer: David Bellamy
Producer: Michael Lloyd
April 5, 1980 (1 week)

When the Bellamy Brothers abandoned their pop formula [see 343—"If I Said You Have A Beautiful Body Would You Hold It Against Me"] and revamped their sound, they went back to their Florida roots to find a band. They remembered Ron & The Starfires, a Top 40/ R & B group that used to play clubs and dances all over the Sunshine State, particularly at the Dade City Teen Center.

The Bellamys asked the band to join them on the road. The group also supported the Bellamys in the recording studio, in contrast to the usual country method of using session musicians. Included in the new Bellamys lineup were bass player Jesse Chambers and his cousin, guitarist Carl Chambers. They played on *The Two and Only* and *You Can Get Crazy*, two albums that yielded "Beautiful Body," the

The Bellamy Brothers

Top Five follow-up "You Ain't Just Whistlin' Dixie," plus the chart-topping "Dancin' Cowboys" [see 388] and "Sugar Daddy."

On the latter tune, Carl's dirty guitar work, marked by heavy "finger noise," came through clearly. "We used to have people come up and say, 'I like that dog barking on that record,'" David laughs. "We'd say, 'Well, okay, whatever you heard,' but I think that's what they were listening to: the finger movement. They thought it was a dog or a cat or something."

"That was just me," shrugs Carl. "I don't know why I played it the way I did. It's just the way it came out, and it felt good at the time, and everybody seemed to like it."

The song itself came from the parking lot of a Howard Johnson's in Knoxville. "We were doing a radio show," David recalls. "The radio station had sent a car or a van or somethin' to come get us, and we were waiting on our limo to show up. I was sittin' there and I saw this girl and this guy arguing. They had the hood of her car up and they were tryin' to get her car running again. He said, 'You know, what you need is a new car,' and she said, 'No, what I need is a sugar daddy.'"

Even if the car didn't work, David was revved up from that spark, and the resulting single hit number one in April of 1980.

374

HONKY TONK BLUES
CHARLEY PRIDE
RCA 11912
Writer: Hank Williams
Producers: Jerry Bradley, Charley Pride
April 12, 1980 (1 week)

The concept of recording an entire album of Hank Williams songs was hardly a new one when Charley Pride released *There's a Little Bit of Hank in Me* in 1980. Hank Williams, Jr., Glen Campbell and Ray Price were among the performers who had previously saluted Williams in that manner, and Moe Bandy had already started his own Hank tribute album when Pride's hit the market.

Since the field had already been mined quite thoroughly, Pride and producer Jerry Bradley hoped to find material that hadn't been covered as often as "Your Cheatin' Heart" or "Cold, Cold Heart." They made an appointment with Ronnie Gant at Acuff-Rose Publishing, the company that held the rights to Hank's catalog.

"When Charley started singing 'Honky Tonk Blues,'" says Bradley, "I thought, 'Well, maybe it can happen.'" They located some of the musicians who had played with Williams during his career, and used them in a move toward authenticity. "We tried to get the original sound and feel," notes Pride, "and we accomplished it, I think."

John Schweers was commissioned to write the title track to *There's a Little Bit of Hank in Me*, which tied the album together musically. Pride settled on such frequently reworked classics as "I'm So Lonesome I Could Cry" and "Mind Your Own Business" [see 702], as well as less familiar titles like "Low Down Blues" and "I Could Never Be Ashamed Of You." The fast-paced "Honky Tonk Blues," featuring the Jordanaires on back-up vocals, represented the album's first single.

"I think [the key to] 'Honky Tonk Blues' was really the way Charley sold the song, the delivery," remarks Bradley. "If you really want to get picky, he had a little trouble with the 's' on it. It sounds like he's singing 'Honky Tonk Blue.' Nobody else ever heard it."

When "Honky Tonk Blues" reached number one on April 12, 1980, it was a historic occasion. It marked the first time that a cover version of one of Hank's songs had reached number one on the *Billboard* country chart.

Only once before had an artist even reached number two with a Hank Williams remake. Linda Ronstadt did it on March 15, 1975, with "I Can't Help It (If I'm Still In Love With You)" [see 212—"When Will I Be Loved"], featuring vocal support from Emmylou Harris.

375

IT'S LIKE WE NEVER SAID GOODBYE
CRYSTAL GAYLE
Columbia 11198
Writers: Roger Greenaway,
Geoff Stephens
Producer: Allen Reynolds
April 19, 1980 (1 week)

With the women's movement in full swing, a curious event occurred for the first time in *Billboard* history on April 19, 1980. On that date, each of the Top Five slots on the country chart was occupied by a female recording artist:

Women, of course, have been an artistic part of the record business since the very beginning. Some sources cite Ada Rehan as the first female recorded, some ten years after Thomas Edison invented the phonograph.

Among country performers, Mother Maybelle Carter might have been the first woman recorded, when she cut tracks with the Carter Family on August 1, 1927, in Bristol, Tennessee. Kitty Wells, who earned a number one record in 1952 with "It Wasn't God Who Made Honky Tonk Angels," is generally regarded as the first significant female solo act among country stars. She blazed the trail for future stars like Patsy Cline and Loretta Lynn, the first female Entertainer of the Year [see 120—"Rated 'X'"].

It's thus appropriate that Loretta's sister topped the chart when women finally dominated the upper echelon. "It's Like We Never Said Goodbye" came from a British songwriter, Roger Greenaway, who had co-written such pop hits as "Long Cool Woman (In A Black Dress)" and "You've Got Your Troubles" with Roger Cook [see 526—"Love Is On A Roll"].

"They'd sent us the tape," Crystal remembers, "and I was riding down the road, and the song came on. I really liked it a lot, and I thought it was my radio playing. It actually was my cassette, 'cause after that, something else came on I recognized. I said, 'What is this?' I just loved it, and I thought it was a song on the radio."

"It's Like We Never Said Goodbye" was Crystal's first number one single after moving from United Artists Records to Columbia. A prior release, "Half The Way," stalled at number two for three weeks, kept out of the top spot by Kenny Rogers' "You Decorated My Life" [see 359] and Waylon Jennings' "Come With Me" [see 360].

UA continued to release material during the transition period, netting three Top Ten records with "When I Dream" (number three), "Your Kisses Will" (number seven) and "Your Old Cold Shoulder" (number five).

376
A LESSON IN LEAVIN'
DOTTIE WEST
United Artists 1339
Writers: Randy Goodrum, Brent Maher
Producers: Brent Maher, Randy Goodrum
Date: April 26, 1980 (1 week)

Until her appearances with Kenny Rogers, people generally recognized Dottie West as a simple country girl. The association made sense, since her biggest record at that time was "Country Sunshine," a song she had originally written for Coca-Cola. It earned her a Clio award and, by popular demand, was released as a single in 1973.

"Country Sunshine" met with unfortunate timing. The record came out around the same time as two blockbuster singles titled "Paper Roses" [see 147] and "The Most Beautiful Girl" [see 148]. "Country Sunshine" stopped at number two on November 24, 1973.

Dottie followed that record with a remake of Diana Ross' "Last Time I Saw Him," hitting number eight, but she failed to connect with the Top Ten again until she hooked up with Kenny. That association netted her two number one singles before she notched her first chart-topper as a solo performer, "A Lesson In Leavin'," which provided listeners with a sharp, new, sassy Dottie.

"It's not like I'm doing anything now that I haven't been doing live since I began singing with Kenny," Dottie told *Billboard*'s Kip Kirby with the release of the *Special Delivery* album. "Kenny draws very sophisticated and contemporary fans, and I had to change my style to fit with him. The album is finally reflecting these changes."

Special Delivery marked West's first effort with Brent Maher and Randy Goodrum. The record company originally sought out Maher to give her a pop edge, and Brent—who'd never worked with country music before—brought in Goodrum to assist.

"'A Lesson In Leavin'' was the second tune that we wrote together," says Maher. "I think the song had a lot of charm to it. It was really quite different, because all the choruses change the lyrics. The chorus starts off the lyric, and by the time it gets to the second chorus, we used the same rhyme in the words, but used different lyrics, which is not your standard format for verse-chorus type songs.

"Then we got in the studio, and Randy and I

originally didn't have that funky, kind of half-time groove to it. We had more or less a straight-ahead country song, and Kenny Malone, the drummer, started playing this funky Paul Simon kind of a groove. Randy and I sort of fell off our seats."

377

ARE YOU ON THE ROAD TO LOVIN' ME AGAIN

DEBBY BOONE

Warner/Curb 49176
Writers: Bob Morrison, Debbie Hupp
Producer: Larry Butler
May 3, 1980 (1 week)

Debby Boone gained a lifelong association with a single song in 1977 when she recorded "You Light Up My Life." The record

Debby Boone

dominated pop music, sold more than four million copies worldwide and locked up the top of the *Billboard* Hot 100 for ten weeks. Unfortunately, its success was also hard to equal.

In addition to its accomplishments in the pop realm, "You Light Up My Life" provided Boone a foundation in country, peaking at number four. In the wake of her first success, she had difficulty recapturing any significant pop attention, and, in fact, her third single, "God Knows," actually charted higher in country music than in pop. As a result, Boone made a calculated attempt to garner further country successes.

"The country audience seemed to have its arms wide open to me," she told Bob Protzman of the Knight-Ridder News Service. "My grandfather was Red Foley, and maybe that caused the country people to like me."

Maybe they liked the pure image cultivated by the daughter of wholesome Pat Boone, or maybe they simply appreciated her smooth vocal delivery. Either way, her forays into country seemed to work.

In 1979, Debby went to number 11 with her remake of Connie Francis' pop hit, "My Heart Has A Mind Of Its Own," and a year later, she nabbed the number one position with "Are You On The Road To Lovin' Me Again." Producer Larry Butler and writers Bob Morrison and Debbie Hupp had all been involved a few months earlier on another number one record, Kenny Rogers' "You Decorated My Life" [see 359]. Hupp's name was misspelled on the Boone record as Debbie Hult.

"Actually, Debbie Hupp came in with the idea," Morrison recalls. "I put a melody first to it, and it wasn't very good. It was a relatively uneventful kind of thing. I fiddled around with it at home and finally got a melody that seemed like it had a little more inspiration involved."

"Are You On The Road To Lovin' Me Again" was one of thirteen songs that Butler submitted to Boone. She had to pick ten of them for an album, and she flew in to Nashville and did her parts in three days.

On the heels of "Are You On The Road . . . ," Boone realized a personal dream. She and husband Gabriel Ferrer (son of actor Jose Ferrer and singer Rosemary Clooney) welcomed their first baby, Jordan Alexander Ferrer, on July 8, 1980.

Boone eventually decided to discontinue her pursuit of a country career—she felt dishonest about it because it wasn't her first love. Instead, she has made at least two TV movies, and toured in a theatrical group.

378

BENEATH STILL WATERS

EMMYLOU HARRIS

Warner Bros. 49164
Writer: Dallas Frazier
Producer: Brian Ahern
May 10, 1980 (1 week)

In 1979, Emmylou Harris released *Blue Kentucky Girl*, an album with strong bluegrass overtones in an era of "crossover" country. Her record label was understandably nervous about the project, but gave her the freedom to go through with it.

"I believe *Blue Kentucky Girl* has a contemporary freshness in its sound," Emmy told *Billboard*'s Kip Kirby. "I think it captures the feeling that comes from the live side of music, of going out with the band. I've always pictured it like walking into a club and hearing songs like these, played by a little bluegrass band where the fiddle player stands up to take his solo break."

Harris' instincts proved successful, both artistically and commercially. Her remake of the Drifters' "Save The Last Dance For Me" ascended to number four; the title track climbed to number six. "Beneath Still Waters" got the nod as the third single.

Emmylou notes: "When I was living in D.C., there was like a secret George Jones society of people who would trade tapes like people trade baseball cards. Anytime you came across something that he had recorded, it was 'Well, have you heard this?'

"In one of those sort of trades, I got this tape. 'Beneath Still Waters' just seemed so classic, so simple, so straightforward and the imagery was beautiful. Also, the melody was so lovely. We cut that in that living room [see 313—"Two More Bottles Of Wine"]. I think it's the second take. It just was perfect."

Blue Kentucky Girl brought Emmylou the second of three Grammies for Best Country Vocal Performance by a Female. The others came for *Elite Hotel* and her 1984 single "In My Dreams." She also earned Grammies for her duet with Roy Orbison, "That Lovin' You Feelin' Again," and for the *Trio* project [see 721—"To Know Him Is To Love Him"].

Following *Blue Kentucky Girl*, Harris delved even more heavily into bluegrass sonorities, with the help of Ricky Skaggs, on *Roses in the Snow*. The package received overwhelming critical acclaim, yielding a Top Ten single with "Wayfaring Stranger" and a Top 20 success with "The Boxer."

379

GONE TOO FAR

EDDIE RABBITT

Elektra 46613
Writers: Even Stevens, Eddie Rabbitt, David Malloy
Producer: David Malloy
May 17, 1980 (1 week)

"Eddie Rabbitt's truly a stylist," says producer David Malloy, "and he knows the little tricks with his voice. He worked many, many hours on those things, and you'll notice on the *Loveline* album, his vocal texture was totally different. We worked on that whole album. I miked him from, like, six feet away. We worked on getting soft vocal sounds, and we really experimented a lot."

The efforts paid off handsomely. After "Suspicions" [see 349] soared to number one in August of 1979, "Pour Me Another Tequila" reached number five the following winter. With the turn of the decade, Rabbitt released the album's third single, "Gone Too Far."

"We wrote that song in the back seat of a car," Rabbitt remembers. "I had a guitar in my hand, and with a lot of the things that we've written together, I come up with these ideas and bring 'em to my partners, and we all get around and write them. We were on our way down to Muscle Shoals to record *Loveline*, and we put it together in the car."

Work on the song began the night before in Malloy's hotel room at the Spence Manor on Music Row. "We were tryin' to get a kind of Steely Dan effect," reports co-writer Even Stevens. "Of course, it was nothing like anything of theirs, but we were just goin' in the studio and experimentin' with a minimal amount of instruments and very clean playing."

"'Gone Too Far' had a jazzy little guitar part that Larry Byrom put on there," adds Malloy. "It was really more of a little pop song than anything. Then Eddie did his wonderful three-part harmonies.

"If Eddie had his way, he would have put harmonies on every line he ever sang in his life. I fought with him constantly to keep harmonies off. I think a lot of it was his insecurity, not thinking that he was a great enough singer—that he needed all those harmonies to make things work. I was always trying to pick and choose where to use them and where not to, so he didn't wear it all out."

"Gone Too Far" debuted in *Billboard* on March 15, 1980, hitting number one two months later.

380
STARTING OVER AGAIN
DOLLY PARTON
RCA 11926
Writers: Donna Summer, Bruce Sudano
Producer: Gary Klein
May 24, 1980 (1 week)

She's best-known as the Queen of Disco, but Donna Summer had a country trick up her sleeve when she wrote "Starting Over Again" with husband Bruce Sudano. The story of a middle-aged couple who break up after thirty years together, it provided a sensitive contrast to the pumping rhythms that characterized such disco singles as "Hot Stuff," "Bad Girls" and "Love To Love You Baby."

"I was surprised to find out that Donna Summer wrote that song," notes Dolly Parton. "That was a song that [producer] Gary Klein and [executive producer] Charles Koppelman brought to the project, and when I heard it, I thought it was great.

"I found out later that Donna Summer is one of the finest writers that I've ever heard, and not just in the disco scene, where she was really big at that time. She's really got a lot of talent, and I was real surprised. No matter what kind of songs she does, there is a lot of talent in that girl."

Gary had produced Summer's duet with Barbra Streisand, "Enough Is Enough (No More Tears)," six months earlier, and "Starting Over Again" proved fairly dramatic. Beginning with just Dolly and keyboard player Michael Omartian, the record built in volume of sound—and volume of musicians—before subsiding again at its conclusion.

"We got pretty dramatic with Dolly, because Dolly is very dramatic," Klein observes, "and I don't mean that in a comical sense. There's a very serious side to her, which I got to know very well. I thought that she could be more dramatic, in terms of the production of her records—not slick, really. A lot of this is perceived as slick, anything cute or out of the

norm, but it was very well thought-out, and very deliberate."

With Summer's name attached, it's not surprising that "Starting Over Again" reached number 36 on the *Billboard* Hot 100, even as it rose to number one on the country chart.

With *Dolly*'s name attached, nothing could be surprising. Born January 19, 1946 in Sevier County, Tennessee, she was the fourth of twelve children. They slept three or four per mattress, and in the wintertime, warmth was provided when one would wet the bed. Just after her thirty-first birthday, that same lady was headlining in Las Vegas.

381
MY HEART/SILENT NIGHT (AFTER THE FIGHT)
RONNIE MILSAP
RCA 11952
Writers: Charles Quillen, Don Pfrimmer/
John Schweers
Producers: Ronnie Milsap, Rob Galbraith
May 31, 1980 (3 weeks)

"Alaska is a place to get well," says songwriter Don Pfrimmer. "Spiritually and economically, you can get well there in a hurry."

Pfrimmer ought to know. A graduate of the University of Montana, he has headed there three different times during an odyssey in which he kept drifting back to Nashville to pursue songwriting. His initial trip to Music City came in 1973, but he didn't have his first hit until Mickey Gilley recorded "The Power Of Positive Drinkin'" in 1978. "That bought me a new car," laughs Pfrimmer, "and got me in debt, 'cause I thought it was easy. Then the dry spell came."

During that spell, Pfrimmer signed a writing deal with Tom Collins at Pi-Gem Music Publishing. Collins had been producing Ronnie Milsap, but they had temporarily gone separate ways by the time Pfrimmer appeared. Desperate for money, Don took his third trip to Alaska, replenishing his finances by working on the pipeline. During that trip, he continued writing, and Collins was able to persuade him to return.

"I got a long distance call from Tom, and he encouraged me to come to Nashville," Pfrimmer explains, " 'cause that's kind of where he thought I belonged. So I did, and I guess I wasn't back in town a month before Charles [Quillen] and I wrote 'My Heart.' "

Though he wasn't producing Ronnie, Collins still pitched "My Heart" to Milsap, who included it on his *Milsap Magic* album.

"I had no idea that record would even be released," Ronnie notes, "much less be number one for three weeks. I thought it was another album cut. That, in some ways, is kind of a clone of 'Back On My Mind Again' [see 345—"Nobody Likes Sad Songs"]. I was playin' around at the piano sayin', 'I need to do a song like that again,' and a couple days later, Charles Quillen [who wrote "Back On My Mind Again"] brought 'My Heart' in."

The record was released as a two-sided single, and Milsap thought the "B" side, "Silent Night (After The Fight)"—written by John Schweers after an argument with his wife about a cat—would be the hit. Instead, "My Heart" emerged as a pleasant surprise, one of only four records released during the '80s to spend three weeks at number one.

ONE DAY AT A TIME
CRISTY LANE

United Artists 1342
Writers: Marijohn Wilkin,
Kris Kristofferson
Producer: Jerry Gillespie
June 21, 1980 (1 week)

The minister must have been surprised when Marijohn Wilkin drove up for counseling in a brand new El Dorado and got out of her car in a mink coat. Her outside opulence masked an inner turmoil that was pulling her apart.

Wilkin was unable to admit her own alcoholism, but she did know that her husband relied too heavily on the bottle, and that he was having an affair. Their marriage was on the rocks.

Her mother had died of a stroke, her business partner, Hubert Long, had passed away,

Cristy Lane

and a friend who tended to her boat also died. On top of that, Dottie West was six months behind in paying back a loan. Things couldn't have gotten much worse.

The minister had never counseled anyone else before, and when Marijohn unloaded her burdens, he gave her some unusual advice. He suggested that she thank God for her problems.

Wilkin followed his advice while driving home, and her tears gave way to laughter as she realized how unbelievable her situation had become. When she got home, she sat down at her piano, and sang the first verse and chorus of "One Day At A Time." "It was literally," she says, "a cry for help."

She called Kris Kristofferson, who had recently had a hit with "Why Me" [see 135], and got him to help her wrap up the song. In 1974, Marilyn Sellars took the first version of "One Day At A Time" to number 19. The song became a gospel standard, but earned greater visibility when Cristy Lane reincarnated it six years later.

A one-time Peoria housewife, Cristy started her career when her husband, Lee Stoller, heard her singing while she was doing the dishes and decided she should be a pro. In 1972, Stoller moved to Nashville, where he started LS Records to market his wife, gaining four Top Ten releases before selling her contract to United Artists. In 1979, the Academy of Country Music named Cristy Lane the Top New Female Vocalist, and the following year, "One Day At A Time" became her only chart-topping single.

Inspired by the telemarketing success of Slim Whitman, Stoller used the song as the centerpiece of a TV-marketed gospel album, recorded in late 1980. It became the first religious LP ever to win the Ampex Golden Reel award for sales of a million copies.

383

TRYING TO LOVE TWO WOMEN
THE OAK RIDGE BOYS

MCA 41217
Writer: Sonny Throckmorton
Producer: Ron Chancey
June 28, 1980 (1 week)

When the Oak Ridge Boys first hit in country music, William Lee Golden was the member with the longest tenure. A native of

Brewton in L.A. (*Lower Alabama*), he joined the group in January of 1965, jumping from a local act, the Pilots Trio.

Considered the Oaks' visionary, Golden was the one who predicted their rise from gospel to country and, eventually, pop acceptance. In time, Golden also became the best-recognized member of the Oak Ridge Boys line-up. On Christmas of 1979, he stopped cutting his hair, and on Thanksgiving of 1980, he stopped trimming his beard. The result was a unique—and much-talked-about—mountain-man appearance.

Between those two image-altering dates, Golden claimed the lead vocal on "Trying To Love Two Women," the first chart-topping Oaks hit to feature him.

"There's a certain kind of song that we look for for each person," says Oak Ridge Boy Duane Allen. "For example, when we looked for songs for William Lee, we had to look for songs that he liked, and he usually picked his own leads. It wasn't a matter of me or anybody else discussing who would do it—it's just that when we heard that song, it sounded like William Lee."

Sonny Throckmorton wrote "Trying To Love Two Women" after a conversation with a neighbor, who confessed that he had been seeing two different women for some time, and was afraid his whole plan would backfire. He told Sonny that he feared he might be shot if one of them figured out the situation, and Throckmorton was immediately struck with the opening line: "Trying to love two women is like a ball and chain."

Once "Trying To Love Two Women" was completed, Throckmorton was actually embarrassed by the song ("I really thought it was a dog, to tell you the truth"), and sang it rather sheepishly for publisher Don Gant, who immediately loved it ("I thought Don was just having an off day"). "Throck" was surprised to find that the Oaks cut it. He was even more amazed when it made the *Together* album, and shocked when they released it as a single. Despite his lack of confidence in it, "Trying To Love Two Women" made a strong debut at number 48 in *Billboard* on April 19, 1980. It went all the way to number one in the summer, ten weeks later.

"After it was a hit and everything, I came to understand why people would like the song," Sonny laughs. "I don't guess I really knew how good the thought was."

The Oaks picked up two more hits from *Together*: "Heart Of Mine" and "Beautiful You" both reached number three.

384

HE STOPPED LOVING HER TODAY

GEORGE JONES

Epic 50867
Writers: Bobby Braddock, Curly Putman
Producer: Billy Sherrill
July 5, 1980 (1 week)

It took three years from the point of conception for "He Stopped Loving Her Today" to finally pay off for songwriters Bobby Braddock and Curly Putman. When it did, it became the most significant single in George Jones' career—more than 25 years after he first started making records.

Putman credits Braddock with the initial idea, although Bobby recalls that it started as a funereal joke.

"We were doing tongue-in-cheek things about 'If you think he looks natural now, you should have seen him two weeks ago,'" says Braddock, "that sort of thing. Then we got kind of serious about it."

"We had to find a way to get around the controversy of the guy being dead," adds Putman. "You do have to kind of have a little finesse."

Johnny Russell was the first to cut "He Stopped Loving Her Today," although Mercury Records refused to release it. The song ended up in the hands of producer Billy Sherrill, who liked the title and the concept but disapproved of what Braddock and Putman had done with it. Sherrill wanted a rewrite, so he called them and requested another verse, in which the woman in the relationship comes back for the man's funeral.

Once Sherrill gave the song his stamp of approval, he still had difficulty convincing Jones to cut it. Jones repeatedly dodged his producer's suggestions until February 6, 1980. Even after cutting it, Jones still doubted it. "As he left my office when I played him the dub, he said, 'Nobody will buy that morbid S.O.B.,'" Sherrill recalls. "I said, 'Okay, George, I'll bet you $100.' I won that one hands down."

Jones eventually paid up after the Fourth of July weekend, when "He Stopped Loving Her Today" reached number one. It also fared well on the awards circuit. Jones won a Grammy, and it earned Single of the Year honors from the Country Music Association, the Academy of Country Music and the *Music City News*.

"Billy Sherrill really believed in the song," says Braddock. "I thought it was pretty good, but not spectacular. George Jones' performance and Billy Sherrill's production have a hell of a lot to do with that record becoming a standard."

385

YOU WIN AGAIN

CHARLEY PRIDE

RCA 12002
Writer: Hank Williams
Producers: Jerry Bradley, Charley Pride
July 12, 1980 (1 week)

"It may seem unusual to you that I was a bit nervous going into the studio to make this album," Charley Pride wrote on the jacket of *There's a Little Bit of Hank in Me*. "After all, it's hardly my first. But it's like trying to describe what my first Opry appearance was like. The happiness, the fright, the awe of the legend itself. I kept thinking, 'I'm doing a legend, someone who's always held in a special place in country's heart.'"

The legend was Hank Williams, one of the first three inductees to the Country Music Hall of Fame when it was established in 1961.

Born September 17, 1923, in Mount Olive, Alabama, Hiram Hank Williams had to work in the streets at an early age, shining shoes and selling peanuts, because his ailing father was unable to fully provide for the family. While conducting business, young Hank learned guitar from a black street musician named Tee Tot.

In 1946, his career headed into full swing when he signed with Fred Rose at Acuff-Rose Publishing. He became one of country music's most prolific hitmakers, and within the next six years, he churned out 36 Top Ten records, including the self-penned standards "Cold, Cold Heart," "Hey, Good Lookin'," "Jambalaya" and "Your Cheatin' Heart."

"You Win Again," Pride's second single from the *Hank in Me* album [see 374—"Honky Tonk Blues"], was written out of Hank's uncontrollable passions for his wife.

"It was his love for Audrey, and his jealousy, that he was going through," says Hank's friend, June Carter Cash. "All of this time, he was turning out 'You Win Again' and 'I Can't Help It (If I'm Still In Love With You),' and pouring his heart out. It was a love that was so consumed with jealousy, and the genius of the man was so confused and mixed up."

When the marriage fell apart, Hank's life did, too. He was fired from the Opry in September of 1952, the same month he married 19-year-old Billie Jean Williams, who later became the wife of Johnny Horton.

Hank died in the back seat of a Cadillac at age 29 on January 1, 1953, headed for a show in Canton, Ohio. The official coroner's report listed the cause of death as a heart attack, though most believe it was either drugs or alcohol.

386

TRUE LOVE WAYS
MICKEY GILLEY
Epic 50876
Writers: Norman Petty, Buddy Holly
Producer: Jim Ed Norman
July 19, 1980 (1 week)

A new decade brought a new approach to Mickey Gilley's recording career. After gaining a national foothold—and seven number one records—with material that mirrored Jerry Lee Lewis, Gilley hooked up with a brand new producer, secured by his publicists, the Brokaw Company.

Jim Ed Norman's very first hit as a producer came with "Right Time Of The Night," a Jennifer Warnes single that reached number five on *Billboard*'s Hot 100 and number 17 on the country chart in 1977. Norman helped revitalize Anne Murray's career [see 337—"I Just Fall In Love Again"], and he also saw a chance to pump new life into Gilley's recording efforts as well.

Norman encouraged him to take more time in the studio, and to explore his potential as a balladeer. Mickey introduced the new sound with "True Love Ways," a song written and first recorded by the late Buddy Holly. The tune was written specifically for Holly's wife, Maria.

"There was an incredible night when *Urban Cowboy* was really starting to explode," remembers Sandy Brokaw. "We had Gilley's jeans coming out, and we played in Dallas/Fort Worth that night. Buddy Holly's widow came out that night, and she said that it was the best cut that anybody'd ever had on that tune. It was a special song to her, because that was the song that was out when he died."

When Gilley's version was released, a Dallas disk jockey took an interest in the similarities of both recordings, and was able to develop a composite that featured portions of each. "That deejay was really a Buddy Holly fan," notes Gilley, "and he said that there was something about the song that always caught him. He discovered that they were in the same key and basically in the same tempo, so he's got me and Buddy singing together, and at the time it was really eerie to me—the same way that it was eerie when I heard Hank Williams and Hank Williams, Jr., singing together on 'There's A Tear In My Beer' [see 734—"Born To Boogie"]."

Holly never appeared on *Billboard*'s country charts during his lifetime, although many of his records, including "Peggy Sue" and "That'll Be The Day," have since been embraced by country radio as "golden oldies." In 1978, Susie Allanson peaked at number seven with a cover of "Maybe Baby."

387

BAR ROOM BUDDIES
MERLE HAGGARD AND CLINT EASTWOOD
Elektra 46634
Writers: Milton Brown, Cliff Crofford, Steve Dorff, Snuff Garrett
Producer: Snuff Garrett
July 26, 1980 (1 week)

"I think you can say that Merle Haggard had a hit and sort of dragged me along," Clint Eastwood told *Rolling Stone*'s Tim Cahill in 1985, referring to his only number one single, "Bar Room Buddies." Merle apparently agreed.

"I almost prostituted myself in some ways," Haggard said in *Newsweek*. He elaborated even further to writer Greg Oates: "[Eastwood, who directed and starred in *Bronco Billy*] shouldn't sell his camera, I'll put it that way. I told him before we started, 'I hope you're a better singer than I am an actor,' but I believe I'm a better actor than he is a singer."

"Bar Room Buddies" appeared in *Bronco Billy*, a film in which Clint portrayed Billy, the owner and star of a traveling Wild West show. Unlike some of his earlier pictures, including *Dirty Harry* and *The Outlaw Josey Wales*, *Bronco Billy* put Eastwood in a more humorous, almost cute, role, one which the critics seemed to appreciate. Apparently, the public wasn't so thrilled about the picture; the soundtrack's three singles fared much better.

Merle Haggard &
Clint Eastwood

Three of the four songwriters of "Bar Room Buddies" had also collaborated eighteen months earlier on the title track from another Eastwood film, *Every Which Way But Loose* [see 335]. Producer Thomas "Snuff" Garrett commissioned "Buddies" for a specific scene in *Bronco Billy*.

"Snuff actually had asked us to write kind of a beer-drinking, buddy-buddy song," explains Steve Dorff, "and Milton Brown wrote the lion's share of that lyric. I did the music, and then we all kind of finished it up."

Initially, the song was intended as a duet between Eastwood and George Jones, but schedules and legal entanglements got in the way, and Haggard became the producers' second choice. Merle also contributed one more single, "Misery And Gin," to the soundtrack. In fact, "Misery" was released on July 5, and scooted to number 31 the week that "Bar Room Buddies" reached the top. "Misery and Gin" eventually peaked at number three.

Eastwood, who credits a Bob Wills concert with introducing him to country music, entered the *Billboard* country chart on two other occasions. In late 1980, he teamed up with Ray Charles on "Beers To You," from the movie

Any Which Way You Can, peaking at number 55. In 1984, he joined T.G. Sheppard for "Make My Day" [see 552—"Slow Burn"], a novelty record that hit number 12.

388

DANCIN' COWBOYS
THE BELLAMY BROTHERS
Warner Bros. 49241
Writer: David Bellamy
Producer: Michael Lloyd
August 2, 1980 (1 week)

Until they were teenagers, Howard Bellamy (born February 2, 1946) and his brother David (September 16, 1950) lived in a Darby, Florida, farmhouse that had neither a telephone nor a television. They did have a radio, though, which David won in a contest, and they found their entertainment in trying to play guitar along with the songs they picked up.

In 1958, they performed in public for the first time, along with their father, Homer, at

Mickey Gilley

the Rattlesnake Roundup in nearby San Antonio, Florida, twenty miles north of Tampa. In 1965, David began playing organ in an R & B act called the Accidents, which opened shows for the likes of Percy Sledge and Little Anthony & The Imperials. Three years later, the Bellamys moved to Atlanta, where they joined a group called Jericho.

"We were with a booking agency out of there," David notes, "and we worked most of the barrooms all over the Southeast. We'd go from Charleston to Atlanta to Birmingham, then over to Mobile and Tallahassee. We used to work all the Southeastern honky-tonks for a week at a time."

They stayed with that band for three years, playing with acts like Brewer & Shipley and the Allman Brothers. The brothers also got their first taste of the recording studio, working with Rodney Mills, whose credits as a producer/engineer include the Classics IV, .38 Special and the Atlanta Rhythm Section. In 1973, David earned a pop hit as the songwriter on Jim Stafford's "Spiders And Snakes."

With that variety of musical styles behind them, Howard and David finally found their niche in country music, and in 1980, their third number one single, "Dancin' Cowboys," paid homage to the lifestyle that evolved.

"That song was sort of an autobiographical song of where we were at, at the time," David explains. "We were like hard and heavy, hittin' the honky-tonk circuit, and it was about the time that *Urban Cowboy* was fixin' to come in, and it was just where we and the band were at that period—on the honky-tonk circuit."

The Bellamys rode "Dancin' Cowboys" (and "singin' horses") onto the *Billboard* country chart at number 66 on May 24, 1980. Ten weeks later, the record galloped to number one.

389
STAND BY ME
MICKEY GILLEY
Full Moon 46640
Writers: Jerry Leiber, Mike Stoller,
Ben E. King
Producer: Jim Ed Norman
August 9, 1980 (1 week)

Gilley's nightclub provided the centerpiece for a movement that became a major trend of the early '80s. "It's just a honky-tonk, but it looks as big as the MGM Grand Hotel or St.

Patrick's Cathedral," wrote Aaron Latham in a 1978 *Esquire* piece titled "The Ballad of the Urban Cowboy."

Record executive Irving Azoff acquired rights from the magazine to use the story as the basis for the movie *Urban Cowboy*, through which John Travolta helped build an already growing interest in Western themes and fashions. A two-album set, the soundtrack used a multiformat approach, featuring such diverse talents as Joe Walsh, Boz Scaggs, Bob Seger, Bonnie Raitt, Linda Ronstadt and Mickey Gilley.

"The album grossed more than $26 million in the U.S. alone," Azoff told the *New York Times* in 1981. "It was Warner Communications' largest-grossing album [in 1980], and I believe it was more profitable than the movie. As a matter of fact, I think it carried the movie."

Urban Cowboy popularized the mechanical bull, a rodeo aid adapted for entertainment at Gilley's. Manager Sherwood Cryer had installed the bull at the club—in spite of Gilley's protests—and it became an immediate sensation. Cryer bought out the rights to manufacture and sell the machine, and clubs all over the country purchased the mechanical bulls at $7,495 apiece.

That fad lasted only a short time, but Gilley's major musical contribution to the film made a lasting impression. Though Epic released "True Love Ways" [see 386] first, Gilley's session on "Stand By Me" was his first with new producer Jim Ed Norman, who matched the song to the movie.

First cut by Ben E. King in 1961, "Stand By Me" was a test of the new artist/producer pairing. During his days with Playboy Records, Gilley had gotten used to recording three songs during each three-hour session. By contrast, Norman worked methodically on "Stand By Me" for more than two days. Gilley was incensed by the third day and stormed out of the studio. Norman pieced together the single from the tracks he had already recorded, and the result was one of Gilley's biggest records ever.

The record debuted at number 63 on Billboard's country chart on May 31, 1980. It crossed over to number 22 on *Billboard*'s Hot 100 (it appeared on the pop chart two weeks before its country debut), and on July 26, 1980, "Stand By Me" and "True Love Ways" gave Gilley the rare accomplishment of having two solo records in country's Top Five simultaneously.

390
TENNESSEE RIVER
ALABAMA
RCA 12018
Writer: Randy Owen
Producers: Harold Shedd, Larry McBride, Alabama
August 16, 1980 (1 week)

On April 12, 1980, a quartet from Fort Payne, Alabama, reached number 17 on the *Billboard* country chart with "My Home's In Alabama" on independent MDJ Records. The day before, RCA signed that same act, Alabama, and within a month, put an album and a new single on the street. Like "My Home's In Alabama," "Tennessee River" paid homage to the group's Southern roots.

"That song was written really from what I thought would be good for a band to do, especially a Southern band," explains Randy Owen, who composed it several years earlier. "I remembered goin' to First Monday, over at Scottsboro, Alabama, which is really like a Trade Day. People take their dogs and their cats and their plows and their peanuts, whatever they've got to sell, and they take 'em to First Monday.

"We drove up and down Sand Mountain. We'd go up to Lookout Mountain, across Fort Payne, to Sand Mountain, and there's the Tennessee River as you're drivin' into Scottsboro. I always looked at the boys on Lookout Mountain kind of like they were mountain men. That's where we lived and everything, so it was kind of like 'Tennessee River and a mountain man/We get together any time we can.'"

While the first verse reviewed his childhood, then-single Owen moved toward a view of the future in the third verse, with hopes for a family. Responding to concerns of producer Harold Shedd and RCA that the track was too long, Alabama deleted the second verse for the single.

"The big thing about the song to me, was to be able to do a little Southern-rock fiddle," says Randy. "At that time, Jeff Cook had just begun to mess with the fiddle a little bit, and I wanted to do the little pick-up we've done on so many songs that's worked so wonderfully."

"Tennessee River" ended one era for Alabama and began a new one. On July 12, the group played its last show at The Bowery in Myrtle Beach, ending a seven-year association with the club. A month later, Alabama became the first band to top the chart with its major label debut.

"The middle verse, to me it didn't make as much sense without that in there," admits a still-amazed Owen. "But what do I know? It's a number one record."

391
DRIVIN' MY LIFE AWAY
EDDIE RABBITT

Elektra 46656
Writers: Eddie Rabbitt, Even Stevens, David Malloy
Producer: David Malloy
August 23, 1980 (1 week)

"Bands make it rock, but the roadies make it roll."

That's the phrase used in billing the 1980 movie *Roadie*, starring Meatloaf and Art Carney. In the end, the film was a flop, but the soundtrack earned substantial attention, with cuts by artists ranging from Pat Benatar to Teddy Pendergrass to Roy Orbison & Emmylou Harris [see 27—"Only The Lonely"] to Eddie Rabbitt, who contributed "Drivin' My Life Away."

Rabbitt plus co-writers Even Stevens and David Malloy first got involved after a call from Steve Wax, a former Elektra executive in charge of the movie's music. He didn't provide Rabbitt with a script or much of an explanation of how the song would be used.

Rabbitt told *Billboard*'s Kip Kirby they had to write "a driving kind of song, not particularly a truck-driving song or a car-driving song, but a song that was just simple . . . about driving. It's not easy writing a song about driving without mentioning a truck, a car or a bus."

They took time out from work on the *Horizon* album to fashion the song, using the roadies' lifestyle as a guide. It took three days of intense effort at their 16th Avenue office in Nashville. "We talked about the roadies themselves," explains Malloy. " 'Who are these guys? They're in these trucks, they drive all the time,' and just kind of got right into it.

"The song really is one step away from 'Subterranean Homesick Blues.' One day, they were playing the old Bob Dylan cut, and my little girl—at the time I think she was nine or ten—comes runnin' in. She says, 'Dad, dad, somebody stole your song.' I laughed so hard,

but if you think about that guitar rhythm, it's fashioned after the Dylan record very much."

After the song was finished, Rabbitt and company were so pleased with the results that they talked Elektra into allowing them to record it for both *Roadie* and the *Horizon* package.

"That was the most magic moment in the studio I've ever heard," reports Stevens. "Everybody was just so good, and the air got absolutely liquid when we were recordin' that. It was so good. I think we got it on the first take."

Though it received minimal exposure in the film, "Drivin' My Life Away" topped the country chart and became Rabbitt's first Top Five single on *Billboard*'s Hot 100.

392
COWBOYS AND CLOWNS/MISERY LOVES COMPANY
RONNIE MILSAP

RCA 12006
Writers: Steve Dorff, Snuff Garrett, Gary Harju, Larry Herbstritt/Jerry Reed
Producers: Snuff Garrett/Ronnie Milsap, Rob Galbraith
August 30, 1980 (1 week)

Ronnie Milsap's fifteenth number one single was his first recorded in Los Angeles. Four writers, including producer Snuff Garrett and Steve Dorff, fashioned "Cowboys And Clowns" specifically for the Clint Eastwood film *Bronco Billy*.

Like Merle Haggard, Milsap cut two songs for the movie, "Cowboys And Clowns" and the title track. Though both of Hag's performances translated to singles, Milsap had only one, but it intertwined even further with Merle's work.

"We actually did 'Bar Room Buddies' [see 387] and 'Cowboys And Clowns' and 'Misery And Gin' all on the same session, in terms of cutting the tracks," Dorff explains. "We had Milsap come in, and Haggard came in on another day, and we did them all at the old RCA Studio on Sunset Boulevard. We cut all the tracks live, and Milsap played on 'Cowboys And Clowns,' which was fun. We did him on one day, and then Haggard came in the next day or a day after that, and did his vocals."

Warner Bros. premiered the film on May 9, 1980, in New Orleans, where one of the highlights included Milsap playing piano while Eastwood and Haggard attempted to perform "Bar Room Buddies." Neither could remember the lyrics, so they fumbled their way through with the aid of cue cards.

"Buddies" made its chart debut that week, and five weeks later, "Cowboys And Clowns" made its first appearance in *Billboard*, on June 21. On August 2, they brushed closely within the Top Ten. Haggard & Eastwood appeared at number four, while Milsap closed in at number six. Four weeks later, Ronnie had a number one single.

The similarities to Haggard's record don't end there. Like Merle, Milsap thought the record could have been stronger.

"I never did feel that I accomplished the kind of performance that I was lookin' for," he says. "I went in and did it according to their schedule. I'd never done anything in Los Angeles before, and I guess I was a little bit anxious to please everybody. My performance on that is not something that I'm too proud of."

393

LOOKIN' FOR LOVE
JOHNNY LEE
Full Moon 47004
Writers: Bob Morrison, Wanda Mallette, Patti Ryan
Producer: John Boylan
September 6, 1980 (3 weeks)

Johnny Lee was hardly a well-known quantity on New Year's Day, 1980, but with the advent of *Urban Cowboy*, he quickly became country music's biggest surprise of the year. Lee was a regular performer at Mickey Gilley's club in Pasadena, Texas, and when the John Travolta picture was released, Lee's major contribution, "Lookin' For Love," was picked up by many radio stations even before it came out as a single.

Songwriter Bob Morrison characterizes "Lookin' For Love" as a "quirky" song, one put together and eventually recorded in unusual circumstances. Wanda Mallette and Patti Ryan taught second grade, and a common look on many of their students' faces—a certain need for love and attention—spurred the title. They took a more adult approach in fleshing out the remainder of the tune, and Ryan sent Morrison a copy through the mail.

"The problem I had with it was the melodic

structure in the chorus," says Morrison. "I felt that they went away from what they basically had, so what I did was tighten it up."

Once they had completed the song via the post office, Morrison cut a demo, but 21 different performers all rejected the composition. At that point, Morrison sent a copy to a friend in California, who took a shot in the dark. "He dropped it off in a big bin of music for *Urban Cowboy*," Morrison notes, "and it got picked out of this big bushel basket and became the centerpiece song quite by accident. We still might be pitching it and having it rejected had that not happened."

"Lookin' For Love" still faced obstacles, though, because after it was recorded, the master tape disappeared. "I'd already done my part in the movie then," remembers Lee, "singing this song from a copy of the tape, but we had to go back and re-record it, and make

Johnny Lee

sure it was exactly the same tempo and everything as the first one we did. To this day, I still don't know if it was somebody's mistake and nobody ever 'fessed up to it, or what the deal was."

"Lookin' For Love" began a three-week stay at number one on September 6, 1980, and two weeks later, it peaked on *Billboard*'s Hot 100 at number five, gaining certification November 11 as a million-selling single.

Says Lee in retrospect: "It made my career."

394
OLD FLAMES CAN'T HOLD A CANDLE TO YOU
DOLLY PARTON
RCA 12040
Writers: Pete Sebert, Hugh Moffatt
Producer: Gary Klein
September 27, 1980 (1 week)

"So many of country things sound corny," says producer Gary Klein, "but to me, country music deals with real basic emotions. Everybody can understand country, and I think that's what makes it attractive to people who live in areas other than the country. Even in New York, so many people like country music because you can understand it. There's a message in it, and it's pretty straightforward. Everybody experiences the feelings of country songs."

A rather simple feeling was embedded in the extremely corny title "Old Flames Can't Hold A Candle To You," but the song worked well enough that it actually succeeded twice. Joe Sun, who worked as a promotion man for the Kendalls and Ovation Records on "Heaven's Just A Sin Away" [see 295], released it in 1978, peaking at number 14.

"Old Flames" caught the ear of Carl Dean when he was listening to the radio one day, and he suggested to his wife, Dolly Parton, that she might want to cut it herself.

"We're always hearing things somewhere else," she explains. "He came home one day and said, 'I heard this song on the radio that I think you ought to hear. I don't know if it's a big hit or not now, but I think that song will be a big hit.'

"Carl's not in the music business at all, and he don't ever get involved in anything that I do, but he does love music. He's not a big country

fan. He flips the radio around—he likes bluegrass, black blues, acid rock, heavy metal, but he's not a big country fan. He was just listening to the radio. He heard this song and just loved it, and so I got it and recorded it."

Dean apparently has a good ear. Dolly's rendition featured her brother, Randy, and Herb Pedersen, who would later join the Desert Rose Band, on back-up vocals. When it peaked in the fall of 1980, it gave her a total of a dozen solo number one records.

Dolly met her husband on the first day she moved to Nashville [see 71—"Joshua"], while doing her clothes at the Wishy Washy laundromat. Two years later, to the day, they were married. A Nashville contractor, Carl Dean remains a reclusive figure in her life—so reclusive, in fact, that his absence from the public eye has become legendary.

395
DO YOU WANNA GO TO HEAVEN
T.G. SHEPPARD
Warner Bros. 49515
Writers: Curly Putman, Bucky Jones
Producer: Buddy Killen
October 4, 1980 (1 week)

The summer of 1980 was one of the hottest in American history, as the city of Dallas, in particular, set a record with 29 consecutive days of temperatures over 100 degrees. Ironically, it was an excellent summer for T.G. Sheppard, who soaked up two back-to-back hits that banked on cool water as a thematic tool.

The first was "Smooth Sailin'," which peaked at number six during the early part of the summer months. Written by Sonny Throckmorton and Curly Putman, the single entered the *Billboard* country charts on April 5. As the single ascended, Throckmorton and Putman earned the Academy of Country Music's Song of the Year award on May 1, for their 1979 Moe Bandy single, "It's A Cheatin' Situation."

Putman also wrote the follow-up to "Smooth Sailin'," Sheppard's fifth number one single, "Do You Wanna Go To Heaven." "Kenny Rogers was hitting big with 'Lucille,' and 'The Gambler' [see 330]," notes Sheppard. "I wanted a record that had sort of a gimmick, as far as the sounds inside of the music. I wanted a great story song."

As it came time for Sheppard to record the *Smooth Sailin'* album, he had an appointment at Tree Publishing with producer Buddy Killen, and Putman was aware of that meeting when he arose in the morning. Weaving baptism and sex together metaphorically, Curly started writing "Do You Wanna Go To Heaven" at home.

"I normally don't do that," says Putman. "Once I'm away from the office, I try to forget it. But, before I came into work, I was fooling around with it a little bit. I had quite a bit of it written, and Buddy and T.G. were together upstairs [at Tree] listening to songs."

Unable to finish what he'd started, Putman turned to fellow songwriter Bucky Jones for help. "I went to lunch, and when I got back, Bucky had finished up a verse that we needed. In the meantime, I went up and sang it for Buddy and T.G., and they liked it immediately. If I'm not mistaken, they cut it that night or the next day."

396

LOVING UP A STORM

RAZZY BAILEY

RCA 12062
Writers: Danny Morrison, Johnny Slate
Producer: Bob Montgomery
October 11, 1980 (1 week)

"Stormy" is an apt description of Razzy Bailey's personal life in 1976. He earned $40,000-50,000 annually by playing "covers" with nightclub bands, but he wallowed in frustration—in that setting, he could never establish his own musical identity.

Bailey had taken to alcohol to assuage his grief, and his marriage ended up on the rocks. He and wife Sandra sought marital help, and when the counselor agreed that she had no choice but to leave Bailey, Razzy mended his ways. Shortly after, they met Cassadaga, Florida, psychic June Mahoney, who predicted that one of his songs would become a hit.

Razzy remained skeptical, but shortly afterward, Dickey Lee cut his composition "9,999,999 Tears" [see 229—"Rocky"], which rose to number three. Record producer/publisher Bob Montgomery felt strongly about Bailey's potential, and worked out an agreement with RCA Nashville division head Jerry Bradley for a four-side contract. The first release under that agreement, "What Time Do

You Have To Be Back To Heaven," reached number nine in 1978.

With four more Top Ten releases behind him, Bailey recorded "Loving Up A Storm," a "cheatin'" song that Danny Morrison and Johnny Slate wrote with the Kendalls in mind.

"Originally, I didn't want to write that song," Morrison remembers. "Johnny thought it was a hit title, and it had been used a lot, and it kind of just evolved. Even after we'd gotten it written, I still wasn't sure that it was a hit song, but the more and more after we got it demoed, I got to where I had a particular fondness for it."

The Kendalls turned it down, but Razzy was interested immediately.

"I heard that song and told Bob Montgomery that I'd like to cut it," Razzy notes, "and he said, 'Well, I don't think you ought to do that kind of song, 'cause we've been doin' positive love songs. I don't know if it's a hit or not for you.' I talked him into lettin' me do it anyway."

Bailey recorded "Loving Up A Storm" for his eponymous album, dedicated to Sandra. During a show at The Palomino Club in Los Angeles, his hunch about the song was confirmed when he received word that the record would be number one in *Billboard*'s October 11, 1980, issue.

397

I BELIEVE IN YOU

DON WILLIAMS

MCA 41304
Writers: Roger Cook, Sam Hogin
Producers: Don Williams, Garth Fundis
October 18, 1980 (2 weeks)

Don Williams once told an audience that "I Believe In You" had "more lyrics that I personally believe in and felt right about than any other song I've ever sung." And rightfully so—Williams created several of the lyrics while he was in the studio.

Songwriter Roger Cook originated "I Believe In You," and held onto the first version for about a year. He remained unhappy with the lyrics, however, and in 1979, he asked fellow songwriter Sam Hogin to help him rewrite it. "He and I sat up until about 5:00 in the morning," says Cook. "We hammered this lyric backwards and forwards until we thought we had something really tight."

The song took shreds of thought from social, political and economic issues and combined them into a simple personal statement. Even with the time they had invested, though, it went through several more alterations, beginning with the demo session. There, they finished up the second verse while they ran it down with the musicians.

Cook played it for producer Garth Fundis, who in turn played it for Williams at the end of a working day in the studio. "I put it on and didn't build any fanfare to it," Fundis recalls. "He sat there at the console and just closed his eyes, and didn't move, listened to the whole song, and as soon as it was over, he just turned to me and said, 'Play it again.'"

Musically, they copied the Cook/Hogin demo almost note for note, but they changed several of the phrases in the original version, including "I believe in rock and roll," "sometimes I don't give a damn" and "the rising cost of getting high." Don also asked the writers for one more change.

"There was not a bridge in that song, until they recorded it," notes Hogin. "A couple days before, they wanted a bridge in the middle part, 'I know with all my certainty . . .,' that part."

"I Believe In You" became Williams' biggest record ever. In addition to topping the country chart, it also hit number 24 on *Billboard*'s Hot 100. On December 2, 1980, *I Believe in You* was certified as his second gold album, and the following October, the Country Music Association named it the Album of the Year.

398
THEME FROM THE DUKES OF HAZZARD (GOOD OL' BOYS)
WAYLON JENNINGS
RCA 12067
Writer: Waylon Jennings
Producer: Richie Albright
November 1, 1980 (1 week)

When work on *Urban Cowboy* [see 389— "Stand By Me"] began, Waylon Jennings was offered several opportunities to take part, either on camera or on the soundtrack. He turned down the producers.

He did get involved, though, in a TV show, "The Dukes of Hazzard," which went on the air with John Schneider [see 594—"I've Been Around Enough To Know"] and Tom Wopat in the leading roles. Jennings worked as the nar-

rator, commonly called "the balladeer," having already contributed to the film that launched it.

"I did a movie called *Moonrunners*," says Waylon, "which had some of the same characters—not the same actors—but it had Uncle Jessie, and Bo and Luke, and I think three or four of them, Roscoe P. Coltrane. I did all the music for the movie, and I also did the narration over the balladeer thing for that. So when they did the spin-off from it, and started the 'Dukes of Hazzard' thing, they called me and asked me if I'd be the balladeer on the pilot."

Once the program went on the air, Jennings had to record new narrations for each new plot, a requirement that cut into his own musical activities. He taped his voice-overs in radio stations all over the country as he toured, or even on the bus. His only on-camera work, though, featured a shot of Waylon, below the neck, with his guitar, while he sang the opening theme.

"They called me and asked me to do that song," he remembers, "so I wrote the song, and sent it out, and they called me back and said, 'We need something in there about bein' modern-day Robin Hoods and fightin' the system.' I just changed a rhyme line, and said, 'fightin' the system like two modern-day Robin Hoods,' so they were happy."

The theme was solid enough that Jennings cut two different versions. One went out over the airwaves every Friday night; the other was featured on his *Music Man* album and released as a single. "Good Ol' Boys" easily hit the top of the country charts, and also became his biggest pop hit, peaking at number 21 on the *Billboard* Hot 100. On December 9, 1980, it was certified as his only million-selling single.

399
ON THE ROAD AGAIN
WILLIE NELSON
Columbia 11351
Writer: Willie Nelson
Producer: Willie Nelson
November 8, 1980 (1 week)

"I think [Willie Nelson] will go down as one of the greatest, if not *the* greatest songwriter ever in country music . . . even greater than Hank Williams," Waylon Jennings told Robert Hilburn in *Billboard*. "He can write the most complex song . . . that will shoot over most people's heads, and then he will turn around and write a little song like 'On The Road Again' that everyone can appreciate."

Willie wrote "On The Road Again," along with several other songs, specifically for Warner Bros.' $11-million picture *Honeysuckle Rose*. Executive producer Sydney Pollack tapped Nelson for the lead after they worked together on *The Electric Horseman* [see 370—"My Heroes Have Always Been Cowboys"].

Willie lacked motivation for writing prior to the picture, but *Honeysuckle Rose* reinvigorated his pen. He started "On The Road Again" during a plane trip with Pollack and director Jerry Schatzberg. They told Nelson they needed a song about touring, and Willie immediately wrote out a perfect four-line chorus on the nearest available paper, to the astonishment of his fellow travelers.

"Even if I had already thought up the song before I got on the plane, I wouldn't have admitted it to Sydney and Jerry," Nelson wrote in his autobiography. "I liked seeing the surprise in their faces. But the fact is, it had never occurred to me until I said those first four words."

The song had no melody for several months, until the day he recorded it in the midst of filming. Willie wanted "On The Road Again" to serve as the movie's title, and several were considered, including *Sad Songs and Waltzes* and *A Song for You*, before *Honeysuckle Rose* came out the winner. The picture emerged on video, however, as *On the Road Again*.

The single debuted in *Billboard* on August 30, 1980, at number 58, and ten weeks later, it topped the country list, while soaring to number 20 on the Hot 100. "On The Road Again" became a signature song for Willie, who, one year earlier, told *Billboard*'s Gerry Wood he had a love/hate relationship with traveling.

"After every tour, I swear it'll be my last. But after I'm home for a couple days, I'm ready to go back on the road."

Willie Nelson

400
COULD I HAVE THIS DANCE
ANNE MURRAY
Capitol 4920
Writers: Wayland Holyfield, Bob House
Producer: Jim Ed Norman
November 15, 1980 (1 week)

"If you go to a social event," says songwriter Wayland Holyfield, "and people ask what you do, and you say you write songs, the inevitable question is: 'Have you written anything that I've heard?' Before 'Could I Have This Dance,' I hated that. Now, I can say 'Could I Have This Dance,' and from a cocktail-party point of view, I'm glad I wrote that."

Actually, Holyfield had already written six number one country records, but the acquaintances who didn't listen to country were left unimpressed by those earlier titles. "Could I Have This Dance" went to number 33 on the Hot 100, giving it wider familiarity.

Part of its "crossover" success can be traced to the *Urban Cowboy* movie [see 389—"Stand By Me"], where "Could I Have This Dance" appeared in the wedding scene. Anne Murray's producer, Jim Ed Norman, was introduced to the song while working with Mickey Gilley at his nightclub. *Urban* music supervisor Becky Shargo couldn't get the film's producer, Irving Azoff, or its director, James Bridges, interested in it, but she played the song for Jim Ed, who fell in love with it immediately.

"I called Irving," notes Norman, "and I think by that time, I'd already embellished it to Anne Murray and Kenny Rogers doing a duet. I don't think Irving even knew what song I was talking about, but it came down to, 'Yeah, if you can get Anne Murray and Kenny Rogers, I'll use it.'"

The first step in production was to work up a demo that would feature the two artists in a rough performance, but discussions with Rogers' management went less smoothly than Norman had hoped. Instead, Murray sang the male lead part and her own harmony, and Jim Ed took that to Azoff and Bridges as a sample of the song's potential.

"They liked it the way it was," Murray remembers. "I said, 'Wait just a second, that was supposed to be a guide track.' I was singing so low because it was for a man's voice. Well, they loved it; they wanted to put it out the way it was, so I said, 'Okay, whatever.'"

Urban Cowboy's backdoor hit has since become a frequent wedding theme.

"That's the most satisfying thing to me," adds Holyfield. "The reason we all started writing was to be able to touch people."

401

LADY
KENNY ROGERS
Liberty 1380
Writer: Lionel Richie
Producer: Lionel Richie
November 22, 1980 (1 week)

The old adage "quit while you're ahead" fits Kenny Rogers during the year 1980. Five years after he first teamed up with producer Larry Butler, Kenny had become the biggest draw in the country music business, and he chose that period to end his artist/producer relationship with Butler.

The year began with "Coward Of The County" [see 364] hitting number one in country and number three pop. A duet with Kim Carnes, "Don't Fall In Love With A Dreamer," surged to number three and number four, respectively; and "Love The World Away," from

the *Urban Cowboy* soundtrack, hit number four and number 14.

His record label prepared a *Greatest Hits* album for the pre-Christmas buying frenzy, and while on top of his game, Kenny looked for a method to energize his creativity. While ending his tenure with Butler, he found a new producer, surprising many by teaming with Lionel Richie from the R & B act the Commodores.

Rogers was enamored with the Commodore hits "Three Times A Lady" and "Easy," and contacted Motown Records founder Berry Gordy to see if the band might be interested in working with him. Gordy conveyed the message to the Commodores, who had been forced to cancel a 96-day concert tour after drummer Walter Orange had a motorcycle accident.

With time on his hands, Lionel flew to meet with Kenny in Las Vegas, where they talked about—among other things—the relationship between Kenny and his wife, Marianne. Richie finished up two songs he had begun a couple of years earlier; one of them, "Lady," he tailored specifically to Rogers' marriage. Both songs ("Goin' Back To Alabama" was the other one) were later cut at Concorde Recording Center in Los Angeles.

"Kenny was so genuine," Richie told Tim Walter in *Billboard*. "I see now why he is where he is. Forget about this superstar stuff—he rolled up his sleeves and said, 'Whatever it [takes] . . . just tell me.'

"I produced Kenny standing side by side with him in the booth. To do two songs, he spent eight-and-a-half hours in that booth and never really took a break. But we got 'em both in one night, and he did a heck of a job."

The result: Kenny's fourth million-selling single, his tenth number one country record, and his first to top *Billboard*'s Hot 100.

402

IF YOU EVER CHANGE YOUR MIND
CRYSTAL GAYLE
Columbia 11359
Writers: Parker McGee, Bob Gundry
Producer: Allen Reynolds
November 29, 1980 (1 week)

Which aspect of Crystal Gayle attracts the most attention? Her compelling vocal quality? Her ability to find strong material? The answer: her hair.

Rarely does one run across an interview with Crystal in which the topic isn't discussed. At times, she has allowed her locks to grow so long that two inches would drag on the ground, but as a rule, she tries to keep it three inches above her heel. As *People* once noted, her hair is just one inch shorter than "Little" Jimmy Dickens!

"It just turned into my trademark," she quipped to Joe Edwards of the Associated Press. "I saw this one person with hair to her knees and that's what I wanted."

While on tour, she washes it every day; when at home, she goes through the ritual every other day. Shampooing and conditioning takes only 20 minutes, but she lets it dry naturally, and that requires about five hours.

Though her hair has contributed to an identifiable visual image, Crystal has profited more by combing through an endless stream of demo tapes in search of the perfect material. While many of the tapes pass through associ-ates before she hears them, her eighth number one single, "If You Ever Change Your Mind," is one that was sent directly to her.

"Songs like that appeal to me," she says. "I love ballads, and I think you can look back and see that with a lot of my songs, when people think of me, they think of ballads, not up-tempos. 'If You Ever Change Your Mind' is just beautifully written. Allen [Reynolds] and I, we get together, we listen to songs and what appeals to us, and we record. That definitely appealed to both of us."

"If You Ever Change Your Mind" was written by Parker McGee, probably best known for writing the first two England Dan & John Ford Coley pop hits, "I'd Really Love To See You Tonight" and "Nights Are Forever."

Earlier that year, Crystal picked up her third Academy of Country Music trophy as Top Female Vocalist. She twice won that award from the Country Music Association, in 1977 and 1978.

Crystal Gayle

403

SMOKY MOUNTAIN RAIN
RONNIE MILSAP
RCA 12084
Writers: Kye Fleming, Dennis Morgan
Producers: Ronnie Milsap, Tom Collins
December 6, 1980 (1 week)

Rarely has a team of songwriters been as hot as Kye Fleming and Dennis Morgan. Beginning with "Sleeping Single In A Double Bed" [see 326] and ending with "Snapshot," they penned at least 23 Top 20 records between 1978 and 1983 for six different artists. Among them were "I Was Country When Country Wasn't Cool" [see 432], "Morning Comes Too Early," "Roll On Mississippi," "All Roads Lead To You" [see 452] and "Smoky Mountain Rain."

The latter was the first of two number one singles for Ronnie Milsap [see 455—"I Wouldn't Have Missed It For The World"], tailored specifically to suit his heritage. "Smoky Mountain Rain" started out as two different songs that were melded together: "Appalachian Mountain Rain" and "I Wonder What She's Doing Now."

"I Wonder What" painted a portrait of a man driving down the interstate, remembering a lost love. "Appalachian Mountain Rain" wove a tale of a rural boy who went to the city and then returned to his sweetheart back home. Neither seemed to work quite right, but publisher/producer Tom Collins suggested Fleming and Morgan combine the two songs for Milsap's upcoming *Greatest Hits* album.

"Knowing that Ronnie's from that area," says Fleming, "it just fit that: 'Hey, wait a minute, we've missed the boat on this. This is *Smoky* Mountain Rain.' We just wanted a story that could be somebody going back to the Smoky Mountains."

Fleming and Morgan wrote "Smoky Mountain Rain" in two days in the middle of a dry spell. It was one of three Top Ten records they completed in the summer of 1980. The others were "Tumbleweed" and "The Best Of Strangers."

"Smoky Mountain Rain," recorded at Woodland Sound Studios, reunited Milsap and Collins, who had parted ways on Milsap's previous album. Ronnie actually played his own piano on the track, and Bergen White enhanced it with a shimmering string arrangement. On December 6, 1980, the record reached the top of the country chart, and it also went to number

24 on the Hot 100. That same month, *Billboard* named Milsap the number one country singles artist of the year.

Ronnie underwent a four-hour surgical procedure at Duke University that December to alleviate nerve damage caused by an eye infection. On the 20th, the *Greatest Hits* album topped the country album chart, one of four "best of" packages in the Top Five.

404

WHY LADY WHY
ALABAMA
RCA 12091
Writers: Teddy Gentry, Rick Scott
Producers: Harold Shedd, Larry McBride, Alabama
December 13, 1980 (1 week)

With a name like Alabama, and two hit singles titled "My Home's In Alabama" and "Tennessee River" [see 390], Fort Payne's budding superstars wisely opted to avoid Southern themes with their second RCA release, "Why Lady Why." Alabama picked it personally, though neither the label nor radio recommended it.

"We knew the song would be a hit," Randy Owen told *Billboard*'s Robyn Wells. "We'd been performing it onstage for [several] years with tremendous response. It was a critical time for us to release a different type of song before we got locked into a stereotype of only singing about states and rivers."

Alabama recorded "Why Lady Why" at Music Mill Recording Studios in Nashville, owned by producer Harold Shedd.

"To me, the main thing, similar to 'Tennessee River,' was the musical arrangement of it," Owen says. "We actually worked on this thing for hours and hours and hours, goin' through doin' the stops and the kicks and the hesitations, and all those kinds of things that make it a unique sound of its own. You don't really hear any songs before or since that sound like it, because of the arrangement."

Bass player Teddy Gentry wrote "Why Lady Why" in early 1978 about, he often says, a racehorse in South Carolina. His co-writer, Rick Scott, played drums for Alabama at the time, although he eventually left the group. On April 1, 1979, Mark Herndon took his place, joining just one year before their ascension to national prominence.

Herndon was actually the fourth drummer in Alabama's history. Cousins Owen, Gentry and Jeff Cook first sang together in 1969, and three years later, they formed Wildcountry, with drummer Bennett Vartanian. The group made its first professional appearance on July 3, 1972, at Canyonland, an Alabama amusement park. Eight months later, the band started a seven-year association with The Bowery, a club in Myrtle Beach. Vartanian left in February of 1976, with another cousin, Jackie Owen, taking his place. Scott took over later that year, remaining another three years.

Wildcountry honed its act in a grueling schedule that sometimes put them on stage for thirteen hours a day at The Bowery with only a half-hour break between sets. They became Alabama when they made their first singles for national distribution, after discovering that several other bands across the U.S. were also named Wildcountry.

405

THAT'S ALL THAT MATTERS
MICKEY GILLEY
Epic 50940
Writer: Hank Cochran
Producer: Jim Ed Norman
December 20, 1980 (1 week)

"I feel like Jim Ed Norman really turned my career around when we started doing songs like 'You Don't Know Me' [see 440] and 'That's All That Matters To Me,'" says Mickey Gilley. "He took me out of Jerry Lee Lewis' shadow."

If Norman deserves credit for Gilley's improved vocal performances, though, Gilley played a major role himself, especially in the case of "That's All That Matters." Written by Hank Cochran, the song had been around for years; in fact, Ray Price cut it in 1964, though it mustered a peak position of only number 34.

"I didn't think at the time that I could really sing that song," Gilley admits, "but Jim Ed said I could, and that it would be a good record for me."

Gilley turned in a strong vocal performance, but after Norman gave him a tape of the track, Gilley was bothered by one line in the song. Several days later, he returned and asked Norman for a chance to go back in the studio and re-record that single line. The producer suggested that Gilley's effort was fine, but Gilley insisted and gave it one more shot. "That's All

That Matters" became his third number one single of 1980, and one of his own personal favorites.

"I've always thought that it was one of my better records," he notes. "I've only had two where I felt like I couldn't go back and re-create. That was one, and the other was 'You Don't Know Me.' I felt like the performance on those two tunes happened to come together at one time, and I was very fortunate to have someone as talented as Jim Ed Norman to do the arrangement and produce those two particular songs. I feel like it's undoubtedly the best record I've ever cut."

Gilley was becoming a hit machine, but records were hardly his only product. His fan club was heavily merchandised in his album sleeves, offering the usual array of Gilley's mugs, tee shirts, belt buckles and bumper stickers. Gilley also offered a book, *Saturday Night at Gilley's*, and an *empty* Gilley's beer can, which cost two dollars.

The brew wasn't as tasty, though, as his performance on "That's All That Matters." "Gilley's Beer will never be any other thing than just a novelty," Mickey confessed to Jennifer Boeth of the *Dallas Times-Herald*.

406

ONE IN A MILLION
JOHNNY LEE
Asylum 47076
Writer: Chick Rains
Producer: Jim Ed Norman
December 27, 1980 (2 weeks)

"Lookin' For Love" [see 393] brought nightclub singer Johnny Lee into a new phase in his career after it appeared in *Urban Cowboy*. Lee wasn't even signed to the Asylum label when the soundtrack was released, and when Asylum threw his single into the marketplace, they quickly pushed the Eagles' "Lyin' Eyes" onto the "B" side.

Lee recorded an album of his own rather quickly, with a need to prove the single was no fluke. "I felt pressure right at first because it was the first time that I'd had a big record," recalls the singer. "I knew that I had to have other big records to remain."

Lee's first choice for a follow-up single was "Do You Love As Good As You Look" [see 415], but the label disagreed. "I thought going from 'Lookin' For Love' to 'Do You Love As

Good As You Look' was a natural," relates Lee, "and as soon as we found out it wasn't gonna be released, the Bellamy Brothers came out with 'Do You Love As Good As You Look,' so I felt a little cheated. But I can't complain. 'One In A Million' was, boom, right up to number one, and I was really pleased to see I had two number one songs in a row."

"One In A Million" reached the top one week after "That's All That Matters" [see 405], bringing Lee and his friend, Mickey Gilley, back-to-back chart-toppers. The two had first met nearly ten years before, while Gilley was working at a Pasadena, Texas, club called The Nesadel. Lee pulled one over on Gilley, falsely claiming they'd worked together before, and, after playing together on stage, Lee remained with Gilley as a singer/trumpet player throughout the '70s. With the advent of *Urban Cowboy*, they toured together incessantly.

"One In A Million" also established a mid-tempo sound and style that would characterize many of Lee's releases. "They were always trying to find the bag I was in," remembers Lee, "and that was always difficult, because I always classified myself as a versatile singer. I like all kinds of different songs, but they were trying to lock me into a bag. To me, the only thing a bag is good for is to carry groceries home in."

407

I THINK I'LL JUST STAY HERE AND DRINK
MERLE HAGGARD

MCA 51014
Writer: Merle Haggard
Producer: Jimmy Bowen
January 10, 1981 (1 week)

Merle Haggard notched his twenty-fourth number one record as a solo performer with "Cherokee Maiden" [see 273] in November of 1976. It took more than four years for him to get his twenty-fifth, "I Think I'll Just Stay Here And Drink."

The period was hardly an unproductive one, though. He earned nine Top Five singles, five of which stopped at number two: "If We're Not Back In Love By Monday," "Ramblin' Fever," "I'm Always On A Mountain When I Fall," "It's Been A Great Afternoon" and "The Way I Am." He also peaked at number four with "From Graceland To The Promised Land," a song he wrote shortly after the death of Elvis Presley [see 291—"Way Down"].

A couple of important events occurred in the meantime that had a huge impact on his music. One of those was his marriage on October 7, 1978, to Leona Belle Williams, his third wife. (Haggard's second wife, Bonnie Owens, served as a bridesmaid at the ceremony.) Exactly three weeks later, the newlyweds entered *Billboard* with their duet recording, "The Bull And The Beaver," which peaked at number 10.

In early 1979, an exhausted Haggard decided to quit the music business. He holed up on his houseboat on Lake Shasta for the better part of six months, and, though he wasn't working, he kept his band on the payroll. It was an expensive way to rekindle his enthusiasm for the business.

A re-dedicated Haggard finally earned his twenty-fifth number one with the experimental "I Think I'll Just Stay Here And Drink." Listed at four minutes and thirty seconds, it featured two drummers, and three lengthy instrumental solos.

"The record companies are always after me to do fast songs," he says. "I didn't know that we had speedometers on records. Anyway, I was trying to write them a fast song.

"Some guy called me one night—I forget who it was—and I invited him up to my house. He said, 'No, I just wanted to call you—I think I'll just stay here and drink,' and he hung up. I thought I'd better write that right quick and get that fast song they need."

Just a few months earlier, Haggard appeared on the cover of jazz magazine *downbeat*, the first country artist ever to do so.

408

I LOVE A RAINY NIGHT
EDDIE RABBITT

Elektra 47066
Writers: Eddie Rabbitt, Even Stevens, David Malloy
Producer: David Malloy
January 17, 1981 (1 week)

On October 24, 1980, Eddie Rabbitt's *Horizon* album became his first to reach number one on the *Billboard* country album chart. Bolstered by "Drivin' My Life Away" [see 391] and "I Love A Rainy Night," it was widely hailed as a throwback to rockabilly, with some justification.

Eddie Rabbitt

Prior to starting the album, producer David Malloy worked on an album for Badfinger. During those sessions, bandmember Tom Evans told Malloy of England's growing fascination with rockabilly.

"I opened up *Billboard* about two weeks later," notes Malloy, "and read this thing about what he was talkin' about. So before we started writin' the *Horizon* music, I went down to the record store and bought the Sun Records collection, and I put on the records for Even and Eddie, and then we started writing."

At the time, Rabbitt went digging through an old Army foot locker he kept with tapes of old songs and fragments of ideas. At the end of one tape, he discovered a repetitive melody with the phrase, "I Love A Rainy Night," and he suggested that to Malloy and co-writer Even Stevens.

Two weeks earlier, Malloy had gotten an idea for a rhythm pattern using alternating fingersnaps and handclaps, and that concept became the centerpiece for the record. The "snaps and claps," however, proved a night-mare in the recording studio. Malloy, Rabbitt and Stevens all tried to do the pattern in various combinations with little success. They even tried a tape loop, and that didn't work.

"We weren't consistent enough to get the sound right every time," Stevens explains, "so the handclaps would sound different every time when we'd alternate back and forth." Finally, they hired percussionist Farrell Morris to handle it. "In about three hours' time," says Malloy, "he laid down two tracks of snaps and two tracks of claps and that was it."

"I Love A Rainy Night" received a boost when Rabbitt signed a deal with Miller beer. He filmed a commercial with the song on November 29, 1980, in Tucson. On New Year's Day, it premiered at halftime during the Rose Bowl (Michigan 23, Washington 6), and the additional exposure helped propel Rabbitt to the top of both the country chart and *Billboard*'s Hot 100.

In March, "I Love A Rainy Night" and "Drivin' My Life Away" were certified as his only two million-selling singles.

409

9 TO 5
DOLLY PARTON

RCA 12133
Writer: Dolly Parton
Producer: Gregg Perry
January 24, 1981 (1 week)

As 1980 came to a close, Dolly Parton added a new line of work to her resumé, taking on an acting role in the motion picture *9 to 5*. Parton played Doralee Rhodes, a naive secretary for a lecherous boss, capably portrayed by Dabney Coleman. Dolly's co-workers and co-stars were Lily Tomlin and Jane Fonda, who hand-picked her for the picture.

"We met by chance while flying on board the same plane to New York," Fonda told Leo Janos in *Cosmopolitan*. "We talked for a while, and I thought, 'That's it—that's Doralee!' I went to see Dolly perform in concert, and I was knocked over. She's sexy and funny and warm. After five minutes, she has you sitting on her knee. You feel comfortable with her, love her, and hug her like an old friend. All those qualities are in her work in the movie."

9 to 5 was aided by a huge publicity campaign, but even more by the snappy title track, which Dolly wrote to overcome boredom on the set.

"The hardest thing was the long wait between shots, the hours you'd sit in make-up and costume and all," she said to *Billboard*'s Kip Kirby. "I thought to myself, 'Now I am not gonna sit around here like this,' 'cause it was the first time in my life that I've ever had to sit

Dolly Parton, from 9 to 5

and do nothin'. I can't embroider or nothin' like that, so I figured if I started writin' songs, it would change my mood. So I started writin' right on the set, and I was amazed at how easily I could do it. That's how I wrote '9 To 5.'"

The movie premiered at Opryland's Roy Acuff Theater in Nashville on December 5, 1980, and opened two weeks later at more than 700 theaters around the country. The record ascended easily to number one on the country chart, but also earned chart-topping status on *Billboard*'s Hot 100, making her the first Nashville-based female since Jeannie C. Riley [see 17—"Harper Valley P.T.A."] to score a number one pop single.

Dolly claimed a Grammy award for "9 To 5," which also became her second million-selling single. Her sister, Rachel Dennison, took the role of Doralee when *9 to 5* became a television series in 1982.

410
I FEEL LIKE LOVING YOU AGAIN
T.G. SHEPPARD
Warner Bros. 49615
Writers: Bobby Braddock,
Sonny Throckmorton
Producer: Buddy Killen
January 31, 1981

Many in the record business are fond of an old cliché: "You can't argue with success."

After "Thinkin' Of A Rendezvous" [see 268] became a number one record in December of 1976, songwriters Bobby Braddock and Sonny Throckmorton collaborated once again. All told, Throckmorton estimates that they have composed only five songs together, but at least three of them have become hits. They generated one of them just a few months after "Rendezvous" peaked, although it took almost four years for the new song to earn its top marks.

"In April of '77, Sonny and I were kicking some ideas around," Braddock remembers. "There was a girl I hadn't talked to in a long time that called me while I was with Throckmorton there at Tree [Publishing]. After talking to her, I thought, 'I Feel You Coming Back Again.'"

In the process of writing that song, Braddock and Throckmorton considered comparing love to a radio station. The idea didn't work in that context, but they were enamored with the concept and put the first idea aside. In half an hour, they had concocted "Fadin' In, Fadin'

Out," which Tommy Overstreet took to number 11 in 1978.

With that task completed, they then turned their attentions to the first song, which Throckmorton later cut for his *Last Cheater's Waltz* [see 357] album. During the recording sessions, however, Sonny realized that singing "I feel you coming . . ." might be misinterpreted. "It was suggested to me that it might be a little risqué," says Throckmorton, "and that we should soften it." Together, the two writers hashed out a new title: "I Feel Like Loving You Again," which proved perfect for Sheppard.

"I love ballads," notes T.G. "I was looking for a real strong ballad that I could build a real great track around, with strings and all this stuff. I love real tight-knit, close harmonies in high keys, and that song lent itself to that."

Released on November 5, 1980, the single entered the *Billboard* country chart on December 6. Eight weeks later, "I Feel Like Loving You Again" became Sheppard's sixth number one record.

411
I KEEP COMING BACK/TRUE LIFE COUNTRY MUSIC
RAZZY BAILEY
RCA 12120
Writers: Johnny Slate, Jim Hurt,
Larry Keith/Danny Morrison,
Jeff Silbar, Sam Lorber
Producer: Bob Montgomery
February 7, 1981 (1 week)

Charley Pride himself once said that he didn't sound as "black" as Razzy Bailey. Bailey grew up with a variety of influences, and they all melded together in a potpourri that relied on a strong country base. His soul sensibilities were underscored even in the name of his backing group—the *RB* Band obviously referred to "Razzy Bailey," but it could have also stood for "rhythm and blues."

R & B figured strongly in his ballad "I Keep Coming Back," a song from three House of Gold songwriters. Razzy and producer/publisher Bob Montgomery first heard the tune on their way into the recording studio.

"We had a 6:00 session," Bailey recalls. "All the songs were picked out, and about 5:45, Johnny Slate come runnin' downstairs and said, 'You gotta hear this song before you go in the studio.' I heard it, and I loved it. I always wanted to do one of those R & B-feelin', country, bluesy ballads, so I said, 'God, yes, let's do it.' So we decided right there on the spur of the moment to do the song."

They actually waited until their next session to cut it, and Slate's co-writers, Jim Hurt and Larry Keith, provided the back-up vocals on the record. Slate's usual co-writer, Danny Morrison, missed out on writing "I Keep Coming Back," since he was involved with the recording session that Bailey was preparing when it was written.

Morrison did get credit on the "B" side, though, writing "True Life Country Music" with Jeff Silbar and Sam Lorber. Like Moe Bandy's "Yesterday Once More" or George Jones' "Who's Gonna Fill Their Shoes," the song chronicled a host of legends, including Waylon Jennings, Crystal Gayle, Kenny Rogers and Charlie Rich.

"We were on a roll, findin' the right songs," says Razzy. "We were just puttin' so much strong stuff on the albums that we couldn't figure out what to put on the 'B' side. So RCA said, 'Hell, let's put 'em both out.' We did that three times in a row, got double-sided number ones."

Both sides debuted at number 57 on November 22, 1980, and by the time they had been in *Billboard* for a dozen weeks, Bailey had his second number one single.

412
WHO'S CHEATIN' WHO
CHARLY McCLAIN
Epic 50948
Writer: Jerry Hayes
Producer: Larry Rogers
February 14, 1981 (1 week)

Charly McClain has a habit of causing headaches. Her first name is a masculine one, and it's presented a stumbling block for many disk jockeys who start working on country stations without really knowing the material.

Named Charlotte Denise McClain at birth, "Charly" was an early nickname among some of her Memphis friends, and while working at a Ramada Inn lounge, many of the patrons likewise picked up on the name. Coincidentally, Epic Records hit upon the name as well when she signed with the label in 1976.

"They thought 'Charlotte McClain' was too common," she says. "It wasn't exciting enough; they wanted something a little more catchy, and someone there suggested 'Charly.' That was okay by me, 'cause by that point, I was used to it."

Her father's illness mistakenly created her interest in recording. He had tuberculosis, and at age eight, she was too young to visit him in the hospital. The three McClain children would sit in the waiting room, though, while their mother went to his room; they taped music on a reel-to-reel recorder for their dad.

Later, while watching an early television awards show, McClain predicted that one day, she would appear on the program. She headed toward that goal when she sang and played bass in her brother's band for six years. At age 17, she became a regular on a Memphis showcase, "The Mid-South Jamboree," and, when Charly joined local group Shylo on stage, their producer, Larry Rogers, took her into the studio to make a demo.

Once with Epic, she cracked the Top Ten in 1978 with "That's What You Do To Me," returning again in 1980 with "Men," and finally hitting number one on "Who's Cheatin' Who." Shylo played the instrumental tracks on the record, though the tune's soap-opera lyrics didn't appeal to McClain.

"When Larry Rogers brought it to me I thought it was kind of corny," she admits, "but they thought it was a hit record, and I said, 'Sure, fine.' The day I recorded that song, it was raining outside, and I still had my raincoat on. I stood there singing it with my hands in my pockets the whole time, and it came off.

"From that time on, I really stopped trying to decide what I thought was a hit or not."

413
SOUTHERN RAINS
MEL TILLIS
Elektra 47082
Writer: Roger Murrah
Producer: Jimmy Bowen
February 21, 1981 (1 week)

Born Lonnie Melvin Tillis in Tampa on August 8, 1932, Mel Tillis grew up in Pahokee, Florida. He played classical violin and drums before he settled on his instrument of choice—a used Sears & Roebuck guitar he purchased from his brother for $25.

Years later, as he approached his fiftieth

birthday, Tillis found himself in the midst of the hottest streak of his career. In total, he amassed 16 consecutive Top Ten singles. The first nine—stretching from "Good Woman Blues" [see 267] through "Coca Cola Cowboy" [see 350]—were all recorded on MCA under the guidance of producer Jimmy Bowen.

Having moved over to Elektra, Bowen brought Tillis along to the label in 1979 and continued the streak. "Blind In Love," "Lying Time Again" and "Your Body Is An Outlaw" were all hits, but Bowen felt he needed a stronger record.

"A lot of artists, sometimes they get too enmeshed in their own publishing companies," Bowen explains. "Even when they go to reach out, other people don't think they're serious and still don't give them their best songs. That's kind of where Mel was at that point, and I just went to Roger Murrah, and said, 'I got to have a hit for Mel Tillis.' He gave me 'Southern Rains,' which he had just written, and Mel liked it."

Like Glen Campbell's "Southern Nights" [see 279], the song succeeded as a celebration of Dixie.

"When I wrote that song, I didn't really sit down to write a 'hit song,'" says Murrah. "I really wanted to say those things, and a good bit of it is just kind of autobiographical. I was in somewhat of a state of homesickness, being in Nashville. I'd moved here from Alabama, so it just kind of threw me into home. As my wife would say, another one of those 'home' songs."

"Southern Rains" became the sixth Tillis recording to find a home at number one. He ended his string with two more Top Ten singles, "A Million Old Goodbyes" and "One-Night Fever." Another pair hit that level within the next two years, "In The Middle Of The Night" and "New Patches."

Based on the performance of 76 singles that hit the *Billboard* chart over three decades, Joel Whitburn's Record Research cited Mel as the twenty-second most successful country performer in history.

414
ARE YOU HAPPY BABY?
DOTTIE WEST
Liberty 1392
Writer: Bob Stone
Producers: Brent Maher, Randy Goodrum
February 28, 1981 (1 week)

Dottie West

He's best known for the controversial costumes he has designed for Cher, but Bob Mackie has also had an impact on country music. In the early '80s, Dottie West paid him $100,000 a year to develop her stage wardrobe, and one of his classic designs for her is the all-white cowgirl outfit—complete with Stetson and holster—that accentuates the cover of her 1981 album *Wild West*.

In fact, Dottie had finished the album and was in Los Angeles with Mackie when she received a phone call from Liberty Records executive Don Grierson, who insisted that he had found another song she ought to add to the album. After she finished with Mackie, she headed to Don's office, where she heard "Are You Happy Baby?" She agreed to cut it.

Meanwhile, Grierson called producer Brent Maher, and played the song for him. "[Co-producer] Randy [Goodrum] was actually out of the country," Maher notes. "He was workin' on *Stir Crazy* with Michael Masser. I talked to Randy and asked if he wanted me to wait until he got back or to go ahead and cut it, and he said, 'Go ahead and cut it.'"

Dottie was on tour at the time with Kenny Rogers and Dave & Sugar, and wasn't available while the instrumental tracks were laid. Maher cut a "scratch" version and played it long-distance for her to make sure the key was workable. Once she gave the go-ahead, he finished the record and waited for her to fly in and overdub her vocals.

"Are You Happy Baby?" went on to be her fourth number one single.

Born in McMinnville, Tennessee, West majored in music at Tennessee Tech, and made her first record in 1959 for Starday. She moved to Atlantic, but Chet Atkins persuaded the label to allow RCA to take her on their roster in 1962. A year later, Jim Reeves had a hit with her composition "Is This Me?," and recorded a Top Ten duet with Dottie, "Love Is No Excuse."

In 1964, West scored another hit with "Here Comes My Baby," which brought her a Grammy award. She has been nominated 19 times, and has racked up 15 Top Ten singles.

415

DO YOU LOVE AS GOOD AS YOU LOOK

THE BELLAMY BROTHERS

Warner Bros. 49639
Writers: Rory Bourke, Jerry Gillespie, Charlie Black
Producers: Michael Lloyd, The Bellamy Brothers
March 7, 1981 (1 week)

They pre-dated Ted Danson's "Cheers" character, Sam Malone, by several years, but many of the Bellamy Brothers' early records are well-suited for Malone's playful vocabulary. "If I Said You Have A Beautiful Body Would You Hold It Against Me" [see 343] might not have won applause from the National Organization for Women, but it did set up a humorous, tongue-in-cheek image for Howard and David.

"We don't put women down," David told Pat Harris in *Country Song Roundup*. "We call our style a 'romantic suggestivity.' As a matter of fact, we get letters from women thanking us for writing tunes like that because they're so romantic."

They tapped the same well again when they recorded their 1980 album *Sons of the Sun*. David wrote the first single, "Lovers Live Longer," based on a headline he read on a gossip tabloid while going through the checkout aisle at a grocery store. "Lovers Live Longer" peaked at number three. NOW couldn't pin the Bellamys down for their follow-up, since they received it from songwriters Rory Bourke, Jerry Gillespie and Charlie Black.

"'Do You Love As Good As You Look' was a song that I got in the mail," David notes. "One of the guys from the publishing company sent it down [to us in Florida], when we were fixin' to go in the studio. We said, 'Well, let's throw that in the batch and cut it,' 'cause it sounded like somethin' we could sing well and sounded like the type of song we were doing at that time."

The song actually got its start in the recording studio, while Black was overdubbing vocal harmonies during a demo session. "A girl walked through the studio," Charlie recalls. "I was informed that they had this idea after she left, so that's where that came from, a walking inspiration there. We surely took the obvious approach on that song, but that was fun."

The writers hesitated about sending it to the Bellamy Brothers, thinking Howard and David wouldn't record something they didn't write themselves. Apparently, it didn't matter. It sounded like a page out of their own songbook, and brought them to number one in March of 1981.

416
GUITAR MAN
ELVIS PRESLEY
RCA 12158
Writer: J.R. Hubbard
Producer: Felton Jarvis
March 14, 1981 (1 week)

Elvis Presley's passing [see 291—"Way Down"] hardly provided an end to his career. On the contrary, Presley records and memorabilia increased in value, and the record-buying public seemed more obsessed than ever with the legend of the King.

That fact was hardly lost on RCA, which set a new record for most sales during a quarter, and in the process, six Presley albums were certified gold or platinum during September and October of 1977, as well as his single "Way Down." Among his million-selling certifications was *Elvis in Concert*, a two-record project that producer Felton Jarvis was finishing up at the time of Presley's demise.

Enhanced by a vocal group that included Janie Frickie, the LP sent Presley to number two in 1978 with his first posthumous single, "My Way." Three more Top Ten singles followed through the end of the decade, and in 1981, nearly four years after his death, the King finally returned to number one through the magic of advanced studio technology.

Jarvis stripped away the instrumental tracks from a number of overlooked Presley recordings, including "You Asked Me To," "I'm Movin' On" and "Guitar Man," retaining the original vocals and rebuilding the tracks with new instrumental sessions. All of the cuts were issued as the *Guitar Man* album, with Jerry Reed, who wrote the song, providing the guitar solo in the title track.

Shortly after completing work on the project, Jarvis suffered a stroke, dying at Nashville's Baptist Hospital two weeks later on January 3, 1981. Unfortunately, Jarvis was unable to witness the success of his efforts, as the "Guitar Man" single reached number one ten weeks later. The follow-up, a cover of Dobie Gray's "Lovin' Arms," would reach number eight in June.

More than ten years after his passing, the Presley mystique lives on. A multitude of album packages have documented just about every aspect of his career, and RCA has on occasion unearthed new, previously-unknown tracks, including outtakes from the Sun days.

Radio station WCVG in Covington, Kentucky, developed an all-Elvis format in 1988, and a Presley fantasy spurred the plot of the movie *Heartbreak Hotel*. Perhaps the strangest event of all was the release of a book, *Is Elvis Alive?*, which questioned the authenticity of his death.

417
ANGEL FLYING TOO CLOSE TO THE GROUND
WILLIE NELSON
Columbia 11351
Writer: Willie Nelson
Producer: Willie Nelson
March 21, 1981 (1 week)

Though Willie Nelson wandered through the wilderness as a recording artist for 15 years after moving to Nashville [see 223—"Blue Eyes Crying In The Rain"], he found stable footing as a songwriter. In his early years, he became part of a group of writers—including Harlan Howard, Hank Cochran and Roger Miller—who frequented Tootsie's Orchid Lounge near the Grand Ole Opry.

Willie emerged with fairly strong credentials, writing Patsy Cline's "Crazy," Faron Young's "Hello Walls" and Ray Price's "Night Life" (Price employed Willie as his bass player). Nelson also wrote "Funny How Time Slips Away," a pop hit for Joe Hinton in 1964 and a country hit for Narvel Felts in 1975. In October of 1973, the Nashville Songwriters Hall Of Fame added Willie to its ranks.

Of all his compositions, Willie cites three as his favorites: "The Healing Hands Of Time," and two songs from the movie *Honeysuckle Rose*—"On The Road Again" [see 399] and "Angel Flying Too Close To The Ground." Willie wrote the latter title during a period in which he and his third wife, Connie, faced some marital problems.

"It's a pretty general theme that can be taken and applied to a lot of different situations," he told Frederick Burger in *Country Rhythms*. "A lot of people have taken it and applied it to their own situation. You could relate it to someone who has died, love affairs or whatever . . . It has a lot of different meanings to a lot of different people who have no idea why I wrote that song."

Willie composed it in 1976, but it took four more years before it saw the light of day in his second motion picture.

"Sometimes I'll keep a song for a while before I release it," he says. "I like to wait until I think it has a chance, because if it's an exceptionally good song and it gets lost in the shuffle, you always wish that you would have waited for a better time to put it out. If you put it out at the wrong time, you've lost a good song."

In this instance, Willie's foresight paid off. Columbia Records released "Angel Flying Too Close To The Ground" as the second single from *Honeysuckle Rose*, and it became his tenth number one record.

418

TEXAS WOMEN
HANK WILLIAMS, JR.
Elektra 47102
Writer: Hank Williams, Jr.
Producer: Jimmy Bowen
March 28, 1981 (1 week)

Following the 1975 mountain-climbing accident that almost claimed his life [see 101—"Eleven Roses"], Hank Williams, Jr., wasn't quite the same performer—and that's exactly the way he wanted things.

Having experimented with a new direction the year prior to his fall, Hank took to a rock-edged sound even more strongly afterward. On his live shows, he followed his own path, even though many concertgoers walked out when he refused to play his father's music. Sometimes the crowd would dwindle to just 200, yet Bocephus played his entire set. He did it his way or didn't do it at all.

Unfortunately, that didn't translate to his records—at least not consistently. His producers continued to dictate some of his material, and in one instance, had him cut the Bee Gees' "To Love Somebody." Finally, while recording the *Family Tradition* album, Hank made sure that his albums mirrored the toughness of his concerts.

"His manager called me and said that Hank wasn't happy with the album and wanted me to come to Muscle Shoals and help him cut some new songs," Jimmy Bowen explained to Ellen Shaw in *Billboard*. "When I got there, I asked Hank what he had written. He said, 'Nobody wants to hear what I write.' I told him they'd have to, 'cause I didn't bring any songs with me. He took me aside and played 'Family Tradition.' I said, 'That'll do it.' We went to the studio

and cut it, and that's how we began working together."

Released in the summer of 1979, "Family Tradition" marked the turning point in Bocephus' career. The record rocketed to number four, and he followed with two more Top Five singles: "Whiskey Bent And Hell Bound" and "Women I've Never Had." "Kaw-Liga" went to number 12, "Old Habits" reached number six, and "Texas Women" brought him back to number one for the first time in nearly nine years.

Hank wrote "Texas Women" after appearing at a nightclub in the Lone Star state. The following day, he penned it as an ode to the ladies he had seen in the audience, weaving in a veritable laundry list of the state's various cities. Included on the *Rowdy* album, "Texas Women" featured a prominent mandolin intro played by Kieran Kane [see 722—"Can't Stop My Heart From Loving You"].

419

DRIFTER
SYLVIA
RCA 12164
Writers: Don Pfrimmer, Archie Jordan
Producer: Tom Collins
April 4, 1981 (1 week)

Country fans often relate to their favorites by their first name only—Tammy Wynette is "Tammy," Waylon Jennings is "Waylon," Willie Nelson is "Willie." Yet Sylvia Kirby is the only performer to ever gain number one records billed consistently under just one name. She scored two, and, coincidentally, both were also one-word titles.

Born December 9, 1956, Sylvia moved from Kokomo, Indiana, to Nashville in January of 1976 with a plan to get started as a secretary. Tom Collins gave her a receptionist job at Pi-Gem Music, and from that position, she began to branch out as a performer. She sang on a number of demos around town, including "Golden Tears" [see 336], and she also sang back-up for Janie Frickie on the road in 1977.

At one point, she tried out for a spot in Dave & Sugar, and even though she didn't get the job, she did impress RCA division head Jerry Bradley, who signed her to the label. When asked if she had experience performing as a solo singer live, she replied, "No, but I learn fast," and she was forced to learn when she opened that year for Charley Pride.

A year later, the western-flavored "Tumbleweed" brought Sylvia her first Top Ten release, and she followed up with "Drifter," which producer Tom Collins felt was essential in establishing an image.

"Sylvia had to me a real pretty face, and a great voice," he notes, "but Crystal Gayle was hot as a pistol, and we didn't want to have another pretty face with long hair. We came up with an idea called 'prairie music': Western-type lyrics with a disco beat."

Sylvia had first heard "Drifter" as a ballad, and it was only the day of the session that Collins decided on the upbeat production. "I wasn't real hot on the idea," she admits, "but once we got in the studio and did it the way Tom heard it in his head, it seemed like that was the only way it should have been recorded."

With backing vocals by the Jordanaires, "Drifter" became the second hit—and title track—from Sylvia's debut album, which yielded a total of four hit singles when both "The Matador" and "Heart On The Mend" went Top Ten later in 1981.

420

YOU'RE THE REASON GOD MADE OKLAHOMA
DAVID FRIZZELL & SHELLY WEST

Warner Bros. 49650
Writers: Larry Collins, Sandy Pinkard
Producers: Snuff Garrett, Steve Dorff
April 11, 1981 (1 week)

David Frizzell & Shelly West titled their first album *Carryin' On the Family Names*. It was appropriate: David was a younger brother to the late Lefty Frizzell, and Shelly called Dottie West "Mom."

"Family" also played a role in their development. Shelly sang back-up on the road with Dottie from 1975 to 1977, where she met Allen Frizzell, another bandmember—and brother to Lefty and David. Allen and Shelly headed to California in 1978, where they teamed up with David and worked two years in nightclubs.

Jack Brumley, brother of former Buckaroo Tom Brumley, signed them to a management

David Frizzell & Shelly West

contract, and then approached record producer Snuff Garrett, who loved the whole family concept. He asked Sandy Pinkard and Larry Collins to write a song for Frizzell and West; they returned with "You're The Reason God Made Oklahoma."

"Snuff had a deal with Casablanca West," Frizzell recalls, "but when we got our product ready, they had to dissolve it, and we were stuck with an album. If I remember right, that was January or February of 1980."

Garrett shopped the album around Nashville and Los Angeles, but was rebuffed by every major label. While working on the soundtrack to *Any Which Way You Can*, Snuff played "Oklahoma" in his car for Clint Eastwood, who asserted "That's a pistol." At Eastwood's direction, the song was included in the movie. "He put it in this really low spot," says co-producer Steve Dorff, "comin' over a truck radio."

"David just knew that it was a hit song," Shelly notes. "With his faith in it, he made me believe in it. At the time, I was so new, and all I could think of was, 'If he's right, it means we're gonna be playin' to big audiences.' I was really scared."

Frizzell's prediction came true. Garrett revived his long-dormant Viva Records and released the soundtrack in late 1980, even before the film's December 12 premiere. Four singles were released ahead of "Oklahoma," but, beginning with KGEN in Tulare, California, radio stations all over the country started playing it off the soundtrack. Viva put it out as a single, and the song no one wanted went to number one.

The duo racked up three more Top Ten singles: "A Texas State Of Mind," "Another Honky-Tonk Night On Broadway" and "I Just Came Here To Dance."

ing artist, Mac didn't chart again until 1983, when "Minimum Love" reached number 41. In the meantime, however, he earned his biggest success by writing "Old Flame."

McAnally had an idea for the song's hook and a sketchy melody, and he felt it would be ideal as a country song. He feared that if he wrote the entire piece alone, it would probably lean a little farther toward a pop tune than it should, so he enlisted a friend named Donny Lowery to help him finish it. Once "Old Flame" was completed, Lowery played a major role in getting Alabama to cut it.

"We'd recorded Donny Lowery's 'Woman Back Home' for *Feels So Right* [see 434], but we'd never met him," Randy Owen explained to Judy Raphael in *Songwriter Connection*. "He was unknown to us. But one night he came on our bus down in Muscle Shoals to thank us and bring us a fruit bow. He said he had a tape with him of the best song he'd ever written. We waited to play it, but we played it on the way back, and we were knocked out by it."

Presenting it personally probably helped Lowery focus the band's attention on the song, although Alabama would have heard "Old Flame" anyway. Producer Harold Shedd had already sent Alabama a tape of "Old Flame" that he had received from Muscle Shoals. That same tape also included the demo of "(There's) No Gettin' Over Me" [see 438].

Alabama was so taken with "Old Flame" that they recorded it at the last minute for the *Feels So Right* album and bumped another song off the record. Then "Old Flame" became the first single, and went on to number one in April of 1981.

"Old Flame" also became an important part of Alabama's concerts. At many shows, audiences have created a tradition in which they flash pocket lighters to call for an encore at the end of an evening, but "Old Flame" engendered a ritual in which ticket-buyers "flick their Bics" in the middle of the song.

421

OLD FLAME
ALABAMA
RCA 12169
Writers: Donny Lowery, Mac McAnally
Producers: Alabama, Larry McBride,
Harold Shedd
April 18, 1981 (1 week)

In 1977, a 19-year-old Alabama native named Mac McAnally recorded his first album. A single, "It's A Crazy World," reached the Top 40 on *Billboard*'s Hot 100. A sporadic record-

422

A HEADACHE TOMORROW
(OR A HEARTACHE TONIGHT)
MICKEY GILLEY
Epic 50973
Writer: Chick Rains
Producer: Jim Ed Norman
April 25, 1981 (1 week)

Alabama

"Songwriting is an emotional purge for me," Chick Rains told Ellis Widner in *Country Rhythms*. "I get rid of a lot of emotion, but it drains me. I get into those dark places in my memory. I write songs that are depressing, sometimes, even to me."

Unlike Merle Haggard, who actually hails from California, Rains is a true "Okie From Muskogee" [see 45]. He moved to Los Angeles in 1966, served in Vietnam, and returned to L.A. in 1972, where one of his songs, "You're The Fingernail On The Blackboard Of My Heart," earned a dubious honor from the *Los Angeles Times* as the Stupidest Song Title of the Year.

Once offered a part in "The Waltons," Rains turned down a spot in the television series to continue his pursuit of music. Eventually, Rains landed a spot in Jim Ed Norman's publishing company, where he turned out "Down To My Last Broken Heart," for Janie Frickie; "Dreams Die Hard," for Gary Morris; and Johnny Lee's number one single, "One In A Million" [see 406].

"A Headache Tomorrow (Or A Heartache Tonight)" became Chick's second number one single when Mickey Gilley took it to the top just four months after "One In A Million" became his first. The alcoholic content of the lyrics was hardly unusual for a country song, but its reference to a pill was. Nonetheless, Gilley encountered no controversies.

"If you listen to the lyrics, the pill that I sing about was aspirin," he explained. "If you have a hangover, you're going to take something to kill the pain, and that's what that particular line was reflecting. I just always thought that the song was a little different, and that it was a cute tune."

During the record's run, Gilley picked up the only Grammy award of his career. "A Headache Tomorrow" entered *Billboard*'s country chart on Valentine's Day in 1981. On February 25, Gilley's "Urban Cowboy" band picked up the trophy for Best Country Instrumental Performance, for "Orange Blossom Special," a track from the *Urban Cowboy* [see 389—"Stand By Me"] soundtrack.

423

REST YOUR LOVE ON ME/I AM THE DREAMER (YOU ARE THE DREAM)
CONWAY TWITTY

MCA 51059
Writers: Barry Gibb/Russ Allison, Dallas
Cody, David C. Hall
Producers: Conway Twitty, Ron Chancey
May 2, 1981 (1 week)

On December 16, 1977, *Saturday Night Fever* opened across America, with John Travolta dancing across the screen to a soundtrack written in part by the Bee Gees. Thirty months later, Travolta had a peripheral effect on country music through his starring role in *Urban Cowboy* [see 389—"Stand By Me"]. The Bee Gees had a more direct impact on the format.

The music on the *Fever* soundtrack made Barry, Robin and Maurice Gibb the hottest act in pop music. In fact, during a couple of weeks in March of 1978, the Bee Gees wrote and/or performed four of the Top Five singles on *Billboard*'s Hot 100. Thus, Johnny Rodriguez received a call from a purported Bee Gee with some skepticism that winter.

Rodriguez was at home when the phone rang, and the caller identified himself as Barry Gibb, calling from Paris. It took some time to convince Johnny that the call was for real, but Barry finally assured Rodriguez of his authenticity and went on to tell the country singer how much he admired his vocal style.

Barry promised to write a song for Johnny, and not long afterward, a tape of "Rest Your Love On Me" arrived in the mail. Rodriguez recorded it for his album *Love Me With All Your Heart*.

At the end of that year, the Bee Gees released their own version of the song as the "B" side to their number one pop record, "Too Much Heaven." "Rest Your Love On Me" appeared on the country chart for 12 weeks, resting at number 39 during its peak.

The Bee Gees' recording caught the attention of Conway Twitty, who cut his own version a couple of years later. Conway's rendition superseded the Bee Gees' peak in its third week on the chart, and eight weeks later, it became his thirtieth number one country single. Shortly afterward, Twitty visited the Bee Gees at their Miami recording studio.

"Before long we were back in their songwriting room, singing country songs," he told

Jack Hurst in the *Chicago Tribune*. "They love country music. They named songs I'd recorded that I'd forgotten about."

Other Bee Gees songs that have charted country include "Islands In The Stream" [see 543], "Buried Treasure," "Eyes That See In The Dark" and "Evening Star," all by Kenny Rogers; Olivia Newton-John's "Come On Over"; Connie Smith's "I Just Want To Be Your Everything"; and Susie Allanson's "Words."

424

AM I LOSING YOU
RONNIE MILSAP

RCA 12194
Writer: Jim Reeves
Producers: Ronnie Milsap, Tom Collins
May 9, 1981 (1 week)

Multitalented as a vocalist and as an instrumentalist, Ronnie Milsap took lessons in his youth on piano, violin and guitar. The first song he ever learned on the six-string was "Am I Losing You," and years later, it provided him with a number one single during a recuperative period.

Ronnie toured quite heavily during 1980, and hadn't been able to take the time to review tapes and come up with enough material to do a new album. RCA wanted an LP, though, and division manager Jerry Bradley engaged him in a conversation in which Milsap started talking about how much he loved the music of Jim Reeves.

Many have recorded albums that paid homage to Hank Williams [see 374—"Honky Tonk Blues"], but rarely if ever had Reeves received such an honor. Milsap and Bradley agreed that a tribute album would keep Milsap product in the marketplace without taxing him to find new songs. It would also give him an opportunity to salute one of his favorite performers—one who had also recorded for RCA years earlier.

The result was *Out Where the Bright Lights Are Glowing*, its title drawn from the first line of Reeves' classic "Four Walls." Milsap also covered nine more of "Gentleman Jim"'s hits, including "He'll Have To Go," "I Guess I'm Crazy" and "Am I Losing You." The only single pulled from the album, the latter tune went to number one in May of 1981.

Milsap contributed to something of a Reeves revival. In 1979-80, RCA gained mileage from Jim's old tracks when they had Deborah Allen overdub new vocals to create "duets" fifteen years after his passing. The Reeves & Allen tandem yielded three Top Ten singles.

Spurred by those successes, RCA dug even deeper to find a series of songs that Reeves and the late Patsy Cline had both recorded in similar keys and at similar tempos. The voices of both stars were linked in the recording studio, and one of those duets, "Have You Ever Been Lonely," created a Top Five single in late 1981.

Hailing from Panola County, Texas, Reeves played minor-league baseball until he was sidelined by a leg injury. His 11-year recording career was cut short by a tragic plane crash near Nashville on July 31, 1964. In 1967, he was inducted into the Country Music Hall of Fame.

425
I LOVED 'EM EVERY ONE
T.G. SHEPPARD
Warner Bros. 49690
Writer: Phil Sampson
Producer: Buddy Killen
May 16, 1981 (1 week)

"We've had three or four songs in our career that when you think of T.G. Sheppard, you think of those songs. I call them signature songs."

That's T.G. Sheppard's way of describing the biggest records in his career, and the *coup de grace* came with "I Loved 'Em Every One." Buoyed by a haunting, minor-chord progression and a catchy, repetitive chorus enumerating romantic exploits, the record, in Sheppard's view, was timed perfectly.

"Country music was really going pop. The cowboy boots and hats and jeans and pickup trucks were really hot. *The Electric Horseman* and soundtracks were *in* in country music, and television was exploiting country music on 'The Tonight Show' and specials."

Various country acts had benefited in the not-too-distant past from hits that crossed over onto the pop charts, including "Somebody's Knockin'," by Terri Gibbs; and, of course, "9 To 5" [see 409], by Dolly Parton. Warner Bros. was likewise ready to capitalize on the trend with Sheppard. T.G. recalls that "they shipped it to pop and country stations at the very same time." As a result, "I Loved 'Em Every One" entered both charts on March 14,

1981, peaking at number 37 in *Billboard*'s Hot 100, while topping the country list on May 16.

"I was totally in shock," says Sheppard of the song's broad-based appeal. "It was our first crossover record, but it wasn't planned that way. We just struck with a great song, a great lyric and a great track."

It was hardly producer Buddy Killen's first crack at the pop charts, though. An Alabama native, Killen was hired by Jack Stapp for $35 a week to pitch songs for Tree Publishing back in 1953. In fact, he was responsible for getting "Heartbreak Hotel" from songwriter Mae Axton to Elvis Presley.

Killen's instrumental recording of "Forever" went to number nine on the pop charts in 1960 for the Little Dippers, and Buddy produced 27 charted singles for soul star Joe Tex, including "Hold What You've Got," "Skinny Legs And All" and "I Gotcha."

As a musician, Killen played bass on such number one country hits as "White Lightning" by George Jones and "Walk On By" by Leroy Van Dyke. He was touring with Hank Williams' Drifting Cowboys when Williams passed away, and he also went on the road with Ray Price and Jim Reeves.

426
SEVEN YEAR ACHE
ROSANNE CASH
Columbia 11426
Writer: Rosanne Cash
Producer: Rodney Crowell
May 23, 1981 (1 week)

Rosanne Cash didn't set out to be a recording artist. Originally, she found greater interest in acting, and majored in drama at Nashville's Vanderbilt University. After heading to California to study at the Lee Strasberg Theatre Institute, she received an offer from Ariola Records in Germany to make an album, which proved a harrowing experience.

Cash went into a deep depression, caused by a severe lack of confidence in her vocal abilities, and it took months to laboriously complete that first project. Not surprisingly, Ariola never released that album, although the company did release Rosanne from the label. Back in the States, the project garnered attention from Columbia Records—ironically, the same label for whom her father, Johnny Cash, recorded.

Columbia didn't release the album either, but had her record a new one instead. She chose as her producer Rodney Crowell, whom she had met at a party on October 16, 1976. Against her mother's wishes, Rosanne struck up a relationship with Rodney, and they married on April 7, 1979.

The previous month, Rodney produced "No Memories Hangin' 'Round," Rosanne's duet with Bobby Bare, at Emmylou Harris' home in Los Angeles [see 313—"Two More Bottles Of Wine"]. Rosanne's first single, it peaked at number 17. Two more singles appeared from the *Right or Wrong* album, and in August of 1980, Cash headed to Davlen Sound in North Hollywood to work on her follow-up album. The first single—and title track—from that release was "Seven Year Ache," a semi-autobiographical song she wrote after a fight with Rodney at a French restaurant on Ventura Boulevard.

"I think it took, like, six months to write it," she remembers. "It started out as a very long poem, and I started it before the argument. I heard Rickie Lee Jones' first album, and I thought, 'God, I love all those street songs. There aren't any songs about bein' on the street in country music. I'd love to write a country street song.'

"Then Rodney and I had the fight, and we left each other on the street. So those things all kind of fell together—this poem, getting inspired by this argument—and I refined this long, long poem into 'Seven Year Ache.'"

It became her first number one record, and also rose to number 22 on *Billboard*'s Hot 100.

Rosanne Cash

427

ELVIRA

THE OAK RIDGE BOYS

MCA 51084
Writer: Dallas Frazier
Producer: Ron Chancey
May 30, 1981 (1 week)

A Texas bar band is responsible for the biggest-selling country record ever made in Nashville.

Eddy Raven had a tour in Texas, and he brought along two of his associates at Acuff-Rose Publishing, Ronnie Gant and Roy Acuff, Jr. One night in Houston, Raven sat with them in the audience while the opening act played, and when that group launched into "Elvira," Gant noted that Acuff-Rose owned the publishing rights to the song.

"I told him he needed to work on that," Raven remembers. "He said, 'You know, [record producer Ron] Chancey's been calling me. The Oak Ridge Boys need a song, and the bass player's raisin' hell, 'cause they don't give him a song that he can star in.' I said, 'Well, this song's perfect. Listen.' About that time, the bass guy is singin', and Ronnie said, 'Well, that's it.' "

"Elvira" already enjoyed a lengthy history. Dallas Frazier wrote it in the mid-'60s after he spied Elvira Street during a drive through Madison, Tennessee. Frazier hit the pop chart with it in 1966, and the song was subsequently cut eight more times from 1967 through 1980, the best-known versions belonging to Kenny Rogers & The First Edition and Rodney Crowell, who took it to number 95 on the country chart. The song finally broke through when Chancey took it to the Oaks.

"Ron called me while we were listening at my house," notes Oak Ridge Boy Duane Allen. "He said, 'I got this crazy idea for a song, and I'm not gonna tell you what it is until I get there,' and he wouldn't tell me what it was until it started playin'.

"I knew the song, but it didn't really hit me until Ron Chancey came in and pitched it directly for us. We knew it would be a hit. We just had never had anything that big."

With Richard Sterban belting out the "oom-papa-mow-mow" 's, "Elvira" easily topped the country chart in its ninth week. It also landed on the Hot 100 that summer, soaring to number five. By August, "Elvira" sold more than a million copies, and has now sold more than 2.5 million.

The Country Music Association and Academy of Country Music both named it the Single of the Year, and "Elvira" also netted the Oak Ridge Boys their only Grammy as a country act.

428

FRIENDS/ANYWHERE THERE'S A JUKEBOX

RAZZY BAILEY

RCA 12199
Writers: Danny Morrison, Johnny Slate/
Razzy Bailey
Producer: Bob Montgomery
June 6, 1981 (1 week)

"It was just a scam," says record producer Bob Montgomery of the song "Friends." "[Danny Morrison and Johnny Slate] conned me out of an advance so they could go to Florida and play golf."

Montgomery unwittingly set himself up. He agreed to give Morrison and Slate the money for their vacation (they told him they needed to get out of town and write in a different atmosphere), and he also introduced them to Lobo, whose beach house they visited. A year earlier, Montgomery had produced Lobo's pop hit "Where Were You When I Was Falling In Love."

"We'd been there three weeks and had not written a song," Morrison recounts. "We had about twenty-five ideas, and just couldn't seem to get anything put together. The last night we were there, we said, 'We've gotta write somethin'.' So we went upstairs and just beat it out, and we had most of the song written, except we didn't have a hook. We didn't know where to go with it. I happened to get lucky from a power stronger than me, who sent down 'Who makes better lovers than friends?' It just all fell in place."

Upon their return to Nashville, Montgomery asked how many songs they had created. When they replied "one," he told them that it better be good. Fortunately for Slate and Morrison, Montgomery loved the song. Reportedly, before Razzy Bailey got it, "Friends" first went to Mac Davis.

"He was gonna record the song," Bailey remembers, "but he wanted part of the [writers' royalties] on it—so the story goes—and they didn't want to give up part of the writing, because they'd already written the song. They kept it for me then."

They ran into one more problem with the song. While Bailey, Montgomery, Slate and Morrison were all out in California, someone from the House of Gold publishing firm pitched "Friends" to producer Jerry Crutchfield, who recorded it with Tanya Tucker and Glen Campbell. Since it had already been reserved for Bailey, Montgomery had to smooth out that wrinkle to keep Tucker and Campbell from releasing it.

"Friends" was backed by "Anywhere There's A Jukebox," a tune that Bailey wrote after an appearance at a Macon, Georgia, club called Nashville South, before he ever signed with RCA.

The result was Bailey's second straight double-sided hit.

429
WHAT ARE WE DOIN' IN LOVE
DOTTIE WEST
Liberty 1404
Writer: Randy Goodrum
Producers: Brent Maher, Randy Goodrum
June 13, 1981 (1 week)

Dottie West's fifth number one single, "What Are We Doin' In Love," was also Kenny Rogers' eleventh and their third chart-topper as a duo, although that fact can't be deduced merely from examining the record label. Kenny's name does not appear anywhere on the record.

"It was obviously me, and I agreed to do it," said Kenny in 1989, long after he had forgotten the matter. "It was Dottie's record, and I didn't need recognition at the time."

"[The record company] really wanted it to be a Dottie West record," concurs producer Brent Maher. "She actually started the song off. She sang the first verse, and he joined on the chorus, and then sang the second verse. He had so many duets going at that time, and they had done a lot of duets together, and that was Kenny's idea. He said, 'I'd love to sing with Dottie, and I love the song. But I don't want to do a duet—I want it to be her record.'"

Maher was the one who originally envisioned the number as a duet, after hearing it at songwriter/co-producer Randy Goodrum's house before a night on the town.

"We were goin' out to a movie or somethin'," Maher remembers. "He said, 'Let me play you this tune I just wrote today.' He started playin'

it, and, man, it just killed me. It was almost like a *West Side Story* kind of melody, really hip [chord] changes.

"He said, 'Who do you think that would be good for?' and I said, 'Man, we ought to cut that on Dottie and get Kenny to go along with it and do a duet.' Kenny came in and they did it all together, and it was quite fun, actually."

"What Are We Doin' In Love" debuted at number 68 on April 4, 1981, one notch below "Elvira" [see 427]. Ten weeks later, the song Dottie characterized in a bio as "the prettiest thing we've done" reached number one.

The following year, the record received a Grammy nomination for Best Country Vocal Performance by a Duo or Group with Vocal. When David Frizzell & Shelly West received similar honors for "You're The Reason God Made Oklahoma" [see 420], it was the first time a mother and daughter had been nominated as competitors in the same Grammy category.

430
BUT YOU KNOW I LOVE YOU
DOLLY PARTON
RCA 12200
Writer: Mike Settle
Producer: Mike Post
June 20, 1981 (1 week)

With her first movie [see 409—"9 To 5"] still doing well at the box office, Dolly Parton scored another career first on February 20, 1981, with her debut as a Las Vegas headliner at the Riviera Hotel. She won over audiences and critics alike, with a show that featured four different sets and a show-stopping imitation of Elvis Presley.

The second number in Parton's Vegas concerts was "But You Know I Love You," a song that became the second single from her *9 to 5 and Odd Jobs* album one month later.

"We were doing songs that dealt with different lines of work," she reports. "We thought that 'But You Know I Love You' dealt with traveling salesmen, with musicians, with a lot of people that travel for different reasons, so that's why we picked it. We were looking for songs in that album that dealt with working people."

"But You Know I Love You" was already a well-established song when Dolly turned in her version. Bill Anderson recorded it in 1969 [see 153—"World Of Make Believe"], and Kenny Rogers & The First Edition took it to the pop charts that same year—naturally, since songwriter Mike Settle was a member of the First Edition.

Mike Post produced the band at that time, and joined Dolly in the studio for the *9 to 5* album. The two had first met when she appeared as a guest on "The Mac Davis Show" in the mid-'70s. "We became instant friends," she says, "so we kind of piddled around in the studio at different times after that. I love working with him. He's so full of life, and magic and talent."

Post is probably best known for his work on television. As a pop artist/producer, he has racked up two Top Ten singles, with the theme from "The Rockford Files" and the theme from "Hill Street Blues." He has also been responsible for the themes to "Magnum, P.I.," "L.A. Law" and "The A-Team."

Post produced one more single from the *9 to 5* album, a working-girl rendition of "The House Of The Rising Sun." It served, somewhat unexpectedly, as a precursor for Dolly's second movie role, in *The Best Little Whorehouse in Texas* [see 490—"I Will Always Love You"].

In the interim, Parton scored two more Top Ten records: "Single Women" and "Heartbreak Express."

431
BLESSED ARE THE BELIEVERS
ANNE MURRAY

Capitol 4987
Writers: Charlie Black, Rory Bourke, Sandy Pinkard
Producer: Jim Ed Norman
June 27, 1981 (1 week)

Beginning in 1979, Charlie Black and Rory Bourke supplied one single per year for Anne Murray. The first was "Shadows In The Moonlight" [see 347], and the string continued in 1980 with "Lucky Me" (a follow-up to her cover of the Monkees' "Daydream Believer") and in 1981 with "Blessed Are The Believers."

"It's just as if a lot of times these guys are writing for me," she says. "That's the way I feel about them. I know they're not—they get together and write these songs the way they hear them and feel them, kind of hoping for the best. But I listen to them, and go, 'Oh, that's for me.'"

That belief held up with "Blessed Are The Believers," a song that drew on the phraseology of the Beatitudes. On this occasion, Black and Bourke co-wrote with Sandy Pinkard in California, at the persuasion of Randy Talmadge, who worked in the Los Angeles branch of the Chappell publishing company.

"Randy and Sandy threw a big party for us," says Bourke. "It was really nice, and Sandy said, 'Well, look, I'll cook you a lamb curry dinner—my specialty.' So we went over to his house, and we ate this wonderful meal; it was just out of this world. We were all sitting around with guitars, and that song just kind of evolved out of the room." "I had sort of a believer idea that was some kind of disjointed thing," adds Black. "I was throwing out words into the air. I think Rory sort of said the rest of the title, and it just suggested the rest of it."

"Randy Talmadge sat there at the table with us the whole time," Bourke continues, "and read a magazine, gave us encouragement—if it wasn't for Randy Talmadge, I don't think that song would have been written in three million years. When it was over, about two hours later, I had to take a walk around the block. I was higher than a kite, just from the beautifulness of the situation."

Murray scored another Top Ten single, "It's All I Can Do," later that year, and her first release of 1982 was another Bourke/Black collaboration, "Another Sleepless Night." That year also brought her Top Ten releases with "Hey! Baby!" and "Somebody's Always Saying Goodbye."

432
I WAS COUNTRY WHEN COUNTRY WASN'T COOL
BARBARA MANDRELL

MCA 51107
Writers: Kye Fleming, Dennis Morgan
Producer: Tom Collins
July 4, 1981 (1 week)

You know you've written a standard when the title becomes a slogan, and many artists have said in one interview or another: "I was country when country wasn't cool."

"I had that idea for about two weeks before we wrote it," explains songwriter Kye Fleming. "I just jotted it down in my notebook. It was in the middle of the *Urban Cowboy* [see 389—"Stand By Me"] stuff, and it just seemed like the right time."

ically, the song was cut in the studio; released on April 16, it was already in *Billboard*'s Top Five when she recorded the album.

Collins flew piano player David Briggs from Nashville to L.A. for the session. Bassist Neil Stubenhaus couldn't get out of an earlier session, and showed up at the end of their booking. Mandrell cut her lead vocal without any bass, and Stubenhaus overdubbed his part during the final 20 minutes.

With George Jones cited in the lyrics, they decided to get another vocalist to join her on the record. At first they considered Ernest Tubb, but then decided on Jones himself. When Mandrell took a flight from L.A. to Nashville, George sat in the seat behind her, and she asked him at that time to participate.

It took Jones only ten minutes in the studio to give Collins a definitive take. "I never will forget his blue jeans," says Collins. "That was the neatest crease in a pair of blue jeans I've ever seen in my life."

Collins and engineer Les Ladd found some old tapes at Woodland Sound with crowd noise and turned the record into a "live" single. It quickly became Mandrell's biggest record.

433

FIRE AND SMOKE
EARL THOMAS CONLEY
Sunbird 7561
Writer: Earl Thomas Conley
Producers: Nelson Larkin,
Earl Thomas Conley
July 11, 1981 (1 week)

Despite a lifelong interest in music, Earl Thomas Conley never took up songwriting until 1968, at age 26. Immediately, however, he pursued the craft with vigor, commuting for two years between his native Portsmouth, Ohio, and Nashville, where he encountered little interest.

In 1970, Conley moved to Huntsville, Alabama, where he continued performing in nightclubs, devoting so much effort to his music that he put his home life in jeopardy. The family survived, though, and Conley set up his future recording career with a visit to a nearby studio. Earl and his brother, Fred, walked in one evening around 9:00 and sprung a tape on studio owner Nelson Larkin, a four-hour-a-night producer who earned his living by selling insurance.

Barbara Mandrell

It took several weeks for Kye to tell songwriter Dennis Morgan and record producer Tom Collins about the idea. "It was a little scary to write," she told *Billboard*'s Edward Morris. "We knew it could be real big or a real joke."

Around Christmas of 1980, Fleming and Morgan went out to California and visited with Barbara Mandrell, who was working on her television show [see 478—" 'Til You're Gone"]. They played five or six songs for Barbara beside her pool, and she reacted strongly to "I Was Country When Country Wasn't Cool."

The song became the centerpiece of *Barbara Mandrell Live*, recorded on June 7, 1981, in the Roy Acuff Theater at Opryland. Iron-

"The tape was awful, compared to today, and I started to tell him that," Larkin recalls. "I said, 'This is bad, but why don't you come back tomorrow?' Usually, that's not my style, and he came back the next day, and so we started a relationship then. There was something there that I liked about him. I liked his voice, and I liked him, for some reason, and just made that split decision."

Larkin released several Conley recordings—including a 1971 remake of "The Night They Drove Old Dixie Down"—on his own Prize label, and the two eventually brought their production team to GRT Records. In 1975, Conley made his first appearance on the *Billboard* country chart, with "I Have Loved You Girl (But Not Like This Before)." Four additional singles charted through 1979, none placing higher than number 67.

Earl moved briefly to Warner Bros., where he charted three more singles, but the label dropped him. In the meantime, Larkin had formed an independent Nashville label, Sunbird Records, and Earl suggested they give it one more try. Larkin bought out ETC's contract, and their first Sunbird session yielded three sides for Conley's *Blue Pearl* album: "Too Much Noise (Trucker's Waltz)," "Silent Treatment" and "Fire And Smoke."

"Silent Treatment" hit number seven in February of 1981, and "Fire And Smoke" topped the chart as a follow-up, a remarkable achievement for a small record company. Both songs were intertwined—Conley wrote the chorus for "Fire And Smoke" in the mid-'70s, but couldn't write the verses until after he penned "Silent Treatment" five years later.

<h1 style="text-align:center">434</h1>

FEELS SO RIGHT
ALABAMA
RCA 12236
Writer: Randy Owen
Producers: Alabama, Larry McBride, Harold Shedd
July 18, 1981 (2 weeks)

"The first time I heard 'Feels So Right' was at a showcase we did after we had signed with RCA," says record producer Harold Shedd, "and I thought, 'Here's one—we've got to do this song.'"

Shedd was the first person outside of Alabama to express interest in "Feels So Right,"

though. Songwriter Randy Owen wrote it in 15 minutes at his parents' house when he was 19 or 20 years old, and in the ensuing decade, he shopped it around Nashville on several occasions. The city's publishers continually told him it was a good start, but it needed a "bridge." Rather than conform, he simply left it as is, and held onto it.

"If something inspires me to write about it, and I can make money from it, well, that's fine," notes Owen, "but I've never written songs just to write a song. Therefore, I've never written a bunch of songs. It has to be inspirational to me before I can get into it."

The inspiration for "Feels So Right" was a former classmate. "I just wrote it about a girl I knew," says Randy. "We always kind of liked one another back in high school, and she was married and I had a girlfriend. After a year or so, she divorced, and one night I was walkin' around the canyon and we just kind of ran into one another, and for a year or two, we had a wonderful thing. Then as a young person, a romantic, I wrote that song one evening."

Even his academic adviser at Jacksonville State University thought the song was just too corny, but Owen's faith in "Feels So Right" never wavered. Alabama used it as the title track for their second RCA album, and the sentiment apparently came through.

"We had people who thought the name of the song was 'Thistle Down,' 'Feels So Tight,' everything, you know," Randy recalls. "But still, they liked the song enough to buy it, and that's really what it's all about. It was a real heartfelt thing for me, a special thing."

Much like Lionel Richie's "Lady" [see 401], the song failed to conform to the usual rhyme scheme that Nashville deems almost sacred. However, it became one of only two Alabama records to stay at number one longer than a week.

<h1 style="text-align:center">435</h1>

DIXIE ON MY MIND
HANK WILLIAMS, JR.
Elektra 47137
Writer: Hank Williams, Jr.
Producer: Jimmy Bowen
August 1, 1981 (1 week)

"Dixie On My Mind" was a positive result of a negative experience Hank Williams, Jr., had to contend with in New York City.

Hank Williams, Jr.

Bocephus played the Lone Star Cafe, a small club at 13th Street and Fifth Avenue in historic Greenwich Village. Closed in 1989, the Lone Star hosted a range of performers, including old rock and roll acts, blues musicians, ensembles of studio players, folkies and country stars trying to build an audience in Manhattan.

The evening that Bocephus played, the crowd was a little more highbrow than he was used to, although it included a couple of guys he invited onto his bus: actor Gary Busey and New York Yankees relief pitcher Rich "Goose" Gossage.

"Goose was loaded, and Gary Busey was loaded," remembers Hank's manager, Merle Kilgore, "and the stage was so small that you could shake hands with the bartender. You could absolutely shake hands with the bartender and be on stage. Hank hated that place."

During the show, Williams literally had Dixie on his mind, and the next day, he flew back to his home in Florida, where he went fishing with Allman Brothers Band guitarist Dickey Betts. Out of his big-city experience, Hank came up with "Dixie On My Mind," but the record caused him a problem when he went back to New York.

Bocephus' commentary on the Big Apple was hardly complimentary. Granted, the city is a hassle to its residents, but he referred to New Yorkers as "squirrels" and "porcupines," and his anti-Manhattan stance kept him from getting any substantial airplay on the city's two country radio stations. In fact, when he returned to do a guest DJ stint at WHN, the station received a bomb threat. As a result, Bocephus was assigned two armed bodyguards.

"That's gonna happen," he said. "They told me when Merle Haggard was there in 1971 he had 'The Fightin' Side Of Me' [see 50] out and they said, 'Oh, we're gonna get you,' and all that kind of stuff. That means you're hot, when that kind of stuff happens."

436

TOO MANY LOVERS

CRYSTAL GAYLE

Columbia 02078
Writers: Mark True, Ted Lindsay,
Sam Hogin
Producer: Allen Reynolds
August 8, 1981 (1 week)

" 'Why Have You Left The One You Left Me For' [see 334] took five minutes to write," says songwriter Mark True, "and 'Too Many Lovers' took two years."

Though True wrote "Why Have You Left The One" on his own, he was signed to Pic-A-Lic as half of a team, with Ted Lindsay, and their partnership yielded "Too Many Lovers" two different times.

"Ted came up with the idea, 'too many lovers, not enough love,'" True explains, "and we wrote the song two years before the hit song that came out. We decided it wasn't any good, and we weren't doin' anything with it. One night I was sittin' around with Sam Hogin, who wrote 'I Believe In You' [see 397] for Don Williams, and I brought up the idea. I always thought it was a great idea, but we didn't write the song right."

"We changed that song around completely," Hogin continues, "and wrote that song real fast—I guess in about an hour. If you could hear the original demo, it was in the bag of a Blondie song. It was like slam-dance music, real fast and punkish."

Crystal Gayle recorded it, but asked the writers for permission to change the title to "These Days," a phrase that appears more often in the song than "Too Many Lovers." Lindsay objected and it went out under the original moniker, though Crystal titled the album *These Days*. It followed "If You Ever Change Your Mind" [see 402] as the second single from the album.

Crystal released one more album for Columbia later in 1981. *Hollywood, Tennessee* was her last before jumping to the smaller Elektra roster, and it yielded a trio of Top Ten singles: "The Woman In Me," "You Never Gave Up On Me" and "Livin' In These Troubled Times."

By the end of 1982, she had added several collaborative efforts to her resumé. Gayle earned a number one duet with Eddie Rabbitt on "You And I" [see 497], and sang with offbeat pop singer Tom Waits in the Francis Ford Coppola film *One from the Heart*. Additionally, she

joined Paul Williams on the theme song to the short-lived ABC series "It Takes Two."

437

I DON'T NEED YOU

KENNY ROGERS

Liberty 1415
Writer: Rick Christian
Producer: Lionel Richie
August 15, 1981 (2 weeks)

On August 15, 1981, Lionel Richie was the hottest figure in pop music. He and Diana Ross held the number one position on the *Billboard* Hot 100 with "Endless Love." At number three that same week was "I Don't Need You," which he produced for Kenny Rogers.

Both were recorded during the same period of time—a grueling period in which Richie divided his days between the Commodores' *In the Pocket* album and Kenny's *Share Your Love*. Lionel worked from 10:00 A.M. to 6:00 P.M. on one project, and then continued from 6:00 P.M. to midnight on the other. When the chance to cut "Endless Love" came up, he had to meet Ross at 3:30 A.M. in Reno.

Despite the crunch, Richie turned out a very successful album for Kenny. The first single, "I Don't Need You," appeared on the country chart on June 20, a week after its debut on the Hot 100.

"As a rule, I find all of my own songs," says Kenny. "I really have a network of people, and when it's time for me to record, I start putting out the feelers and saying, 'Guys, here's what I'm looking for: I need this and I need that.' That song came along in the course of looking through hundreds of songs. It just jumped out at me."

"The selection of the material was most important," Lionel told Ed Harrison in *Billboard*. "It took a month and a half to pick it. I wanted to cross the bridge between contemporary and country. I wanted Kenny's vocals to sound better than ever."

After it topped the country chart, Kenny followed "I Don't Need You" with three more Richie-produced successes. "Share Your Love With Me," "Blaze Of Glory" and "Through The Years" all hit the Top Ten. In return, Rogers provided background vocals on "My Love," from Richie's first solo album.

"It's funny," Kenny notes, "because at the time, I lived in L.A. and Lionel lived in Tuskegee [Alabama]. I kept saying, 'Lionel, this is foolish. You're going to be a major star, and you need to live in California.' So to this day, he thinks it's funny that I talked him into moving from Tuskegee to California, and then a year later, I moved back to Georgia."

438

(THERE'S) NO GETTIN' OVER ME
RONNIE MILSAP
RCA 12264
Writers: Tommy Brasfield, Walt Aldridge
Producers: Ronnie Milsap, Tom Collins
August 29, 1981 (2 weeks)

Tommy Brasfield and Walt Aldridge had been writing songs in Muscle Shoals for a year before they ever showed any to their publisher, but when they finally did present one, it was worth the wait.

Aldridge—a studio guitarist and engineer at FAME Studio—and Brasfield were working for producer Rick Hall on a Mac Davis album when they started "(There's) No Gettin' Over Me." "After the sessions were over," Aldridge recalls, "I'd bounce upstairs where Tom was parked, workin' on the song, and we'd get back into the song. In fact, we got stuck at one point and actually went downstairs to ask Mac if he would help us on the song. Of course, his mind was on the record he was makin'."

They spent an entire week on the song, and once it was completed, they made their first demo, with Aldridge singing lead and playing guitar. Brasfield took the finished product to Nashville. The first artist he approached passed on the song, but he went to Ronnie Milsap's office and played it for Rob Galbraith.

Milsap had already completed an album and turned it in to RCA, but Galbraith thought Ronnie should hear "No Gettin' Over Me," and, along with producer Tom Collins, they decided to make the record quickly. They recorded it about a dozen times, remaining faithful to the demo, but kept the first take. "It seemed like the more we did it, the magic just wasn't there anymore," says Milsap. "We cut it, overdubbed it and finished it the next day and mixed it," adds Collins.

RCA was already pressing copies of "It's All I Can Do," scheduled as the first single from the album, but Milsap was so enthusiastic about "No Gettin' Over Me" that he called division chief Jerry Bradley and asked him to stop the pressing. An incredulous Bradley balked, telling Milsap to bring a copy of the new song by the next morning at 8:30—"but it better be good."

On first hearing, though, Bradley called Indianapolis to stop the pressing, and within two weeks, "No Gettin' Over Me" was pressed and shipped on yellow vinyl.

It became Milsap's biggest single, ultimately yielding his third Grammy award. In addition to its number one status on the country chart, it also spent five weeks at number five on the Hot 100.

439

OLDER WOMEN
RONNIE McDOWELL
Epic 02129
Writer: Jamie O'Hara
Producer: Buddy Killen
September 12, 1981 (1 week)

August 16, 1977, is a day that has gone down in music history through the death of Elvis Presley. Like the rest of America, Ronnie McDowell was deeply disturbed when he heard the news in his hometown of Portland, Tennessee. In fact, McDowell was so upset that he wrote a tribute to Presley, and a few days later, his wife, Karen, wrote $2,800 worth of rubber checks to pay for McDowell to record the song.

The morning after his session, McDowell took five acetates to Nashville, and within a couple of hours, the pop and rock stations were calling their country competitors for a copy of "The King Is Gone." Though the record sold a million copies in a short three weeks, it peaked on the *Billboard* country charts at number 13. It took another four years for Ronnie to finally reach number one.

With the success of "The King Is Gone," McDowell was immediately branded an Elvis imitator; when he imitated Presley on the soundtrack of the Kurt Russell film *Elvis*, the association became even stronger. In 1979, Ronnie hooked up with producer Buddy Killen, who moved him from Scorpion Records to Epic, and in early 1981, he peaked at number two with "Wandering Eyes," written by Jamie O'Hara [see 722—"Can't Stop My Heart From Loving You"].

Around the same time, O'Hara had started dating a lady who surpassed him in years, and one morning, he woke up with inspiration to write "Older Women." Its melody was quite similar to "Wandering Eyes," but McDowell was reluctant to cut it.

"I turned it down the first time, because I didn't think that women would like to be known as 'older,'" McDowell relates, "then he played it for me as I was getting on the elevator to do a session. I listened to it again, and I said, 'You're right, Jamie, that's not a put-down. That's a great positive thing for women over 25.'"

It turned into a positive thing for McDowell, too, when he recorded it in one take, with the Jordanaires on backing vocals. In fact, it worked so well that McDowell and Killen wrote a third song with an almost identical melody: "Watchin' Girls Go By" was released as a follow-up, peaking at number four.

Ronnie
McDowell

440
YOU DON'T KNOW ME
MICKEY GILLEY
Epic 02172
Writers: Cindy Walker, Eddy Arnold
Producers: Jim Ed Norman
September 19, 1981 (1 week)

"You Don't Know Me" was a case of a country song that became a pop hit, only to return under Mickey Gilley's performance as a country single once more.

The idea belonged to Eddy Arnold, who mulled over the title for a couple of years before finally taking it to songwriter Cindy Walker, who helped him work out the storyline. Arnold intended to portray a man who is too shy to approach a woman and stands in the shadows, watching her settle down with another man.

Arnold's recording reached number 10 on the *Billboard* country chart in 1956, and Ray Charles remade it six years later. His version peaked at number two on the Hot 100, nosed out by Tommy Roe's "Sheila."

"I almost laid down and kicked when Jim Ed Norman brought the song in, because I was such a big fan of Ray Charles," notes Gilley. "But Jim Ed said he could promise that it would be a good record. One thing I could always say about Jim Ed: if he said it'd be a good record, you could hang it on the wall, because he'd make it a good record."

Though neither Arnold nor Charles could reach the top position, Gilley gained a number one single with "You Don't Know Me" on September 19, 1981. "Ray Charles had a record on it that I just thought nobody could top," he still maintains. "I picked the thing apart, and I feel like it's the best job that I could do on it. I still don't think I topped it."

Charles' connections with country date back to 1962, when he released two landmark volumes titled *Modern Sounds in Country and Western Music*. Twenty years later, on the heels of Gilley's success with "You Don't Know Me," Charles signed a country deal with Columbia Records.

Ray released a solo album, *Wish You Were Here Tonight,* and followed with a duet album titled *Friendship*. Included was his duet with Willie Nelson on "Seven Spanish Angels" [see 612], as well as collaborations with Hank Williams, Jr., B.J. Thomas and one more with Gilley—"It Ain't Gonna Worry My Mind," which reached number 12 in 1985.

TIGHT FITTIN' JEANS
CONWAY TWITTY
MCA 51137
Writer: Mike Huffman
Producers: Conway Twitty, Ron Chancey
September 26, 1981 (1 week)

"What I have done doesn't impress me at all," says Conway Twitty. "The only thing that counts is that next record. The rest of it, 'Conway did this . . .,' so what? The only thing that's gonna keep [the career] alive is that next record. It's 99 percent song, and it's one percent talent and look, and all those other things in there.

"If there's any so-called secret to my longevity, it lies in that one area right there. When it comes to songs, I've got the patience of Job. I'll go through 3,000 to pick 10 to go on the next album. Some of 'em I hear over and over and over and over, and the really good ones, you can't record 'em all.

"I'll get it down to a 100. That's pretty easy. From 100 down to 50, it's hard, and from 50 down to 30 is really hard, and I hate to let 'em go. I agonize over 'em before I'll turn one of 'em loose."

Among the survivors of Twitty's rigorous trials is "Tight Fittin' Jeans," a barroom variation on the classic theme of love between a wealthy lady and "common" man, in this case a cowboy. Conway loved the song, although his wife, Dee Henry, hates it so much that she turns the station if it comes on while she's in the car.

"Every once in a while," he admits, "you've got to do something for the guys."

That's contrary to the usual ploy that Twitty takes [see 272—"I Can't Believe She Gives It All To Me"], but in this instance, targeting men paid off handsomely. "Tight Fittin' Jeans" debuted at a modest number 71 on July 11, 1981, but in the fall, "Jeans" cloaked the top spot in its twelfth week on the chart.

The song came from Charley Pride's publishing company, and Pride was miffed with his associate, Jim Prater, that he didn't get to record it himself.

"We were standin' in front of some building out in L.A.," Twitty remembers, "some awards show or somethin'. Charley Pride was just jumpin' up and down over that song. Jim said, 'Well, dammit, I pitched it to *you* 15 times and you turned it down.'"

MIDNIGHT HAULER/SCRATCH MY BACK (AND WHISPER IN MY EAR)
RAZZY BAILEY
RCA 12268
Writers: Wood Newton, Tim DuBois/
Raymond Moore, Marcell Strong,
Earl Cage, Jr.
Producer: Bob Montgomery
October 3, 1981 (1 week)

Razzy Bailey's unusual first name first belonged to his father, Erastus. In high school, Erastus' classmates called him Razzy, and he legally bestowed the same monicker on his boy, spelled "Rasie." It was frequently mispronounced, and Bailey altered the spelling to its current double-Z status.

Born near Five Points, Alabama, on Valentine's Day in 1939, Razzy helped his father work as a "truck" farmer, and trucks played a role in his fourth number one single, "Midnight Hauler," albeit for different reasons.

Tim DuBois and Wood Newton actually wrote the song two or three years before Razzy recorded it.

"The entire lyric was written one night as I was following a truck from Tulsa to Stillwater, Oklahoma," says DuBois. "The truck had a little sign on the back of it that said 'Midnight Hauler.' I was just whippin' along followin' him, and about three hours later, I was in Stillwater and had the lyric, and jotted it down after I completed the trip. Wood and I wrote the music to it, and made some minuscule lyric changes several years later, maybe two or three years later."

"Actually, Jimmy Bowen was doin' a soundtrack to a movie," adds producer Bob Montgomery. "They wrote that song for that movie. It was a truck-drivin' kind of movie. So I took it to Jimmy, and Jimmy turned it down, for whatever reason."

It remained unrecorded for a couple of years until Razzy told Montgomery that he wanted to cut a truckin' song.

"I was doin' a lot of one-nighters," remembers Bailey. "I'd been out there for three or four years at this time, but it never ceased to amaze me how much time we spent visitin' with the truckers on the CB. We'd stop, of course, at the truck stops and eat, sometimes take a shower, and always fueled up at truck stops, runnin' all hours of the day and night."

Backed by "Scratch My Back (And Whisper

In My Ear)," "Midnight Hauler" boogied its way to number one in October of 1981, Razzy's third consecutive double-sided hit to top the chart. It was the first time that someone had taken a trio of back-to-back hits to number one since Buck Owens in 1965-66.

Appropriately, Razzy's CB handle is now "Midnight Hauler."

443
PARTY TIME
T.G. SHEPPARD

Warner Bros. 49761
Writer: Bruce Channel
Producer: Buddy Killen
October 10, 1981 (1 week)

"I've never liked to cut records that all sound the same," says T.G. Sheppard. "To keep myself from having burned out over more than fifteen years, I kind of stay fresh with the music. When I feel like I need a change, I'll go out and try different things. I may fail, but at least I'll try, and occasionally you'll connect. When you do, it's worth the gamble."

"Party Time," which was eventually named by *Billboard* among the Top Five country records of 1981, was just such a change of pace. "We were doing a song that was sort of for the good ol' boy," he explains, "a glass of wine, and a girl having fun partyin', and it just gave us a base with the male audience. It showed that we weren't just a slick, romantic guy that sang for girls. We do music for guys, too."

Sheppard picked up "Party Time" from a guy named Bruce Channel, who had earned a number one pop record of his own with "Hey! Baby." Born November 28, 1940, Channel grew up in Texas, gaining a toehold in the business when he played on "The Louisiana Hayride" for six months in 1958. "Hey! Baby" was written with Margaret Cobb, and charted again when it was covered by Jose Feliciano and, later, by Ringo Starr.

"Hey! Baby" didn't regain hit status, though, until 1982, when Channel's friend, Jim Ed Norman, produced a version with Anne Murray which sailed to a country peak at number seven. Channel also wrote several more country hits: "As Long As I'm Rockin' With You" [see 570], by John Conlee; "Don't Worry 'Bout Me, Baby" [see 477], by Janie Frickie; and "Stand Up," by Mel McDaniel.

"Party Time" became T.G. Sheppard's sev-

T.G. Sheppard

enth number one hit, but it was originally slated for Jerry Lee Lewis, who'd asked Tree Publishing to put it on hold. Sheppard heard the song playing in one of Tree's studios when he walked into the company looking for songs, and was dismayed to learn it was already reserved for the Killer.

Says Sheppard: "I told them, 'If anything happens between now and the session, let me know.' For some reason, Jerry Lee Lewis took it off hold, and I cut it."

444
STEP BY STEP
EDDIE RABBITT

Elektra 47174
Writers: Eddie Rabbitt, Even Stevens, David Malloy
Producer: David Malloy
October 17, 1981 (1 week)

Nestled outside the Rocky Mountain community of Nederland, 20 miles from Denver, the Caribou Ranch once included a unique recording facility. Owned by former Chicago producer James Guercio (who founded Country Music Television), Caribou provided artists and musicians with a quiet, secluded environment, affording them a chance to focus on their work with a minimal number of distractions.

Several cabins were located close to the studio, where the performers, musicians and accompanying personnel set up quarters for the period of time it took to complete their projects. Caribou yielded such successful albums as *Chicago X*, Elton John's *Caribou*, Dan Fogelberg's *Nether Lands* and Eddie Rabbitt's 1981 album *Step by Step*.

Each morning, before their noon session, Rabbitt and producer David Malloy would head over to Even Stevens' cabin. Protected from the snow and the cold, they'd light a big fire, and Stevens would prepare breakfast while they mapped out the day's work schedule.

Rabbitt had thirty songs prepared to record for the album, and four or five were already completed as they ended the first of their two weeks at Caribou. At that time, they came up with *Step by Step*'s title track.

The song grew out of a comic routine. The Three Stooges had done a bit (later reprised on "I Love Lucy") in which a man goes crazy and kills someone every time he hears his ex-wife's name. Of course, the name is mentioned several times during the skit—and each time, the man turns into a murderous lunatic, intoning the words "Slowly I turn, step by step, inch by inch . . ."

"I had been doing this for a couple days, and we did it that morning," Malloy notes, "and we keyed it right on there. I remember Eddie and I started doing it. We started this 'first step' thing, and Eddie yelled at Even in the kitchen, 'Even, you better get in here,' so Even stopped. He was cookin' eggs and bacon. Even comes in goin', 'Wouldn't you know it? I'm cookin' and I leave you, and you start this song!'"

"We wrote it in about half an hour in my cabin there," Stevens adds, "and we knew it was wonderful, and went and recorded it. I think it was one of those first take-type deals."

It was also a "crossover"-type deal. "Step By Step" became Rabbitt's fourth consecutive number one country single on October 17, 1981. That same week, it peaked at number five on *Billboard*'s Hot 100, making Eddie the only country star to reach that pop level with three singles in a row during the '80s. "Step By Step" was also the first country video aired by MTV.

445

NEVER BEEN SO LOVED (IN ALL MY LIFE)
CHARLEY PRIDE
RCA 12294
Writers: Norro Wilson, Wayland Holyfield
Producer: Norro Wilson
October 24, 1981 (2 weeks)

In 1981, Charley Pride and producer Jerry Bradley made a mutual decision to end their day-to-day working relationship. At the time, both felt they had lost some of the excitement. Their last two singles, "You Almost Slipped My Mind" and "Roll On Mississippi," stopped at number four and number seven, respectively.

"Jerry and I had agreed that once we went about as far as we could go as co-producers, we might have to change to another producer," recalls Pride. "Jerry sort of handpicked Norro Wilson."

Wilson produced three tracks specifically for Pride's *Greatest Hits* album and played them for Bradley, who still ran the RCA operation. Bradley felt they were good enough to release, but told Wilson he thought they could do better.

"I think he raised the hair on the back of my neck," notes Wilson. "I went and got with Wayland Holyfield, who I think is one of the town's greatest writers, and one of my dearest friends, and I said, 'Dammit, let's just do this.'"

They were specifically shooting for something a bit more energetic and unusual to give Pride a shot in the arm. Holyfield nearly caused an accident when he came up with the title.

"The Sony handheld recorders had just come out, but I didn't have one then," he explains. "I was driving in the car, and I was trying to pull a pencil or a pen out of a bag. I almost hit a car head-on as I was trying to write that line, 'Never Been So Loved (In All My Life).' I almost got killed over Charley Pride."

Once the song was written, Wilson hired D. Bergen White to create the string parts. "His arrangement on that record meant as much almost as the song and the music," Norro says.

The bulk of the single was captured in a live session, rather than a series of overdubs. "All the strings, all the players were there, with a director," notes Holyfield. "This is the way they used to make records in the old, real old days. I think Charley overdubbed his final vocal later sometime, but he was in the studio singing his heart out and it was all just done in a couple or three takes."

With "Never Been So Loved," Pride became only the fourth artist in history to record 25 number one singles.

446
FANCY FREE
THE OAK RIDGE BOYS

MCA 51169
Writers: Jimbeau Hinson, Don August
Producer: Ron Chancey
November 7, 1981 (1 week)

"There's nothing as important to an artist's career as three minutes," says Oak Ridge Boy Duane Allen. "The next most important thing is three *more* minutes of magic."

Finding a three-minute follow-up to "Elvira" [see 427] presented the Oaks with a problem they hadn't counted on. "Elvira" garnered them recognition from pop listeners, yet the

The Oak
Ridge Boys

303

Fancy Free album didn't contain another track that the group felt could appeal to that market. By the same token, another "crossover" record could provide its own problems, since, when country acts attain that kind of attention, Nashville often criticizes them for "going pop."

The Oaks were able to deal with both issues quite easily. "Elvira" got a late start as a pop record, and didn't even enter *Billboard*'s Hot 100 until two weeks before it hit the top of the country chart. They released "Fancy Free" ("one of the most country-sounding songs on the album," according to Duane) shortly after "Elvira" peaked on the pop chart, and thus had two separate records going simultaneously in two different radio formats.

"That," quips Allen, "was a good day to live."

The Oaks first heard "Fancy Free" nine years before they recorded it.

"I never throw away a good song," Duane explains. "I'm highly critical, I think, of songs, and if a song catches my attention, then there's a good shot that maybe it will attract the attention of our fans. I always keep the tape."

"Fancy Free" debuted at number 55 on September 5, 1981. Two months later, the Oaks had their fifth number one record, with Allen singing lead.

Hailing from Taylortown, Texas, Allen gained his formal musical education at East Texas State University. At the same time, he spent three years as the writer, producer, host and salesman for his own one-hour daily gospel radio show on a Paris, Texas, station. Not surprisingly, he became the Oak Ridge Boys' chief businessman after joining in May of 1966.

In the early '70s, Duane wrote a book on gospel music history, and in the '80s, he began renting his antique cars for use in music videos and films. His automobiles now reside in a museum called "Ace On Wheels."

447

MY BABY THINKS HE'S A TRAIN

ROSANNE CASH

Columbia 02463
Writer: Leroy Preston
Producer: Rodney Crowell
November 14, 1981 (1 week)

"Western swing ain't dead; it's Asleep at the Wheel."

So cheered the marketing campaign behind the tenth album released by Asleep at the Wheel. Headed by Ray Benson, the band has seemingly been on the fringe of country success since its formation in rural West Virginia in 1970. Despite its ongoing popularity on the concert trail, the group has managed only one Top Ten single in its history, 1975's "The Letter That Johnny Walker Read."

Benson co-wrote that single with George Frayne (a.k.a. Commander Cody) and Asleep at the Wheel bandmate Leroy Preston, who later left the group, although he continued to write. Preston sent a demo tape of some of his material to Rodney Crowell, who produced two singles off that tape for his wife, Rosanne Cash. They held the nostalgic "I Wonder" for her *Somewhere in the Stars* project, and included Preston's rockabilly piece "My Baby Thinks He's A Train" on *Seven Year Ache* [see 426]. Albert Lee contributed some memorable "chicken-pickin'" guitar work.

"This was half Albert Lee's record, 'cause it's really a guitar-centered song, and Albert really got a chance to stretch out," says Rosanne. "I wasn't at all sure I could sing the song with those octave jumps. It was a style that I wasn't used to singing, and as much as I loved it, it was a bit intimidating to me. It was really like a duet with me and Albert."

By the second verse, the "quirky" single introduces captivating appearances by Emmylou Harris and Jackson Browne cohort Rosemary Butler on backing vocals.

"Rosanne and Rodney were really coming up with some great stuff at that point," notes Emmylou. "You could really sense that they were ready. Of course, I just added an itsy-bitsy, teeny-weeny part. Rosemary Butler is a wonderful singer, great harmonies—she had really done the hard part, and I just came in and added that little tiny thing."

Though the *Seven Year Ache* album was cut in Los Angeles, Cash and Crowell relocated to Nashville in 1981, taking a log home on an 11-acre tract south of the city. Rodney and Rosanne hoped to provide a better environment for their growing family, which included three daughters at that time. "There are too many things goin' on in California," she told Margaret Dick in *Country Song Roundup*. "There are too many temptations for the kids. I'm not saying that every kid out there is on drugs; we just think Nashville has a more stable environment."

Preston worked in a hardware store, but he quit that job when "My Baby Thinks He's A Train" became Rosanne's second number one single.

Mountain," by Claude King (1962); and "Ring Of Fire," by Johnny Cash (1963).

448

ALL MY ROWDY FRIENDS (HAVE SETTLED DOWN)
HANK WILLIAMS, JR.

Elektra 47191
Writer: Hank Williams, Jr.
Producer: Jimmy Bowen
November 21, 1981 (1 week)

The theme of many country stars' lives is one of a wild youth, followed by a repentant, or at least milder, maturity. Hank Williams, Jr., has seen it all firsthand, and many of the people he grew up with—Waylon Jennings, Johnny Cash, Kris Kristofferson, George Jones—became the subject of "All My Rowdy Friends (Have Settled Down)."

Hank characterizes "All My Rowdy Friends" as one of the easiest songs he has ever composed. Four other records debuted higher than "Rowdy" on September 5, 1981, but only one of them, "Fancy Free" [see 446], was able to equal its number one performance.

"Rowdy" also engendered a sequel three years later, "All My Rowdy Friends Are Coming Over Tonight," which went to number 10. "Rowdy II" was accompanied by a landmark video clip, in which Williams called on Porter Wagoner, Leon Redbone, George Jones, George Thorogood, Cheech & Chong and songwriter Paul Williams, among others. It earned airplay on MTV (unusual for a country artist) and brought Bocephus his first Country Music Association award, for Video of the Year.

Like his rowdy friends, Hank insists he's settled down, too, though rumors to the contrary have often circulated. "I smoke a few Salems and drink a little whiskey," he conceded to Barry Bronson in the *Music City News*. "But when it comes to me and my show, we don't put up with any drugs—zero. You don't have 35 people working for you and the success I've had and all the opportunities, and be a pothead. It tees me off that people think that."

Kilgore remains the closest of Bocephus' friends. A friend of Hank's daddy, he met the younger Williams when he was just three days old, but Kilgore was on his way to his own successes. "Love Has Made You Beautiful" took him into the Top Ten as an artist in 1960, and he has also penned three number one singles: "More And More" [see 537—"Night Games"], by Webb Pierce (1954); "Wolverton

449

MY FAVORITE MEMORY
MERLE HAGGARD

Epic 02504
Writer: Merle Haggard
Producers: Lewis Talley, Merle Haggard
November 28, 1981 (1 week)

In 1981, Merle Haggard signed a new, lucrative contract with Epic Records, and the first two albums under the deal brought about a resurgence in his lengthy career. "I Think I'll Just Stay Here And Drink" [see 407] represented his only number one single during a four-year tenure with MCA. He rounded out that agreement with "Leonard" [see 238—"The Roots Of My Raising"] and his live recording, "Rainbow Stew."

In the fall of 1981, Haggard released his frank autobiography, *Sing Me Back Home*, written with Peggy Russell. It chronicled the details of his private life, including his stay in prison [see 1—"Sing Me Back Home"], his romantic feelings for Dolly Parton [see 204—"Always Wanting You"] and memories of his father's death [see 16—"Mama Tried"].

"I'm not sure it was the right thing, putting all my life down in this book," he admitted to *People*'s Dolly Carlisle. "I can see it in people's faces. Now I'm at a disadvantage from the moment I meet someone."

Coinciding with the book's release, though, was the release of his first Epic album, *Big City*. He led off with "My Favorite Memory," which, like the book, detailed a chapter from his private life.

Haggard had been snowed in at his home in California, forcing him to cancel a series of dates in Las Vegas. The song came from that period, in which he and Leona Williams spent thirteen days on his houseboat on Lake Shasta, making snow ice cream and fishing.

Haggard, who describes his 1979 retirement as "male menopause," had become increasingly entranced by the aging process as well as memory.

"The greatest asset a human being has is memory," he explained to Lynne Farrow in *Country Rhythms*. "That's why photography is so popular—it's a memory you can look at. A song is a memory you can listen to, a memory captured in the least amount of words with the simplest explanation and feeling involved in the presentation of it.

"When you look around and see everything change, the only thing that stays the same is that memory, that good time you once had. Sometimes it gets stretched out of proportion, but the main format stays the same."

450

BET YOUR HEART ON ME
JOHNNY LEE
Full Moon 47215
Writers: Jim McBride
Producer: Jim Ed Norman
December 5, 1981 (1 week)

With two number one singles behind him, Johnny Lee continued to mine the *Lookin' for Love* album during 1981, earning his third and fourth hits as "Pickin' Up Strangers" and "Prisoner Of Hope" both rose to number three.

"Pickin' Up Strangers" was actually a late addition to the album, recorded after all the tracks had been agreed upon. Lee recorded the song specifically for the movie *Coast to Coast*, starring Dyan Cannon and Robert Blake, and the record company inserted it in place of "I Can Tell By The Way You Dance" [see 575], which eventually went to number one for Vern Gosdin. Lee's version of "I Can Tell" was included on the first shipment of the *Lookin' for Love* album.

Lee started gaining more exposure as a personality, though, than as a musician. Born in Texas City a day before the Fourth of July in 1946, he grew up on a dairy farm in Alta Loma, Texas. He listened to early rock and roll by Elvis Presley, Jerry Lee Lewis and Chuck Berry; while attending Santa Fe High School, he formed his first band, Johnny Lee & The Road Runners.

His original name was Johnny Lee Hamm, but his father had left before he was born, and Lee dropped his real last name. That fact came out after a 1981 item in *Us* magazine that drew a lawsuit from his paternal parent.

When the Academy of Country Music presented its annual awards on April 30, 1981, Lee picked up the award for Top New Male Vocalist. He also saw "Dallas" star Charlene Tilton for the second time—they had first met during the shooting of *Urban Cowboy*. Johnny

and Charlene talked briefly at the ACM awards, then began a romance when they met up at the 30th anniversary of Dick Clark's "American Bandstand."

The two quickly became a favorite topic of the grocery-store gossip tabloids, and during the same month that "Bet Your Heart On Me" went to number one, they announced their plans to be married on Valentine's Day, 1982. It proved a stormy relationship, played out at the check-out stands for the next two years.

Lee followed up "Bet Your Heart" with four more Jim Ed Norman-produced singles: "Be There For Me Baby," Steve Earle's "When You Fall In Love," Michael Martin Murphey's "Cherokee Fiddle" and "Sounds Like Love."

451

STILL DOIN' TIME
GEORGE JONES
Epic 02526
Writers: John Moffatt, Michael P. Heeney
Producer: Billy Sherrill
December 12, 1981 (1 week)

"Ninety percent of [my success] I owe to other artists that I was raised up listening to: Hank Williams, Roy Acuff, Bill Monroe, Lefty Frizzell," George Jones once told Neil Pond of the *Music City News*. "I got a little bit of them in my phrasing and in my style of singing, and about the other ten percent, I just quit trying to whine like them and put in some of me. And it all comes out George Jones."

The Country Music Association re-affirmed Jones' importance in 1980 and 1981 by conferring on him the title of Male Vocalist of the Year. In the wake of "He Stopped Loving Her Today" [see 394], he became a model of consistency as a recording artist.

The Tom T. Hall-penned "I'm Not Ready Yet" brought Jones to number two. Jones then turned to drinkin' themes with his next two singles: "If Drinkin' Don't Kill Me (Her Memory Will)" (number eight) and "Still Doin' Time," which returned him to number one.

Songwriter Michael Heeney had the seeds of the latter's chorus, with co-writer John Moffat crafting the "honky-tonk prison" motif and providing the verses. For all the song's power, though, producer Billy Sherrill's feeling for the record is far from glowing.

"[Publishing rep] Larry Lee, who spent half his life in the lobby of CBS Records, just brought it by one day from Cedarwood [Publishing]," he says. "Jones happened to be in and Larry brought it in and played it. Nobody did any handstands, but it was about the best of what we had, so we cut it."

With number one singles in the '50s, '60s, '70s and '80s, Jones became the first country star to top the chart in four separate decades.

Jones followed "Still Doin' Time" with a Paul Overstreet composition, "Same Ole Me," featuring back-up vocals from the Oak Ridge Boys. It peaked at number five in the spring of 1982; a year later, George's next solo release, "Shine On," went to number three.

Though his records performed well, the concert facet of Jones' career was soon in disarray once again. He began missing shows, and was arrested twice on chemical possession charges.

On March 5, 1983, Jones married Nancy Sepulveda, credited by many of his friends for bringing about his eventual recovery.

George Jones

452

ALL ROADS LEAD TO YOU
STEVE WARINER
RCA 12307
Writers: Kye Fleming, Dennis Morgan
Producer: Tom Collins
December 19, 1981 (1 week)

With the release of his first album at the end of September in 1982, Steve Wariner became one of few artists whose debut LP was practically a greatest-hits package.

Ten years before, a 17-year-old Wariner appeared at the Nashville Country Club in Indianapolis. Still in high school, he opened a show for Dottie West, who joined him on stage during his set. Later, she asked him to play bass in her band, and a month later, he was on tour, earning his last half-credit of Government for high school through a correspondence course.

Wariner stayed with Dottie for three years, playing bass on "Country Sunshine" [see 376—"A Lesson In Leavin'"]. He moved on to Bob Luman's band for two-and-a-half years, and during his tenure, he earned a recording contract at RCA through his musical idol, Chet Atkins. Chet produced Steve's first four singles, then turned him over to Tom Collins. Two singles later, Wariner earned his first Top Ten record with "Your Memory."

"By Now" reached the same level, and "All Roads Lead To You" led Steve to number one. The lyrical content of those two songs brought comparisons to Glen Campbell's "By The Time I Get To Phoenix" and "Wichita Lineman" [see 23], as did the songs' wide vocal range, and Wariner's talents as a singer/guitarist.

"Tom Collins and I are both fans of those early Jimmy Webb-type records," Steve admitted at that time. "I don't think it's been a conscious effort. I like Glen Campbell, and I've had a lot of people comparing us. I have no problem with that at all, but I don't want to be labeled as a 'sound-alike' or something."

Kye Fleming and Dennis Morgan wrote "All Roads Lead To You" fairly quickly, and Collins initially recorded it with Ronnie Milsap.

"We worked on it for six hours," Tom recalls. "Ronnie just couldn't get it. He tried, he just couldn't get it, so we just canned that particular track. About two months later, I brought the [song] out, Steve liked it, and we went in and cut that track within 45 minutes."

"All Roads Lead To You" reached number one a week before Wariner's twenty-seventh birthday (Christmas Day). It wasn't available on album until the following September, when Steve's first album finally hit the streets.

453
LOVE IN THE FIRST DEGREE
ALABAMA
RCA 12288
Writers: Jim Hurt, Tim DuBois
Producers: Alabama, Larry McBride,
Harold Shedd
December 26, 1981 (2 weeks)

We're country first and crossover second," Alabama bass player Teddy Gentry told *Billboard*'s Robyn Wells. "If crossovers come, that's great, but we'd rather have a number one country song than be lost in the middle of both country and pop charts."

Despite their country leanings, Alabama reached the pop Top 40 on four different occasions: "Love In The First Degree" hit number 15; "Take Me Down" [see 479], number 18; "Feels So Right" [see 434], number 20; and "The Closer You Get" [see 528], number 38.

"I think what caused those songs to cross over was because we were very hot and really getting started at the time," Gentry later suggested to Jim Bohen of the *Morristown Daily Record*. "The pop deejays played us because it was the cool thing to do."

Though the pop audience was just getting familiar with the band, Alabama had become such a country staple that "Love In The First Degree" represented their fifth number one record, coming just 17 months after their first. "Love In The First Degree" was the third single from the *Feels So Right* album, but it had already established itself in many cities when stations began playing it as an album cut. Alabama picked it up from song plugger Ben Hall, who sent it to producer Harold Shedd on behalf of House of Gold publishing and songwriters Tim DuBois and Jim Hurt.

"That was the best two hours I ever spent in my life," DuBois recalls. "I had the idea one morning on the way into work to write, and a guy on the radio mentioned somebody found guilty of murder in the first degree. From that, I got 'Love In The First Degree.'

"I got there, and Jim Hurt had the piece of music that he was fiddlin' with, and I had that idea. We spent about an hour and a half and wrote the first verse and the chorus. Then, that evening, at home, I wrote the second verse, brought it back in the next day, and he loved it. It's almost unfair for it to be that easy."

"Love In The First Degree" helped *Feels So Right* establish a *Billboard* record, when it spent a total of 27 weeks at number one on the country album chart. Alabama broke that mark within a year.

454
FOURTEEN CARAT MIND
GENE WATSON
MCA 51183
Writers: Dallas Frazier, Larry Lee
Producers: Russ Reeder, Gene Watson
January 9, 1982 (1 week)

Since 1975, Gene Watson has maintained a position as one of country music's most consistent hitmakers, taking 21 singles into the Top Ten on *Billboard*'s chart. Surprisingly, only one made it to the top spot, "Fourteen Carat Mind."

Watson first heard the song while listening to demo tapes on his bus after the rest of his band had gone to sleep. He could easily have overlooked it, because it was on an unusual tape configuration.

"I was going through cassettes," he explains, "and I got down to the bottom of the box, and I had this one reel-to-reel tape down there, and I started to slide it back in and forget about it. Then I thought, 'No, I gotta hear it,' so I pulled the reel-to-reel tape recorder out in the bus and hooked it up and put it on. It was Dallas Frazier demoing this song, and I knew during the first verse that I was gonna record that song."

Gene was known for years for his "greaser" hairstyle, but "Fourteen Carat Mind" coincided with a new set of dry curls and a brand new beard. He displayed his fresh look on the cover of the *Old Loves Never Die* album, and "Carat" was the first single.

"The guys in my band had been badgering me for a long time to let my hair grow out and let my beard grow," Watson says, acknowledging that the new 'do debuted at the same time as his only chart-topper. "It was a drastic change, so it sure created a lot of conversation, but as far as I was concerned, it was coincidental."

Watson is a Lone Star native, though his history includes residence in Paris (a town in Texas) and Palestine (Texas, too). He made his first record at age 16, eventually cutting material for Uni Records, Wild World and Resco, which released his 1975 single "Love In The Hot Afternoon." Capitol Records bought the master and reissued it the same year, propelling it to number four.

With that success, Watson was able to give up his Houston job as an auto-body repairman. His vocal tools have instead hammered out a line of traditional-sounding country material, including "Farewell Party," "Should I Come Home (Or Should I Go Crazy)," "You're Out Doing What I'm Here Doing Without," "Memories To Burn" and "Don't Waste It On The Blues."

Gene Watson

455

I WOULDN'T HAVE MISSED IT FOR THE WORLD

RONNIE MILSAP

RCA 12342
Writers: Kye Fleming, Dennis Morgan, Charles Quillen
Producers: Ronnie Milsap, Tom Collins
January 16, 1982 (1 week)

"This album is nostalgic at one point, it's rock 'n' roll, it's country, it's got ballads and it's a little R & B. It's all those things I really like to be."

Such are the words of Ronnie Milsap, describing *There's No Gettin' Over Me*, his fifth gold album. On October 17, 1981, it also became his second release to top the *Billboard* country album chart, thanks to the overwhelming success of the title track [see 438].

Two weeks later, the second single, "I Wouldn't Have Missed It For The World," appeared on the singles chart. It certainly represents the versatility that Milsap strove for. While he is known primarily as a vocalist and pianist, "I Wouldn't Have Missed It" was a guitar-based record.

"Pete Bordonali did the solo on the turnaround," says producer Tom Collins, "and the acoustic guitars and all that, I thought were wonderful, 'cause we doubled and tripled 'em. It had sort of an English type of feel and sound on it."

Collins wasn't just the producer on it; he also suggested the title to the tune's composer, Charles Quillen. Once he got stuck, Quillen took the concept to Kye Fleming and Dennis Morgan, and the song finally took shape. Unfortunately, it also drew a reaction much like "(I'm A) Stand By My Woman Man" [see 258]: a lawsuit.

Tim Williams, a disk jockey at Austin's KOKE, claimed that he had sent Collins a song with the same title.

"Dennis and I were totally out of any of the hassle that went on with that song," recalls Fleming. "I was very upset. We were just carrying on our business as usual. If [Tom] gave us a title, we wrote it." "That [suit] never amounted to much," adds Collins, "because a cliché that I'd heard all my life, I certainly did not rip off. I'd never do that anyway."

Collins and the writers weren't the only ones annoyed by events surrounding the record. "I sang a little too sharp on that," notes Milsap, "so I'm very critical of that, though it's a good song. I just sang live with the band, and there's your record, hoss."

The record hit number one in the country chart and also reached number 20 on *Billboard*'s Hot 100.

456

RED NECKIN' LOVE MAKIN' NIGHT
CONWAY TWITTY
MCA 51199
Writers: Troy Seals, Max D. Barnes
Producers: Conway Twitty, Ron Chancey
January 23, 1982 (1 week)

One of the most fruitful yet least recognized songwriting duos of the '70s and '80s is Troy Seals and Max D. Barnes. Though the two have each racked up a large number of successes in other writing partnerships, most of their early triumphs were joint efforts.

"That was a fluke," Seals insists. "Max D. Barnes lived a couple houses down from me; he'd been a truck driver before. Our kids started playing together, and they were like, 'Well, my daddy's a songwriter, too,' one of those things. So I went down and met him."

Among their collaborations are George Jones' "Who's Gonna Fill Their Shoes," Waylon Jennings' "Drinkin' And Dreamin'" and Keith Whitley's "Ten Feet Away."

Their most consistent supporter, though, has been Conway Twitty. With Loretta Lynn, he made hits out of "I Can't Love You Enough" and "From Seven Till Ten" [see 221—"Feelins'"], two songs that were written on the very same evening. As a solo artist, Twitty culled two number one hits with Seals & Barnes compositions: "Don't Take It Away" [see 342] and "Red Neckin' Love Makin' Night."

"A lot of things we custom-write," notes Barnes. "I don't want to call it manufactured, but if an artist wants a certain type of song, we can do that somehow, like 'Red Neckin' Love Makin' Night.' Conway had asked us to write him a good uptempo, summer-type song, so that's what we did. We wrote that in two nights, and it worked."

Despite Twitty's seasonal intentions, "Red Neckin'" was released during the winter months in 1981. It was a move that Conway had no control over, since he had left MCA Records after making the *Mr. T* album. The label put out "Red Neckin'" while he finished up his first Elektra album [see 468—"The Clown"].

"It had a line in it that said, 'Eat your heart out, Killer,'" Max D. remembers. "That came out when Jerry Lee [Lewis] was in the hospital and in pretty bad shape, and we thought, 'Oh, boy, our timing is terrible.' It had a keyboard ride in it that was really nice, and it was a fun

record. Conway was having fun with it."

As a result, Conway's "Red Neckin'" summer record hit number one in the dead of winter.

457

THE SWEETEST THING (I'VE EVER KNOWN)
JUICE NEWTON
Capitol 5046
Writer: Otha Young
Producer: Richard Landis
January 30, 1982 (1 week)

In 1974, Juice Newton teamed with then-boyfriend Otha Young and Tom Keely to form a country/rock band, Silver Spur, in California. She didn't expect overnight success, but she didn't think it would take seven years to gain a hit record, either.

A year after their formation, Juice Newton & Silver Spur released an eponymous album on RCA, followed by two more group efforts before Keely departed. Dropping the Silver Spur monicker, Newton put out two solo LPs which yielded little more than critical acclaim. Juice thought she had her first hit with "It's A Heartache," but Bonnie Tyler released the same song at the same time and nixed Newton's efforts. Juice did gain a break, though, when the Carpenters scored their only Top Ten country hit in 1978, with her song "Sweet, Sweet Smile."

The 1981 album *Juice* finally brought Newton to the forefront. Her remake of "Angel Of The Morning" hit number 22, while "Queen Of Hearts" went to number 14. Both records reached the Top Five on *Billboard*'s Hot 100. With several options for a third single, they settled on "The Sweetest Thing (I've Ever Known)" after her live performance of that song received an overwhelming response at the annual Country Radio Seminar in 1981.

Young had written the song for Juice back in 1974, although he didn't tell her she was the subject when he first played it for Juice in her hotel room at the American Song Festival in Saratoga.

"The verses started coming to me when we were driving to northern California," Otha recalled to Vernell Hackett in *American Songwriter*. "The car broke down, and I started writing the verses down while we were sitting in a parking lot waiting on someone to come and fix the car. I finished the song over the next few weeks."

"The Sweetest Thing" had first appeared on their 1975 *Silver Spur* album; for *Juice*, they worked up a remixed version, featuring a softer woodwind instrument, and released it as a single. "There were two versions of the song," Juice says. "One had oboe on it, and one had a pedal steel. They're very different instruments, and they give a different character."

"The Sweetest Thing," Juice's first number one single, also helped *Juice* become Newton's first million-selling album.

458
LONELY NIGHTS
MICKEY GILLEY
Epic 02578
Writers: Keith Stegall, Stuart Harris
Producer: Jim Ed Norman
February 6, 1982 (1 week)

Since moving to Nashville in September of 1978, Keith Stegall has contributed regularly to country music's wealth of hit records. He has written "Let's Get Over Them Together," by Moe Bandy featuring Becky Hobbs (number 10); "Hurricane" (number four) and "My Lady Loves Me (Just As I Am)" (number nine), by Leon Everette; "She's Playing Hard To Forget," by Eddy Raven (number 10); and "A Lady Like You," by Glen Campbell (number four).

Stegall also penned Dr. Hook's pop hit "Sexy Eyes" as well as Al Jarreau's "We're In This Love Together," and he co-produced Randy Travis' "On The Other Hand" [see 680]. Nevertheless, Mickey Gilley's "Lonely Nights" was his only composition to reach the top spot.

Stegall had multiple duties with April/Blackwood Music at the time, duping and delivering tape copies for the company during the day, writing mostly in the evening hours. Roger Murrah served as his mentor at the company, and Stegall wrote "Lonely Nights" on Murrah's piano.

"As I recall it, I had part of a verse going," Stegall recalls, "and Stuart Harris was up at the office about 8:00 at night. I said, 'Let me show you what I've got going on this thing,' and went into Roger's office and sat down at that old upright piano and I played him part of what I had. He jumped in there, and in a couple hours we had the song written."

Juice Newton

Tony Brown produced the demo for Stegall and pitched it to Jim Ed Norman, who produced Gilley's single version.

"I thought the song was good," Gilley says. "I got to singing it on some of the dates I was performing in Nevada, at Harrah's and the MGM Grand and Bally's, and the reaction on the song was tremendous. I put it in before it was released as a single, and I knew from the audience reaction that it would be a good record for us."

A native of Wichita, Texas, Stegall is a third cousin to the late Johnny Horton. He made his playing debut at age eight, and paid his dues after moving to Nashville, where he literally lived in a van in front of the April/Blackwood offices for several months after his signing. His dedication paid off in 1985, when he released a self-titled album. The *Keith Stegall* album yielded "California," which peaked at number 13, and "Pretty Lady," which reached number 10.

459

SOMEONE COULD LOSE A HEART TONIGHT

EDDIE RABBITT

Elektra 47239
Writers: Eddie Rabbitt, David Malloy, Even Stevens
Producer: David Malloy
February 13, 1982 (1 week)

"We wanted a 'Halloween-Valentine' kind of song, spooky but romantic," Eddie Rabbitt told *Billboard*'s Kip Kirby when asked about "Someone Could Lose A Heart Tonight." "Until we got it right, it always sounded like Jack the Ripper was on the loose."

Getting it right was the hard part—getting it started was rather simple.

"'Someone Could Lose A Heart Tonight' is one of the few that I actually started on my own," admits songwriter/producer David Malloy. "I was livin' out in L.A. on a little lake, and I started that thing, and I was inspired from the Eagles' record of 'Heartache Tonight.' In fact, I did an album with J.D. Souther, who's a writer on that song. I told him that I really went for that sound on 'Heartache Tonight,' and he said, 'Yeah, we all knew it, and we thought you did a great job on it, too.'"

Buoyed by a pounding, obstinate bassline and scratchy guitar work (created by an electronic alteration, involving drumsticks, a snare drum and guitar), "Someone Could Lose A Heart Tonight" went farther than any other number one single in adapting a rock backbeat for the country medium.

"We weren't really tryin' to push anything on any song out of bounds," offers co-writer Even Stevens. "It just happened to be accepted. We would have done it if it hadn't been accepted, I'm sure. We were always tryin' new things, but we weren't tryin' to push any boundaries or anything. We were just makin' music that we felt."

Like "I Just Want To Love You" [see 328], the final version of "Someone Could Lose A Heart Tonight" didn't emerge until they had already laid down the instrumental tracks.

"We finished writing that song right in the studio as we were recording it," Eddie explains. "We'd go back and change a line because we came up with a better one, as we were doing the master. I'd come back in and listen to the vocal, and I'd say, 'Yeah, the vocal sounds good, but this one line doesn't sound right, or that line doesn't sound right there,' and we'd go back and change it while we were doing it."

"Someone Could Lose A Heart Tonight" was Rabbitt's second single from the *Step by Step* album [see 444]. A third, the Thom Schuyler-penned "I Don't Know Where To Start," hung at number two for three weeks.

460

ONLY ONE YOU

T.G. SHEPPARD

Warner Bros. 49858
Writers: Bucky Jones, Michael Garvin
Producer: Buddy Killen
February 20, 1982 (1 week)

Coming six months after "I Loved 'Em Every One" [see 425] peaked at number one, T.G. Sheppard's "Only One You" sounded remarkably similar to that chart-topper. The single fell into almost the exact same tempo, and featured a lead-guitar riff reminiscent of the previous record.

"Only One You" was written and recorded in a whirlwind of activity. Michael Garvin and Bucky Jones were scheduled to write together at Tree Publishing, but a scheduling conflict forced them to postpone their session until 11:00 P.M. Garvin brought in the germ of "Only One You," and they wrote it in the early morning hours, then played it for Dan Wilson the next morning. They demoed the song immediately, and Wilson phoned T.G. at home and told him to rush in immediately.

"I went down," remembers Sheppard, "and when I was walking down the hallway I could hear them cranking the studio speakers up, and I said, 'Oh, my God.' It was a minor key, like 'I Loved 'Em Every One.' I think it was a Monday, and we recorded it on a Tuesday."

Judy Rodman contributed backing vocals, and ace producer Larry Butler sat in on piano, helping push "Only One You" to the top in its fourteenth week on the country charts.

Sheppard hails from Humboldt, Tennessee, where he was born July 20, 1944. His mother taught piano, and Sheppard (a.k.a. Bill Browder) learned to play guitar and piano before high school. There, he added saxophone, although the marching band director asked him to drop it and carry the flag instead. Meanwhile, he performed with his first group, the Royal Tones, at local dances.

"We paid $14 each for matching white jackets and $1.50 for crests to sew on the lapels," T.G. recalls. "Our idea of a big show was appearing before 500 students at a college."

Sheppard never took his own formal education that far. At age 16, he moved to Memphis, where he performed with Travis Womack. During the same period, he also sang lead for a group called the Embers, recording his first single, "The Girl Next Door," for Sonic Records. He moved on to Atlantic, cutting "High School Days" under the pseudonym of Brian Stacy.

He paid the rent with a job at Lansky Brothers' clothing shop on Beale Street, where the clientele included Charlie Rich, Rufus Thomas and the Bar-Kays.

461

LORD, I HOPE THIS DAY IS GOOD
DON WILLIAMS
MCA 51207
Writer: Dave Hanner
Producers: Don Williams, Garth Fundis
February 27, 1982 (1 week)

Jimmy Swaggart, Jerry Falwell and Jim Bakker probably could have claimed "Lord, I Hope This Day Is Good" as representative of their religious convictions. Then again, so could Norman Vincent Peale or Pope John Paul II.

"Lord, I Hope This Day Is Good" was intended as a morning prayer. Aptly enough, songwriter Dave Hanner started it in the morning, and Don Williams also recorded it in the morning.

"I was actually just feelin' depressed one morning," says Hanner. "I think I'd battled it out with the wife, or somethin', and I went into the room and sat down and started singin' that. The hookline came out, 'Lord, I Hope This Day Is Good,' and I think most of that chorus just came without much thinkin' right then."

A couple of months later, Hanner finished the song, then took it to Mel Tillis, who shied away from its religious message. Don Williams, however, was immediately attracted to

it, especially because it conveyed that message without being heavy-handed.

"Don has fairly strong religious convictions," explains his producer, Garth Fundis, "but we've never wanted to cut gospel or anything like that. But this thing lent itself. Everybody's gone through 'Lord, I Hope This Day Is Good.'"

Williams changed one line in the chorus, then made it the first song he cut during a morning session at Nashville's Sound Emporium Studio. Pat McLaughlin brought a mandolin onto one of Don's records for the first time in a number of years, and the instrumental tracks worked so well that the record ended up running more than four minutes long.

"We knew it was feelin' too good to just put an ending to it," says Garth, "and the band played on. It was probably longer than that. When we've hooked one, we'll just let the band go."

When "Lord, I Hope This Day Is Good" rose to number one, it represented Don's first chart-topping single in more than fifteen months. In the interim, he hit number six with "Falling Again," and number four with "Miracles." Emmylou Harris also joined him on "If I Needed You," which peaked at number three.

Hanner also had another hit during that period. The Oak Ridge Boys took his composition, "Beautiful You," to number three in early 1981.

462

YOU'RE THE BEST BREAK THIS OLD HEART EVER HAD
ED BRUCE
MCA 51210
Writers: Wayland Holyfield, Randy Hatch
Producer: Tommy West
March 6, 1982 (1 week)

"First and foremost, I moved to Nashville to be a songwriter," says Ed Bruce. Over time, that became one of many talents he has used in the entertainment business.

As a writer, Bruce first garnered success in 1965 when Charlie Louvin took "See The Big Man Cry" to number seven on the *Billboard* charts. Ed later followed with "The Man That Turned My Mama On" and "Texas (When I Die)" (Tanya Tucker had Top Five hits with both) as well as "Mammas, Don't Let Your Babies Grow Up To Be Cowboys" [see 305].

Ed Bruce

Former wife and manager Patsy Bruce, meanwhile, built his reputation with New York advertising agencies, and his voice has appeared on jingles for Burger King, United Airlines, McDonald's, the U.S. Armed Services and Maxwell House.

To top it off, Bruce attracted attention from many record labels throughout the years. In the late '50s, he recorded for Sun Records; in the early '60s, he was affiliated with the primarily black Sceptre label; and he finally garnered his first hit single when his own version of "Mammas" charted for United Artists in 1975.

Ed hit his stride, though, when he signed with MCA, where, after several minor hits, he turned in four Top Five singles from 1981 through 1984, the first coming with "You're The Best Break This Old Heart Ever Had." Bruce first heard the song when Wayland

Holyfield played it at a "guitar pull" (a ritual whereby Nashville writers pass a guitar around a circle and perform their most recent material). It was another year before he recorded it, and it proved a perfect vehicle for his gentle bass tonalities.

"Randy Hatch, who is a Vietnam Vet—a paraplegic, as a matter of fact—that was his first so-called major cut," notes Bruce. "I'd known Randy for years, just a good ol' boy, and he was struggling, and it became a number one record."

To add to his jack-of-all-trades status, Bruce branched out into acting once his recording career took off. He appeared in the CBS miniseries *The Chisholms* and the TV special *The Last Days of Frank and Jesse James*, played Tom Guthrie in the eight-month return of "Bret Maverick" in 1982, and hosted the Nashville Network's "American Sports Cavalcade."

463

BLUE MOON WITH HEARTACHE
ROSANNE CASH
Columbia 02659
Writer: Rosanne Cash
Producer: Rodney Crowell
March 13, 1982 (1 week)

"Achingly beautiful" is perhaps the best way to describe "Blue Moon With Heartache." Yet Rosanne Cash remains secretive about its origins. "I really don't know that I want to tell you, or could tell you, where it came from," she says, choosing her words carefully. "It was just a song. I had my catcher's mitt on, and I caught it."

The song was very simple when Rosanne first presented it to bassist/arranger Emory Gordy in her living room in Los Angeles.

"She originally played it on the guitar," Emory recalls, "and I must say—this is no offense to Rosanne's guitar-playing—it leaves a lot to the imagination. That's the positive point about it. We had an electric piano when we were doin' the pre-production. I just got on the piano, and worked through a core system of chords on it that pivoted around a chordal motif, and that's what stuck."

That "chordal motif" became the record's intro, played in tandem by Tony Brown on electric piano and Hank DeVito on steel guitar. At the time, Rosanne found it difficult to settle on a title for the song.

"It remained untitled until the record was mixed, finished—I think it was even pressed before we got a title for that song," she remembers. "The artwork was being held up, so we had these sessions where everybody would try to come up with the title. Rodney [Crowell] and I had just been to a lecture by Tom Robbins, and just read *Still Life with Woodpecker*, and Rodney said, 'Why don't you just call it "Blue Moon With Heartache"?'"

That artsy title first found its way onto a single as the "B" side to "Seven Year Ache" [see 426], but Columbia eventually released it again as the album's third "A" side. It also became Cash's third to hit number one.

Held together loosely by a subtle storyline about a relationship, *Seven Year Ache* brought Rosanne her first gold album on January 6, 1983. In the meantime, she released *Somewhere in the Stars*, bringing two more Top Ten singles, with "Ain't No Money" (number four) and "I Wonder" (number eight).

464

MOUNTAIN OF LOVE
CHARLEY PRIDE
RCA 13014
Writer: Harold Dorman
Producer: Norro Wilson
March 20, 1982 (1 week)

In 1974, Charley Pride released a single that seemed rather appropriate for his own past. "Mississippi Cotton Pickin' Delta Town" [see 196—"Then Who Am I"] painted a picture of the rural South, and its images were so realistic that Pride was concerned that it might have some sort of racial overtones. Producer Jerry Bradley had to promise to throw it out if Pride decided he didn't like it, just to get it recorded.

As it turned out, it was a very successful record, written by someone who knew the setting from his own experience: the late Harold Dorman.

"We grew up in the same hometown," remembers Pride. "Harold worked for the grocery store where we got our groceries every Saturday in Sledge. He was white, and back in those days, we didn't go to school together. We just spoke in passing, so we grew up and I didn't know he wrote songs and he didn't know I sang. Just to show you how life sometimes deals you, it's a very small world."

Even before Pride had his first session, Dorman earned his initial success with a pop/rock song titled "Mountain Of Love." Dorman's own version went to number 21 on the *Billboard* Hot 100 in 1960, and Johnny Rivers traveled to number nine when he remade it in 1964. After Pride cut "Mississippi Cotton Pickin' Delta Town" a decade later, he incorporated both songs into his stage show, demonstrating how a creative writer can often work effectively with very different kinds of material.

"When I would go into ["Mountain Of Love"], the people had such a reaction," Pride remarks. "Norro Wilson was out on the road one day and saw the reaction and said, 'Let's go in and cut that.'"

"Mountain Of Love" climbed to number one on March 20, 1982, and two weeks later, Charley followed up with Kent Robbins' bouncy "I Don't Think She's In Love Anymore." That record stalled at number two in July.

A few weeks later, Pride experienced a more serious near-miss. On August 2, a Cessna airplane hit the tail section of Pride's 16-passenger Fairchild turboprop in Texas.

Razzy Bailey

Weller later produced Razzy on ABC; Bailey recorded for 1-2-3, and he charted for the first time in 1976, on his own Erastus label. His association with RCA, a major label, brought him to the apex of his career, and his fifth number one single came with "She Left Love All Over Me."

"To be honest, I didn't like the song that much when I first heard it," Razzy confesses. "[Producer] Bob Montgomery kept sayin', 'You need to listen to this song, 'cause it's a hit song.' I said, 'It just don't knock me out.'

"The way I heard it was with the writer doin' a flat-top [guitar]. It wasn't a demo, and Bob, as a producer, heard through that. In my opinion, it's a great song, and I really did like the record. I think the arrangement was just as important in the success of that song as the song itself. That little acoustic guitar intro and turn-around in there was a real hook in that song. Of course, I didn't hear that in the demo—it was just a flat-top with no kind of arrangement."

"She Left Love All Over Me" emerged as the first single from Razzy's *Feelin' Right* album, debuting in *Billboard* on December 19, 1981. "She Left Love" left its imprint at number one 14 weeks later.

Razzy followed with "Everytime You Cross My Mind (You Break My Heart)," which peaked at number ten; and "Love's Gonna Fall Here Tonight," which went to number eight. He also cracked the Top 20 with "After The Great Depression" and his remake of Wilson Pickett's "In The Midnight Hour."

The other plane's passengers were killed, while Pride's pilot, Robert Sowers, brought the Fairchild in for a bumpy but safe landing. Six hours later, Pride was on stage at a benefit concert for 500 nuns.

465

SHE LEFT LOVE ALL OVER ME
RAZZY BAILEY

RCA 13007
Writer: Chester Lester
Producer: Bob Montgomery
March 27, 1982 (1 week)

Razzy Bailey was quite familiar with the recording process by the time he signed with RCA Records in 1978. He cut his first record at the age of 10 for a tiny independent label called B & K. He financed his own recording session in the '60s on Peach Records in Atlanta, and he also did the first version of "9,999,999 Tears" [see 396—"Loving Up A Storm"], produced by Joe South, with Freddy Weller and Billy Joe Royal on back-up vocals.

466

BOBBIE SUE
THE OAK RIDGE BOYS

MCA 51231
Writers: Dan Tyler, Adele Tyler, Wood Newton
Producer: Ron Chancey
April 3, 1982 (1 week)

"Elvira" [see 427] opened the Oak Ridge Boys up to an entirely new audience in 1981. When it came time to record another album that fall, they were determined to connect with that audience once more.

Joe Bonsall admitted as much to Bob Allen in *Country Rhythms*: "We were looking for the same kinds of songs, like 'Elvira,' that people could sing along to—songs that had a strong bass part and a strong chorus, like 'Elvira' did. And that's where 'Bobbie Sue' came in. It's sort of a 1982 'Elvira.'"

"Bobbie Sue" started in the words of a two-year-old boy, who couldn't sing "Baa Baa Black Sheep" quite right. He stuttered on the "baa baas," and, as it happened, his father, Dan Tyler, had just left a career in law to become a songwriter. Dan and his wife, Adele, turned their son's mistake into their own good fortune. They co-wrote "Bah-bah-bah-bah-Bobbie Sue" with House of Gold composer Wood Newton, and the publisher then sent a copy of the demo to the Oak Ridge Boys via the postal service.

The group had just finished listening to songs when the mail arrived, and half of them had already left Duane Allen's office when the secretary brought the tape in. They liked "Bobbie Sue" so much that the Oaks cut it at Woodland Sound Studio the following day, trying to make it much like the Coasters' 1958 classic "Yakety Yak."

They were unhappy with the results, though, and waited a couple days before trying again. This time it was magic. They found a groove between "Yakety Yak" and the demo, and producer Ron Chancey added a subtle but important change.

"In the beginning, right at the top of the chorus," recalls Allen, "it was the whole group going 'B-B-B-B-B-Bobbie Sue,' and we put Richard [Sterban] in there doing that [alone] and let him syncopate it a little more."

The Oaks achieved the desired results. "Bobbie Sue" topped the country chart and hit number 12 on the *Billboard* Hot 100.

Their follow-up, "I Wish You Could Have Turned My Head (And Left My Heart Alone)," took the Oaks to number two on October 9, 1982, behind "Yesterday's Wine" [see 489]. One more single, the Eddy Raven-penned "Thank God For Kids," reached number three.

told Lynne Farrow in *Country Rhythms*, referring to his album *Big City*. "It took about two years to write and refine and we worked up a pretty good head of steam. This was probably the first album I ever *tried* on, and there was a bit of depression after it was through."

The title track was one of the last songs added to the *Big City* LP. Longtime friend Dean Holloway had gone with Haggard to West Hollywood, where the album was recorded on Cahuenga Boulevard at Britannia Studios. Holloway became totally disgusted with the city, complaining about the dirty sidewalks of the big city. That's all it took to pique Merle's creative juices.

"I wrote that in about 20 minutes," he told Alanna Nash in *Behind Closed Doors*, "and I went in there and cut it, and put that good old shuffle beat to it. I'd never done a shuffle. I used to hate shuffles, because we had to do them all the time in the clubs. Well, this was the first one I'd done in my whole career, I guess, and it worked."

To say that it worked is an understatement. Kicking off with the twin fiddles of Tiny Moore and Jimmy Belkin, "Big City" became an '80s extension of "Workin' Man Blues" [see 39], lamenting the stress of the rat race and the precarious posture of Social Security.

"Anybody could have sung 'Big City,' I think, and had a hit on it," said Haggard. "It just said what people wanted to hear. They're tired of the slums, and the big scabs, you know? I was."

On July 11, 1983, *Big City* became Merle's first gold album in nine years. It was the third of his career, following *The Best of Merle Haggard* and *The Best of the Best of Merle Haggard*.

Haggard followed "Big City" with "Are The Good Times Really Over (I Wish A Buck Was Still Silver)," yet another commentary on the American economy. Peaking at number two, its melody was quite similar to "My Favorite Memory" [see 449], *Big City's* first single. Not surprisingly, both were written the same day.

467

BIG CITY

MERLE HAGGARD

Epic 02686
Writers: Merle Haggard, Dean Holloway
Producers: Lewis Talley, Merle Haggard
April 10, 1982 (1 week)

"I usually don't get enthused about things I do, but I'm really proud of this," Merle Haggard

---

468

THE CLOWN

CONWAY TWITTY

Elektra 47302
Writers: Charlie Chalmers, Sandra Rhodes, Brenda Barnett, Wayne Carson
Producers: Conway Twitty, Jimmy Bowen
April 17, 1982 (1 week)

"More than writin' a song, it was just an event," says Wayne Carson of "The Clown."

Writing was hardly what Carson had in mind when he went to Arkansas to visit his friends, Charlie Chalmers and Sandra Rhodes, who used to sing with Janie Frickie in a Memphis band. They spent a day fishing, talking and drinking, and by two in the morning, they were all singing together on the front lawn.

"Brenda [Barnett] and I walked down to the river," Carson recalls. "She had this little pixie hairdo, and she'd been in the water. She had that eyeliner and the hair down over her face, real pale skin, and I said, 'You look like a little clown.'

"We sat down with our feet in the water, singin' this little old theme, and then here comes Sandy and Charlie. Some of the local herbs were burning in the air, and we were just having a very mellow late night, we started singing that thing. The more we sang it, the more the words came, and all of a sudden we had the song."

They cut a demo at Castle Studio, and during that session, Carson first visualized the song for Conway Twitty. As it turned out, Conway found the song to his liking and cut it for his debut Elektra album *Southern Comfort*.

Recorded at Sound Stage Studios in Nashville, "The Clown" closed with an appropriate calliope sound, evoking images of the mournful Pagliacci. "Conway had Shane Keister add that at the end," notes producer Jimmy Bowen. "I didn't want it to be too hokey, and I told Conway to be real careful, so he and Shane worked it out. It wasn't too far out, but it was enough."

Once the single was in the can, Bowen faced a crisis during the mastering process. He called from California to Nashville to make an edit in the record, but the plant misunderstood where he wanted the edit made. When he checked in again, they told him that his 4:30 single had been cut to two minutes.

The mistaken pressing was tossed and remade. The correct version debuted at number 46 on January 30, 1982, reaching number one eleven weeks later.

469
CRYING MY HEART OUT OVER YOU
RICKY SKAGGS
Epic 02692

Writers: Carl Butler, Lester Flatt,
Earl Scruggs, Earl Sherry
Producer: Ricky Skaggs
April 24, 1982 (1 week)

At the start of the decade, many in country music hailed the genre as the "Adult/Contemporary Sound of the '80s." Kenny Rogers, Barbara Mandrell and *Urban Cowboy* [see 389—"Stand By Me"], among others, had given the music a glossy pop sheen, and some went so far as to predict the demise of traditional country.

They hadn't counted on Ricky Skaggs. A native of Cordell, Kentucky, Skaggs grew up heavily attracted to the mournful sound of pure mountain harmonies. Ricky made his first record, *Tribute to the Stanley Brothers*, as a 16-year-old contributor to the Clinch Mountain Boys, and, after a procession of jobs in several bluegrass bands, wound up in Emmylou Harris' Hot Band in 1977. He received critical acclaim for his contributions to her 1980 bluegrass album, *Roses in the Snow*. Armed with that credit—as well as tracks from his unfinished *Don't Cheat in Our Hometown* [see 557] album—he secured a deal from Epic Records.

The label signed Skaggs somewhat skeptically. His traditional bent would no doubt limit Epic's ability to market the first album, and one executive even placed a bet that Ricky couldn't sell 50,000 copies within a year of release.

To everyone's surprise, the first Epic release, a cover of Lester Flatt & Earl Scruggs' "Don't Get Above Your Raisin'," soared to number 16. A follow-up, "You May See Me Walkin'," reached number nine. For the third single, Ricky again turned to Flatt & Scruggs, covering "Crying My Heart Out Over You," which had peaked for them at number 21 in 1960.

"I always loved the song," says Ricky, "and had done it a few times in some bluegrass bands. I thought that it came out good when I did it in the studio, but I never really realized that people would like it that much."

Skaggs added a few extra chords in his version, and piano player Buck White suggested they slow it down. When it went on the album, the song was mistakenly credited to songwriter Marijohn Wilkin. Wilkin, in fact, had purchased the copyright as a publisher, along with several other titles, from a friend who needed some money, and she hardly realized she owned it.

Wilkin, White, Epic and Skaggs all came up winners when "Crying My Heart Out" emerged as Ricky's first number one single.

470

MOUNTAIN MUSIC
ALABAMA
RCA 13019
Writer: Randy Owen
Producers: Harold Shedd, Alabama
May 1, 1982 (1 week)

"Mountain Music" is a modern country classic. Its impact is evident through the events that occurred the week it reached number one. On April 29, 1982, the Academy of Country Music named Alabama the Top Vocal Group and Entertainer of the Year; that same day, the *Mountain Music* album simultaneously went gold and platinum for selling one million copies. Two days later, the single gave them half a dozen chart-topping records.

"Mountain Music" took several years to evolve. Randy Owen created the first verse and chorus in 1979, when the band worked at The Bowery in Myrtle Beach. The first verse paid homage to characters out of Southern literature, like Tom Sawyer and Rip Van Winkle.

Owen completed the song in April of 1980, at his home in Alabama. The second verse melded regional games from his childhood, including a form of baseball that used a chalky substance called "chert" rocks, and a tree game called "skinnin' cats."

"I just remembered the mountain music my grandma and grandpa used to play," Randy recalls. "I put the line in about the 'Cajun hideaway,' not knowin' a whole lot about Louisiana, except that I liked Cajun music. Later, I was able to insert Randy Owen into the song. With 'Swim across the river just to prove that I'm a man,' and all those kinds of things, I put a little segment of my life into it, and thus became a real part of the song."

Initially, Alabama recorded "Mountain Music" for the *Feels So Right* [see 434] album, but it didn't feel right. When "Old Flame" [see 421] came along, they held "Mountain Music" back for the next album.

One of their concerns was the arrangement. They started the song with a Southern-rock feel and shifted toward a bluegrass fiddle breakdown, so that the tune sounded much like "Tennessee River" [see 390]. They didn't want criticism for copying one of their own records, but ultimately decided that that arrangement worked best for "Mountain Music."

When they finally cut the definitive version, they recorded almost all of it live, overdubbing only Jeff Cook's fiddle and an electronic box that mimics a cowbell. "We all just went in to the studio, got our guitars, tuned 'em up, and we honed in," says Randy. "I'm really proud of that. That's the way to make records."

471

ALWAYS ON MY MIND
WILLIE NELSON
Columbia 02741
Writers: Wayne Carson Thompson,
Mark James, Johnny Christopher
Producer: Chips Moman
May 8, 1982 (2 weeks)

More than ten years after its conception, "Always On My Mind" found its place in music history in 1982. Wayne Carson, signed to Monument Records in 1971, carried the initial germ of the song for some time and finally decided to write it with guitarist Johnny Christopher in a Memphis recording studio.

"We were red-lining the fun meter," Carson recalls. "We'd been up all night, drinkin' beer and whatever. I was sittin' there playin' the piano, and I started hammerin' around on this thing and we worked on it and worked on it."

When they hit a snag, however, they invited Mark James (who wrote "Suspicious Minds") to help them finish it. After declining initially, James came back with an idea, and they completed the project. Carson recorded it within 24 hours for Monument, but label head Fred Foster refused to release it.

Still, others saw potential. Brenda Lee released it as a single in 1972, and Elvis Presley took it to number 16 in 1973 as the "B" side to "Separate Ways." John Wesley Ryles earned a Top 20 version in 1979, but Willie Nelson never heard the song until Christopher played it for him during sessions for the *Pancho and Lefty* [see 529] album with Merle Haggard.

"I loved the song," Willie reports, "but Merle didn't quite hear it. It probably wouldn't have been a good duet, and we were cuttin' a duet album, so he was probably right in that respect."

Though Haggard nixed "Always," Willie cut a solo version in his new Pedernales Studio in Austin after they finished their album.

"The studio wasn't quite together, and it was soundin' real bad," notes Bobby Wood, who played the very exposed piano parts. "He had a

Willie Nelson

JUST TO SATISFY YOU
WAYLON & WILLIE
RCA 13073
Writers: Waylon Jennings, Don Bowman
Producer: Chips Moman
May 22, 1982 (2 weeks)

"I never thought that song was finished in the beginning," says Waylon Jennings of his composition "Just To Satisfy You." "We were gonna throw it away, but we turned around and wrote another bridge, or another verse, and made it right."

Jennings co-wrote "Just To Satisfy You" around 1960 with Don Bowman, whom he'd previously worked with at KLLL in Lubbock. Bowman had moved to El Paso, but he flew regularly to join Jennings in Phoenix for writing sessions. They wrote four songs in a motel room, and "Satisfy" was one of them.

Waylon recorded the song on several occasions. The first, for A & M Records, was produced by Herb Alpert, with a harpsichord in the arrangement. He also cut it for RCA, as did Bobby Bare, instrumental in getting Chet Atkins to sign Jennings to the label. It never became a hit, though, until Waylon teamed with Willie Nelson to record it for the *Black on Black* album.

"I think Bowman got a hold of Willie when we was doin' those albums together," Jennings says. "He said, 'Do that song, do that song,' so when the album came up, Willie wanted to do that song. It was his idea more than mine."

It proved a timely decision for Nelson when "Just To Satisfy You" followed "Always On My Mind" [see 471] to number one. As a result, Willie spent four consecutive weeks at the top of the chart. More importantly, the occasion marked only the ninth time in history—and the first since 1964—that the same performer sewed up the summit with back-to-back hits.

Later that year, Waylon & Willie released their second duet album, appropriately titled *WW II*. Its lone single, "(Sittin' On) The Dock Of The Bay," peaked at number 13. A year later, they released a third duet album. Originally, it was to be named *Where There's a Will, There's a Way*. Instead, they called it *Take It to the Limit*, and the title track, a cover of the Eagles' pop hit, went to number eight.

The Waylon & Willie collaborations added a new dimension in 1985, with the advent of the *Highwayman* album [see 633].

$60-70,000 piano in there and it sounded like a spinet, but they put a lot of 'highs' on the piano and it ended up soundin' pretty good."

Willie's wife, Connie, and his daughters persuaded him to make "Always" the album's title track and the first single, and it became his biggest record ever. While spending two weeks at the top of *Billboard*'s country chart, it also soared to number five on the Hot 100.

"Always On My Mind" earned three Grammy awards, including Song of the Year, plus two Academy of Country Music trophies and four from the Country Music Association.

473

FINALLY

T.G. SHEPPARD

Warner Bros. 50041
Writer: Gary Chapman
Producer: Buddy Killen
June 5, 1982 (1 week)

To the casual observer, "Finally" might seem to be a typical love song, but it actually works on two different levels. Beneath its surface bubble some very deep-seeded sentiments of spiritual love, and with good reason.

Songwriter Gary Chapman is married to the top star in the world of gospel music, Amy Grant. Born November 25, 1960, in Augusta, Georgia, Grant's command of the contemporary Christian audience is so powerful that her *Straight Ahead* LP remained at number one on *Billboard*'s inspirational album chart for more than a year.

Although he has met with less fervent acceptance, Chapman has also been embraced by the gospel market, and he originally targeted "Finally" for that kind of audience. He produced a demo tape of the song while trying to secure a recording contract, and, as with "Party Time" [see 443], T.G. Sheppard heard the song at Tree Publishing.

"I was in Buddy Killen's office," he recalls, "and I kept hearing this song way back in the chambers somewhere, and I thought it was a beautiful song. When my meeting with Buddy was over, I went back and asked [Tree vice president] Donna Hilley, 'What am I hearing? I want that song.' She said, 'Well, it's a religious album,' and I said, 'That song is mass appeal. It's talking about love, whether it's about God or whatever.'"

Sheppard did make a couple of lyrical changes, and the now-quasi-gospel release found its way to number one.

A few years later, the song became a centerpiece in his live show, as the band would leave Sheppard alone on the stage with a single acoustic guitar to set a dramatic, intimate highlight. The concept came from Joe Gannon, who produced Neil Diamond's *Hot August Night* show—ironic, since Sheppard and Diamond had met years before.

"I was an order-taker in the back of the warehouse," says Sheppard, noting that he worked for Memphis' Hotline Distributors. "One day, the girl up front said, 'There's a guy out here—Neil somebody—to see you.' He had a record on Bang Records. I walked out, and there stood this guy with dirty sneakers, a sweatshirt and hair down to his shoulders, and he said, 'I'm Neil Diamond, I have this new record I'd like for you to distribute for us.' It was 'Solitary Man.'"

474

FOR ALL THE WRONG REASONS

THE BELLAMY BROTHERS

Elektra 47431
Writer: David Bellamy
Producers: Jimmy Bowen, The Bellamy Brothers
June 12, 1982 (1 week)

"For All The Wrong Reasons" represents the start of a new phase in the Bellamy Brothers' career. In 1981, they ended an agreement with Warner Bros. by releasing two singles that never appeared on any album. "They Could Put Me In Jail," a Bob McDill composition that continued their quest for "romantic suggestivity" [see 415—"Do You Love As Good As You Look"], reached number 12. "You're My Favorite Star," blending country music with Jamaican rhythms, became the only reggae record ever to hit the Top Ten on the country chart.

Signing with Elektra Records, Howard and David remained skeptical of working with another producer and persuaded Elektra head Jimmy Bowen to allow them to make their next album, *When We Were Boys*, at home.

"They had a little wooden house, a rehearsal hall with speakers out there," Bowen remembers. "It's the greatest thing you've ever seen. We pulled up a remote truck, and cut the whole album there. We couldn't tell what we had at all 'til we got the hell out of Florida and got back up to the Nashville studio where we mixed it.

"Their house was half the size of [my listening room at home], stuffed with this whole band. It was just a big wall of sound, but we got it back out and isolated tracks and took the technical gear and got noise out of some mikes that didn't belong there and cleaned it up a little bit."

"Bowen came down and played golf," David elaborates, "but he'd come in and oversee the recording, and check everything out, make sure we were doin' it all right. Then he'd go back to Nashville when he was satisfied that we'd put the tracks down."

The Bellamys mixed the album with Bowen at his Sound Stage Studios, using digital equipment for the first time. They tapped as their first single "For All The Wrong Reasons," a song that David wrote after carrying around the chorus' melody for several months. In an unusual twist, the final product featured gospel-tinged harmonies while exploring the topic of infidelity. Despite the seeming incongruity, it worked quite well, propelling Howard and David to their fifth number one country single.

Conway Twitty

475

SLOW HAND

CONWAY TWITTY

Elektra 47443
Writers: Michael Clark, John Bettis
Producers: Conway Twitty, Jimmy Bowen
June 19, 1982 (2 weeks)

The week that "The Clown" [see 468] brought Conway Twitty his first number one single for Elektra Records, the label released "Slow Hand" as a follow-up after discovering that more than 300 radio stations were already playing it off the *Southern Comfort* album.

Written by Nashville tunesmith Michael Clark and Los Angeles veteran John Bettis, "Slow Hand" first gained national exposure one year earlier, when the Pointer Sisters took it to number two on *Billboard*'s Hot 100. Some associates were concerned when Conway decided to cut the record so soon after its pop success, but producer Jimmy Bowen insists that he wasn't among the skeptics. "I always want to push the edge," he says. "I wanted him to go for it. I loved that from day one. We were all nervous about country radio accepting it, but he did it, and then we were safe with it."

Twitty, however, claims that Bowen had a much different reaction at the time.

"He thought I'd lost my mind when I did 'Slow Hand,'" laughs Conway. "Bowen was sittin' there with Dee [Henry] in the control room, goin' 'What's he doin'? What's he doin'?' Dee said, 'Why don't you ask him?' He said, 'No, no, no—I ain't messin' around with nobody that's had that many number one records. But they're gonna accuse me of cuttin' him pop or something.'"

Despite objections, Twitty reasoned that most country fans had never heard the Pointers' version. He also figured that with its Nashville roots, the song would translate well to country. In fact, Clark and Bettis had pitched "Slow Hand" in Music City before the Pointer Sisters ever heard it, but found no takers.

Twitty's rendition erased all doubts. Just two months after the record's release, it made an easy climb into the top spot.

On June 6, Conway made another move that confounded the experts and engendered more than a small amount of snickering in Nashville. He opened Music Village USA, more commonly called "Twitty City." The $3.5-million complex, built on nine acres of land in suburban Hendersonville, encountered a couple of zoning obstacles prior to construction, but it eventually became the third most visited tourist attraction in Nashville.

Included on the grounds are a concert theater and a multi-media show that highlights Twitty's career, as well as the homes of Conway and his offspring. Music Village USA draws 750,000 visitors a year.

476
ANY DAY NOW
RONNIE MILSAP
RCA 13216
Writers: Burt Bacharach, Bob Hilliard
Producers: Ronnie Milsap, Tom Collins
July 3, 1982 (1 week)

Before Ronnie Milsap started making records in Nashville, he had a so-so career doing rhythm and blues [see 165—"Pure Love"]. Milsap cut seven singles for New York-based Scepter Records; in fact, his first, "Never Had It So Good," was written by Ashford & Simpson, known for a series of successful Motown compositions. "Most of the people who heard it," says Ronnie, "thought I was a black artist."

During that period, he worked with Smokey Robinson & The Miracles, Little Anthony & The Imperials and Sam & Dave, among others, and his soul experiences have greatly influenced his country efforts. Nowhere is that more obvious than on "Any Day Now," his remake of a 1962 hit by former Del-Viking Chuck Jackson.

Milsap had long thought of recording the song, and producer Tom Collins brought that notion to the surface when he mentioned "Any Day Now" during a recording session in January of 1982. Milsap immediately started toying with the idea.

"I mentioned it to Charlie McCoy, who was on the session," Ronnie relates. "He said, 'Well, everybody knows that song—what key you wanna do it in?' I said, 'Let's do it in F,' so we go in, and even during the rehearsal, everybody knew the song. After a couple of rundowns, that was an early-on take."

"We cut a basic rhythm track, and it was doin' okay," Collins elaborates. "Then we brought in the Memphis Horns, and they did a 'head arrangement' with Ronnie and I there. Ronnie and me both sort of told 'em what we wanted. Then Bergen White did the strings

after we'd put the background vocals on, and Bergen really enhanced that record. It was one of those records that the more you added to it, the more it took, and we couldn't stop it."

"That's the first song in the studio that I used two tandem 24-tracks," Milsap continues. "We couldn't get everything on one tape, so we used this other tape, a slave tape, and we had to run both machines at the same time to mix. What a slow process, but what a big record it makes."

"Any Day Now" was Milsap's twentieth record to top the country chart, and it also peaked at number 14 on the Hot 100. *Billboard* named it the top adult/contemporary single of 1982.

477
DON'T WORRY 'BOUT ME BABY
JANIE FRICKIE
Columbia 02859
Writers: Bruce Channel, Kieran Kane, Deborah Allen
Producer: Jim Ed Norman
July 10, 1982 (1 week)

When Janie Frickie first hit the *Billboard* country charts in 1977 with "What're You Doing Tonight," she had earned a reputation as the best-known unknown in the business. A session singer at the time, she came to prominence when Larry Gatlin teamed her with Johnny Duncan [see 268—"Thinkin' Of A Rendezvous"] on a single titled "Jo And The Cowboy."

Once Frickie's performances went over the airwaves unidentified, disk jockeys pestered the Columbia promotion staff about the "mystery voice," and she suddenly earned a much greater role on many more records. Billy Sherrill signed her to Columbia Records, forging her first hit with a 1978 remake of "Please Help Me, I'm Falling," the Hank Locklin original that topped the charts for 11 weeks in 1960.

Teaming up with Jim Ed Norman in 1980, Janie went to number two with "Down To My Last Broken Heart," adding two more Top Five records the following year, with "I'll Need Someone To Hold Me (When I Cry)" and "Do Me With Love." Finally, "Don't Worry 'Bout Me Baby," featuring backing vocalist Ricky Skaggs, brought her to the number one position.

The trio of writers was rather impressive, too. Bruce Channel had scored a number one

Janie Frickie

'TIL YOU'RE GONE

BARBARA MANDRELL

MCA 52038
Writers: Tommy Brasfield, Walt Aldridge
Producer: Tom Collins
July 17, 1982 (1 week)

On November 18, 1980, the network premiere of "Barbara Mandrell & The Mandrell Sisters" brought its leading lady into a new career phase. Already one of country music's best-known performers, it pushed her in front of millions of viewers—some of whom hadn't known her work before.

Produced by Sid and Marty Krofft, the variety series emphasized music, but also provided plenty of comedy between Barbara, Louise and Irlene. Barbara came off as "bossy," an exaggeration of their real-life relationships.

The country industry recognized the series' impact, and within eighteen months of the show's debut, Barbara hauled in numerous awards. Between the Country Music Association and the Academy of Country Music, she tallied three trophies as Entertainer of the Year and two as the top Female Vocalist.

Ultimately, the strain of weekly TV spelled an early end to the series. Mandrell sometimes worked fourteen to sixteen hours a day, six days a week. Despite NBC's desire to bring her back for another season, she bowed out, airing her final show on June 26, 1982.

"It was definitely the single most educational thing I've ever done," Barbara explains. "In doing a true variety show, you are called on to do almost everything—from comedy skits to dancing to writing. It was a real challenge. I'm very proud of it and my sisters. I pulled out of the show because I'm not willing to do anything in life halfway, and I felt it would be physically impossible for me to continue at that pace every week."

With the show in full gear, she followed "I Was Country When Country Wasn't Cool" [see 432] with "Wish You Were," peaking at number two in late 1981.

Once freed from her network obligations, Mandrell set to work on her first studio album in nearly two years. Prior to its release, MCA put out "'Til You're Gone," composed by Walt Aldridge and Tommy Brasfield.

"After we wrote 'No Gettin' Over Me' [see 438], we were so fired up we just wrote and

pop record in 1962 with "Hey! Baby," and Kieran Kane would go on to form one-half of the O'Kanes [see 722—"Can't Stop My Heart From Loving You"]. Deborah Allen was likewise a struggling artist, and all three were recording a demo tape when they started the song.

"They were doing a guitar overdub," Allen recalls, "and the three of us were hanging out by the candy machine with nothing to do, so we just started writing. We wrote about half of it, and then I had to go back in and sing. About a week later, Kieran and Bruce and I got back together. We were sitting out on our front porch where [husband] Rafe [VanHoy] and I live, and we wrote the second verse to it."

They took the finished version to Tree Publishing's Don Gant, who drove them to the studio, where Frickie and Norman were working. "We all just barged in and played the song for them," Allen continues. "The next day, I think, they wound up recording it. It was really a lot of fun because it was very spontaneous."

wrote," says Aldridge. "I don't remember specifically writing ''Til You're Gone.' We were writing every night, and had written a lot of songs that were right in that groove."

With saxophonist Ron Eades featured prominently, "'Til You're Gone" became Mandrell's fifth number one single three weeks after her network show ended.

479
TAKE ME DOWN
ALABAMA
RCA 13210
Writers: J.P. Pennington, Mark Gray
Producers: Harold Shedd, Alabama
July 24, 1982 (1 week)

At the time that Alabama first caught on, Nashville had a stigma about groups. Granted, the Statler Brothers and the Oak Ridge Boys had established themselves, but both of those acts were vocal quartets. No successful groups existed in which the vocal band members also played their own instruments. Says Jeff Cook: "It seemed to be the opinion of the major [labels] back then that if you were a band, you would have a hit record and then have internal problems and break up."

Alabama destroyed that line of thinking, and within a few years, many groups emerged in country music. The first of those was Exile, which got its break when Alabama recorded one of their songs.

J.P. Pennington had developed a little musical and lyrical pattern in 1980 around the phrase "Take Me Down." At the time, it had no sexual meaning—no meaning at all—and he dashed off a couple of verses and a chorus and forgot about it.

He and Mark Gray (then a fellow member of Exile) sat down to write one evening at the United Artists Tower on Music Row in Nashville. Exile hadn't been able to match the success of "Kiss You All Over" [see 559—"Woke Up In Love"], and they wanted badly to come up with something that had the same seductive tempo and understated double entendre. Neither came with any specific ideas, and when they hit a dry spot, Pennington suddenly started singing "Take Me Down." Gray fell in love with the idea, and after J.P. played what he already had, Mark developed a bridge to pull it all together.

Exile released its version of "Take Me Down" as a single, though it quickly settled into obscurity. Linda Bloom sent the song from the publisher's L.A. office to producer Harold Shedd a year later, and Shedd played it for Alabama, who were knocked out by it. They captured much of the same flavor while adding a few extra harmony parts in different places, and put a four-and-a-half-minute version on the *Mountain Music* [see 470] album.

After playing the song live, Alabama decided it was too long and chopped a minute out before releasing it as a single. "Take Me Down" debuted at number 38 over Memorial Day weekend in 1982, and leaped to number one eight weeks later.

480
I DON'T CARE
RICKY SKAGGS
Epic 02931
Writers: Webb Pierce, Cindy Walker
Producer: Ricky Skaggs
July 31, 1982 (1 week)

When Ricky Skaggs emerged in 1981 with *Waitin' for the Sun to Shine*, he had only begun to think of himself as a vocalist. Primarily an instrumentalist and harmony singer, Skaggs first learned mandolin at age five, and by the age of ten, he'd added guitar and fiddle to his burgeoning skills.

Ricky gave his first public performance at the age of five, when fans at a Bill Monroe concert in Martha, Kentucky, clamored for Monroe to bring him on stage. Two years later, his instrumental skills brought Skaggs his first musical paycheck: $52.50 for playing "Ruby" and "Honky Tonk Swing" on Flatt & Scruggs' television show.

"I never really started singin' lead until I cut my first album, *Sweet Temptation*," Ricky notes, "and that was kind of like a tryout album to see if I could really hack it in the country music field."

Sugar Hill Records released *Sweet Temptation* in 1979. Though Skaggs still felt a little insecure as a singer, a scant three years later, he picked up the Academy of Country Music's Top New Male Vocalist award, on April 29, 1982. Two days later, he appeared at the ghastly hour of 6:00 A.M. for the opening of the World's Fair in Knoxville.

Another two days later, Epic released "I Don't Care," a song that Webb Pierce had taken to number one for a dozen weeks, beginning July 16, 1955. Pierce didn't actually write "I Don't Care," but he provided Cindy Walker with the title, and she composed it from there. Skaggs received a copy of the song a few years before he recorded it from fellow Hot Band member Hank DeVito, who gave Ricky a compilation tape of Pierce songs, which also included "Honey (Open That Door)" [see 571].

"I always loved the melody in 'I Don't Care'," Ricky recalls. "It was a simple, quick song, but it had a real hope and promise: 'I don't care what you've done in the past. It doesn't matter. I love ya. As long as you'll be mine, we'll make it work.'"

On May 16, 1982, Skaggs became the youngest member of the Grand Ole Opry. On May 29, "I Don't Care" debuted on the *Billboard* country chart at number 52. In its tenth charted week, Skaggs reeled in his second number one single.

481

HONKY TONKIN'
HANK WILLIAMS, JR.
Elektra 47462
Writer: Hank Williams
Producer: Jimmy Bowen
August 7, 1982 (1 week)

Hank Williams, Jr., was just three years old when his father passed away [see 385—"You Win Again"], yet a few visions of Hank, Sr., remain.

"I can remember him just as plain as day," he told *Billboard*'s Gerry Wood, "laying down on the couch and watching TV, and there was a desk I used to bang on with a hammer. And I remember him sitting in an airplane, all legs and hat. And I remember him on a morning radio show. I remember those three snapshots of him, and that's all."

For years, country fans had wanted the younger Williams to be a living snapshot of his father, but he deliberately shunned life as a die-cast copy. Thus, it proved ironic when Bocephus remade several of his father's songs, including "Move It On Over," "Kaw-Liga" and "Honky Tonkin'."

Notes manager Merle Kilgore: "Just like [New York writer] Jim Bessman said, 'Hank Junior doesn't play by the rules, so you can't judge him by the rules.' He wanted to do it his way, but when he proved that he could do it his

way, he went back and did Hank, Sr., stuff, and said 'This'll really knock them off-guard.' But he don't plan it that way, it just happens."

The elder Hank cut "Honky Tonkin'" in his second recording session, and Hank, Jr., originally intended his version as a duet with Tanya Tucker. Unhappy with her performance, he saved the instrumental tracks and did it as a solo record.

It brought new life to his daddy's chestnut, and Hank paid further homage to his father by ad-libbing a couple of lines from "Hey, Good Lookin'" in the tune's chorus. It became his sixth number one single, although it could have easily been the seventh. His prior release, "A Country Boy Can Survive," stalled at number two on April 24, 1982.

Williams set a record that week, though, when *High Notes* entered the *Billboard* country album chart. As a result, eight different Hank, Jr., albums were on the chart simultaneously. That achievement didn't last long—on October 30, *Hank Williams, Jr.'s Greatest Hits* became his ninth album listed.

Hank owns the mark for living entertainers. The late Elvis Presley was the first performer with nine albums listed. He attained that level on January 21, 1978, thanks to the buying frenzy that followed his death [see 291—"Way Down"].

482

I'M GONNA HIRE A WINO TO DECORATE OUR HOME
DAVID FRIZZELL
Warner Bros. 50063
Writer: Dewayne Blackwell
Producers: Snuff Garrett, Steve Dorff
August 14, 1982 (1 week)

"I think anybody who's a brother of a walkin' legend is liable to feel a little inferior," says David Frizzell. "Lefty had just accomplished so many things by the time he was 21 years old, and had just become a world power in country music. There's no way not to feel some sort of pressure.

"I felt he was a very talented man, but I never did feel I had a problem competing with him on a talent level. He did what he did, and I did what I did, and I didn't want to compare those two things."

Anyone else who wanted to make comparisons had to consider David on his own in 1982. Having formed a successful tandem with Shelly West a year earlier [see 420—"You're The Reason God Made Oklahoma"], he finally got the solo hits he had wanted for so long.

David's performing career actually took its roots in Lefty's show. Traveling with his older brother, he played Elvis Presley songs onstage at age 13 at Bakersfield's Rainbow Gardens. He signed with Columbia Records in 1958, but those early recordings did very little to establish him.

After four years with the Air Force, David went through at least five more record deals, none of which paid off. His duets with West, though, brought him into favor, as the Country Music Association and the Academy of Country Music each accorded the duo with a pair of trophies. Both Frizzell and West decided to pursue concurrent solo careers; David's was the first to get off the ground, with "I'm Gonna Hire A Wino To Decorate Our Home."

Dewayne Blackwell, who also wrote the Fleetwoods' "Mr. Blue," created the song and shopped it as a demo for a recording deal. He didn't find any takers, and record producer Snuff Garrett played it for Frizzell one day in his Los Angeles office. Frizzell flipped, and a single phone call secured Blackwell's permission to cut it.

"We recorded it just after that," David notes. "Dewayne came to the session, and we did it just like he had done it."

It became Frizzell's only number one single as a solo artist, although he added two more Top Ten records: "Lost My Baby Blues" and "Where Are You Spending Your Nights These Days."

Sylvia

483

NOBODY
SYLVIA
RCA 13223
Writers: Kye Fleming, Dennis Morgan
Producer: Tom Collins
August 21, 1982 (1 week)

When Sylvia took Kye Fleming and Dennis Morgan's composition "Nobody" to number one, it was a celebration for three friends. The songwriters both worked for Tom Collins at Pi-Gem, the same company where Sylvia got her start as a receptionist [see 419—"Drifter"].

She already had ten songs for her album *Just* *Sylvia*, but she had one more session scheduled to cut new material and see if they had anything stronger. Fleming and Morgan finished up "Nobody" the night before that session, and rushed to the office to give it to Sylvia in the morning. It was so new they hadn't even cut a demo tape.

"They started singing 'Nobody,'" Sylvia recalls, "and by the time they were in the middle of the second chorus, I was singing along with them. It struck me immediately, and I learned the song that morning. We went in at 2:00 and recorded it, and I felt like I was just learning it on the session. It was really a magical kind of thing."

Sylvia also cut "Like Nothing Ever Happened" (a follow-up which peaked at number two) at that session, and "Nobody" was actually relegated to the final 20 minutes. Drummer Buster Phillips, bass player Joe Osborn and guitarist Pete Bordonali laid down the basic tracks on the third take.

"The next day, I started overdubbing," remembers Collins, "and I hear this track and her vocals are good, except maybe one or two words. I stayed in there all day long using Shane Keister and Bobby Ogdin on synthesizer, and we started overdubbing, and Sylvia only had to re-sing two words." The Cherry Sisters (Sheri Huffman, Diane Tidwell and Lisa Silver) also added sassy back-up vocals. "They made that record," says Sylvia.

Released on May 14, 1982, "Nobody" hit number 15 on *Billboard*'s Hot 100, earning a gold record for selling one million copies on December 21.

Sylvia had four more Top Ten singles through 1985, but then took a hiatus from recording to write more personal material. "I didn't have a lot of positive reinforcement as a child," she reflects, "and when I first came to Nashville, a lot of my motivation was fueled by wanting people to accept me. I enjoy singing, but there's got to be a lot more to it now. I want to bring more of me to my music."

484

FOOL HEARTED MEMORY
GEORGE STRAIT
MCA 52066
Writers: Byron Hill, Alan R. Mevis
Producer: Blake Mevis
August 28, 1982 (1 week)

In 1979, George Strait nearly gave up his dream of country stardom. Three trips to Nashville in hopes of landing a recording deal proved futile, and he decided to cash in his chips and live a more secure lifestyle. He agreed to work in Uvalde, Texas, building cattle-auction barns, but he became moody and dejected around the house. A week before George reported to his new employer, his wife, Norma, convinced him that he should stay with music a little longer.

George agreed, and before long, MCA promotion man Erv Woolsey came to his aid. Woolsey, who owned a San Marcos, Texas, club called The Prairie Rose, had heard Strait sing years before and maintained contact with the singer even after he sold the venue. In 1980, he helped Strait hook up with Nashville producer Blake Mevis, and MCA signed George in February of 1981. The label released a track from one of their earliest sessions, "Unwound," as a single, and Strait's unclut-

tered honky-tonk sound quickly soared to number six that summer.

George's first album, appropriately titled *Strait Country*, yielded two more singles, "Down And Out" (number 16) and "If You're Thinking You Want A Stranger (There's One Coming Home)" (number three). Even as those records took off, Strait secured a deal to work on a film for MCA-affiliated Universal Pictures, *The Soldier*.

"It was a real blockbuster movie," George snickers. "You must remember it!"

For the picture, Strait recorded "Fool Hearted Memory," a title that Alan Mevis batted around in his mind for several weeks. When Mevis and co-writer Byron Hill went to work on a song for the movie, it came together quickly.

"We just sat down, and 20 minutes later, there was a song," Alan recalls. "It came so easy, I was a little doubtful I even had a hit. Then it sat on the album like nine months before it got out, and by then I was convinced it wasn't a hit."

The general public had a different perspective, even though few people (if any) saw the movie, or the barroom brawl that the film's producer, Murri Barber, shot in Buffalo with Strait lip-synching on stage. "Fool Hearted Memory" first appeared at number 65 on *Billboard*'s country chart on June 19, 1982. Ten weeks later, Strait earned his first number one single.

485

LOVE WILL TURN YOU AROUND
KENNY ROGERS
Liberty 1471
Writers: Kenny Rogers, David Malloy, Thom Schuyler, Even Stevens
Producers: Kenny Rogers, David Malloy
September 4, 1982 (1 week)

In 1982, Kenny Rogers filmed his first motion picture, *Six Pack*. Though set for release in July, by May, the film still didn't have a song that would also work as a hit record. Kenny's brother, Leland, placed calls to a number of Nashville's finest songwriters to solve their dilemma.

Eddie Rabbitt's partners, David Malloy and Even Stevens, agreed to meet the challenge, and they chartered a bus to meet Kenny on the concert trail. Along the way, they began creating a song, based on the *Six Pack* script. When they arrived at the auditorium, they were so awed by Rogers that they flubbed the song while performing it for him backstage.

Instead, Kenny picked up a guitar, played a simple riff and sang a shred of melody that he had been toying with for some time. Unfortunately, Malloy and Stevens didn't have a tape recorder, and they had promised to see Kenny's show. So, between each song during the concert, they turned to each other in their front-row seats and sang the melody again, ensuring that they wouldn't forget it.

They began the song on the return trip to Nashville, and decided that Thom Schuyler, who had recently signed with their publishing company, should help them. "We stopped, and I called Thom up about midnight," notes Stevens. "I said, 'If you're any kind of song-writer at all, you'll get up, meet us there at the office. We'll get there about two in the morning. We got a great opportunity here and we've got a great start.'"

All three worked through most of the night. Thom, in fact, contributed the original title, "Love Will Turn It Around."

Notes Malloy: "I remember for the melody of the bridge—'It's your heart,' that part—I would imagine myself as Kenny Rogers, holding the microphone, turning my head sideways. That's how that melody came about, imagining myself as him."

"Within about eight or ten hours," Schuyler continues, "that song was started. Then I took it home for the weekend and finished up the lyrics."

Schuyler sang the demo and shipped it overnight to Kenny, who brought Malloy and Stevens in to L.A. to cut the record. The rhythm tracks were recorded three different times, the final one while Kenny took morning tennis lessons. From the time that Leland placed the first phone call, the entire record was finished within a week.

Jerry Reed

486
SHE GOT THE GOLDMINE (I GOT THE SHAFT)
JERRY REED
RCA 13268
Writer: Tim DuBois
Producer: Rick Hall
September 11, 1982 (2 weeks)

"Contempt of court!?"

That exclamation—uttered during the fade-out at the end of both records—provides a clever link between Jerry Reed's first number one single, "When You're Hot, You're Hot" [see 79], and his third, "She Got The Goldmine (I Got The Shaft)."

Unlike the first, "Goldmine" came from an outside writer and was based on a real-life court case, albeit somewhat loosely. Tim DuBois wrote it for the House of Gold publishing company in Nashville several years before Reed actually cut it in Muscle Shoals.

"I had a friend who made the statement one day," relates DuBois, "said his first marriage was like a goldmine, but when they split, she got all the gold and all he got was the shaft.

"That always stuck with me, and I was snowed in one January and just writing by myself. I don't write a lot by myself. In order to write by myself, it has to be something funny that keeps my attention. I wrote that mainly to amuse myself, and Jerry Reed took it and made it his own."

"Goldmine" represented quite a comeback for Reed, who had lost his musical focus in the preceding years. He had become entranced by motion pictures [see 138—"Lord, Mr. Ford"], and in 1981, starred in a short-lived TV series, "Concrete Cowboys." When that program was canceled, it led to a musical recommitment.

Reed studied music theory and woodshedded for the better part of a year, and the work paid off in "Goldmine." It became his first Top Ten single in five years, and his first number one in nine years. Part of the credit belongs to Rick Hall, who had already produced such hits as "One Bad Apple," by the Osmonds; "Baby Don't Get Hooked On Me," by Mac Davis; and "(You're) Having My Baby," by Paul Anka.

Credit is also due to guitarist/vocalist Walt Aldridge (who would go on to form the Shooters) and guitarist Kenny Bell, who played most of the guitars. "That's one of the things that's particularly frustrating as a musician," notes Aldridge, "when you have an artist like Jerry Reed, who everyone assumes plays the guitars on the record. I was playing a lot of the guitars on Rick Hall's sessions at the time. We were, of course, proud of the guitars on that one after it did become a hit."

487

WHAT'S FOREVER FOR
MICHAEL MARTIN MURPHEY
Liberty 1466
Writer: Rafe VanHoy
Producer: Jim Ed Norman
September 25, 1982 (1 week)

A native of Oak Cliff, Texas, Michael Martin Murphey seemed a newcomer to country music in 1982, at least to the general public.

A singer/songwriter, he wrote poetry and short stories as a child, and headed to California at the age of 20 to study writing at UCLA. He ended up performing at Ledbetter's in Westwood, brushing with country-rockers like Jackson Browne, Linda Ronstadt, Jerry Jeff Walker and the Eagles. He also formed a duo with Boomer Castleman, the Lewis & Clark Expedition.

In 1971, Murphey headed to Austin, where he lived for three years during the formative stages of Willie Nelson's "outlaw" movement. During 1972, he made his first appearance in *Billboard*'s Hot 100, with "Geronimo's Cadillac." After moving to Colorado, he went all

the way to number three with "Wildfire." The follow-up, "Carolina In The Pines," reached number 21.

In 1979, Michael moved to Taos, New Mexico. The next year, he co-wrote the script to the movie *Hard Country* and placed "Cherokee Fiddle" on the soundtrack to *Urban Cowboy*, recorded by Johnny Lee. In 1982, his efforts found a more permanent home in country music. "The Two-Step Is Easy" took him to number 44, but a breakthrough—both commercially and personally—occurred with his next single, "What's Forever For," a song he heard songwriter Rafe VanHoy play during a "guitar pull."

"The impact that it had on me at that time is hard to describe," says Murphey. "I thought it was one of the most important love songs I've ever heard. A lot of love songs are written just to exploit people's emotional feelings. But it got down inside the experience, and some of the pain, and some of the troubles that you have to work yourself through. It's not only a wonderful love song that makes people emotional, but it also comes right out and says some things that I've found out are on the minds of an awful lot of people."

VanHoy wrote the song when a couple that he thought would stay together ended up divorcing. At least ten artists covered it before Murphey—including Johnny Mathis, Anne Murray, John Conlee and T. G. Sheppard—yet Murphey's version remains the definitive one. While establishing his country career, the song also returned Murphey to number 19 on the pop chart.

488

PUT YOUR DREAMS AWAY
MICKEY GILLEY
Epic 03055
Writers: Richard Leigh,
Wayland Holyfield
Producer: Jim Ed Norman
October 2, 1982 (1 week)

A fter six straight number one records beginning in 1980, Mickey Gilley's streak ended in 1982 with "Tears Of The Lonely," which peaked at number three. "Tears" was written by Wayland Holyfield, who also wrote Gilley's follow-up, bringing him back to the top spot with "Put Your Dreams Away."

Holyfield co-wrote the song with Richard

Mickey Gilley

Leigh, who had already put together two number one singles for Crystal Gayle, "I'll Get Over You" [see 250] and "Don't It Make My Brown Eyes Blue" [see 292]. Since Leigh penned both of those tunes alone, "Put Your Dreams Away" became his first co-writing venture to reach number one.

"I liked starting off with two CMA-nominated songs—'Brown Eyes' and 'I'll Get Over You,'" says Leigh, "and having written them by myself, that made me feel confident. But I enjoy the fellowship of co-writing a whole lot. I do that almost exclusively now; it's just a lot of fun. I don't have anything to prove to myself."

Leigh characterizes "Put Your Dreams Away" as "less torchy" than his earlier number ones. "I had a little piece of it," he notes, "and had liked Wayland Holyfield a whole lot. We'd always talked about getting together and writ-

ing, and we finally did get together in his office and knocked that one out in a short period of time. He's a good friend with Jim Ed Norman, and we took it over there. Jim Ed liked it a whole lot, and cut it on Mickey."

Gilley recalls, though, that "Put Your Dreams Away" went through several variations before its final version went to vinyl. "The song was rewritten," he says. "I know Jim Ed had taken the tune, and we had worked on it a little bit, and he had them redo some of the lyrics."

On top of a memorable chorus, "Put Your Dreams Away" hinged on an interlocking instrumental passage, ably supplied by Tony Migliore's electric piano and Paul Worley's guitar. Schlitz beer eventually used that same musical theme in a radio commercial while sponsoring the syndicated concert series "Live At Gilley's."

489

YESTERDAY'S WINE

MERLE HAGGARD & GEORGE JONES

Epic 03072
Writer: Willie Nelson
Producer: Billy Sherrill
October 9, 1982 (1 week)

On July 10, 1982, WHN-AM in New York aired a bootlegged copy of "Yesterday's Wine," a song targeted as the first single from Merle Haggard's duet album with George Jones. The station might have jumped the gun, but it wasn't long before the single was released and nearly every other station fell in line.

Haggard had just finished recording another duet album with Willie Nelson [see 529—"Pancho And Lefty"], but that record was put on the shelf because Willie already had a large amount of product in release. Nelson was still credited as the writer in the Haggard/Jones collaboration, though, having written "Yester-

day's Wine" more than ten years earlier for his first concept album.

"We [Willie and his band] were all living in Bandera, out on the golf course in San Antonio," remembers Nelson. "I needed to do an album, and I didn't have anything written. We started putting it together—we recorded a lot of it right on the table there at this big house.

"We did the front part of the *Yesterday's Wine* album—the talking part—then I went to Nashville on a Sunday night, and stayed up all night and wrote seven songs for a Monday session. I was writing off the top of my head all night long, really writing down what I was thinking."

Having completed the *Pancho and Lefty* album in 1982, Haggard chose "Yesterday's Wine" for inclusion in his duet project with Jones.

"Merle brought it to the session, and Jones didn't care what he sang," notes producer Billy Sherrill. "Whoever comes up, or whatever comes up, is fine with him. Merle brought most of the stuff in there, and we just did it."

"Yesterday's Wine" proved to be one of three

**Merle Haggard
& George Jones**

key tracks on the album. "C.C. Waterback" was released as the second single, ascending to number ten. To celebrate the event, Haggard bought 5,095 C.C. Waterbacks (Canadian Club with a water chaser) at Billy Bob's in Fort Worth. It took 40 gallons of whiskey to fill the order, which totaled $12,737.50.

One more track, "No Show Jones," received a large amount of album airplay. Co-written by Jones and Glenn Martin, it took a light-hearted look at the Possum's then-unreliable track record. Though considered as a third single, "No Show Jones" was never released.

490

I WILL ALWAYS LOVE YOU/ DO I EVER CROSS YOUR MIND

DOLLY PARTON

RCA 13260
Writer: Dolly Parton
Producers: Gregg Perry, Dolly Parton
October 16, 1982 (1 week)

With "I Will Always Love You," Dolly Parton became the first artist ever to earn a number one record twice with the same song. The song first rose to the top in 1974 [see 166], and its re-recording for *The Best Little Whorehouse in Texas* was an unplanned occurrence.

Originally, she wrote four new songs specifically for the movie, which already included a musical score penned by Carol Hall. "I Will Always Love You" was also added when the producer needed something for the scene in which Miss Mona (played by Dolly) splits with the sheriff (Burt Reynolds). Three of Parton's creations were scrapped, but "I Will Always Love You" survived.

Whorehouse proved a very painful experience for Dolly. The picture was based on a brothel in La Grange, Texas, called The Chicken Ranch. The bordello was closed in 1973 after Houston newsman Marvin Zindler exposed it, and a Broadway play emerged after Larry King wrote a piece on the establishment for *Playboy*.

Dolly feared that her fans might be upset about the role she had taken, and she frequently danced around the title while publicizing it. The role of Miss Mona proved less traumatic, though, than the actual shooting.

Both King and Hall were concerned that their work would be damaged by the movie, and Reynolds was reportedly edgy about the movie, since his recent roles had been less than successful at the box office.

"I decided, 'I can't deal with this crap,'" Dolly told Robert K. Oermann in *Country Rhythms*, "and chose to stay out of all the squabbling and fighting. And there was a *lot* of it. I sent little notes of apology to Larry King and Carol Hall, saying I was real sorry for any trouble and hard feelings that occurred. I told them I wanted to make 'em proud of the movie, and that I'd do the best I could."

After its appearance in July of 1982, *Whorehouse* bombed with the critics, although it did brisk box office business. Additionally, it yielded a second recording success for Dolly, when she hit number eight the following winter with "Hard Candy Christmas." Still, it remains among her most difficult memories.

After finishing the project, she told Cliff Jahr in *Ladies' Home Journal*: "There is a tiny voice in me that keeps saying, 'This is the last movie that you will ever make.'"

491

HE GOT YOU

RONNIE MILSAP

RCA 13286
Writers: Ralph Murphy, Bobby Wood
Producers: Ronnie Milsap, Tom Collins
October 23, 1982 (1 week)

When Ronnie Milsap first recorded "He Got You," he was quick to point out to those who hadn't heard it yet that the tune was *not* a reworking of the Patsy Cline classic "She's Got You" [see 282].

"When I moved down here, I'd never heard ["She's Got You"]," reports London-born songwriter Ralph Murphy. "When people heard my song on the radio, they came up and said, 'Boy, I bet you're gonna get sued [over] the Patsy Cline song.' I went out and bought a copy and said, 'Holy shit!' It did kind of freak me out. It was nowhere near it musically, but there were certain points it did touch on it [lyrically]."

Murphy wrote "He Got You" with keyboard player Bobby Wood, with whom he had already penned Crystal Gayle's 1979 hit "Half The Way." Murphy, who is primarily a lyricist, developed the idea and then tapped out the basic meter on his leg.

"He didn't have any idea about a groove," Wood recalls. "As he was starting to tell me what it's about, I just started pickin' up what I felt like the lyrics were sayin'. I don't think we've ever been over 30 minutes writin' a song."

They composed "He Got You" specifically for Bobby Whitlock, who had toured with the Rolling Stones and played with Eric Clapton, and had recently moved to Nashville. It was one of a handful of songs Murphy used to try and secure a recording deal for Whitlock, but after finding little success, he gave up on the idea. About that time, producer Tom Collins called, requesting songs for Milsap.

Murphy was to go overseas the next day, but he played "He Got You" for Collins at 5:00 that afternoon. Tom said he would play it for Milsap, and when Ralph checked into his London hotel 24 hours later, a message was waiting: "Loved it. We're gonna cut it."

Milsap closely imitated the demo, and "He Got You" was released as a follow-up to "Any Day Now" [see 476], sailing to number one a week after the Country Music Association awards show in 1982.

Murphy, who started writing at age 15, has a couple of interesting mentors: Tommy Conner, who wrote "I Saw Mommy Kissing Santa Claus," and Roger Cook, author of "I Believe In You" [see 397].

492

CLOSE ENOUGH TO PERFECT
ALABAMA
RCA 13294
Writer: Carl Chambers
Producers: Harold Shedd, Alabama
October 30, 1982 (1 week)

"When I hear a song, I either like it or I don't," says producer Harold Shedd, explaining how he decides if he'll record a song. "When I'm looking for a particular artist, I'm looking for a certain thing. In Alabama's case, we were not lookin' for any beer-drinking, cheatin' kinds of songs. We were lookin' for positive things with positive messages."

Rarely do they come more positive than "Close Enough To Perfect," written by Carl Chambers, who was then a guitarist with the Bellamy Brothers [see 373—"Sugar Daddy"]. He did a little carpentry work for Howard and David, putting up cedar paneling in a tour bus they purchased; Chambers used his wife, Nancy, as an assistant.

"Every time I would put a piece up, she'd find

something wrong with it," Carl laughs, "and I made the quip to her that 'It's close enough to perfect for me.' We just looked at each other, 'cause we knew it was a good hook for a song."

Chambers jotted the title down, and a couple weeks later he wrote the song on behalf of Nancy, who was having trouble dealing with some of his "fringe family" in Florida while he went on the road. "Most people have a tendency to think it's such a pretty song," Carl notes. "Actually, I was very mad when I wrote the song, mad about the way that Nancy was gettin' treated at home."

Ultimately, Chambers' resentment became a long-term funk, and the Bellamys fired him when his attitude created problems in the band. Shortly thereafter, his cousin, Jesse Chambers, also left the Bellamys to play bass with Ricky Skaggs—coincidentally, Skaggs' then-manager, Chip Peay, sued Carl's publishers over the copyright to "Close Enough To Perfect."

Peay had signed a contract for the song in 1981, though Chambers thought he had given the rights to publisher Russ Allison. Ultimately, Peay, Allison and another songwriter all pitched the song to Alabama, and every time, the band kept the demo.

"We to this day are not sure who actually played that song for them first," says Chambers (although Shedd credits Allison). "The lawsuit dragged on for years and years, and I finally gave up part of my money just to get 'em to settle it."

In 1986, Chambers earned another hit, when Skaggs cut "Love's Gonna Get You Someday"—with cousin Jesse playing bass.

493

YOU'RE SO GOOD WHEN YOU'RE BAD
CHARLEY PRIDE
RCA 13293
Writer: Ben Peters
Producer: Norro Wilson
November 6, 1982 (1 week)

"I grew up following the masters, ever since I was knee-high," Charley Pride once told the *Plant City Courier* in Florida. "I listened to Ernest Tubb, Eddy Arnold, Hank Williams, George Jones. I developed my own style by learning from them, not imitating them. B.B. King, Sam Cooke, Brook Benton—there were some of my other favorites. From country, gospel and the blues, which I think is the basis of all American music, I developed my own style."

When Pride first introduced that style, people were quite surprised to hear a black man singing mainstream country music, a medium that has traditionally attracted a white audience. His uniqueness brought all kinds of conjectures, including the rumor that Pride had been "raised by whites."

In fact, he was raised on a steady diet of traditional country music by listening to radio stations WMPS and WREC in Memphis, as well as the Grand Ole Opry. Pride took quite a bit of badgering, too, even from his sister, who couldn't understand why he sang "their music."

Though Charley had made a conscious effort to hang close to the core of country music throughout his career, producer Norro Wilson brought out the soul edges Pride had picked up from B.B. King and Sam Cooke. That was particularly evident on the third single from *Charley Sings Everybody's Choice*, "You're So Good When You're Bad."

"We thought it got down, funky and nasty," surmises Wilson. "We felt like it offered a little different twist for Charley. I tell you what I enjoyed doing with Charley Pride: I enjoyed trying to get some of who he is. He's Charley Pride and he sings white-eyed soul. Now, we've got a lot of white people that sing blue-eyed soul. But still, he's got that in him, a little of that blues, that *naturale* that tends to want to come out, and I enjoyed doing a few of those funky little things with him."

"You're So Good When You're Bad" debuted at number 54 on August 28, 1982, and rose to number one in its eleventh week on the *Billboard* chart.

Nearly seven years later, it received a new bit of attention when the entire single appeared in a romantic scene during an episode of CBS-TV's "Designing Women."

Charley Pride

494
HEARTBROKE
RICKY SKAGGS

Epic 03212
Writer: Guy Clark
Producer: Ricky Skaggs
November 13, 1982 (1 week)

Commercial success has nearly always eluded Guy Clark, but that doesn't bother him. A native of Monahans, Texas, Clark didn't pick up a guitar until age 16, and when he chose music as his life's calling, he did so not for fame or glory, but to satisfy his own creative urges.

Along with his wife, Susanna, Guy moved to California in 1970, signing his first songwriting contract a year later. In 1973, he gave Jerry Jeff Walker "L.A. Freeway." Subsequently, he has penned such hits as "Desperados Waiting For A Train," by Waylon Jennings, Willie Nelson, Johnny Cash and Kris Kristofferson; "Oklahoma Borderline," by Vince Gill; "The Carpenter," by John Conlee; and "She's Crazy For Leaving" [see 802], by Rodney Crowell. His first number one single came when Ricky Skaggs recorded "Heartbroke."

"It was a song I had different parts of over the years," Clark recalls. "I had a couple of verses written in a book that I keep, and I never could figure out where they went. One day I was writing, and I came up with this chorus, and I couldn't figure out where it went, and it floated around for a year or so. Finally, one day, I was going through the book, and I saw the connection. They belonged in the same song, so it's kind of a strange combination of parts, but they just seemed to go together."

"Heartbroke" earned cuts from George Strait and Rodney Crowell, though Guy "thought it was a Chuck Berry tune" when he wrote it. When Clark recorded it himself in Los Angeles, he couldn't find a suitable fiddle player and brought Skaggs out from Nashville. Ricky, unsigned at the time, announced that he intended to record it—if he could ever get a record deal. True to his word, Skaggs rolled it out on his second Epic album, *Highways & Heartaches*.

"I heard Rodney Crowell sing it for the first time at a little ol' club out in California called McCabe's," Ricky remembers. "I got up and sat in with him and sang the high part on the chorus. I just loved the song then, and changed a few words in it, so that it would be palatable to country radio. I've never really understood a lot about what the song says."

495

WAR IS HELL (ON THE HOMEFRONT, TOO)
T.G. SHEPPARD
Warner Bros. 29934
Writers: Curly Putman, Dan Wilson,
Bucky Jones
Producer: Buddy Killen
November 20, 1982 (1 week)

On August 7, 1942, American Marines landed at Guadalcanal, and 40 years later, scenes of World War II were replayed in the strains of country music. Four days after that anniversary, Warner Bros. released T.G. Sheppard's "War Is Hell (On The Homefront, Too)," playing out scenes quite reminiscent of the life-during-wartime film *Summer of '42*.

That movie happens to be among Sheppard's favorites, so "War Is Hell" proved a perfect match once it was completed. "I had lunch with Curly Putman and Dan Wilson," he recalls, "and I told them I wanted a great story song about a young kid losing his virginity. It had to be written just right."

"I think after we got into it, I recognized some of the scenes in it myself," notes Putnam, admitting the similarities to *Summer of*

'42. "When it first started out, I wanted to write another one of those Delta-type songs, kind of like 'Blood Red And Goin' Down' [see 143]. Dan and Bucky Jones and I were at a Mexican restaurant, and we'd had a beer or two, and this title came up.

"The line about 'It was July hot in Georgia' kind of sets up a scene, but then, what made people think about *Summer of '42* was the fact that this young kid was carrying groceries and a war was going on, and there wasn't many men around. I could see that association, but we tried to stay away from that. We definitely weren't trying to rewrite *Summer of '42*."

"This was a very controversial record," Sheppard continues. "'War Is Hell' was written three or four times, re-defined, worked over, looked at, and when I felt like they had it, I recorded it."

Opening with a military snare drum, the single marched dramatically to number one, entering the *Billboard* country charts on September 9, and capturing the number one slot eleven weeks later.

"Buddy Killen had an abundance of great songs over there at Tree Publishing," T.G. explains. "The name of the game is getting the great songs—and sure enough, we did."

496

IT AIN'T EASY BEIN' EASY
JANIE FRICKIE
Columbia 03214
Writers: Shawna Harrington, Mark Gray,
Les Taylor
Producer: Bob Montgomery
November 27, 1982 (1 week)

The year 1982 was one of great importance for Janie Frickie. After scoring her first number one record with "Don't Worry 'Bout Me, Baby" [see 477], she changed producers for the second time in her career, enlisting Bob Montgomery after two albums with Jim Ed Norman.

"They weren't having a whole lot of success saleswise," says Montgomery. "She'd had a couple of pretty good records, but just couldn't get off the ground. [CBS Nashville chief Rick] Blackburn called me and asked if I'd work with her, and I said I'd love to, so we went in."

In the meantime, Frickie shook up her personal life during the summer months. She'd had an engagement ring from manager Randy

Jackson for two years, having first met him when she was a member of the Lea Jane Singers. The group had traveled to Texas to back Johnny Rodriguez during the shooting of the "Austin City Limits" television show, and at that time, Jackson was Rodriguez's road manager.

"Randy says he thinks we ought to put up a monument in the Austin Airport," Frickie told Beryl Reid of *Tune-In* magazine, "because that's where we met. I didn't know who Randy was, and he came out to the airport to meet us. We had our jeans and our boots on. We thought we looked cool, and Randy said, 'Boy, do you all look like a bunch of gringos!'"

After a lengthy courtship, Jackson proposed to Frickie over the telephone during a live call-in program on WSM Radio in Nashville. Two months later, they exchanged vows on September 16, 1982, at a ceremony in Janie's hometown of South Whitley, Indiana. Two days later, her first single with Montgomery entered the *Billboard* country charts.

Montgomery doubled as a producer and as the head of House of Gold Music Publishing, and when he first started looking for material with Frickie, they ran across former Exile member Mark Gray. Mark had been working with some of Montgomery's writers, and when the producer inquired about potential material, Gray sat down at a grand piano in the office and played "It Ain't Easy Bein' Easy" on the spot.

"I remember I got goosebumps," says Frickie. "I knew it was a special song the first time I heard it."

497

YOU AND I
EDDIE RABBITT WITH CRYSTAL GAYLE
Elektra 69936
Writer: Frank Myers
Producer: David Malloy
December 4, 1982 (1 week)

Eddie Rabbitt and Crystal Gayle have song-writer Frank Myers to thank for their first number one duet single. Neither had released a duet before, and "You And I" might never have been recorded if Myers hadn't persisted with Rabbitt's producer, David Malloy.

Myers played guitar for Eddy Raven, and had formed a friendship with Tanya Tucker, whom Malloy was producing for Arista. Myers repeatedly approached the producer with "You And I."

Eddie Rabbitt & Crystal Gayle

Malloy finally sent Myers to visit his father, Jim Malloy, who ran a publishing company. Jim was immediately impressed, and called David to tell him he needed to give the song a listen.

Somewhere along the line, a decision was made that "You And I" would succeed as a duet, and Malloy played the song for Crystal Gayle. As he sat with her, she began singing in the spaces between the melody, developing the call-and-answer style that eventually made its way to disk.

"They wanted me to actually sing a verse," Crystal reports, "but it wasn't in my key. It was way too high, so the only thing I could do was to answer him."

Malloy made one major change in the song after the basic tracks were recorded. "There's two verses before the chorus," he explains. "The second verse is where Crystal comes in and does the answers. Well, it's the same verse twice. Most people don't realize that. I didn't think the song was long enough before it got to the chorus. I copied over the track and extended it."

Malloy and Even Stevens were in the process of building Emerald Sound Studios when the vocal tracks were cut. Rabbitt gave Malloy one take to work with, and the drywall wasn't even up when Crystal added her parts.

"Crystal came in the vocal booth, with the insulation hanging out and everything, and ripped off that vocal in about three minutes," says Malloy. "Then we pulled all the gear back out and finished out the studio."

"We never really sang it together until about six or eight months later, at the Houston Astrodome, after the record was a hit and everything," Rabbitt adds. "We had a gig together where we broke the actual record for attendance: I think, 98,000. It was pretty weird."

"You And I" was used as a love theme on "All My Children."

498

REDNECK GIRL
THE BELLAMY BROTHERS
Warner Bros. 29923
Writer: David Bellamy
Producers: The Bellamy Brothers,
Jimmy Bowen
December 11, 1982 (1 week)

Even after the Bellamy Brothers left Warner Bros. and started releasing product on Elektra [see 474—"For All The Wrong Reasons"], they still owed their prior label more material. The company closed out the agreement with a *Greatest Hits* album, and Warners asked specifically for "Redneck Girl" to round out the collection.

Elektra chief Jimmy Bowen had no difficulty at the time parting with that track. He explains: "I thought, 'Well, I don't know about this little s.o.b.—you can have that one. A song called 'Redneck Girl?' That ain't gonna work.' It turned out to be a great impact record for them. It sold a lot of those *Greatest Hits* albums. I thought it was too strong at the time."

Howard and David recorded "Redneck Girl" using Sam's Tape Truck at their farm in Darby, Florida—appropriate, since part of the inspiration for the song came while they were building their home studio. One of the carpenters got a visit each day at lunchtime from his wife. She drove out to the farm in a pickup truck, carrying a brown paper bag with his midday meal, and a Mason jar filled with iced tea. She stayed with him until lunch hour was over, and that woman reminded David of the redneck girls they frequently saw in the audience while out on tour.

"During *Urban Cowboy* and that period right there, we'd go to Texas, and we could play in Texas every night if we wanted to," David says. "There were honky-tonks on every street corner. All the girls would come up after the show, and they'd take their belts off for you to autograph, and they always had their names on the back of 'em. That's where I got the idea for that song."

"Redneck Girl" debuted at number 77 on the *Billboard* country chart on September 25, 1982. Eleven weeks later, it gave the Bellamys a total of six number one country singles, putting them in first place among all duos, including the Everly Brothers, Conway Twitty & Loretta Lynn and Porter Wagoner & Dolly Parton.

Ironically, the brothers ended up back on Warner Bros. In January of 1983, Elektra/Asylum Records merged its country division with Warners, with the Elektra label personnel placed in charge. The Bellamys already had one last Elektra single, "When I'm Away From You" [see 513], in release at that time. "When I'm Away From You" appeared on their next album, *Strong Weakness*, released on the Warner label, now headed by Bowen. The album also included the song that Bowen had originally given away, "Redneck Girl."

SOMEWHERE BETWEEN RIGHT AND WRONG

EARL THOMAS CONLEY

RCA 13320
Writer: Earl Thomas Conley
Producers: Nelson Larkin,
Earl Thomas Conley
December 18, 1982 (1 week)

When Earl Thomas Conley hit number one on an independent label with "Fire And Smoke" [see 433], he earned plenty of attention in Nashville. The cost of promoting an act at that level often spells the end of a small label, and Sunbird sold his contract to RCA.

"Nipper" first released "You Don't Have To Go Too Far," from Conley's *Blue Pearl* album, but then canned it as a single. In its stead, the company put out "Tell Me Why," which rose to number ten, followed by "After The Love Slips Away," which peaked at number 16. *Fire & Smoke*, Earl's first RCA album, mixed new material with cuts from *Blue Pearl*.

In 1982, Conley released his first all-new package for RCA, *Somewhere Between Right and Wrong*. He suffered from a year-long writing block, and to buy time, he released "Heavenly Bodies," a song that producer Nelson Larkin picked up from two New York songwriters. The record went to number eight.

In the meantime, Conley got back on track as a writer, penning all of the other nine cuts on the album, including the title cut. "It didn't really bother me to go for a year and not come up with somethin' that was great," Earl insists, "because I was writin' all the time.

"But this came along and I said, 'Yeah, this one is right for an uptempo song.' It was really right, 'cause those things are so hard to come up with."

Conley challenged country boundaries with "Somewhere Between Right And Wrong," using a rock and roll backbeat and a punchy horn section. The single was officially released in two different formats—one mix with horns and one mix without—though horns actually appear in both versions. Despite Earl's objections, Larkin also brought in a lyricon (an electronic saxophone), played by Quitman Dennis.

Albany's WGNA refused to play "Somewhere Between Right And Wrong"—as well as "War Is Hell" [see 495]—claiming that it promoted promiscuity. Nevertheless, the record became Conley's second number one single.

WILD AND BLUE

JOHN ANDERSON

Warner Bros. 29917
Writer: John Scott Sherrill
Producers: Frank Jones, John Anderson
December 25, 1982 (2 weeks)

"Wild And Blue" marked the first appearance by John Anderson at the top of the *Billboard* country chart. The *Wild & Blue* album simultaneously represented the last record ever made in Columbia Studio B, one of Nashville's legendary rooms.

Owen Bradley initially built the facility in the '50s, naming it the Quonset Hut, but he sold the studio to Columbia, which renamed it. Record producers Don Law and Billy Sherrill both cut an enormous number of hits in the building, with the likes of Johnny Cash, Tanya Tucker, Tammy Wynette and George Jones, among others.

Frank Jones, who transferred from the Canadian branch of Columbia to Nashville in 1961, worked side by side with Law through much of the '60s. As a team, they raked in 13 number one singles, including Jimmy Dean's "Big Bad John," Flatt & Scruggs' "The Ballad Of Jed Clampett," Marty Robbins' "Devil Woman" and Lefty Frizzell's "Saginaw, Michigan."

"It was very ironic for me," says Jones of the last Studio B session. "It was actually an emotional time for some of the musicians who had been on the session, 'cause some of those guys had been there since probably even before I got there. When you think of all the great records that were cut in there, the history of this place was almost unreal.

"We even had to finish up mixing in another studio. When we were gone from that last session, that was it. They started ripping it down the next morning."

It's appropriate that Jones produced the final master at Studio B, and that it was Anderson's cover of Frizzell's "The Long Black Veil." Anderson was hailed as an heir to Lefty's honkytonk territory, and in "Wild And Blue," he certainly walked a hard-country line.

John Scott Sherrill wrote the song over a six-month period at his home near Franklin, Tennessee. Anderson's sister, Donna, frequented Music City clubs where Sherrill's band, the Wolves In Cheap Clothing (now Billy Hill), played. She had an interest in "Wild And Blue," and introduced the song to her brother, who gave it a Cajun feel and enlisted her to sing back-up vocals.

Warner Bros. released "Wild And Blue" on September 1, 1982, four weeks in advance of the album. Its ascent to number one arrived at the same time as Santa Claus.

501
CAN'T EVEN GET THE BLUES
REBA McENTIRE
Mercury 76180
Writers: Tom Damphier, Rick Carnes
Producer: Jerry Kennedy
January 8, 1983 (1 week)

Several months after purchasing her first tour bus, Reba McEntire found herself in a Dallas repair shop for work on the left front wheel. She had already racked up $20,000 in maintenance, and amid the smell of grease and the sound of hydraulic machinery, she placed a call to her manager. He told her that "Can't Even Get The Blues" had just become her first number one record, and after a short period of disbelief, Reba went into hysterics. Her reaction was justified—it took nine years from her initial discovery to hit the top.

In 1974, McEntire sang "The Star-Spangled Banner" (her favorite song) at the National Rodeo Finals in Oklahoma City. Country singer and quarterhorse-breeder Red Steagall heard her and offered to help her book studio time in Nashville to make a demo. Two years later, Reba nabbed a recording contract with Mercury.

She released her first single, "I Don't Want To Be A One Night Stand," about the same time that she graduated from Southeastern State University in Durant, Oklahoma. Reba married rodeo rider Charlie Battles in June of 1976 and kicked off their honeymoon by visiting radio stations to promote the record.

Despite her enthusiasm, Reba didn't break through with radio until 1979's "Sweet Dreams" [see 269]. She netted her first Top Ten single with 1980's "(You Lift Me) Up To Heaven," and added Top Ten waltzes over the next two years with "Today All Over Again" and "I'm Not That Lonely Yet," the first single from her *Unlimited* album.

"I would have done anything to get her a number one record," says producer Jerry Kennedy. "I knew how hard she was workin' and how much she wanted it." It finally came with

the second *Unlimited* single, one that deviated from her affair with waltzes. Initially, Kennedy had tabbed "Can't Even Get The Blues" for Jacky Ward, but he played it for Reba while they were talking in his office.

"I said, 'Why don't you ever play anything like that for me?'" Reba recalls. "He said, 'You sing ballads, that's your forté.' I said, 'I'd like to sing something uptempo—my shows are awful boring.' That's all I had to sing, was ballads."

As a result, Kennedy gave "Can't Even Get The Blues" to her, and it was the last one they cut for the album.

502
GOING WHERE THE LONELY GO
MERLE HAGGARD
Epic 03315
Writer: Merle Haggard
Producers: Merle Haggard, Lewis Talley
January 15, 1983 (1 week)

If the analogy of "leftovers" in the refrigerator can apply to the recording studio, then maybe that's what Merle Haggard's *Going Where the Lonely Go* album represented. Eight of the ten songs he included in the project were laid down at the same time as his previous LP.

"We did about 24 sides," he explained to Alanna Nash in *Behind Closed Doors*. "Two albums—*Going Where the Lonely Go* and *Big City* [see 467]—were done in the same 48-hour period. We did all those songs, just bam, bam, bam."

It was an extremely productive two days. In addition to two number one singles from the *Big City* album, Haggard netted one more—his thirtieth—with "Going Where The Lonely Go."

As with "Big City," the song was inspired by Merle's buddy, Dean Holloway, during the recording sessions at Britannia Studio. Holloway had left the studio, and as he headed down the street, Haggard asked where he was headed. Holloway's response, "I'm going where the lonely go," triggered Merle's thoughts, and the song was written and recorded before they finished their block of sessions.

With the exception of "Movin' On" [see 216], "Going Where The Lonely Go" followed the usual pattern of inspiration for Haggard.

"I've never just been one to write a song about anything [planned]," he told Vernell Hackett in *American Songwriter*. "Whatever mood I'm in, I sometimes say the songs are handed to me, because [when I write it] it's the first time I've heard it myself.

"I don't have a favorite place to write. I never sit down in a secluded place and write. Usually it happens when I'm in the midst of something and everything is going on around me. That's when something will come to me. You better get it down right then. If you don't, you're in trouble."

It had been more than ten years since his pardon from Ronald Reagan [see 97—"Grandma Harp"], and yet Merle remains imprisoned—albeit by a master of his own choosing. "The hardest part for me is after a performance," he explained to free-lance writer Bob Allen, "when there's people beating on the bus and screaming . . . Sometimes I can't hardly stand it. The only difference in my life now is the size of the cell, and the fact that this one is on four wheels."

Emmylou Harris

503

(LOST HIS LOVE) ON OUR LAST DATE

EMMYLOU HARRIS

Warner Bros. 29898
Writers: Floyd Cramer, Conway Twitty
Producer: Brian Ahern
January 22, 1983 (1 week)

In June of 1982, Emmylou Harris began work on an album project she had considered for several years. Then-husband/producer Brian Ahern took the Enactron Truck on a tour of California, as the Hot Band played dates in Fresno, San Francisco, Petaluma, Santa Cruz and Los Angeles. The resulting tracks were culled for a live album, *Last Date*.

"I must have been crazy to actually think that we could do it and pull it off," she says. "It was an amazingly enormous project, because we were trying to record two albums, old material and new material, and there's a lot of old material I've previously recorded. There's probably a whole album of that."

The live versions of her own hits still remain in the can, and the *Last Date* album emerged as Hot Band remakes of material by Merle Haggard, Gram Parsons and Buck Owens. The whole concept first came about, in fact, when Harris heard Owens' "Buckaroo" on the radio. The band had never played any of the songs in concert before.

"Somehow, if I'm gonna record live, I wanna do new stuff," Emmylou explains. "That to me is more scary, and what you're going for is that feeling of playing a brand new song for the first time and having the tape roll. That was the whole point of *Last Date*: to be the ultimate bar band that you go to see, and you hear all this material that you're not expecting to hear—slightly familiar, but not really."

Most of the material on the album came from the Fresno date. "I think 'Last Date' [see 98] was actually from San Francisco," she says, "but who can remember that? It was all recorded live."

The album also brought a hit with Emmylou's cover of Hank Snow's "I'm Movin' On" [see 160—"Hello Love"]. A year later, she added two more Top Ten singles: "In My Dreams" and "Pledging My Love."

After years in Los Angeles, Emmylou split with Ahern and moved to Nashville in 1983. She began dating songwriter/producer Paul Kennerley, who wrote "In My Dreams" and her 1982 single "Born To Run." Kennerley also co-wrote and produced her 1985 concept album *The Ballad of Sally Rose*. In November of that year, the two were married.

Harris had to wait over four years after "Pledging My Love" for her next Top Ten single, 1988's "Heartbreak Hill."

504

TALK TO ME
MICKEY GILLEY
Epic 03326
Writer: Joe Seneca
Producer: Jim Ed Norman
January 29, 1983 (1 week)

Working primarily at Nashville's Audio Media Studios, Jim Ed Norman developed a successful pattern in recording Mickey Gilley's instrumental tracks. Before Gilley even came in to add his vocals, Norman set the backing tracks with a core rhythm section of Dennis Burnside (keyboards), Eddie Bayers (drums), Joe Osborn (bass), Paul Worley (electric guitar) and Rafe VanHoy (acoustic guitar).

"When we would record, we would come in and try three or four different songs in one day," recalls VanHoy. "We'd work on one song for an hour and a half or two hours, and then, when Jim Ed thought we were kind of getting stale on it, we'd switch to another song, and work on it for a while.

"Then the next day, we'd come in and start on one of those songs we were working on the day before. Sometimes, we'd cut the same song five or six times throughout the week, just looking for some kind of magic energy. The control room would have stacks of two-inch tape practically to the ceiling.

"After we left, Jim Ed and [engineer] Marshall Morgan would have to go through that stuff and edit out this verse and put it with this chorus. We did them so many times, it's hard to know what take we ended up doing."

Obviously, it was a tedious process, but it paid off with Gilley's eighth number one single in a two-and-a-half-year period, when "Talk To Me" reached the top on January 29, 1983. Sunny & The Sunglows had introduced the song in 1963, taking it to number 11 on *Billboard*'s Hot 100.

"Jim Ed asked me about the song," Gilley remembers, "and I used to sing it in the clubs. I thought it was a great song. My only particular problem with that song was that I wasn't up to

vocal quality to really work on the track that much, and Jim Ed cut it and we got it about a half a step too high. I was able to do it, but you could tell there were a few spots I had to strain to get it. A lot of the fans probably never noticed it, but I hear it."

505

INSIDE/CAROLINA DREAMS
RONNIE MILSAP
RCA 13362
Writers: Mike Reid/Kye Fleming, Dennis Morgan, Marie Tomlinson
Producers: Ronnie Milsap, Tom Collins
February 5, 1983 (1 week)

The National Football League's rookie draft of January 27, 1970, holds surprisingly historical significance for country music. The first player picked that day was Terry Bradshaw, an LSU quarterback selected by the Pittsburgh Steelers. The Cincinnati Bengals had the seventh choice, and selected Penn State defensive tackle Mike Reid.

It's the only time that two first-round NFL choices have had an impact on country music. In 1976, Bradshaw went to number 17 with his remake of "I'm So Lonesome I Could Cry." Reid—already citing music as his long-term occupation on draft day—seriously pursued songwriting after five years in pro football. Eight years after his gridiron retirement, he earned his first hit, penning Ronnie Milsap's "Inside."

"I love one-word titles," says Reid, "and that word came to me in the produce section of Kroger's one afternoon. If a title occurs to me that I may want to pursue, the first thing I do is think, 'Does it conjure up a little movie? Do I see people in this song behaving in various ways toward one another?' If you can't see a little movie in there, I generally won't proceed writing it.

"The whole meaning of 'Inside' [had to do with] the way we internalize our feelings toward one another, and we call it love. It seemed to make sense, and seemed to be something I could write, but it was a song that I never particularly expected to have recorded. It just happened to be what Milsap was looking for at the time."

On February 5, 1983, six days after Super Bowl XVII, Reid sacked his first number one single with "Inside," adding that country honor to a slew of football trophies. Among his awards: the 1969 Outland Trophy for outstanding college lineman, unanimous All-American selections, the 1970 NFL Rookie of the Year award, and three All-Pro citings in a short, five-year pro career. In 1987, he was inducted into the College Football Hall of Fame.

Following his sports career, Mike moved to Nashville in 1980 to write for ATV Music. Eighteen months later, at the bidding of publisher Rob Galbraith, he joined Milsap's newly-formed Lodge Hall Music, and "Inside"—Milsap's tenth straight chart-topper—was the first collaborative success.

506
'TIL I GAIN CONTROL AGAIN
CRYSTAL GAYLE
Elektra 69893
Writer: Rodney Crowell
Producer: Jimmy Bowen
February 12, 1983 (1 week)

In 1982, Crystal Gayle left Columbia Records and signed with Elektra, intending to form an association with a smaller label that could provide more personal attention. Ironically, in January of 1983, she found herself at a large company again: Elektra merged with Warner Bros., and suddenly, she was back on a huge artist roster.

At the time, Crystal had released her first Elektra solo recording, "'Til I Gain Control Again," a song that Rodney Crowell had composed in 1976 while a member of Emmylou Harris' Hot Band.

"I wrote that song pretty early in my songwriting career," Crowell says, "and it was just kind of a personal breakthrough. It was in the really early stages of when I moved songwriting out of my head and into my heart. That was a really good move for me, because it made my songs more enduring and more acceptable to people. Although our heads may not have much in common, all of our hearts have everything in common."

Even before "'Til I Gain Control Again" emerged as a single, it touched plenty of his fellow musicians. It's the most frequently recorded of Crowell's compositions, cut by Crowell, Harris, Willie Nelson and Waylon Jennings, among others. Bobby Bare released it as a single in 1979, reaching number 42.

Rodney's version was the only one either Crystal or Jimmy Bowen had heard, though, when they decided to record it for her debut Elektra album, *True Love*—not that it would have mattered.

"I don't care much if something's been recorded before," suggests Bowen. "Other people say, 'Well, I don't want to cut it, somebody else has done it.' But if it hasn't been a recent big hit, what difference does it make? 'Everybody Needs Somebody' with Dean Martin—going back to my first success as a producer—had already been recorded ten or fifteen times. I didn't know it, but it had, so I don't care if it's been recorded before."

Neither did Crystal, although she was unsure about the song at first. "I listened to it, loved it, and said, 'Naw, I don't think that's me,' and tossed it aside," she confesses. "Then Bowen says, 'I think you should try it,' so I said, 'Okay, I'll do it,' and it just fell in place."

Crowell provided backing vocals on the single, which peaked at number one on February 12, 1983.

507
FAKING LOVE
T.G. SHEPPARD & KAREN BROOKS
Warner Bros. 29854
Writers: Bobby Braddock, Matraca Berg
Producer: Buddy Killen
February 19, 1983 (1 week)

"Faking Love" brought together an established male with an up-and-coming female—twice.

Songwriter Bobby Braddock had his first number one single when he wrote "D-I-V-O-R-C-E" [see 12] for Tammy Wynette in 1968. At that time, his "Faking Love" co-writer, Matraca (pronounced "Muh-TRACE-uh") Berg, was less than five years old.

"At the time I met her at Tree Publishing, she was 18 years old," Braddock notes. "I thought she was amazingly good for someone that age. She sang a couple songs she'd written, and I thought she was a good singer and a good writer, so we got together."

Berg developed the title for "Faking Love" after she mistook the title of Tammy's "They Call It *Making* Love," written, coincidentally, by Braddock. A short time after they wrote "Faking Love," T.G. Sheppard recorded the song, but he thought it might work as a duet.

T.G. Sheppard & Karen Brooks

Born in Dallas, Brooks harbored interests in music, art and horses from an early age. Quitting high school, she found work on a ranch in Denton, Texas, where she continued her musical endeavors. She lived for a period of time in Los Angeles before moving to Franklin, Tennessee, around the time she signed with Warner Bros.

"New Way Out" was Karen's biggest solo recording, hitting number 17. She followed it up in 1983 with "If That's What You're Thinking," which peaked at number 21, and "Walk On," which went to number 30. Her only other single to reach the Top 20 was "Tonight I'm Here With Someone Else," which made number 19 in 1984.

508

WHY BABY WHY
CHARLEY PRIDE
RCA 13397
Writers: George Jones, Darrell Edwards
Producer: Norro Wilson
February 26, 1983 (1 week)

When George Jones was a youngster, he used to run down the street naked, as kids will do, and his mother would ask another boy who lived across the road to catch George and bring him back. The neighbor was Darrell Edwards, and years later, both Jones and Edwards collaborated on a number of songs.

Best-known was "Why Baby Why," a tune inspired when Edwards overheard a couple squabbling in their car in Orange, Texas. That song first brought Jones to national acclaim in 1955, and it attracted a wealth of cover versions. Red Sovine & Webb Pierce remade it and took it to number one in 1956, and Hank Locklin took it to number nine that same year. Finally, Charley Pride returned "Why Baby Why" to the top spot 27 years later when working on an album of oldies, appropriately titled *Country Classics*.

Actually, Pride and RCA turned it into a "fake" live recording. The single was shipped to radio with a different version on each side. One contained the version that appeared on the *Classics* album. The other sported the same cut, with added "canned" applause in a few choice spots. The fabricated version was then added to the *Charley Pride Live* album. Most radio stations played the "studio" version.

After hearing "New Way Out" on the radio, he decided that the vocalist, Karen Brooks, would be perfect. "New Way Out" was Brooks' first single, although she had written Rosanne Cash's "Couldn't Do Nothin' Right" and Emmylou Harris' "Tennessee Rose." Sheppard called Brooks at home, and she consented to make "Faking Love" a duet.

"I loved her voice," T.G. remembers, "and then when I met her, I loved her attitude. She's like an Emmylou or a Rosanne. They kind of work at their own leisure. They know who they are, their egos are intact, they have great talent, and I felt Karen was going to be that kind of star, although her career didn't develop after that."

Had Pride had his way, his first hits would have come from Louisville Sluggers instead of Nashville studios. He spent a number of years playing baseball in the Negro Leagues during the '50s, but Charley merely stood by while several of his former opponents found a place in the majors.

"Two players in that league who went on to prominence were Hank Aaron and Ernie Banks," he told Mary Campbell of the Associated Press. "Ernie went straight from the Kansas City Monarchs to the Chicago Cubs. I remember he hit one off me—a home run, in Salina, Kansas, that's still going—and I remember striking him out in Pine Bluff, Arkansas, three years later."

Pride did have his chances. He once earned a $300 bonus to sign with the New York Yankees, but flunked the tryout. He got a tryout with the California Angels in 1961, but didn't make that team, either. Finally, in his last trip to spring training as a player, New York Mets coach Casey Stengel sent him packing for good. Ironically, perhaps, Pride has since been branded "The Jackie Robinson of Country Music."

radio on the cover of 1982's *Listen to the Radio* album. MCA released the title track and "Mistakes" as the first two singles, each peaking at number three. The third, "If Hollywood Don't Need You," conjured up images of Williams' occasional film forays.

Songwriter Bob McDill actually wrote a few different versions of the song. One made reference to Clint Eastwood. The version he played for Don highlighted Williams' pal Burt Reynolds, whose encouragement kept Don from quitting during the *Dancekings* picture.

"I originally had Sally Field in it, too: 'If you see Burt Reynolds, would you shake his hand for me/And tell Sally Field I've seen all her movies,'" McDill recalls. "He took the Sally Field out, because Burt Reynolds was a friend, and Burt Reynolds and Sally Field had just broken up, so he thought that might be in poor taste. He just put Burt Reynolds in there twice."

Recorded in Nashville, "If Hollywood Don't Need You" debuted at number 71, higher than any other new single for the week of December 11, 1982. Three months later, "Hollywood" received top billing on the *Billboard* chart.

509
IF HOLLYWOOD DON'T NEED YOU
DON WILLIAMS
Label: MCA 52152
Writer: Bob McDill
Producers: Don Williams, Garth Fundis
March 5, 1983 (1 week)

Don Williams has appeared in two movies during his career, both of which also featured appearances by Jerry Reed and Burt Reynolds. His "Tulsa Time" [see 331] made the soundtrack of Universal's 1980 release *Smokey and the Bandit II*. Five years earlier, he made his silver screen debut with 20th Century-Fox's *W.W. & The Dixie Dancekings*, a movie that also established his hat as a personal trademark.

"I really had worn hats very little prior to that," says Williams. "But the guy who styled it for me, it was his specialty to style hats to a person's features. And I just little by little got to wearing it more and more until it's like a part of me. I kid about it turning into a growth, but I really don't feel right if I go outside without wearing it. I feel like I'm just not dressed."

Don hung his hat on top of an early-model

510
THE ROSE
CONWAY TWITTY
Elektra 69854
Writer: Amanda McBroom
Producers: Conway Twitty, Jimmy Bowen
March 12, 1983 (1 week)

"The Rose" made its first appearance as the theme song in a 1979 Bette Midler movie of the same name. Based on a composite of tragic rock and roll figures—particularly Janis Joplin—the film was not exactly escapist entertainment, as the central character grappled with addictions to both alcohol and narcotics.

In actuality, the song earned higher recognition than the picture. Midler's version of "The Rose" soared to number three on the *Billboard* Hot 100 in 1980 and secured Grammy nominations for Single of the Year and Song of the Year. In 1983, Conway Twitty revived it as a country single.

"One of my daughters found that song and told me about the movie and all that," relates Twitty. "She brought me the record, and I couldn't understand the words. I'd listen and listen, and I'm really a word person. And if I hear part of a line, I'll pretty well know what the rest of the line is. I couldn't understand it.

"She had to go find the rest of the words for me. I saw these words and it blew my head off. They were beautiful words, and it was a country smash—Conway Twitty all the way."

Twitty recorded it once, with acoustic guitars predominating, but wasn't pleased with the results. After some thought, he added a new track, with Shane Keister playing a dampered electric piano. "He put his hand over behind the keyboard and deadened the strings," explains Conway, "and [got] that clunk-clunk-clunk sound. We did about ten tracks of that or somethin', gettin' that clunk-clunk sound."

Conway never bothered to tell anyone, though, that he intended to turn the record into a recitation. "I went out to make a phone call," laughs producer Jimmy Bowen, "and as I walked back in, he started talkin' that first part, and the engineer [Ron Treat] stopped the tape, thought he was kiddin'. And Conway was dead serious, you know?

"So Conway said, 'Why'd you stop?' and the engineer said, 'I didn't know you were serious.' I said, 'Ron, don't ever stop the tape.' I got all over him, 'cause it worked for Conway to talk it. So we did it again, talked it again, and that was it."

Twitty caught all kinds of flak for "The Rose," but he stifled his critics when it became his thirty-fifth number one country single.

511

I WOULDN'T CHANGE YOU IF I COULD

RICKY SKAGGS

Epic 03482
Writers: Paul Jones, Arthur Q. Smith
Producer: Ricky Skaggs
March 19, 1983 (1 week)

"I want to bridge the gap between contemporary and the pure traditional country," Ricky Skaggs told *Billboard* reporter Kip Kirby in 1981. "There are a lot of people who have just begun getting into country who think what we're doing is new stuff. Sometimes it's hard to hear the country in country music these days. I hope what I'm doing is a way of getting back to the basics again."

Ricky did so, quite obviously, by remaking

older records and releasing his new, updated versions as singles when his career began. Of his first four number one records, three— "Crying My Heart Out Over You" [see 469], "I Don't Care" [see 480] and "I Wouldn't Change You If I Could"—were older songs that had gained favor in the hands of other artists first.

Skaggs first heard "I Wouldn't Change You If I Could" on an album by Reno & Smiley. Don Reno [see 150—"If We Make It Through December"] was an early purveyor of bluegrass, having performed in Bill Monroe's band for a year in the late '40s. Prior to that, he spent seven years with Arthur Smith, who wrote "I Wouldn't Change You If I Could."

"I loved that song," says Ricky. "I just thought it was so cool, and it was a real love song. It was a song that you could really sing to your honey, a butter-up type of song. It really had a lot of promise, a lot of encouragement in it for couples, and I've had people come up and say to me that they sang this song at their wedding, or played the record at their wedding, or fell in love to this song.

"That's great to hear. You work hard out on the road to make a difference in somebody's life. That's really what I'm in this business for. I really am tryin' to make a difference in people's lives through the music."

Ricky's efforts did not go unnoticed—or unappreciated. In October of 1982, the Country Music Association gave him the Male Vocalist of the Year award, just one year after he earned his first Top Ten record. The CMA also presented him with the Horizon award, for the most significant career development that year.

512

SWINGIN'

JOHN ANDERSON

Warner Bros. 29788
Writers: John David Anderson, Lionel A. Delmore
Producers: Frank Jones, John Anderson
March 26, 1983 (1 week)

In 1983, Ralph Emery asked John Anderson why, in his biggest record, he sang "Swangin'," while the female backing singers sang, "Swingin'."

"Someone has to sing it properly," John replied, "and I sure cain't."

"Swingin'," with its small-town praises of amorous neighbor Charlotte Johnson, put Anderson together with frequent writing partner Lionel Delmore—son of Alton Delmore, who registered his own number one single, "Blues Stay Away From Me," as one-half of the Delmore Brothers in 1949.

"I think Lionel had the first basic idea, just a line or two," Anderson told John Wooley of the *Tulsa Daily World*. "We worked on it a long time, but never really felt like it was right. I remember doing some rewriting on the studio floor, and still never knowin' whether it was right or not. I guess you gotta quit somewhere, though."

John first played "Swingin'" for producer Frank Jones with an acoustic guitar. In that format, Frank wasn't particularly impressed, but John was convinced they should record it.

"As we got into the session with the band, it got more and more appealing," Frank says. "The back-up voices got that 'little girl' sound to it, and it just got to be very, very cute."

They continued to build "Swingin'" even further. Anderson enlisted Mike Jordan from his road band to play a rockin' Hammond B-3 organ solo, and they punched up the track with a three-man horn section: tenor sax player Bill Puett, trumpeter Don Sheffield and trombonist Dennis Good.

"Swingin'" was released on the *Wild & Blue* album [see 500], and Warner promotion man Stan Byrd started receiving calls from radio stations nationwide who reported that they were playing it off the album.

"It's the first time ever, I think, we asked 'em not to play a record," Jones laughs. "This was, like, October, and we still wanted to get 'Wild And Blue' up the chart. There was no way we could stop it. By Christmas time, 'Swingin'' was just a smash."

On January 5, 1983, Warners officially shipped "Swingin'" as a single, and it eventually sold 1.4 million copies, the biggest-selling country single in WB history. The Country Music Association recognized the record's success by naming "Swingin'" the Single of the Year and conferring the Horizon Award on Anderson.

John subsequently nicknamed his Martin D-35 guitar "Charlotte."

513
WHEN I'M AWAY FROM YOU
THE BELLAMY BROTHERS
Elektra 69850

John Anderson

Writer: Frankie Miller
Producers: Jimmy Bowen,
The Bellamy Brothers
April 2, 1983 (1 week)

The Bellamy Brothers' history at their farm in Darby, Florida, dates back to the Civil War, when an injured Confederate soldier left his Conway, South Carolina, home to mend. He purchased about 100 acres of land for under 50 cents an acre, and the farm has been passed down from generation to generation.

Two of his great-grandchildren, Howard and David Bellamy, allied with an English songwriter 120 years after the Civil War reached its peak. Frankie Miller sent them a tape of "When I'm Away From You," a song that Kim Carnes had done on *Mistaken Identity*. Immediately struck, they decided to cut it.

"That's a record that almost gave [producer Jimmy] Bowen a heart attack," laughs David, "'cause we cut the first two verses without bass, and he went crazy. He said, 'I can't believe you guys did this. It's like building a house with no foundation.'"

"When I'm Away From You" first appeared in *Billboard* on January 15, 1983, the same week that Warner Bros. and Elektra merged offices [see 498—"Redneck Girl"]. After a dozen weeks on the chart, it cracked the number one position.

Howard and David earned three more Top Ten singles through the end of 1984: "I Love Her Mind," "Forget About Me" (written by Miller with Troy Seals and Eddie Setser) and "World's Greatest Lover." They also flew Miller to the U.S. to co-write a song, and in 1985, that tune, "Lie To You For Your Love," reached number two.

Among the most underrated acts in the business, the Bellamy Brothers have received little fanfare despite their consistent efforts. Of the two, David has the highest profile, writing and singing lead on most of the material. Howard's contribution is not quite as obvious.

"We've done two or three records where Howard has sung lead and I sing harmony," David notes. "It enables us to switch our sound around a little bit, enough to where they know it's us, but it sounds just a little bit different.

"As far as harmony is concerned, we've grown up singing harmony together. I'd sing lead, he'd sing harmony. I'm not sure why. I guess it's 'cause he hears harmony better. I'm not really that good a harmony singer."

The Bellamy Brothers

BELLAMY BROS.

514
WE'VE GOT TONIGHT
KENNY ROGERS AND SHEENA EASTON
Liberty 1492
Writer: Bob Seger
Producers: Kenny Rogers, David Foster
April 9, 1983 (1 week)

Though known as a rock performer through hits like "Night Moves," "Old Time Rock & Roll" and "Rock & Roll Never Forgets," Bob Seger earned surprising success in country music during the spring of 1983. His recording of "Shame On The Moon" reached number 15, and his composition "We've Got Tonight" brought Kenny Rogers and Sheena Easton to number one.

Seger himself earned a pop hit with "We've Got Tonight," taking it to number 13 in 1978, but several other vocalists recognized its potential for country conversion before Kenny recorded it. Dottie West remade it for her album *Special Delivery*, and Conway Twitty also cut it on his *Heart and Soul* LP.

Kenny decided on the song after discussions with Liberty Records head Jim Mazza, and they agreed that it would work well as a duet with Sheena. Kenny called her at home, and it took little time at all for her to agree. A day later, she headed to Kenny's Lion Share Studio, and both of them worked out "scratch" vocals while the musicians laid the basic tracks. A week later, after the rest of the instrumental work was completed, Sheena came back in, and they worked out their final vocals.

"Working with Kenny on our duet, 'We've Got Tonight,' showed me that you don't always have to be in the studio for three months in order to get a hit," Sheena told *Billboard*. "From his first phone call to me to the song being played on the radio took only three weeks, yet it was one my biggest records."

"We've Got Tonight" helped Sheena earn a unique distinction. In March of 1985, *Billboard* presented her with a special award, honoring her as the first artist to crack the Top Five on the magazine's pop, country, adult/contemporary, dance and black music charts.

The song also helped producer David Foster earn a similar honor, as he topped the country, pop and black charts within an eight-month period. Besides "We've Got Tonight," he hit number one with records by Chicago and *Dream Girls* star Jennifer Holliday.

515
DIXIELAND DELIGHT
ALABAMA
RCA 13446
Writer: Ronnie Rogers
Producers: Harold Shedd, Alabama
April 16, 1983 (1 week)

Tommy West, who produced Jim Croce's hits, has called Ronnie Rogers a "blue-jeaned poet." Rogers, in fact, earned his first hit as a songwriter in 1973, the year that Croce died.

That record was Dave Dudley's "Keep On Truckin'." More hits followed, including Dudley's "Me And Ole C.B.," Tanya Tucker's "It's A Cowboy Lovin' Night," and Ed Bruce's "Love's Found You And Me" and "My First Taste Of Texas." Rogers' biggest success came with "Dixieland Delight," a title he fleshed out in rural Fernvale, Tennessee.

"I had me a CJ-5 jeep," he remembers. "I was just ridin' down the road, and the first line, 'Rollin' down a backwoods Tennessee byway/ One arm on the wheel'—that's what I was doin'. I wrote the first half of the song and the chorus."

When he went to the local market, he ran into Chuck Neese, the professional manager for Alabama's publishing company. Neese suggested Rogers should write a song for the band, and Ronnie decided "Dixieland Delight" might fit the bill.

"I went about a week, I guess, and I couldn't get the last half of it together," Ronnie says. "I went out one Sunday afternoon, and I started writin' again, and I looked around and I saw a white-tailed buck deer munchin' on clover, and a red-tail hog sittin' on a limb, a chubby old groundhog, a croakin' bullfrog—I saw all that. So I figured, 'Well, write it down.'"

Rogers cut a simple demo with a friend, featuring just two acoustic guitars and vocals. Producer Harold Shedd played it for Alabama in his studio office, and the group worked up an elaborate arrangement, with Crosby, Stills & Nash–inspired harmonies and their trademark fiddle break [see 470—"Mountain Music"].

Meanwhile, Ronnie himself recorded it for an album on Lifesong Records, but during the session, bass player Steve Schaffer complained that he was sick of the song. Ronnie was irate—until Schaffer explained that he had worked on the record for Alabama for seven hours the day before! Shortly thereafter, a surprised Rogers got to hear the final product.

"It was great," he exclaims. "I took it out to the jeep I'd written it in. I played it for my wife, and we went out and celebrated. Got some new tires, as a matter of fact."

number one, Miller Beer made a deal with the publisher and had the song rewritten as a commercial.

"At that point," says DiPiero, "it stopped being the music business and became like winning the lottery."

516

AMERICAN MADE

THE OAK RIDGE BOYS
MCA 52179
Writers: Bob DiPiero, Pat McManus
Producer: Ron Chancey
April 23, 1983 (1 week)

In late 1980, songwriter Bob DiPiero earned a minor hit single when Reba McEntire covered his song "I Can See Forever In Your Eyes." It only reached number 18, but it was enough that DiPiero received his first check for performance royalties. As many writers do, DiPiero went on a spending spree.

"I went out and bought all these things I didn't have," he recalls, explaining how his shopping trip became "American Made." "I bought a color TV, and a stereo and a camera, and I bought all this stuff on my first BMI check. I didn't buy anything like a Quasar or Motorola, you know, Polaroid, none of that stuff. I bought a Nikon camera and a Mitsubishi TV. It wasn't a Sony TV [like in the song]—it was actually a Mitsubishi, but I couldn't rhyme 'Mitsubishi.' It was killin' me, so I had to change it. So that's basically it: I'm buying all this [foreign] stuff, but my baby's from here."

While DiPiero was writing it, songwriter Pat McManus passed by the room where he was working and ended up contributing to the song. Producer Ron Chancey believed in it, but it took a while before the Oak Ridge Boys became partial to it.

"It was talkin' about all these foreign products," says Duane Allen. "I felt the only way we could make it interesting was to swap the lead around and make it look like each of the guys has got these different things, and I think what we did was what needed to be done to make it a real interesting piece of work. It obviously is not that complicated a song—but things like that, you can do if you're a group that you can't do if you're a solo artist."

The Oaks didn't intend to release "American Made" as a single, but after they played it live a few times, they got such a solid response that they made it the first single and title track of their 1983 album. After their record went to

517

YOU'RE THE FIRST TIME I'VE THOUGHT ABOUT LEAVING

REBA McENTIRE
Mercury 810338
Writers: Dickey Lee, Kerry Chater
Producer: Jerry Kennedy
April 30, 1983 (1 week)

After notching her first number one record with the surprising blues/rock groove of "Can't Even Get The Blues" [see 501], Reba McEntire returned to the waltz tempo that powered many of her prior hits.

"They were the countriest things that were bein' written at the time," says Reba, of her multiple waltzes. "It was the Lee Greenwood/Ronnie Milsap era, where everything was more contemporary—Kenny Rogers and Anne Murray—and we were really lookin' for some country things for me, 'cause that's what I wanted to sing."

Ironically, Reba picked up the country/waltz release, "You're The First Time I've Thought About Leaving," from two former pop performers: Dickey Lee [see 229—"Rocky"] and Kerry Chater [see 817—"If I Had You"]. The two hadn't met in Los Angeles, though; Nashville publisher Bill Hall introduced them when Chater still lived in L.A. but commuted twice a year to Music City.

They wrote it during one of their first co-writing ventures in about three hours. Lee characterizes it as one of the fastest hits he's ever written [see 584—"Let's Fall To Pieces Together"].

"As I remember, it was Dickey's idea, title-wise," Chater notes. "We thought it was a good one and went with it. At the time, I don't remember thinking that it was one of my greatest songs."

"I thought nobody was gonna do that song, even though I loved it," Lee adds. "I had another song that I wanted Reba to hear. I was pretty sure she was gonna do it, so I sent that song to her producer, Jerry Kennedy, and I put this other song ["You're The First Time"] on the tape, just as an afterthought. I knew she wasn't gonna do it, but it was pretty and I wanted her to hear it. As things go, they didn't do the song that I really wanted her to do. They did the other one."

"You're The First Time I've Thought About Leaving" debuted on the *Billboard* country chart on February 5, 1983, and reached number one a dozen weeks later. Reba released only two more singles before leaving Mercury Records: "Why Do We Want (What We Know We Can't Have)" (number seven) and the ironically-titled "There Ain't No Future In This" (number 12).

518

JOSE CUERVO
SHELLY WEST

Warner Bros. 29778
Writer: Cindy Jordan
Producers: Snuff Garrett, Steve Dorff
May 7, 1983 (1 week)

After "Jose Cuervo"'s release in January of 1983, the tequila's manufacturer, Heublein, claimed a sales increase of 27 percent in the ensuing eight months. Songwriter Cindy Jordan had once been named "Miss Jose Cuervo."

Actually, she was crowned before she ever told Heublein about the song. She wrote it in 1977, when she was a cocktail waitress in Torrance, California.

Jordan later entered "Jose Cuervo" in a local country talent search, sponsored by Los Angeles radio station KLAC. The song, originally written for a man, caught the attention of publisher Al Gallico, who acquired the rights and then pitched it to Johnny Duncan. Duncan passed on it, and Jordan rewrote it from a female perspective.

In 1980, Cindy recorded it on Bullhead Records, and after KLAC started playing it, Warner Bros. picked it up. It failed to chart, but it did earn the respect of producer Snuff Garrett. When Shelly West cut her first solo record three years later, Garrett had coproducer Steve Dorff run the song by her.

"Steve used to work out in this little shed in the back of his house, and he played me the tape," Shelly notes. "I thought, 'Man, you expect me to go back to Nashville and play this for my husband?' At least my husband knew a good song when he heard one.

Shelly West

"I liked the melody and what it had to say. I don't know how Cindy did it, but she matched 'em up really well. To me, it had a Hank Williams, Jr., attitude. It sounded like a lot of fun. Why let Hank have all the fun?"

Shelly was certainly in a celebratory mood in May, when the record hit number one. Her next two singles, "Flight 309 To Tennessee" and "Another Motel Memory," reached the Top Ten.

Born in Cleveland to Bill and Dottie West [see 420—"You're The Reason God Made Oklahoma"], Shelly married Allen Frizzell in the late '70s, prior to her duet success with his brother, David. They had a baby daughter, but divorced in 1983. In July of 1985, she married Gary Hood, a television production stage manager.

519

WHATEVER HAPPENED TO OLD FASHIONED LOVE

B.J. THOMAS

Cleveland Int. 03492
Writer: Lewis Anderson
Producer: Pete Drake
May 14, 1983 (1 week)

Though B.J. Thomas was on top of his game when "(Hey Won't You Play) Another Somebody Done Somebody Wrong Song" [see 208] became his first country hit, his personal life was in crisis.

Thomas' father had often told him that people just weren't meant to survive in this life, and those words echoed as B.J. slowly wasted away. He was spending $3,000 a week to feed a cocaine addiction and brushed several times with death. His wife, Gloria, left him.

On January 28, 1976, the road to recovery began when he found Jesus, with Gloria's help. Thomas put his personal life in order, and also recorded several albums specifically for the gospel market. Though he won five Grammies for those releases, he calls it a period of "semi-retirement."

"I had done about 300 days on the road for almost ten years," B.J. says, "and I was just tired of the road, so I stayed home, and Gloria and I worked on the family. We had one child, and then we adopted a little girl, and then Gloria had another little girl, so for about five years, I didn't do very much. The last three years of that five-year period, I was doing maybe twenty dates a year, every now and then."

Several of his records during that time found a home on the country chart, including "Everybody Loves A Rain Song," "Some Love Songs Never Die" and "I Recall A Gypsy Woman," all of which made the Top 40.

Meanwhile, he found frustration with the gospel market, as it judged his clothing and choice of material rather harshly. Many lamented the fact that he still played his earlier "secular" hits in his gospel shows. Frustrated by the constraints, Thomas refocused his attentions on the country market in 1983, hitting number one with his first effort—"Whatever Happened To Old Fashioned Love," a celebration of more innocent days.

"It was written by Lew Anderson," notes B.J. "I've recorded that kind of song a thousand times. I really like that kind of song. Pete

Drake found it and brought it to me, and it really was a great song. There never was any question about us not doing it."

520

COMMON MAN

JOHN CONLEE

MCA 52178
Writer: Sammy Johns
Producer: Bud Logan
May 21, 1983 (1 week)

On May 3, 1975, Sammy Johns peaked at number five on the *Billboard* Hot 100, with "Chevy Van," a tale of a whirlwind romance in small-town America. Released on Atlanta-based GRC Records, the single eventually sold more than three million copies, but when the label encountered legal and financial problems, Johns was unable to capitalize on his success. His follow-up, "Rag Doll," went to number 52, and it wasn't until September 19, 1981, that Johns re-emerged on the country charts with "Common Man."

Surprisingly, the song never would have been created were it not for a dog in heat. Johns owned a pedigree bird dog, Gwen, and once when it was in season, Gwen ran up the street, where a "some o'" dog ("some o' this and some o' that") was ready for a quick romance. Gwen gave birth to ten puppies, and Johns gave away all but one, a dog he named Oreo.

"It was black all over and had white down its belly," Johns remembers. "I loved that dog a whole lot, and the idea for 'Common Man' came from that: my dog ain't got a pedigree. The mother *did* have a pedigree, but Oreo didn't, and I always have that dog to thank for giving me that song."

Once Johns had the inspiration, though, "Common Man" proved a difficult song to finish. "The way it started out was just 'I'm a common man, drive a common car, my dog ain't got a pedigree,'" he recalls. "I started thinking that 'man' and 'car' don't rhyme, plus I had recorded 'Chevy Van,' so I thought I'd just stick 'van' in there—'common man' and 'common van' rhyme. That's when the verses started coming."

Johns' version of "Common Man" peaked at number 50, but two years later, John Conlee recorded a second version, which went all the way to number one. With the song's reference to Budweiser beer, Bud threw a special party for Conlee, who cut a radio spot for the brewery using the "Common Man" melody. Following its success, Conlee received a large number of songs from Nashville's writers embracing the "working man" theme.

"I relate to it," he explains, "because I consider myself a common person. I'm in music, and I do shows, but when I'm at home, I'm in work clothes doing what working people do all the time."

521
YOU TAKE ME FOR GRANTED
MERLE HAGGARD
Epic 03723
Writer: Leona Williams
Producers: Merle Haggard, Ray Baker
May 28, 1983 (1 week)

Born Leona Belle Helton on January 7, 1943, Leona Williams picked up her professional last name from her first husband. A native of Vienna, Missouri, she spent nine months as a member of Loretta Lynn's band in 1966, playing upright bass and singing harmony at a time when Loretta had "Don't Come Home A-Drinkin'" in release.

Her goal, however, was to have her own show, and her own hit records, and a couple of years later, she made her very first single for Hickory Records. During that period, she embarked on a nine-week tour of the Far East and Southeast Asia, at the height of the Vietnam War.

Merle Haggard first heard her on the radio in the early '70s, and immediately became a fan. Not until January of 1975, though, did he finally meet her. Bonnie Owens had quit the road [see 175—"The Old Man From The Mountain"], and Louise Mandrell lasted only six months [see 204—"Always Wanting You"]. Williams was asked to join the band.

Initially, she thought it might help her expand her audience, but it led to even more. Her marriage to Merle [see 407—"I Think I'll Just Stay Here And Drink"] was a rocky one, and Leona wrote "You Take Me For Granted" during a period of confusion.

"Every line in that song is true," she says. "We had just finished a big tour, and I tell you, my feet was hurting, and my back. We had two buses, and Merle's band was in one bus, and he was over in their bus, playing video games.

"I was riding the bus by myself, and I just started writing this song, 'cause it was exactly how I felt. It was like I was the person who got the guys aspirin if they needed it, or a sandwich fix or whatever, going down the road. Every line of it was true."

Haggard never heard it, though, until a recording session at Woodland Studios in Nashville. Between takes, he was trying to make a decision about what tune to record next, and Williams began playing "You Take Me For Granted." He decided on the spot to cut it.

"You Take Me For Granted" was one of two tracks from the Woodland sessions included on the *Going Where the Lonely Go* album [see 502], and it followed the title track to number one.

522
LUCILLE (YOU WON'T DO YOUR DADDY'S WILL)
WAYLON JENNINGS
RCA 13465
Writers: Richard Penniman, Albert Collins
Producer: Waylon Jennings
June 4, 1983 (1 week)

One of Waylon Jennings' biggest supporters never got the chance to see him reach his peak. Jennings met Buddy Holly at KDAV in Lubbock, on a radio show called "Sunday Dance Party." Later, Holly was the first to produce a recording session on Jennings, and he added Waylon as a bass player on the road.

In that role, Jennings had a part in a history-making event. On February 2, 1959, after a show in Clear Lake, Iowa, Waylon gave up his seat on a Beechcraft plane to the Big Bopper [see 54—"Running Bear"], who was suffering from a cold and preferred not to ride the bus to their next show in Fargo, North Dakota. The Bopper, Holly and Richie Valens all died early the next morning in a plane crash.

Holly's style was a hybrid that utilized his affinity for rhythm and blues, and a pure soul singer from that same musical era provided Jennings with a number one country record in 1983. Little Richard went to number 21 with "Lucille" (not to be confused with Kenny Rogers' record [see 280]), and Jennings resurrected it for the album *It's Only Rock & Roll*.

"I'd been playin' with that song for years," says Waylon. "I loved that song, and where I

Waylon Jennings

OUR LOVE IS ON THE FAULTLINE
CRYSTAL GAYLE

Warner Bros. 29719
Writer: Reece Kirk
Producer: Allen Reynolds
June 11, 1983 (1 week)

The story of 1983 in the world of pop music was the influx of Australian music. Men At Work, Olivia Newton-John, Rick Springfield, Air Supply and the Little River Band all helped create an American fascination with the land down under. The movie *Mad Max* didn't hurt, either.

During that summer, Crystal Gayle helped bring a bit of the Aussie spirit to country music, in the guise of her single "Our Love Is On The Faultline."

"I was touring in Australia," she notes, "and had gotten some tapes sent to me, and that happened to be one of them. At the time, I'd listen to all my tapes and exercise, which I was doing in my hotel room. I loved it and couldn't wait to get back to Nashville to play it for [producer] Allen [Reynolds]."

The record provided plenty of kick, thanks to a simple, precise rhythm track propelled by drummer James Stroud and bass player David Hungate, formerly of the Grammy-winning rock band Toto. Most notable, however, is an inspired guitar section from longtime Gayle associate Chris Leuzinger that gives the record its searing flavor.

Leuzinger, who has since become a session player, started working with Crystal when she picked up his group, Peace & Quiet, as her own road band. He stayed with her for some ten years, the last of the original members to leave.

"Faultline" marked the end of an era for Crystal. It was the last in a one-decade stretch of singles produced by Reynolds, who was disenchanted with her move to a new label in 1982 [see 506—"'Til I Gain Control Again"]. Originally, Reynolds cut her entire *True Love* album, but after she submitted it, Elektra made revisions.

"[Label head Jimmy] Bowen wanted her to cut three more songs," says Reynolds, "and I think what he said was, 'three songs that were more country.' But I felt like the album had covered the bases real well, and Crystal came back to talk to me about cuttin' three more songs, and I just didn't want to do it. I didn't

did it out of sync, in the middle, I'd always wanted to do that. It's a pretty ragged record, very ragged, and that was in my last days with bad cocaine, and I can read that all the way through it. It was a great idea, and it came off in spite of what I was doin'."

Jennings' addiction created a series of run-ins with the law, and the habit grew to a point where he was spending $1,500 a day on the drug. He basically blew a $3-million advance from RCA, and it severely affected his recording ability.

"Your attention span is so short," he explains, "and I would get bored immediately, and I'd keep people around the studio for a week at a time, day and night. It'd take me that long to cut one side, because I would go to sleep some, and wake up and see where I was really messed up and didn't do something right. It was a mess. I don't know how I did any of it, really."

want her to yield at that point in her career to that kind of influence from the labels anyway."

Together, Gayle and Reynolds racked up ten number one records. After drifting through several other artist/producer associations, they resumed their collaborations in 1989.

524

YOU CAN'T RUN FROM LOVE

EDDIE RABBITT

Warner Bros. 29712
Writers: Eddie Rabbitt, David Malloy,
Even Stevens
Producer: David Malloy
June 18, 1983 (1 week)

The kitchen at his DebDave publishing company provided a setting for many of Eddie Rabbitt's collaborative efforts with David Malloy and Even Stevens. The three often had coffee and tossed lines around at a formica table with chrome legs. "You Can't Run From Love" is just one of many tunes that came out of those round-robin writing sessions.

Amazingly, none of the three remembers too much about creating the song, except that it was done in the kitchen, and that Rabbitt was highly influential in creating the bridge, or—as some would call it—the "C section." That's not surprising. Lyrically, the record takes off on a time-machine motif, and Rabbitt has long been fascinated with science and science fiction. (In fact, Eddie collected all of the original "Star Trek" episodes.)

"I have a scientific curiosity about the galaxies and quasars and how many light years it is to something," he admits. "Then getting back down the other way into inner space, into subatomic particles and stuff, but, I mean, you can't put that in a song."

In this instance, however, the allusions to futuristic concepts worked perfectly. "That song doesn't have a tremendous feel or anything," Stevens maintains. "It feels good, but it's not something that's mesmerizing, like 'Drivin' My Life Away' [see 391] was, you know, real rockin'. We knew we had to get a killer bridge on that song. We incorporated a lot of synthesizer work on that bridge, too, which wasn't being done a whole lot in country music."

"You Can't Run From Love" brought Rabbitt's total to a dozen number one singles, and peaked on June 18, 1983. The single was the second pulled from his *Radio Romance* album, ultimately an expensive album to create. They had completely finished the first three tracks, but when they listened to the results carefully, they decided that the material was not quite good enough. Rabbitt and company took a razor blade to the masters and started over again. The cost: $12,000.

Eddie had to wait eighteen months before picking up his lucky thirteenth number one single [see 602—"The Best Year Of My Life"]. In the interim, he notched three more Top Ten singles: "You Put The Beat In My Heart," "Nothing Like Falling In Love," and the quirky "B-B-B-Burnin' Up With Love."

525

FOOL FOR YOUR LOVE

MICKEY GILLEY

Epic 03783
Writer: Don Singleton
Producer: Jim Ed Norman
June 25, 1983 (1 week)

Don Singleton was a member of Shylo, a Memphis group that at one time backed Charly McClain. The group featured several singer/songwriters, including Jerry Hayes, who wrote "Rollin' With The Flow" [see 290] and "Who's Cheatin' Who" [see 412]; and Ronny Scaife, who wrote "Men" and "Me And The I.R.S."

Singleton earned a writer's credit on a number one single when Mickey Gilley recorded his composition "Fool For Your Love."

"I didn't 'hear' it," Gilley admits. "I didn't really want to do it at all. It's another song that Jim Ed Norman said was a hit song, and I said, 'Well, if you think it's a hit, I'll do it.' Later, I understood why it was a hit. It was just something that was a fairly well-produced record that Jim Ed was in tune to, and had it not been for Jim Ed, I would have missed that one totally."

"Fool For Your Love" was Gilley's ninth number one record among the first ten singles he released with Jim Ed Norman as producer. It was also his sixteenth number one overall.

Mickey earned one more in a duet with Charly McClain [see 541—"Paradise Tonight"], following up with seven more consecutive Top Ten releases: "Your Love Shines Through," "You've Really Got A Hold On Me" [see 257—"Bring It On Home To Me"], "Too

Good To Stop Now," "I'm The One Mama Warned You About," "You've Got Something On Your Mind," "Your Memory Ain't What It Used To Be" and "Doo-Wah Days."

Though Gilley's success peaked with the *Urban Cowboy* movie [see 389—"Stand By Me"] and the notoriety of his nightclub, that association came to an end in 1987. He terminated his affiliation with manager Sherwood Cryer and took out full-page ads in the *Music City News*, charging Cryer with neglect of the facility.

"Everything must change or grow stagnant," he said in the ad. "My concern was to keep Gilley's at the level, both musically and structurally, that our loyal and long-time patrons have come to expect. My pride in the club is gone. It no longer represents Mickey Gilley, the entertainer."

A Houston court agreed with Gilley, commanding that his name be removed from the facility. Gilley won $17 million as well, after proving he had been defrauded of his percentage on sales of nearly a million T-shirts.

526
LOVE IS ON A ROLL
DON WILLIAMS
MCA 52205
Writers: Roger Cook, John Prine
Producers: Don Williams, Garth Fundis
July 2, 1983 (1 week)

Don Williams stands among Great Britain's top country artists [see 213—"You're My Best Friend"], but that fact didn't help him when MCA released "Love Is On A Roll."

"Everybody in the States knows kind of what 'on a roll' means," explains Don's producer, Garth Fundis. "In England, they didn't understand the phrase. The record didn't do too well there—they thought it meant 'on a bun.'"

How ironic, considering that "Love Is On A Roll" came from English native Roger Cook, who started writing songs in 1959. Five years later, he teamed with Roger Greenaway for the first time, a collaboration that yielded a Top Ten single one year later for the Fortunes, "You've Got Your Troubles." Cook and Greenaway composed a string of pop hits that included the Fortunes' "Here Comes That Rainy Day Feeling," the Hollies' "Long Cool Woman (In A Black Dress)," Carol Douglas' "Doctor's Or-

ders" and the New Seekers' "I'd Like To Teach The World To Sing" (also a Coca Cola commercial).

Having lost his excitement in England, Cook moved to Nashville in February of 1976. His country successes include "Talking In Your Sleep" [see 320], "Livin' In These Troubled Times," "I Believe In You" [see 397] and "Miracles."

Cook and folk/rock artist John Prine got the germ of "Love Is On A Roll" while watching football at Roger's house.

"We started workin' on it, but John was on the road so much, and I liked the tune so much I couldn't help myself, so I started writin' these verses," says Roger. "One day, I presented him with all these verses that I'd written, and he said, 'Wait a minute. Enough's enough. Don't touch that song again 'til I've had a chance to have a go at it.'

"He came back, and he said, 'I've got this middle worked out—"aah, aah, love is on a roll"'—which turned out to be the hook of the song. It was a great little musical hook, and that really cemented the song."

They made a rock-heavy demo, but then decided the song suited Don Williams. Instead of hitting him with their recording, Cook unpacked his ukulele and played it for Don in the middle of a recording session. Don's version topped the American country chart in 1983.

527
HIGHWAY 40 BLUES
RICKY SKAGGS
Epic 03812
Writer: Larry Cordle
Producer: Ricky Skaggs
July 9, 1983 (1 week)

With its central location, Nashville provides an intersection for three major arteries. Interstate 65 runs through Music City in a chain that extends from Gary, Indiana, to Mobile, Alabama; I-24 connects Nashville with both St. Louis and Chattanooga; and I-40 covers nearly the entire continent from east to west, from Raleigh, North Carolina, to Barstow, California.

The latter stretch of concrete has lent its name to two creative endeavors: the Nashville Network's former series "I-40 Paradise," and the Ricky Skaggs hit "Highway 40 Blues." The Skaggs song pays tribute to those musicians who travel America's roadways against insurmountable odds, looking for that one break that might make their names synonymous with Nashville.

Skaggs received "Highway 40 Blues" on a demo tape from songwriter Larry Cordle, a friend from eastern Kentucky. Larry attended school with Ricky's sister, and the Cordles frequently invited Skaggs to play music with them. They even went to the same church, and after Larry joined the Navy, he hooked up with Ricky in Lexington to play "Highway 40 Blues" and several other songs that he'd written.

"I went in and produced a demo session on him," Ricky recalls. "There was a guy that wanted to cut an album on him with these songs, 'cause they were so good. So actually, I produced 'Highway 40 Blues' on Larry before I cut it myself."

Nothing much happened with Cordle's version of the song, and it remained in Ricky's publishing company until the *Highways & Heartaches* album. Ricky's record featured a rash of instrumental solos, as Skaggs experimented with several new musical elements.

"It was an advance for me," Ricky says of the album. "I used the electric guitar in a lot of ways. I used a lot of mandolin. I used banjo a lot. There's a freshness and a movement, kind of a newer direction to *Highways & Heartaches*."

Having played "Highway 40 Blues" live for several months before recording the album, Skaggs knew exactly what kind of direction it needed, and its breezy feel resulted in Ricky's biggest-selling single. Cordle was able to buy a house and a new car, and moved to Nashville.

"Highway 40 Blues" traveled to number one on July 9, 1983, and on October 3, *Highways & Heartaches* fell in line behind *Waitin' for the Sun to Shine* as Ricky's second gold album.

Ricky Skaggs

528
THE CLOSER YOU GET
ALABAMA
RCA 13524
Writers: Mark Gray, J.P. Pennington
Producers: Harold Shedd, Alabama
July 16, 1983 (1 week)

Even as Exile began recording its first country product for Epic Records [see 479—"Take Me Down"], one of the group's original records found a home with Alabama. "The Closer You Get" was created by the same writers—Mark Gray and J.P. Pennington—and appeared on the same Exile album as "Take Me Down," *Don't Leave Me This Way*.

Linda Bloom sent "The Closer You Get" to producer Harold Shedd after Alabama cut "Take Me Down," but when the record debuted in *Billboard* on May 14, 1983, it wasn't the first appearance for the song. Don King released it in 1981 from his *Whirlwind* album, taking it to number 27.

"We knew the Don King version of 'The Closer You Get,'" Shedd admits, "but if you listen to the original version and Alabama's version, they're totally different."

That's quite an understatement. King's rendition was more acoustic, almost in the vein of an S-K-O [see 712—"Baby's Got A New Baby"] single, while Alabama beefed up the song with distorted guitars, a more elaborate arrangement and an altered vocal sound. "We did some technical things vocally," Shedd explains, "where we did some harmonizing and [different] echo and stuff like that. We were always experimenting with new and exciting things, and sometimes it worked."

As with several other Alabama hits, including "Old Flame" [see 421] and "Touch Me

When We're Dancing" [see 698], "The Closer You Get" was the last song to go on the album, but it became the group's tenth number one single two months after it first appeared on the chart.

On February 28, 1984, the record brought Alabama its second Grammy for Best Country Vocal Performance by a Duo or Group; the first came for "Mountain Music" [see 470].

At the same time that "The Closer You Get" began its climb, Gray, one of its writers, made his first appearance as a solo artist. A former member of Exile, he also wrote Janie Frickie's "It Ain't Easy Bein' Easy" [see 496] and Gary Morris' "Second Hand Heart."

As a performer, Mark notched five Top Ten singles during 1984-85, including "Left Side Of The Bed" and "Please Be Love," as well as a duet with Tammy Wynette on "Sometimes When We Touch."

529

PANCHO AND LEFTY
MERLE HAGGARD & WILLIE NELSON
Epic 03842
Writer: Townes Van Zandt
Producers: Chips Moman, Merle Haggard, Willie Nelson
July 23, 1983 (1 week)

Merle Haggard & Willie Nelson

Merle Haggard and Willie Nelson recorded the first of their two duet albums in the space of five days. Each day, they started in the late afternoon and worked in Nelson's Pedernales Studio until 2:00 or 3:00 A.M. The sessions are perhaps best known for Merle's lack of interest in "Always On My Mind" [see 471], but the songs they did record proved fruitful in their own right.

During the sessions, Willie's daughter, Lana, brought a copy of Emmylou Harris' *Luxury Liner* album to the studio about midnight. She played Townes Van Zandt's "Pancho And Lefty," and Willie and Merle's ambitious version emerged as the title track of their own project.

Most of the songs came together rather easily, but Willie and Merle encountered difficulty with "Pancho"'s instrumental bridge. "Actually, that's Chips [Moman] playin' the guitar," says Willie. "Me and Grady [Martin] took a shot at that chorus, and it's so unusual in there that I couldn't get the feel of it. Chips knew more about what he wanted than either one of us, so we let him put it in, and I think he stacked two or three guitar parts on top."

Willie and Merle actually sang together on only the final line, and Merle sang the last verse, which he learned from a track that Willie had already laid down, at 4:00 A.M.

"I'd been asleep about an hour, and I was just completely bushed," Merle recalls. "I couldn't get my bearings, and he had this song and it

seemed like it was half a mile long. It had more words than any song I've ever seen in my life. I said, 'Great, I'll try to learn my part in the morning,' and he said, 'No, let's do it now.' I remember doing it and thinking, 'Well, I'll have to do this over when I wake up,' but I never did have to do it over."

After delaying the album's release for about a year, Epic selected "Reasons To Quit" as the first single, and it went to number six. "Pancho" followed in the summer months, hitting number one in July of 1983.

The first shipment of the album is now a collector's item. Through a printing mistake, the "a" in "Pancho" came out as an "o."

530
I ALWAYS GET LUCKY WITH YOU
GEORGE JONES
Epic 03883
Writers: Tex Whitson, Merle Haggard,
Freddy Powers, Gary Church
Producer: Billy Sherrill
July 30, 1983 (1 week)

After recording an entire duet album with George Jones [see 489—"Yesterday's Wine"], Merle Haggard hooked up with the Possum once more by writing his single, "I Always Get Lucky With You." Haggard co-wrote the song with Freddy Powers, who played guitar in the duet sessions.

Powers insists that Haggard and himself were the only writers involved, despite the label credits for four people. "Merle and I gave away two parts of that song to a guy that works for me and a guy that works for Merle," he explains.

"I wrote it first in about 1978, and then I played it for Merle in about 1980 or '81, and Merle liked the title of it, and liked the song, but he went out on the road one time. He flew with the song, then he finally rewrote it."

"I Always Get Lucky With You" first appeared on Haggard's *Big City* album [see 467], but Merle's manager, Tex Whitson, also pitched the song to producer Billy Sherrill.

"At that point, George and Merle weren't speaking over some falling-out they had," Sherrill notes. "I played it to George. He loved it, and I didn't tell him who wrote it until after he cut it, because he wouldn't have cut it, he was so mad at Merle. After we did it, I told him, but by then, they'd made up. It just came

off real nice, real pretty, and it was real easy to cut."

The CBS publicity department issued a release, stating that it was the first record in which Jones ever broke into falsetto, a claim that Sherrill admits was a stretch. "He just broke his voice a little more than usual," says the producer. "He spread it on a little thick on that one."

"I Always Get Lucky With You" was merely the half-way point of the most successful streak of Jones' career. He followed with eight more consecutive Top Ten records through 1987, including "Tennessee Whiskey" and "She's My Rock," which both peaked at number two.

"You've Still Got A Place In My Heart," "Who's Gonna Fill Their Shoes" and "The One I Loved Back Then (The Corvette Song)" each went to number three. Dating back to "He Stopped Loving Her Today" [see 384], Jones had racked up 15 straight Top Ten singles for the very first time.

531
YOUR LOVE'S ON THE LINE
EARL THOMAS CONLEY
RCA 13525
Writers: Earl Thomas Conley,
Randy Scruggs
Producers: Nelson Larkin,
Earl Thomas Conley
August 6, 1983 (1 week)

When Earl Thomas Conley started having national hits, he encountered an "image problem." Country fans had trouble identifying his name, since it so closely resembled Conway Twitty and Con Hunley. In one instance, a fan even handed him a copy of John Conlee's *Greatest Hits* and asked for an autograph.

If the name wasn't instantly recognizable, the music certainly was. Conley kicked off 1983 with "I Have Loved You, Girl (But Not Like This Before)," a re-recording of his first charted single [see 433—"Fire And Smoke"]. The new version—the third single from *Somewhere Between Right and Wrong*—debuted in *Billboard* on January 15, 1983, and hit number two on April 9. A week later, Alabama kept Earl out of the top spot, as "Dixieland Delight" [see 515] jumped past "I Have Loved You, Girl."

Conley, who has studied Eastern religions

and meditation, frequently speaks of "programming" himself to write, and along with co-writer Randy Scruggs, he programmed himself to create "radio records" for his next album, *Don't Make It Easy for Me*. Conley and Scruggs collaborated on five tunes in the package, and the last of them, "Your Love's On The Line," was pegged as the album's first single.

They wrote the title track [see 564] on a Thursday, with a recording session scheduled for the following Tuesday. Conley hit the road for a pair of concerts on Friday and Saturday, and they settled in on Sunday to create that last song.

"I think it was one of the easiest ones that we wrote," Earl recalls. "'Chance Of Lovin' You' [see 598] had a lot of unfamiliar-type chord changes in it—it's a feel-type record. But 'Your Love's On The Line,' melodically, was inspired by the creativity of 'Chance Of Lovin' You.' We were tryin' a bunch of different things. Every time we got together, me and Randy were just goin' through different riffs of chord changes and stuff, searchin' for things that would work together melodically, at the same time tryin' to come up with some lyric ideas that made sense, too. 'Your Love's On The Line' just fell together real smooth.

"I still love those chords. I wish we hadn't written that song already, 'cause I'd love to do it again."

532

HE'S A HEARTACHE (LOOKING FOR A PLACE TO HAPPEN)
JANIE FRICKIE
Columbia 03899
Writers: Jeff Silbar, Larry Henley
Producer: Bob Montgomery
August 13, 1983 (1 week)

Teaming with producer Bob Montgomery proved a masterstroke in Janie Frickie's career, as she reached a peak in both public popularity and industry recognition. At the time "It Ain't Easy Bein' Easy" [see 496] was in release, she walked off with a standing ovation and a trophy for Top Female Vocalist at the Country Music Association's annual awards show October 11, 1982.

The trophy was only the first. She won the CMA award again the following October, and in the meantime, kept pace with the upper positions on the *Billboard* country chart. She followed "It Ain't Easy Bein' Easy" with "You Don't Know Love," a powerful ballad that featured a duet with male vocalist Bill Warren. That single peaked at number four in the spring of 1983, and her next release, "He's A Heartache (Looking For A Place To Happen)," represented a major change of pace.

"We wanted a high-energy song," Frickie explains. "I was touring with Alabama, and I watched everything they did, and with their high energy on stage, it was magical with the audience. I wanted to try to do that, too. I tried to learn from watching Alabama, and it's stuck with me."

"He's A Heartache" proved the perfect vehicle for an uptempo performance, ably enhanced by Don Gorman's soaring guitar work, but the song was originally intended for another artist. House of Gold had published Juice Newton's record "Love's Been A Little Bit Hard On Me," and Jeff Silbar and Larry Henley wrote "He's A Heartache" with Newton in mind.

"I called her producer, Richard Landis, with the song," recalls Montgomery. "I had Richard's ear, but, for whatever reason, Juice turned it down."

"James Stroud, who was producin' LaCosta—Tanya Tucker's sister—at the time, he was beggin' me," adds Henley. "He wanted to cut it really bad. He wound up callin' [Landis] and askin' him if Juice was gonna cut the song. They released the song to Stroud, and he cut it on LaCosta."

Nothing happened with that version. But Frickie's version performed quite well. It first appeared at number 74 in *Billboard* on May 21, 1983; a dozen weeks later, "He's A Heartache" found a place at number one.

533

LOVE SONG
THE OAK RIDGE BOYS
MCA 52224
Writer: Steve Runkle
Producer: Ron Chancey
August 20, 1983 (1 week)

For 1983's *American Made* [see 516], the Oak Ridge Boys journeyed to Muscle Shoals for the first time to do part of the album.

"They don't care if you spend three hours or twelve hours in the studio that day," says bass singer Richard Sterban. "The studio is yours, and it's up to you. You can spend as much time as you want to, and they are never in a hurry down there."

The Oaks certainly weren't in a hurry, either, with one of the songs they recorded in Muscle Shoals. Their friend and one-time manager, Don Light, first introduced them to "Love Song" three years earlier. They considered the song for each of the three albums prior to *American Made*, but it always ended up in Duane Allen's drawer of good-but-unrecorded material [see 446—"Fancy Free"].

"It had a real long guitar riff in the middle that kept blowin' us away," notes Allen, "but we couldn't hear ourselves doing that song until I got to splicing that tape, and actually cut out about 32 bars that kind of took it off into a different vein.

"Every time I would play it, the guys would say, 'We like it, but . . .' Then I would say, 'What is it about this song you do not like?' and they would say, 'It loses us somewhere in the middle.' Well, we went to the splicing machine and cut out the total entire middle part, which included the guitar turn-around and recitations and a little bit of everything. I just cleaned it up, put it verse/chorus, verse/chorus—that sort of thing—where it would sound like something we would do, and then recorded it immediately."

One unusual portion they did leave intact brought the Oaks down to an *a capella* doo-wop section, with Sterban in a little stair-step bassline. Their bouncy rendition made its first appearance on the *Billboard* country singles chart on June 4, 1983, debuting at number 60. Eleven weeks later, "Love Song" registered at number one.

At the end of the year, the Oak Ridge Boys followed up with "Ozark Mountain Jubilee," featuring William Lee Golden on lead vocals. That single went to number five.

534
YOU'RE GONNA RUIN MY BAD REPUTATION
RONNIE McDOWELL
Epic 03946
Writer: Jeff Crossan
Producer: Buddy Killen
August 27, 1983 (1 week)

Having already established his own reputation by writing a rock radio show called "Star Tracks" for the Westwood One network in Los Angeles, Jeff Crossan tried for several years to crack the Nashville market as a songwriter. Ronnie McDowell finally gave him the break he needed, and several months later, Crossan moved to Music City.

Crossan habitually carries a pocket memo pad, and one day, he discovered that he had written down a simple title, "You're Gonna Ruin My (Bad) Reputation." After writing the song, he gained some interest from Tree Publishing, and when they played it for John Conlee's producer, Bud Logan, he thought it could be a hit, although he also didn't think it was quite right for Conlee.

Tree's song plugger, Tom Long, later played the song when both Dean Dillon and McDowell were in the room at the same time, and Long first offered it to Dillon. Dillon expressed interest, but after he left, McDowell asked for the song, and it eventually wound up on his album *Personally*.

"The demo was so barebones," Crossan recalls. "You could have done anything with it arrangement-wise, and [the singer on the demo] had done kind of a Don Williamsy vocal thing on it."

As a result, the *Personally* version of "Bad Reputation" was recorded as a mid-tempo ballad, and McDowell added it to his show, although he wasn't satisfied. "I knew that the song had merit to it," says McDowell, "and I knew it was a hit song, but it was wrong."

Ronnie worked up a new version with his road band, kicking off with the title and pushing the pace a little faster, and "Bad Reputation" became one of the biggest records of the summer. It debuted in *Billboard* at number 63 on June 11, 1983, and soared to number one after a dozen weeks on the chart.

Crossan also wrote McDowell's follow-up, "You Made A Wanted Man Of Me," which peaked at number three. McDowell earned five more Top Ten hits with Killen as producer through 1986, including "In A New York Minute," "Love Talks" and "All Tied Up." In 1987, they agreed that McDowell should try a new approach, and he moved to Curb Records, where he began producing himself. That brought another Top Ten single when Conway Twitty joined him on a remake of "It's Only Make Believe."

McDowell and his wife still live in Portland, Tennessee, known as "The Strawberry Capital Of The World."

George Strait

535
A FIRE I CAN'T PUT OUT
GEORGE STRAIT
MCA 52225
Writer: Darryl Staedtler
Producer: Blake Mevis
September 3, 1983 (1 week)

George Strait took a unique trip on July 15, 1983. After an interview with the United Stations Radio Network for "The Weekly Country Music Countdown," he was prodded into a short excursion on the world's most maligned subway. Reluctantly, he went with his New York escorts on the shuttle from Times Square to Grand Central Station for a "quickie" view of that commuter landmark.

Upon his return, Strait emerged unscathed from the subway and headed into a waiting limousine—certainly a study in contrasts.

At the time, Strait had ridden five singles into the country Top Ten. In 1983, he had reached that level with "Marina Del Rey" and "Amarillo By Morning," adding to his previous cache [see 484—"Fool Hearted Memory"]. "A Fire I Can't Put Out" hit *Billboard*'s Top 20 the same week that Strait hit Manhattan's subway system, but the record owed more to his Texas roots.

George first went to Nashville in 1977, along with Lone Star songwriter Darryl Staedtler, who was convinced that he could get Strait a recording contract. Staedtler produced six sides for a demo and shopped it around to a number of labels, but each turned him down. The rejection was one of many that Staedtler faced in a lengthy pursuit of the music business.

Having first written at age 15, Darryl lived in Music City for about 15 years, turning in material to at least five different publishing companies. His only Top Ten successes came with the Wilburn Brothers' 1965 release "It's Another World" and Billy "Crash" Craddock's 1975 single "I Love The Blues And The Boogie Woogie," so Staedtler headed to Austin in 1975. When that didn't pan out, he opened a chili parlor, then became a teacher; in 1980, he gave up songwriting altogether and took up a career in real estate.

"A Fire I Can't Put Out" was among the last songs that he wrote, and Strait included it as the final track on his second album, *Strait from the Heart*. Recorded at Owen Bradley's Music City Music Hall, it was shipped as the album's fourth single, and, 27 years after he started writing, "A Fire I Can't Put Out" became Staedtler's first number one record.

536

I'M ONLY IN IT FOR THE LOVE
JOHN CONLEE
MCA 52231
Writers: Deborah Allen, Kix Brooks, Rafe VanHoy
Producer: Bud Logan
September 10, 1983 (1 week)

"I'm Only In It For The Love" was the second Rafe VanHoy composition that reached number one for John Conlee [see 332—"Lady Lay Down"]. In spite of that fact, it actually represented a number of "firsts."

It was the first song that VanHoy and his wife, Deborah Allen, wrote with Kix Brooks (VanHoy later produced Brooks' debut album in 1988). It turned out to be Brooks' first number one, and it was also the first song VanHoy and Allen wrote on their very first synthesizer.

"When we wrote that, we had no idea who we would pitch it to," VanHoy remembers, "because the demo is even more pop-flavored than John's record. Chris Dotson played it for [producer] Bud Logan, and Bud really liked it for John. I never pictured that song for John Conlee, though—I never would have thought to play that for him, but I guess I should have. They cut a great record on it."

With a bouncy tempo and sparse horn arrangement, it was a major change of pace for Conlee, better known at the time for his ballads.

"We've always had a problem, I guess, finding uptempo songs that have much appeal to me," Conlee concedes. "I'm not a downbeat person, I don't think. I *am* laid-back, and I like uptempo songs by other people, but it's hard to find uptempo songs that say something or feel that good to me. That was one that did strike me. We were glad to have it because we've had most of our success with ballads, and it was a bit of a departure for us."

"I thought that was one of the things that was cool about what Bud did with John," adds VanHoy. "Once he had some success with him, he didn't feel like he had to follow any particular formula and play it too safe. He was willing to consider something totally different if it made sense."

In the case of "I'm Only In It For The Love," it made plenty of sense. Its infectious hook carried Conlee to his fourth number one single—and second in a row—on September 10, 1983.

537

NIGHT GAMES
CHARLEY PRIDE
RCA 13542
Writers: Norro Wilson, Blake Mevis
Producer: Norro Wilson
September 17, 1983 (1 week)

Given Charley Pride's athletic history [see 508—"Why Baby Why"], it's tempting to associate "Night Games" with baseball. Songwriters Norro Wilson and Blake Mevis both insist that there's very little reason to do so. "Basically, we just wanted to write a song that Charley would record," says Mevis, "so we made an appointment, sat down and wrote the song."

"Blake had some fabulous ideas with the song," Wilson adds, "and I asserted my energy, and we came up with that song. The title worked, and we wrote around it. I've always maintained that if you're fortunate enough to think up a hit song title, a title will almost write itself."

"Night Games" was Pride's twenty-ninth number one single, and his forty-ninth to hit the Top Ten. He preceded it with "More And More," a remake of a former chart-topping Webb Pierce record, written by Merle Kilgore in 1954. Charley's fiftieth Top Ten single came in 1984 with "Ev'ry Heart Should Have One." The follow-up, "The Power Of Love," was his last bona fide hit with RCA.

Pride left the label in 1986, more than two decades after he first signed. Despite receiving offers, he waited for a year before signing his next deal, with a new company, 16th Avenue Records. It re-teamed him with his former producer, Jerry Bradley, who headed up the company, one arm of the Opryland Music Group. In 1988, Charley netted the label's very first Top Five single, with "Shouldn't It Be Easier Than This."

Pride celebrated his twenty-fifth anniversary as a recording artist in 1990, showing no signs of slowing down.

"I love to sing," he says. "I guess you kind of look at me like Bob Hope. I don't have the money he has, or nothing like that, but I'm just saying, he doesn't need the money, he must be out there because he loves it, and I guess you have to view me that way.

"I can lay off a while, and people say 'Don't you get tired of traveling?' I worked more in 1988 than I did in any other year in my career. Let's face it—I love what I do."

538
BABY, WHAT ABOUT YOU
CRYSTAL GAYLE
Warner Bros. 29582
Writers: Josh Leo, Wendy Waldman
Producer: Jimmy Bowen
September 24, 1983 (1 week)

Unlike Conway Twitty, Crystal Gayle never opened her own food shop [see 44—"To See My Angel Cry"]. But she did pick up her stage name from a hamburger chain.

Originally named Brenda Gail Webb [see 271—"You Never Miss A Real Good Thing"], she faced an identity problem when she signed with Decca Records, which already had Brenda Lee. In an effort to differentiate the Brendas, Gayle's older sister, Loretta Lynn, took it upon herself to find a suitable stage monicker.

After driving past a regional fast food chain in Nashville called Krystal's, Lynn found the right name.

"I thought it was because Crystal signified bright and shiny," Gayle later told Bob Lapham of the *Abilene Reporter-News*.

"Crystal" did have a certain ring to it that transcended its greasy origins, and Gayle was able to adapt her real middle name to lend an air of authenticity. She had become quite accustomed to her stage identity by the time she sided with Jimmy Bowen at Elektra Records in 1982. Bowen produced three tracks on *True Love* [see 523—"Our Love Is On The Faultline"]: "'Til I Gain Control Again" [see 506], "Everything I Own" and "Baby, What About You," written by Josh Leo and former recording artist Wendy Waldman.

Unable to muster success as a pop artist, Waldman found a home in country music. She produced the Forester Sisters and New Grass Revival, sang back-up vocals on Steve Wariner's "Heart Trouble" and "Some Fools Never Learn" [see 643], and co-wrote "Fishin' In The Dark" [see 741] as well.

"We'd worked with Josh and the rhythm section he was with in California, where he did all the Kim Carnes stuff, 'Bette Davis Eyes' and so forth," reports Bowen. "They laid the song on me. I just loved the song, and I played it for Crystal and she loved it immediately."

Recorded at Bowen's Sound Stage Studios and mixed at Emerald Sound, "Baby, What About You" debuted at number 63 on the country chart on July 16, 1983. Ten weeks later, it slipped into the number one position.

539
NEW LOOKS FROM AN OLD LOVER
B.J. THOMAS
Columbia 03985
Writers: Gloria Thomas, Lathan Hudson, Red Lane
Producer: Pete Drake
October 1, 1983 (1 week)

In addition to recording the song, B.J. Thomas also provided the inspiration for "New Looks From An Old Lover." His wife, Gloria, was on the phone one morning when he came into the kitchen, and when her friend at the other end asked how things were going, Gloria responded: "Everything's going great; I'm even getting new looks from my old lover over there."

Gloria had been writing songs and poetry for some time, even co-authoring B.J.'s autobiography. He encouraged her to use the phrase as a song title, and when he recorded his first album for Columbia in Nashville, she wrote the song with Red Lane and Lathan Hudson. B.J., in fact, titled the album *New Looks*.

"When I first heard it," he confesses, "I thought, 'This thing is so country—I don't know if I want to get that country.' So one of the publishers, I think it was Rose Drake, sent a tape the next morning to Kenny Rogers. When I found that out, I wanted to do it immediately. Gloria and I still get a big kick out of knowing that we had a number one record together."

"New Looks From An Old Lover" was the second single pulled from the album, following "Whatever Happened To Old Fashioned Love" [see 519], and Thomas initially planned to release "The Wind Beneath My Wings" as the third. He never got the chance: four weeks after "New Looks" hit the market, Gary Morris released "Wings."

Instead, Thomas released "Two Car Garage," which hit number three; and "The Whole World's In Love When You're Lonely," a Fred Knobloch [see 712—"Baby's Got A New Baby"] composition that reached number 10. He also teamed with Ray Charles on "Rock And Roll Shoes."

Legal problems between his label and a business associate presented a snag, though, and several more releases failed to equal those successes. "They were wanting me to be a lot more country than I was comfortable with," he says, "so we just took the time and decided what we wanted to do with the music."

With his chameleon-like ability to excel in a variety of styles, Thomas decided to return to mainstream pop music. First evidence came when he recorded the theme song to the TV sitcom "Growing Pains." He redid it once with Jennifer Warnes and again with Dusty Springfield.

B.J. Thomas

540

DON'T YOU KNOW HOW MUCH I LOVE YOU

RONNIE MILSAP

RCA 13564
Writers: Michael Stewart, Dan Williams
Producers: Ronnie Milsap, Tom Collins
October 8, 1983 (1 week)

Ronnie Milsap got mixed results in the spring of 1983 with his rockin' single "Stranger In My House." It brought songwriter Mike Reid a Grammy for Best Country Song, and also took Milsap as high as number 23 on *Billboard*'s Hot 100. Milsap earned his only Academy of Country Music award that spring for Top Male Vocalist.

"Stranger In My House" peaked at number five on the country chart, a good showing in anyone's book, but, because of its atypically searing quality, not up to Milsap's usual performance. In fact, it ended Ronnie's string of ten straight number one singles, one of the ten best streaks in chart history.

Milsap bounced right back, however, with the second single from the *Keyed Up* album, "Don't You Know How Much I Love You." Ronnie picked it up from Dan Williams and Mike Stewart, a couple of jingle singers who work out of Nashville. Stewart, in fact, did the vocal work on the zydeco-influenced Lemon Clorox

commercials of 1989 ("Those lemons they roll, those lemons they bounce . . .").

"Mike Stewart's an insane guy," Ronnie highlights, "one of those kind of dancin' fools like James Brown around the office, and real crazy and real creative. Dan Williams is, too, both those guys. For a while they were around here doin' things with us.

"They had brought me this song, and there was a master done on that by some young group lookin' for a label deal, and it was done a couple of steps higher, some young singer that could sing way up there. So I took it in and took it down to the key of G, where I could sing it."

"Don't You Know How Much I Love You" debuted at number 60 on July 23, 1983, sliding into number one a dozen weeks later.

"That's one of those songs, along with 'Stranger In My House,' where I started working with [engineer] Kyle Lehning [producer of Dan Seals and Randy Travis], one of my all-time favorite people," says Milsap. "What a great guy, great producer, engineer—he has tremendous instincts and hears better than anyone I've ever been around."

Another Milsap associate hit a significant point with "Don't You Know How Much I Love You." It was the tenth of Milsap's number one records produced by Tom Collins.

541

PARADISE TONIGHT

CHARLY McCLAIN & MICKEY GILLEY

Epic 04007
Writers: Mark Wright, Bill Kenner
Producer: Chucko Productions
October 15, 1983 (1 week)

In 1983, many of country music's artists were looking for duet partners to record with. At the time, Mickey Gilley had a handful of tunes that he wanted to record with a female performer, and when he made a guest appearance with Charly McClain on NBC's TV series "CHiPs", he thought he'd found the right combination.

"That was the very first time that Mickey and I had ever really talked," Charly says, noting that she reacted positively. "Really, to be perfectly honest, I was just trying to be nice, because I thought duets were really more hassle than they were worth."

McClain had recorded an earlier duet in 1979, teaming up with Johnny Rodriguez on "I Hate The Way I Love It." The single peaked at number 16 on the *Billboard* charts, but coordinating both artists' schedules had been a nightmare, creating her aversion to collaborations.

About three months later, McClain was in Nashville recording material at The Music Mill. Her manager, John Lentz, found out Gilley was in town as well, and he headed over to Audio Media, where the Texas singer was recording. Instead of reminding him of the

Charly McClain & Mickey Gilley

duet, Lentz simply asked Gilley to drop by and say hello, but once he arrived, the duet came about rather quickly.

Both songwriters were in the studio at the time, and made a few lyrical changes to convert the song to a duo. Gilley had to learn the song on the spot, with producer Norro Wilson (credited on the label as "Chucko Productions") spoon-feeding Gilley the harmony parts. "I learned the harmony line like a lead line," Mickey confesses, "because I didn't know how to sing harmony."

Gilley thought it would be merely a rehearsal, to see if they might record a duet later. In fact, Wilson took the vocals from that session, mixed it all together, and placed the duet on McClain's *Paradise* album. Shortly afterward, McClain started dating soap star Wayne Massey [see 621—"Radio Heart"], and when the label wanted the duet as a single, Massey convinced her it was the right move.

It proved so successful that McClain and Gilley followed up with an entire duet album, *It Takes Believers*, earning another Top Five single with their remake of Roy Orbison's "Candy Man."

542
LADY DOWN ON LOVE
ALABAMA
RCA 13590
Writer: Randy Owen
Producers: Harold Shedd, Alabama
October 22, 1983 (1 week)

Alabama waited seven years to record "Lady Down On Love," a song that Randy Owen composed during his most prolific week as a songwriter. That same week, in 1976, he put the finishing touches on "Tennessee River" [see 390].

Alabama was booked at the Red Carpet Inn in Bowling Green, Kentucky, and part of their usual routine included a little give-and-take with the audience. A large group of ladies occupied one particular table, and when the band asked them why they were all there together, the women replied that they were celebrating a divorce.

"They pointed to a girl down at the other end," Owen remembers. "She didn't look like she was celebratin', so I said somethin' to her about it, and she said, 'Well, I'd really rather be at home with my husband and be in love.' That really struck me, because I thought it was unique. Most of the time when people divorce, it's like, 'That turkey, I wish I'd never married him.'

"She said, 'You know, this is the first time I've been out on my own since I was 18, and I really don't know how to act.' That was the first line of 'Lady Down On Love,' and bein' a person who'd been away from home a lot, I just turned this thing around and wrote the second verse from the side of a man, and how he would have felt in the same situation—since it was probably a man's fault, anyway. My feelings are very strong pro-women. Most of the time, if there are any problems, it's usually the man's fault."

Initially, Owen hoped that Johnny Rodriguez would record "Lady Down On Love," though he never got a reply from any of Johnny's associates. That turned out for the best, since Alabama released it as the third single from the album *The Closer You Get*. Owen played the guitar himself, recording it four times and using parts of two different takes.

Strings were arranged for "Lady Down On Love" by Kristin Wilkinson, who had just ended a long-term relationship the same day she heard it for the first time. "To me," says Owen, "that's the greatest strings I've ever heard in my life."

In the end, the sad sentiment powered the record to number one.

543
ISLANDS IN THE STREAM
KENNY ROGERS & DOLLY PARTON
RCA 13615
Writers: Barry Gibb, Robin Gibb, Maurice Gibb
Producers: Barry Gibb, Karl Richardson, Albhy Galuten
October 29, 1983 (2 weeks)

After signing a recording deal with RCA that many have estimated at $20 million, Kenny Rogers chose an unusual recording partner in the guise of producer Barry Gibb, one-third of the Bee Gees [see 423—"Rest Your Love On Me"]. The result was *Eyes That See in the Dark*, ten separate songs written by the brothers Gibb specifically for Kenny.

Among the ten was "Islands In The Stream," originally planned as a solo recording. By the time of release, it emerged as a duet with RCA labelmate Dolly Parton.

"That was the cream on the cake for me," Gibb said, shortly after the album's release, "because Dolly is my favorite female singer at the moment. I think she's just amazing.

"It came together quite unusually. We were looking for the right female singer to record with Kenny, bearing in mind he'd recently done a duet with Sheena Easton [see 514—"We've Got Tonight"]. This needed to be a little more unusual. Kenny and Dolly had never done a duet before, although they'd sung on television together. Once it was suggested, it was the only way to go. Being in the studio with the two of them was a great experience. They're very loose with each other, very relaxed. They did all the vocals live. There were no separate overdubs from each artist."

Not surprisingly, the dream combination was an instant winner with both country and pop radio. "Islands" simultaneously topped both charts for two weeks on its way to racking up a slew of awards. Rogers & Parton earned the American Music Award for Best Country Single, while the Academy of Country Music cited them for Single Record of the Year and Vocal Duet of the Year.

On October 18, 1983, "Islands" joined "Elvira" [see 427] as one of only two country records ever certified by the Recording Industry Association of America as platinum singles, for sales over two million.

Eyes That See in the Dark held several other successes for Kenny. "Buried Treasure," a song the Gibbs wrote for Kenny and his wife, Marianne, reached number three, while "Evening Star" peaked at number 11. Both featured Larry Gatlin & The Gatlin Brothers Band as guest vocalists. "Buried Treasure"'s flip side, "This Woman," also earned a number 23 peak on *Billboard*'s Hot 100.

544

SOMEBODY'S GONNA LOVE YOU
LEE GREENWOOD

MCA 52257
Writers: Don Cook, Rafe VanHoy
Producer: Jerry Crutchfield
November 12, 1983 (1 week)

By the time he earned his first number one single, Lee Greenwood had already earned distinction as the Country Music Association's

Male Vocalist of the Year, an honor he accrued with two years of wall-to-wall country hits.

Greenwood first appeared as a relative unknown, debuting on the *Billboard* country charts on September 19, 1981, with "It Turns Me Inside Out"—a year after he first met producer Jerry Crutchfield. "I couldn't quite decide how to approach this," Jerry reports, "because I knew it was gonna take the right song material. Quite a while passed, maybe ten or eleven months, before Lee and I got back together, but I never lost the enthusiasm, because I knew that I was listening to a voice that was unbelievably great."

Jerry's brother Jan provided "It Turns Me Inside Out," which peaked in some markets as it debuted in others. As a result, it only reached number 17 on the national charts, but stayed in the Top 100 for 22 weeks.

Thanks to Greenwood's smoky vocal quality, and a quivering vibrato, the single drew comparisons to Kenny Rogers, and the CMA nominated the composition for Song of the Year during 1982.

In the meantime, Greenwood continued to set himself apart as a talented vocalist. He followed "Inside Out" with "Ring On Her Finger, Time On Her Hands," another ballad that peaked at number five. MCA released Lee's debut album, *Inside Out*, in April of 1982, and it brought two more Top Ten singles, "She's Lying" and "Ain't No Trick (It Takes Magic)," both of which went to number seven.

Kenny Rogers cut another song that Greenwood wrote for the album, "A Love Song," which peaked at number three. A second Greenwood album produced yet another Top Ten hit with "I. O. U." in the spring of 1983, and on August 20, Greenwood entered the *Billboard* charts with the title track, "Somebody's Gonna Love You."

Written by Rafe VanHoy and Don Cook, the tune benefited from a dreamy vocal arrangement that VanHoy's wife, Deborah Allen, had suggested for the demo before it was eventually submitted to producer Jerry Crutchfield.

"Jerry basically chose all the songs for us and would send them to me to see if I liked them or not," explains Greenwood. "Instantly, I liked that record. It was kind of a James Taylor approach to the music. Ronnie Milsap had a lot of records like that, and I liked that a lot."

As the song scaled the country charts, Lee picked up the Male Vocalist trophy from the CMA in October, and just one month later, "Somebody's Gonna Love You" became his first number one single.

ONE OF A KIND PAIR OF FOOLS

BARBARA MANDRELL

MCA 52258
Writers: R.C. Bannon, John Bettis
Producer: Tom Collins
November 19, 1983 (1 week)

Barbara Mandrell's sixth number one single was a family effort. Her brother-in-law, R.C. Bannon [see 317—"Only One Love In My Life"], brought fellow songwriter John Bettis onto Barbara's yacht on Old Hickory Lake, where they spent five days writing songs in the middle of winter.

One evening, they collaborated on "One Of A Kind Pair Of Fools." John suggested they write lyrics around the title "Too Hot To Sleep." Once they finished that number, they envisioned "Too Hot To Sleep" for Barbara, and decided that "One Of A Kind" would be better suited for her sister, Louise.

"When we came off the boat, we played both of 'em to Louise first," R.C. recalls. "She said, 'Oh, I hope Barbara doesn't like "Too Hot To Sleep" 'cause I would love to record that.' So we went down to Barbara's house that afternoon and we sang her both songs, and she said, 'Well, "Too Hot To Sleep" sounds like Louise— I'd like to cut "One Of A Kind Pair Of Fools." ' It just flip-flopped on us as writers."

Louise reached number 10 with "Too Hot" in the summer of 1983. Barbara then put out "One Of A Kind," and it topped the chart in November.

Approximately ten months later, on September 11, 1984, Barbara and her two children were nearly killed when another car jumped lanes and hit hers head-on. She suffered a severe concussion, and rumors abounded that she would never work again.

Mandrell, of course, couldn't be kept away too long. On January 3, she held a press conference to quell the rumors, and on June 10, she returned to live performances with an appearance at the *Music City News* awards. On September 6, 1985, she had her third child.

She continued to make hit records, too. Following "One Of A Kind Pair Of Fools," Barbara added eight more Top Ten singles through the end of the '80s, including "Happy Birthday Dear Heartache," "Only A Lonely Heart Knows," "Fast Lanes And Country Roads" and "I Wish That I Could Fall In Love Today."

Barbara Mandrell

546

HOLDING HER AND LOVING YOU
EARL THOMAS CONLEY
RCA 13596
Writers: Walt Aldridge, Tommy Brasfield
Producers: Nelson Larkin,
Earl Thomas Conley
November 26, 1983 (1 week)

In 1975, when Earl Thomas Conley and Nelson Larkin still lived in Huntsville, Alabama [see 433—"Fire And Smoke"], they frequently headed to Muscle Shoals to hang out with some of that area's musicians. They formed a friendship with songwriter Tommy Brasfield; despite their camaraderie, Brasfield never pitched a song to Conley until 1983, when he finally felt that he had written one suited to Earl's musical personality.

"Tommy and I had a friend that was actually goin' through that painful situation at that time," co-writer Walt Aldridge notes. "We were talkin' about this guy one night, and tryin' to put ourselves in his place and imagine what it's like to be in that sad situation, and the song was born of it."

When Brasfield took the song to Nashville, Conley and producer Larkin were preparing for a rough recording session. Earl wanted to use his band in the studio, but the night before, things had not progressed well. They decided that evening to use session players the next day, but only after a drawn-out argument. Larkin wasn't particularly thrilled about the songs they planned to cut, and decided to attend the session out of duty.

Larkin was about to head to the studio when Brasfield came into his office, promising a hit for Conley. Larkin tried to put off listening to the demo, but at Tommy's insistence, he put the tape in his cassette player. Nelson didn't like the first song, but he let the tape run while he gathered up material, and after hearing the first few lines of the next track, "Holding Her And Loving You," he knew he had a hit.

Getting Earl to listen wasn't easy. Nelson showed up at the session 15 minutes late, and Earl didn't want to hear anything new. They worked on the other two songs, and after things went smoothly, Conley consented to listen. After hearing just three lines, he decided to cut it.

The musicians played it through just twice, and Earl, who was getting sick, promised to come back and do another vocal when he felt better. Larkin, however, didn't want another performance.

After hitting number one, "Holding Her And Loving You" earned respect for Aldridge and Brasfield from their peers: the Nashville Songwriters Association named it the Song of the Year.

547

A LITTLE GOOD NEWS
ANNE MURRAY
Capitol 5264
Writers: Charlie Black, Rory Bourke,
Tommy Rocco
Producer: Jim Ed Norman
December 3, 1983 (1 week)

Records rarely gain the kind of media attention given "A Little Good News." The song became the topic of newspaper columns, editorials and feature stories, calling attention to Anne Murray, the three songwriters and the negative sway of news. So strong was its message that then-Vice President George Bush used lyrics from "A Little Good News" in a political speech.

Rory Bourke wasn't even supposed to be working with Charlie Black and Tommy Rocco the morning they wrote it, but his scheduled writing partner canceled at the last minute. When he joined the other two, they were watching Bryant Gumbel on "The Today Show."

"It was one of those periods where every story was worse than the one before it, bombings and kidnappings," remembers Black. "We were sitting there with that first cup of coffee and I was saying, 'Golly, have you been listening to the news? I just can't stand it anymore; it hurts to turn on the TV.'"

"It's an interesting song from the standpoint that there was no idea," Bourke suggests. "We got to the end, to where it says, 'Nobody O.D.'d, nobody died in vain.' We looked at each other, and said, 'Gee, we've got to have an idea for a title,' so Charlie said, 'We sure could use a little good news today.' The title was the last thing written."

Once the number was completed, the trio harbored doubts about its commerciality. "We believed in the song," Rocco reports. "We thought we had written a great song, but we didn't think anyone would want to cut it."

Murray raised a few eyebrows, though,

when she accepted it whole-heartedly. Her singles had never embraced social topics before, although some of her early album tracks had. "I just thought it had to be sung," she explains. "My God, was it ever pertinent, and, unfortunately, it's every bit as pertinent today as it was then."

"A Little Good News" proved a blockbuster at the awards shows. The Country Music Association named it Single Record of the Year, and the album also won top honors. In addition, the song was the third to bring Murray a country vocal Grammy, following "Love Song" and "Could I Have This Dance" [see 400].

And now for the bad news: the record was the last in the Bourke/Black string of annual Murray singles [see 431—"Blessed Are The Believers"].

548
TELL ME A LIE
JANIE FRICKIE
Columbia 04091
Writers: Barbara Wyrick, Mickey Buckins
Producer: Bob Montgomery
December 10, 1983 (1 week)

"Tell Me A Lie" developed as the fourth single—and third to hit number one—from Janie Frickie's album *It Ain't Easy*. The song had actually appeared before when Sami Jo cut a pop version at Fame Recording Studios in Muscle Shoals. Entering the *Billboard* Hot 100 on February 9, 1974, the original eventually peaked at number 21 on the MGM South label.

Frickie can thank her husband, Randy Jackson, for keeping the original song fresh in her memory. "Randy had that on his tape of all-time favorite songs that we would carry around and listen to all the time," she says. "We had listened to that song for a long time, and I remembered that song from its earlier days. We still have the original record at home with Sami Jo singing it."

After she first co-wrote the song with Mickey Buckins, Barbara Wyrick moved to Nashville, where she toured as a backing vocalist with Ronnie Milsap and signed as a songwriter with Maypop Music. Five weeks after "Tell Me A Lie" went to number one on the country chart, she scored again when "In My Eyes" [see 553] turned the trick for John Conlee.

The recording sessions for "Tell Me A Lie" also proved quite memorable. During the mid-'70s, Frickie had done an endless stream of jingles in Memphis for the Tanner Agency, resulting in radio station I.D.s and a large number of commercials. One of her co-workers was Judy Rodman [see 679—"Until I Met You"], who sang on all three of Frickie's number one singles from the *It Ain't Easy* album.

"We used to room together in Memphis before I got married," notes Rodman, "and I hadn't worked with Janie in years and years. I didn't sing with her after she left Memphis until I sang with her on that record, so that was a lot of fun."

"We were just striving singers, trying to do what we love most," says Frickie of their Memphis partnership, which included a nightclub stint in a group called Phase II. "We enjoyed it, but you could get in a rut real easily just singing commercials day after day after day. There was a variety, because everything was different, but you had to punch a time clock. It was like a factory."

549
BLACK SHEEP
JOHN ANDERSON
Warner Bros. 29497
Writers: Daniel D. Darst, Robert Altman
Producers: John Anderson, Lou Bradley
December 17, 1983 (1 week)

Many country hopefuls dream of someday working on the Grand Ole Opry, but John Anderson literally worked *on* the Opry. After leaving his native Apopka, Florida, in 1972, he took a string of day jobs in Music City while spending his nights performing downtown on lower Broadway. One of those day jobs included shingling the Opry when the new auditorium was under construction [see 156—"There Won't Be Anymore"].

John signed his first recording contract with the tiny Ace of Hearts label in 1974. The deal yielded no hits, but it did display his knack for picking material. He recorded "What Did I Promise Her Last Night," which eventually became a Top Ten single for Mel Tillis. In 1977, Anderson moved on to Warner Bros.

Even then, development came slowly. Two years passed before "Your Lying Blue Eyes" became John's first bona fide hit. In 1980, he cracked the Top Ten for the first time with "1959." The following year, "I'm Just An Old Chunk Of Coal (But I'm Gonna Be A Diamond Someday)" took him to number four, and he sang that song in his first Opry appearance. Critics considered Anderson a savior for traditional music, the second coming of Lefty Frizzell. Admittedly, however, his first musical influences were rock acts like the Rolling Stones and Steppenwolf.

"I've gotten the chills listening to Merle Haggard and George Jones," he would tell John Milward at *USA Today*. "But one show that really got to me was Alice Cooper's 'Welcome To My Nightmare.'"

By the summer of 1983, Anderson had a total of eight Top Ten singles under his belt, including "I Just Came Home To Count The Memories," "Would You Catch A Falling Star" and "Goin' Down Hill." On August 24, Warner Bros. released "Black Sheep," destined to earn a place as his third chart-topping single. The song had Hollywood ties. It was written by actor/songwriter Danny Darst, who also wrote "Roll On, Big Mama" [see 206], and movie director Robert Altman, associated with the Oscar-winning films *M*A*S*H* and *Nashville*.

Since "Black Sheep," Anderson has mustered only three Top Ten singles: "Let Somebody Else Drive" (a Mothers Against Drunk Driving favorite), the Walt Aldridge-penned "She Sure Got Away With My Heart" and "Honky Tonk Crowd."

Unhappy with previous management agreements, he now handles his own business affairs.

550

HOUSTON (MEANS I'M ONE DAY CLOSER TO YOU)

LARRY GATLIN & THE GATLIN BROTHERS BAND

Columbia 04105
Writer: Larry Gatlin
Producers: Jerry Crutchfield, Larry Gatlin
December 24, 1983 (2 weeks)

Though they started out hot with their Columbia debut [see 358—"All The Gold In California"], Larry Gatlin & The Gatlin Brothers Band suffered through an inconsistent period for the next three and a half years.

Only three records ("Take Me To Your Lovin' Place," "What Are We Doin' Lonesome" and "Sure Feels Like Love") managed to crack *Billboard*'s Top Ten between 1980 and 1983—until the group put together a surprising swing tune, "Houston (Means I'm One Day Closer To You)."

"Actually, I started that song as a ballad," notes Larry. "We'd been singing at the Cheyenne Frontier Days, and I started it and sang part of it at a performance that night. I didn't think much about it, and didn't finish it, and one day, about three days before the Houston Rodeo, my brothers said, 'Why don't you write something about the Houston Rodeo?'

"So I rewrote it. Instead of using Cheyenne, I used Houston, but I thought they wouldn't want to hear anything like a little old ballad. They'd want to hear something like a Texas swing, so I rearranged it, and they absolutely loved it that night at the rodeo. We recorded it, and it went to number one."

The town holds special significance for the oldest Gatlin brother, who attended the University of Houston on a football scholarship. A wide receiver, Larry Gatlin saw little action—he played behind two successive All-Americans, Kenny Hebert and Elmo Wright ("He was the first one that started doing the dance in the end zone"), who later played for the Kansas City Chiefs.

The Gatlins followed "Houston" with "Denver," but on December 10, 1984, Larry checked into the CareUnit of Orange, California, for treatment of drug abuse. After his release in January, the Gatlins played at President Ronald Reagan's Inaugural Ball, and four years later, they returned to play at the Ball for George Bush, who named the Gatlins one of his favorite acts.

The group added three more Top Ten records for Columbia ("The Lady Takes The Cowboy Every Time," "She Used To Be Somebody's Baby" and "Talkin' To The Moon") before signing with the Universal label in 1988.

551

YOU LOOK SO GOOD IN LOVE

GEORGE STRAIT

MCA 52279
Writers: Rory Bourke, Glen Ballard, Kerry Chater
Producer: Ray Baker
January 7, 1984 (1 week)

When George Strait and record producer Ray Baker brought in session singers to overdub background parts on his *Right or Wrong* album, the group included Judy Rodman [see 679—"Until I Met You"], who confided to a couple of her fellow singers that she felt sorry for Strait.

"He had great pitch, and I loved his preciseness," Judy explains. "His voice, on the tape, had a good sound. But I didn't think he'd ever make it, 'cause he was just too shy."

Naturally, that very album became Strait's first gold record and yielded three number one singles. Judy appeared on two of them: "Let's Fall To Pieces Together" [see 584] and "You Look So Good In Love."

Kerry Chater [see 817—"If I Had You"] had introduced West Coast songwriter Glen Ballard to Rory Bourke on a trip to Nashville, and when Bourke headed out to Los Angeles several months later, the three got together to write in the demo studio at MCA Music. Rory suggested "You Look So Good In Love" as a title, and a day later, they returned to the studio to demo the finished song.

"It wasn't really long enough," Rory recalls. "We were goin' in the elevator, and I looked at Kerry. I said, 'Do we dare do something as corny as a recitation in this song?' He says, 'Oh, no, man.' I said, 'Yes,' so Glen and I basically wrote the recitation while Kerry was runnin' down the song to sing it."

Recording the vocal for the demo took 45 minutes. Every time that Chater arrived at the recitation, he burst into laughter.

Record producer Ray Baker was hardly laughing, though, when he heard it. He had listened to 150 tapes in his den at home on a rainy day in Nashville, and within the first 30 seconds of "You Look So Good In Love," he knew he had to cut it. Strait wasn't so sure. He didn't like the recitation, and Baker finally promised him that if after recording it George still wasn't convinced, they could erase the master and "send it to magnetic heaven."

The song survived and became the first single from *Right or Wrong*. George must have changed his mind about it, too—he later bought a racehorse and named it Looksgoodinlove.

552

SLOW BURN

T.G. SHEPPARD

Warner Bros. 29469
Writers: Tommy Rocco, Charlie Black
Producer: Jim Ed Norman
January 14, 1984 (1 week)

Working with producer Buddy Killen, T.G. Sheppard earned eight consecutive number one records from 1981 to 1983. With the release of his first *Greatest Hits* album, he included a brand new track, his remake of Nilsson's "Without You." The original version, which Sheppard promoted [see 214—"Tryin' To Beat The Morning Home"], hit number one on *Billboard*'s Hot 100 for four weeks in 1972, but the remake managed to reach only number 12 on the country chart.

For the first time in five years, Sheppard turned to another producer for his next album, choosing Jim Ed Norman. Jim Ed had played piano on the Eagles' 1975 recording "Lyin' Eyes," and had arranged material on many of their LPs, including *Hotel California* and *Desperado*.

"We were looking for that kind of song where we could do the same Eagles kind of harmonies and instrumentation," says Sheppard, "that real open airiness, and great moving parts with harmonies, and Tommy Rocco and Charlie Black came through."

In fact, Rocco and Black had labored over "Slow Burn" several times, and the song finally clicked when they were up against a deadline for a demo session. They wrote it on a Tuesday, cut the demo on Wednesday, and sent it to Norman on Friday. Jim Ed cut it with Sheppard the following week.

"It was one of those kinds of things like 'Finally' [see 473]," notes T.G. "You know when you've got one. It's a gut feeling. You know it, the musicians know it, they pick better on it. It's a kind of electricity, and everything just falls into place. You can cut it in 30 minutes. It just happens. You don't have to force it or work on it.

"'Slow Burn' was that kind of record. When the count-off started, and the guys started reading the charts, it just fell right in there. I think it was a one-take song."

Though "Slow Burn" was their only number one single together, Norman and Sheppard proved quite successful in their brief, two-album association. Spurred by a line from the movie *Sudden Impact*, Sheppard cut "Make My Day" with actor Clint Eastwood, and followed with three Top Ten singles: "Somewhere Down The Line," "One Owner Heart" and "You're Going Out Of My Mind."

553

IN MY EYES

JOHN CONLEE

MCA 52282
Writer: Barbara Wyrick
Producer: Bud Logan
January 21, 1984 (1 week)

A one-time resident of Muscle Shoals, Alabama, Barbara Wyrick moved to Nashville in the early part of the '80s, and ended up on the road as a back-up singer for Ronnie Milsap. She gained her first number one record as a songwriter on December 10, 1983, when Janie Frickie covered "Tell Me A Lie" [see 548], and six weeks later, she picked up her second chart-topping release with John Conlee's recording of "In My Eyes."

Conlee tabbed the single as the title track to his seventh album, and he dedicated it to his wife, Gale, on the back of the album. "It just seemed to say a lot about our feelings about each other," explains Conlee. "In fact, it was probably my favorite song on the album."

The couple met through Conlee's booking agent, Bill Goodwin. Gale was the sister of Goodwin's wife, and she was introduced to John at one of his concerts. After a year-and-a-half courtship, they married on April 25, 1982. She already had a daughter, and the couple added a girl (in May of 1983) and a boy (in February of 1986). The marriage had little effect on Conlee's work schedule.

"Before I was married, I didn't go out for 300 days a year—on purpose," he says. "I never intended to, and essentially, we set a goal of doing 125 to 130 dates a year. That was the same before I was married and since I was married.

"As far as the way I do it, there hasn't been a lot of change; the way I feel inside, there *has* been a change. I have a desire to be home even more than before, and I was always a homebody.

"That's the biggest negative to me about what I do—not doing shows, but just not being home. If there were that magic button to push to just zap you back to your house at night, and then the next day, zap you back to do the show, that would be ideal."

The Conlees live outside of Nashville on a 32-acre farm, and Conlee has also taken over the financial responsibilities for his parents' 250-acre farm in Kentucky. It's definitely a family business: John's mom handles all the books for both the farms and Conlee's musical activities.

554

THE SOUND OF GOODBYE
CRYSTAL GAYLE

Warner Bros. 29452
Writer: Hugh Prestwood
Producer: Jimmy Bowen
January 28, 1984 (1 week)

Songwriter Hugh Prestwood waited until age 30 to leave El Paso for a musical future in New York. A teacher by day and club performer by night, he moved to the Big Apple when a woman he knew asked him for some songs for a demo she was recording for CBS. Though she was never signed, the producer liked the material, and it was just enough to prod Prestwood into taking the plunge in the early '70s.

Jackie DeShannon and Judy Collins were among the first to cut Hugh's songs in 1979, and Judy later played a role in his first chart-topping country song, "The Sound Of Goodbye." Prestwood wrote it in 1981.

"That was when my second marriage was falling apart," he says, "and that was very much a part of that song. I was having a conversation at some point, and I just remember thinking, 'We're not saying it, but it's like we're saying goodbye.' I wrote down this idea that it sounds like goodbye, and then wrote the song."

It took three years for "The Sound Of Goodbye" to edge onto the airwaves. Prestwood's publishers pitched the song over and over, receiving no interest, but when Hugh went to Nashville, Judy Collins suggested he set up an appointment with producer Jimmy Bowen.

Prestwood gave Bowen a tape with three or four songs, including "The Sound Of Goodbye," but by the time he showed it to Crystal, Bowen couldn't remember where the song had come from. Prestwood's demo had apparently been transferred to another tape, but the "contact" information wasn't.

"It was just a tape with a song on it, and nothing else," says Crystal, "no phone number, nothing. Bowen said, 'Well, let's just record it, and after we record it we'll find out who wrote this thing,' so we did."

Fortunately, engineer Ron Treat later walked into another studio where a friend was working with a copy of the demo. The other engineer told Ron it belonged to Prestwood, and all the paperwork was then finished up, allowing the record's release.

"Everybody was afraid of it at first," remembers Bowen, "They thought it was too strong for country radio. I knew it was country—it was just a little stronger than they were used to."

At the start of 1984, "The Sound Of Goodbye" made a strong showing at number one.

555

SHOW HER
RONNIE MILSAP

RCA 13658
Writer: Mike Reid
Producers: Ronnie Milsap, Tom Collins
February 4, 1984 (1 week)

Following the success of "Inside" [see 505], Mike Reid found Ronnie Milsap was always willing to listen to something he'd written, and it started a string in which Milsap cut eleven Reid singles through the end of the '80s.

"We both like the same old records and the same records that are out there now," Reid explained to *American Songwriter*'s Vernell Hackett in 1984, "the same kind of people. I'm certainly not an artist like Ronnie, but our piano-playing styles are even similar."

Besides sharing Milsap's musical preferences, Reid also benefited from proximity. As a writer for Milsap's publishing company, he had an opportunity to be around Ronnie often, and could create songs that appealed to Milsap's specific interests. Such was the case with the third Reid single.

"I loved the song that James Ingram had out called 'One Hundred Ways' on [Quincy Jones'] *The Dude*," Milsap explains. "I thought, 'God, what a song. If I had a song like that . . .' I was around here in my office building just ravin' about that song, and I'd have 'em play it. Reid was around here, and he said, 'Hell, Milsap, if you like that, I can write somethin' like that.'"

That's exactly what Mike did. After a conversation at home with his wife, Sue, he com-

Ronnie Milsap

THAT'S THE WAY LOVE GOES
MERLE HAGGARD
Epic 04226
Writers: Sanger D. Shafer, Lefty Frizzell
Producers: Merle Haggard, Ray Baker
February 11, 1984 (1 week)

"That's The Way Love Goes" made its second trip to number one exactly ten years after Johnny Rodriguez first turned the trick [see 154] with the very same song. It was one of the last hits written by Lefty Frizzell, who tended to write with "Whitey" Shafer only when a good idea "popped up."

"That was one day we actually set out to write," notes Shafer. "We went up to Dallas Frazier's cabin. I kind of had the first part of it, and I sang it to Lefty, and he said, 'That's the way love goes.' I thought that was great, so we wrote that one. We wrote 'I Never Go Around Mirrors' the same day."

Haggard actually cut "That's The Way Love Goes" four or five times through the years before he finally got a version he liked. He tried different tempos, band line-ups and arrangements, but it never quite came together until he teamed up with producer Ray Baker, whom he had known since the mid-'60s.

Their first session together yielded a number one single, "You Take Me For Granted" [see 521], but Baker was frustrated when subsequent sessions took up huge chunks of time without results. "They're great musicians," Baker says of the Strangers, "but they don't get in a hurry about things, and I was used to getting budgets and being frugal with the money we spent."

Baker persuaded Merle to try using a group of studio musicians, but it took even more persuasion to get him to come in at 10:00 A.M. to record.

"He had an apartment out there [in the Nashville suburbs] on Old Hickory Lake with Leona," notes Baker, "and I said I'd come out and bring him down to the studio. I figured that if I could get him down to the studio in the morning, all these guys that hung around him at night would be asleep and couldn't bug him. Merle likes to have people drop by; he just can't say no to anybody.

"We just went in there and cut, and it was so easy. Even Merle was amazed how great it came off. We cut three records in about two hours and twenty minutes."

posed "Show Her." "We had a little glass of wine and got to talkin': for everyone who's in some sort of relationship—whether it's a marriage or just a meaningful relationship—it's a difficult thing to make 'em work smooth all the time.

"We were talkin' about that, and it occurred to me that our true selves are more what we *do*, not always what we *say*. So out of that, I was sittin' at the piano, and I had that little melody.

"I wasn't sure about an idea like that for a song. It's not necessarily one that jumps out and says, 'Write me, write me.' It was not a great title, but I think the song worked."

"Show Her" reached number one on February 4, 1984, exactly one year after "Inside" first took Reid to the top.

One of them was "That's The Way Love Goes," which brought Haggard his very first Grammy for Best Country Vocal Performance by a Male.

557
DON'T CHEAT IN OUR HOMETOWN
RICKY SKAGGS
Sugar Hill 04245
Writers: Ray Pennington, Roy E. Marcum
Producer: Ricky Skaggs
February 18, 1984 (1 week)

"The worst numbers you can have is number 21, number 11 and number two," suggests Ricky Skaggs. "They're the dreaded numbers of life."

Ricky refers to chart numbers. When a record peaks at one of those numbers, it has narrowly missed the Top 20, Top Ten, or number one.

Such was the case for Ricky on October 29, 1983. He reached number two with "You've Got A Lover," but had the misfortune of being behind "Islands In The Stream" [see 543], which stayed at the top for two weeks.

"'Lover' was so destined to go number one," Ricky sighs, "but 'Lover' just could not keep the momentum and go to number one after [Kenny and Dolly tied it up]. That just broke my heart, but that's kind of one of those that got away."

"Don't Cheat In Our Hometown," released just ten days later, didn't get away. Skaggs had heard the Stanley Brothers' version years before on an album on King Records. During his tenure with Emmylou Harris' Hot Band, Ricky played it several times for artists like Waylon Jennings and Willie Nelson in hotel rooms, when the musicians were hanging out in the middle of concert tours.

On another occasion, the Hot Band ran into Kris Kristofferson and Rita Coolidge at a television taping in Germany, and once again, they ordered up food and traded songs in the motel. Kristofferson responded positively to "Don't Cheat In Our Hometown," and Ricky felt that if a songwriter of Kristofferson's stature liked it, he should consider recording it.

Skaggs *did* record it, with the Hot Band, and made it the title track of an album on Sugar Hill Records, although it took several years for the project to be released [see 571—"Honey (Open That Door)"].

"I've never been one to do cheatin' and drinkin' songs," Ricky admits, "and I don't really consider this song a cheating song. It's sayin' 'Don't cheat,' and I guess the guy in the song really hit home. I got to thinkin' about what it would be like to know your wife had run off with your best friend, and how he would have to look his friends in the eye in a little small town where everybody knows what's goin' on. I had a tender spot in my heart for the guy in that song."

558
STAY YOUNG
DON WILLIAMS
MCA 52310
Writers: Benny Gallagher, Graham Lyle
Producers: Don Williams, Garth Fundis
February 25, 1984 (1 week)

"I believe in songs and I don't like to do anything to a song other than put a frame around it," Don Williams once told Nashville writer Kelly Delaney. "Anything I feel is a distraction from the song, I just try to avoid. And so I try to have songs that I feel are good enough that I don't have to come up with a super slick instrumentation to make it happen."

That very basic approach worked well for Don on his 1983 album *Yellow Moon*. The first single, "Love Is On A Roll" [see 526], took him to number one on July 2. Four weeks later, "Nobody But You" made its first appearance on the *Billboard* country chart, finally peaking on October 22 at number two, just behind "Lady Down On Love" [see 542]. The album's third release, "Stay Young," brought Williams the fifteenth chart-topping single of his solo career.

The record resulted, in part, from a corporate decision by Almo/Irving Music to open a Nashville division in the early '80s. Producer Garth Fundis now runs his own operation out of Almo/Irving's office, but in 1983, the company gave him "Stay Young."

"They had the West Memphis catalog and they had Rondor Music out of England," notes Fundis. "David Conrad is the fellow who was runnin' the office, so he didn't need to sign writers for a couple of years. He had all these great copyrights to work with.

"He'd go through and find things that might work for artists in town, and that was one of the first songs he brought me. It was just one of those neat little songs that had a good message to it: keep goin', don't slow down."

"Stay Young" represented the first number one country single for Graham Lyle, a British songwriter. Graham was formerly with McGuinness Flint, a band that hit the *Billboard* Hot 100 once in 1971, with "When I'm Dead And Gone." During the '70s, he teamed up with Benny Gallagher, also from McGuinness Flint, as a pop recording act. However, the twosome had better luck as writers (they penned the title track of Art Garfunkel's *Breakaway* album). Lyle has gone on to write a string of Tina Turner hits, including "What's Love Got To Do With It," "Typical Male" and "We Don't Need Another Hero." Other country successes include "Straight To The Heart" [see 709], "Joe Knows How To Live" [see 786] and "Maybe Your Baby's Got The Blues" [see 745].

559

WOKE UP IN LOVE
EXILE
Epic 04247
Writer: J.P. Pennington
Producer: Buddy Killen
March 3, 1984 (1 week)

When Exile first emerged on the country charts during 1983, the band had already notched a number one pop single five years earlier. "Kiss You All Over" spent an entire month at the top of *Billboard*'s Hot 100, beginning September 30, 1978, and the song finished up as one of the Top Five pop records of the entire year.

"Kiss You All Over" sold more than four million copies worldwide, but a year later, the group was on a downhill slide. Lead vocalist Jimmy Stokely left the group, and Exile charted only two more singles. "I think the song was so big that it just sort of did us in," guitarist J.P. Pennington said later.

Two years after their ascension to the top of the pop world, Exile struggled just to find work. They played locally in their hometown of Lexington, Kentucky, losing almost all contact with the record industry in Los Angeles. The one man who retained faith in the band was manager Jim Morey, a partner in Gallin Morey Associates—the same company that handled Dolly Parton.

Morey suggested to Nashville producer Buddy Killen that he work with the band, and Killen jumped at the chance. At one time, he had cut "Kiss You All Over" in a session with Bill Anderson and had remained a fan of the group.

Killen brought Exile to his downtown Nashville club, The Stockyard, on several occasions, to showcase the band for local record executives. It took a year before CBS division head Rick Blackburn signed the group to Epic.

Their first single, "The High Cost Of Leaving," entered *Billboard*'s country chart on August 20, 1983, eventually peaking at number 27. They followed up with "Woke Up In Love."

"J.P. has said that he had that title for several years," notes bass player Sonny Lemaire. "He couldn't get anything going with it, and one day, all of a sudden, it just came to him, the idea of how to write the song—basically, a music hook and everything. He was out driving, he said he went home and completed the song in about half an hour."

Pennington's 30 minutes of labor eventually paid dividends when "Woke Up In Love" brought Exile its first number one country single.

560

GOING GOING GONE
LEE GREENWOOD
MCA 52322
Writer: Jan Crutchfield
Producer: Jerry Crutchfield
March 10, 1984 (1 week)

"That was the last of the slow songs," says Lee Greenwood of his second number one single, "Going Going Gone." Actually, Greenwood continued to record ballads even after that single, but he consciously made a break from the dramatic arrangement that characterized "Going Going Gone" as well as earlier hits like "It Turns Me Inside Out" [see 544—"Somebody's Gonna Love You"] and "Ring On Her Finger, Time On Her Hands."

"It was the third Jan Crutchfield hit we had," notes Greenwood, who was born October 27, 1942. "'It Turns Me Inside Out' was the first, and 'She's Lying' was the second. He also wrote 'Statue Of A Fool' [see 35] for another Scorpio named Jack *Greene*. 'It Turns Me Inside Out' was his next big hit with Lee *Green*-wood, so there was kind of a similarity there.

"Jan came into the office, and played it for me on his guitar. He's this big coal-miner type of guy—real rough-looking—but he has such a tender way of putting things."

When Crutchfield first played the song live for Greenwood, he punctuated parts of the verse by slamming his guitar, and after some explanation, he conveyed an image of a loud, heavily-orchestrated rhythm that would contrast with the easy nature of the melody. "We tried to capture that feeling," offers Greenwood, "and I think we did. Maybe that made the difference."

As "Going Going Gone" drove into the Top Ten, two other significant events occurred for Lee. On February 24, 1984, *Somebody's Gonna Love You* became his first gold record, and four days later, as Joan Rivers and Boy George exchanged barbs on the national broadcast, Greenwood grabbed the Grammy award for Top Country Vocal Performance by a Male, with his performance on "I.O.U."

The follow-up to "Going Going Gone" failed to repeat as a number one record, but it proved just as important in many other ways. Greenwood wrote "God Bless The U.S.A." in the wave of patriotism that followed when a Soviet plane downed a South Korean flight on September 1, 1983, killing 269 people. His anthemic performance achieved a number seven peak, and also earned Song of the Year honors from the Country Music Association.

Lee Greenwood

561

ELIZABETH

THE STATLER BROTHERS

Mercury 814881
Writer: Jimmy Fortune
Producer: Jerry Kennedy
March 17, 1984 (1 week)

Elizabeth Taylor occupies an influential position in American culture: as a headlining actress, a leading combatant in the fight against AIDS and a woman with her own perfume. Taylor also inspired the Statler Brothers' second number one single—with a movie she starred in 28 years earlier.

The Statlers are ardent fans of the cinema, a fact that rings true in their songs "The Movies" and "Whatever Happened To Randolph Scott," and they often unwind from performances by watching old films on their tour bus. On one occasion, they picked the 1956 film

Giant, starring Rock Hudson, James Dean and Taylor. Group member Jimmy Fortune latched onto the actress' first name, and, inspired by the beauty of the word, wrote a song to match.

Fortune was the newest member of the group, having joined after ill health forced Lew DeWitt off the road. DeWitt suffered from Crohn's disease, a rare condition aggravated in his case by the stress of constant touring. He took time off the road in 1982, with Fortune replacing him temporarily, and DeWitt rejoined the group at the *Music City News* awards on June 7. It proved to be his final appearance with the Statlers, as he announced his retirement, and Fortune was named to replace him.

"We were looking for someone who would fit in with us personally," says Don Reid, "and someone who would fit in with us professionally. We wanted to enhance the sound—not change the sound, because we had fans with us that we didn't want to go off and leave, of course. We feel like Jimmy fit the bill there, and it was just a very smooth transition from the very first."

"They had to go through a lot of press conferences because of [the change]," DeWitt told Donna DeLaney of *Country Song Roundup*. "I felt really bad about it, but there was nothing I could do. My doctor told me it was either [quit] or I was going to be in a lot of trouble."

After several years of recuperation, DeWitt recorded a solo album in 1985. Crohn's disease claimed Lew's life during his sleep on August 15, 1990, at his home in Waynesboro, Virginia.

562
ROLL ON (EIGHTEEN WHEELER)
ALABAMA
RCA 13716
Writer: Dave Loggins
Producers: Harold Shedd, Alabama
March 24, 1984 (1 week)

Many hailed it for its relationship with the George Orwell novel, but the year 1984 also marked the 100th birthday for a very special dog. "Nipper" went down in history for his interest in the gramophone. His English owner, Francis Barraud, took note of Nipper's fascination with the talking machine, and painted a true-to-life scene of the dog cocking its ear in front of the contraption, calling it "His Master's Voice." Four years after he buried the dog on Eden Street in Kingston, Barraud sold the painting to a London executive. It was spotted in his office by Eldridge Johnson, of the Victor Talking Machine Company, and Nipper quickly became associated with Victor Records, and later, RCA.

The centennial of that world-renowned pup started in extraordinary fashion for RCA. On the first Thursday of the year, the company shipped a single from its best-selling act, Alabama. The same month, the label also rolled out a million copies of the *Roll On* album, making it the first Nashville album "shipped platinum."

The title track satisfied Alabama's desire for a "truckin'" song. With five buses and four semis hauling the group's road show, they were in constant contact via CB radio with drivers who asked them to cut something specifically for truckers. Alabama decided to oblige them, but they put additional restrictions on it. They wanted something with a positive message, possibly even a connection

with family. The first song they decided to record for the album was a Dave Loggins composition called "Wheels" [see 756].

"We had that song on hold for a long time," reports producer Harold Shedd. "We had it on hold when 'Roll On (Eighteen Wheeler)' [another Loggins song] came along, and then we opted for 'Eighteen Wheeler' instead of the other song."

Alabama had "Roll On" for a year before they finally released it, doing a huge amount of production for the final track. They recorded a truck engine for the intro outside of The Music Mill early one morning, and ended the record with a unique echo effect. In addition to the album cut, four different versions were released for radio.

Whichever version radio stations settled on, they couldn't go wrong. The hopeful message of "Roll On" easily drove it to number one by the end of March.

563
LET'S STOP TALKIN' ABOUT IT
JANIE FRICKIE
Columbia 04317
Writers: Rory Bourke, Rafe VanHoy,
Deborah Allen
Producer: Bob Montgomery
March 31, 1984 (1 week)

"Let's Stop Talkin' About It" was one of two songs written during the course of a week by Rory Bourke, Rafe VanHoy and Deborah Allen, in their first trial as a songwriting trio. The other song, "Baby I Lied," proved a monster record when Allen cut it on her own.

Had Bourke done things his way, "Let's Stop Talkin'" might never have been written in the first place. The idea initially came from him, but it became apparent immediately that the song didn't fit the traditional country mold.

"All of our material kind of leans toward the progressive side anyway," says VanHoy of his longtime partnership with Allen, "and we wanted to do things that weren't so typically country. It felt a little more pop than Rory was comfortable with—not because he didn't feel good about writing it, but he hadn't had a lot of luck getting songs like that recorded.

"Deborah kept saying it was a hit title, and Rory was dragging his feet. Rory said, 'I'll you right now, if you want to do it, we'll do it, but I think we're wasting our time.'"

Allen then made a bet with Bourke, promising the record would go to number one. If she was right, Bourke owed her and VanHoy a dinner at Nashville's expensive Julian's Restaurant; if Bourke was right, they would treat him.

Allen recorded both "Let's Stop Talkin' About It" and "Baby I Lied" under a contract with Capitol Records. The label released neither, and dropped her from the roster. Bob Montgomery was impressed with "Baby I Lied," and tried to get rights to record that song.

"They were kind of holding on to it," Montgomery remembers, "because they had a deal cooking with RCA. They also had 'Let's Stop Talkin' About It', and I wrangled that one out of them."

Eventually, RCA bought the master to "Baby I Lied," which became a number four country single for Allen, crossing over to number 26 on *Billboard*'s Hot 100. She also went to number two with her follow-up, "I've Been Wrong Before," charting at the same time as Janie Frickie's version of "Let's Stop Talkin'," which peaked at number one.

"We never collected on our dinner with Rory," says VanHoy of the earlier wager, "but I'm sure if we pressed him, he would oblige."

564
DON'T MAKE IT EASY FOR ME
EARL THOMAS CONLEY
RCA 13702
Writers: Earl Thomas Conley,
Randy Scruggs
Producers: Nelson Larkin,
Earl Thomas Conley
April 7, 1984 (1 week)

With the release of *Blue Pearl* [see 433—"Fire And Smoke"], critics labeled Earl Thomas Conley's music as "thinking man's country." Never one to stay in one place for long, he purposely expanded on the introspective angle for the *Don't Make It Easy for Me* album, masking meanings in a musical and lyrical sheen that de-emphasized the personal nature of his work.

The messages still existed, however, in a number of the songs, most notably the title track. Conley wrote it about personal challenges.

"A lot of us make it hard for ourselves, just

for the challenge of it," he explains. "Some people will say, for instance [they want to be rich], and yet at the same time have a deep fear of having money, and a deep unworthiness about havin' money, so that's a blockage right there. You can't have anything if you've got a counter-belief that blocks it. So this song is about the challenges of life, and we painted it into a love relationship with a girl."

Changing the storyline for *commercial* reasons proved a personal breakthrough for Conley, since he combatted his own personal fears about money and success. They stemmed from his youth in Portsmouth, Ohio, when he felt degraded and humiliated by living in poverty.

While casting aside that psychological stone, Conley also tested the limits of the country format, as he had done earlier in "Somewhere Between Right And Wrong" [see 499]. Be-

E.T. Conley

tween its throbbing bassline and searing guitars, "Don't Make It Easy For Me" simply rocked out—and rightly so, since Conley imagined himself moving on stage with his guitar as he wrote it. In fact, it rocked so much that RCA asked a Nashville station to test the first pressing, and had the record toned down before it was released.

"As far as I'm concerned, we lost some of the feeling, some of the drive," Earl laments. "It kind of lost some of the energy when we had to quiet it down so much for country radio."

Apparently, there was quite enough left. "Don't Make It Easy For Me" became Conley's fifth number one single.

565

THANK GOD FOR THE RADIO

THE KENDALLS

Mercury 818056
Writers: Max D. Barnes,
Robert John Jones
Producer: Blake Mevis
April 14, 1984 (1 week)

It's been called "a blend that's never bland." The Kendalls introduced their unique family harmonies in a series of singles that were unusual for a father/daughter team—cheatin' records [see 295—"Heaven's Just A Sin Away" and 327—"Sweet Desire"]. Royce and Jeannie tired of temptation, though, and eventually put out the word to Nashville's songwriters not to send them any more songs about two-timing romance.

Though occasional cheatin' themes snuck through, the Kendalls started rounding out their repertoire with successive releases, and through 1982, a total of ten singles reached the Top Ten. Among them: "I'm Already Blue," Dolly Parton's "Put It Off Until Tomorrow," "Teach Me To Cheat" and "If You're Waiting On Me (You're Backing Up)."

They recorded the latter two in 1981, after leaving Ovation Records for Mercury. Their career stalled, though, and they went two years without another hit. In an experimental move, the Kendalls recorded their 1983 album *Movin' Train* with three different producers. Brian Ahern cut four tracks in California, while additional sessions were directed by Jerry Gillespie in Muscle Shoals and Blake Mevis in Nashville.

Included was "Thank God For The Radio,"

written by Max D. Barnes and former Ovation employee Robert John Jones. "He had the idea, 'Thank God For The Radio,'" says Barnes, "and we talked about the fact that there was 'Thank God For Kids.' It was in a different direction and everything. But we didn't think we were gonna get a record on that, because the Oaks had had that similar title a year or two before."

They almost didn't get a cut with the Kendalls, but Royce and Jeannie insisted on it, even though none of their producers were interested.

"Finally," says Royce, "we were doin' our last three songs in Nashville, and Blake Mevis tried to get us to do some other song. Come to find out, somebody else had just cut it and it was on their album, so we didn't want to cut that. I said, 'Well, we're gonna do this song,' so we just laid it down. I had told Jeannie I thought it was a number one song, and I was right on that particular one."

The *Billboard* charts bore that out in the spring of 1984.

566

THE YELLOW ROSE

JOHNNY LEE WITH LANE BRODY

Warner Bros. 29375
Writer: Public Domain
Producer: Jimmy Bowen
April 21, 1984 (1 week)

Johnny Lee was in the process of his divorce from Charlene Tilton [see 450—"Bet Your Heart On Me"] when his work with Lane Brody brought his fourth number one single.

Brody had been Lee's labelmate in 1977, when he cut a number 15 hit on "Country Party." A native of Racine, Wisconsin, Lane first made waves in Chicago, where she sang jingles for McDonald's, Juicy Fruit and Kentucky Fried Chicken. She also worked as a model, turning down an offer to be a *Playboy* centerfold.

Following releases on the GRT label, Brody met entertainment executive Steve Wax, who became her manager. Wax got her a guest shot on "Taxi," as well as vocal work in the TV movies *Country Gold* and *Gift of Life*. In 1983, she earned a number 15 country hit with "Over You," from the movie *Tender Mercies*.

In the meantime, the producers of a new NBC night-time soap, "The Yellow Rose," picked Lane to sing the theme song for the program. Wax then asked Brody who she would like as a vocal partner, and, after first selecting a former partner named Thom Bresh, she suggested Johnny Lee.

"I just happened to be in L.A.," Johnny remembers. "When it came down to do it, I had to leave right after the session and fly someplace to do a concert that night."

NBC wanted the theme to appear on an album, and Brody and Lee agreed, but only if they could rewrite the lyrics. Neither took credit for their part, and they worked on it down to the wire, taking time out from a recording session while producer Jimmy Bowen met elsewhere with Conway Twitty, whom he was also recording.

"I ended up sitting on Conway's Gremlin in the parking lot of the studio, trying to rewrite my part of the song," recalls Lee, "and Lane was at the other end of the studio, rewriting hers. We finally, within an hour or so, had the lyrics down, and we cut it."

At first, it was slated as the "B" side of Lee's solo single, "Say When," but Brody had already sparked some interest by talking with disk jockeys about the song. Once the label realized that fact, Warner Bros. began working "The Yellow Rose." It peaked at number one just three weeks before the TV program's final episode aired.

567
RIGHT OR WRONG
GEORGE STRAIT
MCA 52337
Writers: Arthur Sizemore, Haven Gillespie, Paul Biese
Producer: Ray Baker
April 28, 1984 (1 week)

When Merle Haggard released his 1970 album *A Tribute to the Best Damn Fiddle Player in the World*, he turned an 18-year-old Texas boy named George Strait on to the music of Bob Wills. Combining honky-tonk styles with the big-band sound of the day, Wills became "The King of Western Swing," and one of his own chestnuts pulled Strait out of a jam in 1983— 50 years after Wills organized his Texas Playboys.

Having recorded his first two albums with producer Blake Mevis, Strait decided to make a change in the midst of the third. He scrapped the project and started over again with Ray Baker, but they faced a deadline problem.

Lane Brody & Johnny Lee

MCA had already released a fourth single from *Straight from the Heart* [see 535—"A Fire I Can't Put Out"] and wanted the new album quickly.

They selected a dozen songs for the project and spent two intense days recording it at Nashville's Woodland Sound Studio. With nine behind them, they needed only one more, but discarded the remaining three. They had only 20 minutes left on their final session, and Baker suggested they try a song that he had seen George play on a live date: Wills' "Right Or Wrong."

"There was a guy on the session named Johnny Gimble, a great fiddle player," says Baker, "and I knew that Johnny used to play with Bob Wills. He was right in the middle of all that Western swing stuff. I gave Johnny the freedom to do what he wanted to. He was just great on that fantastic intro and turnaround. I think he had as much to do as anybody with making that record a hit."

Once Gimble (named Instrumentalist of the Year by the Country Music Association in 1975, 1986, and 1987) taught the song to the rest of the musicians, they required only two takes to get the final, short (2:02) performance. With the album's basic tracks completed, Strait headed out of the studio to his waiting tour bus, and hit the road with his Ace in the Hole Band. "Right Or Wrong" emerged as the title track and second single from the album, debuting at number 61 on the *Billboard* country chart on February 11, 1984. It took a dozen weeks to reach the chart pinnacle.

568
I GUESS IT NEVER HURTS TO HURT SOMETIMES
THE OAK RIDGE BOYS
MCA 52342
Writer: Randy Vanwarmer
Producer: Ron Chancey
May 5, 1984 (1 week)

Five years before the Oak Ridge Boys recorded his song "I Guess It Never Hurts To Hurt Sometimes," Randy Vanwarmer enjoyed a brief fling in the Top Ten of the *Billboard* Hot 100. He reached number four with his ballad "Just When I Needed You Most" in 1979. Subsequent singles, however, failed to even come close.

"After that first record, I kind of wanted to move away from that soft thing a little bit," Randy says. "I was young, not real experienced in the business, and I've since learned that if you do something well, that's what you should do. It took me about eight or nine years to realize that. I really feel that 'Just When I Needed You Most,' if it were released today, would be a country record."

"Just When I Needed You Most," in fact, has gained airplay on some country stations as an "oldie," but his introduction into the market came through the Oak Ridge Boys. Vanwarmer had written "I Guess It Never Hurts To Hurt Sometimes" one Christmas Eve for his father, who had died several years before. He recorded it on one of his albums, but it never emerged as a single.

"My wife sent it to [then-MCA chief] Jim Foglesong," Vanwarmer recalls, "and he gave it to [Oaks producer] Ron Chancey. Ron played it on his boat that summer, and his wife fell in love with that song. When they went in to make the next Oaks record, she asked if the Oaks would cut it just for her, just to play on the boat, so Ron kind of said, 'Okay.'"

Of course, the Oaks liked the song as well, and they cut a version very similar to Vanwarmer's. "I Guess It Never Hurts To Hurt Sometimes" reached number one during the spring of 1984, and later that year, Cal Smith called the Oaks and asked them to sing the song at Ernest Tubb's funeral, as per E. T.'s last request.

The song spurred Vanwarmer to move in 1985 to Nashville, where he later signed as an artist with 16th Avenue Records. He has written several more hits for others as well, including the Oaks' 1988 release "Bridges And Walls" and Michael Johnson's "I Will Whisper Your Name."

569
TO ALL THE GIRLS I'VE LOVED BEFORE
JULIO IGLESIAS & WILLIE NELSON
Columbia 04217
Writers: Albert Hammond, Hal David
Producers: Richard Perry, Albert Hammond
May 12, 1984 (2 weeks)

In 1989, Joel Whitburn's Record Research cited Willie Nelson for a most unusual accomplishment: he's the country artist who has hit the *Billboard* country chart with the most vocal partners. Willie charted duets with 20 different partners (although two, Leon Russell and Hank Wilson, were the same person [see 352—"Heartbreak Hotel"]), including Waylon Jennings, Kris Kristofferson, Ray Price and Mary Kay Place. His most unusual pairing teamed Willie with Latin superstar Julio Iglesias.

"My wife, Connie, and I were in London last fall, and we heard Julio on the radio," Willie told Russell Shaw in *Billboard* during 1984. "I liked his music immediately. Connie suggested that I record with him, and I thought it was a good idea."

"I phoned [manager] Mark Rothbaum," Nelson further elaborated in his autobiography, "and said, 'Try to find out who Julio Iglesias is and see if he wants to cut a record with me.' Mark found Julio in Los Angeles. Julio said, sure, he'd like to do a song with me. I didn't know Julio was selling more records at that time than anybody in the world."

Pairing a Latin romantic with a Texan redneck was hardly an easy task. Producer Richard Perry had brought Albert Hammond in as an associate producer, and Hammond found the perfect song in his own catalog. He had written "To All The Girls I've Loved Before" with Hal David in 1976, originally intended for Frank Sinatra. Iglesias liked it, and took it to Nelson's Austin studio, where they cut the vocal track in about two hours. After the session, Willie and Julio shared dinner, including two bottles of Spanish wine. Julio then took the tape back to Los Angeles, where he worked further to improve his English on the final product.

"To All The Girls" was an overwhelming success. It spent two weeks atop *Billboard*'s country chart, and went to number five on the Hot 100, selling a million copies in the process. The Country Music Association named Willie & Julio the Vocal Duo of the Year, and the Academy of Country Music named the record the Single of the Year. In September of 1984, Julio placed five titles on *Billboard*'s pop album chart simultaneously.

Originally, Columbia pressed their remake of "As Time Goes By," from Willie's *Without a Song* album, as a follow-up, although it was pulled after a few copies were shipped to radio. Willie and Julio didn't hook up again until their duet on "Spanish Eyes," from Nelson's 1988 album *What a Wonderful World*.

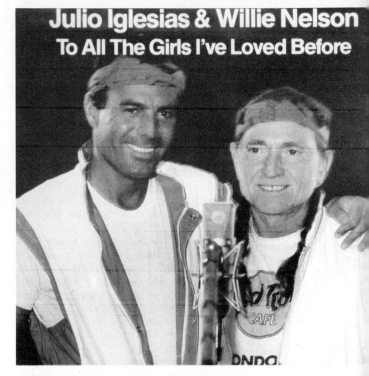

Julio Iglesias & Willie Nelson
To All The Girls I've Loved Before

570

AS LONG AS I'M ROCKIN' WITH YOU
JOHN CONLEE
MCA 52351
Writers: Kieran Kane, Bruce Channel
Producer: Bud Logan
May 4, 1984 (1 week)

Born October 7, 1949, in the Queens borough of New York City, Kieran Kane grew up in Mount Vernon and traveled upstate often as a youngster. He frequented rodeos and heard plenty of country music on jukeboxes, but it was his brother who turned him on to bluegrass when he was 13.

After high school, Kieran spent a couple of years studying at Boston University and Suffolk University, but he gave up his education to devote more time to music. He opened for acts like the Steve Miller Band and the Flying Burrito Brothers, and in 1971, he moved to Los Angeles, where he formed a band called Knuckles.

Kane struggled through L.A.'s joints for several years, until he met Deborah Allen at one of his shows. She and then-boyfriend Rafe

VanHoy suggested he move to Nashville, and when a friend decided to move to Music City in 1979, Kane went with him.

It didn't take long for Kieran to find success in Nashville. He began playing mandolin on many of Hank Williams, Jr.'s records (most notably "Texas Women" [see 418]), but he earned even more acclaim as a songwriter. He penned a 1980 Johnny Duncan single, "Play Another Slow Song," and earned a number one record when Janie Frickie cut "Don't Worry 'Bout Me Baby" [see 477]. An Alabama album cut, "Gonna Have A Party," earned significant airplay in 1982, and the prior year, Kane cut one solo album, which included two Top 20 hits: "You're The Best" and "It's Who You Love."

His second number one single came with "As Long As I'm Rockin' With You," a song first included on his solo album. He co-wrote the song rather quickly with Bruce Channel one summer morning while his wife prepared their lunch. Kane wanted it released as a single, but Elektra didn't feel it was the best material available. Three years later, John Conlee covered it successfully.

"I loved the sentiment in that song," Conlee notes. "I guess everybody who has a relationship and gets married hopes that it is forever, and that you will share the young life and the rocking chair days, and that's what I've got on my mind, too."

Two years later, Kane joined with Jamie O'Hara to form the O'Kanes [see 722—"Can't Stop My Heart From Loving You"].

571
HONEY (OPEN THAT DOOR)
RICKY SKAGGS
Sugar Hill 04394
Writer: Mel Tillis
Producer: Ricky Skaggs
June 2, 1984 (1 week)

Though Ricky Skaggs first earned national prominence with the 1981 album *Waitin' for the Sun to Shine* [see 480—"I Don't Care"], he already had eight albums behind him when he signed with Epic Records, including two albums that paired him with his friend, Keith Whitley, on Rebel Records. He was also working on another, *Don't Cheat in Our Hometown* [see 557], which proved instrumental in his Epic deal.

"[*Don't Cheat*] was cut for Sugar Hill," Ricky explains. "I had a two-album deal with Sugar Hill, and I was still workin' with Emmylou Harris when I did the album. When I was tryin' to get a major deal, I played some of these tracks for CBS, tellin' 'em, 'Look, you can't have it. This is for another label, but when I'm finished with this album, I'm free.'

"I played 'Honey (Open That Door),' 'Don't Cheat In Our Hometown' and 'Don't Step Over An Old Love' (a duet with Dolly Parton), so the strength of that album, and *Sweet Temptation*, is really what got me signed at CBS. 'Honey (Open That Door)' was one of the keys to getting me signed."

Prior to the Epic deal, Skaggs finished eight of the tracks—including "Honey"—at Emmylou's house, with Brian Ahern's Enactron Truck [see 313—"Two More Bottles Of Wine"]. Skaggs primarily used members and ex-members of the Hot Band, plus the Whites. The Sugar Hill agreement, however, contained no contractual deadline, so before he finished the album, he recorded *Waitin' for the Sun to Shine*. Ricky then added two more tracks, "Uncle Pen" [see 590] and "A Wound Time Can't Erase," while simultaneously cutting *Highways & Heartaches* in Nashville.

Even as Epic began to release tracks from *Highways*, the label entered negotiations with Sugar Hill for rights to *Don't Cheat in Our Hometown*, and after about eighteen months of dickering, they agreed to put it out under a joint Sugar Hill/Epic label.

"Honey," an old Webb Pierce tune that Skaggs picked up from Hank DeVito, provided Mel Tillis his first number one single as a songwriter in a dozen years [see 109—"I Ain't Never"]. Between the song's 1979 recording date and its February 28, 1984, release date, Skaggs took back-up singer Sharon White as his marital honey, on August 4, 1981.

572
SOMEDAY WHEN THINGS ARE GOOD
MERLE HAGGARD
Epic 04402
Writers: Leona Williams, Merle Haggard
Producers: Merle Haggard, Ray Baker
June 9, 1984 (1 week)

"I appreciate everything Merle Haggard did, like listen to my songs," says his ex-wife, Leona Williams. "I never played him very many, but what I did play for him I wanted to be real good. It was one of my dreams to write a song good enough for him to record."

Merle cut several of her songs, and the two that were released as singles both reached number one: "You Take Me For Granted" [see 521] and "Someday When Things Are Good." The latter, in fact, was recorded during the same three-hour session that yielded his previous number one record, "That's The Way Love Goes" [see 556].

"Someday When Things Are Good" reflected Leona's inner state at the time. Her on-again, off-again marriage to Merle had been a heavy burden, and her two sons had been uprooted several times and enrolled in different school systems. She became frustrated both as a mother and a wife.

"I had left so many times that I finally got to the point where I said, 'I'm not gonna leave anymore,'" she explains. "I had Noel, Merle's son, and I was trying to keep him straight, and also Marty, he would come stay with us some, and I kept thinking, 'Gosh, someday when things are good I'm gonna leave.' I kept writing this down. We had this big bathroom, and I had my pen and my notepad there. Of all places, I started writing it there."

A few weeks later, she previewed the song for Haggard on the bus before a show in Fresno. "Merle and I were getting along that day and everything was great," she recalls. "I hated to play it for him because I was afraid he'd read between the lines, but he really liked it."

As the song promised ("Someday when things are good, I'm gonna leave you"), Leona left and filed for divorce in 1983. A year later, the song went to number one.

Since that time, Williams has moved back to Vienna, Missouri, where she lives on a farm with her husband, Dave Kirby—a former member of Haggard's band, the Strangers.

573
I GOT MEXICO
EDDY RAVEN
RCA 13746
Writers: Eddy Raven, Frank J. Myers
Producers: Eddy Raven, Paul Worley
June 16, 1984 (1 week)

Eddy Raven earned his first number one single in the summer of 1984, and it only took fourteen years to do it!

Raven moved from Louisiana to Nashville in the summer of 1970, and songwriting, rather than recording, was his primary objective. As it turned out, writing also kept food on his table throughout most of the period. Don Gant got him started at Acuff-Rose Music, and one of Raven's happiest moments came when Roy Acuff cut his song "Back In The Country."

Raven wrote a number of Top Five singles, including "Touch The Morning" and "Country Green," for Don Gibson; and "Sometimes I Talk In My Sleep," for Randy Cornor. He first hit the *Billboard* country chart as a recording artist in 1974, and steadily churned out singles throughout the decade on a variety of labels. Until 1981's *Desperate Dreams*, however, he was unable to crack the Top 20; with that album, four singles did the trick.

Raven recorded another album for Elektra Records, but it was never released. Instead, he took a year-and-a-half hiatus to realign his management, establish his own publishing company and gain a new recording contract with more "creative control" (Raven was released from his Elektra contract when Elektra and Warner Bros. merged in January of 1983). In the meantime, the Oak Ridge Boys scored a Top Five single by recording his "Thank God For Kids."

Eddy wrote a number of songs during his time off, and "I Got Mexico" appropriately offered a vacation-like message.

"'I Got Mexico' was one of the songs I wrote while I was off, and I wrote that specifically to be my 'comeback' song, I guess," says Eddy. "A lot of those thoughts went through my mind while I was there. You daydream a lot.

"It's just a song I wanted to write about my fantasy to be there, and get away from it all. It was an escapist song. Everybody at one time in their life wants to tell society and the powers that be exactly what that song says: 'I don't need you/I got Mexico.'"

"Eddy played me the song at his house in Hendersonville," recalls producer Paul Worley. "I knew from the minute he played that song for me it was a number one record."

574
WHEN WE MAKE LOVE
ALABAMA
RCA 13763
Writers: Troy Seals, Mentor Williams
Producers: Harold Shedd, Alabama
June 23, 1984 (1 week)

The last song that Alabama recorded for the *Roll On* [see 562] album came from a songwriter new to Nashville. Mentor Williams had first earned attention with "Drift Away," recorded by Dobie Gray as a pop hit in 1973. Narvel Felts cut the same song as a country record that same year, taking it to number eight in *Billboard*. Williams returned to the country chart when Alabama cut "When We Make Love."

"Mentor had just moved to town," recalls co-writer Troy Seals. "He'd been in L.A. for several years, and had produced Dobie, and 'Drift Away,' and we'd become friends. He'd just moved to Nashville, and I said, 'Well, the best that I can do for you is just write with you. Come on down to the house.' We never thought the song was there. We had about three different choruses, and found that one."

The song brought a new flavor to Alabama ballads. The keyboard intro gave their records a fresh texture, and lead vocalist Randy Owen cracked and moaned a little more than in previous singles, creating a powerful romanticism.

RCA released "When We Make Love" on April 6, 1984, and it debuted fifteen days later in *Billboard* at number 51. In its tenth charted week, the single edged into number one.

As the primary singer, Owen is, for many, the major focal point of Alabama. Though record companies were initially skeptical about signing a country group [see 479—"Take Me Down"], some suggested that Owen should bill himself as a solo artist. He refused in the hopes that the band would be successful, and made a personal pact, promising to abandon his musical career if the band couldn't make it by the time he turned 30.

Owen reached that milestone on December 13, 1979. One week earlier, "I Wanna Come Over" peaked at number 33 on independent MDJ Records [see 390—"Tennessee River"], the group's first single to reach the Top 40.

Remaining with the band, Randy has become Alabama's chief spokesman and the guiding force behind many of their charitable efforts. Alabama has raised untold millions for a vast array of causes, most notably through their June Jam series.

Alabama

575

I CAN TELL BY THE WAY YOU DANCE (YOU'RE GONNA LOVE TONIGHT)
VERN GOSDIN

Compleat 122
Writers: Sandy Pinkard, Rob Strandlund
Producer: Blake Mevis
June 30, 1984 (1 week)

Somewhere along the line, the press dubbed Vern Gosdin "The Voice."

Born August 5, 1934, in Woodland, Alabama, Vern was the sixth of nine children. On Saturday nights, he went to sleep to the sounds of the Opry, dreaming that one day he might take the stage himself. In his teens, Vern and two brothers plied their family harmonies on a gospel radio program at WVOK in Birmingham.

He tried briefly to start a country career in Atlanta, then moved to Chicago, where he ran the D & G Tap (Buford Pusser, later the inspiration for *Walking Tall*, was the club's bouncer). Vern relocated in 1960, forming a bluegrass group called the Golden State Boys with his brother, Rex. The Golden State Boys later became the Hillmen, led by Chris Hillman, and the brothers recorded an album with ex-Byrd Gene Clark in 1967. After Hillman joined the Byrds, he cut Vern's "Someone To Turn To" in the movie *Easy Rider*.

Eventually, Gosdin quit the music business and moved back to Georgia, founding his own glass and mirror company. He was able to support himself by working only nine hours per week. Music still called, however, and Gosdin shelled out $8,000 of his own money to record "Hangin' On" and "Yesterday's Gone." After hearing a demo tape, Emmylou Harris consented to add harmony vocals, and both records became hits for Elektra in 1976-77.

Moving from label to label, Gosdin attained seven more Top Ten releases in the ensuing years, including "Till The End," "Dream Of Me," "If You're Gonna Do Me Wrong (Do It Right)" and "Way Down Deep." Finally, "The Voice" appeared at number one with a song he had held onto for two years, "I Can Tell By The Way You Dance." Gary Morris had recorded the song, and although he didn't have a hit with it, Gosdin shied away from it. He was concerned that it rocked too much, but he showed it to producer Blake Mevis, when Mevis wanted to record uptempo material.

"I didn't want to cut another Vern Gosdin ballad," says Mevis. "That's where he'd always been. I wanted people to say, 'I didn't know that he could sing like that.' It's just like when you're gonna buy a suit—you don't buy a blue pin-striped suit if you've got one in the closet."

576

SOMEBODY'S NEEDIN' SOMEBODY
CONWAY TWITTY

Warner Bros. 29308
Writer: Len Chera
Producers: Conway Twitty, Dee Henry, Jimmy Bowen
July 7, 1984 (1 week)

"Somebody's Needin' Somebody" was the first of Conway Twitty's number one singles to credit Dee Henry as a co-producer. A longtime production assistant, Dee has since become Conway's wife, and wields a great deal of influence in attending to the nuts and bolts of his career.

"She makes every step I make," explains Conway. "She is involved in everything that I do, except the creative process. She knows as much about the boards in these control rooms as the engineers do, and anything technical like that she knows. The creative end of it, I handle; all the rest of it, she handles, and does it well.

"All that other stuff's important, too, and she's got a good ear for songs. She listens to every song I do, just as many times as I do, and I appreciate a female's ear."

Henry also provided a female touch to the production on "Somebody's Needin' Somebody," Twitty's first number one record since "The Rose" [see 510], four singles earlier. "I think it's a great country song," Conway said in the *Twitty City Times*. "There's a lot of lonely people out there, and this song covers exactly that."

Twitty's three prior releases performed well, though they failed to add to his list of chart-topping hits. Ricky Skaggs contributed backing vocals to "Lost In The Feeling," which stopped at number two behind "He's A Heartache (Looking For A Place To Happen)" [see 532] and "Love Song" [see 533].

Conway remade the Eagles' "Heartache Tonight," using the Osmond Brothers as back-up singers, and it peaked at number six. Another remake, of Lionel Richie's "Three Times A

Lady," made it to number seven.

"Somebody's Needin' Somebody" helped Conway earn recognition as *Billboard*'s number one country singles artist for 1984. Such honors have been infrequent for Twitty, since most of his awards have come for his duets with Loretta Lynn. He's never won a single Country Music Association trophy as a solo artist, but that doesn't bother him.

"If you're one of those artists who keeps runnin' up and down those awards steps," he says, "[it's the] same old face, and people are thinkin', 'Goddamn it, I don't care who wins it as long as he don't, or she don't.' I don't wanna be one of those."

577
I DON'T WANT TO BE A MEMORY
EXILE

Epic 04421
Writers: J.P. Pennington, Sonny Lemaire
Producer: Buddy Killen
July 14, 1984 (1 week)

Just prior to the band's signing in 1983, Exile earned a reputation in Nashville for its country songwriting prowess. Group members Les

Taylor and J. P. Pennington earned a number of hits recorded by other performers in a relatively short period of time. Dave & Sugar took "Stay With Me" to number six in 1979, Janie Frickie topped the charts with "It Ain't Easy Bein' Easy" [see 496], and Alabama took two of their songs to number one: "Take Me Down" [see 479] and "The Closer You Get" [see 528].

At the time, Exile was in the process of regrouping. Two years after "Kiss You All Over" [see 559—"Woke Up In Love"] reached number one on *Billboard*'s Hot 100, the band had returned to Lexington, Kentucky, playing nightly at The Rebel Room, a small bar in a local bowling alley.

Through determination alone, the band stayed together during that period, honing its vocal harmonies and working diligently on songwriting. J.P. Pennington was the only original member of the band remaining (the group was formed as the Exiles in June of 1963), and he formed a strong writing bond with Sonny Lemaire, who joined during January of 1978.

Their initial collaboration resulted in "The High Cost Of Leaving," their first country single; their next team effort became their second number one, "I Don't Want To Be A Memory."

Exile

"After we finished 'High Cost Of Leaving,' J.P. and I had this idea," recalls Lemaire. "We were just kind of on a roll. It pretty much just wrote itself; we did it in maybe half an hour or 45 minutes, and it was quick. It was fun, and it was just one of those simple songs that was easy to write once you locked into the idea."

While "Memory" topped the country chart, Huey Lewis & The News had a Top Five album on *Billboard*'s LP chart, further underscoring Exile's knack for recognizing a hit song. The first single from Lewis' *Sports* album was "Heart And Soul," which had been the title track of a 1981 Exile package.

"I pulled off to the side of the road the first time I heard it, because I thought it was us," notes Lemaire. "We made them a good demo."

578
JUST ANOTHER WOMAN IN LOVE
ANNE MURRAY
Capitol 5344
Writers: Patti Ryan, Wanda Mallette
Producer: Jim Ed Norman
July 21, 1984 (1 week)

Before she ever took music as a serious vocational pursuit, Anne Murray went to work as a phys-ed instructor in the Canadian school system. Singing just seemed so natural that she rarely considered the possibility of earning money with her voice.

Learning about her talent hardly came about in a normal manner, anyway. She was nine years old, riding in the backseat with her mother and aunt, singing along with a Gogi Grant song on the radio. Her aunt remarked at what a lovely voice the youngster had; as it turned out, Aunt Kay was tone deaf.

She was right, though. Murray's smooth vocal delivery proved to be the hallmark of her career, and producer Jim Ed Norman worked carefully to frame her in the best possible light.

"I had historically done things with Anne that used the lower part of her range rather than the higher part," he relates. "I really was enamored with the more relaxed quality that came, and her ability to communicate in that relaxed style.

"After doing records that way for several years, there's a tendency for it to sound the same—there's a homogenized kind of quality that comes to it. There's not a lot of tension,

there's not a lot of challenge that goes on between artist and listener. So later on, we began to voice things 'up' to get some of that rasp and angst."

Both styles contrasted effectively in "Just Another Woman In Love," which moved between smooth, relaxed verses and a soulful chorus. Murray, the former gym instructor, received the song from Patti Ryan and Wanda Mallette, a couple of teacher/songwriters who had also written "Lookin' For Love" [see 393] four years earlier.

"I can remember being on a plane and going through tapes," she recalls, "and I heard this and I just went, 'Oh, boy.' I still just love this tune. I love to sing it, I even love to listen to it. Usually, I don't listen to my records, unless it's for a reason."

Coincidentally, Norman had simultaneously combed through thousands of tapes for material, and "Just Another Woman In Love" was one he wanted her to hear. With both artist and producer in agreement, they recorded the song for *A Little Good News* [see 547]. After debuting April 28, 1984, it reached number one in its lucky thirteenth week on the *Billboard* chart.

579
ANGEL IN DISGUISE
EARL THOMAS CONLEY
RCA 13758
Writers: Earl Thomas Conley, Randy Scruggs
Producers: Nelson Larkin, Earl Thomas Conley
July 28, 1984 (1 week)

When Earl Thomas Conley released *Don't Make It Easy for Me*, *USA Today* hailed its cross-pollinated texture as "Nashville meets Fleetwood Mac." By the time the fourth single had run its course, his publicists proclaimed Earl "The Michael Jackson of Country Music."

On July 23, 1984, RCA threw a party for Earl at The World's End on Church Street in Nashville to celebrate a milestone that Jackson had never achieved. In fact, Elvis Presley, the Beatles, Bruce Springsteen—no one in any format had previously done what Earl did with the album. *Don't Make It Easy for Me* yielded four number one singles on the *Billboard* country chart. The fourth came with "Angel In Disguise."

"[RCA executives] Randy Goodman and Joe Galante were in a club listening to somebody—a possible recording artist from somewhere," says Conley, recalling "Angel" 's origins. "They came upon this waitress, and said, 'Wow! She's just an angel in disguise!' That's the way they told me about it. So they said, 'Man, you need to write a song about that,' and they gave me the idea."

"'Angel In Disguise' had the keyboard riff thing in it that just worked for that song," adds producer Nelson Larkin. "Earl and Randy [Scruggs] used to bring in the worst demos for me to listen to when they wrote, on a little [cassette machine]. Sometimes it was hard until you got in the studio to know what you had, but I think the keyboard player that we had on that session really pulled that thing together. It's got a distinguishable sound, and Earl sang it well."

Ironically, less than a decade earlier, Conley felt as if he were spinning his wheels. Having tried to conform to others' rules and suggestions of how to write successful songs, he felt robbed of his individuality. Any acceptance seemed somehow hollow, and he went through what he describes as a "psychological collapse."

"I had to figure out where I wanted to go with my life," Earl says. "I got into meditation. Now I've turned my life completely around just simply by asking myself a few questions and not accepting everything to be fact until I questioned it. I'll do that as long as I'm on Earth . . . I can create a good reality for myself, or I can create a bad one. At least I have a choice now."

580

MAMA HE'S CRAZY
THE JUDDS
(WYNONNA & NAOMI)
RCA 13772
Writer: Kenny O'Dell
Producer: Brent Maher
August 4, 1984 (1 week)

In May of 1979, Naomi Judd brought her family to Nashville. Two years earlier, daughter Wynonna had gone into a recording studio for the first time, and Naomi spent several years on Music Row looking for a deal.

A number of record labels and executives turned them down. Songwriter Kenny O'Dell, however, took an interest. He met several times with Wynonna (a Franklin High School student, still in braces) and Naomi to try and help them develop. Ultimately, he wrote a song specifically for the Judds.

"Workin' out of home, I fell into a groove where my wife and I would have lunch around 2:00," he remembers. "There was this soap opera on TV at the time, a short-lived one called 'Texas,' a take-off on 'Dallas.' I had my legal pad there by me to write down lines and anything that came off the dialogue, and 'Mama, He's Crazy' was one of the dialogues they had on this particular show."

O'Dell used it as the basis for a song, and played it for the Judds at their next meeting. Wynonna, age 18, had her first boyfriend, and the song was quite appropriate, but Kenny didn't get to hear what they did with it. Soon afterward, they drifted apart.

Naomi worked as a nurse at Williamson County Hospital, where the facility admitted one Diana Maher after an auto accident. Naomi gave her a tape, made with a $30 K-Mart tape recorder, and Diana forwarded it to her father, record producer Brent Maher. On March 2, 1983, Maher took the Judds to RCA for a live audition with the label. As a result, they signed a recording contract and set to work on a mini-album with six songs.

"They love everything from bluegrass to the Andrews Sisters and Bonnie Raitt-type stuff," Maher notes. "We worked for almost a year before we ever went in the studio, just trying to narrow it down and find the marrow of the bone. What kept coming back was 'Mama He's Crazy'—that was our country foundation—and 'Had A Dream,' which was more of a rhythmic, country-funk type of area."

"Had A Dream" was released first, peaking at number 17, and "Mama" followed, riding all the way to number one.

"We were just doing what we were doing," shrugs Wynonna, "and it happened to happen."

581

THAT'S THE THING ABOUT LOVE
DON WILLIAMS
MCA 52389
Writers: Richard Leigh, Gary Nicholson
Producers: Don Williams, Garth Fundis
August 11, 1984 (1 week)

The *Cafe Carolina* album added a new texture to Don Williams' music, with the light and

Don Williams

breezy air of sax player Jim Horn, an L.A. session man who relocated to Nashville. "That's The Thing About Love" marked Horn's first major contribution after the move, though he'd worked on country records before [see 316—"I Believe In You"].

"That's The Thing About Love" emerged from a songwriting session pairing Richard Leigh and Gary Nicholson. After a lengthy, unproductive day, Leigh cued up a Ray Charles record to change the mood and ease their frustration.

"We just fell back into that 'Brown Eyes' [see 292] kind of feel," notes Leigh. "It said somethin' about the eagle and the dove, and that sort of stuff, and the title just blurted out. There wasn't any reason why—it wasn't inspired or anything, it just sort of popped out. We had a fun time just writing a song about how funny love is, how odd it is, and how it's full of contradictions, and how universal those contradictions are."

The demo they played for producer Garth Fundis included a sax solo, and Don decided

they should try to emulate that sound.

"Jim Horn had just moved to town," says Fundis, "and had called me a couple weeks prior and introduced himself. We talked, and he was just a great guy. So we called Jim Horn, and he came in, and when horn players come in, they have to overdub to the track. Of course, we were cuttin' live, and he walked in, all the musicians are there, and he's like, 'Are we cuttin' live? Great.' Two or three takes, and we had it. It was pretty much all live."

Williams added one more number one single after changing record labels in 1985 [see 685—"Heartbeat In The Darkness"]. He continued his usual string of Top Ten hits as well, including gems like "We've Got A Good Fire Goin'," "Then It's Love," "I Wouldn't Be A Man," "One Good Well" and "I've Been Loved By The Best."

A long-term back problem (caused by trying to lift too many Coca-Cola cases as a teenager) forced Don off the road for a 17-month period, during which he considered quitting the record business. Luckily, he decided to stay with it.

582

STILL LOSING YOU
RONNIE MILSAP

RCA 13805
Writer: Mike Reid
Producers: Ronnie Milsap, Rob Galbraith
August 18, 1984 (1 week)

Ronnie Milsap's twenty-fifth number one single took a great deal of effort from everyone concerned. Even at the start, songwriter Mike Reid encountered a lengthy struggle, one he happily pursued because he loved his working title, "Still Losing You." "I liked that combination of words," he says. "It was a title, though, that you could write a couple of different ways."

Reid put it through numerous rewrites, including one in which he actually added 20 seconds to the song by deleting a major section. "When you took the bridge out," he explains, "it convoluted the arrangement, so we put the bridge back in. I tend to think too much and outsmart myself, and it takes a long time to have things settle down. That song was a *long* time settlin' down."

Milsap didn't find "Still Losing You" any easier.

"I just couldn't get the sound or the mood," he says. "It seemed too tense; it didn't seem relaxed. I didn't beat it to death, but on three different days, I'd make that one of the songs on the session that I wanted to try, and on the third try, it came off real good."

Ronnie enhanced it with a 32-second synthesizer introduction, reminiscent of Steve Winwood's pop hit "While You See A Chance." Shane Keister, who scored Jim Varney's first movie, *Ernest Goes to Camp*, worked up a "head arrangement" in the key of C, and tacked it onto the beginning when the record was completed. Keister's arrangement appeared on the album, but the single shipped without it.

"You'll notice," Ronnie points out, "that same intro is on Dan Seals' intro to 'You Still Move Me' [see 706]. It's the same thing. [Engineer] Kyle [Lehning] loved it so much he said, 'Milsap, I'm gonna do it again.'"

Though "Still Losing You" hit number one, a change in record company personnel kept it from being bigger than Milsap had hoped. A new president came in and wiped out Ronnie's plans to market it pop; Ronnie had hoped "Still Losing You" would gain a smattering of airplay on pop stations and thus set up "She Loves My Car," a record with Top 40 potential. Instead, "She Loves My Car" (Milsap spent $125,000 to do a video for the song) was relegated to the "B" side of his follow-up, "Prisoner Of The Highway," which hit number six on the country chart.

583

LONG HARD ROAD (THE SHARECROPPER'S DREAM)
THE NITTY GRITTY DIRT BAND

Warner Bros. 29282
Writer: Rodney Crowell
Producers: Paul Worley, Marshall Morgan
August 25, 1984 (1 week)

"Long Hard Road" seems an appropriate title for the first number one single by the Nitty Gritty Dirt Band. NGDB gave its first live performance in Orange County, California, on May 13, 1966—eighteen years earlier.

In the interim, the group went through several personnel changes and fifteen albums. In 1970, their single "Mr. Bojangles" found a home in the Top Ten on the pop chart, but they never came close again until 1979, when "An American Dream" reached number 13. By that time, they had shortened the group name to The Dirt Band.

In the meantime, they took on several supporting roles. They worked on the Clint Eastwood movie *Paint Your Wagon*, sang back-up on Michael Martin Murphey's "Wildfire" and worked under the pseudonym of the Toots Uncommons on Steve Martin's "King Tut."

Their 1972 album *Will the Circle Be Unbroken* was a landmark three-album set—their first gold record, and a package that united West Coast "hippies" with traditional country artists like the Carter Family, Doc Watson, and Roy Acuff.

Commercial consistency remained elusive for the Dirt Band until manager Bill McEuen, swamped by his work on Steve Martin's movie career, had Chuck Morris take over. Morris insisted they put the "Nitty Gritty" back in the group name and suggested they concentrate on the country market. In 1983, "Shot Full Of Love" reached number 19, and the group followed it up with "Dance Little Jean," their first Top Ten country record. "Long Hard Road" then took them to the top.

Rodney Crowell, who wrote "An American Dream," also penned "Long Hard Road." He based the song on stories he had heard from his parents, who were raised by sharecroppers before they moved to Houston after the Depression. "My dad did construction work," Rodney recalls, "but they always spoke very vividly and longingly for the days when they lived on the farm and ran barefooted."

NGDB persuaded Ricky Skaggs to play fiddle on "Long Hard Road," the first track they cut for the *Plain Dirt Fashion* album. Originally, it was intended for release on Capitol Records, but they switched labels in the middle of the album, and it ended up on Warner Bros.

"It was our first number one record of all time, ever, on any chart," notes Dirt guitarist Jeff Hanna, "so it holds a special place in our hearts. We were stoked."

584
LET'S FALL TO PIECES TOGETHER
GEORGE STRAIT
MCA 52392
Writers: Dickey Lee, Tommy Rocco, Johnny Russell
Producer: Ray Baker
September 1, 1984 (1 week)

George Strait picked up his fifth number one record from the man who wrote Buck Owens' first. Johnny Russell earned his first success in the record industry by writing "Act Naturally," and he's been a part of the country business ever since. With aspirations as a recording artist, he has placed 28 singles on the *Billboard* chart through the years, but only one of them—1973's "Rednecks, White Socks And Blue Ribbon Beer"—made the Top Ten.

One of Russell's most disappointing moments came when Mercury Records failed to release an album that he strongly believed in. He recorded "Song Of The South" [see 805], "He Stopped Loving Her Today" [see 384] and "You'll Be Back (Every Night In My Dreams)," among ten cuts, but Mercury deemed the material too weak.

Fortunately, Johnny didn't miss out with "Let's Fall To Pieces Together." Songwriter Tommy Rocco had suggested that title to four or five other writing partners, but all of them had passed on it. One day at the Welk publishing offices, he heard Dickey Lee and Johnny Russell writing in another office and decided

he wanted to work with both of them. He "crashed in," sang three lines of the chorus, and Russell chimed in with a fourth line. Russell and Lee dropped the song they had started and set to work on the new idea.

"We got it pretty well put together real quick," Russell reports. "Then over the next few days, we polished it and worked on it. When you write with Dickey Lee, you rewrite and you rewrite, because you walk in his office, and he says, 'Are you sure you wanna say it this way? Are you happy with this line?' As a matter of fact, I wouldn't be surprised if he called me now to ask if I was happy with the first line of 'Let's Fall To Pieces Together.'"

They first sent the song to producer Billy Sherrill for George Jones, but were rebuffed. Next, they approached producer Blake Mevis about recording it with Strait, although nothing happened then, either. Strait liked the song, though, and when he picked Ray Baker as his producer [see 567—"Right Or Wrong"], Baker agreed with George on its potential. They saw that potential fulfilled on September 1, 1984.

585
TENNESSEE HOMESICK BLUES
DOLLY PARTON
RCA 13819
Writer: Dolly Parton
Producers: Mike Post, Dolly Parton
September 8, 1984 (1 week)

The queen of positive thinkers, Dolly Parton went through several setbacks during the early '80s. They included a gynecological problem, the painful filming of *The Best Little Whorehouse in Texas* [see 490—"I Will Always Love You"], and a threat on her life that prompted Parton to cancel a tour in the summer of 1982.

Dolly picked herself up, though, and went back to work. At the end of 1983, she released an album of rock and roll covers, *The Great Pretender*, going to number three with "Save The Last Dance For Me." She talked briefly about a role in *Superman III*, but ended up getting $3 million to star alongside Sylvester Stallone in *Rhinestone*.

Rhinestone was the culmination of a seven-year effort by songwriter Larry Weiss to bring "Rhinestone Cowboy" [see 220] to the screen. Three production deals and six different scripts fell by the wayside before 20th Century-Fox accepted the final draft. By the time of its release, the producers shortened the title to *Rhinestone*, although Weiss and his composition received onscreen credit. Dolly rolled up her sleeves and put in endless hours on the project.

"She's just a tireless worker," says Herb Pedersen, who provided backing vocals on the soundtrack. "This girl would come out to the studio and record with us all day, and then at night, she'd go to these fabulous dinners in L.A. and hang out with all these actors. The next day, she'd be out there in her jeans and sweatshirt, workin' real hard with the players again."

The movie turned out to be a disaster. Its humorous segments generally failed to produce laughs, although critics tended to laugh at Stallone's attempts at singing. Moviegoers, like Stallone, merely groaned.

Despite the script's shortcomings, the movie did produce a few solid musical moments, as Dolly wrote 13 of the 14 tunes that appeared on the soundtrack. "Tennessee Homesick Blues" was the first single, paying homage to the Smoky Mountains, where she was raised. Entering *Billboard*'s country chart on June 9, 1984, it ascended to number one just

Jim Glaser

after Labor Day, when *Rhinestone* was already being shown as a feature film on cross-country flights.

Rhinestone yielded two more hits: "God Won't Get You" hit the Top Ten, and Floyd Parton sang "Waltz Me To Heaven," which Waylon Jennings turned into a hit the following year.

586
YOU'RE GETTIN' TO ME AGAIN
JIM GLASER
Noble Vision 105
Writers: Pat McManus, Woody Bomar
Producer: Don Tolle
September 15, 1984 (1 week)

"You're Gettin' To Me Again" was the final step in a dream that took thirty years to mold. Having worked for years as a member of Tompall & The Glaser Brothers Band, Jim Glaser was already fairly established in the record business. In 1959, the Glasers backed Marty Robbins [see 251—"El Paso City"] on his number one record "El Paso," and in 1963, they sang behind Johnny Cash on "Ring Of Fire," which also hit the top.

The Glasers wanted badly to make a name for themselves as a separate act, and hit with a handful of successes over the years—"Rings" went to number seven in 1971, and "Lovin' Her Was Easier (Than Anything I'll Ever Do Again)" hit number two ten years later. But they got sidetracked by their ownership of both an artist-management firm and the publishing company that owned the copyrights to "Gentle On My Mind" and "Woman, Woman" (which Jim Glaser wrote for Gary Puckett & The Union Gap). As a result, the Glaser Brothers disbanded in 1973 and stayed apart for six years.

Jim had first appeared on the *Billboard* charts as a solo artist in 1968, and by 1979, he was still looking for the right break when he met a pop promotion man for A & M Records named Don Tolle. An Atlanta resident, Tolle wanted to develop his own label, but it wasn't until 1982 that he could muster enough financial support to get Noble Vision off the ground.

Glaser was his first artist, and the company fared unusually well for an independent. Four singles from *The Man in the Mirror* all made dents in the Top 40, and the fifth, "You're Gettin' To Me Again," finally made number one. Unfortunately, Noble Vision was unable to duplicate their success.

"Don lost the financial backing," notes Glaser, "and that's the sad thing about independents. Even though the label had four Top Ten records and an album that had been on the charts for a year and a half, we still were not in the black. It costs a lot to promote that heavily."

Noble Vision's distribution was picked up by MCA, although that relationship lasted a very short time before the deal was annulled. Glaser, meanwhile, has also done well as a back-up vocalist, appearing on such hits as "Watchin' Girls Go By," by Ronnie McDowell, and the Sylvia hits "Drifter" [see 419] and "Tumbleweed."

587

LET'S CHASE EACH OTHER AROUND THE ROOM
MERLE HAGGARD
Epic 04512
Writers: Merle Haggard, Freddy Powers, Sherill Rodgers
Producers: Merle Haggard, Ray Baker
September 22, 1984 (1 week)

Merle Haggard was in a bit of a slump as a songwriter until somewhere around the beginning of the '80s. Two different occurrences helped break that block. One was a challenge that Leona Williams unconsciously issued during their marriage; the other came from a rekindled friendship with Freddy Powers.

Haggard and Powers first met each other around 1961. Haggard was playing in Las Vegas at the Nashville Nevada Club as a guitarist for Wynn Stewart, while Powers was working down the street at the Showboat, opening for comedian Spike Jones. That was a few years before Haggard broke as a recording artist, and they lost touch with each other until about 1980.

"Willie Nelson's been a lifelong friend of mine," says Powers. (Freddy played a prominent role on Willie's *Somewhere Over the Rainbow*.) "I was up at his house, and we met up there with Merle, all together, and started talking. The first thing we knew, we realized that we'd been kind of buddies way back a long time ago, before he'd become Merle Haggard."

Their friendship renewed, Haggard and Powers began writing together rather frequently. "I Always Get Lucky With You" [see 530] was their first collaboration to see the light of day, appearing on the *Big City* album [see 467]. Haggard's first Powers-written single came in 1984 on "Let's Chase Each Other Around The Room."

"Merle and I wrote that one time comin' out of Canada on the bus, goin' to the CMA awards," Powers remembers. "We were working together on the road, and one night, this girlfriend of mine who also sang in the band, Sherill Rodgers, she just made the comment, 'When we get to Nashville I'm gonna chase you around the room,' or something like this. Merle and I picked up on it and wrote that song."

Haggard inserted "Let's Chase Each Other" onto the *It's All in the Game* album, recorded entirely at Nashville's Eleven-Eleven Sound. The band included members of the Strangers, augmented by Powers on rhythm guitar, Bobby Wood on keyboards and Mike Leech on bass. The single entered the *Billboard* chart on July 14, 1984, with the song and the album each settling into the number one spot on their respective charts ten weeks later.

588

TURNING AWAY
CRYSTAL GAYLE
Warner Bros. 29254
Writer: Tim Krekel
Producer: Jimmy Bowen
September 29, 1984 (1 week)

"Crystal Gayle's *Cage the Songbird* album is one of my favorite albums that I've worked on since I've been in Nashville," says producer Jimmy Bowen. "Crystal sang great. She was pregnant. Sometimes, you get 'em at the right point in the pregnancy, they'll sing great. Of course, she always does."

While working on the very last track of the album on August 22, 1983, an unusual event occurred that would make *Cage the Songbird* a very memorable album for Crystal.

"We were actually mixing 'I Don't Wanna Lose Your Love' in the studio when I started having these back pains," she laughs . . . now. "I thought, 'This chair is awfully uncomfortable!' I didn't realize it, but I was in labor. I'd never been that way before."

Though Crystal and husband/manager Bill

Gatzimos had taken classes for natural childbirth, their daughter was a "breach baby" and had to be delivered by cesarean section. Named Catherine Claire, she made "I Don't Wanna Lose Your Love" a very special release. Pulled as the second single from the album, the song spent two weeks at number two in the spring of 1984, edged out by "To All The Girls I've Loved Before" [see 569].

Gayle's follow-up, "Turning Away," brought her back to number one. "It's just so fun," she says, "just a little rock and roll song there. It's totally unlike any of the other songs I've recorded."

Crystal picked up "Turning Away" from Nashville writer Tim Krekel. Long a force on the Music City club scene, Krekel signed briefly with Arista Records with his rock trio, the Sluggers. They released one album, *Over the Fence*, in 1986.

"'Turning Away' was kind of a riff song," assesses Bowen. "The whole record is kind of a riff. Like 'The Sound Of Goodbye' [see 554], it was musically pretty different for country radio, and people were afraid of it, too."

Crystal released one more single from the *Cage the Songbird* album: "Me Against The Night" soared to number four at the close of 1984.

Her next album—the last with Bowen—contained four songs produced by Los Angeles veteran Michael Masser, whose credits include both Diana Ross and Whitney Houston. The title track, "Nobody Wants To Be Alone," and "A Long And Lasting Love" both attained a Top Five plateau.

589

EVERYDAY
THE OAK RIDGE BOYS
MCA 52419
Writers: Dave Loggins, J.D. Martin
Producer: Ron Chancey
October 6, 1984 (1 week)

Given their gospel heritage [see 314—"I'll Be True To You"], the Oak Ridge Boys shied away for years from country singles that might have an overt gospel message. They wanted to make sure that their audience realized they had made a commitment to country music.

The Oak Ridge Boys

The gospel influence was almost always apparent, however, in their harmonies.

"It's funny," producer Ron Chancey told *Billboard* in 1984. "Sometimes still we'll be in the studio, and I'll say, 'Hey, you guys are gospeling out.' It's kind of a private joke between us; they'll ask me, 'Are we gospeling out too much, Ron?' Not that there's anything wrong with it, but it doesn't work in a lot of the songs."

One it *did* work in is "Everyday." Songwriter Dave Loggins concocted the song specifically for the Oak Ridge Boys after hearing one of their records on the radio while driving into MCA Music. He switched off the sound and started singing the chorus *a capella*. Once he arrived at the publishing house, Dave played what he had for fellow writer J.D. Martin. It took a week and a half for them to finish "Everyday."

"He was real honed in on the fact that we were gonna write a song for the Oaks, right from the beginning," recalls J.D., "and I think it's unusual for both of us to write with a specific act or artist in mind. Usually, I will try to write a good song, no matter who I think would fit it.

"In that case, it was real obvious that that's what we were doin'. It was fun, because we would try to imagine the bass parts and all the harmonies and all of that."

Once Loggins and Martin finished the song, they sent it to the Oaks, who were finishing up work on the *Deliver* album. Unfortunately, they were a few days too late, and the album went out without "Everyday." The song was held back and later released as one of two new cuts on the group's *Greatest Hits 2*. In this instance, by "gospeling out," the Oak Ridge Boys secured their tenth number one single.

lie, in the Monroe Brothers; and later with his band, the Kentuckians, which became the Blue Grass Boys.

Commonly referred to as "The Father of Bluegrass," Monroe had a heavy influence on Ricky Skaggs, as did former Blue Grass Boys Lester Flatt & Earl Scruggs, Don Reno, Red Smiley and Carter Stanley. Despite its lengthy heritage, bluegrass music had accounted for only one number one country single prior to Ricky Skaggs: Flatt & Scruggs hit the top in 1963 with "The Ballad Of Jed Clampett."

Skaggs came up with bluegrass chart-topper number two by covering one of Monroe's classics, "Uncle Pen." Monroe wrote it as a tribute to his uncle, Pen Vandiver, a fiddler and mandolin player who helped Monroe learn to play and later took him to local dance halls to show off his budding talents. Ricky recorded "Uncle Pen" to help fill out *Don't Cheat in Our Hometown* [see 557] when Epic Records picked up rights to the album from Sugar Hill [see 571]. Ricky had been ending his concerts with the song, and the response was so overwhelming that he felt certain it had potential.

Once the album was finished, Ricky knew he wanted "Uncle Pen" to be a single, but he also felt that it would make a poor choice for a *first* single. In the meantime, a number of radio stations, starved for uptempo material, started playing it off the album. Though the first two singles from *Don't Cheat in Our Hometown* reached number one, Skaggs still faced a battle with the record company, which harbored doubts about the commercial potential of a bluegrass release.

"I told 'em I'd totally take the blame for whatever happens," Ricky recalls. "I just felt like it was a big record. People were lovin' it out on the road."

Ricky's forecast for the record proved correct. It hit number one on October 13, 1984, eight days after the album went gold.

590
UNCLE PEN
RICKY SKAGGS
Sugar Hill 04527
Writer: Bill Monroe
Producer: Ricky Skaggs
October 13, 1984 (1 week)

It's been called "country music in overdrive." Bluegrass originated in Kentucky, in the hands of Bill Monroe, who melded blues, jazz and folk music, and leaned heavy on fiddle, mandolin and banjo. During the '30s, Monroe perpetuated the sound with his brother, Char-

591
I DON'T KNOW A THING ABOUT LOVE (THE MOON SONG)
CONWAY TWITTY
Warner Bros. 29227
Writer: Harlan Howard
Producers: Conway Twitty, Dee Henry,
Jimmy Bowen
October 20, 1984 (1 week)

With a songwriting ability that has propelled him for more than three decades, Harlan Howard is the dean of Nashville songwriters.

Born in Michigan, Howard started writing by listening to the Grand Ole Opry and creating new lyrics for the melodies. In 1958, Charlie Walker's recording of "Pick Me Up On Your Way Down" became his first Top Ten single, launching a line of hits that stretches into five different decades.

Early successes included "Busted," "I Fall To Pieces," "Heartbreak U.S.A.," "Excuse Me (I Think I've Got A Heartache)," "Heartaches By The Number" and "I've Got A Tiger By The Tail." Twenty years later, many of those old chestnuts were rediscovered, bringing new life to "Life Turned Her That Way" [see 762], "She's Gone, Gone, Gone" and "Above And Beyond" [see 835]. He continued to write new material, however, and even as Nashville resurrected those tunes, Howard fashioned new classics like "Why Not Me" [see 600], "Somebody Should Leave" [see 619] and "Somewhere Tonight" [see 751].

Conway Twitty was the first to reintroduce Howard's music, by recording "I Don't Know A Thing About Love." The two were longtime friends, since Howard had been instrumental in Conway's switch in the mid-'60s from rock and roll to country [see 248—"After All The Good Is Gone"]. Though Conway had included many of Harlan's songs on his albums, he'd never released one as a single before.

Howard wrote the "I Don't Know A Thing About Love" in the summer of 1983, while fishing at night on Center Hill Lake, a man-made reservoir in Nashville.

"Fishing is kind of like an automatic thing," explains Howard. "You don't have to think about it, so your mind kind of drifts away. I was thinking about the moon, the astronauts landing up there, and I was thinking about those old Tin Pan Alley love songs, giving the moon so much power. I just got to playing around with the thought in my mind.

"I always kept a writing pad in the boat, and I had enough sense to throw some of it down, and then when I came home, I continued to doodle with it. I never took it serious until way down at the bottom. There's a part where it gets slightly religious, and the moon says, 'Don't ask me, there's somebody above me that you need to talk to.' Then when I wrote that part I said, 'Wow! I really like this song.'"

Howard had a "Don Williams fixation" with the tune, but Williams never cut it. Instead, it ended up in Twitty's hands, and at the top of the *Billboard* chart.

592

IF YOU'RE GONNA PLAY IN TEXAS (YOU GOTTA HAVE A FIDDLE IN THE BAND)

ALABAMA

RCA 13840
Writers: Dan Mitchell, Murry Kellum
Producers: Harold Shedd, Alabama
October 27, 1984 (1 week)

Shortly after Alabama left The Bowery [see 390—"Tennessee River"], the group embarked on its first major concert tour, and part of their journey took them through Texas. The Longhorn State is like no other, and the Fort Payne foursome was devastated by their reception. Patrons at the clubs where they played spent less time listening and more time dancing.

"We would cry when we would get home from the club that night," lead vocalist Randy Owen told Pam Alloway of the *Beaumont Enterprise*. "[But a record company executive] said if they don't dance to your music out there, they don't like you."

That advice came from RCA promotion man Wayne Edwards, and it helped the group realize that their music had made an impact in country music's largest market. The dancers, in fact, hoped that Alabama would play a fiddle tune, and songwriters Dan Mitchell and Murry Kellum knew that little story when they decided to write "If You're Gonna Play In Texas (You Gotta Have A Fiddle In The Band)" specifically for the group. Manager Dale Morris brought it to Alabama on a demo tape that included two other songs.

"We were lookin' for a song that would use a fiddle," recalls producer Harold Shedd. "After 'Tennessee River' and 'Dixieland Delight' [see 515], it became a trademark, so we wanted to do some of those things. If it's working, you don't want to get too far away from that. You gotta touch home base. That was somethin' that we could put a fiddle on that would not sound manufactured or contrived."

Though fiddle chores belong to Jeff Cook in concert, session player Blaine Sprouse took up the bow on the record, and it hit number one on October 27, 1984—19 days after Alabama became the first act to win the Country Music Association's Entertainer of the Year award three times in a row.

"If You're Gonna Play In Texas (You Gotta

Have A Fiddle In The Band)" holds a unique mark as the longest title ever to reach number one. It's a close race with "If I Said You Have A Beautiful Body Would You Hold It Against Me" [see 343]. Both require 14 words, and 51 letters, but "If You're Gonna Play In Texas (You Gotta Have A Fiddle In The Band)" uses three additional characters for punctuation.

593
CITY OF NEW ORLEANS
WILLIE NELSON
Columbia 04568
Writer: Steve Goodman
Producer: Chips Moman
November 3, 1984 (1 week)

After "Always On My Mind" [see 471] went to number one in 1982, Willie Nelson had to wait two-and-a-half years for his next chart-topping solo hit. In the interim, he earned number one duets with Waylon Jennings [see 472—"Just To Satisfy You"], Merle Haggard [see 529—"Pancho And Lefty"] and Julio Iglesias [see 569—"To All The Girls I've Loved Before"].

He added four Top Ten records as a solo star, including "Let It Be Me" and "Last Thing I Needed First Thing This Morning," two singles off *Always On My Mind* which peaked at number two. "Little Old Fashioned Karma" and "Why Do I Have To Choose" also reached the Top Ten.

Willie returned to number one on his own with "City Of New Orleans," a 14-year-old song written by Chicago folk artist Steve Goodman after his marriage in February of 1970. He went with his new bride, Nancy, to meet her grandmother in Mattoon, Illinois, taking a train called the City of New Orleans on the Illinois Central line.

While Nancy slept, Steve jotted down notes about the passing scenery, and when he returned to Chicago, he discovered that that particular train would be shut down unless ticket sales increased. Goodman blended it all into a song, and then recorded "City Of New Orleans" on his eponymous debut album. Arlo Guthrie heard it, and turned it into a pop hit in 1972.

Willie heard that version, as well as Sammi Smith's 1973 cut, and invited comparisons by recording it himself.

"I've got a lot of guts," he laughs. "I did

'Georgia' [see 312] after Ray Charles did it, and I did 'Blue Eyes Crying In The Rain' [see 223] after Roy Acuff. A good song never dies."

Unfortunately, a good songwriter does. Goodman passed away from leukemia on September 20, 1984, leaving "City Of New Orleans" and David Allan Coe's "You Never Even Called Me By My Name" as his best-known compositions. On November 3—the same date that "New Orleans" became Willie's fifteenth number one record—54 artists paid tribute to Goodman with a show at the Pacific Amphitheatre in Costa Mesa, California. The roster included Jackson Browne, Jimmy Buffett, Emmylou Harris, Nelson, Rosanne Cash and Rodney Crowell.

"City Of New Orleans" earned a Grammy the following February for Country Song of the Year.

594
I'VE BEEN AROUND ENOUGH TO KNOW
JOHN SCHNEIDER
MCA 52407
Writers: Dickey Lee, Bob McDill
Producer: Jimmy Bowen
November 10, 1984 (1 week)

In the summer of 1981, John Schneider—known to many as Bo Duke, from "The Dukes of Hazzard" [see 398]—traversed a trail from TV to radio. His tenor rendition of Elvis Presley's "It's Now Or Never" soared to number four on the country chart, simultaneously climbing to number 14 on the *Billboard* Hot 100. His follow-up, a more countrified "Them Good Ol' Boys Are Bad," hit number 13 in country music.

Schneider's vocal career stalled there. Subsequent singles, treading the same stratum as "It's Now Or Never," never caught on, in part because they were geared toward teenagers. By the same token, Schneider's Friday night prime-time slot worked against him.

"It's understandable that the record industry isn't interested in people from Hollywood who they think are making records in their spare time," he admitted to *Billboard*'s Kip Kirby. "I probably shouldn't have gotten into recording when I did, because the music really didn't deserve to be taken seriously."

Unwilling to throw in the towel on his musical career, Schneider secured producer Jimmy

John Schneider

GIVE ME ONE MORE CHANCE
EXILE

Epic 04567
Writers: J.P. Pennington, Sonny Lemaire
Producer: Buddy Killen
November 17, 1984 (1 week)

With their first country album behind them, Exile quickly followed in 1984 with a new album, *Kentucky Hearts*, and the first single, "Give Me One More Chance," became their third number one record during the 1984 calendar year.

Kicking off with the chorus, the words run by so rapidly that it almost sounds like a foot-race. Nevertheless, bass player Sonny Lemaire suggests that recording the harmony parts wasn't as difficult as one might guess: "Actually, rhythmically, the way those words flow together, you can say them quickly. I think it's one of the few songs we've written where it was fun playing with the words rhythmically, and it just came out that way."

"Give Me One More Chance" credits Lemaire and J.P. Pennington as writers, but Lemaire notes that the whole band—including drummer Steve Goetzman, guitarist Les Taylor and keyboard player Marlon Hargis—contributed to the feel.

"I think we'd been messing around in rehearsal with that kind of a beat, with Steve playing drums like that, and it kind of triggered the musical idea for the song. A lot of times in rehearsal, instrumentally we would just play certain things, and I know that J.P. and I were really looking for something to write like that."

The first verse used the word "confidant," and Lemaire adds that it garnered a large response from inside the industry. "For some reason, we got a lot of comments from other artists about it. They really liked it; it seemed like an odd word to use in a country song at the time. It was fun to write—no earth-shaking sentiment about it—and we basically wrote it in about two or three hours."

Released in July of 1984, "Give Me One More Chance" debuted on the *Billboard* country chart August 11. Fourteen weeks later, it became Exile's third consecutive number one release.

"I have to think that quite possibly we were in the wrong style of music for twenty years," Pennington later told Thomas Goldsmith of *The Tennessean*.

Bowen, who had just left Warner Bros., to work on an album with him. John paid for it out of his own pocket and looked for material in Nashville. He was frustrated when publishers repeatedly pitched him songs in the same vein as "It's Now Or Never," and after going through demo after demo at Welk Music, he finally told company rep Bob Kirsch to play him a song that he really liked but wouldn't think was suited for Schneider. Kirsch pulled out an eight-year-old song, "I've Been Around Enough To Know," and Schneider immediately decided to record it.

Jo-El Sonnier had originally cut a Cajun version, partially translated into French, for Mercury in 1975, and writers Bob McDill and Dickey Lee had given up hope of ever having it recorded again. When Bowen arrived at MCA, he had John's single released in an unusual manner. Realizing Schneider's teen-idol image, MCA shipped 75 copies to radio stations with no identification on the label. Only three programmers recognized Schneider—many thought it was George Strait—but they all committed to play it.

"I've Been Around Enough To Know" required 16 weeks to reach number one, but it brought Schneider a new respectability in the process.

For Pennington, country success was practically inbred. His mother, Lily Mae Ledford, had performed with an all-girl string band called the Coon Creek Girls, and his father emceed a radio show, "The Renfro Valley Barn Dance." Pennington's uncle, the late Red Foley, is a member of the Country Music Hall of Fame.

596

YOU COULD'VE HEARD A HEART BREAK

JOHNNY LEE

Warner Bros. 29206
Writer: Marc Rossi
Producer: Jimmy Bowen
November 24, 1984 (1 week)

"You Could've Heard A Heart Break" first hit the *Billboard* country charts on January 8, 1983, when Roy Clark's backing band, Rodney Lay & The Wild West, took it to number 53.

Johnny Lee never heard the song in its first release, though, and when a song plugger approached him at the Spence Manor on Music Row in Nashville, Johnny related very well to the story he heard.

"You gotta hear this song," the agent told Lee. "This kid, Marc Rossi, wrote it. He's going through a divorce; he just wrote this song, and I think it's a hit for you."

"I just liked the song," Lee remembers. "It was one of those times when I was listening to hundreds of songs. I had a big box full of tapes up in my room, and that particular song just happened to stick in my mind."

That was a lucky break for Lee, who took the tune all the way to number one without realizing that it had ever been recorded before. However, for several years, it seemed like it would be Lee's last lucky break. His follow-up, "Rollin' Lonely," went Top Ten in 1985, and he also charted satisfactorily with "Save The Last Chance" and "They Never Had To Get Over You."

By the middle of 1986, he was without a record label and attempted to get out of his management agreement with Sherwood Cryer, who had also managed Mickey Gilley. "Mickey and I signed a ten-year contract with this guy," says Lee. "Then later on, when I was ready to get my part of my money, he said, 'Well, you don't have any money; I'll see what you owe me.' I didn't even get paid for *Lookin'*

for Love [see 393]. The album went gold, and I wrote the song 'Annie,' and I never saw a dime of any of that money. It ended up he had me under a 90-year contract at 50 percent, which wouldn't have been bad if I was getting my 50 percent, but I wasn't."

Things turned around, though, when he remarried in 1987. Two years later, he signed a ten-album deal with Curb Records, appropriately naming the first *New Directions*. During 1990, Maverick Press released his biography.

"I was very lucky to have the first opportunity," Johnny says of his career. "I feel like I earned the second opportunity."

597

YOUR HEART'S NOT IN IT

JANIE FRICKIE

Columbia 04578
Writers: Michael Garvin, Bucky Jones, Tom Shapiro
Producer: Bob Montgomery
December 1, 1984 (1 week)

"All of the songs that Bob produced were in the same type of 'contemporary country' bag," says Janie Frickie of the five number one records she recorded with producer Bob Montgomery. "They were not stone-traditional country, and those songs were my best records out of my whole career. That's what I'm best at."

Following "Let's Stop Talkin' About It" [see 563], Frickie remained in a high-energy mode with "If The Fall Don't Get You," peaking at number eight in the summer of 1984. "Your Heart's Not In It" returned her to number one for the sixth time in her solo career.

"That's just a good, strong ballad with a very meaningful message to it," Janie assesses. "It sort of touches the heart, and women and men can both relate to songs like that. That's the kind of songs that I like to do the most."

Michael Garvin wrote "If Your Heart's Not In It" with frequent collaborators Bucky Jones and Tom Shapiro.

"That first part of that chorus—'I can't take your body if your heart's not in it'—that kind of hit me one day," Garvin recalls. "I had a little garage studio at the time, and it just kind of fell in front of me. I went to Bucky and Tom with it. We do a lot of writing together, and they dug it, and we fleshed it on out."

After committing to the song, Janie waited six months to record it.

Born December 19, 1947, Frickie grew up in a rural home near South Whitley, Indiana. After studying at the University of Indiana, she acquired a teaching degree in Memphis, where she first started singing sessions. After graduation, she moved to Los Angeles, back to Memphis, and finally to Nashville, where she became one of the hottest session singers in town.

She sang jingles for Coors, Pizza Hut, American Airlines, 7-Up and Red Lobster, among others, but also earned a reputation singing on records. Her credits include "I'd Really Love To See You Tonight," by England Dan & John Ford Coley; "Still The One," by Bill Anderson; "It's A Cheatin' Situation," by Moe Bandy; "I'll Get Over You," by Crystal Gayle [see 250]; and, of course, the series of duets with Johnny Duncan [see 268—"Thinkin' Of A Rendezvous"].

598
CHANCE OF LOVIN' YOU
EARL THOMAS CONLEY
RCA 13877
Writers: Earl Thomas Conley,
Randy Scruggs
Producers: Nelson Larkin,
Earl Thomas Conley
December 8, 1984 (1 week)

Born October 17, 1941, the third of eight children, Earl Thomas Conley inherited some of his musical penchant from his relatives.

"We'd sit around and listen to the radio when I was a kid," he remembers. "We had a big ole tube-type Philco, and my father was into Jimmy Martin, Bill Monroe and Hank Williams. The most memorable times were when my uncle would come over. My dad wasn't allowed to drink in the house, so they'd sit in the car and listen to the Grand Ole Opry. Watching them listen to the music and seeing how it affected them influenced me, too."

The effect that country music had on his classmates also influenced Earl. When they thumbed their noses at "hillbilly" songs, Conley likewise drifted toward other music. ETC ("Tom," as they called him then) grew enamored of Nat King Cole, Brook Benton, Elvis Presley and Jerry Lee Lewis, and he later developed interests in the Rolling Stones, the Eagles and Elton John, among others.

Such diverse influences partially explain his unique brand of country music. In 1984, these styles bubbled to the surface in "Chance Of Lovin' You," the first single from his *Treadin' Water* album. "We were goin' for a different type sound," notes producer Nelson Larkin. "The way Earl writes, with his chord progressions, he writes a lot of minor chords and makes it work, where a lot of artists can't make it work."

Conley co-wrote the song with Randy Scruggs during the period in which they completed "Don't Make It Easy For Me" [see 564], "Your Love's On The Line" [see 531] and "Angel In Disguise" [see 579]. In fact, during seven writing sessions, they were able to craft half a dozen songs.

Though Conley had written it earlier, the single ended up in the middle of a time crunch. Earl's heavy tour itinerary made it difficult to set a cohesive recording schedule, and RCA pushed him and Larkin to meet release dates for the project. Despite Larkin's displeasure with the results ("I was not particularly satisfied with the drum sound [or] the mix"), "Chance Of Lovin' You" checked in during the final month of 1984 as Earl's fifth consecutive number one single.

Simultaneously, Earl joined Gus Hardin on a duet, "All Tangled Up In Love," which peaked at number eight.

599
NOBODY LOVES ME LIKE YOU DO
ANNE MURRAY WITH DAVE LOGGINS
Capitol 5401
Writers: James Dunne, Pamela Phillips
Producer: Jim Ed Norman
December 15, 1984 (1 week)

In 1984, Dave Loggins quickly became one of the hottest songwriters in Nashville. He turned out number one hits with Alabama's "Roll On (Eighteen Wheeler)" [see 562] and the Oak Ridge Boys' "Everyday" [see 589], plus the Nitty Gritty Dirt Band's "I Love Only You" and Don Williams' "Maggie's Dream."

Nonetheless, he was little-known to the general public. His only hit as a vocalist had come ten years earlier when "Please Come To Boston" reached the Top Ten on *Billboard*'s

Dave Loggins &
Anne Murray

Hot 100. He gained his second hit in a duet
with Anne Murray.

At the time, Capitol Records wanted Murray to cut a duet with someone possessing
"marquee value." "I don't know who they
talked to," she says. "I remember hearing
Elton John and Paul McCartney and all those
people, and time went by, and I went, 'Now, can
I sing with the person I want to sing with?'"

She had been hearing Dave Loggins on
demos for several years, and often expressed
to producer Jim Ed Norman a special attraction
to Dave's voice. He suggested she might want
to try singing "Nobody Loves Me Like You Do"
with Loggins.

"She was right in there with that," Jim Ed
notes. "She was so enamored of David's voice,
I don't think she batted an eye. She was very,
very excited, so I called David, and he said,
'Yeah, that sounds kind of interesting.'"

A couple of weeks later, Norman called Log-

gins at MCA Music's demo studio and asked
him to head to the airport. A ticket was already
waiting, and Loggins flew up to Toronto to
work on the track that afternoon. He learned
the song on the plane and did a scratch vocal
with Anne in the studio. Later, once Murray's
part was finished, he recorded his final vocal in
Nashville.

Despite a lack of "marquee value," the rec-
ord was an overwhelming success. "Nobody
Loves Me Like You Do" ascended to number
one in December of 1984. The following Octo-
ber, the Country Music Association named
Murray and Loggins the Vocal Duo of the Year.
Loggins became the only artist ever to win a
CMA vocal trophy without a record deal.

"I tried to entice him into [signing]," says
Norman, "but we never could quite get it together, and I just came to the conclusion that
he really wasn't interested. He's doing so well
as a writer, I can understand why."

600

WHY NOT ME
THE JUDDS
(WYNONNA & NAOMI)

RCA 13923
Writers: Harlan Howard, Sonny
Throckmorton, Brent Maher
Producer: Brent Maher
December 22, 1984 (2 weeks)

Once the Judds overwhelmed listeners with "Mama He's Crazy" [see 580], RCA set them to work on a full album to follow their mini-LP. After assembling material, producer Brent Maher felt they still needed something with a strong, mid-tempo groove, and he turned to songwriter Harlan Howard.

Harlan wanted to go fishing, but they decided to set up a Sunday writing session at Howard's home. They didn't have any strong ideas, and Harlan suggested they call Sonny Throckmorton, who had recently moved from Texas back to Nashville and lived just a few blocks away. Throck protested ("Man, this is *Sunday*") and then came over as a favor to Harlan. He brought along the foundations of "Why Not Me."

"I had had the melody for a long time," Sonny notes. "I had reached a point in my career where I just kind of quit workin' at it that much. I was tryin' to write it as 'How 'Bout Me,' but I couldn't ever get anything."

Howard had recently heard another song called "How About Me" and altered the title, although he still had doubts about it.

"'Why Not Me' wasn't a great title, and 'What About Me' wasn't either," Harlan explains. "To get a really good record, you've gotta write a hell of a song when you're dealing with a title that average. The only thing I know to do with songs like 'Why Not Me' and 'Busted'—which I never thought was a good title—is to put the title in there often so that people remember it. The weaker the title, the more you gotta hear it."

Howard concocted the lyrics to the song around the Judds' personalities, rather than any real-life events. Maher and Throckmorton pieced together the musical elements, and Brent then took a tape to guitarist Don Potter.

The day that Maher arrived, Potter had just found a slide that he hadn't slipped on his finger for years, and when Brent played the song, Don joined in and added a bent note that became a signature in the instrumental hook.

Maher also created another unusual texture: he gave his guitar to keyboard player Bobby Ogdin, who slapped the back of the six-string in place of a kick drum.

The result: the Judds' second consecutive number one single, and their second consecutive Grammy-winner.

601

DOES FORT WORTH EVER CROSS YOUR MIND
GEORGE STRAIT

MCA 52548
Writers: Sanger D. Shafer, Darlene Shafer
Producers: Jimmy Bowen, George Strait
January 5, 1985 (1 week)

Having changed producers prior to his *Right or Wrong* album [see 567], George Strait again found someone new to sit behind the glass for his follow-up album, *Does Fort Worth Ever Cross Your Mind*. In this instance, he turned to Jimmy Bowen, who joined MCA in May of 1984, just a few months before Strait went into the recording studio.

"He came to see me, and told me he had sixteen tracks cut that he wasn't gonna put his voice on," Bowen recalls. "He didn't like 'em. We talked about how I thought he should record. He went back, got some songs, including 'Fort Worth,' and we went in and cut ten songs in three days, which is rare for us. We usually record five days to get 'em in."

Whitey Shafer wrote "Does Fort Worth Ever Cross Your Mind" eight years earlier, with help from his wife at the time, Darlene.

"I lived in Fort Worth for a long time," he remembers, "and it seemed like Fort Worth was always in the shadow of Dallas. I just wanted to do somethin' about the two cities, and I had a pretty good melody goin'. My ex-wife had a little saying 'Does Fort Worth ever cross your mind?,' and the title of that sounded really good."

Moe Bandy recorded the song first, and Keith Whitley also cut it, although Keith's version was never released. Shafer caught Strait's ear by playing him Whitley's version, although Reba McEntire could have conceivably beaten George to it.

"After the album had come out," George recalls, "Reba said, 'Yeah, I considered doin' that song,' but she said that she didn't want to

406

do a song with beer in it, or somethin' like that. So she passed on the song."

Released as the first single from the album, "Fort Worth" first appeared at number 74 in *Billboard* on September 29, 1984. It made for a happy New Year when it slid into number one in the first week of '85, Strait's fifth consecutive single to top the chart.

His three-day project with Bowen also garnered accolades from his industry peers, as both the Country Music Association and the Academy of Country Music named *Does Fort Worth Ever Cross Your Mind* the Album of the Year.

602
THE BEST YEAR OF MY LIFE
EDDIE RABBITT

Warner Bros. 29186
Writers: Eddie Rabbitt, Even Stevens
Producers: Even Stevens, Eddie Rabbitt,
Jimmy Bowen
January 12, 1985 (1 week)

Ironically, Eddie Rabbitt released "The Best Year Of My Life" in the midst of perhaps the worst year of his personal life. Eddie and his wife, Janine, had a son, Timmy, on August 12, 1983, at Williamson County Hospital in Franklin, Tennessee. Timmy was born with a rare birth defect, biliary atresia, which affects the body's ability to eliminate waste products.

"We were going up to the hospital five and six days a week for about two years there," says Rabbitt, "which is an awful pressure when you do it. The career had to go on the back burner. I wasn't writing, and with some of those projects, I just wasn't into it."

Transferred to Nashville's Vanderbilt University Hospital, Timmy generated medical bills in excess of $400,000. Eddie found little pleasure outside of food, and gained 55 pounds during that period. Ultimately, little Timmy underwent a liver transplant, but a couple of days later, on July 16, 1985, he passed away.

"The Best Year Of My Life" was released in the middle of that period, but Rabbitt wrote it at the beginning, when the weight of Timmy's defect hadn't yet sapped him of his strength and enthusiasm.

"That was a song that I had written two months before Eddie and I got together [to write]," Even Stevens remembers. "David [Malloy] had quit bein' Eddie's producer at that

point, and I was producin' him, and I coproduced that album with Jimmy Bowen and Eddie.

"I had written a song called 'Best Year Of My Life,' and brought it in. It wasn't really done. I showed Eddie the song, and we rewrote the song, basically. It was just a real positive love song idea."

At the time, Rabbitt had just started working with Nautilus equipment and running two miles a day. He was in the best shape of his life, and honestly felt the emotions that surrounded "The Best Year Of My Life."

Rabbitt recorded much of the *Best Year of My Life* album at Emerald Studios, then owned by Stevens and Malloy. Modeled on various features from studios in Los Angeles, Muscle Shoals and Caribou [see 444—"Step By Step"], Emerald opened in 1983, with Stevens producing Engelbert Humperdinck for the first complete Emerald album.

Studio ownership took more time and money than they anticipated, so Stevens and Malloy sold Emerald a few years later.

603
HOW BLUE
REBA McENTIRE

MCA 52468
Writer: John Moffat
Producer: Harold Shedd
January 19, 1985 (1 week)

Reba McEntire's recording of "How Blue" was almost a trade-off with George Strait for "Does Fort Worth Ever Cross Your Mind" [see 601] . . . almost. Reba turned down "Fort Worth" over its reference to beer (incidentally, she also passed up "On The Other Hand" [see 680]) before Strait heard it. George never did hear "How Blue" prior to its release, although it was originally intended for him. Instead, it wound up in the hands of producer Harold Shedd, who earmarked it for Reba.

John Moffat, a former athlete/pre-med student/comedy writer/advertising executive, moved to Nashville from Indianapolis in November of 1979, after winning the Kentucky Fried Chicken amateur songwriting contest. Until he landed "Still Doin' Time" [see 451], Moffat toiled for a mere $200 a month (rent was $150). "How Blue," his second number one composition, came out of a musical curiosity.

"That was just kind of an experiment in a

Reba McEntire

Shedd suggested she change the word "breast" to "chest," and Reba decided to cut it.

"I would've passed on it," she says, "and I'm glad that Harold had the foresight to know a good song. I like to sing real deep songs that have stories to them, and 'How Blue' is just a good-feelin' song, which usually makes a monster song. I don't see that sometimes."

She recorded "How Blue" in the same session as "Somebody Should Leave" [see 619].

604

(THERE'S A) FIRE IN THE NIGHT
ALABAMA
RCA 13926
Writer: Bob Corbin
Producers: Harold Shedd, Alabama
January 26, 1985 (1 week)

From 1979 to 1982, the Corbin/Hanner Band repeatedly attempted to find a niche in the country music business. The Pittsburgh quintet placed half a dozen singles on the *Billboard* chart, although only two—"Livin' The Good Life" and "Everyone Knows I'm Yours"—managed to climb as far as number 46.

Eventually, group leaders Bob Corbin and Dave Hanner disbanded the unit and carried on as songwriters. Both of them had already proven themselves in that field: Hanner had written a couple of hits [see 461—"Lord, I Hope This Day Is Good"], and Corbin's credits began to add up. Two Mel Tillis records started things off: "Blind In Love" and "In The Middle Of The Night." Corbin later supplied Don Williams with "I'll Never Be In Love Again" and gave Alabama hits with "Can't Keep A Good Man Down" [see 644] and "(There's A) Fire In The Night."

"I think as nearly as I can recall, I came up with the hook line first and I just built the song around it," Corbin says of the latter tune. "I think I drew on my experiences from the years playing, and I thought it might appeal to Alabama, because they did the bars for a long time before they made it. It's kind of like bein' out on the road. It starts out, 'Runnin' scared/Wonderin' what I'll do when I'm through tonight.'

"I think I was just drawin' on my own experience. I tried to keep the song general enough so that anybody that was just out on their own, or whatever, would associate with it."

Corbin worked down to the wire on the song

bluegrass area, which I had no experience in, and no business being in," he explains. "I was kind of goin' into my bluegrass period, I guess."

"How Blue" was about the only song that Harold Shedd and McEntire agreed on in the process of recording the *My Kind of Country* album. Shedd wanted to take Reba in a more contemporary direction, while Reba wanted a traditional slant, and she eventually sought out songs for herself at the suggestion of MCA executive Jimmy Bowen.

Even in the case of "How Blue," Reba had her doubts when Harold presented it to her. They had gone over material for an entire day, and an exhausted Reba had reservations about the song because it was written from a man's viewpoint. Harold suggested she make some lyrical changes, but she put it off until the next morning. After she took in a night's rest, prior to a demo session for Tillis' publishing company, and his wife, sick with the flu, begged him to stop. Mrs. Corbin must have felt much better when Bob's song found its way to Alabama. Corbin did the demo with harmonies quite similar to what they would probably record, and it emerged as the fourth number one single from the *Roll On* [see 562] album, Alabama's fifteenth chart-topping hit overall.

In 1989, "Fire In The Night" appeared in the movie *Roadhouse*, starring Patrick Swayze.

605

A PLACE TO FALL APART
MERLE HAGGARD
& JANIE FRICKIE
Epic 04663
Writers: Merle Haggard, Willie Nelson, Freddy Powers
Producers: Merle Haggard, Ray Baker
February 2, 1985 (1 week)

On Saturday, October 27, 1984, "A Place To Fall Apart" debuted on the *Billboard* country chart, a duet pairing Merle Haggard with Janie Frickie. That same weekend, Epic Records sponsored a three-hour program—"The Merle Haggard Story," his first network radio special in ten years.

"A Place To Fall Apart" actually fell together in a series of events, beginning with Willie Nelson and songwriter Freddy Powers. "I had that idea," recalls Powers, "and Willie and I were down in Austin. I told him I had a hell of an idea, so Willie and I fooled around with it in the car one afternoon, throwing a couple of lines around."

The second part of the chain came on the same bus trip with Haggard that yielded "Let's Chase Each Other Around The Room" [see 587]. "We were in the Opryland Hotel," says Powers. "Merle had been writing all these Leona Williams songs when they split up, and he said, 'I wish I could write me one little song, and just get her off my mind—finalize it.' He wanted to tell her what he thought in a song."

Powers suggested he forget about melodies and rhymes, and simply write everything he wanted to say in a letter. The first line of the note read, "Leona, I'll probably never see you eye-to-eye again," which became the first line of "A Place To Fall Apart."

"We extracted the song right out of the middle of the letter," Merle notes. "It was

really a neat way of writing a song, because it had no air of being contrived at all. It was real, the letter being of a real nature.

"Then," he laughs, "we burned the letter."

"A Place To Fall Apart" and "Natural High" [see 623] were both recorded at Eleven-Eleven Sound in Nashville, with vocal support from Janie Frickie. "We got hold of Janie at the last minute or so, and got her to overdub some things," reports producer Ray Baker. "I remember Merle just asked her to kind of ad-lib—'Don't pick a line and sing harmony to it, just kind of go in and shut your eyes and feel it'—and she did."

606

AIN'T SHE SOMETHIN' ELSE
CONWAY TWITTY
Warner Bros. 29137
Writers: Jerry Foster, Bill Rice
Producers: Conway Twitty, Dee Henry
February 9, 1985 (1 week)

Eddy Raven made his second appearance on the *Billboard* country chart in November of 1974, when he introduced a song written by the prolific Jerry Foster & Bill Rice team.

"We had somebody in mind or whatever when we wrote the song," recalls Rice, "because it has an awful lot of range in the song, and it's not an easy song to sing. Raven did a marvelous job on it, but not everybody can sing that song."

Despite Raven's performance, the record only went to number 46 and was promptly forgotten. Years later, however, Dee Henry got a copy of Raven's recording and fell in love with it.

"She thought it would be a good record for me," notes Conway Twitty, "and she played it for me. I really liked Eddy Raven's singin', and I loved his record on it, but I called to get Bill Rice's demo on it. I wanted 'em both, 'cause I love Bill's singin', and I love his writin'. Nobody's closer to a song than the writer, and I always want to hear what they feel. If they can get that thing exactly right, then I'll go into the studio and cut it exactly like that."

Twitty did all of his work on "Ain't She Somethin' Else" before word could get back to Rice about it. He found out that Conway was recording the song strictly by accident while taping demos with his wife, Sharon, at Sound Stage Studio A.

"It was really very strange," says Rice. "Jimmy Bowen was in studio B, the smaller studio, cutting Conway. We didn't know it at the time, but anyhow, their musicians had just taken a break and they came out while I was walkin' through the hall, gettin' a cup of coffee.

"One of the musicians hollered and said, 'Rice, we just cut one of your songs, man, and I mean it came off like gangbusters.' I didn't even know anything of it, and they told me what song it was. I thought Conway did a really, really good job on it."

The general public apparently agreed with Rice. Twitty's version of "Ain't She Somethin' Else" made its first chart appearance in November of 1984—exactly ten years after Raven debuted it. In its fourteenth week, the record became Conway's thirty-eighth number one single.

607

MAKE MY LIFE WITH YOU
THE OAK RIDGE BOYS
MCA 52488
Writer: Gary Burr
Producer: Ron Chancey
February 16, 1985 (1 week)

In 1982, songwriter Gary Burr broke into the record business in an unusual way. He sent a tape to Nashville from his home in Connecticut, and actually got a response. The first song on the tape was "Love's Been A Little Bit Hard On Me," and publisher Bob Montgomery sent Burr a contract and got Juice Newton to record it. It took nearly three more years before Burr earned his second hit.

"Most of the love songs I write," Gary explains, "are 'she broke my heart, so I shot her,' those kinds of things. My publisher came to me and said, 'You know, these are all fine. These are fun songs, but I sit home at night and wish that just once you'd write a positive love song like 'You're great, I love you.' I could sell that.'

"So I went home, and I wrote 'Make My Life With You.' I had been toying with the rhyme of 'it ought to be up to me.' I liked that rhyme, but I couldn't get anywhere with that, so I used the rhyme [a little differently], and I gave it to my publisher. He was very happy that it was a positive love song, and he was absolutely right—he went out and sold it immediately."

The Oak Ridge Boys recorded "Make My Life With You" in their own Acorn Recording Studio for their *Greatest Hits 2*. They were already quite familiar with Burr, since they had done four or five of his songs previously.

"None of them made the album," notes the Oaks' Duane Allen, "and it wasn't because of the quality of the song—unless the quality was so good that we just didn't get it good enough."

Burr spent five years with Pure Prairie League, and after "Make My Life With You" hit number one, hits seemed to come more frequently, even though he didn't leave Connecticut for Nashville until 1989. He earned successes with "That's My Job" (Conway Twitty), "Burned Like A Rocket" (Billie Joe Royal) and "The Vows Go Unbroken" (Kenny Rogers).

Burr admits that he still writes too few positive love songs: "There's just so many 'I love you' songs. The world don't need more of 'em. Somebody has to fill the niche of psycho-killer songs, so I take that burden on myself."

608

BABY'S GOT HER BLUE JEANS ON
MEL McDANIEL
Capitol 5418
Writer: Bob McDill
Producer: Jerry Kennedy
February 23, 1985 (1 week)

Having first signed with Capitol Records in 1976, Mel McDaniel entered a new phase in his career in 1984. Jim Foglesong came in as the head of the label's Nashville division during a major shakeup, and he suggested that McDaniel try working with producer Jerry Kennedy.

"It was the first song on the first session that we did," McDaniel says of "Baby's Got Her Blue Jeans On." "I did not ever dream that it would be a number one song. Jerry kept saying it was a hit, my wife kept saying it was a hit, my band kept saying it was a hit. I believe in everything that we record, and always hope for the best, but you never know when that one's gonna be there."

Songwriter Bob McDill carried around the melody and the guitar riff in his head for several months when he originally wrote the song, all the while trying to come up with a substitution for the "Blue Jeans" title. "It sounded dated at first," he recalls, "and I was afraid to use it, but it sounded just right."

McDill pitched two different arrangements of the song for several years and was turned down by just about all of Nashville's producers, until Kennedy snatched "Blue Jeans" for McDaniel. A thumping cowbell and Pete Wade's translation of McDill's guitar riff created a rhythmic groove that's become a trademark for McDaniel records.

"That's the kind of music I grew up with," says Mel. "It's gotta have a real good, feel-good snap."

McDaniel first performed on stage on Halloween, 1958, in Okmulgee, Oklahoma. Living briefly in Nashville, he moved to Anchorage, Alaska, where he honed his performing skills at King X's Lounge before returning to Tennessee. This time around, he started writing for Combine Music and singing demos (including "A Tear Fell," later recorded by Billy "Crash" Craddock).

Once signed by Capitol, McDaniel scored five Top Ten singles prior to "Blue Jeans," three of which were also McDill compositions: "Louisiana Saturday Night," "Right In The Palm Of Your Hand" and "I Call It Love."

On January 11, 1986, Mel McDaniel became the 62nd member of the Grand Ole Opry.

Mel McDaniel

609

BABY BYE BYE

GARY MORRIS

Warner Bros. 29131
Writers: Gary Morris, Jamie Brantley
Producers: Jim Ed Norman, Gary Morris
March 2, 1985 (1 week)

Gary Morris can trace his career as a country singer directly to Jimmy Carter's 1976 bid for the presidency. Morris appeared frequently on the campaign trail with the former Georgia governor as a performer, and after he won the election, Carter invited Gary to perform at a special White House reception for the Country Music Association. Norro Wilson attended that event, and when Morris showed up at Warner Bros. two years later with a demo tape, Wilson was the head of A & R. He remembered Gary's performance, and signed the singer immediately.

His third single for the label, "Headed For A Heartache," established Morris instantly, reaching number eight in 1981. Two more singles hit the Top 20, then Gary reeled off a string of seven consecutive Top Ten records, including "Velvet Chains," "The Love She Found In Me," "The Wind Beneath My Wings" (named Song of the Year by both the Country Music Association and the Academy of Country Music) and "You're Welcome To Tonight" (a duet with Lynn Anderson).

Having used four different production teams to create his first two albums, Gary turned to Jim Ed Norman for the third, *Faded Blue*, with an eye toward capturing the energy of his live shows.

"He wanted to create more of a 'band' kind of sound, rather than the stand-up singer," Norman says. "That was really, I think, what was behind 'Baby Bye Bye.' He wrote that song with his guitar player, Jamie Brantley, and it was a piece of material that, from the beginning, had a real nice character and feel to it."

"The record is—as are a lot of the songs that I've written—about surface versus the interior of a human," Gary explains. "That's about pretty women on the outside and beautiful people on the inside. A lot of times, people will confuse the baggage they were given when they were born with what they've got—heart and soul—inside them. That song talks about women who may think they're gonna be young and beautiful forever, and the price they ultimately may have to pay for that."

Morris intended it as a summer record, but Warner Bros. held it back as a single until two others had already been pulled from the album. On March 2, 1985, "Baby Bye Bye" became Gary's first number one single.

viewed it for his fellow Statlers. "It was good for a wedding," surmises lead singer Don Reid, "but it was also good for a record."

Fortune's arrival brought the total number of Statlers to six. The original foursome made its first appearance at the Lynhurst Methodist Church near Staunton, Virginia, in the late '50s, but even before that, one Joe McDorman had preceded Don Reid in the quartet's informal line-up. McDorman would later rejoin the Statlers on a gospel track.

It took the Statlers a dozen years to score their first number one single on the *Billboard* charts [see 311—"Do You Know You Are My Sunshine"], but Fortune wrote two [see 561— "Elizabeth"] within a year. Both of Fortune's compositions earned Song of the Year honors from the *Music City News*—ironic, considering the Statlers hadn't expected him to write.

"He didn't know he could write, either," says Reid. "He had never really written before. He kept talking about it, we encouraged him to do so, and he found out he had talent down there he hadn't tapped yet."

As a group, the Statlers won the *Music City News* trophy for Vocal Group of the Year 16 times in 17 years. In fact, the quartet has been making country records longer than any other headlining group in the business.

"I think we did pioneer some things for groups," notes Reid. "I don't want to sound immodest, but when we came along in the '60s, if you were a group in country music, you were 'ooh-wah, ooh-wah' behind somebody. We didn't want that—we wanted to be up front."

610

MY ONLY LOVE

THE STATLER BROTHERS

Mercury 880411
Writer: Jimmy Fortune
Producer: Jerry Kennedy
March 9, 1985 (1 week)

It could have scored a "90+" on "American Bandstand," but "My Only Love" earned a "16" on the Statler Brothers' scale. The group has a unique system of evaluating material from one to four; when each member's score is totaled up, the highest-rated songs get cut for their albums. Invariably, the songs that notch the maximum "16" end up as singles.

Jimmy Fortune wrote "My Only Love" specifically for a wedding at which he was to sing, but before the bridal performance, he pre-

611

CRAZY FOR YOUR LOVE

EXILE

Epic 04722
Writers: Sonny Lemaire, J.P. Pennington
Producer: Buddy Killen
March 16, 1985 (1 week)

"Charley Pride came up to me one time and he just absolutely loved 'Crazy For Your Love,'" remembers Exile's bassist Sonny Lemaire. "I think it was the wordplay in the verses; he really loved the way it fit together."

Pride wasn't the only listener captivated by "Crazy For Your Love." Released in November of 1984, the song debuted on *Billboard*'s country chart on December 8, just three weeks after "Give Me One More Chance" [see 595] peaked at number one. The following March, the record became Exile's fourth consecutive number one single.

"When we came up with the hook and figured out exactly how we wanted to write it, it was a lot of fun," says Lemaire of his collaboration with J.P. Pennington. "Some of the words and the phrases that were used in it, and the way the melody just kind of flowed along with the lyrics, it was fun. At the time, I think it was one of my favorites."

Exile's trademark sound—in evidence on "Crazy On Your Love"—was a hybrid of a wide range of influences. Lemaire cites Elvis Presley and Hank Williams among his early favorites, but other members had fewer country ties in their listening habits. Keyboard specialist Marlon Hargis and guitar player Les Taylor list such black influences as Motown and James Brown, while drummer Steve Goetzman followed session sidemen like Larry Londin and Steve Gadd. Pennington cites George Gershwin as his primary influence.

"If somebody would have told me in 1972 that I was gonna be in a country band with a number one record, I would have beat them to death . . . with an Iron Butterfly record," Pennington told Alanna Nash in a 1984 interview for *Country Rhythms*.

Nevertheless, Exile was embraced so quickly that 1985 brought them the second of three consecutive Academy of Country Music nominations for Top Vocal Group.

Much of that success can be traced directly to the Pennington/Lemaire collaboration. Pennington was already having his songs recorded when Sonny first joined the band in 1978, and it was Australian songwriter/producer Mike Chapman (of "Kiss You All Over" [see 559—"Woke Up In Love"] fame) who inspired Lemaire's progress.

"I was scared to death to play my songs for anybody," Sonny recalls, "and he helped boost my morale for songwriting more than any other person at the time."

612

SEVEN SPANISH ANGELS
RAY CHARLES
WITH WILLIE NELSON
Columbia 04715
Writers: Troy Seals, Eddie Setser
Producer: Billy Sherrill
March 23, 1985 (1 week)

Ray Charles & Willie Nelson

In 1982, Ray Charles signed a recording contract with Columbia Records out of Nashville [see 440—"You Don't Know Me"], leading to a series of four country albums over the next four years. Only one of them, *Friendship*, was a major success. A collection of duets with ten different performers, it hit number one on March 23, 1985, the same date that Ray earned his only number one country single, "Seven Spanish Angels."

The original concept for this song, a Mexican-flavored tragedy, belonged to Eddie Setser, who wrote frequently with Troy Seals. After much resistance, Seals helped craft the song with Willie Nelson in mind.

"We started writing, hoping we could emulate Marty Robbins and 'El Paso,'" Seals explains. "We didn't think we had a song like that,

but that whole flavor of the Southwest and cowboys. Of course, the chorus is kind of an old wives' tale, an old story that's been handed down."

Seals and Setser sent the finished demo to Willie, who liked it, but wanted to wait until a future date to record it. They also sent a copy to Billy Sherrill, who was producing *Friendship*. Sherrill envisioned "Seven Spanish Angels" for Ray Charles and Ronnie Milsap, but Milsap didn't want to cut it.

In the meantime, Sherrill found out that Willie liked it and asked Nelson to record it with Charles. Ray cut the basic tracks in Nashville, took it to Texas to add Willie's voice, and then sent the tape back to Sherrill, who added strings and backing voices in Music City.

In the process, Sherrill made a major deletion that clouded the song's storyline.

"The song was like two movements," he explains. "One of 'em was the 'Seven Spanish Angels' thing, and the boy and the girl and the soldiers comin' and shootin'. Then, it went into some sort of a refrain and another melody that explained it all—why the angels, why there were seven, and all that.

"I called Troy and said, 'Hey, man, this is like a book, not a song. It's like you gotta sit down and take notes.' We just wiped out the whole other end of it, and ended up leavin' you in the dark about what it meant—which I think contributed to the beauty of the song."

Kenny Rogers

613

CRAZY

KENNY ROGERS

RCA 13975
Writers: Kenny Rogers, Richard Marx
Producers: Kenny Rogers, David Foster
March 30, 1985 (1 week)

With his 1984 album *What About Me?*, Kenny Rogers picked up a trio of songs from a then-unknown songwriter. Richard Marx contributed the title track (performed by Kenny with James Ingram and Kim Carnes), as well as "Somebody Took My Love" and "Crazy," a tune he co-wrote with Rogers.

"Richard and I probably wrote the first line or two of ["Crazy"]," Kenny confesses, "and I just couldn't get started on it. Richard went home and probably wrote 90 percent of this song, and came back, and I may have changed two or three words.

"This is a song I do not deserve credit for being on, but I like it so much I'm gonna take credit anyway, 'cause I was there for part of it. But Richard Marx really wrote that song. We've laughed about it. Every time we talk, I say, 'Richard, I did "Crazy" last night, and I'm trying to figure out which line it was I wrote in there.' I can't figure it out yet, and usually I can spot my lines."

"Crazy" first appeared on *Billboard*'s country chart on December 22, 1984, at number 69. Kenny had to wait another fourteen weeks before the record reached number one.

Another two years later, Marx was on his own, having sung as a back-up vocalist for Kenny, as well as for Lionel Richie, Madonna and Dolly Parton. He also forged a place on rock radio with "Don't Mean Nothin'," and secured a pop/rock solo career with hits like "Hold On To The Nights," "Satisfied" and "Right Here Waiting."

"Richard used to hang around the studio when Lionel and I would work together," Rogers recalls, "and he was one of those extremely talented guys. He can sing [back-up] with me and kind of sound like me; he can sing with Lionel and kind of sound like Lionel; he can sing with Michael Jackson and sound like Michael Jackson. You need that—you don't want someone whose voice is so obvious and so definite that it distracts from the lead."

While "Crazy" made its run for number one, Jackson, Richie, Rogers and 46 other artists (including Waylon Jennings and Willie Nelson) participated in the landmark U.S.A. For Africa single "We Are The World," recorded on January 28, 1985, following the American Music Awards.

614

COUNTRY GIRLS
JOHN SCHNEIDER
MCA 52510
Writers: Troy Seals, Eddie Setser
Producer: Jimmy Bowen
April 6, 1985 (1 week)

Control—that's the difference between John Schneider's first vocal success, "It's Now Or Never" [see 594—"I've Been Around Enough To Know"], and the three-year streak that began in 1984.

"The Broadway-style delivery and big power voice were what CBS and Scotti

Brothers bought as my image," Schneider told *Billboard*'s Kip Kirby, referring to the earlier period. "I would be given eleven songs before a session and told to pick ten, and then they'd ask me what day next week I'd like to come in and sing them. That was the extent of my involvement."

Producer Jimmy Bowen allowed John the opportunity to make his own decisions about arrangements, songs and keys—after all, Schneider was investing his own money on their first collaboration—and the results came closer to Schneider's musical heart.

"He'd ask me ahead of time, 'What instruments do you hear on this song?'" John remembered. "And I'd tell him a clarinet and a trombone and a trumpet, and he'd say, 'Great, we'll get them. What do you hear on this song—violins?' And I'd say, 'No, not really,' and we wouldn't use them. It was very flattering to me as an artist."

Once Schneider landed "I've Been Around Enough To Know," he was better able to tune Nashville songwriters to the kind of songs he wanted. Many immediately created material specifically for John, as was the case with "Country Girls," the follow-up single.

"I've had the good fortune to sit with John," says songwriter Troy Seals, "and he's just a great guy. When he came to Nashville, he was real honest. He knew he already had the image that he had, but it didn't take long to know him and know what he felt like doin'."

Based on those meetings, Seals got together with songwriter Eddie Setser to craft "Country Girls." "We liked the feel of the song, and were tryin' to write something for John that would work," Troy explains. "We really had no idea that he'd do it, but the song expresses our sentiment exactly: you don't have to be from Kentucky to like country girls."

"Country Girls" first appeared in *Billboard* on January 5, 1985, at number 58. Three months later, it slipped into number one.

615

HONOR BOUND
EARL THOMAS CONLEY
RCA 13960
Writers: Charlie Black, Tommy Rocco, Austin Roberts
Producers: Nelson Larkin, Earl Thomas Conley
April 13, 1985 (1 week)

Charlie Black, Tommy Rocco and Austin Roberts emerged as three of the most prolific songwriters in Nashville during the early to mid-'80s. Black and Rocco both hooked up as writing partners during the prior decade, while working for Ricci Moreno's publishing company. Rocco calls himself an "old Italian boy from Philadelphia" ("My daddy thought I was a hill-a-billy") and Moreno convinced him initially to go under the pseudonym of Skippy Barrett.

Roberts started writing with Black and Rocco after moving to Nashville around 1983. Once affiliated with the cartoons "Scooby Doo" and "Josie And The Pussycats," Austin earned a couple of pop hits during the '70s: "Something's Wrong With Me" and "Rocky" [see 229]. He wrote Lee Greenwood's Grammy-winning "I.O.U.," and then scored three number one singles with Black and Rocco: "Strong Heart" [see 684], "100% Chance Of Rain" [see 664] and "Honor Bound."

"The idea for 'Honor Bound' had laid around for a long time," Black remembers. "I hit Rocco with it a couple of times, and we thought, 'Yeah, that's good, we'll look at it.' We moved on to something else, but Rocco said, 'You know, what about that idea? That was good, we could do somethin' with that.' Austin saw the whole story when he heard the title, and so we started from there."

Conley tapped "Honor Bound" as the only "outside song" included on the album *Treadin' Water*. Earl accepted it as a vocal challenge, and performed it so well that many of his fans assumed that he had written it himself.

"That was one of the songs that we cut with the band that I had to do a lot of work on to get it soundin' right," admits producer Nelson Larkin. "Earl's vocal performance was good, and all that, but track-wise, I always thought it could be a lot better."

Despite Larkin's reservations, "Honor Bound" debuted at number 68 on the *Billboard* country singles chart on January 5, 1985. Fourteen weeks later, it became Roberts' first chart-topper, Black's sixth, Rocco's fourth, and Conley's eighth.

616

I NEED MORE OF YOU
THE BELLAMY BROTHERS
Curb 52518

Writer: David Bellamy
Producers: The Bellamy Brothers,
Steve Klein
April 20, 1985 (1 week)

For their 1984 album, *Restless*, the Bellamy Brothers took a new approach. "We were kind of burnt out on California and Nashville, as far as recording and everything," explains David Bellamy. "We just wanted to try something different and take it a little easy."

Consequently, they headed to North Miami Beach to work at Criteria Sound Studios, a facility that opened in 1956 and has yielded at least 120 gold and platinum albums. The studio's credits include records by Julio Iglesias, Exposé and Crosby, Stills & Nash. In fact, several of the musicians, arrangers and engineers on *Restless* worked directly on pop albums by the Bee Gees and Gloria Estefan & Miami Sound Machine. The Bellamys' co-producer also maintained ties to the studio.

"Steve Klein was an engineer at Criteria," David notes. "He worked on a lot of the early John Cougar albums, and he helped me and Howard produce the album. We wanted to stay at the beach for a few weeks, and we went down there and kind of took it easy. *Restless* was a good album to cut down there. It went real smooth and it was laid-back."

The Bellamys led off the album with "Forget About Me" and "World's Greatest Lover" [see 513—"When I'm Away From You"], pulling "I Need More Of You" as the third single. David had been haunted by the melody for about six months before he wrote lyrics to it.

"We released 'I Need More Of You' in Europe," David recalls, "and it started to do real well. It was a pop record in Europe, so we talked to [Jimmy] Bowen and the guys up there [in Nashville] and said, 'Well, let's release it here and see if it does any good.'

"It was the biggest record from that *Restless* album. It turned out to be real big. After that, Bowen said, 'We're gonna start using Austria for a test market.'"

On April 20, 1985, "I Need More Of You" returned the Bellamys to number one for the first time in two years. Each of their next three singles came close to repeating that feat, but stalled at number two: "Old Hippie," edged out of number one by "Love Don't Care (Whose Heart It Breaks)" [see 630] and "Forty Hour Week" [see 631]; "Lie To You For Your Love," nudged out by "Nobody Falls Like A Fool" [see 649]; and "Feelin' The Feelin'," upstaged by "Once In A Blue Moon" [see 668].

and you go out and you have a ball.

"I guarantee you it's inspired a lot of women, 'cause they'll come to the concerts and hold up signs saying, 'We're having a girls' night out.'"

617

GIRLS NIGHT OUT
THE JUDDS
(WYNONNA & NAOMI)
RCA 13991
Writers: Brent Maher,
Jeffrey Hawthorne Bullock
Producer: Brent Maher
April 27, 1985 (1 week)

In February of 1985, the Judds made Grammy history. They were nominated in the general category for Best New Artist, and, though they didn't win, they were the first Nashville act nominated for that award since Jeannie C. Riley [see 17—"Harper Valley P.T.A."] in 1969. Instead, they took home the Grammy for Best Country Duo or Group with "Mama He's Crazy" [see 580].

In the meantime, Wynonna and Naomi were already charting their third number one single, "Girls Night Out." Credit for the song belongs to Judds producer Brent Maher and the otherwise-unknown Jeffrey Hawthorne Bullock, a Cheyenne, Wyoming, resident who occasionally fishes for trout with Maher. Bullock and his wife had gone to Nashville, where he did some finishing work on a few songs he'd written. The couple stayed at the Maher residence, and Brent started the song as they prepared to dine out one evening.

"I picked up my guitar, and there was a rhythm pattern, and this melody just fell out," Brent remembers. "Jeff and his wife, Tina, kind of started dancin' around the room." At Tina's urging, Brent and Jeff went to work on it, and fashioned "Girls Night Out."

"I think I started writin' the verses first, and the choruses just sort of blurped out," Maher continues. "I wrote it just to be a little ditty, and it turned out to be a much bigger record than what I ever thought it would be. Actually, when I turned the record in, I never thought that would be a single. I just thought it was a really good-feel kind of a deal, but it turned out to be, in the early part of the Judds' career, a real anthem for them, especially at concerts. When they went into 'Girls Night Out,' the place would go crazy."

"There are a lot of women out there who don't have a date on Friday night," Wynonna explains. "I've been there. So what do you do? You get together with your girlfriends. You sit and talk about how ornery and trouble-making men are, and you forget about your troubles

618

THERE'S NO WAY
ALABAMA
RCA 13992
Writers: Lisa Palas, Will Robinson,
John Jarrard
Producers: Harold Shedd, Alabama
May 4, 1985 (1 week)

In April of 1985, *People* magazine readers named Alabama their favorite group, topping such pop acts as Hall & Oates, the Pointer Sisters and Huey Lewis & The News. By May, Alabama earned an even weightier distinction, tying Sonny James' long-standing record of 16 consecutive number one country singles [see 86—"Here Comes Honey Again"].

The song that did the trick was "There's No Way," which came directly from Alabama's own publishing company, Maypop Music.

"I was hanging around Maypop at that time, typing contracts and sort of helpin' out," recalls songwriter Will Robinson. "Lisa Palas and John Jarrard were over there writing, and [manager] Chuck [Neese] wanted me to get together with them.

"I had the idea for the melody already written and a couple lines for the chorus, and I ran it by 'em and we just sort of finished it right there. Because it was Alabama's company, it got sent to them. Almost everything was getting sent to them automatically, and then a couple months later we got a call back from Randy [Owen]. He wanted to put it on hold."

Robinson, Palas and Jarrard had to sweat it out, though, once Alabama took "There's No Way" into The Music Mill for the recording session. The musicians the band hired couldn't seem to make it work, and after several hours, they gave up on the song. That night, the writers were contacted with the news that the song wasn't coming off, and it looked bleak.

"There was one little thing they were doin' wrong, it turned out, on the chorus," Robinson explains. "Just in the words, 'There's no way.' There's three chords there, and for some reason, the pickers that they were using weren't hearing it. The next day, they got new pickers, with the leader being David Briggs.

When he came in, he heard what they were tryin' to do and then he heard the demo, and he immediately knew what was wrong. They cut it and it came out great."

Initially, the band had thought of "There's No Way" strictly as an album cut, but it came off so well that producer Harold Shedd and RCA Records persuaded Alabama to release it as a single.

619
SOMEBODY SHOULD LEAVE
REBA McENTIRE
MCA 52527
Writers: Harlan Howard, Chick Rains
Producer: Harold Shedd
May 11, 1985 (1 week)

Reba McEntire began to come into her own as a recording artist on the album *My Kind of Country*. She suggested to producer Harold Shedd that they avoid recording the album with a string section, and became adamant about it when informed that strings would cost an additional $10,000. Reba also started selecting her own material [see 603—"How Blue"], and manager Bill Carter set up one of her first song-finding appointments, with songwriter Harlan Howard.

She drove with husband Charlie Battles to Howard's house, and after a half hour of small talk, they sat down to listen to songs. Harlan played several "ditties," and Reba diplomatically passed on them. Satisfied that she wanted something better, Howard pulled out his ace.

"He played me 'Somebody Should Leave,' and big ol' tears come up in my eyes," she remembers. "The hair was just standin' up on my arms, and the tears were runnin' down my cheeks. ("She sat bolt-upright in that chair like she'd been pinned by a Sumo wrestler," says Howard.)

"When it got through, I blinked away the tears and I said, 'Can I have that song?' He said, 'I thought you'd like that one.' He was testin' me the whole time. If I'd have liked those other ones, he wouldn't have played me 'Somebody Should Leave.' That was his cherished baby. He was very protective of it."

Harlan guarded "Somebody Should Leave" with good reason: it was personal. He started it with Chick Rains on a 75-mile drive to Center Hill Lake, and, as they discussed the status of his marriage, Howard remarked, "It looks to me like somebody should leave." Rains thought it would make a good title, and they wrote the first verse and chorus before they arrived at their destination, where Rains jotted it down on a legal pad.

After fishing on Howard's houseboat until midnight, they finished the song on the sundeck the next morning. Harlan decided he wanted someone with a traditional orientation—hopefully Reba—to record it.

"I knew that it was quite country," he says. "Hell, you're married, you got babies, you're gettin' a divorce, and all that good country stuff that I dearly love. I know that's important."

620
STEP THAT STEP
SAWYER BROWN
Capitol 5446
Writer: Mark A. Miller
Producer: Randy L. Scruggs
May 18, 1985 (1 week)

It wasn't "The Tonight Show," and it wasn't Publishers' Clearinghouse—but it did involve Ed McMahon.

In September of 1983, Sawyer Brown auditioned for a new syndicated TV show called "Star Search." At the end of the program's first year, the band copped the $100,000 first prize—and a recording contract.

The band came together from three different sections of the country. Guitarist Bobby Randall and bassist Jim Scholten grew up in Michigan; vocalist Mark Miller and keyboard player Gregg Hubbard were high school classmates in Apopka, Florida; and percussionist Joe Smyth came from the Maine Symphony.

All found their way to Nashville between 1979 and 1981, taking on roles in singer Don King's backing band. They shared an apartment, and, after leaving King's employment, worked as many as 300 days on the club circuit in a single year. After a scant two years, Sawyer Brown (they took the name from a street west of Nashville) gained national attention from its "Star Search" berth.

They capitalized on their exposure quickly. Their first single, "Leona," hit number 16, and they embarked in the spring of 1985 on a 42-city tour, opening for Kenny Rogers & Dolly Parton. Concurrently, they released their second single, "Step That Step."

Miller, a high school "jock," hadn't begun writing songs until age 21. He created "Step That Step" one night while driving the group on its grueling club routine. While his bandmates slept, he came up with the tune to keep himself awake at the wheel, a song about the determination needed to make it to the top.

That's exactly where "Step That Step" went, too. When it hit number one in May of 1985, Miller had his first chart-topping record just two years after he started writing. Sawyer Brown also scored Top Ten singles with "Used To Blue," "Betty's Bein' Bad," "This Missin' You Heart Of Mine" and their remake of the George Jones classic "The Race Is On." Still, some critics dismissed the band's music as "bubblegum country."

"We'd rather be called bubblegum than terrible," they told Vernell Hackett in *Country News.* "[We] think they call us that because [our music] is not hard-core country. It's not real serious. It doesn't really say anything, it doesn't make any big statement—it's just a lot of fun."

621
RADIO HEART
CHARLY McCLAIN
Epic 04777
Writers: Steve Davis, Dennis Morgan
Producer: Norro Wilson
May 25, 1985 (1 week)

"I think she's got the most magical little identity in her voice I ever heard," says producer Norro Wilson, in reference to Charly McClain. "You don't have to like how she sings, how high she sings, how loud she sings, but the minute you hear her sing, you say, 'Oh, that's Charly McClain.' I think that's what it takes to be a success in our business—to have pipes that have that immediate identity."

In 1981, McClain came under the direction of Wilson, following five years with producer Larry Rogers, and, as a result, her records became more consistent. She gained five consecutive Top Ten hits in 1981 and 1982, including "Sleepin' With The Radio On" and "Dancing Your Memory Away," but when she began making duets with Mickey Gilley [see 541— "Paradise Tonight"], Charly's solo success tailed off.

In the meantime, she married Wayne Massey, former star of "One Life To Live," on July 16, 1984. Massey, who had earned a recording deal of his own, proved instrumental in her next number one record, "Radio Heart."

"He originally had picked that song for himself," Charly notes. "We had just met with Rick Blackburn at CBS, the president of the label. He said I had to have a hit record out soon, and that according to some sort of survey, 75 percent of my record buyers are women—which they felt was unusual for a female singer—so they wanted a song that would relate to a woman."

At a later date, Massey literally picked his flu-ridden wife up out of her bed and carried her into their music room, where he forced her to listen to "Radio Heart." She reluctantly agreed to cut it, but she also points to the major role that he played even during the recording process.

"If Wayne had not been in the studio, it wouldn't have come off like it did. That was really the first song that he was involved in, and he really helped me when I went in for the final vocal. He'd walk out on the floor and say, 'You gotta get mad, this guy left you with kids; you're mad and you've got to make it sound that way.' It worked."

McClain and Massey sang several duets together as well, including "With Just One Look In Your Eyes" and "You Are My Music, You Are My Song." In 1988, Charly signed with Mercury Records, where Massey took over as her permanent producer.

622
DON'T CALL HIM A COWBOY
CONWAY TWITTY
Warner Bros. 29057
Writers: Debbie Hupp, Johnny MacRae,
Bob Morrison
Producers: Conway Twitty, Dee Henry,
Ron Treat
June 1, 1985 (1 week)

Songwriter Johnny MacRae didn't decide to follow music until he was in the last five years of a fifteen-year stint with the Navy. One of his shipmates had a relative at KFWB radio in Los Angeles, and through that connection, MacRae earned his first recording and publishing contracts.

His own records did very little. MacRae did work, however, on Bobby "Boris" Pickett's novelty hit "Monster Mash."

"I was one of the Crypt-Kickers," he says. "I played electric razor, ratchet wrench and chains, blew bubbles on it. We got to doin' the background and Gary Paxton produced it. We were doin' the 'wah-oohs,' and I said, 'Why don't we sing 'Wah-ooh, tennis shoe?' Gary says, 'That don't make any sense, Johnny,' and I said, 'I don't think any of it does, Gary.' I don't think anybody knows that [line], but it's just plain as day if you're looking for it."

In June of 1963, MacRae moved to Nashville, where he drifted from publisher to publisher. In 1972, he ended up at Combine Music, where he became a vice president before leaving a dozen years later. MacRae helped cultivate the talents of younger writers like Bob DiPiero, John Scott Sherrill and Pat McManus, but he also wrote a number of country hits, many with frequent collaborator Bob Morrison. Among his singles were George Jones' "Shine On," Reba McEntire's "(You Lift Me) Up To Heaven," Mel Tillis' "One Night Fever," Charly McClain's "That's What You Do To Me," Conway Twitty's "I'd Love To Lay You Down" [see 372] and Conway's duet with Loretta Lynn, "I Still Believe In Waltzes." After forming his own company, Johnny picked up hits with Highway 101's "Whiskey, If You Were A Woman" and John Conlee's "Mama's Rockin' Chair," plus two more number one records: Ricky Van Shelton's "Living Proof" [see 839] and Twitty's "Don't Call Him A Cowboy."

"I wrote the chorus just when the *Urban Cowboy* thing was happening," says Johnny. "Everybody had on a cowboy hat and jeans. It was the 'in' thing. I never could get started on that song right. I wrote two or three versions of it, you know, and just didn't like 'em."

MacRae showed Debbie Hupp his idea, and after she went home to Louisville, she called him with appropriate lyrics. Bob Morrison helped shore up the melody, and suddenly, they had a very workable song.

"Conway's kind of a controversial guy," says Morrison. "He has been known to have records that hang it all out there, so it worked out good for him."

Conway debuted "Don't Call Him A Cowboy" in *Billboard* on March 16, 1985, and after a dozen weeks, he rode high in the saddle at number one.

623

NATURAL HIGH
MERLE HAGGARD
Epic 04830
Writer: Freddy Powers
Producers: Merle Haggard, Ray Baker
June 8, 1985 (1 week)

When "Natural High" went to number one in June of 1985, it represented Merle Haggard's fifty-second week at the top during his career—the equivalent of a full year of number ones!

The singer/songwriter didn't write his own hit in this instance; instead, it came from his friend, Freddy Powers. Visiting Willie Nelson's Pedernales Ranch, Powers started the song in Texas after a simple phone call.

"There was a jazz singer that I was running around with named Debbie DeFazio," says Powers, "and she was always 'up.' I called her up and said, 'You know, you're always just on a natural high,' and I thought about that title, and wrote it down on a piece of paper." Powers finished it up on a plane trip out to Lake Tahoe, where he was meeting Haggard. Notes Powers: "Merle heard 'Natural High' the first time and said, 'That's a number one song right there.'"

Like "A Place To Fall Apart" [see 605], the song was enhanced in the studio with a last-minute appearance by Janie Frickie. She was walking through a Music Row-area parking lot with her husband/manager Randy Jackson when they bumped into Haggard.

"Merle was at Shoney's Inn, on his bus," she remembers, "and he had just recorded these songs. He said, 'Come on up here; I want you to listen to some tapes.' We liked the songs, and he said, 'Well, how about you coming in and doing some things on 'em?' So we went right in and did it."

One other last-minute addition to the record was Lloyd Lindroth, a harpist who was friends with Powers. They ran across him in the lobby of the Opryland Hotel, and invited him to join them when they laid the basic tracks in the recording studio.

"I'm thinking 'What in the hell are we gonna do with a harp?'" admits producer Ray Baker. "That guy shows up, and he's got his harp, and he's sitting out there with all those hillbilly pickers, but it just so happened that we cut 'Natural High.' I couldn't have thought of a better sound to have on that record."

624

COUNTRY BOY
RICKY SKAGGS
Epic 04831
Writers: Tony Colton, Ray Smith, Albert Lee
Producer: Ricky Skaggs
June 15, 1985 (1 week)

As he did with "You've Got A Lover" in 1983 [see 557—"Don't Cheat In Our Hometown"], Ricky Skaggs just missed on his first attempt to register his ninth number one single. "Something In My Heart" stopped at number two, right behind "Ain't She Somethin' Else" [see 606]. The second try, however, nabbed the desired number one status, plus an Entertainer of the Year trophy.

Ricky Skaggs

The vehicle was "Country Boy," a rollicking, smoldering composition that British guitarist Albert Lee introduced in 1971, as a member of Heads, Hands And Feet. In the '60s, Lee's hot-picking influenced rock musicians like Jimmy Page of Led Zeppelin and Steve Howe of Yes. Since leaving Heads, Hands And Feet, Albert has played with Jackson Browne, Joe Cocker and Eric Clapton.

Lee took root in country music, replacing James Burton in Emmylou Harris' Hot Band in 1976. He contributed to her hits "Making Believe" and "Two More Bottles Of Wine" [see 313], among others, and also appeared on "Lovin' Only Me" [see 824], "My Baby Thinks He's A Train" [see 447] and the *Trio* album [see 721—"To Know Him Is To Love Him"].

After playing on the original version of "Country Boy," Albert added the song to his own *Hiding* album. In 1982, Karen Brooks reversed gender, calling it "Country Girl," on *Walk On*, and Skaggs made the song the title cut of his 1984 release.

"The track was done on the first take," says Ricky. "We did another track just for safety, to see if we could beat it, and it never ever felt as good as the first one. That's the type of song that you just can't keep going over and over again. I mean, it would kill you—the drummer would pass out."

"Country Boy" is the only number one single to have something in common with Porky Pig: a brief section of the "Looney Tunes Theme" in its lengthy instrumental section. The song also lent itself to one of country music's most innovative videos, when Bill Monroe joined Skaggs on Times Square in New York. Even Hizzoner, Mayor Edward Koch, made a brief appearance in the clip.

In October of 1985, the Country Music Association named Ricky the Entertainer of the Year, thanks in large part to Albert Lee's lightning-quick composition.

625

LITTLE THINGS
THE OAK RIDGE BOYS
MCA 52556
Writer: Billy Barber
Producer: Ron Chancey
June 22, 1985 (1 week)

In the early summer months of 1985, American pop radio gave plenty of space to British artists like Phil Collins, Wham!, the Power Station, Tears For Fears and Paul Young. Just one year earlier, Young had inadvertently thwarted the Oak Ridge Boys' plans to do their own British-flavored release.

"I wanted to do something electronically, drums and so on," recalls Duane Allen. "I even wanted to go to London to do it, but I was not in majority control with those ideas. So what I did was search through a bunch of English [song] catalogs, and I found this song by Paul Young, 'Come Back And Stay.'

"We were in Muscle Shoals to record it, and I got a call from MCA Records, who said, 'The latest single from Paul Young's premiere American album is "Come Back And Stay." ' I just sunk, 'cause I thought we had something."

Allen still clung to his idea, but they had to find a new song to use as a vehicle. During the sessions for the *Step On Out* album, fellow Oak Joe Bonsall received that song, "Little Things," in the mail.

"Since it was different, we decided to make it a real high-tech-sounding song for that period of time," says Allen. "It worked. It was a number one song. It was a different song. It was cut that way—people expect that kind of a record out of us every once in a while."

As they did in "Elvira" [see 427] and "Bobbie Sue" [see 466], the Oaks gave bass vocalist Richard Sterban a separate, melodic counterpoint in the *a capella* breakdown. Sterban, who owns country music's lowest vocal cords, hails from Camden, New Jersey, across the river from Philadelphia.

Sterban grew fascinated with the low sounds of J.D. Sumner of the gospel act the Blackwood Brothers. Years later, after a stint with Joe Bonsall in the Keystone Quartet, Richard worked alongside Sumner in the Stamps Quartet, singing back-up for Elvis Presley.

In 1972, Sterban replaced Noel Fox in the Oaks. Around 1975-76, when the Oaks opened a show for Freddy Fender in Phoenix, he became the centerpoint of a concert trend for the group. When he broke into one of his trademark bass tones, the female portion of the audience erupted. "It took me a while to get over it," Sterban confesses. "Now I kind of almost expect it."

A one-time clothing salesman for Gimbel's, he is the most fashion-conscious group member. He's also a co-owner of the Nashville Sounds baseball team [see 262—"The Games That Daddies Play"], a launching pad for major league All-Stars Don Mattingly, Willie McGee and Chris Sabo.

SHE KEEPS THE HOME FIRES BURNING

RONNIE MILSAP

RCA 14034
Writers: Dennis Morgan, Don Pfrimmer,
Mike Reid
Producers: Ronnie Milsap, Rob Galbraith,
Tom Collins
June 29, 1985 (1 week)

In May of 1975, Ronnie Milsap hit number one with "Daydreams About Night Things" [see 222], a song linking labor and love. Ten years later, Milsap tapped that same theme again with a single from his *Greatest Hits, Volume 2,* "She Keeps The Home Fires Burning."

It had been several years since Milsap re-leased a single that didn't lean toward an adult/contemporary style, and producer Tom Collins specifically set out to find a solid country song to demonstrate that Ronnie still had it in him. Unfortunately, when it came down to the wire, Tom hadn't yet come up with anything they were happy with.

As he did with "Smoky Mountain Rain" [see 403], Collins decided to graft two songs together. Songwriter Don Pfrimmer had written a lyric that still needed a melody. Meanwhile, Mike Reid and Dennis Morgan had constructed "She Keeps The Home Fires Burning," a melody that Collins loved with a lyric he found uninteresting. The writers literally melded the two songs in a side room at GroundStar Laboratory while Milsap worked on other material.

"Larry Londin was just beatin' on the drums, and you could hear Ronnie singin' and we were off in a little room just smokin' cigarettes," Pfrimmer recalls. "It required a total rewrite, and the ink wasn't dry and they hit the door and said, 'Are you done?'

"'Well, hey, yeah, we been sittin' here waitin' on you for an hour.' And I'll never forget Ronnie, 'cause the smoke in this little, bitty room, it just billowed out. It knocked him backwards out of the door. They got a big can of Lysol spray and sprayed it in there. Anyway, he listened to the song and said, 'I love it. Let's go for it.'"

Ronnie Milsap

The title, of course, was reminiscent of the 1915 World War I anthem, "Keep The Home Fires Burning." The new Milsap recording first appeared in *Billboard* at number 53 on April 6, 1985. It won Nashville's weekly chart battle on June 29.

627

SHE'S A MIRACLE
EXILE

Epic 04864
Writers: J.P. Pennington, Sonny Lemaire
Producer: Buddy Killen
July 6, 1985 (1 week)

Touring some 220 days a year, Exile found that success in country music required a rigorous schedule. Writing while on the road proved almost impossible for J.P. Pennington and Sonny Lemaire, and because of that, they would simply make skeletal notes of their ideas and flesh them out once they could set aside time at home to write together. Among the ideas that became particularly rewarding was "She's A Miracle," a song about a girl named Nicole Lemaire.

"I had a sentiment about my daughter," explains Sonny, "and that phrase, 'She's A Miracle,' just fit her to a tee. It's loosely written about just that kind of sentiment, but obviously it was interpreted as a man talking about his wife or his girlfriend or whatever—however you feel special about someone."

The tracks for "She's A Miracle" were laid down in Nashville's Soundshop Recording Studio during 1984, and, as with their songwriting, Pennington and Lemaire had to squeeze in sessions whenever they could.

"Since we write our own stuff, and record our own stuff, it was a lot of extra work for us, with all the touring that was happening," says Lemaire. "It was real difficult to rehearse every song. With a lot of the stuff that we took into the studio, we didn't have an arrangement. We had to work it up in the studio."

Soundshop is owned by Buddy Killen, who produced the first three Exile country albums. Killen also owned Tree Publishing, which published the band's self-written material, and Lemaire suggests it was a very compatible situation.

"I think it was a common background," he notes. "Besides the country influences, there were a lot of R & B influences. Buddy produced

Joe Tex [see 425—"I Loved 'Em Every One"], and a wide variety of black artists. We grew up heavily immersed in Motown, and we just kind of clicked.

"Buddy is a real 'song' person, and he helped the songs in the studio, creating that magic when the tracks went down."

Killen also persuaded Exile to contribute to tracks for another of the artists he worked with. The band played all the instruments and sang the backing vocals on Ronnie McDowell's "Love Talks." Released in the summer of 1985, the record peaked at number nine.

628

FORGIVING YOU WAS EASY
WILLIE NELSON

Columbia 04847
Writer: Willie Nelson
Producer: Willie Nelson
July 13, 1985 (1 week)

"That's sort of a generalized song, I guess," says Willie Nelson of "Forgiving You Was Easy." "I could probably apply it to a dozen situations in my life. As far as the exact reason I wrote it, I don't really remember right now."

He does remember *when* he wrote it, though. Willie was cutting a duet album with Faron Young, under the production guidance of Fred Foster [see 834—"Nothing I Can Do About It Now"]. They needed another song for the album, *Funny How Time Slips Away*, and the day after they discussed getting new material, Nelson came back with "Forgiving You Was Easy."

Faron remembers it, too.

"I did [a new version of] 'Four In The Morning' [see 93] by myself," recalls Young. "Willie said, 'I'm gonna do this one by myself,' and he cut 'Forgiving You Was Easy' at that session, but it's not on that album. He held on to it, and put it out for his own single."

"Forgiving You Was Easy" debuted at number 70 in *Billboard* on April 13, 1985. Thirteen weeks later, on July 13, it edged into the number one position. That same day, Bob Geldof's Live Aid concerts, jointly televised from London and Philadelphia, raised millions for the African famine. It also provided Willie with the idea for Farm Aid.

"Bob Dylan, on Live Aid, said we should do something for the farmers," Nelson explained to *Billboard*'s Gerry Wood, "and I figured that was a good idea. I figured we'd do a concert and that would be the end of it, and we'd go on to the next big town and do something else. Getting into it, I found that this is a serious problem that could undermine this whole country's economic structure if something is not done to help the farmer."

Nelson held the first of his Farm Aid concerts on September 22, at the University of Illinois in Champaign, with help from a long list of musicians—Merle Haggard, Tanya Tucker, Foreigner, John Cougar Mellencamp, Vern Gosdin and John Conlee, to name just a few. Telecast live via the Nashville Network, the show raised $10 million in pledges, and Willie wrote the first of many checks to the National Council of Churches.

Willie, who personally signed every check drawn on the fund, also held more Farm Aid shows, in 1986, 1987 and 1990.

629

DIXIE ROAD
LEE GREENWOOD

MCA 52564
Writers: Don Goodman, Mary Ann
Kennedy, Pam Rose
Producer: Jerry Crutchfield
July 20, 1985

Lee Greenwood recorded "Dixie Road" specifically for his first *Greatest Hits* album. That LP meant a great deal to Greenwood, who years earlier doubted that he'd ever record again.

Lee signed with Paramount Records and moved to Los Angeles, where the city experienced an earthquake on his very first day in town, February 9, 1971. Though a natural occurrence, it served as an omen for the fate of his contract. "It was kind of a shady deal," he remembers. "I think everybody knew it was not destined to get off the ground; I didn't know it, I was just the artist."

Gulf + Western purchased Paramount, and Greenwood's record, "My First Day Alone Without You," was never released. By the same token, the new management refused to let Greenwood out of his five-year contract. With Lee unable to pursue his dream, his finances fell into disarray and many of his belongings were repossessed.

Desperate and depressed, Greenwood went to work frying poultry in a fast-food establish-

ment called Dixie Chicken. The job lasted only three months before he moved on to a series of jobs in Montana, San Diego and Las Vegas. Years after Dixie Chicken, "Dixie Road" represented his third number one single.

Mary Ann Kennedy, Pam Rose and Don Goodman had written the song four years earlier, around the same time they composed "Ring On Her Finger, Time On Her Hands" [see 544—"Somebody's Gonna Love You"]. At a recording session, Kennedy asked Greenwood to listen to the song, although she didn't think he would be interested. Instead, he thought it was perfect.

"'Dixie Road' was a typical country story about boy meets girl," he says. "He wants to go on and be a star, and she doesn't want to hold him back. When I heard it, I said, 'How come you held it so long? Why didn't you give it to somebody?' So they gave it to me."

Following Lee's singles "Fool's Gold" and "You've Got A Good Love Comin'," "Dixie Road" was more typically country than any of his previous singles. "Everybody will send you a song just like the one you just recorded, normally," he explains. "When you get something that's different, and you record it, that's the one that will keep you hot on the charts."

630

LOVE DON'T CARE
(WHOSE HEART IT BREAKS)
EARL THOMAS CONLEY

RCA 14060
Writers: Earl Thomas Conley,
Randy Scruggs
Producers: Nelson Larkin,
Earl Thomas Conley
July 27, 1985 (1 week)

Earl Thomas Conley benefited from an impressive country lineage in developing many of his hits during the '80s. After breaking with Lester Flatt in 1969, Earl Scruggs formed the Earl Scruggs Revue; the line-up included two of his sons, Randy and Gary Scruggs.

The Scruggs brothers broke away from the Revue in the summer of 1980 to form their own band, and Randy became a co-owner of Scruggs Sound Studio in Nashville. Conley cut part of the *Blue Pearl* album there, leading to a long-term partnership.

"Randy had done an acoustic guitar thing on 'Fire And Smoke' [see 433] and 'Silent Treatment,'" Earl recalls. "One thing led to another, and we thought we should write together some. We started tryin' maybe one or two songs per album, and got up to five on the *Don't Make It Easy for Me* album." They co-wrote seven for *Treadin' Water*, including the first single, "Chance Of Lovin' You" [see 598], and the third, "Love Don't Care (Whose Heart It Breaks)."

"I believe that's a fact—love don't care whose heart it breaks," Earl emphasizes. "It didn't care when it broke my heart. Love's pretty one-sided sometimes. She's either loving you more [or you love her more]. There's a defense and an offense goin' on with love all the time, I feel like. Someone's always winnin' and someone's always losin'. If people stay together, I guess, it's turnin' around on both people, and they're havin' their time, and their turn, of bein' on offense or it wouldn't last very long. When you lose, man, love is a pretty cruel thing."

"We cut it on the same session as 'Chance Of Lovin' You,'" producer Nelson Larkin adds. "If you listen to that thing, we kind of changed the harmony sounds on those two sides. They're a

little different, the way we did the harmony, which is an integral part of Earl's sound."

"Love Don't Care" became the fifth number one single for Conley and Scruggs as co-writers. In the meantime, Randy enhanced his reputation in Nashville by expanding into record production. He produced Earl's 1988 album *The Heart of It All*, as well as several Sawyer Brown albums. Scruggs also worked on the Nitty Gritty Dirt Band classic *Will the Circle Be Unbroken, Volume II*.

631
FORTY HOUR WEEK (FOR A LIVIN')
ALABAMA
RCA 14085
Writers: Dave Loggins, Don Schlitz, Lisa Silver
Producers: Harold Shedd, Alabama
August 3, 1985 (1 week)

Randy Owen spoke for Alabama with the release of the *Forty Hour Week* LP: "The

Alabama

album is a dedication to the people we admire most—the working people, people who do their work and live by their word. That's the kind of people that raised us, picking cotton and working in the mills. We come from people that worked hard for a living and we're proud of them."

Indeed, Fort Payne, Alabama, bills itself as the "Sock Capitol of the World," and the three members of the group who hail from that region—Randy, Teddy Gentry and Jeff Cook—collectively handled such jobs as picking cotton, laying carpet, factory work and on-air radio shifts. When they labored at The Bowery [see 390—"Tennessee River"], the forty-hour week became a thing of the past; they sometimes put in as many as eighty hours onstage in a seven-day period.

Naturally, Alabama was immediately attracted to "Forty Hour Week," a song that rightfully required a bit of work to make it gel. Initially, Lisa Silver and Dave Loggins labored on the tune at MCA Music in Loggins' office, situated next to Don Schlitz's office. That particular day, Schlitz had run out of ideas and was literally roaming the halls looking for someone to write with. Once Silver and Loggins had taken "Forty Hour Week" as far as they could, they pulled Don in to finish it.

"I really like the song," says Schlitz. "It's a tribute to working people, very pure and simple—the people that really get things done. There's some nice little personal lines that we etched in their minds. One concerns the cop out on the beat, and that's for my dad."

Loggins played the song for Owen in Huntsville, Alabama, and when it hit the "Hello, America" salute, Randy pictured flags waving in the breeze. He ultimately added a few notes from "America The Beautiful" to close out the record. Once it hit number one, "Forty Hour Week" set a new mark, giving Alabama 17 chart-topping singles in succession.

A few detractors point out that a holiday single, "Christmas In Dixie," reached only number 35 in 1982, but as *Billboard*'s Paul Grein wrote, "only a Scrooge would count that against them."

632
I'M FOR LOVE
HANK WILLIAMS, JR.

Warner Bros. 29022
Writer: Hank Williams, Jr.
Producers: Jimmy Bowen,
Hank Williams, Jr.
August 10, 1985 (1 week)

"I get a lot of my ideas from the newscasts or the headlines, you know," Hank Williams, Jr., once told John Lomax III in *Country Rhythms*. "I try to write something that will get me excited, that'll get them [listeners] excited. That way, if I have a view or a feeling on it, I can hopefully write it or project it better than somebody that's making it up."

Hank pulled together a rather large list of headline issues for his 1985 release "I'm For Love." Among them: Mothers Against Drunk Driving, the farm crisis, the pill and anti-smoking legislation.

"Hank watches a lot of television, and he's up on all these current affairs and everything," explains manager Merle Kilgore. "We were together in downtown Sacramento, sitting in a hotel room, waiting for one of his girlfriends to show up, flying in. He wrote this song for her."

Williams' initial instinct was to take the song to Johnny Cash, but Kilgore talked him into keeping it for himself. Hank used it to kick off the fiftieth album of his career, cleverly-titled *Five-0*. In October of 1985, it became the ninth of his albums to go gold, and by 1989, the total had surged upward to fifteen gold albums.

"I'm For Love" was Bocephus' first number one single in three years, though he fielded eight Top Ten releases in the interim. Among them were "Gonna Go Huntin' Tonight," which combined his favorite pastime with the pursuit of women; "Leave Them Boys Alone," the last hit to feature Ernest Tubb; and "Attitude Adjustment," a record banned by a few radio stations who deemed it too violent.

Williams followed "I'm For Love" with "This Ain't Dallas," which peaked at number four and gave a nod to J.R. Ewing and the gang at South Fork.

Hank succeeded in part because of the spontaneous nature of his recordings, first captured when he teamed with producer Jimmy Bowen.

"Very little was planned," Bowen reported to Ellen Shaw in *Billboard*. "He'd bring in these songs on little pieces of paper, napkins and things. He'd keep them in his guitar case or a little box he carried around with him. He'd pull out a song or part of a song and play it for the guys on his guitar."

Willie Nelson,
Waylon Jennings,
Kris Kristofferson,
Johnny Cash

633

HIGHWAYMAN

WAYLON JENNINGS, WILLIE
NELSON, JOHNNY CASH,
KRIS KRISTOFFERSON

Columbia 04881
Writer: Jimmy Webb
Producer: Chips Moman
August 17, 1985 (1 week)

"Highwayman" represents reincarnation—on more than one level! When he first composed the song, Jimmy Webb intended it as a study in the evolution of a soul. "When I wrote ["Highwayman"]," he told *Billboard*, "it was in England after a very vivid dream I had of being a highwayman who was pursued and then hanged. Up until then, I hadn't thought much about past lives."

Webb first recorded it for his own 1977 album, *El Mirage*, and a couple of years later, Glen Campbell titled one of his own albums

after it. "Highwayman" was reincarnated much more successfully when Waylon Jennings, Willie Nelson, Johnny Cash and Kris Kristofferson were all recording a Christmas show in Switzerland.

"We were singing together every night," Cash recalled to Katy Bee in *Billboard*, "and these songs got to feeling really good. Willie and I talked about doing a duet album together, but I told him I didn't want to stand in line to get a duet album out with him. So Kris, Waylon and all of us started talkin' about doin' this thing together."

The *Highwayman* album became a monumental project at producer Chips Moman's studios and Woodland Sound Studios in Nashville. Exactly half of the ten cuts featured all four vocalists, while the others represented a variety of duos and trios, with outside help on one cut from Johnny Rodriguez. How they settled on "Highwayman" remains a bit of a mystery.

"I think all of us had heard that song once," says Waylon. "I had it, and John had it, and Willie may have had it. I don't think Kris had it. I had tried to figure out a way to cut that song. I loved that song, and then all of a sudden, I thought, 'No wonder, it's four different people,' which made it perfect."

They first performed "Highwayman" onstage together at Willie Nelson's Fourth of July Picnic in 1985. They also did it (with Glen Campbell filling in for Kristofferson) at Farm Aid in September of 1985.

"Highwayman" won the Grammy award for Country Song of the Year in February of 1986, and the record was named the year's top single by the Academy of Country Music.

Buoyed by the gold success of the *Highwayman* album, Jennings, Nelson, Cash and Kristofferson recorded *Highwayman II* in 1989.

634
REAL LOVE
KENNY ROGERS & DOLLY PARTON
RCA 14058
Writers: David Malloy, Richard "Spady" Brannon, Randy McCormick
Producer: David Malloy
August 24, 1985 (1 week)

The magic of Kenny Rogers & Dolly Parton was too much to confine to "Islands In The Stream" [see 543]. In 1984, the duo hooked up for a seasonal album, *Once Upon a Christmas*, and an accompanying holiday television special, "A Christmas to Remember," that aired on December 2.

They paired for a major tour in 1985, and portions of their concerts in Seattle and Portland were taped for an HBO special, "Kenny Rogers And Dolly Parton Together." At the time, they were en route to their second chart-topping duet, "Real Love."

After years of work with Eddie Rabbitt, David Malloy was called on to produce Dolly's *Real Love* album, and the title track was the only song he wrote for it. "Dolly told me that Kenny owed her a favor because of 'Islands In The Stream,'" recalls Malloy, "and I said, 'Well, let's cash in on that favor and do a big duet.'"

Malloy gave some thought to Dolly's personality and general image in fashioning a general direction for the album, and that direction directly affected the breezy nature of "Real Love."

"To me, she's kind of this goodwill ambas-

sador," he says, "spreading a little joy and happiness, so I wanted an album that was up and energetic, and you had to have dancy kind of melodies, 'cause Dolly sounds good when the melodies really move.

"The tricky part with Kenny and Dolly is that Dolly sounds good when the melodies move around kind of quick. Kenny does not sound good on melodies like that. Kenny needs a longer note to get the sound of his throat established. When Kenny sings a real quick little melody, he sounds like ten other guys. You have to let him stretch out a little bit so you can establish who he is."

With those particulars in mind, Malloy co-wrote "Real Love" with Spady Brannon and keyboard player Randy McCormick, and cut Rogers' vocals at Sunset Sound in Los Angeles. Malloy did some "touch-up" work, though, before the track was finished.

"I ended up going in with a vocal pitch and re-pitched some of his words in the second verse," Malloy confides. "I never did tell him that."

A month after their HBO special, Kenny & Dolly went all the way to number one with "Real Love."

635
LOVE IS ALIVE
THE JUDDS (WYNONNA & NAOMI)
RCA 14093
Writer: Kent M. Robbins
Producer: Brent Maher
August 31, 1985 (1 week)

"If you can conceive it and you can believe it, you can achieve it." That motto will go down in history as one of several that Naomi Judd introduced to her daughters, Wynonna and Ashley. While Ashley was more prone to accept her mother's directions—inspirational, but very strict—Wynonna wasn't, and she and Naomi fought frequently in the pre-stardom years when the Judd family resided in Franklin, Tennessee.

During that period, both mother and daughter seriously contemplated suicide. An on-again, off-again relationship with her boyfriend [see 801—"Change Of Heart"] compounded Naomi's desires to end it all, but she decided against it, because of the kids. At one point, Wynonna considered a self-induced demise after a fight in which Naomi banished her from the house. Wynonna lived for two months with her father in Florida before returning.

Fortunately, Wynonna and Naomi shared a common goal: country stardom. Once conceiving and believing brought results, their circumstances forced a reconciliation. "When I say country music saved us, I'm not kidding," Wynonna told Laura Fissinger in *McCall's*. "Suddenly we were on the road together in each other's faces 24 hours a day. We *had* to work it out."

As they repaired their relationship on the road, the Judds became the first country act to gain four number one singles from their first full-length album, a distinction attained with "Love Is Alive."

Songwriter Kent Robbins had an "in" with the Judds' producer, Brent Maher, since both had offices in the same building when Maher first met Wynonna and Naomi [see 580—"Mama He's Crazy"]. Shortly after his introduction to the duo, Maher took Robbins out to his car to play their demo tape, then challenged Kent to write some material for them. Robbins' first contribution was a track for their introductory mini-LP, "Isn't He A Strange One."

"'Love Is Alive' is one of the few things that I wrote with the artist in mind, and actually had the artist that I had in mind do it," Kent says. "'Isn't He A Strange One' had kind of a funky, lilting groove to it, and 'Love Is Alive' is actually a Son of 'Isn't He A Strange One.' I went for that same type of feel, and the 'Son Of' turned out to be bigger than the original."

636
I DON'T KNOW WHY YOU DON'T WANT ME
ROSANNE CASH
Columbia 04809
Writers: Rosanne Cash, Rodney Crowell
Producer: David Malloy
September 7, 1985 (1 week)

On February 23, 1983, Rosanne Cash occupied a seat at the Shrine Auditorium in Los Angeles, where her single "Ain't No Money" [see 463—"Blue Moon With Heartache"] was nominated for Best Country Vocal Performance by a Female. Juice Newton came out the winner that evening, for "Break It To Me Gent-

ly" [see 641—"You Make Me Want To Make You Mine"]. The next day, Rosanne's loss inspired a new song.

"I was drivin' down Hollywood Boulevard," she recounts, "and I was very tongue-in-cheek, saying, 'I got my new dress, I got my new shoes/I don't know why you don't want me,' just writing this little ditty and being very sarcastic.

"So I went home and I showed Rodney [Crowell] what I had, and he said, 'This is good enough to make into a real song. Why don't we write it together?' So we did."

Rosanne went two-and-a-half years between albums, and she waited until April of 1984 to record "I Don't Know Why You Don't Want Me." It emerged as her only number one single produced by someone other than Crowell. Frequent Eddie Rabbitt cohort David Malloy had produced an album for Rodney that Warner Bros. never released, and through that association, Malloy took the reins on Rosanne's next project.

"Arrangement-wise, what I basically added to that song was that little round on the end," David says. "I thought we should round it four times and end it. But Rosanne had written a little answer thing like that. She wrote it out that way, and so we cut it.

"I worked very hard on her vocals for a long time. I really tried to get them outstanding, and obviously, it did pay off. She was wonderful. I loved Rodney and Rosanne, and still do. They're some of my very favorite people, very charismatic, and it's just an absolute joy to have worked with them."

Cash's friend Vince Gill added backing parts to the record, and on September 7, 1985, it hit number one. Ironically, that same week, Rosanne contributed vocals to his Top 40 single, "If It Weren't For Him," which eventually reached the Top Ten.

Even more ironic, "I Don't Know Why You Don't Want Me"—the song written after a Grammy loss—earned a Grammy.

637
MODERN DAY ROMANCE
THE NITTY GRITTY DIRT BAND
Warner Bros. 29099
Writers: Kix Brooks, Dan Tyler
Producers: Paul Worley, Marshall Morgan
September 14, 1985 (1 week)

The Nitty Gritty Dirt Band titled its 1985 album *Partners, Brothers and Friends*, dedicating it to the memory of Steve Goodman [see 593—"City Of New Orleans"]. The band line-up included five members at the time, but the Dirt trail included thirteen previous members. The best-known was Jackson Browne, one of the six founders that hung around McCabe's Guitar Shop in Orange County, California.

Of the five, Jeff Hanna, Jimmy Ibbotson and Bob Carpenter have all handled the vocal lead at different times, but Ibbotson got that part on the group's first four Top Ten country hits. "I said, 'Hey, man, I been singin' lead in this band for a long time,'" Hanna laughs. "'Next time we hear a hit, how 'bout I sing it?'

"We heard 'Modern Day Romance,' and we thought it was really cool, because even though I'm the one that's accused of having the more sort of smooth voice, that was a real *country* tune."

"It's kind of a quirky song, a little different, a little off-the-wall," adds producer Paul Worley. "It's one of those songs that had been around for the *Plain Dirt Fashion* album [see 583—"Long Hard Road"], and we really liked it, but we didn't cut it. We put it on the back burner, but then the song popped up again for the second album. We were listenin' to it, and I think even at the beginning we listened to it, said, 'I don't know,' put it back again.

"Right at the end of the second album, the song popped up again, and we said, 'You know, this song keeps poppin' up. There must be somethin' to it. We really oughta cut it.'

"We all liked 'Modern Day Romance' a whole lot. But we were tryin' to be cerebral about it, when really we should have just gone ahead, as we ended up doin'—followin' our gut feelings about the song."

The Nitty Gritty Dirt Band preceded "Modern Day Romance" with their Top Five singles "I Love Only You" and "High Horse," and followed it with Top Tens "Home Again In My Heart," "Partners, Brothers And Friends" and "Stand A Little Rain."

The latter song had been released by May 13, 1986, when the band held a special concert celebrating "20 Years Of Dirt."

638
I FELL IN LOVE AGAIN LAST NIGHT
THE FORESTER SISTERS
Warner Bros. 28988

Writers: Paul Overstreet, Thom Schuyler
Producers: J.L. Wallace, Terry Skinner
September 21, 1985 (1 week)

Pop or rock music had the McGuire Sisters, the Supremes or Bananarama, but country music never had a successful girl group until the advent of the Forester Sisters. Hailing from Lookout Mountain, Georgia—the same area that spawned Alabama [see 390—"Tennessee River"]—they started singing in church as youngsters. After college, Kathy, June and Kim started working with a number of bands, but finally decided to make themselves the focus and hire others to work for them. Christy joined her sisters in 1982, turning the trio into a quartet.

While they were performing at a Lookout Mountain festival, a songwriter approached the Forester Sisters with a song called "Yankee Don't Go Home." It inspired them to seek a recording contract, and in December of 1983, they recorded a demo tape in Muscle Shoals. That tape found its way to Warner Bros. A & R representative Paige Rowden, resulting in a showcase for the label's executives. That night, Warners offered them a singles deal, and they signed on July 31, 1984.

The following January, the Foresters released their first single, "(That's What You Do) When You're In Love." Surprising many, it quickly scaled its way into *Billboard*'s Top Ten, and Warners commissioned an album. The sisters came up with "I Fell In Love Again Last Night," written by Thom Schuyler and Paul Overstreet at a time when many of Thom's friends had marriages failing.

"When you really get down to it, as trite as it may seem, married people need to stay in love," Schuyler offers. "They need to care about one another, and they need to excite one another emotionally and physically, and all sorts of things. That's what Paul and I wanted to write about, falling in love again with the person you married."

Shelly West cut the song first on an album, but it came to prominence when the Foresters picked it up.

"For our first album, we went around to the different publishing houses, and we'd divide up two-and-two," Christy Forester remembers. "On that particular day, we all four ended up at a publishing company called the Writers Group, and they played us this song. It had a different beat. It was slower, and we heard a quicker beat to it, but we knew right away that we liked it a lot, because it had a high 'chill-bump factor.'"

639

LOST IN THE FIFTIES TONIGHT (IN THE STILL OF THE NIGHT)

RONNIE MILSAP

RCA 14135
Writers: Mike Reid, Troy Seals,
Freddy Parris
Producers: Tom Collins, Ronnie Milsap,
Rob Galbraith
September 28, 1985 (2 weeks)

In the mid-'50s, Freddy Parris and the Five Satins recorded "In The Still Of The Nite" [*sic*] in a church basement in New Haven, Connecticut. By the time it found success on the Ember label, Parris was stationed with the Army in Japan.

"In The Still Of The Nite" only reached number 24 on *Billboard*'s Hot 100 chart, but it was twice reissued and outlasted many of the records that surpassed it in its first appearance. Through the years, the record accumulated multi-millions in sales.

"I think that, as much as any song, defined the whole genre of '50s songwriting," says Nashville writer Mike Reid. In that capacity, "In The Still Of The Nite" served as the centerpiece for a retrospective salute to the doo-wop era three decades later.

"I grew up in the '50s," says Reid's co-writer, Troy Seals, "and at that point, I was playin' rock and roll. Now, '50s rock and roll is country music, and from time to time, I'll sit down and pull out the golden oldies and listen. My wife's got all these albums—Jerry Lee Lewis, Fabian, Buddy Holly, Fats Domino—and they're just great. I came up with that title ["Lost In The Fifties Tonight"], and 'In The Still Of The Nite' just fit that song. It could've been 'Oh, What A Night' by the Dells."

Even though "Lost In The Fifties Tonight" was a derivative work, Reid and Seals figured that they would work out an equitable split once they found out who wrote it. In the meantime, they pitched it to Ronnie Milsap, who decided instantly to cut it. As it turned out, Parris was the sole writer, but his publisher worked out a deal in which Freddy got half the writers' cut, rather than one-third.

"I ran down Freddy Parris," Reid reports. "He was in a position where he appreciated the use of the song, and appreciated the money, so it turned out to be a wonderful experience. He more than deserved whatever he got out of it."

Milsap and Bruce Dees overdubbed a series of background "shoo-be-doo-wop"'s, and the record was an instant success, one of only two singles to spend two weeks at number one during 1985. It generated a pair of Grammy awards and Academy of Country Music recognition as Song of the Year.

640

MEET ME IN MONTANA

MARIE OSMOND WITH DAN SEALS

Capitol 5478
Writer: Paul Davis
Producers: Paul Worley, Kyle Lehning
October 12, 1985 (1 week)

"Meet Me In Montana" was a landmark record for both of its featured performers. Marie Osmond hadn't topped the country charts for a dozen years [see 147—"Paper Roses"], while Dan Seals hadn't topped any chart since "Love Is The Answer" hit number one on *Billboard*'s adult/contemporary list in 1979.

With four Top Ten country records under his belt, Seals had begun to re-establish himself. Marie, meanwhile, had already made country records for a couple of different labels prior to her Capitol signing, to little avail. Her successful duets and prime-time series with brother Donny were far in the past.

"With Marie, we knew we had a battle to fight," admits producer Paul Worley. "She and I and her record company and her manager knew that we had to fight to bring her back, and that song came in."

Paul Davis, who had a couple of Top Ten hits himself on the Hot 100, wrote "Meet Me In Montana" while on tour in the state. On the bus, he listened heavily to Merle Haggard's *Big City* [see 467] album, with its title track praising the Treasure State. It helped him appreciate the landscape's natural beauty, and, after Arista Records turned down Davis' own recording of the song, he sent a demo of "Meet Me In Montana" in duet form to Capitol. A & R man Lynn Shults sent it on to Worley, who thought Dan Seals could pull it off with Marie.

Seals agreed, though it took about six months to coordinate both artists' schedules. Finally, Osmond and Seals spent three hours at Audio Media Recorders working out their vocals.

"I didn't add a note or take away a note, for

the most part, from the way Paul did the song," says Seals. "I love Paul's writing, and the harmony parts are pretty difficult if you start pulling it apart. To sit down and write something like that, with the trills and harmony together, and make it work, is very difficult."

The record was mixed while both artists were on the road, and appeared on Marie's *There's No Stopping Your Heart* [see 658] album, as well as Dan's *Won't Be Blue Anymore*. On October 13, 1986, one year after "Meet Me In Montana" reached number one, the Country Music Association named Marie Osmond & Dan Seals the Vocal Duo of the Year.

Marie Osmond & Dan Seals

641

YOU MAKE ME WANT TO MAKE YOU MINE

JUICE NEWTON

RCA 14139
Writer: Dave Loggins
Producer: Richard Landis
October 19, 1985 (1 week)

Born February 18, 1952, at the Lakehurst, New Jersey, naval base, Judy Kay Newton didn't stay in the Garden State long. Her father, Charles, had a military occupation, and he soon moved the family to Virginia Beach, where Juice picked up her unusual nickname—now her legal name. She doesn't know why it was given to her, and for several years, she refused to divulge her real name.

Juice's last name links her as a direct descendant of Sir Isaac Newton, the English scientist and mathematician who created the theory of gravity, as well as calculus and algebra's dreaded binomial theorem. Unlike that ancestor, Juice figured on a musical career, one she headed toward as a teenager, listening to her brother's rhythm & blues records.

She got her first guitar as a freshman at Virginia Beach's First Colonial High School. Her mother gave her a $120 Espana acoustic guitar, "a Christmas, birthday and all-events gift for the entire year." Following graduation, Juice went to California, enrolling in Foothill College in Los Altos Hills. There she met Otha Young [see 457—"The Sweetest Thing (I've Ever Known)"] and formed Dixie Peach, a group that evolved into Juice Newton & Silver Spur.

When Newton's records found favor with the public, they were hardly traditional country, but she was embraced by the format nonetheless. On the heels of the *Juice* album, she released *Dirty Looks*, which brought her a Top Ten pop record with "Love's Been A Little Bit Hard On Me." The follow-up, a remake of Brenda Lee's "Break It To Me Gently," took her to number two on the country chart, behind "You're So Good When You're Bad" [see 493] and "Heartbroke" [see 494]. "Break It To Me Gently" brought Juice a Grammy for Best Country Vocal Performance by a Female. She waited another two-and-a-half years before her next Top Ten record, Dave Loggins' composition "You Make Me Want To Make You

Mine," which went all the way to number one.

"It's a fun song, long title," she says. "We just felt that it would be a fun song to add to the record. It's very up. It's not something that you have to concentrate on—it's just a pleasant sort of listening song."

642
TOUCH A HAND, MAKE A FRIEND
THE OAK RIDGE BOYS
MCA 52646
Writers: Homer Banks, Raymond Jackson, Carl Hampton
Producer: Ron Chancey
October 26, 1985 (1 week)

In the mid-'70s, the Oak Ridge Boys made a very difficult shift from gospel to country music [see 314—"I'll Be True To You"]. The Oaks' work in the gospel field had long been admired by both fans and critics alike, as they piled up four Grammies in religious categories. In 1976, Johnny Cash kept them from quitting.

"John encouraged us to stick with it," Richard Sterban told Kelly Delaney in *Billboard*. "He told us that we really did have a great show and that there was a market for our music. He said, 'I know it and you know it, but nobody else knows it yet. No one will ever find out if you give up. You just have to hang in there and weather the storm—your day will come.'"

Nearly a decade later, with their situation drastically altered, the Oaks were able to return to their gospel roots more easily than on prior country singles [see 589—"Everyday"]. They included occasional gospel material on their albums; in 1985, they successfully covered the Staple Singers, a black gospel act that had turned to mainstream R & B.

The Staples hit number one on *Billboard*'s Hot 100 with "I'll Take You There" (1972) and "Let's Do It Again" (1975), also reaching the Top 40 in 1974 with "Touch A Hand, Make A Friend."

"I've loved that as long as I've loved the Staple Singers," says Duane Allen, "which is as far back as I can remember listenin' to music. We eventually *had* to record a Staple Singers song because we loved 'em so much. When that song was pulled off an old album and pitched to us, it was a natural."

It was the first song the Oaks ever cut in their own Acorn Recording Studio, although others, including "Everyday" and "Make My

Life With You" [see 607], came out earlier. Like those, "Touch A Hand" rose to number one.

Joe Bonsall provided the tenor voice in the group's harmonies. A Philadelphia native, he ran with a street gang as a teenager. Joe changed his life after a "rumble," and ended up in several gospel quartets. In 1973, he became the last member to join the Oak Ridge Boys before their eventual switch to country music.

643
SOME FOOLS NEVER LEARN
STEVE WARINER
MCA 52644
Writer: John Scott Sherrill
Producers: Tony Brown, Jimmy Bowen
November 2, 1985 (1 week)

"You're only as good as your last record." That hackneyed phrase has haunted many artists through the years, and about 1983, that included Steve Wariner. After "All Roads Lead To You" [see 452] reached number one, four subsequent singles failed to crack the Top Ten. Only "Kansas City Lights" (number 15) even came close.

Wariner decided to toughen up his sound, and turned to producer Tony Brown for his *Midnight Fire* album. The title track—the first Wariner single on which he played his own guitar solo—brought Steve back to number five, and his remake of Bob Luman's "Lonely Women Make Good Lovers" hit number four.

In the process of making the album, Wariner considered a John Scott Sherrill song called "Some Fools Never Learn," but Wariner and Brown felt a little edgy. "It was a story song," Brown explains. "Steve had never done a song of that nature. It also had that line in there, 'Damn my eyes,' and we were wonderin' if his fans would give him flak for that. Those reasons were basic paranoia, from a producer and artist standpoint."

Paranoia won out, and they skipped over the song, but Wariner held a tight grip on "Some Fools."

"I just kept it in my briefcase for a year and a half," Steve laughs. "We cut the album, and then my contract was up, and as things worked out, I decided to leave RCA, and I went to MCA. When I got over to MCA, that was one of the first songs that I decided to do."

MCA released "What I Didn't Do" and

"Heart Trouble" first, and both songs reached the Top Ten. "Some Fools Never Learn" returned Steve to the top spot, nearly four years after his first number one single. In the process, it confirmed Wariner's expectations.

"'Some Fools' is the only song I've ever recorded," Steve notes, "that the minute we finished and walked out of the studio, I told Tony Brown, 'That's gotta be a number one record.' I've never said that about any other record I've ever cut."

It was the first number one record written by John Scott Sherrill, now with Billy Hill. "It involved some women," he explains, declining to reveal "Fools"'s personal origins. "That was a long time ago. I think I'm in the clear now."

Steve Wariner

644
CAN'T KEEP A GOOD MAN DOWN
ALABAMA
RCA 14165
Writer: Bob Corbin
Producers: Harold Shedd, Alabama
November 9, 1985 (1 week)

Once you've spent hours and hours—or days and days—working on a writing project, it's difficult to have any objectivity about it. Bob Corbin is a perfect example with "Can't Keep A Good Man Down."

"I was right at the end of my term for a publishing agreement," he recalls. "There's a certain number of songs that you have to turn in—not all the time, but sometimes, and in my case, there was. I had four songs to turn in. I had three finished, and 'Can't Keep A Good Man Down' I just threw off in about three days. I thought it was a piece of shit. For me, it was just fulfilling my obligation so I could get my next draw.

"When we demoed it, I apologized to the studio guys. I said, 'Now, this isn't a great song or anything,' but we finished it, and they were all saying, 'Hey, we think this is great.' The guy who was head of the publishing company, that was the one he liked. He said, 'I'm gonna give this to Alabama.' And I said, 'No, give the others to Alabama. Don't give 'em that one, 'cause it'll embarrass me.'

"Luckily for me, he didn't take my advice. That just goes to show you that songwriters aren't always the best judges of their own material. I'm real happy, but up until this day, I don't get it."

The first night that Alabama had the demo, Randy Owen, Mark Herndon and Teddy Gentry cranked it in their tour bus, while Jeff Cook tried to catch some sleep in the back. After more than ten consecutive plays, Cook ran up front and told them he knew his part already so they could shut it off.

Born August 27, 1949, Cook is the most versatile musician in the group, capable on guitar, keyboards, fiddle and bass. His first performance came at age six, when he belted out "Hound Dog" at school. By his teens, he had progressed to his first two groups: the Viscounts and J.C. & The Chosen Few. In 1970, Jeff earned a degree in electronics, and he put all of his talents together when he built his own recording studio in Fort Payne, used primarily for Alabama's pre-production work.

645

HANG ON TO YOUR HEART

EXILE

Epic 05580
Writers: J.P. Pennington, Sonny Lemaire
Producer: Buddy Killen
November 16, 1985 (1 week)

"As a writer, I run into other artists that aren't songwriters," J. P. Pennington told *The Tennessean*'s Thomas Goldsmith during 1986. "They always want something that's positive and uptempo."

Historically, that style was a hallmark of Exile's singles, and "Hang On To Your Heart" fell right in line with their prior releases.

"I don't think it was intentional at first," surmises bassist Sonny Lemaire. "It was just the way things were coming out. I think that we hit so hard with 'Woke Up In Love' [see 559] that the record company realized, 'Hey, this is a neat formula; it's working.' On the albums, not everything was 'up.' We had ballads and other things, but I suppose the record company just locked into a tried-and-true formula for a while."

That strategy proved successful in providing Exile with their sixth consecutive number one record—"Hang On To Your Heart," the title track and first single from their third Epic album. Though pleased by the achievement, Lemaire couldn't have applauded the single's success: both wrists were in casts when it hit *Billboard*'s number one position on November 16, 1985.

"We were getting a little more contemporary in the songs at that point," notes Lemaire. "I think 'Hang On To Your Heart' was a reflection of our R & B background, with the melody and the way it flows."

Their interest in soul music provided a unique counterpoint in Exile's development as a country act. When Epic executive Rick Blackburn first saw the group at The Stockyard, they played a five-song Motown medley. And when the label introduced them to the country industry at the Exit/In during Country Music Week in 1983, he persuaded Exile to perform the medley once more.

"People talked about that for years," says Lemaire. "We kind of discussed whether we should do it or not, but it was such a strong piece of material, and we're a band with all kinds of musical roots. That was just one thing that we did. Why deny your roots?"

Exile never received a backlash for its "non-country" offering. The medley included "I Can't Help Myself (Sugar Pie, Honey Bunch)," "Reach Out, I'll Be There," "Ain't Too Proud To Beg," "My Girl" and "Signed, Sealed, Delivered."

646

I'LL NEVER STOP LOVING YOU

GARY MORRIS

Warner Bros. 28947
Writers: Dave Loggins, J.D. Martin
Producer: Jim Ed Norman
November 23, 1985 (1 week)

"The music that I really grew up with is R & B," says producer Jim Ed Norman. "The music I was always most enamored with was the music made by Gamble & Huff and Thom Bell. Goin' all the way back to workin' with the Eagles as an arranger, if you listen to the first four beats of 'Take It To The Limit' and the first four beats of 'If You Don't Know Me By Now' by Harold Melvin & The Bluenotes—my goal was not to be able to tell them apart, unless you had perfect pitch."

Like Norman, Gary Morris holds a strong affinity for "groove music," and both of them had long been familiar with "I'll Never Stop Loving You" when they decided to record it for Morris' *Anything Goes . . .* album. J.D. Martin and Dave Loggins had written the song during the same week as "Everyday" [see 589], and actually envisioned it as a pop record before it ended up in Morris' hands.

"'I'll Never Stop Loving You' was one of those stream-of-consciousness kinds of things," J.D. recalls. "Dave started spouting some wonderful lines. We ended up cutting the demo of the song and tearing it down until we finally ended up with a song that was four-and-a-half or five minutes long. Then when Gary did the song, he even eliminated some more, so it doesn't have all the original lyrics in it. But he definitely got the story, the feelings across."

Morris brought in guitarist Gary Hooker from his band, GMO, to play on the record. Hooker ran through it a couple of times to get warmed up, but Morris told him not to play anymore. They had recorded those takes, unknown to Hooker, and he had played exactly what was needed.

"A lot of times, people come up and say,

'Gary, how did you get that guitar sound?'" Morris notes. "Really all we did was take the Strat and plug it straight into the recorder—no effects or anything—and play it. It's such a good-sounding guitar. A lot of people have forgotten how good some guitars sound."

Between the clean guitar sound and its infectious groove, "I'll Never Stop Loving You" was one of the most energetic records of 1985. It cruised to number one on November 23.

647

TOO MUCH ON MY HEART
THE STATLER BROTHERS

Mercury 884016
Writer: Jimmy Fortune
Producer: Jerry Kennedy
November 30, 1985 (1 week)

None of the Statler Brothers are named Statler, and only two of them (Don and Harold Reid) are brothers. The monicker dates back to 1964, when they first went on tour with Johnny Cash [see 24—"Daddy Sang Bass"] and picked the name off a box of facial tissues.

Manufactured in Massachusetts, the Statler brand is pretty much a regional product ("We have some because our fans send them to us," notes Don Reid, "and we have boxes sitting all around the office"), and the Statlers have frequently told reporters that they could have just as easily been named the Kleenex Brothers.

Recorded under an alter ego as "Lester 'Roadhog' Moran & His Cadillac Cowboys," *Alive at Johnny Mack Brown High School* displayed the band's sense of humor in even greater abundance, and the Statler love for puns characterized their 1967 hit "You Can't Have Your Kate And Edith Too," 1979's "How To Be A Country Star," and 1982's "Whatever." They took a more serious route on their fourth number one single, "Too Much On My Heart," their only chart-topper to feature the group singing unison lines.

"I think it's one of the heavier messages that we've done," surmises Don Reid. "It's a love song, in a way, but it's almost a thing where you say you can get too much love sometimes."

For their writing skills, Kurt Vonnegut once dubbed them "America's Poets" in the pages of *Country Music* magazine, and beginning in 1969, the Statlers established an annual Fourth of July celebration, "Happy Birthday,

The Statlers

U.S.A." Their affiliation with Jerry Kennedy, dating back to 1970 [see 311—"Do You Know You Are My Sunshine"], is the longest-running artist/producer relationship in Nashville.

"First off, Jerry's been successful," Reid says, explaining their loyalty, "and secondly, he's a good friend. We feel comfortable with Jerry. We think of him as a fifth Statler."

The same emotions underscore the longevity among the four actual Statlers. "I think we basically like each other," Don posits. "We would be friends if we weren't in business together. I think that is the reason we're still together—we enjoy what we're doing, and that's basically it."

648

I DON'T MIND THE THORNS (IF YOU'RE THE ROSE)
LEE GREENWOOD
MCA 52656
Writers: Jan Buckingham, Linda Young
Producer: Jerry Crutchfield
December 7, 1985 (1 week)

"The only other 'rose' song that I remember being so strong was the one that Gary Morris sang—'Give her thorns and she'll find the roses,'" says Lee Greenwood, referring to Morris' "The Love She Found In Me." "When I saw him sing that on the Academy of Country Music Awards show, the song itself drew applause from the audience when he broke into the chorus.

"When I heard 'I Don't Mind The Thorns (If You're The Rose),' I felt the same emotion. It was a wonderful endorsement of a relationship between a man and a woman, and flowers are, of course, what we use to just say a message of love without saying it. It's better than candy, probably, or just a card, but flowers really say it well. There's a fragrance to them, there's an element of tenderness, and when the chorus comes around, it moves you. I knew it was a hit the first time I heard it, and there was no way I was going to lose that song."

In fact, Greenwood gave the song the type of smoky interpretation only he could deliver, and it easily became his fourth number one single. Greenwood's unique vocal approach was actually developed by mistake during his years as a Las Vegas performer.

"The way they build those clubs," he sneers,

"they're really no better than the honky-tonks in Texas or anywhere else."

During one period, Greenwood worked four years without a single day off, performing in a rock show seven nights a week. During the daytime, he dealt cards at the blackjack tables on an eight-hour shift, sometimes putting in an extra four hours of overtime. The stress and the smoke simultaneously proved costly and beneficial.

"I got so tired that my voice just got to be hamburger," Lee recalls. "My range decreased from three octaves to less than an octave. I could hardly talk in the morning and could barely get the notes out at night."

Mel Tillis' bass player, Larry McFaden, first spotted Greenwood singing in a Reno piano bar, and later suggested that Lee come to Nashville to record. Greenwood paid for his own first-class ticket, leading to his demo sessions and his deal with MCA. The raspiness he acquired in Nevada proved an ideal match for "I Don't Mind The Thorns."

649

NOBODY FALLS LIKE A FOOL
EARL THOMAS CONLEY
RCA 14172
Writers: Peter McCann, Mark Wright
Producers: Nelson Larkin,
Earl Thomas Conley
December 14, 1985 (1 week)

Songwriter Peter McCann calls "Nobody Falls Like A Fool" a "transition song." A Connecticut native, McCann started making records for Motown in 1971, moving to Los Angeles four years later.

In 1977, McCann attained national fame, first by penning Jennifer Warnes' "Right Time Of The Night," then for his own recording of "Do You Wanna Make Love." Both hit the Top Ten of the *Billboard* Hot 100, while seeing country action as well. Warnes' recording reached country's Top 20, while three versions of "Do You Wanna Make Love"—by Bobby Smith, David Wills and Buck Owens—hit the country chart in the ensuing two years.

In 1985, Peter earned two more country hits. Janie Frickie took his composition "She's Single Again" to number two; and Earl Thomas Conley cut "Nobody Falls Like A Fool." McCann wrote the chorus on the latter tune in Los Angeles with Nashville songwriter Mark

Wright. The two made a point of getting together again to finish it, after Peter moved to Nashville in April of 1985.

"There are some people out in L.A. who will say that I was always writing country music and didn't belong in L.A.," McCann laughs. "There's some guys in Nashville that say, 'Well, he's a pop writer and doesn't belong down here.'"

Conley and his producer, Nelson Larkin, weren't particularly enamored with "Nobody Falls Like A Fool" at first, but RCA pressured them into recording it for Earl's *Greatest Hits* album. At the session, Larkin told the musicians that he wasn't thrilled about it, and they worked on ways to improve it, including a tempo change.

"The tracks went down great," Larkin says. "When Earl sang it, he tried to sing it a little different than he usually sings. That night, we went over to my house. It was late at night, we got my wife up. She said she liked it, but that Earl was tryin' to sing too high. We convinced ourselves that it was a good song, got all our resentments out, and went back in and put a vocal on it."

Keyboard player Ron Oates introduced them to Dee Murray and Nigel Olsson, of Elton John's band. They added background harmonies, and eight months after McCann finished writing it, "Nobody Falls Like A Fool" rose to number one—Conley's tenth chart-topping single.

650

THE CHAIR
GEORGE STRAIT
MCA 52667
Writers: Hank Cochran, Dean Dillon
Producers: Jimmy Bowen, George Strait
December 21, 1985 (1 week)

"Sixty or 70 percent of the time, George Strait just fools me completely on the songs he likes to sing," says producer Jimmy Bowen. "He's right, obviously, but I never know it until he cuts 'em. [Production assistant Don] Lanier and I used to have a joke. We'd give George 30 songs and see which ones he was gonna like. We were right half the time, but 'The Chair'—I thought for sure he wouldn't want to do it."

In fact, Strait took an immediate liking to "The Chair." It was the ninth Dean Dillon song to appear on a Strait album, the fourth

released as a single, and the first to hit number one.

"'The Chair' was written off the west coast of Palm Beach, Florida, with Hank Cochran, on Hank's boat, the Legend," Dillon remembers. "That song came literally out of thin air. We had gone down to Florida with the intention of writing, and we got down there and had written three or four songs. I was just sitting there in a chair, lookin' at Hank, and he was twiddling his thumbs, and out of the clear blue sky, I said, 'Well, excuse me, but I think you've got my chair.'"

Had Bowen controlled Strait's career more closely, George might never have even heard the song, since the producer didn't think he would like it. The two started working together on *Does Fort Worth Ever Cross Your Mind* [see 601], forming a relationship that Strait sees as crucial to his artistic growth.

"Bowen's philosophy is that if he's in there callin' all the shots, then it becomes his album and not the artist's, when it should be the other way around," George explains. "It was quite a change for me, goin' with Bowen, because it put more responsibility on my shoulders as far as workin' with the musicians. It gave me the freedom to choose my own material, and to have the songs arranged and sound the way that I wanted them to sound."

The new sound was much more raw, particularly on the two singles that preceded "The Chair." The changes were on target, too. Both "The Cowboy Rides Away" and "The Fireman" hit the Top Ten, and "The Chair" gave Strait a dozen Top Ten records in a row.

651

HAVE MERCY
THE JUDDS
(WYNONNA & NAOMI)
RCA 14193
Writer: Paul Kennerley
Producer: Brent Maher
December 28, 1985 (2 weeks)

The Judds picked up their fifth number one single, "Have Mercy," from a former member of the British advertising community. In 1976, the punk explosion took England by storm, and while Paul Kennerley was attracted to bands like the Stranglers and the Sex Pistols, he also took an interest for the first time in country music. He was hooked by a Waylon

The Judds

Jennings record, which struck him as country-meets-the Rolling Stones.

Kennerley started investigating the idiom's roots and wanted to write some country material. Since his background didn't provide him with the type of experience he felt he needed to write appropriate lyrics, he turned to American history for his first projects. The results were two concept albums, *White Mansions* and *The Legend of Jesse James*, through which he met Jennings and Emmylou Harris.

Emmylou cut his song "Born To Run" in 1981, and Paul started visiting Nashville frequently, moving there permanently in 1983. He has since written such hits as "Chains Of Gold," for Sweethearts of the Rodeo; "In My Dreams," for Emmylou; and "Blue Side Of Town," for Patty Loveless.

Kennerley has had his largest successes, however, with the Judds. He penned five of their singles during the '80s, four of them hitting number one. The first was "Have Mercy," although he actually gave them "Cry Myself To Sleep" [see 705] first.

"Once they cut 'Cry Myself To Sleep,' I actually tried to write a song for them," says Paul. "It's the first time I'd ever written a song specifically for an artist. I felt I had a measure of them, since they'd done another song.

"Brent Maher, who I'd just recently met, called me up and was very encouraging. He's one of those producers that would come along and seek you out and sort of goad you along a little bit. In the case of 'Have Mercy,' I really tried to write something that had that rhythm & blues flavor."

Maher went over to Kennerley's house to hear "Have Mercy," and then headed to Jackson, Mississippi, where the Judds were appearing, to play it for them on their bus.

"The first time they heard it," he says, "they just jumped up and down. I think the line that really grabbed Wynonna was 'I could hear you was playin' Haggard and Jones.'"

"Have Mercy" became the Judds' fifth chart-topper in December of 1985.

652

MORNING DESIRE
KENNY ROGERS
RCA 14194
Writer: Dave Loggins
Producer: George Martin
January 11, 1986 (1 week)

"I look for songs that say what every man would like to be able to say, and every woman would like to hear," says Kenny Rogers. "If you do that, that's a common denominator that's hard to ignore. Men buy [those songs] for women, and women buy 'em for themselves."

Among the songs Rogers views in that manner is "Morning Desire," one he personally commissioned. Needing a concept for material on his forthcoming album, he turned in 1985 to Bruce Springsteen's "I'm On Fire" for inspiration. "It was a great-sounding record," says Kenny, "real open-sounding, but very simple, not a lot of instrumentation, not real busy."

Kenny placed a call to Nashville, and invited songwriter Dave Loggins to visit him at the Rogers estate in Georgia. If Dave could provide him with a cross between "Something's Burning" (the First Edition "thing with the heartbeat in it") and "I'm On Fire," it was almost guaranteed to appear on the album.

"So he came to my farm in Georgia, and I put him in my guesthouse," Rogers recalls. "We played some golf and we hung around for a while, and I said, 'Okay, now you have to go to work,' and I put him in there and wouldn't let him come out until he had written me this song."

All told, Loggins spent about a day and a half at Kenny's house, and "Morning Desire" fulfilled all of Kenny's expectations.

"I loved the song, I loved the feel, I loved everything about it," Kenny maintains. "Except there was this one lyric in there that just came out of left field and bothered me, and that was the thing about thunder and horses' hooves. Dave said, 'Really? That's one of my favorite lyrics!' and [Kenny's wife] Marianne said, 'Mine, too.' Marianne's always right when it comes to those kinds of things."

Kenny followed their instincts and left the line in, eventually agreeing with them. Ex-Beatles producer George Martin recorded an array of compelling sounds, and Kenny called on jazz guitarist Stanley Jordan to cap the record with an angelic solo.

On October 14, 1985, the video clip for "Morning Desire" became the first to premiere on a Country Music Association awards telecast. After the turn of the year, it became Rogers' eighteenth number one single.

653

BOP
DAN SEALS
EMI America 8289
Writers: Paul Davis, Jennifer Kimball
Producer: Kyle Lehning
January 18, 1986 (1 week)

Dan Seals grew up a fan of Hank Williams and Ernest Tubb, but first found national success in pop music, rather than country. His duo England Dan & John Ford Coley swiped the number two spot on the *Billboard* Hot 100 in 1976 with "I'd Really Love To See You Tonight," and over the next three years, they enjoyed five more Top 40 hits, most of them recorded in Nashville.

In 1982, with the partnership behind him, Seals decided to try his hand at country music—his first love—and the following year, he reached the country Top 20 with "Everybody's Dream Girl." Beginning with "God Must Be A Cowboy" in 1984, he reeled off four straight Top Ten records, including "My Baby's Got Good Timing" (number two).

Seals completed the transition from unfulfilled pop performer to country stardom with his *Won't Be Blue Anymore* album. "Meet Me In Montana" [see 640] took him to number one with Marie Osmond, and "Bop" became his first chart-topper on his own. Having made a commitment to more mainstream country with the earlier records, Dan took a surprising turn back toward a pop style with "Bop."

Initially, Capitol executive Lynn Shults brought the song to producer Kyle Lehning when the album was all but completed. Lehning immediately relayed a copy to Seals, and they decided to add it to the record . . . if they could.

"They were holding 'Bop' in Hollywood for a new movie that was coming out," Dan remembers. "I guess it was something like *Dirty Dancing*, and this went on for a week or two. We continued to want to do the song, and evidently that scene fell through, because Paul [Davis] called back and said, 'Do it.'"

They tried to stick closely to Davis' demo,

performed with a drum machine and Synclavier, but they changed the key. Davis worked hand in hand with Lehning into the wee hours of the morning, re-programming the machines and re-recording the tracks in Nashville's Masters Touch Studio.

Seals later came off a lengthy tour and sang his part just three times. Despite its rockin' overtones, country stations picked "Bop" up off the album, and Capitol released it as a single. After it hit number one on the country chart, the record soared to number 42 in *Billboard*'s Hot 100.

In 1986, the Country Music Association named "Bop" the Single Record of the Year.

654

NEVER BE YOU

ROSANNE CASH

Columbia 05621
Writers: Tom Petty, Benmont Tench
Producers: Rodney Crowell,
David Thoener
January 25, 1986 (1 week)

Though he's a fan of George Jones, and has recorded with Roy Orbison as a member of the Traveling Wilburys, Tom Petty probably doesn't come to most people's minds when they think of country music. The leader of the Heartbreakers, he's better known for making rock hits like "Don't Do Me Like That," "Don't Come Around Here No More" and "Free Fallin'."

Petty has left an imprint on the country charts, however. He contributed as a vocalist to Hank Williams, Jr.'s "Mind Your Own Business" [see 702], and wrote three country hits: Orbison's "You Got It"; "Thing About You," by Southern Pacific; and "Never Be You," by Rosanne Cash.

Cash first recorded one of Petty's songs, "Hometown Blues," for her *Seven Year Ache* [see 426] album, and Petty stopped by the studio at that time to meet her. Rosanne became friends, as well, with Heartbreaker keyboardist Benmont Tench, and that friendship led to her involvement with "Never Be You."

"They were making a soundtrack for *Streets of Fire*," she explains. "Jimmy Iovine was producing it, and Tom Petty had this song on it, with Benmont. So they called me up and asked

Rosanne Cash

me if I wanted to sing the song on the soundtrack, and I said, 'Sure,' and I went to L.A. and I did it. It was Tom and a band, but it just never got right, and there were legal problems."

As a result, someone else performed it on the soundtrack, but Rosanne held onto the song. She later recorded it at New York's Record Plant with a band that included Tench, John Cougar Mellencamp guitarist Larry Crane, session bass player Willie Weeks, and drummer Anton Fig, a member of Paul Shaffer's "Late Night With David Letterman" band. The record became Rosanne's fifth number one single.

Originally, it wasn't even part of the *Rhythm & Romance* album, but a new Columbia Records executive wanted to push Rosanne pop and got her to record two more songs for the project. Original producer David Malloy was already committed to do a Dolly Parton album [see 660—"Think About Love"], so Cash cut "Never Be You" and "Hold On" (a Top Five single) with Rodney Crowell producing. *Rhythm & Romance*, which took more than a year to make, also yielded a Top Five hit with "Second To No One."

655

JUST IN CASE
THE FORESTER SISTERS
Warner Bros. 28875
Writers: J.P. Pennington, Sonny Lemaire
Producers: J.L. Wallace, Terry Skinner
February 1, 1986 (1 week)

When four sisters from the same family are all competing for a limited number of lead vocals, one can almost bet there'll be a fair amount of arguing. Such is the case with the Forester Sisters, although they're usually able to resolve the situation internally.

"The question one time was, 'Can we have a little more say in our vocals?'" producer J.L. (Jerry) Wallace recalls. "We were like, 'What does that mean?' They asked this in a Warner Bros. meeting, and we said, 'What does that mean?' And they said, 'Let us fight.'"

Out of their fighting, the Foresters are able to come up with a strong vocal harmony. The evidence is "Just In Case," a song that first appeared on Exile's *Kentucky Hearts* album.

"I'm not sure which came first," says Exile's Sonny Lemaire, who co-wrote it with J.P. Pennington. "But at the time, we had a tour manager that would say his name—we were jokin' about it—was Justin Case. I think it dawned on me that it would be a neat kind of thing to write about. I don't remember how it came about, but I just remember that funny phrase, laughin' about it, checkin' into a hotel room and signin' in as Justin Case. But I don't know which came first—the song or his idea."

The Foresters didn't hear the Exile version, though, until after they had already recorded the song. Instead, they were introduced to it by another performer who would later record his own hits, including "Like Father, Like Son" and "Give Me His Last Chance."

"Right after we got our record deal," Christy Forester explains, "we went to Knoxville, Tennessee, and did a show called 'Pickin' At The Paradise,' which was part of the Nashville Network's programming at that time. Lionel Cartwright was a part of that show, and his band did 'Just In Case.' At that time, we were lookin' for material, and we remembered really likin' the song when we heard it. It was uptempo, and everybody got into it."

Wallace and co-producer Terry Skinner purposely cut a version which was almost identical to the Exile one, with Wallace handling the guitar solo. The result was the Foresters' second number one single.

656

HURT
JUICE NEWTON
RCA 14199
Writers: Jimmy Crane, Al Jacobs
Producer: Richard Landis
February 8, 1986 (1 week)

"I was never even exposed to country music as a kid," says Juice Newton. "But club owners would say, 'You have an accent—you must be a country singer.' I'd say, 'No, but does that mean we'd have the job?' If that's what they wanted, that's what I'd be. So I'd go buy Patsy Cline and Brenda Lee records and learn the songs. And I found I had a knack for it."

Juice also had a knack for turning old pop songs into new country hits. She did it first with "Angel Of The Morning" [see 457—"The Sweetest Thing (I've Ever Known)"], and later with "Break It To Me Gently" [see 641—"You Make Me Want To Make You Mine"]. She turned the trick once again in 1986 with "Hurt."

Timi Yuro introduced the song in 1961, reaching number four on the *Billboard* Hot 100. It also landed on the pop chart in remakes by Little Anthony & The Imperials and the Manhattans.

Newton wasn't the first to bring it into country music. Connie Cato reached number 14 with "Hurt" in 1975, and Elvis Presley took it to number six in the spring of 1976. Juice added it to her *Old Flame* album, relying very little on the original for her interpretation.

"I was familiar with the tune," she explains, "but I didn't know it intimately. I was vaguely familiar with the song, and my version's somewhat different, because I know that in the original there's a spoken part, and I don't do that. That's not in my personality, so I made the decision early on that that's not how I would interpret the song."

"Hurt" reached number one on February 8, 1986, the highest chart position for any version in the song's history.

The *Old Flame* album proved a goldmine. In addition to "You Make Me Want To Make You Mine" and "Hurt," it yielded four Top Ten singles: "Old Flame," "Both To Each Other (Friends & Lovers)" [see 691], "Cheap Love" and "What Can I Do With My Heart." In late 1987, Newton picked up one more Top Ten record on "Tell Me True."

Her relationship with Otha Young went by the wayside on a personal level, although they remained friends and musical partners. Juice married polo pro Tom Goodspeed in 1986.

657
MAKIN' UP FOR LOST TIME
CRYSTAL GAYLE & GARY MORRIS
Warner Bros. 28856
Writers: Gary Morris, Dave Loggins
Producer: Jim Ed Norman
February 15, 1986 (1 week)

"It was a really good song—a stupid project, but a really good song." That's an accurate assessment by one of Crystal Gayle's closest associates.

He speaks, of course, of "Makin' Up For Lost Time," a velvet duet combining Crystal's talents with those of Gary Morris. The song was recorded specifically for the "Dallas" soundtrack, the "stupid project" that Warner Bros. hoped to tie in with the TV show.

The initial threads of the single came to-

gether in the midst of a Broadway show. Morris made his stage debut on November 30, 1984, where he appeared along with Linda Ronstadt in *La Boheme*. Nashville songwriter Dave Loggins made a couple of trips to New York during *La Boheme*'s run, and got together with Morris to write. "Makin' Up For Lost Time" stemmed from one of those collaborative sessions.

"I actually thought that [Ronstadt and I] might record it when I wrote it," Morris recalls. "Then Warners came to me and wanted me to do a duet for a special project with Crystal. They had Crystal on the label, and I said, 'Well, I got this one song—if she likes it, we can do a duet,' and it worked out real well for us."

By the time Gary recorded a demo, Crystal had already been confirmed as his duet partner. He went into the studio with Judy Rodman [see 679—"Until I Met You"], who provided the voice that Gayle would learn the song from.

"We hadn't gotten together before the session," Crystal reports. "We go into the studio, we sing together, and that's the result. We did not go back in and do anything over. We did the song, and played off each other. Fortunately, we both have strong voices to sing together. I can sing loud with Gary as well as he can."

"Makin' Up For Lost Time" performed well enough that Gary and Crystal reunited for an entire duet album, *What If We Fall in Love?*, in 1987. Included was their new theme song for the daytime soap opera "Another World." They introduced it on the show together in the early part of April; Morris appeared on "Another World" for only one day, while Gayle guested for an entire week, portraying herself in a plot in which she was stalked by a killer. "Another World" peaked at number four.

658
THERE'S NO STOPPING YOUR HEART
MARIE OSMOND
Capitol 5521
Writers: Michael Brook, Craig Karp
Producer: Paul Worley
February 22, 1986 (1 week)

When "Donny & Marie" debuted on ABC-TV on January 16, 1979, the Osmond siblings were quickly differentiated: Marie was "a little bit country," and Donny was "a little bit rock

Marie Osmond

and roll." Though she had moved on to host "Ripley's Believe It Or Not" ten years later, Marie made it clear that the country label applied.

"I love country," she said. "When we had the variety series, I did a lot of different kinds of music. That's just the format of variety TV shows. But long before that, I had decided country was for me. I love the music. And I like the fact that women can be successful in country music, and that there's some longevity to a country singer's career."

She drove that fact home with her comeback duet, "Meet Me In Montana" [see 640], and quickly followed it with another catchy song. "There's No Stopping Your Heart" came from New Jersey songwriter Michael Brook. Under his real name, Michael Bonagura, Brook later gained recognition as one-third of Baillie & The Boys, with "Oh Heart" and "Long Shot."

Bonagura's publisher had supplied a demo of the song to Capitol Records, where Terry Choate took an interest and forwarded it to Osmond's producer, Paul Worley. "It was a

male vocal on the demo," notes Worley, "and it was a good demo. I fell in love with the song immediately. Marie happened to be in town, and we ran out to her hotel room near Opryland and played the song for her and she got excited about it, too."

They used "There's No Stopping Your Heart" as the title track for Marie's album, although Worley contacted Ed Seay to remix it before the single's release. "We even did some editing and moved some musical intros around," says Worley, "so that the single version, which everybody heard, is not on the LP."

The new version (with an accompanying video produced by brother Alan Osmond) debuted in *Billboard* on November 11, 1985, and topped the country chart three months later. Another single from the album, "Read My Lips," made it to number four.

Marie compared her more recent successes to the days of "Paper Roses" [see 147]: "I was under the tutelage of a lot of great people. Now, I get to capitalize on that experience, and I feel like I'm more of a contributor."

YOU CAN DREAM OF ME
STEVE WARINER
MCA 52721
Writers: Steve Wariner, John Hall
Producers: Tony Brown, Jimmy Bowen
March 1, 1986 (1 week)

Besides his work as a singer and guitarist, Steve Wariner has several other talents: he paints, he does magic in some of his stage shows (including a disappearing-bra trick), and he is particularly proud of his songwriting. Wariner wrote his first single, "I'm Already Taken," and has had songs covered by Bob Luman and Conway Twitty. "You Can Dream Of Me" marked his first composition to hit number one.

"That's a big steppin' stone, or goal achieved, for me," he assesses. "Since I was 16, I'd been tryin' to write what I thought was a really good song, and I think I finally felt legitimate as a writer after havin' a number one."

Steve co-wrote "You Can Dream Of Me" with John Hall, best known as the lead vocalist for Orleans, a group that copped two Top Ten pop hits: "Dance With Me" and "Still The One" (Bill Anderson turned the latter song into a number 11 country single in 1977). Wariner's then-manager Don Light told Steve in 1985 that he might want to meet Hall.

"I'd been hearin' about John Hall from different people, who were sayin' that we should get together and write," Steve notes, "and then I met John one night at the Bluebird Cafe. We set up a time to write and became friends right off the bat."

Hall had the chorus to "You Can Dream Of Me" already written from one of their first co-ventures. Steve "flipped out over it," and they engaged in the proverbial give-and-take at Wariner's house until they had fleshed out the verses. Orleans (comprising Hall and brothers Lance and Larry Hoppen) contributed backing vocals to Wariner's recording, and MCA signed the band to a short-lived recording contract.

"That was a big step for Steve, to do a song that was leaning toward a pop/contemporary sound," says producer Tony Brown. "The chord structure was very pop, and the way it was written was a very pop lyric, but Steve sort of kept it in the country mainstream. It had that little Orleans flare to it, which I thought was a pretty interesting mixture."

THINK ABOUT LOVE
DOLLY PARTON
RCA 14218
Writers: Spady Brannon, Tom Campbell
Producer: David Malloy
March 8, 1986 (1 week)

"Think About Love" was the third single from Dolly Parton's *Real Love* album. The first, "Don't Call It Love," went to number three in the winter of 1985, and the title track [see 634] was the second chart-topping release Parton recorded with Kenny Rogers. Though it was the third song released, "Think About Love" was actually the first song that producer David Malloy earmarked for the project.

"I usually lock on one song and use that as the 'access,'" Malloy says, "and I kind of move to the left and to the right of that particular song when I'm picking songs for an artist. That was my key song—total Dolly."

Maybe, but not *totally* Dolly. Malloy had a great deal of control over the project, and Parton wrote only four of the album's ten songs.

"I only met with Dolly twice before we went into the studio," he notes. "I had just two hours of time with her the whole time, ever, before I went into the studio to make the album. I basically never had a chance to get with her. I picked all the songs and everything and assembled the demos in order, how I would sequence the album and everything, and said, 'This is how I hear it.' She looked at me and said, 'Let's do it your way.'"

That way was pretty successful. "Think About Love" zipped into the country chart on November 30, 1985, and reached the summit the following March. The *Real Love* album also yielded a fourth single, "Tie Our Love (In A Double Knot)," which peaked at number 17.

"She's one of the greatest people I've ever had the honor of working with," gushes Malloy. "The way you see her and the way she is on television and all that is the way she is every time I ever was around her, just absolutely wonderful.

"My dad had worked with Dolly and Porter [Wagoner] [see 181—"Please Don't Stop Loving Me"] years before as an engineer, and I never had met her or anything, but she was just an absolute delight. She would come into the studio and sing these incredible vocals, always on pitch."

I COULD GET USED TO YOU
EXILE

Epic 05723
Writers: Sonny Lemaire, J.P. Pennington
Producer: Buddy Killen
March 15, 1986 (1 week)

Exile devoted 21 seconds to a musical intro-duction before a single voice was heard in the strains of "I Could Get Used To You." Though most country records take only eight to ten seconds to develop, lengthy intros be-came something of an Exile trademark, as the band played for 18 seconds on "Crazy For Your Love" [see 611], 16 in "She's A Miracle" [see 627], 19 in "Hang On To Your Heart" [see 645], and a whopping 32 in "I Can't Get Close Enough" [see 752].

"As a band, it's kind of neat to set the song up musically first somehow," observes bass player Sonny Lemaire. "We try to sound like Exile from the start of the song, and it's fun trying to establish a musical hook along with the lyrical hook."

In the case of "I Could Get Used To You," Exile reeled in its seventh straight number one country single.

"J.P. [Pennington] had that hook," says Lemaire. "I went over to his house, and he said, 'Man, I got this idea,' and he sang the hook, and I was just so knocked out with the melody. It was all ready for a chorus, and it was just exciting. I loved the sentiment involved in it, and we wrote it real quick—a couple of hours."

"I Could Get Used To You" ascended to the top of *Billboard*'s chart just six weeks after the Forester Sisters reached number one with "Just In Case" [see 655], another Pennington/ Lemaire composition. In October, their co-writing efforts earned an award from BMI, the songwriters' performing-rights organization, as the top country writers of the year.

"It proves to me that we weren't a fluke," Pennington told Nashville journalist Bob Mil-lard. "To me, the biggest thrill has been follow-ing up one number one with another."

"We were real open to one another, and we could bounce ideas off one another and not be afraid to hear that they wouldn't work," Lemaire assesses. "J.P. and I didn't socialize together a lot, but when we wrote together, we could stay there for hours. Nothing else would come into focus."

WHAT'S A MEMORY LIKE YOU (DOING IN A LOVE LIKE THIS)
JOHN SCHNEIDER

MCA 52723
Writers: Charles Quillen, John Jarrard
Producers: Jimmy Bowen, John Schneider
March 22, 1986 (1 week)

"Songs are like kids. You don't ever give up on them."

Songwriter John Jarrard offered that nugget of wisdom to *Tune-In*'s Eda Galeno while dis-cussing one of his compositions, "What's A Memory Like You (Doing In A Love Like This)." The song lay around for three years before it attracted interest, making it the sec-ond late-bloomer that John Schneider brought to the public [see 594—"I've Been Around Enough To Know"].

The song enjoyed a flurry of activity at the time that Schneider recorded it. Moe Bandy and Conway Twitty also cut versions, and Steve Wariner had intended to do it as well. When John first heard the demo, he thought it was the best song he had ever come across, and Wariner, upon realizing Schneider's pas-sion for it, let go of the song and cleared the way for John to cut it.

Schneider made his powerful rendition the title track for his third MCA album, and the single hit *Billboard* at number 71 on December 14, 1985. In its fifteenth charted week, it set-tled into the number one position. Any doubts that country fans had about his sincerity and devotion to the format had been erased by that time. John's two previous singles, "It's A Short Walk From Heaven To Hell" and "I'm Gonna Leave You Tomorrow," reached the Top Ten, with the latter eliciting comparisons to Merle Haggard.

John further underscored his commitment to a career in country music while recording his *A Memory Like You* album. "The Dukes of Hazzard," in which he first appeared on Janu-ary 26, 1979, was canceled. Schneider booked studio time in the summer of 1985, but when an episode featuring Waylon Jennings brought solid ratings, CBS tried to revive the show, with shooting to begin the week that Schnei-der was in the studio. John refused to cancel his sessions, and "Dukes" made its final prime-time appearance on August 16.

Born April 8, 1945, in Mount Kisco, New

York, Schneider worked in both acting and music for much of his life. He had his first lead role at age eight, in a school performance of *Fiddler on the Roof*, and in sixth grade, joined the school chorus. His resumé later expanded with summer stock roles in *Bye Bye Birdie* and *The Wizard of Oz*. At age fourteen, his mother took him to Atlanta, where he continued to develop his creative ambitions. He appeared in a Marine documentary, a Disney production and *Smokey and the Bandit* prior to "Dukes."

Lee Greenwood

663

DON'T UNDERESTIMATE MY LOVE FOR YOU
LEE GREENWOOD
MCA 52741
Writers: Steve Diamond, Steve Dorff,
Dave Loggins
Producer: Jerry Crutchfield
March 29, 1986 (1 week)

On April 30, 1966, the Young Rascals topped *Billboard*'s Hot 100 with "Good Lovin'," the first of two number one pop singles. Twenty years later, a near-Rascal earned his fifth number one in country music, as Lee Greenwood checked in with "Don't Underestimate My Love For You."

Greenwood's connection with the Rascals came when he toured in the mid-'60s with Sandu Scott & The Scotties. Greenwood had signed up as a sax player, lured by the chance to tour with the band in the Caribbean and make an appearance on "The Ed Sullivan Show." As fate would have it, the group folded in New York, when Scott decided to get married, and two of the remaining members asked Greenwood to form a new band along with them.

Greenwood knew, however, that he had a guaranteed income in Vegas and declined the offer. While he went back to Nevada, the two ex-Scotties—Dino Danelli and Felix Cavaliere—went on to pop stardom with the Young Rascals.

Two decades later, Greenwood's fifth number one in country music came with "Don't Underestimate My Love For You," a tune with a somewhat unlikely title. "A very strange title," admits songwriter Steve Dorff, "a very strange song. The whole thing about that record was strange."

Dorff and Steve Diamond wrote the first part of the song in Los Angeles, developing the title and the melody, but they ran into trouble on some of the verses. "We were kind of banging our heads against the wall," says Dorff, "and Steve said we should see if Dave Loggins wanted to write the lyric."

Diamond and Loggins had already done some writing together, and a copy of the song was sent to Nashville, where Loggins rewrote many of the lyrics. Once the song was completed, Loggins also sang the demo that was submitted to Greenwood.

"Dave Loggins to me is the James Taylor of Nashville," notes Greenwood, "and we're very good friends. He's sent me several songs that I've recorded. His writing talent is just incredible. The only trouble with the way he writes is that sometimes he writes songs that other people can't sing, because he sings them so damn well."

Lee performed admirably on "Underestimate," though, entering the *Billboard* country chart on December 28, 1985. Three months later, the song peaked at number one.

664

100% CHANCE OF RAIN

GARY MORRIS

Warner Bros. 28823
Writers: Charlie Black, Austin Roberts
Producer: Jim Ed Norman
April 5, 1986 (1 week)

Born December 7, 1948, in Forth Worth, Texas, Gary Morris made an early commitment to athletics, and he has excelled in that area. At age eleven, he played in the Little League World Series. He was strong safety on the football team at Cisco Junior College in Texas, and that squad went to one of only three bowl games that existed for junior colleges.

"Winning might not be everything," he told Kelly Delaney in *Country Song Roundup*, "but losing is nothing. That all translates to music, because I feel confident, prepared, and I know I'm gonna do okay. Doing the best I can—that attitude came from athletics."

Gary came out a winner on a musical level at the beginning of 1986. On February 22, his duet with Crystal Gayle, "Makin' Up For Lost Time" [see 657], resided in *Billboard*'s Top 20, as did a solo effort, "100% Chance Of Rain."

"Charlie Black and Austin Roberts wrote it, and Jim Ed Norman played it for me," Gary says of the latter record. "When I first heard it, I thought I'd record it. The way it gets your attention—'8:00 A.M., radio on, just for a little noise/Empty house, I just needed to hear the sound of another voice'—would just draw 'em in. I knew that if I could sing it, it would be a good record, and it worked."

Six weeks after it entered the Top 20, "100% Chance Of Rain" cracked the top spot, but it also brought a black cloud to the visual side of Morris' musical career. During the making of a video clip for the single, there was

no rain in sight, so the production team had to resort to man-made water.

"I swore after doin' that I'd never do another song about rain," Gary asserts. "I stood outside and got sprayed by a 40,000-gallon truck with a fire hose on it. I swore my next song would be about sunshine and the islands, so that if we did a video, I'd have to go somewhere romantic and lay in the sun."

Subsequently, he had roughly seventeen shows rained out when the song was at its peak, including one indoor date when a storm knocked out the power. The band jokingly renamed that tour the Rain Tour.

665

SHE AND I

ALABAMA

RCA 14281
Writer: Dave Loggins
Producers: Harold Shedd, Alabama
April 12, 1986 (1 week)

"She And I" isn't really Alabama—at least, not in total.

RCA planned a *Greatest Hits* album for the group, including a hodge-podge of material—some of their earlier number one records, live renditions of "My Home's In Alabama" and "Tennessee River" [see 390], plus two new songs. Teddy Gentry, Randy Owen and road manager Greg Fowler wrote one of the new tracks, "The Fans." RCA country chief Joe Galante suggested "She And I" as the other.

Gentry, for one, wasn't particularly thrilled about the song at first listen, but trusted Galante's judgment anyway. The label had a tight deadline for the album, and Alabama had to head into the recording studio with little advance notice. Owen had the group's organization contact band member Jeff Cook, whom Randy believed was vacationing in Tallahassee. As it turned out, though, Cook was in St. Thomas and didn't think he could get back to Nashville in time. Alabama had to tab songwriter Dave Loggins as a replacement.

"She And I" featured a barrage of unique sounds. Most talked-about was a strange drum effect, by which the echo for each drumbeat—instead of "decaying"—ends with a pop. "We reverse-gated echoes and did tricks like that," explains producer Harold Shedd. "A lot of technical things made that record unique."

Ricky Skaggs with Elvis Costello

The record also conjured up shades of Elvis Presley's "Suspicious Minds" when it faded out on the ending, only to return to full volume before fading a second time. Nearly two minutes were clipped from the album version when "She And I" was released as a single, and it climbed to number one on April 12, 1986, its twelfth week on the *Billboard* country chart.

In August, *Alabama's Greatest Video Hits* broke new ground as the first country video certified platinum.

Teddy Gentry ultimately decided that "She And I" was a better record than he had initially imagined. Born January 22, 1952, Gentry picked up the bass practically overnight; he was originally a rhythm guitarist. But when his high school group entered a battle-of-the-bands contest and needed a bass player, Gentry woodshedded for two days—the group went on to win.

Gentry's family didn't have indoor plumbing, or even an outhouse, and Teddy's rise from poverty to national fame has helped to brand Alabama as an example of an authentic American dream.

666

CAJUN MOON
RICKY SKAGGS
Epic 05748

Writer: Jim Rushing
Producer: Ricky Skaggs
April 19, 1986 (1 week)

Ricky Skaggs took on a truckload of pressure to follow up his *Country Boy* [see 624] album. During the spring of 1985, he left with his band for its first European tour and decided to do it in grandiose fashion. After warming up on the European mainland, Skaggs arranged to record a live album when they arrived at the Dominion Theatre in London. With those plans laid, Ricky went even further, and shot the entire series of shows for a concert video.

Knowing that a lot of money was being spent, and that much rode on his performance, Skaggs played before a crowd in a country where he had never even headlined before. He gave it all he had and got back . . . polite applause.

After the first London show, Ricky was nervous. Maybe they'd miscalculated. Maybe the music didn't translate to England as well as they thought it would. Maybe he didn't give a good performance.

The next day, his fears were washed away. He received overwhelming critical approval. Some of his associates explained that English audiences were simply more reserved than American crowds. With that understanding, Skaggs felt much more at home the second night, and he estimates that 90 percent of the *Live in London* album came from that show.

The album contained several highlights. Rocker Elvis Costello joined Ricky on stage for a rendition of "Don't Get Above Your Raisin'." The record also yielded three singles. The first, "You Make Me Feel Like A Man," and the third, "I've Got A New Heartache," both reached the American Top Ten. Sandwiched between them was Ricky's tenth chart-topping single, "Cajun Moon."

Ricky picked up the song from Jim Rushing, whom he had signed to his publishing company in 1984. A native of Lubbock, Rushing learned some of the fine points of writing from Bob McDill, and went on to create "Pittsburgh Stealers," for the Kendalls; "Nothing Sure Looked Good On You," for Gene Watson; and Ricky's 1988 single "Thanks Again."

Skaggs more or less commissioned "Cajun Moon," asking Rushing for something with a southern Louisiana feel. Though Ricky liked the song, he never pictured it as a single until his wife, Sharon White, insisted it was a hit. Sharon was right. "Cajun Moon" debuted at number 68 on January 11, 1986, and danced its way to number one fifteen weeks later.

667

NOW AND FOREVER (YOU AND ME)
ANNE MURRAY
Capitol 5547
Writers: David Foster, Jim Vallance, Randy Goodrum
Producer: David Foster
April 26, 1986 (1 week)

After an eight-year artist/producer relationship, Jim Ed Norman and Anne Murray parted company with the release of the *Heart Over Mind* album in 1985. Following the lead-off duet with Dave Loggins [see 599—"Nobody Loves Me Like You Do"], Murray went to number two with "Time Don't Run Out On Me" and reached number seven with "I Don't Think I'm Ready For You," from the movie *Stick*.

Norman had become the head of Warner Bros. in Nashville, and, though the label had allowed him to produce *Heart Over Mind* for Capitol, he needed to follow his new path. He left behind an impressive legacy with Murray, though: on June 10, 1985, *Heart Over Mind* became her tenth gold album.

Anne decided in the meantime to move in a pop direction, and recorded her next release,

Something to Talk About, with a trio of separate producers: Jack White, Keith Diamond and David Foster. Foster's "Now And Forever (You And Me)" was the album's first single, co-written with Randy Goodrum [see 337—"I Just Fall In Love Again"] and Jim Vallance, best known for his work with Canadian rock musician Bryan Adams.

"David came into the studio, and I hadn't heard anything," Anne laughs. "I hadn't heard anything on tape, anything, and he said, 'Okay, this is how it goes,' and he hummed it. He said, 'This is how it goes, do you like it?' I said, 'Yeah, I like it, but it has no words.' 'Well, we'll get some.'

"He put down a drum track, and did a whole rhythm track all by himself with this machine. Anyway, he went away, and he called, or I called, Randy Goodrum and asked him to write some words to it. Next thing you know, we had a tune, but we're talking about building it from scratch."

Mr. Mister's Richard Page interweaved a vocal part on the chorus, and Murray had a song she felt would work well as a pop record. Instead, it peaked at number 92 on *Billboard*'s Hot 100, hitting number one on the country chart.

Murray's large collection of memorabilia (including gold records, Grammys, Junos, etc.) has long been in storage in her house, but it finally found a home of its own. In the summer of 1989, her hometown of Springhill, Nova Scotia, opened the Anne Murray Center.

668

ONCE IN A BLUE MOON
EARL THOMAS CONLEY
RCA 14282
Writers: Tommy Brasfield, Robert Byrne
Producers: Nelson Larkin, Earl Thomas Conley
May 3, 1986 (1 week)

On March 22, 1986, Earl Thomas Conley registered the first number one country album of his career, when his *Greatest Hits* reached the top spot in *Billboard*. Ironically, Conley doesn't like the album. The early material brought back unpleasant personal memories, and he couldn't listen all the way through.

"It's kind of embarrassing," he muses, "although I loved the older stuff that I did. God forbid anyone should ever lose their innocence to that degree, that they can't look back and laugh at themselves. It's like old photographs, you know. I guess it does give you a more well-rounded view of the person—a little more well-rounded than I like to look at."

Conley added two new songs to the package: "Nobody Falls Like A Fool" [see 630] and "Once In A Blue Moon." Co-written with "Holding Her And Loving You" [see 546] writer Tommy Brasfield, "Once In A Blue Moon" was the first country hit penned by Muscle Shoals musician Robert Byrne, who had recorded a few albums for Mercury in the '70s and who had written songs for Dr. Hook, the Captain & Tennille and Johnny Rivers.

The publisher tried to get Byrne and Brasfield to rewrite the second line in the chorus. Though they tried, the song didn't work without the line, and they shopped the original version around Nashville.

"I remember playin' it for Steve Wariner," says Byrne, "and he didn't 'hear' it. I've gotten to the point where I like to play things for Steve, 'cause everything I've played for him has gone to number one. I say, 'Hey, Steve, just do me a favor and pass on this thing.' I've got a little superstition happenin' here."

As with "Holding Her," Brasfield played the song for Earl's producer, Nelson Larkin, who then forwarded it along to Conley, even though they already had the two songs they needed for the *Greatest Hits* album. They bumped one of those songs to make room for "Blue Moon."

"When I first heard it, it was like 'Holding Her And Loving You,'" Earl notes. "It was a definite number one single, I thought, right off the bat."

On May 3, the *Billboard* charts proved Conley correct. In July of 1989, *Greatest Hits* became Earl's first gold record.

Judd, with the release of *Rockin' with the Rhythm*. "I really tried to stretch myself as a vocalist, and we also tried some songs that are different from anything else we've ever done before."

The second single pulled from the album proved that the Judds had netted quality material: "Grandpa (Tell Me 'Bout The Good Old Days)" eventually nabbed a pair of Grammy awards, for Best Country Vocal Performance by a Duo or Group, and Best Country Song.

Ironically, Jamie O'Hara, who wrote "Grandpa," never knew any of his grandparents, paternal or maternal. All had passed away before he was born, and he now calls the song therapeutic, suggesting that it filled a void in his personal life.

"I'd been working very regularly around that time," O'Hara recalls. "I was in a songwriting groove, and woke up one morning, and that's the song that came out. 'Grandpa' was a gift that songwriters get every once in a while, if you're putting in your work."

Within a week, he played the song for producer Brent Maher, specifically with the Judds in mind.

"To hear 'Grandpa' and not like it, you've got to have a stone for a heart," Brent insists. "It just hit me so hard, and I met with the girls a couple days later, and I played it for them. Wynonna got these big ol' blurry tears in her eyes, and we knew pretty much well off that it was gonna be a strong song for them."

The timing was incredible. Naomi had recently lost her own father, Glen Judd, and on hearing the song, she fell to pieces as well.

"I knew that when we cut the record, there would be no way we were ever gonna miss," Maher adds. "It was just one of those songs that works from the first time you heard it."

"Grandpa" entered the *Billboard* country chart at a stellar number 52 on February 15, 1986, three days after *Rockin' with the Rhythm* was certified as the Judds' second gold album. It reached number one a dozen weeks later.

669

GRANDPA (TELL ME 'BOUT THE GOOD OLD DAYS)

THE JUDDS (WYNONNA & NAOMI)

RCA 14290
Writer: Jamie O'Hara
Producer: Brent Maher
May 10, 1986 (1 week)

"I feel more comfortable with my voice on this album than I ever did before," said Wynonna

---

670

AIN'T MISBEHAVIN'

HANK WILLIAMS, JR.

Warner Bros. 28794
Writer: Harry Brooks, Andy Razaf, Fats Waller
Producers: Jimmy Bowen, Hank Williams, Jr.
May 17, 1986 (1 week)

On May 9, 1978, the Longacre Theater in New York brought a musical revue to Broadway. *Ain't Misbehavin'* celebrated the creative legacy of Thomas "Fats" Waller, an influential bluesman who invented the "stride" piano. The production featured some thirty of his compositions, including "Honeysuckle Rose," "'T'ain't Nobody's Biz-ness If I Do," "I'm Gonna Sit Right Down And Write Myself A Letter," and, of course, "Ain't Misbehavin'."

The latter was the first major success for an unusual vocalist named Louis Armstrong, who performed it in an all-black revue in Harlem titled *Hot Chocolates*, which opened during 1929. Waller, born in New York in 1904, composed the song at his home on 133rd Street in Harlem, with the aid of Andy Razaf. The rest of *Hot Chocolates* was already mapped out, but the producers needed a theme to complete the show. Waller already had the melodic idea somewhat sketched out, and the song was put together in just 45 minutes. In 1943, Waller rendered his own interpretation of "Ain't Misbehavin'" in the movie *Stormy Weather*.

The song was probably an unlikely candidate for country success, but Hank Williams, Jr., happened to hear it one day, and "Ain't Misbehavin'" stuck in his head. As a result, he put it on record, and it emerged as the third single from his *Five-0* album [see 632—"I'm For Love"]. Hank turned to Jerry McKinney for an unusual soprano sax solo, and the single version, which lopped off more than a minute of music, behaved rather well—it reached number one on May 17, 1986, in its thirteenth week on the *Billboard* country chart.

Bocephus' musical versatility might have surprised some, but his musical heritage explains his unusual mix of material, which includes blues, pure pop, hard country and Southern rock.

"I was born right into it," Williams told Michael Bane in *Billboard*. "When I was growing up, there were some super people over at the house. Perry Como would be there. Fats Domino would be there. Jerry Lee Lewis, Charlie Rich, Al Hirt—I was around them all the time."

"Ain't Misbehavin'" was the last single in Hank's eleven-album association with producer Jimmy Bowen. He subsequently teamed up with Jim Ed Norman and Barry Beckett, whose first production, "Country State Of Mind," brought Hank to number two for two weeks, behind Conway Twitty's "Desperado Love" [see 686] and Reba McEntire's "Little Rock" [see 687].

671
TOMB OF THE UNKNOWN LOVE
KENNY ROGERS
RCA 14298
Writer: Micheal Smotherman
Producer: George Martin
May 24, 1986 (1 week)

"One year I'm weird and eccentric, and the next year I'm brilliant."

That's songwriter Micheal Smotherman's explanation for a sometimes hot/sometimes cold career. The "eccentric" label probably got started early, when his mother misspelled Micheal's name on his birth certificate.

Heading from Oklahoma to Los Angeles in the late '70s, Smotherman hooked up with Billy Burnette, who played country dates on occasion with his father, rockabilly pioneer Johnny Burnette. Johnny's friend, Roger Miller, hired Smotherman to play piano, and when he heard some of the songs that Micheal wrote, he persuaded Waylon Jennings and Glen Campbell to record them. It was then that Micheal took writing seriously.

"I had always assumed," he explains, "that if something came naturally to me, it must not be worth anything."

Once he indulged his new-found skill, Smotherman racked up successes like Campbell's renditions of "Can You Fool" and "I'm Gonna Love You"; Earl Thomas Conley & Anita Pointer's duet, "Too Many Times"; and Michael Martin Murphey's "Never Givin' Up On Love."

His only number one came with "Tomb Of The Unknown Love," a song he describes as a "Celtic psychodrama." Kenny Rogers had seen Smotherman perform at a benefit, and expressed an interest in two of his songs. Micheal sent those two on a tape, along with three others, including "Tomb."

Rogers recorded it for *The Heart of the Matter*, an album produced by former Beatles producer George Martin. "George is the consummate producer," says Herb Pedersen (now with the Desert Rose Band), who sang back-up on the record. "He never gets in your way. He knows what he wants, and he gets it as delicately and as forcefully as necessary. You always walk out of there feeling terrific, 'cause he not only makes you feel good about what you're doing, but he gets the best out of you."

RCA nixed future Rogers/Martin collaborations, but Kenny's records continued to perform well as he ended that particular contract. "Twenty Years Ago" and "I Prefer The Moonlight" hit number two, and "The Factory" also reached the Top Ten. After a switch to Reprise, he connected with the Top Ten again in 1989, on "The Vows Go Unbroken."

Kenny secured his twentieth number one single by teaming with Ronnie Milsap on "Make No Mistake, She's Mine" [see 736].

672
WHOEVER'S IN NEW ENGLAND
REBA McENTIRE
MCA 52767
Writers: Kendal Franceschi,
Quentin Powers
Producers: Jimmy Bowen, Reba McEntire
May 31, 1986 (1 week)

In January of 1987, Reba McEntire earned her first gold album, and on February 24, she picked up her first Grammy award. Both revolved around her fifth number one single, "Whoever's In New England."

Portraying a married couple in the South, the song sent a businessman on frequent trips to Boston. "Whoever's In New England" could be taken two ways. One interpretation suggests that the trips are a smokescreen for the husband to visit another woman.

Reba explained her own interpretation to the *Boston Globe*'s Steve Morse, when she started shooting the video at the city's Logan Airport on January 30, 1986: "The song is all about a woman's imagination. I've gone through the same thing when my husband was in the rodeo. I'd be sitting around thinking, 'What's he doing tonight? Where is he?' Then I'd call his hotel, but he wouldn't be there. So you get a roaming imagination even though he might just

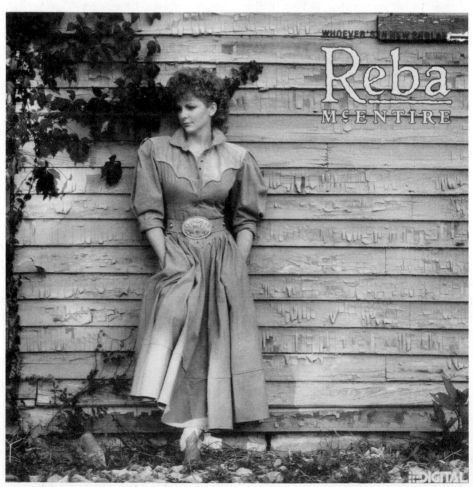

be on his way back to the hotel."

Pat Higdon, then with the Oak Ridge Boys' Silverline/Goldline publishing companies, brought the song to production assistant Don Lanier's office.

"Different people tell me different stories about what the feelin's was on that song," Reba reports. "Some say that [then-husband] Charlie [Battles] didn't want me to record it, some say that I didn't want to record it. I promise you, the first time I heard that song, I loved it.

"Don Lanier is always wearin' a baseball cap, and when he finds a song he likes, his eyebrows will totally disappear underneath that baseball cap. I get chills, just goosebumps deluxe. Pat played several songs and then played 'Whoever's In New England.' I looked at Don. His eyebrows disappeared, and I was just chillin' out."

Producer Jimmy Bowen usually cuts an entire album in the space of one week, and after they'd gotten halfway through a week of recording, Reba's voice started to wear out. "New England" was the last song she had to cut, and she doubted if she could pull it off.

Bowen remembers: "I'm goin', 'Aw, do it—it'll be great, it'll be great.' So she did it, and it ended up bein' a number one record. That song took her from bein' a country-singles radio artist into bein' a record-seller."

673
HAPPY, HAPPY BIRTHDAY BABY
RONNIE MILSAP
RCA 14286
Writers: Margo Sylvia, Gilbert Lopez
Producers: Ronnie Milsap, Tom Collins,
Rob Galbralth
June 7, 1986 (1 week)

When Ronnie Milsap "doo-wopped" his way to number one with the award-winning "Lost In The Fifties Tonight" [see 639], RCA's Nashville chief Joe Galante realized they had the foundation for a strong concept album. Though "Lost In The Fifties" was recorded for *Ronnie's Greatest Hits, Volume 2*, it also became the title track for Milsap's follow-up LP.

"I'm such a fan of '50s music," Ronnie sighs. "You're always a fan of whatever it was in high school that put you there, the music that you loved when you were in high school, whether it's Glenn Miller or Ernest Tubb or Michael Jackson. That music's special to you."

"Happy, Happy Birthday Baby" was particularly special for Milsap. As a vocalist/guitarist in his high school band, the Apparitions, he had sung it at a number of dances in Raleigh, North Carolina. A Boston-based family group, the Tune Weavers, introduced it in 1957.

Lead singer Margo Sylvia and her brother, tenor Gilbert Lopez, wrote it, and it went all the way to number five on *Billboard*'s pop chart. Even before Milsap chose a few suitable oldies for his *Lost in the Fifties Tonight* concept album, he and his wife, Joyce, had discussed doing "Happy, Happy Birthday."

"It was fun to do," says Ronnie. "Those kinds of songs—to me, that's what makin' records is all about. It's supposed to be fun. You go in there two or three times and there's the record.

"Jim Horn came over and played saxophone on it. Bruce Dees and I did all those background vocals one track at a time. There was some mystique about those voices on 'Lost In The Fifties.' It had 22 tracks of background vocals on it that were mixed down to stereo, and 'Happy, Happy Birthday' had probably about the same number again, just goin' in there singin' the high parts. The bass parts are always the fun parts on those '50s things."

Milsap's rendition first appeared at number 53 on the *Billboard* country singles chart on March 8, 1986, edging into number one a lucky 13 weeks later. On October 13 (lucky again!), the Country Music Association named *Lost in the Fifties Tonight* the Album of the Year.

674
LIFE'S HIGHWAY
STEVE WARINER
MCA 52786
Writers: Richard Leigh, Roger Murrah
Producers: Tony Brown, Jimmy Bowen
June 14, 1986 (1 week)

In 1977, a burgeoning Steve Wariner declined to record a song that he heard a year later on his car radio. Then, it was Anne Murray performing "You Needed Me," but Steve has never harbored any regrets about letting that one slip away.

"I thought it was a girl's song," he says, "and I still think it's more of a female lyric."

In 1986, the tables turned when Steve found a hit with a song that a number of other performers had passed up. "Life's Highway," a "message song" of hope for the future, excited songwriters Richard Leigh and Roger Murrah when they created it, but it endured several years of rejections from some of Nashville's top artists.

"I had that sort of a folkie kind of a melody and didn't know what to do with it, thought it should be kind of spiritual in direction," notes Leigh, explaining the song's roots. "Roger had this title, 'Life's Highway', and I thought it was great, and the song just seemed to jump out. We squirted lines, and the next thing we knew, we had a song. We went down and did a demo of it the same day."

Though others turned it down, songwriter Paul Craft believed in "Life's Highway" and intended to cut it with Tony Brown, in a co-production deal with another artist. When that deal didn't pan out, Brown decided that the song might work for Wariner.

"I remember the day I walked in his office," recalls Steve. "I just flipped out over this song. As soon as he played me the demo, we turned the player off, dialed the phone, made the call and put 'Life's Highway' on hold for me."

"It had a little bluegrass sound to it," Brown continues, "and it was a bit ethereal for a Steve Wariner record, but we both loved it. We cut it 'cause we thought it was a song with high integrity."

Despite Brown's fears that his cohorts at MCA would shy away from its lyrical stance, "Life's Highway" earned strong marks at the company, and it became the title track for Wariner's fourth album. The single easily hit number one during the same week that country listeners converged on Nashville for Fan Fair.

The Forester Sisters

675

MAMA'S NEVER SEEN THOSE EYES
THE FORESTER SISTERS
Warner Bros. 28795
Writers: J.L. Wallace, Terry Skinner
Producers: J.L. Wallace, Terry Skinner
June 21, 1986 (1 week)

"On our first album, I think we had only two slow songs and everything else was up-tempo, which is rare, really," notes Christy Forester of the Forester Sisters. "But I think that had a lot to do with the success of the album, 'cause so much of it was real uptempo stuff."

That's certainly true of the album's fourth single, "Mama's Never Seen Those Eyes," written by the Foresters' producers, Terry Skinner and J.L. Wallace. The two came up with the idea for "Mama's" while mixing material from the second of the three four-song sessions that yielded the album. By that point, they'd worked long enough with engineer Steve Melton that he had a feel for their musical theories, so Skinner and Wallace left some of the material in Melton's hands while they ducked out of the control room for a breather.

"We'd gotten separated in some way, and we were shootin' pool or somethin'," Wallace notes. "I had this chorus to 'Mama's Never Seen Those Eyes.' I called Terry and said, 'Hey, listen to this.' He said, 'Yeah, that's good. Let's fiddle with this.'

"So we sat out on the cutting board at Studio B at Muscle Shoals Sound Studio and wrote the tune in about 12 or 13 minutes. He had a guitar stuck in one of the booths back there, and we just grabbed it and went for it.

"Everything came, the little lines and we had it all. We needed to cut that tune on the Foresters. We had '(That's What You Do) When You're In Love' [see 638—"I Fell In Love Again Last Night"], which was a real heavy fiddle tune, and we didn't have another fiddle tune."

Since "Mama" was in the title, the Foresters felt it might be too close to "Mama He's Crazy" [see 580], and Skinner and Wallace had to talk them into recording it. Warner Bros. also had to be convinced. The label initially planned to release the track as the "B" side of "Just In Case" [see 655], but the producers talked them into holding it back. Thanks to radio interest, "Mama's Never Seen Those Eyes" emerged as a rare fourth single, the third from the Foresters' debut LP to reach number one.

676

LIVING IN THE PROMISELAND
WILLIE NELSON
Columbia 05834
Writer: David Lynn Jones
Producer: Willie Nelson
June 28, 1986 (1 week)

For several months beginning in April of 1980, Florida's population swelled with the arrival of new immigrants from Cuba. These new residents were part of a mass exodus—one approved by Fidel Castro that caused great controversy in the U.S. It also provided the starting point for "Living In The Promiseland," a song that took Willie Nelson to number one half a dozen years later.

"The Cuban thing was goin' on and the Cubans were supposed to get all these things and they weren't gettin' anything," recalls songwriter David Lynn Jones. "I don't know why we were promisin' anything in the first place beyond freedom.

"But it was all the boat people from Vietnam, too, and I suppose subconsciously, that's what inspired the song, because the song isn't about America the Great or America the Beautiful. It's about America the Dream, and it's whatever you make it. A lot of people come here thinkin' it's one thing and find something else."

Jones wrote about two-thirds of "Promiseland" in 15 minutes, and then simply dropped it. A few years later, though, business maneuvers forced its completion. Jones was cutting an album in California with producer Bob Johnston, but before they could finish the project, the record label went bankrupt. In the aftermath, he tried to find a new publisher, and when he did, David agreed to submit not only the songs he had finished, but also any unfinished works.

That included "Living In The Promiseland." Jones had forgotten the song, but a musician mentioned it during a demo session for his new publisher. He finished the tune during the final five minutes before they cut it, and within two weeks, it was in Willie Nelson's hands.

Bee Spears, Willie's bass player, had a tape with eight of Jones' songs on it, and he played it for Nelson during a round of golf. Willie invited David to sing "Promiseland" on the first Farm-Aid show [see 628—"Forgiving You Was Easy"], and then recorded it in Austin the following week.

It hit number one on June 28, 1986, and the

next week, "Promiseland" was featured on network television during the re-dedication ceremonies for the Statue of Liberty.

A year later, David Lynn Jones notched his only Top Ten single as a performer, "Bonnie Jean (Little Sister)."

677

EVERYTHING THAT GLITTERS (IS NOT GOLD)
DAN SEALS

EMI America 8311
Writers: Bob McDill, Dan Seals
Producer: Kyle Lehning
July 5, 1986 (1 week)

Dan Seals followed up "Bop" [see 653] with "Everything That Glitters (Is Not Gold)," a stark contrast to the techno-inspired dance groove of its predecessor. Because it was a departure, the record holds a special place in Seals' heart.

"We didn't have another 'Bop,'" he says, "and that would be the normal thing you'd want to have, to follow that same yellow brick road. 'Bop' showed me that the people liked the stuff that I do most of the time."

Seals had written "My Baby's Got Good Timing" earlier with Bob McDill, and "Everything That Glitters" was their second or third attempt to work together. Both hail from Texas (Dan from McCamey and Dallas; Bob from Beaumont), and that shared background started a discussion that led to the rodeo tale of "Glitters."

Dan recalled a story from his youth about a married couple that split up. The father kept the kids, and since that was an unheard-of situation in Seals' neck of the woods, it always perplexed Dan. As an adult, Seals relived a part of that story. He separated from his wife, Andrea, for several months, and for most of that time, their children lived with him. Though he managed to salvage his marriage, Seals was able to relate to the permanent break-up in "Glitters."

"To this day, it's probably the most respected song in my mind that I've ever written," says Seals. "It's a timeless story, it's unique. And when I put the yodel [not a true yodel, but certainly a break between his natural and falsetto voice] in it, that set it apart. It's like each piece—the storyline's great, the mel-

ody's great, but the yodel thing made it special. I grew up listenin' to Roy Rogers and Gene Autry, yodeling, and to be able to use it in a song—and actually make it a part of the song, instead of tacking it on as an additive—I figured would be good."

Seals didn't anticipate that "Everything That Glitters" would become a single, but it received an overwhelming response from his associates. When Seals roped in his third number one single, it came on an appropriate date. The first rodeo took place on the Fourth of July in 1883, in Pecos, Texas. "Glitters" reached number one on the *fifth* of July.

678

HEARTS AREN'T MADE TO BREAK (THEY'RE MADE TO LOVE)
LEE GREENWOOD

MCA 52807
Writers: Roger Murrah, Steve Dean
Producer: Jerry Crutchfield
July 12, 1986 (1 week)

Lee Greenwood's musical talents were in-bred. Mother Bliss played piano professionally, while father Eugene had been a sax player during his enlistment with the Navy. A year after Lee's birth in Los Angeles, however, his parents divorced, and the youngster went along with his older sister, Patricia, to live with their grandparents on a farm near Sacramento.

At the time, Lee's talents in both music and baseball made him consider each field as a possible vocation, and at the age of 12, he was already playing saxophone professionally. A year later, though, his mother remarried, and Greenwood moved to Anaheim for two years. During that period, he took up sax with Del Reeves' country band. Reeves would go on to have a number one country single in 1965 with "Girl On The Billboard."

Returning to Sacramento, Greenwood formed his own group, the Moonbeams, and went on to develop yet another, the Apollos. That band played up and down the West Coast, eventually landing a one-year contract in Las Vegas. But when the rest of the group headed off for Hawaii in February of 1963, Greenwood remained in Nevada, where he became a vocalist, bandleader, show-tune writer and arranger.

With that background, most of Greenwood's

records leaned toward the dramatic, but in 1986, he culled a more countrified release as the third single from his *Streamline* album. Steve Dean and Roger Murrah wrote "Hearts Aren't Made To Break (They're Made To Love)" in October of 1984, and producer Jerry Crutchfield originally picked it for recording artist Craig Dillingham. Instead, Jerry cut it with Greenwood, and MCA tapped it to follow "I Don't Mind The Thorns (If You're The Rose)" [see 648] and "Don't Underestimate My Love For You" [see 663].

"There were stronger songs on the album," Lee says, admitting his own reluctance to make it a single. "The only reason we went for it was that Nashville wanted that kind of country song. It was really slow and easy, and I was surprised it went to number one."

Judy Rodman

679

UNTIL I MET YOU

JUDY RODMAN

MTM 72065
Writer: Hank Riddle
Producer: Tommy West
July 19, 1986 (1 week)

When Mary Tyler Moore opened her own label in Nashville during 1984, MTM Records signed Judy Rodman first. The company named former Jim Croce producer Tommy West as its senior vice president, and hired Meredith Stewart, from Loretta Lynn's Coal Miner's Music, to run the publishing company. Rodman, West and Stewart had already begun to play a role in the label's first number one single.

Rodman moved to Music City during 1980, leaving Memphis, where she had already established herself as a jingles singer of some renown. In Memphis, she roomed and sang with another vocalist named Janie Frickie [see 548—"Tell Me A Lie"], and after her relocation, Rodman built her resumé with commercials for Kellogg's, Chevrolet, McDonald's and Piedmont, among other companies. She also provided "oohs" and "aahs" to a lengthy list of country hits that includes "Only One You" [see 460], "You Look So Good In Love" [see 551], "I'll Come Back As Another Woman" and "Shine On."

Doing back-up work for Ed Bruce, Judy impressed West, who produced that session. He suggested they try to get her a recording deal, and he put up his own money to record five songs on a demo. Stewart gave them one of the five, "Until I Met You," a song that had appeared previously on one of Loretta's LPs.

After signing with MTM, Rodman included the song on her debut album, and the label pulled it as the fourth single. The record received a boost from the Academy of Country Music. Shortly after the release of "Until I Met You," the ACM named Judy the Top New Female Vocalist.

"Reba McEntire told me backstage at the Academy of Country Music awards that she had thought about cuttin' that, too," Judy reports. "The song had been around for years and years, and it just bided its time."

Judy earned three more Top Ten singles for MTM: "She Thinks That She'll Marry," "Girls Ride Horses Too" and "I'll Be Your Baby Tonight," written by her most notable fan, Bob Dylan.

The daughter of an air-traffic controller, Rodman had her flight in the top stratosphere of the country chart abruptly grounded when MTM was sold off. She signed as a writer with Dave Loggins' Pied Piper Music, intending to improve those skills and create more of her own material for her next record deal.

680

ON THE OTHER HAND

RANDY TRAVIS
Warner Bros. 28962
Writers: Paul Overstreet, Don Schlitz
Producers: Kyle Lehning, Keith Stegall
July 26, 1986 (1 week)

"You never know what can happen if you just show up for work." So says Paul Overstreet, who stayed in bed late one morning when he didn't feel well and mulled over the possibility of canceling a writing session with Don Schlitz. Don called the house, and told Paul he'd keep working anyway, but Overstreet dragged himself in to work on a song called "Greedy Heart."

They hit a snag with a line, and Schlitz started running down their options. In the middle of his list, he set up a new idea with "On the other hand . . .," and Paul immediately chimed in "there's a golden band." They took off on that tangent, and dashed off a song that brought them a little pride. They envisioned "On The Other Hand" in the grasp of Merle Haggard, George Jones or, perhaps, Dan Seals, and song plugger Pat Higdon relayed it to Seals' producer, Kyle Lehning.

"Pat came in a few days later," Don recalls, "and said, 'Kyle really likes the song, but he doesn't hear it for Danny [Seals]. He hears it for this new guy he's recording named Randy Travis.' We're looking at Pat, and saying, 'Randy what? What's this about?'"

Travis—a.k.a. Randy Bruce Traywick—worked at the time as a singer, cook and dishwasher at the Nashville Palace, a nightclub at the outskirts of the Opryland complex, owned by his manager, Lib Hatcher. Traywick had recorded a live album at the Palace, with the help of Keith Stegall, himself an artist affiliated with producer Lehning. Stegall played the album for Lehning, and when Warner Bros. A & R chief Martha Sharp caught Traywick's act, she pushed for a recording contract—signed in February of 1985—for three singles. Sharp also renamed her new artist "Randy Travis."

Lehning and Stegall cut four songs on Randy, including "Prairie Rose," which ended up on the soundtrack to *Rustlers' Rhapsody*; and "On The Other Hand," which peaked at a meager number 67 in the fall of 1985, although it lingered on the chart for a dozen weeks.

A second single, "1982," took Travis to stardom, shooting to number six and allowing him

to quit the Palace job. Warner Bros. then re-released "On The Other Hand." This time, it debuted at number 64—higher than before—and hit number one in fourteen weeks.

681

NOBODY IN HIS RIGHT MIND WOULD'VE LEFT HER

GEORGE STRAIT
MCA 52817
Writer: Dean Dillon
Producers: Jimmy Bowen, George Strait
August 2, 1986 (1 week)

"Nobody In His Right Mind Would've Left Her": the title might prove humorous to left brain/right brain theorists, but it was also quite profitable for songwriter Dean Dillon. It only took a half-dozen years to turn out that way.

Dillon (his real name, given him by his adoptive parents, was Rutherford) signed as an artist with RCA Records in 1979, and he remained with the label over a four-year period. In 1980, he wrote a song with parentheses in the title—"Nobody In His Right Mind (Would've Left Her)"—during a plane trip from Texarkana back to Nashville.

"The plane got in late that night, and I went on to bed," Dean remembers. "I got up the next morning, and there was one particular chord in that song that I had never played in my life. My fingers, when I picked up the guitar that morning, just went to that chord, so I know that was a divine gift there. I mean, there's no other way."

Shortly after hooking up with record producer Blake Mevis [see 484—"Fool Hearted Memory"], George Strait came across the song and recorded it. About the same time, however, RCA released Dillon's recording as a single, and it reached number 25, his best chart showing to date. As a result, MCA scrapped plans to release Strait's version, and that recording never came out.

"I was always crazy about the song," George says. "I thought it was great, so whenever I was able to, we just went back in and recut it completely. We didn't use the old tracks at all. We just re-did the whole thing. I know it's on one of Keith Whitley's albums [*L.A. to Miami*], and I believe Blake was cuttin' it on Keith at the same time that we were doin' it in the studio."

Strait's version appeared in *Billboard* on May 17, 1986—one day prior to his thirty-fourth birthday—and reached number one after a dozen weeks on the chart. George had little cause for celebration, though. During June, his daughter, Jenifer, died in a car accident. When he accepted his second Country Music Association Male Vocalist of the Year award from Dolly Parton, Linda Ronstadt and Emmylou Harris on October 13, he dedicated the trophy to Jenifer's memory.

682

ROCKIN' WITH THE RHYTHM OF THE RAIN

THE JUDDS (WYNONNA & NAOMI)

RCA 14362
Writers: Don Schlitz, Brent Maher
Producer: Brent Maher
August 9, 1986 (1 week)

"I've been very fortunate to write a couple of rain songs," says songwriter Don Schlitz. "The first song Brent Maher and I ever wrote together was 'Rockin' With The Rhythm Of The Rain.' And Donny Lowery and I wrote a song for the Nitty Gritty Dirt Band, called 'Stand A Little Rain,' and if you see a couple of clouds in the sky, you can almost flip through your radio dial and hear one of those songs. I always pray for rain—it helps the airplay."

Ironically, "Rockin' With The Rhythm Of The Rain" debuted on the *Billboard* country chart on May 24, 1986, the same week that Gary Morris' "100% Chance Of Rain" [see 664], which produced some negative rain experiences, disappeared from the list.

"Rockin' With The Rhythm" was tailor-made for the Judds. Maher lived five minutes from the house they used to own in Franklin, Tennessee, and when he came over, he frequently found the Judd clan rocking in their front porch swing. The awning was made of tin, and they loved to sit out on the porch whenever a gentle rain appeared. Brent brought that little scenario out during conversation the first time he

The Judds

got together with Schlitz to write.

"We didn't have any ideas whatsoever to write with," Maher recalls. "I'd never written with Don, and we didn't know much about each other, other than the stuff that we'd heard. That was the first tune that we'd ever written together. We sat down and just kind of talked for a couple of minutes. I started playin' that kind of a shuffle groove, and Don said, 'What's that? I love that.'

"We really wrote that one fast. That song probably didn't take an hour and a half to write. It literally fell out. We had our little blaster there that we were workin' on and writin' on, singin' parts into, and even at that stage, I really felt that that would be a big record for them. It was just so right for the Judds."

"Rockin' With The Rhythm Of The Rain" stormed the number one position in a dozen weeks, reaching its peak position on August 9, 1986. Two months later, the *Rockin' with the Rhythm* album reached the platinum mark on October 7—the Judds' second million-selling package.

683

YOU'RE THE LAST THING I NEEDED TONIGHT

JOHN SCHNEIDER

MCA 52827
Writers: David Wills, Don Pfrimmer
Producers: Jimmy Bowen, John Schneider
August 16, 1986 (1 week)

As with "What's A Memory Like You" [see 662] and "I've Been Around Enough To Know" [see 594], "You're The Last Thing I Needed Tonight" had been around for four or five years before John Schneider unlocked its magic and turned it into a number one record.

Don Pfrimmer wrote the song in his basement with David Wills, and a pair of Georges both tried to record it.

"It was cut by George Jones, first of all, and it just never happened," Pfrimmer recounts. "It just didn't come off, so it didn't make the album. That killed me. Then George Strait cut it, and the same thing happened. It didn't make the album, either."

Schneider's version proved the song's merit, tipping in at number one in 1986. Over the next year, Schneider registered three more Top Ten singles: "At The Sound Of The Tone," "Take

The Long Way Home" and "Love, You Ain't Seen The Last Of Me." Despite his best efforts to maintain dual careers in music and acting, he called it quits with music in 1987.

"John Schneider is a real good actor, and that's what he really is," suggests producer Jimmy Bowen. "He became a very successful country singer, but deep down, bein' out on the road on a bus, playin' one-nighters, is not what this 'actor' wanted to do, really.

"He's a genius. He can write movies, he can be a playwright, screenwriter, he's a director, he's a producer. He's just one of those kinds of people. He's got 18 things goin' at once.

"But he doesn't like to do anything half-assed. He missed acting. He did what I thought of as his 'farewell tour.' He went out with torn Levi's and a T-shirt, and all of a sudden, this kid is out doin' a rock and roll show. He fixed it so he'd *have* to go back and be an actor. I've never seen anybody do that—it was quite amazing."

Schneider turned up in a number of TV movies in the ensuing years. In 1990, he emerged once again on a prime-time series, "Grand Slam," with comedian Paul Rodriguez.

684

STRONG HEART

T.G. SHEPPARD

Columbia 05905
Writers: Tommy Rocco, Charlie Black, Austin Roberts
Producer: Rick Hall
August 23, 1986 (1 week)

When T.G. Sheppard hooked up with producer Rick Hall in 1985, it marked a reunion of two old friends. During the early '70s, in his role as a radio promotion man, Sheppard had worked many of the pop singles Hall produced for Mac Davis and the Osmonds. In fact, Sheppard was actually in the studio when Hall produced Davis' "Hell Of A Woman" and Paul Anka's "Having My Baby."

Together, Sheppard and Hall earned Top Ten releases with "Doncha?" and "In Over My Heart," finally returning to number one after a two-and-a-half-year absence with "Strong Heart."

Tommy Rocco, Austin Roberts and Charlie Black wrote the song in Black's backyard, around the same time that they penned "Honor Bound" [see 615]. Mark Gray recorded it for

an album, and his producer, Steve Buckingham, suggested that Hall should do it with T.G. Based on a market study, Columbia Records wanted to change the song to a second-person form—"(*You* Must Have A) Strong Heart"—but the songwriters declined.

Cut at Fame Recording Studios in Muscle Shoals, the ballad proved timely for Sheppard, who was going through a divorce from his wife, Diana.

"I felt a lot of guilt after being married for 21 years," he says. "The marriage failed—which was my fault—because the career took precedence. It shouldn't have, but it did.

"I personally started relating to my music from that point on. Before, I would cut songs that I felt everyone could relate to—it wasn't important that I related to it as much as *they* did. But all of a sudden, I started stretching as a singer, doing things vocally, and having more feeling for the music, because I was relating myself to the song."

"Half Past Forever (Till I'm Blue In The Heart)," "You're My First Lady" and "One For The Money" rounded out Sheppard's series of Hall-produced singles, each of them stopping at number two.

In the meantime, Sheppard developed a series of diversions outside of music. He became the official spokesman of T.G. Sheppard's Folgers Racing Team; opened a bed-and-breakfast (Moon Mountain Lodge) and a Mexican restaurant (North of the Border) in the Smoky Mountains; and helped develop Guitars & Cadillacs, a Kansas City nightclub.

685

HEARTBEAT IN THE DARKNESS
DON WILLIAMS
Capitol 5588
Writers: Dave Loggins, Russell Smith
Producers: Don Williams, Garth Fundis
August 30, 1986 (1 week)

Don Williams must have an appreciation for the defunct Amazing Rhythm Aces. He employed former Ace guitarist Barry "Byrd" Burton on "Good Ole Boys Like Me" and "It Must Be Love" [see 356], and he benefited from former Ace lead vocalist Russell Smith with "Heartbeat In The Darkness."

Smith calls his music "rhythm and bluegrass." "I got tired of people goin', 'What kind of music do you play?,' and that's close to what it is. I like a lot of backbeat, I like the blues—but I'm a real countrified kind of a voice, most of the time. 'Rhythm and bluegrass' is the closest I've come to describing it."

Russell developed his double-pronged approach as a youngster in middle Tennessee, where his radio picked up the Grand Ole Opry on WSM and the latest R & B on WLAC. Both musical styles were embraced by the Amazing Rhythm Aces when they formed in 1972, although they didn't settle on their monicker for another two years.

The band came to prominence in 1975 with the Smith-written "Third Rate Romance," and added single successes with "Amazing Grace (Used To Be Her Favorite Song)" and their Grammy-winning "The End Is Not In Sight (The Cowboy Tune)."

The group disbanded in 1981 when oil prices soared and made their road show too expensive. Smith opted for a solo career, but he has fared better as a songwriter, penning John Conlee's "Old School," T. Graham Brown's "Don't Go To Strangers" [see 719], Highway 101's "Honky Tonk Heart" and "Heartbeat In The Darkness."

"That was just kind of a 'Can't Buy Me Love' attitude," Russell says of the latter tune, "tryin' to feel what was really important in life, instead of just money and things. Love is more important than things."

Producer Garth Fundis happened to stop by the publishing company at the time Smith and Dave Loggins were writing the song, and slipped into their workroom just long enough to say hello. They showed him what they'd come up with on "Heartbeat," and he asked Smith and Loggins to think about Don Williams when it was finished.

Initially, they weren't sure it was right for Williams, but they brought it to Garth two days later, and Don turned their "rhythm and bluegrass" offering into a number one single.

686

DESPERADO LOVE
CONWAY TWITTY

Warner Bros. 28692
Writers: Michael Garvin, Sammy Johns
Producers: Conway Twitty, Dee Henry,
Ron Treat
September 6, 1986 (1 week)

When it rolled into the top spot during the weekend after Labor Day, "Desperado Love" set a new standard for country chart performance. The record made Conway Twitty the first artist to rack up 40 number one singles. Since Twitty got his start doing rock and roll material, it's somehow appropriate that his fortieth came from Sammy Johns, a singer/songwriter who caught attention in 1975 with his pop hit, "Chevy Van" [see 520—"Common Man"].

"A bunch of things happened in my life, and things weren't going too well," Sammy remembers. "I was losing my house, and that's a very depressing thing to have happen, when you just can't pay for the place that you've grown to love.

"I was sittin' there drinkin' beer after beer, and I was thinkin', 'Is there any way I can turn this into a song and not make people so depressed that they'd want to go drink beer, too? What's my feeling here? I'm desperate. Yes, I'm very desperate to keep this house,' and then I said, 'Desperate, maybe I can take the desperate feeling and make the house into a woman.' So instead of having a desperate love for my house, I turned it into a desperado love for a woman.

"We lost the house, but it turned out to be the best thing anyway, 'cause I've changed wives and changed houses."

The first verse finished, Sammy got together with songwriter Michael Garvin in Nashville, completing the song in a rather quick session. Conway didn't contact them until he had already recorded it, and Garvin was particularly happy with the cut: he had always wanted to land a song with Twitty.

"One nice thing about him and T. G. Sheppard [see 460—"Only One You"] both," says Garvin, "they both wrote me letters to thank me for the song, which I thought was awfully nice. Most artists don't do that."

Three subsequent singles almost added to Twitty's list of number one records. "Fallin' For You For Years" (shut out by "Cry Myself To Sleep" [see 705]), "Julia" (beaten by "It Takes A Little Rain" [see 723]) and "I Want To Know You Before We Make Love" (stymied by "Fishin' In The Dark" [see 741]) each hit number two. Four more Top Ten singles, including "That's My Job" (number six), "Goodbye Time" (number seven), "Saturday Night Special" (number nine) and "I Wish I Was Still In Your Dreams" (number four), followed, and Conway rounded out the '80s with 72 Top Ten hits.

Basing his findings on the *Billboard* chart, Joel Whitburn's Record Research cited Twitty among the five top country recording artists of all time.

687
LITTLE ROCK
REBA McENTIRE
MCA 52848
Writers: Pat McManus, Bob DiPiero,
Gerry House
Producers: Jimmy Bowen, Reba McEntire
September 13, 1986 (1 week)

Reba McEntire made her first record during her late teens as a member of the Singing McEntires, a family group that also featured her sister, Susie, and her brother, Pake. That first single was a tribute to her grandfather, rodeo rider John McEntire, and the group sold all 350 copies that it had pressed.

By 1986—a little more than a decade after the Singing McEntires folded—two members of the trio had found national record deals. Reba was in her tenth year as a recording artist, and Pake emerged on RCA. His first single, "Every Night," debuted in January of 1986 and reached number 20. He followed with "Savin' My Love For You" (number three) and "Bad Love" (number 12). Pake also joined Karen Staley as a background singer that summer on Reba's number one single, "Little Rock."

"Little Rock" was written in Nashville by WSIX-FM disk jockey Gerry House with Bob DiPiero and Pat McManus, who previously collaborated on "American Made" [see 516].

"We went to lunch—which is a big Nashville songwriter tradition—and we were there for about three hours, just dragging our feet," DiPiero remembers. "Gerry said that on the way to the restaurant, he was driving behind this car from Little Rock. We kind of just toyed around with that. That's just one of those songs that we banged out in about an hour—then we continued having lunch. It was a gift from God."

"Little Rock" almost became a kind of Nightmare On Music Row, Part II for Reba. A year earlier, she had committed to record "She's Single Again," but through a publishing company mix-up, she and Janie Frickie both cut it around the same time. Frickie released it as a single first.

It happened again with "Little Rock." The publishers gave it to both Reba and Janie, and McEntire flew into a rage. It was an honest mistake, and she worked out the problem with Frickie's producer, Bob Montgomery. Reba got to keep it, and turned in one of her most energetic performances.

688
GOT MY HEART SET ON YOU
JOHN CONLEE
Columbia 06104
Writers: Dobie Gray, Bud Reneau
Producer: Bud Logan
September 20, 1986 (1 week)

Before he secured a recording contract from ABC Records in 1976, Kentucky native John Conlee was already a Nashville resident, working on pop station WLAC. His stint there helped him understand some of the more elusive aspects of the music business, but it also left an imprint on his vocal style.

"Training my voice to speak on the radio, in some subconscious way, affected the way I phrase songs," he reports. "I have tapes of my singing prior to radio, and then after being in radio two or three years. That's when whatever my style is developed on its own."

After that style brought four consecutive number one singles in 1983 and 1984, Conlee continued to leave his stamp on country stations. Three more records went into the Top Ten: "Way Back," which peaked at number four; "Years After You," number two; and "Working Man," number seven. "Blue Highway" slipped to number 15, and "Old School" ended John's association with MCA with a number five single.

Moving to Columbia Records, Conlee went to number 10 with "Harmony," and returned to the top with "Got My Heart Set On You." The tune was written by Dobie Gray, who had notched a number five single on *Billboard*'s Hot 100 in 1973 with "Drift Away." That song was adapted for a country audience that same year by Narvel Felts, who took it to number eight.

" 'Got My Heart Set On You' is an uptempo type thing that appealed to me a lot," says Conlee. "I liked what it had to say. I happened to be at a radio station in Nashville that helped to break 'Drift Away' for [Dobie], so he's a friend—but the song was there."

Conlee earned two more Top Ten records under his Columbia deal, with "The Carpenter" and "Domestic Life," and in 1988, he moved over to Opryland Music's 16th Avenue Records.

"If I never have another hit, there are people in the industry who know us for being song people, and doing great songs," John reflects, evaluating his career. "That's the reputation I want to cultivate. I want to be known for that more than anything else—for doing quality stuff."

689

IN LOVE
RONNIE MILSAP
RCA 14365
Writers: Mike Reid, Bruce Dees
Producers: Ronnie Milsap, Tom Collins,
Rob Galbraith
September 27, 1986 (1 week)

After his debut on "Inside" [see 505], song-writer Mike Reid emerged among the elite tunesmiths in Nashville. By the end of the decade, his list of hit records swelled to approximately twenty titles, including Willie Nelson's "There You Are," Tanya Tucker's "I'll Come Back As Another Woman," Conway Twitty's "Fallin' For You For Years" and Don Williams' "I Wouldn't Be A Man."

Mike's highest output, however, came by placing material with Ronnie Milsap. Eleven singles in all hit the Top Ten, including his duet with Ronnie, "Old Folks," which stopped at number two in 1988, just behind "Eighteen Wheels And A Dozen Roses" [see 771].

Reid and RCA considered a recording deal on the basis of that single, but ultimately, Mike decided he was quite content to stay off the road and concentrate on his writing.

Instead, his songs have gone on the road in the hands of other Nashville vocalists, eight of them having reached number one. The sixth of those came in 1986 with "In Love," a song co-written by Bruce Dees, Milsap's vocal assistant on "Lost In The Fifties Tonight" [see 639 and 673—"Happy, Happy Birthday Baby"].

"Bruce Dees is a great guitar player," Mike says, "and that was about the seventh rewrite of that song. Along the way, it was a ballad, then it was midtempo, and then it was a rock and roll song. Whenever I started to think too much about it, it turned into a contrived thing. Bruce did such wonderful things on the demo with his guitar work—things that were crucial to the sound of the record and the song—that he had to get part-writer credit on it."

"We did that record a couple of times," Milsap reports. "I did it the first time with a live drummer, and I didn't like the way it felt, so I went to a drum machine.

"A lot of folks were talkin' about the record,

and [producer] Tony Brown mentioned that he loved that song so much that when he did 'Small Town Girl' [see 714], it's the same kind of thing in front of that, that same haunting thing. Different key, different tempo, different sound—but it's the same licks."

690

ALWAYS HAVE, ALWAYS WILL
JANIE FRICKIE
Columbia 06144
Writer: Johnny Mears
Producer: Norro Wilson
October 4, 1986 (1 week)

"Always Have, Always Will" became the seventh number one single for Janie Frickie—a rather impressive accomplishment for a woman who expressed reluctance at the prospect of signing a recording deal.

At the outset, Frickie remained content to work as a studio vocalist with the Lea Jane Singers, where she earned more than $100,000 per year singing on both jingles [see 597—"Your Heart's Not In It"] and commercial recordings. The success of her singles with Johnny Duncan, however, spurred interest from CBS staff producer Billy Sherrill, who offered her a contract.

"They really did have to push me into signing with Columbia," admits Frickie. "I was intent on being a back-up singer and staying that way."

She changed her mind, however, when CBS Records president Bruce Lundvall showed up backstage at a convention in Nashville, where Frickie was performing in the band at the Municipal Auditorium. "I was on the pay phone making a phone call," she relates, "and he tapped me on the shoulder, and said, 'Are you gonna sign a contract with us or not?' That's how they finally got me; I realized they really did want me."

Settled into her position as a solo artist, Frickie made a couple of changes with the release of her 1986 *Black & White* LP. First, she ended her three-album partnership with producer Bob Montgomery, teaming with veteran Norro Wilson. The result was a new sound, heavy on the blues, and that particular style carried her to number one with "Always Have, Always Will." On October 4, *Black & White* became Janie's only LP to reach number one on the *Billboard* country album chart.

"Always Have, Always Will" also produced a subtle change in the spelling of Frickie's name, which was originally spelled "Fricke." Since she was constantly being called "Frick" on a number of awards shows by everyone from Phil Collins to Charlie Daniels, she added the extra "i" to her last name to alleviate the pronunciation problems.

Meanwhile, Frickie had already expanded as an entrepreneur. After making her own stage apparel as a hobby, she introduced a line of clothing and accessories in 1985. By 1988, her fashions were reportedly carried in 200 to 300 stores.

691

BOTH TO EACH OTHER (FRIENDS & LOVERS)

EDDIE RABBITT & JUICE NEWTON

RCA 14377
Writers: Jay Gruska, Paul Gordon
Producer: Richard Landis
October 11, 1986 (1 week)

"It's their song," laughs Eddie Rabbitt, "but I'm kind of annoyed at them for putting it out."

The topic is "Both To Each Other (Friends & Lovers)," a single that Gloria Loring & Carl Anderson released on USA Carrere within a week of Rabbitt & Juice Newton. Loring, in her role as Liz Chandler, had introduced the song on the "Days of Our Lives" soap. Rabbitt wasn't too familiar with it at first, although his producer was.

"Richard Landis played me the song," Eddie recalls. "I liked it, and since he was recording with Juice Newton also, we thought it might be a neat song to do as a duet. I didn't realize it came out of a soap opera until I got home and I was playing the demo for my wife, and she said, 'That's in my soap opera.'"

The song had already been on the show for six months, though, and Landis didn't think it would be released as a single. Richard and Eddie figured that with the exposure on daytime TV, the song had a ready-made market. They checked once more with the publisher, who led them to believe that there would be no single coming out from the cast of "Days Of Our Lives."

Instead, Loring secured a deal with the Canadian Carrere label, and her duet with Anderson debuted on *Billboard*'s Hot 100 on July 5, 1986. One week later, the Rabbitt/Newton collaboration appeared on the country chart. Both went up the charts simultaneously, Loring's version peaking at number two on September 27, 1986; Rabbitt & Newton topped the country list two weeks later.

"I don't blame them," explains Eddie. "I just wish they would have told us they were planning to do that, 'cause I wouldn't have put out the single. I don't cover anybody."

"Both To Each Other" was Rabbitt's second duet to reach number one. Ironically, the other duet, "You And I" [see 497], also appeared in a soap opera, "All My Children."

"Both To Each Other" was also part of a duet bonanza for songwriter Paul Gordon. While both versions of that song earned success, Peter Cetera and Amy Grant released another of his compositions, "The Next Time I Fall," a number one pop single.

692

JUST ANOTHER LOVE

TANYA TUCKER

Capitol 5604
Writer: Paul Davis
Producer: Jerry Crutchfield
October 18, 1986 (1 week)

When "Just Another Love" reached number one on October 18, 1986, it marked Tanya Tucker's return to the top spot after an absence of more than ten years [see 261—"Here's Some Love"].

In the interim, she cruised through her early and mid-20s attracting an avalanche of publicity—much of it the unwanted gossipy kind. She was linked romantically with a string of beaus that included actor Don Johnson, now-deceased pop star Andy Gibb, boxer Gerry Cooney and, of course, Glen Campbell.

Her romance with Campbell was extremely overplayed by the press, with the couple setting Valentine's Day, 1982, as their wedding date. It never happened, and, in the aftermath, Campbell remains reluctant to even mention it.

During that period, the two collaborated on several projects, including a duet on "Dream Lovers." Glen also sang backing vocals on two of Tanya's solo hits, "Pecos Promenade" (number 10, 1980), from the movie *Smokey and the Bandit II*; and "Can I See You Tonight" (number four, 1981). "Feel Right" went to number 10

Tanya Tucker

business people. It's hard to do it all. Songwriting takes a lot out of you; it's mind-depleting. It really works your head, especially the way you have to get into a certain mood to write a song."

After a three-year absence from recording, Tanya signed a new contract with Capitol Records in 1985. Six months later, she was back with a bang—and with some new songs written by Paul Davis. He and Paul Overstreet co-authored "One Love At A Time," which reached number three, and Davis also wrote "Just Another Love," which featured himself and Vince Gill as supporting vocalists.

693

CRY

CRYSTAL GAYLE
Warner Bros. 28689
Writer: Churchill Kohlman
Producer: Jim Ed Norman
October 25, 1986 (1 week)

The circumstances surrounding Crystal Gayle's performance of "Cry" are somewhat similar to the force that gave "I Don't Wanna Lose Your Love" [see 588—"Turning Away"] a sense of magic: childbirth.

In the midst of recording the *Straight to the Heart* [see 709] album, Crystal underwent a cesarean section in the delivery of her son, Christos. She remained in bed for six weeks prior to the surgery, and several studio bookings were canceled because of it. Once the baby was born, she required another three to four weeks of recuperation while the sutures healed. During the post-surgery period, producer Jim Ed Norman had a sudden flash regarding the album while driving to work.

"I said to myself, 'There's something that I still have not captured that I really like about Crystal's voice,'" he remembers, "that torch-like part of what she does, the bluesy part. Literally, within seconds of making that particular observation, the song 'Cry' popped into my head."

Norman called Crystal at home, and had no trouble convincing her to remake the Johnnie Ray classic. "I grew up singing the song," she notes, "so I didn't even ask for a lead sheet."

Restless Heart's Dave Innis was included among the musicians Norman assembled for the session, and he came away with a new appreciation for the talents of the small but

in 1983, and Tanya co-wrote Hank Williams, Jr.'s hit "Leave Them Boys Alone."

"Harlan Howard always says I'm a songwriter trying to get out of a singer's body," comments Tucker on that endeavor. "All my friends that are songwriters know I can do it—but I'm the one that's kind of lackadaisical about it.

"I should do more and get more involved. But it's so hard when you're trying to keep your career in line, your life in order, your records at the top, and deal with the fans and deal with mighty vocalist. "I was just amazed at how big her voice was in the studio," Innis says, "'cause she was there the entire time, and really worked hard with the group. I mean she sang it through, it must have been 25 times before we got the track, and she was in there from the word 'go.'"

"We recorded it in two different keys," Gayle adds. "I do that a lot of times. My voice is never awake in the mornings. I go in and record something. After they learn the song and get familiar with it, I say, 'Well, let's try it in another key and see how it feels.'"

They tried a few tricks, like adding tremolo to the guitars, to create a bridge between a period sound and a contemporary interpretation.

Crystal wasn't the first to bring "Cry" to the country audience. Lynn Anderson notched a number three single [see 85—"How Can I Unlove You"] in 1972. Gayle eclipsed that mark by taking it all the way to the top.

694

IT'LL BE ME
EXILE

Epic 06229
Writers: Sonny Lemaire, J.P. Pennington
Producer: Buddy Killen
November 1, 1986 (1 week)

Beginning with "Woke Up In Love" [see 559] and ending with "I Could Get Used To You" [see 661], Exile put together seven consecutive number one singles in a short two years.

The string came to a halt, though, when Epic chose the third single from the *Hang On to Your Heart* album. Originally titled "I Got Love (Super-Duper Love)," "Super Love" entered *Billboard*'s country chart on April 5, 1986, but it managed only a number 14 peak position, leaving the group admittedly disappointed.

"I really liked the song," laments co-writer Sonny Lemaire. "I mean, it wasn't anything earth-shaking, but it was fun.

"J.P. and I had been writing one day, and not really accomplishing anything. I had the guitar, and he said, 'We need something really different, kind of off-the-wall or something,' and it just came out—bang!

"I hit a D7 guitar chord, and sang, 'Baby, I'm off the wall, up a creek,' and he looked at me, and said, 'Goin' down the wrong way on a one-

way street,' and we both laughed. The song kept flowing and flowing.

"When we got to rehearsal the next day, we didn't even know how the guys were gonna react to it, but they loved it. It was real R & B–ish at the time for country music. I loved the track on the record, and it was disappointing—radio stations wouldn't play it because it was not country enough at the time.

"Subsequently, it's gone on to become one of the most requested songs we've ever done."

"Super Love"'s failure to reach number one was a mere glitch in the band's progression, though. Exile hurriedly released a follow-up ballad, closer to country's mainstream. "It'll Be Me" was the first song Pennington and Lemaire wrote when they went to work on the *Hang On to Your Heart* album. Returning Exile to number one, it proved a wise choice as a single, "Taylor"-made for one member of the group.

"We wrote that song specifically for Les Taylor's voice," Lemaire admits. "Les is a real soulful singer—not that J.P. isn't—but Les has more range than J.P. has vocally, and we really wrote it for Les."

695

DIGGIN' UP BONES
RANDY TRAVIS

Warner Bros. 28649
Writers: Paul Overstreet, Al Gore
Producer: Kyle Lehning
November 8, 1986 (1 week)

Randy Travis embodies the meaning of the familiar phrase "overnight success." After ten years of diligent nightclub work with the guidance of manager Lib Hatcher, Randy finally stopped washing dishes [see 680—"On The Other Hand"] in March of 1986. Seven months later, he was a country music phenomenon.

In October, his *Storms of Life* album went gold, while the Country Music Association honored Randy with the Horizon award and named "On The Other Hand" the Song of the Year. The following spring, the Academy of Country Music cited "Other Hand" as Song and Single of the Year, and named *Storms of Life* the Top Country Album. In February of 1987, *Storms* became the first debut country album in history to sell a million copies within a year of release.

Randy Travis

when Warner Bros. commissioned an album from Travis once "On The Other Hand" took off.

Gore was tending his garden when he received the phone call, informing him that Randy planned to record "Bones."

"How can you not record a song that's figured out how to use the word 'exhuming?'" laughs producer Kyle Lehning. "You gotta cut that."

"Bones" rattled the number one position the week after Halloween of 1986. Travis reached number two with the fourth *Storms* single, "No Place Like Home."

696

THAT ROCK WON'T ROLL
RESTLESS HEART
RCA 14376
Writers: John Scott Sherrill, Bob DiPiero
Producers: Tim DuBois, Scott Hendricks,
Restless Heart
November 15, 1986 (1 week)

At its inception, Restless Heart possibly had more doubts about its future than did RCA division head Joe Galante. Nashville is frequently skeptical of country bands with more than a hint of rock or pop overtones, and Restless Heart leaned heavily away from the traditional side.

If Music City itself took a wait-and-see attitude, though, country radio embraced the band (lead vocalist Larry Stewart, keyboardist Dave Innis, guitarist Greg Jennings, bassist Paul Gregg, drummer John Dittrich) immediately. The group started rehearsing for the first time in 1983, and in January of 1985, Restless Heart debuted on the *Billboard* country chart with "Let The Heartache Ride." They rode it all the way to number 23, extremely respectable for a first effort.

Each of Restless Heart's next three singles—"I Want Everyone To Cry," "(Back To The) Heartbreak Kid" and "Til I Loved You"—vaulted it into the Top Ten. With its second album, the group cemented its presence, launching its first number one single with "That Rock Won't Roll."

Originally, songwriters Bob DiPiero and John Scott Sherrill co-wrote the song with a Nashville session player, basing it on one of his guitar patterns.

"The guitar lick was kind of cool, but the

The third single from the album, "Diggin' Up Bones," possesses a title that might sound appropriate for Halloween, but Paul Overstreet and Albert Gore (no relation to the Tennessee senator) wrote it on Thanksgiving Day of 1983.

Overstreet visited the Gore house for turkey, and the two commenced to grind out a pair of songs. After that, Paul offered up the title to "Diggin' Up Bones," though he hadn't connected the phrase with any specific meaning. "I told him I needed a concept," Albert remembers, "so he sang me a line or two, then I sang a line, and it just fell in place. It didn't take long. I wish they all came that easy."

Gore, who started in the business as an engineer in 1964 for Starday, had worked the board for such artists as Red Sovine, George Morgan and Porter Wagoner & Dolly Parton, and his biggest songwriting success took more than two years to see the light of day. Overstreet originally intended to hold on to "Bones" and record it himself, but he relinquished it song wasn't happenin'," DiPiero remembers. "It just kind of laid there. We never demoed it, we never pursued it, and eventually, the guy took his guitar lick back, and put it in a movie. Then we took back the title, and one day we were just foolin' around, and we came up with that intro guitar lick that's on there now."

Producer Tim DuBois brought the song to a session during pre-production for the *Wheels* album, and when the band worked it up, he felt it had all the earmarks of a giant record. Restless Heart still harbored doubts.

"We thought 'That Rock Won't Roll' was too pop to be played on country radio," admits Dave Innis, "and, frankly, we didn't know if we wanted to release a song that was that 'pop' for fear of being labeled a pop act when we were really trying to be a country act."

Nevertheless, the single caught on quickly, and took them to number one within two years of their chart debut. Laughs Larry Stewart: "The five of us all looked at each other, and said, 'Yeah, I knew it all along.'"

697
YOU'RE STILL NEW TO ME
MARIE OSMOND
WITH PAUL DAVIS
Capitol 5613
Writers: Paul Overstreet, Paul Davis
Producer: Paul Worley
November 22, 1986 (1 week)

"Please remember," Marie Osmond admonished John Andrew Prime of the *Shreveport Times*, "I do *not* do duets all the time."

It might have seemed that way, though, in 1986. Once "Paper Roses" [see 147] established her, Marie racked up a pair of Top Ten pop duets with Donny Osmond in the '70s: "I'm Leaving It (All) Up To You" and "Morning Side Of The Mountain." She returned to the top of the country chart with Dan Seals in 1985 on "Meet Me In Montana" [see 640], and a year later worked with Paul Davis on "You're Still New To Me."

Davis had re-established his name as a songwriter with "Montana." He first appeared on the country chart in 1975 with "Ride 'Em Cowboy." After pop hits with "I Go Crazy," "Sweet Life," "Cool Night" and "'65 Love Affair," he found a new home in Nashville, writing "Montana," "Bop" [see 653] and "Just Another Love" [see 692].

"You're Still New To Me" was his first appearance as a featured vocalist on a number one country single, but not his last. He also joined Tanya Tucker and Paul Overstreet on "I Won't Take Less Than Your Love" [see 759].

Initially, Davis wrote and demoed "You're Still New To Me" for a solo artist, but after he pitched it to Marie, it quickly became a duet number. "I think Marie, or maybe her manager, came up with the idea of doing it as a duet," recalls producer Paul Worley. "We thought of Dan Seals, but that wasn't to be."

Seals had two solid reasons for declining. He didn't tour with a female singer on the road, so he wouldn't be able to perform it live. Plus, he had an album of his own out, and didn't want to take a risk that a duet would dent the sales of a potential solo single.

Instead, Marie sang with Davis, and the results were magic—especially since the record came out after a near-tragedy. On July 30, 1986, Paul was shot during a robbery attempt in a parking lot on Nashville's Music Row. As he recovered, "You're Still New To Me" hit number one in its thirteenth week on the chart.

The duet also coincided with another important partnership: Marie married her second husband, Brian Blosil, on October 29,

698
TOUCH ME WHEN WE'RE DANCING
ALABAMA
RCA 5003
Writers: Terry Skinner, J.L. Wallace,
Ken Bell
Producers: Harold Shedd, Alabama
November 29, 1986 (1 week)

Michael Jackson, David Bellamy and Harlan Howard all claim to have written songs that seemingly came from a power greater than themselves. Terry Skinner asserts that "Touch Me When We're Dancing" has similar origins: "It was almost like a channeling effect—like the signal's out there and you just have to be in the right place to receive it."

The right place for "Touch Me When We're Dancing" was the road between Nashville and Muscle Shoals. Skinner and J.L. Wallace returned one evening from Music City to their home in Alabama via Interstate 65 and took a shortcut, turning off at the Pulaski exit in Tennessee.

"Wallace was 'cuttin' Z's,'" Skinner remembers. "In that geographical location, you can't pick up diddly-squat on the radio, so I turned it off, and it was just the hum of the car, and the hum of Wallace. Maybe everything was just right. It was almost like this little melody and the first line was just floatin' in the air."

Skinner woke Wallace and sang it for him. The next morning, they called co-writer Kenny Bell and finished it.

"We cut it initially on a subsidiary label that RCA was tryin' out called Free Flight," notes Wallace. "The name of our group was Bama, and 'Touch Me' came out before *Ala*bama had signed with RCA."

The Bama version hit number 86 on *Billboard*'s Hot 100 at the end of 1979. In the summer of 1981, the Carpenters covered it, reaching number 16 on the Hot 100 and number one on the adult/contemporary chart.

Five years later, Alabama publishing rep Kevin Lamb called Skinner from Nashville, and scheduled lunch in Muscle Shoals. Over red beans and rice, they discussed potential hit material for an album that the group had almost finished, and decided on a Bama song called "Summer Nights." Lamb played it for producer Harold Shedd, who liked it, and then had a copy of the tape made for Randy Owen. That tape also included "Touch Me When We're Dancing"; and when Randy heard the song, he decided to cut it that day.

At the time Alabama recorded it, several members didn't even know it had been done before. That last-minute addition became the first single from their album *The Touch*, and their twentieth single to top the country chart.

699

IT AIN'T COOL TO BE CRAZY ABOUT YOU
GEORGE STRAIT
MCA 52914
Writers: Dean Dillon, Royce Porter
Producers: Jimmy Bowen, George Strait
December 6, 1986 (1 week)

"I had 'It ain't cool to be crazy about you . . .'—I had that much of the song for a long time, and I never could come up with nothing else," remembers songwriter Dean Dillon of a tune that he eventually submitted to his occasional golfing buddy, George Strait. "A lot of times, you'll get just so much of a phrase, and

you got to play it around in your head, and it may take years. You have to study it and get the groove down in your head before you can actually attempt to put it down on paper."

For "It Ain't Cool," Dillon also had to acquire the services of co-writer Royce Porter. Dillon and his wife went to visit Porter and his wife at home, and while the ladies engrossed themselves in girl talk, Dean and Royce headed out to Porter's 34-foot houseboat.

"We sat back on the couch and picked up a guitar and was fiddlin' around, throwin' some ideas around," Porter recounts. "Dean had this idea, 'It Ain't Cool To Be Crazy About You,' and he'd been workin' on it, or thinkin' on it, for two or three months. He did that first part—'It ain't cool to be crazy about you/It ain't suave or debonaire'—and I said, 'Son, get back and give me the guitar.'

"We jumped right on it, and I guess about an hour later we finished that song and took it up to the house and played it for Kimmy and Shirley. They said, 'Uh-huh—that'll pay for the houseboat.'"

The following day, Dillon's publisher, Larry Butler, was so enamored with the song that he produced a demo session immediately, just so he would have a chance to work with it.

"I'm not sure about this," says Strait, "but I believe Mac Davis had a hold on that song about the same time we were gonna get it. Finally, he released the song, and so we did it. I think [producer Jimmy] Bowen was cuttin' Mac at the same time, too."

Strait's recording imitated the demo rather closely, with John Jarvis' melancholy piano work providing the song's musical foundation. Though many, including Bowen, were surprised that Strait selected it, "It Ain't Cool To Be Crazy About You" easily reached number one in December of 1986.

700

HELL AND HIGH WATER
T. GRAHAM BROWN
Capitol 5621
Writers: T. Graham Brown, Alex Harvey
Producer: Bud Logan
December 13, 1986 (1 week)

As 1986 began, T. Graham Brown resolved to "be a great human being, a wonderful cat, have a Masters Of The Universe doll named after me, have three number one singles, have

T. Graham Brown

my own Saturday morning cartoon show, and triple my watchings of 'The Andy Griffith Show.'"

Whether or not he actually accomplished some of the other goals, His T-Ness can prove partial success in one area. He earned *one* number one record that year, and it came during the last three weeks of 1986.

A native of tiny Arabi, Georgia, Brown became a hot property in Nashville shortly after moving there in 1982. He sang jingles for the likes of McDonald's, Disneyland and Budweiser, and provided the vocal work for many of the demos in town. In fact, it was Brown's voice that Randy Travis heard when he listened to the demo of "1982" [see 680—"On The Other Hand"].

Two Capitol executives took notice of his talents, and in 1984, T. Graham signed with the label. He copped a Top Ten single with his second release, "I Tell It Like It Used To Be," in the fall of 1985; during the next year, he hit the Top Five with "I Wish That I Could Hurt That Way Again" and finally reached the desired number one spot with "Hell And High Water."

Brown wrote the song with Alex Harvey, best known for composing "Delta Dawn," "Reuben James" and "Baby, Baby (I Know You're A Lady)" [see 47]. Both men were signed to the same publishing company, and after picking up on a line from one of T.'s songs, Harvey suggested that they write together.

Though initially intimidated, Brown finally consented to go to Harvey's house on a Wednesday morning. Alex's wife would fix breakfast, they'd write the song and head out to the golf course. Instead of writing the song they intended to, they composed "Hell And High Water" after breakfast, and though both ended up crying, they had doubts about the song. They played it for Alex's wife, who also broke into tears.

The publisher pitched the song for seven or eight months, with little interest, but when T. Graham signed with Capitol, he took it into Muscle Shoals Sound Studio. It represented his first number one single, and helped him partially fulfill his earlier resolution.

701

TOO MUCH IS NOT ENOUGH
THE BELLAMY BROTHERS WITH THE FORESTER SISTERS
Curb 52917
Writers: David Bellamy, Ron Taylor
Producer: Emory Gordy, Jr.
December 20, 1986 (1 week)

For those who like to classify, "Too Much Is Not Enough" might be considered a "group duet." The combination of the Bellamy Brothers and the Forester Sisters seemed a natural, based on their interactive history.

"We met them at Fan Fair, I guess in 1985," remembers Christy Forester, "and they came up to us and said, 'Well, which one of y'all are kin to the Holtzhowers?' We've known about them all our lives, and they'd heard about us."

The Foresters' great-uncle had moved to Florida years before to make a living in truck farming, and their dad went down to visit on occasion. As it turned out, Dean Holtzhower, cousin to the Foresters' father, taught David and Howard Bellamy in Sunday school.

After meeting at Fan Fair, the Bellamys asked the girls to sing backing vocals on a record for them. Naturally, the Foresters agreed, and Howard and David sent them a demo to learn.

In the meantime, the Bellamys had already cut tracks on "Too Much Is Not Enough." David had written the song in Cologne, West Germany, during a snowstorm, with the assistance of their piano player, Ron Taylor. It occurred to the Bellamys to turn that song into a duet with the Foresters, instead of the other song they originally sent to the sisters.

At that point, the record bogged down in the legal department. Neither the Foresters' label nor Curb was particularly helpful in getting all the paperwork taken care of. Notes David: "We had Curb calling in and saying, 'No, I won't spend any more money to bring the girls into the studio. How much can it be to bring 'em from Chattanooga to Nashville?'"

Ultimately, Howard and David paid for the Foresters to come into the studio, and spent two hours getting the vocals down in one mammoth session. "It was difficult gettin' six voices on a single record," recalls producer Emory Gordy. "Howard ended up singin' bass." "Yeah," David adds. "He had the Richard Sterban part."

David and Kim Forester shared the vocal leads. Once the track was finished, David persuaded Gordy and Jimmy Bowen to get the master ready to release, even though the legal departments were still dragging their feet.

"Of course, after the labels, the lawyers, and everybody heard it," says David sarcastically, "it was their idea all along."

The result was an energetic single, which debuted in *Billboard* on September 27, 1986, at number 51. It rose to number one thirteen weeks later, and provided the foundation for a joint concert trek—appropriately billed as the Brothers & Sisters Tour.

702
MIND YOUR OWN BUSINESS
HANK WILLIAMS, JR.

Warner Bros. 28581
Writer: Hank Williams
Producers: Hank Williams, Jr.,
Barry Beckett, Jim Ed Norman
December 27, 1986 (2 weeks)

"Mind Your Own Business" was the culmination of a long-time goal that Warner Bros. had for Hank Williams, Jr. The label wanted an "event record," one that would pair him with one or more name performers and create a bit of excitement, simply because of the aggregate name value. When it happened with "Mind Your Own Business," it was almost by mistake.

Bocephus' father wrote the song and cut it at Nashville's Castle Recording Studio on March 1, 1949, just three months before his debut on the Grand Ole Opry. Hank, Sr.'s version peaked at number five later that same year. No one had really planned to cut the song when Hank, Jr., began work on the *Montana Cafe* album in 1985.

"Hank, at one point during the recording, said 'I kind of like this song; what do you think about this?'" recalls co-producer Jim Ed Norman. "When doing it, we cut a track on it and had it all together, and then realized that it just didn't get off the dime with Hank singing it all the way down, that it was just Hank doing another one of his dad's songs. He'd done that before. I remember Hank's feeling was, 'People have already heard that from me.'"

Norman suggested instead that they turn "Mind Your Own Business" into an event record. Hank specifically wanted Reverend Ike, a black evangelist from New York. The Reverend, surprised by the request, consented, but begged off the verse he was assigned about preaching.

Instead, Willie Nelson took that particular verse, recording his part with Norman at Chicago's Universal Studio. Barry Beckett traveled around the country to cut the other special guests: Reverend Ike (at New York's Atlantic Studios), Reba McEntire (at RMS in Las Vegas) and Tom Petty (at Schnee Studios in North Hollywood).

"Reverend Ike was probably the most fun to work with on that project," says Beckett. "He's got a lot of energy, and it all came out on that one verse. I love what Petty did—he was really funky on it—and Reba, I've never heard her in such high voice."

"Mind Your Own Business" helped propel *Montana Cafe* to gold status, and Hank made a noteworthy gesture: he sent a gold record to each of his four special guests.

703

GIVE ME WINGS
MICHAEL JOHNSON
RCA 14412
Writers: Rhonda Fleming, Don Schlitz
Producer: Brent Maher
January 10, 1987 (1 week)

Michael Johnson's musical history is a veritable cornucopia. Learning guitar from his brother, Paul, at age 13, he found rocker Chuck Berry and jazzman Charlie Byrd among his sources of inspiration. At 21, he spent a year in Barcelona, studying with classical guitarist Graciano Tarrago. Upon his return to the U.S., Johnson toured for another year with John Denver in the Chad Mitchell Trio.

His debut album emerged in 1971 under the guidance of producers Phil Ramone (known for his work with Billy Joel and Paul Simon) and Peter Yarrow, of Peter, Paul & Mary. In 1978, Johnson scored three pop hits: "Bluer Than Blue," "Almost Like Being In Love" and "This Night Won't Last Forever."

Michael ended up in yet another musical category in the winter of 1985, signing (without a demo tape) to RCA Records' country division. The move represented quite a contrast to the high-brow approach of his classical training, and he certainly noted the irony.

"There's a kind of [discussion]," he mused, "like 'What happened? Did he sell his limo and buy a truck?' Really, there's always been a schizophrenia in my career between the records I make and what I do when I perform live."

Johnson signed with RCA via producer Brent Maher, and the first country single out of the gate was a logical choice: a Top Ten duet with Sylvia (whom Maher produced) on "I Love You By Heart." Two singles later, he ascended to the top of the chart with the Don Schlitz/Rhonda Fleming composition "Give Me Wings."

"We spent two days on it," Don remembers. "'Give Me Wings' was an important song to both of us personally. It's one of those wonder-

Michael Johnson

ful songs that can be personal to the writer, and still communicate an idea in a positive way to the listener. The song has to do with being sensitive and strong at the same time—sometimes you have to be strong enough to let something go."

Maher had written "Rockin' With The Rhythm Of The Rain" [see 682] with Schlitz, and while he was looking for songs at MCA Music, Brent stuck his head in Don's office just to say hello. Schlitz and Fleming were in the middle of "Give Me Wings," and Maher liked it so much, he committed to it, even before it was finished. Michael liked it, too, and the results were simply captivating.

704

WHAT AM I GONNA DO ABOUT YOU
REBA McENTIRE
MCA 52922
Writers: Doug Gilmore, Bob Simon, Jim Allison
Producers: Jimmy Bowen, Reba McEntire
January 17, 1987 (1 week)

On October 13, 1986, Reba McEntire picked up country music's ultimate prize: the Country Music Association's Entertainer of the Year award. Even as a youngster, Reba coveted CMA trophies—she used to practice acceptance speeches when she went to bed at night.

Naturally, she was moved by her victory, and took out an ad in *Billboard* with a pledge: "Wherever I can get a foot in the door for country music, my boot will be there for all of us . . . We will do our best to carry the banner for country music."

As country's reigning queen, she first carried the flag with "What Am I Gonna Do About You," a single that debuted in *Billboard*'s country chart two days before the CMA bestowed its honor. Reba had first considered it for her *Whoever's in New England* [see 672] album. She was uncertain about it, held it back, and then reconsidered it for her follow-up LP.

"Sometimes you don't know," she admits. "You have to live with things for a long time. 'Cause if you're in a macho-woman mood, you'll pass on some songs that are real tender, and if you're in a real teary-eyed mood, you'll pass on some real strong songs. If anything's even one-hundredth good, I keep it and listen to it again another day."

Reba listened again on her bus during a concert tour, and two bandmembers, Leigh Reynolds and Narvel Blackstock, overheard the tape. They convinced her to take a closer listen, and she eventually recorded it and made it the album's title track.

"What Am I Gonna Do About You" ranked among Reba's most adventurous performances to that point, too. She filled it with more vocal embellishments—passing notes, graces notes and "curlicues"—than on any prior single.

"A lot of people have always calmed me down on those curlicues and said I'm doin' too many, but I like 'em," she states. "They say, 'Well, you sound like you're tryin' to imitate Dolly Parton.' I say, 'I am—I like Dolly Parton. Why not? That's what I like to do.'

"Now Jimmy [Bowen] gives me the freedom. He used to get on me, too, said I was getting a little carried away with curlicues. I said okay, and then slipped 'em back in."

705

CRY MYSELF TO SLEEP
THE JUDDS
(WYNONNA & NAOMI)
RCA 5000

Writer: Paul Kennerley
Producer: Brent Maher
January 24, 1987 (1 week)

"Cry Myself To Sleep" had been around for several years before it reached the top of the *Billboard* country chart. Had it been up to Paul Kennerley, he might never have even pitched it to Wynonna and Naomi Judd.

"The Judds didn't exist when I wrote 'Cry Myself To Sleep,' and that was really just an experiment," Paul explains. "I'd been doing so much wordy writing for a couple of concept albums [see 651—"Have Mercy"]. I really wanted to get away from that and get down to a basic, almost like a Don Gibson, kind of writing—a sad song, but at a fast tempo, with a stripped-down lyric. That was how I started out with 'Cry Myself To Sleep,' and it had a very bluesy sort of a lick."

Initially, Kennerley played the demo for Emmylou Harris, at the same time he played her "In My Dreams" [see 503—"(Lost His Love) On Our Last Date"]. Harris chose to record "In My Dreams," which brought her a Grammy award; though she liked "Cry Myself To Sleep," she didn't feel it was right for her. Once the Judds emerged, she encouraged Paul to take that song to them. Kennerley didn't particularly see it as a good match, but he got a chance to play it for their producer, Brent Maher, anyway.

"My publisher kept telling me about Brent Maher," Paul recalls, "and I'd heard the Judds' first two records, and he said, 'Well, we'll have to get you two guys together.' I think he bought Brent a $14 breakfast and drove him out to my house. I played him a few things that I thought would be good for the Judds—country-type things—and then I said, 'Well, I'll just play you this anyway, but I don't suppose it's what you want.' It was 'Cry Myself To Sleep.'"

Maher liked it immediately and played it for the Judds, who in turn decided to record it. "Cry Myself To Sleep" debuted at number 48 on October 18, 1986, peaking at number one in its fifteenth week on the chart.

"Thank you very much, Emmylou Harris," quips Maher. "I'd better pay her money for that," Kennerley pipes in.

"Cry Myself To Sleep" succeeded as the fourth number one single from the Judds' *Rockin' with the Rhythm* album. The other three were "Have Mercy," "Grandpa (Tell Me 'Bout The Good Old Days)" [see 669] and the title track [see 682].

YOU STILL MOVE ME
DAN SEALS

EMI America 8343
Writer: Dan Seals
Producer: Kyle Lehning
January 31, 1987 (1 week)

"You Still Move Me" deals with the standard country theme of temptation. But it does so in a poignant manner, unlike any other song that has struggled with the topic. The protagonist meets with a past love, contemplates their prior relationship and forces himself to return to his wife. He hopes his spouse will never recognize that his feelings for his "ex" still remain.

"That's a powerful idea," says producer Kyle Lehning. "It's a beautiful tune. Sometimes those kinds of things, people don't want to talk about, but everybody feels them. I think that really strikes a lot of chords."

Seals conceived the chorus to "You Still Move Me" in the basement of a South Carolina nightclub where he was appearing. His guitarist, Joe Stanley ("a mountain man, just an old trapper who's into livin' off the land"), came into the room, and, after tears started welling up in his eyes, encouraged Dan to finish it.

"Personally, the way I look at that song, I think it's the first time I started puttin' together the things that I learned while workin' with Bob McDill [see 677—"Everything That Glitters (Is Not Gold)"]," Seals suggests. "Bob has the ability to, within a few words, bring out pity, pathos, any number of feelings from a person—not because of the rhymes, but just because of the specific words involved.

"I finished 'You Still Move Me,' and I had two ways to go with it. I had it written as 'You still move me, though I'd never let you know.' I consciously made a decision to write it 'I'd never let *her* know.' I felt it made the song a lot stronger by changin' the direction."

After Seals recorded it for his *On the Front Line* album, his record company called him in Canada during a tour to tell him they wanted to release "You Still Move Me" as the first single. Despite his reservations—Seals felt an up-tempo record like "Three Time Loser" [see 738] was a better choice to introduce the album—"You Still Move Me" proved quite successful. In its fifteenth week on the Billboard country chart, it became his fourth number one record.

LEAVE ME LONELY
GARY MORRIS

Warner Bros. 28542
Writer: Gary Morris
Producers: Gary Morris, Bruce Albertine,
Steve Small
February 7, 1987 (1 week)

Gary Morris has maintained an impressively eclectic career—both in his musical choices and his artistic mediums. Besides making hit records, he has added experience in theater and on television to his credentials.

On November 30, 1984, Gary debuted in an off-Broadway production of *La Bohème* in New York that co-starred Linda Ronstadt; that engagement came just three months after he first

Gary Morris

appeared on the Grand Ole Opry. In 1986, Morris took the role of blind country singer Wayne Masterson for thirteen episodes of ABC-TV's "Dynasty II: The Colbys," playing on screen with Emma Samms, Charlton Heston, Barbara Stanwyck and Ricardo Montalban. It dramatically increased his recognizability among non-country fans.

In the wake of "Dynasty II," he strove for an acoustically-oriented project with *Plain Brown Wrapper*, which yielded his fifth number one single, "Leave Me Lonely."

"I wrote that for the *Plain Brown Wrapper* album, which, for me and my own personal taste, was my best album to date at that time," Gary offers. "I really liked the album a lot. It was right after doin' 'The Colbys'; there was a lot of glitz and glamour and stuff that accompanied the L.A. lifestyle, and I'd had a bellyful of it. Thus came the album. 'Leave Me Lonely' was just a statement that I wanted some space from that, and it worked."

On November 30, 1987—three years to the date after the start of *La Bohème*—Morris returned to New York to take the place of Colm Wilkinson in a Broadway production of *Les Misérables*. He gained a positive response in the Big Apple, though it might have cost him at country radio. When he came back with another country album, it failed to earn the kind of response his prior records had.

Gary, however, remains undaunted: "I'm here to live my life, do my music, and hopefully have some people that like it enough to go buy it. I'm gonna do different things, and make some music that people wanna have. If they wanna have it, I'll get to keep makin' music—if not, I'll be a professional hunter."

708

HOW DO I TURN YOU ON
RONNIE MILSAP
RCA 5033
Writers: Mike Reid, Robert Byrne
Producers: Ronnie Milsap, Tom Collins,
Rob Galbraith
February 14, 1987 (1 week)

On Valentine's Day of 1987, Ronnie Milsap received a very special present: "How Do I Turn You On" became his thirtieth number one single. The feat vaulted Milsap into third place on *Billboard*'s career list, past the performer who helped him get his start in country music,

Charley Pride [see 165—"Pure Love"]. Ronnie joined Merle Haggard and Conway Twitty as the only artists to reach the 30 mark through the end of the '80s.

"How Do I Turn You On" might have been a surprise to many. It certainly was to songwriters Mike Reid and Robert Byrne, who never envisioned it as a country record.

"We wrote that thing and demoed it with a DeBarge kind of feel," notes Byrne. "We thought we'd pitch it in L.A., to maybe a young, black-type artist, and Rob Galbraith [one of Milsap's co-producers] really loved that song. We had no intention of playing that for anybody in Nashville, 'cause we figured we'd get laughed out of town. Ronnie Milsap was the only guy that could do anything with that thing."

"I'd had the title and the music and the melody and the chords for a long time," Reid adds. "My original intent was to try to write it in a tender side of 'how do I get you to fall in love with me,' as opposed to really just the obvious thing that people might imagine when they hear that title.

"I either was not a good enough writer at the time or couldn't find it, and Robert Byrne, who's a great writer from Muscle Shoals, heard the song and loved it and went and wrote the lyric. It turned out a little more in the obvious sense than I'd hoped. Still, I think "How Do I Turn You On" worked."

It wouldn't have come off, however, if Galbraith hadn't been so adamant about recording it. Producer Collins wasn't particularly enamored with the song, and even Milsap needed a nudge from Rob to give it a shot.

"I was on the session," Byrne reports, "and as soon as Ronnie heard himself sing it, it was like you could tell he was gettin' into it, and he wouldn't have given you two cents for it before. Rob ended up tellin' me it was his favorite song on the album."

709

STRAIGHT TO THE HEART
CRYSTAL GAYLE
Warner Bros. 28518
Writers: Graham Lyle, Terry Britten
Producer: Jim Ed Norman
February 21, 1987 (1 week)

In "Straight To The Heart," Crystal Gayle falls closer to Tina Turner than to her sister,

Loretta Lynn. There's good reason for that: English songwriters Graham Lyle and Terry Britten form the same team that penned Tina's Grammy-winning "What's Love Got To Do With It."

Martha Sharp, from Warner Bros.' A & R department, was the first to run across the tune, and she supplied it to producer Jim Ed Norman, who also headed the label's country division. "I just thought it was great," Norman says. "The demo of the song had some of that drum-machine kind of character that we ended up using on the record for Crystal." Adds Gayle, "I just loved the feel of it—when I heard it, I loved the intro."

The "intro," in fact, takes a bluesy, sultry approach before the chugging drum machine speeds up the pace. Jim Horn's sax solo makes it an even more uncharacteristic country hit.

"Pitching the song to Crystal, she was, like, 'Well, I don't know about that,'" Norman recounts. "Then she finally grew, I think, to really like it and feel good about it. But it was one of those kinds of records that was just literally built from the ground up, starting with the drum machine and adding to it. I remember it being painstaking, nonstop."

"Straight To The Heart" entered the *Billboard* country chart the week before Thanksgiving of 1986, eventually peaking at number one a week after Valentine's Day of '87. It marked the start of a Happy New Year for the singer, too.

Gayle saw the culmination of a longtime dream with the opening of Crystal's For Fine Jewelry & Gifts. Located in the Belle Meade Shopping Plaza, near Nashville's upper-crust residential area, the shop is unusual for country's entrepreneurs. Rather than carrying run-of-the-mill souvenir T-shirts and coffee mugs like the majority of star stores do, Crystal's features a classy mixture of Waterford crystal, attractive necklaces and fine silver.

The following year, Crystal experienced a first: co-headlining with Loretta in September at Lake Tahoe. The show was so enjoyable that they went on a lengthy series of tours together, and made plans to record an album with their sister, Peggy Sue.

710
I CAN'T WIN FOR LOSIN' YOU
EARL THOMAS CONLEY
RCA 5064

Writers: Robert Byrne, Rick Bowles
Producers: Nelson Larkin,
Earl Thomas Conley
February 28, 1987 (1 week)

Despite his prior billing as an introspective songwriter [see 564—"Don't Make It Easy For Me"], Earl Thomas Conley turned his attention to other areas of record-making with his 1986 album *Too Many Times*. He wrote only three of the tracks, none of which were released as singles.

RCA picked the title cut as the first release, pairing Conley with Anita Pointer of the Oakland-bred rhythm and blues group Pointer Sisters. It seemed an unlikely duo, although the Pointers did win a country Grammy award in 1975 for their recording of "Fairytale." "Too Many Times" made it to number two on November 1, 1986, but it stalled there behind "It'll Be Me" [see 694]. Because the record was a duet, it technically didn't halt Earl's string of consecutive number one singles, which stood at that time at nine. The tenth number one single came with his follow-up, "I Can't Win For Losin' You."

"We literally wrote it for Ray Charles," says songwriter Robert Byrne. "We kind of were messin' around. 'I Can't Stop Loving You' [see 108] was a Ray Charles hit, and 'Born To Lose' and all these things, and we ended up tryin' to put all these titles together and make a 6/8, kind of R & B feel, which that song was. The verses were real conversational, and we wrote it for Ray, note-for-note, lyric-for-lyric. They held it for a while and passed on it, and Earl made a great record on it."

Earl cut the song at the insistence of Nelson Larkin's wife, Mary, and it emerged as one of the album's highlights.

"I think *Too Many Times* is my best album, as far as vocals go," he assessed. "The vocals are just so much smoother and polished and there's a lot more presence on them. It seems that I take much more control of each individual song than I ever have.

"I looked for songs that I could have written myself and felt myself. Every one of the songs makes some kind of statement. There were times in 'Can't Win For Losin' You' where I would break down and couldn't sing it because I could relate to it so much."

On November 29, "I Can't Win For Losin' You" debuted on the *Billboard* chart at a respectable number 58. A lucky 13 weeks later, Earl won out with his tenth number one solo single in succession.

711

MORNIN' RIDE

LEE GREENWOOD

MCA 52984
Writers: Steve Bogard, Jeff Tweel
Producer: Jerry Crutchfield
March 7, 1987 (1 week)

The name "Lee Greenwood" is represented in numerology by the number 11, and that held a great deal of significance in Lee's seventh number one record. Greenwood had an office building constructed on Music Row in Nashville, and the address turned out by accident to be 1111 16th Avenue. He recorded parts of his *Love Will Find Its Way to You* album at 1111 Sound Studios, also by coincidence.

"Mornin' Ride" became a number one single, and, when Lee later released his eleventh album, *Greatest Hits Volume Two*, the single was one of eleven tracks he purposely included.

The sessions for *Love Will Find Its Way to You* featured an incredible array of back-up singers, including Judy Rodman, Dave Loggins, Vince Gill and Restless Heart's Larry Stewart. Gill and Stewart both contributed to "Mornin' Ride," a sexually blatant celebration of the waking hours.

"There've been many songs that have been questioned regarding lyric content," Greenwood concedes. "In fact, if you go back to [Tennessee Ernie Ford's 1955 hit] 'Sixteen Tons,' at the end they had the word 'damn' in it, and they had to go back and take it off. When we came up with 'Mornin' Ride,' it was obviously a connotation of sexuality, but you have to think of other songs, like 'She Left Love All Over Me' [see 465]. Today it seems more acceptable. When we put it in our shows, it became pretty popular with the girls, who like that tongue-in-cheek humor."

"Mornin' Ride" was Greenwood's last collaboration with producer Jerry Crutchfield, as Jimmy Bowen stepped in for his next project. "Jerry is a great artist," Lee assesses, "and I work well with an emotional guy, someone who understands my emotions." Bowen likewise proved beneficial, helping Greenwood continue his string of Top Ten singles in 1987, with "Someone," "If There's Any Justice" and "Touch And Go Crazy."

During much of his recording career, Greenwood remained available to appear in jingles; in addition to his country work, he did commercials for McDonald's, Coors and Nestles Crunch. He eventually moved from his eponymous building on Music Row to a new office—with the address, coincidentally, of 13*11* Elm Hill Pike.

712

BABY'S GOT A NEW BABY

S-K-O

MTM 72081
Writers: J. Fred Knobloch, Dan Tyler
Producer: James Stroud
March 14, 1987 (1 week)

S-K-O started out in the mid-'80s as a trio of songwriters, dedicated to growing as recording artists, but still committed to providing new material for other performers. And many of those other performers had cut songs written by (Thom) Schuyler, (Fred) Knobloch and (Paul) Overstreet.

Their compositions included "16th Avenue," "Hurricane" and "I Don't Know Where To Start," by Schuyler; "The Whole World's In Love When You're Lonely" and "Used To Blue," by Knobloch; and "On The Other Hand" [see 680], "You're Still New To Me" [see 697] and "Same Ole Me" by Overstreet.

When they formed, Schuyler, Knobloch & Overstreet grappled with a question of image: Should they publicly position themselves as three songwriters who happen to perform together? Or, should they play down their credentials and make the group their only focal point? Ultimately, they decided to keep their writing craft at the forefront.

"I think that's one of the fascinations of show business: what's going on backstage," Knobloch explained. "You know, that's the hardest thing to get, the backstage pass. [People like] knowing who plays on a record and who wrote it, and all that stuff."

All three recorded as solo artists prior to S-K-O, although Knobloch was the only one to gain hits. "Why Not Me" reached the Top 40 on the *Billboard* Hot 100 (with his last name spelled "Knoblock"), and he also gained two Top Ten country singles: "Memphis" and "Killin' Time," the latter a duet with Susan Anton.

The first Schuyler, Knobloch & Overstreet release, "You Can't Stop Love," reached number nine. Knobloch wrote their second, "Baby's Got A New Baby," with Dan Tyler. Tyler had the title, Fred had the musical idea,

and they fit it together during one of many writing sessions. They wrote the bridge—or "C section"—at a later date, and Fred took personal pride in inserting a rare minor-11th chord into it. "Baby's Got A New Baby" became only the second single to hit number one on the MTM label [see 679—"Until I Met You"].

Around the same time, Overstreet departed for a solo career, and Craig Bickhardt took his place, making the group S-K-B. They had one more Top Ten single, "Givers And Takers," and then disbanded the trio in 1989, partly because they wished to spend more time with their families.

713

I'LL STILL BE LOVING YOU
RESTLESS HEART
RCA 5065
Writers: Pat Bunch, Pam Rose, Mary Ann Kennedy, Todd Cerney
Producers: Tim DuBois, Scott Hendricks, Restless Heart
March 21, 1987 (1 week)

When Restless Heart took "I'll Still Be Loving You" from the country chart to number 33 on *Billboard*'s Hot 100, it marked the first time since "To All The Girls I've Loved Before" [see 569] that a country hit also reached the Top 40 on the pop chart. The record earned Restless Heart its first Grammy nomination, but it was a struggle from start to finish.

Songwriters Pam Rose and Mary Ann Kennedy have co-written hits for Janie Frickie, Lee Greenwood and Crystal Gayle, and worked together in an all-female quartet called Calamity Jane. As Kennedy Rose, they signed a recording contract with Sting's Pangaea label.

They wrote "I'll Still Be Loving You" at the home of Todd Cerney, husband of former *Billboard* country editor Kip Kirby.

"We didn't have any neat stuff like synthesizers and drum machines, and he had a roomful," Kennedy explained to the *Bluebird Cafe News*. "We sat down at the synthesizers and Pam started this progression. And then Todd started playing along on the guitar, and I started singing. And we worked for a few hours and had [the music]."

Mary Ann decided on the title and a general lyrical framework, but couldn't piece together the details. The song languished for a year, until they contacted songwriter Pat Bunch. It took her less than a half-hour to finish it. The writers then pitched "I'll Still Be Loving You" to Kenny Rogers, who passed on it.

Restless Heart had its own problems making the song work. Though producer Tim DuBois recognized its potential, the group remained uneasy about the match. "The demo was all done with synthesizers," Tim explains, "and we felt like it was too short."

Lead vocalist Larry Stewart and guitar player Greg Jennings refused to give up on it. Finally, Jennings suggested a "James Taylorish" guitar arrangement, and they added an acoustic instrumental bridge.

"It's not your standard three-chord song," says group member Dave Innis. "It's fairly intricate work, and we really worked on that song for a long, long time before it ended up in its final form. It didn't want to be recorded—it really was tough to do."

Their efforts paid off royally. In addition to its number one/crossover status, "I'll Still Be Loving You" has become a popular wedding song.

SMALL TOWN GIRL
STEVE WARINER
MCA 53006
Writers: John Jarvis, Don Cook
Producers: Tony Brown, Jimmy Bowen
March 28, 1987 (1 week)

During 1986, Steve Wariner greatly expanded his musical associations. Besides pairing with Orleans [see 659—"You Can Dream Of Me"], he worked with guitarist Larry Carlton to fashion a new theme song to the sit-com "Who's The Boss?" (that version ran from the fall of 1986 through 1989). Steve teamed with Nicolette Larson on the Top Ten single "That's How You Know When Love's Right," and he turned to singer/songwriter John Wesley Ryles for a Top Five single, "Starting Over Again."

Just before Christmas, Steve introduced a former Rod Stewart band member as a songwriter. John Jarvis played keyboards for Stewart on "Tonight's The Night," "You're In My

Restless Heart

Heart" and "Passion," also contributing to sessions by Stevie Nicks and Stephen Bishop, among others, before moving to Nashville. There, Jarvis has played on records such as "Hey, Bartender," "All My Ex's Live In Texas" [see 727], "The Last One To Know" [see 748], "Too Much Is Not Enough" [see 701] and "What I'd Say" [see 804]. His songwriting credits include "I Wish I Was Still In Your Dreams," "Julia" and "Working Without A Net."

Jarvis wrote the music for "Small Town Girl" at the home studio of co-writer Don Cook, who supplied all of the song's lyrics. It juxtaposed the frenetic energy of New York with the peaceful demeanor of a rural girl, and Wariner first heard it near a Nashville shopping mall.

"I popped John's demo of that into my car player when I was goin' down Franklin Road over by 100 Oaks," Steve recalls. "John's a great keyboard player, and he had all these neat parts on the keyboard. I really liked the demo, and I could hear me doin' it."

But Steve almost didn't do it.

"It's one of those typical stories where the session was basically over," says Jarvis of Steve's recording. "It had been on the list of songs to do, but we hadn't gotten to it. I begged, and everybody agreed to stay over an extra 20 minutes, and we sort of whipped it together. It's one of those 'by-the-hair' kinds of recording sessions: 'You've got two takes— we'll get it or not get it.'"

"Small Town Girl" was Steve's fifth number one single.

715

OCEAN FRONT PROPERTY
GEORGE STRAIT
MCA 53021
Writers: Dean Dillon, Hank Cochran,
Royce Porter
Producers: Jimmy Bowen, George Strait
April 4, 1987 (1 week)

On February 14, 1987, George Strait created a milestone for country music. His album *Ocean Front Property* appeared at number one on the *Billboard* country album chart, the first package ever to debut in the top spot. The feat was fueled both by Strait's growing popularity and by interest created from the title track, already poised that week at number 21. The song's roots went back to one of his earlier singles, "The Chair" [see 650].

Dean Dillon and Hank Cochran wrote "The Chair" on a trip to Florida. Royce Porter was supposed to join them on that excursion, but the song had already been completed by the time he arrived. Collectively, they wrote sixteen songs on that trip, and when they returned to Nashville, Dillon booked time at Wild Tracks Studio to record demos.

Porter and Cochran both contributed to the session, but once the songs that involved them were finished, about 8:00 P.M., they wandered off to another office in the studio.

"I asked the engineer where they were," Dillon remembers, "and he said they were in the back room writing a song. I said, 'They ain't gonna write no song on my session without me,' so I went back in the room, and they had the first verse pretty well together. They told me if I could come up with a bridge and a last verse, everything would be hunky-dory, so I jumped right in."

An hour later, Porter, Cochran and Dillon had "Ocean Front Property," although they were the last to recognize its potential.

"We were not all that impressed with it," Porter maintains. "We liked it, but we didn't think it was near as big a record as it turned out to be. It's like Boudleaux Bryant, who walked into Wesley Rose's office and threw a tape down on his desk, and said, 'Do somethin' with this—if you can.' It turned out to be 'Rocky Top.'"

Strait saw "Ocean Front Property"'s value, though, and held onto the song for a year. On a plane back to Tennessee just before the session, he came up with an interweaving fiddle/steel guitar pattern, and Johnny Gimble and Paul Franklin created the exact interlocking melody he desired.

The result: Strait's tenth number one record. And, George notes impishly, "It's big in Arizona."

716

"YOU'VE GOT" THE TOUCH
ALABAMA
RCA 5081
Writers: Will Robinson, John Jarrard,
Lisa Palas
Producers: Harold Shedd, Alabama
April 11, 1987 (1 week)

Almost exactly two years after they supplied Alabama with a single that helped the group tie Sonny James' record for the most consecutive number one records [see 618—"There's No Way"], Will Robinson, John Jarrard and Lisa Palas provided the song that set the current mark at 21, " 'You've Got' The Touch."

"It was just a situation where John had an idea, which was 'You've Got The Touch,' and I went out and wrote a melody," Robinson reports. "It sounded like an Alabama idea, something they might do if we could hook it, so I wrote the melody and we came back and added some lines and just finished up.

"We sent it to 'em, and that was put on hold for about a year, and we didn't hear anything else about it. When they went in the studio, we got a call saying they wanted a lyric sheet on 'You've Got The Touch' sent over, and that's how we found out."

Alabama clinched it with a sensitive performance, eliminating a tempo change in the process, and " 'You've Got' The Touch" combined with "Touch Me When We're Dancing" [see 698] to furnish a theme for their album *The Touch*. The title could have used a little touch-up when the album went to the printers, though. Originally, the writers intended it to go out with parentheses—"(You've Got) The Touch"—but a typo went unchecked, and the parentheses were replaced by quotation marks.

" 'You've Got' The Touch" was released after a unique occurrence—Alabama lending back-up vocals to Lionel Richie's "Deep River Woman." The single took Richie to number 10 on the country chart.

Alabama followed " 'You've Got' The Touch" with the autobiographical "Tar Top." When "Tar Top" halted at number seven in the fall of 1987, it became the first Alabama single since "My Home's In Alabama" in 1980 to stop short of the top spot.

Nineteen eighty-seven was also the last year of bachelorhood for drummer Mark Herndon. A self-proclaimed Army brat, Herndon was born May 11, 1955, in Massachusetts, but lived out his youth in several states. Mark didn't even take up drums until he was in college, and he knew almost nothing about country music when Alabama hired him—he got the job partly for his abilities, and partly because he showed up for the audition on time.

717
KIDS OF THE BABY BOOM
THE BELLAMY BROTHERS
Curb 53018
Writer: David Bellamy
Producer: Emory Gordy, Jr.
April 18, 1987 (1 week)

The Bellamy Brothers

When David Bellamy wrote "Old Hippie," he had no idea that he was serving as a spokesperson for part of the "thirtysomething" generation. In fact, it took brother Howard to persuade him that they should record it. And it took MCA division chief Jimmy Bowen to decide "Old Hippie" should be a single.

Weaving together pieces of nostalgia—Woodstock, John Lennon's death, Vietnam—"Old Hippie" depicted an aging relic of the '60s, grappling with his own physical changes and the movements that altered his society. After the song reached number two, the Bellamy Brothers waited before recording "Kids Of The Baby Boom," a tune David frequently referred to as "Son of 'Old Hippie.'"

"'Baby Boom' was the lines that were left over from 'Old Hippie,' basically," David says. "I wrote both of those songs the same day. We were in Miami, cuttin' the *Restless* album [see 616—"I Need More Of You"]; I had gotten the idea for 'Old Hippie' when I was down there, and had written about fifteen verses to it. One of the lines that I edited out was something about 'Kids Of The Baby Boom.' I liked that line, and I was working on trying to get another melody, and maybe another idea that was the same, but different. That's when I came up with 'Kids Of The Baby Boom.'"

Whereas "Old Hippie" came close, "Kids Of The Baby Boom" went all the way to number one, the tenth Bellamy single to reach that plateau. Seventeen months later, "Old Hippie III" appeared, better known as "Rebels Without A Clue." The single completed a nostalgia trilogy that resulted in three Top Ten singles.

Five other singles took the Bellamys to the Top Ten through the end of the '80s: "Crazy From The Heart," "Santa Fe," "I'll Give You All My Love Tonight," "Big Love" and "You'll Never Be Sorry."

Despite their 25 Top Ten singles—a record for a duo—the Bellamys remain family guys. In fact, their mother, Frances, is their bookkeeper. According to David, she acquired that post "after somebody else spent the first million, of course. We just give her all the money—she gives us a little allowance."

718

ROSE IN PARADISE
WAYLON JENNINGS
MCA 53009

Writers: Stewart Harris, Jim McBride
Producers: Jimmy Bowen,
Waylon Jennings
April 25, 1987 (1 week)

During 1985, Waylon Jennings celebrated his twentieth anniversary with RCA Records. Jennings had cut 14 number one singles for the label (a fifteenth, "Highwayman" [see 633], was released on Columbia), but it had been a couple of years since his last [see 522—"Lucille"].

In the meantime, Waylon had racked up six more Top Ten singles, including "America," "Waltz Me To Heaven" and "Drinkin' And Dreamin'," which peaked at number two. During 1985, however, he ended his relationship with RCA and signed with MCA, where he kicked off the agreement with "Working Without A Net" and "Will The Wolf Survive."

His fourth single for the label, "Rose In Paradise," earned Jennings his sixteenth number one record. The song appeared on Waylon's second MCA album, *Hangin' Tough*—but was discovered just after he finished the first, by producer Jimmy Bowen's associate, Don "Dirt" Lanier.

"He played it for me, and I said, 'Where were you two weeks ago?'" laughs Waylon. "So I said, 'You're a good songfinder, now let's see how good a hen you are. I want you to sit on that song for a year until I record again.'"

"Rose In Paradise" actually sat around for several years before Jennings cut it. "The demo was one of the reasons," he explains. "It sounded long and draggy, but I knew there was something in that song. I reversed the arrangement on that thing."

Waylon followed "Rose" with two more Top Ten releases, "Fallin' Out" and "Rough And Rowdy Days." The latter came from his "audiobiography," *A Man Called Hoss*, which he promoted with a series of one-man concerts.

On December 12, 1988, Jennings underwent triple bypass surgery at Nashville's Baptist Hospital. His private room was located across the hall from Johnny Cash, who had heart surgery himself exactly one week later.

During 1989, Waylon returned to his usual duties, which also included the marketing of Waylon's West Texas Barbecue Sauce. Two of his cousins do most of the work for the company, while his wife, Jessi Colter, is a vice president.

Though he has diversified, Waylon insists he's not quite ready to give up his best-known career: "I don't think I've done all the things I can in music yet. I still get just as big a kick out of music—especially the recording part of it—as I ever did."

719
DON'T GO TO STRANGERS
T. GRAHAM BROWN
Capitol 5664
Writers: J.D. Martin, Russell Smith
Producer: Bud Logan
May 2, 1987 (1 week)

When asked to describe his music, T. Graham Brown frequently calls it "Otis Redding meets George Jones." That made him a logical candidate to record something from Russell Smith, who calls his own material "rhythm and bluegrass" [see 685—"Heartbeat In The Darkness"].

The two hooked up on "Don't Go To Strangers," a song that Brown calls "one of the bluesiest things we do." Smith co-wrote it with J.D. Martin, incorporating his standard R & B approach on the title.

"It was just a song," Russell says, matter-of-factly, "kind of against the grain of country music at that point, and just kind of a lonely song. It's like a guy that was waitin' around for somebody to open their eyes and see what was there. I wanted to inject a little Staple Singers into it."

"'Don't Go To Strangers' has the personality of Russell Smith imprinted all over it," Martin adds. "It's like one of those days when I was there to assist. It was a neat feeling, but it's really Russell's style—that blues, sort of R & B thing. I feel like I acted as the editor or the musical arranger."

Martin was disappointed at first when he found out that the publisher had given the song to His T-Ness. After all, Brown was an unknown quantity, and J.D. feared the song might simply get lost. T., however, turned in a hot performance at Nashville's Woodland Sound Studio, sparked by flashy guitar licks from Brent Rowan.

By the time the record hit the streets, Brown had 150 concert dates set for 1987 as an opening act for Kenny Rogers (at times, the bill also included Ronnie Milsap [see 736—"Make No Mistake, She's Mine"]). "Don't Go To Strangers" emerged as the fourth single from T.'s debut album, and the second to top the chart.

720
THE MOON IS STILL OVER HER SHOULDER
MICHAEL JOHNSON
RCA 5091
Writer: Hugh Prestwood
Producer: Brent Maher
May 9, 1987 (1 week)

"I've always felt like the things that make a lot of my songs special also tend to make them slightly off-center," surmises songwriter Hugh Prestwood. "I'm a hard person to get cuts on, but if they do it right, usually the record does well."

Such was the case with "The Moon Is Still Over Her Shoulder." An unusual opening guitar riff makes the downbeat confusing the first time you hear it, but that hook helped make the song particularly memorable.

"The basic idea came from a book called *Dinner at the Homesick Restaurant*, by Ann Tyler, who wrote *The Accidental Tourist*," Prestwood explains. "There's a little passage in this book about a woman who's remembering someone that she went to high school with, and that she can't ever imagine her being any older than that.

"It was just so well-said, that I was really struck by that idea that you might remember somebody from a certain time when they were younger, better than you would later on. It struck me that it would be nice to put that into a relationship, with a guy who continues to see his wife as it was when he first fell in love with her."

Prestwood waited three years from the time he wrote it to see "The Moon Is Still Over Her Shoulder" find its niche. Michael Johnson got a hold of it, then played it for producer Brent Maher.

"I loved it," Brent relates, "but what really convinced me was that my wife came out of the kitchen and said, 'That is a marvelous song.' That song really speaks to her, and it's one of the ultimate love songs."

Johnson's *Wings* album featured many of the same musicians who played on "Bluer Than Blue" [see 703—"Give Me Wings"], but also featured guitarist Don Potter, who created—along with Michael—a dual-acoustic centerpiece for the project. That type of "core sound" for the album proved a winner with country listeners, as "The Moon Is Still Over Her Shoulder" became the second chart-topping single from the package on May 9, 1987, in its fifteenth week on the *Billboard* country chart.

Within the next eighteen months, Johnson notched three more Top Ten records: "Crying Shame," "I Will Whisper Your Name" (written by former pop vocalist Randy Vanwarmer) and "That's That," another Prestwood composition.

721

TO KNOW HIM IS TO LOVE HIM
DOLLY PARTON, LINDA RONSTADT, EMMYLOU HARRIS

Warner Bros. 28492
Writer: Phil Spector
Producer: George Massenburg
May 16, 1987 (1 week)

It took nine years for the long-awaited *Trio* album to finally see the light of day.

The first shreds of groundwork were laid in 1974, when Linda Ronstadt's "I Can't Help It (If I'm Still In Love With You)" [see 212—"When Will I Be Loved"] featured a still unknown

Emmylou Harris as a backing vocalist. Within the next year, Dolly Parton met Ronstadt at the Grand Ole Opry, and between the three of them, they discovered they had the proverbial "mutual admiration society."

They harmonized in public for the first time on the premiere of the short-lived "Dolly" syndicated TV show [see 202—"The Bargain Store"], and that same year, Dolly joined Emmylou on "When I Stop Dreaming," a cut from the *Luxury Liner* album.

That song provided something of a focal point when the concept for the *Trio* album began to take shape. After singing "When I Stop Dreaming" and "Light Of The Stable" at a private meeting, the three decided an entire album was necessary. They met at Parton's Nashville home for several days in January of 1978 to formulate the project.

The sessions were recorded with the intention of releasing them through Asylum Records. But once the trio's record labels and assorted lawyers got more deeply involved, the project turned into a fiasco. Too much outside advice soured the album, and several years later, it looked like a dead deal.

As a result, expectant fans had to settle for

Linda Ronstadt,
Emmylou Harris,
Dolly Parton

occasional glimmers. Dolly had already paired with Linda on "I Never Will Marry," and she also teamed up with Emmylou on the *Roses in the Snow* cut "Greener Pastures." Four trio tracks emerged in the interim, spread over a variety of albums: "Mister Sandman," "Evangeline," "Even Cowgirls Get The Blues" and "My Blue Tears."

Beginning on Parton's birthday in 1986, the project took hold once again, only this time, they were able to complete it over an eleven-month period. "To Know Him Is To Love Him" was the only release to reach number one, although three others carried the threesome into the Top Ten: "Telling Me Lies," "Those Memories Of You" and "Wildflowers."

Of a possible sequel, Parton told *Billboard*'s Gerry Wood, "The chances of that happening again, with the three of us trying to find that kind of time, are pretty slim."

722

CAN'T STOP MY HEART FROM LOVING YOU
THE O'KANES

Columbia 06606
Writers: Jamie O'Hara, Kieran Kane
Producers: Kieran Kane, Jamie O'Hara
May 23, 1987 (1 week)

Take two songwriters disappointed with the state of their careers, throw them together in an attic, and what do you get? If the writers are Kieran Kane and Jamie O'Hara, you get a new duo, bent on simplicity—and a number one record.

Both Kane and O'Hara write for Tree Publishing, and they originally teamed up to pool their talents on a few demo tapes and peddle songs to the established artists in Nashville. They recorded songs on an eight-track machine in Kane's attic, and soon discovered they had a common interest in simple—very simple—songs.

Kane and O'Hara started writing together, making more demos, and then decided they might have the basis for an album. They approached their publisher, who financed their endeavor. But the duo soon realized that sticking to basics is tougher than it appears—or sounds.

"Most of our time in the studio is spent first adding, then paring back," O'Hara explains. "We'd do a track, work on it for days, then literally decide to strip it back to vocals and guitar. I think we both began to appreciate the power of understatement."

With its sparse arrangements, repetitive lyrics and infrequent chord changes, the O'Kanes' material caught on from the outset. Their first single, "Oh Darlin'," hit number 10; the follow-up, "Can't Stop My Heart From Loving You," went all the way to number one.

The verse of that song remains on one chord until the very last line, and when they shopped it around Nashville, they received numerous rejections on the grounds that the song was too simple. The O'Kanes needed a measure of confidence just to stay with their stripped-down approach.

The O'Kanes

"Growing up in the Nashville songwriting community, there's a lot of rules that we've had to shed along the way to get to that," O'Hara points out. "Getting to this simplicity has been harder than it seems, actually, because you have to go out on a limb a little bit."

The O'Kanes racked up four more Top Ten hits from their first two albums: "Daddies Need To Grow Up Too," "Just Lovin' You," "One True Love" and "Blue Love."

723
IT TAKES A LITTLE RAIN
(TO MAKE LOVE GROW)
THE OAK RIDGE BOYS
MCA 53010
Writers: James Dean Hicks, Roger
Murrah, Steve Dean
Producer: Jimmy Bowen
May 30, 1987 (1 week)

Three writers, four vocalists, a producer, another artist and a backing musician. The story behind "It Takes A Little Rain (To Make Love Grow)" is a tangled one.

"I was just drivin' down the road one day and I got the title," says James Dean Hicks, who decided to develop the idea with Roger Murrah and Steve Dean. "I think at the time, we had Barbara Mandrell in mind. We got the melody, but as it turned out, she didn't need any more ballads. We had the melody and the title and a few lines and just stopped."

"About eight months later," Dean continues, "Jimmy and I were gettin' ready to write and we came across this tape that we had made that day eight months before. We listened to it and got real excited about it again, so we brought it to Roger and said, 'Hey, let's finish this thing.'"

That same week, Hicks and Murrah also completed "This Crazy Love" [see 737]. Apparently, two demos were made for "It Takes A Little Rain," one of them featuring Steve Sanders, then a guitarist in the Oak Ridge Boys' backing band.

"'It Takes A Little Rain' obviously was a hit from the [first] demo," says Oak Duane Allen, "but Steve Sanders brought me a tape the next day of 'It Takes A Little Rain' with him singin' it on another demo that Tom Collins had hired him to cut independently.

"The version with Steve Sanders was so good that on the tape that I ultimately made of

'It Takes A Little Rain,' I incorporated most of the licks that Steve had in his demo of the song."

Tabbed as the first single from *Where the Fast Lane Ends*, "It Takes A Little Rain" easily rose to number one on May 30, 1987.

Other events at the time weren't so easy. Their biography, *The Oak Ridge Boys: Our Story*, was released in March, the same week William Lee Golden was asked to leave the group. Sanders, who had decided to quit their band, was asked to replace Golden; on May 11, one hour before they announced Sanders' appointment, Golden filed a $40-million lawsuit.

Ultimately, the Oaks pulled through, but for the short run, they certainly endured . . . a little rain.

724
I WILL BE THERE
DAN SEALS
EMI America 8377
Writers: Tom Snow, Jennifer Kimball
Producer: Kyle Lehning
June 6, 1987 (1 week)

Songwriter Tom Snow owns a long list of pop hits, including "Let's Hear It For The Boy" (Deniece Williams), "He's So Shy" (the Pointer Sisters), "After All" (Cher & Peter Cetera), "Alibis" (Sergio Mendes) and "You Should Hear How She Talks About You" (Melissa Manchester).

Snow's songs have also drifted into country music, particularly Dolly Parton's "Don't Call It Love" [see 660—"Think About Love"] (a song that first appeared on Kim Carnes' *Mistaken Identity* album) and Moe Bandy's "You Haven't Heard The Last Of Me" (initially on Anne Murray's *Heart Over Mind*). Snow's first country number one, however, came with "I Will Be There," a song he never envisioned as a country recording.

Originally, Tom carved out the melody and a musical track, working at his home studio in Los Angeles. Jennifer Kimball, who co-wrote Dan Seals' hit "Bop" [see 653], had the good fortune of crossing Snow's path at the time.

"She was over visiting my wife one afternoon," Tom recalls. "I was in my studio. She said, 'Oh, that sounds good.' I hadn't quite finished working on the track and the melody, and then when I did, I called her and said, 'You wanna take a shot at writing the lyrics with me?' We sat down and hammered out a lyric."

"I Will Be There" languished on the shelf for several years until Snow appointed his daughter to work with his catalog. When Seals' producer, Kyle Lehning, took a trip to California to look for material, she set up an appointment with him, and the song found a place on Dan's *On the Front Line* album.

"'I Will Be There' was put on the album specifically because it was the only uptempo song I could find that had decent lyrics that were positive and made sense," Dan says. "The most difficult thing in this business is finding an uptempo song from a publishing company that means something. Writers write ballads; groups write fast songs. Very, very rarely do you find an uptempo song from a writer, and Tom Snow has made a living writing great uptempo songs."

Though Seals' guitar player, Joe Stanley [see 706—"You Still Move Me"], handled the solo parts, Restless Heart's Greg Jennings played electric guitar on the session, with Baillie & The Boys providing background harmonies.

725
FOREVER AND EVER, AMEN
RANDY TRAVIS
Warner Bros. 28384
Writers: Don Schlitz, Paul Overstreet
Producer: Kyle Lehning
June 13, 1987 (3 weeks)

When Warner Bros. released "Forever And Ever, Amen" on March 25, 1987, the label kicked off a campaign that would generate the first single to spend three weeks at number one since "Lookin' For Love" [see 393]. "Amen" picked up two Grammy awards, and earned honors from both the Country Music Association and the Academy of Country Music as the Single and Song of the Year. Like the award-winning "On The Other Hand" [see 680], Randy Travis received it from songwriters Don Schlitz and Paul Overstreet.

"My wife's son would say to her, 'Mommy, I love you forever and ever, amen,'" says Schlitz of the song's origins. "I was going over to write with Paul one night, and I told him the idea for the song, 'I'm gonna love you forever and ever, amen.' He loved it, and we sat on his porch.

"We put candles out that night. He didn't want to turn on the porch light, 'cause it would attract too many bugs. So we put candles out,

and I'm sprawled out on his porch, with my legal pad and pencil, trying to get enough light to write out the words. We spent a couple of hours working on the song, just knowing all along that it was a hit, went in the next day, and [recorded a demo] with voice and guitar."

To the song's sentiment, they added a humorous nod to Overstreet's wife, Julie, a hairstylist when she first met Paul. She had once mistakenly turned a relative's hair green, and they turned that inside joke into a line about balding women.

They hustled "Forever And Ever" over to Warner's Martha Sharp, who screens much of Travis' material, and, quips Schlitz, "the rest is *Billboard* history."

Warner Bros. released the *Always & Forever* album [see 746—"I Won't Need You Anymore"] on May 4, and two months later, it had already sold more than a million copies. On July 11, it became the first country album to reach the Top 20 of the *Billboard* pop album chart since Kenny Rogers' *Eyes That See in the Dark*, in November of 1983.

On June 4, 1988, *Always & Forever* completed a remarkable run: 43 weeks at the top of the country album chart. That easily eclipsed the previous mark of 28 weeks at number one, for Alabama's *Mountain Music*.

726
THAT WAS A CLOSE ONE
EARL THOMAS CONLEY
RCA 5129
Writer: Robert Byrne
Producers: Nelson Larkin,
Earl Thomas Conley
July 4, 1987 (1 week)

"I'm probably the hardest singer in this town to write for," Earl Thomas Conley once proclaimed to Vernell Hackett in *American Songwriter*. "Not because I'm so different or because of my style, but for my emotions, my feelings. I have to be able to feel the song and believe in it. It's along the same lines that Hank Williams had, the feelings and the emotions he could put into a song."

Songwriter Robert Byrne obviously tapped a sensitive vein in Earl's being. Conley covered three of his songs in consecutive solo singles: "Once In A Blue Moon" [see 668], "I Can't Win For Losing You" [see 710] and "That Was A Close One."

"We were both headin' in the same direction at that particular time, I guess," Earl suggests. "Everything he was writin' that I recorded, I said, 'Yeah, I believe this.' By believin' it, I felt that when I recorded it, I could be convincing, and everyone else would know that I believed it. That's how hit records come about."

Earl may have had faith in "That Was A Close One," but Byrne had his doubts about its acceptability for a mass audience.

"That was such a personal song," Robert explains. "I went into a demo session over at Fame [Recording Studio, in Muscle Shoals], and almost didn't demo it, because I thought it was too personal. I just tagged it on the end of the session. All the other stuff that I believed in never saw the light of day, all the other songs that I thought were hits.

"We ended up demoing that thing, and the guys played so well on the demo. Everybody inspired each other. We ended up pitchin' that song to Earl. I still thought it was pretty personal stuff, but Earl loved it. I just thought that nobody would have any use for it, that everybody would say 'So what?'"

Conley recorded "That Was A Close One" at the same session as "I Can't Win For Losing You." While he was out of town on tour, producer Nelson Larkin went back in and inserted a relieved-sounding "Whew!" (Earl would probably call it contrived) after the second chorus.

Byrne's "personal" song ended up a personal highlight for everyone involved in the record, on Independence Day of 1987—the date it reached number one.

727

ALL MY EX'S LIVE IN TEXAS
GEORGE STRAIT
MCA 53087
Writers: Sanger D. Shafer,
Lyndia J. Shafer
Producers: Jimmy Bowen, George Strait
July 11, 1987 (1 week)

Both Whitey and Lyndia (pronounced "Linda") Shafer believe in fate, and it certainly played a role in their marriage. Before they met, Lyndia was a divorced, working mother of three in Pennsylvania; the continuous strain of her situation was starting to sap her strength. After some tears and a prayer of desperation, she turned on the TV and hap-

E.T. Conley

pened to catch "Austin City Limits," a concert show she had never seen before.

Whitey Shafer was the featured guest, and, though she didn't know his name, she liked his voice and filed it in her mind. A short time later, she heard the same voice on the radio and dashed off a letter ("This is so unlike me!") to the disk jockey, who put her in touch with Whitey's publisher, Acuff-Rose, in Nashville.

Whitey sent her some records and sheet music, and soon appeared at a show in the Keystone State. Lyndia's mother bought her the first two tickets issued for that date, and she was able to meet Whitey in September of 1981. The following January, they were married.

Lyndia's first hit as a songwriter came five years later, when Whitey supplied a title—"All My Ex's Live In Texas"—that could have spelled disaster in some marriages.

"That was a fun song to write," says Whitey. "I was kinda writin' my biography. I changed the names to protect the guilty. I do have some ex's in Texas. Thank God they live down there.

It's not really why I live in Tennessee, but it's a good kicker for the song."

Whitey had used the "ex's/Texas" rhyme before in a different song, with a different context, but it was never recorded. He came home from a golf tournament one day with the new variation, and Lyndia joined him in fleshing out the idea: "The *Mobil Travel Guide* and Whitey's melody, and away we went!" They blended in Texarkana, Abilene, Galveston and Temple; Whitey tossed in the Brazos River, which George Strait later changed to the personally-relevant Frio River.

The resulting record was a shoo-in at number one. Whitey drove up to New York for the Grammy awards in March of 1988. Though he didn't win, he and Lyndia had gained a nomination for Best Country Song. "All My Ex's Live In Texas" also brought Strait his only Grammy nomination.

728

I KNOW WHERE I'M GOING
THE JUDDS
(WYNONNA & NAOMI)
RCA 5164
Writers: Don Schlitz, Craig Bickhardt,
Brent Maher
Producer: Brent Maher
July 18, 1987 (1 week)

She was just 18 when the Judds' career took off [see 580—"Mama He's Crazy"], and Wynonna Judd subsequently went through a period of soul-searching, confused by the turn of events that made her life a source of public curiosity. During that time, she turned to Judd guitarist Don Potter for counsel, and his guidance led to a spiritual dedication. To many, "I Know Where I'm Going" reflected that commitment.

"People don't have to interpret it that way," Wynonna notes. "They can just see it as another song to boogie to, and if that's all they get from it, that's fine. But when you get right down to it, that's exactly what I was feeling."

"There's a definite spiritual tone in it," songwriter Don Schlitz concurs, "but we did not want to hit anybody over the head with it. Sometimes, the less you say—or the more subtly you say something—the more effective it is."

When Schlitz and Brent Maher started "I Know Where I'm Going," they had no idea

where they were going with it. Maher had a rough guitar lick and a melody, and introduced the pattern to his partner. Schlitz made a tape of it and frequently popped it into his car's cassette deck over the course of several months. He couldn't get anything going, but when they met again, Maher suggested the spiritual angle, along the lines of the Impressions' "People Get Ready."

"That attitude turned Don on like a freight train rollin' down the line," says Maher. "All of a sudden, lyrics just started pourin' out of him, and we had it written. The problem was, we couldn't come up with a chorus. We couldn't come up with anything melodically that was any good."

Brent played what they had for Wynonna and Naomi, whose reaction was "Great, but . . ."

Schlitz and Maher tried several more times to rewrite it, but never succeeded. Finally, when Don took a trip to California, Brent took the song to a third writer, Craig Bickhardt.

"I thought that the problem was in the bridge," Craig says, "so really, all I did with that song was rewrite the melody on the bridge, the [section that starts] 'Don't you want to come . . .' That's the only contribution I really had to that song."

Apparently, it was enough.

729

THE WEEKEND
STEVE WARINER
MCA 53068
Writers: Bill LaBounty, Beckie Foster
Producers: Tony Brown, Jimmy Bowen
July 25, 1987 (1 week)

Oregon native Bill LaBounty initially tried his hand at a musical career in Los Angeles, but in 1975, he made his first trip to Nashville, destined to become his future home. There, Michael Johnson had a pop hit with his song "This Night Won't Last Forever." Still, LaBounty continued to thrash it out in L.A., notching occasional singles like Robbie Dupree's "Hot Rod Hearts" and "Brooklyn Girls."

In 1984, a publisher introduced LaBounty to songwriter Beckie Foster, intending for them to write together. They immediately hit it off—although they wrote very little—and eventually married. Disenchanted with L.A., they relocated that year in Nashville, where Bill found immediate success when Sawyer

Brown cut "Used To Blue" and "Heart Don't Fall Now" (the latter co-written by Beckie). In 1987, they picked up their first number one single with "The Weekend."

"When you write, you might play one riff over and over again," notes LaBounty, "and I was singing to this riff. I must have sung 'The Weekend,' because Beckie came in and said, 'Did you say "The Weekend?"' I don't remember saying that, but the song came together from what she *thought* she heard me say. We wrote it real late at night—in our pajamas."

A friend named Randy Hart handles keyboards for Steve Wariner, and he played a tape of "The Weekend" for his employer on the tour bus. Steve had just finished recording his *It's a Crazy World* album, but he liked the song so much that he scheduled an extra session, cutting "The Weekend" as well as "Hey Alarm Clock" and "Small Town Girl" [see 714]. With the basic tracks laid down, producer Tony Brown brought LaBounty in to add extra keyboard layers.

"We wanted to make sure we copied his demo verbatim 'cause it was so perfect," says Tony. "We even had Bill bring in his synthesizer to make sure we got the same exact patch, the same program, 'cause every synthesizer sounds a little bit different."

LaBounty also contributed harmony vocals. "Talk about high, the harmony on that record is getting' up there," Wariner jokes. "Bill was standin' on chairs."

"The Weekend" made its *Billboard* debut during the weekend of April 25, 1987, and hit number one exactly three months later.

730

SNAP YOUR FINGERS
RONNIE MILSAP
RCA 5169
Writers: Grady Martin, Alex Zanetis
Producers: Ronnie Milsap, Rob Galbraith,
Kyle Lehning
August 1, 1987 (1 week)

Chet Atkins usually gets the glory, but Grady Martin certainly ranks among the top session guitarists ever to pick up a six-string in a Nashville studio. Perhaps best known for the "fuzztone" guitar he mistakenly created on Marty Robbins' "Don't Worry" [see 20—"I Walk Alone"], Martin has played on hundreds of hits, including "El Paso," "I Fall To Pieces,"

Floyd Cramer's "Last Date" [see 98] and the original version of "Guitar Man" [see 416]. In 1979, he joined Willie Nelson's band.

Grady's most significant work as a songwriter came in 1962, when he and Alex Zanetis worked on "Snap Your Fingers" at 10:00 P.M. for a 4:00 A.M. recording session with R & B singer Joe Henderson. Martin wrote all but four lines in the song, which they finished in less than 90 minutes, and Henderson earned a Top Ten pop record with it.

"Snap Your Fingers" has had a lengthy history, too. Barbara Lewis, Dean Martin and Sammy Davis, Jr., have covered it, and it has also appeared three times on the *Billboard* country chart. Dick Curless introduced it in 1971; three years later, Don Gibson took it to number 12. Finally, in 1987, Ronnie Milsap resurrected it as a number one single.

"Ronnie wanted to cut that," reports producer Kyle Lehning, "and brought it in and played it on piano. Rob [Galbraith] and I both loved it and thought it was a great idea. It was a real interesting record to make, 'cause it was a melting pot of styles."

"Snap Your Fingers" was the first single culled from the *Heart and Soul* album, Milsap's first LP recorded entirely with digital equipment. The track appeared in *Billboard* at number 48 on May 23, 1987. With little difficulty, "Snap Your Fingers" reached number one in its eleventh charted week.

Born January 17, 1929, near Chappel Hill, Tennessee, Martin was inspired to take up his craft by the music that piped into his family's house from the Grand Ole Opry. At 15, he went to Nashville, where he made his Opry debut in 1946 as a fiddler. His first recorded success came with Red Foley's 1950 hit "Chattanoogie Shoeshine Boy," and Grady went on to record with Hank Williams, Bing Crosby, Henry Mancini, and with perhaps his most vocal supporter, Merle Haggard.

731

ONE PROMISE TOO LATE
REBA McENTIRE
MCA 53092
Writers: Dave Loggins, Lisa Silver,
Don Schlitz
Producers: Jimmy Bowen, Reba McEntire
August 8, 1987 (1 week)

In 1987, Reba McEntire surprised friends, family and fans with her divorce from eleven-year husband Charlie Battles. In an unusual twist, her publicists issued a press release making the split public knowledge, and in the process, indicated that Reba preferred not to discuss the subject. It was a strong move—McEntire got the media's support and sympathy, and didn't have to talk about the divorce publicly until she was ready.

At the time, Reba had the third single from the *What Am I Gonna Do About You* [see 704] album in release. The second, "Let The Music Lift You Up," had peaked at number four. The third, "One Promise Too Late," came from Dave Loggins, Lisa Silver and Don Schlitz, the same trio that wrote "Forty Hour Week (For A Livin')" [see 631].

" 'One Promise Too Late' was the exact opposite [of 'Forty Hour Week']," says Schlitz. "Lisa Silver and I were working on the song, and Lisa had a real neat melody and I had some words, and we got to the bridge, and were stuck. Dave Loggins, on that day, was walking

Michael Martin Murphey

around the hall, and we said, 'Dave, come be a bridge-buster.' So he came in, and we knocked that sucker out."

The demo tape apparently reached Reba at an opportune moment. She was contemplating the divorce at the time, and reacted strongly to the song's message about marital misgivings.

"I was in a depressive mood," she remembers. "On the album, right before the mixing stage—or maybe right after the mixing stage—I saw [MCA executive] Bill Catino in West Virginia. He came on the bus, and I played him the album. He said, 'Good God, Reba, you gettin' a divorce or somethin'?' I had filed two days before, or I was thinkin' about it or somethin', and he didn't know. The next time he saw me, he said, 'Man, I can't believe I said what I said,' but I told him he was pretty perceptive. When you're in a depression, that's the kind of songs you want to sing."

Her emotional rendition of "One Promise Too Late" secured her eighth number one single, and Reba hardly let her personal upheaval crimp her professional life. On October 28, she won overwhelming critical approval for a performance at Carnegie Hall.

732

A LONG LINE OF LOVE
MICHAEL MARTIN MURPHEY
Warner Bros. 28370
Writers: Paul Overstreet, Thom Schuyler
Producers: Steve Gibson, Jim Ed Norman
August 15, 1987 (1 week)

On the heels of "What's Forever For" [see 487], Michael Martin Murphey became a regular presence in country music, with successive hits like "Still Taking Chances," "Will It Be Love By Morning," "I'm Gonna Miss You, Girl" and "From The Word Go." Surprisingly, for a singer/songwriter, many of them—including both his number one records—came from other writers.

"I've always had a problem writing love songs that were sort of generic, that reached everybody," Michael explains. "So I've turned to other writers for those kinds of songs. Since those are the kinds of songs that make up the staple of radio, my number one songs have come from other places."

"A Long Line Of Love" came from songwriters Thom Schuyler and Paul Overstreet. Schuyler, invited to sing at his brother-in-law's wedding, had started it specifically for that event.

"I wrote the chorus and the first verse," Thom recalls. "We were getting closer and closer to the wedding date, and I couldn't bring myself to finish the song, so I got together with Paul. We finished the song rather hurriedly, and I went up and tried it out at the wedding, and a lot of tears fell. It was a very appropriate wedding song."

"'Long Line Of Love' is a pretty straightforward piece of material," says Murphey. "It's part of the revival of tradition, in a sense that country music's strength has always been that it was family music.

"When I first recorded that song, there were actually people who said, 'Man, don't put that out—that's too corny.' I said, 'What do you mean? What's corny about it?' 'Well, it talks about family. It's too sentimental.'

"What's wrong with our society when you can't say, 'My grandfather loves my grandmother,' that tradition is important to me, that my family supported me for years? These are things that have become so foreign to us because almost two out of three marriages in this country end in divorce.

"This song brings back the warmth, but it also says, 'When times get hard, we don't give up,' and to me, that's one of the most important lines. If you want to make a family tradition and love work, it's something you've got to work hard on."

733
WHY DOES IT HAVE TO BE (WRONG OR RIGHT)
RESTLESS HEART
RCA 5132
Writers: Randy Sharp, Donny Lowery
Producers: Tim DuBois, Scott Hendricks,
Restless Heart
August 22, 1987 (1 week)

If Restless Heart has been plagued during its history, it's been through a chronic misinterpretation of the band's beginnings. Producer Tim DuBois started assembling the group with admittedly self-serving intentions.

"I conceived the idea as an outlet for my material," Tim concedes. "I was writing material that I was havin' trouble gettin' recorded—country acts felt like it was too pop, pop acts thought it was too country, and it just

kind of fell between the cracks. The idea in the beginning was to build a vehicle for some of my songs, and some of my close friends' writing. Some people have made it out as if it was a very, very cold and calculated thing. There's much more involved, though, than that."

Restless Heart originally went under the working title of the Okie Project. DuBois, coproducer Scott Hendricks and Greg Jennings had met at Oklahoma State University in 1975. In 1978, Hendricks met Oklahoma native Paul Gregg, while working at Opryland. When Restless Heart was formed in 1983 [see 696— "That Rock Won't Roll"], Jennings and Gregg were recruited, along with Okies David Innis and Verlon Thompson, plus a "token Yankee": drummer John Dittrich.

"I think a lot of people have the idea that I went out and hired five guys, stuck 'em in the studio, and there was your band," says DuBois. "Instead, it developed over many months of time in the studio, working together. A lot of us had known one another. It *was* premeditated, but there was a lot more of a garageband spirit from the beginning."

Thompson quit—just as Restless Heart prepared to record its first album—and Larry Stewart stepped in to handle lead vocals. Even at that time, the group considered recording "Why Does It Have To Be (Wrong Or Right)," but they passed on it because it sounded too much like Exile.

They turned it down again on the second album. But when they delivered the project to RCA, the label complained that the album had too many ballads and asked the band to find two substitute songs. At that time, Gregg stepped forward and threatened to quit if they didn't give "Why Does It Have To Be" a shot.

With a number of alterations, they molded the song into their own, and came up with their third chart-topping single in the process.

734
BORN TO BOOGIE
HANK WILLIAMS, JR.
Warner Bros. 28369
Writer: Hank Williams, Jr.
Producers: Barry Beckett,
Hank Williams, Jr., Jim Ed Norman
August 29, 1987 (1 week)

Hank Williams, Jr., was recording the *Born to Boogie* album before he even had a song titled "Born To Boogie." Bocephus maintains his office in Paris, Tennessee, with a home on the Tennessee River, and after visiting a friend by boat, he came up with the song in a rush around 2:30 A.M. Later that morning, he went into the office to put the song down on a tape recorder.

In the recording studio, "Born To Boogie" proved a booger.

"We were having a hard time keeping the pulse right," notes co-producer Jim Ed Norman. "I asked Hank if he'd ever worked with a drum machine, and he hadn't up until that point. We set a clock track and used a drum machine through there to help anchor the song. Then it ended up staying on the record. If you listen to the record to this day, you've got that backbeat/handclap thing which is actually from the drum machine."

"It took us about six hours to cut it," adds co-producer Barry Beckett, "not that everybody was playing wrong. It was a hard shuffle, difficult to get, and to keep that much power going for that period of time. That was a heck of a song, and most of the takes, everybody was getting tired before the end of it. So I guess everybody got mad at me. They eventually said, 'We're gonna get this take, do or die.' That's actually the defiant kind of attitude that's on the record: 'We dare you to tell us this is not right.'"

"Born To Boogie" eventually earned the approval of the public at large. On August 29, 1987, it became the tenth number one single in Hank's career. That year, Bocephus also received some long overdue recognition. Both the Academy of Country Music and the Country Music Association named him the Entertainer of the Year. He repeated that feat the next year in the CMA and the next two years in the ACM.

Hank also earned a coup at the CMA presentation in 1989 for "There's A Tear In My Beer," an "event record" [see 702—"Mind Your Own Business"] that teamed him— through the magic of overdubbing—with his late father. "Tear In My Beer" grabbed both the Vocal Event of the Year and Video of the Year trophies.

735
SHE'S TOO GOOD TO BE TRUE
EXILE
Epic 07135

Writers: Sonny Lemaire, J.P. Pennington
Producer: Buddy Killen
September 5, 1987 (1 week)

Fifteen years after Charley Pride took the same title to number one [see 113], Exile's "She's Too Good To Be True"—a completely different song—also hit the top of the *Billboard* country charts. In fact, the band's Sonny Lemaire hadn't heard Pride's similarly-titled recording.

"J.P. [Pennington] and I were in Nashville on a Sunday night," Lemaire remembers, "and we needed a song to cut Monday. He had a rough outline of a melody, and we went over to Soundshop Studio B, and wrote that song Sunday night. It took us several hours to write it, and hammer it out, and then we cut it the next day."

Though it came from the same album, "She's Too Good" trailed the previous single, "It'll Be Me" [see 694], by ten months. It was an unusually long gap between records, primarily because work on the *Shelter from the Night* album [see 752—"I Can't Get Close Enough"] took longer than expected.

"We were still writing for the next album, and had to have product out there," notes Lemaire. "That's one of my all-time favorite songs that we've recorded, and we just really believed in that song, and it worked."

Even before "She's Too Good To Be True" became a single, Exile underwent the first of several personnel changes. Marlon Hargis left the group, and was replaced on keyboards by Lee Carroll, who had spent two-and-a-half years on the road with the Judds. Carroll took part in the recording sessions for *Shelter from the Night*, but his addition wasn't the last alteration in Exile's line-up.

In August of 1988, Les Taylor dropped out of the band to pursue solo projects. Paul Martin, who had sung on a few commercial jingles with Pennington, was selected as a replacement. At the beginning of 1989, Pennington likewise left the group. Taylor and Pennington had traditionally handled lead vocals on all of Exile's material, and that role went in their absence to Lemaire and Martin.

"It was real scary at first," admits Lemaire, "because we had to really look at ourselves and decide if it's what we want to do—you know, *can* we do it? Immediately, we felt camaraderie between the four of us."

The new Exile alignment emerged on Arista Records in 1990, with an appropriately-titled album: *Still Standing*.

736

MAKE NO MISTAKE, SHE'S MINE

RONNIE MILSAP
& KENNY ROGERS

RCA 5209
Writer: Kim Carnes
Producers: Rob Galbraith, Kyle Lehning
September 19, 1987 (1 week)

Kim Carnes' friendship with Kenny Rogers dates back to 1966, when she joined the New Christy Minstrels. She wasn't particularly fond of folk music, and quit three different times before leaving the group for good. Her brief membership yielded two important contacts, though. One, fellow Minstrel Dave Ellingson, became her husband; the other was Kenny.

As a member of the First Edition, Rogers was the first to cut one of Kim's songs, "Where Does Rosie Go." Her stock as a songwriter continued to build throughout the '70s, but she remained unknown to the general public as a performer until her 1978 duet with Gene Cotton, "You're A Part Of Me."

Carnes gained greater acclaim, though, when Kenny asked her and Ellingson to write a concept album. Titled *Gideon*, it yielded a lone single in 1980, the Rogers & Carnes duet "Don't Fall In Love With A Dreamer." The track hit number three on the country chart, and number four on *Billboard*'s Hot 100. A year

later, Carnes bowled over the pop audience with "Bette Davis Eyes," topping the chart for nine weeks.

She had to wait until 1984 for her next significant hit, teaming once again with Kenny, plus James Ingram, on "What About Me?" She followed with another duet, this one pairing her with Barbra Streisand.

Carnes received that opportunity quite unexpectedly when Streisand's producer, Jon Peters, called and suggested that Kim write something for a duet. Within ten minutes, she was at the piano constructing "Make No Mistake, He's Mine," which became their single.

Two years after its release, Kenny once again brushed with Carnes' career, when he re-recorded that song. Rogers and Ronnie Milsap were touring during 1987 and needed a song that they could perform together on stage during the show. Milsap searched in vain for the right song, and Kenny finally decided to redo "Make No Mistake."

They made the record together with the band, although later, both Kenny and Ronnie overdubbed different sections, leaving producers Rob Galbraith and Kyle Lehning to piece together the best performances.

RCA released the duet in advance of both albums, Milsap's *Heart and Soul* and Kenny's *I Prefer the Moonlight*. The single reached number one about a month after both LPs were released. Carnes, incidentally, sang backing vocals on the title track to Kenny's album, which peaked at number two.

Kenny Rogers &
Ronnie Milsap

THIS CRAZY LOVE
THE OAK RIDGE BOYS
MCA 53023
Writers: Roger Murrah,
James Dean Hicks
Producer: Jimmy Bowen
September 19, 1987 (1 week)

When songwriter James Dean Hicks first moved to Nashville, he picked up the telephone book and found a listing for Tom Collins Music. Hicks had always liked the songs that Tommy Collins wrote for Merle Haggard [see 91—"Carolyn" and 238—"The Roots Of My Raising"]. He was hired and worked there for two weeks before discovering that *Tommy* Collins and *Tom* Collins were two separate people.

Hicks picked up his second number one record with "This Crazy Love," a song he co-wrote with TCM associate Roger Murrah. "I had a crazy little acoustic guitar lick that I came upon, and it really knocked me out," James remembers. "I took it to Roger, and 'This Crazy Love' just started to sing around the lick—so we started to get a melody goin'." "We kind of wanted to do somethin' with a little edge on it," Roger adds.

"This Crazy Love" ended up in the hands of the Oak Ridge Boys, and Duane Allen was particularly tuned in to the demo when he cued it up. But he was expecting "It Takes A Little Rain" [see 723]. MCA head Bruce Hinton had sent a copy of that song to a hotel where the Oaks were staying during a tour. Several people had told Allen that "It Takes A Little Rain" was a hit, and when the tape came in, he ran to the parking lot and popped it into the cassette deck on their bus.

"There was no label on the tape at all," Duane notes. "It was just a blank tape in a blank box. I kept lookin' for 'It Takes A Little Rain,' and I didn't notice that it wasn't cued up to the beginning. Whoever listened to it prior to sending it didn't rewind it, so the tape was on the second song."

That song was "This Crazy Love." Allen liked it, but he didn't feel sure about it for the group and sent it to Waylon Jennings. Waylon also liked it, but didn't record it. "It Takes A Little Rain," of course, was the first song on the demo, and the Oaks ended up cutting both. They selected "This Crazy Love" as the second single from *Where the Fast Lane Ends*, and it became the Oaks' fifteenth number one.

THREE TIME LOSER
DAN SEALS
EMI America 43023
Writer: Dan Seals
Producer: Kyle Lehning
September 26, 1987 (1 week)

Dan Seals boasts an impressive family tree. His brother, Jimmy Seals, made up half of the pop duo Seals & Crofts; his father, Waylon, played occasional bass with Bob Wills and Ernest Tubb; cousin Chuck Seals wrote Ray Price's "Crazy Arms" [see 77—"I Won't Mention It Again"]; cousin Troy Seals [see 157—"There's A Honky Tonk Angel"] is a member of the Nashville Songwriters Hall of Fame; and cousin Johnny Duncan owns three number one hits.

Dan was involved with another relative—his daughter, Holly—when he penned his sixth number one single (fifth as a solo performer), "Three Time Loser." Holly was appearing in a television project, "Snowbird," that helps adults deal with kids. Dan got the idea for the song on the way to the TV studio, then finished it up while waiting in his car in the WSM parking lot.

" 'Three Time Loser' was not an important idea," Seals maintains. "But I had felt that way in my life at school. Man, I never could get it together. I'd get hung up on some girl, and I'd always get the one I didn't want, and I just felt like a loser most of the time. I didn't date a lot in school, and then on the road, music took a lot of my life away. There wasn't any time. I took a daytime job, too."

Dan and record producer Kyle Lehning picked "Three Time Loser" as one of seven Seals-written songs for the *On the Front Line* album. They recorded it as a guitar-heavy tune, with Larry Londin on drums and David Hungate on bass. The finished product mixed the band with electronic technology.

"Actually, what you're hearing is Larry Londin's drum part programmed into the drum machine," Lehning notes. "There were some discrepancies between the bass, and the way the whole thing went together. It was a very difficult tune to do, but Larry's part was brilliant, so what I did was just listen to what he played and transcribe it into the drum machine."

As a result, the record jacket credits Londin as "scientist" and Lehning as "hunchback."

"The science of the thing was Larry's creative process," Kyle explains. "The hunchback work was me sitting there, meticulously punching buttons and reproducing his part on the drum machine."

"Three Time Loser" clicked in at number 57 when it debuted on the *Billboard* country chart on June 27, 1987. Three months later, it topped out at number one.

Naturally, we all wanted to sing lead on it, too."

The group offered five more singles through the end of the '80s, including "Lyin' In His Arms Again," "Letter Home," "Sincerely," "Love Will" and "Don't You." The Foresters became the first artists since the debut of the 100-position *Billboard* chart [see 136—"Love Is The Foundation"] to take each of its first thirteen charted records into the Top Ten.

739

YOU AGAIN
THE FORESTER SISTERS
Warner Bros. 28368
Writers: Don Schlitz, Paul Overstreet
Producers: James Stroud, Barry Beckett
October 3, 1987 (1 week)

With three number one singles behind them, the Forester Sisters just missed their chance for a fourth with "Lonely Alone." That record hit number two in October of 1986 behind "Always Have, Always Will" [see 690], then stayed there the following week when "Both To Each Other" [see 691] skipped over it. They did reach the top with their next release, teaming up with the Bellamy Brothers for "Too Much Is Not Enough" [see 701], then stalled at number five with "Too Many Rivers." The Foresters notched their fifth chart-topper with "You Again," written by Paul Overstreet, who penned their first [see 638—"I Fell In Love Again Last Night"], and Don Schlitz.

"We wrote that the day after we wrote 'On The Other Hand' [see 680]," Schlitz reports. "That came from a line that, I think, [songwriter] Mike Reid had told me about—the You Again Syndrome. You've been married for awhile and you wake up in the morning and you look at your spouse and go, 'Oh, you again.'

"You have to deal with that, and you make the best of it. When the best of it is made, I think people can celebrate the fact that, 'Yeah, I'd choose you again.'"

The Forester Sisters first heard "You Again" while they were doing sessions at Woodland Sound Studio—unusual, since they prefer not to preview new material while they're recording other songs.

"We try not to let that happen," says Christy Forester, "but they had sent it over for us to hear, and it was kind of like 'I Fell In Love Again Last Night.' It's one of those songs that when you hear it, it just tugs at your heart."

740

THE WAY WE MAKE A BROKEN HEART
ROSANNE CASH
Columbia 07200
Writer: John Hiatt
Producer: Rodney Crowell
October 10, 1987 (1 week)

Rodney Crowell took a break from producing Rosanne Cash when she did her *Rhythm & Romance* album [see 636—"I Don't Know Why You Don't Want Me"]. Crowell felt he was placing her in a musical rut, and also wanted to refocus on his own solo career, having already produced albums for a number of other performers. Rodney returned to the studio with Rosanne to cut *King's Record Shop*, in which he had a formative hand. It replaced a *Greatest Hits* release.

"I was driving home one night," Crowell told Jan Hoffman in the *Village Voice*, "and all of a sudden, out of the sky, a thunderbolt flashed into my mind, and I said to myself, 'Rose is an artist! And really good [artists] don't put out *Greatest Hits* records.' So I came home, and after about three hours of 'I Will Not Be Denied,' [Rosanne] started leading me around and we began to conceive what turned into *King's Record Shop*."

The first single from the album came with "The Way We Make A Broken Heart." Songwriter John Hiatt also wrote Rosanne's *Somewhere in the Stars* single "It Hasn't Happened Yet" and the Desert Rose Band's "She Don't Love Nobody."

"Several years ago, John Hiatt was doing this record in town," Rosanne says. "It was a very odd record, and he asked me to sing 'The Way We Make a Broken Heart' with him, so I went and did it with him, and it was a very strange duet. We never actually sang together. I don't know if the record ever came out, but that song never came out.

"But I held onto the song, thinking that I wanted to do it someday. When we did *King's Record Shop*, there was some discussion as to whether I should do it as a duet or do it alone; we finally decided that I should do it alone.

"It just turned out so beautiful, and I loved the record so much. Steuart Smith's guitar solo is lovely. Ry Cooder had recorded it, and he had gotten Bobby King and his guys to sing back-up, so we got them to sing back-up on my record, too. That turned out very cool—an 'Under The Boardwalk'-type thing, but also Patsy Cline a little bit, too."

Rosanne Cash

741
FISHIN' IN THE DARK
THE NITTY GRITTY DIRT BAND

Warner Bros. 28311
Writers: Wendy Waldman, Jim Photoglo
Producer: Josh Leo
October 17, 1987 (1 week)

In 1986, after the Nitty Gritty Dirt Band celebrated its twentieth anniversary [see 637—"Modern Day Romance"], multi-instrumentalist John McEuen left the band for a solo career. The remaining members—Jimmy Ibbotson, Jeff Hanna, Jamie Fadden and Bob Carpenter—had much to prove to themselves with their next album, *Hold On*.

"We were as insecure as anybody would be when a guy that's been in a band for twenty years and is highly visible leaves," relates Hanna. "You always wonder if folks are gonna react to you in the same way. But they seem to have bought it, so we're happy about that."

First evidence that the Dirt Band could survive without McEuen came with "Baby's Got A Hold On Me," which peaked at number two in the spring of 1987. Their follow-up, "Fishin' In The Dark," fared even better.

Former pop vocalist Jim Photoglo wrote the melody to "Fishin' In The Dark" in 1986, about a year after moving from Los Angeles to Nashville. He took it to co-writer Wendy Waldman, who had been listening to Garrison Keillor's "Prairie Home Companion," and she announced that she wanted to make it a song about fishing. Photoglo skeptically rolled his eyes, but he let her do her lyrical wonders, and Waldman definitely "hooked" it.

Josh Leo, a close friend of Waldman, took over production midway through the *Hold On* album, and "Fishin'" was the first song he brought to the Dirt Band.

"We really love writin' our own songs," says Hanna, "and a lot of the hits we've had, we've written. But this one *sounded* like we wrote it or it was written for us—it had 'Dirt Band' written all over it. It just blew our minds.

"We cut it immediately. The record company liked it so much they wouldn't put it out as the first single. They wanted to use it as a clean-up hit, more or less. They gave it an RBI."

By 1989, the Nitty Gritty Dirt Band—once inconsistent hit-makers—held a streak of fifteen consecutive Top Ten singles. That same year, they created a landmark album with *Will the Circle Be Unbroken, Volume II*. Featuring

an all-star supporting cast that included Johnny Cash, John Denver, Ricky Skaggs and Bruce Hornsby, among others, it captured the Country Music Association Album of the Year award.

742

SHINE, SHINE, SHINE
EDDY RAVEN
RCA 5221
Writers: Bud McGuire, Ken Bell
Producers: Don Gant, Eddy Raven
October 24, 1987 (1 week)

On December 19, 1986, a number of TV viewers saw Eddy Raven introduce "Shine, Shine, Shine" on the syndicated "Dance Fe-

ver." RCA Records wasn't pleased. It had pegged the title cut from *Right Hand Man* as the second single off the album, and had little thought of releasing "Shine, Shine, Shine" at all. In the end, Raven won out. The song generated a strong response at his live shows and radio picked it up off the album, so RCA let it out as the fourth single—Eddy's second to reach number one.

Songwriter Kenny Bell created a small part of the song one evening, but didn't think much of it until a stagnant writing session the next day. He left for about 30 minutes, and started listening to the tape in his car. Bell took it back to his writing session, and worked out the rest of the song with Bud McGuire, eliciting surprising comparisons to Jackson 5 with the "ABC"-ish intro.

"That comes from years of workin' with Rick Hall [in Muscle Shoals]," Bell notes.

"When I first started there, we did the Os- monds, and the early Osmond stuff did kind of copy the Jacksons, and that's where that came from. That's a Jacksons-by-way-of-Osmonds-by-way-of-Muscle Shoals kind of thing—a lot of 'by-way-of's."

Songwriter Mickey Newbury heard the tune at Larry Butler's office and suggested it was perfect for Raven. The publisher sent it, and Raven agreed to record it. But producer Paul Worley wasn't excited about it, so it didn't make the *Love and Other Hard Times* album.

"I played it for a year on the bus and never got tired of it," says Raven.

For his next album, Eddy persuaded his mentor, Don Gant, to come out of retirement. It was the last record Gant produced before he passed away.

It also ended a three-year period between chart-topping hits for Raven [see 573—"I Got Mexico"], although it was hardly a dry run. Eddy racked up eight Top Ten singles in the interim, including "She's Gonna Win Your Heart," "You Should Have Been Gone By Now," "Sometimes A Lady" and "You're Never Too Old For Young Love."

743

RIGHT FROM THE START
EARL THOMAS CONLEY
RCA 5226
Writers: Billy Herzig, Randy Watkins
Producers: Nelson Larkin,
Earl Thomas Conley
October 31, 1987 (1 week)

"I always wanted to be in the movies," Earl Thomas Conley told Wanda Stanley of the *Jeffersonville News* in Indiana. "We would go to the movies, I was probably ten years old or so. I think we'd get to go . . . maybe twice a year. John Wayne was my hero."

Earl made it in the movies—although not on screen—in 1989, when *Road House*, starring Patrick Swayze, used "Right From The Start," the fourth single from *Too Many Times*.

"That song came in through the mail," notes producer Nelson Larkin. "My secretary, Sarah, found the song, said it was a hit, and we cut it. We put it on the album just for her 'cause she'd done a lot of good things for Earl and me. But we never had any intentions of it bein' a single."

"Right From The Start" was penned by two songwriters from Texas, Billy Herzig and Randy Watkins, who had never had a major cut before. The record sported more of a rhythm and blues flavor than anything Conley had done previously, and it took him to number one on Halloween of 1987. The record also marked the end of Earl's in-studio relationship with Larkin.

"We're great friends," says Larkin. "It's kind of like a husband-and-wife deal. We fought occasionally, but we were the type of people that if we had a fight, hey, the next morning we were friends again.

"RCA always wanted somebody else to produce him. Earl was gettin' pressured, and actually, I've forgotten what we got into it about. He says, 'Well, I'm just gonna produce my next album by myself.' He'd said that a hundred times, and I said, 'It's about time you did one by yourself,' somethin' like that."

"We had a groove," Conley reflects on their 14 number one singles. "We knew each other. We could read each other's minds without talkin'. You get people that you just gel with, and something magic happens. Nelson, all those years, was that kind of a situation."

Larkin continued producing Billie Joe Royal after his split with Conley, who remained signed to RCA through Larkin's production company. Conley turned to long-time partner Randy Scruggs [see 630—"Love Don't Care (Whose Heart It Breaks)"] and Emory Gordy, Jr., for his next album.

744

AM I BLUE
GEORGE STRAIT
MCA 53165
Writer: David Chamberlain
Producers: Jimmy Bowen, George Strait
November 7, 1987 (1 week)

"I want to reach the point where people hear my name and immediately think of real country music," George Strait told *Billboard*'s Kip Kirby when he debuted in 1981. "I think what I'm doing is a little bit different from everything else that's out on the radio, and I'd like to keep it that way."

Strait differentiated himself by digging into Western swing at a time when traditional sounds were hardly in vogue. By the end of the decade, traditional was the rule, rather than the exception, a trend that George's success had helped to create. In 1987, Strait perpetuated his swing motif with "Am I Blue." He obtained it from David Chamberlain, a writer whose only previous Top Ten single was a 1977 Billie Jo Spears release, "I'm Not Easy."

"I was born and raised in Fort Worth, in the Bob Wills area, and grew up on swing," says Chamberlain. "I just basically used the word 'blue,' and went after it. You take a word, like 'wall,' you're gonna come up with 'Hello Walls,' 'Four Walls,' you're gonna come up with the songs eventually.

"I did 'blue' that way—'Blue Orleans,' 'Am I Blue,' 'Have I Got Some Blues For You,' 'It Was Blues To Me'—on and on." "Am I Blue" is the best-known title from Chamberlain's blue period.

"It took a while to write it," he remembers. "I really had George Strait in mind, and he turned it down twice."

Rarely has a country rhythm section played any tighter than the "Am I Blue" studio ensemble, which included drummer Owen Hale and bassist Lee Sklar. George still speaks of the record rather matter-of-factly: "It was just one of those little swing tunes that I enjoy doin' so much. I used to do all swing if I could in the old days, when we were playin' the clubs. We almost did four hours of Wills and whatever else we could do."

"Am I Blue" became Strait's fifth consecutive number one record, and Chamberlain couldn't have been happier. In 1986, Strait had pressed up David's song "Stranger Things Have Happened" as a single, but Larry Boone released the song first. MCA scrapped "Stranger Things" and put out "It Ain't Cool To Be Crazy About You" [see 699] instead.

745
MAYBE YOUR BABY'S GOT THE BLUES
THE JUDDS (WYNONNA & NAOMI)
RCA 5255
Writers: Troy Seals, Graham Lyle
Producer: Brent Maher
November 14, 1987 (1 week)

Traditionally, the Judds record each of their albums twice. First, Wynonna and Naomi take the songs they plan on cutting into the recording studio to make a simple demo with just themselves, producer Brent Maher and guitarist Don Potter. Once they've demoed the entire album, they eliminate any songs that don't work, then record the remainder once more with a full band. The Judds broke from that tradition with "Maybe Your Baby's Got The Blues."

Maher commissioned the song, more or less. British songwriter Graham Lyle was set to come to Nashville to write with Troy Seals, and Troy's publisher, David Conrad at Almo/Irving Music, told Brent he'd try to get the two writers to come up with something for Wynonna and Naomi.

"We were just writin' and got in on that song and it felt real good," recalls Troy. "Graham loves country, and he comes to write country—he truly does. We were workin' on 'Maybe Your Baby's Got The Blues' and Brent Maher came by the door and heard it, and said, 'What's that?'"

Seals introduced Brent and Graham, then the writers pulled up their guitars and played their unfinished version of "Maybe Your Baby's Got The Blues." Maher was suitably impressed, and invited them to come over to his Creative Workshop Studio at the end of the day to play it for Wynonna and Naomi. They completed the song after Brent left.

"At 6:00," Maher recounts, "they rolled in the studio, brought their guitars and sat down and played 'Maybe Your Baby's Got The Blues.' We just threw it on a little blaster, with Graham and Troy singin' it, and the girls liked it. That evening, we did a demo on it, and it sounded so great that we decided to keep it."

Thus, the Judds recorded the song only once for their album, although they did add other instruments in a later session. They released it as the third single from the *Heartland* album, following their Top Ten remake of "Don't Be Cruel" [see 275—"Moody Blue"] and "I Know Where I'm Going" [see 728]. "Maybe Your Baby's Got The Blues" became the Judds' tenth number one single.

746
I WON'T NEED YOU ANYMORE (ALWAYS AND FOREVER)
RANDY TRAVIS
Warner Bros. 28246
Writers: Troy Seals, Max D. Barnes
Producer: Kyle Lehning
November 21, 1987 (1 week)

"It seems like some of the things that have been the biggest moneymakers, and the biggest hits, have been things that just kind of happened," says award-winning songwriter Max D. Barnes. "Some songs, we sit around and labor with for weeks, knowin' that we got somethin', and they're still layin' on the shelf somewhere. Then some things we'll write in a few hours and they'll be hits."

"I Won't Need You Anymore," a song Barnes penned with frequent collaborator Troy Seals in 1981, fell in among their quickly-written projects. George Jones recorded it at that time for the *Still the Same Ole Me* album, and a guitar/vocal demo that Seals recorded found its way into the hands of Randy Travis and his producer, Kyle Lehning, several years later when Travis started working on his second album.

Seals and Barnes had written the title cut for Travis' first album, *Storms of Life* [see 695—"Diggin' Up Bones"], and "I Won't Need You Anymore" earned the same distinction, when Travis picked out a phrase from the first line and dubbed the album *Always & Forever*. That theme held double significance since the first single, "Forever And Ever, Amen" [see 725], tread the same territory of infinite devotion.

Travis dedicated the album to his manager, Lib Hatcher, signing it "Always and forever. Love, Randy." That message further fueled speculation about the relationship between artist and mentor, who share a converted log cabin in Ashland City, Tennessee.

"I'm his manager," Hatcher insisted to Kathy Haight of the *Charlotte Observer*. "I'm not his girlfriend, not his wife, not his mother. I'm his best friend."

That friendship caused rifts in two separate families. Hatcher first heard Travis in 1976 at a talent contest at Country City U.S.A., a club she owned in Charlotte. She made him a regular performer at the club, then purchased a new venue, taking Travis along to The Nashville Palace [see 680—"On The Other Hand"] in 1981. In the process, Hatcher's husband divorced her, and Travis encountered disapproval from his father for sharing a home with Lib, although Randy has since made up with his dad.

Hatcher's years of belief paid off handsomely, when Travis' first two albums sold more than five million copies combined. On September 20, 1987, Warner Bros. recognized Randy's achievements, presenting him a two-year-old quarterhorse—named, appropriately enough, Platinum.

LYNDA
STEVE WARINER
MCA 53160
Writers: Bill LaBounty, Pat MacLaughlin
Producer: Tony Brown
November 28, 1987 (1 week)

They titled it "Lynda," but Bill LaBounty and Pat MacLaughlin could have easily called their collaboration "The Spiderman Song."

"I've never asked Bill," offers Steve Wariner, "but I think that song was written about Lynda Carter, 'cause he's talkin' about Spiderman and Wonder Woman. I guarantee you it's Lynda Carter."

"That's coincidental," LaBounty insists, "but I met Lynda Carter real early on. I think Pat came up with the name Lynda and the 'Y' spelling. Maybe it was a subconscious thing.

"But the Spiderman line—Steve almost didn't sing it 'cause he thought it was too far-out. Then he changed his mind, and that line sort of makes the song. That's the part that everybody always remembers—the 'I'll be your Spiderman.'"

LaBounty first spotted MacLaughlin, a native Iowan, performing in Nashville. Bill called Pat the next day to tell him what a great show he had given, and they ended up writing together. "Lynda" was one of their first collaborations, and they finished it within two hours—except for one line. It took another month before they finally came up with that line.

"It started out to be a funny song," Bill says, "kind of a non-sequitur lyric, just goofy things that have a gist of a meaning, but not really. But then the chorus was just a simple romantic chorus.

"We thought it was funny, because we thought the lyrics were about this Mad Max sort of future world, after the end of civilization. It was like 'If the world explodes, I'll still love you,' and then it goes back to the chorus: 'But we'll ignore it.' I really don't know what it means. We thought it was a joke, and we actually didn't think that anybody would really want to record the song. It's one of those songs where you get together and play around and say, 'Well, that was good for today; tomorrow, we'll write a real song.'"

Guitarist Steve Gibson added an array of guitar riffs on the demo, and producer Tony Brown copied many of them note-for-note on the final product. Wariner added his own impressive guitar solo. Despite concern that it rocked too much for country radio, "Lynda" danced to number one in November of 1987.

748

SOMEBODY LIED
RICKY VAN SHELTON
Columbia 07311
Writers: Joe Chambers, Larry Jenkins
Producer: Steve Buckingham
December 5, 1987 (1 week)

Ricky Van Shelton earned his first number one record three years after leaving Grit, Virginia, for the uncertain surroundings of Nashville. Ricky and his wife had planned to move to Music City when they could save enough money, but Bettye landed a job as a corporate personnel director in the Tennessee capital, and her new income would support them both.

On December 27, 1984, they headed into town on Interstate 40, and Ricky played house-husband in a rental property not far from Opry-land. During the day, he practiced his vocal work and his songwriting, and worked up demos on a four-track machine in his basement. By night, he made the rounds of the Nashville club circuit, particularly a joint called the Nashville Palace, where he met dishwasher/Warner Bros. recording artist Randy Travis [see 680—"On The Other Hand"].

In the meantime, Bettye established a friendship with Linda Thompson, and when Linda heard Ricky rehearsing in the basement, she asked for one of his tapes. She took it home to her husband, columnist Jerry Thompson of *The Tennessean*, who eventually persuaded Columbia Records executive Rick Blackburn and producer Steve Buckingham to hear Shelton.

On June 19, 1986, the two execs caught Ricky's live act at The Stock Yard, a downtown club owned by Buddy Killen. Within two weeks, Ricky walked into a full-fledged recording studio for the first time in his life. He cut three songs on that session: "Wild-Eyed Dream," "Somebody Lied" and a cover of Ernest Tubb's "Thanks A Lot."

Columbia released "Wild-Eyed Dream" first; it reached number 24, and Shelton's second single, "Crime Of Passion," hit the Top Ten. The third, "Somebody Lied," became his

Ricky Van Shelton

first to top the chart. Conway Twitty's nephew, Larry Jenkins, co-wrote "Somebody Lied" in 1985, and it first appeared on Twitty's *Don't Call Him a Cowboy* album [see 622].

"When I got signed to CBS, Steve Buckingham already had that song squirreled back," says Shelton. "He goes through so many tapes, and [he comes across] songs that he thinks are just good songs, but he's got nobody at CBS that he thinks they're good for. So he'll set it back, waitin' for the right person. That's what he had done with 'Somebody Lied.'"

The song fit Shelton perfectly, and it hit number one in its sixteenth week on *Billboard*'s country chart.

749

THE LAST ONE TO KNOW
REBA McENTIRE
MCA 53159
Writers: Matraca Berg, Jane Mariash
Producers: Jimmy Bowen, Reba McEntire
December 12, 1987 (1 week)

Singer/songwriter Matraca [pronounced "Muh-TRACE-uh"] Berg describes her un-

K.T. Oslin

usual first name with the same term she applies to her music: "exotic hillbilly."

"I do have a relative that has that name," she adds, "a distant cousin. I think it's just a made-up hillbilly name. They do that up there."

"Up there" is Kentucky, where her mother, a former background vocalist, came from. Her mom moved to Nashville after Matraca's Aunt Sudie ("There's another name!") established herself as a session singer, and Matraca was born in Music City.

"I've always known I was gonna write songs," she says. "I thought I was gonna be a lawyer for a brief period, but, since I didn't make it out of high school, it wasn't very likely. I've always made up songs, ever since I was about four years old, so it was a pretty natural progression."

Berg earned her first number one record at age 18 [see 507—"Faking Love"] and figured that writing songs must be a pretty easy way to make a living. It didn't take long before reality set in, however, and she headed to Louisiana with a rock and roll band. After returning to Nashville, Matraca wrote for Merit Music on a song-by-song basis, and a week after her mother died, she recorded a demo of "The Last One To Know."

Three years later, Berg had gone to write for Warner Bros.' publishing house, and nothing had come of her song. Merit hired a new "song plugger," Mike Wood, who ran across the tape and pitched it around Nashville.

"They didn't tell me about it," Matraca notes. "I heard a rumor out on the street that I had a Reba McEntire cut and it was gonna be a single, and I came there. I said, 'Is this true?' It was a nice surprise."

Reba made "The Last One To Know" the title track of her 1987 album, recorded at Emerald Sound Studio. When she first cut it, however, she purposely added an extraneous word to the chorus, only to later realize it made no sense. She went back and re-recorded her vocal; the last take she did cemented Berg's second chart-topping song.

750

DO YA'
K.T. OSLIN
RCA 5239
Writer: K.T. Oslin
Producer: Harold Shedd
December 19, 1987 (1 week)

On August 8, 1987, *80's Ladies* first appeared on the *Billboard* country album chart at number 15, the highest debut ever for a female country artist's first album. The mark belonged to Kay Toinette Oslin, but at age 45, she was hardly a newcomer to show biz.

Born in Crossitt, Arkansas, Oslin wound up her high school years in Houston, where her classmates at Milby High School voted her "Miss Beatnik." Following a couple years of drama at Lon Morris College, she joined Guy Clark in the '60s to form a folk trio, then recorded a duet album with Frank Davis in Los Angeles that never hit the market.

Returning to Houston, K.T. picked up work in the chorus of a 1966 traveling production of *Hello, Dolly!*, and in July of '67, she took an 80th Street apartment on Manhattan's Upper West Side. From there, she garnered roles in *West Side Story* and *Promises, Promises*, then drifted into studio vocal work and commercials.

In the early '80s, Kay T. Oslin (as shown on the record label) appeared briefly on the *Billboard* country chart with an Elektra Records single, "Clean Your Own Tables." Though she had already written "80's Ladies" and "Younger Men"—cuts from her later debut album—the label prevented her from recording such "radical" material.

Disappointed with her initial country showing, Oslin returned to commercial work in the Big Apple, where she woke up one morning fearful that a hemorrhoid commercial would be her legacy. A stockbroker aunt from Austin invested $7,000 in her talents, and in 1985, K.T. moved to Nashville. In January of '86, she showcased her talents at a local club, attracting interest from record producer Harold Shedd, who wanted to sign her as a songwriter. They demoed some songs, and Shedd then pitched her tape to RCA, who ultimately signed her to a recording deal.

"80's Ladies," K.T.'s second RCA single, hit number seven in 1987, and she followed with "Do Ya'," cut originally at a faster tempo. Oslin still hadn't finalized her RCA agreement while making the album. Depressed, she one day started playing her songs at half-tempo. At that point, she decided "Do Ya'" worked better at the slower speed, and she re-cut the song in one take at her next session.

"Do Ya'" first appeared on the *Billboard* country singles chart on September 12, 1987, at number 64. In its fifteenth week, it carried K.T. to the number one position for the first time.

751
SOMEWHERE TONIGHT
HIGHWAY 101
Warner Bros. 28223
Writers: Rodney Crowell, Harlan Howard
Producer: Paul Worley
December 26, 1987 (2 weeks)

Minnesota's Paulette Carlson padded around the streets of Nashville for about ten years before finding success. When the brass ring finally appeared, Paulette found herself in the only band in country music to feature a female lead vocalist.

Carlson had a brief recording deal with RCA in 1983-84, but little happened. After the label released her, she decided to assess her situation pragmatically. Producer Paul Worley convinced her she needed a manager, and put her in touch with Chuck Morris, who already worked with the Nitty Gritty Dirt Band.

Morris had a concept for a country group fronted by a woman, and Paulette was the perfect choice. Their connections landed drummer Cactus Moser, bassist Curtis Stone and guitarist Jack Daniels (yes, that's his real name), and the resulting conglomerate chose Highway 101 as its monicker.

Initially, the group met some resistance. MCA almost signed them, but ultimately declined. Finally, Worley approached Warner Bros. division chief Jim Ed Norman. "I said, 'Look, this is something that I really believe in, and we're havin' trouble gettin' anywhere with it,'" Worley reports. "He said, 'If you really believe in it, you have my support—let's go make some records.'"

They headed into the studio three different times before recording something that satisfied them. That song, "The Bed You Made For Me," brought instant results after its debut in January of 1987. It shimmied its way to number four, and Warner Bros. "upped" their singles deal and rushed Highway 101 into the studio to cut an album. Their second release, "Whiskey, If You Were A Woman," got as far as number two. A third, "Somewhere Tonight," fared even better.

Rodney Crowell had the basic idea two years earlier, then teamed with Harlan Howard in an effort to emulate the Buck Owens/Harlan Howard songs of the early '60s. Harlan felt Rodney had done most of the work, and promised to make sure it got recorded. He gained some major interest, too.

"Randy Travis had cut 'Somewhere Tonight' for Warner Bros. a couple of times," Paulette recalls, "and I don't think that he felt it was right for him. They decided not to put it on the album, for some reason."

Warner executive Martha Sharp liked the song, and salvaged it for Highway 101. Less than a year after the group's debut, "Somewhere Tonight" became their first number one single.

752
I CAN'T GET CLOSE ENOUGH
EXILE
Epic 07597
Writers: Sonny Lemaire, J.P. Pennington
Producer: Elliot Scheiner
January 9, 1988 (1 week)

With the release of their *Shelter from the Night* album in 1987, Exile ended a long-running association with producer Buddy Killen in favor of Elliot Scheiner. Known for his production work with former Eagle Glenn Frey and Ashford & Simpson, Scheiner had also accrued credits as an engineer for Billy Joel, Olivia Newton-John and Steely Dan.

"That's what intrigued us," says bass player Sonny Lemaire, "that this guy who captured Grammys with his engineering work on the Bruce Hornsby album would accept us and want to work with us."

Not surprisingly, Hornsby contributed one song to the LP, "Fly On The Wall," which he co-wrote with Elton John's longtime lyricist, Bernie Taupin. Exile wrote seven of the ten cuts on the album, and one of them, "I Can't Get Close Enough," went on to become their tenth number one single.

"I'm just real proud of that song," notes Sonny. "It's one of those sentiments that really just says it all: you just can't get close enough. I'm real proud of the melody, and I'm real proud of the lyric."

"I Can't Get Close Enough" is the only number one country single ever recorded in Connecticut. The sessions were held in Stamford, an exclusive community about ten miles north of the New York stateline.

"We didn't just say 'Let's go to Stamford,'" Lemaire laughs. "Elliot lives there, right outside of Stamford, and he wanted to record at home. Initially, we thought we'd record in New York, but we found a studio, the Carriage House. It's in a gorgeous residential area up there, and Stamford is not a cheap place to live."

Exile took on a grueling schedule to make the record. During May of 1987, they toured on weekends, flying to LaGuardia Airport in New York City on Monday mornings. The group would then commute to Connecticut for four solid days of recording before flying back out again for the next weekend. They kept up that pace for a month, continued touring through the end of the summer, and finally went to L.A. to finish the project.

"We had a great time, but that album killed us," comments Lemaire. "I was home five days from May to September."

In addition to "I Can't Get Close Enough," *Shelter from the Night* yielded four more singles, with "Just One Kiss" peaking at number nine in July of 1988.

753
ONE FRIEND
DAN SEALS
Capitol 44077
Writer: Dan Seals
Producer: Kyle Lehning
January 16, 1988 (1 week)

In September of 1988, Dan Seals released a greatest-hits album, titled *The Best*. The record featured eleven songs—ten previous Top Ten singles and one "new" release, "One Friend." In actuality, "One Friend" had previously appeared on Dan's *San Antone* album, timing out at 1:55.

"From the moment it first came out," Seals recalls, "people at the record company would say, 'We ought to make a Hallmark card production out of that. It should come out at Christmas time, but it just don't fit our format of commerciality, because it ain't long enough.' A two-minute song ain't got a chance in this business."

"One Friend" did have a chance, in large part because Capitol Records promotion director Paul Lovelace believed in it so strongly. Seals, at one point, tried to lengthen the song, but it ended up sounding "redundant." Lovelace was able to make it work.

"Paul had always loved the tune," notes producer Kyle Lehning. "He'd gotten married, and for his marriage, he'd edited the thing together and made it into a longer song. Paul said, 'You guys gotta hear this, and maybe think about doin' this and puttin' it out.'

"[The first version] had no drums, just acoustic guitars, Danny and some strings. We listened to [Paul's edit and decided to] cut it again, and change the arrangement and beef it up: add some drums to it, put a little instrumental section to it. We went back in and made a new record out of a song that was on a previous album."

Adds Seals: "The reason it was so successful was not only because the lyrics were good—that played a part—but also because it came out around Christmas. It's a very sensitive time. People want to feel something. 'Rot until you puke' just don't fit on the radio. You start looking for meaningful things. That song had it, and it was requested on the radio.

"Nowadays, people come up many nights and say, 'We got married to that song.' It feels so good to have a song that people want to use on such a special day, that those lyrics are what they want to say to each other."

754
WHERE DO THE NIGHTS GO
RONNIE MILSAP
RCA 5259
Writers: Mike Reid, Rory Bourke
Producers: Ronnie Milsap, Rob Galbraith,
Kyle Lehning
January 23, 1988 (1 week)

"Where Do The Nights Go" was a very special record for Ronnie Milsap, since it featured an enchanting series of solo parts and acoustic fills by the master, Chet Atkins. Noted as a producer [see 167—"I Don't See Me In Your Eyes Anymore"], Atkins lost interest in playing the corporate game and left his executive position with RCA to return to making music. The guitar, after all, had brought him to Nashville in the first place.

Few can boast the incredible track record that Atkins enjoys. He had a few single hits as an instrumentalist, most notably 1965's "Yakety Axe," a take-off on Boots Randolph's "Yakety Sax" that propelled Atkins to number four. As a sideman, he played on hundreds of hit records, including Elvis Presley's "Heartbreak Hotel" [see 352], the Everly Brothers' "Bye, Bye Love," Don Gibson's "Oh, Lonesome Me" and the George Jones & Ray Charles single "We Didn't See A Thing."

"These stars want me on their records sometimes," says Chet, "and usually I don't even let 'em pay me. I just have 'em make a donation to the W.O. Smith School of Music that teaches music to underprivileged kids."

Atkins' presence on "Where Do The Nights Go" was a special treat for both Rory Bourke and Mike Reid, who wrote the song. They also teamed up for Gene Watson's "Back In The Fire" and Don Williams' "I Wouldn't Be A Man."

"At that time, we were gettin' together a couple of times a week," Bourke recalls. "'Where Do The Nights Go' was one of our sort of regular writing sessions, and as I remember it, we were working on verses and didn't really have the full idea on that. We worked on it a couple of times, and then that idea finally snapped in."

"It was melodically, at the time, something of a stretch for us," concurs Reid. "The title came out of just sittin' there with a groove and a melody."

Milsap recorded "Where Do The Nights Go," adhering closely to the demo's style ("Although," admits Reid, "we didn't have Chet Atkins"). The record checked in at number 61 on October 24, 1987, clearing number one thirteen weeks later.

755
GOIN' GONE
KATHY MATTEA
Mercury 888874
Writers: Patrick Alger, Bill Dale,
Fred Koller
Producer: Allen Reynolds
January 30, 1988 (1 week)

On April 1, 1967, the Country Music Hall of Fame and Museum officially opened permanent headquarters along Music Row in Nashville. Members had been added to the Hall of Fame annually since 1961, providing a tribute to well-established careers, but in the case of Kathy Mattea, the Hall represented a starting point.

Hailing from Cross Lanes, West Virginia, Mattea sang and played guitar in a collegiate bluegrass group called Pennsboro. When the bandleader set off for Nashville, Kathy went, too, landing a job as a tour guide at the Hall of Fame. Intent on writing songs for a living, she supported herself in a variety of occupations, particularly as a waitress at T.G.I. Friday's

Kathy Mattea

near Vanderbilt University; as a vocalist on demo sessions for as little as $10; and as a back-up singer for Bobby Goldsboro.

Kathy soon recognized that Nashville held more interest in her vocal work than her compositions, and she sought the help of a voice teacher, Phoebe Brinkley. As her session work increased, her voice appeared on many of the demos circulating around town, leading to a 1983 recording contract with Mercury Records. Producer Allen Reynolds—then planning to sever any relationships with major record labels—put off selling his recording studio for the chance to work with her, although Kathy herself nearly quit too soon.

Two albums and seven singles failed to signal a clear musical direction, and when Mercury went through an executive overhaul, the label froze recording funds just as Mattea started work on the third album. Frustrated, she considered packing it in, but ended up recording the pivotal *Walk the Way the Wind Blows*. It yielded a quartet of Top Ten singles—"Love At The Five & Dime," the title cut, "You're The Power" and "Train Of Memories." With her next album, *Untasted Honey*, Kathy savored her first number one single, "Goin' Gone."

"We sweated gettin' that song," Reynolds reports. "It was out by Nanci Griffith on one of her albums on Rounder Records. Meanwhile, the Forester Sisters cut it, but their label ended up chuckin' it. There were other people that were interested in that song anyway, so we were really glad that it still hadn't found a home when it came time for us to record. That's also among the reasons it was the first single off that album."

756

WHEELS
RESTLESS HEART
RCA 5280
Writer: Dave Loggins
Producers: Tim DuBois, Scott Hendricks,
Restless Heart
February 6, 1988 (1 week)

When Restless Heart topped the *Billboard* country chart with the title track from the *Wheels* album, they became only the second band in country music history to earn four number one singles from the same album. "(There's) A Fire In The Night" [see 604] made Alabama the first. Ironically, Restless Heart's fourth chart-topping hit was an Alabama reject [see 562—"Roll On (Eighteen Wheeler)"].

"Our whole first album was passed on by Alabama—seriously!" says Restless Heart keyboard player Dave Innis. "All of the songs that we recorded were Alabama-pitched rejects. That kind of stuff happens all the time. We passed up a song that was pitched to us by John Scott Sherrill and Bob DiPiero. They ran it by us, and we said, 'Naw, it's not us.' Shenandoah recorded it, called 'Church On Cumberland Road' [see 814]. It was number one for two weeks for them, and we turned it down. I guarantee you that if we passed on it, Alabama heard it first.

"But some things are right for some artists and not for another. Had Restless Heart recorded that song, it wouldn't have been a number one record probably, because it wouldn't have been our personality. That's why you either take a song or pass a song."

In the case of "Wheels"—the first song they chose for their second album—Restless Heart didn't even hear the song until the Bellamy Brothers had already recorded it for the *Howard & David* album. They didn't find out that the Bellamys had done it until they had already committed to record it—then they refused to listen to the Bellamy version, because they didn't want that performance to influence their own arrangement.

Ultimately, "Wheels" proved appropriate for the group. Both Innis and Larry Stewart consider songwriter Dave Loggins a personal friend, and the song's "highway" theme had become a routine part of the band's existence.

"[It seems like] we've been traveling from town to town, never really stopping except to set up and play," notes Innis. "Then it seems like we're off to another town, and that's what 'Wheels' is about—living on the road."

In March of 1988, Restless Heart picked up their first gold record for the *Wheels* album. Comically, their management company gave John Dittrich a misspelled plaque, incorrectly awarded to *Jim* Dittrich.

757
TENNESSEE FLAT TOP BOX
ROSANNE CASH
Columbia 07624
Writer: Johnny Cash

Producer: Rodney Crowell
February 13, 1988 (1 week)

As the daughter of Johnny Cash, one might assume that Rosanne Cash had an easy "in" to the record business. In fact, her heritage was something of a burden for Rosanne during much of her life.

As a youngster, Rosanne was teased by her classmates in Ventura, California, for having a hillbilly as a father, and she had fits when he tried to force her to learn 100 country classics. She eventually accepted her parental ties, though she refused to draw on them in her career. Rosanne didn't secure Johnny's help to get a recording contract, even though she ended up signing with Columbia Records [see 426—"Seven Year Ache"], where Johnny also recorded.

She did tour with Johnny briefly during the '70s, but she made music her own way. She purposely separated her career from her father's at the start, and when she began to ease up, Rosanne recorded "That's How I Got To Memphis" as a duet with her father for the *Somewhere in the Stars* album. On *King's Record Shop*, she turned in a new, "sonically updated" version of "Tennessee Flat Top Box," a 1962 hit for Johnny that had peaked at number 11. She knew that he'd recorded it, but didn't realize her dad had also written it.

"I'd known the song my whole life," she says, "and I thought something I'd known my whole life has gotta be public domain. But Rodney [Crowell] kept saying, 'You know, I think your dad wrote this tune.' So he got the tape from the Country Music Hall of Fame archives, and it turned out that my dad *had* written it. I went, 'Well, of course, who else could have written this song?' It was immensely satisfying to sing it, having known it since I was three. It was like singing a lullaby that you'd heard from your childhood."

In *Billboard's* February 13, 1988, issue, "Tennessee Flat Top Box" reached number one on the country chart. Johnny took out a full-page ad that week, thanking his daughter for remaking it.

"A lot of people have made such a big deal out of the fact that you didn't know that I wrote 'Tennessee Flat Top Box' when you recorded it," the ad read. "I'm glad you didn't.

"I could never put into words how much it meant to me that you recorded my song. Your success with 'Tennessee Flat Top Box' is one of my life's greatest fulfillments. I love you, Dad."

758

TWINKLE, TWINKLE LUCKY STAR

MERLE HAGGARD

Epic 07631
Writer: Merle Haggard
Producers: Ken Suesov, Merle Haggard
February 20, 1988 (1 week)

Merle Haggard celebrated the twenty-fifth anniversary of his first appearance in *Billboard* during the last week of 1988. Earlier in the year, "Twinkle, Twinkle Lucky Star" became the thirty-eighth number one single in that lengthy period of time.

"Earlier on, his voice was higher and he sang songs in a higher key," notes steel player Norm Hamlet. "I think now that he's mellowed, he's actually better. We've lowered the keys, some of them, and he seems to have more body, more quality. He's always had that, but it just seems to come out better now."

Haggard tested his range in "Twinkle," displaying a bit of doo-wop influence in a record that contained a rather unusual trumpet solo. Merle wrote it on his houseboat at a time when his frequent co-writer, Freddy Powers, was sleeping in his own houseboat on Lake Shasta.

"This one morning," Merle recounts, "I was thinking about how Bob Wills and Tommy Duncan had written the words to old fiddle tunes. I thought about this old fiddle tune called 'Twinkle, Twinkle Little Star.' I worked and worked, and I finally realized there just wasn't no way to write no words with that thing. So, I just wrote a 1955 rock-and-roll style 'Twinkle, Twinkle Lucky Star.'

"I had it about half-written, and I went over to wake Freddy up, and Freddy said he had a cold or something. I said, 'Well, I'm writing a number one song—you're gonna be sorry.' As luck would have it, I was right."

"Twinkle" marked the first time that Ken Suesov (pronounced "SUE-uh-sov") ascended to the top as a producer. Suesov had worked at Tom Jones' Britannia studio in Hollywood as an engineer, contributing to Merle's *Big City* album [see 467] and Shelly West's "Jose Cuervo" [see 518].

In the nearly three years that had transpired since his last number one [see 623—"Natural High"], Haggard earned several other Top Ten hits: the autobiographical "Kern River" (number 10), "I Had A Beautiful Time" (number five) and "A Friend In California" (number nine). Nineteen eighty-seven marked the first

time since his chart debut that he didn't earn a Top Ten single.

Merle followed up "Twinkle, Twinkle Lucky Star" with "Chill Factor," the seventeenth Top Ten record of his career.

759

I WON'T TAKE LESS THAN YOUR LOVE

TANYA TUCKER WITH PAUL DAVIS & PAUL OVERSTREET

Capitol 44100
Writers: Paul Overstreet, Don Schlitz
Producer: Jerry Crutchfield
February 27, 1988 (1 week)

With her return to prominence in 1986, Tanya Tucker displayed an incredible amount of consistency. After "Just Another Love" [see 692] reached number one, she garnered a number two release, with "I'll Come Back As Another Woman"; a number eight single, with "It's Only Over For You"; and another number two, with "Love Me Like You Used To."

Tanya's next release returned her to number one, and it proved to be a very special record, particularly for songwriter Paul Overstreet. Frequent writing partner Don Schlitz had first conceived the idea for "I Won't Take Less Than Your Love," and offered to let Paul write it alone. Overstreet insisted they work together on it, though, and they finished it up about 10:00 one evening on Paul's front porch—the same place they wrote "Forever And Ever, Amen" [see 725] for Randy Travis.

Schlitz played the song on a guitar for producer Jerry Crutchfield, who instantly recognized it as a perfect vehicle for a trio.

"We tried a couple different things," Tucker remembers. "We were gonna do George Jones, we were gonna do Don Williams, and I decided, 'Hey, I got two of the greatest singers in Nashville, two of the greatest writers, why not do it with them?' I'd rather do it with some unknowns than do it with someone that's well-known. That way, I can introduce the fans to some people that I like."

Indeed, it was a pivotal record for Overstreet. At the time they submitted the song to Crutchfield, Overstreet was one-third of Schuyler, Knobloch & Overstreet [see 712—"Baby's Got A New Baby"]. He had just made the decision to leave that ongoing trio when

Crutchfield called to ask if he'd like to take part in this short-term assembly. Within a year, Overstreet was on his way to a successful solo career.

"The song really puts it all in a nutshell about life in general," surmises Tucker, "and we all sang a different verse that really goes with our lives. Paul Davis talking about the farmer, because that's what he wants to be; me talking about the mother and the son, because I'm very family-oriented; and Paul Overstreet talking about the Lord, which he's very involved with. Each of the verses fit us so well, and everything fell into place."

760

FACE TO FACE

ALABAMA

RCA 5328
Writer: Randy Owen
Producers: Harold Shedd, Alabama
March 5, 1988 (1 week)

With their 1987 album *Just Us*, Alabama put themselves on the line as songwriters, composing each of the album's nine tracks. They selected "Tar Top" as the first single [see 716—" 'You've Got' The Touch"], and followed with "Face To Face," a song that differed from any Randy Owen had ever written before. Usually, Owen writes his songs only after being inspired by a specific event [see 434—

"Feels So Right"]. In this instance, though, he had a melodic progression before he ever conceived the first line. It led to a passionate rendering of an explicit subject.

"The feeling behind the song is real simple," Owen explains. "Over the years, it's been my experience that you can make love in every position in the world, but it usually ends up bein' face to face when it has real meaning. If you really care for that person, you really enjoy seein' them enjoy the feeling as much as you enjoy what you're feeling.

"The line on the song that sums it up to me—I went on and on tryin' to find somethin' like a conclusion, like a climax, if you will—was, 'We happen face to face.' That's how simple it was, but it took forever to work that up. Not I or you, but '*We* happen face to face.' "

After years of resisting duets, Alabama felt that a female voice might complement Owen's performance and solidify the image of two people becoming one. They wanted a lady to add just a few lines at the end of the record, and considered several other people before deciding on K.T. Oslin. Owen had become a fan of her single "80's Ladies," and they also realized that this move could be easily accomplished—K.T. worked with producer Harold Shedd, and also recorded for RCA. The guys weren't even around when she laid down an experimental vocal track.

"We didn't know if we would use it when we did it," says Shedd. "We didn't know if the guys would like it or not, but as it turned out, it did add a little touch to it."

761

TOO GONE TOO LONG
RANDY TRAVIS

Warner Bros. 28286
Writer: Gene Pistilli
Producer: Kyle Lehning
March 12, 1988 (1 week)

"I think one of Randy Travis' appeals as an artist is this kind of an angel/devil thing," notes producer Kyle Lehning. "He's got this real sweet side, but, at the same time, there's a sort of glint in his eyes. There's something crazy about 'Too Gone Too Long.' Randy has a really interesting sense of humor, and I think there's an irony to that tune."

"Too Gone Too Long" came to Randy from a source that might seem unusual on the sur-

Randy Travis

face: a native of urban Fairview, New Jersey, whose resumé connects him with Spanky & Our Gang, Bette Midler and the Manhattan Transfer. Gene Pistilli penned Spanky's only Top Ten hit, "Sunday Will Never Be The Same"; started the Transfer with Tim Hauser in 1972; and composed two Midler songs, "Gave My Soul To Rock 'N' Roll" (for *The Rose*) and "Pretty Legs And Great Big Knockers" (for *Art or Bust*). "Knockers" co-writer Teddy Irwin convinced Pistilli to try Nashville, and Gene moved in 1985, giving himself two years to make it.

"Too Gone Too Long" emerged as a single at the end of his deadline, although the legwork went into it a year earlier. Pistilli started the song with a vision of an Eagles-like midtempo harmony number, doused it with the Western swing of Bob Wills, then recorded a demo that he compares to Doc Watson. After numerous rejections, Gene took the song to Margie Hunt at Columbia Records the day before Thanksgiving in 1986.

"Gene Watson was supposed to do a duet album with George Jones," Pistilli explains. "So I went over to see Margie, and I played her the song, and she said, 'That album's not gonna happen soon, if it happens at all. You oughta try to get this song to Randy Travis.' I literally said, 'Randy who?' She said, 'You'll know his name real soon.'"

Pistilli had one more appointment left for 4:00, and nearly blew it off, but forced himself to see Almo Music's David Conrad. Conrad mentioned Travis as well, and took the song that night to Warner Bros.' Martha Sharp, who needed to find one more song for Randy's second album.

Randy recorded "Too Gone Too Long" in a last-minute session that Sunday. It became his fifth number one record—and his second with a Thanksgiving heritage [see 695—"Diggin' Up Bones"].

762

LIFE TURNED HER THAT WAY
RICKY VAN SHELTON

Columbia 07672
Writer: Harlan Howard
Producer: Steve Buckingham
March 19, 1988 (1 week)

As a youngster, Ricky Van Shelton preferred the Beatles and the Rolling Stones to Roy

Acuff and Buck Owens, but a trip to a service station with his brother, Ronnie, changed that outlook. More than twenty people—from teens to senior citizens—were picking guitars and swapping songs there, and Shelton heard something special.

"I started fallin' in love with country music in the middle of the '60s," he says. "By 1970, I was totally hooked."

Along the way, Ricky missed a 1967 hit for Mel Tillis. When he finally heard it twenty years later, "Life Turned Her That Way" turned into a number one single.

"I think it kind of fits my philosophy," says songwriter Harlan Howard, explaining the song's good-woman-gone-bad storyline, a composite of several ladies he knew. "I do believe that in most relationships, if there's a bad guy, it's the guy. If anybody's gonna cheat, normally it's the guy. If anybody loses their ego and has to go out and get in an affair, it's the guy, in most cases. That's just the way it is. Most of the heartaches in this world seem to occur to women."

Howard first gave the song to "Little" Jimmy Dickens, noted for novelty records like "Take An Old Cold 'Tater (And Wait)" and "A-Sleeping At The Foot Of The Bed." Though Harlan liked Dickens' ballads, he correctly figured that the song wouldn't be a hit.

Dickens threw it on the "B" side of "May The Bird Of Paradise Fly Up Your Nose," a novelty tune that became his only number one single in 1965. Mel Tillis heard "Life Turned Her That Way," and, despite Howard's misgivings ("Jimmy Dickens sung the hell out of it"), Mel took it to number 11 in 1967.

Ricky never heard Tillis' version, but Steve Buckingham played it for him when they worked on Shelton's first album, and they recorded it, with one major alteration.

"Mel's version of 'Life Turned Her That Way' was a waltz," Ricky explains. "Steve and I changed it to 4/4 time, and actually, after we changed it, we found out from Harlan that he wrote it in 4/4. We didn't know that—we just thought it would sound better that way."

763

TURN IT LOOSE
THE JUDDS
(WYNONNA & NAOMI)
RCA 5329

Writers: Don Schlitz, Craig Bickhardt, Brent Maher
Producer: Brent Maher
March 26, 1988 (1 week)

"Traveling," says Wynonna Judd, "gives us a chance to be so plugged in to middle America, to the folks that are the salt of the earth. The album *Heartland*, that's exactly where that title came from—the heartland, the people who are the foundation, who keep this great country running."

Traveling figured heavily for the Judds on a very unusual day, August 27, 1988. They performed in San Diego during the afternoon for President Ronald Reagan, then flew to the heartland to appear with Randy Travis at the Iowa State Fair in Des Moines. They kept their audience waiting only an extra five minutes that windy night, and their repertoire included their latest number one record, "Turn It Loose."

"I really get aggravated at people that are cool and reserved," Wynonna says. "The person in the front row who's sitting there with his girlfriend, and everything—I'm always saying to people, 'Don't be so concerned with being cool.' 'Turn It Loose' is exactly that message—'Excu-u-use me, but . . .'—and put on your shouting shoes. If you think about it, you go out and you purchase a pair of shoes, and they're really, like, outrageous, then it changes your attitude. Or you put on something that just makes you want to go out in the streets and direct traffic. That was exactly the song's message."

"Attitude" was exactly what Brent Maher and Craig Bickhardt had in mind when they wrote "Turn It Loose." Bickhardt had the basic "groove music" for the tune, and they proceeded to write it specifically as a performance song for the Judds.

"We weren't thinkin' about a single or anything," notes Maher. "We were just thinkin' it would be fun to write something like that, that we could have a real attitude about, and just have them really enjoyin' it on stage. We could almost envision them acting it out on stage while we were writin' it."

"Turn It Loose" reached number one on March 26, 1988, and by the time they reached Iowa five months later, the Judds owned a piece of history. They formed Pro Tours, making them the first female act to own its own booking agency (Loretta Lynn *co*-owned an agency with Conway Twitty [see 87—"Lead Me On"]).

764

LOVE WILL FIND ITS WAY TO YOU

REBA McENTIRE

MCA 53244
Writers: Dave Loggins, J.D. Martin
Producers: Jimmy Bowen, Reba McEntire
April 2, 1988 (1 week)

On October 12, 1987, Reba McEntire established a new Country Music Association record when she took home her fourth consecutive trophy for Female Vocalist of the Year. The following March 21, she set the same mark with the Academy of Country Music. That week, the Gallup Youth Survey cited Reba among teens' ten favorite female singers— even more popular than Pat Benatar, Stevie Nicks and Cyndi Lauper. Two weeks later, she earned her tenth number one single with "Love Will Find Its Way To You."

"The way that came about," says songwriter J.D. Martin, "I was in the studio just practicing the piano one day, and I had that opening introduction worked out. Dave [Loggins] walked in the room while I was playin' that, and from that kind of introduction, we started writing the song.

"I thought that song would never make it on country radio. The original demo sounded a little more pop. It was more keyboard-oriented, and she did it with guitars, which helped take it back into country, I guess. But it was one of those tunes that I never knew what to do with."

McEntire was immediately drawn to the song, as she often is with Loggins compositions. The first time she went to MCA Music to see Loggins, he played her ten songs, and she took nine to record.

"I'm a big fan of Dave Loggins—his singin', his writin', everything about him," Reba admits, "and we needed an uptempo tune real bad. I don't do uptempo stuff as good as everything else. To me, when I do an uptempo song, I have to make it lilt like a woman will twist when she's walkin' down the street. Sometimes the band will [play it choppy], and I don't like it choppy. I want some swing to it, a little bounce, so I can kind of walk across stage while I'm singin'."

Martin used to occupy the stage as a member of Tanglefoot, a Midwestern band based in Aspen. After making an album in 1978 with Paul Rothchild (who produced albums by the Doors and Janis Joplin), Tanglefoot relocated to Nashville in 1980. There, the group broke up; Martin became one of the city's premier songwriters, and, briefly in 1986, a recording artist for Capitol Records.

765

FAMOUS LAST WORDS OF A FOOL

GEORGE STRAIT

MCA 53248
Writers: Dean Dillon, Rex Huston
Producers: Jimmy Bowen, George Strait
April 9, 1988 (1 week)

"Famous Last Words Of A Fool" first appeared on the *Billboard* country chart on November 12, 1983. Songwriter Dean Dillon made that recording, which went to number 67. It marked the last single Dean recorded for RCA. He had to wait another five years to make a record, returning briefly on the Capitol label.

As Dillon prepared his first Capitol album, George Strait gave "Famous Last Words Of A Fool" new life.

"That was written right after my first ex-wife left me," Dean recalls. "She left me that song, evidently, 'cause she took everything else I had."

Initially, Strait and producer Jimmy Bowen recorded simply as a "piece of business." The latter is a phrase Bowen uses regularly, and he often cites Conway Twitty's "That's My Job" to make his point.

"I ask artists to find three or four songs that are just perfect for country radio," Bowen explains. "The rest of the album should be pieces of business, that show off the artist's talent. They cause the album to be a show, with an open and a close, so that there's pace to an album. You can put it on and listen to it and be entertained, re-live the concert experience.

"Occasionally, a piece of business turns out to be a hit. That's when you really sell records."

" 'Famous Last Words' is one of my favorite songs that I've done," George adds. "It wasn't really a big, impact-type record for me, but it was such a pretty song. I don't think it really caught on like I thought it would."

"Famous Last Words Of A Fool" had a big enough impact that the same month it hit number one, the album *If You Ain't Lovin' (You Ain't Livin')* was certified as Strait's tenth gold album. The only album that hadn't gone gold was his Christmas record.

On May 5, Strait released *George Strait Live!*, a 52-minute video shot on New Year's Eve of 1986, at a sold-out show at Reunion Arena in Dallas. He received a platinum video award for that project. In 1989, he opened George Strait's Texas Connection near Music Row in Nashville, where all of the gold and platinum awards remain on display.

766

I WANNA DANCE WITH YOU

EDDIE RABBITT

RCA 5238
Writers: Eddie Rabbitt,
Billy Joe Walker, Jr.
Producer: Richard Landis
April 16, 1988 (1 week)

"I Wanna Dance With You" represented something of a comeback for Eddie Rabbitt as a songwriter. Though he earned a number one single with Juice Newton on "Both To Each Other" [see 691], he hadn't actually written a chart-topping song for three years.

The death of his son, Timmy, had caused him to pull away from his work and concentrate more on the family. Once he and Janine had another (healthy) son, Tommy, in 1986, Eddie was ready to devote his attentions to music once more.

Actually, Rabbitt didn't fare too badly in the interim. The *Best Year of My Life* album and *Rabbitt Trax* yielded a total of two number one singles and three more Top Ten records. He experimented on *Rabbitt Trax* in particular, recording side two in New York with producer Phil Ramone, noted for his work with Billy Joel and Paul Simon. Eddie cut side one with Juice's producer, Richard Landis, who stayed with Rabbitt through the next album as well.

Coming out of his personal depression, "I Wanna Dance With You" demonstrated Rabbitt's rediscovered energy for music. He composed it with guitar player Billy Joe Walker, Jr., at the studio console during a recording session. Eddie's father used to play fiddle and accordion in an Irish band in Jersey, and Eddie affects the dialect when explaining his father's contributions.

"We were at a dance one time, and he pointed to a fat, ugly girl down in the corner, down a row of empty chairs. Everybody was out dancing, she was sittin' there by herself.

"He said to me, something to the effect of,

'See that girl down there? Now, that's a shame that nobody's dancin' with her. She's a lonely girl. I'll tell you somethin'. When you grow up, the best thing you can do is go over and ask that girl to dance. It only takes three or four minutes out of your life, and you're gonna make her whole night, and you'll be more of a man if you do something like that.'

"At the time, I thought, 'Yuck, who'd wanna dance with her?' But when I grew up, I saw the wisdom of his words, that to make someone else happy is to make yourself happy. So with that in mind, I wrote the song 'I Wanna Dance With You.'"

767

I'LL ALWAYS COME BACK

K.T. OSLIN

RCA 5330
Writer: K.T. Oslin
Producer: Harold Shedd
April 23, 1988 (1 week)

K.T. Oslin's songwriting career started in 1978, while she was touring the Southeast with an electronic band. At a cafe in Due West, South Carolina, Oslin noticed a line scrawled on the wall of the ladies room: "I ain't gonna love nobody but Cornell Crawford."

K.T. didn't know Cornell, but the name intrigued her, and she concocted a storyline and a melody around that piece of American graffiti. Oslin didn't write again for a year, then waited another six months to compose her third song. Finally, two years after "Cornell," she wrote a song she really liked and, to her surprise, found herself working toward a goal she never imagined.

"I thought I had as much chance of becoming a songwriter as I did of becoming a shepherd in Manhattan," she told Dennis Hunt of the *Los Angeles Times*. "Me, a songwriter? What a laugh!"

Nashville's female set took her quite seriously, however. Gail Davies recorded "'Round The Clock Lovin'" in 1981, and Sissy Spacek cut "Lonely But Only For You" (with Rodney Crowell producing) in 1983. K.T. also landed cuts with Dottie West, Judy Rodman and the Judds.

Around 1982, Oslin's writing took on new dimensions with the aid of a drum machine. She first wrote "Younger Men" [see 750—"Do

Ya'"] with a mechanical aid, then wrote "I'll Always Come Back" and "80's Ladies."

"I just kept on writing and I kept getting better," K.T. said to Hank Gallo of the *New York Daily News*. "And I got better as a singer. And I kept listening to the radio and I said, 'There ain't nothing on here that I can't compete with. I may not be better, but I can compete with that.'"

Given the chance by RCA, K.T. backed up that bold statement in 1988—ten years after "Cornell Crawford" prodded her songwriting journey. "I'll Always Come Back"—tying in unique images of sheep and boomerangs—brought her back to number one on April 23 for the second time. One month earlier, the *80's Ladies* album went gold, and in May of 1989, it hit the platinum level after selling a million copies.

768

IT'S SUCH A SMALL WORLD
RODNEY CROWELL & ROSANNE CASH
Columbia 07693

Writer: Rodney Crowell
Producers: Tony Brown, Rodney Crowell
April 30, 1988 (1 week)

All the elements of Rodney Crowell's first number one single were in place for several years. Nashville had been pulling for him since the release of his first album, ten years earlier, and many had hoped for a duet with Rosanne Cash for almost as long. In addition, the song that brought him to the top, "It's Such A Small World," was written about five years before its release.

"Rosanne found out I had never been to a Broadway play," Rodney recalls. "This was '83, I think, and it became a mission to her: 'You've never been to a Broadway play? Well, come on.' So she set it all up, brought me to New York, got second-row seats for a play called *Nine*, and I was blown away by live performance, by the dialogue.

"I went back to where we were staying and sat down and wrote this song. I had it in mind that I wanted to write a song that was dialogue, one person speaking to another."

"My dad had this incredible penthouse on Central Park South," Rosanne continues, "which had this incredible view of the park,

Rodney Crowell & Rosanne Cash

Highway 101

and all the way down Central Park West. Rodney would sit on this balcony and write all day long. He goes, 'I want you to help me write this song,' and I said, 'Aw, I'm gonna go to Bloomingdale's—you write it.' Hindsight, I'm thinking, 'How stupid!'"

Rodney immediately pegged it as a duet to record with Rosanne, but their first effort didn't work. He brought the song in to producer Tony Brown when they started work on his *Diamonds & Dirt* album.

"He played 'It's Such A Small World' for me, and I said, 'God, that's a hit,'" Brown says. "We cut it, and Rodney said he still didn't like the way we cut it, but he was in the mood to just be a team player. He says to this day that he still doesn't like the version that we did.

"We decided after hearing it that it should be the first single. We thought, 'Let's be scientific about this: if Rodney Crowell's gonna be a star, what better from a brand new album than a duet with Rosanne? It's a guaranteed hit.'"

769
CRY, CRY, CRY
HIGHWAY 101
Warner Bros. 28105
Writers: John Scott Sherrill, Don Devaney
Producer: Paul Worley
May 7, 1988 (1 week)

Anyone who saw the title before they heard the song might have thought that Highway 101's "Cry, Cry, Cry" was a reworking of Johnny Cash's very first recording on Sun Records. In fact, the song was relatively new when publisher Woody Bomar first played it for producer Paul Worley.

"I wrote that with Don Devaney," remembers John Scott Sherrill. "He's one of my favorite people in the world. He's a character, an absolute off-the-wall character. At times he'll

519

be talking to you and just take off all his clothes—not because he's being sexual or anything. It's just that the feeling of clothing becomes too much to handle, so you're writing a song with him, and you turn around, and he won't have any clothes on."

Devaney is perhaps best known for writing "Someone Loves You Honey" [see 307] for Charley Pride. "Cry, Cry, Cry" came rather quickly once he teamed up with Sherrill—and Devaney kept his clothing on throughout the process.

"We had that idea—'It's a little creek now, but when the rain comes down, it's gonna be a ragin' river'—and a melody to go with it," John Scott elaborates, "and I thought that was one of the greatest opening lines I'd ever heard in my life. We just sat down and banged it out at the little upstairs room at Combine Music. We didn't have the chorus until Devaney said, 'Cry,' and I said, 'Cry,' and he said, 'Cry.'"

Highway 101 recorded the song the same week as "Somewhere Tonight" [see 751], in between concert dates as an opening act for George Strait. A year later, they lofted it into the *Billboard* country chart at number 49 in its first week, February 13, 1988. A dozen weeks after that, "Cry, Cry, Cry" dropped into the number one slot.

In the interim, Highway 101 picked up honors from the Academy of Country Music for Vocal Group of the Year. They were so certain that they wouldn't win that bandmember Curtis Stone went on his honeymoon instead of attending the show. That program started a trend: Highway 101 captured the Vocal Group trophies from both the ACM and the Country Music Association for 1988 and 1989.

770

I'M GONNA GET YOU

EDDY RAVEN

RCA 6831
Writer: Dennis Linde
Producer: Barry Beckett
May 14, 1988 (1 week)

Eddy Raven occasionally calls himself "The Rodney Dangerfield of Country Music." If he gets little or no respect, the same could be said of the Cajun music he grew up with.

Raven played with Buckwheat Zydeco in his youth, as well as the Rocking Cajuns, the Swing Kings and the Boogie Kings, among others. Likewise, he played the blues with Johnny and Edgar Winter, but gave up that pursuit because he didn't like the chemically-supported atmosphere.

Keyboard player Barry Beckett hoped to capture some of Raven's influences when he took over as Eddy's record producer after the death of Don Gant [see 742—"Shine, Shine, Shine"]. Beckett received an advance from RCA to produce five sides on Raven, and three appeared on *The Best of Eddy Raven*: "I'm Gonna Get You," "Joe Knows How To Live" [see 786] and "'Til You Cry."

"I told him that I wanted to totally change him, takin' a little of the calypso out, and introducin' some new elements," Beckett explains. "A lot of people had overlooked the fact that he knows the blues well, 'cause he's from a part of Louisiana where the blues came out of.

"I wanted to get a little bit more blues in him, if possible, and get those tracks crackin', get a harder sound on the tracks. I started lookin' for a good Cajun song. I had been down to [Louisiana] about six months earlier, and I went around and heard some of the music in the dance halls. I couldn't understand why nobody could cut a good Cajun hit."

Beckett came across songwriter Dennis Linde's "I'm Gonna Get You." Billy Swan was the first to release it, hitting number 63 in 1987. Raven and Beckett mirrored Linde's demo, and further enhanced it with Mike Lawler imitating a Cajun accordion on synthesizer. "We put the Cajun words and the Cajun attitude in it," Raven notes, "and gave it that little loose drum sound, and it became a big record."

"I'm Gonna Get You" snapped in at number 57 on the *Billboard* country chart for the week of February 13, 1988. Thirteen lucky weeks later, it rocked and rollicked its way into the number one position.

771

EIGHTEEN WHEELS AND A DOZEN ROSES

KATHY MATTEA

Mercury 870148
Writers: Paul Nelson, Gene Nelson
Producer: Allen Reynolds
May 21, 1988 (2 weeks)

Brothers Paul and Gene Nelson wrote "Eighteen Wheels And A Dozen Roses" about their aunt and uncle, Hop and Louise Langley, of Washington, North Carolina. When the Nelsons visited the Langley household in their youth, Hop was usually on the road, and Louise frequently spoke of the day when he could retire and trade in his truck for a Winnebago.

Once he received his gold watch, the Langleys did just that, and in 1984, Paul and Gene—now writing songs in Nashville—decided the final drive of a retiring trucker could provide an interesting storyline. They concocted the title, then left it for a year, finally completing "Eighteen Wheels And A Dozen Roses" in 1986. In the process, they substituted their grandfather's name, Charlie, for Hop.

Pat Higdon of Warner Bros. Music put together a lengthy tape of the Nelsons' material, and gave it to Kathy Mattea, who found "Eighteen Wheels" in the middle. Kathy then played several of the songs for producer Allen Reynolds. She told Reynolds that she liked "Eighteen Wheels" best, and after hearing the tape, he agreed that it was a winner. She assumed that with the "truckin'" theme, a man would record it, and when Mattea asked Allen who he thought should do it, he insisted that she cut it.

Like the Reynolds-produced "Don't It Make My Brown Eyes Blue" [see 292], "Eighteen Wheels" went down in one take. "It was no problem," Allen recalls. "It just fell right into place, and when we came in and listened to the playback, everybody said, 'Yeah, that's the cut.' Kathy said, 'That was easy. What are we gonna do next?' It's a funny thing how some of those special ones come together that way."

Even while "Goin' Gone" [see 755] broke out, radio stations picked up "Eighteen Wheels" off the *Untasted Honey* album, with Jay Phillips of Oklahoma City's KXXY leading the push to make it a follow-up single. "Eighteen Wheels" spent two weeks at number one, the first record by a solo female artist to do so since "You're The Only One" [see 348]. At the time "Eighteen Wheels" peaked, Kathy was on tour with her band in Europe.

"When we left, things were normal," she told Neil Pond of the *Music City News*, "but when we came back, the phones were smokin' and everybody was going nuts."

"Eighteen Wheels" earned Single Record of the Year honors from the Country Music Association and the Academy of Country Music; the ACM also named it the Song of the Year. In addition, the title appeared in the dialogue of the film *Rain Man*.

772
WHAT SHE IS (IS A WOMAN IN LOVE)
EARL THOMAS CONLEY

RCA 6894
Writers: Bob McDill, Paul Harrison
Producers: Emory Gordy, Jr., Randy L. Scruggs, Earl Thomas Conley
June 4, 1988 (1 week)

After a lengthy series of hits with Nelson Larkin [see 743—"Right From The Start"], Earl Thomas Conley teamed with Randy Scruggs [see 630—"Love Don't Care (Whose Heart It Breaks)"] to produce *The Heart of It All* in 1988. Doubting themselves, they also secured the assistance of Emory Gordy, Jr. Conley wrote just three songs for the project, turning to Bob McDill for the first single, "What She Is (Is A Woman In Love)."

"I don't know how many months we worked on 'What She Is,' off and on," says McDill of his collaboration with Paul Harrison. "It's so deceptively simple. It sounds like Earl Thomas made it up when he walked in the studio, but that's the hardest thing to achieve—that simplicity—and say something, too.

"Earl's cut just knocked us out. Believe it or not, he was actually apologetic, because he thought he hadn't phrased it the way I phrased it on the demo. But his version was better. The way he phrased it took it to another level. No apologies were required."

"Earl was having problems with the phrasing," Gordy confirms, "and we went in and made our own little demo of it, and finally Earl got comfortable with the phrasing. Earl's not one to copy someone else's phrasing. He has his own way of delivering it, and when he does deliver it to his satisfaction, it's definitely his for the rest of eternity."

Conley felt the song was somewhat chauvinistic, since it depicted the woman in a saintly manner, selflessly devoted to her man and willing to put up with his lack of consideration.

"I can relate to this song," Earl admits, "'cause I went through that with my own family, my own life and everything. I've always been dedicated to her, but not as much as she was dedicated to me. Lookin' at it from where I'm at right now, I don't think that she deserves to sit at home and put up with all this shit, you know. Nevertheless, that's the way the old school was. I knew that an awful lot of people who are out there still feel this way. And I thought the song was very commercial."

Earl was right. "What She Is" was his fifteenth number one single.

773

I TOLD YOU SO
RANDY TRAVIS
Warner Bros. 27969
Writer: Randy Travis
Producer: Kyle Lehning
June 11, 1988 (2 weeks)

Born May 4, 1961, in Marshville, North Carolina, Randy Travis came by his love of country music honestly. In 1968, his father Harold drove to Nashville to record a self-composed song called "A Lonely Shadow." A year later, young Randy took up the guitar himself, and in short order, he and brother Ricky cemented a duo, playing fiddler conventions, parties and Moose halls.

By age 14, though, Travis moved to a new beat, one that took him to the edge of disaster. He consumed alcohol, acid, Quaaludes and/or speed on a daily basis. Travis broke into a van, stole from a grocery store, totaled four cars and led a quartet of policemen on a 130-mile-an-hour chase.

Fortunately, Randy had just the right guidance at just the right time. After quitting high school, he gained employment with Lib Hatcher [see 746—"I Won't Need You Anymore"], and she stood behind him at his lowest point. With Travis set for a now-customary court appearance, even his attorney thought that he would receive a minimum five-year sentence. But because Hatcher provided gainful employment and believed so strongly in him, the court gave Randy one more chance. Still, the judge warned him, "If you come back, bring your toothbrush, 'cause you're going to stay."

Travis believed him, and turned himself around practically overnight.

"I probably would have been dead by now, probably would have been killed," Travis told Jack Hurst in the *Waterbury Republican*. "Three of the people that I ran around with are dead. Two of them were shot, and one was killed in a car wreck. And another one's doing 101 years."

At Hatcher's bidding, Travis took his music talents seriously for the first time, and at 17, he

started writing songs, although he didn't come up with any "keepers" for about five years. His first hit as a writer came on his second album with "I Told You So."

Darrell Clanton recorded it in 1985, as a "B" side, and Randy wanted to record it as well for his own debut album. He didn't receive too much encouragement, though, and put it aside until the next album. It emerged as the fourth single—and fourth number one—off the disk.

Travis has also had songs recorded by Ricky Skaggs, Gene Watson and Earl Clark.

774

HE'S BACK AND I'M BLUE
THE DESERT ROSE BAND
MCA/Curb 53274
Writers: Michael Woody,
Robert Anderson
Producer: Paul Worley
June 25, 1988 (1 week)

The six members of the Desert Rose Band own such an impressive list of credentials that media profiles of the group frequently turn into a lengthy name-dropping exercise. Their collective resumé features work with Linda Ronstadt, Benny Goodman, Rod Stewart, Ricky Nelson and the Byrds.

Byrds alumnus Chris Hillman, in fact, is the central figure in the California-grown ensemble. Hillman's country credits go back to the Golden State Boys, a folk/bluegrass group that included Vern Gosdin and that later changed its name to the Hillmen. In the mid-'60s, the Byrds enjoyed a prominent position in the emerging folk/rock scene, with "Mr. Tambourine Man," "Turn! Turn! Turn!" and "Eight Miles High," later recording a landmark album in the country/rock movement, *Sweetheart of the Rodeo*.

After the Byrds flew their separate ways, Hillman winged his way through a series of solo, duo and trio efforts, including a pair of albums for Sugar Hill Records: 1982's *Morning Sky* and *Desert Rose*. Hillman and Herb Pedersen both appeared on Dan Fogelberg's 1985 album *High Country Snows*, and that album paved the way for the Desert Rose Band. (The album's timing also spared Pedersen from having to appear on screen as a band member in the movie *Rhinestone* [see 585—"Tennessee Homesick Blues"].)

When Fogelberg prepared a summer tour,

he asked Hillman and Pedersen to develop an acoustic act to open the shows, and they reeled in guitarist John Jorgenson and bassist Bill Bryson. After the tour, steel player Jay Dee Maness and drummer Steve Duncan joined them for a Los Angeles street festival. They continued to play scattered club dates, and after an engagement at The Palomino in February of 1986, Curb Records' Dick Whitehouse persuaded the group to sign a recording deal.

The Desert Rose Band's second single, "Love Reunited," reached number six; and their next, "One Step Forward," peaked at number two. They took the final step with "He's Back And I'm Blue," a song that Hillman received from his longtime friend, Michael Woody.

"This is before the Desert Rose Band was an entity," notes Hillman. "I was laid up with a broken hip, and I got this cassette from Michael. I loved that song, and a year later, the Desert Rose Band started to make some waves, and I remembered the song. I had the cassette in my office, and we cut it."

775
IF IT DON'T COME EASY
TANYA TUCKER
Capitol 44142
Writers: David Gibson, Craig Karp
Producer: Jerry Crutchfield
July 2, 1988 (1 week)

Tanya Tucker is easily among the most controversial figures in the current generation of country stars. From her romantic endeavors [see 692—"Just Another Love"] to her movement into a country/rock hybrid [see 261—"Here's Some Love"], nearly every move she's made has drawn both headlines and criticism.

That was also true in February of 1988, when Tucker checked into the Betty Ford Center to conquer a cocaine and alcohol addiction. "Personally, I didn't think I had a problem," she told Neil Pond of the *Music City News*. "But my friends and my family thought I did—and if they were worried about it, something must have been wrong. I think they overreacted a lot, but no way around it—that stuff's not good for you, period. It's like saying, 'OK, I want to take some strychnine now.'"

In spite of that particular event, Tanya's career remained as strong as ever, bringing her a number one single (her ninth) just before Independence Day.

"'If It Don't Come Easy' was a song that I didn't like at first," she confesses, "and I went ahead and cut it, but after I cut it, I really liked it. I liked the words. I really liked what it had to say, because I'm not one to sing poor-little-me songs."

Tanya agrees with the suggestion that the song is like a country equivalent of the self-help book *Women Who Love Too Much*.

"I think the attitude was great for women out there that relate to that," she explains. "I've had a lot of women tell me the song gave them strength, and made them feel like hanging in there, or they wanted to hang in there and they realized they shouldn't. If it don't come easy, let it get out the door."

"If It Don't Come Easy" was Tanya's third number one record in less than two years, and she asserts that she felt no pressure in her return to prominence. "I probably should have, but I have a way of just letting it roll off my back. Later on, I get to thinking about it, and go, 'Wow, that was a close one; I'm really glad it worked out like it did.'"

776

FALLIN' AGAIN
ALABAMA
RCA 6902
Writers: Teddy Gentry, Greg Fowler,
Randy Owen
Producers: Harold Shedd, Alabama
July 9, 1988 (1 week)

Though group members Randy Owen, Jeff Cook and Teddy Gentry all consider themselves songwriters, "Fallin' Again" represented the first Alabama single since "Why Lady Why" [see 404] on which Gentry participated as a writer. It was also the first hit co-written by road manager Greg Fowler.

"I think a lot of other things replaced my writing time during the first three or four years that things started really happening for us," Gentry told Larry Rhodes in *American Songwriter*. "That's easy to do until . . . you can hire competent people you can trust to take care of all that.

"For a long time, I got to where I was trying to be involved in the [Alabama] T-shirt design and a lot of other things, but I've started writing again. I really enjoy writing, and whether I was successful or not, I think I would still do it."

"Fallin' Again" was actually composed during Gentry's dry period, around 1982. He started the song before a concert, worked on it with Fowler after the show, and finished it off with Owen the next day. Half a dozen years later, "Fallin' Again" emerged as the third single from the *Just Us* album.

Coincidentally, the first three songs recorded for the project—"Fallin' Again," "Tar Top" and "Face To Face" [see 760]—were all done at the same session, and Owen was the only member of Alabama present that day.

"I had some time off during the holidays,"

Randy says. "In fact, it was right around my birthday, and it was rainin', about the worst rain I ever drove through in my life. I had a new Corvette at the time, and I drove to Nashville, and I said I never wanted to drive a Corvette again. I traded it for two pickup trucks.

"Really, I just gathered together some of the people that I knew that work together good, and I wanted to go in and cut those tracks. I had spent a lot of time studyin' them and how to approach them, so that if we wanted to go in and cut 'em ourselves, we could do it. We decided to leave 'em the way they were."

"Fallin' Again" marked the last single from a dozen albums produced for Alabama by Harold Shedd, who moved on to head PolyGram Records in an amicable parting.

777

IF YOU CHANGE YOUR MIND
ROSANNE CASH
Columbia 07746
Writers: Rosanne Cash, Hank DeVito
Producer: Rodney Crowell
July 16, 1988 (1 week)

Most of Rosanne Cash's songs come straight from life experiences or observations. Rarely are they "crafted," but one of those exceptions comes with "If You Change Your Mind." She wrote it with a former member of Emmylou Harris' Hot Band, Hank DeVito, who also penned Emmylou's "Tennessee Rose" and Juice Newton's "Queen Of Hearts."

"Hank had started it," Rosanne reports, "and Hank and I are real close friends. He said, 'I wanna write this song for the Everly Brothers—do you wanna help me finish it?' I said, 'Sure,' so he came over, we finished the song. We had a very definite perspective of what we were writing and who we were writing it for.

"It wasn't lyrically deep or probing. It was very stylized for them. So Hank and I demoed it, and said to Rodney [Crowell], 'You wanna hear this song Hank and I wrote for the Everlys?' I played it for Rodney, and he said, 'Naw, you gotta keep that for yourself, or I quit.'"

Cash recorded the song at Sixteenth Avenue Sound on March 3, 1987, at the same session in which she cut "The Way We Make A Broken Heart" [see 740]. "If You Change Your Mind" first appeared in *Billboard* on April 2, 1988, with the "It's Such A Small World" duet [see

768] poised at number seven. Rosanne's solo single hit number one fifteen weeks later.

While cutting the demo for "If You Change Your Mind," Rosanne examined some of De-Vito's artwork, and found a hand-colored photograph he had taken of King's Record Shop—an oldies store owned by Pee Wee King's brother, Gene, and located at 240 West Jefferson Street in Louisville.

Rosanne persuaded DeVito to let her use it as the cover for the album; Hank took a picture of her and had it stripped into the photograph to produce the jacket. On March 2, 1988, Bill Johnson of the CBS art department was officially given a Grammy award for Best Album Package for *King's Record Shop*. It was the first Nashville-produced record ever to receive that honor.

Vern Gosdin

778

SET 'EM UP JOE
VERN GOSDIN
Columbia 07762
Writers: Hank Cochran, Vern Gosdin,
Dean Dillon, Buddy Cannon
Producer: Bob Montgomery
July 23, 1988 (1 week)

Though Vern Gosdin earned a number one single in 1984 [see 575—"I Can Tell By The Way You Dance"], that feat hardly guaranteed future success. Two years later, he found himself without a record deal at all.

Gosdin followed with "What Would Your Memories Do" and "Slow Burning Memory," both peaking at number 10. He released five more singles for independent Compleat Records, but each one peaked lower than the one before. Finally, in 1986, Compleat bit the dust. A year later, Merle Haggard extended an offer for Vern to work on an album to be marketed on TV, but Merle's friend and frequent co-writer, Hank Cochran, stepped in.

"Merle had talked to Vern about comin' out to his studio in California," recounts producer Bob Montgomery, "and I think he was gonna do that, but Hank Cochran brought him up to me. Hank and I got to talkin', and I told him I'd like to try to do somethin' with Vern."

Columbia Records advanced enough money to cut a few sides on Gosdin. Montgomery recorded five songs, and one, "Do You Believe Me Now," was released as a single, peaking at number four in 1988. They added another five

songs to round out Vern's first Columbia LP, *Chiseled in Stone*. The follow-up single, "Set 'Em Up Joe," returned him to number one.

"That was written in Gatlinburg, Tennessee," reports co-writer Buddy Cannon. "Hank has a cabin up there on the Little Pigeon River, and Vern and Dean Dillon and I went up to visit with Hank and to write some songs specifically for the album.

"We wrote about ten or twelve songs on that particular outing. We were sittin' there around the fireplace of Hank's cabin, tryin' to think of somethin' to write. Dean spouted out the two opening lines of the song, and it just kind of took off from there. About an hour later we had the song."

Unintentionally, the song evolved into a salute to "Walkin' The Floor Over You," and "the original E. T." "I've always loved Ernest Tubb," says Dillon, "and I know Hank and Vern and Buddy have a mutual admiration for him, and respect. He was just a great pioneer in country music."

Written in 1941, "Walkin' The Floor" existed before *Billboard* ever had a country chart, but the reference propelled "Set 'Em Up Joe" to number one almost fifty years later.

779

DON'T WE ALL HAVE THE RIGHT

RICKY VAN SHELTON

Columbia 07798
Writer: Roger Miller
Producer: Steve Buckingham
July 30, 1988 (1 week)

Roger Miller has made numerous personal revolutions in his musical life, rising from the in-law of a country comedian to a recording star and Broadway-show writer.

Much of Roger's inspiration for a music career came directly from his relationship with Sheb Wooley, the man behind "The Purple People Eater," "That's My Pa" (a number one country single in 1962) and the theme for "Hee Haw." Wooley was also an in-law, and Miller no doubt derived some of his humorous songwriting talents from his relative's example.

On his second trip to Nashville, Roger took on a job as bellhop at the Andrew Jackson Hotel downtown, and pestered the country artists who stayed there to listen to his songs. He also hung out at Ralph Emery's tapings at WSM and beat the streets of Music Row—whatever it took to be heard.

Finally, he connected in 1958. After joining Ray Price's band, his employer recorded Roger's "Invitation To The Blues" as the flip side to "City Lights" [see 195]. "Invitation" went to number three. A year later, Roger earned two more hits: "Billy Bayou," by Jim Reeves, and "Half A Mind," by Ernest Tubb.

Roger ultimately excelled as a recording artist, garnering eight Top Ten singles from 1964 through 1966, including "King Of The Road," "Dang Me" and "Chug-A-Lug." His efforts netted a phenomenal eleven Grammy awards in 1965-66. Twenty years later, Miller earned a distinction as the first country writer to win a Tony award, for his score to the Broadway production *Big River*.

Since 1980, two of Roger's own records have yielded successful remakes: "Husbands And Wives," for David Frizzell & Shelly West; and "Don't We All Have The Right" (originally the flip side of his 1970 single "South"), for Ricky Van Shelton.

"The way Steve Buckingham and I do songs, we'll just have a little jam session in Steve's office with acoustic instruments," Ricky says. "If these songs work playin' acoustically, then we'll take 'em into the recording studio."

During one of those sessions, guitar player Steve Gibson suggested "Don't We All Have The Right," and after they secured a copy, everyone agreed on it. Columbia pulled it as the fifth single from Shelton's debut album, and "Don't We All" reached number one in its thirteenth week on the chart.

780

BABY BLUE

GEORGE STRAIT

MCA 53340
Writer: Aaron Barker
Producers: Jimmy Bowen, George Strait
August 6, 1988 (1 week)

Like many who entered their teens during the height of the Beatles years, George Strait began his musical pursuits by thrashing out rock and roll tunes in a Pearsall, Texas, garage band. His high school group worked up covers of "Gloria" and "Louie Louie," among others, but they "never really got out of the garage."

Following his graduation, George signed up with the Army, where he spent three years. They stationed him in the Midwest and then transferred him to Hawaii, where he shuffled papers in the payroll and disbursement division. A general at his base organized a country band during his tenure, and that event prodded Strait to give performing a serious look.

"I always wanted to be a singer," George says. "Always. But I never really knew how to get into it. I'm not sure what hit me, though—I just know that one day in Hawaii, I decided to really get serious about it."

Strait got a "thumbs up" at his audition, and spent his last year in the service making music. Six months after his stint ended, he returned to San Marcos, where he enrolled at Southwest Texas State University. George posted notices on school bulletin boards, advertising his vocal services, and wound up with the Ace in the Hole Band.

It's a bit of a stretch from "Louie Louie" to country stardom, but Strait made that jump, and as a result, he boosted a fellow Texan by recording "Baby Blue." San Antonio songwriter Aaron Barker had been in the business seventeen years when Strait cut it, and Barker actually wrote "Baby Blue" about five years before the single was released.

"I never even dreamed the thing would be recorded," Barker told Steve Bennett of the *San Antonio Light*. "I've pitched more songs to

Nashville than you can shake a stick at—songs that I've thought were much more commercial—and here this little song goes number one."

Strait had heard the song a couple of years earlier, and played the demo frequently on his bus in the interim. Finally, he recorded it for the *If You Ain't Lovin' (You Ain't Livin')* album, and released it as the second single.

"I tell you," Barker asserted, "George Strait has done more for me in three minutes and 32 seconds than anyone else has in seventeen years."

781

DON'T CLOSE YOUR EYES
KEITH WHITLEY

RCA 6901
Writer: Bob McDill
Producers: Garth Fundis, Keith Whitley
August 13, 1988 (1 week)

Sandy Hook, Kentucky, native Keith Whitley held a lifelong love for country music, but he got to sing it professionally only after detouring through a bluegrass side route.

Keith played guitar at age six, hit West Virginia radio waves at age nine, and joined teenager Ricky Skaggs in Ralph Stanley's band six years later. Both Whitley and Skaggs made their recording debuts in 1971, on the album *Cry from the Cross*.

Keith toured from 1974 to 1977 with Stanley, then joined J.D. Crowe & The New South as lead vocalist at age 21. Finally, in January of 1983, he moved to Nashville to pursue his country ambitions, landing a recording contract with RCA Records. The album *A Hard Act to Follow* put him onto the *Billboard* country chart, but his real breakthrough came with 1986's *L.A. to Miami*, as "Miami, My Amy" reached number 14. Three more singles— "Ten Feet Away," "Homecoming '63" and "Hard Livin'"—took him into the Top Ten.

Whitley recorded another entire album, set to release in September of 1987, but once the project was completed, he shelved it. "I just didn't feel like it was as strong an album as I needed," he said. "I thought it was a good album, but I just didn't feel it was the great album that I needed at this point in my career."

RCA agreed to let Keith co-produce a new record, and he quickly settled on Garth Fundis, in large part because of a tape that

George Strait

Garth had sent that included Bob McDill's "Don't Close Your Eyes."

"It came from a scene in *California Suite*," McDill recalls, "when Maggie Smith, the English actress—her longtime lover is gay, but they've gone to California. She's nominated for an Oscar. He's gay, she's very lonely and afraid, and in one scene, she knows that he has homosexual lovers, and she fears that he sometimes makes love to her and dreams about these homosexual lovers. So she says to him, 'Tonight, don't close your eyes.'

"I thought, 'Gee, wow, great.' Of course, five years later, that comes to fruition. It's a slow business."

Keith first heard "Don't Close Your Eyes" in October of 1987 and recorded it in November. Nine months later, it brought him his first number one record.

782

BLUEST EYES IN TEXAS
RESTLESS HEART

RCA 8386
Writers: Tim DuBois, Dave Robbins,
Van Stephenson
Producers: Tim DuBois, Scott Hendricks,
Restless Heart
August 20, 1988 (1 week)

After the *Wheels* album netted four number one singles and a gold record [see 756], Restless Heart felt pressure when it came time to start the next album at Nashville's Omnisound Studios.

"Once you establish yourself as an artist and have a career going, you constantly have to try and grow and expand and do somethin' you haven't done," offers group member Dave Innis. "You can't just do the same thing over and over again, or people are gonna move on to someone that's doin' somethin' new and innovative.

"At the same time, you're always scared to death that you're gonna fall flat on your face. You know, it's art, and it's fun, and it's a journey. It's also my bread and butter, and everyone else in the group is the same way. I lose sleep over it. We all wanna do somethin' great, and we all want to do somethin' that continues to put meat on the table. You're only as good as your last record."

Restless Heart met expectations with *Big Dreams in a Small Town*. To kick off the record, RCA culled "Bluest Eyes In Texas" as a single, a tune that highlighted the band's lush, tenor harmonies. The song came direct from the collective pen of producer Tim DuBois, Van Stephenson and Dave Robbins, a trio that authored Restless Heart's very first single [see 696—"That Rock Won't Roll"]. They had the band in mind from start to finish as they wrote it.

Restless Heart already shared fans with artists ranging from Randy Travis to Hank Williams, Jr., to Kiss, but "Bluest Eyes" brought them a new respect from a group of fans known as Texans.

"We went from unknown act to superstars in one record in the state of Texas," Innis assesses, "and we end our shows with 'Bluest Eyes In Texas' when we're down there. It was really easy to record, and it was somethin' that everybody in the band wanted to do, which is a rarity. We usually have one dissenting vote on

everything, but not that time."

The record briefly introduced Paul Gregg as a solo vocalist on a single line—"Where did I go wrong?"—and in August of 1988, the "Bluest Eyes In Texas" brought Restless Heart their fifth number one record.

783

THE WANDERER
EDDIE RABBITT

RCA 8306
Writer: Ernest Maresca
Producer: Richard Landis
August 27, 1988 (1 week)

Early rock and roll fans probably never would have guessed that Dion DiMucci would provide a basis for future country hits. Both as a solo performer and the lead vocalist of Dion & The Belmonts, Dion was closely linked to such familiar titles as "A Teenager In Love," "Runaround Sue" and "Abraham, Martin And John."

Two of his biggest records translated into successful country recordings. Billy "Crash" Craddock took "Ruby Baby" [see 192] to the top of *Billboard*'s chart in 1974, and Eddie Rabbitt duplicated that feat with "The Wanderer."

The record was part of a minor trend that saw a revitalization of the rock and roll sound from 1955 to 1965. Songs like "In The Still Of The Night" [see 639—"Lost In The Fifties Tonight"], "It's All Over Now," "It's Only Make Believe," "Hello Mary Lou" and "I Feel Fine" all enjoyed a renaissance in country music during the two years before and after Rabbitt's recording.

"I hadn't even noticed that anybody was doing the old '50s kind of rock things," Rabbitt insists. "It really wasn't the idea or the point of it at all. I just wanted to do something I remembered from when I first started listening to the radio and diggin' the music.

"When I started to think about girls and music what I remember is being up in a friend's room, a guy named Jack Tracy. I used to hang out there and bounce basketballs on the floor and tell stories, and I remember hearing 'The Wanderer' up in his room, and I thought it was so cool."

"The Wanderer" actually won a sort of minicontest. In paying homage to his past, Eddie considered it alongside Roy Orbison's "Ooby Dooby" [see 27—"Only The Lonely"].

"I listened to it," Rabbitt recalls, "and I said, 'Well, if I have my choice between the two, I'd rather do "The Wanderer."'" There's more meaning to it. 'Ooby Dooby' turned out to be 'ooby dooby, ooby dooby, ooh wah, ooh wah,' and I thought 'The Wanderer' would be stronger lyrically!"

Dion's recording also had an ability to speak for an entire generation. "I think 'The Wanderer' signified not only a period of time," Rabbitt enthuses, "but it made a statement about rock and roll comin' on—the image, the look, that whole thing."

784
I COULDN'T LEAVE YOU IF I TRIED
RODNEY CROWELL
Columbia 07918
Writer: Rodney Crowell
Producers: Tony Brown, Rodney Crowell
September 3, 1988 (1 week)

"I have to be honest with myself," admits Rodney Crowell, evaluating "I Couldn't Leave You If I Tried." "It's not one of the greatest songs I ever wrote, but they don't have to all be *War and Peace*."

Such was the major lesson of *Diamonds & Dirt*. Crowell and his friend, Donivan Cowart, blew into Nashville in the early '70s on the advice of a crook who promised them a deal with Columbia Records. The deal, of course, never materialized, and Crowell and Cowart lost their shirts.

Cowart headed to Arizona, and Crowell settled into Nashville, ready to take control of his destiny. He washed dishes at T.G.I. Friday's [see 755—"Goin' Gone"], but hung up his towel in 1972 and struggled through the next several years on the dimes and dollars he could accrue through music. In 1975, Brian Ahern recruited him for Emmylou Harris' Hot Band.

Emmylou highlighted many of his songs on her albums, and Rodney emerged as a songwriter and record producer of note, simultaneously pursuing a solo career. His albums *I Ain't Livin' Long Like This*, *But What Will the Neighbors Think* and *Rodney Crowell* brought only minor successes, and Warner Bros. eventually canned his fourth album.

Crowell then moved to Columbia, releasing the rock and roll–tinged *Street Language*, with similar results: critical success and commercial failure. Perplexed, Rodney turned to his former piano player, Tony Brown, for advice.

Tony suggested a simple approach: "I said, 'Listen to all your tunes and be real smart—think radio. You've had hits by everybody but yourself, so you know you can write hits.' We just started goin' through stuff, and 'I Couldn't Leave You If I Tried' sounded like a hit to me, so we wrote that one down. We just compiled what we thought were ten mainstream country songs."

Buoyed by the success of his duet with Rosanne Cash [see 768—"It's Such A Small World"], Crowell notched his first solo hit with "I Couldn't Leave You If I Tried."

"I call that a physical song," Rodney says. "To me, that's a dance record, what we called the country shuffle. I wrote 'I Couldn't Leave You' in a short sitting, and that's one of those songs where my mind had nothing to do with it—it was strictly physical."

785
(DO YOU LOVE ME) JUST SAY YES
HIGHWAY 101
Warner Bros. 27867
Writers: Bob DiPiero, John Scott Sherrill, Dennis Robbins
Producer: Paul Worley
September 10, 1988 (1 week)

When Nancy Reagan got her Just Say No campaign off the ground in the fight against drugs, she probably never envisioned that it would lead to a number one country record. John Scott Sherrill wasn't particularly enamored with Nancy. He told writing partner Bob DiPiero that he wanted to take the Just Say No campaign and twist it into a song title, "Just Say Yes."

"[It's not that he's pro-drug;] John was just anti-Nancy," declares DiPiero. "Nancy Reagan had nothing to do with that song, and she probably wouldn't want to know about it. It was just us havin' fun that day."

Along with Dennis Robbins, they turned the title into a love song and then submitted it to Highway 101. Warner Bros. knew the story behind it, and felt skittish about the title. They offered "Do You Love Me" as an alternative, but when the writers found that unacceptable, both parties arrived at a compromise: "(Do You Love Me) Just Say Yes." "Now," Sherrill laughs, "we're always putting parentheses in the song titles we submit to them."

That was only the first change. When the band took "Just Say Yes" into the recording studio, they discovered the melodic range created problems for Paulette Carlson. The solution, which the writers approved, was unique. "I took the lead melody and made it a harmony," Paulette explains, "and took one of the secondary parts and made it the lead vocal."

The band itself provided another area of contention. After two minutes and 23 seconds, the vocal parts were finished, although the group played for more than a minute before fading out.

"We really believed in the music," says Worley, "and believing that the band identity is an important part of Highway 101, we had to fight. There were forces within the promotion department of the record company that were worried about it: 'Oh, the disk jockeys will hate it—they'll say, "The vocals are over, so the record ought to be over."' We fought over that for about two weeks."

The record went out with the instrumental section intact, and provided Highway 101 with its third number one single. The Berklee School of Music also gave its approval: "Just Say Yes" was used as a case study of a perfect marriage of words and melody.

Eddy Raven

786

JOE KNOWS HOW TO LIVE
EDDY RAVEN
RCA 8303
Writers: Graham Lyle, Troy Seals,
Max D. Barnes
Producer: Barry Beckett
September 17, 1988 (1 week)

"Joe Knows How To Live" can be favorably compared to Eddy Raven's first number one single, "I Got Mexico" [see 573]. Both songs utilize a Caribbean feel, and both use an island setting to offer a fantasy escape from the rat race.

"Joe is very much alive in our minds," says songwriter Troy Seals. "[Co-writer] Max [Barnes] and I never could afford to do that. We were always burdened with families and responsibilities. But Joe is very much alive in our minds. It's a thing that we thought about, basically, like 'Drinkin' And Dreamin',' another thing of ours that Waylon [Jennings] had out. That guy would hit the table, drink a little bit, and pretend."

"Troy had the idea for it," Max continues, "and he came over to my house, and we wrote on it, at it, turned it wrong-side out and pulled it back through itself, and all these things. It was one of several songs that we were workin' on at that period of time."

While their work was still in progress, Seals had another writing session, with Graham Lyle. Troy was still unhappy with the melody in the chorus, and played it for Graham, who asked if he could work on it. With the approval of both Troy and Max D., Lyle took "Joe" home, made some changes and brought it back the next day. With a little more effort, Seals and Lyle gave it the finishing touches.

The Nitty Gritty Dirt Band first cut the song, but David Conrad at Almo/Irving Music thought Raven might do a more definitive version. Years before, Raven had taken Ronnie Milsap's place at the King of the Road Motel [see 165—"Pure Love"], and Conrad had briefly played guitar with Eddy. Conrad sent a demo of "Joe Knows How To Live" to producer Barry Beckett, who also thought it could be done "more Ravenesque."

"The song was perfect for us," Raven states, "and we wound up with a really good record on it. I'm glad they didn't play all the ad-libs that I put into the end of the song. It's nice that someone used some discretion. I got clever at the end—I was probably a bit risqué, I'm sure, when it got to the part about Betty and Momma."

Betty notwithstanding, "Joe" lived for a week at number one.

787
ADDICTED
DAN SEALS

Capitol 44130
Writer: Cheryl Wheeler
Producer: Kyle Lehning
September 24, 1988 (1 week)

Hailing from the Baltimore area, Cheryl Wheeler made her way to Rhode Island in 1976, establishing a presence on the Newport folk scene. In 1985, North Star Records was founded specifically to showcase her recording talents, and Cheryl's first two albums created a critical buzz that filtered through Los Angeles and Nashville. In Music City, a booking agent heard one of her albums, and producer Kyle Lehning was prodded into giving her a listen. After listening to Wheeler's first two albums, Kyle suggested to Dan Seals that he record one of her songs, "Addicted," a song she wrote in Pawtucket.

"I had been talking to my sister on the telephone," Wheeler remembers, "and she was having this very stormy relationship with a man, and had been for a long time. In the process of this conversation, she said, 'I don't know what to do. I feel like I'm addicted to a real bad thing.'

"I was so struck with that sense of feeling like you're addicted. Everybody—at least all women—have done that, and I was so moved by her predicament, and so empathetic, that after she hung up the phone, I started writing 'Addicted.' Most of the song is just reminiscent of what she told me in the phone conversation about how she was feeling."

" 'Addicted' just amazed me," says Seals. "The lyrics on it were so true. I felt a little funny about singin' it at first, because it was a woman's song, and I didn't know if I could sing a song like that. But when I sang it, it was like 'This guy understands what a woman goes through'—and I'm here to tell you it ain't true! I *don't* understand what a woman goes through, but I understand a damn good song!"

"In Dan's version, there was a verse cut out," Wheeler adds. "I always knew that that last verse shouldn't be there, but it never occurred to me that the answer was to just merely stop singing it. That's Kyle. As he says, 'You shouldn't spend a lot of time polishing a turd.' "

As a result of "Addicted" 's success, Wheeler signed with Capitol in 1989. "I've since told my sister to have as miserable a life as possible," she jokes. "It's done wonders for me."

788
WE BELIEVE IN HAPPY ENDINGS
EARL THOMAS CONLEY WITH EMMYLOU HARRIS

RCA 6632-7
Writer: Bob McDill
Producers: Emory Gordy, Jr.,
Randy L. Scruggs
October 1, 1988 (1 week)

"We Believe In Happy Endings" had been around for more than a decade when Earl Thomas Conley and Emmylou Harris took it to number one.

"That happened at the last minute," reports producer Emory Gordy, Jr. "Emmylou came in, and she had this song. We sat down and did an arrangement right there on the spot and just proceeded to do it, turned on the tape machine and left 'em alone."

Actually, "Happy Endings" was a bit more complicated than that. Harris had consented to record with Conley for his album *The Heart of It All*, and received three or four songs on a tape of prospective duets. She liked those songs, but "Happy Endings," first recorded by Johnny Rodriguez, kept nagging at her.

"I love Johnny's version of it," Emmylou says. "I think he's one of our better singers, and that was my favorite of all the things he's done. I always thought that would just make a beautiful duet."

When she showed up in the studio, she suggested the song, and everyone involved agreed on recording it. Conley, however, harbored doubts about working with Emmylou.

"I was nervous," Earl confesses, "because I've always idolized her, and never felt like we necessarily fit in the same ballpark. We did as far as the craft, but I didn't know if the two worlds would fit together. My voice was so much rougher and dirtier and all this stuff, and hers is so immaculately clean that I really almost panicked."

Emmylou told Earl to forget about differences and simply "feel" the song.

"People have too much of an idea that voices have to sound similar to sound good," she explains. "There's an amazing beauty, I think, that comes with dissimilar voices. Earl and I sound great together, and the thing that makes us sound great together is that we are so different."

Their vocal differences provide a certain irony, since personal differences, caused by cabin fever, led songwriter Bob McDill to create the song in the first place. "It was a year we had a rough winter," he recalls. "My wife and I were snowed in and couldn't even get out of the driveway for a couple weeks. We were arguing, and snapping each other's heads off, and the idea for 'We Believe In Happy Endings' came out of that situation."

789

HONKY TONK MOON
RANDY TRAVIS
Warner Bros. 27833
Writer: Dennis O'Rourke
Producer: Kyle Lehning
October 8, 1988 (1 week)

A Boston native, Dennis O'Rourke has alternately called Fort Lauderdale, Ireland and Nashville home. He spent eleven years singing Irish folk music in pubs, and lists "bartender" on his resumé. But he swore for years that he'd never write a song with the phrase "honky-tonk." Naturally, his first hit came with "Honky Tonk Moon," which arose from a trip to a health club.

"Floyd Cramer's song, 'Last Date' [see 98 and 503], came on the radio," Dennis remembers. "I'd always liked that song very much, but I never could understand the title. I thought that was such a mundane title for a nice piece of music. A line popped into my head that it should be called 'Honky Tonk Sunset,' or something like that, because that's what it sounded like to me."

O'Rourke developed the chorus of "Honky Tonk Moon" by the time he reached the spa, and held onto the idea while he exercised. After returning home, Dennis wrote the bulk of it in 30 minutes, recalling a handful of his favorite bars—places he had frequented as a patron or entertainer. He distilled them into images of a country tavern, complete with pool table, jukebox and screen door.

"I wrote the song about honky-tonks," O'Rourke notes, "and drinking's not mentioned at all. Of course, cigarette smoking is, which is probably worse than beer drinking. But I got a boot out of bringing off that image of a nice evening in the country and a little honky-tonk, without mentioning swilling down warm beers."

After playing the song in clubs for a year, Dennis borrowed $5,000 to cut it on a four-song demo with keyboardist/producer Dennis Burnside, who tried to pitch O'Rourke as an artist. Burnside found no takers, but he dubbed a copy of "Honky Tonk Moon" onto a separate cassette. Without telling his client, he left a copy on the desk of Warner Bros. A & R executive Martha Sharp when she was out of her office.

Sharp gave it a listen, then forwarded the tape to Randy Travis and producer Kyle Lehning. They recorded "Honky Tonk Moon" in early 1988, with Burnside transcribing his solo on the demo from the key of G to F#.

Playboy readers named "Honky Tonk Moon" the top country single of the year.

790

STREETS OF BAKERSFIELD
DWIGHT YOAKAM & BUCK OWENS
Reprise 27964
Writer: Homer Joy
Producer: Pete Anderson
October 15, 1988 (1 week)

The longest span ever between two number one country records by the same recording artist was set by Elvis Presley, who waited nineteen years between his chart-topping "Jailhouse Rock," in 1958, and "Moody Blue" [see 275], which reached number one in 1977.

Elvis hit the top of *Billboard*'s Hot 100 in the interim, though, which makes Buck Owens' achievement all the more spectacular. After "Made In Japan" [see 102] in 1972, Buck had to wait sixteen years before he returned to number one with Dwight Yoakam on "Streets Of Bakersfield." It's the second longest gap between two number one country records by the same performer.

Owens had intended to give up the performing life altogether when he retired in 1980, but Yoakam rekindled an interest in Buck's music.

"People would send me articles in which he talked more about me than he did about himself," says Owens. "I had never met him, yet he dedicated his first album to me."

In September of 1987, Yoakam appeared unannounced at Buck's Bakersfield office and persuaded Buck to perform with him onstage. "Waylon and Willie and I go back thirty years," notes Owens. "I never got up with them. I never got up with anybody, but I felt very comfortable with Dwight."

In January of 1988, Buck was asked to be a part of the Country Music Association's thirtieth anniversary television special, representing the Bakersfield Sound with Merle Haggard. When Hag bowed out, Owens asked if he could substitute Yoakam. The CMA wanted a song about the town sometimes called "Nashville West," and Owens picked "Streets Of Bakersfield" from a 1972 album of his.

Homer Joy, an aspiring songwriter from Arkansas, first wrote it after heading out to Bakersfield to pitch songs to Owens. It took ten days for Joy to get past the secretary. In the interim, he composed the song—with its opening line, "You don't know me, but you don't like me"—while walking the streets of Bakersfield.

After performing it on the CMA show, Yoakam and Owens sang "Streets Of Bakersfield" again at the Academy of Country Music awards. A couple of disk jockeys taped the performance on their VCRs and wanted to program the duet on their stations. As a result, Yoakam put the song on his *Buenas Noches from a Lonely Room* album, and it became Yoakam's first number one single.

791

STRONG ENOUGH TO BEND
TANYA TUCKER
Capitol 44188
Writers: Beth Nielsen-Chapman,
Don Schlitz
Producer: Jerry Crutchfield
October 22, 1988 (1 week)

Born October 10, 1958, Tanya Tucker hails from the same West Texas town of Seminole as Larry Gatlin. Her move toward an entertainment career began at the age of nine, when her father, Beau, placed an incredible amount of trust in the youngster's talent. Asked if she'd like to be an entertainer or continue her education, Tanya opted for a chance to sing, and Beau Tucker moved the family to Nevada in search of an opportunity for his daughter.

Even before her first recording deal [see 130—"What's Your Mama's Name"], Tucker had already appeared in the Sydney Pollack-directed movie *Jeremiah Johnson* (starring Robert Redford and Will Geer). She later gained a role in the TV movie *Georgia Peaches*.

In October of 1988, Tanya observed several milestones. The one-time teenage phenom (formerly dubbed "The Texas Tornado") reached her thirtieth birthday. She secured two nominations in the Country Music Association awards, for Female Vocalist of the Year and Vocal Event of the Year (with Paul Davis & Paul Overstreet). In addition, she nabbed her tenth number one single, "Strong Enough To Bend."

"Strong Enough" was Tucker's second number one record written by Don Schlitz [see 759—"I Won't Take Less Than Your Love"], and the single also featured co-writer Beth Nielsen-Chapman in a supporting vocal role. As Overstreet had done after "I Won't Take Less Than Your Love," Nielsen-Chapman went on to sign an artist agreement.

"I really, really enjoyed that song," says Tanya. "Beth's just a wonderful singer and a wonderful writer, and I'm glad to see her getting a break, and feel like I've helped with that, too. 'Strong Enough To Bend' is just the epitome of what love should be, I think the love that we all strive for."

As Tucker strives to do with all her singles, the song conveyed a very positive viewpoint. It also displayed a maturity that contrasted sharply with the image of the party girl who grew up on the magazine covers at the grocery check-out counter.

"L.A. was a fun town, and I had friends up the cuckoo," she recalls. "It wasn't musically fruitful, but I was having a great time. It was a thing I went through, but now looking back on it, it's like [I was] a different person."

792

GONNA TAKE A LOT OF RIVER
THE OAK RIDGE BOYS
MCA 53381
Writers: John Kurhajetz, Mark Henley
Producer: Jimmy Bowen
October 29, 1988 (1 week)

On June 8, 1987, Steve Sanders made his first live appearance as an official member of the Oak Ridge Boys [see 723—"It Takes A Little Rain"] during the *Music City News* awards show.

Sanders was already an entertainment veteran. As a teenager, he performed on Broadway, in *The Yearling;* on film, in Otto Preminger's *Hurry Sundown;* and on TV, on "The

Ed Sullivan Show" and "To Tell the Truth." Musically, his resumé included stints with Alvin Lee and Steve Winwood, plus rhythm guitar for the Oaks' backing band. Steve also wrote "Live In Love," the "B" side to the Oak Ridge hit "Bobbie Sue" [see 466].

Once he joined, Sanders contributed to the sessions for *Heartbeat*, a transitional album that yielded but one hit, "True Heart." That song came up at the last minute, when the Oaks asked Don "Dirt" Lanier, an associate of producer Jimmy Bowen, for something uptempo. He brought them two songs: they recorded "True Heart," and asked him to save the other one, "Gonna Take A Lot Of River," for the next album. Subtitled "Mississippi, Monongahela, Ohio," "Gonna Take A Lot Of River" was catchy, both musically and lyrically.

"I could not forget the word 'Monongahela,'" says Duane Allen, "and all that summer, I went around singin' it, and I tried to pronounce that word. I finally learned how to pronounce it correctly, then I couldn't ever forget it.

"That's the reason that we named the album, the tour and everything *Monongahela*, because once you know how to pronounce it, you never forget it. I figured if it worked that way on me, why not do it for everybody like that?"

"This is the first Oak Ridge Boys single where I've gotten to sing lead," Sanders noted in an MCA bio. "I really love this song. It's real uptempo, a happy kind of thing. I've been working thirty years in show business, and this chance means all the world to me. I live for this kind of opportunity."

"Gonna Take A Lot Of River" gave the Oaks their sixteenth number one single, and Sanders quickly stepped into a higher profile with the *Monongahela* album. The second and third singles—"Bridges And Walls" and "Beyond Those Years"—also featured him as lead vocalist. Each record hit the Top Ten.

793

DARLENE
T. GRAHAM BROWN
Capitol 44205
Writers: Mike Geiger, Ricky Ray Rector, Woody Mullis
Producer: Ron Chancey
November 5, 1988 (1 week)

In the mid-'70s, Anthony Graham Brown bluffed his way into a movie. He ended up

playing a redneck in Richard Pryor's *Greased Lightning.* In the mid-'80s, he made an appearance with John Schneider in *The Farm,* and in the fall of 1988, T. earned his third movie role, in *Heartbreak Hotel.*

At the same time, His T-Ness racked up his third number one single, "Darlene." Songwriters Mike Geiger, Ricky Rector and Woody Mullis created the song from a simple groove, and Delbert McClinton [see 313—"Two More Bottles Of Wine"] was among the first to record it. When Brown heard McClinton's version, he took a copy of the tape into the recording studio, where producer Ron Chancey was working with him on the *Come As You Were* album. As it turned out, Chancey had brought a copy of the same song to the same session; since they were on the same wavelength, they decided they had to cut it.

"It was just catchy," Brown notes, "but I'd always said I'd never cut a song with a girl's name in the title of it, 'cause I thought it was real corny to do. I told Chancey, 'The only thing I hate about this song is it's got a girl's

name in it.' He said, 'You know, the two biggest records I ever had had girl's names in 'em— "Elvira" [see 427] and "Bobbie Sue" [see 466].' So we went in and cut it, put it out, and damn, it went to number one."

It did so on November 5, 1988. The three singles that preceded "Darlene"—"Brilliant Conversationalist," "She Couldn't Love Me Anymore" and "The Last Resort"—each reached country's Top Ten, as did the follow-up, "Come As You Were." As a result, nine out of T. Graham Brown's first ten singles had hit that chart level.

T. Graham is certainly a one-of-a-kind personality, and he enjoys a suitably one-of-a-kind nickname: His T-Ness. The name was coined by Michael Garvin, a co-writer of Brown's first hit, "I Tell It Like It Used To Be" [see 700]. Brown showed up late for a demo session, prompting Garvin to comment, "Oh, His T-Ness has finally arrived."

"I thought that was great," His T-Ness laughs. "I could definitely use that. So I've just kind of hung on to that."

794
RUNAWAY TRAIN
ROSANNE CASH
Columbia 07988
Writer: John Stewart
Producer: Rodney Crowell
November 12, 1988 (1 week)

As a youngster, Rosanne Cash wrote poems and short stories, and she has continued to do so since becoming a recording artist. She places so much emphasis on her writing that she's been prone to discount her vocal work.

"When I was making albums where I had only one or two of my own songs on them, I felt like I didn't have a total right to make the album," she explained to *American Songwriter*. "With *King's Record Shop*, I finally came to terms with singing as a valid interpretive art."

Appropriately, Cash turned to another songwriter, John Stewart, for the album's fourth single. A onetime member of the Kingston Trio, Stewart had also written "Daydream Believer," a pop hit for the Monkees and a country hit for Anne Murray. His contribution to Rosanne was "Runaway Train."

"Larry Hamby, who's in the A & R department at CBS, played me Mary-Chapin Carpenter's version of it, and I sat in his office and cried," Rosanne recalls. "I thought it was such a brilliant song, so that's how we came across it. We were heavily influenced by Mary-Chapin Carpenter's arrangement.

"Actually, it didn't have a bridge when we heard it. I didn't care, but Rodney [Crowell] really wanted it to have one, so he called up John and asked if he'd write a bridge for it. He said, 'Yeah,' and we recorded it."

The session occurred on March 25, 1987, and also included Cash's performance of "Tennessee Flat Top Box" [see 757]. On November 12, 1988, "Runaway Train" gave Rosanne her tenth number one single. It also set a chart record, making her the first female solo artist to register four number one country singles from the same album.

Exactly one month later, Rosanne gave birth to Carrie Kathleen, the fourth daughter in the Crowell/Cash household. Yet one week later, on December 19, her father, Johnny Cash, underwent successful open heart surgery.

Despite her heritage, and her obvious acceptance by country fans, Rosanne receives letters that suggest she's "ruining" country music.

"I always have," she laughs. "Some of 'em I pin up on my bulletin board. Some of 'em, if they really piss me off, I'll answer 'em. My self-esteem isn't that fragile that they're gonna make me go crawl in a corner."

795
I'LL LEAVE THIS WORLD LOVING YOU
RICKY VAN SHELTON
Columbia 08022
Writer: Wayne Kemp
Producer: Steve Buckingham
November 19, 1988 (2 weeks)

"Star"-dom fit Ricky Van Shelton long before he ever signed a recording contract. During his youth, Shelton affixed stars to his school notebooks and model cars and airplanes. Since then, he's added a star to his guitar, and incorporated the astral symbol into jackets and belt buckles.

Shelton hasn't gone "star crazy," however. Though he has collected numerous awards, he insists that he's unconcerned about winning or losing them. Likewise, Ricky hasn't gone out of the way to showcase himself on record. Instead of dazzling with vocal fireworks, he delivers his songs straight and true, with powerful conviction.

"I was brought up singin' gospel music," Shelton explains. "Gospel singers sing from the heart, and you don't have any time to put anything into it but your feelings. I just open my mouth and it comes out that way. It's like when I'm singin', my soul takes over. Music is the voice of the soul, without a doubt."

Ricky bared more of his vocal soul with his second four-star collection, 1988's *Loving Proof* [see 839—"Living Proof"], from which CBS pulled Wayne Kemp's "I'll Leave This World Loving You" as the first single.

Kemp wrote the song around 1972, and recorded it as the "B" side to "Honky Tonk Wine," his biggest single as a recording artist. Ronnie Milsap recorded it on his *A Legend in My Time* album in 1975, and Kemp cut it again as a single for Mercury Records in 1980. Once more, Wayne featured the song on a 1984 TV-advertised album, *Past, Present & Future*, which also included a later George Strait hit, "The Fireman" [see 650—"The Chair"].

Ricky heard one of those earlier versions, but didn't consider recording it until producer

Steve Buckingham suggested it. Shelton knew the song as a waltz, although he recorded it in 4/4 time (so did Milsap), as he did with "Life Turned Her That Way" [see 762].

"When you take a waltz, if it'll work in 4/4, that makes it a brand new song," Ricky suggests. "You phrase it different, enunciate it different, you say it totally different—and it becomes a brand new song."

796
I KNOW HOW HE FEELS
REBA McENTIRE
MCA 53402
Writers: Rick Bowles, Will Robinson
Producers: Jimmy Bowen, Reba McEntire
December 3, 1988 (1 week)

Beginning June 11, 1988, Reba McEntire spent eight weeks atop the *Billboard* country album chart with *Reba*. The album surprised many of her fans. It featured a remake of Aretha Franklin's "Respect" and a cover of the classic "Sunday Kind Of Love." The latter, suggested by her personal publicist, Jennifer Bohler, reached number five on the country singles list.

With Reba reaching the pinnacle of country music, some fans feared that she might be "going pop." She quelled some of their concerns with the second single from the album, "I Know How He Feels."

"Originally, it was written as a male version, 'I Know How *She* Feels,'" reports Will Robinson, one of two writers. "It was the same lyric, but there were some different lines in the chorus and the second verse."

Kevin Lamb and Cliff Williamson of Maypop Music played it for Terry Skinner and J.L. Wallace, who were producing the Forester Sisters. They liked the song, but asked if Robinson and co-writer Rick Bowles could fashion a new set of lyrics for a female to sing.

"It turned out, after we finished, to be a better female song," Will continues. "It seemed to work better. Then we sent it out to Reba. It had been on hold for the Forester Sisters and for Judy Rodman, but those just never materialized, luckily for us. Then Reba cut it."

"That was after [my] divorce," McEntire notes, "and I really contemplated about whether I would sing it or not, because I thought people might interpret it as saying that

Ricky Van Shelton

I had regrets about the divorce, which I don't. Once I make a decision, it's the right thing to do, and there's no turnin' back.

"When I say somethin', I've thought about it for a long, long time, and that's the way it is. I didn't sing it because that's the way I felt. I sang it because it was a good song, and I knew it was a hit."

Reba's recording featured an unusual production technique. There were no drums whatsoever through the first verse and first chorus, although the arrangement grew as the record progressed.

"I Know How He Feels" debuted in *Billboard* at number 59 on September 10, 1988, and reached number one a dozen weeks later.

797
IF YOU AIN'T LOVIN' (YOU AIN'T LIVIN')
GEORGE STRAIT
MCA 53400
Writer: Tommy Collins
Producers: Jimmy Bowen, George Strait
December 10, 1988 (1 week)

Songwriter Tommy Collins has frequently been confused with Tom Collins, the man who produces Barbara Mandrell and Ronnie Milsap. So it surprised the former Collins when the latter Collins called him long distance. Tommy joked that Tom was probably calling to sue him, but, in fact, Tom was simply looking for songs.

Tommy has been a valuable source of songs for many, particularly Merle Haggard [see 238—"The Roots Of My Raising"], but his first hits as a recording artist and a writer came during the middle '50s. He registered four Top Ten hits in 1954-55: "You Better Not Do That," "Whatcha Gonna Do Now," "Untied" and "It Tickles." He also went Top Ten in 1966 with "If You Can't Bite, Don't Growl." George Strait rejuvenated one of Collins' songs from 35 years back, "If You Ain't Lovin' (You Ain't Livin')."

"I wrote the song in 1953," Tommy remembers. "There wasn't any particular event. It was the idea that I had that love is more important than riches and things, possessions. I was beginnin' to hear a lot about people becomin' wealthy in the music business, and people were tellin' me how much money some of those men had, and I really wasn't impressed. I thought the best thing in life was to find love, or to have someone."

Collins had signed with Capitol Records at the time, but he wasn't recording yet, so he submitted the song to Cliffie Stone at Central Songs. Faron Young got a crack at it, and his version spent three weeks at number two in early 1955.

Strait considered the song while recording an album with producer Ray Baker. Ray secured a copy of it from Collins and George recorded it then, but it was shelved when he decided to run with a new producer [see 601—"Does Fort Worth Ever Cross Your Mind"].

"We just put it off for a few albums," says Strait. "Finally, the song came back to mind, and we just went in there and did it. I always thought it was a really neat song."

Collins, who used to share an apartment with Ferlin Husky, can thank Husky for his professional name. He was named Leonard Sipes at birth, but Capitol wanted a simpler name for their solo artist. When Leonard volunteered to head out during one of Husky's recording sessions to pick up food for the musicians, someone asked for a Tom Collins. Husky gave Sipes that name, and it stuck.

He works rarely, if at all, in the U.S., but Collins still tours Europe twice a year.

798

A TENDER LIE
RESTLESS HEART
RCA 8714
Writer: Randy Sharp
Producers: Tim DuBois, Scott Hendricks, Restless Heart
December 17, 1988 (1 week)

Restless Heart vocalist Larry Stewart explained the differences between *Big Dreams in a Small Town* and the group's prior albums to Bob Allen in *Country Music*: "It's a lot more just us, as a band . . . Before, when we did our harmony vocals, we would pair off in twos and take turns recording our parts. We'd really struggle to get each word, each syllable, perfect. This time, we just all got around the microphone together and did all our parts at the same time, just like we do on stage."

For the album's second single, Restless Heart turned to songwriter Randy Sharp, who had written "Why Does It Have To Be (Wrong Or Right)" [see 733], plus Karen Brooks' "New Way Out" [see 507—"Faking Love"].

The group first heard "Tender Lie," as did producer Tim DuBois, while sifting through tapes of potential material on an airplane from Los Angeles to Nashville. If anyone came across something he liked, he would pass it along to someone else to hear on a Walkman.

"I got halfway into the first chorus of 'A Tender Lie' and just started freakin' out," remembers Dave Innis. "I took the tape and gave it to Larry, and said, 'Man, this is a smash—please tell me you hear this song.' He heard it and said, 'I agree. This is it.'"

DuBois agreed, too. In fact, he calls "A Tender Lie" his favorite of Restless Heart's records—high praise, since DuBois actually wrote several of them himself.

"I couldn't wait until the plane got down so I could call Randy up and say, 'For God's sake, don't play that song for anybody else,'" DuBois says. "I mean, it had that kind of effect on me. It's a great song, and I think we cut a great record on it."

Not every member of the band was crazy about "A Tender Lie"—not because they didn't appreciate it, but because it's so simple that they weren't particularly challenged by the instrumental parts. By the same token, Restless Heart recognized the song's appeal, and the record went on to become the group's sixth straight number one single.

Restless Heart's next release broke that string, as "Big Dreams In A Small Town" peaked at number three. Another single from the *Big Dreams* album, "Say What's In Your Heart," reached number four.

799

WHEN YOU SAY NOTHING AT ALL
KEITH WHITLEY
RCA 8637
Writers: Paul Overstreet, Don Schlitz
Producers: Garth Fundis, Keith Whitley
December 24, 1988 (2 weeks)

When Keith Whitley released his *L.A. to Miami* album, he could possibly have landed a couple of number one records. Instead, George Strait took home a chart-topping single with "Nobody In His Right Mind Would've Left Her" [see 681], and Randy Travis did the same with "On The Other Hand" [see 680], written by Don Schlitz and Paul Overstreet.

"We always had a runnin' joke that they wanted me to cut another one of their songs and get the first crack at a single on it," Whitley noted. "So we were very happy when I heard 'When You Say Nothing At All.'"

"That was a day where we just went in the office and tried to just stay there until we came up with something," Overstreet recalls. "It was one of those things where you start messing around with the guitar and humming, and something sparks, you know, 'When You Say Nothing At All.' We just sat down and tried to write a song around it."

"Sometimes actions speak louder than words, as the old saying goes," adds Schlitz, "and we just found another way to say that. Sometimes if you listen carefully enough with your eyes, you can hear a whole lot more than you hear with your ears. Keith did a great job singin' that song—he truly sang it from the heart."

"When You Say Nothing At All" debuted in *Billboard* at number 61 on September 17, 1988. In its fifteenth charted week, it reached the top spot and, because *Billboard* magazine skips an issue at the Christmas holiday, it held there for a second week.

Whitley's *Don't Close Your Eyes* [see 781] album sold 500,000 copies by the following summer, and it represented a major change in his recording process. Co-producing with

Keith Whitley

Garth Fundis, they recorded fourteen songs for the project; of the ten that made it, seven of Whitley's performances were delivered on the first take.

"[Before], a very important part of Keith Whitley was not comin' across on the records," Keith said. "My fans would say, 'We love your records, but you're so much better live.' So that's one of the first things that I told Garth when we started workin' together—that there was somethin' that came across in my live shows that had not been captured on record."

800

HOLD ME
K.T. OSLIN
RCA 8725
Writer: K.T. Oslin
Producer: Harold Shedd
January 7, 1989 (1 week)

The years 1988 and 1989 belonged to K.T. Oslin on country music's awards-show caravan. Beginning with her 1988 Grammy award for "80's Ladies" [see 750—"Do Ya'"] and ending at the '89 Academy of Country Music ceremony, where she walked off with Top Female Vocalist, Oslin won a total of eight awards between the ACM, the Country Music Association and the Grammys.

At the '89 ACM awards, her second album, *This Woman*, took Album of the Year honors. K. T. loosely formatted the release as a concept album, deriving its flavor from *80's Ladies*.

"It's the next logical musical step for her," RCA's Nashville chief, Joe Galante, explained to *Billboard*'s Edward Morris. "It enlarges on the themes of the first album. She's written three songs for each of the characters in '80's Ladies': the smart one, the pretty one, and the borderline fool."

Like its predecessor, *This Woman* sold more than a million copies by the decade's end, although the first single, "Money," brought an inauspicious start, topping out at unlucky number 13. RCA selected an unusual—even for K. T.—second single: "Hold Me" departed from standard A-B-A-B song form, contained large sections of recitation and lasted more than four and a half minutes.

"K. T.," assesses producer Harold Shedd, "has a real knack for knowing what to do with her material."

The lady that Tom T. Hall dubbed "everybody's screwed-up sister" pulled off a major coup with "Hold Me," when, despite its lack of respect for usual "hit standards," the record trotted to number one during the first week of 1989. Less than two months later, the song

The Judds

garnered Oslin a pair of Grammys: for Best Country Vocal Performance by a Female and Best Country Song. Particularly intriguing is the fact that "Hold Me" is about marriage—yet Oslin has never said "I do."

"I . . . write from a personal point of view," K.T. told Dennis Hunt in the *Los Angeles Times*. "I see what my friends are going through, how they react to relationships. I learn from watching people and try to put it in terms that music fans would find interesting."

This Woman bred two more Top Ten singles in 1989: "Hey Bobby" (number two) and the title track (number five).

801

CHANGE OF HEART
THE JUDDS
RCA 8715
Writer: Naomi Judd
Producer: Brent Maher
January 14, 1989 (1 week)

In 1988, The Judds released their first *Greatest Hits* album, featuring two new singles: "Give A Little Love" and "Change Of Heart." The first stalled at number two in August. The second was written by Naomi Judd during a personal crisis and first recorded five years earlier.

Naomi penned it for her boyfriend, Larry Strickland, to sing to her. A former background singer for Elvis Presley, Strickland was the first man that Naomi met when she moved the family to Nashville in 1979 [see 580—"Mama He's Crazy"]. After a rocky five-year romance, their relationship hit an all-time low.

Bob Millard quotes Naomi in his unauthorized biography, *The Judds Story*: "He broke my heart. I stayed up three days and three nights, couldn't eat or sleep, and I wrote 'Change Of Heart.' The song just came out beginning to end."

Wynonna and Naomi performed the song at the live audition that got them signed to RCA. Shortly afterward, Strickland proposed to Naomi, though she turned him down. They went a year and a half without seeing each other before he returned to her life.

In the meantime, producer Brent Maher insisted that the Judds record "Change Of Heart" for their debut mini-album. "I can't count the times," he says, "that people would come up to me and say, 'Gosh, you guys should

have put that song out as a single.' " At the suggestion of RCA division chief Joe Galante, they re-recorded it for the *Greatest Hits* album, and the new version turned out even better than the first.

"We'd grown a lot," Maher explains. "Wynonna has grown a lot vocally. We felt we could cut the track a little bit better, a little bit more dynamic, and we raised the key up a half-step."

The new cut of "Change Of Heart" appeared as a single in October of 1988, and it received an extra push when Wynonna and Naomi performed it live during the Country Music Association awards show. Both vocalists were on edge—Wynonna was in the spotlight more than for any other song, performing without her guitar; Naomi could see Strickland in the first few rows of the audience.

Three months later, the record went to number one. On May 6, 1989, "Change Of Heart" had a happy ending—Naomi and Larry were married.

802

SHE'S CRAZY FOR LEAVIN'
RODNEY CROWELL
Columbia 08080
Writers: Rodney Crowell, Guy Clark
Producers: Tony Brown, Rodney Crowell
January 21, 1989 (1 week)

"I enjoy storytelling that is really deep and involved," says Rodney Crowell, "but by the same token, human beings are funny, you know. I am a serious guy, and I guess I'm what you'd call a deep thinker, but I'm just as shallow and silly, too."

Rodney let his silly side take command on the third single from the *Diamonds & Dirt* album, "She's Crazy For Leavin'," written with longtime buddy Guy Clark.

"I had a version written years ago," Guy notes, "and it never did quite gel. It wasn't quite finished or somethin'. It didn't hang together really good. And when Rodney was producin' an album of mine called *South Coast of Texas*, we were getting the songs together, tryin' to figure out what we were gonna do, and just playin' songs. I played part of that one, and we said, 'Yeah, that really works—but let's rewrite it.' So we sat down and went back over it and put it in its current form, then went ahead and recorded it."

The Dirt Band's John McEuen also cut it for

a solo project, and Steve Wariner recorded it for the *Life's Highway* album with producer Tony Brown, who played keyboards on Guy's record.

"I tried to get MCA to release it off Steve's album," Tony remembers. "They wouldn't put it out, so when Rodney was goin' through all of his songs [see 784—"I Couldn't Leave You If I Tried"], he brought that up again, and I told him I always thought it was a hit. We were makin' important decisions just right off the top of our heads. Rodney said, 'I always liked that, too. Let's cut it, it fits right in with the mood of the whole album.'"

They intended to quickly lay down the basic tracks, hustle Rodney out of the studio before he could second-guess himself, and finish up the record later. Ultimately, "She's Crazy For Leavin'" sounds almost like it came fresh from the concert stage.

"It's such a visual episode," Rodney suggests. "It's almost like a cartoon. It would be fun to go hear somebody play that live. Plus, the album is basically a live recording, with very little overdubbing. It's just the musicians counting the song off, and playing it—just like they would on stage."

803
DEEPER THAN THE HOLLER
RANDY TRAVIS

Warner Bros. 27689
Writers: Paul Overstreet, Don Schlitz
Producer: Kyle Lehning
January 28, 1989 (1 week)

Randy Travis brushed with tragedy on January 17, 1989. On their way to promote *The Youth Yellow Pages* at a Tennessee school, Travis and manager Lib Hatcher swerved to avoid another automobile and wound up in a ditch. Both emerged unscathed from the accident, and two days later, Randy appeared on the nationally-televised Presidential Inaugural Gala, ushering in George Bush. The following week, Travis racked up his eighth number one single, with "Deeper Than The Holler."

"Back home in Mississippi, there were a lot of hollers," notes songwriter Paul Overstreet. "In Tennessee there are, too. I've always liked that word 'holler,' and Don Schlitz and I just wanted to write something that just compared country images to the city."

"We were kind of writing our own version of 'Ain't No Mountain High Enough,' from a slant that we understood," Schlitz adds. "I don't live at the foot of the Rocky Mountains, and I've never lived right on the ocean, so when I hear songs like 'Climb Every Mountain,' I don't understand that.

"But I do have hills in the backyard, and the pine tree looks plenty tall to me. 'Deeper Than The Holler' is just a very simple, very direct song. There's kind of a hidden wink to my wife in the second verse with the reference to Broadway. My wife's an actress and knows everything about all the Broadway musicals. Sometimes when we're talkin' music, we're talkin' from two different planets, so there's a little wink there to her."

Ever since "On The Other Hand" [see 680], Travis and producer Kyle Lehning have listened to everything that Schlitz and Overstreet have sent them. "Deeper Than The Holler" received a quick approval, though it took some effort to produce the final version.

"By the time I finished that and was ready to mix it, it was just full of instrumentation," Kyle explains. "There was a lot of sorting out of stuff to get that record finished. In fact, I think that breakdown section—where the band drops out, and it's just Randy and acoustic guitars and background vocals—was actually done in the mix. We never played it that way, but just decided to make the change at that point, and it worked real well."

The ultimate understatement.

804
WHAT I'D SAY
EARL THOMAS CONLEY

RCA 8717
Writers: Robert Byrne, Will Robinson
Producers: Emory Gordy, Jr.,
Randy L. Scruggs
February 4, 1989 (1 week)

A simple phone call hooked up Will Robinson and Robert Byrne as songwriters. Robinson commuted several times from Nashville to Muscle Shoals, where they wrote at Byrne's lakeside home. Their first song, "She Doesn't Cry Anymore," emerged as Shenandoah's first Top Ten record. T.G. Sheppard cut their second, and their third, "What I'd Say," became Earl Thomas Conley's fifteenth consecutive number one single.

"We were really proud of that," says Will. "It

was one of those things that was sort of a gamble, but it worked. There probably weren't many artists that could have done that besides Earl, because of that line 'Go to hell.'"

"I never thought anybody in Nashville would cut that," Byrne continues. "You can say 'hell' in songs, but it's pretty tough to say 'go to hell.' I played it for Earl, just for him to hear it. I never thought there was any way he'd end up recordin' it. I gotta hand it to [division president] Joe Galante and everybody at RCA for havin' the balls to release it, because they could have gotten a lot of flak."

"I said, 'Man, I gotta cut this,'" notes Earl, recalling his first reaction. "A lot of people said, 'What are you gonna do about sayin' "hell" three times on the radio?' I said, 'Well, if they feel that strongly against it, let it flop.' Show me one person that hasn't felt like this. I don't care if he's a preacher—everybody's felt like sayin' this, and most people have said this."

Producer Emory Gordy, Jr., once edited the word "friggin'" out of the single version of the Bellamy Brothers' "Old Hippie," only to later hear the word on network television, in the movie *All of Me*. Though worried about its acceptance, Gordy wanted to see "What I'd Say" released, in spite of the "go to hell" line.

"'You can eat crackers in my bed any day' is a lot more offensive," Emory explains. "I can name a lot more offensive songs than 'What I'd Say.' That's just a well-written, musical song. I was pleased with the arrangement that the musicians had done, and it would be a shame to let it go simply because there might be two or three people out there that wouldn't like the phrase 'Go to hell.'"

805

SONG OF THE SOUTH
ALABAMA
RCA 8744
Writer: Bob McDill
Producers: Alabama, Josh Leo
February 11, 1989 (1 week)

A student of the South, Bob McDill portrayed a Depression-era Dixie in "Song Of The South." Though not old enough to have experienced it, McDill relied on written research and word of mouth in depicting a poverty-stricken family and its sense of good fortune with the advent of the New Deal.

"I'm really proud of that song," Bob says. "I

think it's one of the best things I've ever done. [Alabama] did leave out the middle verse, and I was disappointed at first, but I think that it's probably good.

"You can kind of see the hookworm and the malnutrition take over in that verse. That's probably a little too much for the public. Nobody likes to think that it could have been that bad, but it certainly was. Especially in the South, people really suffered: malnutrition, scurvy, beriberi, rickets, hookworm. In fact, when the draft for World War II was called, half the young men from the South were rejected for diseases and conditions resulting from malnutrition. It was pretty severe."

Written in 1980, "Song Of The South" engendered interest immediately. Johnny Russell took it to number 57 in 1981, and Tom T. Hall and Earl Scruggs reached number 72 the following year with a bluegrass version. McDill still believed in the song, and when RCA asked him to contribute to the *Signatures* songwriter album in 1988, he recorded "Song Of The South" as a ballad. Initially, RCA planned to release it as a single, but division head Joe Galante decided the song might work for Alabama.

"Oddly enough," Alabama's Teddy Gentry told Melinda Joiner of the *Huntsville Times*, "the first time I heard 'Song Of The South,' I didn't like it. The line 'Sweet potato pie and shut my mouth' may be the best line in the song, but being from the South, I just didn't particularly like it.

"I mean, I love sweet potato pie, but that's something Northerners *think* we say, and we don't. We worked on the song all day, and by late afternoon, we got the fiddle in there and gave it kind of a Cajun sound. The whole mood of the song changed, and I liked it better."

The single debuted at number 50 over Thanksgiving weekend in 1988, and reached number one eleven weeks later.

806

BIG WHEELS IN THE MOONLIGHT
DAN SEALS
Capitol 44267
Writers: Bob McDill, Dan Seals
Producer: Kyle Lehning
February 18, 1989 (1 week)

When he split with John Ford Coley [see 653—"Bop"], Dan Seals agreed to a deal in which he could keep his "England Dan" moniker. In exchange, he promised to take on any financial obligations that might surface in connection with the pop duo's name. Unknown to Seals, their former manager left a trail of unpaid back taxes and lawsuits, and the Internal Revenue Service went to Dan for restitution. He lost his house, his van . . . everything, including his pride.

Though he was able to rebound, Seals understandably exercised caution as he rebuilt his career. In fact, he refused to purchase a tour bus—traveling in a cramped van instead—until 1987, when he already had more than three years of country hits under his belt.

Seals' touring lifestyle was something of a dream come true, a fact underscored by his autobiographical "Big Wheels In The Moonlight," in which the singer dreams of shaking the small town dust off his shows and hitting the road in a big rig.

"We were just plunkin' around on a piece of melody he had," remembers co-writer Bob McDill, "and somehow he said something that I thought was something that he thought was something that I thought was something. We misunderstood each other in the conversation, but out of that, the phrase 'Big Wheels In The Moonlight' came up."

"We started talkin'," Seals adds, "about what it's like in a small town, growin' up along the highway, layin' in bed, listenin' to the trucks changin' gears. I could tell if they were gonna eat at the city cafe. Our town had one red light, and usually the truckers would stop and eat, or they'd just keep changin' gears and get goin' out of sight."

McDill continues: "We thought, 'Wow! What a hoot! A truck-driving song. This'll be hilarious, a real funky, contemporary, truck-driving song.' 'Cause there hadn't been one in years and years.

"I'll be darned—as soon as we got the thing written, the charts got covered up with these truck-driving songs all of a sudden. The wheels turn so slowly that by the time the thing came out, it wasn't as inundated as it might have been."

After debuting at number 61 on November 21, 1988, "Big Wheels In The Moonlight" rolled into *Billboard*'s top spot in its fifteenth week on the country chart, February 18, 1989, giving Seals eight consecutive chart-topping singles. The streak ended with his follow-up: "They Rage On," again written by Seals and McDill, peaked at number five on June 10.

807
I SANG DIXIE
DWIGHT YOAKAM
Reprise 27715
Writer: Dwight Yoakam
Producer: Pete Anderson
February 25, 1989 (1 week)

"Country music has always been a spontaneous, metamorphic tradition," Dwight Yoakam told Bud Scoppa in *Us* magazine, admitting that his own rambunctious honky-tonk contains "covert sociopolitical overtones."

That a self-proclaimed "hillbilly" would describe a rural-generated musical form with such polysyllabic verbiage clashes head-on with the "Beverly Hillbillies" stereotype that many outsiders foist upon country music and its people. Elevating the music above that stereotype is a mission that Yoakam has chosen.

Born in Pike Floyd Holler, Kentucky, Yoakam grew up primarily in Columbus, Ohio, although the family returned to the Holler on weekends to visit relatives. Enamored with the music of Lefty Frizzell and Buck Owens, Yoakam headed to Nashville in 1976 to sign a recording contract. Labels weren't interested in his traditional bent, however, and he ended up in California, where he spent half-a-dozen years as a trucker.

"Driving for a living gives you a lot of time to think and be alone," Dwight says. "I enjoy being alone, and find a great deal of creative energy in solitude."

But Yoakam hasn't remained alone in his fervor for pure country. He slowly built a reputation among younger, rock audiences in California, and got a second chance at a label deal. This time, his whiny hillbilly voice earned Top Five singles with his cover of Johnny Horton's "Honky Tonk Man" and "Guitars, Cadillacs," both from his first album. In 1987-88, he launched four more Top Ten efforts, and finally hit number one by teaming with Buck Owens [see 790—"Streets Of Bakersfield"].

Dwight reached the top once more by following up with "I Sang Dixie," lifted off *Buenas Noches from a Lonely Room*. Described by some as a concept album, Yoakam insists that *Buenas Noches* is more "thematic." "I get moody; I kill someone; then I get religion in the end," he told Holly Gleason in *Billboard*, summarizing the plot on side one. "This record's more me—there are expressions of me that people haven't heard before."

Though pulled from side two, and though it didn't figure into the song cycle, "I Sang Dixie" also investigated death, and succeeded despite country radio's predisposition toward positive love songs.

"Believe me," Yoakam told Peter Watrous of the *New York Times*, "the record company didn't exactly love getting a record full of death and murder."

808

I STILL BELIEVE IN YOU
THE DESERT ROSE BAND

MCA/Curb 53454
Writers: Chris Hillman, Steve Hill
Producer: Paul Worley
March 4, 1989 (1 week)

"We're one of the few acts that do everything ourselves," says Chris Hillman of the Desert Rose Band's recording efforts. "We don't bring in any studio players, we don't bring in studio singers. There's a lot of groups out there that do that. The Byrds did that, even. 'Mr. Tambourine Man' [see 774—"He's Back And I'm Blue"]—that was the one song we didn't all play on. Roger McGuinn played on it, and we used session players—Leon Russell, all kinds of people. But with Desert Rose— what you hear [on record] is the band you see on stage."

The Desert Rose Band specializes in infectious, energetic material, but, for reasons unknown, their uptempo records haven't gained the number one chart positions that their ballads have. At the end of 1988, for example, T. Graham Brown's "Darlene" [see 793] left "Summer Wind" dangling at number two. In June of 1989, "She Don't Love Nobody" peaked at number three, and in September, their cover of Buck Owens' "Hello Trouble" stopped at number 11. "I Still Believe In You," a ballad, reached the chart pinnacle.

" 'I Still Believe In You' is basically a love song," assesses Hillman. "It didn't really apply to me or Steve Hill in our personal lives. We just created this scenario of a guy that is in love and whatever happens in the relationship—'I still believe in you.' "

"We had been recording a lot of midtempo-type tunes," explains Herb Pedersen. "We got to this one, it was like, 'Okay, slow it down— take it easy, and get a real good reading on it.'

"With ballads, you spend a little more time on each word coming out of your mouth. You're singing slower, and I think that was at the point where John [Jorgenson] and I started taking a little more time with our monitor set-up in the studio for our backgrounds."

Using a pair of out-of-phase Auratone speakers, they rigged up a method of recording their vocals without headphones, creating a more realistic situation in the studio.

Along with Southern Pacific, Highway 101 and Dwight Yoakam, the Desert Rose Band has helped to rekindle a West Coast country trend, arguably missing since the days of the Bakersfield Sound [see 91—"Carolyn"].

809

DON'T YOU EVER GET TIRED (OF HURTING ME)

RONNIE MILSAP

RCA 8746
Writer: Hank Cochran
Producers: Ronnie Milsap, Rob Galbraith, Tom Collins
March 11, 1989 (1 week)

Ronnie Milsap made experimentation a hallmark of his '80s recordings, and one songwriter who provided Ronnie with many of the vehicles for his creativity benefited from Milsap's help. Mike Reid appeared on RCA's *Signatures* album—which highlighted five different writers and their material—and Milsap joined him on "Old Folks." That single went to number two in 1988.

Milsap's next effort was "Button Off My Shirt," a synthesizer-based song that peaked at number four in the New Traditionalist Era. On the heels of that record's success, Milsap went to work on a more mainstream country effort.

"We'd struggled to get some airplay on 'Button Off My Shirt' in certain areas," Ronnie admits, "and I think [RCA executive] Joe Galante, at that time, was lookin' for something a little bit more country, and I said, 'I can do that.'"

The result was the 1989 LP *Stranger Things Have Happened*. For the first single, Milsap appropriately came up with a country chestnut, "Don't You Ever Get Tired (Of Hurting Me)." Ray Price released the first version, which peaked at number 11 in 1966. Fifteen years later, Ray hit the same position in a remake with Willie Nelson.

"I probably wouldn't have [covered] that," says Ronnie, "except that I was tryin' to write some songs, and I was workin' with Don Schlitz and Hank Cochran. In the midst of that thing with Hank, I asked him what was his favorite song, and he mentioned 'You Comb Her Hair,' by George Jones. I said, 'Man, I know that was '63 and these new fans probably don't know it, but I'm not gonna touch it.' Then he mentioned 'Don't You Ever Get Tired (Of Hurtin' Me).'"

"Ronnie has such a great vocal range," notes producer Tom Collins. "When he goes up at the end on this song, it totally is fantastic. When Milsap gets a hold of a song, and it's really him, no one else has done it the way he's done it. That makes it a whole new song, as far as I'm concerned."

Milsap's new oldie cracked the top spot in March of 1989. A solid country follow-up, "Houston Solution," rose to number four.

810

FROM A JACK TO A KING

RICKY VAN SHELTON

Columbia 08529
Writer: Ned Miller
Producer: Steve Buckingham
March 18, 1989 (1 week)

Record buyers who want a Ricky Van Shelton album often encounter confusion finding his material: stores almost always have his material in stock, but it's frequently misfiled. Shelton has become accustomed to the problem: as a youngster, his mailman often delivered his letters to the wrong address.

When he lived in Grit, Virginia, another Ricky Shelton lived on the same rural route, and, to avoid the mail problem, his mother suggested that Ricky add his middle name, Van. In the long run, record retailers, disk jockeys and reporters have mistakenly assumed that Van Shelton is his last name.

Though Shelton encounters semantic confusion, he has set himself apart stylistically as something of a "remake king." Each of his first four number one singles had been recorded before, and he earned his fifth chart-topper with yet another cover, of "From A Jack To A King."

"That's a great tune," says Ricky. "Back in

the mid-'60s, when I started becomin' interested in country music, I started singin' that song. We were lookin' for somethin' like that for the album, and [my wife] Bettye mentioned it to me one day. She suggested 'Jack To A King,' and I said, 'Bingo.' Immediately I called Steve Buckingham up. I mentioned 'Jack To A King'; he said yes. We loved it."

"From A Jack To A King" entered the *Billboard* country chart during the first week of 1989, debuting at number 42. Ten weeks later, it took Shelton to the top, eclipsing the track record of Ned Miller's original version, which spent four weeks at number two in 1963.

Shelton worked as a pipe-fitter prior to his move to Nashville [see 748—"Somebody Lied"]—ironic, since Miller held a similar job thirty years earlier. Miller also worked in air conditioning and refrigeration, prior to managing a Vernal, Utah, taxi company.

Ned moved to California in 1956, gaining his first hit seven months later when Bonnie Gui-

tar recorded his song "Dark Moon." After he scored with his own version of "From A Jack To A King," Miller wrote his only two other hits, "Invisible Tears" and "Do What You Do, Do Well." With the help of his wife, Sue, Ned also penned "Behind The Tear," a number one record for Sonny James in 1966.

811

NEW FOOL AT AN OLD GAME
REBA McENTIRE
MCA 53473
Writers: Steve Bogard, Rick Giles, Sheila Stephen
Producers: Jimmy Bowen, Reba McEntire
March 25, 1989 (1 week)

When Dolly Parton released her *Dolly* album in 1979, Reba McEntire gave it a listen at

her sister Susie's apartment in Stillwater, Oklahoma. Reba liked the record, but it also gave her something to shoot for. She hoped that someday, she'd be accepted widely enough that she could title one of her own albums with her first name.

With the approval of producer Jimmy Bowen, McEntire got her wish with the *Reba* album [see 796—"I Know How He Feels"]. The second number one record from the package, "New Fool At An Old Game," was, for all intents and purposes, a slice out of her own life.

"It's a song a lot of people can relate to," she explains. "There's a lot of divorced people in the world, and they may be in a relationship for ten or fifteen years, and then they're back into dating, just like a teenager, and they're like 'Aah! Things have changed!' Everything's so open nowadays, and they don't know what to do about it. I thought everybody could relate to it, and they did."

That included Reba, who had learned first-hand about re-entering the dating pool [see 731—"One Promise Too Late"]. In September of 1987, she moved from Oklahoma to Nashville and established Reba's Business, appointing former bandmember Narvel Blackstock as her manager.

A romance blossomed, although Reba kept it fairly private. Finally, on June 3, 1989, she and Narvel tied the knot in a ceremony for family and a few friends in Lake Tahoe. The following week, they spent part of their honeymoon at Fan Fair in Nashville. The family expanded rather quickly, too: in February of 1990, Reba gave birth to a baby boy, Shelby Stephen.

Meanwhile, McEntire moved through 1989 and into the new decade in strong fashion. She achieved her thirteenth chart-topping single with "Cathy's Clown" [see 827], and established a new record for female artists when *Sweet Sixteen* topped *Billboard*'s country album chart for eleven weeks in a row. The album's second single, " 'Til Love Comes Again," peaked at number four.

On January 19, 1990, Reba made her silver screen debut in the horror film *Tremors*.

812
BABY'S GOTTEN GOOD AT GOODBYE
GEORGE STRAIT
MCA 53486

Writers: Tony Martin, Troy Martin
Producers: Jimmy Bowen, George Strait
April 1, 1989 (1 week)

When George Strait released the *Beyond the Blue Neon* album in 1989, he told Bob Allen in *Country Music*: "I think it's the best I've ever done. I felt excited when I came out of the studio, like I'd accomplished something I'd wanted to accomplish for a long, long time."

If that was good news for George, it was less than ideal for his friend, songwriter Dean Dillon, even though Dean was involved with the album's first single. Strait, still searching for material, had Dillon visit his Nashville office to play some of his latest songs. In the process, Dean also handed George "Baby's Gotten Good At Goodbye." The writers, Tony and Troy Martin, were new, although their father, Glenn, had a lengthy history in the business [see 81—"I'm Just Me"]. "Baby's Gotten Good At Goodbye" was the last song recorded for the album, and it had a direct effect on the only Dillon song tabbed for the project.

"I did Dean's song in the studio and just didn't hook it, I didn't feel like," George explains. "It [didn't really fit] well with the rest of the album, and right at the end of the session, I said, 'Look, we've got a little time—let me go ahead and cut "Baby's Gotten Good At Goodbye." ' So we went ahead and cut it, and Dean's cut got thrown off the album. It was terrible to have to tell him that.

"Dean's song was a good one, but there's some songs that are like that. You go in there, and they just don't come off, and it just didn't. When he found out that it was a song that he brought me that bumped his off, I think it kind of upset Dean, but after a while he understood."

"That shows you that Dean really loves George," surmises producer Jimmy Bowen. "They're really good friends, and Dean just had to accept that that's life. But Dean's had a lot of George Strait songs."

"Baby's Gotten Good At Goodbye" debuted at number 50 on the *Billboard* country chart dated January 21, 1989. Ten weeks later, the single tipped in at number one on April Fools' Day.

Four weeks later, *Beyond the Blue Neon* became the seventh George Strait album to top the country chart, following *Right or Wrong* [see 567], *Something Special*, *#7*, *Ocean Front Property* [see 715], *Greatest Hits, Volume Two* and *If You Ain't Lovin' You Ain't Livin'* [see 797].

813

I'M NO STRANGER TO THE RAIN

KEITH WHITLEY

RCA 8797
Writers: Sonny Curtis, Ron Hellard
Producers: Garth Fundis, Keith Whitley
April 8, 1989 (2 weeks)

With the release of the *Don't Close Your Eyes* [see 781] album, RCA Records felt Keith Whitley was on the verge of superstardom. The country record industry had long recognized his potential, but alcohol created problems for him during sessions for his first two RCA albums.

"It just came down to the point of us having to say, 'Keith, get your life together or go find another home,'" RCA's Joe Galante told *Billboard*'s Edward Morris. "To his credit, he did go out and wrestle with the devil, and he won."

Keith seemingly lived his life "on the edge." At age 17, he escaped a 120-mile-per-hour car crash that killed a friend, and two years later, he drove off a cliff into a frozen river, escaping with just a broken collarbone. "I guess there was a little streak of self-destructiveness in me," he admitted, "'cause I grew up with fast cars, motorcycles and drinkin', and it all went hand-in-hand.

"[I used to think that] in order to be successful in this business, I had to emulate some of the people who had been idols of mine—people like Lefty Frizzell and George Jones. I thought drinkin' was part of it, but I found out the hard way that it's not."

After apparently conquering his demons, Whitley released "I'm No Stranger To The Rain" as the third single—and third to reach number one—from *Don't Close Your Eyes.*

"That song is kind of autobiographical for me," Keith suggested. "Although I didn't write the song, I could very well have written it. It really deals with survival. The line in that song that made me know I wanted to record it comes in that first verse: 'I fought with the devil/Got down on his level/But I never gave in/So he gave up on me.' I could really identify very strongly with that particular line."

Unfortunately, Keith's devils beat him a month after "I'm No Stranger" hit number one. On May 9, 1989, his brother-in-law found Keith's lifeless body at 12:30 P.M. Whitley registered a blood alcohol level of .477—nearly five times the minimum level for intoxication in Tennessee.

814

THE CHURCH ON CUMBERLAND ROAD

SHENANDOAH

Columbia 68550
Writers: Bob DiPiero, John Scott Sherrill,
Dennis Robbins
Producers: Rick Hall, Robert Byrne
April 22, 1989 (2 weeks)

Songwriter Bob DiPiero calls "The Church On Cumberland Road" a "hillbilly 'Get Me To The Church On Time.'"

DiPiero, in fact, came up with the idea on a trip to England, where he provided backing vocals on a series of recording sessions for an RCA record by Mark Germino. DiPiero had never been to Great Britain before, and took great interest in its centuries-old architecture.

"They took me to this English pub," Bob remembers. "We were stayin' there for a couple of hours and kind of poured out of the place, like, at night, after all this ridiculous English beer. There was a church across the street, a big ol' church. I think it was like 600 years old or somethin', a big old stone church, and I remember goin' up and kind of hugging it. I hugged this church with the old stone and decided I wanted to write a song about this church."

Back in Nashville, DiPiero drove across the Cumberland River on his way home, and settled on the title. He fleshed out the song with John Scott Sherrill and Dennis Robbins, then submitted it to their publisher, Woody Bomar. In turn, Bomar took their prized composition and gave it to Muscle Shoals' Robert Byrne. Woody then announced to the writers that he had secured a Shenandoah cut.

"We said, 'A what?'" Sherrill laughs, in retrospect. "But now we have a little more faith in him when he does that."

Byrne and Rick Hall, though jointly credited on all of the ten cuts on Shenandoah's *The Road Not Taken*, each produced half the album. Byrne received songwriter credits on five of the tunes, and "The Church On Cumberland Road" was the only song he produced that he didn't write. Byrne sifted through hundreds of songs from Nashville publishers, and after he brought "Cumberland Road" back, Hall suggested that they drop it.

Notes Shenandoah's lead vocalist, Marty Raybon: "Rick said, 'Well, I don't want y'all to

Shenandoah

cut that—it's got drinkin' in it, and there just ain't nobody that lays out drinkin' all night and goes to church.'"

Hall really protested when Columbia's Bob Montgomery announced that "Cumberland Road" would be a single. The label won out, and so did Shenandoah—and Hall—in the end. "Cumberland Road" brought the band its first chart-topping record.

815

YOUNG LOVE
THE JUDDS
RCA 8820
Writers: Paul Kennerley, Kent Robbins
Producer: Brent Maher
May 6, 1989 (1 week)

Anyone who read the title "Young Love" before they heard the Judds' recording might have thought it was a cover of the 1957 Sonny James classic [see 80—"Bright Lights, Big City"]. In fact, songwriter Paul Kennerley, who started the tune, had never heard of James' record (it wasn't a hit in England) until he started playing his own number for some of his music business friends. One of the first was Judd producer Brent Maher.

"I remember drivin' up to Paul Kennerley's house right before I was goin' on vacation in the summer [of 1988]," Brent recalls. "My son was with me, and Paul was in this really cheerful mood, strolled out of his garage with his guitar in hand.

"He started strumming: 'She was sittin' cross-legged on the hood of her Ford/Filin' down her nails with an emery board.' He started rattlin' off the whole first verse. It was a picture-perfect scenario of what used to go on—and it still goes on, like in our little town here of Franklin [Tennessee]. Every Friday and Saturday night, I can drive around Franklin Square, and it's full of kids sittin' on top of pickups, checkin' each other out."

Maher asked Kennerley to consider writing it for the Judds, but by the time Brent returned from his vacation, Paul hadn't progressed any further. "I knew the layout of the song and what was happening," Paul reflects, "but I couldn't get the meat and potatoes of the lyric, all that detail stuff that needed doing. I just couldn't focus on it."

Kennerley's publisher, David Conrad, wanted to see the song finished, and once it appeared that Paul would never complete it himself, Conrad suggested that he team up with Kent Robbins.

"I jumped right in," Robbins says. "[Paul] had that goin', the first two lines. When I heard that, I went 'O-kay.' Over about three days there, we came up with all those verses. It's sort of a long story—the record's about 4:20."

The length didn't stop it from succeeding. "Young Love" hit number one on May 6, 1989, the same date that Naomi Judd got married [see 801—"Change Of Heart"]. The following week, the title was revised on the *Billboard* chart to "Young Love (Strong Love)": the publisher wanted to differentiate the song from Sonny James' recording.

816
IS IT STILL OVER?
RANDY TRAVIS
Warner Bros. 27551
Writers: Ken Bell, Larry Henley
Producer: Kyle Lehning
May 13, 1989 (1 week)

Randy Travis had reason for concern early in his career. In a discussion with producer Kyle Lehning ("I certainly respect country music, but I'm not an aficionado"), Randy mentioned his reverence for "Lefty," to which Lehning responded "Lefty who?" Travis expected anyone in the business would automatically know Lefty Frizzell [see 260—"If You've Got The Money, I've Got The Time"], and had to wonder if he'd sided with the right producer.

"He was gracious enough to trust me a little bit," laughs Kyle, "and he immediately gave me Lefty Frizzell's *Greatest Hits* album, which I've listened to many, many times. Now I see where all these guys came from."

"These guys" include Merle Haggard and George Jones, two of Travis' biggest influences. More than a trace of his predecessors can be found in the grooves of Randy's ninth number one single, "Is It Still Over?"

The song came from Ken Bell and Larry Henley, who would get together weekly to write material. In one of their sessions, they finished early in the day, and Henley, who had recently broken up with a girlfriend, decided to get her on the phone: "I think I'll call her and see if we're still over." Bell heard a title in Henley's quip, and the next time they met, they set to work on "Is It Still Over?"

"We wrote the whole thing in 20 or 25 min-

utes," Larry recalls. "Ken came by, we laughed, we were on the floor rollin' around while we was writin' that song. We put a little writers' tape down that day with all the mistakes and all the laughter on it. Kenny had a session, and had to go to work. I went to lunch, and I ran into [Warner Bros.'] Martha Sharp at lunch, and I said, 'I think I've got a song for Randy Travis. How can I get it to you?'"

Martha told him that if he wanted to pitch something to Randy, she needed it that day. Since they didn't have a demo tape made up, Bell gave her the embarrassing work tape, and that entry garnered Henley and Bell a Randy Travis single. It took five or six different sessions before Randy and Kyle could get a musical track that they liked, cutting most of "Is It Still Over?" with a live band.

817
IF I HAD YOU
ALABAMA
RCA 8817
Writers: Kerry Chater, Danny Mayo
Producers: Barry Beckett, Alabama
May 20, 1989 (1 week)

In the late '60s, Gary Puckett & The Union Gap emerged among pop's top acts with five Top Ten singles, including "Woman, Woman," "Young Girl" and "Lady Willpower." Twenty years later, the band's bass player, Kerry Chater, had risen to the top among Nashville songwriters.

Chater left The Union Gap in 1970, drained from the seemingly endless touring. He had always wanted to be a writer anyway, and concentrated his efforts in that area.

Living in Los Angeles, Kerry made periodic jaunts to Nashville to work with the city's writers. The first trip to bring success came when he boarded a plane to write with Rory Bourke and Charlie Black, but didn't even let them know he was coming until he reached the Dallas airport. The result of that visit was Jennifer Warnes' hit "I Know A Heartache When I See One," and Chater later created "I.O.U.," for Lee Greenwood; "You Look So Good In Love," for George Strait [see 551]; "You're The First Time I've Thought About Leaving," for Reba McEntire [see 517]; and "What She Wants," for Michael Martin Murphey.

Chater co-wrote "If I Had You" with Acuff-

Rose songwriter Danny Mayo, but that song nearly missed getting recorded. Alabama producer Barry Beckett had listened to a number of songs, none of which he felt were right for the group. He decided to leave, but told Mayo's publisher he'd listen to one more song. That's when they pulled out "If I Had You," and Beckett decided to show it to Alabama.

"I didn't know whether Randy Owen would like it for sure," remembers Barry, "but it was real simple, it's easy to do in a show, and it was right for the girls."

Alabama put the song on hold, but didn't do anything with it for several months. The writers and publishers grew nervous about the group dropping the song from the album. "Finally," says Chater, "one of the publishers ran into Randy Owen at a party and said, 'I hate to ask, but how is that song comin'? Are you gonna do it?' He said, 'Well, we didn't cut it on our last session.' The publisher was real disappointed for a few seconds, then Randy told him, 'We didn't cut it—we *smashed* it.'"

Aptly spoken: "If I Had You" became Alabama's twenty-fifth number one record.

818

AFTER ALL THIS TIME
RODNEY CROWELL
Columbia 68585
Writer: Rodney Crowell
Producers: Tony Brown, Rodney Crowell
May 27, 1989 (1 week)

If familiarity breeds contempt, then Rosanne Cash and Rodney Crowell have a ready-made explanation for their often-stormy marriage. Despite their efforts to maintain a certain distance between their separate solo careers, their relationship has intertwined in numerous ways. They have written a number of songs together, and have provided a sounding board for each other; Rodney has produced most of Rosanne's hits; they both recorded "It's Such A Small World" [see 768]; and each has written songs about the other, like Cash's "Seven Year Ache" [see 426] and Crowell's "After All This Time."

Rodney started the latter tune in 1978, prior to their marriage. He spent a great deal of time with Willie Nelson during that period, and wrote the first two verses with Willie's unique style in mind. After Rodney and Rosanne moved in together, the notebook disappeared, and Crowell didn't see it again until they established a Nashville office in the mid-'80s.

He recalls: "I was unpacking some boxes that had just been sitting since we moved from L.A. to Nashville and found the old notebook, and remembered. It was as if five minutes had passed, so I finished the song."

With seven years elapsing from the song's start to finish, Crowell titled it "After All This Time," then waited several more years before recording it as one of three ballads on the *Diamonds & Dirt* album.

"I thought it was one of Rodney's best-written pieces, but it didn't have any of the signs of what turntable hits are usually made of," assesses producer Tony Brown. "It's over four minutes long, it's slow, but it's got neat hooks in it. We cut it, and I knew it was a real important song for Rodney. But I had no idea that it would be poppin' up in Song of the Year nominations. I think years from now, because of songs like 'After All This Time' and "Til I Gain Control Again' [see 506], they'll be namin' streets after Rodney in Nashville."

"After All This Time" picked up a Grammy award for Best Country Song for 1989, and set a new mark as well. When it reached the top of the chart over Memorial Day, Crowell became the first person ever to write, produce and perform four number one country singles from the same album.

819

WHERE DID I GO WRONG
STEVE WARINER
MCA 53504
Writer: Steve Wariner
Producers: Jimmy Bowen, Steve Wariner
June 3, 1989 (1 week)

Steve Wariner's musical efforts have often involved his family members. He learned to play guitar as a youngster when his father, Roy, practiced with a band in the living room. In the bedroom, Steve played along as they did Hank Williams and George Jones tunes. Eventually, Steve gave his first public performance playing in his dad's band.

Even before that, Steve and his brother, Terry, built their own "instruments." Steve cut guitar bodies out of cardboard and used yarn for strings. Terry, meanwhile, converted oatmeal packages into drums.

Terry later joined Wariner's road band as a

drummer and backing vocalist, but eventually strapped on the guitar. He has also provided backing vocals on many of his brother's records, including 1988's "Hold On (A Little Longer)," which hit number six. Two prior singles from the same album, "Baby, I'm Yours" and "I Should Be With You" (the title track), hit number two.

Steve's brother David came into the picture on Wariner's next album, *I Got Dreams* [see 837]. A graphic artist, David contributed to the LP's jacket design. Steve chose the self-penned "Where Did I Go Wrong" as the first single from the package.

" 'Where Did I Go Wrong' was a gift from somewhere," he notes. "I wrote it in about 30 minutes. I was on tour with Reba McEntire, in the dressing room while she was on, and it came from somewhere and I started writin' it down."

Wariner cut the song with producer Jimmy Bowen at Soundstage Studio in Nashville, achieving an unusual sound when Billy Walker, Jr., tuned up an Ovation 12-string guitar.

"I was watchin' him right before he was gettin' ready to cut it," Steve remembers, "and I saw he was puttin' the capo way down on the neck—I think it was like the tenth or twelfth fret. Then he started playin' that little—it sounds like a mandolin—part. It amazed me to watch him do that. It's so far down, I couldn't understand why it didn't sound out of tune. But a lot of people think it's a mandolin."

Supporting vocalist Mac McAnally developed a vocal "swap" for the end of the record, as he and Wariner trade parts while the song fades out. On June 3, 1989, "Where Did I Go Wrong" went right to number one.

820

A BETTER MAN
CLINT BLACK
RCA 8781
Writers: Clint Black, Hayden Nicholas
Producers: Mark Wright, James Stroud
June 10, 1989 (1 week)

When Clint Black debuted with "A Better Man," he repeatedly earned comparisons to Merle Haggard. Clint has his mother, Ann Black—and Hag—to thank for his introduction to country music.

When Clint was just seven, Mom specially requested a song from KIKK Radio in

Clint Black

Houston, and allowed Clint and his three older brothers to stay up late until that song came on the radio. The station played her request, hooking Clint as a country fan with "Okie From Muskogee" [see 45].

Like Merle, Black emerged as a singer/songwriter, although he hails from the other side of the U.S. Black was born in Long Branch, New Jersey—Bruce Springsteen territory—where his father briefly worked. The family returned to Houston within six months, and during his teens, Clint started playing bass in his brother's band and entertaining at family events. He spent several years on Houston's club circuit, and the song that launched his national career—"a tribute to a dying romance"—paid homage to a girl he had dated for seven years.

"We were friends first, for years, before we ever started datin'," Clint explains, "and I'd like to think we still are friends. I just knew the relationship wasn't gonna work, and I'd just started co-writin' with my guitar player, Hayden Nicholas. He had a musical idea; I sat down with him, and he showed it to me. As soon as I heard it, I asked him to play it again. The second time around, the words rolled off my tongue—'I'm leavin' here a better man/For knowin' you this way . . .' He knew what I was goin' through at the time, and nothin' more needed to be said. We sat down and started workin' on it."

"A Better Man" appeared on the *Billboard* country chart on February 18, 1989. Sixteen weeks later, the record edged into the number one position, making Black the first artist since Freddy Fender to reach the top with his first charted single [see 201—"Before The Next Teardrop Falls"].

821

LOVE OUT LOUD
EARL THOMAS CONLEY
RCA 8824
Writer: Thom Schuyler
Producers: Emory Gordy, Jr.,
Randy L. Scruggs
June 17, 1989 (1 week)

When "Love Out Loud" reached number one on the *Billboard* country chart in June of 1989, Earl Thomas Conley's achievement went all but unnoticed. ETC registered sixteen consecutive number one singles, a feat superseded only by Alabama [see 631—"Forty Hour Week"]. With "Love Out Loud," Conley tied Sonny James [see 86—"Here Comes Honey Again"] for the second longest string of chart-toppers.

"I was quite pleased with 'Love Out Loud' when I initially wrote it," says Thom Schuyler. "I did a very simple, James Taylor-ish kind of demo with acoustic guitar, and pitched it to another artist on the same label as Earl. That artist and his producer had the song on hold for about eighteen months."

When that artist finally recorded it, "Love Out Loud" ended up the tenth song on a nine-song album. Schuyler was understandably upset.

"I got on the phone and called the appropriate people and sort of regurgitated my ill feeling," Schuyler notes. "They understood my state of mind enough to say, 'Let us work on this, we like the song.' They took it to Earl and his producers, and they made what I thought was a wonderful record of it."

"When I first heard this song, I said, 'Yeah,'" Conley relates, "'cause there's so many people that don't like to use the word 'love' cheaply,

and that seldom ever say the word. Even when they feel it, they're afraid to say 'I love you.' I don't know if they're afraid it'll become a watered-down thing, or if they're really not sure they love somebody enough to deserve the word. But there's an awful lot of people that can't say it, yet feel it tremendously."

Conley had enough ballads for *The Heart of It All*, and went into pre-production with Emory Gordy, Jr., and Randy Scruggs to try and find a new arrangement. Schuyler's "folky" demo became more of a rocker in the process.

At the time, Earl vocally admitted his desire to see his string of number one records continue, but it wasn't in the cards. He released "You Must Not Be Drinking Enough"—first recorded by Don Henley on *Building the Perfect Beast*—as the fourth single from his album. It stopped at number 26; Conley's winning streak stopped at sixteen.

822

I DON'T WANT TO SPOIL THE PARTY
ROSANNE CASH
Columbia 68599
Writers: John Lennon, Paul McCartney
Producers: Rodney Crowell,
Rosanne Cash
June 24, 1989 (1 week)

Despite her earlier opposition to a *Greatest Hits* album [see 740—"The Way We Make A Broken Heart"], Rosanne Cash released *Hits 1979-1989* on the heels of her successful *King's Record Shop* package.

"After ten years, it was time," Cash explains. "I like the symmetry of doin' it in a ten-year period. This is the first one I've had out. The record company's asked me about it before, and I never wanted to do it—I really hated the idea. But to compile ten years' worth of work, I thought it was worth it. Also, I'm proud that I've got ten years' worth of this kind of work to put together on an album."

Five months into her pregnancy [see 794—"Runaway Train"], Rosanne went with husband/record producer Rodney Crowell to Ronnie Milsap's GroundStar Lab to cut three new songs in August of 1988. Two of them—"Black And White" and "I Don't Want To Spoil The Party"—appeared on the *Hits* project. The latter, when released as a single, became the first country version of a Beatles tune to reach number one.

"I'm a die-hard Beatles fan," Rosanne admits. "I was president of a Beatles fan club when I was 12. Rodney and I had talked about doing this song. We'd been to Telluride and seen Bela [Fleck], Mark O'Connor, Edgar Meyer, Jerry Douglas, and Pat Flynn. All those guys play together, and we thought it would be so cool to do this song with them. We did it with Pat Flynn and Steuart Smith and Barry Beckett, so it was really an amazing band. Edgar played his beautiful stand-up bass, you know. It was cool."

John Cowan of New Grass Revival helped out on backing vocals, and "I Don't Want To Spoil The Party" coincided with the twenty-fifth anniversary of the Fab Four's invasion of America. It wasn't the first time that the Beatles impacted the country chart: Johnny Rodriguez had a Top Ten version of "Something" in 1974, Anne Murray took "I'm Happy Just To Dance With You" to number 23 in 1980, and Sweethearts of the Rodeo collected a Top Ten remake of "I Feel Fine" in 1989.

823
COME FROM THE HEART
KATHY MATTEA
Mercury 872766
Writers: Susanna Clark, Richard Leigh
Producer: Allen Reynolds
July 1, 1989 (1 week)

With "Come From The Heart" poised at number 23 on May 10, 1989, songwriter Richard Leigh jokingly vowed: "If it doesn't go number one, I'll eat my guitar." Luckily, Richard's teeth and frets all remain intact—"Come From The Heart" reached the top in its twelfth week on the *Billboard* country chart.

Leigh and Guy Clark's wife, Susanna, wrote "Come From The Heart" two years earlier on the second day of a two-day writing session. They spent the first day laboriously piecing together a ballad that didn't quite gel, and the process was so draining that Richard had thoughts of canceling the second session. Nevertheless, they proceeded to work on the same song once more, with the same fruitless results.

"We started talkin' about, 'You know, we're just tryin' too hard,'" Richard recalls. "That's one of the lines in the song: 'Sometimes in life and love, there's such a thing as tryin' too hard.'

"That reminded me of this odd little thing I heard in a club one time that I've never forgotten. A guy yelled out to the woman singin' on the stage, 'That's it, Diane! Come on, sing like you don't need the money!'"

Using that phrase to open the chorus, Leigh and Clark cruised through "Come From The Heart" in less than an hour. Though others echoed their enthusiasm for the song, they struggled a bit getting it recorded, until Don Williams finally nabbed it for his *Traces* album. Kathy Mattea liked it as well, but, because of licensing regulations, had to wait a year before she could record it. At the end of that year, she selected "Come From The Heart" as the first song to cut for her own *Willow in the Wind* project.

"There's something real universal to it," Kathy told Dan Spalding of the *Warsaw Times-Union* in Indiana. "It's one of those songs that, the first time I heard it, I laid down on the middle of the floor and said, 'I can't believe it!' I thought it was a masterpiece."

Mattea's signature vocal work added luster, framed by an arrangement that highlighted Mark O'Connor on mandolin.

Kathy's previous two singles, "Untold Stories" and "Life As We Knew It," both peaked at number four.

824
LOVIN' ONLY ME
RICKY SKAGGS
Epic 68693
Writers: Even Stevens, Hillary Kanter
Producers: Steve Buckingham,
Ricky Skaggs
July 8, 1989 (1 week)

The years 1986 to 1988 were a trying period for Ricky Skaggs. His son, Andrew, was shot in the mouth by a trucker while riding in a car with his mother in August of 1986. Eight-year-old Andrew rebounded from that incident.

In the meantime, Ricky managed only two Top Ten records—"Love's Gonna Get You Someday" and a duet with Sharon White, "Love Can't Ever Get Better Than This"—out of seven consecutive singles. Ricky rebounded as well.

In 1989, he wrapped up a grueling period in which he simultaneously produced Dolly Parton's *White Limozeen* [see 844—"Yellow Roses"] and his own *Kentucky Thunder* album.

"I'll never do that again to my wife and my

Ricky Skaggs

Stevens reports. "It wasn't for her. So Ricky said, 'Fine, I'll record it.'"

"Lovin' Only Me" represented a slight departure for Ricky. For the first time, he called on a co-producer, choosing Sweethearts of the Rodeo producer Steve Buckingham. He also brought the key down and sang in a lower register than on previous singles.

"Lovin' Only Me" first appeared in *Billboard* at number 70 on April 8, 1989, reaching number one in its fourteenth charted week.

825

IN A LETTER TO YOU

EDDY RAVEN

Universal 66003
Writer: Dennis Linde
Producer: Barry Beckett
July 15, 1989 (1 week)

In 1989, Jimmy Bowen launched a new record label, Universal Records, with an impressive roster of already-established recording artists. Just one year later, he dissolved the company and took most of those performers to Capitol. In the interim, Universal racked up two number one singles, both belonging to Eddy Raven. The first, "In A Letter To You," was the fifth chart-topping record in Raven's career.

Raven took "In A Letter To You" from songwriter Dennis Linde, whom he called specifically after their success with "I'm Gonna Get You" [see 770]. Linde scored his first hit with Elvis Presley's "Burning Love," and also added "Had A Dream (For The Heart)," by both Elvis and the Judds; Gary Morris' "The Love She Found In Me"; and Don Williams' "Walkin' A Broken Heart."

Eddy decided on the first hearing to cut "In A Letter To You," but he placed a call to the publisher to warn them that they might get sued, since the song sounded so much like Don Williams' "Then It's Love." As it turned out, Linde had written that, too.

"It was a light lyric, but it was such a drivin' thing," Raven says of "Letter." "That's the first thing I said [to producer Barry Beckett]: 'These lyrics don't make a lot of sense.' He said, 'Yeah, but just remember two or three people rollin' around out there in the grass high on dope, or somethin'.' I said, 'Well, it makes sense to me now.'"

Eddy paid the musicians triple scale to

family," Skaggs insists. "That was the hardest thing. Sharon was pregnant and pretty much spent six months of the pregnancy all by herself, 'cause I was in the studio every day that I was home. If I was workin' on the coast, I'd fly in to Nashville and do some work through the day and fly out to do a show that night. I mean, it was crazy."

It was all worth it, though, as Ricky's efforts provided a double comeback. Dolly earned her first number one record as a solo artist in four years [see 424—"Why'd You Come In Here Lookin' Like That"] and Ricky earned his first in three years, with "Lovin' Only Me."

Former Eddie Rabbitt associate Even Stevens wrote "Lovin' Only Me" with Hillary Kanter, a one-time back-up singer for Julio Iglesias. Stevens thought the song would do well for Dolly and called Hazel Smith, at Ricky's office, to try and schedule an appointment with Skaggs. It took several months to fit Even in, but Ricky was enamored with the song and suggested to Dolly she cut it.

"She thought it was a better song for a man,"

record it during three days of sessions for the *Temporary Sanity* album in early January, 1989. On April 22, "In A Letter To You" debuted on the *Billboard* country chart, and in mid-July, it vaulted to number one.

"The lyrics don't say that much," Beckett affirms, "but when you've got Raven singin' 'em, then it sounds authentic. Some of the good artists would not have brought that thing off that well, 'cause the lyric is pretty simple."

Born Edward Garvin Futch on August 19, 1944, Eddy picked up the "Raven" monicker when he made his first record for the Cosmos label in Georgia. Unknown to Eddy at the time, "Raven" prefigured in his own genealogical history. A dying Cherokee boy had been adopted into his family and nursed back to health. The boy assumed the Futch name, but his Cherokee name, when translated, was Raven.

826
WHAT'S GOING ON IN YOUR WORLD
GEORGE STRAIT
MCA 53648
Writers: David Chamberlain,
Royce Porter
Producers: Jimmy Bowen, George Strait
July 22, 1989 (1 week)

"I go by the hook only," says songwriter David Chamberlain of his writing process. "If somebody gives me a hook—'Just Once I Didn't Think Twice' or 'Take This Job And Shove It' [see 300]—any kind of hook, I pretty much will have it there."

Speaking with Chamberlain is dangerous, since any phrase can and will be used against you in a song. For instance, while he was simply walking down the street, the words from a passerby—"What's goin' on in y'all's world?"—provided the hook for a song that he co-wrote with Royce Porter.

"We wrote it on my boat," notes Porter. "We write a lot on my boat [see 699—"It Ain't Cool To Be Crazy About You"]. I bought a new boat, an 'Ocean Front Property' [see 715] boat. I've got a 43-footer. I think we wrote that song in the winter of '88 on that boat. It was just one of those that when we wrote it, we knew it was a hit."

"What's Going On In Your World" was the highest-debuting single on the *Billboard* chart during the week that ended April 29, 1989. Almost three months later, it popped into the

magazine's number one position, giving George ten straight chart-topping records. Despite his successes, Strait remains a trifle insecure about his abilities to cut hits.

"I still get nervous when I go in the studio," he confides. "I only go in there once a year, and it's not somethin' you can really get used to, I don't think. The studio musicians are used to it, but they're in there every day. For me, it's a different thing every year. You want to try to impress them, as well as everybody else, with your material. You don't want to go in there with a bunch of material that they're gonna just hate to do. That's kind of a way you can gauge how your album's goin'—if *they're* excited about it, then you know you've got somethin'."

827
CATHY'S CLOWN
REBA McENTIRE
MCA 53638
Writer: Don Everly, Phil Everly
Producers: Jimmy Bowen, Reba McEntire
July 29, 1989 (1 week)

When Reba McEntire was three years old, in 1957, the Everly Brothers came seemingly out of nowhere to captivate America. Phil and Don netted eight Top Ten country hits over the next two years, including four number one singles: "Bye Bye Love," "Wake Up Little Susie," "All I Have To Do Is Dream" and "Bird Dog."

They also topped the pop chart three times, the last coming in 1960 with "Cathy's Clown," a record that never appeared on the country chart. "Cathy's Clown" was the first Everly release after they moved from Cadence Records to Warner Bros., and was written in Nashville after a concert tour. Don borrowed from the marching cadence of "The Grand Canyon Suite" and crafted the lyric after a story that his father had conveyed about an old girlfriend named Marion who used to tease him.

The Everly's upbeat, playful number ultimately emerged as their biggest pop record, but even they were probably surprised by the mournful version that Reba turned out nearly thirty years later.

"I didn't think of changing it over like that," Reba admits. "I have to say that back in 1980 or '81, I had a manager who played me the song. Dolly Parton sang it, and I thought, 'Golly, why didn't I get this first?' She never used it. I asked the publisher why she didn't do it, but they didn't know."

In August of 1988, Acuff-Rose sent her Dolly's version once more, and, satisfied that Dolly had never released it, Reba took "Cathy's Clown" to producer Jimmy Bowen. They cut it for her *Sweet Sixteen* album.

"As it turned out, I did the overdubs on it the week after we recorded it, like at 3:00 in the morning," says Reba. "I wanted to do the harmony on it. I wouldn't let Suzy [Hoskins-Wills], my back-up harmony singer, do it at all, 'cause I wanted that one. It was just my little baby. I had just pampered it and pampered it, and I wanted to sing it."

After a lengthy commercial dry spell, the Everlys parted ways in July of 1973, but ten years later, they reunited with a live concert in England. In 1986, Phil and Don returned to number 17 on the country chart with "Born Yesterday."

828

WHY'D YOU COME IN HERE LOOKIN' LIKE THAT

DOLLY PARTON

Columbia 68760
Writers: Bob Carlisle, Randy Thomas
Producer: Ricky Skaggs
August 5, 1989 (1 week)

The three years that followed Dolly Parton's "Think About Love" [see 660] saw her further diversify her already wide-ranging business and entertainment roles.

On May 3, 1986, Dolly lent her name to the Silver Dollar City amusement park chain. The park in her native Sevier County, Tennessee, became Dollywood—an obvious play on the Hollywood sign set in the hills of Los

Dolly Parton

Angeles—and attendance jumped from 758,000 in 1985 to 1.3 million in 1986.

The long-awaited *Trio* project [see 721—"To Know Him Is To Love Him"] finally saw the light of day in 1987, and the same year brought the debut of Parton's TV variety show, "Dolly." ABC signed her for $44 million—the biggest deal in television history—and she laughed off the sum with her usual charm: "It takes a lot of money to make me look this cheap."

Unfortunately, ABC's investment was an embarrassment to both the network and to Dolly. The show debuted on September 27, 1987, and the following May, it aired for the last time. Reportedly, it improved after some of the first installments, although by then, many viewers had already written it off.

While the show was still on the air, Dolly released her first solo album under a new contract with Columbia. *Rainbow*—keyed by a duet with Smokey Robinson—fared about as poorly as *Dolly*. Since *Trio* had performed so well, holding down the number one position on the country album chart for five weeks, she decided to reinvestigate her roots.

Thus, she set to work on *White Limozeen*, co-writing two tracks with Mac Davis and enlisting Ricky Skaggs to produce it. The album hit the stores on June 9, 1989, but on April 25, Columbia released "Why'd You Come In Here Lookin' Like That" in advance. Dolly received the song on a demo tape from Buddy Sheffield, a Mississippi songwriter who also wrote some of her TV scripts. "Why'd You Come In Here" was the last song on the tape, and, it turned out, the only one he didn't write—he had added it to the demo as a favor to a friend.

Jo-El Sonnier provided Cajun accordion on Dolly's session, and "Why'd You Come In Here" represented a comeback when it reached number one, more than three years after Parton's previous solo chart-topper.

Patty Loveless

829
TIMBER I'M FALLING IN LOVE
PATTY LOVELESS
MCA 53641
Writer: Kostas
Producer: Tony Brown
August 12, 1989 (1 week)

"I tell people I'm a combination of Linda Ronstadt, Loretta Lynn and Ralph Stanley."

The Ronstadt influence in Patty Loveless' music comes through in her first number one single, "Timber I'm Falling In Love." The Loretta influence runs much deeper.

Like Lynn, Patty Ramey hailed from a small Kentucky town (Pikeville), and was affiliated with the Wilburn Brothers (after Loretta left their road show [see 92—"One's On The Way"]). Teddy Wilburn didn't feel that then-teenaged Patty was mature enough to record, and when she married Wilburn drummer Terry Lovelace, she moved with him to North Carolina (Patty changed the spelling of her last name when people repeatedly asked if she was related to porn star Linda Lovelace). In fact, Patty claimed Loretta as a relative, although she didn't use the connection as an "in," and kept it secret until Lynn blurted it out on "Nashville Now" in 1989.

Patty stayed away from Nashville for almost ten years, working first in nightclubs, then making a decision to give it up. After a fluke stage appearance, however, she discovered that country music had shifted back to a sound that suited her.

Loveless came to Nashville in 1985, and, two weeks after she recorded a demo, Patty signed with MCA. She waited three years to produce her first Top Ten single, "If My Heart Had Windows." Three more singles reached that level—"A Little Bit In Love," "Blue Side Of Town" and "Don't Toss Us Away"—but her first number one came in 1989 with "Timber I'm Falling In Love."

Kostas, the writer behind "Timber," is a Greek immigrant who ended up in Bozeman, Montana, before the age of ten. Prior to Loveless' *Honky Tonk Angel* album, Kostas bowled over producer Tony Brown with his writing and ended up with three songs on the album. "He wrote 'Timber' later on," explains Patty. "It had such a Buddy Holly feel that I thought it could work for us."

Loveless nailed it on the first take in the recording studio, and Vince Gill later added harmony vocals, but Brown had to fight to get it out as a single. "Everybody thought it was too silly and too simple," he says. "Let's face it: some of our greatest hits of all time weren't necessarily all serious."

Kostas also wrote Patty's Top Ten follow-up, "The Lonely Side Of Love."

Byrne took the resulting demo to Rick Blackburn and Larry Hamby at Columbia Records, and the label gave the group a "thumbs up," asking them to finish an entire album.

"CBS wasn't all that excited about them," Byrne insists. "CBS sort of throws it out there to see if it'll stick. If it does, then they get behind it."

Shenandoah's first two singles did little to generate any excitement, but a third, "She Doesn't Cry Anymore," brought the group to number nine in the spring of 1988. "Mama Knows" followed it to number five; with the band still traveling in a van and hauling a trailer, "The Church On Cumberland Road" [see 814] drove them to number one.

Shenandoah's next release, "Sunday In The South," took a similar path, journeying to the top by the end of summer.

"I remember the very first time we heard it, in Rick Hall and Robert Byrne's office there at FAME," says Raybon. "We heard 'Sunday In The South,' and every one of us turned around and said, 'Man, I grew up like that.'

"I can really honestly and truly relate to that. It really sounded a whole lot like us, as far as our backgrounds and the way our families were—goin' to church, all-day singin', that kind of thing."

830

SUNDAY IN THE SOUTH

SHENANDOAH

Columbia 68892
Writer: Jay Booker
Producers: Rick Hall, Robert Byrne
August 19, 1989 (1 week)

Vocalist Marty Raybon, drummer Mike McGuire, bassist Ralph Ezell, keyboardist Stan Thorn and guitarist Jim Seales never intended to secure a recording contract. Performing as the MGM Band, they invited Muscle Shoals compadre Robert Byrne to hear them play, just to show off some of their individual songs. During the set, they encouraged Byrne to join them onstage; he declined but remained in the audience.

Rick Hall had always liked Byrne's songwriter demos, and had extended an open invitation for Robert to produce any act he believed in through Hall's FAME Productions. After the show, Byrne told Shenandoah that he wanted to work with them in the recording studio, and the band with no formal aspirations suddenly had a window of opportunity.

831

ARE YOU EVER GONNA LOVE ME

HOLLY DUNN

Warner Bros. 22957
Writers: Chris Waters, Tom Shapiro, Holly Dunn
Producers: Chris Waters, Holly Dunn
August 26, 1989 (1 week)

A native of San Antonio, Texas, Holly Dunn brought a wealth of musical experience with her when she moved to Nashville in August of 1979. After singing frequently for her father's Church Of Christ congregation and appearing at a variety of high school talent competitions, Holly landed a gig in 1975 with the Freedom Folk Singers, a group that tied in with the Bicentennial. She moved on to the Hilltop Singers and then appeared solo at numerous local hangouts. In the meantime, she attended Abilene Christian University.

It took a little time for Holly to get off the ground in Music City. Five years after she established residence, she finally earned her first hit by writing Louise Mandrell's Top Ten single "I'm Not Through Loving You Yet." Shortly thereafter, MTM Records signed her as a recording artist. By 1987, Dunn had netted the Top New Female Vocalist trophy from the Academy of Country Music, plus the Horizon award from the Country Music Association—primarily for "Daddy's Hands," a song she wrote as a Father's Day gift to her dad.

Five more Top Ten records increased Holly's recognizability, including "A Face in The Crowd" (her duet with Michael Martin Murphey) and "Love Someone Like Me," which peaked at number two. MTM folded in late 1988, about the same time she wrote "Are You Ever Gonna Love Me" with Tom Shapiro and her brother, Chris Waters. When she signed with Warner Bros. the following February, Dunn immediately started recording *The Blue Rose of Texas*, and made the song the first track on the album.

"Tom came in with the melody and I had an idea lyrically," she remembers, "and we rolled with it. I wanted an uptempo song with sort of a pseudo-positive message to it to round out the *Blue Rose* project, and that's what we came up with.

"Of all the songs on the album, it was the one that worried me the most, 'cause I felt like it was certainly the most middle-of-the-road song that I'd put out in quite some time. Most of my stuff tends to be traditional-sounding. We could've gone really far away musically with this song from the kind of records that I normally put out."

By the summer—ten years after Holly moved to Nashville—"Are You Ever Gonna Love Me" became her first number one single.

832

I'M STILL CRAZY
VERN GOSDIN
Columbia 68888
Writers: Vern Gosdin, Steve Gosdin,
Buddy Cannon
Producer: Bob Montgomery
September 2, 1989 (1 week)

On October 9, 1989, the Country Music Association cited "Chiseled In Stone" as Song of the Year. Thirteen years before it was actually written, songwriter Max D. Barnes conceived the idea in honor of his son, who died in a car accident. When he showed the idea to Vern

Gosdin, Vern co-wrote it about his divorce. The record reached number six in November of 1988.

Divorce played a key role in Gosdin's album *Alone*, his follow-up to the *Chiseled in Stone* album.

"All the songs I wrote for the [*Alone*] album came from a divorce," Gosdin told Shawn Williams in the *Music City News*. "Max D. Barnes wrote 'Alone.' I thought it was one of the greatest songs I'd ever heard. It just gets to me. There's a line in there that just knocks me out—'Then a chill crawled all over me.' I told Max, 'I'll kill you if you put another line like that in a song!'"

Columbia Records tapped "I'm Still Crazy" as the first single from *Alone*.

Holly Dunn

"We wrote that song sometime in the summer of '88," notes co-writer Buddy Cannon. "Vern was over at my house one night. We're neighbors, and we're always tryin' to come up with a new song idea when he's around, so we were sittin' around my kitchen table there, and that one was just kind of born. We didn't start out with an idea or anything."

Gosdin and Cannon finished the first verse and the chorus that evening, but when they got stuck, they decided to wait until later to finish the song.

"Well," Buddy recounts, "Vern went out on the road to work a date, and his son, Steve Gosdin, plays in his band. Vern and Steve got to messin' with that out on the road, and Steve kicked in most of the last verse, so it was kind of written in two different places. When they got back off the tour, they had 'I'm Still Crazy' finished. That's the first song Steve's ever had recorded, and one of the first ones he ever wrote."

"I'm Still Crazy" first appeared in *Billboard* during Memorial Day weekend of 1989, debuting at number 68. Over Labor Day weekend, it reached number one.

833

I WONDER DO YOU THINK OF ME
KEITH WHITLEY
RCA 8940
Writer: Sanger D. Shafer
Producers: Garth Fundis, Keith Whitley
September 9, 1989 (1 week)

At 9:45 A.M. on May 9, 1989, producer Garth Fundis concluded an interview for this book, and mentioned that he was rushing to ready a new Keith Whitley album for fall release. At the same time, at a different location, Keith was speaking on the phone with his mom. Three hours later, Whitley had passed away [see 813—"I'm No Stranger To The Rain"].

In the ensuing weeks, RCA speeded up the production process even further, and on June 9, the first single, Whitey Shafer's "I Wonder Do You Think Of Me," hit the streets. Originally, Keith had wanted to release Lefty Frizzell's collaboration with Shafer, "I Never Go Around Mirrors," as a single from the *Don't Close Your Eyes* [see 781] album.

Keith greatly admired Lefty, and on his way to the studio to record "Mirrors," he actually stopped by the cemetery where Frizzell was

buried—less than a quarter of a mile from the home Whitley shared with Lorrie Morgan—and stood in the rain over Lefty's grave, reciting the lyrics to "Mirrors."

Despite Keith's emotional rendition of the song, RCA felt it wouldn't work for radio, and encouraged him to find a similar, but more commercial, song. That's when Keith came up with "I Wonder Do You Think Of Me," which Lorrie approved for release after Whitley's passing.

"When I first got married to Lyndia [see 727—"All My Ex's Live In Texas"]," Shafer remembers, "she sold her house and bought me an electric piano, and that's the first melody I came up with. I never could find any idea, or any words, that I wanted to put to that song. But every once in a while, I'll just play an old melody if I'm in a certain mood, and words will fall into that melody.

"About 1986, I came up with that song. Keith was gonna put it out as a single, regardless of the circumstances, but it's kind of [ironic] the way it is now. It kind of hits the nail on the head."

"I Wonder Do You Think Of Me" landed at number 48 in its first week in *Billboard*, June 24, 1989. It required only a dozen weeks to reach number one.

834

NOTHING I CAN DO ABOUT IT NOW
WILLIE NELSON
Columbia 38 68923
Writer: Beth Nielsen Chapman
Producer: Fred Foster
September 16, 1989 (1 week)

After more than a decade of practically unabated success, Willie Nelson hit a major slump after "Living In The Promiseland" [see 676] hit number one in 1986. He waited more than two years before making the Top Ten again with "Spanish Eyes" [see 569—"To All The Girls I've Loved Before"]. Willie waited more than three years to earn his twentieth chart-topping release, "Nothing I Can Do About Now," pulled from his album *A Horse Called Music*.

The LP teamed Nelson with his long-time friend, Fred Foster. The owner of the defunct Monument label, Foster was the first—or one of the first—to sign Dolly Parton, Roy Orbison, Larry Gatlin and Kris Kristofferson, among others. The label dated back to 1959, when Billy Grammer went to the Top Five with "Gotta Travel On."

Though Monument was dormant for several years, Foster reactivated it in 1982 with the release of *The Winning Hand*, a double-album that featured a variety of duets between Parton, Nelson, Kristofferson and Brenda Lee. The album netted a hit, with Dolly & Willie's "Everything's Beautiful (In Its Own Way)."

Foster had gone through a traumatic bankruptcy when he and Nelson hooked up on *A Horse Called Music*. Willie called Fred in Nashville to set up a game of golf, during which Foster played him a demo of the title track. Willie booked studio time for the following week and they cut that song, then proceeded to do an album's worth of material.

Foster picked up the first single, "Nothing I Can Do About It Now," from songwriter Beth Nielsen Chapman. "I ran into her in the parking lot," he recalls, "and asked her if she had anything uptempo for Willie. She said, 'No, but I'll write something.'"

"We listened to probably a hundred songs," Willie continues, "and we did two of Beth Nielsen Chapman's songs. That track was cut in Nashville. Actually, Beth sang the original vocal on it. Then they came down to Austin, and I added my vocal and Beth sang harmony with me. She really sort of laid it out there for me to follow."

Another Nelson single, "There You Are," reached the Top Ten.

As Willie watched the *Horse Called Music* album return him to the top, he also put together a new cable venture, the Cowboy Television Network.

835
ABOVE AND BEYOND
RODNEY CROWELL
Columbia 68948
Writer: Harlan Howard
Producers: Tony Brown, Rodney Crowell
September 23, 1989 (1 week)

On May 16, 1989, songwriter Harlan Howard offered a prediction for Rodney Crowell's "Above And Beyond": "It will be a Top Five hit. Rodney told me at least a year ago it was going to be a single, but, to tell you the truth, I kind of gave up on it, 'cause they'd put out so many records from this album."

Rodney Crowell

Harlan's skepticism was understandable: four singles preceded "Above And Beyond" from *Diamonds & Dirt*, despite Crowell's original intentions to release it first.

"The first song we cut on the album was 'Above And Beyond,'" explains producer Tony Brown. "We cut that, and everybody said 'That's a hit.' Then we cut 'I Couldn't Leave You If I Tried' [see 784], and everybody said 'That's a number one, too.'

"We definitely wanted to make 'Above And Beyond' the centerpiece of the album, to give us a direction. We cut it first on purpose, to set the mood and the tone of the album. That way, the rest of the songs wouldn't take too big a departure from mainstream country."

Buck Owens achieved a hit with the song first, taking it to number three on the *Billboard* chart back in 1960. Rodney—then nine years old—learned to sing it at that time, and years later, got a chance to co-write "Somewhere Tonight" [see 751] with Howard. When Rodney held back on "Above And Beyond," Owens asked if it was going to be issued as a single; if not, then he wanted to re-record it himself!

After Crowell's recording finally hit the streets in June of 1989, it exceeded Howard's expectations, reaching country's summit in September. In the process, Rodney set a standard as the first country artist to gain five number one singles off an album. *Diamonds & Dirt* went on to gold certification in March of 1990.

"Five number ones on that album was definitely a peak," Rodney concedes, "but it's not the last peak for me. There'll be other peaks, and I'm not gonna try to break my own record consciously. Songs are songs, you know. Once I write them or record them, I just have to let them go. I can't get my ego involved in it."

836
LET ME TELL YOU ABOUT LOVE
THE JUDDS
RCA 8947
Writers: Carl Perkins, Paul Kennerley, Brent Maher
Producer: Brent Maher
September 30, 1989 (1 week)

Jackson, Tennessee, resident Carl Perkins holds an influential position in music, thanks to his pioneering rockabilly efforts on the Sun label. Carl's "Blue Suede Shoes" became a number one country record in 1956, and stopped at number two on the *Billboard* pop charts.

Perkins has contributed only two more Top Ten country singles as an artist: "Boppin' The Blues" and "Dixie Fried." He's been an important contributor as both a guitarist and songwriter on many other records, especially "Daddy Sang Bass" [see 24] and "Let Me Tell You About Love."

"Carl's one of the most wonderful people on the planet," producer Brent Maher enthuses, "and he's so into his music. If he sits down and plays you 'Blue Suede Shoes,' he will play it with as much heart and soul as he did twenty-five or thirty years ago."

Maher and Don Potter co-produced a Perkins album, and out of that association, Brent suggested to Carl that they try to write together. Finding time was a problem, but Maher had a writing session scheduled with Paul Kennerley and correctly predicted that Perkins would be welcome. "To have Carl Perkins in your kitchen," says Paul, "is quite exciting."

"I think it was on a Saturday," Maher recounts. "Carl drove up from Jackson, and we sat down, and I'll tell you, the place was loaded with groove. He started playin' that great little rockabilly groove, and we started singin' and chantin'. That's just a fun song. If you want to dissect a lyric and say, 'Are you serious?,' that's one to dissect."

Maher added the melody to Perkins' pickin', and Kennerley came up with the title "Let Me Tell You About Love." Finally, they concocted a series of verses that pulled together five romantic couples from history and literature.

"We did a demo and had Carl in the garage at the house," Kennerley reports. "We had a two-car garage, and one side of it I converted into a little demo studio for myself, a sixteen-track thing. The other side of it was an empty, cold garage. We put Carl out there and did this little track, and it was fantastic."

Perkins also contributed his guitar licks to the actual record, the Judds' fourteenth to reach number one.

The '90s started for Wynonna and Naomi on a sour note. Naomi woke up ill on New Year's Day, then visited the doctor that week. Physicians discovered she possessed a rare, incurable strain of hepatitis. The Judds kept it fairly private until October 19, when they announced that Naomi would have to give her final concert tour in 1991.

837

I GOT DREAMS

STEVE WARINER

MCA 53665
Writers: Steve Wariner, Bill LaBounty
Producers: Jimmy Bowen, Steve Wariner
October 7, 1989 (1 week)

Steve Wariner

"I Got Dreams" represented Steve Wariner's ninth number one single, but it also represented a first for country music. Wariner improvised a George Benson-like "scat" solo in the center of the record, vocally doubling a line he played on guitar.

Louis Armstrong first popularized "scat"—nonsensical phrases used in an improvised vocal solo—in 1926, purportedly when he forgot the words to a song he was recording. Jazz singers Ella Fitzgerald and Mel Torme also employed scat frequently.

Unless one counts Roger Miller's quirky "Dang Me," which reached number one twenty-five years earlier, "I Got Dreams" was the first number one country single to feature that kind of performance. Wariner co-wrote the song with Bill LaBounty, and the scat element was there practically from the beginning.

"While we were makin' the little rough work tape, as we had written it, I was just kind of foolin' around, doin' the scat singin'," Steve says. "I don't know why. I was just messin' around, and Bill said, 'Yeah, I love that.' When I was workin' with Chet Atkins years ago [see 452—"All Roads Lead To You"], he always loved that, when I would scat. He always said, 'You ought to do more of that on record,' so that's kind of why I did it, too."

"'I Got Dreams' kind of came together quickly," LaBounty continues, "and it was more of a groove approach to the music, which you don't hear too much of in country. But Steve is one artist who's really into the rhythmic feel, and I've always liked that about him.

"That was just something where I had the music, and the feel. I knew I was gonna write with Steve the next day, so I sort of got it ready. In fact, I even had the title—I was thinkin' 'I Got Dreams' at the chorus line."

When Wariner came over to Bill's house, they each had an idea to work with. Steve had a ballad started, but he decided he'd rather work on LaBounty's groove. Writing around a drum-machine pattern, they wrapped up the song in under three hours.

838

KILLIN' TIME

CLINT BLACK

RCA 8945
Writers: Clint Black, Hayden Nicholas
Producers: James Stroud, Mark Wright
October 14, 1989 (1 week)

The seeds of Clint Black's debut album were planted in early 1987. He needed to hire a band for a one-time performance, and reluctantly accepted a group whose guitarist reminded him of Cyndi Lauper. By the time their lone rehearsal rolled around, she had left the band, replaced by a Houston guitar player who had recently returned from Los Angeles, Hayden Nicholas.

Blown away by his playing, Black pulled Nicholas aside during a break and told Hayden how desperately he wanted to make a good demo. Nicholas owned an eight-track studio at home, and they worked out an agreement to record some material there. After their first session, it became apparent that Black and Nicholas were on a similar musical wavelength—they wrote a song, "Straight From The Factory," that evening.

In May, Black took a demo tape to a Houston record promoter, Sammy Alfano, hoping to find a manager. Two days later, Alfano had arranged for a one-on-one performance at the office of ZZ Top manager Bill Ham. In turn, Ham signed Clint to a management deal, and, within three months, Black inked another deal, landing with RCA Records.

The process of making the first album showered a mixture of emotions on Clint. There were plenty of exciting possibilities for his future, but in the short run, he had to endure the frustration of waiting.

"We were about halfway through the album production," Clint recalls, "and Hayden and I were drivin' off to some gig north of town. We were always talkin' about, 'There's a lot goin' on, but there's not a lot goin' on around here . . . yet.' We had a lot of time on our hands, and I said, 'Yeah, this killin' time is killin' me.' We looked at each other, our eyes got real big, and we knew we had a hook."

"Killin' Time" became the title track for Black's debut album, released April 29, 1989. After the success of "A Better Man" [see 820], "Killin' Time" emerged as Clint's second single, hitting number one during the week of the Country Music Association awards show. By that time, the *Killin' Time* album had reached number one on the *Billboard* country chart and gone gold as well. For his efforts, the CMA honored Black with the Horizon award for new and/or developing acts.

839

LIVING PROOF
RICKY VAN SHELTON

Columbia 68994
Writers: Johnny MacRae, Steve Clark
Producer: Steve Buckingham
October 21, 1989 (1 week)

With five consecutive number one singles under his belt, Ricky Van Shelton stopped short of his sixth. His version of the Felice and Boudleaux Bryant composition, "Hole In My Pocket," didn't get past number three in the summer of 1989.

Ricky returned to the top, however, with the fourth single from the *Loving Proof* album, "Living Proof." Originally, Shelton planned "Living Proof" as the album title, but board-

room discussions at CBS altered his blueprint. Hank Williams, Jr.'s biography, written by Michael Bane, carried the same title, and label executives wanted to avoid any possible confusion.

"It wouldn't have gotten mixed up," Shelton laments, with 20/20 hindsight. "If people had bought *Living Proof*, they would have been buyin' it for me. There was no danger in it getting mixed up. I wish I hadn't listened to 'em now."

The album did well enough under the *Loving Proof* banner. The Recording Industry Association of America certified it gold in December of 1988, and readers of the *Music City News* named it the Album of the Year in 1989. Ricky picked up a total of four awards at the *Music City News* ceremony, including Male Artist of the Year, and two trophies for "I'll Leave This World Loving You" [see 795]: Single Record of the Year and Video of the Year.

Johnny MacRae co-wrote "Living Proof" with Steve Clark, a Lexington, Kentucky, native who signed to MacRae's Hide-A-Bone Music publishing company. They created it in a frequent meeting place—MacRae's secluded cabin at Kentucky Lake, about 25 miles southeast of Paducah.

"Steve came down for a week," Johnny remembers. "We go up there and fish and write. It's away from telephones, it's away from everything, and it's a great place to work. In fact, most of the success I've had in the last few years has been songs written there, just because of that relaxed atmosphere."

"Living Proof" hit number one on October 21, 1989, in its fourteenth charted week. The single first appeared on the *Billboard* country chart on July 22, at number 95. Only one number one record ever debuted at a lower rung: Freddy Fender's "Before The Next Teardrop Falls" [see 201].

840

HIGH COTTON
ALABAMA

RCA 8948
Writers: Roger Murrah, Scott Anders
Producers: Josh Leo, Alabama
October 28, 1989 (1 week)

On April 10, 1989, Charlie Daniels and Carl Perkins presented Alabama with a very special award, when the Academy of Country Music cited the band as the Artist of the Decade.

No one could dispute the honor. In their first ten years of national acceptance, Alabama sold 40 million records, won two Grammy awards [see 528—"The Closer You Get"], picked up 13 ACM trophies and earned eight more honors from the Country Music Association. *Billboard* named Alabama the top country artist every year from 1982 through 1985.

The group closed out the decade with their twenty-sixth number one single, "High Cotton," written by Roger Murrah and Scott Anders. The duo had penned the Oak Ridge Boys' "Ozark Mountain Jubilee" in 1983; "High Cotton" was actually written around that period of time, but Anders had dropped out of the business before Alabama picked it up. The song brought him back into the music industry to write for Murrah's publishing company.

"Scott and I had a mutual friend, when my wife and I first moved to Franklin," says Murrah, recalling their first meeting. "We lived in this little apartment below the landlady's son, and Scott was a friend of theirs. He played guitar and he was into music, so they thought we might be good acquaintances. One thing led to another and we became real good friends. He's a carpenter by trade, and we wrote quite a few songs together."

Like his "Southern Rains" [see 413], Murrah's "High Cotton" paid homage to Dixie, a theme that has succeeded frequently for Alabama. As it turned out, the song became the rope in a friendly tug-of-war between Barry Beckett and Josh Leo, who each produced half of the *Southern Star* LP.

Beckett had produced the song for Murrah several years earlier, when Roger was pursuing a recording deal. Mark Wright, an A & R man for RCA, reminded Beckett of the tune, but he cut so much material on Alabama that he never quite got around to recording "High Cotton." Barry thought he would save it for the band's next album—until Leo asked for "High Cotton" when he couldn't find enough songs for *his* half of *Southern Star*.

Laughs Beckett: "Of course, I kidded him a little bit, and said, 'No, get out there and find some songs, Josh.' So eventually, he had a hard time findin' songs, and I said, 'Here, take the song . . . but you owe me.'"

841

ACE IN THE HOLE
GEORGE STRAIT

George Strait

MCA 53693
Writer: Dennis Adkins
Producers: Jimmy Bowen, George Strait
November 4, 1989 (1 week)

Merle Haggard has his Strangers, Barbara Mandrell has her Do-Rites, and Mel Tillis has his Statesiders. The difference between those bands and George Strait's Ace In The Hole Band is that the those three artists named their groups after their early hits. In Strait's case, the band name came *before* the song.

Songwriter Dennis Adkins, a music industry veteran who has lived and worked in both Nashville and Bakersfield, didn't tailor "Ace In The Hole" to Strait's group. In fact, he had already written half the song before he ever made the connection. Despite the obvious link, "Ace In The Hole" didn't win instant approval from George.

"I believe the song had been pitched to me before and I passed on it," Strait admits. "It was one of those that just kind of got aced out for some reason or another, but Dennis pitched it to me again, and it caught my ear.

"So we went in there and did it. It doesn't have anything to do with the band, but I thought it was kind of a neat twist. The band is named Ace In The Hole, and the song is the same thing. I caught a little flak on not bringin' the band in to cut it, but at the time, it just wasn't right for that to happen."

As it was, Strait garnered a hot instrumental performance from the assembled studio band; he further enhanced the sound by using saxophone player Steve Marsh in tandem with some of the steel guitar and fiddle lines. With its clever ploy and infectious rhythm, "Ace In The Hole" dealt George his eighteenth number one single in November of 1989. During the Grammy awards in February, Bud Light debuted a new commercial that featured "Ace In The Hole" as its theme song.

Strait didn't pick up any honors that night, but he finally aced the Country Music Association awards the previous October: after five straight nominations, George was named Entertainer of the Year.

Quiet and reserved, Strait hadn't been picked by more than a handful of insiders, owing to a stage show that was short on gloss, but long on music. Still, when he accepted the award, he declared what many voters already felt: "I truly believe audiences go away entertained."

842

BURNIN' OLD MEMORIES
KATHY MATTEA

Mercury 874672
Writers: Larry Boone, Gene Nelson, Paul Nelson
Producer: Allen Reynolds
November 11, 1989 (1 week)

When Larry Boone went to Florida Atlantic University on a baseball scholarship, he possessed All-American dreams, but a knee injury doused his athletic intentions. Boone went on to collect a physical education degree, with several journalism courses thrown in, and first considered sportswriting as a living. That idea didn't last long. In the early '80s, he moved to Nashville and ended up singing at the Country Wax Museum on Music Row, right across from the Country Music Hall of Fame [see 755—"Goin' Gone"].

After losing his scholarship, Boone paid his way through school by playing at a Boca Raton steakhouse, where another aspiring musician, Gene Nelson, had played a couple years before. After his move to Music City, Boone met

Nelson, and they began writing together—along with Gene's brother, Paul—penning forty or fifty songs in a year's time.

About twenty of those tunes have since been recorded, including "Old Coyote Town," by Don Williams, and "Burnin' Old Memories," picked up by Kathy Mattea. Boone and the Nelsons wrote the latter title when they were stumped on another tune.

"We really didn't have any direction to go with the other song," says Larry. "I threw this title out, and everybody said, 'Yeah, let's write it.' I had the chorus, where the hook lays, and so we just jumped on it and wrote the song real fast."

A number of performers put "Burnin' Old Memories" on hold, including Ricky Van Shelton and Janie Frickie, and it went unrecorded for three years. Despite Allen Reynolds' encouragement, Kathy Mattea was reluctant to record it, but during a session for the *Willow in the Wind* album, they ran through three songs, and still had time remaining for another. Reynolds brought up "Burnin' Old Memories" again; this time, Mattea agreed to try it.

They did it on the first take, with Ricky Skaggs alumni Ray Flacke and Bruce Bouton trading electric guitar and steel licks. Ultimately, it followed "Come From The Heart" [see 823] as a single, and Kathy sang it on the Country Music Association awards show in October of 1989—the same night she won the Female Vocalist of the Year trophy. Two months later, "Burnin' Old Memories" hit number one.

One year earlier, Larry Boone earned his first Top Ten single as a recording artist, with "Don't Give Candy To A Stranger."

843

BAYOU BOYS
EDDY RAVEN

Universal 66016
Writers: Frank J. Myers, Troy Seals, Eddy Raven
Producer: Barry Beckett
November 18, 1989 (1 week)

"I've been trying for years to marry the Creole, Cajun, Caribbean reggae sound, put it all together," Eddy Raven said, shortly after completing *Temporary Sanity*. "I finally got what I think is the answer with 'Zydeco Lady' and 'Bayou Boys.'

"We've got the steel-drum sound the islands have, with a groove and drive and lyrical cadence that the Cajun music gives you, and we haven't put the fiddles in it. But we've got the accordion sound with the synthesizer. I call it, affectionately, my electric Cajun music. This album is the first time that I've come out of a session feeling I've finally taken that next step for Cajun music."

"Bayou Boys" was a semi-autobiographical song, documenting a carousing Louisiana youth. Raven carried the idea for two years, and suggested it to his guitarist, Frank Myers. Finally, with a deadline approaching for the *Temporary Sanity* album, they tried to fashion it one night at Eddy's house, although he wasn't pleased with the results.

Myers, however, thought they should cut it, and took the song to producer Barry Beckett, who felt it was incomplete. Myers kept suggesting the song during the session, and Raven finally told him if they were going to do it, it needed a rewrite.

"In between cuts, while they were re-doin' some stuff in the control room, Troy Seals came in," Raven remembers. "We'd been doin' 'Zydeco Lady' and 'Island' [two songs Seals and Raven co-wrote], and we went to eat lunch and talked about it. We got back to the studio with about 30 minutes to go, and I said, 'Let's go work on this song.'

"I told Frank to get the guitar, and I completely rewrote the lyrics right there. Troy was there. He didn't want to take a piece of the songwriting credit, but I said, 'Aw, you're here—shit, you bought us lunch.' So Troy got in on that deal, and he had a couple of ideas. He came up with that line about 'Told each other secrets/Wore each other's clothes.' He started that chain of thought."

"Bayou Boys" and "Risky Business" edged out another song for the last two spots on the album. After Raven went on a Cajun package tour during the summer, the electric Cajun sound of "Bayou Boys" brought him his second number one on the Universal label.

Dolly Parton and Ricky Skaggs worked together on several occasions prior to his producing of her *White Limozeen* album. He performed on her remake of the Beatles' "Help!" for an album a decade earlier, and she joined him in a duet on Ricky's *Don't Cheat in Our Hometown*. He was a logical choice as producer once she decided to renew her mountain roots.

"He had a better understanding of who I am," Dolly explained to William Stadiem in *Interview*, "because he grew up in eastern Kentucky, very similar to the way we did, and his people are like my people. He knows that Appalachian music, the Irish-English-Dutch influence that came there to the Appalachian mountains. And I felt that if I was gonna do a true country album in a big way again, it was important to have somebody who has an understanding of my roots."

The second single to come from *White Limozeen* was "Yellow Roses," a tune that Parton wrote alone for the project. "I remember her playin' me some songs that she'd written when we were lookin' for songs for the album," Skaggs notes. "She said, 'Well, here's one you might like.' And when I heard it, I said, 'Yeah, I like that a lot—that's really country.'

"One of the things that I felt was real important to that song was strings. I had never cut strings before on any record in my life. I've done fiddle things, but had never used a string ensemble. When I heard 'Yellow Roses,' I said, 'That's the Dolly of old—that's the '60s Dolly right there.' We wanted to get the old string sound from those early Nashville records."

"Yellow Roses" reached number one during the Thanksgiving weekend in 1989, about the same time that Dolly's fourth movie, *Steel Magnolias*, hit American theaters. Dolly remains a talent of many dimensions.

"Everybody wants to be successful at whatever their inner dream is," she philosophizes. "I'm not near finished with what I want to do yet. I want to be somebody that left something good behind for somebody else to enjoy."

844

YELLOW ROSES
DOLLY PARTON
Columbia 69040
Writer: Dolly Parton
Producer: Ricky Skaggs
November 25, 1989 (1 week)

845

IT'S JUST A MATTER OF TIME
RANDY TRAVIS
Warner Bros. 28841
Writers: Brook Benton, Belford
Hendrickson, Clyde Otis
Producer: Richard Perry
December 2, 1989 (1 week)

Prior to 1989, only two Randy Travis singles ever hit the *Billboard* country chart without reaching the Top Ten. Travis released the first, "She's My Woman," under his real name, Randy Traywick, in 1978. Produced by Joe Stampley on Paula Records, it stalled at number 91. The second, "On The Other Hand" [see 680], managed only a number 67 peak position, although the record easily eclipsed its initial performance when re-released by Warner Bros.

Travis and associates gambled in 1989 with an unusual single titled "Promises." Recorded with just vocals and an acoustic guitar, the highly dissonant song stopped at number 17 after eight weeks on the chart. "Promises" represented Randy's first non-Top Ten release in four years, so the first single from his next album was crucial.

Travis came up with "It's Just A Matter Of Time," a song he recorded with pop producer Richard Perry (whose credits include Barbra Streisand, the Pointer Sisters, Carly Simon and "To All The Girls I've Loved Before" [see 569]) for a compilation album titled *Rock, Rhythm & Blues*. Warners singled out Travis as the only country contributor in a ten-cut line-up that included Elton John, Chaka Khan, Michael McDonald and Christine McVie, among others.

Perry tried to recapture the sound of the late-'50s pop classics, and had Travis re-learn Brook Benton's original version of "It's Just A Matter Of Time" practically note-for-note.

"It's just about as close to pop as you're ever going to hear from me," Randy told Peter Reilly of *Stereo Review*. "Perry's purpose is to show the influence that country has had on rock. You can hear that when you listen to Hank Williams."

Despite Perry's Los Angeles ties, they recorded "It's Just A Matter Of Time" in Nashville, using mostly Music City session players. Perry himself sang the bass parts. Randy was so pleased with the results that he persuaded Warners to include the track on his own *No Holdin' Back* LP. They released it as the album's first single; it debuted in *Billboard* at number 44 on September 23, 1989. Ten weeks later, "It's Just A Matter Of Time" reached number one, twenty months after Benton passed away [see 67—"Endlessly"].

Travis' release represented the third go-around for "It's Just A Matter Of Time" on the country chart. Sonny James took it to number one in 1970 [see 49], and Glen Campbell released it in 1985, reaching number seven.

846

IF TOMORROW NEVER COMES
GARTH BROOKS
Capitol 44430
Writers: Kent Blazy, Garth Brooks
Producer: Allen Reynolds
December 9, 1989 (1 week)

"If I have any talent at all," says a modest Garth Brooks, "it's from God, and my mom, who was on Capitol Records also."

Garth's mother, Colleen Carroll, recorded for the label in the mid-'50s without success, then married and settled in Oklahoma. Garth came along on February 7, 1962, and grew up in Yukon, giving his first performance at a fourth-grade talent show. After a brief fling with a local act called the Nyle, Brooks played 24 hours a week at Shotgun's Pizza Parlor, while pursuing an advertising degree at Oklahoma State University. In 1985, he headed to Nashville for the first time, but stayed only 23 hours before returning home.

"I thought the world was waiting for me," Brooks now laughs, "but there's nothing colder than reality. I wouldn't trade that experience for the world; it's what I needed, but I knew I was coming back."

His return came two years later, with a group called Santa Fe. After a month, the band disintegrated, but Garth rolled up his sleeves and went to work on his dream. He sang on numerous demo sessions around town, and ended up with a Capitol recording deal after playing a Nashville Entertainment Association showcase.

The label released Brooks' eponymous debut album, produced by Allen Reynolds, on April 12, 1989, with half of the record's ten cuts written by Garth. His first single, "Much Too Young (To Feel This Damn Old)," debuted inauspiciously at number 94 on March 24. Sixteen weeks later, the record peaked at number eight, eliciting vocal comparisons to George Strait.

Brooks followed with another self-penned tune, "If Tomorrow Never Comes," in which the singer contemplates his own death, and how he'll be perceived by his widow, Sandy.

"This song means a lot because of friends I have lost in the past," he assesses. "It makes the statement, 'If tomorrow never comes, have I done my job?' I passed that idea by a thousand songwriters until Kent Blazy realized the potential of the song, and we wrote it."

Garth Brooks

The day before the recording session, bass player Mike Chapman welcomed a baby into his family, and he plastered pictures of his son all over the music stand. "If Tomorrow Never Comes" took on another meaning for the musicians, and their sensitive rendition resulted in a number one single for Brooks in December.

847

TWO DOZEN ROSES
SHENANDOAH
Columbia 69061
Writers: Robert Byrne, Mac McAnally
Producers: Rick Hall, Robert Byrne
December 16, 1989 (1 week)

When the MGM Band [see 830—"Sunday In The South"] signed with Columbia Records, the group and producer Robert Byrne made an effort to find a new, permanent mon-

icker. Byrne ran a contest in the Muscle Shoals area with little success, and ultimately, the name came down to a last-minute decision.

"We was called down to Rick Hall's office at FAME studios," explains vocalist Marty Raybon, "and was told at 5:00 that at 5:30 our first record was goin' to press. They said we had two names, and we had to pick either one of 'em, because if we didn't, *they*'d pick it, and we'd have to stick with what they gave us. The names were Shenandoah and the Rhythm Rangers. We just couldn't really see ourselves as the Rhythm Rangers."

After "Mama Knows" took Shenandoah into Top Five territory for the first time, the label chose "The Church On Cumberland Road" [see 814] as a single. In the process, they put off releasing the group's second choice, "Two Dozen Roses." With two number one singles under their collective belt, Shenandoah finally pulled that song in the fall of 1989.

Hall, Byrne and the band were all quite familiar with Muscle Shoals resident Mac

McAnally, whose writing credits included Alabama's "Old Flame" [see 421], T.G. Sheppard's "You're My First Lady" and Ricky Van Shelton's "Crime Of Passion," among others. Hall asked McAnally and Byrne to write something specifically for Shenandoah, and Mac got started while taking care of his kids. Once he got them to sleep, he stepped out on the porch, and the first line of "Two Dozen Roses" popped into his head. He immediately associated it with Raybon, and then finished writing it with the band in mind.

Byrne—sensitive about having too many of his songs recorded by the group—didn't play it for Shenandoah. Instead, McAnally gave it to Hall on a day that Robert wasn't around. Once they decided to cut it, however, Byrne handled production on the record.

"Two Dozen Roses" first appeared at number 61 on the *Billboard* country chart on September 16, 1989. Exactly three months later, Shenandoah collected its third consecutive number one single.

848

A WOMAN IN LOVE
RONNIE MILSAP
RCA 9027
Writers: Doug Millett, Curtis Wright
Producers: Ronnie Milsap, Rob Galbraith, Tom Collins
December 23, 1989 (2 weeks)

The '80s closed out on an "up" note for both Ronnie Milsap and a former Vern Gosdin associate, Curtis Wright. Milsap earned his thirty-fifth number one single, putting him third on the all-time list behind Conway Twitty, with forty chart-topping hits, and Merle Haggard, with thirty-eight.

Number thirty-five for Milsap came with "A Woman In Love," the first number one single written by Wright. A Pennsylvania native, Curtis moved to Nashville in January of 1987, and within eighteen months, he picked up a job with Vern Gosdin's road band, playing guitar and bass and singing harmony. Wright also joined his boss on the *Alone* album, providing back-up vocals on his hits "I'm Still Crazy" [see 832] and "That Just About Does It."

Wright quit Gosdin's band in December of 1989, the same month that he earned his number one record, penned during his first year in Nashville.

"Doug Millett and I got together, as we often do, just to go over some ideas and things," Wright recalls. "He brought out this kind of a road map, if you will, of a song, and played it for me. He wanted me to work on it with him, and I listened to it. Maybe I wasn't in the right frame of mind, but it didn't do a whole lot for me.

"We sat down, and as we got into the thing, it kind of opened up like a book. We hashed out a little melody and a verse and chorus and a bridge, and it just kind of happened. It was a great idea, and at the time, Earl Thomas Conley had out his song called 'What She Is (Is A Woman In Love)' [see 772]. I thought the song was two or three years away from anyone doin' anything with it. It goes to show you, you can easily be wrong."

Signed to Willin' David Music (owned, in part, by former Elvis Presley piano player David Briggs), Wright never imagined that Ronnie Milsap would take to his composition; he considered the artist and the song an illogical matchup. He was wrong about that, too—Ronnie snapped up "A Woman In Love."

Milsap supported the single with his first video since "Lost In The Fifties Tonight" [see 639], which was also his first video made in Nashville.